DATE DUE

DEMCO 38-296

STUDIES IN INTERNATIONAL SPACE LAW

Books By or Edited by the Same Author

1. *General Principles of Law as Applied by International Courts and Tribunals*, London: Stevens & Sons, 1953. Grotius Classic Reprint Series No. II, Cambridge: Grotius Publications, 1987. li + 490 pp.

2. *The Law of International Air Transport*, London: Stevens & Sons; New York: Oceana, 1962. xlii + 726 pp. Chinese translation, *Guoji Hangkong Yunshu Fa*, Beijing: CAAC Publications Division, 1996. 19 + 364 pp.

3. (ed.) *International Law: Teaching and Practice*, London: Stevens & Sons., 1982. xxix + 287 pp.

4. (ed. with E. D. Brown) *Contemporary Problems of International Law: Essays in honour of Georg Schwarzenberger on his eightieth birthday*, London: Stevens & Sons, 1988. xxvi + 371 pp.

Studies in
International Space Law

Bin CHENG

Licencié-en-droit (Genève); Ph.D., LL.D. (London);
Hon.LL.D. (The Chinese Univ., Hong Kong); FRAeS
Officier, Ordre des Palmes Académiques (France);
Santos Dumont Medalist (Brazil)

Emeritus Professor of Air and Space Law, University of London;
Visiting Professor of Law, University of Detroit Mercy

Sometime Dean of the Faculty of Laws,
and Chairman of the Board in Studies in Laws, University of London;
Chairman of the Air Law Committee, International Law Association

CLARENDON PRESS · OXFORD
1997

eat Clarendon Street, Oxford OX2 6DP

ord New York

Bangkok Bogota Bombay
Buenos Aires Calcutta Cape Town Dar es Salaam
Delhi Florence Hong Kong Istanbul Karachi
Kuala Lumpur Madras Madrid Melbourne
Mexico City Nairobi Paris Singapore
Taipei Tokyo Toronto Warsaw
and associated companies in
Berlin Ibadan

Oxford is a trade mark of Oxford University Press

Published in the United States
by Oxford University Press Inc., New York

© *Bin Cheng 1997*

British Library Cataloguing in Publication Data
Data available

Library of Congress Cataloging in Publication Data
Data available
ISBN 0–19–825730–9

1 3 5 7 9 10 8 6 4 2

Typeset by Hope Services (Abingdon) Ltd.
Printed in Great Britain
on acid-free paper by
Biddles Ltd., Guildford and King's Lynn

To Katharine Kam-Pui
And to Theodore Yao-Yüan and Veronica Yao-Hwa

Preface

I am very grateful to the Oxford University Press for having suggested to me the publication of a collection of my writings on international space law. For this purpose, I have selected altogether 26 articles written over a span of some 40 years, beginning with one which was actually published the year before mankind first succeeded in reaching outer space. The selection covers, I would like to think, a fair range of the more important aspects of international space law.

It is hoped that this book will be of interest to not only those concerned with outer space and space law, including all those involved directly or indirectly in the ever-growing space industry, but also all international lawyers, for the birth and growth of international space law, itself but a branch of international law, offer a unique insight into the nature and sources of international law itself.

The publication of this book coincides with the fortieth anniversary of Sputnik I which marks the beginning of the space age, and the thirtieth anniversary of what has sometimes been labelled Book I of the *corpus juris spatialis*, namely, the 1967 Space Treaty (Treaty on Principles Governing the Activities of States in the Exploration and Use of Outer Space, including the Moon and Other Celestial Bodies). The Treaty, accepted by the vast majority of States of the world, including all the super-, co-operative, or near-space powers, lays down the overall legal framework for all space activities, whether governmental or non-governmental, and for all subsequent legal developments relating to outer space.

I wish to take the opportunity of the publication of this book to acknowledge my long-standing debt of gratitude to a number of persons and institutions. First, I would like to mention UCL (University College, London University), which I joined as a student in 1945, and as a member of the staff in 1950, when George W. Keeton was concurrently Dean of the Faculty of Laws and Head of Department, and Georg Schwarzenberger was in charge of the teaching of international law. During Keeton's Headship, they jointly pioneered and pursued a very far-sighted and at the time highly original policy of expanding the study of international law from being that of a single subject to one of its many specialized branches. Looking back, I am particularly grateful for their warm encouragement and unstinting support already early in my teaching career to pay special attention to the subjects of Methods and Sources of International Law and Air and Space Law, in addition to General

International Law. In that connection, I would like also to record my gratitude to the Rockefeller Foundation which, during the period 1958–61, made me a very generous grant to assist me in my research in space law.

Four years after George Schwarzenberger very belatedly received his chair in International Law, the University in 1966 saw fit to confer on me the personal chair of Professor of Air and Space Law. It was a gesture which I particularly appreciated, especially for the sake of the subject in question. However, it made no difference to my academic interests or my academic duties, which were spread over the whole field of international law. Already well before his retirement in 1975, I was taking over most of Professor Schwarzenberger's teaching duties, except his course on International Economic Law. After his retirement, the task and privilege of leading the team of international lawyers at University College fell to me. For their warm support and friendship, I shall always remain grateful. However, perhaps acting on the principle of *ex re sed non ex nomine*, or maybe just out of inertia, being fortunate enough not ever having had to apply for any post, I never troubled to seek a change in my title. Nevertheless, my own experience convinces me that, in pursuing any special interests in international law, it is essential to remain firmly attached to the discipline as a whole. At the same time, I find that, in this way, the pursuit of special interests can in turn greatly enhance one's understanding of the entire international legal system.

Professor Ian Brownlie in his perceptive article on 'Problems of Specialization' has rightly drawn attention to the dangers of studying specialized areas of international law without regard to international law as a whole.[1] This warning amply justifies—if justification be required—the repeated reminders in the following pages that international space law forms part of international law, and the constant forays into various aspects of general international law.

In venturing from international law into outer space, I recall with gratitude the always unsparing help and advice I was privileged to be able to receive from the start from the late Professor Sir Harrie Massey, FRS, the world renowned authority in space research, who was Quain Professor of Physics at UCL from 1950 to 1975. Of course, all errors are my own.

I have reproduced the various papers in this volume essentially in the form in which they were first published. This does not mean that there have not been here and there, where necessary, some minor adjustments and consolidations, and the addition of a few tables and other illustrations. For permission or concurrence to reproduce the various materials in this volume, I am greatly indebted to Sweet & Maxwell Ltd in respect of Chapters 1, 3, 4, 5, 6, 12, 21, the Epilogue, parts of Chapter 11 (which first appeared in *Current Legal Problems*), and Chapter 10 (*Year Book of World Affairs*); the British Institute of International and Comparative Law in respect of Chapter 2

---

[1] In B. Cheng (ed.), *International Law: Teaching and Practice*. (1982), pp. 109–13.

(*International and Comparative Law Quarterly*), the Indian Society of International Law in respect of Chapter 7 (*Indian Journal of International Law*), and parts of Chapter 21 (*Essays on International Law in Honour of Krishna Rao*); the Institute of Public International Law and International Relations of the University of Thessaloniki in respect of Chapters 8 and 13 (*Thesaurus Acroasium*), the Director of the *Journal du Droit international (Clunet)* in respect of Chapter 9 (*Journal du Droit international (Clunet)*); Oceana Publications, Inc, in respect of Chapter 11 (*Manual on Space law*); the McGill University Institute and Centre of Air and Space Law in respect of Chapter 14 (*Annals of Air and Space Law* and *Earth-Oriented Space Activities and Their Legal Implications*); Elsevier Science Publishers B.V. in respect of Chapters 15, 16, and parts of Chapter 24 (*Encyclopedia of Public International Law*); Kluwer Law International in respect of Chapters 17 (*Air and Space Law: De Lege Ferenda*), 20 (*Essays in Honour of Judge Taslim Olawale Elias*), 22 (*The Highways of Air and Outer Space over Asia*); 23 (*AIR and Space LAW*), and 24 (*Essays in Honour of Wang Tieya*); the European Space Agency in respect of parts of Chapter 22 (*Proceedings of an International Conference on Earth Observation from Space and Management of Planetary Resources*); the American Institute of Aeronautics and Astronautics, Inc, in respect of Chapter 18 (*Space Law Colloquium*); and the *Journal of Space Law* in respect of Chapters 19, 25, and parts of Chapter 14 (*Journal of Space Law*).

My special thanks are due to Mr Miklos Pinter, Chief, Cartographic Section, LPD, of the United Nations Department of Public Information, for supplying me with UN maps Nos. 1267x and 1268x, being maps on the RB–47 flight on 1 July 1960, and map No. 1270x regarding Soviet flights off the US coast, with permission on behalf of the Publications Board to reproduce them; to Mr Nandasiri Jasentuliyana, Deputy to the Director General, United Nations Office at Vienna, and Director, Office for Outer Space Affairs, United Nations, for his friendly and always ready support and assistance throughout the years; and to the successive Directors, Librarians and members of the institute and library of the London University's Institute of Advanced Legal Studies for their many years of unfailing help and assistance.

Finally, I wish to express my grateful thanks to the Publishers and Printers, and the many people involved in seeing the volume through the press.

London, August 1996

B.C.

Summary Contents

PART I

INTERNATIONAL LAW AND SPACE LAW

Chapter

PART II

THE UNITED NATIONS AND OUTER SPACE

PART III

UNITED NATIONS TREATIES ON OUTER SPACE

PART IV

OUTER SPACE, ASTRONAUTS, AND SPACE OBJECTS

PART V

MILITARY USE OF OUTER SPACE

PART VI

COMMERCIAL USES OF OUTER SPACE
AND INTERNATIONAL LAW

EPILOGUE

APPENDIX

Table of Contents

PART I
INTERNATIONAL LAW AND SPACE LAW

PART III
UNITED NATIONS TREATIES ON OUTER SPACE

**Chapter 14: The Legal Regime of Airspace and Outer Space:
the Boundary Problem**
Functionalism versus Spatialism: the Major Premises   425

PART V
MILITARY USE OF OUTER SPACE

PART VI
COMMERCIAL USES OF OUTER SPACE
AND INTERNATIONAL LAW

EPILOGUE

Abbreviations and Acronyms*

A	PCIJ Judgments and Orders, Series A
A/	UN Doc.: docs. of GA
A/AC.98/	UN Doc.: docs. of *Ad Hoc* Committee on Outer Space
A/AC.98/C.1/	UN Doc.: docs. of *Ad Hoc* Committee on Outer Space's Scientific and Technical S.-C.
A/AC.98/C.2/	UN Doc.: docs. of *Ad Hoc* Committee on Outer Space's Legal S.-C.
A/AC.105/	UN Doc.: docs. of COPUOS
A/AC.105/PV.	UN Doc.: COPUOS' *procès verbaux*
A/AC.105/C.1/SR	UN Doc.: SR of COPUOS' Scientific and Technical S.-C.
A/AC.105/C.2/SR	UN Doc.: SR of COPUOS' Legal S.-C.
AASL	*Annals of Air and Space Law*
A/B	PCIJ Judgments and Orders, Series A/B
ABAJ	*American Bar Association Journal*
ABM	anti-ballistic missile
ABM Treaty	Treaty on the Limitation of ABM Systems, USA–USSR, Moscow, 1972
A/C.1/	UN Doc.: docs. of UN GA Committee I
A/C.1/SR	UN Doc. SR of UN GA Committee I
A/CONF.62/	UN Doc.: docs. of UNCLOS III
ADAS	*Annales de droit aérien et spatial* (*AASL* in French)
Add.	Addendum
ADIZ	Air Defense Identification Zone [US]
Adv. Op.	Advisory Opinion
AFDI	*Annuaire Français de Droit international*
AJIL	*American Journal of International Law*
Annuaire de l'Institut	*Annuaire de l'Institut de Droit international*
App.	Appendix
A/RES/	UN Doc.: resolutions of UN GA

---

* In the book in order to avoid repetition, where the context makes it clear that a document being cited is a UN document, only the UN document reference or symbol is normally given, omitting any specific mention of the fact that it is a UN document, or of the UN organ from which it emanates, as the latter can be easily identified from the document reference.

ASIL Proc.	*Proceedings of the American Society of International Law*
ASL	*AIR (& Space) LAW*
A/SPC/00/SR	UN Doc.: SR of the 00th session of UN GA's Special Political Committee
Astronauts Agreement	Agreement on the Rescue of Astronauts, the Return of Astronauts and the Return of Objects Launched into Outer Space, London, Moscow and Washington, 22 April 1968
B	PCIJ Judgments and Orders, Series B
BBC	British Broadcasting Corporation
Bernhardt (ed.), *Ency. PIL*	R. Bernhardt (ed.), *Encyclopedia of Public International Law*
BMD	ballistic missile defence
BMEWS	Ballistic Missile Early Warning System
BYIL	*British Year Book of International Law*
C.	UK Doc.: Command Papers, C. 1 to 9550 (1870–99)
CADIZ	Canadian Air Defence Identification Zone
Calif. LR	*California Law Review*
Can. YBIL	*Canadian Yearbook of International Law*
CCIR	International Radio Consultative Committee
Cd.	UK Doc.: Command Papers, Cd. 1– 9239 (1900–18)
CENTO	Central Treaty Organization
CERN	European Organization for Nuclear Research (*Conseil Européen pour la Researche nucléaire*)
cf.	compare
Ch.	chapter
Cheng, 'Custom'	Bin Cheng, 'Custom: The Future of General State Practice In a Divided World', in R. St. J. Macdonald and D. M. Johnston (eds.), *The Structure and Process of International Law* (1983), pp. 513–54 [N.B.: pp. 545 and 546 have been transposed.]
Cheng, *General Principles of Law*	Bin Cheng, *General Principles of Law as Applied by International Courts and Tribunals* London: Stevens (1953); Cambridge: Grotius Classic Reprint Series, No. II (1987).
Cheng (ed.), *International Law*	Bin Cheng, (ed.), *International Law: Teaching and Practice* London: Stevens (1982)

Cheng, *The Law of Transport*	Bin Cheng, *The Law of International Air Transport* London: Stevens (1962)
Cheng, 'Nature and Sources of International Law'	Bin Cheng, 'On the Nature and Sources of International Law', in B. Cheng (ed.), *International Law: Teaching and Practice* (1982), pp. 201–33
Cheng, 'The Right to Fly'	Bin Cheng, 'The Right to Fly', 42 *Grotius Society Transactions* (1956), pp. 99–131
Chicago Convention, 1944	Convention on International Civil Aviation, Chicago, 1944
Chicago Proceedings	US Department of State, *Proceedings of the International Civil Aviation Conference, Chicago, Illinois, Nov. 1–Dec. 7, 1944* (1948)
Chs	chapters
CLP	*Current Legal Problems*
Clunet	*Journal du Droit international privé (Clunet)*
Cm.	UK Doc.: Command Papers, Cm. 1– (1986–)
Cmd.	UK Doc.: Command Papers, Cmd. 1–9889 (1919–56)
Cmnd.	UK Doc.: Command Papers, Cmnd. 1–9927, (1956–86)
Com.	Committee
COPUOS	Committee on the Peaceful Uses of Outer Space
COSPAR	ICSU Committee on Space Research
CSAGI	ICSU's Special Committee for the IGY
DBS	direct broadcasting by satellite
DC/	UN Doc.: docs. of UN Disarmament Commission
DC/SC1/	UN Doc.: docs. of UN DC S.-C. 1
Dec. & Op.	Mixed Claims Commission, United States–Germany (1922), *Consolidated edition of Decisions and Opinions* (Washington DC, GPO, 1928, 1933, 1940)
Dept. of State Bull.	*Department of State Bulletin*
Doc.	Document
docs.	documents
DWB	See USIS *DWB*
E/CN . . ./	docs. of the Economic and Social Council
ELDO	European Space Vehicles Launchers Development and Construction Organization
Ency.	*Encyclopaedia*
Ency. Brit.	*Ency. Britannica*
Ency. PIL	R. Bernhardt (ed.), *Encyclopedia of Public International Law*

ENEA	European Nuclear Energy Agency
EOSAT	Earth Observation Satellite Co.
ERTS	Earth Resources Technology Satellite
ESA	European Space Agency
esp.	especially
ESRO	European Space Research Organization
EUROCHEMIC	European Company of the Chemical Processing of Irradiated Fuels
EURATOM	European Atomic Energy Community
FAGS	Federation of Astronomical and Geophysical Services
ff.	following pages, etc.
FOBS	Fractional Orbital Bombardment System
GA	General Assembly (of the United Nations)
GAOR	UN GA Official Records
Gen.	1. General 2. Genesis (Old Testament)
General Principles of Law	Cheng, *General Principles of Law*
Geo. Wash. LR	*George Washington LR*
GPO	1. General Post Office 2. Government Printing Office
Hague *Recueil*	Académie de droit international de La Haye, *Recueil des Cours*
H.C. Deb. 5 s., col.	UK Doc.:*Parliamentary Debates* (Hansard), House of Commons, Official Report, Fifth Series, column
HCR	*Hague Court Reports*
Hudson, *Int. Leg.*	M. O. Hudson (ed.), *International Legislation* (9 vols., 1931–50)
IAF	International Astronautical Federation
id.	*idem* (the same person or word)
IAEA	International Atomic Energy Agency
IATA	International Air Transport Association
ibid.	*ibidem* [in the same place as that referred to immediately above]
ICAO	International Civil Aviation Organization
ICAO Doc.	ICAO Document
ICBM	intercontinental ballistic missile
ICJ	International Court of Justice

ICJ Rep.	*Reports of Judgements, Advisory Opinions and Orders of the ICJ*
ICLQ	*International and Comparative Law Quarterly*
ICSU	International Council of Scientific Unions
IFN Treaty	Treaty between the USA and the USSR on the Elimination of Their Intermediate-Range and Shorter-Range Missiles, Washington, 1987
IFOV	instantaneous field of view
IGA	Agreement on Co-operation in the Detailed Design, Development, Operation and Utilisation of the Permanently Manned Civil Space Station between the Government of the United States of America, Governments of Member States of the ESA, the Government of Japan, and the Government of Canada (also known as the Intergovernmental Agreement), Washington, 29 September 1988
IGC	International Geophysical Co-operation
IGY	International Geophysical Year
IISL	International Institute of Space Law of the IAF
ILA	International Law Association
ILC Ybk	*International Law Commission Yearbook*
ILQ	*International Law Quarterly*
ILR	*International Law Review*, for instance, *Netherlands ILR*
Int. Aff.	*International Affairs*
Int. Aff. (Moscow)	*International Affairs* (Moscow)
Int. Org.	*International Organization*
INTELSAT	International Telecommunications Satellite Consortium; which, upon the coming into force of the Definitive Agreements, became the International Telecommunications Satellite Organization
ISMA	International Satellite Monitoring Agency
ITC	International Telecommunication Convention
ITU	International Telecommunication Union
JAGJ	*Judge Advocate General Journal*
JAG LR	*Judge Advocate General LR*
JALC	*Journal of Air Law and Commerce*
Jasentuliyana and Lee, *Manual*	Nandasiri Jasentuliyana and Roy S. K. Lee (eds.), *Manual on Space Law*. Dobbs Ferry, NY: Oceana (4 vols., 1979–81)

JBL	*Journal of Business Law*
JDI	*Journal du Droit international*
JIL	*Journal of International Law*, for instance, *Indian JIL*
JRAeS	*Journal of the Royal Aeronautical Society*
JSL	*Journal of Space Law*
Keesing's	*Keesing's Contemporary Archives*
Korean JASL	*Korean Journal of Air and Space Law*
L.	UN Doc.: docs. of limited distribution
Liability Convention	Convention on International Liability for Damage Caused by Space Objects, London, Moscow and Washington, 29 March 1972
LJ	*Law Journal*, for instance, *Cambridge LJ*
loc. cit.	*loco citato* [at the place or reference previously given, but not necessarily at the same page(s)]
LoNP	League of Nations Publication
LNTS	League of Nations Treaty Series
LR	*Law Review*, for instance, *Harvard LR*
MIDAS	Missile Defence Alarm System
MOL	Manned Orbiting Laboratory
Moon Treaty	Agreement Governing the Activities of States on the Moon and Other Celestial Bodies, New York, 18 Dec. 1979
Moore, *International Arbitration*	J. B. Moore, *History and Digest of the International Arbitrations to which the United States has been a party, etc.* Washington (6 vols., 1898)
mSv	milliSievert
n.	note
NASA	National Aeronautics and Space Administration
NATO	North Atlantic Treaty Organisation
N.B.	*nota bene* (note well)
NBC	National Broadcasting Company [US]
Nielsen's *Report*	Fred. K. Nielsen, *American and British Claims Arbitration, under the Special Agreement, concluded between the United States and Great Britain, Aug. 18, 1910. Report of Fred. K. Nielsen.* Washington, US GPO (1926).
nem. con.	*nemine contradicente* [with no one dissenting]
nn.	notes

NOAA	National Oceanic and Atmospheric Administration
OECD	Organization for Economic Co-operation and Development
OEEC	Organization for European Economic Co-operation
Off. Text	*Official Text*
Off. Rec.	*Official Record*
op. cit.	*opere citato* [in the work previously cited]
PCIJ	Permanent Court of International Justice
PUOS/C.2/DG	UN Doc.: COPUOS conference room papers/Legal S.-C./Drafting Group
PUOS/C.2/WG	UN Doc.: COPUOS conference room papers/Legal S.-C./Working Group
PUOS/C.2/70/ WG. . ./CRP. . .	COPUOS/Legal S.-C../70th Session/Working Group . . ./conference room papers
PV	*Procès-verbaux*
q.v.	*quod vide* [which see]
RDILC	*Revue de droit international et de législation comparée*
Registration Convention	Convention on Registration of Objects Launched into Outer Space, New York, 14 Jan. 1975
Rev. belge dr. int.	*Revue belge de droit international*
Rev. Gén. Air	*Revue générale de l'air*
RFDA	*Revue française de droit aérien (et spatial)*
RGDIP	*Revue générale de droit international public*
RIAA	United Nations, *Reports of International Arbitral Awards*
RICNT	Revised Informal Composite Negotiating Text
RIL	*Review of International Law*
RR	Radio Regulations
s.	section
S/	UN Doc.: docs. of the UN Security Council
§	1. section 2. numbered clause
SAMOS	Satellite and Missile Observation System
S.-C.	Sub-Committee
sect.	section

Schwarzenberger, *Int. Law*	G. Schwarzenberger, *International Law* (4 vols., 1945–86)
SDI	Strategic Defense Initiative
Senate Symposium (1958)	US Senate, *Space Law*. A Symposium prepared at the Request of Honorable Lyndon B. Johnson, Chairman, Special Committee on Space and Astronautics, 85th Congress, 2nd Sess., Dec. 31, 1958. Washington: US GPO (1959)
Senate Symposium (1961)	US Senate, *Legal Problems of Space Exploration: A Symposium*. Prepared for the use of the Committee on Aeronautical and Space Sciences, US Senate. 87th Congress, 1st Sess., Senate, Doc. No. 26. Washington: US GPO (1961)
Ser.	Series
SI Corp	Spot-Image Corporation
SIPRI	Stockholm International Peace Research Institute
Space Treaty	Treaty on Principles Governing the Activities of States in the Exploration and Use of Outer Space, including the Moon and Other Celestial Bodies, London, Moscow and Washington, 27 Jan. 1967
Space Law Colloquium	IISL, *Proceedings of the Colloquium on the Law of Outer Space*
SPOT	*Satellite probatoire pour l'observation de la terre*
S/PV	UN Doc.: *procès-verbaux* of the UN Security Council
SR	summary records
ss.	sections
SSR	Soviet Socialist Republic
Sub-Com.	Sub-Committee
Suppl.	Supplement
Tenn. LR	*Tennessee LR*
Thesaurus Acroasium	Institute of International Public Law and International Relations of Thessaloniki, *Thesaurus Acroasium*
TIAS	US Doc.: *Treaties and Other International Acts Series*
UAR	United Arab Republic
UK	United Kingdom
UKAEA	UK Atomic Energy Authority
UKTS	UK Doc.: *Treaty Series*
UN	United Nations

UNCOPUOS	COPUOS
UNCLOS III	Third UN Conference on the Law of the Sea
UN Doc.	United Nations docs.
UNESCO	United Nations Educational, Scientific, and Cultural Organization
UNIDIR	United Nations Institute for Disarmament Research
Univ.	University
UNTS	UN Treaty Series
UNYB	*United Nations Year Book*
UPU	Universal Postal Union
US	United States (of America)
USA	United States of America
USAF	US Air Force
US GPO	US Government Printing Office
USIS	US Information Service (London [unless otherwise specified])
USIS *DWB*	USIS, *Daily Wireless Bulletin*
USIS, Off. Text	USIS, Official Text
USSR	Union of Soviet Socialist Republics
UST	US Doc.: *United States Treaties and Other International Agreements*
Ven. Arb. 1903	J. H. Ralston and W. T. S. Doyle, *Venezuelan Arbitrations of 1903, etc.* Washington, 1904
WG.	Working Group
WMO	World Meteorological Organization
WHO	World Health Organization
WP	working paper
YBASL	*Yearbook of Air and Space Law*
YBIL	*Yearbook of International Law*
YBWA	*Yearbook of World Affairs*
ZLW	*Zeitschrift für Luft-(recht) (und Weltraumrecht(sfragen))*

Glossary of Foreign Words and Technical Terms

ab initio	from the beginning
anti-ballistic missile	missile to intercept a ballistic missile during its flight trajectory
a contrario	by or from contraries (of an argument based on contrast)
addendum (*pl.* addenda)	an addition to be incorporated (into a document or book)
ad hoc	for the sake of a particular case
ad hominem	directed at a particular person (instead of in accordance with rules of general application)
a fortiori	with all the more reason
animus	mind, a state of mind, intention (often used in conjunction with *corpus* to denote the psychological element of a number of legal concepts, such as 'Occupation', q.v.)
animus domini	(in international law) the intention of holding a territory as one's own, as its sovereign (one of the two constituent elements of 'Occupation' as a title to territory—see *corpus*)
apogee	the point in the orbit of an earth satellite where it is furthest from the earth
ASAT	a weapon to destroy satellites in outer space
casus belli	an act or situation provoking or justifying war, or deemed to be such
clause compromissoire	arbitration clause
clausula rebus sic stantibus	clause which is claimed by the adherents of this doctrine to be implicit in all agreements and treaties that an agreement applies for as long as things remain essentially as the parties at the time of the conclusion of the agreement had assumed that they would be, and circumstances have not fundamentally changed
conflict of laws	that part of the municipal law of each State which deals with the application of the law to private law cases involving a foreign element, such as a

	contract concluded abroad; also known as private international law, and used by extension to describe such rules as exist in international law to deal with similar cases involving more than one system of municipal law
consensus	general agreement (of views, etc.); also procedure that has grown up in the United Nations of adopting resolutions, etc., by general agreement without a formal vote
consensus ad idem	meeting of the minds; actual agreement on the matter at issue; identity in the views of the parties concerned
consuetudo	established usage, the material element of a legally binding custom
consuetudinis	genitive of *consuetudo*
contra	of the opposite view
corpus	1. an important body or collection of writings, or texts. 2. the material element, as distinguished from the psychological element *animus*, in a number of legal concepts, such as 'Custom', or 'Occupation', q.v.
corpus juris spatialis	*corpus* of space law
custom	used in Article 38(1)(b) of the ICJ Statute almost synonymously with 'customary law' when it refers to the Court applying 'international custom, as evidence of a general practice accepted as law', meaning thus 'customary international law', q.v., but the term is often used in practice to mean established usage (*consuetudo*, q.v.), or even simple usage
customary international law	used variously to mean international law based on custom, i.e., established usage (*consuetudo*, q.v.), that is generally accepted as law (*opinio juris*, q.v.), or the whole body of international law other than treaties or general principles of law, or simply the whole body of international law other than treaties synonymously with the term 'general international law', q.v.
data	the raw signals including imagery generated from an observation satellite
de facto	in fact
de jure	in law
de lege ferenda	from the standpoint of *lex ferenda*

de lege lata	from the standpoint of the *lex lata*
démarche	(in diplomacy) an approach or mild representation
détente	easing of strained relations, esp. between States
dies ad quem	the day until which
domestic law	see 'municipal law'
en passant	by the way
erga omnes	applicable, opposable, or in relation to or *vis-à-vis* all
et passim	and at various places throughout the work, chapter, or section referred to
et seq.	and the following (pages, articles, paragraphs, etc.)
Fractional Orbital Bombardment System	weapon system which employs missiles that behave rather like an artificial satellite with a low orbit except that they are designed to re-enter the earth's atmosphere and home on their targets before they complete a single orbit
general international law	in a narrow sense, it means the whole body of international law other than treaties and the general principles of law, as referred to in Article 38(1) of the ICJ Statute. In a broad sense, it includes also the general principles of law. In the latter sense, it embraces the whole body of rules of international law that are applicable to all subjects of international law, as distinguished from treaties which are binding on only the contracting parties. Together they constitute the international legal system, q.v.
geostationary orbit	a circular orbit at an altitude of 35,800 km above the earth's equator. A satellite placed in this orbit revolves round the earth at a speed which corresponds to the rotation of the earth with the result that the satellite appears to be stationary above the earth
geosynchronous orbit	same as geostationary orbit, q.v.
Greek gift	something given with a treacherous purpose
idem.	the same author or word
in absentia	in (his, her or their) absence
in abstracto	in the abstract

Inadimplenti non est adimplendum	nonfulfilment of a treaty obligation is justifiable in regard to a contracting party who fails to fulfil his part of the bargain
Inclination (orbit)	the angle of inclination of the orbital plane of a satellite to the earth's equatorial plane
in esse	in being
in medio	to be found halfway down or towards the middle
in principio	to be found near the top or beginning
in concreto	in the concrete
in fine	to be found towards the end
in posse	in the state of being a possibility
in situ	in its actual place; on the spot
in statu nascendi	in the state of being born
inter alia	among other things
international law	the system of legal rules, principles and procedures which apply between and among international persons, q.v. Term used often to mean either 'general international law', q.v., or the 'international legal system', q.v.
international legal personality	capacity to bear rights and duties under international law
international legal system	legal system of the international legal and political order operative among the subjects of international law, q.v. It comprises both the rules, principles and procedures of general international law in the broad sense of the term, q.v., which apply to all the subjects of international law, q.v., and those created by treaties which apply only between the contracting parties
inter partes	between the parties
international persons	entities possessing international legal personality, i.e., mutually recognized sovereign States, and such other entities as have been granted, or recognized as possessing, international legal personality, q.v.
inter se	as between or among themselves/the parties
ipso facto	by that very act or fact
ipso jure	by the law itself; simply by operation of the law
jure gestionis	(a State entering into a transaction or acting) not in a sovereign and political capacity, but like any ordinary individual or entity involved in a commercial, entrepreneurial or managerial activity, thus being governed by the same rules—cf. *jure imperii*.
jure gentium	by or under the law of nations, q.v.

jure imperii	(a State entering into a transaction or acting) in its sovereign and political capacity and therefore coming under the rules applicable to it as such, enjoying, for instance, sovereign immunity—cf. *jure gestionis*
jurisaction	the concrete or physical element of State jurisdiction, q.v., being the legal power recognized in international law actually to set up machinery to make, implement and enforce, and physically to make, implement and enforce its laws, judicial pronouncements, and other legally binding decisions—cf. jurisfaction
jurisfaction	the normative element of State jurisdiction, q.v., being the legal power recognized in international law to make laws, render judicial pronouncements, and adopt other decisions with legally binding force—cf. jurisaction
jus cogens	peremptory norms of the law which invalidate provisions in agreements between contracting parties that contravene them
lacuna (pl.: lacunae)	a gap (in the law)
lapsus calami	slip of the pen
lapsus linguae	slip of the tongue
law of nation	international law, q.v.
leges ferendae	plural of *lex ferenda*
lex	law, or more specifically legal rules, as distinguished from *jus* the latter referring to the whole legal system, or specific parts of it, or the concept of law itself
lex ferenda	the law that is yet, or (in one's opinion) ought, to be made
lex fori	the law of the country to which the court belongs
lex inter partes	(having the force of) law (i.e., legally binding) between the parties
lex lata	the law as laid down; i.e., existing law, as distinguished from *lex ferenda*, q.v.
lex loci	the law of the place, i.e., country (where something takes place)
lex loci delicti commissi	the law of the place where the wrong was committed
lex non scripta	the unwritten law
lex patriae	the law of the national State of a person, whether individual or corporate

locus	place/location (where an activity or event takes or took place)
locus delicti	the place where the wrong was committed
locus standi	a right to be heard or intervene in a given matter
lucrum cessans	loss of profit (in the computation of damages)
milliSievert	a unit of radiation dose, based on a milliGray multiplied by a quality factor that characterizes the damage done by the particular radiation
mirabile dictu	wonderful to relate; miraculously
modi vivendi	plural of *modus vivendi*
modus vivendi	a way of living, co-existing or coping with one another (*pl.*: *modi vivendi*)
municipal law	name given by international law to the national law of a State, also referred to as the domestic, or national law of a State
mutatis mutandis	(in comparing different cases or situations), once the appropriate adaptations have been made
nemine contradicente	with no one dissenting
node	either of the two points where the orbit of a satellite intersects the plane of the orbit of the earth
non	no
Notstand	state of necessity (*l'état de nécessité*), justifying the defence or plea of necessity
nullum crimen sine lege	there is no crime/no act should be considered a crime/ without a pre-existing law making the act a crime
obligatio imperfecta	imperfect obligation, i.e., obligation that is lawful and binding, but not enforceable
occupatio bellica	belligerent occupation under the law of war which, as such, does not confer title to territory
occupation	recognized mode in international law of acquiring title to *territorium nullius*, q.v., provided that the occupation is effective and with *animus domini*, q.v.
occupatio pacifica	occupation by one State of the territory or part of the territory of another under the law of peace with the latter's consent, and without *animus domini*, q.v., for the purpose of, for instance, securing the performance of a treaty or guaranteeing a loan
opinio communis juris generalis	a common or unanimous *opinio juris generalis*

opinio conditionalis juris generalis	a conditional *opinio juris generalis*
opinio generalis juris	a general *opinio juris*, i.e., one held by the generality of the subjects of international law
opinio generalis juris generalis	a general *opinio juris* among the subjects of international law that the rule is one of general international law. It is usually made up of the concurrent *opiniones individuales juris generalis* of the generality of States, and in fact represents general international law, q.v. Thus Article 38(1)(b) of the ICJ Statute speaks of 'a general practice accepted as law'. Contrary to a view sometimes advanced, it is not a tacit agreement among States
opinio individualis juris generalis (pl.: opiniones individuales juris generalis)	the *opinio juris* of an individual subject of international law that the rule is one of general international law
opinio juris (pl.: opiniones juris)	in municipal laws, which are hierarchical legal systems, where the force of the law comes from the legal sovereign of the political order, it means subjective awareness or knowledge on the part of the person or persons concerned that a given rule is one that is legally binding under the law of the land, and consequently it implies the consciousness of a legal duty to comply with it. It is an essential constituent element of custom, q.v., together with *consuetudo*, q.v., the latter enabling the subject to know of the existence of the rule. In international law, however, which is a horizontal legal system, where States are sovereign and equal and are under no superior law-making authority, it means primarily a State or other international person's acceptance or recognition, tacit or express, of a given rule as a valid and binding rule of general international law, acceptance or recognition which can be conclusively deduced from the pronouncement or conduct of that State or international person concerned, and which is invocable (*opposable*) against that State or international person on the basis of consistency or reciprocity. Since what makes a rule of general international law, q.v., binding is simply because States accept it as legally binding, *opinio juris* is thus in fact what determines the existence and content of rules

	of general international law. State practice or usage serves to provide evidence of what it is
opinio juris consuetudinis	acceptance or recognition of a rule as one of customary law
opinio juris de lege ferenda	acceptance or recognition of a rule as one *de lege ferenda*, q.v.
opinio juris de lege lata	acceptance or recognition of a rule as one of the law in force
opinio juris generalis	acceptance or recognition of a rule as one of general international law
opinio juris sive necessitatis	acceptance or recognition of a rule as binding either because it is the law or because it is considered necessary to do so
opiniones	plural of *opinio*
opiniones individuales juris generalis	plural of *opinio individualis juris generalis*
opinio obligationis conventionalis	acceptance or recognition of the binding character of a rule as a matter of contractual or treaty obligation
opposabilité	see *opposable*
opposability	see *opposable*
opposable	(of a statement or conduct which is) of the nature that it can in law be invoked against (a State or other international person); hence: *opposabilité*. Sometimes anglicized to 'opposable' and 'opposability'
orbital parameters	parameters defining the orbit of a satellite
pace	with due deference to
pacta de contrahendo	plural of *pactum de contrahendo*
pacta tertiis nec prosunt nec nocent	agreements do not create any rights, nor can they impose any legal obligations on third parties (without their consent)
pacta sunt servanda	agreements are to be kept
pacta tertiis	short for *pacta tertiis nec prosunt nec nocent*
pactum (pl.: pacta)	agreement, treaty or contract
pactum de contrahendo (pl.: pacta de contrahendo)	an agreement to negotiate with a view to concluding a further agreement. Such an agreement does not oblige the parties necessarily to succeed in reaching agreement, but does oblige them to negotiate in good faith with a genuine desire to reach agreement
pactum tacitum	tacit treaty or agreement, of which international custom, q.v., is sometimes said to be an example, but see *opinio generalis juris generalis*

parking slot	popular expression to denote a position in the geostationary orbit where a satellite can be placed without causing interference with the operation of other satellites in the same orbit
passim	to be found at various places throughout the cited text
per se	by or in itself
perigee	the point in the orbit of an earth satellite that is closest to the earth
prima facie	at first sight
primary data	the raw signals including imagery generated from an observation satellite
pro tanto	to that extent; for so much
pro subjecta materia	in so far as the subject-matter under discussion is concerned
procès-verbal (*pl.* procès-verbaux)	written report of proceedings or memorandum; minutes
public international law	international law; term used in particular to distinguish it from private international law, i.e. conflict of laws q.v.
qua	In the capacity of
quid pro quo	something in return for something else
quod vide	which see
ratione materiae	by reference to the subject-matter
ratione personae	by reference to the parties or persons concerned
ratione temporis	by reference to time
ratione instrumenti	by reference to the type of instruments used
ratione loci	by reference to the place or location
re	in the matter of
res communis (*pl.*: *res communes*)	in Roman law, it means a thing that is for the use of all because it is not subject to private ownership, but the term often overlaps with *res publicae* which in addition implies not only State sovereignty but also ownership. In international law, as in this work, in order to avoid confusion, the term is often used to denote common ownership or sovereignty by two or more States. *Res extra commercium*, q.v., is used for the other meaning of the word
res communis omnium	*res communis*, q.v., under the common sovereignty of all States
res communis usus	*res communis* in terms of use

res derelicta	derelict, a thing voluntarily abandoned by its owner with the intention of not retaking it
res extra commercium	things outside commerce, i.e., not subject to private ownership or transaction. Used in international law, it means object, space or territory which is not subject to national appropriation, but is open to use by all. Cf. *res communis*
res incorporales	incorporeal effects, things which exist only in contemplation of law, but have no physical existence (such as a legal right, interest or obligation)
res inter alios acta	in full form, *res inter alios acta alteri nocere non debet*, a transaction between third parties ought not to injure a person's legal position; a matter which in law is of concern only to others
res judicata	a thing or matter which has been finally decided on its merits by a court of competent jurisdiction. Such a matter cannot be litigated again between the same parties
res nullius	term borrowed from Roman law, where it means a thing without an owner. Used in international law to mean territory without a sovereign recognized as a subject of international law, and hence susceptible in law of being acquired by a subject of international law
restitutio in integrum	reparation to make the victim of a wrong completely whole again; or restoration of a situation to what it would probably have been but for the wrongful act or the act in question. It is not just the restoration of the *status quo ante*, q.v.
semble	it seems
sensu lato	in its broad meaning; broadly speaking
sensu stricto	in its narrow meaning; strictly speaking
si	yes
sic	thus, meaning that this is exactly what was said or how it was written
sine die	without an appointed date (when business/meeting will be resumed)
sine qua non	an indispensable condition
Sputnik	each of a series of Soviet artificial earth satellites launched from 1957. Sputnik I, launched on 4 October 1957 was the first man-made object to reach outer space

State jurisdiction the recognized power of a State in international law, divisible into three types, namely, territorial, quasi-territorial and personal, to exercise the functions of a State (including legislative, judicial and executive) over respectively (i) its national territory, (ii) ships and aircraft of its nationality, space objects of its registry, and all means of transport capable of operating in areas not subject to the jurisdiction of any State, and (iii) its nationals, individual or corporate. It comprises two elements, jurisfaction, q.v., and jurisaction, q.v.

status mixtus traditional international law distinguishes between the state of peace and the state of war, to which respectively apply the law of peace and the law of war. *Status mixtus* signifies a situation where the distinction becomes unclear, especially when parts of the law of war have to be applied even though a state of peace nominally exists

status quo the state of things as they are; the existing state of affairs

status quo ante the state of things as they were before

subjects of international law those that are directly subject to international law, i.e. primarily mutually recognized sovereign States, but also such other entities that have been granted, or recognized as possessing, international legal personality, q.v. Same as international persons, q.v.

sub voce under the word

sub spe rati (treaties/instruments that have been signed and are) waiting for their ratification/completion (and coming into force, when the possibility of their being ratified and coming into force has not been ruled out)

synchronous orbit same as geosynchronous orbit, q.v., though not confined to the earth

terra firma (*pl.: terrae firmae*) dry land, firm ground

terra nullius land that is *res nullius*, q.v.

territorium commune humanitatis territory with the status of common heritage of mankind, a relatively new concept in international law; for details, see Index

territorium extra commercium territory that is *res extra commercium*, q.v.

territorium nullius	territory that is *res nullius*, q.v.
travaux préparatoires	preparatory work; preliminary papers, particularly those leading to the conclusion of a treaty or the adoption of a piece of legislation
treaty	consensual agreement concluded under international law between subjects of international law with a view to creating binding obligations, whatever its form and whatever its particular designation, whether called treaty, agreement, convention, protocol, declaration, exchange of notes or others
troika	a Russian vehicle with a team of three horses abreast—idea advocated by Soviet Premier Khrushchev that in all international matters, there should always be an equal representation of East, West and the Third World, especially between East and West
tu quoque	thou too—a retort charging the other party with doing the same thing as oneself
urbi et orbi	to the city and the world; to everyone home and abroad
via	by way of
vœu	a wish, or recommendation. In the League of Nations Assembly, the ordinary unanimity rule was bypassed by the rule that decisions consisting of a *vœu* required only a simple majority, a device frequently resorted to. The French words *invitation*, *recommendation* were also used instead of *vœu*. The accent is on the non-binding character of the decision
volenti non fit injuria	no infringement is done to a person's rights if he has consented to what has been done

Table of Cases

List of Figures, Maps, Plates, and Tables

Introduction

Like space flights, of which it is but an inevitable concomitant, space law has come into existence only in the second half of the twentieth century. When the subject was first discussed, there were some who greeted it with considerable scepticism or even derision. At the other extreme, there were also many who entertained fanciful expectations that in space there would soon be an entirely new heavenly order, free from all terrestrial strife and governed by a matching celestial law.

Today space is part of our daily life. We take for granted such things as satellite weather pictures, crackle-free transoceanic telephone conversations, satellite television with live broadcasts from the other side of the earth and even from outer space, images of the edge of the visible universe courtesy of the Hubble space telescope, global positioning navigation devices not only for ships and aircraft, but also for motor vehicles and intrepid explorers. From a more specialized angle, space has opened entirely new doors for all kinds of commercial, industrial, and scientific enterprises, ranging from agriculture, astronomy, through communications, environmental protection, fishery, the prospecting for and conservation of natural resources, medical and pharmaceutical research, as well as diverse manufacturing processes relying on a gravity-free environment, to telecommunications, and the management of zoological nature reserves, just to mention some. At the same time, while rocketry, which is at the heart of space flights, has completely revolutionized military strategy, observation from space has also brought about a vital breakthrough in the disarmament process by providing an effective means of verification.

In anticipation, as well as in the wake, of these technological advances, an appreciable body of space law has meanwhile grown apace. If one may say so, it is a law of a very down-to-earth nature on the whole. The present collection of studies, written over a period of some 40 years starting from the very beginning of the space age, covers a good part of the major developments in international space law during this period.

Needless to say, space law is definitely not a law governing, or intended to govern, our relations with extraterrestrial beings, notwithstanding all the efforts being made to search for extraterrestrial life and to contact extraterrestrial intelligence. Nor is it an autonomous system of law operating independently in outer space, unattached to any earthly authority or political order.

In brief, space law is merely a term of functional classification. It refers to that part of existing legal systems on earth which relates to outer space or to activities in or involving outer space. Up to the present, the legal system that has been most directly concerned is, inevitably, that of public international law; for to borrow a dictum from Judge Max Huber in the *Palmas Case* (1928), territorial sovereignty under international law 'serves to divide between nations the space upon which human activities are employed'.[1] But already in a few countries, specific rules relating to space activities have already been enacted, whilst the scope of application of certain rules of domestic law have in some instances been tentatively extended to activities in outer space. The result is that, alongside international space law, there are at the same time various systems of domestic space law.[2] However, especially when speaking of the world as a whole, such domestic space laws are still at a very early stage of growth, although in time they will no doubt expand rapidly and extensively, particularly among those States with space capabilities.

For the moment at least, the most important branch of space law is undoubtedly international space law, and it is with international space law that the following studies are concerned. Since not everyone who is interested in space law is familiar with international law, it has been found necessary, over the years, not only constantly to emphasize that international space law forms an integral part of public international law,[3] but also on many occasions to dwell at some length on various related aspects of international law, especially its nature and sources.[4] Moreover, it has been found useful sometimes to make explicit the premises on which one's views on international law are based.[5] In turn the study of space law has helped considerably to throw light on many aspects of international law. Some of these lessons learnt are discussed in the Epilogue and several of the other chapters.

In the light of what has just been said, Part I groups together a number of papers on the relationship between international law and space law. Chapter 1, written soon after the publication of the then highly exciting news that the United States and the Soviet Union were both going to launch the world's first artificial earth satellites as part of their programmes for the International Geophysical Year (1 July 1957–31 Dec. 1958), examines some of the international law problems which the forthcoming space age was likely to encounter. Chapter 2, the appearance of which coincided with the launching of Sputnik I, continues the theme, while assessing the legal aspects of the then raging controversy provoked by the release in the West of unmanned high altitude 'meteorological' balloons over various Soviet-bloc countries. These balloons, likened to miniature satellites, carried sophisticated photographic and other

---

[1] 2 *RIAA*, p. 829, at p. 839.   [2] Cf. Ch. 14 below, Fig. XIV.1 below.
[3] See, e.g., Ch. 13, s. I.A; Ch. 14, s. II.
[4] See, e.g., Ch. 8, s. V; Ch. 13, s. I *passim*; Ch. 14, ss. III–V; Epilogue.
[5] See, e.g., Ch. 14, s. III; Ch. 20, 5. I.

recording equipment, and were designed to fly over a number of Soviet-bloc countries, before landing their equipment and recordings somewhere in the Pacific or in North America. The controversy provided a foretaste of the disputes to come.

Chapters 3 and 4 further explore the possibility of comparisons and analogies in related fields. They review respectively the development of international air law and the rules of international co-operation and control in the field of nuclear energy in order to see how these two cognate branches of international law may provide lessons for the future development of international space law. In fact, if nothing else, they can respectively give much food for thought for those who support the US attitude towards the problem of delimiting the frontier between airspace and outer space,[6] and the US interpretation of the term 'peaceful'.[7] The comparison with nuclear energy is particularly relevant in view of the growing demand on the one hand for the greater spread of space technology so that it may be used 'for the benefit and in the interests of all countries', in the words of Article I of the 1967 Space Treaty, and the increasing concern on the other hand for international security arising from the amount of space technology that is capable of both civil and military use.[8]

Chapter 5, through a re-examination and a reclassification of the concept of State jurisdiction, seeks to demonstrate that international law and international treaties, such as the United Nations Charter, are in principle applicable to outer space from the very beginning and do not need, contrary to what was then a very prevalent view, to be specifically extended to it.

After a somewhat faltering start, which itself has a lesson to impart,[9] the United Nations has played a crucial rôle in the development of international space law. Part II is devoted in particular to this rôle of the United Nations, including its related agencies. Chapter 6 provides from the legal point of view a general survey of the work of the United Nations in the space field, as well as an examination of certain related and very specific issues and disputes which the United Nations was dealing with at the time. Among these were the problem of the allocation and control of radio frequencies, the legality of the use of reconnaissance satellites, which was related to the question of the definition and delimitation of outer space, and the military use of outer space. The dispute in and outside the United Nations between the Soviet Union and the United States over two aerial incidents which occurred in 1960 provided the basis for a clear and fundamental distinction being drawn between the legality of peripheral and penetrative reconnaissance in international law. This distinction is crucial in determining the legality of reconnaissance by means of

---

[6] Cf. Ch. 14 below.   [7] Cf. Ch. 19 below.
[8] Cf. S. E. Doyle, *Civil Space Systems: Implication for International Security* (1993), a UNIDIR sponsored study.
[9] Cf. Epilogue, ss. III and IV.C.

satellites, provided of course that it is possible to define the boundary between national airspace and outer space.

The task of elaborating rules on space law in the United Nations is performed principally by the Legal Subcommittee of the General Assembly's Committee on the Peaceful Uses of Outer Space (COPUOS). To start with, the exact composition and the voting procedure of COPUOS were the subject of intense bargaining between East and West. When it finally started work in the early sixties, a controversy arose immediately between the Soviet Union and the United States as to whether it was better to develop space law through treaties or General Assembly resolutions. As the West had a comfortable majority in the General Assembly at that time, it was the United States that favoured General Assembly resolutions. It was the United States that was putting forward the view that General Assembly resolutions, apart from being much more expeditious to adopt, and enjoying much greater flexibility, were legally just as effective as treaties. Its delegate stated in the Legal Sub-Committee:

international agreements were not the only *sources of law*. As stated in Article 38 of the Statute of the International Court of Justice, . . . the growth of *customary law* as evidenced by State practice should also be taken into consideration. When a *General Assembly resolution* proclaimed principles of international law . . . and was adopted unanimously, it *represented the law as generally accepted in the international community*.[10]

It was this statement and the general United States stance at the time that prompted the title of Chapter 7, namely: 'United Nations Resolutions on Outer Space: "Instant" International Customary Law?'.

Chapter 7 in no way questions the well-known truism that under the UN Charter, General Assembly resolutions are not legally binding except in budgetary and administrative matters. However, in trying to get to the heart of the matter, the conviction is reached that *opinio juris* in international law, which is a horizontal legal system, differs in meaning from *opinio juris* in municipal law, which is, as a rule, hierarchical in character. Whereas in a hierarchical system, a rule of customary law requires both *opinio juris* and usage, in a horizonal legal system such as international law, where all the subjects of the system are at the same time its law-makers, the essential constituent element of a rule of general international law, or what, as the US delegate reminds us, Article 38 of the ICJ Statute calls 'international custom', is (to use the terminology of Article 38 again) its being generally 'accepted as law'—as a rule of general international law. All that is needed, therefore, is an *opinio generalis juris generalis* among States. The rôle of practice, instead of being constitutive, becomes essentially evidentiary. This leads thus to the phenomenon of the one-element general international law, and from there to the possibility of

---

[10] A/AC/105/C.2/SR.20 (22.4.63), pp. 10–11. Italics added.

instant general international law, inasmuch as the *opinio generalis juris gener-*
alis of States is capable of instantaneous formation and change. The fact that
general international law is still called customary international law or simply
international custom by the ICJ Statute and, out of habit, by many international lawyers explains the use of the expression one-element custom and the
much misunderstood 'instant custom'.

In the light of this finding, the answer to the question asked in the title is
that, whilst General Assembly resolutions are not, save in the exceptions mentioned, in themselves legally binding, a specific resolution which, in clear,
explicit, and unequivocal language, indicates that the intention is to proclaim
what members of the General Assembly, without dissent, *already accept as a*
rule of general international law may well be said to furnish adequate evidence
that a new rule of general international law is in existence. This is so not only
inter se among UN members, but, in view of the dominant position which the
United Nations occupies at the moment, it will doubtless be claimed by its
members as also valid *erga omnes*.[11] In such cases, the binding force of the new
rule is not derived from the resolution, but because it is accepted as law—as a
rule of general international law—by the generality of States. However, in
none of the General Assembly resolutions on outer space then being examined, is the wording found to be anywhere near to conveying such an intention. They are all essentially for the 'guidance' of States.

Unfortunately the journal in which the article was first published is not
always available in some of the smaller international law libraries, but this
does not appear to have deterred some critics from voicing criticisms without
having seemingly ever seen the article and still less read it. They seem mostly
either to ignore the question mark in the title and take the title to be a statement, or assume the writer's conclusion to be in the affirmative. On those
assumptions, some reject the concept of 'instant' international law by arguing
inconsequentially and at length the truism that General Assembly resolutions
are in principle not legally binding. Others rather offhandedly dismiss the
concept of instant 'customary' international law on the mere ground that it is
a contradiction in terms, ignoring that there is a figure of speech known as
oxymoron, and sadly unaware, it would appear, of the fact that the traditional
term customary international law, used as the equivalent of general international law, is increasingly being recognized as a misnomer, because by far the
greater part of general international law is not based on custom in the sense
of long practice. As Judge Sir Robert Jennings has pointed out, 'it is not custom at all, and never was'.[12] More cynically, yet other detractors choose to

---

[11] It may perhaps be mentioned that, while treaties are not binding on third parties without their
consent (Vienna Convention on the Law of Treaties, 1155 UNTS 331, Art. 34), rules of general
international law, as Art. 38 of the ICJ Statute recognizes, are made by the generality of States. Cf.,
e.g., Ch. 8, s. V.D; Ch. 14, S.IV. On the rôle of the dominant section, cf. Epilogue, s. III.

[12] 'The Identification of International Law', in Cheng (ed.), *International Law*, p. 3, at p. 6. See
also Professor R. R. Baxter (as he then was), 'Treaties and Custom', Hague *Recueil* (1970–1),

cast dark shadows of suspicion on the concept of instant international law as a Third World plot to give greater weight to General Assembly resolutions— obviously not knowing that it was the United States which first put forward the idea that General Assembly resolutions can represent international 'customary' law. So much for scholarship!

Twenty years after the initial study, this theme of a living general international law consisting in the *opinio generalis juris generalis* of States that can respond instantaneously to changes, a proposition which is well demonstrated in space law, is taken up again and further explained in the wider context of the nature and sources of international law in the following chapter on the United Nations and the Development of International Law Relating to Outer Space.[13] The main objective of this chapter is to examine the procedure followed in the United Nations for the development of international space law and of principles relating to various space activities, as well as UN's achievements in this area up to that point. Such achievements by then include General Assembly resolutions 1721, 1884, 1962 and 37/92, and the five treaties prepared by COPUOS.[14] Chapter 8 concludes with some reflections gained from this survey of the UN experience on the conditions governing international rule-making in general.

Part III contains detailed studies of the drafting history and provisions of four of the five treaties relating to outer space drafted by the United Nations. First and the most important among them is the 1967 Space Treaty, which establishes the main legal framework for the peaceful exploration and use of outer space. Next follows chronologically the 1968 Agreement on the rescue and return of astronauts in an emergency, and the return of stray space objects, which is largely a treaty of a humanitarian character. The third treaty is the 1972 Convention on International Liability for Damage Caused by Space Objects which in practice ranks in importance next to the 1967 Space Treaty. Whereas the 1967 Space Treaty represents the ground rules agreed upon at the dawn of the space age by the two super-space-powers for the future exploration and use of outer space, in the drafting of which the other members of COPUOS and of the UN had in practice little say, the Liability Convention was more democratically drafted within COPUOS. From a purely legal perspective, the latter can be said to be the greatest triumph for COPUOS. It embodies rules and procedures which ensure that a dispute concerning the principle and extent of liability for damage caused by a foreign space object can, as between the contracting parties, be finally resolved, if

---

p. 25: 'The time factor as a separate element in the proof of custom now seems *irrelevant*' (at p. 67, italics added); 'If all States were today to declare that the state of the law is that foreign states are not entitled to immunity in national courts, that would be the law, even though it had theretofore been acknowledged that the law is just the opposite' (at p. 44).

[13] See Ch. 8, ss. IV and V.

[14] The text of all these treaties and resolutions, plus resolutions 41/65 and 47/68, are reproduced in the Appendix below.

necessary, by a third party, notwithstanding any obstructionist tactics on the part of the defendant, all within carefully laid down time limits. This compares well with the International Law Commission's early abortive attempt to draw up an arbitration code. Moreover, the Liability Convention is probably the first treaty in a non-commercial matter in which the Soviet Union agreed to the principle of third-party settlement of disputes. Besides, from the technical point of view, the Liability Convention is probably the best drafted of all the five UN treaties relating to outer space.

The same cannot be said of the 1979 Moon Treaty, which is the subject of Chapter 12, the last chapter in Part III. This remark is not to minimize, still less to ignore, but to draw attention to, and to sympathize with, the enormous difficulties faced regularly by negotiators of especially multilateral international treaties. In face of such difficulties, the achievements of COPUOS since its formation have been remarkable. Indeed the Moon Treaty has the high distinction of being the first instrument officially to declare a part of the world to be in law the common heritage of mankind, thus beating at the post by a nose the 1982 UN Convention on the Law of the Sea, which accords the same status to the deep ocean bed and subsoil. All five UN treaties on outer space are in force. The 1975 Registration Convention is the only one not separately dealt with in Part III, but it is treated extensively in several other parts of this volume.[15]

Part IV deals in some detail with the definition and legal status of respectively outer space, astronauts and space objects, including the problems of jurisdiction over astronauts, space objects, and installations on celestial bodies, in the light of both general international law and the several UN treaties relating to outer space. Over all these topics, there remains today a considerable amount of ambiguities and uncertainties, mostly due to a lack of sufficient official notice of, or interest in, the matter, or a shortage of international legislative time,[16] but in the case of the delimitation of outer space primarily because of strong opposition to its being resolved at the moment.

Chapter 13 provides an overview of the whole field. Chapter 14 examines at some length the question of the definition and delimitation of outer space in the light of the major premisses of international law, and argues for an early resolution of the issue. Chapters 15 and 16 cover the legal status of respectively astronauts and space objects. Chapter 17 suggests that nationality be conferred on space objects, as in the case of ships and aircraft, in order to remove some of the present anomalies.

From the outset, as its name implies, the remit of COPUOS is confined to the *peaceful* uses of outer space. The Soviet Union in particular was keen to keep the work of COPUOS and the UN's Disarmament Commission separate.[17] However, the 1967 Space Treaty has succeeded in including an Article

---

[15] See Ch. 8, s. II.B.4; Ch. 13, s. IV.C; Ch. 16, s. V; and Ch. 24, s. II, ss. H and I.
[16] See esp. Ch. 18.   [17] Cf. also Ch. 6, s. VI.

IV which bans certain weapons from outer space and reserves celestial bodies to uses that are exclusively for peaceful purposes. Considerable misconception surrounds Article IV, with many believing that the restrictions which apply to celestial bodies extend to the whole of outer space. Military use is in fact the prime motive behind space research, and space has almost from the very beginning been used extensively for military purposes, such as reconnaissance and telecommunications, and will certainly be used in any armed hostilities involving intercontinental ballistic missiles and similar or related weapons. For this reason, the misconception surrounding Article IV may well be one of the factors contributing to (a) the argument that the word peaceful means non-aggressive, and not non-military, notwithstanding the clear precedents pointing to the contrary of the Antarctic Treaty and the numerous treaties in the field of nuclear co-operation for peaceful uses,[18] and (b) the refusal to have outer space properly defined and delimited, in case such delimitation may hamper future military activities.

Part IV is devoted to the study of the military use of outer space. Chapter 19 deals with the meaning of the term 'peaceful' especially in the context of Article IV of the 1967 Space Treaty, whilst Chapter 20 discusses the legality of using outer space for military purposes under both general international law, and relevant international agreements.

Finally, Part VI covers various aspects of the commercial uses of outer space, an area of ever-increasing importance. Chapters 21 and 22 deal respectively from the international law point of view with the use of communications satellites and remote sensing satellites, two of the most important commercial uses of outer space.

Article VI of the 1967 Space Treaty introduces the novel concept that States are responsible for 'national activities in outer space', not only those carried on by governmental agencies, but also those by non-governmental entities. The latter are further to be subject to 'authorization and continuing supervision by the appropriate State Party'. The exact meaning and scope of Article VI are far from clear. A similar provision is found in the Moon Treaty. Liability for damage caused by space objects is covered separately by Article VII of the Space Treaty, and of course much more comprehensively in the 1972 Liability Convention. Chapters 23 and 24 deal with two different aspects of the problems of responsibility and liability from the standpoint of both general international law and the relevant UN space treaties, namely, launch activities, and national, especially non-governmental, space activities. Finally, in an overall survey of the whole field of international space law, Chapter 25 seeks to pinpoint, particularly from the perspective of the future commercial development of space, those areas of law which require clarification, improvement, and further regulation, and thus stand in need of new treaties.

---

[18] Cf. Ch. 4, esp. ss. IV ff.

To conclude this collection of studies, there has been included, as an Epilogue, an essay on the Contribution of Air and Space Law to the Development of International Law. In it, among other things, are set out certain lessons that can be learned from the observation of the birth and growth of air and space law in the twentieth century, lessons which may well assist us in our understanding of the nature, and the conditions for the future development, of the international legal system as a whole.

PART I

INTERNATIONAL LAW AND SPACE LAW

1

In the Beginning: the International Geophysical Year

In the 1956 volume of *Current Legal Problems*, the annual publication of the Faculty of Laws of London University's University College, I published, a year before Sputnik I, a paper on 'Recent Developments in Air Law'[1], the first part of which on Airspace Sovereignty and Earth Satellites may serve as a suitable introduction to this collection of studies in international space law which I have written over the years. It appears as follows with minor adjustments.

Among recent developments of especial interest in the field of air law—I wrote in 1956—is that of high altitude or interplanetary flight. It seems that, with the announcement by the United States Government on 29 July 1955,[2] and by the Soviet Government four days later,[3] of their respective intentions to launch artificial earth satellites during the forthcoming International Geophysical Year (1 July 1957–31 Dec. 1958),[4] a consideration of the legal aspects of space flight should no longer be postponed.[5]

I. The Principle of Airspace Sovereignty

Article 1(1) of the 1944 Chicago Convention on International Civil Aviation[6] provides:

The contracting States recognize that every State has complete and exclusive sovereignty over the airspace above its territory.

---

[1] 9 *CLP* 1956 pp. 208–20. Reproduced by kind permission of Sweet & Maxwell Ltd.

[2] By Dr Detler Bronk, President of the National Academy, and Dr A. Waterman, Director of the National Science Foundation, on behalf of President Eisenhower. The existence of an 'Earth Satellite Vehicle Programme' was first disclosed by the US Secretary of Defense Forrestal on 30 Dec. 1946.

[3] By Professor Leonid Sedlor, Head of the Commission on Interplanetary Communications, the existence of which was made public in April 1955.

[4] Cf. Sir Harold Spencer Jones, 'The Internatianal Geophysical Year', 53 *The Listener* (1955), p. 231.

[5] The writer wishes to acknowledge his indebtedness to Professor H. S. W. Massey, M.Sc., Ph.D., FRS, of University College, London, who kindly read this section and made a number of valuable comments. Naturally the writer alone is responsible for the views expressed and any error which may herein be found.

[6] 15 UNTS, p. 295.

Almost identical provisions are to be found in the various multipartite treaties on civil aviation which the Convention has superseded.[7] Today, there appears to be little doubt that this principle, repeatedly affirmed in treaties and in municipal statutes,[8] is declaratory of existing international law. The territorial sphere of a State's jurisdiction, therefore, extends upwards into space and downwards to the centre of the earth, the whole in the shape of an inverted cone. This jurisdiction, it must be emphasized, is *ratione loci* in respect of the airspace and not *ratione materiae* in respect of the air therein.[9]

This territorial jurisdiction over the airspace is dependent upon a State's sovereignty over the subjacent territory, including the territorial sea.[10] In relation to the territorial sea, the International Court of Justice, in the *Anglo-Norwegian Fisheries Case* held: 'It is the land which confers upon the coastal State a right to the waters of its coasts.'[11] It may be said that, similarly, it is a State's sovereignty over a portion of the earth's surface which confers upon it a right to the superincumbent airspace. It follows that there can be no airspace sovereignty over *terra nullius* or the high seas,[12] nor any claim to sovereignty over the airspace above a State's vessels[13] on, or aircraft[14] over, the high seas, or above its diplomatic premises or warships in foreign countries.[15] On the whole, it would appear that, where the frontiers of a State are not disputed, the delimitation of the lateral limits of its airspace does not present any unusual difficulty.[16]

As to the upper limits of a State's territorial sovereignty, it seems, however, that there is considerable uncertainty. In view of the general acceptance of the

---

[7] Convention on the International Regulation of Aerial Navigation, Paris, 1919, Art 1(1) (11 LNTS, p. 173); Ibero-American Convention on Aerial Navigation, Madrid, 1926, Art. 1(1) (Hudson, 3 *Int. Leg.*, p. 2019); Convention on Commercial Aviation, Havana, 1928, Art. 1 (Hudson, 4 *Int. Leg.*, p. 2354).

[8] See E. Nys, 'Droit et aérostats,' 34 *RDILC* (1902), p. 501.

[9] This distinction was made already in 1906 by Westlake, 21 *Annuaire de l'Institut* (1906), p. 298, but confusion persists even today.

[10] Cf. Havana Convention, 1928, Art 1(2). See also Paris Convention, 1919, Art. 1(2); Chicago Convention 1944, Art. 2.

[11] *ICJ Rep. 1951*, p. 116, at p. 133.

[12] Cf. Art. 12 of the Chicago Convention, 1944. Limitation of space does not permit the discussion here of the legal problems raised by air defence identification zones such as those established by Canada and the US.

[13] Cf. rejection of the theory that vessels are floating parts of a State's territory in *Chung Chi Cheung* v. *The King* [1939] A.C. 160.

[14] The cumulative effect of Arts. 3 and 4 of the Italian Code of Navigation of 1942 suggests an assertion of Italian sovereignty over airspace above Italian ships on, and Italian aircraft over, the high seas, or over *terra nullius*. It is submitted that such a claim of sovereignty would be without foundation in international law, as the entire airspace above the high seas must be regarded as free and that above *terra nullius* as being without a sovereign. Cf. similarly, the draft Chilean Aeronautical Code, 1947, Arts. 4 and 5.

[15] Cf. *Asylum Case*, *ICJ Rep. 1950*, p. 266.

[16] See further B. Cheng, 'The Right to Fly', 42 *Grotius Society Transactions* (1958), p. 99; Cheng, *The Law of International Air Transport*, pp. 120–2. A curious case is Greece which claims a territorial sea of three miles, but a territorial airspace seaward of 10 miles.

principle of a State's exclusive and complete sovereignty over its airspace, it is not intended here to reopen the discussion, which reached its height at the turn of the century, whether airspace above a State's territory is free to all nations,[17] or whether it is free but subject to the right of self-preservation of the subjacent State,[18] or whether it is merely limited to a 'territorial belt' like the territorial sea[19] or subject to the right of innocent passage by aircraft of foreign States.[20] The problems at issue are, on the one hand, the meaning and the upper limits of airspace, and, on the other hand, the status of the space beyond.

II. The Definition of Airspace

As to the meaning of the term airspace, it would appear that, in the absence of any legal definition or authoritative interpretation, the rule of interpretation enunciated by the Permanent Court of International Justice in the *Eastern Greenland* case (1932) may well be followed. In that case, the Court was asked to interpret the meaning of the term Greenland used in various diplomatic documents, and it held: 'The natural meaning of the term is its geographical meaning'.[21] The natural meaning of the term airspace in the Paris and Chicago Conventions is, therefore, its geophysical meaning, denoting the space where air is to be found.

Here it is worth remembering that 'air is a mixture of gases and is not a chemical compound.'[22] It is a physical phenomenon rather than a scientific definition with fixed properties. Even though half of the air in the earth's atmosphere may be below a height of 5.8 kilometres,[23] 'there is plenty of evidence for the existence of highly rarefied air at four hundred miles above sea level'.[24] For that reason, Professor J. C. Cooper's statement that 'above 60 miles beyond the earth's surface (approximately 100 kilometres) what we term a vacuum exists',[25] and his conclusion that 'the "airspace" is part of the lower atmospheric region',[26] are both open to question.

---

[17] Cf. E Nys, 'Droit et aérostats', 34 *RDILC* (1902), p. 501, or 19 *Annuaire de l'Institut* (1902), p. 86; 21 ibid. (1906), p. 297.

[18] Cf. P. Fauchille, 'Le domain aérien et le régime juridique des aérostats', 8 *RGDIP* (1901), p. 414; 19 *Annuaire de l'Institut* (1902), p. 19; 21 ibid. (1906), p. 321.

[19] Cf. for: instance, Hans Oppikofer, 'International Commercial Aviation and National Administration', *Enquiries into the Economic, Administrative and Legal Situation of International Air Navigation*, LoNP, 1930, No. C.339, M.139, 1930, VIII, p. 112. Peru, at one time, declared the freedom of the air above 3,000 metres.

[20] Cf. Westlake, Corsi, 21 *Annuaire de l'Institut* (1901), pp. 299–300.

[21] A/B 53, p. 52.

[22] J. R Partington, 'Atmosphere', 2 *Ency. Brit.* (1945), p. 640.

[23] Ibid, p. 641.

[24] P. White, 'Atmosphere', 1 *Chambers' Ency.* (1950), p. 740.

[25] 'High Altitude Flight and National Sovereignty', 4 *ILQ* (1951), p. 411, at p. 415; or 13 *IATA Bulletin* (June 1951), p. 46.

[26] 4 *ILQ* (1951), p. 414.

The argument in support of this restrictive interpretation of the term 'airspace', as used in the Paris Convention, 1919, and in subsequent international treaties, is based on the definition of aircraft in the Annexes to the Paris Convention, 1919,[27] and the Chicago Convention, 1944,[28] as 'all machines which can derive support in the atmosphere from the reactions of the air'. According to this interpretation, airspace is limited to 'the region of space where the "air" was present in . . . sufficient quantities to support flight in the balloons or airplanes which were regulated by the Convention'.[29] The same restrictive interpretation was adopted by Mr Oscar Schachter, Director of the General Legal Division of the United Nations Office of Legal Affairs, in a paper read at the Hayden Planetarium Symposium on Space Travel.[30] This interpretation of the term airspace, which fixes the upper limits of airspace by the maximum altitude attainable by aircraft, besides being highly artificial, raises many difficulties. First of all, the strict definition of aircraft as used in the Annexes to the Paris and Chicago Conventions, adopted subsequently to the respective Conventions, need not necessarily have been exclusive in the minds of the framers of the Conventions, if it were present in their minds at all. Other international agreements[31] and a number of municipal statutes[32] use definitions of the term 'aircraft' which may well be extended to cover flying machines, such as rockets[33], which do not depend on the 'lift' from the air. Secondly, is the maximum altitude envisaged in this restrictive interpretation, the theoretical height which an aircraft, even at the drawing board stage, may attain or that actually reached? Finally, as has been pointed out in a different context, 'the maximum altitudes attained by aircraft are debatable for two reasons: (1) they are broken every month or so, and (2) the exact figures are usually classified as security information.'[34] It thus seems inconceivable that the

---

[27] 4 *ILQ* (1951), p. 413.　　　　　　　　　　　　　　　　[28] Annexes 6, 7, and 8.

[29] Cooper, loc.cit. in n. 25, 17 above, p. 413.

[30] 'Legal Aspects of Space Travel', 11 *Journal of the British Interplanetary Society* (1952), p. 14: The most reasonable rule would seem to be one that defines the airspace in terms of the atmospheric elements necessary to ' "lift" aircraft.'

[31] E.g., Pan-American Sanitary Convention, Havana, 1924, Art. 2 defines aircraft as 'any vehicle which is capable of transporting persons or things through the air, including aeroplanes, seaplanes, gliders, helicopters, airships, balloons and captive balloons' (Hudson, 2 *Int. Leg.*, p. 1308).

[32] E.g., US: Civil Aeronautics Act, 1939, s. 1, 1(4): ' "Aircraft" means any contrivance now known or hereafter invented, used, or designed for navigation of or flight in the air'; French Aerial Navigation Law of 31 May 1924, Art. 1: 'For the purpose of this law, aircraft means any vehicle which is able to rise or to fly in the air.' See similarly, draft Argentine Aeronautics Code, 1951, Art. 35; Canadian Aeronautical Act, 1919, s. 6(1); Dominican Civil Aerial Navigation Law, 1949, Art. 3; Egyptian Air Navigation Regulation, 1935, Art. 1(2); Guatemalan Civil Aviation Law, 1949, Art. 9. The Brazilian Air Code of 1939 (Art. 18) does not even limit the definition to machines capable of flight in the air; it includes all machines capable of flight and navigation in *space* as such. Cf. also the draft Chilean Aeronautical Code, 1947, Art. 10.

[33] Cf. e.g. O. G. Sutton, *The Science of Flight* (1949), ch. 6: 'The Ultimate Flying Machine', pp. 163 ff.

[34] M. W. Rosen and R. B. Snodgrass, 'The High Altitude Sounding Rocket', in R. L. F. Boyd and M. J. Seaton (ed.), *Rocket Exploration of the Upper Atmosphere* (1946), p. 46, at p. 47.

framers of the Paris and Chicago Conventions, in using the term airspace, wished to link it with such an uncertain quantity and to fix its limits by the maximum altitude attainable by aircraft or that they wished to 'peg' the upper reaches of their national territory to such a variable factor as the latest official altitude record. If, indeed, there is a correlation between the term airspace and the strict definition of aircraft as used in the Annexes to the Paris and Chicago Conventions, the connecting link consists in, it is submitted, the word 'atmosphere' used in the definition and not in its reference to the 'lift' to be derived from the air. Airspace, or the atmosphere, is the frame of reference by which aircraft is defined but is not itself delimited by it. To argue otherwise would be to put the cart before the horse.

The correct interpretation of the term airspace appears, therefore, to be still the natural one of the region where air is to be found, whether ozonized, ionized or—rarefied! In other words, airspace is synonymous with atmosphere, including all its various layers, the troposphere, the ozonosphere, the ionosphere, and, to some extent, the exosphere.[35] Support for his view may be drawn from both international agreements and municipal statutes. In fact, the Paris Convention itself considered airspace as equivalent to atmospheric space,[36] and the terminology of the Paris Convention in this respect has been adopted in a number of municipal statutes.[37]

[35] See S. K. Mitra, *The Upper Atmosphere* (1952), pp. 2–3. In other methods of classification, the stratosphere takes the place of the ozonosphere. Cf. G. P. Kuiper (ed.), *The Atmospheres of the Earth and Planets* (1949), Introduction pp. 2, 8. See further methods of classification, M. Nicolet, 'Dynamic Effects in the High Atmosphere', in G. P. Kuiper (ed.), *The Earth as a Planet* (1954), pp. 644 ff.

[36] In Art. 1(1) of the Paris Convention, 1919, the French and Italian equivalents of the term airspace were respectively '*espace atmosphérique*' and '*spazio atmosferico*', in other words, atmospheric space. The Spanish text of the Havana Convention, 1926, used the term '*espacio aéreo*', while that of the Madrid Convention, 1926, referred to sovereignty over the '*espacio atmosférico*'. Although no official text of the Chicago Convention has yet been agreed upon in French and Spanish, the Lexicon published by the International Civil Aviation Organization considers as the French and Spanish equivalents of the term 'airspace', '*espace aérien*', or '*espace atmosphérique*', and '*espacio aéreo*'. Airspace, atmospheric space, *espace aérien, espace atmosphérique, espacio aéreo, espacio atmosférico*, and *spazio atmosferico* must, therefore, be considered as synonymous and identical.

[37] Most municipal statutes follow the formulation of Art. 1(1) of the Paris Convention. The following States used the term airspace: Chile, Costa Rica, Dominican Republic, Egypt, Guatemala, Honduras, Iran, US. The following States use the term atmospheric space: Bolivia, Colombia, Ecuador, Nicaragua, Spain. The United Kingdom Air Navigation Act, 1920, reaffirmed national sovereignty to the superincumbent 'air', while the Brazilian Air Code of 1938 referred simply to the 'space' above Brazilian territory. The draft Argentine Aeronautical Code of 1951 asserts sovereignty over the space above Argentine territory, 'unlimited in height', but the official commentary of this particular provision considers that it is in accordance with both the Paris Convention, Art. 1(1), and the Chicago Convention, Art. 1(1).

III. The Upper Limits of Airspace

Having arrived at the conclusion that terrestrial airspace is considered by States in both international agreements and their municipal laws to be in law synonymous with the earth's atmosphere, the question arises as to its exact upper limit. Here it would seem that geophysicists are still uncertain of the answer, although their knowledge of the upper atmosphere has in recent years considerably increased.[38] It appears that on the fringe of the earth's atmosphere there lies a belt of considerable thickness where, because of the decreasing density of the atmosphere with increasing height, particles travelling upwards become more and more free from the risk of collision with one another. Many of these particles which soar upwards quickly turn about under the influence of gravity and fall into denser layers of the atmosphere below,[39] whilst others manage to escape into outer space.[40] The scene is not unlike that of the spray from an ornamental fountain, with some lighter particles of water being carried away in the breeze while the bulk return to the basin below. The middle of this effervescent region is taken as the base of the exosphere. One authority puts this baseline or 'critical level' at between 500 and 1,000 kilometres above the earth's surface,[41] whilst another at between 450 and 550 kilometres.[42] But, of course, it is to be understood that this baseline or 'critical level' is not a sharp or well-defined line in the ordinary sense of the term, its height may vary considerably according to the regions and the seasons, and its determination may involve a certain amount of arbitrariness. Indeed, this question appears to be still so highly controversial among geophysicists that some of the most eminent among them are of the opinion that it is scientifically impossible to trace the outer limit of the earth's atmosphere, if such an outer limit exists at all from the scientific standpoint.

The matter appears, therefore, supremely vague, and there can be no doubt that an international agreement fixing a precise upper limit to airspace sovereignty at a definite height, be it 100, 200, 500, or 1,000 kilometres, would be infinitely preferable. But such an agreement requires the consent of the States concerned and would be binding only on those States which have agreed to it. In view of the numerous difficulties and delays encountered by States in their efforts to reach agreement on the much more mature and well-established subject of the inner and outer limits of the territorial sea, once thought to be the

---

[38] See e.g. G. P. Kuiper (ed.). *The Atmospheres of the Earth and Planets* (1949); S. K. Mitra, *The Upper Atmosphere* (1952); G. P. Kuiper (ed.), *The Earth as a Planet* (1954); R. L. F. Boyd and M. J. Seaton (ed.), *Rocket Exploration of the Upper Atmosphere* (1954).

[39] Lyman Spitzer, Jr., 'The Terrestrial Atmosphere Above 300 km', in Kuiper, op. cit. (1949) in n. 38 above, p. 213, at p. 222.

[40] Ibid., pp. 241 ff.

[41] Ibid., p. 223. Cf. Boyd and Seaton, op. cit. in n. 38 above, and Mitra, op. cit., ibid.

[42] M. Nicolet, 'Dynamic Effects in the High Atmosphere', in Kuiper, op cit. (1954) in n. 38 above, p. 645.

ripest topic for international codification, the chances of an early international agreement on the upper limit of the territorial airspace would appear to
be more than remote. Perforce, the only criterion available and acceptable is
the physical limit of the earth's atmosphere, however uncertain and ill defined
this may be. A more precise knowledge of this subject will, moreover, certainly
result from the many experiments to be carried out in the forthcoming
International Geophysical Year.

On this basis, the opinion may be ventured that, from the legal point of
view, the upper limit of airspace, and hence of territorial sovereignty, should
coincide with the above-mentioned critical level in the earth's atmosphere, if
this should ultimately prove amendable to scientific calculation and ascertainment, while the exosphere, the outer limit of which appears to be even
more uncertain, may perhaps be regarded as a contiguous zone, by adopting
an analogy with maritime law. Assuming the height of this critical level to be
1,000 kilometres, it does not seem, however, that this assertion of State sovereignty is excessive if it is remembered that the mean radius of the earth is more
than six times this distance, i.e., 6,371.221 kilometres.[43] In other words, the
height of a State's airspace sovereignty would be less than one sixth of the
depth of its subterranean sovereignty.[44]

IV. The Legal Status of Outer Space

On the other hand, there seems to be no possible justification for recognizing
any extension a State's sovereignty beyond the earth's atmosphere into outer
space, except through effective occupation of another planet or star or parts
thereof, in virtue of a new rule, yet to be established, of general international
law or treaty law. The effect of the latter will, however, be limited only to States
consenting thereto. The view has been put forward by one writer that the
'upper limit of sovereignty is so to speak determined by the law of gravity',
and is to be found at the point where the earth's attraction stops.[45] The following quotation from a popular work on *Interplanetary Flight* by an eminent
writer affords a ready answer to this proposition:

Man is still essentially a two-dimensional creature . . . It is, therefore, perhaps not
surprising that some very curious ideas persist about gravity—one of the commonest
being that it ceases, more or less abruptly, at a definite distance from the earth . . .
Strictly speaking, no point in the Universe is 'beyond the earth's gravity'

---

[43] C. W. Allen, *Astrophysical Quantities* (1955), p. 105.

[44] For subsequent developments, see Ch. 14 below, esp. s. X: The Limit between Outer Space
and Territorial Space.

[45] Ming-Min Peng, 'Le vol à haute altitude et l'article 1 de la Convention de Chicago, 1944',
12 *Revue du Barreau de la Province de Quebec* (1952), p. 277; or 6 *RFDA* (1952), p. 390.

which decreases as the inverse square of the distance and so becomes zero only at infinity.[46]

In fact, any claim to State sovereignty in outer space, unrelated in its location to the earth itself, raises formidable difficulties, if it is remembered that the earth is rotating at the velocity of .465 km/s at the equator,[47] at the same time, it is moving round the sun at 29.77 km/s,[48] and, in addition to these, it is sharing with the sun and the rest of the solar system a velocity of about 20 km/s relative to the neighbouring stars in the general movement of the solar system towards a point in the constellation Hercules.[49]

In contrast to outer space as such, terrestrial airspace, by reason of the earth's atmosphere forming part and parcel of our planet and rotating with it, constitutes a fixed adjunct to a nation's territory and can be considered to be an integral part of it.

For these reasons, outer space must be regarded as free. Whilst a State may claim personal or quasi-territorial jurisdiction over individuals or vehicles possessing its nationality travelling in outer space, it cannot claim territorial sovereignty over any portion thereof, unless a contrary rule is, at some future date, established in international law either by treaty or as a matter of general international law. The freedom of outer space is thus closely analogous to that of the high seas. On the basis of the same analogy, it might perhaps be argued that a State would have a similar right to prevent hovering outside its airspace,[50] especially in the fringe region, the right of hot pursuit into,[51] and the right of self-defence against any unlawful attack[52] from, outer space.

V. Artificial Satellites and Space Travel

It follows from the conclusions so far reached that a State would at any time be at liberty to launch rockets, artificial satellites, space stations or space ships from its own territory, *terra nullius* or the high seas into the atmospheric space above these regions or into outer space. As long as these instruments or machines can be projected into their extraterrestrial orbits or paths without passing through the atmospheric space of any foreign State, no serious problem of international law would seem to arise directly from such activities.[53] On the other hand, if it is proposed, as seems to be the present United States

---

[46] A. C. Clarke (1950), p. 7.
[47] C. W. Allen, op. cit. in n. 43 above, p. 105: v = 46511 cm/s.　　　　　　　[48] Ibid.
[49] See Harold Jeffreys, 'Earth', 7 *Ency. Brit.* (1955), p. 830, at p. 831.
[50] Cf. G. Schwarzenberger, 1 *International Law* (1949), pp. 159 ff. on hovering in maritime law.
[51] See the case of *The I'm Alone* (1933, 1935), 2 *RIAA*, p. 1609.
[52] See Cheng, *General Principles of Law*, pp. 77 ff.
[53] The Soviet plan, announced in April 1955, was to build a space station which would revolve round the earth beyond the terrestrial atmosphere.

plan,[54] to launch the satellites into an orbit two or three hundred miles from the surface of the earth, then it almost becomes inevitable that these satellites will travel through the airspace of States situated along their orbits. If this were the case, the tacit or express consent of those States the airspace of which is traversed will be required in order that there may not be even a technical violation of their sovereignty.[55]

Express consent or an international agreement would naturally eliminate any doubt as to the right of passage. The question is, however, to what extent, in international law, tacit consent may be inferred. In these days when national frontiers are heavily draped by various types of curtains, it may be worth remembering that the world did once, for a relatively short spell, enjoy an extremely liberal regime in the matter of transit and communication. During the second half of the nineteenth century, the requirement of passports for entry and exit of nationals and foreigners alike was rapidly dropped by one country after another,[56] although this was reintroduced in an even more rigorous manner after the outbreak of the First World War. Having regard to this, it might perhaps be said that, to the extent that it is not expressly prohibited by international law[57] or by the municipal law of the country concerned,[58] the entry of foreigners or objects from a foreign State is tacitly permitted. Thus in the early days of aviation, foreign aircraft were frequently allowed freedom of passage without let or hindrance.[59] Even today, meteorological balloons, which technically fall under the definition of aircraft,[60]

[54] As explained by Dr Bronk and Dr Waterman on 29 July 1955, and subsequently amplified in Brussels by Professor M. Nicolet, Executive Secretary of the International Committee of Scientists, co-ordinating the activities of the International Geophysical Year.

[55] An interesting point was raised in the *Trail Smelter Case* (1938, 1941), 3 *RIAA*, p. 1905, where the emission of smoke from a Canadian factory which caused substantial damage in the United States, besides being a nuisance in international law, constituted an infringement of the sovereignty of the United States. The tribunal, however, considered that it was beyond its jurisdiction to decide this issue (p. 1932).

[56] Cf. Egidio Reale, 'Le problème des passeports', 50 Hague *Recueil* (1934), p. 89, at pp. 105 ff.

[57] If earth satellites can be considered as aircraft, then Art. 8 of the Chicago Convention, 1944, prohibiting the flying of a pilotless aircraft into a foreign country without the latter's permission would be applicable. The various types of artificial earth satellites details of which have so far been released do not appear, however, to fall within the definition of aircraft in the Annexes to the Chicago Convention; cf. n. 28 above. Cf. also *Trail Smelter Case*, loc. cit. in nn. 55 above, and 65 below.

[58] Cf. the more liberal definition of aircraft in many municipal statutes, n. 32 above.

[59] See 38 *Clunet* (1911), pp. 1152–3, concerning German balloons carrying officers and photographic apparatus which flew freely over Belgium and the Netherlands in 1911.

[60] Cf. nn. 28 and 32 above. They would fall outside the definition in those cases where municipal statutes incorporate in the definition either the element of navigability (e.g., Canada, Chile, Finland, US) or the capability of being used as a means of transport (e.g., Argentina, Brazil, Finland). The second element may, however, be liberally interpreted to include meteorological instruments.

Indeed, some of the meteorological balloons, launched from various parts of the world by the US in 1956 in its 'Operation Moby Dick', and subsequently described in a United States Note (8 Feb. 1956) as 'miniature satellites', measured in diameter from 30 feet to 120 feet, and the larger ones among them were capable of carrying a payload of 1,500 lbs. Moreover, the course of their flight round the world, though not truly controllable, was fairly predictable, thanks to the regular

frequently drift into foreign countries and Hertzian waves are constantly being directed at a foreign State or beamed through its atmosphere. It is true that there have been protests against the release of balloons from foreign countries and against foreign broadcasts, but essentially these protests relate to the contents of the balloons or the substance of the broadcasts rather than to any technical violation of airspace.[61]

The view may, therefore, perhaps be ventured that, provided the intention to launch the artificial satellites, together with all relevant details, is communicated well in advance to all States concerned and to be overflown, and no objection is raised thereto, a tacit consent may probably be inferred.[62] The announced intention of the United States to make known beforehand the wavelength of the radio instruments to be carried in the artificial satellites and to make available to the world all the data to be gathered from the experiment,[63] together with the readiness of the Soviet Union expressed three days later to co-operate in the United States project,[64] may be taken as an indication that perhaps no insuperable difficulty will be encountered in this direction.

But, insofar as the State from which pilotless aircraft (including balloons), intercontinental ballistic missiles, artificial satellites or space vehicles are launched is concerned, whether by a government or by private individuals, a special point must be remembered. This is that 'a State owes at all times a duty to protect other States against injurious acts by individuals from within its jurisdiction,'[65] and *a fortiori* must refrain from such acts itself.[66] It must therefore ensure that its own aircraft, rockets, artificial satellites, or space ships, whether travelling within or outside the earth's atmosphere, must not be injurious for foreign States or their nationals,[67] and it must also ensure the same

pattern of behaviour of the jet streams in the earth's lower atmosphere. The Soviet Union, which did not object to the passage of conventional meteorological balloons, protested (4 Feb. 1956) against the flight of this type of outsized weather balloons, which carried photographic and radio equipments, as well as other meteorological instruments, over its territory. See further the next two footnotes.

[61] On the position of conventional meteorological balloons, outsized meteorological balloons like those described in the preceding n., and propaganda balloons, see further Ch. 2 below, and Cheng, 'The Right to Fly', 42 *Grotius Society Transactions* (1956), p. 99.

[62] The United States undertaking of 8 Feb. 1956, in reply to the Soviet protest of 4 Feb., mentioned above in n. 60, at least 'provisionally . . . to avoid the launching of additional balloons which, on the basis of known data, might transit the USSR' shows that a mere Press release (8 Jan. 1956), which has not been communicated to foreign Powers, intimating such intention, would not be a sufficient basis to infer acquiescence, even though such an announcement *urbi et orbi* has raised no immediate objection from any State. The statement of the US Secretary of State in a Press conference on 7 Feb. 1956 that the legal position was extremely obscure can only be taken as an euphemistic admission of a possible or technical breach of Soviet airspace sovereignty.

[63] See *Keesing's* (1955), 14337.

[64] M. Khrushchev, in Moscow, on 1 Aug. 1955 (ibid.).

[65] *Trail Smelter Case* (1938, 1941), 3 *RIAA*, p. 1905, at p. 1963.

[66] See Cheng, *General Principles of Law*, pp. 83 ff.

[67] In the explanatory section of the US announcement of 29 July 1955, it was stated: 'The satellite itself will orbit around the earth for a period of days, gradually circling back into the upper atmosphere, where it will eventually disintegrate harmlessly.'

by legislation or otherwise in regard to those launched by private individuals from within its jurisdiction. Any failure in this duty would entail responsibility under international law. With this safeguard, it may perhaps be hoped that, as in the early days of aeronautics, astronautics, at this experimental stage, may yet enjoy a short spell of freedom from frontier restrictions, at least until it becomes of direct military or commercial significance.

2

International Law and High Altitude
Flights: Balloons, Rockets,
and Man-made Satellites*

I. Introduction

'A mystery wrapped in an enigma,' Sir Winston Churchill's aphorism about
Russia, was recently borrowed by the United States Secretary of State John
Foster Dulles to describe the position of high altitude flights in international
law. This was at a news conference[1] held two days after the United States had
received a protest from the Soviet Union against the flight of balloons,
released by United States military organs and other organizations, over Soviet
territory.

As the United States reply of 8 February 1956 recalled, details of a United
States Air Force meteorological survey, which has already been in progress for
two years and commonly known as 'Moby Dick', had been given in a
Department of Defense News Release on 8 January 1956. Large plastic balloons, 'in effect miniature "satellites",' the News Release (Nos. 9–56) stated,
'will carry meteorological instruments, including cameras and radio equipment to record and telemeter atmospheric information' above 30,000 feet.
Apparently, some 4,000 balloons had already been released, mostly in the
United States, but, with the co-operation of other governments, also from
Brazil, Panama, Scotland, Japan and Okinawa. The announcement ended by
saying that additional research stations would be opened in Europe, Alaska
and Hawaii during 1956. A corresponding announcement was made in Oslo
on 3 February 1956, giving details of forthcoming Norwegian participation in
an international programme of meteorological research, which included the
use of large balloons carrying 400 lbs. of instruments, including photographic
apparatus, round the earth's surface at an altitude of 80,000 to 90,000 feet.[2]

* First published in 6 *ICLQ* (1957), pp. 487–505; reproduced in *Senate Symposium* (1958), pp.
184–98, and *Senate Symposium* (1961), pp. 141–55, where unfortunately the numbering of the
footnotes was altered and the footnote numbers, together with all the cross-references, became
completely mixed up. Reproduced from the *ICLQ* by kind permission of the British Institute of
International and Comparative Law.

[1] The writer is indebted to the US Information Service, London (USIS) for an extended report
of the news conference, as well as other relevant documents.

[2] *The Times* (London), 4 Feb. 1956.

Since it was estimated that the balloons would most likely land their instruments somewhere in the Pacific area, they were evidently intended to take advantage of the powerful high altitude jet streams which regularly blow in a west-east direction in the Northern Hemisphere and expected to traverse the airspace of countries between Norway and the Pacific.

The European part of the programme was, however, quickly cut short by the Soviet protest to the United States on 5 February 1956. This was followed by a further note of 18 February, in which the Soviet government charged the United States with attempted aerial photography of Soviet territory.[3] Meanwhile, protests to the United States government were sent by Albania, Bulgaria, the Communist Chinese Government, Czechoslovakia, the Eastern German Government, Hungary, Mongolia, Poland and Rumania, while the Soviet government protested also to the Federal German government and Turkey.[4] Representations were also made by Sweden to Norway and the United States.[5] In addition, some Eastern European countries lodged complaints against the United States with the Secretary-General of the United Nations and the European Office of the International Civil Aviation Organisation.

In their replies of 8 and 11 February respectively, both the United States and Turkey undertook, in view of the Soviet objection, to suspend provisionally the further release of meterological balloons which, on the basis of known data, might cross into Soviet territory. But Mr Dulles, in his Press conference on 7 February 1956, maintained that, although there was no clear rule of international law on the subject, the United States felt that it had the right to send these balloons. He said: 'We would be disposed to be respectful to the strong views of any country which was opposed to it . . . We would do this, not as a matter of their right but as a matter of decent, friendly relations.'

Soviet writers have not, however, been slow in pointing out that, in its official communications, the United States has not asserted any strict right of one State to fly such balloons into the airspace of another State.[6] Indeed, notwithstanding what has just been mentioned, the whole emphasis of Mr Dulles's

---

[3] This charge had previously been made verbally by Soviet spokesmen at a Press conference held in Moscow, on 9 Feb. 1956.

[4] See *Keesing's* (1955–5), 14723A.

[5] In its reply of 12 Mar. 1956 to the Swedish representation of 6 Mar. 1956, the US government referred to its previous announcement of 8 Jan. 1956, and stated that since early Feb. 1956, no balloons had been launched which might pass over Swedish territory. A State Department statement issued on 12 Mar. 1956, disclosed that 'the reply stated that the United States had carefully considered the objections of the Swedish Government and expressed [the] hope that the latter's concern had now been met' (USIS *DWB*, 13 Mar. 1956, p. 3).

As to the warning issued by the Austrian Minister of the Interior, see *The Times* (London), 6 Feb. 1956.

[6] A. Kislov and C. B. Krylov, 'State Sovereignty in Airspace', 3 *Int. Aff.* (Moscow, Mar. 1956), p. 35, at p. 43.

Press conference was on the obscurity of international law on the subject of high altitude flights by balloons and artificial satellites.[7]

This studied hesitancy on the part of the United States Secretary of State on the legal position may perhaps be interpreted as a euphemistic admission that the United States did not have an absolute right to fly these camera-carrying balloons over the territory of another State. The Soviet allusion to the possibility of the tables being turned, even though it was in respect of propaganda balloons,[8] probably did not pass unnoticed. Here it is worth pointing out that, because of the relative geographical position of the Soviet Union and the United States, the west-east direction of the jet streams in the Northern Hemisphere, and these jet streams being strongest in the North Pacific, the United States is in a much more vulnerable position than the Soviet Union in regard to balloon flights, whether for aerial reconnaissance or other purposes in time of peace or offensive operations in time of war.

The United States in fact had a foretaste of balloon warfare towards the end of the Second World War. In the period of a few months, some 900 to 1,000 Japanese paper balloons, armed with incendiary and anti-personnel bombs, reached the United States almost as far east as Detroit.[9] Yet these were much inferior to modern balloons which, made of low-cost polythene, measure, in the larger models, some 164 feet wide and 230 feet high, carry in their gondolas a payload of up to 1,500 lbs. and can easily circumnavigate the globe. The course of their flights round the world, while not truly controllable, is fairly predictable thanks to the regular pattern of behaviour of the jet streams which carry them forward at speeds varying from 50 to 300 miles an hour. From the military standpoint, their cost of a few thousand dollars is next to nothing compared with the $8 million for a B–52 jet bomber, and they share with ballistic missiles the inestimable advantage of not having to be manned. Both balloons and rockets will no doubt be adaptable for the delivery of the recently developed pocket-size thermonuclear weapons, once accuracy is achieved.[10] These considerations throw into perspective the more serious side of the diplomatic storm which raged round these balloons, in addition to the obvi-

[7] E.g., 'The question of the ownership of the upper air is a disputable question, and also of the ether above the air'; 'The legal position is quite obscure'; 'What the legal position is, I wouldn't feel in a position to answer, because I do not believe that the legal position has even been codified'; 'There is no clear international law on the subject'. Indeed, his first answer in this connection was: 'I wish I could tell you' what was the position under international law, of balloons and circling satellites. To be historically accurate, however, it should perhaps be mentioned that his reference to his international law 'getting a bit rusty' related to the position of radio broadcasts and not balloons, contrary to what a reading of the report in *The Times* (London) of 8 Feb. 1956, may suggest.

[8] Note of 5 Feb. 1956.

[9] See 'What the "Balloon Scare" Is All About' *The United States News and World Report* (17 Feb. 1956), p. 27.

[10] On 20 Feb. 1957, the United States Secretary of Defense Charles E. Wilson announced that 'nuclear capability will . . . be incorporated into our surface-to-air defence systems, including Nike-Hercules and Talos', i.e., two types of guided missile (USIS, 20 Feb. 1957).

ous desire to exploit the incident for the purpose of political propaganda and discrediting President Eisenhower's 'open sky' plan of aerial inspection,[11] and these considerations must be taken into account in gauging the general attitude of States—which, after all, are the law-makers in the society of nations—towards the law of high altitude and space flights.

As regards space vehicles, the ultimate instrument of robot warfare, they will move freely in the upper atmosphere or outer space, while targets on the surface of the earth will revolve mechanically, inexorably and inescapably into their line of vision and fire. It is perhaps not surprising, therefore, to find that a recent publication in the Soviet Union, *Thoughts on Air Strategy*, ends with the reflection that: 'Today's giant air bases will become bomber cemeteries in a future war.'[12] The significance of this observation need hardly be stressed, as it is reputedly from the weighty pen of Grand Marshal Pavel F. Zhigarev, who was for many years Commander-in-Chief of the Soviet Air Force until he was transferred in January 1957, according to unconfirmed reports, to take charge of the Soviet airline Aeroflot.[13]

II. 'Flight Craft' and 'Flight Space'

What then is the position of high altitude flights by balloons, rockets and man-made satellites in international law? Consideration must first be given to the legal regime of the airspace and the outer space, which together may be called 'flight space',[14] while the term 'flight craft' may be applied to all devices capable of flying in 'flight space'.

The former term may, in this context, be preferable to airspace because flight may be conducted, or at least may shortly be conducted, in space where there is no air, or too little air to justify the use of the term airspace.[15] The

---

[11] Cf. 'Aerial Inspection Plan and Air Sovereignty', 24 *Geo. Wash. LR* (1956), p. 565.

[12] See 'The Last Weapon But One', 11 (3) *Aviation Week* (1956), p. 190; cf. also the remarks of Dr Wernher von Braun, development operations chief of the US Army Ballistic Missile Agency, to the Association of the US Army at Washington's Sheraton-Park Hotel, on 26 Oct. 1956,11 (12) *Interavia* (1956), p. 967: 'Satellites As Weapons'. See also F. I. Ordway, 'The Surface-to-Surface Missile, Today and Yesterday', ibid., p. 974, and F. Romano's paper read before the 7th International Astronautical Congress in Rome in Sept. 1956, *The Times* (London), 20 Sept. 1956.

[13] It is significant that the recent statement of the British government on defence, which announced the 'biggest changes in military policy ever made in normal times', pins its faith entirely on the development and use of ballistic missiles.

[14] See J. C. Cooper, *Air Law: Subject Matter, Terminology, Definition* (1951), p. 13; Alex Meyer, *Legal Problems of Flight into Outer Space* (1952), pp. 4 ff.

[15] Prof. Josef Kaplan, Chairman, US National Committee for the International Geophysical Year (IGY), disclosed, on 11 Sept. 1956, in a paper read at the Barcelona conference held to make final preparation for the IGY (reprinted, in part, under the title 'The IGY Rocket and Satellite Program', 11 (12) *Interavia* (1956), p. 933), that the first US earth satellites to be launched in 1957 from the east coast of Florida at Cape Canaveral will be spherical in shape, about 20 inches (50.8 cm.) in diameter, weighing approximately 21.5 pounds (9.8 kg.). It will revolve about the earth in an apparent latitude range of about 40 degrees of either side of the equator and will move in its

introduction of the term flight craft also appears justified, because a widely accepted definition, used, for instance, in the Annexes to the Paris Convention for the Regulation of Aerial Navigation of 1919 and the Chicago Convention on International Civil Aviation of 1944, limits aircraft to 'any machine which can derive support in the atmosphere from the reactions of the air.' This definition of aircraft *sensu stricto*, while it includes both instruments which are lighter than air, like balloons and airships, and those which are heavier than air, like gliders and aeroplanes, does not apply to devices such as rockets, earth satellites and other space vehicles. Even though they may perhaps fall within a *sensu lato* definition of aircraft as used in certain systems of municipal law,[16] the term flight craft has the advantage of obviating any ambiguity.

III. Physical Structure of Flight Space

Physically speaking, flight space, which means space in which flight is possible, denotes (a) airspace and (b) outer space. *Airspace* is space where air is normally to be found[17] and is, therefore, identical with atmospheric space. Each planet or star that possesses an atmosphere thus has its own airspace, each airspace being co-extensive with the corresponding atmosphere.[18] *Outer space*, which includes interplanetary and interstellar space, means space between the innumerable planets and stars, beyond their respective atmospheres where these exist.[19] The line of demarcation between terrestrial atmosphere and the outer space is at present still controversial among geophysicists, some of whom even doubt whether it can be defined at all, but views have been put forward that it lies roughly somewhere between 500 and 1,000 kilometres, i.e., between 310 and 620 miles.[20]

elliptical path from between 200–300 to perhaps 800–1,500 miles (320–485 to 1,300–2,400 km.) from the earth.

[16] See the writer's 'Recent Development in Air Law', 9 *CLP* (1956), p. 208, at pp. 211–212 [Ch. 1 above, s. II *in medio*].

[17] See ibid., pp. 210 ff. [s. II]; cf. *contra* J. C. Cooper, 'High Altitude Flight and National Sovereignty', 4 *ILQ* (1951), p. 411; see, however, his 'Legal Problems of Upper Space', *ASIL Proc* (1956), p. 85, at pp. 87 and 91.

[18] Cf. G. P. Kuiper (ed.), *The Atmospheres of the Earth and Planets* (1949).

[19] It is to be noted that in the 1967 Space Treaty and in subsequent treaties drawn up by the United Nations on outer space, the term 'outer space' is always used to denote not only interplanetary and interstellar space outside the earth and its atmosphere, but also all the celestial bodies which may be found in that vast region. Thus the 1967 Space Treaty uses constantly the phrase 'outer space, including the moon and other celestial bodies'; see further Ch. 9 below.

[20] See loc. cit. in n. 16 above, pp. 213 ff. [Ch. 1, s. III, above] and authorities cited therein. Lt. D. M. Draper, Jr., USNR, in his paper on 'Satellites and Sovereignty', believes that the margins are between 10,000 and 18,000 miles (*The JAG Journal* (Sept.–Oct. 1956), p. 23); Mr P. K. Roy, Head of the Legal Division of ICAO, is of the view that the margins are between 1,500 and 60,000 miles (*ASIL Proc.* (1956), p. 94). See further Ch. 14 below.

IV. Legal Status of Flight Space

As to its legal status, flight space may again be divided into (a) airspace and (b) outer space. *Airspace* itself may be sub-divided into (i) airspace above State territories (i.e., national airspace), (ii) airspace above the high seas, and (iii) airspace above *terra nullius*, both terrestrial and extraterrestrial. It does not seem disputed today that each of these three types of airspace partakes of the status of the subjacent surface territory.

As regards the legal status of *outer space*, it seems slightly dogmatic at present to assert that it 'is and must always be a *res extra commercium* incapable of appropriation'[21] like the high seas. It has, in this connection, to be remembered that the freedom of the high seas is not based on any transcendental logic. As Professor R. Y. Jennings said, 'any student of the history of international law knows that the establishment of the rule of the freedom of the seas was not brought about merely by Grotius's assertion of it, but also as the result of a long and complicated historical development which eventually made it the acceptable rule for maritime States at a time when they were strong enough to impose it.'[22] In other words, the freedom of the high seas is an agreed status, and no such consensus of States, which is, after all the real basis of international law,[23] can be said to exist in respect of outer space, inasmuch as States have hardly begun to bring their mind to bear on this problem.[24] No *lex lata* exits until a general consensus of States is achieved either tacitly or expressly. In the development of the law of outer space, States will be free to agree to any one of the following solutions: (a) fixing the upper limit of their national airspace below the upper limit of the terrestrial atmosphere, (b) extending the upper limit of national airspace beyond the upper limit of the terrestrial atmosphere to a given height in outer space, (c) declaring the whole or parts of extraterrestrial space *res nullius*, (d) treating the whole or parts of it as *res extra commercium*, or (e) creating an entirely new regime for an

---

[21] C, W. Jenks, 'International Law and Activities in Space', 5 *ICLQ* (1956), p. 97, at p. 104; Meyer, op. cit. in n. 14 above, p. 7; cf., however, Cooper, loc. cit. (1956) in n. 25, 17 above, pp. 90 ff.

[22] 'Some Aspects of the International Law of the Air', 75 Hague *Recueil* (1949), p. 509 at p. 584, n. 1.

[23] PCIJ: *The Lotus* (1927), Ser. A, No. 10, p. 18.

[24] A report on the subject was submitted to the 10th Session of the Assembly of ICAO, the membership of which now in 1957 numbers 70. The Assembly has yet to study the report. The Soviet Union and a number of the Eastern European countries are, however, not members of ICAO in 1957.

Cf. also the useful discussion on the subject by the American Society of International Law, *ASIL Proc.* (1956), pp. 84 ff.; the matter was also raised at the 47th Conference of the International Law Association meeting at Dubrovnik in 1956 and is being studied by the Air Law Committee of that Association. Furthermore, two papers were read, one by A. A. Cocca (Argentina), the other by A. G. Haley (USA), on the legal aspect of space travel at the 7th International Astronautical Congress held in Rome, Sept. 1956. See also W. R. Sheeley, 'Remarks on Space Law', 17 *Alabama Lawyer* (1956), p. 370.

unprecedented situation, since it may conceivably be questioned whether the void is a *res* at all, even though one can of course have *res incorporales*.

Whatever is said now would, therefore, be primarily conjectural or *de lege ferenda*. But in a system of international law which is essentially earth-bound and land-minded, in which both the territorial sea and the national airspace are regarded as mere appurtenances of land territory,[25] it may be expected that this traditional attitude, in addition to considerations of military security and commercial advantage, will strongly influence the views of States in the development of the law of extraterrestrial space.

On the one hand, strong exception will probably be taken to any floating spheres of territorial jurisdiction in outer space, independent of any reference to land territory. In particular, just as States at present do not recognize claims to a column of national airspace above ships or aircraft flying the flag of a State, they will probably also refuse to recognize claims to a zone of national or territorial space round a State's spacecraft. Witness the fear already expressed lest the potential enemy of a State 'squat' on its continental shelf.[26]

On the other hand, States may not perhaps object to treating other planets and stars, including their atmospheric space, as *res nullius*, capable of appropriation through effective occupation by individual States. There might even be general acquiescence in or agreement on the extension of national territory beyond the terrestrial atmosphere by the geometrical projection of the lateral limits of national airspace into outer space. However, in view of the fact that assertions of national sovereignty at extreme heights become increasingly less definable and meaningful even for States of continental dimensions, it may not be an unreasonable conjecture that States will subject the whole of outer space to the same regime as the high seas, with possibly an extended contiguous zone consisting of the outer fringes (the exosphere) of the terrestrial atmosphere.[27]

V. The Right to Fly

It is, however, not necessary to await a final definition of the status of every part of the flight space before determining the right of a State's flight craft to fly in it. In this regard, the entire flight space falls simply into two categories: (a) national flight space and (b) free flight space. *National flight space* is, at present, limited to terrestrial national airspace. *Free flight space* represents such portions of flight space as are not subject to national sovereignty and today

[25] See loc. cit. in n. 16 above, p. 209 [Ch. 1 above, s. I *in principio*], and cf. ICJ: *Anglo-Norwegian Fisheries Case, ICJ Rep. 1951,* p. 116, at p. 133, and PCA: *Grisbadarna Case* (1909), 1 *HCR,* p. 487, at p. 491.

[26] Cf. *Abu Dhabi Oil Arbitration* (1951), 1 *ICLQ (1952),*), p. 47, at p. 257.

[27] See loc. cit. in n. 16 above, p. 215 [Ch. 1 above, s. III *in fine*].

includes airspace above the high seas, airspace above *terra nullius* and extraterrestrial space; for, insofar as the right to fly is concerned, no difference exists between airspace above the high seas and airspace above *terra nullius*. Consequently, whether outer space is assimilated to the high seas (i.e., *res extra commercium*) or to *terra nullius*, the position would not be essentially different.

No State may, in time of peace, exercise jurisdiction over the flight craft bearing the nationality of another State in the whole of free flight space without the latter's consent, acquiescence or tolerance, except in the case of piracy *jure gentium*[28], or on the ground of self-defence.[29] Thus, if balloons, rockets, earth satellites and space vehicles are launched from national territory, *terra nullius* or the high seas, they are entirely free, from the standpoint of international law, to fly, at any altitude inside national airspace, airspace above the high seas or *terra nullius*, or in outer space, without requiring permission from foreign States.

On the other hand, because of the exclusive and complete sovereignty of the territorial State therein,[30] no flight craft may fly in, into or through a State's national flight space without its permission, acquiescence or tolerance, at no matter what altitude. Notwithstanding what Mr. Dulles said in his Press conference on 7 February 1956, it does not appear that this principle is today seriously disputed.

VI. Permission, Acquiescence, Tolerance and Estoppel

Permission by a State to fly in, into or through its national airspace may of course be given expressly or tacitly. Express permission raises no special problem.[31] The whole 'mystery' of the subject lies in determining the existence of tacit consent, and may be approached from three angles: (1) State flight craft, (2) civil flight craft and (3) duty of the State from which flights are made.

---

[28] Cf. *The Le Louis* (1817), 2 Dodson 210.

[29] See ibid., and Cheng, *General Principles of Law*, pp. 77–97.

[30] See loc. cit. in n. 16 above, pp. 208 ff. [Ch. 1 above].

[31] Cf. the joint programme of cosmic research by means of balloons started in October 1952, at Aligarth, in Uttar Pradesh, sponsored by the US National Geographical Society, India's Moslim University and the Bartol Foundation of the Franklin Institute in Philadelphia (USIS *DWB*, 12 Oct. 1952, p. 4), and the collaboration between Professor C. F. Powell of Bristol University and Soviet Physicists in balloon flying expeditions in the Arctic and in European Russia further south to carry out similar research into cosmic radiation, *The Times* (London), 5 Oct. 1955.

See also the Agreement between the United Kingdom and the United States of 21 July 1950, for the establishment in the Bahama Islands of a Long-Range Proving Ground for Guided Missiles, and subsequent agreements relating thereto, Cmd. 8109 (1950), Cmd. 8485 (1952), Cmd. 8881 (1953), Cmd. 9565 (1955), Cmd. 9810 (1956), Cmd. 9811 (1956). See further the writer's 'The Right to Fly,' 42 *Grotius Society Transactions* (1956), pp. 99–131.

A. State Flight Craft

What is a State flight craft and what is its position in international law? Article 3 of the Chicago Convention on International Civil Aviation, 1944, despite its ambiguity, affords some guidance. This Article provides, in its paragraph (b), that 'aircraft used in military, customs and police services shall be deemed to be State aircraft', and, in the next paragraph, that 'no State aircraft of a contracting State shall fly over the territory of another State or land thereon without authorization by special agreement or otherwise, and in accordance with the terms thereof.'

It is doubtful whether the above definition of State aircraft is intended to be exhaustive. The Air Transport Committee of the International Civil Aviation Organization, in its *Classification of International Civil Aircraft Operations*,[32] seemed to consider all government owned and operated aircraft as State aircraft. But if consideration is given to the corresponding provision in the Paris Convention on Aerial Navigation of 1919 (Article 30), the drafting history of the Chicago Convention,[33] the corresponding provision in the Chicago Interim Agreement on International Civil Aviation, 1944 (Article VIII, section 3), two subsequent multipartite conventions concluded under the auspices of the International Civil Aviation Organization,[34] and other provisions of the Chicago Convention itself (Articles 5, 77–9), it would appear that only aircraft engaged in military, customs and police services are to be considered as State aircraft, prohibited from flying into the national airspace of another country without special permission. Other aircraft, even belonging to or operated by the State, are considered as civil aircraft and assimilated to private aircraft insofar as any rights and privileges which private aircraft may enjoy,[35] without prejudice, however, to any privileges and immunities which may inure to them as State property.[36]

On the basis of this interpretation, the regime established by the Chicago Convention is not substantially different from that under customary international law. Thus all flight craft engaged in activities implying the exercise of State jurisdiction, i.e., *jure imperii*, may not enter foreign territory without special permission. They constitute State flight craft *sensu stricto* and would certainly include those engaged in aerial reconnaissance. Permission to enter foreign national flight space can generally not be presumed and unauthorised

---

[32] ICAO Doc. 6895-AT/695, 26/8/49.

[33] *Chicago Proceedings*, pp. 555, 586, 671,679, 1381.

[34] Geneva Convention on Rights in Aircraft, 1949 (310 UNTS 151; ICAO Doc. 7620), Art. XIII, and Rome Convention on Surface Damage, 1952 (310 UNTS 131; ICAO Doc. 7364), Art. 26.

[35] Cf. Paris Convention on Aerial Navigation, 1919 (11 LNTS 173), Art. 30; see further B. Cheng, 'State Ships and State Aircraft', 11 *CLP* (1958), pp. 225–57, and also J. C. Cooper. 'National Status of Aircraft', 17 *JALC* (1950), p. 292, at p. 309.

[36] Cf. *Civil Air Transport Inc.* v. *Central Air Transport Corporation* [1953] A.C. 70; and Aristeides, 'The Chinese Aircraft in Hong Kong', 4 *ILQ* (1951), p. 159.

entry, except perhaps cases of distress,[37] would be considered as unjustified violations of national territory. On the other hand, public flight craft other than State flight craft *sensu stricto* are treated as civil flight craft subject to the law of civil aviation.

The distinction between these two types of public flight craft is admittedly not clear and it may well be a matter of dispute whether meteorological services operated by the armed forces are *jure imperii* or *jure gestionis*. To some extent, the answer may depend upon the immediate use to be made of the information obtained. Thus, in time of war, when the information is required for the planning of day-to-day operations, a neutral State may be led to consider that such meteorological flights constitute an integral part of a belligerent's military efforts and object to their intentional passage over its territory as being in violation of its territory and neutrality. On the other hand, in time of peace there may be a general tolerance of such flights for the general promotion of human knowledge and mutual convenience. In the case of non-photographic weather balloons, it would seem that such general acquiescence probably exists.

In its reply on 11 February 1956 to the Soviet Union, the Turkish government expressed astonishment that the Soviet Union should protest against the use of meteorological balloons as Soviet balloons had been found on Turkish territory several times, and the United States government in its second note of 1 March 1956 pointed out that, at the time of the Soviet protests, Soviet balloons were found in the United States, Finland, Germany, Iran, Japan and Turkey. 'It is illogical,' the United States note said, 'that the Soviet Government should desire one rule for itself and another for the rest of the world.' From this limited point of view, Mr Dulles would be correct in saying that a State is estopped from demanding the cessation by other States of activities in which it is itself indulging.[38] For the same reason, it may be said that States no longer protest against the passage of radio waves from foreign stations through their national airspace. The comment of Soviet writers to these *tu quoque* arguments has been merely to label them as 'absurdities.'[39] But the fact that the Soviet government, in its note to the United States government of 18 February 1956 maintained that 'the flights of these balloons over the Soviet Union have nothing in common with meteorological research but pursue quite different aims' may perhaps be interpreted as meaning that the Soviet Union had no objection to 'genuine' meteorological balloons that were not a danger to aviation or threat to security.

---

[37] See further Cheng, *General Principles of Law*, pp. 75–7; Resolution 927 (X) of the General Assembly of the United Nations; O. J. Lissitzyn, 'The Treatment of Aerial Intruders', 47 *AJIL* (1953), p. 559.

[38] See further Cheng, *General Principles of Law*, pp. 141–9.

[39] Loc. cit. in n. 6 above, pp. 43–4.

The lesson to be drawn from the 1956 balloon incident would seem to be that, while States do not generally object to certain innocuous and innocent high altitude flights by public and private flight craft of other States for accepted purposes, they retain technically the right to stop such flights whenever they consider that their interests are adversely affected,[40] provided of course that they themselves do not claim such privileges in the airspace of other States. But it would seem that no implicit consent can be inferred from the absence of immediate objection from foreign States to such announcements *urbi et orbi* as that of the United States Department of Defense of 8 January 1956 which was not communicated to foreign States.

On the other hand, the view may be ventured that when details of any proposed flights are officially communicated well in advance to all States to be overflown and no objection is raised thereto, a tacit consent may probably be inferred. Thus, in regard to the proposed launching by the United States of artificial earth satellites in the forthcoming International Geophysical Year (1 July 1957–31 Dec. 1958), its announced intention of making known beforehand the wavelength of the radio instruments to be carried and of making available to the world all the data to be gathered from the experiment, together with the readiness the Soviet Union expressed shortly afterwards to co-operate in the project may be taken as an indication that no objection in principle will be made by the Soviet Union to the actual passage of these instruments through its airspace.[41] Announcements of similar experiments by means of space vehicles and high altitude rockets have also been made by the Soviet Union[42] and the United Kingdom.[43]

B. Civil Flight Craft

As has just been explained, civil flight craft include those owned and operated by the State as well as those of private individuals. Here it should be mentioned that, in the writer's view, private individuals are not, at present and as a general rule, subjects of international law and, in their private capacity, are incapable of committing an international unlawful act.[44] As such, they cannot violate the sovereignty of a foreign State, whatever the purpose of their flights.

[40] See Cheng, *General Principles of Law.* pp. 52–68.
[41] See loc. cit. in n. 16 above, p. 220 [Ch. 1 above, *in fine*]; Kaplan, loc. cit. in n. 15 above, cf. also A. E. Haley, 'Space Law—Basic Concepts', 24 *Tenn. LR* (1956), p. 643.
[42] See loc. cit. in n. 16 above, p. 220 [Ch. 1 above, *in fine*]; Prof. Igor Bardin said at the IGY Barcelona final planning conference in September 1956 that details concerning the Soviet plans to launch one or more earth satellites during the IGY would be given to all countries as soon as possible so that the Russian satellite programme could be integrated into the international programme for 1957 (*The Times* (London), 12 Sept. 1956).
[43] See *inter alia* F. E. Jones and H. S. W. Massey, 'Rocket Exploration of the Upper Atmosphere', 177 (4510) *Nature* (1956), p. 643.
[44] See Cheng, *General Principles of Law*, pp. 163–217.

On the other hand, individuals are subject to municipal law and, in conducting such flights, come prima facie under the laws of their own State, the
State of registration of the flight craft, the State from which such flights originate, and any State or States flown over or otherwise affected, for instance
through collision.[45] Thus in September 1953, when the International Council
of Churches proposed to float balloons from Germany over areas of Eastern
Europe with translations of the Christian Bible, while the United States
Department of State, to which the matter was referred, was of the view that
'no authorization is required of the United States Government,' it advised the
United States High Commissioner in Germany that 'the Council should seek
to obtain the approval of the appropriate German authorities.'[46] These, however, were by no means the first propaganda balloon flights in recent years; for,
at a 'Great Peace Rally' organized by the London *Daily Worker* in November
1948, so-called 'Peace Balloons' were released in Trafalgar Square and many
were reported to have landed in Holland and Germany.[47]

As to the permissibility of such flights over foreign territory, it depends
essentially upon the latter's municipal law. In this regard, it may be worth
remembering that the world did once, especially in the second half of the nineteenth century, enjoy a large measure of economic liberalism and, as late as
1911, even military aircraft were sometimes able to fly freely over foreign territory.[48] Even today, it may be said of any country which upholds the principle of *nullum crimen sine lege* that flights by foreign civil flight craft will be
presumed to be permitted unless expressly prohibited. However, even where
the entry of such flights may be tacitly presumed, they must furthermore comply in all other respects with local law, such as regulations concerning the
flight craft themselves, their personnel, the carriage of instruments, including
photographic apparatus, the rules of the air, the dropping of objects, etc.[49]

In the case of public flight craft, every State should, in principle, refrain
from violating the municipal law of a friendly power, especially in the operation of civil flight craft into its territory. But where the matter is trivial and the
enforcement of the law is difficult or impracticable, for instance, in the case of
pilotless flight craft, unless the local State is determined to make of it a major
diplomatic issue or, under traditional international law, to treat it as a *casus
belli*, there may sometimes be no remedy, except by means of retaliation—
retortion or reprisals. This is also the case of wireless telegraphy, where, in the
early days of its development, States often protested in vain against the passage of radio waves across their airspace or their 'ether,' a term then widely
used. Ineffectual representations or protests thus gradually give way to tolerance and even acquiescence, so that protests against foreign broadcasts are

---

[45] Cf. PCIJ: *The Lotus* (1927), Ser. A, No. 10.   [46] USIS *DWB*, 3 Sept. 1953, p. 6.
[47] *Daily Worker*, 19 Nov. 1948, p. 1.
[48] See loc. cit. in n. 16 above, p. 218, n. 17 [Ch. 1 above, n. 59].
[49] Cf. Chicago Convention, 1944, Arts. 9–13, 30, 36, 68.

today based generally on their hostile or subversive nature rather than on any technical violation of national airspace.

What has just been said is true in an even larger measure with regard to flights by individuals in their private capacity; for, provided that they do not infringe local law, they can afford altogether to ignore the laws of foreign States, if they succeed in not falling then or later into their hands. Apart from its duty to protect foreign States from injurious acts emanating from its territory, hereafter to be mentioned, a State incurs no direct responsibility for the acts of private individuals in its territory, has no duty to ensure their compliance with foreign laws, and, in the absence of treaty provisions, no obligation to surrender or extradite them to foreign States the law of which they may have violated. Thus it would seem that it would be perfectly lawful for a State to buy secret information concerning foreign States from private individuals operating on their own initiative within its territory and abroad, as long it is not itself otherwise directly or indirectly concerned with such operations. This may perhaps be taken as an indication that 'Operation Moby Dick' which was openly conducted by the weather service of the United States Air Force with the co-operation of a number of European countries, was not, contrary to the Soviet assertion, intended as a mission of aerial reconnaissance of Soviet territory even though the cameras carried could incidentally take pictures of the terrain flown over;[50] for such activities could be much more conveniently and appropriately left to private initiative and enterprise.

If the State from which such private flights are initiated is not in principle directly responsible therefor, still less would a State be responsible for similar acts by its nationals acting in their private capacity in a foreign country. This is the case of the propaganda balloons of which the Soviet Union complained. The United States attitude has always been that 'it is not directly or indirectly participating' in the launching of such balloons and, therefore, 'denied any United States Government responsibility.'[51]

While the United States government may be politically correct in saying that 'in the Soviet Government Note [of 4 February 1956] there is an apparent confusion between a publicized meteorological operation and previous Soviet allegations concerning the launching of propaganda balloons,'[52] a close examination of the Soviet notes shows, however, that the Soviet Union recognized a juridical distinction between the camera-carrying balloons— consistently referred to as those launched by 'United States military organs'—

---

[50] Mr Dulles's Press conference, 7 Feb. 1956: 'When you fly at 50,000 feet or thereabouts you generally find cloud conditions underneath, and there is some recording, I believe, photographically of certain cloud conditions. It would be quite accidental, I believe, if the photograph happened to pick up anything significant on the ground'. Statement of US Air Force Secretary Donald A. Quarles, issued on 11 Feb. 1956: '. . . In certain of experiments the balloons carry photographic equipment to record instrument readings and to take pictures of the underlying cloud formations and terrain features' (USIS *DWB*, 13 Feb. 1956, p. 3).

[51] Note of 8 Feb. 1956.   [52] Ibid.

and propaganda balloons—referred to with equal consistency as those launched by 'United States organizations.' While the Soviet government considered both types of balloon as constituting a danger to aircraft 'flying along Soviet domestic routes and on international routes,'[53] it specifically charged only those balloons launched by 'United States military organs' with 'gross violation of Soviet airspace'.

With regard to propaganda balloons launched by 'United States organizations',[54] the Soviet Notes constituted much more a *démarche* or at most a representation than a formal protest, 'noting' merely that, despite previous 'approaches' to the United States government, the latter 'has so far taken no measures to stop these actions of United States organizations.' It is significant that in the final paragraph of the first Soviet note to the United States registering its 'determined protest', its demand for 'immediate cessation' referred only to 'the said inadmissible acts by the United States military organs' and no mention was made of those by 'United States organizations', in respect of whose activities it merely alluded suggestively four paragraphs earlier to 'what would arise' if the tables were turned. In other words, the Soviet Union did not appear to have held the United States directly responsible for the propaganda balloons, and no such responsibility can be said to exist, in law, in the absence of direct or indirect participation.

C. Duty of the Territorial State

Whilst a State does not bear direct State responsibility for the acts of private individuals in its territory, it 'owes at all times a duty to protect other States against injurious acts by individuals from within its jurisdiction,'[55] and must *a fortiori* itself refrain from such acts. In regard to propaganda balloons, the Soviet Union was, therefore, correct in not relying on the argument of possible breaches of territorial sovereignty but stressed their possible danger to other aircraft and persons and property on the ground. This rule appears also to be admitted by the United States; for Mr Dulles in his Press conference stated: 'In the main, it is a recognized practice to avoid putting up into the air anything that which [sic] could interfere with any normal use of the air by anybody else.'

But, as the Trail Smelter Arbitral Tribunal said, 'the real difficulty often arises rather when it comes to determine what, *pro subjecta materie* [sic], is deemed to constitute an injurious act,'[56] and in a case concerned with the emission of fumes, the Tribunal held that the territorial State is responsible 'when the case is of serious consequence and the injury is established by clear

---

[53] As regards camera-carrying balloons, see the second Soviet note of 18 Feb. 1956.
[54] Presumably admitted as private; cf. *contra*, loc. cit. in n. 6 above, p. 39.
[55] *Trail Smelter Case* (1938, 1941), between Canada and the US, 3 *RIAA*, p. 1905, at p. 1963.
[56] Ibid.

and convincing evidence.'[57] Whether balloon flights constitute a danger to
aviation has been a point of some controversy among the parties concerned.
The United States Department of Defense in its News Release of 8 January
1956, maintained that 'experience has . . . shown that balloon flights are not a
hazard to aviation when flown at altitudes above 30,000 feet. Since commercial aviation and most military aviation are presently conducted below 30,000
feet, balloons are prevented from floating below this level by safety devices'
and, in its reply to the Soviet Union of 8 February 1956, the United States
government declared its readiness 'to explain further to the Soviet
Government the safety measures incorporated in the project'.

In its note of 18 February 1956, the Soviet government maintained that the
United States explanation was 'in contradiction to established factual data'.
The actual situation is probably indicated by a statement by United States
authorities, based on experiments made by the United States Air Force and
analyses made by the Massachusetts Institute of Technology. It would appear
that the chances of and the possible harm arising from aircraft colliding with
any kind of balloon are 'infinitesimally small'. The only tangible danger is that
an aircraft may run into the load of weather instruments as it is rising past levels used by commercial aircraft or drifting down by parachute.[58] But, whatever may be the actual or potential danger of balloon flights, if they are
conducted by a State, the State would appear to be responsible, even if only
morally,[59] for any loss or injury suffered by foreign States and their nationals.
Insofar as such flights are operated by private individuals, it will no doubt be
a matter of dispute whether the danger involved for foreign States and their
nationals is of a sufficiently serious character to entail the responsibility of the
State from which such flights originate. Czechoslovakia, Hungary, and
Poland, in their protests to the United States, all alleged specific incidents,
some fatal,[60] but these charges have been vigorously denied by Crusade for
Freedom, an American private organization responsible for the leaflet balloons released by Radio Free Europe, on account of the diminutive weight of
the balloons (2 lbs.) and of their load of leaflets (2–7 lbs.) and the altitude of
their flights (18,000 feet).[61] It should, however, perhaps be mentioned that in
this dispute the Federal German government did not consider itself involved
vis-à-vis the Soviet Union; for, in its reply of 6 March 1956 to the Soviet
protest, it stated that, as a result of investigations which had been carried out,
'it was established that no air balloons for the spreading of political or other
propaganda in the USSR were launched from the territory of the Federal

---

[57] *Trail Smelter Case* (1938, 1941), between Canada and the US, 3 *RIAA*, p. 1905, at p. 1965.
[58] *The New York Times*, 6 Feb. 1956.
[59] That is to say, assuming the flight to have been, in all respects, lawful. Cf. American–British
Claims Arbitral Tribunal (1910): *William Hardman Case* (1913), Nielsen's *Report*, p. 495, at p.
497; *Cadenhead Case* (1914), ibid., p. 505, at p. 508. If the flight is unlawful, there will be a legal
duty to repair integrally the consequences of the unlawful act.
[60] *Keesing's* (1955–6), 14723A.   [61] *The Times* (London), 7 Feb. 1956.

Republic.' Leaflet balloons had apparently been directed only at 'captive countries' in Eastern Europe and not at the Soviet Union itself.[62]

D. Pilotless Aircraft

In connection with the duty of the territorial State, a special word must be said about pilotless aircraft and other pilotless flight craft, such as rockets and earth-satellites. Article 8 of the Chicago Convention provides that:

No aircraft capable of being flown without a pilot shall be flown without a pilot over the territory of a contracting State without special authorization by that State and in accordance with the terms of such authorization. Each contracting State undertakes to insure that the flight of such aircraft without a pilot in regions open to civil aircraft shall be so controlled as to obviate danger to civil aircraft.

Each of the two sentences of this loosely drafted Article is open to a variety of interpretations.

1. *Permissibility of Pilotless Flights.*   It should first be noted that the first sentence, in subjecting pilotless flights to special authorization, refers only to national airspace and not to free flight space. It does not, therefore, apply to pilotless flights over the high seas, *terra nullius*, or in outer space.

To the extent that it is needed, the requirement of special authorization may be interpreted as referring to any one of the following three types of pilotless flight:

(i) Flights from one contracting State to another contracting State. In other words, each contracting State is under a duty to prohibit such flights from its territory into that of another contracting State, without the latter's special authorization. This interpretation is, however, not strictly in conformity with the text.

(ii) Flights within the territory of a single contracting State. This is strictly literal interpretation, but one which, in view of the specific duty imposed by the second sentence of the Article, renders the first sentence somewhat redundant.

(iii) Flights governed by the Convention. This interpretation is probably most in conformity with the intention of the parties. Article 8 thus becomes an exception clause to all treaty provisions between the contracting States to the Chicago Convention which grant the aircraft of one another transit or traffic rights, leaving pilotless flights in the realm of customary international law.

2. *Control of Pilotless Fights.*   The scope of each contracting State's duty to control pilotless flights may be one or more of the following:

[62] Ibid.

(i) In respect strictly of its own territory. This is a literal, but rather unlikely interpretation of the two sentences of Article 8 taken together.

(ii) In respect of all aircraft bearing its nationality wherever they may be. This is a possible, though not the most probable, interpretation of the intention of the parties, since it would leave unregulated pilotless aircraft which have not been registered and therefore, have no nationality.

(iii) In respect of all flights originating from its territory, which may take place wholly within national airspace or partly within it and partly within free flight space and/or foreign airspace including (or excluding?) airspace belonging to non-contracting States to the Chicago Convention.

It would appear, therefore, that even given the most liberal scope, Article 8 does not, in any significant manner, impose upon the contracting States to the Chicago Convention any obligation additional to their duty under general, alias customary, international law. It should, furthermore, be noticed that Article 8 does not prohibit pilotless flights in regions open to civil aviation, but merely requires them to be subject to control. Even if Article 8 were extended to apply to all types of flight craft, contracting States to the Chicago Convention may continue to allow pilotless flights, whether by balloons, rockets or earth-satellites, from their territories, provided they are so controlled as to obviate danger to civil aircraft.

VII. Conclusion

The obligation of States under general international law to control flights originating from their territory is thus perhaps even wider than that under the Chicago Convention and it may not perhaps be unreasonable to hope that with this safeguard a large measure of freedom may be allowed by States to high altitude flights by foreign States and their nationals for the purpose of scientific research, whether by aircraft, rockets or man-made satellites, so that the solving of the mystery of the upper atmosphere, of which so little is known, shall not be unduly retarded because of the mystery of the law.[63] In so doing, may these words of His Holiness Pope Pius XII in a recent address[64] serve both as a guide and a challenge:

The Lord God, who implanted in man's heart an insatiable desire for knowledge, did not place any limit on his efforts at conquest when He said: 'Subdue the earth' (Gen. 1, 28). It was rather the whole of creation which He offered for the human spirit to penetrate and thus understand more and more profoundly the infinite greatness of the Creator.

[63] In this connection, mention should perhaps be made of the US proposal to the Soviet Union in its note of 1 Mar. 1956 of a joint programme of meteorological research through the World Meteorological Organisation.

[64] Address at Castel Gandolfo to the delegates to the 7th International Astronautical Congress in Rome, 1956.

3

From Air Law to Space Law*

I. Introduction

In a subject such as space law, it is especially important to keep one's feet on the ground if the discussion is not to lapse into a branch of science fiction. The recipe for successful law-making, like government in general, is the art of the possible. Idealistic proposals which ignore the realities of international life can do more harm than good[1] to an emergent branch of the law where many urgent problems require international good will and co-operation for their solution.

The purpose of this chapter is to examine what has so far been achieved in air law, and the possibility of extending to outer space principles and standards that have already gained wide acceptance in the sphere of aerial navigation. In particular, attention will be focused on four basic principles underlying the Chicago Convention on International Civil Aviation, 1944,[2] to which in 1960, 77 States were parties. These four principles are (i) airspace sovereignty, (ii) nationality of aircraft, (iii) certain conditions to be fulfilled by aircraft engaged in international aerial navigation, their crews and passengers, and (iv) international co-operation and facilitation.[3]

II. Airspace Sovereignty

A. Principle

Following the precedent set by the Paris Convention on the Regulation of Aerial Navigation, 1919,[4] the contracting States to the Chicago Convention, 1944, recognize in its first Article that 'every State has complete and exclusive sovereignty over the airspace above its territory.' Although prior to the First

---

* First published in 13 *CLP* (1960), pp. 228–54. Reproduced by kind permission of Sweet & Maxwell Ltd.

[1] Cf., e.g., Ph. C. Jessup and H. J. Taubenfeld, 'Outer Space, Antarctica, and the United Nations', 13 *Int. Org.* (1959), p. 363, at p. 363: 'Some of the current spate of writing about outer space is so highly imaginative as to discourage serious students of international organization and law from pursuing detailed studies of very real problems which now confront the United Nations.'

[2] 15 UNTS 295; ICAO DOC. 7300.

[3] See further Cheng, *The Law of International Air Transport*, pp. 119–70.

[4] 11 LNTS, p. 173.

World War there was considerable discussion as to the exact legal status of the airspace above a State's territory, after the First World War the principle of airspace sovereignty became so widely accepted by States both in their municipal laws and in their diplomatic and treaty practice that it seems safe to conclude that it is now a well-recognized rule of general, *alias* customary international law.[5]

Article 2 of the Chicago Convention, 1944, specifies, for the purposes of the Convention, the lateral limits of airspace sovereignty by defining the meaning of State territory. Moreover, although the Convention makes no express reference thereto, it appears by implication to accept also the proposition that there is no national sovereignty over the airspace above the high seas and *terra nullius* which constitutes, therefore, free flight space.[6]

The Chicago Convention, 1944, does not, however, define the term airspace. Doubt may thus arise regarding the upper limit of national airspace. It would be well here to follow the rule of interpretation enunciated by the Permanent Court of International Justice in the *Eastern Greenland Case* (1933). In that case the Court had occasion to interpret the meaning of the term Greenland used in various diplomatic documents. It held that 'the natural meaning of the term is its geographical meaning.'[7] The natural meaning of the term airspace in the Paris and Chicago Conventions should, therefore, also be its geophysical meaning, denoting space where air is to be found.[8] Airspace is thus synonymous with atmospheric space, this being, moreover, clearly the intention of the framers of the Paris Convention, 1919.[9]

The territorial scope of a State's jurisdiction, as recognized in international air law, extends, therefore, upwards into space and downwards to the centre of the earth, the whole in the shape of an inverted cone. The sides of each cone are formed by straight lines projected downwards to the centre of the earth and upwards into space. As the earth is very nearly a true sphere, there will be neither gaps nor overlapping in between these inverted cones.

This principle of airspace sovereignty, well recognized in air law, is equally applicable to space law. But the identification of airspace with the earth's atmosphere leaves undefined the exact upper limits of national sovereignty. Such a definition, while hitherto unimportant in air law, is one of the first and most important problems that have to be tackled in space law.

The existing legal position has been well summed up by Lord Hailsham in the House of Lords:

---

[5] See further the writer's 'Recent Developments in Air Law', 9 *CLP* (1956), p. 208, Part I: Airspace Sovereignty and Earth Satellites [Ch. 1 above].

[6] See further the writer's 'International Law and High Altitude Flights: Balloons, Rockets and Man-Made Satellites', 6 *ICLQ* (1957), p. 487, at pp. 492–4 [Ch. 2, s. IV above].

[7] PCIJ: Ser. A/B 53, p. 52.   [8] See loc. cit. in n. 5 above, at pp. 210–3 [Ch. 1 above, s. II].

[9] In Art. 1(1) of the Paris Convention, 1919, the French and Italian equivalents of the term airspace were respectively '*espace atmosphérique*' and '*spazio atmosferico*', in other words, atmospheric space.

Her Majesty's Government consider that sovereignty over space above national territory cannot extend indefinitely up-wards. It cannot, however, be said that international
law has yet determined the exact limit to be placed on the extension of sovereignty
upwards or what legal regime should apply in realms of outer space to which sovereignty does not extend. There are still too many unsolved problems in this field to justify the adoption at present of any sweeping legal propositions, in whatever direction
they tend.[10]

This statement is interesting in that it (i) confirms the principle of airspace
sovereignty; (ii) affirms that national sovereignty cannot extend indefinitely
upwards; (iii) recognizes that there is no exact delimitation of the upper limit
of national sovereignty; (iv) considers that the legal regime of outer space is
yet undecided, but at the same time (v) implies that national sovereignty does
not now extend to outer space.

As regards the upper limit of airspace, it hardly needs to be recalled that the
atmosphere of the earth does not end abruptly, but becomes thinner and thinner with every increase in height until its particles no longer fall back regularly
towards the earth and it gradually disappears into the space beyond. A frontier belt exists, known as the exosphere, which varies in width and in height
according to the season and the region of the world, but its base is estimated
to lie generally at about 300–500 miles above the surface of the earth. If the
principle of airspace sovereignty is taken literally, and States do not otherwise
either expressly or tacitly agree on a different limit, it may perhaps be said that
this base of the exosphere constitutes the upper limit of national airspace.[11]

This is not to say, however, that this rather ill-defined twilight region of
almost 200 miles provides a satisfactory delimitation of the upper limit of
national sovereignty. If, as Judge M. Huber has so rightly said in the *Palmas
Case* (1928), territorial sovereignty 'serves to divide between nations the space
upon which human activities are employed,'[12] any frontier which is not
unequivocal is bound to be a source of controversy. The most urgent task in
space law is, therefore, to secure a general agreement among States fixing the
precise upper limit of national sovereignty.

With effects limited to themselves, the parties to such an agreement are at
liberty to choose any arbitrary distance as the extreme height of national
space, which need not necessarily coincide with the limits of the terrestrial
atmosphere. In such an agreement the contracting States may also, as among
themselves, by consent and mutual recognition dispense with the condition of
effective occupation otherwise regarded by international law as indispensable
to a valid title to territorial sovereignty.[13] A somewhat similar situation may

---

[10] 11 June 1959, 216 H.L. Deb. 5 s., col. 975.
   [11] See loc. cit. in n. 5 above, at pp. 213–5 [Ch. 1, s. III above].   [12] 2 *RIAA*, p. 829, at p. 839.
   [13] Cf. ibid., at pp. 838–40, and pp. 869–71; see also PCIJ: *Eastern Greenland Case* (1933), Ser.
A/B 53, and ICJ: *Minquiers and Ecrehos Case, ICJ Rep. 1953*, p. 53; cf. also G. Schwarzenberger,
'Fundamental Principles of International Law', 87 Hague *Recueil* (1955), chs. 3, 4, and 5, and id.,
1 *Int. Law* (3rd ed., 1957), pp. 299 ff.

be found in the claim by maritime States to the continental shelf adjacent to their coast. Thus in the Geneva Convention on the Continental Shelf, 1958,[14] the term continental shelf is defined in a manner which differs from its purely geological concept (Article 1), and the condition of occupation, 'effective or notional', is expressly waived (Article 2(3)).

Doubt has, however, sometimes been expressed as to whether States may, even by agreement, extend their national sovereignty beyond the terrestrial atmosphere. It is said that, because of the rotation of the earth, its orbit around the sun and the movement of the solar system and the whole universe, the position of extraterrestrial space is forever changing. This consideration, though at first sight weighty,[15] cannot, however, be regarded as decisive upon reflection.

First, this argument overlooks the fact that the surface of the earth itself also shares in these perpetual movements of all heavenly bodies, including what we call 'immovables', which, no lawyer will likely dispute, are susceptible of possession. Secondly, it ignores the fact that frontiers are, as often as not, merely a matter of geometrical construction. Take, for instance, the meridian line of a boundary river, a straight baseline, the outer limit of the territorial sea and the lateral limits of national airspace. These are all purely notional lines drawn by reference to certain geographical features on this planet which itself is constantly moving. The continuous flow of the water or air enclosed by these notional lines in no way affects their legal validity as national frontiers. There seems, therefore, to be no reason why geometrical lines drawn by reference to specific features on the surface of the earth which enclose a portion of extraterrestrial space cannot constitute valid national frontiers. What is indispensable is that there must be a point of reference consisting in a piece of national territory on *terra firma* which is—at least this is the case up to now—located on this planet; for man is essentially geocentric and, when it comes to national territory, very land-minded.

In fine, there is nothing inherently impossible in law or in geophysics which prevents States agreeing to an upper limit of national sovereignty beyond the atmosphere of the earth. In the United States a distance of 10,000 miles has been mentioned,[16] and, if States so agree, they are free to choose, with effects limited to those which consent to or recognize it, either this or any other figure, whether above below the natural limit of the terrestrial atmosphere.

---

[14] UN Doc. A/Conf. 13/L. 52–L. 55; Cmnd. 584 (1958); cf. also L. C. Green, 'The Geneva Conventions and the Freedom of the Seas', *CLP* (1959), p. 224, at p. 228.

[15] Cf. loc. cit. in n. 5 above, pp. 216 ff. [Ch. 1 above, s. IV, *in medio*], and loc. cit. in n. 6 above, p. 493 [Ch. 2, s. IV above].

[16] Mr Loftus E. Becker, Legal Adviser of the Department of State before the Special Committee on Space and Astronautics, US Senate, 6–15 May 1958. National Aeronautics and Space Act, *Hearings*, pp. 333–4: 'I would say 10,000 miles could well be taken as an outside limit, although we have never taken any exact position on the point.'

This does not imply, however, that agreement among States on the subject will be easy or that the fixing of the upper limit of national sovereignty at a height well beyond the terrestrial atmosphere is necessarily in the interests of scientific exploration or the peaceful use of outer space.

From this point of view, the efforts of the two Geneva Conferences of 1958 and 1960 on the regime of the high seas to revise the width of the territorial sea are instructive for two reasons. First, they show that even portions of the high seas which are otherwise *res extra commercium*, that is to say, objects which in law are not subject to appropriation by individual States, may be validly occupied to the extent to which such occupation is agreed to or recognized by other States—for any extension of the existing width of the territorial sea involves in effect an encroachment on the high seas. Secondly, if States wrangle so long over a few miles of the territorial sea, it will certainly be rash for anyone to suggest that they would, without difficulty, agree upon the exact height of their national sovereignty.

The foremost consideration that will influence the attitude of States in reaching a decision on this subject will be, as Soviet writers have already pointed out, that of national security.[17] While it is true that in these days of reconnaissance earth satellites and intercontinental ballistic missiles with nuclear warheads, any system of national defence based purely on physical distance seems ruefully obsolete, yet if the history of air law offers any guide, States will most probably prefer to claim the greatest height practicable as the limit of their national space, leaving it to subsequent arrangements by agreement to remove or abate such obstacles and inconveniences as may be created by this vertical division of space.[18] For the present, as the United Kingdom Government has so clearly Stated,[19] States are finding that there are yet too many unsolved problems to warrant the adoption of a rigid attitude towards the subject and resigning themselves temporarily to 'wait and see'.

During this period of uncertainty the two space powers will doubtless busy themselves with gathering the hay while the orbits of their satellites are still unobstructed. The situation recalls that before the First World War, when States had not yet made up their minds as to the precise regime to be applied in their national airspace, and German reconnaissance balloons were for a time flying freely over the Low Countries. The side that is the first to be satisfied with its winnings, or alternatively the first to be frightened by the rate it is losing its chips, will presumably then kick the table over and ring down the space curtains.

---

[17] Cf. A. Galina, 'On the Question of Interplanetary law', 7 *Sovetskoe Gosudarstvo i Pravo* (1958), p. 52; English translation by F. J. Fieger and J. R. Thomas, reprinted in *Senate Symposium* (1959), p. 508, at pp. 513–4: 'The result at which we arrive thus reduces to the fact that the outer altitude limit of State sovereignty must be established in such a manner as to protect the State against encroachments on its territorial sovereignty, on its independence.'

[18] Cf. B. Cheng, 'The Right to Fly', 42 *Grotius Society Transactions* (1956), p. 99, at pp. 105 ff.

[19] See n. 10 above, and also n. 16 regarding the United States.

But while the sky is literally the limit of national sovereignty, it would appear, on the other hand, that States would refuse to recognize spacecraft as artificial islands, drifting hither and thither, each with its own enveloping territorial space. This view is based on the increasingly territorial character of national sovereignty, whereby the territorial sea and national airspace are both regarded as appurtenances to land territory, and the general abandonment of the legal fictions that ships and diplomatic premises are extraterritorial portions of national territory. The net result would be that space lying outside recognized national space would in law become incapable of appropriation by individual States. Then, in a roundabout way, outer space, not because of its ever-changing position, but because it is not delimited by reference to territory on the surface of the earth, would achieve the same status as the high seas as *res extra commercium*.[20]

But extraterrestrial bodies such as the moon and the planets must prima facie be regarded as *res nullius* which, like the New World and the continent of Africa at one time, are susceptible of being appropriated as national territory through effective occupation.[21] The requirement of effective control justifies the statement made in the United States that 'neither Russia nor anyone else could claim the moon merely by planting a flag on it'.[22]

Moreover, titles to territory, to be absolute, require the recognition of other States.[23] This consideration accounts for the sometimes seeming moderation of territorial claims made by States. Thus the Soviet Union, after the landing of Lunik I on the moon, declared that 'there will be no territorial claims'.[24] Indeed, it frequently occurs that States do not lay claims to a territory in which they have an interest, and yet refuse to recognize the territorial claims of any other State.[25] In case of dispute, the better claim—in terms of actual display of sovereignty and foreign recognition—prevails.[26] Thus it also follows that the longer a country exercises the functions of a State over a territory, the more difficult it becomes for other States to dispute its title. From this point of view, there may perhaps be more than a grain of truth in what Dr von Braun was reported to have said: 'It is quite possible that within two years the Russians would be able to put a "bus load of astronauts" into space . . . If we

---

[20] See text between n. 15 and n. 17 above.   [21] See n. 13 above.

[22] Mr Loftus E. Becker, reported in *The Times* (London), 7 Mar. 1959.

[23] Cf. G. Schwarzenberger, 1 *Int. Law* (3rd ed., 1957), pp. 299 ff.

[24] Prof. A. Topchiev, Deputy Chairman of the Soviet Academy of Sciences, Press Conference, 15 Sept. 1959, reported in *The Times* (London), 15 Sept. 1959.

[25] Cf. the 1912 Protocol between Norway, Russia and Sweden regarding Spitzbergen which, owing to the First World War, did not, however, come into effect; cf. T. Niemeyer and K. Strupp, 1 *Jahrbuch des Völkerrechts* (1948/49), p. 142.

[26] Cf. *Palmas Case* (1928) 2 *RIAA*, p. 829, at pp. 838–9: 'If a dispute arises as to the sovereignty over a portion of territory, it is customary to examine which of the States claiming sovereignty possesses a title . . . superior to that which the other State might possibly bring forward against it.'

continue at this leisurely pace we will have to pass Russian Customs when we land on the moon.'[27]

The successful conclusion of a treaty in 1959 freezing for 30 years all territorial claims to Antarctica, which shall remain demilitarized,[28] might encourage the hope of a similar agreement in respect of outer space. But, while such an agreement is certainly possible, its probability is doubtful. It might, indeed, be thought that the Antarctic Treaty became possible only when rocketry and space exploration had deprived that continent of much of the strategic importance which its possession was at one time thought capable of conferring.

This scepticism does not imply that the restriction of outer space, including all extraterrestrial bodies, to peaceful uses is not regarded as eminently desirable from the standpoint of humanity at large. The doubt is based on the fact that rocketry and space exploration are proving to be of vital military significance, involving the necessity to review and revise every aspect of strategic planning. Unless it be within the context of a much wider political accommodation between East and West, any effort to restrict outer space to purely peaceful uses appears to be no more than a pious hope and any lip-service declaration subscribed to by States, for instance, in the form of a unanimous Resolution of the General Assembly of the United Nations, would amount to little more than Declaration I of the First Hague Peace Conference of 1899. In this Declaration the contracting Powers agreed to 'prohibit, for a term of five years, the discharge of projectiles and explosives from balloons or by other new methods of a similar nature'. When the time came for the renewal of this undertaking at the Second Hague Peace Conference of 1907, as Pearce Higgins summed it up, 'the development in the science of aerostatics since 1899 caused several States which had supported the Declaration in 1899 either to refrain from voting or to oppose the proposal'.[29]

It would appear, therefore, that no matter how attractive proposals for the internationalization of outer space may seem, States are most likely to insist on a relatively high ceiling to their national sovereignty, leaving any inconveniences that may arise therefrom to be ironed out by subsequent agreements.

B. Consequences

Once national space is defined, the result will be that no flight craft may fly in, into, or through another State's national space without its permission, acquiescence or tolerance, at no matter what altitude.[30] This is the position of national airspace in present-day air law, and it is implicitly confirmed in the Chicago Convention, 1944, in addition to its Article 1, by, *inter alia* its Articles

---

[27] *The Times* (London), 31 Oct. 1959.
[28] The Antarctic Treaty, 1 Dec. 1959, 402 UNTS 71; Cmnd. 913 (1959).
[29] *The Hague Peace Conferences* (1909), p. 489.
[30] See loc. cit. in n. 18 above, pp. 494 ff.

3 (State aircraft), 5 (non-scheduled flights), 6 (scheduled air services), 7 (cabotage) and 8 (pilotless flights). Furthermore, once an aircraft has been permitted to fly into or over the territory of another State, the machine, its crew, and passengers must comply with local laws and regulations. This consequence of the principle of airspace sovereignty is expressed in many of the provisions of the Chicago Convention, 1944, which, moreover, leaves the contracting States a large measure of discretion as to the substance of these laws and regulations.[31]

So far there has been little opposition to the passage of foreign artificial earth satellites over national territories. The initial perigees and apogees of the orbits of Sputnik I, Discoverers I, II, V, VII, XI and the Soviet Space Ship are, respectively, 142–588, 99–605, 142–220, 136–450, 100–520, 109–380 and 193–230 miles. These are all wholly or partly in the earth's atmosphere—at least the upper regions thereof—and, assuming that the sovereignty of States skyward is conterminous with the terrestrial atmosphere and, therefore, extends to approximately 300–500 miles, within the national airspace of the countries over which they pass.

The lack of protest about these satellites up to now hardly affects the principle of airspace sovereignty; for those States which directly or indirectly took part in the International Geophysical Year, and those now taking part in the work of COSPAR (the Committee on Space Research of the International Council of Scientific Unions), can be said to have given their implied consent. For the rest, the passage of such satellites through national airspace depends on the tacit acquiescence of the States over which their orbits pass. It would be erroneous otherwise to conclude that a legal right of innocent passage has already arisen in favour of artificial satellites, similar to the right of innocent passage of merchant ships through foreign territorial seas.

As the Permanent Court of International Justice has pointed out in the case of *The Lotus* (1927), in order to speak of a duty of abstention under international customary law, it is essential to prove not only the existence of a practice or usage (*consuetudo*) but also a conviction on the part of States in general that the practice is legally binding (*opinio juris sive necessitatis*). 'For only if such abstention were based on their [States] being conscious of having a duty to abstain would it be possible to speak of an international custom.'[32] At present, it can hardly be said yet that States are of the view that they have a legal right to launch satellites through the airspace of other States or that they are under a legal duty to suffer the passage of foreign artificial satellites through their own national airspace.

---

[31] See further ss. III, IV, and V below.
[32] PCIJ: Ser. A 10, p. 28; see also ICJ: *Asylum Case, ICJ Rep. 1950*, p. 266, at p. 276, and *US Nationals in Morocco Case, ICJ Rep. 1952*, p. 176, at p. 200.

It has already been suggested that States may at any time raise the barriers of national sovereignty to space exploration.[33] When that happens, spacecraft may pass over the territory of foreign States only with their consent and, in doing so, must comply with any condition that they may impose.

C. Privileges exchanged

It follows from the concept of airspace sovereignty that the first objective in any aeronautical agreement is to exchange the right to fly, to which all other concessions become subordinated.

In this regard the Chicago Convention, 1944, first distinguishes between State aircraft and civil aircraft. State aircraft are those 'used in military, customs and police services' (Article 3). The test is therefore functional and does not depend on ownership. Aircraft owned by the contracting States which do not fall within the above definition are, for the purposes of the Convention, regarded as civil aircraft to which alone the Convention applies.[34] In addition, the Convention excludes from its operation pilotless aircraft which are not permitted to overfly the territory of another contracting State without a special authorization by that State (Article 8).[35]

Of manned civil aircraft, the Chicago Convention, 1944, for the purpose of conferring the right to fly, distinguishes between commercial and non-commercial flights. Commercial flights are those which carry passengers, cargo or mail for remuneration or hire, and are subdivided into scheduled and non-scheduled flights.

In respect of non-commercial flights, the Convention grants a fairly liberal right for aircraft bearing the nationality of any of the contracting States to fly into the territory of other contracting States or to fly across it with or without a stop. No right of entry or transit is granted in respect of scheduled air services, while that granted in respect of non-scheduled commercial flights is rather nominal. Consequently, commercial flights, whether scheduled or non-scheduled, may be performed over the territories of other contracting States only on the basis of supplementary treaties, both multilateral and bilateral— at present primarily bilateral.[36] Economic rights other than commercial carriage, for instance, various types of aerial work such as aerial survey or crop dusting, are not included in the Chicago Convention, 1944, nor generally granted on a treaty basis.

As regards space flights, a distinction must thus be made between military agreements among States closely integrated one with another which co-operate in the development of military missiles and space vehicles of military

---

[33] See text to, before, and after n. 15 above.
[34] See further B. Cheng, 'State Ships and State Aircraft', 11 *CLP* (1958), p. 225.
[35] See further loc. cit. in n. 6 above [Ch. 2 above].
[36] See loc. cit. in nn. 3 and 18 above. On cabotage, see s. IV.B below, *in fine*.

application, and general conventions designed to include the totality or the majority of States for the peaceful uses of outer space.

In any proposed International Convention for the Peaceful Exploration and Exploitation of Outer Space it is to be expected, therefore, that its scope would be limited to the equivalent of civil aircraft, although, in the nature of things, it would be impracticable, at least for the present, to exclude unmanned civil spacecraft, even if special regulations may have to be devised to ensure their safe operation.

In regard to civil spacecraft, manned or unmanned, States will probably have little objection to purely scientific flights across their national space, subject to safeguards which they may wish to establish in the interest of national security. Indeed, so far, States may be said to have behaved with commendable liberality in this regard.

Until national satellites can be launched, so that there is no case for protectionism, States may also be liberal regarding the passage of foreign meteorological, communication, or navigational satellites, even when they are performing services for financial considerations. On the one hand, encouragement may be derived from the comparative ease with which, during the inter-war period, rights for commercial flights were granted by, for instance, Latin-American countries when they themselves did not dispose of sufficient air transport facilities. On the other hand, the attitude, during the same period, of some States which were situated along certain trunk air routes, such as Turkey and Persia, may give rise to the fear that a strategically situated State might exploit its geographical location for the purpose of extracting countervailing gains in return for the right of passage. Where a sufficient degree of international goodwill exists, parties to an eventual International Convention might even agree to allow the launching of foreign civil spacecraft from within their territories.

Once, however, rocketry becomes as common as aeronautics, then commercial rivalry may well create a situation which now weighs heavily on international civil aviation. Every privilege will then be granted only against commensurate advantages being given in return.[37]

Even when the right of entry, departure, and transit, especially commercial entry and departure for the purpose of bringing in and taking out passengers and/or cargo, has been granted, attention must be turned to ancillary privileges without which the right itself may be deprived of much of its meaning.

Thus, under the Chicago Convention, 1944, contracting States grant one another, in respect of their scheduled air services, national treatment in the matter of prohibited areas and, in respect of all flights, equal treatment as among the contracting States, in the application of temporary restriction or prohibition of flying in exceptional circumstances (Article 9).

---

[37] See loc. cit. in nn. 3 and 18 above.

Moreover, in respect of all flights, the standard of national treatment and equal treatment as among all contracting States is accepted:

• in the application of air regulations (Article 11);
• in the conditions governing the use of 'all air navigation facilities, including radio and meteorological services, which may be provided for public use for the safety and expedition of air navigation' (Article 15);
• in 'charges that may be imposed or permitted to be imposed by a contracting State for the use of . . . airports and air navigation facilities' (Article 15);
• in the regulation or prohibition of the carriage of dangerous articles by aircraft over a State's territory (Article 35).

In addition, the following ancillary privileges are exchanged:

• prohibition of 'fees, dues or other charges' being 'imposed by any contracting State in respect solely of the right of transit over or entry into or exit from its territory of any aircraft of a contracting State or persons or property thereon' (Article 15);
• temporary exemption from duty 'subject to the customs regulations of the State' of 'aircraft on a flight to, from, or across the territory of another contracting State' (Article 24);
• exemption from customs duty, inspection fees or similar charges of fuel, lubricating oils, spare parts, regular equipment and aircraft stores on board an aircraft of a contracting State or imported into the territory of a contracting State for incorporation in or use on an aircraft of another contracting State engaged in international air navigation (Article 24);
• exemption of the aircraft of another contracting State or its owner or operator during an authorized entry into or transit across the territory of another contracting State, while engaged in international air navigation, from any claim, seizure, detention or interference by the territorial State or any person therein, on the ground of an alleged infringement of any patent or registered design rights (Article 27);
• mutual recognition of certificates of airworthiness and certificates of competency and licences issued or rendered valid by the contracting State in which an aircraft is registered, provided that the requirements under which such certificates or licences were issued or rendered valid are equal to or above the minimum standards which may be established from time to time by the International Civil Aviation Organization (Article 33);[38]
• duty of each contracting State in the territory of which an aircraft of another contracting State has met with an accident 'involving death or serious injury, or indicating serious technical defect in the aircraft or air navigation facilities':

---

[38] See s. V.A below.

(a) to 'institute an inquiry into the circumstances of the accident, in accordance, so far as its laws permit, with the procedure which may be recommended by the ICAO';[39]

(b) to afford the contracting State in which the aircraft is registered 'the opportunity to appoint observers to be present at the inquiry'; and

(c) to 'communicate the report and findings' of the inquiry to the State of registration (Article 26);

• duty of each contracting State in the event of an aircraft (whether or not, it would appear, registered in another contracting State) in distress in its territory:

(a) 'to provide such measures of assistance . . . as it may find practicable';

(b) 'to permit, subject to control by its own authorities, the owners of the aircraft or authorities of the State in which the aircraft is registered to provide such measures of assistance as may be necessitated by the circumstances'; and

(c) when undertaking search for missing aircraft, to 'collaborate in coordinated measures which may be recommended from time to time' by the ICAO (Article 25).[40]

Most of the ancillary privileges which have been evolved in relation to civil aviation appear applicable *mutatis mutandis* to civil spacecraft, including a liberal use of the standard of national treatment and equal treatment as among the contracting States in the application of flight regulations, use of ground facilities, including tracking facilities. Other privileges may well include exemptions from charges or dues imposed solely in respect of the right of transit, from customs duties on the spacecraft or its stores, fuel, spare parts and equipment, from seizure, detention or interference based on alleged infringement of patent or registered design rights, mutual recognition of minimum standards of safety, mutual co-operation and assistance in the recovery of unmanned spacecraft which have re-entered the terrestrial atmosphere, or manned spacecraft in distress or involved in accidents.[41]

III. Nationality of Flight Craft

The second important principle accepted by parties to the Chicago Convention, 1944, is that enunciated in Article 17:

Aircraft have the nationality of the State in which they are registered.

The practical importance of this principle is that it opens the way to rights and liabilities being grafted directly on to the aircraft, irrespective of the nationality of its owner or operator.

---

[39] See s. V.A below. [40] See s. V.A below.

[41] See below Ch. 9 on provisions subsequently adopted in the 1967 Space Treaty, Ch. 10 on the Astronauts Agreement, and Ch. 12 on the Moon Treaty.

Moreover, nationality being one of the most important devices for the allocation of objects of international law to the various subjects of international law,[42] the attribution of a nationality to aircraft also simplifies the task of resolving which is the subject of international law most directly concerned with a given aircraft. Rights and duties under international law in respect of aircraft may then be created directly and attached to the State the nationality of which the aircraft possesses.

Thus, under Article 12 of the Chicago Convention, every contracting State is obliged to ensure 'that every aircraft carrying its nationality mark, wherever such aircraft may be, shall comply with the rules and regulations relating to the flight and manoeuvre of aircraft' in force at any given place, including, over the high seas, rules of the air established by the ICAO,[43] and 'each contracting State undertakes to insure the prosecution of all persons violating the regulations applicable.'[44] Moreover, certificates of airworthiness (Article 31), licences for radio transmitting apparatus (Article 30 (*a*)), and of the operating crew (Articles 30 (*b*) and 32), are to be those issued or rendered valid by the State in which the aircraft is registered.[45]

At present, spacecraft have been launched only by States, and the problem of nationality has hardly arisen; for every State is directly responsible for spacecraft owned, operated or launched by it. But in the absence of recognized nationality for spacecraft, the subject of international law primarily responsible for spacecraft owned, operated or launched by private individuals, including commercial concerns, will be the State where the spacecraft are launched rather than the State of which their owners or operators are nationals.[46] There is, on the whole, much to be said for extending the institution of nationality based on registration to spacecraft, leaving the territorial State responsible merely for failure to exercise due diligence in preventing the launching of unregistered spacecraft that may injure the rights of other States, or those of their nationals.[47]

IV. Conditions to be Fulfilled by Flight Craft, their Crews and Passengers

The Chicago Convention, 1944, imposes a number of conditions with which aircraft of contracting States engaged in international air navigation, their crews and passengers must comply, especially when over the territory of another contracting State.

---

[42] See Schwarzenberger, 1 *Int. Law* (3rd ed., 1957), pp. 354 ff.   [43] See s. V.A below.
[44] See further B. Cheng, 'Crimes on Board Aircraft', 12 *CLP* (1959), p. 177.
[45] Cf. also Arts. 39–42.   [46] Cf. loc. cit. in n. 6 above, pp. 498 ff. [Ch. 2, s. VI.B above].
[47] See further Ch. 17 below: Nationality for Spacecraft?

A. Conditions Regarding the Instruments of Flight

As has already been mentioned,[48] the benefits exchanged among the contracting States under the Chicago Convention, 1944, do not extend to State
aircraft and pilotless aircraft. These aircraft may not overfly the territory of
another contracting State without special authorization. Moreover, 'every aircraft engaged in international navigation shall bear its appropriate nationality and registration marks' (Article 20) and 'shall be provided with a certificate
of airworthiness issued or rendered valid by the State in which it is registered'
(Article 31). When in or over the territory of another contracting State, it may
'carry radio transmitting apparatus only if a licence to install and operate such
apparatus has been issued by the appropriate authorities of the State in which
the aircraft is registered. The use of radio transmitting apparatus in the territory of the contracting State whose territory is flown over shall be in accordance with the regulations prescribed by that State' (Article 30(*a*)). Under
Article 36 of the Convention, 'each contracting State may prohibit or regulate
the use of photographic apparatus in aircraft over its territory.'

Article 34 of the Convention prescribes that 'there shall be maintained in
respect of every aircraft engaged in international navigation a journey log
book . . . in such form as may be prescribed from time to time pursuant to this
Convention.'[49] In addition, under Article 29 of the Convention, 'every aircraft
of a contracting State, engaged in international navigation,' must carry the following documents:

 (*a*) its certificate of registration;
 (*b*) its certificate of airworthiness;
 (*c*) the appropriate licences for each member of the crew;
 (*d*) its journey log book;
 (*e*) if it is equipped with radio apparatus, the aircraft radio station licence;
 (*f*) if it carries passengers, a list of their names and places of embarkation
       and destination;
 (*g*) if it carries cargo, a manifest and detailed declaration of the cargo.

B. Conditions Governing the Type of Operation

It follows from the exclusion of State aircraft and pilotless aircraft from the
scope of the Chicago Convention, 1944, that the benefits conferred by the
Convention inure only to manned civil aircraft bearing the nationality of a
contracting State, whether owned or operated by a contracting State or by private individuals. An important duty accepted by the contracting parties which
may be of especial significance in any international agreement on the peaceful
uses of outer space is that found in Article 4:

---

[48] See s. II.C above.   [49] See s. V.A below.

Each contracting State agrees not to use civil aviation for any purpose inconsistent with the aims of this Convention.

The Chicago Convention, 1944, also prohibits the carriage of munitions of war or implements of war without the permission of the State flown over (Article 35). Moreover, each contracting State reserves the right, for reasons of public order and safety, to regulate or prohibit the carriage in or above its territory of other articles (Article 35). In this connection, mention has already been made of the power of each contracting State to prohibit or regulate the use of photographic apparatus in aircraft over its territory.[50]

Apart from these general restrictions, the right to fly granted under the Chicago Convention, 1944, varies according to the type of operation in which an aircraft is engaged. Cabotage and scheduled commercial services depend on special authorization of the States flown over, while non-scheduled commercial flights (i.e., most charter flights) are subject to such regulations, conditions or limitations as the State overflown may consider desirable. Only private flights not carried out for remuneration or hire are more or less free from restrictions as regards the right of entry and transit.[51]

C. Conditions Governing the Operating Crew

Article 32(*a*) of the Chicago Convention, 1944, provides that 'the pilot of every aircraft and the other members of the operating crew of every aircraft engaged in international navigation shall be provided with certificates of competency and licences issued or rendered valid by the State in which the aircraft is registered.' Moreover, when an aircraft registered in one contracting State is in or over the territory of other contracting States, 'radio transmitting apparatus may be used only by members of the flight crew who are provided with a special licence for the purpose, issued by the appropriate authorities of the State in which the aircraft is registered' (Article 30(*b*)).

D. Entry and Departure

Article 10 of the Chicago Convention, 1944, permits every contracting State to require all foreign aircraft entering or leaving its territory to do so only at designated customs airports. Under Article 5 of the Convention, notwithstanding the right of transit non-stop granted in respect of non-scheduled flights, a State may nevertheless, by virtue of the same Article, require the aircraft of another contracting State flying over its territory to effect a landing. Moreover, although Article 5 grants the right of entry and transit to aircraft of other contracting States engaged in non-scheduled flights without the need of obtaining prior diplomatic permission, it at the same time permits each

---

[50] See s. IV.A above.   [51] See II.C above.

contracting State, 'for reasons of safety of flight, to require aircraft desiring to proceed over regions which are inaccessible or without adequate air navigation facilities to follow prescribed routes, or to obtain special permission for such flights.'[52]

In addition, Article 9 of the Convention authorizes contracting States to establish prohibited areas or temporarily to restrict or prohibit flying over the whole or any part of their territories 'in exceptional circumstances or during a period of emergency, or in the interest of public safety.'

'The laws and regulations of a contracting State as to the admission to or departure from its territory of passengers, crew, or cargo of aircraft, such as regulations relating to entry, clearance, immigration, passports, customs, and quarantine shall be complied with by or on behalf of such passengers, crew or cargo upon entrance into or departure from or while within the territory of that State' (Article 13). 'The appropriate authorities of each of the contracting States shall have the right, without unreasonable delay, to search aircraft of the other contracting States on landing or departure, and to inspect the certificates and other documents prescribed by this Convention' (Article 16).[53]

Moreover, in order that aircraft of the contracting States may enjoy certain of the customs exemptions granted by the Convention, they must comply with the pertinent customs regulations of the territorial State (Article 24). Likewise, spare parts and spare equipment in storage in another contracting State for use or installation in the repair of an aircraft of a contracting State benefit from the exemption, in the former State, from claims, seizure, detention or interference on the ground of alleged infringement of patent or registered design rights only if 'any patented part or equipment so stored shall not be sold or distributed internationally in or exported commercially from the contracting State entered by the aircraft' (Article 27 (*b*)).

E. Observance of Aeronautical Regulations

Under the Chicago Convention, 1944, there is not only a right, but also a duty incumbent on every contracting State, to ensure that, first, every aircraft flying over or manœuvring within its territory shall comply with its aeronautical regulations and, secondly, every aircraft bearing its nationality wherever it may be shall comply with the aeronautical regulations there in force (Article 12). Furthermore, the use of radio transmitting and photographic apparatus in the territory of the contracting State whose territory is flown over shall be in accordance with the regulations prescribed by that State (Articles 30 (*a*), and 36).

The various conditions enumerated above governing civil aircraft of the contracting States to the Chicago Convention, 1944, when engaged in inter-

---

[52] Cf. also Art. 68 regarding scheduled flights.   [53] See s. IV.A above.

national navigation are admittedly of a rather technical and detailed nature which are further elaborated in international standards and recommended practices made by the International Civil Aviation Organization.[54] For this reason, they may not be entirely suited to space flights. Yet, certain of the conditions of a more or less general character may provide useful analogies.

Thus, with regard to the instruments of flight, the exclusion of spacecraft used in military, customs, and police services appears to be eminently appropriate. Moreover, the need for every spacecraft to be clearly identified by advance notice of launching and radio signals is a matter of some urgency and importance; for it might well help to prevent a tragedy of errors in a period of political tension when a misguided rocket can easily trigger off a cosmic war. The use of radio and photographic apparatus, including the choice of radio frequencies, is also a matter which cries out for regulation. In fact, at the 1959 Administrative Radio Conference of the International Telecommunication Union the Radio Regulations established at Atlantic City, 1947, were extensively revised and for the first time include allocations of radio frequencies for space and earth-space transmission services. The same Conference also adopted a recommendation (No. 35) for the convening of an Extraordinary Administrative Radio Conference during the latter half of 1963 with an agenda which will pay special attention to telecommunication problems arising out of space research.[55]

Furthermore, while the carriage of log books and other documents may be, at the present juncture, rather premature, an undertaking by contracting States to a general convention on outer space not to use civil spacecraft for any purpose inconsistent with the peaceful exploration and exploitation of outer space must be regarded as highly desirable. A general prohibition of the carriage of munitions of war, implements of war, and other dangerous articles by spacecraft when over the territory of other contracting States to such an agreement can only be considered as sound common sense.

Again, while it may be premature now to lay down hard-and-fast rules concerning the crew and passengers of spacecraft, it would, however, be hardly out of place to reserve the right of the States overflown to establish prohibited areas and temporarily to forbid or regulate the passage of space vehicles across their territories in time of emergency or other exceptional

---

[54] See s. V.A below.

[55] Cf. A. Henry, 'The Administrative Radio Conference', *Telecommunication Journal (ITU)* (1960), p. 40*e*, at p. 41*e*; E. Wenk, 'Radio Frequency Control in Space Telecommunications', US Senate Committee on Aeronautical and Space Sciences, 86th Congress, 2nd Session, Committee Print (1960), which, in its Appendix G (pp. 149 ff.), reproduces the provisional text (Jan. 1960) of Art. 5 (Frequency Allocations, 10 Kc/s to 40 Gc/s) of the 1959 Radio Regulations; cf. also the International Telecommunications Convention, Geneva, 1959, and its successive amendments at Montreux; Malaga–Torremolinos, 1973; and Nairobi, 1982. In 1989, at Nice the ITU Constitution was separated from the Convention. See further Tania L. Masson-Zwaan, 'International Telecommunications and ITU Developments', in C. J. Cheng and P. Mendes de Leon (eds.), *The Highways of Air and Outer Space over Asia* (1992), pp. 99–108.

circumstances. Moreover, when and if astronautical regulations are drawn up, whether nationally or internationally, it would again be only right that they should be observed.

V. International Co-operation and Facilitation

The fourth basic principle accepted by the contracting parties to the Chicago Convention, 1944, is that of mutual co-operation and facilitation in the development of international air transport. This principle finds expression in three different directions: (i) standardization of aeronautical regulations and procedures, (ii) provision of the infrastructure of international aerial navigation, and (iii) the mutual facilitation of international air transport.

A. Standardization

In the sphere of international standardization, rules and regulations relating to civil aviation present the obvious starting point. General obligations undertaken by the contracting States to the Chicago Convention, 1944, may be found in Articles 12, 28, and 37, relating to the rules of the air, communication procedures, codes, markings, signals, lighting and other operating practices and rules, aeronautical maps and charts, and, generally, uniformity in 'regulations, standards, procedures, and organization in relation to aircraft, personnel, airways and auxiliary services in all matters in which such uniformity will facilitate and improve air navigation.' Other provisions which are also relevant are Articles 14 (sanitary regulations), 23 (customs and immigration procedures), 25 (search and rescue), 26 (investigation of accidents), 29 (documents), 33 (certificates of airworthiness and certificates of competency) and 35 (definition of munitions of war or implements of war for the purpose of prohibited carriage).

The principal method to achieve this international standardization is through the quasi-legislative and pre-legislative procedures of the International Civil Aviation Organization, under which fifteen Annexes to the Chicago Convention, 1944, five Procedures for Air Navigation Services (PANS), various Regional Supplementary Procedures (SUPPS) and three international treaties have been adopted and are still operative.[56]

One of the topics not covered by these documents is the duty assumed by the contracting States under Article 14 of the Convention to prevent the spread of disease. Primary responsibility in this field now rests with the World Health Organization. Under its constitution the WHO enjoys a quasi-legislative power similar to that of the ICAO Council. On 25 May 1951, the

---

[56] See further B. Cheng, 'Centrifugal Tendencies in Air Law', 10 *CLP* (1957), p. 200, at p. 203; and id., loc. cit. in n. 3 above, pp. 63–76.

Fourth World Health Assembly unanimously adopted the International Sanitary Regulations (WHO Regulations No. 2),[57] which entered into force on 1 October 1952. Additional regulations were adopted by the Eighth World Health Assembly in 1955,[58] and the Ninth Assembly in 1956.[59] A consolidated edition of the Regulations containing these additions was published in 1957.[60] For most States, these are the relevant regulations applicable to international air travel.

In the realm of space flights a great deal of work has already been done by the International Council of Scientific Unions during and since the highly successful International Geophysical Year. Even the duty to prevent the spread of disease finds an echo in the agreement adopted to sterilize all space vehicles that may otherwise contaminate extra-terrestrial bodies.

Once it is decided to draw up a general agreement to regulate the peaceful exploration and exploitation of outer space, the contracting States may do well to agree also on the setting up of an international organization similar to the ICAO established under the Chicago Convention, 1944. Such a World Organization for Outer Space (WOFOS) will then be able to continue the work hitherto performed on a non-governmental level by the International Council of Scientific Unions.

B. Infrastructure

Under Article 28 of the Chicago Convention, 1944:

Each contracting State undertakes, so far as it may find practicable to:
  (*a*) Provide, in its territory, airports, radio services, meteorological services and other air navigation facilities to facilitate international air navigation, in accordance with the standards and practices recommended or established from time to time, pursuant to this Convention . . .

Under Article 69, if the ICAO Council considers that the airports or other air navigation facilities, including radio and meteorological services, of a contracting State are not reasonably adequate for the safe, regular, efficient and economical operation of international air services, present or contemplated, the Council may make recommendations for the purpose of finding means by which the situation may be remedied. In addition to the adoption of relevant international standards and recommended practices, the most concrete way whereby the ICAO can help in improving the infrastructure of international civil aviation is through its administrative function in operating joint financing schemes in support of air navigation services and facilities. To date, three separate arrangements are in operation, all in the North Atlantic area:

---

[57] WHO, *Technical Report Series*, No. 41 (1951).
[58] WHO, 64 *Off. Rec.* (1955), pp. 84–6.   [59] WHO, 72 *Off. Rec.* (1956), pp. 80–3.
[60] WHO, *International Sanitary Regulations* (Annotated ed., 1957).

(i) North Atlantic Ocean Stations, (ii) air navigation services in Greenland and the Faeroes, and (iii) air navigation services in Iceland.

Apart from the adequacy of the infrastructure of international civil aviation, there is the problem of its availability. Article 15 of the Chicago Convention, 1944, thus lays down the standard of national treatment and equal treatment as among the contracting States in the use, 'by aircraft of every contracting State, of all air navigation facilities, including radio and meteorological services, which may be provided for public use for the safety and expedition of air navigation . . .'

Then there is the problem of charges for the use of airports and other air navigation facilities. Again, Article 15 of the Convention imposes the standard of national treatment in favour of aircraft bearing the nationality of other contracting States, subject to the right of the ICAO Council to review such charges and to make recommendations thereon for the consideration of the State or States concerned. The matter of airport and air navigation facilities charges has, however, been, in practice, an extremely thorny problem and two conferences were held, one on airport charges in 1956,[61] the other on route facilities charges in 1958.[62] A number of recommendations were adopted by each conference, without affecting unduly the discretion of member States to proceed as they were wont.

Mention may, however, perhaps be made of two abortive proposals in regard to the provision of the infrastructure of international civil aviation made by the Interim Assembly of the Provisional International Civil Aviation Organization prior to the establishment of the ICAO. These were:

(i) the establishment of an international agency supported by contributions of member States to provide, operate and maintain all communications facilities and ground aids, but excluding airports, over all or certain international civil air routes, and

(ii) the establishment of a common fund for the provision of airport and other air navigation facilities to which all member States contribute.[63]

When the ICAO was set up, the ICAO Council which had been requested to examine these proposals reported to the ICAO Assembly in 1950 that the first proposal was neither realistic nor desirable and that the second proposal had in fact been superseded by the joint support programme of the Organization.[64]

Be that as it may, experience has shown the greater need for adequate ground facilities in space programmes and the considerably higher costs required for their installation and operation. Under the circumstances, States entering into a general agreement on outer space may perhaps be induced to

---

[61] *Proceedings*, ICAO Doc. 7745, APC/1 (1956), 3 vols.
[62] *Proceedings*, ICAO, Doc. 7874, RFC/1 (1958), 2 vols.
[63] ICAO Doc. 1811, A/40; see also ICAO Doc. 7462–C/870 (1954), Appendix V, pp. 61 ff.
[64] ICAO Doc. 4968, A4–P/1, p. 61.

give further thought to these two schemes as applied to the peaceful exploration and exploitation of outer space, thereby circumventing the difficulties
which airport and route facilities charges have given rise to in international
civil aviation.

C. Facilitation

Under Article 22 of the Chicago Convention, 1944:

Each contracting State agrees to adopt all practical measures, through the issuance of
special regulations or otherwise, to facilitate and expedite navigation by aircraft
between the territories of contracting States, and to prevent unnecessary delays to aircraft, crews, passengers and cargo, especially in the administration of the laws relating
to immigration, quarantine, customs and clearance.

As the ICAO has pointed out,

the basic aim of the Organization in the field of Facilitation is to achieve, to the maximum degree consistent with the public interest, free and unimpeded passage of aircraft
and the crews, passengers, baggage, cargo and mail that they carry on international
flights. The principal means by which this aim can be accomplished are simplified and
uniform procedures, amendments to regulations which may delay or restrict the movement of international traffic, and continuing efforts on the part of airport authorities
and operators of international flights to reduce ground delays to a minimum.[65]

Of all the topics in the Chicago Convention, 1944, examined above, perhaps
only Facilitation appears slightly remote when applied to space research and
exploitation. Yet it can hardly be denied that the same spirit of goodwill which
underlies the field of Facilitation in international air transport will be even
more urgently required if international co-operation in man's newly con-
quered dimension is to achieve its maximum effect.

VI. Conclusion

It is indeed far from the intention of this chapter to suggest that space law is
but air law writ large, or that principles and standards accepted in air law may
be mechanically transposed to the field of space law. It is hoped that this chapter may have, in some small way, contributed to stimulate discussions of the
subject of space law along concrete rather than speculative, and practicable
rather than idealistic, lines, so that those actually called upon to cope with
such problems may find therein, instead of a cloud of glorious aspirations, a
few historical pointers to order in outer space.

[65] ICAO, *Aims and Objectives of ICAO in the Field of Facilitation*, ICAO Doc. 7891–C/908
(1958), p. 3.

4

International Co-operation and Control:
from Atoms to Space*

I. Introduction

Outer space shares with the atom this common feature. Harnessed for peaceful use, they each can yield mankind hitherto undreamed of benefits; abused for military purposes, they may spell the end of the human race. How to control their exploitation for military ends and to promote international co-operation in their peaceful use is one of the most pressing problems of our time. Indeed, some may even say that man's very survival depends on the solution to this problem.

One of the major difficulties in finding an entirely satisfactory solution lies in the fact that in both cases developments for peaceful purposes can be either of direct military benefit or easily diverted surreptitiously to warlike use. Consequently, in any scheme of international co-operation for peaceful use, it is necessary to provide for safeguards. The experience which has been gained in this direction in the nuclear field will obviously be of practical value to similar schemes of international co-operation and control regarding outer space.

The validity of the nuclear analogy for outer space extends in fact beyond matters of public law to a host of problems of private law, such as patent rights, warranties, and liabilities. Editorial space, however, allows only for the consideration in this chapter of the main forms of international co-operation which have so far been established in the nuclear field and the principal safeguards which have been incorporated in them.

II. International Control of Nuclear Weapons

While much has been heard of the desideratum that nuclear energy and outer space should only be used for peaceful purposes, it is obvious that at present the most advanced and energetic research in both fields by those States which have such capabilities is directed towards military ends. The series of nuclear tests carried out by the Soviet Union in 1961, and the urgent need felt imme-

* First published in 15 *CLP* (1967), pp. 226–47. Reproduced by kind permission of Sweet & Maxwell Ltd.

ERRATA SLIP

p. 350, text, line 3 from base: 'into' *read* 'in'

INDEX

p. 772, col. 2, under 'Agreement Relating to the International . . .', line 4: 'Operation' *read* 'Operating'.

p. 773, col. 2, line 4 from base: 'Bagotá' *read* 'Bogotá'.

p. 774, col. 2, line 16: '600–15' *read* '600–1'.

p. 778, col. 2, under 'East-West relations': *add* '119–20'.

p. 781, col. 2, under 'hierarchical and horizontal legal systems': *add* '433,'.

p. 781, col. 2, under 'IMO, . . .': 'IMO' *read* 'INMARSAT'.

p. 783, col. 2, under 'personal scope': *add* '384, *385*,'.

p. 784, col. 2, under 'launchn activities': 'launchn' *read* 'launch' indented.

p. 784, col. 2, under 'international liability for damage . . ., mesure of compensation': 'mesure' *read* 'measure'

p. 786, col. 1, last line but one: *add* ', *and under* United States'.

p. 787, col. 1, line 17: *add* 'outer void space'.

p. 788, col. 1, under 'non-militarization, celestial bodies, Space Treaty': *add* '248,' and ', 532'.

p. 788, col. 1, 6 lines from base: 'IV.iii,' *read* '55–7'.

p. 788, col. 2, lines 4 and 5: *add* '248,' and ',*532*'.

p. 788, col. 2, under '*opinio juris*, ascertainable without difficulty': *add* ', 679'.

p. 790, col. 1, line 17: *add* ', outer void space'.

p. 792, col. 1, line 1, after '*see*': delete 'I'.

p. 792, col. 2, under 'resolution v. treaty in . . .': *move* 'third-' to next line.

p. 793, col. 2, under 'recovery and return, military space objects, *q.v.* ': *add* '*above*'.

p. 794, col. 1, under 'spatialism, boundary between . . .': '*q.v. under* functional versus spatial delimitation', *read* (functional versus spatial delimitation), *q.v.*'.

p. 795, col. 2, under 'Art. IV . . .': *add* '*248,* ' and '*532,* '.

p. 795, col. 2, under 'Art. VI . . .': *add* '*635,* '.

p. 796, col. 1, line 2: 'ares' *read* 'areas'.

p. 796, col. 1, under 'Treaty on Principals *(cont.)*: universality,': *after* 'principle' *add* 'of'.

p. 796, col. 2, 14 lines from base: *read* 'United Nations resolutions and principles . . .'.

p. 797, col. 1, under 'United Nations resolutions and principles . . .': 'related to space' *read* 'relating to outer space'.

diately afterwards by the United States to resume atmospheric tests in order not to be left behind in the nuclear arms race, bears witness to at least the first half of this observation. Evidence for the remaining half may be found in the fact that, without the numerous artificial satellites which it has in orbit, the United States might well have failed to detect the high-altitude tests made by the Soviet Union in this series for the purpose of developing anti-missile missiles. This incident underscores the military significance of outer space and shows that the demilitarization of outer space is likely to be every bit as difficult as nuclear disarmament. Also illustrative of this point is the United States' 'space needles' experiment which was launched in October 1961 notwithstanding a chorus of protests from many eminent space scientists.

Insofar as nuclear weapons are concerned, it would appear that their use is illegal under international customary law only if, and to the extent to which, they produce effects which may be classified as those of poison or poisoned weapons.[1] But even if the use of nuclear weapons as such were illegal, their possession, manufacture and testing must in themselves be considered as lawful, in the light of current State practice, provided that no appreciable injury were caused to foreign States, including their inhabitants or their property.[2]

Negotiations have, however, been going on for years in and outside the United Nations seeking ways to restrict or to ban, by agreement, the possession, manufacture or testing of nuclear weapons, but so far they have produced no positive results. The two world blocs, East and West, are well entrenched behind their respective slogans: 'No control without disarmament' and 'No disarmament without control.' The crux of the problem seems then to lie in the matter of control.

While it is true that both sides have been doing a great deal of political fishing in the rather muddy waters of control, yet, at least in regard to controlling the possession of nuclear arms, a real obstacle does exist. This is the fact—recognized by both sides, it would appear, only in 1955—that 'in the present state of scientific knowledge it is impossible to detect existing stocks of nuclear arms'.[3] This means that even if a complete or partial nuclear disarmament agreement were successfully concluded, while it may be possible to control the actual amount of nuclear arms destroyed by the respective parties, there is no possibility, at present, of verifying the nuclear devices remaining in the possession of the parties.

It does not seem, however, that the same is true of a ban on the manufacture of nuclear weapons, known as a 'cut-off'. In this case, the States concerned agree not to produce any more fissionable material for weapon purposes from a given date onwards, and to exploit nuclear energy in future

---

[1] See G. Schwarzenberger, 'The Legality of Nuclear Weapons', 11 *CLP* (1958), p. 258.

[2] See *Trail Smelter Arbitration* (1935, 1941), Award II, 3 *RIAA*, p. 1905, at p. 1963; cf. Cheng, *General Principles of Law*, p. 130.

[3] United Kingdom Foreign Office, *The Search for Disarmament* (1960), p. 39.

only for peaceful uses. As will be seen later, methods of control have been devised to prevent projects of international nuclear co-operation for peaceful purposes from being diverted to military use. There is no reason to believe that, once a cut-off has been effected, such methods and procedures, with suitable adaptations, may not be used to prevent subsequent exploitation of nuclear energy from being channelled to purposes of war. It would appear that here the problem is no longer one of the impossibility of effective control, but one of the acceptability of the proposed control methods and procedures, or perhaps more simply the will to effect such a cut-off.

This applies with even greater force to any agreed ban on nuclear tests. A Conference of Experts from the two power blocs met at Geneva in 1958. It reported that, with a distribution of approximately 160–70 land-based control posts and about ten ships, and the use of aircraft, it would be feasible both to detect and to identify most nuclear tests, apart from devices of small yield tested underground, over ten kilometres in the atmosphere or deep down in the ocean.[4] These gaps, however, did not take long to close; for by the end of 1959 'methods of control had been worked out for tests in the oceans, in the atmosphere, and up to the greatest distance in outer space.[5]

The Conference of Experts was followed by one conference after another for the purpose of finding an agreement to ban all nuclear tests. The fate of these discussions at Geneva is too well known to require further mention. The latest Soviet line is 'No foreign spies on Soviet soil', but it may be recalled that the Anglo-American offer of a ban on atmospheric tests without 'on-site' controls was no more successful in stopping the 1961 series of Soviet tests.

The inevitable conclusion must therefore be that the failure of the two blocs to agree on either a cut-off of the production of nuclear weapons or a ban on nuclear tests is due not to any technical difficulties in instituting control, but to the absence of a fundamental political settlement between them without which no effective disarmament is conceivable.[6]

The position is not greatly different in respect of outer space. Various proposals have been made to limit outer space to purely peaceful uses, the most important of which remains that put forward by President Eisenhower in September 1960 in his address to the General Assembly of the United Nations.[7] So far, these proposals have been largely lost in the many disarmament packages that have been presented by the East and the West.

A resolution (1721 (XVI)) adopted by the General Assembly on 20 December 1961, commends to States the principle that 'outer space and celestial bodies are free for exploration and use by all States in conformity with international law, and are not subject to national appropriation.' While the

---

[4] Cmnd. 551 (1958).   [5] Op. cit., n. 3, above, p. 34.
[6] See Epilogue below, s. IV: Conditions Governing International Rule-Making.
[7] See B. Cheng, 'The United Nations and Outer Space', 14 *CLP* (1961), p. 247, at p. 277 [Ch. 6 below, s. VI, *in fine*].

recommendation that both outer space and extraterrestrial bodies be treated as *res extra commercium* in international law[8] is worthy of attention, it is perhaps also significant that the resolution does not specify that they should be open only to peaceful exploration and use.

Indeed, if regard is had to the fact that both the United States and the Soviet Union keep strictly silent about each other's artificial satellites, some orbiting above their territories at heights which may well be regarded as within their national airspace, it would appear that neither side at the moment wishes to take any step that might lead to the disruption of its own programme of space exploration which it would be naïve to think can be free from military implications.[9]

III. Co-operation for Mutual Defence Purposes

The development of rules of international law, whether customary or treaty law, is essentially a function of the degree of integration between the States concerned. Thus, whereas between the Eastern and the Western blocs it has not been possible to establish any limitation on the military use of nuclear energy or outer space, within each of the two camps co-operation and control are not only possible but can also be far-reaching, whether for defence or peaceful purpose. Thus, among NATO countries, under a treaty signed in Paris on 22 June 1955, the United States and other NATO countries undertake to make available to NATO atomic information relating to defence.[10] The United States also concluded bilateral agreements of a similar nature with a number of countries, including Canada, Germany, the Netherlands, and Turkey.

By far the most extensive in scope is, however, the Agreement concluded between the United States and the United Kingdom on 3 July 1958, for Co-operation on the Uses of Atomic Energy for Mutual Defence Purposes.[11] This Agreement was made possible only after the 1958 amendment of the United States Atomic Energy Act of 1954. The scope of the 1958 agreement was further extended by an amendment of 7 May 1959.[12] It was this agreement which enabled the nuclear propulsion plant to be transferred to the United Kingdom for the building of *H. M. S. Dreadnought*.

Limitation of space permits here only a brief outline of the main features of this agreement which will, however, give some indication of the type of co-operation possible between States within the same power bloc.

[8] See B. Cheng, 'From Air Law to Space Law', 13 *CLP* (1960), p. 228 [Ch. 3 above].
[9] Ibid., p. 234 [Ch. 3 above, s. II.A *in fine*], and loc. cit. in n. 7 above [Ch. 6 below, loc. cit.].
[10] UKTS No. 21 (1956), Cmd. 9799.
[11] UKTS No. 41 (1958), Cmnd. 537; this supersedes the previous agreement of 15 July 1955 (UKTS No. 52 (1955), Cmd. 9555).
[12] UKTS No. 72 (1959), Cmnd. 859.

A. Forms of Co-operation

These fall into three categories:

(i)   exchange of classified information regarding nuclear defence and nuclear weapons, save the bomb itself (Article II);

(ii)   transfer by sale of a complete submarine nuclear propulsion plant by the United States to the United Kingdom (Article III), together with all patent rights and licences connected therewith (Art. IX(B)), and the necessary nuclear fuel for a period of ten years; and

(iii)   exchange of nuclear materials and the transfer by the United States to the United Kingdom of certain non-nuclear parts of atomic weapons (1959 amendment).

The second and third forms of co-operation exist only in the agreement between the United Kingdom and the United States, and not in the other agreements, which relate exclusively to atomic information.

B. Safeguard and Conditions

Of the conditions incorporated in the agreement to safeguard the interests of the parties, the following may be mentioned.

1. *Automatic Reservation.* The most important limitation on the obligations undertaken by the parties is the fact that the duty to make available information, material or equipment under the agreement is subject to the right of the supplying State to determine that this measure 'will promote and will not constitute an unreasonable risk to its defence and security' (Article I). Moreover, under Article II, only such information 'as is jointly determined to be necessary' is supplied or exchanged.

2. *Exclusively Military Use.* Except by mutual agreement, information, material, or equipment supplied under the agreement shall be used 'exclusively for preparation or implementation of defence plans in the mutual interests of the two countries' (Article V(C)).

3. *Security regulations.* Classified information and any materials or equipment made available under the agreement must not be transferred to unauthorized persons or, with the exceptions stated in Article VII, beyond the jurisdiction of the recipient State (Article VI(C)). Furthermore, such information, materials, and equipment are to be accorded full security protection under applicable security arrangements between the parties and applicable national legislation and regulations of the parties (Article VI(A)).

4. *Responsibility for Use and 'Hold harmless' Clause.* In the use or application of any information, material, or equipment made available under the agreement, the recipient State assumes full responsibility (Article IV). With particular reference to the nuclear submarine plant supplied by the United

States to the United Kingdom, the latter 'shall indemnify and hold harmless the Government of the United States against any and all liabilities whatsoever (including third-party liability) . . .' (Article III(E)).

While these agreements relating to mutual defence were in the first instance designed to cover the military applications of nuclear energy, they may in fact be extended to include also the military uses of outer space. Thus, among the classified information to be exchanged, the general provision in these agreements lists the following items:

1. the development of defence plans;
2. the training of personnel in the employment of and defence against atomic weapons and other military applications of atomic energy;
3. the evaluation of the capabilities of potential enemies in the employment of atomic weapons and other military applications of atomic energy.

All these items potentially refer also to defence and defence systems against, or making use of, ICBMs, artificial satellites, and space vehicles. The agreement between the United Kingdom and the United States mentions in addition information relating to 'the development of delivery systems' of atomic weapons (Article II(A)). Rocketry may be said to fall well within this category.

Moreover, both the conditions and safeguards provided for in these agreements and the provisions relating to the transfer of the submarine propulsion plant in the Anglo-American agreement afford useful precedents as to how similar co-operation may take place in the military uses of outer space.

IV. Cooperation for Peaceful Uses

In co-operative arrangements for the peaceful use of nuclear energy, the main concern is to prevent the diversion of the nuclear information, material, and equipment made available under the respective agreements to military use, thus leading to a spread of the possession of nuclear weapons. A more or less elaborate system of control is therefore generally included. The lesson to be learned in this sphere will be important: (i) in the event of an agreement being reached on the 'cut-off' of nuclear production for military purposes, or (ii) in case similar schemes are established for co-operation in the peaceful use of outer space. International co-operation in the peaceful uses of nuclear energy operates, roughly speaking, on four different levels:

1. Universalist international institutions,
2. Regional and sectional international institutions,
3. Bilateral agreements, and
4. Joint enterprises.

A. Universalist International Institutions

On the universalist level, mention should be made of the proposal first put forward by the United States in 1946, known as the 'Baruch Plan.'[13] According to this proposal, an international authority would be set up which would own all fissile material in trust for the world, and own, operate, and manage all facilities for handling dangerous amounts of such materials. When a control system was in full operation, the manufacture and use of atomic weapons would be banned and existing stocks disposed of. This plan, known also as the Atoms for Peace Plan, was, however, not accepted. However, ten years later, following another United States proposal made originally by President Eisenhower on 8 December 1953, the treaty of 26 October 1956, succeeded in setting up the International Atomic Energy Agency (IAEA).[14]

The point has sometimes been made that failure to accept any proposal to internationalize outer space would merely be repeating the error of 1946 when a splendid opportunity of ensuring that nuclear energy would be used only for peaceful purposes was missed. From this point of view, to treat the position of outer space today and that of nuclear energy in 1946 as comparable would be a gross error, for in 1946 the United States had a monopoly of the actual manufacturing process of the atomic bomb. Had the Baruch Plan been accepted, even if all the existing stocks of the bomb were destroyed, the monopoly then enjoyed by the United States would have been perpetuated. Soviet opposition to the Plan was, therefore, inevitable. Consequently, if any proposal for the internationalization of outer space has a better chance of success today, it would hardly be on account of the lesson of the Baruch Plan, but because of the approximate parity in space technology between East and West. A striking illustration of this proposition is Premier Khrushchev's suggestion, contained in his message of congratulation to President Kennedy after Colonel John H. Glenn's successful flight into space on 20 February 1962, that the Soviet Union and the United States should collaborate in space research.[15] Indeed, international co-operation in space research has existed almost from the beginning on a fairly wide basis either through existing international agencies, such as the International Telecommunication Union and the World Meteorological Organization, or on a non-governmental level through the International Council of Scientific Unions and especially its committee on space research COSPAR.[16] It was in fact an offer made by the United States

[13] UN Atomic Energy Commission, *Off. Rec.*, 1st Year, 1st Meeting, No. 1, p. 4, at pp. 7 ff.; see also US, *Atoms for Peace Manual*, S.Doc. No. 55, 84th Cong., 1st Sess. (1954).

[14] See further s. V.A below.

[15] See also the concrete proposals made in answer thereto by President Kennedy in his letter to Premier Khrushchev of 7 Mar. 1962 (*The Times* (London), 19 Mar. 1962, p. 12; USIS (London), *Off. Text*, 19 Mar. 1962), following his preliminary reply of 22 Feb. 1962.

[16] See further loc. cit. in n. 7 above, at pp. 248 ff. [Ch. 6, s. II below].

to representatives of COSPAR in March 1959 which led subsequently to the successful launching of the first British artificial satellite UK.1, named 'Ariel,' by a United States Delta rocket from Cape Canaveral on 26 April 1962.

B. Regional and Sectional International Institutions

On the regional and sectional level, there is a plethora of organizations and institutions. Without being exhaustive, mention may first be made of CERN, the European Organization for Nuclear Research, with its seat at Geneva, established by the treaty of Paris of 1 July 1953.[17] The counterpart to CERN in the Soviet bloc is the Joint Institute for Nuclear Research at Dubna, Moscow Region, which was established by a treaty of 26 March 1956,[18] later supplemented by a Statute of the Joint Institute dated 23 September 1956.[19] Concurrently with the establishment of the European Economic Community, the Six by the treaty of Rome of 25 March 1957, also created EURATOM (the European Atomic Energy Community).[20] On 1 February 1958, by decision of OEEC, the European Nuclear Energy Agency (ENEA)[21] was set up. Furthermore, in June 1959, the CENTO Institute of Nuclear Science, originally opened in March 1957 at Baghdad as the Baghdad Pact Nuclear Centre, was reopened in Teheran.

In the field of space research, a number of western European countries and Australia are signatories to the London Convention of 29 March 1962, for the establishment of a European Launcher Development Organization (ELDO), with headquarters in Paris. Separate from ELDO is ESRO which is still in its formative stage, membership of both organizations not being identical. ESRO stands for the European Space Research Organization and is intended to be a purely scientific body. Its headquarters will probably also be in Paris.

C. Bilateral Agreements

Bilateral programmes of co-operation have principally been initiated by the United States, the United Kingdom, the Soviet Union, and Canada. They have concluded a number of bilateral agreements with other States for the purpose of nuclear assistance. It should perhaps be added in this connection that a bilateral agreement on co-operation in space research has also been concluded between the United Kingdom and the United States.[22] As at

[17] UKTS No. 3 (1960), Cmnd. 928.
[18] See H. W. Dewey, 'Soviet Russia's Role in International Cooperation for Peaceful Use of Atomic Energy', in E. B. Stason, *Atoms and the Law* (1959), p. 1405, at p. 1408; March agreement reproduced, p. 1490.
[19] Ibid., p. 1493; IAEA, *Multilateral Agreements* (1959), p. 29.
[20] IAEA, *Multilateral Agreements* (1959), p. 79; application has since been made by the United Kingdom to join EURATOM.
[21] IAEA, *Multilateral Agreements* (1959), p. 201.
[22] UKTS, No. 116 (1961), Cmnd. 1572.

present, this agreement does no more than provide a framework for 'a series of experiments [to be] cooperatively planned and conducted by designated agencies of the two Governments.' But its potentialities have been fully demonstrated by the successful launching of 'Ariel,' referred to above.

D. Joint Enterprises

As for joint enterprises, these are institutions of municipal law established by agreement among a number of States. Examples within this category are the European Company of the Chemical Processing of Irradiated Fuels, more briefly known as EUROCHEMIC,[23] the joint operation of the Halden Boiling Water Reactor in Norway,[24] and the high temperature gas-cooled reactor project, known as 'Dragon',[25] located in the United Kingdom.

These joint enterprises vary in their organization. In the case of EURO-CHEMIC, it is a joint stock company under Belgian law. In the other two cases, no separate legal entity has been created, the Norwegian Institute of Atomic Energy and the United Kingdom Atomic Energy Authority operating the respective projects on behalf of the member States. In the former project, there is a Committee of Representatives of the contracting States, whereas in the latter there is a Board of Management. A common feature of all three joint enterprises is the fact that they all function under the auspices of ENEA, the European Nuclear Energy Agency.

The various joint enterprises serve usually very specific and limited purposes. The other programmes of co-operation, whether bilateral or multilateral, have generally speaking a number of common features which may be conveniently examined together.

V. Objectives and Functions

Essentially, the objectives of all these programmes consist in promoting the development of the peaceful uses of nuclear energy in the territories of the participating States.

A. Multilateral Co-operation

The functions of IAEA are probably the widest and also the least specific. Essentially, IAEA acts as a clearing-house and a centre of co-ordination, whether it be for the exchange of scientific and technical information, the exchange and training of scientists, the securing of services, materials, equip-

---

[23] IAEA, *Multilateral Agreements* (1959), p. 211.
[24] Ibid., p. 233.　　　　　　　　　[25] Ibid., p. 249.

ment or facilities, or the adoption of common safety regulations.[26] CERN at Geneva and the Joint Institute of Nuclear Research at Dubna, on the other hand, are essentially research centres, each with its own laboratories and scientists. By its statute, the reports of CERN are to be published and therefore available to both members and non-members, whereas the statute of the Joint Institute merely provides that the results are to be available to members. Whilst the Rome treaty establishing EURATOM also has provisions for the creation of a Joint Nuclear Research Centre, both EURATOM and ENEA stress the economic and industrial aspects of nuclear energy. One result of the establishment of EURATOM is the creation of a common market in nuclear materials and equipment comprising the territories of the Six, and among its functions is that of facilitating the investment of capital in nuclear industries within the common market.

B. Bilateral Co-operation

Bilateral agreements for co-operation in the peaceful uses of nuclear energy have been concluded by the United States, the United Kingdom, the Soviet Union, and Canada with a number of third States. Generally speaking, these agreements may be divided into two categories, those relating to research reactors and those relating to power reactors, known often as the research bilaterals and the power bilaterals.[27] In practice, however, it seems more apt to distinguish between those which are simply research bilaterals and those which are combined research-and-power bilaterals. Research bilaterals entered into by the United Kingdom include agreements concluded with the Federal Republic of Germany (1956),[28] Sweden (1957)[29] and Portugal (1958),[30] to which may be added the simplified agreements with Norway (1957)[31] and Denmark (1960).[32] Coming within the category of research-and-power bilaterals are those agreements of the United Kingdom entered into with Italy (1957),[33] Japan (1958),[34] EURATOM (1959)[35] and Spain (1960).[36]

Mention should also be made of the two agreements concluded by the United Kingdom in 1955 with, respectively, the United States[37] and

---

[26] Cf. B. G. Bechhoefer and E. Stein, 'Atoms for Peace: The New IAEA', in Stason, op. cit., n. 18, above, p. 1361.

[27] Cf. R. B. von Mehren, 'The United States Bilateral Program', in *Progress in Nuclear Energy*, Ser. X (ed. H. S. Marks, 1959), p. 198; since R. B. von Mehren's article has already given an excellent account of the American practice, the present survey will be essentially limited to United Kingdom bilaterals.

[28] UKTS, No. 33 (1956), Cmd. 9842; No. 7 (1958), Cmnd. 375.

[29] UKTS, No. 67 (1957), Cmnd. 290.   [30] UKTS, No. 30 (1958), Cmnd. 513.

[31] UKTS, No. 65 (1957), Cmnd. 277.   [32] UKTS, No. 46 (1960), Cmnd. 1127.

[33] UKTS, No. 21 (1958), Cmnd. 458.   [34] UKTS, No. 6 (1959), Cmnd. 625.

[35] UKTS, No. 28 (1959), Cmnd. 702.   [36] UKTS, No. 50 (1961), Cmnd. 1427.

[37] UKTS, No. 55 (1955), Cmd. 9560; No. 3 (1956), Cmd. 9677; No. 35 (1956), Cmd. 9847.

Belgium.[38] The layout of these two treaties differs, however, from that of sub-sequent United Kingdom research-and-power bilaterals and they have not been included in the ensuing survey of the general pattern of United Kingdom bilateral agreements in the field of nuclear co-operation. First, as regards the information to be exchanged between the parties, these two agreements appear to be much wider in scope than other bilaterals in that they seem to include also the exchange of classified information. The fact, however, is that, among research-and-power bilaterals, these two treaties were the only ones concluded before the December 1956 revision of the *Tripartite Declassification Guide*, undertaken jointly by Canada, the United Kingdom, and the United States.[39]

But there are also other circumstances which set these two agreements apart from the others. The special relationship between the United Kingdom and the United States in this respect need hardly be mentioned. Thus, regarding the sale and purchase of materials for purposes other than research (i.e., for use in power reactors), this treaty, unlike other United States bilaterals, says no more than that they may be arranged by agreement between the parties. Moreover, the parties seem content with no further safeguards than their own reciprocal guaranties which, in substance, resemble those subscribed to, mostly unilaterally, by the recipient State in the other research-and-power bilaterals.

As for the agreement with Belgium, wherein the United Kingdom under-takes to supply material for both research and power reactors, although cer-tain safeguards are provided for, especially in relation to the fuel so supplied and to any special nuclear material derived therefrom, these safeguards are not as developed as those found in subsequent United Kingdom research-and-power bilaterals. From this point of view, it should perhaps be mentioned that, as the Preamble to the treaty with Belgium states, 'a special relationship' in the nuclear field also exists between the two countries. This relationship finds expression in the detailed provisions in the agreement concerning the sale of uranium and thorium ores and concentrates to the Combined Development Agency which is a joint agency of the Canadian, United Kingdom, and United States governments.

Before embarking on the following survey of the rest of the United Kingdom bilateral agreements in nuclear co-operation it should be added that, on the part of the United Kingdom, many of the rights acquired and duties assumed under these agreements are to be exercised or carried out, as the case may be, by the United Kingdom Atomic Energy Authority (UKAEA).

[38] UKTS, No. 80 (1955), Cmd. 9632; No. 23 (1956), Cmd. 9794.
[39] See US, *Progress in Peaceful Uses of Atomic Energy, July–December 1957* (1958), p. 199.

C. Research Bilaterals

1. *Scope*. In these bilaterals, the parties undertake to exchange unclassified research information concerning the peaceful uses of atomic energy, and to assist each other, to such extent as is practicable, in the procurement of materials, equipment and other requisites for their atomic energy research and development programmes. On its part, the United Kingdom agrees that UKAEA will supply, or assist the other party in obtaining from the United Kingdom, research reactors and the fuel for research reactors to such extent and on such commercial terms as may be agreed. It further agrees that UKAEA will process, or assist the other party in arranging for the processing in the United Kingdom of, used fuel from research reactors operating in the other State on terms to be agreed upon, and will assist in training personnel sponsored by the other party.

Subject to certain reservations, the recipient of such unclassified information is entitled to use it freely for its own purposes and to communicate it to a third party. But it is also stipulated in these agreements that the State or agency supplying information, material, or equipment under their provisions is not responsible for the accuracy or completeness of such information, or the suitability of such information, material, or equipment for any particular use or application, or for the consequences of their use or application in the recipient State. This does not imply, however, that contracts made pursuant to these bilateral agreements may not contain such guarantees, and British bilaterals, in contradistinction to United States bilaterals, generally say so expressly.

Among British research bilaterals, the agreement with Portugal further contains, with respect to nuclear fuel supplied under the agreement, a 'hold harmless' clause whereby the Portuguese government undertakes to indemnify and hold harmless the United Kingdom government and UKAEA against any and all liability (including third-party liability) from any cause whatsoever arising out of the possession or use of such fuel, after it had been delivered to the Portuguese authorities.

2. *Safeguards*. In both research and research-and-power bilaterals, 'since'—in the words of these agreements—'it is the intention of the contracting parties that the information exchanged and the material and equipment supplied shall be used solely for the promotion and development of the peaceful uses of atomic energy,' a number of controls and safeguards are included in them in order to prevent the information, material, and equipment so supplied from being diverted to military use. Indeed, the two simplified British research bilaterals with Denmark and Norway are concerned purely with controls and safeguards, respectively, nuclear co-operation with these countries having been regulated by non-governmental agreements between their national atomic energy authorities.

In view of the system of safeguards embodied in the Statute of IAEA and the ENEA Security Convention of 1957,[40] all United Kingdom research bilaterals refer to the possibility of the parties eventually agreeing to controls and safeguards being administered by IAEA or by ENEA. Until this happens, however, five specific safeguards are laid down:

(i) any reactor, reactor component, or any uranium, thorium or plutonium obtained under these agreements or any plutonium or U–233 derived from the use of research reactors or fuel obtained under these agreements shall be used only for purposes coming within the agreement concerned (in the agreement with Portugal this condition has been merged with the guaranties undertaken by the Portuguese government);

(ii) any processing of fuel supplied by the United Kingdom Atomic Energy Authority (UKAEA) must be carried out by the said Authority or by facilities approved by it;

(iii) except by agreement between the parties, no alteration shall be made of the form and content of such fuel after its removal from the reactor and before its delivery to the said Authority or to such processing plants as have been approved by it;

(iv) records must be maintained relating to burn-up of reactor fuel obtained under these agreements and power levels of operation of reactors using it, and periodical reports must be made to UKAEA;

(v) representatives of UKAEA may from time to time inspect the condition and employment of any part of any fuel supplied under these agreements and observe the operation of any reactor using any part of such fuel.

Finally, the recipient State in these agreements usually subscribes to three guaranties to the effect that:

(i) the above safeguards shall be maintained;

(ii) no reactor, reactor component or material supplied under these agreements or material derived therefrom will be used for any military purpose; and

(iii) no such equipment or material will be transferred to unauthorized persons or beyond the jurisdiction of the recipient State.

D. Research-and-power Bilaterals

1. *Scope.* Everything that is to be found in the research bilaterals is also to be found in these agreements. Their scope is, however, enlarged to include unclassified information on the practical application of atomic energy. References to reactors and reactor fuel now extend to power reactors as well as research

---

[40] See s. VI below.

reactors, except that the duty of UKAEA to supply or to assist the recipient State in obtaining fuel applies primarily to research and power reactors obtained from the United Kingdom. The supply of additional fuel for other reactors depends on contracts to be agreed upon between the parties. Moreover, in addition to processing used fuel from research and power reactors operating in the recipient State, UKAEA will also assist it 'in the design, construction and operation of facilities for the manufacture of fuel . . . and for the processing of used fuel' in the recipient State itself. Mention may also be made of the rather special character of the agreement between EURATOM and the United Kingdom (1959), an agreement which provides for mutual collaboration between equals rather than unilateral assistance. Additional items to be found only in that agreement include references to mutual technical advice by the secondment of experts or otherwise between UKAEA and the Commission of EURATOM (Article V), and the undertaking by the two authorities concerned to encourage and facilitate the granting of sub-licences by persons holding licences to patents which they own, and to make available to each other, on commercial terms, licences under all patents owned by them relating to the manufacture of fuel (Article IV).

United Kingdom research-and-power bilaterals contain the same provision as the research bilaterals regarding the free use of information exchanged, and responsibility for the use made of the information, equipment and material supplied. And except for the agreement with EURATOM where the matter is to be further discussed (Article XIV), they all have a hold harmless clause regarding any fuel supplied to the recipient State. The agreement with Spain (1960) contains in this connection an oblique reference to the conventions on third-party liability for damage attributable to radioactivity, then under study by IAEA[41] and OEEC[42].

2. *Safeguards*. Like the research bilaterals, most combined bilaterals also envisage the possibility of controls being administered one day by IAEA or by ENEA.[43] The agreement with EURATOM merely says, however, that IAEA or ENEA 'might be asked to assist.' Meanwhile, again with the exception of the treaty with EURATOM where a special arrangement exists (Article XIII), these agreements all provide for the following three groups of safeguards:

(a) *Safeguards relating to the sale of fuel*. Here the combined bilaterals incorporate the various safeguards which are already to be found in the research bilaterals, although the system of inspection is now integrated with the general safeguards. But, in addition, two further conditions are found.

---

[41] IAEA, Draft International Convention on Minimum International Standards Regarding Civil Liability for Nuclear Damage.

[42] Now the Convention on Third-Party Liability in the Field of Nuclear Energy, Paris, 29 July 1960, Cmnd. 1211 (1960). See further IAEA, *International Conventions on Civil Liability for Nuclear Damage* (1966).

[43] See s. VI below.

First, fuel purchased from the United Kingdom must be used only in reactors obtained from or approved by the United Kingdom. Secondly, the amount of fuel to be supplied shall not exceed that needed for the full loading of such reactors, plus whatever quantity is required for the efficient and continuous operation of such reactors, known sometimes as the 'pipeline.'

(b) *General safeguards*. These general safeguards are for the specific purpose of ensuring that equipment and material supplied under these agreements are not diverted to military use. First, the United Kingdom is given the right to examine the design of equipment or facilities which are to be made available to the other contracting State or persons under its jurisdiction pursuant to these agreements or in which any material obtained from the United Kingdom or special nuclear material derived therefrom is to be used or processed. Secondly, a more elaborate system of inspection than that in research bilaterals is instituted, under which United Kingdom representatives shall have 'access at times to all places and data, and to any person . . . for the purpose of accounting for source material or special nuclear material so supplied and source material or special nuclear material derived from the use of material or equipment so supplied.' Thirdly, the recipient State undertakes to maintain operating records, and to make them available when required, so as to ensure that 'an accurate account shall at all times be kept of source material and special nuclear material derived from the use of material or equipment supplied' under these agreements.

(c) *Additional safeguards relating to special nuclear material*. Special nuclear material, the meaning of which is defined in these agreements, derived from the use of any material or equipment supplied under them, shall be at the disposal of the respective recipient States under a number of additional safeguards. First, the storage of any surplus quantity of such material is subject to the control of the United Kingdom Atomic Energy Authority (UKAEA). Secondly, if the recipient State wishes to dispose of any of this surplus material, UKAEA has an option to purchase it. Thirdly, the transfer of any surplus not so purchased shall be subject to the agreement of the United Kingdom.

Finally, as in research bilaterals, there is a general undertaking on the part of the recipient State to use the material and equipment obtained under these agreements, as well as any material derived therefrom, solely for peaceful ends, and not for any military purposes; not to allow any of them to be transferred to unauthorized persons or beyond the jurisdiction of the recipient State; and to observe the safeguards stipulated in the respective agreements. Moreover, in each of these combined bilaterals where safeguards are provided for, there is a provision enabling the United Kingdom to terminate the agreement if it considers that the other party, after having been called upon to take corrective steps, has failed to comply with the safeguards in the treaty. In this event, any fuel or special nuclear material supplied under the agreement concerned (though it would appear not any special nuclear material derived therefrom) shall be returned to the United Kingdom, subject to compensation at current prices.

United States bilaterals[44] which, of course, are far more numerous, differ but little in their essential features from British bilaterals. Mention may, however, perhaps be made of the fact that in some of the earlier United States research bilaterals, the fuel is only leased, instead of being sold, to the recipient State. In general, more stringent and specific restrictions are contained in United States agreements, whether research or power, regarding the quantity and quality of fuel that may be supplied to the recipient State. This is probably due to the fact that, whereas United Kingdom power reactors use natural uranium as fuel, United States power reactors use enriched uranium. But it may be recalled that United Kingdom combined bilaterals also contain a quantitative limitation, restricting the duty to supply fuel primarily to British-supplied reactors, a limitation not found in United States power bilaterals.

Insofar as the Soviet Union is concerned, its bilateral agreements on the peaceful use of nuclear energy are predominantly research bilaterals.[45] An interesting pointer is the oft-repeated Soviet contention that Soviet bilateral agreements, in not providing for a system of control, do not violate the sovereignty of the States receiving nuclear assistance, whereas Western agreements are mere instruments of imperialism. Soviet bilaterals are, however, extremely brief, requiring for their implementation further agreements between the parties. As these supplementary agreements are not made public, it is difficult to assess whether the Soviet programme of bilateral co-operation contains effective safeguards against the diversion of special nuclear material derived especially from power reactors to military use.

It is, of course, well known that power reactors produce nuclear material in quantity and quality that are also suitable for the manufacture of atomic weapons. This fact emphasizes the need for effective control, if the circle of the atomic arms club is not to be further widened,[46] and lends importance to the safeguards which have previously been discussed.

VI. Safeguards Administered by International Agencies

It will be recalled that most of the United Kingdom bilaterals refer to the possibility of adopting safeguards to be administered by various international

[44] See loc. cit. in n. 27 above.
[45] See G. Ginsberg, 'The Soviet Union and International Cooperation in the Peaceful Use of Atomic Energy', 54 *AJIL* (1960), p. 605; and n. 18 above.
[46] Cf. Resolution A 1665 (XVI), adopted unanimously by the UN General Assembly on 4 Dec. 1961, on the Prevention of the Wider Dissemination of Nuclear Weapons.

agencies.[47] Such systems are to be found in the Statute of IAEA, in the Rome Treaty establishing EURATOM, and in the Convention sponsored by OEEC on the Establishment of a Security Control in the Field of Nuclear Energy,[48] which is directly linked to ENEA.

The actual methods of control in these multilateral agreements resemble, to a remarkable degree, the various safeguards to be found in United Kingdom and United States research-and-power bilaterals,[49] such as examination of the design of specialized equipment and facilities, including nuclear reactors, approval of the means to be used for the chemical processing of irradiated materials, maintenance and production of operating records, progress reports, limiting the use of special nuclear material recovered or produced as by-product to purely peaceful purposes, and control over any surplus quantity of such special fissionable material. In each case, the ultimate sanction consists in either the suspension or the withdrawal of the assistance given by the international agency concerned.

What is, however, the most interesting feature of these schemes is the system of inspection taken over from bilateral agreements. In every case, an inspectorate of a truly international character is to be created. In the ENEA Security Treaty and in EURATOM, the inspection system is further reinforced by a procedure designed to overcome the recalcitrance of any contracting or member State. In the former case, the Control Bureau may apply to the President of the Tribunal set up under the Treaty, and in the latter case the EURATOM Commission may apply to the President of the Court of the European Communities, each for the purpose of obtaining a warrant to carry out the inspection. In both instances, the respective Presidents must give a decision within three days.

What is perhaps the furthest step yet taken in this direction is the power which Article 81, paragraph 4, of the 1957 Rome Treaty establishing EURATOM has conferred on the EURATOM Commission:

If there is danger in delay, the Commission may itself issue a written order, in the form of a decision, to the effect that the inspection be carried out. Such order shall be submitted without delay to the President of the Court of Justice for subsequent approval.

VII. Conclusion

The experience of international co-operation and control in both the military and peaceful uses of nuclear energy can provide valuable lessons in the regulation of the future exploration and exploitation of outer space, where the problems of dual use are likely to be equally complex.

---

[47] See nn. 40 and 43 above.   [48] Paris, 20 Dec. 1957; UKTS No. 8 (1960), Cmnd. 971.
[49] See s. V.D.2 above.

Without aspiring to procedures which may be acceptable only within a supranational community like EURATOM, the systems of inspection administered by international agencies in the field of nuclear energy, as found in the Statute of IAEA and in the ENEA Security Treaty, if allowed to operate, will provide helpful precedents not only for similar schemes of international cooperation and control in the peaceful uses of outer space but also for any effective plan of general disarmament without which there is no real hope in the effective demilitarization of either nuclear energy or outer space.

5

The Extraterrestrial Application of International Law*

I. Introduction

At the dawn of the space age, doubt in one form or another was often expressed, not least by various Members of the United Nations, whether international law as such was from the very beginning applicable to outer space. Thus some 'stressed that there was as yet no international law governing outer space,'[1] while others were 'not sure that international law, as we know it on earth, can or ought, *mutatis mutandis*, to be extended to outer space.'[2]

This hesitancy towards the 'extension' of international law to outer space is due sometimes to a romantic notion that is well illustrated by the following passage from a speech of the Indian delegate:

My delegation cannot contemplate any prospect other than that outer space should be a kind of warless world, where all military concepts of this earth should be totally inapplicable. The limitative connotations inherent in the imperfections of our present-day international law should not be transported into outer space . . . It seems to us that many of our concepts of international law and those based on national considerations which have necessarily become a part of the mental make-up and attitudes of men and nations should be radically revised. When the day comes that men of various nations, through international co-operative efforts, journey into outer space and celestial bodies, many old concepts will have to be forgotten and will, indeed, be out of place in outer space. There should be only one governing concept, that of humanity and the sovereignty of mankind.[3]

* First published in 18 *CLP* (1965), pp. 132–52. Reproduced by kind permission of Sweet & Maxwell Ltd.

[1] United Arab Republic, A/C.1/SR.1342 (2.12.63), p. 163; France, ibid./SR.1345 (5.12.63), p. 183; 'an international law of outer space had yet to be created'.

[2] India, A/AC.105/PV.3 (20.3.62), p. 63; Brazil, A/C.1/SR.1346 (5.12.63), pp. 190–1; Brazil, A/AC.105/PV.24 (22.11.673), p. 21; cf. also F. R. Schick, 'Problems of a Space Law in the United Nations,' 13 *ICLQ* (1964), p. 969, at p. 977; R. H. Mankiewicz, 'Some Thoughts on Law and Public Order in Space', *Can. YBIL* (1964), p. 258, at pp. 260–1.

[3] A/AC.105/PV.3 (20.3.62), pp. 63–6 (see also text to n. 7 below); Mexico, A/AC.105/PV.6 (23.3.62), p. 26 (see also text to n. 4 below). Cf. M. S. McDougal and others, *Law and Public Order in Space* (1963), p. 46: 'As matters stand today there is ample evidence that as we push out into the environment of the earth we are almost certain to carry the disunited world arena with us'.

But there are also more down-to-earth considerations.[4] Among them is one which is of particular relevance to the present discussion. It has been referred to by several delegates to the United Nations.[5] As another Indian delegate has put it, because the United Nations General Assembly in its resolution 1721A (XVII) of 20 December 1961,[6] the first substantive resolution on outer space adopted by the General Assembly, has 'commend[ed] to States for their guidance' not only the principle that 'international law, including the Charter of the United Nations, applies to outer space and celestial bodies,' but also the principle that outer space and celestial bodies are not subject to national appropriation, what is necessary is 'to define to what extent international law would operate and to what extent sovereign rights have to be waived.'[7] Hence, as the United Arab Republic delegate has suggested, 'a study should be made to determine precisely what rules of international law or practice were applicable to outer space.'[8]

It seems appropriate, therefore, in any study of international space law first to examine whether and, if so, the extent to which international law as such is from the beginning extraterrestrially applicable to outer space and celestial bodies. It is proposed to look at first the position under general international law (alias, customary international law) and next the extent, if any, to which this position has been affected by two among the first substantive resolutions on outer space adopted by the General Assembly of the United Nations, namely, resolution 1721A (XVI) of 20 December 1961,[9] and resolution 1962 (XVIII) of 13 December 1963,[10] which in themselves, are without binding force. The former 'commends to States for their guidance,' *inter alia*, the principle that 'international law, including the Charter of the United Nations, applies to outer space and celestial bodies.' The latter 'solemnly declares that . . . States should be guided' by, among others, the principle that their activities in the exploration and use of outer space and celestial bodies shall be carried on in accordance with international law.[11] The position under the 1967 Treaty of Principles Governing the Activities of States in the Exploration and Use of Outer Space, Including the Moon and Other Celestial Bodies (the Space Treaty),[12] will be discussed in Chapter 8 on the Space Treaty.[13]

---

[4] See, further, Brazil (2.11.63), Schick, and Mankiewicz, loc. cit. in n. 2 above; Mexico, loc. cit. in n. 3 above.

[5] Amongst others, Mexico, A/AC.105/PV.6 (23.3.62), p. 26; France, A/AC.105/C.2/SR.3 (30.5.62), p. 5; Bulgaria, A/AC.105/C.2/SR.6 (6.6.62), p. 4.

[6] *UNYB* (1961), p. 35. Text reproduced below as Appendix II.1. See further s. IV below.

[7] A/AC.105/PV.13 (13.9.62), p. 6.

[8] A/AC/105/C.2/SR.18 (18.4.63), p. 4; similarly Brazil, A/C.1/SR.1346 (5.12.63), p. 191.

[9] Loc. cit. in n. 6 above; reproduced below as Appendix II.1. See also s. IV below.

[10] GAOR Annexes (XVIII) 28, p. 27; see Appendix II.3, and also s. IV below.

[11] For an analysis of the status of these two resolutions, see further B. Cheng, 'United Nations Resolutions on Outer Space: "Instant" International Customary Law?', 5 *Indian JIL* (1965), p. 23, pp. 40 ff. *et passim* [Ch. 7 below, s. X *et passim*].

[12] Annex to A/RES/2222 (XXI), *GAOR* (XXI), Suppl. No. 16; see Appendix I.1.

[13] See below Ch. 9, s. V.A: The Extraterrestrial Application of International Law.

II. Position under General International Law

Since States are still the normal subjects of international law, and the attribution, delimitation and regulation of the competence of States in their mutual relations represent the most important function of international law,[14] a discussion of the extraterrestrial limits of the various types of State jurisdiction under international law will, it is submitted, afford a clear picture of the extent to which international law is *ipso jure* applicable extraterrestrially.

For this purpose, it appears convenient to make use of a classification of the notion of State jurisdiction which I first adopted in a paper on 'Crimes on Board Aircraft', published in 1959.[15] This classification divides State jurisdiction into three types, namely, territorial, quasi-territorial, and personal,[16] and separates each into two distinct elements, for which two new terms had to be coined, namely, jurisfaction and jurisaction.[17] I believe that this classification affords a clearer insight into the notion of State jurisdiction, which at present often appears to be highly complex and confused. Moreover, it is hoped that by means of a schematic presentation of the various component elements of State jurisdiction in the accompanying Table V.1[18] the extent to which international law has been applicable to outer space, from even before the first sputnik, becomes readily apparent.

First, it may be helpful briefly to explain the essentials of this classification.

A. Types of State Jurisdiction

1. *Territorial Jurisdiction.* Territorial jurisdiction is the sum total of the powers of a State in respect of a portion of *terra firma* under its governmental authority, including all persons and things therein, and the extraterritorial activities of such persons. It is generally derived from territorial sovereignty, but may also be derived from treaties, as in the case of mandated, trust, or leased territories. It may also come from *occupatio pacifica* or *bellica*.

---

[14] See Ch. Rousseau, 'Principes de droit international public', 93 Hague *Recueil* (1958), p. 369, at pp. 394–5. The lectures were devoted to a study of State jurisdiction. See also A. M. Stuyt, *The General Principles of Law as Applied by International Tribunals to Disputes on Attribution and Exercise of State Jurisdiction* (1946).

[15] 12 *CLP* (1959) p. 177, at pp. 181 ff.

[16] See also G. Schwarzenberger, *A Manual of International Law* (6th ed., 1976), pp. 74–5. Cf. different systems of classification, op. cit. in n. 14 above and n. 17 below, and G. Schwarzenberger, 1(1) *Int. Law* (1957), pp. 183 ff.

[17] Cf. the American Law Institute, which three years later in its *Restatement of the Law—The Foreign Relations Law of the United States—Proposed Official Draft* (1962) suggested a similar distinction between jurisdiction to prescribe and jurisdiction to enforce. This was adopted in the Second Edition (1965). However, jurisfaction covers more than merely jurisdiction to legislate, and jurisaction more than mere law enforcement. The Third Edition of the *Restatement* (1987) has since reverted to a tripartite division of jurisdictions to prescribe, to adjudicate and to enforce.

[18] Cf. the present writer's 'Inter Astra Silent Leges?—Prolegomena to Jural Cartography,' 30 *GLIMS* (Michaelmas, 1961), p. 18.

2. *Personal Jurisdiction.* Personal jurisdiction is the sum total of the powers of a State in respect of individuals or corporate bodies or business enterprises having its nationality or otherwise enjoying its protection or owing it allegiance, wherever they may be. Pirates *jure gentium* may also be said to come under the extraordinary personal jurisdiction of all States.

3. *Quasi-territorial Jurisdiction.* In between territorial jurisdiction and personal jurisdiction stands *quasi-territorial jurisdiction.* This is the sum total of the powers of a State in respect of ships, aircraft and spacecraft (to the extent to which they are also granted legal personality) having its nationality or registration. Its powers over pirate vessels *jure gentium* come also under this heading. Quasi-territorial jurisdiction differs from personal jurisdiction in that it extends not only to the craft in question but also to all persons and things on board, including the activities of such persons, whether on board the craft or elsewhere.

B. Elements of State Jurisdiction

By its nature, jurisdiction may be separated into two distinct elements, the normative element and the physical or concrete element. *Jurisfaction*[19] denotes the normative element of jurisdiction and represents the power of a State[20] to adopt valid and binding legal norms or decisions and to apply or concretize them with binding effect through its appropriate organs, whether judicial or otherwise. The spheres of validity or operative force of these norms or decisions may be delimited *ratione loci* (territorial), *ratione instrumenti* (quasi-territorial), or *ratione personae* (personal).

Jurisaction, on the other hand, is the physical or concrete element of State jurisdiction and denotes the power of a State, at any given time or place, physically to perform any governmental function, be it the act of actually making, applying, implementing or enforcing laws, such as holding a legislative assembly, conducting an administrative inquiry, setting up a tribunal, or arresting a wanted person. From this point of view, the validity of jurisaction presupposes jurisfaction, but it is possible to have jurisfaction without jurisaction.

Attempts have sometimes been made to express the distinction underlying this division of State jurisdiction into jurisfaction and jurisaction by differentiating between the *enjoyment* or possession of State jurisdiction and the *exercise* of State jurisdiction. Thus it is frequently said that a State *enjoys* concurrent personal jurisdiction over its nationals even when they are in a

---

[19] If preferred, jurisdiction *sensu stricto* or, following the American Law Institute (see n. 17 above), jurisprescription, though, on account of discrepancies in interpretation, the latter term may be a source of confusion.

[20] This is so in the case of State jurisfaction. It may otherwise be the power of any authority, in which case the power may be restricted merely to the concretisation (in the kelsenian sense) of pre-existing legal norms.

foreign State. It is then said that, as long as its nationals are in the latter State, the former State may not, or alternatively it is said that it simply cannot, exercise this personal jurisdiction over them. This description is, however, a hopeless confusion of words.

For, in the situation described above, the national State both *enjoys* and is entitled to *exercise* concurrently its *personal jurisfaction* over its nationals even while they are in a foreign country and, therefore, subject to the latter's territorial jurisfaction as well as its territorial jurisaction. The national State may thus enact laws making its nationals abroad liable to national income tax, requiring them to register with the local consuls or recalling them for military service. Its courts, moreover, have judicial jurisfaction over them: their judgments will be binding on them. In fact, the national State's personal jurisfaction over its nationals is limitless in its geographical, or one may say cosmographical, scope, and this personal jurisfaction may be exercised concurrently with the local State's territorial jurisfaction and jurisaction.

But, on account of the exclusive character of jurisaction and the hierarchy of different types of jurisaction,[21] *while, and* at the place *where*, an individual is under the territorial or quasi-territorial jurisaction of another State, his national State does not enjoy, and may not exercise, *personal jurisaction* over him, inasmuch as personal jurisaction must cede precedence to territorial and quasi-territorial jurisaction. It may not, for instance, attempt to arrest him or kidnap him. Any such attempt by a State to exercise personal jurisaction at a place which is subject to the territorial or quasi-territorial jurisaction of another State would normally be an infringement of the right of the latter and a violation of international law.

Such personal jurisaction may, however, be exercised from outside spheres of territorial or quasi-territorial jurisaction of other States. This has the effect, of course, of restricting such exercise of personal jurisaction to only its legislative and judicial form, and of excluding executive jurisaction. In practical terms, this means that a State may, in its own territory (or in *territorium nullius*), pass laws applicable to its own nationals who are in foreign countries, or on board foreign craft that are not in its own territory, and even try them *in absentia*, but it may not send its officers to where they are in order to arrest them.

Moreover, when and where its nationals are not subject to the territorial or quasi-territorial jurisaction of any other State, then the national State's personal jurisaction comes fully into its own. For example, when they are in *territorium nullius*, the national State, if it wishes, is entitled to set up machinery there to enact laws to govern their conduct, arrest them for the purpose either of bringing them home for trial or trying them there and then by an ad hoc tribunal, and even to carry out the sentence there.

---

[21] See text to n. 25 below.

The legality and validity of acts of jurisaction depend, therefore, not only on their nature and the person *vis-à-vis* whom they are carried out, but also, most important of all, on their *locus*.[22] This factor is, however, sometimes ignored by those who belittle the importance and urgency of a clear-cut frontier between territorial space and outer space and who advocate the functional approach to the regulation of activities in and relating to outer space.[23]

The above presentation of the concept of State jurisdiction allows, it is submitted, a more precise and accurate explanation of the notion of State jurisdiction. Indeed, only by distinguishing between jurisfaction and jurisaction is it possible to bring out in their entirety the logical consequences of the judgment of the Permanent Court of International Justice in *The Lotus Case* (1927).[24] In that decision the World Court rejected the territoriality of criminal law as a binding rule of international law and affirmed in effect the universal scope of territorial jurisfaction and the overriding character of territorial jurisaction.

Almost inevitably, therefore, jurisfaction is most of the time concurrent, while in respect of jurisaction, at any given time and place, there must always be only one authority which prevails over all others. Once jurisaction is separated from jurisfaction, the hierarchical order of the various types of jurisaction emerges in its full simplicity. In the absence of any treaty or other consensual arrangements whereby this state of affairs is modified,[25] whenever a conflict arises, territorial jurisaction overrides all other types of jurisaction, while quasi-territorial jurisaction overrides personal jurisaction.

This distinction between jurisfaction and jurisaction has been found helpful in elucidating the problems arising from potential negative and positive conflicts of criminal jurisdiction in relation to offences on board aircraft.[26] It will be seen from the accompanying Table V.1 that, in conjunction with the classification of State jurisdiction into territorial, quasi-territorial and personal jurisdiction, it is also useful in answering many of the questions regarding the extraterrestrial application of international law.

It is apparent from the Table, for instance, why it would not be strictly correct to say that, because of 'the total absence of any territorial sovereignty in outer space, it should be recognized that no State might exercise any kind of jurisdiction in outer space';[27] for, even in the absence of territorial sovereignty, whenever their nationals or spacecraft are in outer space or have landed on celestial bodies, States are perfectly entitled to exercise either personal or quasi-territorial jurisdiction over them, as the case may be. Thus the seventh

---

[22] See below, n. 49 and text thereto.   [23] See below, n. 35 *in fine*.   [24] A 10.

[25] E.g., in the case of extraterritorial rights and consular jurisdiction.

[26] See, in addition to loc. cit. in n. 12 above, Report of the Royal Aeronautical Society Air Law Group Steering Committee to the Minister of Aviation on *Crimes and Offences on Board Aircraft* (1962), copies of which are obtainable by application to the Secretary of the Society; see also Sir R. Wilberforce, 'Crime in Aircraft', 67 *JRAeS* (1963), p. 175.

[27] India, A/AC.105/C.2/SR.2 (29.5.62), p. 4.

Table V.1. STATE JURISDICTION*

TYPE	TERRITORIAL	QUASI-TERRITORIAL	PERSONAL
OBJECT	*Terra firma* (terrestrial or extra-terrestrial) including adjacent maritime belt, subsoil and superjacent space	Ships, aircraft and spacecraft	Individuals, corporate bodies and business enterprises
MATERIAL SCOPE	In respect of the whole territory, including all its resources, all persons and things therein, and the extraterritorial activities of all such persons, whether individual or corporate	In respect of the craft themselves and all persons and things therein, including the activities of such persons, individual or corporate, whether on board the craft or elsewhere	In respect of individuals, corporate bodies and business enterprises, and all property, rights and legal interests belonging to them, wherever they may be
SOURCE	*International customary law:* sovereignty, law of war and *status mixtus*, including self-defence and reprisals. *Treaties* with, and *recognition* or *acquiescence* of, other international persons, *e.g.* protectorates, leased, mandated and trust territories	State jurisdiction over flag-craft and pirate vessels *jure gentium*. Right to flag under *international customary law* may be based on nationality of owner or charterer, other 'genuine link,' and registration. It may also be derived from *consent*, *recognition* or *acquiescence* of other international persons	*International customary law:* State jurisdiction over nationals, including corporate bodies and business enterprises endowed with nationality, other persons owing allegiance, and pirates *jure gentium*. *Treaties* with, and *recognition* or *acquiescence* of, other international persons, *e.g.*, jurisdiction over protected persons

ELEMENT	JURISFACTION	JURISACTION	JURISFACTION	JURISACTION	JURISFACTION	JURISACTION
HIERARCHY AND PRECEDENCE (*Jurisfaction*)	On a par with other types of jurisfaction		On a par with other types of jurisfaction		On a par with other types of jurisfaction	
HIERARCHY (*Jurisaction*)		First		Second		Third
PRECEDENCE (*Jurisaction*)		In case of conflict, overrides quasi-territorial and personal jurisaction		In case of conflict, gives way to territorial jurisaction but overrides personal jurisaction		In case of conflict, gives way to both territorial and quasi-territorial jurisaction
GEOGRAPHICAL SCOPE	Limitless (terrestrial and extraterrestrial)	National territory of a State, other territory for the international relations of which it is responsible, and territory under its *occupatio pacifica* or *bellica*	Limitless (terrestrial and extraterrestrial)	Over flag-craft anywhere outside territories subject to the territorial jurisaction of other recognised international persons	Limitless (terrestrial and extraterrestrial)	Over all individuals, corporate bodies and business enterprises subject to a State's personal jurisdiction outside territories or craft subject to the territorial or quasi-territorial jurisaction of other recognised international persons

Table V.1. *cont.*

RELEVANCE TO SPACE LAW	Extraterrestrially applicable	Stresses the urgent need of clearly delimiting national space from outer space. Will also apply to extra-terrestrial territories, once sovereignty established and recognised in accordance with existing rules of international law	Extraterrestrially applicable	Applicable to national spacecraft in outer space	Extraterrestrially applicable	Applicable to nationals and other persons or entities subject to a State's personal jurisdiction even when they are in outer space

* For a more compact version of this table see p. 441.

principle in General Assembly resolution 1962 (XVIII), at least in its first part, is merely an expression of existing international law when it says:

The State on whose registry an object launched into outer space is carried shall retain jurisdiction and control over such object, and any personnel thereon, while in outer space.

Quite rightly, this principle recognizes that the quasi-territorial jurisdiction of the State of registry extends not only to the vehicle, but also to all personnel on board irrespective of their nationality, with quasi-territorial jurisaction over-riding personal jurisaction. As a result of man's penetration into space, all the rules of international law governing the attribution and exercise of quasi-territorial and personal jurisdiction become fully applicable extraterrestrially whenever spacecraft and nationals of members of the international society venture beyond the terrestrial airspace. They are also subject to the extraterrestrial effects of territorial jurisfaction exercised from national territories on the earth.

As yet, only territorial jurisaction is not found in outer space or on celestial bodies. Consequently, the rules of international law governing the positive aspects of the exercise of territorial jurisaction (that is to say, where, how and *vis-à-vis* whom it *may* be exercised) are, as a matter of *fact* but not *law*, not yet extraterrestrially applicable, except those governing the acquisition of territorial sovereignty and jurisdiction. Rules such as those governing the expropriation of private property belonging to foreigners, for instance, would have no application on the moon, even when there is a fair-size population there, until territorial sovereignty has been established and recognized.

But, in addition to rules of international law governing the attribution and positive exercise of quasi-territorial and personal jurisdiction, all the rules governing the negative aspects of all three types of jurisdiction are already fully applicable to outer space and celestial bodies, that is to say, all the rules indicating when, where, how, and *vis-à-vis* whom they may *not* be exercised. Thus, until and unless territorial sovereignty has been established and recognized in outer space or on celestial bodies, no State will be entitled to exercise territorial jurisaction there. In the absence of territorial jurisaction, quasi-territorial jurisaction becomes supreme. None but the flag-State, however, is entitled to exercise quasi-territorial jurisaction over any spacecraft, or persons and things on board them, extraterrestrially. If such persons are not subject to the quasi-territorial jurisaction of any State, then only the national State may normally exercise personal jurisaction over them. Any attempt to exercise jurisaction in outer space or on celestial bodies in excess of these limits will be an infringement of the right of either the flag-State or the national State of the individual, as the case may be, and a violation of international law.

What has been said above suffices to show why it would be difficult to sub-scribe to the view of the Austrian delegate when he was reported to have said that:

It was not known which part of international law applied to the moon; in his opinion none did.[28]

III. Res Communis, Res Nullius, Res Extra Commercium

The Austrian delegate was quite correct, however, when he said:

International law . . . nowhere defined the status of a *res communis omnium*.[29]

But this was not for the reasons which he had given. The real reason is that under general, alias customary, international law there is no *res communis omnium*, an object under the joint sovereignty of all subjects of international law. In addition to territories under the territorial sovereignty of recognized subjects of international law, only two other types of territory exist, namely, on the one hand, *res nullius*, that is to say, territory not subject to the territorial jurisdiction of any recognized subject of international law but susceptible of national appropriation, and on the other hand, *res extra commercium*, that is to say, territory not subject to national appropriation, like the high seas.

As regards the possible establishment of territorial sovereignty in outer space and over celestial bodies, the question therefore is whether outer space and over celestial bodies constitute *res communes omnium, res nullius* or *res extra commercium*.

In discussions in the United Nations, many national delegates have referred to outer space and celestial bodies as *res communes omnium*, but only a few have drawn the logical consequences from the concept of collective sovereignty or joint *dominium*. Paradoxically, it was at the same meeting where the Soviet delegate had read into the minutes of the Legal Sub-Committee the statement of the Soviet government issued on 3 June 1962, regarding the United States announcement of a programme of high altitude nuclear tests over the Pacific, that the Roumanian delegate, speaking of the danger of analogies, said:

The concept of *res communis usus* might, if applied to outer space, be used to hinder the use of space for research by any State on the ground that it was common property.[30]

Indeed, after the controversial United States high altitude nuclear test of 9 July 1962 over Johnston Island, delegates from the Soviet bloc did not fail to invoke the concept of *res communis* as an ad hoc argument in order, on the one hand, to condemn the action of the United States and, on the other hand, to support the Soviet draft declaration of principles governing outer space submitted to the Legal Sub-Committee on 6 June 1962.[31] The Soviet draft, *inter*

---

[28] A/AC.105/C.2/SR.5 (5.6.62), p. 6.   [29] Ibid.   [30] Ibid./SR.4 (4.6.62), p. 10.
[31] A/AC.105/C.2/L.1.

alia, provided for prior consultation and co-ordination before any measure is carried out which might hinder other States in the exploration and use of outer space. Thus the Czechoslovak delegate said on 14 September 1962:

The United States delegation is worried about a Soviet veto over national programmes of other countries. However, every State in the world and the international community as a whole has the right of veto over actions of a certain State which would violate the principle that outer space is *res communis*.[32]

There is, however, no basis for considering that, under general international law, outer space or celestial bodies are under such a regime where action by one State is subject to the veto of another. What, then, is the legal status of outer space and celestial bodies under general international law? Here a distinction is necessary between celestial bodies on the one hand and outer space on the other.

A. Outer Space

For reasons which the present writer has fully explained elsewhere,[33] *outer space*, meaning the void between celestial bodies (including the earth and their atmospheric space), constitutes, under existing international customary law, *res extra commercium* in that it is not subject to national appropriation.

The question then arises as to the present limit between territorial space over which the subjacent State exercises territorial sovereignty and jurisdiction and outer space which is *res extra commercium*. In the absence of any express international agreement making such a demarcation, territorial space must be deemed to be at least conterminous with territorial airspace (i.e., atmospheric space) over which States undoubtedly exercise territorial sovereignty. At a time before space flights began, the present writer, on the basis of geophysical factors, had estimated the upper limit of airspace to lie at a height of between 500 and 1,000 kilometres (i.e., between 310 and 620 miles) above the surface of the earth.[34] Since then, it appears that a general practice has grown up among States interpreting airspace as meaning space in which navigation by conventional aircraft is possible and outer space as space where artificial satellites are able to orbit, thus bringing the frontier down to approximately 50 miles (80 km), with a possible margin of 25 miles (40 km) either

---

[32] A/AC.105/PV.16 (14.9.62), p. 12; USSR, ibid./PV.15 (14.9.62), p. 10; cf. Soviet Doctrine, R. D. Crane, 'Soviet Attitude Toward International Space Law', 56 *AJIL* (1962), p. 685, at 696.

[33] See the present writer's 'Recent Developments in Air Law', 9 *CLP* (1956), p. 208, at pp. 215–7 [Ch. 1 above, s. IV]; 'International Law and High Altitude Flights: Balloons, Rockets and Man-Made Satellites,' 6 *ICLQ* (1957), p. 487, at pp. 492–4 [Ch. 2 above, s. IV]; 'From Air Law to Space Law', 13 *CLP* (1960), p. 228, at p. 234 [Ch. 3 above, s. II.A *in fine*].

[34] See loc. cit. in n. 33 above (1956), pp. 213–5 [Ch. 1 above, s. III]; (1957), pp. 491–2 [Ch. 2 above, s. III]; (1960), pp. 230–1 [Ch. 3 above, s. II.A *in principio*.]

way.[35] This development may be regarded either as the interpretation of an existing rule of international law by the practice of States,[36] or the emergence of a new rule of customary (i.e., general) international law modifying a previous one.[37]

[35] J. C. Cooper, who rightly believes in the importance of a frontier between national space and outer space, in 1951 estimated that the area of 'air-lift' extended to a height of 60 miles (*ILQ* (1951), p. 411). In 1956 (*ASIL Proc.* (1956), p. 84), he was of the view that atmospheric (and territorial) space coincided with the area of 'air-lift' and proposed that sovereignty should be further extended to 300 miles to cover the area of 'air-drag,' designating this area 'contiguous space,' and that the space beyond should be declared free (see also his address before the British Branch of the International Law Association, 7 *ICLQ* (1958), p. 82). In a letter published in *The Times* (London), 7 Sept. 1957, he suggested that it might be necessary to raise the 300-mile limit to 600 miles.

A. G. Haley, in the late 'fifties adopted a line suggested by Theodore von Kármán in 1957, later termed the Kármán primary jurisdictional line, which divided the aeronautic from the astronautic regions. In the present state of technology, this line is said to be located at approximately 52 miles (see further Haley, *Space Law and Government* (1963), pp. 75 ff.).

G. P. Zhukov, 'Conquest of Outer Space and Some Problems of International Relations', *Int. Aff.* (Moscow, 1959), p. 88, reprinted in *Senate Symposium* (1961), p. 1072, at p. 1083: 'in my opinion, the extent of State sovereignty should not include the space where the first sputniks travelled.'

L. Lipson and N. de B. Katzenbach, *American Bar Foundation Report to NASA* (1960), reproduced in *Senate Symposium* (1961), p. 779, at p. 794: frontier lies between 12 miles and 100 miles from earth surface. The authors support the conclusion of the UN Ad Hoc Committee (1959) that the boundary problem was not susceptible of priority treatment and its suggestion of a functional approach to the regulation of activities in space (at p. 798). See the present writer's comment on the Ad Hoc Committee's conclusion in 'The United Nations and Outer Space', 14 *CLP* (1961), p. 247, at pp. 259 ff. [Ch. 6 below, s. IV].

G. P. Zadorozhnij, 'Osnovnye Problemy Nauki Kosmicheskogo Prava' (Basic Problems of Cosmic Law), in Ye. Korovon (ed.), *Kosmos I Mazhdunarodnoe Pravo* (*The Cosmos and International Law*) (1962), p. 23, at p. 46, sets sovereignty below the zone in which satellites orbit (cited in Haley, op. cit., p. 85, n. 24).

David Davies Memorial Institute, *Draft Code of Rules on the Exploration and Uses of Outer Space*: '25 miles is probably the outside limit of effective aerodynamic lift', 'while 70 miles is indicated as the present limit of effective orbiting', 50 miles suggested as 'the limit of sovereignty and the beginning of outer space'.

J. C. Cooper in communications within the International Law Association, published in the Report of the Air Law Committee to the Tokyo Conference, 1964, indicated his willingness to support 'an upper boundary of national airspace at an altitude of 75 miles, with limited and controlled rights of passage for spacecraft in a zone between altitudes of 25 miles and 75 miles' (ILA, *Report of the 51st Conference, Tokyo* (1964), p. 678, at p. 682).

A. Meyer in the same correspondence emphasized that 'a borderline between airspace and outer space must be fixed at some future time', and was willing to support a numerical limit of 80 km. above sea level, though he would be prepared to agree that, until traffic into outer space developed further, the frontier problem did not as yet call for priority consideration at this moment (ibid., p. 688, at p. 692).

McDougal and others, op. cit. in n. 3 above, prefer the functional approach and call the attempt to seek boundaries 'a comedy of errors'; cf. the present writer's comment in review in 16 *Univ. of Toronto LJ* (1965), pp. 210–3, and the present writer's intervention in the Space Law Section in International Law Association, *Report of the 51st Conference, Tokyo* (1964), pp. 638–43.

Cf. also C. W. Jenks, 'Le droit international des espaces célestes—Rapport préliminaire', in Institut de droit international, 50 (I) *Annuaire de l'Institut* (1963), p. 128, at pp. 318 ff., and comment thereon by A. Meyer, loc. cit. above, p. 692.

[36] Cf. *Temple of Preah Vihear Case*, *ICJ Rep. 1962*, p. 6.

[37] See Mexico, loc. cit. in n. 38 below. On international customary law, see loc. cit. in n. 11 above.

The evidence for saying that States now accept a fairly low limit of territorial space is their attitude towards the problem of the right of passage of orbiting satellites and, particularly, towards reconnaissance satellites. A careful scrutiny of the discussions on outer space in the United Nations reveals that States appear to be in general agreement that orbiting satellites in their orbits never enter airspace and, therefore, the problem of the right of passage through foreign territorial airspace does not arise, except possibly during launching and re-entry.[38]

Furthermore, even when delegates from the Soviet bloc are at their most vehement in their attack on United States reconnaissance satellites,[39] they never query the premise of Western delegates who defend their use, that these satellites operate in outer space outside the territorial space of any State.[40] Their arguments are either that espionage is itself contrary to international law and the United Nations Charter,[41] even if carried out from the high seas,[42] or that it is contrary to the friendly relations among nations.[43] Some have also made use of the *ad hominem* argument of the existence of the United States Air Defense Identification Zones (ADIZ) over the high seas.[44] Although the Hungarian delegate at one point spoke of such activities being 'perpetrated in "zones" which were unquestionably subject to the sovereignty of the subjacent State,'[45] it should be mentioned that these Identification Zones are themselves established over the high seas and are only lawful to the extent to which they do not violate the principle of the freedom of the high seas.[46] In any event, the

[38] Canada, A/AC.105/PV.4 (21.3.62), p. 26: 'Under the concept of outer space now being developed, as long as a spacecraft stays within outer space it is safely proceeding in an area which we might describe as the "high seas" of the air.' The Mexican delegate seemed to consider that this was the result of space powers and non-space powers alike generally accepting a lowering of the previous upper limit of territorial space, A/AC.105/C.2/SR.18 (18.4.63), p. 7. The Mexican view may well be, strictly speaking, the more correct interpretation.

[39] Their use is most probably not one-sided. Cf. a reported conversation between Mr Khrushchev and Mr W. Benton, US delegate to UNESCO on 28 May 1964, when the former was said to have spoken of the superiority of the photographs taken from Soviet space satellites, *The Times* (London), 30 May 1964, p. 8.

[40] Cf. also G. Zhukov, 'Space Espionage Plans and International Law', *Int. Aff* (Moscow, 1960), p. 53, reproduced in *Senate Symposium* (1961), p. 1095; Zhukov and Zadorozhnij, loc. cit. in n. 35 above; Crane, loc. cit. in n. 32 above, pp. 704 ff.

[41] Cf. USSR, A/AC.105/C.2/SR.17 (17.4.63), p. 7; Czechoslovakia, A/C.1/SR.1294 (7.12.62), p. 238; Hungary, A/AC.105/C.2/SR.26 (1.5.63), p. 4.

[42] USSR, A/C.1/SR.1289 (3.12.62), p. 216: 'As to the reference to observation from the high seas, the analogy would hold good only for observing what was taking place on the high seas and not for spying on particular countries'; Bulgaria, A/C.1/SR.1296 (10.12.62), p. 246.

[43] Cf. USSR, A/AC.105/C.2/SR.22 (24.2.63), p. 5.   [44] USSR, ibid.

[45] Ibid./SR.26 (1.5.63), p. 5.

[46] Cf. the present writer's 'The Right to Fly', 42 *Groutius Society Transactions* (1956), p. 99, at p. 102; and the Soviet protest against the pursuit of, and warning shots fired at, a Soviet aircraft (with the Soviet President on board), by a French fighter aircraft in a French ADIZ off the Algerian coast on 9 Feb. 1961, Ch. Debbasch, 'La zone contiguë en droit aérien,' 24 *Rev. Gén. Air* (1961), p. 249, though both Debbasch and J. T. Murchison, *The Contiguous Air Space Zone in International Law* (1956) probably need qualification as to their views on the status of air defence identification zones in international law.

existence of ADIZ off the Alaskan coast did not seem to have prevented Soviet reconnaissance aircraft from flying sometimes as close as five miles from what is United States territory.[47] The absence of serious incidents in such cases, and the return of the two survivors from the RB–47 shot down off the Soviet coast in 1960,[48] are largely due to the existence of well-defined outer limits of the territorial seas off the coasts of Alaska and of the Kola Peninsula.[49]

A precise frontier between territorial space and outer space is equally important; for unless the frontier is clearly delimited, conflicts of jurisdiction can easily and legitimately occur which at all times would be difficult to resolve and in times of international tension may quickly escalate into major crises. The establishment of an authoritative frontier, which must be widely accepted in order to be of value, can only be achieved by means of a multilateral treaty; and this appears to be an eminently opportune juncture to seek such an international convention, inasmuch as there is already substantial agreement on a fairly low limit.[50]

B. Celestial Bodies

While outer space constitutes *res extra commercium* under existing international customary law, the same cannot be said of celestial bodies. They are *terrae firmae* and there is no reason why they cannot in law be brought under national sovereignty through effective occupation and foreign recognition, unless by international agreement States bind themselves not to do so.[51]

Here arises the problem of the two resolutions of the General Assembly, resolution 1721A (XVI) adopted on 20 December 1961,[52] and resolution 1962 (XVIII) adopted on 13 December 1963.[53]

---

[47] USA, during RB–47 debate, S/PV.883 (26.7.60), p. 30, at pp. 33–34, and see Map 1 annexed to S/PV.881. See further B. Cheng, 'The United Nations and Outer Space,' 14 *CLP* (1961), p. 247, at p. 272 [Ch. 6 below, s. V.B. *in fine*]; O. J. Lissitzyn, 'Some Legal Implications of the U–2 and RB–47 Incidents', 56 *AJIL* (1962), p. 135, at p. 141.

[48] On the RB–47 incident, see Cheng, loc. cit. in previous n. at pp. 268–272 [Ch. 6 below, s. V.B].

[49] On the legality of peripheral reconnaissance as opposed to penetrative reconnaissance, see ibid., at pp. 262 ff. [Ch. 6 below, s. V]; and intervention at Tokyo Conference, loc. cit. in n. 35 above, *in fine*.

[50] See further ibid. and the present writer's review of McDougal et al., loc. cit. in n. 35 above, *in fine*.

[51] See loc. cit. (1956) in n. 33 above, p. 215 [Ch. 1 above, s. IV, *in principio*]; (1957), pp. 493–4 [Ch. 2 above, s. IV]; (1960), pp. 234–5 [Ch. 3 above, s. II.A *in medio*].

[52] Loc. cit. in n. 6 above.

[53] GAOR Annexes (XVIII) 28, p. 27; the text is reproduced as Appendix II.3 below.

IV. Resolutions 1721A (XVI) and 1962 (XVIII)

The former resolution commends to States 'for their guidance' not only the principle that international law applies to outer space, but also that 'outer space and celestial bodies are . . . not subject to national appropriation.' As some delegates have not failed to point out, the second principle contradicts the first, at least insofar as celestial bodies are concerned.[54] Inasmuch as it has already been established that the first principle embodied in resolution 1721A is merely declaratory of international customary law, the question arises, therefore, whether the second principle is a valid and effective exception to the first, to the extent to which it contradicts it. There is, moreover, resolution 1962 (XVIII), which incorporates a Declaration of Legal Principles Governing the Activities of States in the Exploration and Uses of Outer Space. The Declaration enunciates nine principles in all. The introductory part of the Declaration and the first four principles of the Declaration are as follows:

The General Assembly solemnly declares that in the exploration and use of outer space States should be guided by the following principles:
1. The exploration and use of outer space shall be carried on for the benefit and in the interests of all mankind.
2. Outer space and celestial bodies are free for exploration and use by all States on a basis of equality and in accordance with international law.
3. Outer space and celestial bodies are not subject to national appropriation by claim of sovereignty, by means of use or occupation, or by any other means.
4. The activities of States in the exploration and use of outer space shall be carried on in accordance with international law, including the Charter of the United Nations, in the interest of maintaining international peace and security and promoting international co-operation and understanding.

The third principle of resolution 1962 raises, therefore, the same problem as the second principle of resolution 1721A.

The answer in both cases depends on the legal force of these two resolutions. The present writer has elsewhere examined this question and arrived at, *inter alia*, the following conclusions.[55] Both resolutions are in themselves without binding force. The language they use is not such as would estop members of the United Nations from denying that the principles they incorporate are binding. The various undertakings of member-States to respect these principles have been given mostly on the very assumption that these resolutions are mere recommendations and appear to constitute, generally speaking, no more than mere statements of intention. Two or three States, having declared that they regard these principles as declaratory of international customary law, might perhaps be precluded from denying their binding character in their

---

[54] See nn. 5 and 7 above.   [55] See loc. cit. in n. 11 above [Ch. 7 below].

inter se relations. Finally, perhaps the only binding element attached to these principles is to be found in the prior agreements between the two super-powers which made these two resolutions possible. These prior agreements represent *modi vivendi* between the super-powers regarding outer space, and the one preceding resolution 1962 incorporates, it would appear, also a *pactum de contrahendo* to translate eventually the principles embodied in the Declaration into binding treaties.

Inasmuch as these two resolutions lack binding force, on the one hand, it may be said that the extraterrestrial applicability of international law and the legal status of outer space and of celestial bodies under existing international customary law have not been affected by them. On the other hand, it may per-haps also be pointed out that, although celestial bodies remain in principle susceptible of appropriation, the *modi vivendi* between the super-powers may lead them, and the two resolutions may lead others, not to recognize any claims to sovereignty put forward either individually by States or collectively through intergovernmental agencies.[56] In view of the decisive importance of recognition, especially by the dominant elements of international society, in titles to territory,[57] this policy of the super-powers, if adhered to in practice,[58] may effectively prevent the establishment of territorial sovereignty on celestial bodies, in much the same way as the 1959 Antarctic Treaty has succeeded, for the time being at least, in freezing territorial claims to different parts of that continent.[59] All this amounts, however, to no more than saying that the prin-ciple of non-appropriation of celestial bodies enunciated in resolutions 1721A and 1962 may in time, if adhered to and upheld by members of the United Nations, including both super-powers, become a rule of international cus-tomary law, but, as yet, cannot be considered as one of existing international law.

V. Conclusions

In brief, State jurisdiction may be divided into three types (territorial, quasi-territorial and personal) and separated into two elements (jurisfaction and jurisaction). All three types of jurisfaction of States, whether with or without space capabilities, are already capable of being exercised with extraterrestrial effect. In addition, States with space capabilities may actually exercise quasi-territorial and personal jurisaction in outer space and on celestial bodies. As

---

[56] Cf. the first principle of Brussels resolution on the Legal Régime of Outer Space (1963) of the Institut de droit international, which foresees the exclusion of 'any kind of appropriation', 50 (II) *Annuaire de l'Institut* (1963), p. 369; see C. M. Chaumont, 'La résolution de Bruxelles', *Rev. belge dr. int.* (1965), p. 15, at pp. 19 ff.

[57] Cf. G. Schwarzenberger, 'Title to Territory', 51 *AJIL* (1957), p. 308, at pp. 316–8.

[58] Cf., however, Crane, loc. cit. in n. 32 above, at p. 699, especially n. 49.

[59] See loc. cit. (1960) in n. 33 above, at p. 235 [Ch. 3 above, s. II.A, *in fine*].

yet there is no territorial sovereignty in outer space or on celestial bodies and consequently there is no warrant for the extraterrestrial exercise of territorial jurisaction. All the rules of international law governing the attribution and exercise of all types and all elements of State jurisdiction are fully applicable extraterrestrially. There is no reason to believe that outer space and celestial bodies are, under existing international law, *res communes omnium* implying joint sovereignty of all States and a right of veto to each. Outer space constitutes in fact *res extra commercium*, and only quasi-territorial, and perhaps in exceptional circumstances also personal, jurisdiction (both jurisfaction and jurisaction) may be exercised there. This emphasizes the importance and urgency of a clearly defined boundary between outer space and territorial space where the subjacent State is entitled to exercise exclusive territorial jurisaction and where it would be unlawful for any other State to attempt to exercise any type of jurisaction. Such delimitation can, however, only be carried out by means of an international agreement. Meanwhile the practice of States appears to have narrowed this boundary, if not to a line, at least to a zone of about fifty miles in height overlying a lower zone of approximately 25 miles of (it would seem) undisputed national airspace above the surface of the earth (or, perhaps more accurately, sea level). Notwithstanding resolutions 1721A and 1962, however, celestial bodies constitute *res nullius* and for that reason no State, even if a landing has been made, is at present entitled to exercise territorial jurisaction there; but there is in law no reason why territorial sovereignty may not be acquired on celestial bodies in accordance with ordinary rules of international law. But, in fact, claims to territorial sovereignty on celestial bodies may be frustrated by the refusal of the major powers having space capabilities to recognize such claims. In order effectively to bar such claims in law, however, what is needed is another international treaty. Inasmuch as outer space and celestial bodies are of concern to all States, whether having space capabilities or not, it would seem to be in the interest of every State to seek the early conclusion of a general treaty on the boundary between national space and outer space and another on non-appropriation of celestial bodies, even though ultimate success must depend on their being acceptable to, and accepted by, the majority of space powers and both super-powers.[60]

---

[60] This chapter first appeared in 1965. On relevant subsequent developments, see esp. Chs. 9, 12, 13 and 14 below.

PART II

THE UNITED NATIONS
AND OUTER SPACE

6

The United Nations and Outer Space*

I. Introduction

The United Nations and its specialized agencies have so far played a useful, though subordinate, role in co-ordinating the efforts of nations in space research,[1] which is now rapidly moving beyond the purely exploratory stage into the phase of military and commercial exploitation.

In the military field, apart from the development of military missiles and satellites providing general information which may be of military value, such as the geodetic satellites, the United States was reported in November 1959 to have placed contracts for its first space vehicle, known as the Dyna-Soar, which is intended eventually to be capable of carrying bombs and of shooting down missiles and satellites. In 1960, it successfully launched on 24 May and 20 December two infra-red missile detector satellites, being part of the Missile Defense Alarm System (MIDAS). By means of photocells which, already in the summer of 1958, were said to be capable of detecting the heat emissions from ballistic missiles a few seconds after they had been launched more than 1,000 miles away, MIDAS will operate in conjunction with the Ballistic Missile Early Warning System (BMEWS) and provide a warning some thirty minutes before impact, instead of the fifteen minutes afforded by BMEWS alone. Moreover, a reconnaissance satellite containing photographic and related equipment, the SAMOS II (Satellite and Missile Observation System), was successfully put into orbit on 31 January 1961, from Point Arguello, California.[2]

* First published in 14 *CLP* (1961), pp. 247–79. Reproduced by kind permission of Sweet & Maxwell Ltd. The writer wishes to takes this opportunity of acknowledging his indebtedness to the Rockefeller Foundation for a generous grant to assist his research in space law, particularly in the preparation of this chapter and several of the subsequent chapters.

[1] Cf., *inter alia,* the following UN documents: *Report of the Secretary General on Para. I(a) of General Assembly resolution 1348 (X111)* [of 13 Dec. 1958, establishing the *Ad Hoc* Committee], A/AC.98/4 (16.6.59), *Report of the Ad Hoc Committee on the Peaceful Uses of Outer Space,* A/4141 (14.7.59); Economic and Social Council (ECOSOC) (X111), General Review of the Development and Co-ordination of the Economic. Social and Human Rights Programmes and Activities of the UN and the Specialised Agencies as a Whole, *24th Report of the Administrative Committee on Co-ordination to ECOSOC,* E/3368 (10.5.60), Part V: 'Peaceful Uses of Outer Space'. and Annex 11.

[NB: This chapter was written in 1961. For discussions of subsequent developments in the UN in the field of space law, see in particular the following two chapters in Part II, and the chapters in Part III below.]

[2] 'SAMOS in Orbit,' *Flight* (11 Feb. 1961), p. 171.

In the commercial sphere, even in 1949, the President of the Executive and Liaison Commission of the Universal Postal Union (UPU) said that the postal rocket was then 'being secretly studied in various laboratories.'[3] Ten years later, a postal rocket safely delivered, 100 miles from ship to shore, 3,000 letters bearing ordinary stamps franked with the imprint 'USSm Barbero.'[4] On 21 October 1960, the American Telephone and Telegraph Co. applied to the United States government for permission to put a space telephone exchange into orbit within a year,[5] and a group of five private industrial concerns in the United Kingdom, on 2 February 1961, formed the British Space Development Co. as a 'springboard' for the commercial exploitation of space.[6] A fortnight later, Mr Bevins, the United Kingdom Postmaster-General, announced that it had been decided to erect a large steerable aerial system for satellite communication tests.[7]

The problem now is the manner in which the United Nations and its specialized agencies will be able to co-ordinate and assist this development, and the extent to which they will be able to regulate and control it, so that man's conquest of space leads him not to his last arena in his internecine struggle for power but ushers in a new era of wondrous achievements in human well-being and progress.

II. Financial Assistance and Data Clearing

Of the specialized agencies, three deserve special mention for their contributions to space research: the United Nations Educational, Scientific and Cultural Organisation (UNESCO), the World Meteorological Organisation (WMO) and the International Telecommunication Union (ITU).

UNESCO's contribution has been primarily financial, in the form of grants to the International Council of Scientific Unions (ICSU), the international non-governmental organization responsible for the International Geophysical Year 1957–8 (IGY) and the subsequent International Geophysical Co-operation (IGC), approximately $100,000 to the ICSU's Special Committee for the IGY (CSAGI) over a period of four years and an annual subvention of about $20,000 to the Federation of Astronomical and Geophysical Services (FAGS).[8] As is well known, the first satellites, both Russian and American, were launched as part of the IGY programme of research. UNESCO has, however, also plans for a more active part in the co-ordination of scientific

---

[3] 'The UPU and Commercial Aviation', 10 *IATA Bulletin* (1949), p. 102, at p. 107.

[4] *The Times* (London), 9 June 1959; cf. also experiment of German Rocket Society (*The Times* (London), 25 May 1959).

[5] *The Times* (London), 22 Oct. 1960.   [6] *The Times* (London), 3 Feb. 1961.

[7] *The Times* (London), 16 Feb. 1961.

[8] *Appraisals of UNESCO's Programmes for the ECOSOC* (1960), p. 88.

efforts of its members in space research[9] and for the use of space vehicles in furthering its educational and cultural aims and purposes.[10]

By comparison, the work of WMO in this field has been more substantive. From its inception (1951), WMO took an active part in the organization of IGY and was instrumental in changing the name from the Third International Polar Year. The Second Congress of WMO, meeting in Geneva in 1955, approved the IGY meteorological programme and invited its members to carry it out.[11] On its recommendation, the WMO Executive Committee in 1956 established the IGY Meteorological Data Centre within the WMO Secretariat,[12] at the same time inviting all meteorological services to supply the Centre regularly with data from their IGY stations.[13] As a result, nearly sixteen million observations taken by some 3,000 meteorological stations over the 550 days of the IGY were catalogued by the Centre and recorded on approximately 16,000 Microcards which are now available at cost to WMO members and the public in complete or partial sets or individually.[14] The material they contain is, and will continue to be, of enormous interest for research of all types for a long time to come.

In addition, WMO is also currently paying close attention to the use of earth satellites for meteorological observation. On 23 March 1960, a Panel of Experts submitted to the WMO Executive Committee a report on the Study of the Atmosphere and Atmospheric Phenomena by Means of Artificial Satellites, to which was added an addendum[15] on 10 June after the successful launching of TIROS I on 1 April 1960. Previously, on 31 March 1959, Dr Wexler had submitted a report on Meteorological Satellites to WMO,[16] the gist of which was that WMO should consider steps 'to promote the use of meteorological satellite data, to ensure rapid dissemination of such data to the meteorological services and to facilitate use of the data in meteorological diagnosis and prognosis.'[17]

The Panel of Experts, however, in its Report regarded the problem of meteorological telecommunication as more immediate from the standpoint of both

---

[9] Cf. 54 EX/Decisions 6.9 (June 1959); Report of Director-General to the 55th session of the Executive Board (55 EX/8); 55 EX/Decisions 5.5 (Nov.–Dec. 1959); also the work of UNESCO in oceanographic research, *Report on the Results of the Intergovernmental Conference on Oceanographic Research, Copenhagen, July 1960*, 11C/PRG/7 (7 Oct. 1960).

[10] Resolution 1.1322 on the use of satellites to combat illiteracy adopted unanimously by the General Conference on 10 Nov. 1960, 11 C/Resolutions (Prov.), p. 11; this rather futuristic resolution may perhaps best be regarded as a posthumous tribute to the originator of the idea, M. Gaston Berger, killed a week previously in a car accident (*The Times* (London), 11 Nov. 1960).

[11] Resolution 23 (Cg.–II); see also WMO, *IGY 1957–58 Meteorological Programme*, Doc. No. 55, IGY.1 (1956).

[12] Resolution 13 (EC–VIII).   [13] Resolution 14 (EC–VIII).

[14] Cf. WMO, IGY 1957–58 Meteorological Data Centre, *Report No. 7* (*Microcards of IGY Meteorological Data* 1957); sample card distributed with 9 *WMO Bulletin* (July 1960); 'Microcards of IGY Meteorological Data', 8 ibid. (1959), p. 153, and 10 ibid. (1961), p. 38.

[15] WMO, EC–XII/Doc. 29, and EC–XII/Doc. 29, ADD.1.

[16] Appended to EC–XIV/Doc. 29.   [17] EC–XII/Doc. 29, p. 10.

frequency allocation and improvement in technique.[18] It took note of the fact that ITU was then concerned with the allocation of frequencies in connection with space exploration and urged that WMO should take action in time to present the case of meteorological telecommunication adequately at the Extraordinary Radio Conference to be convened by ITU in 1963 to consider the needs of space telecommunication.[19]

III. Radio Frequency: Allocation and Control

A. Allegations of Treaty Violation Not Proven

From every angle, telecommunication is crucial to the exploration and exploitation of outer space.[20] It is not surprising, therefore, to find here the first treaty law made specifically in relation to outer space. It has sometimes been asserted that frequencies used by some of the artificial satellites constituted actual violations of international treaties in force at the time or have resulted in interference with transmissions on internationally protected frequencies. Thus, Mr A. G. Haley, with reference to SPUTNIK I, said:

The first overt or actual violation of the rules and regulations promulgated pursuant to international treaties was occasioned by the USSR's use of the frequencies of 20•005 and 40•002 megacycles . . . The experimental station of the United States National Bureau of Standards, station WWV in Lanham, Md., has the assigned frequency of 20•0 megacycles. The ITU has assigned a guard band of 10 kilocycles on each side of this frequency to prevent interference with station WWV's operations. The signals of the Soviet satellites at 20•005 megacycles were 5 kilocycles within this zone of interdiction.[21]

Similarly, Mr M. Aaronson wrote:

It is estimated that interference with radio services took place approximately three times in twenty-four hours as the Soviet earth satellite appeared in the airspace over the United Kingdom.[22]

These statements, which unfortunately have gained currency,[23] have, however, not been confirmed by the responsible authorities in the United States and the United Kingdom. In reply to the question: 'Whether in the opinion of the National Bureau of Standards the use of the frequency of 20•005 mc/s by the Soviet satellites is in violation of the assignment of frequency made by

---

[18] EC–XII/Doc. 29, p. 6.   [19] See below text to n. 49.
[20] See a most informative survey by E. Wenk, *Frequency Control in Space Telecommunications* (1960).
[21] 'Law of Outer Space—Radio Control Urgently Needed', *Senate Symposium* (1957), p. 458, at p. 459.
[22] 'Space Law', ibid., p. 273, at p. 280.
[23] Cf. Wenk, op. cit., n. 20 above, p. 40 and p. 94.

ITU to Station WWV,' Mr Allen Barnabei, Communications Liaison Officer of the United States National Bureau of Standards, said categorically:

No, the band 19990 to 20010 kc/s may be used for earth space research purposes.[24]

Insofar as the United Kingdom is concerned, the GPO Radio Services Department, in answer to an inquiry made by the writer, wrote on 14 October 1960:

Although the possibility of interference from satellite transmissions and their associated ground stations to normal radiocommunications cannot be dismissed, no reports of such interference have been received by the Post Office up to the present time.

Similarly, the writer was informed by letter dated 12 October 1960, by the Engineering Information Department of the British Broadcasting Corporation:

We ourselves have not experienced any interference of this kind [i.e., from transmissions associated with space exploration] to our Broadcast transmissions in either the Domestic or External services.

B. Nature of International Frequency Regulation

It is not possible here to enter into a detailed examination of the international law of telecommunication. Suffice it to say in this context that its nature is essentially co-ordinative and recommendatory rather than determinative and mandatory. Thus, under the successive international telecommunication conventions,[25] the duties of the contracting parties are limited to ensuring that all radio stations under their jurisdiction 'are operated in such a manner as not to result in *harmful interference* to the radio services or communications of other Members or Associate Members [of ITU] . . . which operate in accordance with the provisions of the Radio Regulations.' The Atlantic City Radio Regulations, 1947, which were operative until superseded on 1 May 1961, by the Geneva Radio Regulations, 1959, also provided merely:

A country, member of the Union, shall not assign to a station any frequency in derogation of either the table of frequency allocation given in this chapter or the other provisions of these Regulations, except on the express condition that *harmful interference*

---

[24] Letter to the writer dated 28 Oct. 1960. The writer wishes to take this opportunity of acknowledging the kind assistance given to him by the UK and US authorities herein referred to and by Mr Edward W. Allen, Chief Engineer, US Federal Communications Commission, as well as the Royal Swedish Embassy in London which, in a letter to the writer dated 29 Dec. 1960, with reference to a United Press dispatch published in the *New York Times* of 14 Oct. 1957, stated: 'Contact with the Stockholm Police Force, as well as with other interested parties, has failed to bring to light any evidence of SPUTNIK I having disturbed radio conversations between police headquarters and radio patrol cars.'

[25] Thus, those adopted at Atlantic City, 1947 (Art. 44 (1)), 193 UNTS, p. 188; Buenos Aires, 1952 (Art. 45 (1)), Cmnd. 520 (1958); Geneva, 1959 Art. 47 (1), ITU ed.

shall not be caused to services carried on by stations operating in accordance with the provisions of the Convention and of these Regulations.[26]

Apart from verbal changes, the same provision is found in the Geneva Radio Regulations, 1959.[27]

'Harmful interference' was furthermore specifically defined in the Atlantic City Radio Regulations, 1947, as:

Any radiation or any induction which endangers the functioning of a radio-navigation service or of a safety service or obstructs or repeatedly interrupts a radio service operating in accordance with these Regulations.[28]

The same is true of the Geneva Radio Regulations, 1959, which in fact qualify the latter part of this definition by adding the word 'seriously,' even though they now include also interference 'seriously degrading' a radio service.[29] In a footnote, the term 'safety service' was specified in the Atlantic City Regulations as meaning:

Any radio service, the operation of which is directly related, whether permanently or temporarily, to the safety of human life and the safeguarding of property . . .[30]

Although no such definition is found in the Geneva Radio Regulations, 1959, a similar one is included in Annex 3 to the International Telecommunication Convention, Geneva, 1959, to which the Geneva Radio Regulations are annexed.[31]

These Radio Regulations are not, therefore, intended to prevent the sharing of duly allocated, assigned, and registered frequencies by other stations which do not cause 'harmful interference'. And even where alleged 'harmful interference' has occurred, although in principle an obligation exists in respect of the station sharing a frequency assigned to another immediately to 'suspend operations upon receipt of advice of this harmful interference,'[32] the matter is to be settled primarily between the two administrations concerned.[33] The Geneva Radio Regulations, 1959, have in fact introduced now the possibility of direct co-ordination between the operating organizations, subject to agreement by the administrations concerned.[34] If the matter cannot be settled by direct agreement between the administrations concerned, it may be reported

[26] Art. 3, § 3 (No. 88), 194 UNTS (1954), p. 5, at p. 27 (emphasis added).
[27] Art. 3, § 3 (No. 115), ITU ed.   [28] Art. I, s. IV (No. 69).
[29] Art. I, s. III (No. 93): '. . . or seriously degrades, obstructs or repeatedly interrupts a radio service operating in accordance with these Regulations.'
[30] No. 69.1.
[31] 'Any radiocommunication service used permanently or temporarily for the safeguarding of human life and property' (No. 313, n. 1), ITU ed., p. 72.
[32] Atlantic City Radio Regulations (RR), 1947, Art. 11, s. IV(5) (No. 339); similarly Geneva RR, 1959, Art. 9, s. IV(5) (No. 611).
[33] Atlantic City RR, 1947, Art. 14, §§ 1–4 (Nos. 383–9); Geneva RR, 1959, Art. 15, §§ 1–11 (Nos. 704–14).
[34] Geneva RR, 1959, Art. 15 § 4 (No. 707).

to the ITU International Frequency Registration Board,[35] whose powers, however, consist merely in investigating the dispute and issuing 'a report containing its findings and recommendations for the solution of the problem.'[36] What happens if the administrations concerned decline to accept the findings and recommendations of the Board is now stated with unabashed candour in a new paragraph introduced into the Geneva Radio Regulations, 1959:

In a case where, as a result of a study, the Board submits to one or more administrations suggestions or recommendations for the solution of a problem, and where no answer has been received from one or more of these administrations within a period of thirty days, the Board shall consider that the suggestions or recommendations concerned are unacceptable to the administrations which did not answer. If it was the requesting administration which failed to answer within this period, the Board shall close the study.[37]

If, after all these indecisive encounters, an administration still finds a need and the will and stamina to persevere with the vindication of its legal rights, arbitration is in principle possible. But even after the latest revision of the text of the International Telecommunication Convention at Geneva, in 1959, the arbitral procedure set out in Annex 4 of the Convention is of a type which, as the Advisory Opinion of the International Court of Justice in the *Interpretation of Peace Treaties Case* (1950) has shown, may easily be stultified by the wilfulness of one of the parties to the dispute. For, although provision exists for the Secretary-General of ITU to select the third arbitrator in case of disagreement between the two national arbitrators as to the choice, no remedy is provided in case one of the parties wilfully refuses to appoint its own arbitrator.[38]

Last, but not least, it should be recalled that, in successive international telecommunication conventions, the following reservation is always maintained:

Members and Associate Members retain their entire freedom with regard to military radio installations of their army, naval and air forces.[39]

It would follow, therefore, that there is a long way to go yet before the assertion may justifiably be made that the frequency of 20•005 mc/s used by SPUT-NIKS I, II and III constituted an infringement of the Atlantic City Radio Regulations, 1947, or of the International Telecommunication Convention, Atlantic City, 1947, as revised in Buenos Aires in 1952. Even though it be true

[35] Atlantic City RR, 1947, Art. 14, § 6 (No. 391); Geneva RR, 1959, Art. 15, § 13(2) (No. 717).
[36] Atlantic City RR, 1947, Art. 11, s. VII, § 18 (No. 355); Geneva RR, 1959, Art. 9, s. VII, §§ 44–5 (Nos. 623–33).
[37] Art. 9, s. VII, § 46 (No. 634).
[38] See *ICJ Rep.* 1950, p. 221, and comments thereon in the writer's *General Principles of Law*, pp. 151–5.
[39] Atlantic City ITC, 1947, Art. 47(1); Buenos Aires ITC, 1952, Art. 48(1); Geneva ITC, 1959, Art. 50(1).

that ICSU's Special Committee for the IGY (CSAGI) did recommend the use of the 108 mc/s channel for space research by means of artificial satellites, this choice had no binding force and was recognized fully at the time to be both arbitrary and temporary.[40]

C. Purpose of and Need for Frequency Control

In pointing out the lack of effective sanction behind international frequency allocations, the intention is not to belittle their importance, but merely to show that parties to international telecommunication agreements have intended to create not an international licensing authority for the mandatory distribution of the frequency spectrum, but an international co-ordinating centre to facilitate the avoidance of mutual interference. For radio interference is usually a two-way traffic—apart from the special case of radio astronomy— and any operating station which interferes with another will itself suffer from the interference. Except where the intention is to jam the broadcast of another, it is therefore to be assumed that every State wishes to ensure the maximum freedom from interference in telecommunication.

Especially in the field of space research, it would indeed be difficult to imagine any State using for its satellites a frequency which is already occupied, without the gravest deliberation and reasons and at the risk of jeopardizing the success of these incalculably expensive experiments, costly in terms of both money and scientific efforts. The problem of frequency control in space research consists, therefore, not so much in preventing space and earth-space radio communications from interfering with other transmissions, but rather in clearing certain portions of the radio spectrum so as to protect these communications from interference that might lead not merely to the failure of these experiments, but also serious danger to property, life, and even international peace owing to some malfunctioning in the control of space vehicles. This need is even greater in the case of radio astronomy where there is no control over the frequencies of cosmic signals which are, moreover, of extremely feeble intensity.[41]

It is not surprising, therefore, to find that the United Nations *Ad Hoc* Committee on the Peaceful Uses of Outer Space, in its Report submitted to the General Assembly of the United Nations in the summer of 1959,

strongly urges that ITU and the States members of the 1959 Administrative Radio Conference of ITU allocate adequate frequencies for space programmes, with adequate bandwidths for the foreseeable needs of space programmes in the next three years.[42]

[40] See op. cit. in n. 20 above, at p. 40.
[41] Cf. ibid., pp. 61 95.; also J. H. Oort, 'Radioastronomy: An Open Window on the Universe', 26 *Telecommunication Journal* (Oct. 1959), p. 210; and below, n. 47.
[42] A/4141, para. 69, p. 45; see also below, text to nn. 47–49.

When the Administrative Radio Conference met in 1959, it had before it rec-
ommendations which had been formulated earlier in the year by the
International Radio Consultative Committee (CCIR) at Los Angeles[43] and
COSPAR of ICSU, the latter forwarded to ITU by its President, Professor
H. C. van de Hulst, on 13 August 1959.[44]

The Administrative Radio Conference met at Geneva from 17 August 1959
to 21 December 1959. Simultaneous with the second half of the Radio
Conference, the Plenipotentiary Conference also met at Geneva. *Inter alia*,
the latter produced a new International Telecommunication Convention while
the former a new set of Radio Regulations. The Convention entered into force
on 1 January 1961 between parties having deposited their instruments of ratification or accession,[45] while the Radio Regulations, which are annexed to the
Convention, on 1 May 1961.[46]

For the first time, the Radio Regulations earmark specific frequency bands
for space and earth-space services and radio astronomy observations,
although far from always being on an exclusive basis. The important point,
however, especially in the case of radio astronomy which, even though it is
revealing to man some of the most deeply hidden mysteries of the universe,[47]
does not carry the glitter of a military bonus and has to compete with powerful commercial interests for a place in the already highly congested radio spectrum, consists in the international recognition of the new status of these
various forms of space research. In fact, in addition to the Radio Regulations,
the Administrative Radio Conference, 1959, adopted, *inter alia*, two recommendations (Nos. 31 and 32) designed to further the cause of radio astronomy.[48] Furthermore, the Conference also recommended (No. 36) 'that an
Extraordinary Administrative Radio Conference be convened, in principle
during the latter part of 1963' to consider the technical progress in the use of
radio communication for space research, to re-examine the frequencies allocated for this purpose and, if necessary, to adopt rules for the identification
and control of radio emissions from space vehicles.[49]

Thus, the oldest specialized agency of the United Nations[50] takes the lead
in being the first to have introduced a set of rules of international treaty law
relating to activities in space.

But it would now appear that, in addition to frequency allocation, what is
one of the most urgent problems in this field at the moment is an improvement

---

[43] Docs. 437 (Revised) (27.4.59); 531–E (22.4.59); 538–E (22.4.59), annexed to *Report of Secretary-General on Para. 1 (a) of GA Resolution 1348S (XIII)*, A/AC.98/4 (16.6.59), Annexes II to V.

[44] Reproduced op. cit. in n. 20 above, at pp. 47–8.

[45] Art. 22 (No. 295).   [46] Art. 45, § 1 (No. 1629).

[47] Cf. R. H. Brown and A. C. B. Lovell, *The Exploration of Space by Radio* (1958); also Prof. M. Ryle's lecture on 10 Feb. 1961, at the Royal Astronomical Society, 'The Theory of Universe', *The Times* (London), 11 Feb. 1961.

[48] *Radio Regulations,* ITU ed. (1959), pp. 607 and 608.   [49] Ibid., p. 613, at p. 614.

[50] Founded in 1865 as the International Telegraphic Union.

in radio technology and in the legal and administrative machinery so that
there may be a far stricter control over the use of the radio spectrum than has
so far been achieved nationally or internationally. Thus, Colonel James D.
Flashman, Directorate of Communications, USAF, wrote:

Under concepts by which the frequency spectrum is now used, it is just not possible to
guarantee that any portion of the spectrum will be interference free, regardless of
national or international intentions or agreements. Controls which would make this
guarantee possible simply do not exist . . . Without positive control, virtually all our
activities in space communications and electronics will be conducted in an atmosphere
of calculated risk, subject to the whim of the negligent, inexperienced or inept co-user
of the spectrum, within whose power it is to wreck completely an operation upon
which the prestige of an entire nation may rest . . . [A] spectrum user must at least be
equipped with the tools necessary for him to gage precisely and continuously the total
effect of his radiations upon the electromagnetic spectrum.[51]

Here then is an even greater challenge facing the Extraordinary Radio
Conference in 1963,[52] all radio engineers, and the radio administrations of the
world.

IV. Blind Spot in the Sky

In the United Nations itself, the path into space has proved truly steep.
Following proposals made by the United States in January[53] and July[54] 1957,
and a Soviet counter-proposal put forward in March 1958,[55] the General

---

[51] 'Positive Control of the Electromagnetic Spectrum', *USAF Signal Magazine* (May 1959),
quoted op. cit. in n. 20 above, p. 87, at 88.
[52] See n. 49 above.
[53] Mr Lodge, US delegate, GA (XI), 1st Com., A/C.1/SR 821 (14.1.57), p. 41.
[54] Mr Stassen, US, UN Disarmament Commission, 5-Power Sub-Committee, 25 July 1957.
'Keeping the Peace in Outer Space' (*The Times* (London), 26 July 1957); 'US Proposes Controls
on Space Missiles be in Disarmament Pact', United States Information Service, London (USIS),
Off. Text, 26 July 1957; *Report on the Proceedings of the Sub-Committee of the UN Disarmament
Commission, London, March 18–September 6, 1957*, Cmnd. 333 (1957), pp. 9–10, 17; formalised
in Working Paper on Proposals for Partial Measures of Disarmament submitted to the Sub-
Committee by Canada, France, the UK and the US, on 29 Aug. 1957, DC/SC.1/66, Cmnd. 333
(1957), 96, at 98: 'VI—The Control of Objects Entering Outer Space: All parties to the convention agree that within three months after the entry into effect of the convention they will co-operate in the establishment of a technical committee to study the design of an inspection system
which would make it possible to assure that the sending of objects through outer space will be
exclusively for peaceful and scientific purposes.' See also the US proposal of 2 Sept. 1958, to the
General Assembly (A/3902).
[55] At a Press conference in Moscow on 15 Mar. 1958, the Soviet government announced a 4-
point proposal: (1) a ban on the use of outer space for military purposes and an undertaking to
launch rockets only as part of an international programme. This was dependent on (2) elimination of foreign military bases, (3) control, through the United Nations, of the first two points, and
(4) creation of a United Nations body for international co-operation in space research (*Sunday
Times* (London) 16 Mar. 1958). Proposal submitted to the General Assembly on 17 Mar. 1958
(A/3818); see also below, nn. 118 and 121.

Assembly on 13 December, 1958, approved a revised twenty-power draft resolution on the establishment of an eighteen-member *Ad Hoc* Committee on the Peaceful Uses of Outer Space.[56] This Committee, which met in May and June 1959,[57] was boycotted by the Soviet Union, Czechoslovakia, and Poland; nor did India and the United Arab Republic attend.[58] Its Report[59] was considered by the General Assembly at its XlVth session.[60] As a result thereof, the General Assembly decided on 12 December 1959,[61] to establish a twenty-four-member Committee on the Peaceful Uses of Outer Space and to convene an international scientific conference in 1960 or 1961 for the exchange of experience in space research. Apparently cold-shouldered again by the Soviet bloc, this new Committee, which was due to report to the XVth session of the General Assembly, has yet made little headway at the time of writing; nor has apparently a date been fixed for the projected scientific conference.

Among the terms of reference of the *Ad Hoc* Committee[62] (and also of the new Committee[63]) was the study of the ways and means to encourage space research and of the legal problems which might arise. The Report of the *Ad Hoc* Committee, at least in regard to problems of space law,[64] is distressingly disappointing. It divided these problems into those 'susceptible of priority treatment'[65] and those which were not,[66] and classified among the latter the problem of 'determining where outer space begins'[67] and the legal regime of extraterrestrial bodies.[68]

As regards the first problem, the Report cannot be reproached for having said that it might not be '*susceptible of* priority treatment,' inasmuch as States

---

[56] Draft resolution, A/C.1/L.220/Rev. (21.11.59); approved by the First Committee, 24 Nov. 1958, GA (III) A/C.1/SR 995, pp. 245–6; adopted by the General Assembly, 13 Dec. 1958, GA (XIII) A/PV 792; text of resolution 1348 (XIII), GA (XIII), Off. Rec., Supp. No. 18 (A/4080), pp. 5–6. Cf. H. J. Taubenfeld, 'Consideration at the United Nations of the Status of Outer Space'. 53 *AJIL* (1959), p. 400.

[57] A/AC.98/SR 1–6; A/AC.98/Agenda 1–3; documents A/AC.98/1–4; working papers A/AC.98/L 1–L 13; Technical Committee A/AC.98/C.1/SR 1–2, 14 (3–13 being closed meetings); Legal Committee A/AC.98/C.2/SR 1–5 and working paper A/AC.98/C.2/L 1. Cf. P. C. Jessup and H. J. Taubenfeld, 'The United Nations *Ad Hoc* Committee on the Peaceful Uses of Outer Space', 53 *AJIL* (1959), p. 877.

[58] 'Space Inquiry Boycotted by Communists', *The Times* (London), 7 May 1959.

[59] A/4141 (14.7.59).

[60] At its 803rd Plenary Meeting, 22 Sept. 1959, the General Assembly on the recommendation of its General Committee (A/4214), included the *Ad Hoc* Committee Report as item 25 in the agenda of the XIVth session. The First Committee considered this item at its 1079th to 1081st meetings on 11 and 12 Dec. 1959.

[61] At the 1079th meeting of the First Committee, a draft resolution (A/C.1/L 247) was submitted by twelve powers, including the UK, US and USSR, which, as amended by a Belgian proposal (A/C.1/L 289), was adopted *nem. con.*; see *Report of the First Committee on the Report Ad Hoc Committee*, GA (XIV) A/4351 (12.12.59). This Report was adopted by the General Assembly on 12 Dec. 1959, without discussion (GA (XIV) A/PV 856, p. 752). For text of resolution 1472 (XIV), see GA (XIV), Off. Rec., Supp. No. 16 (A/4354), pp. 5–6.

[62] Resolution 1348 (XIII); see above, n. 56.   [63] Resolution 1472 (XIV); see above, n. 61.
[64] A/4141, pp. 63 ff.   [65] Ibid, pp. 63 ff.   [66] Ibid, pp. 67 ff.
[67] Ibid, pp. 67 ff.   [68] Ibid, pp. 69 ff.

may find it hard to achieve a general agreement. But it could hardly have been with candour that '[t]he Committee noted that the solution of the problems which it had identified as susceptible of priority treatment was not dependent upon the establishment of such limits.'[69] The Committee became positively misleading when it expressed the belief that, with the practice of artificial satellites so far passing freely through the airspace of other States,

there may have been initiated the recognition or establishment of a generally accepted rule to the effect that, in principle, outer space is, on conditions of equality, freely available for exploration and use by all in accordance with existing or future international law or agreements.[70]

This passage is equivocal. It may be utterly meaningless in simply saying that no State may claim to exercise exclusive territorial sovereignty over a portion of outer space that is not merely an extension upwards of its airspace—a proposition which not many will deny. Or, read in its context, this passage may be calculated fallaciously to suggest that a rule of international customary law already exists obliging States as a positive legal duty to permit the so-called 'innocent passage' of foreign non-military satellites through their national airspace. I have previously had occasion to deal at length with the error of this view so that it is not necessary here to repeat the relevant reasons.[71] Suffice it to say that at the most there is only a non-binding usage to this effect.[72]

The refusal of the *Ad Hoc* Committee to face the problem of separating national airspace (or space)[73] from outer space means that it was itself uncertain of the precise geographical scope of its own terms of reference. In other words, the Committee did not purport to know whether it was dealing with problems five miles from the surface of the earth, 50 miles, 500 miles, or 5,000 miles! The explanation of the Committee's evasive stand, can, however, be easily found. When this issue was first raised in its Legal Sub-Committee, there was unanimous support for the Chairman in deciding to omit all references to

---

[69] A/4141, p. 68.   [70] Ibid., p. 64.

[71] Cf. the writer's 'Recent Developments in Air Law', 9 *CLP* (1956), p. 208, Part I: Airspace Sovereignty and Earth Satellites [Ch. 1 above]; 'International Law and High Altitude Flights: Balloons, Rockets and Man-Made Satellites', 6 *ICLQ* (1957), p. 487 [Ch. 2 above]; 'The Right to Fly', 42 *Grotius Society Transactions* (1958), p. 99; ILA, *Report of the 48th Conference New York* (1958), p. 250; 'Problems of Space Law', 7 *The New Scientist* (1960), 1256; 'From Air Law to Space Law', 13 *CLP* (1960), p. 228 [Ch. 3 above].

Cf. also Sweden's criticism of the *Ad Hoc* Committee's Report on this score, 11 Dec. 1959, GA (XIV) A/C.1/PV 1079.

[72] Cf. Schwarzenberger, *A Manual of International Law*, 1 (1960), pp. 2 and 27–9.

[73] While I believe that the present upper limit of national airspace is conterminous with the terrestrial atmosphere, I am of the opinion that, contrary to a very prevalent view, it is not impossible in law by agreement between the States concerned, not only to bring down this limit, but also to *extend* national sovereignty to a greater height from the surface of the earth, although it would not be possible to claim as national territory a portion of outer space that is not a mere extension of national airspace. Therefore, by agreement national space may extend beyond national *air*space. See loc. cit., n. 71 above, esp. 13 *CLP* (1960), p. 228, at p. 230 ff. [Ch. 3 above, s. II.A]. In practice, 'national airspace' will mostly mean also 'national space'.

military problems in the Committee's Report.[74] As the determination of the boundary between national space and outer space, the inevitable first step in any rational approach to the legal problems of outer space, depends ultimately on the security interests of States—as writers and representatives of the Soviet bloc have not failed to point out—it would appear that, therefore, the Committee decided not only to close its eyes to this basic issue, but also to rationalize and to justify this blind spot in its vision of the heavens.

V. Reconnaissance and Surveillance Satellites

Any system of international regulation of activities in space which pretends to turn a blind eye to their military aspects is foredoomed. Three problems, in particular, require to be considered: reconnaissance from space, surveillance from space, and the disarmament or demilitarization of outer space and extraterrestrial bodies. These three problems may, however, be resolved into two in the sense that surveillance from space, if not consented to, is equivalent to reconnaissance and, if agreed to, forms part of disarmament. The shooting down by the Soviet Union of two United States aircraft, the U–2 on 1 May 1960, 1,250 miles inside the Soviet Union, and the RB–47 on 1 July 1960, over the Barents Sea, illustrates admirably the position in international law of two different types of reconnaissance: penetrative and peripheral.

The distinction between penetrative and peripheral reconnaissance was drawn in a statement made by the United States Secretary of State, Mr Herter, soon after the U–2 incident. Having first mentioned that since the beginning of the Eisenhower Administration the President, under the National Security Act, 1947, had put into effect directives to gather intelligence for the defence and protection of the free world, Mr Herter continued:

Under these directives, programmes have been developed and put into operation which have included *extensive aerial surveillance* by unarmed civilian aircraft, *normally of a peripheral character but on occasion by penetration.*[75]

This distinction must be taken to mean that penetrative reconnaissance involves unauthorized entry into the territory of the foreign State concerned,[76] or at least espionage in the course of an otherwise legitimate flight,

---

[74] A/AC.98/C.2/SR 5, p. 8.

[75] USIS, Off. Text, 10 May 1960, p. 2 (emphasis added); cf. also censored version of US Secretary of Defense Gates' testimony before US Senate Foreign Relations Committee on the U–2 incident when he was reported to have referred freely to the vital information obtained during the previous four years by US photographic reconnaissance over the Soviet Union, 'Another Alert Ordered for US Forces,' *The Times* (London), 3 June 1960.

[76] See B. Cheng, 'International Law and High Altitude Flights: Balloons, Rockets and Man-Made Satellites', 6 *ICLQ* (1957), p. 487 [Ch. 2 above], and cf. Lissitzyn, 'The Treatment of Aerial Intruders', 47 *AJIL* (1953), p. 559.

while peripheral reconnaissance is effected by means and devices situated outside the boundary—the periphery—of that State's territory. Such devices need
not, of course, be an aircraft or a satellite. Thus, it was reported in 1957 that:

The United States had been 'tapping' Russia's missiles secrets for more than two years
with powerful long-range radar and other equipment based near the Black Sea resort
of Samsun in Turkey . . . The equipment was said to have a range up to 1,000 miles.[77]

The very different position which these two types of reconnaissance, penetrative and peripheral, occupy in international law further stresses the crucial
importance of a clear demarcation between the national airspace or space of
a State forming part of its territory and outer space over which its territorial
sovereignty no longer extends.

A. Penetrative Reconnaissance

The facts of the U–2 incident, including the trial of the pilot of the aircraft, are
already too well known to need repetition here,[78] except perhaps to offer a possible explanation of the timing of that ill-fated flight, since this has aroused a
great deal of speculation and criticism.[79] In view of the fact that the aircraft
was timed to be over the Soviet Union early in the morning of 1 May, when military parades would take place in different parts of the Soviet Union, it may be
conjectured that those who planned the flight expected that for that reason the
U–2 would be able to gain valuable information regarding the disposition of
Soviet forces and details of their latest weapons and other equipment.

On 18 May 1960, the Soviet Union addressed an urgent request to the
Security Council to consider the 'aggressive acts' of the United States.[80] The
Security Council, when convened, declined to adopt the Soviet proposal to

---

[77] *The Times* (London), 21 Oct. 1957; see also below under *Peripheral reconnaissance*.

[78] See *Keesing's*, pp. 17425–30, and 17667–8. A highly informative and critical account is the
NBC telefilm, 'The U–2 Affair,' broadcast on BBC television on 2 Jan. 1961; cf. also Soviet
Booklets (No. 76), *Trial of American U–2 Spy Pilot* (London, 1960), containing a summary of the
proceedings against Powers, the U–2 pilot. Briefly, an unarmed and unmarked US U–2 aircraft,
capable of flight at a height (over 20,000 metres) thought at the time to be beyond the range of
Soviet anti-aircraft defences, several similar flights having previously been made over the Soviet
Union, was piloted by Powers on 1 May 1960, with over two tons of photographic and electronic
equipment, on a reconnaissance mission flying from Pershawar in Pakistan across Afghanistan
into the Soviet Union at a point 20 km south-east of Kirovabad (Tajikistan) heading in a more or
less straight line for Archangel, Kandalaksha, and Murmansk, via Dushame, the Tyuratum
Cosmodrome near the Aral Sea, Chelyabinsk, Sverdlovsk, and Kirov, thus passing over a number of important military and industrial sites, before flying on to land at Bodö in Norway. At
about 20–30 miles south or south-east of Sverdlovsk, the U–2 was brought down by Soviet fire.
Power parachuted, and was captured, put to trial, convicted and imprisoned. See further n. 99
below. [Powers was eventually released in 1962 in exchange for Rudolph Abel, a Soviet master spy,
and published his account of the flight under the title *Operation Overflight* (1970).]

[79] Cf. criticisms voiced by the US Senate Foreign Relations Committee in *Events Relating to
the Summit Conference*, 86th Cong., 2nd sees., Report No. 1761 (28 June 1960), pp. 22 ff; also
'Unhappy Landing', first leader, *The Times* (London), 9 May 1960.

[80] S/4314 (18.5.60), S/4315 (19.5.60), and S/4315/Corr. 1 (20.5.60).

condemn the U–2 flight as an 'aggressive act'.[81] Instead, the Security Council proceeded to the consideration of a resolution proposed by Argentina, Ceylon, Ecuador and Tunisia on 23 May 1960,[82] that is to say, five days after the Soviet complaint had been received. As the Soviet delegate said:

True, the four-Power resolution is a separate item on our agenda. But we all know that it came into being as a result of the Security Council's debate on the item put forward by the Government of the U.S.S.R. Consequently, whether or not that is the intention of the authors of the draft resolution, every one of us, and the public as a whole, will regard the two questions as directly interconnected.[83]

This resolution, adopted on 27 May 1960, (a) recommends that international problems be settled by peaceful means, (b) appeals to member governments to refrain from the use or threats of force in their international relations and to respect each other's sovereignty, territorial integrity and political independence, and (c) requests the governments concerned to continue their efforts to achieve general and complete disarmament under effective international control.[84] According to one's predilection, this platitudinous and equivocal resolution may be construed as mildly condemning either the flight of the U–2 or the shooting down of an unarmed aircraft, or both. But the legality of penetrative reconnaissance remained unresolved.

Commenting on the U–2 incident, Senator Fulbright, Chairman of the United States Senate Foreign Relations Committee, was reported to have said on 28 June 1960, that the gravest mistake in the whole episode was President Eisenhower's assumption of responsibility for the flight. Senator Fulbright said:

If chiefs of State begin the practice of personally admitting the violations of each other's sovereignty, the orderly conduct of international affairs will quickly become impossible—as, indeed, it did in Paris last month.[85]

That Senator Fulbright is absolutely correct in his view that the U–2 flight constituted a violation of Soviet territorial sovereignty is so elementary a point in international law that it would be merely flogging a dead horse to labour it here,[86] except perhaps to add a word on the United States official

---

[81] Soviet draft resolution S/4321 (23.5.60); consideration by the Security Council, 23–6 May 1960, SC (XV) S/PV 857–60.

[82] S/4323 and S/4323/Rev. 2.   [83] SC (XV) S/PV 861, p. 16 (26.5.60).

[84] S/4328 (XV) adopted on 27 May 1960, SC (XV) S/PV 863, *nem. con.*, Poland and the USSR abstaining.   [85] *The Times* (London), 29 June 1960.

[86] Cf. Cheng, loc. cit. in n. 237 above [Ch. 2 above], and Q. Wright, 'Legal Aspects of the U–2 Incident', 54 *AJIL* (1960), p. 836, at p. 853. See an opposite view by Mr S. M. Beresford, Special Counsel, Committee on Science and Astronautics, US House of Representatives, 'Surveillance Aircraft and Satellite: A Problem of International Law', 27 *JALC*. (1960), p. 107, at p. 113: '. . . U–2 flights were not invasions of Soviet airspace.' It would be of interest to know Mr Beresford's view on the legality of such a flight over the United States undertaken by a similar Soviet aircraft on a similar mission.

In the NBC telefilm referred to above in n. 78, Senator Fulbright said, *inter alia*: 'Now I think one of the most serious things too growing out of this was our endeavour, on the part of our people, to justify these flights.'

admission, and President Eisenhower's assumption, of responsibility for the flight.

In his statement to the Supreme Soviet on 5 May 1960, breaking the news of the U–2 flight to the world, Mr Khrushchev said:

I do not doubt President Eisenhower's sincere desire for peace. Reason must guide us.[87]

After the United States had denied any intentional violation of Soviet airspace, Mr Khrushchev in his speech winding up the three-day session of the Supreme Soviet on 7 May, when he first revealed that the pilot was captured and alive, still conceded:

I fully admit that the President did not know that a plane was sent beyond the Soviet frontiers and did not return,

even though he added the quip: 'But this should make us even more watchful.'[88] Late the same afternoon the United States Department of State issued a statement which not only admitted that the U–2 was on a deliberate espionage flight but also vaunted that such flights had been made regularly during the past four years:

As a result of the inquiry ordered by the President, it has been established that in so far as the authorities in Washington are concerned there was no authorization for any such flight as described by Mr Khrushchev. Nevertheless, it appears that in endeavouring to obtain information now concealed behind the Iron Curtain a flight over Soviet territory was probably undertaken by an unarmed civilian U–2 plane . . . It is in relation to the danger of surprise attack that planes of the type of unarmed civilian U–2 aircraft have made flights along the frontiers of the free world for the past four years.[89]

In a statement made by Secretary of State Herter two days later (9 May), even the exculpation of 'the authorities in Washington' was withdrawn. He said that, although 'specific missions of these unarmed civilian aircraft have not been subject to Presidential authorization,' authority for such flights was derived from directives issued by the President under the National Security Act, 1947.[90] In his Press statement of 11 May, the President himself added:

. . . ever since the beginning of my Administration I have issued directives to gather, in every feasible way, the information required to protect the United States and the free world . . .[91]

In Moscow Mr Khrushchev was reported to have said on the same day: 'I was horrified to learn that the President had endorsed these acts.'[92]

This open and defiant admission of responsibility for the U–2 flight by the Administration and by the President himself meant that (to use President

[87] Quoted in NBC telefilm, cited in note 78 above.   [88] *The Times* (London), 9 May 1960.
[89] USIS, Off. Text, 9 May 1960.   [90] USIS, Off. Text, 10 May 1960, p. 2.
[91] USIS, Off. Text, 11 May 1960.   [92] *The Times* (London), 12 May 1960.

Eisenhower's own words as contained in his statement of 11 May 1960, in explaining the nature of intelligence activities)[93] the 'regular, visible agencies of the Government' which should normally be 'divorced from' such 'below-the-surface' activities, instead of dissociating themselves from these activities when they had been discovered, blatantly took credit for them as if nothing in the world had happened. Little wonder the Russians felt that insult was being added to injury. Salt was well rubbed into the wound when on 12 May the United States government handed to the Soviet government a Note in which it was said:

In its Note the Soviet Government has stated that the collection of intelligence about the Soviet Union by American aircraft is a "calculated policy" of the United States. The United States Government does not deny that it has pursued such a policy for purely defense purposes.[94]

The point of international law, illustrated rather dramatically by the U–2 incident, that penetrative reconnaissance is an infringement of the legal rights of the State spied on remains highly relevant even though U–2 flights have been discontinued. This is evident from the following passage in President Eisenhower's broadcast to the American people on 25 May 1960, after his return from the abortive Summit Conference in Paris:

In fact, before leaving Washington [for the Conference], I had directed that these U–2 flights be stopped. Clearly their usefulness was impaired . . . Furthermore, *new techniques, other than aircraft, are constantly being developed.*[95]

If these new techniques refer to reconnaissance satellites such as MIDAS and SAMOS,[96] then the question whether their flights over the Soviet Union constitute penetrative or peripheral reconnaissance can again only be answered if we know what is the precise upper limit of Soviet national space.

B. Peripheral Reconnaissance

Two facts seem hardly in doubt in regard to the RB–47 incident, even though they have not been fully admitted by the respective protagonists responsible for them. First, here was another unarmed United States military aircraft clearly engaged in carrying out reconnaissance over military installations along the Soviet coast bordering on the Barents Sea, but the difference with

---

[93] USIS, Off. Text, 11 May 1960.   [94] USIS, Off. Text, 13 May 1960.
[95] USIS, Off. Text, 26 May 1960, p. 3 (emphasis added). In hearings before the Senate Foreign Relations Committee on the events leading to the summit conference, US Secretary of Defence Gates confirmed the suspension of U–2 flights, but intimated that the loss of a valuable source of intelligence would be compensated by other means of which he did not speak in specific terms. *The Times* (London) correspondent in his dispatch interpolated: 'the reconnaissance satellites?' (*The Times* (London), 3 June 1960).
[96] See above, second paragraph of this chapter.

the U–2 incident was that the RB–47 was never intended to penetrate into Soviet airspace.[97] What was involved was peripheral reconnaissance. Secondly, the aircraft, which never penetrated Soviet airspace, was shot down over the high seas by Soviet fighters after they had failed to force it into Soviet airspace.[98]

If, on 1 May, the Americans were lulled by four years of immunity,[99] what the Russians failed to realize on 1 July was that, thanks to NATO's northern radar chain and other mobile radar stations, every move of the RB–47, even though it maintained complete radio silence, was known to the United States military authorities.[100] Thus, significantly, in his letter to Prime Minister Macmillan, Mr Khrushchev wrote on 5 August 1960:

[97] Cf. 'Testing Russian Radar Screens,' *The Times* (London), 20 July 1960.

[98] Cf. United States delegate Lodge's speech before the Security Council giving an account, with the aid of two maps showing the planned route and the course actually followed by the RB–47, 25 July 1960, SC (XV) S/PV 881 and maps; see also below, notes 100 and 101. The two maps, UN maps Nos. 1267x and 1268x are, herein, reproduced with kind permission from the UN Publications Board. The first map, chart 1, shows the planned route of the RB–47, whilst chart 2 is a detailed map of both the planned and the actual paths of the aircraft, as well as of the point where it was shot down.

[99] See above, n. 75. There is some controversy as to the height at which the U–2 was intercepted. An interesting point in the proceedings against the pilot (op. cit. (1960), n. 78 above) is the seeming Soviet anxiety to establish that the U–2 was hit at its maximum altitude of 68,000 feet (pp. 18, 29, 35, and 59). But a caption to the frontispiece (a map showing the course of the U–2), while saying that Powers was flying at 68,000 feet over Afghanistan, states that, when over the Soviet Union, 'he was then flying at *nearly* 67,000 feet' (p. 2; emphasis added). According to US intelligence sources in the NBC telefilm (see note 78 above): 'As Powers neared Sverdlovsk, he reported a flame-out in his jet engine and began to descend to the altitude at which it was possible to restart his engine in the air. The last communication with Powers was about 40,000 feet . . . [The plane] . . . had been forced down by a mechanical failure and not shot down by a rocket at 70,000 feet as the Soviets later claimed.' In view of the fact that it was known that the Russian T–6, T–7, and T–8 anti-aircraft missiles with respectively radar, inertial and infra-red guidance were capable of altitudes of between 60,000 feet (T–6) and eighteen miles (T–8) (see *The Times* (London), 7 May 1960), even though the NBC telefilm gave the maximum altitude of the U-2 as 90,000 feet, it would not appear impossible that the Russians did succeed in scoring a near-hit and wing the U–2 at an altitude nearing 67,000 feet. The last time a U–2 flew across the Soviet Union without being intercepted, even though detected by Soviet radar, was on 9 April 1960, according to Mr Khrushchev ('Skandal-Pie in the Sky', *Sunday Times* (London), 15 May 1960). Maybe what the Americans did not count on was not that the Soviet Union did not have the missiles with an adequate range but radars which could furnish instantaneously data of the course of the aircraft sufficiently precise for the missiles to home on their target; cf. below, n. 100.

[100] Cf. 'How the RB–47 was Tracked', *Sunday Times* (London), 31 July 1960. What the events seem to suggest, however, is that the co-ordination and the interpretation of the monitored data from ground and mobile stations are not instantaneous, but take a long time. This may at least be a partial explanation why eleven days after the shooting down of the RB–47, the State Department still refused all comment on the ground that a full report was awaited (*The Times* (London), 12 July 1960), but on the twelfth day (12 July) the White House Press Secretary, Mr James Hagerty, was able to state: 'The American RB–47 plane was over international waters and at no time flew over Soviet territory . . .' (USIS, Off. Text, 12 July 1960). On the same date, the United States answered the Soviet Note regarding the RB–47 and maintained that the RB–47 was never less than about 30 miles from Soviet land territory (USIS, Off. Text, 13 July 1960). A full account of the incident was presented by the US delegate to the Security Council on 25 July (see above, n. 98).

You, like the statesmen of the United States, insist that the RB–47 plane did not violate the Soviet border. And what, Mr Prime Minister, are your reasons for this? You did not fly this plane. You *did not see, nor could you track, this aircraft*. The pilots that flew the shot-down aircraft *did not report* to you about their flight or *bearings*. Why do you argue so categorically about things which you *cannot know* for sure?[101]

The answer, however, had already been given on 26 July 1960 by the United States representative at the United Nations, Mr Cabot Lodge, after the Soviet Union had brought the matter before the Security Council on 13 July:[102]

I explained yesterday that the United States possesses scientific devices which followed the RB–47 throughout its flight. I am sure that Soviet military authorities would like to know all about these devices, but I can assure you that the United States is not going to give them that satisfaction and it is not going to divulge our military secrets.[103]

Indeed, in the case of the RB–47, the United States was so sure of its facts and of the strength of its legal position that it proposed to the Security Council that the incident should be either investigated by a commission of inquiry or adjudicated upon by the International Court of Justice.[104] The Soviet Union vetoed this proposal[105] and subsequently, on 20 August 1960, placed its complaints arising from the U–2 and the RB–47 incidents before the XVth session of the General Assembly.[106] But with the release by the Soviet Union of the two surviving airmen from the RB–47 after the Kennedy Administration had taken office in 1961,[107] it seems safe to assume that both incidents are now closed.[108] It may even be a fair conjecture that the U–2 pilot might soon be released from prison and expelled by the Soviet Union in order not to present too obvious a contrast between these two incidents. The United States government, on the other hand, appears anxious that these two cases be clearly distinguished one from the other. Thus, President Kennedy in his first telecast Press conference on 25 January 1961, when he announced the release by the

---

[101] *The Times* (London), 6 Aug. 1960. Actually the British Prime Minister had already said in a written reply in the House of Commons on 26 July 1960: 'The aircraft's flight plan did not take it within fifty miles of Soviet territory at any point. We were ourselves able to determine the position of this aircraft, and we have reliable evidence to show that it did not go within thirty miles of the coast. Our information fully tallied with the United States estimate' (627 H.C. Deb. 5 s., *col. 111*). The same information was given a day before (25 July) by Sir Pierson Dixon in the Security Council (S/PV 881, p. 9, at p. 10). Emphasis in *The Times* report added.

[102] Soviet complaint of 13 July 1960 (S/4384; S/4385), considered on 22 (S/PV 880), 25 (S/PV 881), 26 July (S/PV 882, 883), and 8 Aug. 1960 (S/PV 884).

[103] SC (XV) S/PV 883, p. 31.   [104] S/4409/Rev. 1 (26.7.60).

[105] SC (XV) S/PV 883, p. 39 (26.7.60). Mr Kuznetsov, the Soviet delegate, said: 'The United States proposal can be interpreted only as an attempt to deprive the Soviet Union of its sovereign right to take whatever steps are necessary to ensure the inviolability of its frontiers, and to transfer the right to an international commission or to the International Court. It is legitimate to ask what self-respecting State would agree to so glaring an infringement of its sovereign rights.'

[106] Doc. A/4446.

[107] 'Russia Releases Survivors of RB–47', *The Times* (London), 26 Jan. 1961.

[108] 'Mr Khrushchev on Forgetting the U–2', *The Times* (London), 2 Jan. 1961, referring to Mr Khrushchev's various New Year toasts.

Map VI.1 PLANNED AND COMPLETED ROUTE OF THE U-2 FLIGHT OVER THE SOVIET UNION ON MAY 1960

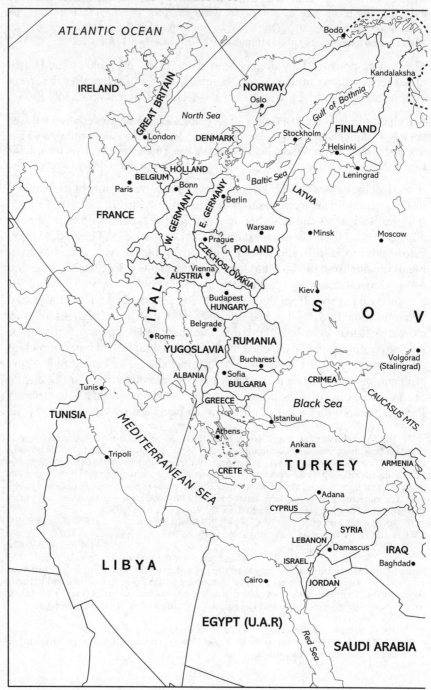

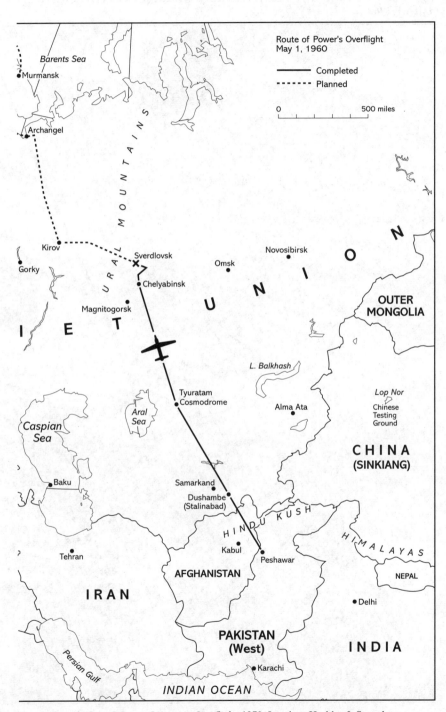

Source: Francis Gary Powers, *Operation Overflight*, 1970. London: Hodder & Stoughton

Map VI.2 PLANNED ROUTE OF THE RB-47 AIRCRAFT ON ITS FLIGHT ON 1 JULY 1960

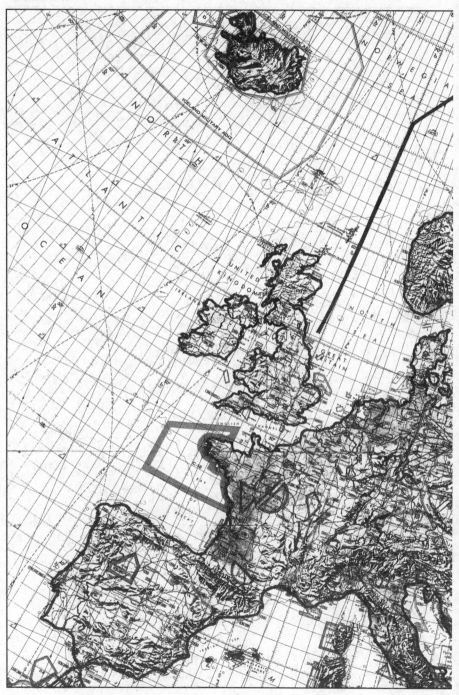

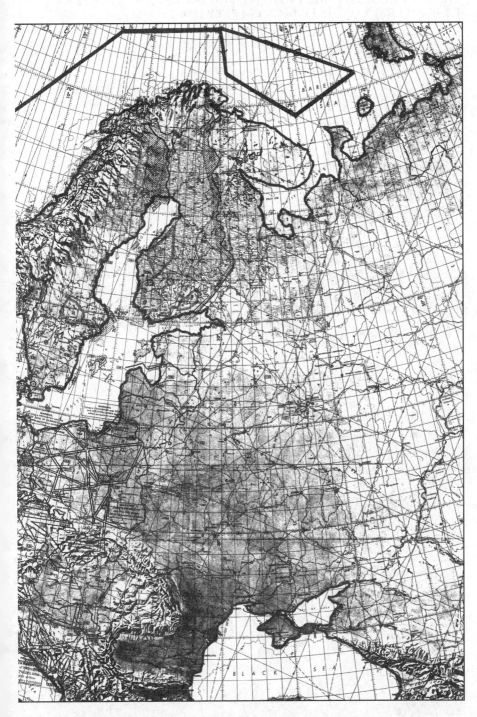

Source: UN Doc. S/PV.881/Add.1 (25.7.60), Annex, Chart No.1. UN map No. 1267x. Reprinted by kind permission of the UN Publications Board.

MAP VI.3 DETAILED FLIGHT PATH (PLANNED AND ACTUAL) OF THE RB–47 AIRCRAFT ON ITS FLIGHT ON 1 JULY 1960

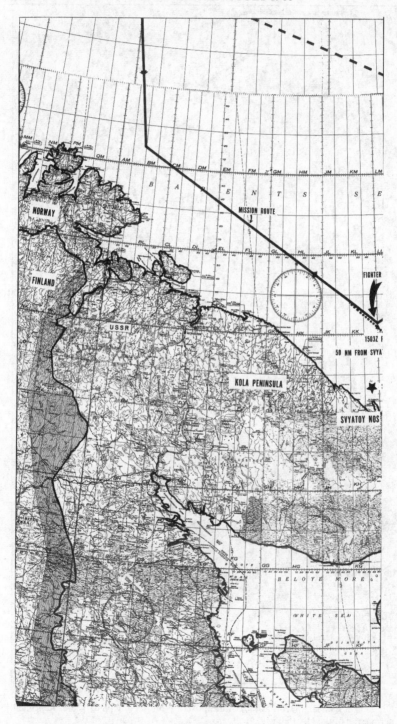

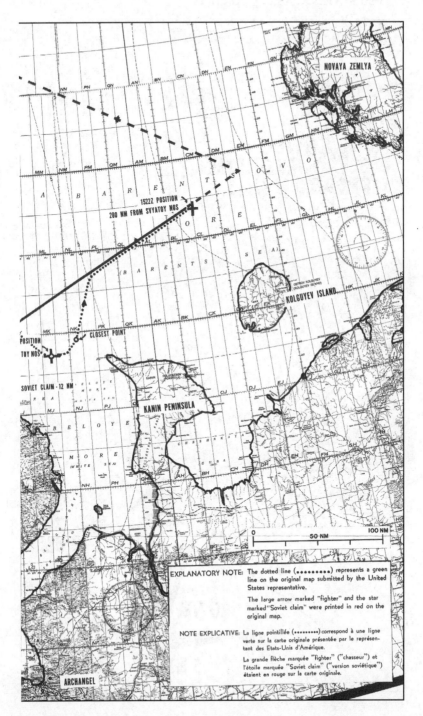

Source: UN Doc. S/PV.881/Add.1 (25.7.60), Annex, Chart No.2. UN map No. 1268x. Reprinted by kind permission of the UN Publications Board.

MAP VI.4 USSR PERIPHERAL RECONNAISSANCE FLIGHTS OFF THE UNITED STATES ALASKAN COAST

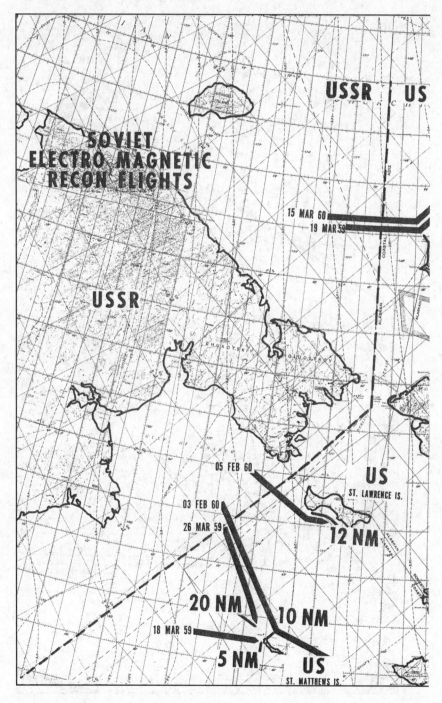

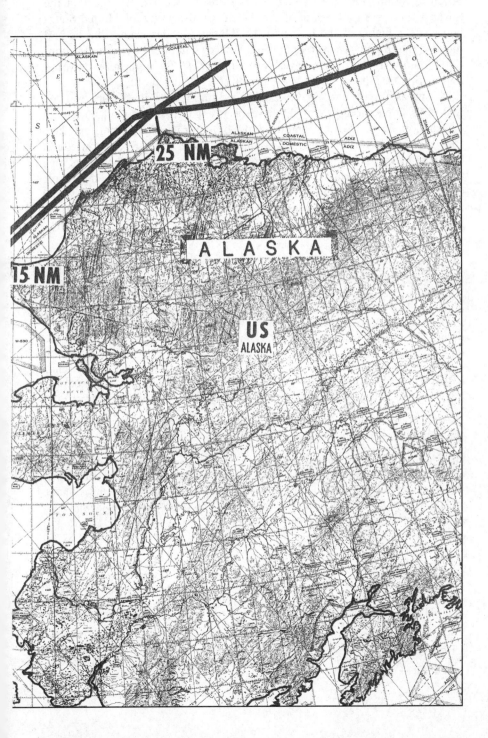

Source: UN Doc. S/PV.883/Add.1 (27.7.60). Chart 1. UN map No. 1270x. Reprinted by kind permission of the UN Publications Board.

Soviet government of the two survivors from the RB–47, stressed that the Soviet Union was fully aware of the distinction drawn by the United States between the flights of the U–2 and the RB–47. He also stated that he had directed that flights *penetrating* Soviet airspace would not be resumed, a continuation of President Eisenhower's order in 1960.[109] By implication, it would appear that peripheral reconnaissance will still be carried out.

Be that as it may, it seems well established that if the RB–47 were over the high seas, even though it might have been engaged in reconnaissance, its destruction by the Soviet Union would be contrary to international law. Indeed, the legality of peripheral reconnaissance was implicitly acknowledged by both the British and the United States delegates to the United Nations, and not disputed by the Russians. Thus, Sir Pierson Dixon, during the debate on the RB–47 incident, said that the Security Council would have to be 'in virtually permanent session' if Britain were to make an issue of every separate occasion when she was 'overlooked, or overheard by the Soviet Union.'[110] He mentioned in particular:

We in the United Kingdom have for a long time known that Russian reconnaissance aircraft carry out intelligence-gathering flights . . . Similarly, we in the United Kingdom are frequently subjected to the annoyance of seeing Soviet trawlers, which we know are fitted up with electronic and technical equipment required to intercept radio transmissions in the United Kingdom, in close proximity to our own territorial waters, or in close proximity to areas where naval exercises or Western military research activity is carried out . . . The same thing applies to the numerous unidentified submarines recently found lurking in the neighbourhood of United Kingdom naval exercises and, indeed, in suspicious circumstances which suggest that they are carrying out electronic intelligence operations within fifty miles of the coast of the United Kingdom.[111]

And, in his speech of 26 July, Mr Lodge, the United States delegate, with the aid of maps and photographs, pointed out:

[T]he Soviet Union has been sending these electronic reconnaissance planes regularly off the coast of Alaska, as close as five miles from our territory, to gather intelligence on our radars and other electronic signals . . . The difference between the United States and the Soviet Union is that we shoot their aircraft with cameras; they shoot ours with guns and rockets and kill or imprison our crews.[112]

---

[109] USIS, Off. Text, 26 Jan. 1961, p. 2.   [110] SC (XV) S/PV 881 (25.7.60), 9, at 13.

[111] Ibid., 12. Cf. also the UK Prime Minister's statement in the House of Commons on 19 July (627 H.C. Deb. 5 s., col. 257) and the Minister of Defence Mr Watkinson's written answer to a question on the same subject on 20 July (ibid., *cols. 48–9*). Mr Macmillan, in his statement on 19 July, said: 'These flights and these movements by sea are perfectly legal under international law,' referring to reconnaissance activities of both sides (ibid., col. 259).

[112] SC (XV) S/PV 883 (26.7.60), p. 30, at pp. 33–4, and maps issued under Add. 1 (27.7.60). Chart 1, UN map No. 1270x, reproduced here with kind permission from the UN Publications Board, shows a number of Soviet peripheral reconnaissance flights along Alaska in 1959 and 1960, and their nearest point from the US coast.

The pointed difference in the legality of penetrative reconnaissance and of peripheral reconnaissance leads us back to the fundamental importance of clearly delimiting the upper limits of national space, a problem deliberately eschewed by the United Nations *Ad Hoc* Committee on the ground that it is not essential to the continued peaceful use of outer space;[113] for reconnaissance by means of an artificial satellite is lawful if the latter's orbit lies outside the national space of the State spied on, but illegal if it penetrates within.

VI. Demilitarization and Disarmament

To turn from reconnaissance to the demilitarization of outer space is to enter into the opaque, confused, and frustrating history of disarmament in the United Nations. So far, there is not a gleam of light on the horizon. The two poles are represented by the respective slogans of no disarmament without control and no control without disarmament.

Insofar as the establishment of the *Ad Hoc* Committee on the Peaceful Uses of Outer Space[114] and of its successor[115] deserves to be so regarded, they are the only fruits that several years of efforts in this field have borne. The seeds were sown by a United States proposal to set up a technical committee to study the design of an inspection system for objects entering into space, put forward in 1957.[116] Pollination came from a Soviet counter-proposal presented first in March 1958[117] and subsequently in November 1958 to the General Assembly.[118] But up to now [1961, see n. 1 above *in fine*] the twenty-four-power Committee has made little headway.

As regards the banning of military activities in outer space, again the United States succeeded in being the first to have introduced such a proposal before the Political Committee of the General Assembly on 14 January 1957.[119] The Soviet counter-proposal[120] was limited initially to the banning of

---

[113] See above, nn. 67–74, and text thereto.   [114] See above, text to n. 56 ff.

[115] See above, text to n. 61.   [116] See above, nn. 53–4.   [117] See above, n. 55.

[118] A/C.1/L.219/Rev. 1 (18.11.58), Soviet proposal to establish an international committee for co-operation in the study of cosmic space for peaceful purposes of eleven members (USSR, US, UK, France, India, Czechoslovakia, Poland, Roumania, UAR, Sweden, Argentina).

[119] Loc. cit. in n. 53 above: 'Renewed negotiations should strive towards the following objectives . . . fourthly, to ensure that research and development activities concerning the propulsion of objects through outer space would be devoted exclusively to scientific and peaceful purposes'; see also ibid. para. 13 (p. 42).

[120] See UK, *Report on the Proceedings of the Sub-Committee of the United Nations Disarmament Commission, London, March 18–September 6, 1957*, Cmnd. 333 (1957), App. I, DC/112: Fourth Report of the Sub-Committee of the Disarmament Commission (1 Aug. 1957), Annex 1, DC/SC.1/49: Soviet Proposal on the Reduction of Armaments and Armed Forces and the Prohibition of Atomic and Hydrogen Weapons (18 Mar. 1957), p. 25 ff. At this stage, the Soviet Union apparently held the view that it was the nuclear warhead that mattered and not the missiles or rockets themselves (see ibid., p. 10). The date 18 Mar. 1956, given on p. 25 as that of the Soviet proposal is an obvious misprint (see p. 23 where the date of Doc. DC/SC.1/49 is given as 18 Mar. 1957; cf. also ibid., p. 6, para. 4).

rockets suitable for use as nuclear weapons, but it was subsequently broadened to include the military use of outer space in general.[121]

However, other obstacles stand between the Soviet bloc and the Western powers. Both sides usually present their schemes as part of a 'package proposal', and each then recriminates against the other for picking and choosing from the 'package' those items which it finds attractive without agreeing to their accompanying conditions. Thus, the Western proposals always stress control and inspection which the Russians regard as nothing more than 'legitimized espionage'. The Russians, in turn, always link their disarmament proposals with the question of 'foreign bases' which the Western powers consider as red herrings.

Perhaps in a flush of success immediately after the launching of SPUTNIK I, Mr Khrushchev was reported to have expressed Soviet willingness to discuss directly with the United States the problem of space control independently of general disarmament, provided that agreement could be reached on 'peaceful co-existence'.[122] Secretary of State Dulles almost simultaneously made an announcement expressing willingness to separate space control from general disarmament, on condition that the 'associates' of the United States agreed,[123] and the Political Committee of the General Assembly was so informed.[124] But in the subsequent official version of the Soviet proposal the word 'disarmament' appeared instead of 'peaceful co-existence'.[125]

Another snag is the not unnatural dislike on the part of Soviet Union of finding itself in a numerical minority in the United Nations. It prefers, therefore, either a direct approach between the two hegemonic powers, itself and the United States, as its October 1957 proposals show,[126] or a tripartite arrangement consisting of the Soviet bloc, the Western bloc, and the 'neu-

---

[121] See above, n. 55. See also Soviet draft resolution before the First Committee of the General Assembly, A/C.1/L.219 (7.11.58); this part of the Soviet proposal was subsequently dropped in favour of A/C. 1/L.219/Rev. 1 (18.11.58), q.v. above, n. 118.

[122] The proposal was made in the course of an interview in Moscow with Mr James Reston, the chief Washington correspondent of the *New York Times* (*The Times* (London), 9 Oct. 1957); see also ibid., 12 Oct. 1957.

[123] *The Times* (London), 9 Oct. 1957.

[124] Mr Lodge, US delegate, GA (XII) A/C.1/SR 866, p. 5, at p. 7: 'The four Powers proposed that a technical committee should be established to work out an inspection system which would ensure the use of outer space exclusively for peaceful purposes. If there was general agreement to conduct such a study on a multilateral basis, the United States was prepared to participate without awaiting the conclusion of negotiations on the other substantive proposals' (10.10.57).

[125] 'Unhelpful Attitude of Russians', *The Times* (London), 12 Oct. 1957.

[126] See above, n. 122. A State Department statement issued on 8 Oct. 1957 referred to Mr Khrushchev's proposal for a direct United States–Soviet study of the control of objects entering outer space and after recalling the Western proposal of 29 Aug. (see above, n. 54), pointed out that what was proposed was a 'multilateral international study and not a bilateral study between the United States and the USSR and that the United States would not be disposed to consider any alteration of this aspect of the proposals' (*The Times* (London), 8 Oct. 1957). See also reply from Soviet Embassy to United States Congressman Victor Anfuso of 5 Jan. 1960 (*Flight*, 15 Jan. 1960, pp. 67–8).

trals'. Failure to accept the Soviet tripartite concept in the formation of the *Ad Hoc* Committee on the Peaceful Uses of Outer Space resulted in the Soviet bloc boycotting it.[127] The Soviet Union had wanted an eleven-member Committee consisting of four Western powers, four Soviet-bloc countries and three 'neutrals'.[128] The ratio in the eighteen-nation *Ad Hoc* Committee that was established was: 13:3:2.[129] In the composition of the twenty-four-nation Committee,[130] which was created as a result of a resolution sponsored jointly by the Soviet Union and the United States,[131] it has been reported that the ratio of 12:7:5 involved in fact an acceptance of Soviet terms by the Western powers. This was perhaps for the sake of securing that the new creation should be born in wedlock between East and West, for they had originally proposed the ratio of 12:5:7 and were not prepared to go beyond 12:6:6.[132] Unfortunately for the child, this *mariage de convenance* did not last and it is suffering from the usual consequences of parted parents: neglect and abandonment.

In principle, the United States has consistently rejected the 'two sides' concept. During the discussion leading to the formation of the *Ad Hoc* Committee, the United States delegate to the United Nations said:

There are no 'two sides' to outer space. There are not—and never have been—'two sides' in the United Nations . . . We do not . . . accept the idea of 'two sides'—and, frankly, we don't understand it.[133]

The Soviet 'two sides' concept and struggle for parity scored a point, however, when the Conference of Foreign Ministers, shortly before the XIVth session of the General Assembly in 1959, recommended the formation of a ten-nation committee on disarmament to replace the previous five-power Sub-Committee. Whereas the latter was composed of the Soviet Union in the midst of four Western powers (Canada, France, United Kingdom, United States), the ten-nation Disarmament Committee is based on equality between the 'two sides': five NATO powers on one side (Canada, France, Italy, United Kingdom, United States) and five Warsaw-Pact countries on the other (Bulgaria, Czechoslovakia, Poland, Roumania and the Soviet Union).[134]

---

[127] See above, n. 58.   [128] See above, n. 118.

[129] Argentina, Australia, Belgium, Brazil, Canada, Czechoslovakia, France, India, Iran, Italy, Japan, Mexico, Poland, Sweden, USSR, UAR, UK, and US.

[130] Albania, Argentina, Australia, Austria, Belgium, Brazil, Bulgaria, Canada, Czechoslovakia, France, Hungary, India, Iran, Italy, Japan, Lebanon, Mexico, Poland, Roumania, Sweden, USSR, UAR, UK, and US.

[131] See above, n. 61.

[132] Cf. 'Soviet Wins Point in UN Space Talk', *New York Times*, 9 Dec. 1959, p. 184.

[133] Mr Lodge, US delegate, during the debate on the establishment of the *Ad Hoc* Committee, 24 Nov. 1958, USIS, Off. Text, 25 Nov. 1958, p. 2; the account in GA (XIII), A/C.1/SR 994, p. 235, is slightly abridged.

[134] The Ten-Power Disarmament Committee owes its origin to an agreement reached between the Foreign Ministers of France, UK, US, and the USSR during a conference held in Geneva in Aug. 1959 (see Misc. No. 14 (1959), Cmnd. 868). In consequence of this statement, the four

The meeting of this Committee began on 15 March 1960, and on 1 April the United States Chief of Delegation, Mr F. Eaton, proposed that the United States and the Soviet Union—the only two powers with space capabilities—should agree on the banning of space weapons and accept a system of control as a pilot scheme for more ambitious projects at some future date.[135] The Soviet Union alleged, however, that this proposal was aimed at control without disarmament. The Committee adjourned on 20 April and reconvened on 7 June. On 27 June, the five Warsaw-Pact powers, accusing the Western powers of insincerity, withdrew from the Committee.[136] On the same day, the Soviet Union requested the inclusion in the agenda of the Xvth session of the General Assembly of an item on disarmament.[137]

Meanwhile, the eighty-two-member Disarmament Commission, which had not met since 10 September 1959, was convened on 16 August 1960, and on 18 August unanimously recommended to the General Assembly that the ten-nation Disarmament Committee should 'continue in being and be convened whenever deemed necessary'.[138] After having considered the Report of the Commission, the General Assembly adopted three resolutions which were all related to nuclear weapons. The first 1176 (XV), adopted on 27 December 1960, aimed at preventing further dissemination of nuclear weapons. The other two, 1177 (XV) and 1178 (XV), adopted respectively on 27 and 28 December 1960, were concerned with the suspension of nuclear tests.[139]

This leads us to the latest and perhaps the most important proposal that has yet been made in the United Nations regarding outer space, namely, that made by President Eisenhower before the General Assembly on 22 September 1960. After recalling the recent example of the Antarctic Treaty of 1959[140] and the missed opportunity of 1946 when the Soviet Union turned down the United States Atoms for Peace Plan for placing atomic energy under international control,[141] President Eisenhower proposed:

1. We agree that celestial bodies are not subject to national appropriation by any claims of sovereignty.

---

governments made a joint statement on 7 Sept. 1959, about the establishment of this Committee (see UK, *Verbatim Reports of the Ten-Power Disarmament Committee, 15 March–29 April 1960, and 7–27 June 1960*, Cmnd. 1152 (1960)).

[135] TNCD/PV 14, Cmnd. 1152 (1960), p. 267, at p 270.

[136] TNCD/PV 47 (27.6.60), Cmnd. 1152 (1960), pp. 879 ff.

[137] A/4385 (27.6.60) and Corr. 1 (29.6.60).

[138] 16 Aug. (DC/PV 66), 17 Aug. (DC/PV 67, 68), 18 Aug. (DC/PV 69, 70), 1960; resolution of 18 Aug. (DC/182/Corr. 1); Report to General Assembly of 26 Aug. 1960 (A/4463), referred on 10 Oct. 1960, to First Committee which reported to the General Assembly on 20 Dec. 1960 (A/4680).

[139] A/RES/1576, 1577 and 1578 (XV).

[140] 1 Dec. 1959, Cmnd. 913 (1959), 402 UNTS 71; cf. P. C. Jessup and H. J. Taubenfeld, *Controls for Outer Space and the Antarctic Analogy* (1959).

[141] Presented by US delegate, Mr Bernard M. Baruch (thus also known as the Baruch Plan), at the first meeting of the UN Atomic Energy Commission, 14 June 1946, Off. Rec., 1st Year, 1st Meeting, No. 1, p. 4, at pp. 7 ff.

2. We agree that the nations of the world shall not engage in warlike activities on these bodies.
3. We agree, subject to appropriate verification, that no nation will put into orbit or station in outer space weapons of mass destruction. All launchings of space craft should be verified in advance by the United Nations.
4. We press forward with a programme of international co-operation for constructive peaceful uses of outer space under the United Nations . . .[142]

There are some unexplained features in these proposals. For instance, why limit the ban of territorial claims and warlike activities to extraterrestrial bodies and not extend it to outer space in general? Moreover, does it mean that the proposed restriction on the launching of spacecraft applies (a) to only weapons of mass destruction, but not other types of weapon, and (b) to putting such weapons into orbit or station in outer space, but not to these and other weapons aimed directly at another State?

Furthermore, too much stress must not be placed on the Antarctica analogy and the so-called missed opportunity of the Atoms for Peace Plan. Insofar as the 1959 Antarctic Treaty is concerned, it is only realistic to think that agreement proved feasible only when success in rocketry considerably downgraded that continent's strategic value, so that it is not altogether a valid precedent for outer space, at least for the present. As for the Atoms for Peace Plan, one needs only to reflect on the failure of the Western powers to prevent France from building and testing what have sometimes been unkindly called antiquated atomic bombs in order to realize that, even with all the hindsight and experience of the last fourteen years, the chance of the Plan being accepted in 1947 seems today no better than it was then. Indeed, if the Soviet Union had accepted the Plan in 1947, what would be the odds of its having by now reached parity with the United States in the know-how of thermonuclear weapons?

Yet, notwithstanding these observations and reservations, the Eisenhower proposal represents the most far-reaching that has been made by either side up to date in relation to outer space. Moreover, bearing in mind that there is now approximate parity between the East and West in space technology, as

---

[142] USIS, Off. Text (22.9.60), pp. 5–6. The Official Records of the General Assembly, GA (XV) A/PV 868 (22.9.60), p. 45, at p. 48, list the second sentence of item 3 as a separate item 4 (para. 58), while removing what appears in the text as item 4 to para. 59, thus not forming part of the actual proposals. The USIS text appears to make better sense and both USIS, London, and the Department of State, Washington, D.C. (letter to the writer from Mr John N. Washburn, Acting Assistant Legal Adviser, dated 6 Apr. 1961), insist that it is to be taken as correct. On the other hand, the United Nations Chief of the Official Records Editing Section says: 'I have checked with the sound track . . . and have ascertained that the text printed by us corresponds exactly to what the speaker said . . .' (relayed to the writer by letter from the UN Information Centre, London, dated 17 Mar. 1961). It would seem, therefore, that there was a *lapsus linguae* in the actual delivery of the speech which the United States delegation to the UN failed to correct in the provisional records.

compared with the absence of nuclear parity in 1947, there is strength in the remarks prefacing the Eisenhower proposal:

National vested interests have not yet been developed in space or in celestial bodies. Barriers to agreement are now lower than they will ever be again. The opportunity may be fleeting. Before many years have passed, the point of no return may be behind us . . . We must not lose the chance we still have to control the future of outer space.[143]

It matters little whether this or any other proposal is eventually adopted by the United Nations. The fact remains that outer space offers mankind in general, the United Nations in particular, and the space powers specifically, not only a technological, but also a commensurate political and moral challenge. For unless we succeed in composing our differences, we shall not have peace on earth or in space, without which we will go on facing the constant danger of a cosmic war that threatens to wipe mankind off the surface of the earth.

[143] GA (XV) A/PV 868 (22.9.60), p. 45, at pp. 47–8 (paras. 56 and 58).

7

United Nations Resolutions on Outer Space: 'Instant' International Customary Law?*

I. Introduction

The General Assembly of the United Nations has no legislative power. Nevertheless, two of its resolutions on outer space, resolution 1721A (XVI) of 20 December 1961 and resolution 1962 (XVIII) of 13 December 1963, have often been hailed as 'the first chapter in the book of space law'.[1] The purpose of this chapter is to examine the legal status of these resolutions. It is hoped that, in doing so, some light may also be shed on the nature of the so-called international 'customary' law.

II. United Nations and Outer Space

Following proposals made by the United States in January and July 1957 and a Soviet counter-proposal put forward in March 1958, the General Assembly of the United Nations, on 13 December 1958, approved a twenty-power draft resolution on the establishment of an eighteen-member *Ad Hoc* Committee

---

* First published in 5 *Indian JIL* (1965), pp. 23–48; reprinted in Cheng (ed.), *International Law*, pp. 237–62. Reproduced by kind permission of the Indian Society of International Law.

[1] Thus, regarding resolution 1962, Canadian delegate, A/C.I./SR.1346 (5.12.63), p. 189; See also, e.g. R. N. Gardner, 'Outer Space: A Breakthrough for International Law', 50 *ABAJ* (1964), p. 30; cf. *contra* F. B. Schick, 'Problems of a Space Law in the United Nations', 13 *ICLQ* (1964), p. 969. As regards resolution 1721 A, see e.g. O. Schachter in M. Cohen (ed.), *Law and Politics in Space* (1964), pp. 96 ff., and M. S. McDougal, ibid., p. 115; C. W. Jenks, 'Le droit international des espaces célestes—Rapport préliminaire', 50 *Annuaire de l'Institut* (1963), pp. 321 ff.

The effects of Resolution 1962 were the subject of a lively discussion in the Space Law Committee and at the Tokyo Conference (1964) of the International Law Association. See the report of Prof. Goedhuis, Rapporteur of the Space Law Committee to the Tokyo Conference, which includes a Memorandum of the learned Rapporteur on Resolution 1962 and the text of replies to the Rapporteur's Questionnaire received from various Members of the Committee, including Dr M. Bodenschatz, Prof. P. Chauveau, Prof. J. C. Cooper, Dr. E. Fasan, Av. G. Guerreri, Dr E. Huber Prof. O. J. Lissitzyn, Prof. A. Meyer, Dr E. Pépin, Dr M. Zylicz, and Dr G. Zhukov. Opinions differed greatly among members of the Committee as to whether the resolution was binding. See also the discussions at the Conference on the Committee's draft resolution A (ILA), *Report of the 51st Conference, Tokyo* (1964), pp. 622–776).

on the Peaceful Uses of Outer Space. This Committee, which met in May and June 1959, was, on account of its membership, boycotted by the Soviet Union, Czechoslovakia, and Poland; nor did India and the United Arab Republic attend. Its Report was considered by the General Assembly at its XIVth Session. As a result thereof, the General Assembly decided on 12 December 1959 to establish a twenty-four-member Committee on the Peaceful Uses of Outer Space.[2] This new Committee also met with difficulties. The Soviet bloc was still dissatisfied with its composition and, moreover, wanted the unanimity rule to be applied, instead of the majority rule applicable to all subordinate organs of the Assembly. At the insistence of the United Kingdom government, it eventually met for the first time on 27 November 1961 in order to transact certain formal business before its two-year term expired. After adopting a report[3] to the General Assembly, the Committee adjourned *sine die*.

III. Resolution 1721 (XVI)

While the Assembly's First Committee was considering the Outer Space Committee's Report, a five-part draft resolution was submitted by Australia, Canada, Italy, and the United States.[4] This was subsequently revised and resubmitted by all the members of the Outer Space Committee, including the Soviet Union.[5] Behind this draft resolution, therefore, stood an agreement between the two space powers.[6] It was really this agreement which broke the deadlock between them regarding outer space co-operation in the United Nations. With this underlying agreement between the two space powers, it was hardly surprising that the twenty-four-nation draft was adopted unanimously by the First Committee on 11 December 1961 and then by the General Assembly on 20 December 1961 as resolution 1721 (XVI).[7] The fifth and last part (Part E) of the resolution continued the existence of the Outer Space Committee and enlarged its membership to twenty-eight.

Part A of the resolution incorporated in substance certain suggestions made by President Kennedy in his address before the General Assembly on 25 September 1961.[8] Its operative part is worded as follows:

---

[2] For developments up to 1961, see the present writer's 'The United Nations and Outer Space', 14 *CLP* (1961), p. 247 [Ch. 6 above].

[3] A/4987.   [4] A/C. 1/L.301.   [5] A/C.1/L.30/Rev. 1 and Corr. 1.

[6] Cf. Mr Khrushchev's message to President Kennedy of 20 Mar. 1962, (see n. 17 below), in which he said: 'I regard as a positive fact that at the XVIth session of the United Nations General Assembly, the Soviet Union and the United States found it possible to agree on the proposal about the initial principles of space legislation, which was then unanimously approved by all the Members of the United Nations.' See also Soviet delegate, A/C.1/SR.1214 (11.12.61), p. 268 (para 12).

[7] A/5026; text also in *UNYB* (1961), p. 35, herein reproduced below as App. II.1. Cf. also P. K. Kartha, 'Some Legal Problems Concerning Outer Space', 3 *Indian JIL* (1963), p. 1.

[8] Cf. also ILA, *Report of the 49th Conference, Hamburg* (1960), p. 245.

The General Assembly,

. . .

1. *Commends* to States for their guidance in the exploration and use of outer space the following principles:

(a) International law, including the Charter of the United Nations, applies to outer space and celestial bodies;

(b) Outer space and celestial bodies are free for exploration and use by all States in conformity with international law and are not subject to national appropriation

. . .

Resolution 1721A (XVI) thus has no pretension to being binding. It merely 'commends' to States 'for their guidance' certain principles. This, of course, does not prejudice the issue whether either or both of the principles it so commends to States may or may not already be binding on States under existing international law.[9] While many Member States refrained from pronouncing on the legal status of resolution 1721A, some did explicitly refer to it as a mere recommendation.[10] The principles it commends to States were, however, expressly 'supported' by some,[11] and 'subscribed to' by the United Kingdom.[12] The Soviet Union and the United States seemed to have gone further and, at least at one point, treated the resolution as binding, the former apparently because the resolution had been adopted unanimously by the General Assembly,[13] the latter, it would seem, for the same reason,[14] and because it considered the resolution to be declaratory of international customary law.[15] It is questionable, however, whether the above-mentioned view of the Soviet Union, which was expressed only once, can be treated as representative of its general attitude towards General Assembly resolutions.[16] In any event, the much longer period of gestation of General Assembly resolution 1962 (XVIII) has afforded Member States more opportunities to make

---

[9] See the present writer's 'The Extraterrestrial Application of International Law', 18 *CLP* (1965), p. 132 [Ch. 5 above].

[10] E.g. France, A/AC.105/PV.3 (20.3.62), p. 48; Romania, ibid./PV.8 (27.3.62), pp. 13–15; see also n. 16 below.

[11] E.g., Poland, A/AC.105/C.2/SR.6 (6.6.62), p. 7; Soviet Union, ibid./SR.7 (7.6.62), p. 5.

[12] A/AC.105/PV.3 (20.3.62), pp. 33–40; A/AC.105/C.2/SR.3 (30.5.62), p. 3.

[13] A/AC.105/C.2/SR.14 (19.6.62), p. 2: Resolution 1721 A (XVI) laid down certain principles which were binding upon all States . . . Members of the United Nations had clearly shown, by their unanimous approval of the resolution, that they recognised the need to lay down binding legal principles.'

[14] A/AC.105/PV.2 (19.3.62), pp. 13–15.

[15] A/AC/105/C.2/SR.20 (22.4.63), pp. 10–11. See below text to n. 53.

[16] USSR: 'The fact is the declaration we are proposing would be a binding international instrument while a resolution of the General Assembly [referring to resolution 1721], in accordance with the provisions of the Charter, is merely a recommendation', A/AC.105/PV.10 (10.9.62), 41; 'General Assembly resolution 1721 (XVI) . . . unfortunately is not yet a legal obligation on the part of States . . .', ibid./PV.15 (14.9.62), p. 11; 'resolution 1721 (XVI), like all other General Assembly resolutions, was merely a recommendation', A/C.1/SR.1289 (3.12.62), p. 215.

See further *sub voce* 'contradictions and inconsistencies' under the entry 'Admission' in the Index to the present writer's *General Principles of Law*.

clear their attitudes on this subject, and it will probably be more helpful if their position is examined with reference primarily to resolution 1962 which, moreover, in substance incorporates the two principles contained in resolution 1721A.

IV. The Outer Space Committee

Resolution 1721 (XVI), in addition to continuing the existence of the Outer Space Committee and enlarging its membership from twenty-four to twenty-eight, *inter alia* invited the Outer Space Committee 'to study and report on the legal problems which may arise from the exploration and use of outer space'. The expanded Outer Space Committee met for the first time on 19 March 1962. It could hardly have done so in more propitious conditions. Apart from the agreement reached between the two space powers the previous December, which was what made resolution 1721 possible and really enabled the Committee to begin work, less than a month before, on 20 February, Mr Khrushchev, in his congratulatory message to President Kennedy, on the successful completion of a three-orbit space flight by Colonel J. Glenn, had suggested that the two countries should co-operate in their space efforts. Two days before the meeting began, President Kennedy, in response to the above message, sent Mr Khrushchev a letter containing specific proposals. And on 20 March a very positive reply was received in which Mr Khrushchev accepted all the proposals except the one on the setting up of tracking stations in each other's territory. He also proposed joint tracking and the signing of two treaties, one on assistance to and return of astronauts, and the other on space law.[17]

At the opening session of the Outer Space Committee, the following statement was made by the Chairman:

I should like to place on record that through informal consultations it has been agreed among the members of the Committee that it will be the aim of all members of the Committee and its Sub-Committees to conduct the Committee's work in such a way that the Committee will be able to reach agreement in its work without need for voting.[18]

This is the beginning of the procedure of 'consensus'. In other words, every member of the Committee and of the Sub-Committees was given a veto. But in fact, as it was stressed by almost all the delegates, the essential point was agreement between the two space powers. The Indian delegate was merely voicing a general sentiment when he said:

---

[17] Cf. below, text to nn. 24 ff. On US–USSR co-operation in space, cf. J. Simsarian, 'Outer Space Co-operation in the United Nations', 57 *AJIL* (1963), p. 854, at pp. 860–1.

[18] A/AC.105/PV.2 (19.3.62), p. 4.

This was a wise decision because no solution which is not acceptable to the two space Powers can be implemented.[19]

This observation is only too true in the light of the experience of the Outer Space Committee.

In the course of 1962, a number of proposals were submitted. Four in particular were intended to set out basic principles governing the activities of States in the exploration and use of outer space, those of the Soviet Union of 6 June 1962,[20] the United Arab Republic of 14 September 1962,[21] the United Kingdom of 4 December 1962,[22] and the United States of 8 December 1962.[23]

There were a number of points on which these various proposals, especially the American, British, and Soviet ones, were in agreement; but there were also items in the Soviet draft, in particular paragraph 8, prohibiting reconnaissance satellites, and paragraph 6, which would have given the space powers a right to veto each other's space activities, which met with strong United States opposition.

V. Treaty Versus Resolution

But there was also strong disagreement between the two space powers regarding the form in which these principles were to be set out. The Soviet Union wanted a treaty.[24] The United States, on the other hand, was equally adamant that it wanted a General Assembly resolution and not a treaty. States within the Soviet bloc all solidly supported the Soviet position. Among the others, some at first also favoured a treaty, but most, if not all, eventually became at least resigned to the United States standpoint.

VI. Superpower Dominance

If the Soviet-United States agreement underlying resolution 1721[25] finally enabled the Outer Space Committee to begin work, and the Committee did so in propitious circumstances,[26] the atmosphere in the Committee and especially in its Legal Sub-Committee was soon darkened by the controversy between the two space powers over the United States high-altitude nuclear tests over Johnston Island in June and July 1962. The Soviet government's

---

[19] A/AC.105/PV.13 (13.9.62), p. 7; cf also Poland, A/AC.105/C.2/SR.6 (6.2.62), p. 6; Soviet Union, A/AC.105/PV.15 (14.9.62), p. 29.
[20] To the Legal Sub-Com., A/AC.105/C.2/L.1; cf n. 17 above.
[21] To the Outer Space Com., A/AC.105/L.6.
[22] To GA Com. I, A/C.1/879.   [23] To GA Com. I, A/C.1/881.
[24] See above n. 16, text to n. 17, and below nn. 32 ff.
[25] See n. 6 above.   [26] See text preceding n. 17.

statement on these tests, issued on 3 June 1962, was read into the minutes by the Soviet delegate and circulated as the first document of the two Sub-Committees.[27] Little headway was made on the legal side for a whole year. When the second session of the Legal Sub-Committee adjourned on 3 May 1963, no agreement was in sight.

However, in the course of the summer, the Moscow Test Ban Treaty was signed[28] and a series of bilateral arrangements were reached between the United States and the Soviet Union on co-operation in outer space.[29] By the time the fourth session of the Outer Space Committee opened on 9 September 1963, there was a complete change in atmosphere and it was then evident that agreement between the two space powers on the legal problems of space activities was imminent. The Committee held only four meetings and then adjourned, leaving the two space powers to continue their negotiations, assisted and attended by a few others. It would appear that after agreement had been reached between the two space powers, the original intention was to bring the text from what the French delegate pointedly called the 'secluded places' where it was negotiated, straight to the First Committee of the General Assembly. It was subsequently decided, however, that the proposal should 'make a stop' in the Outer Space Committee in order, it would appear, to collect the signatures of all the other members of the Committee. To this end, the Committee met on 22 November 1963[30] with the understanding seemingly that no amendment would be entertained. In the event, the proposal was adopted unanimously first by the Outer Space Committee, then by the First Committee and finally by the General Assembly itself (13 December 1963), without a word being changed or a comma disturbed, to become resolution 1962 (XVIII):

Declaration of Legal Principles Governing the Activities of States in the Exploration and Use of Outer Space

The General Assembly,

. . . .

Solemnly declares that in the exploration and use of outer space States should be guided by the following principles:

---

[27] A/AC.105/C.1/1 (5.6.62), and A/AC.105/C.2/1 (5.6.62).

[28] (5.8.63), 480 UNTS 43; 2 *ILM* (1963) p. 889. The USSR and the US further expressed their intention not to station in outer space any objects carrying nuclear weapons or other kinds of weapons of mass destruction. Consequently, GA resolution 1884 (XVIII) of 17 Oct. 1963 solemnly called on all States similarly not to do so (A/RES/1884 (XVIII)).

[29] Transmitted to the UN by letter of 22 Aug. 1963 from the permanent representatives of the Soviet Union and the United States (GAOR Annexes (XVIII) 28, p. 1).

[30] A/AC.105/PV.24, as printed in GAOR Annexes (XVIII) 28, p. 14. All future references to A/AC.105/PV.24 are to this version. As regards the substance of the draft resolution, cf. the Resolution on the Legal Status of Outer Space adopted unanimously by the Institut de Droit international on 11 Nov. 1963 at Brussels, 50 (II) *Annuaire de l'Institut* (1963), p. 361. For full text of resolution 1962, see App. II.3 below.

1. The exploration and use of outer space shall be carried on for the benefit and in the interests of all mankind.

2. Outer space and celestial bodies are free for exploration and use by all States on a basis of equality and in accordance with international law.

3. Outer space and celestial bodies are not subject to national appropriation by claim of sovereignty, by means of use or occupation, or by any other means.

4. The activities of States in the exploration and use of outer space shall be carried on in accordance with international law, including the Charter of the United Nations, in the interests of maintaining international peace and security and promoting international co-operation and understanding.

5. States bear international responsibility for national activities in outer space, whether carried on by governmental agencies or by non-governmental entities, and for assuring that national activities are carried on in conformity with the principles set forth in the present Declaration. The activities of non-governmental entities in outer space shall require authorization and continuing supervision by the State concerned. When activities are carried on in outer space by an international organization, responsibility for compliance with the principles set forth in this Declaration shall be borne by the international organization and by the States participating in it.

6. In the exploration and use of outer space, States shall be guided by the principle of co-operation and mutual assistance and shall conduct all their activities in outer space with due regard for the corresponding interests of other States. If a State has reason to believe that an outer space activity or experiment planned by it or its nationals would cause potentially harmful interference with activities of other States in the peaceful exploration and use of outer space, it shall undertake appropriate international consultations before proceeding with any such activity or experiment. A State which has reason to believe that an outer space activity or experiment planned by another State would cause potentially harmful interference with activities in the peaceful exploration and use of outer space may request consultation concerning the activity or experiment.

7. The State on whose registry an object launched into outer space is carried shall retain jurisdiction and control over such object, and any personnel thereon, while in outer space. Ownership of objects launched into outer space, and of their component parts, is not affected by their passage through outer space or by their return to the earth. Such objects or component parts found beyond the limits of the State of registry shall be returned to that State, which shall furnish identifying data upon request prior to return.

8. Each State which launches or procures the launching of an object into outer space, and each State from whose territory or facility an object is launched, is internationally liable for damage to a foreign State or to its natural or juridical persons by such object or its component parts on the earth, in air space, or in outer space.

9. States shall regard astronauts as envoys of mankind in outer space, and shall render to them all possible assistance in the event of accident, distress, or emergency landing on the territory of a foreign State or on the high seas. Astronauts who

make such a landing shall be safely and promptly returned to the State of registry of their space vehicle.

Resolution 1962 involves a compromise between the two space powers in matters not only of substance, but also of form. This was revealed by, among others, the Indian delegate to the Outer Space Committee at the one-meeting session of 22 November 1963, called to endorse the agreement between the two super-powers:

Many of the points in dispute between the space Powers have been cleared up and an agreed paper is now before us. There is also agreement in regard to the form which the legal principles should take. They are first to be formulated as a declaration in a General Assembly resolution, and then in the future, as appropriate, to be translated into international agreements.[31]

From this point of view, it should be mentioned that the United States had already at an earlier stage agreed that, in addition to a treaty on liability as proposed by the United States, there should also be a treaty on assistance to and return of astronauts and space vehicles. From the above statement of the Indian delegate, it would appear that what the Soviet Union and the United States had agreed upon was that the remaining principles contained in resolution 1962 should, eventually, also be incorporated in legally binding treaties. What can only be surmised as one of the possible reasons which finally persuaded the Soviet Union to agree to the use meanwhile of a General Assembly resolution for enunciating the principles governing space activities is the cumbersome and politically rather uncertain procedure of treaty-making under the United States Constitution.

VII. Binding and Non-Binding Declarations

The original Soviet disagreement with the United States in matters of form was based on the premises that, in the opinion of the Soviet government, (i) the agreed principles of space law should be embodied in a legally binding instrument,[32] and (ii) General Assembly resolutions lacked binding force.[33] But the Soviet proposal to call the treaty a Declaration was the source of some confusion; for some delegates thought that 'there was no great difference between a declaration . . . and a General Assembly resolution.'[34] And the Canadian delegate seemed to have distinguished three types of instrument, namely, 'merely a General Assembly resolution', 'a declaration', and a bind-

---

[31] A/AC.105/PV.24, p. 21; repeated in substance in Com. I, A/C.1/SR.1343 (3.12.63), p. 168.
[32] See above nn. 16, and 24.   [33] See above n. 16.
[34] Mexico, A/AC.105/C.2/SR.18 (18.4.63), p. 8; cf. also USSR when agreement was imminent between the two super-powers (see text to nn. 29 above ff.): 'everyone agrees that there should be a declaration now' (A/AC.105/PV.20 (9.9.63), p. 29).

ing treaty or convention.[35] But declarations do not constitute a separate legal category. A treaty may call itself a declaration and is no less binding for being so called. A General Assembly resolution which chooses to assume the name declaration is not thereby rendered legally more binding than any other recommendation. This fact was well recognized in a Memorandum of the United Nations Office of Legal Affairs on the 'Use of the Terms "Declaration and Recommendation" ':

3. In United Nations practice, a 'declaration' is a formal and solemn instrument, suitable for rare occasions when principles of great and lasting importance are being enunciated, such as the Declaration on Human Rights. A recommendation is less formal.

4. Apart from the distinction just indicated, *there is probably no difference between a 'recommendation' or a 'declaration' in United Nations practice as far as strict legal principle is concerned.* A 'declaration' or a 'recommendation' is adopted by resolution of a United Nations organ. As such it cannot be made binding upon Member States, in the sense that a treaty or convention is binding upon the parties to it, purely by the device of terming it a 'declaration' rather than a 'recommendation'. However, in view of the greater solemnity and significance of a 'declaration', it may be considered to impart, on behalf of the organ adopting it, a strong expectation that Members of the international community will abide by it. Consequently, in so far as the expectation is gradually justified by State practice, a declaration *may* by custom become recognized as laying down rules binding upon States . . .[36]

The operative word in the last sentence of this quotation is, of course, 'may'. In this connection, it may be pointed out that the Universal Declaration of Human Rights was not recognized as binding on States when it was adopted,[37] and still is not so regarded.[38]

The distinction between a treaty-declaration and a resolution-declaration was also clearly pointed out by the Australian delegate:

His delegation appreciated fully the difference between a resolution adopted by the General Assembly, whether expressed as a recommendation or as a declaration, and an instrument in the nature of a convention or legally binding declaration, duly executed and ratified by Governments . . . [*A*] *resolution or declaration by the General Assembly was certainly not law-making in the sense that a treaty, convention or declaration formally ratified by Governments was.*[39]

While the Australian delegation at first agreed with the Soviet Union that the declaration of basic principles should be in the form of a binding treaty,[40]

---

[35] A/AC.105/C.2/SR.21 (23.4.63), p. 8.

[36] E/CN.4/L.610 (2.4.62), pp. 1–2. Italics added. Cf. text to n. 89 below.

[37] See the present writer's 'International Law in the United Nations', 8 *YBWA* (1954), p. 170, at p. 185.

[38] Cf. text to n. 76 below.   [39] A/AC.105/C.2/SR.23 (25.4.63), p. 4, italics added.

[40] A/AC.105/C.2/SR.11 (14.6.62), p. 6.

it subsequently was persuaded that 'there might . . . be great advantages, especially in that new field of law, in making a start with instruments in resolution form, in which unanimity could be achieved without loss of flexibility. Full legal form could be developed later . . .'[41]

The main argument advanced in favour of a General Assembly resolution was its simplicity. Thus, with reference to the Soviet proposal for a treaty on assistance to and return of astronauts and space vehicles,[42] the United States delegate said:

Preparing a treaty and obtaining the required number of ratifications was a time-consuming process, whereas the Legal Sub-Committee was in a position to act immediately by preparing a draft resolution for action by the General Assembly.[43]

Later, speaking on the Soviet draft declaration of basic principles, particularly its paragraph 9 which also dealt with the subject of assistance and return, he further remarked:

[The United States government] did not believe action for assistance and return should be delayed for the drafting, signature, ratification and entry into force of a treaty or international agreement. The applicable principles were clear and should be readily agreed by Governments for incorporation into a simple declaration.[44]

In repeatedly stressing the difficulties in concluding international agreements, it is not impossible that the United States had in mind particularly the difficulties in its own constitutional process of treaty-making, including the possibility of the consent and advice of the US Senate being required, even though it is not to be doubted that the procedure for adopting Assembly resolutions is much simpler. The United States delegate said, moreover:

[His delegation] was convinced that the shared humanitarian and scientific concerns of the international community were such that States would willingly comply with such a resolution.[45]

However, in law a world of difference exists between a legally binding instrument and one the observance of which depends wholly on the good will of the States concerned. As the French delegate pointed out:

The United States proposal doubtless held out the promise of more rapid results, while the method advocated by the USSR would have the advantage of conferring incontestably binding force on any regulation adopted. It was quite possible that with time the current enthusiasm about the achievements of astronauts might wane. When damage was caused by a space vehicle which made an emergency landing, the State in whose territory he landed might be tempted to treat the astronaut involved as a criminal, to arrest him and to impound the space vehicle. *A General Assembly resolution*

---

[41] A/AC.105/C.2/SR.23 (25.4.63), p. 4.   [42] See n. 17 above.
[43] A/AC.105/C.2/SR.1 (28.5.62), p. 9. The US subsequently agreed that there should also be a treaty on the subject; cf. above text after n. 31.
[44] A/AC.105/C.2/SR.7 (7.6.62), p. 10.   [45] A/AC.105/C.2/SR.1 (28.5.62), p. 8.

might in such circumstances not be a legally operative instrument for ensuring different treatment.[46]

VIII. Effects of General Assembly Resolutions

Indeed, hardly any delegate attempted to attribute binding force to a General Assembly resolution,[47] especially one which had not been unanimously accepted. There was, however, at least among some delegates, a feeling that special significance attached to a unanimous resolution. Thus when the draft declaration of principles was presented to the First Committee, the Soviet delegate appeared to have made a unanimous acceptance of the draft resolution of the General Assembly a condition of the Soviet undertaking to respect the principles contained in it:

The Soviet Union . . . undertook also to respect the principles enunciated in the draft declaration if it were unanimously adopted.[48]

The United Kingdom delegate also drew the following distinction between an ordinary resolution and an unanimously adopted resolution:

Although as stated by the USSR delegation, resolutions of the General Assembly were not—save in the exceptional cases provided for in the Charter—binding upon Member States—a resolution, if adopted unanimously, would be most authoritative. [49]

The Indian delegate went further. In his opinion,

A declaration had moral force and, when adopted unanimously, was generally accepted as part of international law.[50]

It is, however, difficult to see how this view can be justified. Under Article 18 of the United Nations Charter, resolutions of the General Assembly, even in 'important matters', only require a two-thirds majority. Legally and

---

[46] A/AC.105/C.2/SR.9 (12.6.62), p. 2; emphasis added.

[47] On effects of GA resolutions, see *inter alia*, R. Bindschedler, 'La délimitation des compétences aux Nations Unies', 108 Hague *Recueil* (1963), p. 305; F. A. Vallat, 'The Competence of the United Nations General Assembly', 97 ibid. (1959), p. 203; A. J. P. Tammes, 'Decisions of International Organs as a Source of International Law', 94 ibid. (1958), p. 265; M. Virally, 'La valeur juridique des recommandations des organisations internationales', 2 *AFDI* (1956), p. 66; D. H. N. Johnson, 'The Effects of Resolutions of the General Assembly of the United Nations', 32 *BYIL* (1955–56), p. 97; G. Schwarzenberger, *International Law*, I (2nd ed., 1949), pp. 539 ff.; F. B. Sloan, 'The Binding Force of a "Recommendation" of the General Assembly of the United Nations', 25 *BYIL* (1948), p. 37. See also G. I. Tunkin, *Droit international public* (1965), pp. 101–12.

[48] A/C.1/SR.1342 (2.12.63), p. 161.

[49] A/AC.105/C.2/SR.17 (17.4.63), p. 9; and ibid./SR.24 (29.4.63), p. 13.

[50] A/AC.105/C.2/SR.22 (24.6.63), p. 10; cf., however, India, A/C.1/SR.1294 (7.12.62): 'The best procedure would be to establish multilateral agreements, as a resolution of the General Assembly would not have the same kind of legal obligation on States.'

constitutionally, no special virtue attaches to a unanimous vote, even though politically it may be of significance. The political aspect of the unanimous vote in the twenty-eight-member Outer Space Committee[51] was thus emphasized by the Soviet delegate, when the United States delegate, at one point, hinted that the Committee should revert to the normal majority rule of United Nations organs, though obviously what the Soviet Union particularly had in mind was unanimity between the two super-powers:

Twenty-six signatures on this document would have no value; there must be twenty-eight signatures. Even if all of us, including the Soviet Union, the countries of Asia, Africa and Latin America—which are in principle in favour of signing the declaration—sign, if there is no signature of the United States, the whole endeavour would have no result. It is clear that without agreement of the United States it is impossible to resolve such a problem. [52]

The United States delegate put forward, however, the following explanation of the possible legal significance of a unanimous vote. In his view,

A General Assembly resolution would be the most appropriate instrument for a declaration of general principles. Some delegations had argued that only an international agreement signed by governments would be legally binding. International agreements were not, however, the only sources of law. As stated in Article 38 of the Statute of the International Court of Justice, decisions of international tribunals and the growth of customary law as evidenced by State practice should also be taken into consideration. When a General Assembly resolution proclaimed principles of international law—as resolution 1721 (XVI) had done—and was adopted unanimously, it represented the law as generally accepted in the international community.[53]

The same was said by the Canadian delegate of the draft of what later became resolution 1962:

The legal principles contained in it reflected international law as it was currently accepted by Member States.[54]

IX. 'Instant' International Customary Law?

It would appear to be the contention of the United States delegate that international 'customary' law, i.e., general international law applicable *erga omnes*, maybe created instantly by means of unanimously adopted resolutions of the General Assembly. How far is this possible? At this juncture, it may be appropriate to re-examine the traditional concept of the constitutive elements of

---

[51] See above n. 18.   [52] A/AC.105/PV.15 (14.9.62), p.28; cf. also above n. 19.
[53] A/AC.105/C.2/SR.20 (22.4.63), pp. 10–11.
[54] A/C.1/SR.1346 (5.12.63), p. 189; cf. also India, above n. 50.

international customary law.[55] The orthodox view is that a rule of customary law has two constitutive elements: (i) *corpus*, the material or objective element, and (ii) *animus*, the psychological or subjective element. The *corpus* of a rule of customary law is the existence of a usage (*consuetudo*) embodying a rule of conduct. The *animus* consists in the conviction on the part of States that the rule embodied in the usage is binding (*opinio juris*). This view finds expression in Article 38(1)(b) of the Statute of the International Court of Justice which speaks of the Court applying 'international custom, being evidence of a general practice accepted as law'.

There is a school of thought, the principal exponent of which at present is doubtless Professor Guggenheim,[56] which disputes the reality and consequently the requirement of the subjective element of *opinio juris*. But both the Permanent Court of International Justice[57] and the International Court of Justice[58] have in a number of cases stressed the importance of the subjective element of *opinio juris*.[59] Indeed, it should perhaps be pointed out that by the so-called 'psychological' element of *opinio juris*, it is intended to mean not so much the mental process or inner motive of a State when it performs or abstains from certain acts,[60] but rather the *acceptance* or *recognition* of, or *acquiescence* in, the *binding character of the rule* in question implied in a State's action or omission, or in other words, its being *a rule of the general law binding on all*.[61] It is not without reason that the Statute of the World Court

---

[55] Cf. *inter alia* E. Suy, *Les acts juridiques uinilatéraux en droit international public* (1962), Ch. VII; G. Tunkin, 'Remarks on the Juridical Nature of Customary Norms of International Law', 49 *Calif. LR* (1961), p. 419; Sir Gerald Fitzmaurice, 'The Law and Procedure of the International Court of Justice: General Principles and Sources of Law', 1951–4, 30 *BYIL* (1953), p. 1; 1954–9, 35 ibid. (1959), p. 183; P. Guggenheim, 'Contribution à l'histoire des sources du droit des gens', 94 Hague *Recueil* (1958), p. 5; Sir Hersch Lauterpacht, *The Development of International Law by the International Court* (1958), Ch. 28; I. C. MacGibbon, 'Customary International Law and Acquiescence', 32 *BYIL* (1957), p. 115; G. Schwarzenberger, I (1) *International Law* (1957), Ch. 2; B. Cheng, *General Principles of Law*, Introduction; J. Kunz, 'The Nature of Customary International Law', 47 *AJIL* (1953), p. 662; P. Guggenheim, 'Les deux éléments de la coutume en droit international', 1 *Etudes en l'honneur de G. Scelle* (1950), p. 275; C. Rousseau, *Principes généraux du droit international public* (1949), pp. 815–62; M. Sørensen, *Les sources du droit international* (1946) pp. 84 ff.; H. Kelsen, 'Théorie du droit international coutumier', *Rev. intern. de la théorie de droit* (1939), p. 253; L. Kopelmanas, 'Custom as a Means of the Creation of International Law', 18 *BYIL* (1937) p. 127.

[56] Loc. cit. (1950) in n. 55 above and 1 *Traité de droit international public* (1953), p. 45; cf. also Kelsen and Kopelmanas, loc. cit. in n. 55 above.

[57] E.g., *The Lotus Case* (1927), A 10, p. 28.

[55] E.g., *Asylum Case, ICJ Rep. 1950*, p. 266, at p. 276; *Right of Passage Case, ICJ Rep. 1960*, p. 6, at pp. 42–3.

[59] See also Suy, op. cit. in n. 55 above; Guggenheim, loc. cit. (1958) in n. 55 above, at pp. 52–3; Lauterpacht, op. cit. in n. 55 above, at 380; Schwarzenberger, op. cit. in n. 55 above, at pp. 39 ff.; Kunz, loc. cit. in n. 55 above, at p. 665.

[60] Cf., e.g., Guggenheim, loc. cit. (1953) in n. 55 above, at 47; Sørensen, op. cit. in n. 55 above, at p. 110.

[61] Cf. Suy, op. cit. in n. 55 above, at p. 229; See also J. Basdevant, 'Règles générales du droit de la paix', 58 Hague *Recueil* (1936), p. 475, at p. 513.

speaks of 'international custom, being evidence of a general practice *accepted as law*.'

However, Article 38(1)(*b*) of the Statute would have been even more correct if it had said, 'international custom as evidenced by a general practice accepted as law'; for it is not the custom or customary rule of international law which is evidence of the general practice, but rather the general practice accepted as law that provides evidence of the customary rule.[62]

Indeed, it may be permissible to go further and say that the role of usage in the establishment of rules of international customary law is purely evidentiary: it provides evidence on the one hand of the contents of the rule in question and on the other hand of the *opinio juris* of the States concerned. Not only is it unnecessary that the usage should be prolonged, but there need also be no usage at all in the sense of repeated practice, provided that the *opinio juris* of the States concerned can be clearly established. Consequently, international customary law has in reality only one constitutive element, the *opinio juris*. Inasmuch as States are their own law-makers, where there is a general *opinio juris* among them, there is a rule of general international law. It is true that in the case of a rule without usage, objection might be taken to the use of the term custom or customary. But whether in such a case one speaks of international customary law or general international law or an unwritten rule of international law becomes purely a matter of semantics. In fact, the International Court of Justice, instead of referring to 'international customary law', has increasingly been using the term 'general international law' which in reality is a broader and much more accurate description.

It should, however, be pointed out that in municipal law it would ordinarily not be possible to have a legally binding custom without usage; for in municipal law it is not the *opinio juris* of individual subjects of the legal system that is decisive but the *opinio generalis juris* of the specific locality, trade, profession, or grouping concerned as a whole. To this *opinio generalis juris* the general law of the community gives its blessing and lends the weight of its own authority, resulting in a symbiosis between the *opinio* of the specific section of society concerned and that of the law-makers for the body politic as a whole. Such *opinio generalis juris* can normally be established and ascertained only through a general and usually also prolonged practice within the specific section of society in question.

But in international law, the possibility of general international law without usage becomes obvious if it is remembered that in international society States are their own law-makers.[63] From the analytical point of view, the binding

---

[62] Cf. e.g., Ch. de Visscher, 'La codification du droit international', 6 Hague *Recueil* (1925), p. 325, at p. 352, n. 1.

[63] Cf. PCIJ: *The Lotus Case* (1927), A 10, p. 18: 'The rules of law binding upon States therefore emanate from their own free will as expressed in conventions or by usages generally accepted as expressing principles of law . . .'

force of all rules of international law ultimately rests on their consent, recognition, acquiescence, or the principle of estoppel. If States consider themselves bound by a given rule as a rule of international law, it is difficult to see why it should not be treated as such insofar as these States are concerned, especially when the rule does not infringe the right of third States not sharing the same *opinio juris*.[64] The *Asylum Case*[65] and the *Right of Passage Case*[66] have shown that it is possible for such *opinio juris* to exist among a limited number of States or even between two States so that, besides rules of universal international customary law, one finds also local and even bipartite international customary law.[67]

From this point of view, there is no reason why an *opinio communis juris* may not grow up in a very short period of time among all or simply some Members of the United Nations with the result that a new rule of international customary law (or unwritten rule of international law) comes into being among them. And there is also no reason why they may not use an Assembly resolution to 'positivize' their new common *opinio juris*. In such a case, without prejudice to the question whether he was right in regard to resolution 1721A, the United States delegate was merely stating a truism when he said:

When a General Assembly resolution proclaimed principles of international law . . . and was adopted unanimously, it represented the law as generally accepted in the international community.[68]

What he would obviously be correct in saying is that when a General Assembly resolution proclaims principles recognized, albeit not long since, by Members of the United Nations as principles of international law, and is adopted unanimously, it represents the law as generally accepted in the United Nations. In such an event, the binding force of these principles comes not from the resolution, but from their acceptance by Member States as part of international law. They are, therefore, binding even before the resolution, although the resolution helps to establish their existence and contents.

This indeed was the view of the Italian delegate to the Legal Sub-Committee:

His delegation did not . . . feel that the binding force of the principles would be undermined by the mere fact that they were enunciated in the form of a General Assembly resolution. In international law, rules were binding primarily because States considered themselves bound by such rules, whatever their origin. From that view

---

[64] Cf. the interesting but slightly different distinction between *consuetudine introduttiva* (introductory or innovative custom) and *consuetudine abrogativa* (abrogatory or repealing custom) by Morelli in his *Nozioni di diritto internazionale* (1958), pp. 25–6; see also Suy, op. cit. in n. 55 above, at pp. 260 ff.

[65] *ICJ Rep. 1950*, p. 266.   [66] *ICJ Rep. 1961*, p. 6.

[67] 'It is difficult to see why the number of States between which a local custom may be established on the basis of long practice must necessarily be larger than two' (ibid., at p. 39).

[68] See above n. 53.

point, recommendations of the General Assembly undoubtedly had binding force. In any case, recommendations of the General Assembly had the function of identifying, and even of eliciting participation in the formation of, the rules exacted by the awareness of the international community to certain basic needs—an awareness which was the primary and fundamental source of international law.[69]

In such cases, resolutions of the General Assembly fulfil 'the function of identifying' the latent *opinio juris* of Member States of the United Nations.[70] They serve as midwives for the delivery of nascent rules of international law which form within the United Nations. While the resolutions do not in themselves create binding legal obligations, Member States voting in favour of those resolutions of either a law-finding or a fact-finding character may, on the basis of the principle of good faith,[71] be prevented from denying the veracity of what is stated in the resolutions.[72] This was the view of the Permanent Court of International Justice in respect of certain resolutions of the League Assembly. The Court, in the case of the *Monastery of St Naoum* (1924), for instance, regarded as conclusive the votes cast by States directly concerned in favour of an Assembly resolution recognizing the competence of the Principal Allied and Associated Powers to settle the frontiers of Albania.[73]

[69] A/AC.105/C.2/SR.20 (22.4.63), p. 7. See also the idea of the 'living law' in the drawing up of the Statute of the World Court, the present writer's *General Principles of Law*, pp. 16–19; cf. too R. Ago's 'spontaneous law' in his 'Science Juridique et droit international', 90 Hague *Recueil* (1956), p. 849, or *Scienza Giuridica e Diritto Internazionale* (1950); see also P. Chauveau, loc. cit. in n. 1 above under *Valeur obligatoire de la Déclaration du 13 Décembre 1963*. A distinction has, however, to be made between those who attach decisive importance to the general *opinio juris* of States and those who identify law with social needs or necessities; see Rousseau, op. cit. in n. 55 above, pp. 832–3. Thus, M. S. McDougal and others in their *Law and Public Order in Space* (1963), pp. 115 ff., seem to equate *opinio generalis juris* with what they call 'general community expectations' (see also, e.g., p. 227) with a rather elastic interpretation of who are 'authorised general community spokesmen'; see also M. Cohen, op. cit. in n. 1 above, at p. 13, for whom the decisive factor appears to be the 'common interest of mankind'.

As the Italian delegate has pointed out, however, while social necessities may be the material forces behind the formation of the rule, the nominative and juridical element comes from the response of States to these needs and their consequent acceptance of the rule designed to meet them. Social necessities act on the will of States; the will of States bring forth rules of international law (cf. n. 63 above). To attempt to bypass the will of States would be to miss out the most vital link in the international law creating process.

[70] On international law-determining agencies or evidence of rules of international law, see Schwarzenberger, op. cit. (1957) in n. 55 above, pp. 25 ff.; on GA resolutions as elements of international law-determining agencies, see Johnson, loc. cit. in n. 47 above, pp. 116–7; cf. however, Schachter, loc. cit. in n. 1 above, p. 98.

[71] See the present writer's *General Principles of Law*, pp. 137 ff.

[72] Cf. also Vallat, loc. cit. in n. 47 above, p. 231. As a possible example of a fact-finding resolution, cf. GA resolution 195(III) of 12 Dec. 1948 on Korea, para. 2, *UNYB* (1948–9), p. 290, in which the General Assembly '[d]eclares that there has been established a lawful government (the government of the Republic of Korea) having effective control and jurisdiction over that part of Korea where the Temporary Commission was able to observe and consult and in which the great majority of the people of all Korea reside, that this Government is based on elections which were a valid expression of the free will of the electorate of that part of Korea and which were observed by the Temporary Commission; and that this is the only such Government in Korea.' This resolution was adopted by a vote of 46 to 6, with 1 abstention.

[73] PCIJ: B 9, p. 13; see further Schwarzenberger, op. cit. (1949) in n. 47 above, pp. 539 ff.

However, in order to speak of a law-finding resolution, there must have existed, first of all, the necessary *opinio communis juris* among Members of the United Nations that what they are enunciating in the resolution represents binding rules of international law. Secondly, the wording of the resolution must not merely identify clearly the contents of the rules in question, but must also unequivocally express this *opinio communis juris*. These conditions appear to have been satisfied, at least formally, in the case of General Assembly resolution 96(I) of 11 December 1946 wherein unanimously,

The General Assembly . . . affirms that genocide is a crime under international law.[74]

This resolution was reaffirmed by the General Assembly on 21 November 1947.[75] Unlike the proposed International Covenants on Human Rights intended to render obligatory some at least of the provisions of the non-binding Universal Declaration of Human Rights,[76] the subsequent Genocide Convention of 9 December 1948 assumes genocide to be a crime under international law and merely provides for its 'prevention and punishment'. In its Article 1, 'the contracting parties confirm that genocide is a crime under international law.'[77] Thus, whatever 'crimes under international law' may mean,[78] it is difficult to see how any United Nations Member may now dispute that genocide is one of them.

The same cannot, however, be said of the Assembly resolution 95(I) 'affirming' the so-called 'principles of international law recognised by the Charter of the Nuremberg Tribunal'; for there the Assembly deliberately and rather subtly declined to use either the word 'reaffirm' as found in the original United States proposal or the word 'confirm', thus indicating clearly a lack of consensus among United Nations Members as to the binding character of the Nuremberg principles as rules of general international law.[79]

---

[74] A/64/Add. 1, p. 188; *UNYB* (1946–7), p. 254.

[75] Resolution 180(II), A/519, pp. 129 ff.; *UNYB* (1947–8), pp. 219–20.

[76] Resolution 217 (III), A/811, of 10 Dec. 1948. See above n. 37. Cf. also M. S. McDougal and G. Behr, 'Human Rights in the UN', 58 *AJIL* (1964), p. 603.

[77] 78 UNTS p. 277; cf. *Reservations to the Genocide Convention, ICJ Rep. 1951*, p. 15, at p. 23: 'The origins of the Convention show that it was the intention of the United Nations to condemn and punish genocide as "a crime under international law" . . . The first consequence arising from this conception is that the principles underlying the Convention are principles which are recognised by civilised nations as binding on States, *even without any conventional obligation*' (emphasis added).

[78] Cf. loc. cit. in n. 37 above, pp. 186–7; G. Schwarzenberger, *The Frontiers of International Law* (1962), Ch. 8: The Problems of an International Criminal Law.

[79] Cf. loc. cit. in n. 37 above, p. 186; Viscount Maugharn, *UNO and War Crimes* (1951), pp. 102 ff.; R. K. Woetzel, *The Nuremberg Trial in International Law* (1962), p. 15 (both these writers have, however, in their quotation of the resolution reproduced the word 'reaffirm' used in the original proposal). See also Kunz, loc. cit. in n. 55 above, p. 669.

X. Resolutions 1721A and 1962

What has been said of General Assembly resolution 95(I) affirming the Nuremberg principles applies all the more to resolutions 1721A (XVI) and 1962 (XVIII). The former expresses no view as to the legal status of the two principles which it 'commends to States for their guidance'.[80]

Although the title of the latter is 'Declaration of Legal Principles Governing the Activities of States in the Exploration of Outer Space,' this does not mean that the principles are necessarily binding in law. For example, in innumerable treaties, States have developed a vast number of optional rules of conduct in the field of international economic relations[81] and international air transport.[82] These optional rules are legal in character, but their binding force is potential (*in posse*) rather than actual (*in esse*). They may be made binding by the consent of States, either unilaterally or *inter se* through international agreement, but they are not binding in themselves. It would be conducive to greater clarity if, following the example of Professor Schwarzenberger, one were to call these norms not rules, but optional principles or standards of international law.[83] In this sense, resolution 1962, to the extent to which it is not restating existing rules of international law, merely expresses non-binding standards of international law governing the activities of States in the exploration of outer space.

This conclusion is confirmed by the operative part of the resolution, in which one merely finds that the General Assembly

Solemnly declares that in the exploration and use of outer space States should be guided by the following principles . . .

The General Assembly does not declare that States are actually bound by these principles. Any State which votes in favour of this resolution can hardly be said, therefore, to have estopped itself from saying that these principles are mere guidelines for States and are not legally binding.[84]

Thus, in regard to resolutions 1721A and 1962, the French delegate has in both instances not failed to point out their non-binding character.[85] France was particularly critical of the way agreement was reached in the case of resolution 1962. When the draft was being considered in the Assembly's First Committee, the French delegate made it clear that,

[80] See above text following n. 8.
[81] See Schwarzenberger, op. cit. in n. 78 above, Ch. 9: The Principles and Standards of International Economic Law.
[82] See the present writer's *The Law of International Air Transport*.
[83] See G. Schwarzenberger, 1 *A Manual of International Law* (1960), p. 39; and op. cit. in n. 81 above.
[84] Cf. Bindschedler, loc. cit. in n. 47 above, p. 345.
[85] In respect of resolution 1721, see A/AC.105/PV.3 (20.3.62), p. 48.

while supporting the principles set forth in the draft declaration . . . , he wished to stress that the latter could not be looked on as more than a *statement of intention; legal obligations stricto sensu could only flow from international agreements*, and an international law of outer space had yet to be created.[86]

This last point was also made by the United Arab Republic delegate,[87] while the Czechoslovak delegate said that his delegation 'would have preferred a more binding document'.[88]

Upon final analysis, the position of Australia is similar, and throws interesting light on the character of these 'legal principles' contained in the Declaration as being *potentially* rather than *actually* binding. For, while the Australian delegate wanted to 'emphasise that Australia for its part will continue to conduct its activities in outer space in accordance with these principles', he said equally clearly on the other hand that,

in our view a General Assembly declaration of *legal principles* cannot itself be creative of legal duties.

He went on to say, however:

[I]t is equally not the Australian delegation's view that such a General Assembly declaration can have no part in the development or creation of international law. It is our view that a declaration of legal principles by the General Assembly, especially if universally adopted and adhered to in practice, may be valuable evidence of international custom, which in turn is a most important source of law .[89]

This merely confirms that until the necessary *opinio juris* develops ('if universally adopted'), accompanied by the requisite usage ('and adhered to in practice'), such a 'declaration of legal principles' remains recommendatory.

The Australian position also shows that there is nothing incompatible in a State declaring its intention to comply with the principles contained in the resolution, while treating the resolution itself as a mere recommendation. Consequently, both in regard to resolution 1721 and resolution 1962, when a Member State merely says that it 'supports',[90] 'subscribes to',[91] 're-endorses',[92] 'would be scrupulously guided by' or 'would conscientiously respect',[93] 'intends

---

[86] A/C.l/SR.1345 (5.12.63), p. 183.   [87] A/C.1/SR.1342 (2.12.63), p. 163.

[88] A/C.1/SR.1345 (5.12.63), p. 182.

[89] A/AC.105/PV.24 (22.11.63), p. 18, italics added; see also A/AC.105/C.2/SR.23 (25.4.63), p. 4. Cf also above text to n. 36.

[90] E.g., with reference to resolution 1721, n. 11 above; with reference to resolution 1962, France, n. 86 above; Canada, A/AC.105/PV.24 (22.11.63), p. 17; Austria, ibid., 20; UK, A/C.1/SR.1342 (2.12.63), p. 164.

[91] E.g., with reference to resolution 1721, UK, n. 12 above.

[92] E.g., with reference to resolution 1721, USA, A/AC.105/PV.2 (19.2.62), pp. 13–15.

[93] Italy, both with reference to resolution 1962, respectively A/AC.105/PV.24 (22.11.63), p. 20 and A/C.1/SR.1342 (2.12.63), p. 164. Was a difference intended by saying 'to respect' instead of 'to be guided by'?

to respect',[94] or even 'is prepared to respect',[95] the principles embodied in the resolution, it does not mean that it is thereby legally bound by them.[96]

It is not disputed, however, that even if a resolution remains a mere recommendation, States are free by consent to bind themselves to the principles it embodies. A State may thus be bound by a unilateral declaration which it has made to another.[97] Furthermore, even where the declaration does not amount to a binding obligation, a State having given an assurance to another as regards its national policy, may by the principle of good faith, incur a legal duty to notify the latter of any change of policy,[98] which in this case probably means that such a State may not revise its policy without first raising the issue in the United Nations. But whether a Member State, by the statements of its representatives in the United Nations, has in fact incurred either one or the other of these obligations must depend on each individual case. Certainly, it does not appear possible to generalize, either from the unanimous votes of the General Assembly or the general support for these two resolutions among Member States, that they are binding on Member States or that they create any legal duty.

It remains finally to examine three statements made by representatives of Member States in the Assembly's First Committee when the draft declaration was introduced. These statements, which present certain special features, were made on behalf of the United States, the Soviet Union, and Canada.

The United States delegate, who spoke first, in effect introduced the draft declaration, and, in the provisional records of the First Committee, he was reported to have stated:

[The United States government] considered that the legal principles contained in the draft Declaration reflected international law as accepted by Members of the United Nations, and it was prepared to accept them. However, the Declaration was only a first step . . . [99]

---

[94] E.g., with reference to resolution 1962, UK, A/C.1/SR.1342 (2.12.63), p. 164.

[95] E.g., with reference to resolution 1962, USA, A/C.1/SR.1342 (2.12.63), p. 159.

[96] Thus in an admittedly rather ambiguous passage in his speech winding up the discussion in the Outer Space Committee, when the draft of what later became resolution 1962 was introduced there, the Soviet delegate said: 'I must remark with great satisfaction that the majority of the members of the Committee who took part in the debate did not challenge the propositions included in the draft declaration, and consequently it may be assumed that they are acceptable to all the members of the Committee. Therefore, giving all the remarks made here their due, *I think we must assume*—indeed, those who made the remarks proceeded on this assumption—that in the matter of international legal regulation *it is impossible to compel any State to accept a particular proposition, if for any reason it is still not prepared to do so*' (A/AC.105/PV.24 (22.11.63), p. 23, italics added). Cf. also, as regards the US, text to nn. 100 ff. below.

[97] Cf., e.g., the Ihlen declaration in the *Eastern Greenland Case* (1933), PCIJ: A/B 53, p. 71; see further Schwarzenberger, op. cit., (1957) in n. 55 above, Ch. 30. See also *International Status of South-West Africa Case*, *ICJ Rep. 1950*, p. 128, at pp. 135–6 and 142; but cf. dissenting opinions of Judge McNair (p. 146, at p. 161) and Judge Read (p. 164) to appreciate the difficulties in interpretation.

[98] See further the present writer's *General Principles of Law*, pp. 137 ff.

[99] A/C.1/SR.1342.Prov. (2.12.63), p. 3; see also above nn. 15 and 53, with reference to resolution 1721A.

It is interesting to observe that in the final version of the official records, this passage has been amended to read as follows:

[The United States government] considered the legal principles contained in the operative part of the draft declaration reflected international law as accepted by Members of the United Nations. The United States intended to respect them and hoped *the conduct they recommended* in the exploration of outer space would become the practice of all nations. However, the declaration was only a first step . . .[100]

As amended, this United States statement is self-contradictory, unless in the opinion of the United States, international law itself has merely recommendatory rather than binding force. Without seeking in any way to minimize this contradiction, it seems that the United States government basically agreed that the resolution would be a mere recommendation, though it considered the principles it contained to be declaratory of international law as accepted by United Nations Members and was prepared to respect them.

The Soviet delegate who spoke next said:

The United States representative had said that in his Government's view the legal principles contained in the draft declaration reflected international law as accepted by the Members of the United Nations and that the United States for its part intended to respect them. The Soviet Union, in its turn, undertook also to respect the principles enunciated in the draft declaration if it were unanimously accepted.[101]

Finally, the Canadian representative, referring to the draft declaration, stated:

[T]he legal principles contained in it reflected international law as it was currently accepted by Member States. It was significant in that connexion that the two major space Powers had declared their intention, provided the draft declaration was approved by the General Assembly, to conduct their activities in outer space in conformity with these principles. His Government also undertook to do so.[102]

It is interesting from this point of view that both the Soviet and the Canadian representatives interpreted the United States statement as no more than a declaration of an intention to respect[103] the principles of the draft Declaration. The Soviet undertaking was interpreted by the Canadian representative to mean the same thing, and the Canadian commitment was no more than an undertaking to do likewise. Under the circumstances, it may be wondered whether these undertakings are more than, as the representative of France has put it, mere 'statements of intention,'[104] or whether they amount to statements of policy on which other Member States are in law entitled to rely until they hear to the contrary,[105] or whether they have the effect of binding these States to the principles contained in the Declaration.

---

[100] A/C.1/SR.1342 (2.12.63), p. 159, italics added.
[102] Ibid./SR.1346 (5.12.63), p. 189.
[104] Cf. n. 86 above.
[101] A/C.1/SR.1342 (2.12.63), p. 161.
[103] Cf. n. 94 above.
[105] Cf. n. 98 above.

If the binding effect of these undertakings is not entirely beyond doubt, what about the United States[106] and Canadian statements that the principles contained in the draft Declaration reflected international law as accepted by Members of the United Nations?[107] While this conclusion seems obviously unwarranted as regards many United Nations Members, yet, are not the United States and Canadian governments estopped from asserting that they were in error[108] at least insofar as they themselves were concerned; for while they could not speak for the other Members of the United Nations, they surely could speak for themselves.[109] But even if the answer were in the affirmative, it may still be asked whether they are so estopped *vis-à-vis* all the United Nations Members or only those which consider themselves for the same or any other reason bound. If only *vis-à-vis* the latter, then the number of States so bound appears to be no more than a handful, at least at the time when the resolution was adopted, namely, the United States, Canada, and perhaps India and the Soviet Union.

XI. Conclusions

It may finally be helpful to summarize the conclusions, some perhaps only tentative, reached in this chapter.

1. International customary law (*alias* general international law in the narrow sense of the term, i.e., the unwritten rules of international law applicable *erga omnes* minus the general principles of law) requires only one single constitutive element, namely, the *opinio juris* of States. General international law in its broad meaning includes the general principles of law.

2. This assertion that international customary law requires only one single constitutive element does not mean that usage or practice is not a normal element of rules of international customary law, but usage or practice, instead of being a constitutive and indispensable element, merely provides evidence of the existence and contents of the underlying rule and of the requisite *opinio juris*.

---

[106] See also above nn. 15 and 53, with reference to resolution 1721A.

[107] Cf. also India, text to n. 50 above; but the Indian position there was with respect to unanimously adopted resolutions of the General Assembly in general rather than these principles in particular. Cf., however, also quotation in n. 50, and op. cit. in n. 16 above *in fine*.

[108] While not sharing this view, it may be of interest to mention in this context H. Kelsen's initial error theory, according to which during the initial period of most rules of customary law, the parties concerned must always be acting in error, but such 'errors' do not matter (H. Kelsen, loc. cit. in n. 55 above, and id, *General Theory of Law and State* (1945), p. 114); cf., however, Kunz, loc. cit. in n. 55 above, at p. 667.

[109] Cf. *West Rand Gold Mining Co. Ltd.* v. *The King* [1905] 2 K.B. p. 391, at p. 406: 'whatever has received the common consent of civilized nations must have received the assent of our country.' There is no reason why the Canadian and US statements cannot be considered as expressions of the newly formed individual *opinio juris* on the subject of those two countries.

3. The essence of general international customary law is the *opinio generalis juris generalis* of States.

4. Rules of particular or local international customary law may exist between two or more States, provided the requisite *opinio communis juris* exists between them.

5. The contents of rules of international customary law may change according to the relevant *opinio juris* of States at any given time.

6. There is no reason why a new *opinio juris* may not grow overnight between States so that a new rule of international customary law (or unwritten international law) comes into existence instantly. This shows that international law is a living law, and explains how changes take place.

7. Except in constitutional matters relating to the administration and finances of the Organization, resolutions of the United Nations General Assembly are merely recommendatory.

8. Provided that the intention is expressed articulately and without ambiguity, there appears to be no reason why an Assembly resolution may not be used as a means for identifying the existence and contents of a new *opinio juris*.

9. Such a law-finding resolution is itself still without binding force, but provides strong evidence of the existence and contents of the rule of law it states, and Member States voting for it may even be estopped from denying what it avers.

10. The wording of General Assembly resolution 1721A and 1962 falls short, however, of that required for law-finding resolutions.

11. Some Member States clearly stated their view that resolutions 1721A and 1962 were merely recommendatory.

12. Some Members made statements supporting both resolutions, but these statements do not necessarily mean that those which made them are thereby legally bound by these resolutions.

13. A number of Member States stated that they would respect or observe the principles contained in these resolutions, but some at least among them made it clear that they were not thereby legally bound by them.

14. A few said they 'undertook' to respect these principles. To what extent their position differs from those referred to under paragraph 13 above is uncertain.

15. Two or three States considered these principles as declaratory of existing international law. It would appear that these States might be regarded as estopped from denying this status to these principles if they were invoked against them; but it may be wondered whether such a rule of particular international customary law would not operate only among States which share the same *opinio juris* or at most only among States which consider themselves bound by this rule for one reason or another.

16. The general conclusion would therefore be that resolutions 1721A and

1962 are not legally binding on any Member State of the United Nations *qua* Assembly resolutions. The principles they enunciate are for the most part only optional, and in themselves non-binding, principles and standards. A few States *might*, however, be considered legally bound by these optional principles either because of their unilateral undertakings to be so bound or because of their acceptance of these principles as rules of existing international law. But even assuming that they are so bound, the extent to which they are bound both *ratione personae* (as among which States?) and *ratione temporis* (whether and how they may release themselves from the obligations assumed?[110]) remains an open question.

17. The real consensual elements and strength in these two resolutions are probably to be found in the agreements between the two space powers which made their unanimous adoption by the General Assembly possible.[111] In the absence of further details concerning these behind-the-scene agreements, it would appear that they might be in the nature of *pacta de contrahendo*[112] which draw up merely the heads of agreement between the parties and envisage their eventual translation into duly executed international treaties, when appropriate.[113]

18. The two space powers may well be held to be bound meanwhile by these *pacta de contrahendo* to observe the principles contained in these two resolutions in their *inter se* relations.[114] These principles represent a *modus vivendi* between them regarding outer space.

19. Experience has shown that unanimity between the two super-powers, which alone have effective space capabilities at present, is an essential condition of agreement on legal principles governing activities in space.

20. There is, however, often an assumption that what is good for the super-powers is also good for international society at large.

21. Once agreement is reached between the super-powers, there is a tendency to take the agreement of the other States for granted.

22. There is a tendency, especially in the Doctrine of international law, to make rather facile claims of universal binding force for such agreements between super-powers.

---

[110] Cf. Schachter who believes resolutions such as resolution 1721A to be an expression of 'law', and, in extolling their superiority over treaties for certain purposes, said: 'Moreover, the declarations do not appear to imply the degree of permanent commitment characteristic of treaties; declarations can be changed by a later Assembly and, consequently, they have a suppleness which may be highly desirable in areas of rapid changes' (loc. cit. in n. 1 above, at p. 99).

[111] Cf. n. 6 above and text immediately preceding n. 30 above.

[112] Cf. Schwarzenberger, op. cit. in n. 55 above, pp. 440 ff.; the present writer's *General Principles of Law*, pp. 117 ff.

[113] Cf. n. 31 above.

[114] Cf. the present writer's *General Principles of Law*, pp. 109–11 (Duty of parties to treaties *sub spe rati*) and pp. 140–1 (Duty in certain circumstances to maintain the *status quo*). The principles in question may well be applicable here.

23. In view of the conclusions reached in the course of this chapter, it would seem highly misleading and undesirable if the impression were allowed to be created that resolutions 1721A and 1962 are actually binding generally on Members of the United Nations and even non-members, especially by attaching to them some meaningless label such as 'soft law'. Pseudo-law can be the worst enemy of the Rule of Law.

24. Notwithstanding possible internal constitutional difficulties and the usual dilatoriness of States in ratifying agreements, it seems that in the long run the conventional procedure of making international law by treaties will still prove the most straightforward and direct method, and certainly the one most free from eventual controversies and difficulties. It is indeed much to be hoped that the present 'maximum area of agreement that is possible' on the future legal regime of outer space as represented by resolutions 1721A and 1962 will be speedily transformed into legal obligations binding on the maximum number of States.

8

The United Nations and the Development of International Law Relating to Outer Space*

I. Introduction

The United Nations celebrates this year 1985 its fortieth anniversary. One of its most important achievements during the first 40 years of its existence is its rôle in the development of international space law since man first entered outer space 28 years ago with the successful launching of Sputnik I. However, the United Nations almost drifted into this rôle, if not exactly by accident, at least by default. Its organ principally responsible for this achievement is the General Assembly's Committee on the Peaceful Uses of Outer Space (COP-UOS), whilst the official organ established by the United Nations under Article 13(1)(*a*) of its Charter for the 'progressive development of international law and its codification' is of course the International Law Commission.

So far, thanks mainly to work carried out by, in or in the corridors of COP-UOS, the United Nations has adopted four substantive General Assembly resolutions and five treaties in the field of international space law. Together they constitute a most remarkable example of deliberate rule-making to cover an entirely new field, in every sense of the term, of human activities and of international law. The rules that the United Nations has helped to bring forth are the ground rules which operate in man's latest New World, this time one of infinite dimensions.

The work of the United Nations in the development of international space law is worthy of attention, first, obviously, because of the intrinsic importance of this new branch of international law. Secondly, since the United Nations is likely to remain the main forum for the future development of general international space law, as opposed to specialized international space law such as that of international telecommunications law through the International Telecommunication Union, an understanding of the process whereby its work

* Lectures delivered in 1985 at the Institute of International Public Law and International Relations of the University of Thessaloniki, and first published in 16 *Thesaurus Acroasium* (1990), pp. 49–121. Reproduced by kind permission of the Institute, publishers of the *Thesaurus Acroasium*.

has been carried out will doubtless be of help in shaping its future approach to the subject.

Last but not least, a study of the subject may provide us with a useful insight into the nature of general international law and the process of its formation; for in the development of space law in the United Nations one witnesses in effect, in almost laboratory conditions, the birth and growth of an entirely new branch of international law. We may also learn something of the conditions governing the formation of its rules.

In my lectures at this Institute six years ago on 'Outer Space: The International Legal Framework: The International Legal Status of Outer Space, Space Objects and Spacemen',[1] I have already dealt with the substance of much of the international space law elaborated by the United Nations. On this occasion, we shall be concentrating our attention on the second and third aspects of the subject as mentioned above.

II. Achievements to Date

As mentioned before, the United Nations has so far elaborated the texts of five treaties on the law of outer space and, in addition, passed four resolutions of direct relevance to the substantive law.

A. Resolutions

First, the four General Assembly resolutions. These are chronologically as follows.

1. *Resolution 1721 (XVI) of 20 December 1961.*[2]   This resolution, in its Part A(1), 'commends' to States 'for their guidance in the exploration and use of outer space' the following principles:

(*a*)   International law, including the Charter of the United Nations, applies to outer space and celestial bodies;
(*b*)   Outer space and celestial bodies are free for exploration and use by all States in conformity with international law and are not subject to national appropriation.[3]

Paragraph (*a*) is a mere re-statement of the existing position in international law in the sense that there has never been any suggestion that the sphere of application of either general international law or the Charter of the United

---

[1] See B. Cheng, 'Outer Space: The International Legal Framework—The International Legal Status of Outer Space, Space Objects and Spacemen', 10 *Thesaurus Acroasium* (1981), p. 41 [Ch. 13 below].

[2] A/5026; text also in *UNYB* (1961), p. 35 [Appendix II.1 below].

[3] See B. Cheng, 'United Nations Resolutions on Outer Space: "Instant" International Customary Law?', 5 *Indian JIL* (1965), p. 23, at pp. 24 ff., reprinted in B. Cheng (ed.), *International Law* (1982), p. 237, at pp. 238 ff. [Ch. 7 above, s. III].

Nations is restricted to this planet. They regulate the activities of States and of members of the United Nations wherever such activities may be deployed, whether on earth or in outer space.[4]

Paragraph (*b*), on the other hand, is a different story. Whilst the first part of the paragraph may be true, the second half may not be entirely so.

At the time of the resolution, 1961, while outer space as such, inasmuch as it is neither *terra firma* nor an appurtenance of *terra firma*, was probably already considered an international *res extra commercium* not subject to national appropriation, just like the high seas, the same could hardly be said of celestial bodies which, being *terrae firmae*, had no reason not to be considered as international *res nullius* susceptible of being reduced to national sovereignty through effective occupation.[5] The postulated principle, insofar as it relates to celestial bodies, can, therefore, only be regarded as *de lege ferenda*. Its legal status depends consequently upon that of the resolution in which it is enunciated.[6] Attention may also be drawn to the fact that the resolution merely '*commends*' the principle 'to States *for their guidance*', without any claim to the principle being one of international law and, consequently, legally binding, a point which is often overlooked, not only in respect of this resolution, but also in discussions on General Assembly resolutions in general.[7]

From the substantive point of view, however, there can be little doubt of the political importance of the principle in so far as it relates to outer space and especially celestial bodies.

2. *Resolution 1884 (XVIII) of 17 October 1963.*[8] The Soviet Union and the United States having, after the successful conclusion of the Moscow Nuclear

---

[4] See further B. Cheng, 'The Extraterrestrial Application of International Law', 18 *CLP* (1965), p. 132 [Ch. 5 above].

[5] See Cheng, 'Outer Space: The International Legal Framework', loc. cit. in n. 1 above, at p. 41, ch. I, s. 8 [Ch. 13 below, s. I.H.]. As regards the appropriateness of the use of the term *res* in relation to outer space, it is true that in 1957 in the paper 'International Law and High Altitude Flights: Balloons, Rockets and Man-Made Satellites', 6 *ICLQ* (1957), p. 487, at p. 493 [Ch. 2 above, s. IV], while stating that, if States so wanted, there was no reason why they could not, when it came to outer space, instead of using any of the existing categories of legal status of territory, decide on the 'creation of an entirely new régime for an unprecedented situation', I did throw in, for good measure, the remark, 'since it may be doubted whether the void is a *res*.' However, while this terminological doubt would be sufficient to set States thinking along new lines, if they wished to create an entirely new legal régime for outer space, it is more than questionable whether it can thereby be the basis of a new régime. States having in fact chosen for outer space a régime which is that of *res extra commercium*, this terminological nicety can hardly be enough *per se* to bring about for outer space a special legal régime, and to prevent the term *res* from being applied to this vacuous new environment (Cf. M. Lachs, *The Law of Outer Space* (1972), p. 48). After all, Roman law did end up recognizing *res incorporales* (Cf. P. F. Girard, *Manuel élémentaire de droit romain* (1929), pp. 272 ff.). On spatial classification of world territory under international law, see B. Cheng, 'The Legal Régime of Airspace and Outer Space: The Boundary Problem—Functionalism versus Spatialism: The Major Premises', 5 *AASL* (1980), p. 323, pp. 335–8 [Ch. 14 below, s. VI].

[6] See further ss. IV, and V.J below.   [7] See further s. V.J below.

[8] A/RES/1884 (XVIII). For text, see text to n. 123 below [App. II.2 below].

Test Ban Treaty on 5 August 1963, declared their intention not to station in outer space any objects carrying nuclear weapons or other kinds of weapons of mass destruction, this resolution of the General Assembly 'solemnly calls on all States' similarly not to do so. However, since the actions on the part of the United States and the Soviet Union are mere expressions of intention and not legally binding undertakings, the 'solemn call' in this resolution to other States, irrespective of the legal effect of General Assembly resolutions in general, can only be regarded as exhortative.

3. *Resolution 1962 (XVIII) of 13 December 1963*.[9]   This resolution represents a major breakthrough in the development of international space law. It resulted basically from an understanding between the then only two space powers, the Soviet Union and the United States, on the ground rules to be observed, not only by themselves but by all States, in the exploration and use of outer space, following their agreement on the Nuclear Test Ban Treaty. With scarcely any consultation with the other members of COPUOS, this understanding was translated into the Declaration of *Legal* Principles Governing the Activities of States in the Exploration and Use of Outer Space, which is the subject of this resolution.[10] In this resolution, which was adopted unanimously as was also the case with the two resolutions previously referred to, the General Assembly 'solemnly declares that in the exploration and use of outer space States should be *guided*' by the principles enunciated therein. All the principles proclaimed in this resolution were subsequently incorporated, many of them verbatim, into the 1967 Treaty on Principles Governing the Activities of States in the Exploration and Use of Outer Space, including the Moon and Other Celestial Bodies. Although the introductory clause of the declaration still uses the language of mere exhortation in saying that 'States should be *guided* by the following principles', the title of the Declaration labels the principles it proclaims as '*legal*'.

Moreover, both the history of the resolution and its contents suggest that its authors intended that it should provide the ground rules for the future exploration and use of outer space, and that the substantive rules, if not some of its embellishments such as paragraph 1 on the 'benefit' and 'interests of all mankind', shall be law *in statu nascendi*, law in the nascent state. Examples are the principles of international responsibility for national activities in outer space (para. 5), jurisdiction of the State of registry over objects launched into outer space (para. 7), international liability for damage caused by objects launched into outer space (para. 8), and the re-affirmation of the principle of no national appropriation of outer space or celestial bodies (para. 3).

---

[9] A/RES/1962 (XVIII) [App. II.3 below]. See also text to n. 125 below.
[10] See Cheng, 'United Nations Resolutions on Outer Space', loc. cit. in n. 3 above, at pp. 28–30 [Ch. 7, s. VI].

4. *Resolution 37/92 of 10 December 1982 on Principles Governing the Use by States of Artificial Satellites for International Direct Television Broadcasting.*[11] The title of the resolution is in a sense self-explanatory. It will be noted, however, that a gap of nineteen years exists between this resolution and the previous one, during which period the United Nations proceeded by way of treaties in its development of international space law. In all, as will be seen shortly, five treaties were drawn up by COPUOS during the intervening years. The direct broadcasting by satellite (DBS) resolution represents, therefore, a return to a previous method of elaborating principles governing the activities of States in the exploration and use of outer space.

However, whereas the principles proclaimed in the resolution of 1963 were said, in the title of the Declaration, albeit not in the text, to be 'legal principles', and there were a number of pointers of the intention of their authors that they should one day become law, the 1982 resolution, both in its title and its text, studiously—in fact, deliberately—avoided the epithet 'legal'. Furthermore, whilst hitherto COPUOS followed the procedure of consensus in all its work, and the final product, be it in the form of a simple resolution or of a treaty text, was always approved in the end by the General Assembly without a vote, with the DBS principles, matters were different. By 1982 COPUOS had been working for some ten years on a declaration of principles governing the use of DBS, as well as a treaty on such principles. However, the Report of the Legal Sub-Committee for its 21st Session (1–19 Feb. 1982) did not even mention its work in this area.[12] The Report of COPUOS for the 37th Session of the General Assembly the same year said it had established a Working Group to consider the matter and various suggestions were being considered, 'but agreement was not reached.'[13] When COPUOS' report reached the General Assembly's Special Political Committee, the Greek delegate did remark, however,

that a consensus had been reached on a working paper submitted by Sweden, with the sole exception of a sentence contained in paragraph 2 of the draft principle on consultation and agreement among States.[14]

But revolt was obviously already afoot; for he went on to say:

Greece attached the greatest importance to the principle of consensus which had so far governed the work of the Committee and no effort should be spared to preserve it. To

---

[11] A/RES/37/92; 22 *ILM* (1983), p. 451 [App. II.4 below].
[12] A/AC.105/305.   [13] A/37/20, Suppl. No. 20, p. 10.
[14] A/SPC/37/SR.17 (3.11.82), p. 11. According to the US delegate, 'intensive informal negotiations' among COPUOS members during the previous two years had made 'consensus on a comprehensive text' achievable for the first time, but those 'rejecting consensus were apparently unwilling to deal with two sensitive issues, namely, international legal responsibility of States regarding the content of broadcasting and the requirement of prior consent, through a non-prejudiced reference to the international law on those matters' (A/SPC/37/SR.34 (22.11.82), p. 10).

that should be added the obvious consideration that it was preferable to have a text accepted by everybody rather than one rejected by some of the very countries whose actions it was designed to regulate.[15]

In fact a draft resolution on DBS (A/SPC/37/L.5) sponsored by a number of Third World countries had already been circulated on 21 October 1982. Notwithstanding the above open plea and doubtless numerous ones in the corridors, the Brazilian delegate to the Special Political Committee at its 33rd meeting on Friday 19 November 1982 formally submitted a revised version of the draft resolution (A/SPC/37/L.5/Rev.1), sponsored by 20 essentially Third-World countries.[16] According to him:

The draft set of principles contained in [the] draft resolution . . . had reflected the views of virtually all Member States and had been endorsed by the Group of 77 at UNI-SPACE 82.[17]

Behind-the-scenes efforts to secure consensus had obviously failed. The draft resolution was adopted by the Special Political Committee at the following meeting on Monday 22 November 1982. The vote was 88 to 15, with 11 abstentions.[18] In the Plenary of the General Assembly the vote was 107 votes for, 13 against, and 13 abstentions. The majority consisted of essentially Third-World and Soviet-bloc countries or, in other words, according to some system of classification, States from the Second-, Third- and Fourth-Worlds. Belgium, Denmark, the Federal Republic of Germany, Iceland, Israel, Italy, Japan, Luxembourg, the Netherlands, Norway, Spain, the United Kingdom, and the United States voted against. Australia, Austria, Canada, Finland, France, Greece, Ireland, Lebanon, Malawi, Morocco, New Zealand, Portugal and Sweden abstained. Iran, which abstained in the Special Political Committee, joined the majority in the Plenary. France and Portugal had previously voted against the resolution in the Special Political Committee.

B. Treaties

Secondly, the United Nations has been responsible for elaborating a number of treaties of fundamental importance to international space law for adoption by States. Five such treaties have so far been adopted.[19] All have come into force, although their legal impact may not all be the same.

1. *Treaty on Principles Governing the Activities of States in the Exploration and Use of Outer Space, including the Moon and Other Celestial Bodies, 27 January*

---

[15] Ibid.   [16] A/SPC/37/SR 33 p. 7.   [17] Ibid.   [18] A/SPC/37/SR.34, p. 14.
[19] The texts of all five treaties are conveniently to be found in the booklet *The United Nations Treaties on Outer Space* published by the United Nations in 1984, Sales No. E.84.I.10 [all reproduced under App. I below].

1967.[20]   The 1967 Treaty is the first and doubtless also the most important of these five treaties. The impetus behind the conclusion of this treaty was the successful 'soft' landing by the Soviet Union of its automatic station Luna IX on the moon on 3 February 1966, after three failures the previous year. Speaking from his ranch in Texas on 7 May 1966, President Johnson announced that the United States, which had hitherto opposed the development of international space law through treaties, would seek a treaty through the United Nations to prevent any nation from claiming sovereignty over the moon or any other celestial bodies and that the exploration thereof would be for peaceful purposes only. Consultations with the Soviet Union took place on 11 May when an outline of twelve points which, in the opinion of the United States, should be included in a 'celestial bodies treaty' was handed to the latter. The response of the Soviet Union was prompt. On 30 May, it requested the 'Conclusion of an international agreement on legal principles governing the activities of States in the exploration and conquests of the Moon and other celestial bodies' to be included in the agenda of the 21st session of the General Assembly. The text of a Soviet draft treaty followed on 16 June 1966. Whilst both drafts and their successive amendments were considered in the Legal Sub-Committee of COPUOS, in the course of which the United States agreed to enlarge the scope of the treaty to include also outer space, the really crucial discussions took place directly between the two space powers until they were able to present an agreed text in the form of a 43–power sponsored draft resolution to the First Committee of the General Assembly on 15 December 1966 for it to be adopted unanimously four days later by the General Assembly itself on 19 December 1966 in resolution 2222 (XXI). The actual treaty itself was then opened for signature on 27 January 1967 simultaneously in London, Moscow, and Washington DC, the capitals of the three Depositary States. The treaty requires the ratifications of five Signatory States in order to come into force, which must, however, include those of the three Depositary States, namely, the Soviet Union, the United Kingdom, and the United States.

The 1967 Space Treaty provides a legal framework for man's exploration and use of outer space and, in doing so, transforms into binding legal obligations the various principles first enunciated in resolution 1962 (XVIII),[21] whilst adding others. *Inter alia*, it defines the legal status of outer space and of celestial bodies (both *res extra commercium*) (Article II), partially demilitarizes outer space (Article IV(1)), reserves celestial bodies wholly for 'peaceful purposes' (Article IV (2)), establishes the principle of States Parties' 'international responsibility' for 'national activities in outer space', even those carried on by non-governmental entities (Article VI), holds the launching State Party

---

[20] See further B. Cheng, 'Le Traité de 1967 sur l'espace/The 1967 Space Treaty', 95 *JDI* (1968), p. 532 [Ch. 9 below]. See also s. VI.A below.

[21] See s. II.A.3 above.

liable for damage caused by space objects to another State Party or its nationals (Article VII), postulates that States Parties register the objects they launch into outer space and submits space objects and their personnel in outer space and on celestial bodies to the jurisdiction and control of the State of registry (Article VIII).

Attention may be drawn to the fact that, although practically all the provisions of the 1967 Treaty are capable of being made into rules of general international law, and were in fact intended by many of the States involved to be such, most of them remain worded merely as treaty undertakings assumed between the contracting Parties.

2. *Agreement on the Rescue of Astronauts, the Return of Astronauts, and the Return of Objects Launched into Outer Space, 22 April 1968.*[22]   Alas 1967 saw the first fatalities in space exploration. On 27 January, three United States astronauts died when fire broke out on board Apollo I before take-off. On 24 April, Colonel Vladimir Kamorov of the Soviet Union perished in Soyuz I on landing. Never before in the history of the United Nations has a request of the General Assembly to one of its Sub-Committees to prepare the text of a multipartite treaty been implemented with such alacrity as in the case of the 1968 Astronauts Agreement. On 3 November 1967, the General Assembly requested COPUOS 'to continue with a sense of urgency its work on the elaboration of,' *inter alia,* 'an agreement on assistance to and return of astronauts and space vehicles'. On 13 December 1967, an agreed text was circulated at the request of the Soviet and United States delegations to members of the Legal Sub-Committee of COPUOS, which met the following day. It then took no more than another five days for the draft treaty to reach the General Assembly on 19 December when it received the unanimous commendation of the General Assembly there and then, even though many a delegate was unhappy with the haste.

The Astronauts Agreement is essentially a one-sided undertaking by the contracting States to notify both the launching authority and the Secretary-General of the United Nations if they receive information or discover that an astronaut or a space object has made an emergency or unintended landing in territory under their jurisdiction, on the high seas or in any other place not under the jurisdiction of any State. They further undertake to search, rescue, and return the astronaut unconditionally if within their territory, and render such assistance they can if outside. Search and return of space objects are, however, only upon request and, in that event, at the launching authority's expenses. The contracting States' duties are in respect of all astronauts and space objects, whether or not belonging to another contracting State. The Soviet Union was the prime mover behind the Agreement, and it would

---

[22] See further B. Cheng, 'The 1968 Astronauts Agreement', 23 *YBWA* (1969), p. 185 [Ch. 10 below].

appear that, in order to gain especially British support, it dropped for the first time its strong opposition to inter-governmental space organizations being given some standing in these treaties. The result is that, under Article 6 of the Agreement, such organizations would be recognized as 'launching authorities' within the meaning of the term under the Agreement, provided that the organizations concerned have declared their acceptance of the rights and obligations provided for in the treaty and a majority of the States of the respective organizations are contracting parties to the Agreement and to the 1967 Space Treaty. This formula is followed in all subsequent treaties on outer space concluded under the auspices of the United Nations.

3. *Convention on International Liability for Damage Caused by Space Objects, 29 March 1972.*[23]   What goes up must come down: so the saying goes. From the very beginning of the space age, one of the many very real fears among the ordinary people and among States, especially among the non-space powers, has been the danger of space objects falling within their country and thereby causing personal injuries or material damage. Although Article VII of the 1967 Space Treaty does stipulate that the launching State is internationally liable for damage caused by its space objects, what concerned the authorities was the lack of definition of the modalities of this liability and the absence of any pre-established machinery to determine with binding authority, in case of dispute, the principle and extent of liability. They were hoping, at one time, that the question of assistance to astronauts and that of liability would be given at least equal priority by the United Nations, and were very disappointed when the former was acted upon first. The latter's chance came in 1971 when there were signs of increasing co-operation between the two major space powers and of even what might be the beginning of a period of East-West *détente*. After nine years of discussion, agreement was finally reached on the text of the liability Convention and it was approved by the General Assembly on 29 November 1971 in resolution 2777 (XXVI). The Convention was opened for signature on 29 March 1972.

The 1972 Liability Convention is, from the technical point of view, perhaps the best drafted of all the legal instruments on outer space produced so far by the United Nations. It defines the circumstances in which a launching State or inter-governmental organization becomes liable, lays down the procedure for the presentation of claims and, above all, provides relatively effective means for resolving disputes regarding the settlement of claims.

4. *Convention on Registration of Objects Launched into Outer Space, 14 January 1975.*[24]   Closely related to the question of liability for damage

[23] See further B. Cheng, 'Convention on International Liability for Damage Caused by Space Objects', in Jasentuliyana and Lee (eds.), 1 *Manual* (1979), p. 83 [Ch. 11 below].

[24] Cf. A. A. Cocca, 'Convention on Registration of Objects Launched into Outer Space', ibid., p. 173; B. Cheng, 'Spacecraft, Satellites and Space Objects', in Bernhardt (ed.), 11 *Ency. PIL* (1989), p. 309 [Ch. 16 below].

caused by space objects and that of international responsibility for national space activities is the problem of identification of space objects and the entities that launch them. While there are those who, basing themselves primarily on analogy with ships and aircraft, deem it important that space objects should also bear visual identification marks, it was soon realized that at the present stage of the technology, identification depends much more on knowing and tracking the basic orbital parameters of objects launched into space. General Assembly resolution 1721B (XVI) adopted in 1961 called upon States to furnish information on launchings promptly to COPUOS and requested the Secretary-General to maintain a public registry of the information supplied. Such information was, however, to be furnished on a voluntary basis.

The Registration Convention (A/Res/3235 (XXIX)) provides for two separate forms of registration, both mandatory, of every 'space object launched into earth orbit or beyond' (excluding thus objects not intended to go into orbit, such as ballistic missiles), the two registers being seemingly for different purposes. First, each object must be registered in a national registry and in one national registry alone, even when there may be several launching States. Since the contents of the national registry are left to each States concerned, they may or may not be useful for identifying the objects recorded in the registry. National registration serves in this case more or less the same function as nationality in the case of ships and aircraft in ensuring that a juridical link exists between every object in outer space and some one State on earth through which benefits as well as duties can be grafted onto the space object or the State or both,[25] such as jurisdiction, international responsibility, observance of international treaties, and so forth. The Registration Convention provides also for institutional registration in the case of space objects launched by inter-governmental organizations, although how some of these purposes may, in such an event, be served may be somewhat difficult.[26]

The Convention creates, in addition to national and institutional registration, a United Nations Registry maintained by the Secretary-General to whom each State of registry must furnish, 'as soon as possible', specific items of information concerning each object carried on its registry. It is this information that will, in most cases, help to identify objects in earth orbit or beyond, both while they are in outer space and when they have returned to earth, rather than what may be left of the physical markings on the debris in the event of an accident, even though metallurgical tests can also prove useful.

[25] Compare the position of aircraft, Cheng, *The Law of International Air Transport*, pp. 128 ff., and see further Cheng, loc. cit. in n. 24 above [Ch. 16 below, also Chs. 17 and 18].

[26] On the problems of so-called 'international registration' of aircraft, see B. Cheng, 'Nationality and Registration of Aircraft—Article 77 of the Chicago Convention', 32 *JALC*, (1966), p. 551; 'Nationality of Aircraft Operated by Joint or International Agencies', 2 *YBASL* (1966), 5; 'Memorandum on Nationality and Registration of Aircraft' in ILA, *Report of the 52nd Conference, Helsinki* (1966), p. 268.

5. *Agreement Governing the Activities of States on the Moon and Other Celestial Bodies, 18 December 1979.*[27]   One of the first concerns of many nations at the very beginning of the space age was to prevent the spread of colonialism to outer space. This concern resulted first in paragraph (b) of General Assembly resolution 1721 of 1961,[28] and subsequently in Article II of the 1967 Space Treaty.[29] Unbeknown maybe to most members of COPUOS at the time, a little over six months after the Space Treaty was opened for signature in January, Mr Arvid Pardo, the Maltese Ambassador to the United Nations, launched an entirely new concept in international law when in August 1967 he proposed, on behalf of his government, that the sea-bed and ocean floor beyond the limits of present national jurisdiction should be declared 'a common heritage of mankind', and, as such, to be used exclusively for peaceful purposes and administered by an international authority for the benefit of all peoples and of present and future generations. The concept fired the imagination particularly of developing countries. On 15 December 1969, the United Nations General Assembly adopted resolution 2574D by 62 votes in favour (primarily developing nations), 28 against (industrialized nations), with 28 abstentions, declaring a moratorium on sea-bed exploitation.[30] The following year, on 17 December 1970, in resolution 2749 (XXV), the General Assembly 'solemnly declare[d]':

The sea-bed and ocean floor, and the subsoil thereof, beyond the limits of national jurisdiction (hereinafter referred to as the area), as well as the resources of the area, are the common heritage of mankind.[31]

General Assembly resolutions are, however, mere recommendations and are not legally binding.[32] It was left to the Third United Nations Conference on the Law of the Sea (UNCLOS III) to draw up an international treaty to translate this concept into treaty law, and to set up 'the Authority' to 'organise and control activities in the Area'.

The concept was quickly seized upon by those interested in the development of international space law. In 1970, Argentina presented to the Legal Sub-Committee of COPUOS a Draft Agreement on the Principles Governing Activities in the Use of the Natural Resources of the Moon and Other Celestial Bodies, the first article of which boldly proclaims that 'the natural resources of the Moon and other celestial bodies shall be the common heritage of mankind.'

In what can only be regarded as a move to head off the Argentine initiative, the Soviet Union on 27 May 1971 proposed the addition of a new item on the

---

[27] See further B. Cheng, 'The Moon Treaty: Agreement Governing the Activities of States on the Moon and Other Celestial Bodies within the Solar System other than the Earth, December 18, 1979', 33 *CLP* (1980), p. 213 [Ch. 12 below].

[28] See s. II.A.1 above.   [29] See s. II.B.1 above.

[30] A/RES/2574D (XXIV); 9 *ILM* (1970), 422.

[31] A/RES/2749 (XXV); 10 *ILM* (1971), 220.   [32] See s. V.J, V.J below.

agenda of the forthcoming session of the United Nations General Assembly, namely, the Preparation of an International Treaty Concerning the Moon. A few days later it submitted its own draft Moon Treaty. The Soviet draft betrayed evidence of great haste in its preparation. It was essentially a rehash of the relevant provisions of the 1967 Space Treaty, was limited to the Moon, and did not deal with the problem of resources. However, being linked to a formal proposal of a new agenda item in the General Assembly itself, once the agenda item was approved, it took precedence over the Argentine proposal in deliberations in COPUOS' Legal Sub-Committee in that the Soviet proposal was taken as the basic document for purposes of discussion. This was no doubt what the Soviet initiative was intended to do.

Basically, two different forces were at work. On the one hand, the essentially non-space developing countries, which, with especially an eye to the difficulties that were being encountered at the slow-moving UNCLOS III, wanted primarily to have the new concept of the common heritage of mankind accepted for at least some portion of the universe in some legally binding document, saw the preparation of the moon treaty as precisely such an opportunity. On the other hand, while the Soviet Union was the chief opponent of any mention of common heritage of mankind, the United States, without wishing to be seen, perhaps at least at that stage prior to its walk-out from UNCLOS III, as rejecting such an eye-catching concept especially over such a barren waste as the moon, treated the whole exercise more or less as one of damage control.

The end result was somewhat predictable. Both sides can claim that they have achieved their respective objectives, with the success of the developing countries being perhaps more nominal than real. Article 11(1) of the treaty declares:

The moon and its natural resources are the common heritage of mankind, which finds expression in the provisions of this Agreement, in particular in paragraph 5 of this article.

The prime objective of the developing countries has in this way been secured, but the very subtle wording of this paragraph, known as the Austrian formula in honour of its begetter, means that common heritage of mankind is no more than a short-hand label for the provisions of the treaty. These provisions, in fact, amount to relatively little. In particular, if one turns to paragraph 5, one finds that it says:

States Parties to this Agreement hereby undertake to establish an international régime, including appropriate procedures, to govern the exploitation of the natural resources of the moon as such exploitation is about to become feasible . . .

The obligation to establish an international regime consists, therefore, in no more than that of a *pactum de contrahendo*. Meanwhile, it has been clearly maintained by at least one of the super-space powers, namely the United States, that the Moon Treaty does not establish a moratorium on exploitation. In any event, no space power of any significance has rushed to ratify the treaty.

III. Procedure

A. The Organs

As has been mentioned before, the main organ for the development of international space law is COPUOS, and perhaps more specifically its Legal Sub-Committee. The predecessor of COPUOS was the eighteen-member *Ad Hoc* Committee on the Peaceful Uses of Outer Space established by resolution 1348 (XIII) of the United Nations General Assembly on 13 December 1958. The *Ad Hoc* Committee, which met in May and June 1959, was, on account of its membership, boycotted by the Soviet Union, Czechoslovakia and Poland; nor did India and the United Arab Republic attend. Its Report was considered by the General Assembly at its XIVth Session. As a result thereof, the General Assembly decided on 12 December 1959 by resolution 1472 (XIV) to establish COPUOS, albeit with a membership then of only twenty-four. Among the terms of reference of COPUOS, as of the *Ad Hoc* Committee, is the study of the ways and means to encourage space research and of the legal problems which might arise.

In order to discharge this dual function, COPUOS has two plenary Sub-Committees, namely, the Scientific and Technical Sub-Committee and the Legal Sub-Committee. Legal matters are, as to be expected, discussed primarily in the Legal Sub-Committee.

However, in its infancy, COPUOS met the same difficulty as the *Ad Hoc* Committee. The Soviet bloc was still dissatisfied with its composition and, moreover, wanted the unanimity rule to be applied, instead of the majority rule applicable to all subordinate organs of the General Assembly. At the insistence of the United Kingdom government, it eventually met for the first time on 27 November 1961 in order to transact certain formal business before its two-year term expired. After adopting a report to the General Assembly, the Committee adjourned *sine die*.

Meanwhile, the political climate between the two superpowers changed quite dramatically. While the Report of COPUOS was before the Assembly's First Committee, a five-part draft resolution was submitted by Australia, Canada, Italy, and the United States.[33] This was subsequently revised and resubmitted by all the members of COPUOS, thus including the Soviet Union.[34] Behind this draft resolution, therefore, stood an agreement between

---

[33] A/C.1/L.301.   [34] A/C.1/L.301/Rev. 1 and Corr. 1.

the two super-space powers.[35] It was really this agreement which broke the deadlock between them regarding outer space co-operation in the United Nations. With this underlying agreement between the two space powers, it was hardly surprising that the twenty-four-nation draft was adopted unanimously by the First Committee on 11 December 1961 and then by the General Assembly on 20 December 1961 as resolution 1721 (XVI).[36]

The fifth and last part (Part E) of the resolution continued the existence of COPUOS and enlarged its membership to twenty-eight. It moreover invited COPUOS *inter alia* 'to study and report on the legal problems which may arise from the exploration and use of outer space . . .'[37]

B. Consensus

The enlargement of COPUOS and the strengthening of the Soviet bloc component in its composition was not the only concession made to the Soviet Union in order to secure its co-operation. From the start, being in the minority, the Soviet Union had wanted the unanimity rule to be applied in COPUOS, instead of the majority rule applicable to all subordinate organs of the United Nations General Assembly.

When the expanded COPUOS met for the first time on 19 March 1962, the following statement was made by the Chairman at the opening session:

I should like to place on record that through informal consultations it has been agreed among the members of the Committee that it will be the aim of all members of the Committee and its Sub-Committees to conduct the Committee's work in such a way that the Committee will be able to reach agreement on its work without need for voting.[38]

Thus formally began the informal procedure of 'consensus' which eventually spread to many other organs of the United Nations.[39]

Some six months later, during discussions of the draft which led eventually to resolution 1962 (XVIII),[40] the United States delegate to COPUOS hinted that the Committee should revert to the normal majority rule of United Nations organs, but as the Soviet delegate emphasized:

Twenty-six signatures on this document would have no value; there must be twenty-eight signatures. Even if all of us, including the Soviet Union, the countries of Asia,

[35] In a message to President Kennedy on 20 March 1962, Mr Khrushchev said among other things: 'I regard as a positive fact that at the XVIth session of the United Nations General Assembly, the Soviet Union and the United States found it possible to agree on the proposal about the initial principles of space legislation, *which was then unanimously approved by all the Members of the United Nations*' (italics added).

[36] See s. II.A.1 above.   [37] Cf. s. VI.C below.   [38] A/AC.105/PV.2 (19.3.62), p. 2.

[39] Cf. Guy de Lacharrière, 'Consensus et Nations Unies', *AFDI* (1968), p. 6; A. D'Amato, 'On Consensus', 8 *Can. YBIL* (1970), p. 104; S. Bastid, 'Observations sur la pratique du consensus', in W. Wengler (Festschrift für), 1 *Multitudo Legum Jus Unum* (1973), p. 11.

[40] See s. II.A.3 above.

Africa and Latin America—which are in principle in favour of signing the declaration—sign, if there is no signature of the United States, the whole endeavour would have no result. It is clear that without agreement of the United States it is impossible to resolve such a problem.[41]

What the Soviet Union particularly had in mind was doubtless to ensure that no conclusion could or should ever be reached against its wishes.

Consensus is of course a form of unanimity, but it is no longer necessarily a numerical unanimity, nor even necessarily a decision *nemine contradicente*, one without a dissenting vote, as no vote is taken. What it does mean is that no decision will be taken against the strong objection of any member; in particular no decision will be taken without the concurrence of any member that really matters. In other words, it requires the unanimity of the dominant section in a given situation. It is a subtle way of bypassing the rigid one-State one-vote rule. *En passant*, it may be of interest to observe that, while the one-State one-vote rule is sometimes defended on the ground that it is egalitarian and democratic (presumably by analogy with the one-man one-vote principle in municipal society), there are in the United Nations no fewer than 31 States with a population of under one million, when at the same time there are at least seven countries with a population of over 100 million, including China with a population of nearly 1,000 million. If the one-man one-vote principle is democratic, can the one-State one-vote principle also be democratic, when the vote of each person in the former countries counts for over 100 times that of his neighbour in the latter countries? In any event, in the initial days of the development of space law, what really mattered was agreement between the then only two space powers. Thus the Indian delegate to COPUOS, when the hint of a possibility of returning to the majority principle, defended the decision to follow the procedure of consensus and said:

This was a wise decision because no solution which is not acceptable to the two space powers can be implemented.[42]

He was no doubt voicing a general sentiment; for the question came up again only after 20 years had lapsed, during which time, to borrow the words of the United States delegate to the General Assembly's Special Political Committee, consensus it had become:

the foundations upon which the United Nations had built substantial achievements in the field of outer space.[43]

However, the consensus procedure remains an informal procedure. It was departed from, much to the chagrin of the United States, in the case of reso-

---

[41] A/AC.105/PV.15 (14.9.62), p. 28.

[42] A/AC.105/PV.13 (13.9.62), p. 7; cf. also Poland, A/AC.105/C.2/SR.6 (6.2.62), p. 6; Soviet Union, A/AC.105/PV.15 (14.9.62), p. 29.

[43] A/SPC/37/SR.34 (22.11.82), p. 10. The occasion was the US explanation of its vote against the draft which eventually became resolution 37/92 (see s. II.A.4 above.)

lution 37/92 on Direct Television Broadcasting by Satellites, which was adopted by the General Assembly on 10 December 1982, by 107 votes to 17, with 13 abstentions.[44] As the United States delegate to the Assembly's Special Political Committee said, in explanation of the United States' vote against the draft of the resolution:

Never before had a group of sponsors, however great the difficulty in achieving consensus [in COPUOS], considered it appropriate to ask a voting majority in the Organization to adopt principles regarding activities in outer space which had exceeded consensus.[45]

The procedure of consensus requires a great deal of behind-the-scenes consultation, especially among the parties 'directly concerned', to use the expression found in Article 79 of the United Nations Charter. At one time, the proceedings of COPUOS and of its Legal Sub-Committee were fairly fully reported, those of the former in verbatim records and those of the latter in summary records. However, looking back at the fairly detailed records of the proceedings of the Legal Sub-Committee of those days, one almost gets the impression that, at least during its formal proceedings, the Sub-Committee spent more time discussing how it should carry out its work than on the substance of space law. The reason is simply because the most critical part of the negotiations was always carried out behind the scenes, either directly between the two super-space powers, as was very much the case at the beginning, or among those who considered themselves 'the only ones that really matter'. Sometimes the situation could get into such a stage that, notwithstanding pleas from the Rapporteur and the Chairman, no one would discuss the really critical issues faced by the Sub-Committee in open session.[46]

At the beginning, with the publication of the proceedings of COPUOS and its Sub-Committees, at least in mimeograph form, this situation was relatively apparent or transparent. However, towards the end of the sixties, no doubt in order to adjust to realities, the Legal Sub-Committee turned itself into a Working Group more and more often. Since then, as, in the name of economy, the proceedings of Working Groups are not published, even in summaries or in mimeograph form, what actually transpires becomes more and more opaque. In addition, there are all these 'informal consultations' which do not get reported at all.[47]

Thus, in the case of the Moon Treaty, whilst COPUOS' Chairman on opening the 22nd Session of the Committee on 18 June 1979 was voicing his despair at the lack of progress in the matter by the Legal Sub-Committee after

---

[44] See s. II.A.4 above.   [45] A/SPC/37/SR.34 (22.11.82), p. 10.

[46] See further Cheng, 'Convention on International Liability for Damage Caused by Space Objects', loc. cit. in n. 23 above, at pp. 89–90 [Ch. 11, s. III.F.3 below].

[47] Compare, for instance, what was said by the Greek and United States delegates as quoted in n. 14 above with what was found in the Report of COPUOS on the progress on the principles on DBS.

more than eight years of discussion, the next thing one finds is a simple entry in the so-called verbatim records, without any fanfare or record of any discussions, that the draft Treaty relating to the Moon in the draft report of the Committee was adopted by consensus without a vote on 3 July, i.e., 15 days later,[48] without anyone being any the wiser as to what actually happened.

C. The Route

The normal procedure is for matters to be discussed first in the Legal Sub-Committee, and when agreement has been reached, the draft is then submitted to COPUOS, from where it would go to the First Committee, or more recently to the Special Political Committee, of the General Assembly before reaching the General Assembly itself, although there are not infrequently exceptions.

Thus the proposal that eventually became General Assembly resolution 1721 (XVI) of 20 December 1961, the first substantive resolution relating to the law of outer space adopted by the General Assembly,[49] was submitted directly to the First Committee, without going through COPUOS or any of its sub-committees, albeit by all members of COPUOS. With the very important resolution 1962 (XVIII) of 13 December 1963 containing the Declaration of Legal Principles Governing the Activities of States in the Exploration and Use of Outer Space, which was essentially negotiated directly between the two super-space powers, assisted and attended upon sometimes by a few others, at what the French delegate to COPUOS pointedly called some 'secluded places', the draft was to have also gone straight to the First Committee. It was subsequently decided, however, that the proposal should 'make a stop' in COPUOS in order, it would appear, to collect the signatures of all the other members of the Committee. To this end, the Committee was convened and the draft submitted to it, with the understanding seemingly that no amendment would be entertained. It was adopted unanimously by COPUOS, then by the First Committee and finally by the General Assembly, without a word being changed or a comma disturbed.[50]

In the case of the 1967 Space Treaty,[51] more or less the same happened. After a year of rather inconclusive discussion on assistance, liability and especially priorities, the Legal Sub-Committee, when its Fifth Session opened in July 1966, brushed everything aside in order to consider various drafts of a treaty on the legal regime of celestial bodies and outer space which the superpowers had just submitted to it. Although it was able during its Fifth Session to comment on these drafts, the crucial negotiations took place directly between the two super powers and behind the scenes. Agreement once

---

[48] See Cheng, 'The Moon Treaty', loc. cit. in n. 27 above, at pp. 216–8 [Ch. 12, s. II.E below].
[49] See s. II.A.1 text to nn. 33–6 above, and s. V.H.2 below.
[50] See s. II.A.3 above, and s. V.H.2 below.   [51] See s. II.B.1 above.

reached, the text was submitted on Thursday, 15 December 1966, by a 43-power draft resolution directly to the First Committee, bypassing COPUOS. The draft was adopted without objection by the First Committee on Saturday, and received the unanimous commendation of the General Assembly on Monday.

The 1968 Astronauts Agreement[52] is another exception that proves the rule. A text was 'negotiated backstage' by the super-space powers and thrust upon the United Nations, which was then given less than a week to consider and approve it. The Legal Sub-Committee had merely a day and a half and COP-UOS itself only a Saturday morning to discuss it, although both succeeded, even in such a short time, to bring significant improvements to the draft. This time it was the First Committee that was bypassed. On this occasion, a number of countries did point out, however, that the consideration by the General Assembly of resolutions that had not been examined by one of the Main Committees and not been inscribed on the agenda in accordance with the rules of procedure should not be allowed to become a precedent.[53]

Insofar as treaties drawn up by the United Nations are concerned, the first three treaties were all in the form of draft treaties 'commended' to States by General Assembly resolutions. The treaties were then at a later date opened for signature in the depositary States. The Registration Convention and the Moon Treaty are simply opened for signature at United Nations Headquarters in New York.

D. The Principle of Universality

One of the controversies at the time was the circle of States which were entitled to become parties to these treaties. Since the treaties were being drawn up by the United Nations, the general inclination was to limit the treaties to members of the United Nations, the so-called 'United Nations family'. It has to be remembered, however, that at the time, especially during the period of negotiations leading to the 1967 Space Treaty, apart from the question of Chinese representation in the United Nations, there were a number of friends and allies of the one bloc not being recognized by States of the other bloc and being kept out of the United Nations, such as East Germany and the two Vietnams. While the United States favoured the United Nations family approach, the Soviet Union was adamant on opening the treaties to 'all States'—the so-called principle of 'universality'. This difference remained one of the major obstacles that held up the negotiations of the first treaties. In the end the United States gave in to the Soviet view.[54]

[52] See s. II.B.2 above.

[53] See further Cheng, 'The 1968 Astronauts Agreement', loc. cit. in n. 22 above, at pp. 195–7 [Ch. 10 below, s. IV *in fine*].

[54] See Cheng, 'The 1967 Space Treaty', loc. cit. in n. 20 above, at pp. 554 and 556, esp. nn. 77 and 82 [Ch. 9 below, s. III.C, esp. nn. 77 and 82]; Cheng, 'The 1968 Astronauts Agreement', loc.

This explains the unusual procedure for the opening of the early treaties for signature and their final clauses; for not only was the United Nations not used as the depositary of signatures, ratifications, and accessions, but the treaties were each given also not one but three depositary States, namely, the Soviet Union, the United Kingdom, and the United States. The first three treaties were consequently opened for signature simultaneously at London, Moscow, and Washington. The result was that governments and countries like Nationalist China and South Vietnam were able, if they so wished, to sign and ratify the treaties in Washington, and the German Democratic Republic in Moscow.

It could of course also have been because of the fact that Communist China was finally seated in the United Nations in 1971 and the two Germanies were both admitted to the Organization in 1973, as well as to the lesser importance attached to the two subsequent treaties, that in the case of the 1975 Registration Convention and of the 1979 Moon Treaty, the treaty texts, once approved by the General Assembly, became immediately 'open for signature by all States at United Nations Headquarters in New York'.

Each of the five treaties drawn up by the United Nations requires only five ratifications in order to come into force. The importance attached to the first two treaties and to acceptance of them by the space powers before they can come into force is marked by the requirement in them that among the five ratifying States must be the three designated depositaries. Thus whilst the 1967 Space Treaty and the 1968 Astronauts Agreement cannot come into effect without the acceptances of the Soviet Union, the United Kingdom, and the United States, the 1972 Liability and 1975 Registration Conventions, as well as the 1979 Moon Treaty, can. In fact, the Moon Treaty was brought into force by the ratifications of the following States: Chile, the Philippines, Uruguay, the Netherlands, and Austria. Treaties are of course binding only upon States that have actually accepted them, by signature (where a treaty does not require ratification), by signature and ratification (where a treaty requires signatures to be ratified), or by adhesion or accession (where a treaty permits adhesion or accession by non-signatories). All the five treaties relating to outer space concluded under the auspices of the United Nations require signatures to be ratified and permit adhesion or accession.

IV. Resolutions v. Treaties

Ever since the very beginning, there was a debate within COPUOS on the best method of developing international space law.[55] There was in particular

---

cit. in n. 22 above, at p. 191 [Ch. 10 below; s. III.B, text to n. 30]; Cheng, 'Convention on International Liability for Damage Caused by Space Objects', loc. cit. in n. 23 above, text to nn. 25 and 45, and p. 99 [Ch. 11 below, text to nn. 28 and 49, and s. V.A.2].

[55] See loc. cit. in n. 3 above [Ch. 7 above], and s. VI.A below.

strong disagreement between the two super-space powers on this issue when COPUOS began work in earnest in 1962 and was considering a number of proposals for formulating basic principles governing the activities of States in the exploration and use of outer space. Bearing in mind that in principle no State can be bound by a treaty without its consent, the Soviet Union which was in the minority in the United Nations at the time, understandably wanted a treaty so that it would not be bound by rules to which it had not given its consent. A treaty would also ensure that everyone would be effectively bound by whatever has been agreed upon. The United States, on the other hand, which, with its friends and allies, was still able then to command easily a two-thirds majority in the United Nations, was equally insistent that it wanted a General Assembly resolution and not a treaty. States within the Soviet bloc not unexpectedly all solidly supported the Soviet position. Among the others, some at first also favoured a treaty, but most, if not all, eventually became at least resigned to the United States standpoint.

The Soviet position was based on the premises that, in the opinion of the Soviet government, (a) the agreed principles of space law should be embodied in a legally binding instrument, and (b) General Assembly resolutions lacked legally binding force.[56]

One of the principal arguments advanced in favour of General Assembly resolutions was its simplicity. Thus, with reference to the Soviet proposal for a treaty on assistance to and return of astronauts and space vehicles, the United States delegate said:

Preparing a treaty and obtaining the required number of ratifications was a time-consuming process, whereas the Legal Sub-Committee was in a position to act immediately by preparing a draft resolution for action by the General Assembly.[57]

Later, speaking on the Soviet draft declaration of basic principles, particularly its paragraph 9 which also dealt with the subject of assistance and return, he further remarked:

[The United States government] did not believe action for assistance and return should be delayed for the drafting, signature, ratification and entry into force of a treaty or international agreement. The applicable principles were clear and should be readily agreed by Governments for incorporation into a simple declaration.[58]

An extension of the argument of simplicity is that of flexibility. Thus, while the Australian delegation at first agreed with the Soviet Union that the

---

[56] See for instance, USSR: 'The fact is the declaration we are proposing would be a binding international instrument while a resolution of the General Assembly [referring to resolution 1721], in accordance with the provisions of the Charter, is merely a recommendation', A/AC.105/PV.10 (10.9.62), p. 41; 'General Assembly resolution 1721 (XVI) . . . unfortunately is not yet a legal obligation on the part of States . . .', ibid./PV.15 (14.9.62), p. 11; 'resolution 1721 (XVI), like all other General Assembly resolutions, was merely a recommendation', A/C.1/SR.1289 (3.12.62), p. 215.

[57] A/AC.105/C.2/SR.1 (28.5.62), p. 9.   [58] A/AC.105/C.2/SR.7 (7.6.62), p. 10.

declaration of basic principles should be in the form of a binding treaty,[59] it subsequently was persuaded that,

there might . . . be great advantages, especially in that new field of law, in making a start with instruments in resolution form, in which unanimity could be achieved without loss of flexibility. Full legal form could be developed later . . .[60]

In the development of the law, two distinct forms were thus clearly contemplated: General Assembly resolutions and treaties. However, this in no way means that they are the same in form or in legal effect. In fact, the same Australian delegate said very clearly on the same occasion:

His delegation appreciated fully the difference between a resolution adopted by the General Assembly, whether expressed as a recommendation or as a declaration, and an instrument in the nature of a convention or legally binding declaration, duly executed and ratified by Governments . . . [A] resolution or declaration by the General Assembly was *certainly not law-making* in the sense that a treaty, convention or declaration formally ratified by Governments was.[61]

However, while standing on the same side—so to speak—as his Australian colleague, the United States delegate to the Legal Sub-Committee took a slightly, although not necessarily contradictory line. In his view:

A General Assembly resolution would be the most appropriate instrument for a declaration of general principles. Some delegations had argued that only an international agreement signed by governments would be legally binding. International agreements were not, however, the only sources of law. As stated in Article 38 of the Statute of the International Court of Justice, decisions of international tribunals and the growth of customary law as evidenced by State practice should also be taken into consideration. When a General Assembly resolution proclaimed principles of international law—as resolution 1721 (XVI) had done—and was adopted unanimously, it represented the law as generally accepted in the international community.[62]

In the end, as we have seen, the Soviet Union and its supporters acquiesced in the United States position, and three substantive resolutions were adopted[63] before switching over to the treaty mode. Five treaties were agreed upon between 1966 and 1979[64] before the General Assembly, where the West no longer commands a majority and the Group of 77 more or less holds sway, in 1982 reverted once more to passing resolutions, and doing so on this occasion by majority vote instead of consensus.[65]

---

[59] A/AC.105/C.2/SR.11 (14.6.62), p. 6.   [60] A/AC.105/C.2/SR. 23 (25 4 63), p. 4.
[61] A/AC.105/C.2/SR.23 (25.4.63), p. 4; italics added.
[62] A/AC.105/C.2/SR.20 (22.4.63), pp. 10–11.   [63] See s. II.A above.
[64] See s. II.B above.   [65] See s. II.A.4 above.

V. The Legal Status of General Assembly Resolutions and the Nature of General International Law

A. International Norms in 'Their Infinite Variety'

The late Judge Richard Baxter wrote on 'International Law in Her Infinite Variety'.[66] Indeed, if one were to widen the circle and take into account not only legally binding norms governing the behaviour of States, but also other norms of behaviour, be they political, moral, or social, operating within international society, the variety becomes even more formidable. Therefore, if we are not to be confused in our approach to the subject, it becomes vital that we distinguish the different varieties and do not mix them up.

B. Norms Outside the International Legal System

In the first place, we must recognize that there are many norms operating within international society that do not fall within the international legal system, even when they may be of a juridical nature. Here, let it be recalled that the Permanent Court of International Justice clearly did not endorse Hans Kelsen's monist theory of the relationship between international law and municipal law. In the *German Interests in Polish Upper Silesia Case* (Merits) (1926), the Court stated unequivocally:

From the standpoint of International Law and of the Court which is its organ, municipal laws are merely facts . . .[67]

Rules of municipal law do not form part, therefore, of the international legal system.

In addition, there are also norms of a non-juridical nature which do not form part of the international legal system. I refer here to rules or even agreements of a purely political, social, or moral nature without any implication that their breach would also be a violation of a legal obligation. What store States set by their non-legal commitments is a question the answer to which depends obviously on the country concerned and on circumstances. Sometimes, non-legal commitments can be regarded as less compelling than legal ones. Thus, when the government in South Vietnam was on the point of collapse, in order to assuage the fears of Americans as the consequences of the 'solemn commitments' that the United States had given to that government, the United States Secretary of State Dr Henry Kissinger assured the nation that such commitments as existed were 'not legal, but only moral'.

On other occasions, non-legal commitments may well be treated as even more important than legal ones. This, for instance, may well be the view of

[66] 29 *ICLQ* (1980), p. 549.   [67] A.7, p. 19.

some of the signatories to the Final Act of the Conference on Security and Co-operation in Europe signed by 35 States in Helsinki on 1 August 1975, commonly known as the Helsinki Final Act.[68] One of the Final Clauses of the Final Act makes it quite clear that the Final Act is not a treaty by saying:

The Government of the Republic of Finland is requested to transmit to the Secretary-General of the United Nations the text of this Final Act, *which is not eligible for registration under Article 102 of the Charter of the United Nations*, with a view to its circulation to all the members of the Organization as an official document of the United Nations.[69]

At the same time, the Final Act does not fail to emphasize its own importance as a political commitment in its ultimate paragraph:

Wherefore, the undersigned High Representatives of the participating States, *mindful of the high political significance which they attach to the results of the Conference*, and declaring *their determination to act in accordance with the provisions contained in the above texts*, have subscribed their signatures below: . . .[70]

In many ways, there are parallels between legal commitments and political commitments, especially in the sense that they are all commitments. However, they operate each within its own framework, with mostly different rules on formation, validity, breach, suspension, termination, and sanctions. Social scientists whose interest is in finding out how international society works often see no special significance in legal norms compared with other social norms. For lawyers, however, it is vital that we distinguish legal rules from rules of other social disciplines, even though we should never lose sight of the social context in which our legal rules operate. Failure to distinguish legal rules from norms belonging to cognate disciplines would deprive law of its specificity and in due course destroy it and its special effect altogether. Many newfangled approaches to international law by both political scientists and international lawyers tend in this direction in trying to bring under the umbrella of law all kinds of non-legal factors and forces in society, such as national and international goals, politics, economics, public opinion, pressure groups, and so forth that clearly lack any *opinio juris*, and in often ignoring and even rejecting any distinction between *lex lata* and *lex ferenda*.

C. International Law is Exclusively a Law of International Persons, made by International Persons, for International Persons

The norms we are looking at are those belonging to a legal system, and not norms of a political, moral, or social character. This is a legal system that operates in a society composed exclusively of international persons, i.e., entities endowed with international legal personality. This is in fact a truism in the

---

[68] 14 *ILM* (1975), p. 1292.   [69] Italics added.   [70] Italics added.

sense that international legal personality means the capacity to bear rights and duties under international law. Non-international persons may have benefits and burdens indirectly conferred or imposed on them, but they have no direct legal rights or obligations under international law, inasmuch as they would have no capacity to bear rights and duties under international law.

Confusing the rôle that is actually played or, in the speaker's opinion, that ought to be played in international relations by the entity in question with the technical problem of its legal status in international law, a fairly fashionable fallacy at the moment consists in maintaining that important multinational corporations and/or all individuals ought to be, or already are, international persons. The truth is that present-day international persons are, with at most only one or two exceptions, primarily States, i.e., territorially organized political entities recognized as sovereign and independent (i.e., subject to no other earthly authority), together with a number of inter-State organizations to which international legal personality has been granted.[71] Since membership of these organizations is normally limited to States, the basic unit of international society remains, therefore, the sovereign and independent State.

The law which regulates relations in international society is basically, therefore, one of States, by States, and for States. In particular, it is not derived from any superior temporal authority, since States are by definition sovereign and independent. Nor in a multi-religion, multi-ideological, and multi-cultural society, is it directly derived from any supposedly divine source or is identifiable with some individual system of secular natural law, whatever its contents may be. Instead, as the Permanent Court of International Justice said in the case of *The SS Lotus* (1927), 'Rules of law binding upon States . . . emanate from their own free will . . .'[72]

This is not to say that rules of international law, including international space law, cannot trace their *material* or ultimate source, i.e., inspiration, to some spiritual, humanitarian, altruistic or other wise and laudable origin. But they can equally be inspired by materialistic, selfish, ulterior, or other base motives. Indeed all laws must have been made for one reason or another; for no law is ever made gratuitously for no purpose. Even pure window-dressing can serve very real political ends, and placebos meet genuine needs. The point, however, is that no ideas, however sensible, just, and compelling can by their mere sensibleness, justice, and compelling nature be *ipso facto* considered part of the law. In every society, a rule becomes a legal rule only when it has been received as such by the law-maker. International society is no exception. Inasmuch as it is a society of equals, its law is a horizontal system, in which

[71] See Cheng, 'The Future of General State Practice In a Divided World', in R. St. J. Macdonald and D. M. Johnston (eds.), *The Structure and Process of International Law* (1983), p. 513 (hereinafter cited as 'Custom'), at pp. 516 ff. N.B.: in the book, pp. 545 and 546 have been transposed, and are wrongly paginated.

[72] A.10, p. 18.

the law-makers are themselves the subjects of the legal system.[73] Rules are rules of international law only when they have the acceptance of the generality[74] of the subjects of international law, through consent, recognition, acquiescence, or estoppel. What has to be remembered is, therefore, that international law is a law made exclusively by the subjects of international law. The different procedures whereby subjects of international law make rules of international law, or alternatively the products of these different procedures, are generally known as the *formal* sources of international law, as opposed to its *material* sources.

D. Treaties and General International Law Distinguished

There is a very prevalent fallacy that treaties and general international law are merely two different forms of rules of international law, or two formal sources of international law different only as regards their form, and that ultimately both are agreements, one express the other tacit. It follows from this that, since general international law requires only general, and not unanimous, consent in order to be binding on all subjects of international law, a treaty which is generally accepted by a large number of parties is also universally binding. I have already dealt with this problem at some length in my paper on 'Custom' in Professors Macdonald and Johnston's *The Structure and Process of International Law* (1983), where a fuller account can be found.[75]

It suffices here simply to point out that treaties and general international law are different in their nature, in the process of their formation, and in their legal effect. Treaties are consensual agreements between subjects of international law, designed to produce legally binding effect solely between the contracting parties, conferring neither legal rights nor imposing legal obligations (to be distinguished from benefits and practical adverse effects) on third parties without their consent. *Pacta tertiis nec prosunt nec nocent.* Treaties are sources of *legal obligations* for the contracting parties, and, under the principle *pacta sunt servanda*, which is a general principle of law as well as a rule of general international law, are as legally binding on the parties as a legal rule (*lex inter partes*), but they are *not sources of law*, law in the sense of the body of norms with legally binding effect on *all* subjects of the legal system (*erga omnes*). They are to be distinguished as to their nature and effect from rules of general international law. Thus, none of the five treaties relating to outer space drawn up under the auspices of the United Nations, in their capacity as treaties, affects the legal rights and duties of non-parties.

This point of view, which is sometimes regarded as 'old-fashioned' by self-styled 'progressive' international lawyers, happily now finds confirmation in

---

[73] See Cheng, 'Custom', loc. cit. in n. 7 1 above, at pp. 519 ff.
[74] See further s. V.H.2 below.
[75] See Cheng, 'Custom', loc. cit. in n. 71 above, at pp. 526 ff.

provisions of the 1969 Vienna Convention on the Law of Treaties, many of the provisions of which are considered to be declaratory of general international law. Thus, Article 34 proclaims clearly:

A treaty does not create either obligations or rights for a third State without its consent.

This article is, however, without prejudice to Article 38 which states:

Nothing in articles 34 to 37 precludes a rule set forth in a treaty from becoming binding upon a third State as a customary rule of international law, recognised as such.

This leads us to the nature of customary international law, or what the Permanent Court of International Justice sometimes called, and what the International Court increasingly calls 'general international law'. There is no doubt that a number of the treaty rules relating to outer space have become 'customary' international law, particularly those found in the 1967 Space Treaty, such as the status of outer space and celestial bodies as *res extra commercium* (Article II), jurisdiction of the State of registry (Article VIII), and possibly the principle of international responsibility for national space activities (Article VI), and international liability for damage caused by objects launched into outer space (Article VII). The process of this metamorphosis, which is often not properly understood, will be discussed below.[76]

E. The International Legal System and General International Law Distinguished

It may be appropriate first also to distinguish between on the one hand the international legal system as such and on the other hand general international law meaning the totality of rules within the international legal system that are of general application, i.e., applicable to all subjects of the legal system, in other words, *erga omnes*. The international legal system as such is a wider concept comprising all norms having legal force with the system. Coming within the international legal system would be not only rules of *general* international law, but also *regional* or *sectional* international laws which are particular to specific regions or sections of international society that subscribe to them, as well as treaties which, as we have just seen, are legally binding only on those that have consented to them. It is important to bear in mind this distinction between on the one hand the international legal system as such and on the other hand the more limited body of rules of general application that is increasingly being referred to as *general* international law,[77] even though the situation can often be somewhat unclear because particularly the term international law is sometimes used to refer to the international legal system as a whole and sometimes to only general international law, and the term general

---

[76] See s. V.I below.   [77] See further ss. V.F and V.G below.

international law is used to include both the so-called customary international law and the general principles of law. The accompanying chart seeks to set out the overall position.

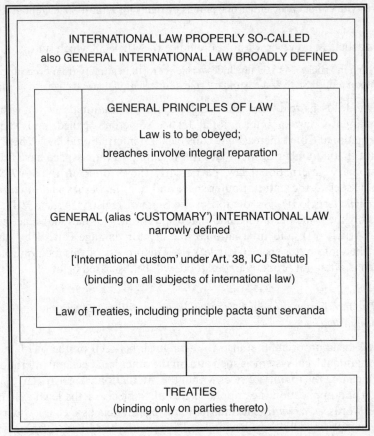

Figure VIII.1. THE INTERNATIONAL LEGAL SYSTEM

F. Nature of General International Law

General international law then consists of those rules of the international legal system that are applicable *erga omnes* to all subjects of international law. I have already also dealt with the topic at some length elsewhere,[78] from where further details can easily be found. It suffices here to point to some of the relevant conclusions.

[78] See Cheng, 'Custom', loc. cit. in n. 71 above, and B. Cheng, 'Nature and Sources of International Law', in B. Cheng (ed.), *International Law* (1982), p. 203.

Remaining within the above definition of what is general international law, the term is nevertheless capable of several slightly different acceptations. In its widest meaning, it extends to the totality of non-treaty rules within the international legal system. It then becomes synonymous with the sum of the unwritten rules of international law, the *lex non scripta*, provided that one is careful in excluding oral treaties from this category of rules of international law[79] or *lex*. In this sense, it would embrace both what the Statute of the International Court of Justice calls in its Article 38(1)(*c*) 'the general principles of law . . .', as well as what it calls in its Article 38(1)(*b*) 'international custom . . .' Quite often, the term general international law is used in this meaning.

However, since the Statute of the Court has recognized that the general principles of law form a special category[80], a great deal of the time, the term general international law is used to designate the remaining category of norms within the international legal system as defined in Article 38, namely, 'international custom'—in other words customary international law. In this sense, the designation general international law is often preferred to customary international law, inasmuch as it is being increasingly realized that much of what is called customary international law is not based on custom at all, to the extent to which custom implies long usage.

There is no doubt that much of international law has evolved through long practice of States which gradually accepted it as behaviour reflecting adherence to a legal rule. As the Permanent Court of Justice put it in the case of *The Lotus* (1927):

The rules of law binding upon States . . . emanate from their own free will as expressed . . . by usages generally accepted as expressing principles of law and established in order to regulate the relations between these co-existing independent communities or with a view to the achievement of common aims.[81]

Article 38(1)(*b*) of the International Court's Statute calls this portion of international law more briefly, though not necessarily very elegantly, 'international custom, as evidence of a general practice accepted as law'. It would probably be more correct to speak of international custom (in the sense of a rule of international customary law), as *evidenced by* a general practice accepted as law.

However put, what is clearly expressed in the Court's judgment and its Statute is that rules of international law can be found in usages or general practice *generally accepted by States as law or as expressing principles of law*. This form of law, which is quite common also in municipal law, is usually known as custom or customary law. In municipal law, custom is applied always subject to the will of the law-making authority, the power that is of the body politic in question, which obviously requires the underlying rule, before

---

[79] See s. V.D above.   [80] See Cheng, *General Principles of Law*.   [81] A.10, p. 18.

it can be applied and enforced, to be well evidenced by clear and consistent usage, both in its own interests and the interests of those to be subjected to such a rule. But, unless one is involved in a non-legal or even non-normative context where usages are observed *per se* as rites or rituals, what is enforced by the legal order is the *rule of conduct underlying or evidenced by the usage, and not the usage as such*. In this sense, when one speaks of customary law, one usually refers to its two constituent elements, the material one, the *corpus*, consisting in the usage or general practice, the *consuetudo*, and the psychological one, the *animus*, consisting in what is known as the *opinio juris* or sometimes called the *opinio juris sive necessitatis*. The latter element, in its municipal law context, which would almost always be a hierarchical legal system with superior legislative, judicial and law-enforcement authorities above the subjects, is usually translated as a sense of legal obligation or a sense of being legally bound. This is natural because in a hierarchical legal system, the customary rule, since it has not been directly made by the law-maker, becomes a rule which has the force of law only when sanctioned and authorized by the law-maker, or recognized as such by the judicial or law-enforcement authorities. It is a rule that is above the subjects, even though they may have been and are instrumental in initiating and preserving it.

The position is, however, different in the international legal system, which is horizontal as opposed to hierarchical, where all the primary subjects are sovereign and equal, with no superior law-making, judicial or law-enforcement authority above them. In assessing the nature of general international law in international society, it is necessary, therefore, not to import municipal law analogies lock, stock, and barrel. In international law, as the Permanent Court of International Justice in the above passage quoted from the judgment in the case of *The Lotus* said, rules of international law emanate from the free will of States. To quote the judgment further, 'rules of law binding upon States' are simply what are 'generally accepted as expressing principles of law'. Unlike custom in municipal law, in the case of general international law, it is this general acceptance by the subjects of the legal system who are at the same time its law-makers which makes the law, which confers on the rule its legal force. There is no need for some hierarchically superior law-making authority or judicial authority to authorize its application or to recognize its applicability as a rule of law. If, therefore, we are to use the municipal construction of custom as consisting in usage and *opinio juris* and apply it to general international law, what must be taken into account is this very important difference which we have just mentioned. *Opinio juris* in the case of general international law is no longer the sense or conviction that the rules in question impose legal obligations, which is a not unusual attitude in face of rules made by a superior authority, but simply, in the words of the Permanent Court, acceptance of the rules as 'expressing principles of law', and not as principles of some cognate social discipline such as politics or

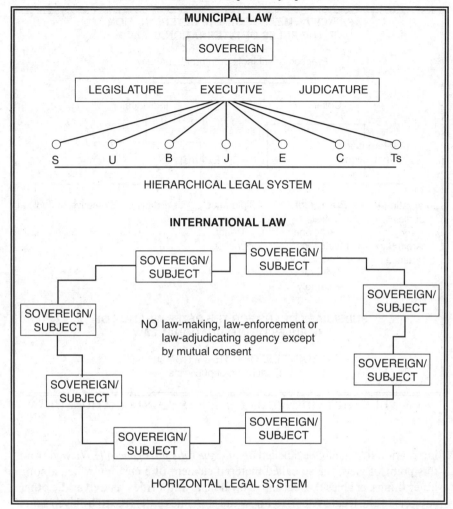

Figure VIII.2. HIERARCHICAL AND HORIZONTAL LEGAL SYSTEMS

morality, or as expressing no consistent principle at all. The legal principle or rule in question can be an authorizing one, conferring a right, just as it can be one of prohibition, imposing a legal obligation.

G. The Essence of General International Law

It follows from what has just been said that the essence of general international law is this acceptance by the generality of States of a given rule as a rule of international law of general application to all subjects of the legal system. This general acceptance of a rule (or rules) as a rule (or rules) of general

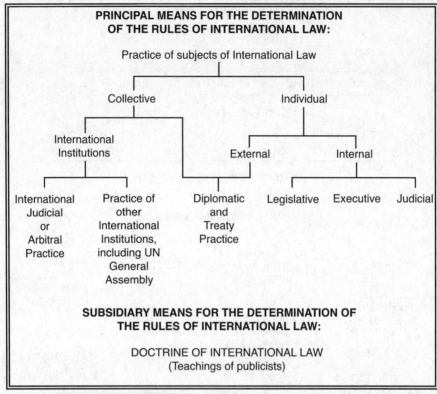

Figure VIII.3. THE EVIDENCE OF THE RULES OF INTERNATIONAL LAW

international law may be labelled *opinio generalis juris generalis*. Viewed from this point of view, the so-called material element of a custom, which among other things, enables the legislative or judicial authorities, as well as the other subjects of the legal system, to know the contents of the rule to be given sanction to, no longer has the same importance in the international legal system; for whatever the generality of States accept as rules of international law will nevertheless be rules of international law, whether their contents be well or less well known. What in municipal law is an indispensable constituent element serves in general international law merely as, in the words of Article 38(1)(*b*) of the International Court's Statute, 'evidence'. The essence of general international law is, therefore, States' *opinio generalis juris generalis*. Usage is merely evidentiary. To say so is not, as some critics of this view have said that I have done, to do away altogether with usage or State practice in the ascertainment of rules of general international law. All that I am, and have been, saying is that *general acceptance* is the essence or quintessence of general international law; usage or general practice is merely a means, and not necessarily the only means, of establishing its existence. Whenever and however we can prove the existence of a general acceptance by States of a rule as a rule of general application in the international legal system, we have a rule of general international law, whether or not there is also usage. In many ways, this was more or less what the United States delegate to COPUOS' Legal Sub-Committee was saying.[82] He also reminded us that after all, Article 38 of the Statute of the International Court of Justice speaks of 'judicial decisions and teachings of the most highly qualified publicists of the various nations, *as subsidiary means for the determination of rules of law.*' This is not to say, however, that usage is not generally speaking the *primary means* for the purpose. The position is set out in the accompanying chart on the evidence of rules of international law.

H. The Formation of Rules of General International Law

Two further points in this connection need to be examined. First, how does this *opinio generalis juris generalis* come about? Secondly, why general acceptance and not unanimous acceptance? When we have answered these two questions, we will also be able to see more clearly the distinction between treaties and rules of general international law as to their legal nature and effect.

1. The Genesis of Opinio Generalis Juris Generalis

(a) *Opinio individualis juris generalis.* In what is basically a very decentralized horizontal legal system, every State, in its dual capacity as simultaneously a subject and a law-maker of the system, having decided to join and remain within the system, has constantly to make up its own attitude towards each rule of international law, and to comport itself accordingly. This is what Judge Guy de Lacharrière, formerly Chief Legal Adviser of the French Ministry of Foreign Affairs for many years, called so aptly in his well-known book of that title, *La politique juridique extérieure*[83] of States, the policy of their external legal relations. The opening sentence of the book succinctly captures the picture:

Les politiques juridiques des différents Etats, en dépit de la diversité ou de la contradiction de leurs contenus, ont en commun la volonté des gouvernements concernés de déterminer leurs conduites en fonction de leurs propres objectifs, c'est-à-dire de leurs intérêts nationaux tels qu'ils les apprécient.[84]

---

[82] A/AC.105/C.2/SR.20 (22.4.63), pp. 10–11, quoted in s. IV above *in fine*, text to n. 62.

[83] (1983).

[84] P. 13. 'The policies of their external legal relations of different States, notwithstanding the diversity and the contradictions in their conents, have in common the will of the governments concerned to shape their conduct in accordance with their own objectives, that is to say with their national interests as they see them' (translation).

This would be the first step in the formulation of a State's own conception of what is to be the content and scope of a given rule of general international law, its own individual *opinio juris generalis*, in other words its *opinio individualis juris generalis*, in respect of that rule. Contrary to what is often maintained by critics of *opinio juris*, it is totally different from motives. When the Soviet Union launched Sputnik I in October 1957 without seeking the permission of the States overflown, either before or after the launch, the inference must be that, according to the Soviet concept of international law, there is no rule against its orbiting its artificial earth satellite round the earth, the motives why the Soviet Union launched Sputnik I being here totally irrelevant. The principle of reciprocity and non-contradiction which is inherent in the nature of a system of rules applicable to all means that this Soviet stance is opposable in law to the Soviet Union—that it can be invoked against the Soviet Union.[85] This Soviet stance which we distil from its conduct is taken to be the Soviet Union's *opinio individualis juris generalis* in the matter. *Opinio individualis* is thus essentially an inference, one which can be drawn from the words as well as the deeds of a State, words or deeds of such a nature that the inference can be invoked in law against that State as its accepted view of the law concerning the matter in question. In the end, of course, it must be the totality of a State's conduct that counts, be it commission or omission, acts or utterances. Where the evidence is not wholly consistent or conclusive, each party would no doubt rely on such evidence that is favourable to its own cause.

(b) *Concurrence of parallel opiniones individuales juris generalis.* An *opinio individualis juris generalis* is only what a State considers the law to be. It does not make a rule of international law as such. It represents the will of only one State. Where the formation of treaties differs from the formation of rules of

---

[85] In order to dispel some misunderstanding to which the notion of opposability (a term borrowed from the French *opposable* and *opposabilité*), it may be explained that it is not an attempt to *apply* the Kantian 'categorical imperative' to international law (cf. A. Carty, *The Decay of International Law* (1986), p. 22). The notions of generality, reciprocity and non-contradiction are inherent in the concept of law. They form some of the working premisses of the law underlying in fact the general principles of law. By virtue of them, anyone within a legal system who accepts a rule as a rule of law also accepts that it is applicable to oneself and to others in general (the very idea of *erga omnes*), unless one considers oneself to be above the law or immune from its application. Consequently and particularly in international law, where States are themselves also the lawmakers, a State's conduct evidencing acceptance of a given rule or a particular acceptation of a given rule becomes opposable to that State. This opposability may well fit in with L. Fuller's 'inner morality of the law' or 'principles of legality' (see his *Morality of Law* (1969)), which may well in turn, in terms of purely legal justice, fit in with Kant's basis of morality. However, what must be remembered is that these principles or premisses are essentially procedural or structural in character governing the working of the legal system, rather than substantive relating to the content of the actual norms of behaviour. In highlighting the element of opposability, one is, therefore, far from saying that all law, perhaps still less international law, implying and including thereby all its substantive rules, finds its philosophical foundation in morality, Kantian or otherwise. After all, it is said that there is honour among thieves, who, if sufficiently numerous and well organized, will obviously have also their own 'law' applicable, with its own 'inner morality', *inter se* and operating outside society's legal system.

general international law is this. Whereas in the formation of treaties, there is a meeting of the wills of the contracting parties to produce an agreement with binding effect in law on themselves. In the formation of general international law, what is required is not a meeting of wills, that is, not an agreement. Instead, all that is needed is a concurrence of individual and unilateral wills running in parallel on the part of the generality of States. In other words, what is required is a concurrence of parallel *opiniones individuales juris generalis* in sufficient numbers to constitute what may be regarded as an *opinio generalis juris generalis*—in other words, a general concurrence on what the law is, not only between or as among themselves (*inter se*), but in respect of all subjects of the international legal system (*erga omnes*). Once such a general concurrence can be said to exist, a new rule of international law has come into existence.

Until then, any novel *opinio individualis juris generalis* has no legal force and, to any extent to which it departs from any existing rule of international law, may be validly treated as illegal by other States. In fact, other States may often find themselves obliged to voice their dissent, especially when their rights and interests are affected, if they are not to be considered as having acquiesced or even concurred in this departure from the existing rule,[86] or otherwise precluded from contesting it as happened to the United Kingdom in the *Anglo-Norwegian Fisheries Case* (1951) in regard to Norway's straight baselines.[87]

2. *General or Universal Acceptance Required?*[88] The question whether a rule of general international law needs the concurrent *opiniones* of all subjects of the international legal system, or only the generality of them was raised during the drafting of the Statute of the Permanent Court of International Justice, when the original proposal for Article 38(1)(b) spoke of 'the *common* practice of nations, accepted by them as law'.[89] Eventually it was decided, in addition to stylistic changes, to substitute '*general* practice' for '*common* practice'. The question came up in the *North Sea Continental Shelf Cases* (1969) before the International Court of Justice. There too, the Court spoke only of the requirement of '*general recognition* that a rule of law or legal obligation is involved,' although the Court did add that the practice denoting such recognition should include 'that of States whose interests are specially affected'.[90]

In reality, in the making of rules of general international law, notwithstanding claims by Soviet writers that, all States being equal, unanimous

---

[86] Compare from this point of view the lack of opposition to the US President Truman's continental shelf Proclamation, 1945, with, for instance, the vigorous protest on the part of the USA against the 1970 Canadian Arctic Waters Pollution Prevention Act (Cheng, 'Custom', loc. cit. in n. 71 above, at pp. 536 ff.).

[87] *ICJ Rep. 1951*, p. 116, at pp. 138–9.

[88] See Cheng, 'Custom', loc. cit. in n. 71 above, at pp. 538–48.

[89] See Baron Descamps's original proposal, in Cheng, *General Principles of Law*, 1. at pp. 11–2.

[90] *ICJ Rep. 1969*, p. 3, at p. 43.

acceptance is required, it is always the will of the dominant section that prevails, like in the making of all laws. In many ways, this is merely stating a truism; for those who are able to make their will prevail in a given situation must be reckoned *pro tanto* to be the dominant or prevailing section within that grouping, and conversely unless that section of society is able to make its legislative will prevail, it would not qualify as the dominant section. Basically, the dominant section consists of those who have the *capability*, the *intention*, and the *determination* of making their will prevail. Whilst, in general, those whose interests are specially affected, should be among those that accept the rule, yet in the end it is one's capability, intention, and will to uphold one's *opinio individualis juris generalis* that count. From this point of view, Soviet writers on international law and other ultra-consensualists protest in vain that, although this may be what happens in practice, this practice is against the principle of equality of States. However, it may be pointed out that the principle of equality of States means only equality before the law. It does not necessarily apply to law-making. Thus in municipal law, the principle of equality before the law has never included universal suffrage as an indispensable element. There is no reason why it should in international law.[91]

The weighing of States in the formation of legal norms in the international legal order is most dramatically demonstrated in the field of space law. Space law accentuated this phenomenon because, at the beginning of space exploration, there were only two States with space capabilities, the Soviet Union and the United States.

In surveying the history of COPUOS, we have already seen that, although the *Ad Hoc* COPUOS was first established in 1958 and made into a permanent Committee the following year, it was only in 1961 that COPUOS began work in earnest. Among the factors which enabled COPUOS to operate were first, as we shall see later,[92] its changed composition and secondly its decision, which we have already mentioned,[93] to proceed by consensus. This in a sense requires the agreement of all its members, or, put another way, the absence of dissent from any of its members. But, as it was stressed by almost all the delegates at the time, the essential point was agreement between the two space powers.

At one stage in the career of COPUOS, at a time when the United States was still commanding an easy majority in the United Nations and its various committees, the United States hinted that the Committee and its sub-committees should revert to the normal majority rule of United Nations organs. The Soviet delegate, even though what he had in mind was no doubt primarily the positive votes of both super powers and not just the vote of the United States, said with candour and a great deal of truth:

---

[91] Cf. s. III.B above.　　[92] See s. VI.C below.　　[93] See s. III.B above.

Twenty-six signatures on this document would have no value; there must be twenty-eight signatures. Even if all of us, including the Soviet Union, the countries of Asia, Africa and Latin America—which are in principle in favour of signing the declaration, sign, if there is no signature of the United States, the whole endeavour would have no result. It is clear that without agreement of the United States it is impossible to resolve such a problem.[94]

The operative part of this statement is the last sentence: 'without agreement of the United States it is impossible to resolve such a problem.' And as it was a question of space law, what was true of the United States was no doubt also true of the Soviet Union. But this certainly would not be true of every member of the then twenty-eight-strong Committee, and still less of every member of the United Nations. In law-making, some States are definitely more equal than others.

In practice, this was clearly shown by the manner in which the various United Nations General Assembly resolutions promoting the development of space law were arrived at. Especially in the early days of space exploration, the substantive provisions of each and every one of the resolutions were based primarily on direct agreement between the two space powers. Thus in the case of the first of these resolutions, namely resolution 1721 (XVI) adopted by the General Assembly on 20 December 1961, although the draft had nominally been submitted by all the members of COPUOS,[95] according to Mr Khrushchev's message of 20 March 1962 to President Kennedy, it really stemmed from an agreement between the two space powers.[96]

As for resolution 1962 (XVIII) adopted by the General Assembly on 13 December 1963, which contained the Declaration of Legal Principles Governing the Activities of States in the Exploration and Use of Outer Space,[97] the precursor of the 1967 Space Treaty, what happened was that when the fourth session of COPUOS opened on 9 September 1963, it was clear that agreement between the two space powers on the basic legal issues in the exploration and use of outer space was imminent. As a result, the Committee held only four meetings and then adjourned, leaving the two space powers to continue their negotiations, assisted and attended upon by a few others. It would appear that after agreement had been reached between the two space powers, the original intention was to bring the text from what the French delegate pointedly called the 'secluded place' where it had been negotiated, straight to the First Committee of the General Assembly, thus bypassing COPUOS. It was subsequently decided, however, that the proposal would 'make a stop' in

---

[94] A/AC.105/PV.15 (14.9.62), p. 18.　　　[95] See ss. II.A.1 and III.C above.

[96] In his message, Mr Khrushchev said: 'I regard as a positive fact that at the XVIth session of the United Nations General Assembly, the Soviet Union and the United States found it possible to agree on the proposal about the initial principles of space legislation, *which was then unanimously approved by all Members of the United Nations*' (A/AC.105/2; italics added). See also Soviet delegate, A/C.1/SR.1214 (11.12.61), p. 268 (para. 12).

[97] See s. II.A.3 above.

COPUOS in order, it would appear, to collect the signatures of all the other members of the Committee. To this end, the Committee met on 22 November 1963 with the understanding seemingly that no amendment would be entertained. At this meeting, the Indian delegate, presumably one of the select few privileged to attend the behind-the-scenes negotiations of the space powers, said:

Many of the points in dispute between the space powers have been cleared up and an agreed paper is now before us.[98]

In the event, the proposal was adopted unanimously first by COPUOS, then by the First Committee and finally by the General Assembly itself without a word being changed or a comma disturbed to become resolution 1962 (XVIII).

What one finds in this case, therefore, is a resolution which purports to state the 'legal principles governing the activities of States in the exploration and use of outer space' being in essence drafted exclusively by agreement between the, then only two, space powers. The other Members of the United Nations and of the world virtually took no part in determining either their content or their formulation. Whilst it is true that at the time, only the two super powers had space capabilities, yet even then many others had the potential of acquiring such capabilities. Moreover, a number of the principles in the resolution were applicable to all States, including those which had no space pretensions whatsoever, such as the principle governing liability for damage caused by objects launched into space. Furthermore, even before the resolution was adopted, the view had already been expressed by some that:

[t]he legal principles contained in [the draft resolution] . . . reflected international law as it was currently accepted by Member States.[99]

If so, this means that rules of general international law intended for general application were being drawn up by agreement exclusively by two States, even though many States may be regarded as being 'specially affected'.

It may be said in this case that what was agreed upon by these two States was nevertheless adopted unanimously by the General Assembly of the United Nations with the result that, whatever may be the effect of General Assembly resolutions in general and this resolution in particular, this resolution did receive the approbation of all the Members of the United Nations. And, probably for this reason, there were States which attached great importance to the fact that this was a resolution that had been adopted unanimously.[100]

---

[98] A/AC.105/PV.24 (22.11.63), p. 21; repeated in substance in Committee in, A/AC.1/SR.1343 (3.12.63), p. 168.

[99] E.g., Canada, A/AC.1/SR.1346 (5.12.63), p. 189.

[100] E.g., USA, A/AC.105/C.2/SR.20 (22 .4.63), pp. 10–11; see further s. V.J.5 below.

However, in the first place, this does not take into account the fact that United Nations membership is still not universal. Switzerland is a notable exception, on which a rule of general international law would no doubt be regarded as binding. Secondly, to reason in this way is to ignore the reality of the situation. Thus one has only to look at the next substantive General Assembly resolution on outer space, namely Resolution 2222 (XXI) adopted on 19 December 1966.[101]

This resolution 'commended' the text of the treaty on outer space drawn up by COPUOS to 'all States' for their signature, ratification and accession. The treaty was based substantially on the Declaration in resolution 1962 (XVIII). Although, this time, there was some more discussion in COPUOS on the text of the draft treaty, which became in due course the 1967 Space Treaty, the crucial issue at all times was whether the provisions were acceptable to the Soviet Union and the United States, and much of the negotiation took place directly between them. Once they were able to reach agreement, then the rest became largely a formality. Agreement was announced on 8 December 1966. A 43-power draft resolution incorporating the agreed text was submitted on 15 December 1966. It came before the First Committee on 17 December, and the Plenary of the General Assembly on 19 December 1966. One can but sympathize with the Tanzanian delegate to the General Assembly when he sounded, as he said he wanted to do, a 'note of discord', in complaining that the General Assembly had been given too little time to consider the draft treaty. 'It is probable,' said he, 'that the completed draft . . . has not yet been seen by many of the Foreign Offices of the delegations represented here.'[102] In this case, he did not wish to stand in the way of the General Assembly which then proceeded to adopt the resolution unanimously. Yet, with due respect to the States concerned, would it have mattered very much had Tanzania and some of the States whose Foreign Offices had not yet had a chance of seeing a complete text of the draft treaty or resolution abstained or even voted against the resolution?

Not really, as long as there was a two-thirds majority for the resolution to be adopted. What was legally relevant in this instance was not the size of the vote. What was to become legally binding was the treaty and not the resolution, and what would make the treaty legally binding were the requisite signatures and ratifications. The treaty requires only five ratifications in order to come into force, but these must include the ratifications by the three depositary governments, namely, the Soviet Union, the United Kingdom, and the United States.[103]

Whilst in principle the treaty will be binding only on those States that are parties to it, there are nevertheless provisions in the treaty which purport to be legal rules of a general nature applicable *erga omnes*, or what the International

---

[101] See s. II.B.1 above.   [102] A/PV.1499 (Prov.) (19.12.66), p. 66.
[103] See s. II.B.1 above.

Court of Justice in the *North Sea Continental Shelf Cases* called provisions of 'a fundamentally norm-creating character such as could be regarded as forming the basis of a general rule of law.'[104] A typical example is Article II of the Space Treaty which provides:

Outer space, including the moon and other celestial bodies, is not subject to national appropriation by claim of sovereignty, by means of use or occupation, or by any other means.

There is much evidence to indicate that many States, parties to the Treaty, believe Article II to be declaratory of general international law. The question then is how does such a provision in a treaty transform itself into a rule of general international with binding effect even on non-parties. As we shall presently see, this metamorphosis of a treaty provision into a rule of general international law is possible. What is required is the emergence of an *opinio generalis juris generalis* in regard to this article among either the contracting States or non-contracting States. As among the contracting States, there would be a switching over on their part from their previous *opinio obligationis conventionalis vis-à-vis* the article to a new *opinio juris generalis*. But what is required to establish an *opinio generalis* in this connection is that there must be among States holding such *opiniones individuales*, not only those 'whose interests are specially affected', as the International Court of Justice said, but also those which have the capability, the intention and the will to uphold Article II as a rule of general international law. In other words, we need not only States which are disposed to observe Article II (whether through favour or fear), but also, above all, States which are able, willing, and determined enough effectively to challenge any breach thereof by others, for example, any dissentient who attempts to appropriate any portion of the moon or outer space. Together they constitute the dominant section in this instance, with the latter forming its hard core. It is in this sense that it is said that rules of general international law are made by the dominant section of international society. It was in a similar context that Professor Brigitte Stern found a new meaning for the expression *opinio juris sive necessitatis*:

L'*opinio juris* traduit ainsi l'idéologie dominante de la société internationale [quoting R. J. Dupuy, 'Coutume sage et coutume sauvage' in *Mélanges Ch. Rousseau* (1974), 80], intégrée par tous, si elle est voulue par certains et subie par d'autres. Et peut-être qu'ainsi l'expression si souvent torturée d'*opinio juris sive necessitatis* prend tout son sens; selon leur situation de pouvoir dans la société internationale, les Etats participeront volontairement à l'élaboration de la coutume internationale, soit en ayant le sentiment de créer du *droit*, soit en ayant le sentiment d'obéir à une *nécessité*, celle-ci résultant précisément de la volonté des premiers.[105]

---

[104] *ICJ Rep. 1969*, p. 3, at p. 42. This is not necessarily to agree with the Court's terminology. Even purely contractual provisions create norms, albeit only *inter partes*.

[105] 'La coutume au coeur du droit international: Quelques réflexions', *Mélanges Reuter* (1981), p. 479, at p. 499: '*Opinio juris* thus reflects the dominant ideology of international society,

In this connection, it is interesting to contrast Article II of the Space Treaty with the more ambitious attempt in the 1979 Moon Treaty to declare the moon and other celestial bodies within the solar system other than the earth, as well as their resources, 'the common heritage of mankind'.[106] Now, both the Space Treaty and the Moon Treaty were drafted, at least nominally, by COPUOS. Both went through the same procedure for adoption by the General Assembly, and each was adopted by the General Assembly by acclamation or consensus without a vote. Both require only five ratifications to come into force. The only apparent difference, from the procedural point of view, is that, unlike the Space Treaty which requires the ratifications of the three depositary States, the Soviet Union, the United Kingdom, and the United States, among the five in order to come to force, the Moon Treaty does not require the ratification of any specific State. Both treaties are now in force. The Moon Treaty came into force on 11 July 1984, having been ratified by then by Austria, Chile, the Netherlands, the Philippines, and Uruguay.

However, without any disrespect to any of these five countries, if it is claimed that since the Moon Treaty is now in force, the moon and other celestial bodies in the solar system other than the earth have thereby been, as a matter of general international law legally, validly and with binding effect *erga omnes*, transformed into the common heritage of mankind, such a claim will hardly be credible.

In contrast, disregarding what effect General Assembly resolution 1721 (XVI) may or may not have in the matter, the moment the Space Treaty, having previously been ratified by a number of other States, came into force on 10 October 1976, when the three depositary States ratified it simultaneously, if it was claimed there and then that Article II of the Space Treaty placing outer space and celestial bodies beyond national appropriation had become also a rule of general international law, such an assertion would in all probability have been sustainable. But it is quite evident that this effect could not have sprung from the mere fact that when the Space Treaty came into force on 10 October 1967, there were 17 parties to it instead of there being only 5 to the Moon Treaty. For to borrow and adapt what the Soviet delegate had said in a slightly different context,[107] in the case of a rule of this nature, its acceptance by the United States and the Soviet Union is of crucial importance. And yet this would certainly not be true of just any or every member of international society.

integrated by everyone, if it is wanted by some and submitted to by others. And maybe it is in this way that the expression *opinio juris sive necessitatis*, which is so often subjected to various torturous interpretations, finds its full meaning: States voluntarily take part in the elaboration of customary international law, either having the feeling that they are actually making the *law*, or having the feeling that they have to bow to *necessity*, a necessity created by the will of the former—everyone according to its own power position in international society' (translation).

[106] See s. II.B.5 above.
[107] See A/AC/PV. 15 (14.9.62), p. 18; quoted in s. V.H.2, text to n. 94 above.

All this points to the conclusion that in the making of rules of general international law, the weight of States certainly is not equal. Unanimity is not required. What is needed is that the preponderant weight of States should be behind a given norm before it can be pronounced a rule of general international law. How the weight of different States is to be calculated varies with the subject matter, the context and the circumstances, if it can be calculated with precision at all; but the important point if we are to understand the process of international law-making is openly to recognize that this difference does exist and may legitimately be taken into account, instead of treating it as heretical or taboo, because it seemingly flies in the face of the principle of sovereign equality. Its recognition will also help us to understand how international law is able to sustain itself in an essentially horizontal and self-governing society: it is supported by the dominant section.

In fact, it may be said that inside the United Nations, the dominant section consists, in each given case, in the majority which can muster sufficient votes to have a motion constitutionally adopted. But the problem of our times is whether and how far this purely numerical 'dominant section' within the United Nations corresponds with the dominant section in the real world outside. Even within the United Nations, it would be well to remember the difference between what is required for the adoption of a resolution in the General Assembly and what is required for the adoption of a decision or recommendation in the Security Council.[108]

I. The Metamorphosis of Treaty Provisions into Rules of General International Law

The formation of treaties being different from the formation of rules of general international law, the question may well be asked how can treaty provisions become rules of general or customary international law as mentioned in Article 38 of the 1969 Vienna Convention on the Law of Treaties. The answer is in fact quite simple, as we have already partially indicated. It all depends on the attitude of States.

In the first place, it may be mentioned that, contrary to a fairly wide misconception, contracting parties to a treaty do not normally regard the treaty provisions to which they have subscribed as rules of general international law applicable even to non-parties. At the same time, they are all, as shown by Article 34 of the Vienna Convention, of the view that they are not bound by treaties to which they are not parties. In short, contracting parties to a treaty entertain *vis-à-vis* its provisions not an *opinio juris generalis*, but only an *opinio obligationis conventionalis*, that is to say, the view that these provisions possess the force of a contractual obligation, but not the force of a rule of law. The dif-

---

[108] Cf. s. III.B above.

ference lies not in the degree of bindingness, which is the same in both cases, but in the personal scope of applicability and the different legal framework for treaties as compared with that for rules of general international law. Treaties are applicable only between the contracting parties; legal rules are applicable to all subjects of the legal system. The former are subject to rules now re-stated in the Vienna Convention on the Law of Treaties. The legal framework for the latter is quite different and much less well stated.

Treaty provisions are transformed into rules of general international law whenever it can be established that there is in regard to any particular treaty provision an *opinio generalis juris generalis*. Normally, this would involve the contracting parties themselves changing their attitude towards the provision in question. But, as we have just seen, in the end what is required is the accep-tance of the rule as one of general international law by the dominant section of society, whether or not contracting parties.

In this regard, before any rash conclusion is drawn that all the five treaties relating to outer space concluded under the auspices of the United Nations, including each and every one of their provisions, have all become rules of gen-eral international law, it may be worthwhile pointing out that all five treaties contain a withdrawal clause permitting the contracting States to withdraw from the treaty, i.e., to denounce it, by written notice. Before any such con-clusion can be drawn, therefore, it is necessary to reflect what would be the purpose of a withdrawal clause if a State that has effectively withdrawn from the treaty in accordance with its withdrawal clause remains bound by its pro-visions on account of their having become rules of general international law. However, there is no doubt that, when the generality of States have, as Article 38 of the Vienna Convention says, 'recognised' the treaty provisions as expres-sions of general international law, then they are binding on third States. Save for the origin of the rules being different, the formation of rules of general international law derived from treaty provisions is the same as that of any other rules of general international law derived from other sources.

J. Instant General (alias 'Customary') International Law and General Assembly Resolutions

1. *Concept Further Explained.*   It follows from what has already been said regarding the horizontal nature of the international legal system, and the effect that this has on the rôle of *opinio juris* in international law as compared with municipal law,[109] that the quintessence of general international law con-sists in an *opinio generalis juris generalis* in international society. This being the case, notwithstanding the fact that the contents of much of this law are to be ascertained from usages in States practice, such usages are not legally

---

[109] See ss. V.F and V.G above.

indispensable to the legal existence or validity of a rule of general international law. An *opinio generalis juris generalis*, the existence of which has been established by any other means, is just as valid as one the existence of which is attested by usage.

Whereas, in days gone by, prolonged practice was required even in the international sphere in order for the configuration of an underlying rule to be delineated, today, modern conditions, including an altogether much faster tempo of international life, continual scientific and technical advances of world impact taking place at unprecedented speed, means of supersonic transport and instant communications, and mass media with global coverage, often present nations simultaneously with problems which require immediate responses, among which legal ones no less than others. Thus the launch by the Soviet Union of Sputnik I on 4 October 1957 gave rise immediately to, amongst others, a host of legal problems which require answers. For instance, when Sputnik I was passing over a State's territory, was it orbiting outside the territorial space of that State or was it in transit through the latter's national airspace? In the latter event, was it doing so as a matter of right, or only permitted to do so on sufferance, or was it trespassing? These were questions which immediately faced the legal adviser of every ministry of foreign affairs. In due course, each State must formulate its own *politique juridique extérieure*, its own *opinio individualis juris generalis*, in the matter. Should there be general concordance among the various *opiniones individuales juris generalis*, an *opinio generalis juris generalis* and a new rule of international law would have grown up. Thus four and a half years later, the Canadian delegate to COP-UOS was already able to say:

Under the concept of outer space now being developed, as long as a spacecraft stays within outer space it is safely proceeding in an area which we might describe as the 'high seas' of the air.[110]

This statement was not very well put, inasmuch as the crux of such a problem is whether the area in which the spacecraft finds itself is or is not outer space, but what the Canadian delegate obviously meant was that, under international law as it had by then developed, all satellites that remained in orbit were considered as beyond national airspace and to be in outer space, thus outside the territorial jurisdiction of the subjacent State. What clearly emerges is that in the formation of rules of general international law, the time factor is not of crucial importance.[111]

It was in this meaning that in 1965 I first used the expression 'instant customary international law' and asked the question whether United Nations resolutions on outer space were examples of it in an article entitled 'United

---

[110] A/AC.105/PV.4 (21.3.63), p. 26.
[111] Cf. ICJ, *North Sea Continental Shelf Cases*, *ICJ Rep. 1979*, pp. 42–3; Dissenting Opinion of Judge Tanaka, p. 177; Dissenting Opinion of Judge Lachs, p. 230.

Nations Resolutions on Outer Space: "Instant" International Customary Law?' and published in Volume 5 of the *Indian Journal of International Law* (1965), pp. 23–48.

There are many who welcome the concept, including the late Professor (later Judge) Richard Baxter who thought the expression 'felicitous', but there are also quite a few who are sceptical.

2. *Those Who Refute an Idea by Simply Giving it a Bad Name.* Thus one or two summarily dismiss the notion of instant customary international law without any further reasoning, leaving one to wonder if they have actually read the article, apart from having seen the title, sometimes perhaps not even the title as a whole, including the question mark. The most obvious are those who pedantically or naïvely take the oxymoron expression ' "instant" custom' absolutely literally, *au pied de la lettre*, in utter grammatolatry, and thereupon reject the *concept itself* offhandedly as being self-contradictory, and therefore not worthy of consideration, thus betraying not merely intellectual arrogance, but also total ignorance of the fact that for some time now, as Judge Jennings has said: '. . . most of what we [including, he might have added, Article 38(1)(*b*) of the Statute of the International Court of Justice] perversely persist in calling customary international law is not only *not* customary law: it does not even faintly resemble a customary law.'[112] Some do so by linking it to General Assembly resolutions adopted after the developing countries have gained ascendancy in the General Assembly by their superior number, and pooh-poohed it, without further ado, as merely a device invented by the developing countries to give legally binding force to such resolutions. In the first place, those writers in the industrialized West who now assume such a dismissive attitude towards General Assembly resolutions appear to be blissfully ignorant or oblivious of the numerous pronouncements by governments and writers in the West extolling the virtue of General Assembly resolutions as a means of actually bringing about new rules of international law relating to outer space, at a time when the United States commanded a comfortable two-thirds majority in the Assembly.

Thus in discussions in the Legal Sub-Committee of COPUOS which led eventually to General Assembly resolution 1962, the United States delegate said:

A General Assembly resolution would be the most appropriate instrument for a declaration of general principles. Some delegations have argued that only an international agreement signed by governments would be legally binding. International agreements were not, however, the only sources of law. As stated in Article 38 of the Statute of the

---

[112] R. Y. Jennings, 'The Identification of International Law', in B. Cheng (ed.), *International Law*, p. 3, at p. 5. See also R. R. Baxter, 'Treaties and Custom', 129 Hague *Recueil* (1970–1), pp. 25–106. The reference to ' "instant" customary international law' as 'this felicitous expression' is in n. 46 on p. 69.

International Court of Justice, decisions of international tribunals and the growth of customary law as evidenced by State practice should also be taken into consideration. When a General Assembly resolution proclaimed principles of international law—as resolution 1721 (XVI) had done—and was adopted unanimously, it represented the law as generally accepted in the international community.[113]

What else is this but a pronouncement, the expression of an *opinio juris,* that General Assembly resolutions make instant customary law? But of course this was in the halcyon days when the United States and friends commanded a clear majority in the General Assembly. The period went right back to the founding of the United Nations, a high water mark of which was the adoption of the United States' Acheson Plan (named after the United States Secretary of State Dean Acheson) to extend some of the functions, and hopefully also some of the powers, of the Security Council in the maintenance of international peace and security to the General Assembly through the Uniting for Peace Resolution. Many international legal writers in the West are still ritualistically singing its praise, however useless it may have proved to be.[114]

The tables have, however, now been turned, and some writers in the West are beginning to swing the pendulum to the other extreme, blindly knocking aside any possible differences of opinion as machinations of the Third World. The irony of course is that the gravamen of my article on 'instant' customary international law was to show that many of the claims made for the legally binding effect of General Assembly resolutions by the United States in particular and others as well were unwarranted and that, whilst 'instant' international law rules were possible, General Assembly resolutions in general and the two General Assembly resolutions on outer space examined in particular did not as such bring forth instant international law. Meanwhile, with the passage in 1982 of General Assembly resolution 37/92 on Direct Broadcasting by Satellites by a majority vote,[115] the United States cannot but deplore this departure from the consensus rule which at one time it opposed,[116] and find cause to regret some of its earlier pronouncements on the value of General Assembly resolutions. This may perhaps be an object-lesson in the possible boomerang effect of so-called 'dynamic' interpretations of the law, whether by States or by writers.

3. *Those Who Flog the Wrong Horse.*   A second group of sceptics of instant customary international law may or may not have read the article in question; for they too appear to ignore what the term stands for. However, unlike the first group who appear merely interested in giving a dog a bad name in order

---

[113] A/AC.105/C.2/SR.20 (22.4.63), pp. 10–11; see also O. Schachter in M. Cohen (ed.), *Law and Politics in Space* (1964), p. 96, at p. 99.

[114] See B. Cheng, 'International Law in the United Nations', 8 *YBWA* (1954), p. 170, at pp. 180–2.

[115] See section II.A.4 above.   [116] Cf section III.B above.

to get it hanged—in this case by glibly and blindly attributing false motives to the concept, the second group do adduce legal reasoning and arguments in an attempt to throw doubt on the notion. Unfortunately, some, not unlike those in the first category, seem either not to have read the article beyond the title, or, having read it, to have grossly misunderstood it; for they too assume, like the first group, that the thesis of the article was to assert that General Assembly resolutions are automatically instant customary international law. However, unlike the first group, they do then go on to explain at length why General Assembly resolutions, except in organizational and budgetary matters, are merely recommendations and are not legally binding, seemingly in refutation of imaginary arguments of mine which in reality I have never made! From this point of view, it is to be regretted that they have not had an opportunity of reading the article, or, having read it, they have failed to understand it, because, as the saying goes, they are flogging a dead horse—and the wrong one at that; for the very purpose of the article was to combat the euphoria generated by initial resolutions on outer space adopted by the United Nations, and to set out what was considered to be the precise legal position of especially General Assembly resolutions 1721A and 1962.[117]

4. *Original Conclusions Recalled.*   Although the above article, having been reproduced *in toto* as an Appendix to *International Law: Teaching and Practice* (1982), should now be more accessible, it may nevertheless be worthwhile repeating hereunder a few of its conclusions:

6. There is no reason why a new *opinio juris* may not grow overnight between States so that a new rule of international customary law (or unwritten international law) comes into existence instantly. This shows that international law is a living law, and explains how changes take place.

7. Except in constitutional matters relating to the administration and finances of the Organization, resolutions of the United Nations General Assembly are merely recommendatory.

8. Provided that the intention is expressed articulately and without ambiguity, there appears to be no reason why an Assembly resolution may not be used as a means of identifying the existence and contents of a new *opinio juris*.

9. Such a law-finding resolution is itself still without binding force, but provides strong evidence of the existence and contents of the rule of law it states, and Member States voting for it may even be estopped from denying what it avers.

10. The wording of General Assembly resolution 1721A and 1962 falls short, however, of that required for law-finding resolutions.

11. Some Members clearly stated their view that resolutions 1721A and 1962 were merely recommendatory.

---

[117] See ss. II.A.1 and 2 above, and Cheng, 'United Nations Resolutions on Outer Space', loc. cit. in n. 3 above [Ch. 7 above].

12. Some Members made statements supporting both resolutions, but these statements do not necessarily mean that those which made them are thereby legally bound by these resolutions.

13. A number of Member States stated that they would respect or observe the principles contained in these resolutions, but some at least among them made it clear that they were not thereby legally bound by them.

14. A few said they 'undertook' to respect these principles. To what extent their position differs from those referred to under 13 above is uncertain.

15. Two or three States considered these principles as declaratory of existing international law. It would appear that these States might be regarded as estopped from denying this status to these principles if they were invoked against them; but it may be wondered whether such a rule of particular international customary law would not operate only among States which share the same *opinio juris* or at most only among States which consider themselves bound by this rule for one reason or another.

16. The general conclusion would therefore be that resolutions 1721A and 1962 are not legally binding on any Member State of the United Nations *qua* Assembly resolutions. The principles they enunciate are for the most part only optional, and in themselves non-binding, principles and standards. A few States *might*, however, be considered legally bound by these optional principles either because of their unilateral undertakings to be so bound or because of their acceptance of these principles as rules of existing international law. But even assuming that they are so bound, the extent to which they are bound both *ratione personae* (as among which States?) and *ratione temporis* (whether and how they may release themselves from the obligations assumed?[118]) remains an open question.[119]

As the above quoted conclusions clearly show, the question of 'instant' customary (or unwritten or general) international law (Conclusion 6) could not be more distinctly separated from the legal effects of General Assembly resolutions, and as regards the latter, the position could hardly have be put with less ambiguity.

5. *Effects of General Assembly Resolutions and the Importance of the Wording and of the Voting Pattern.*   However, one should always beware of falling into doctrinal dogmatism. United Nations' General Assembly resolutions on outer space should alert us to at least the *possibility* of rules of general international law being brought instantly to life through General Assembly reso-

---

[118] Original n. 109 [Ch. 7 above, n. 110]: 'Cf. O. Schachter who believes resolutions such as resolution 1721A to be an expression of "law", and, in extolling their superiority over treaties for certain purposes, said: "Moreover, the declarations do not appear to imply the degree of permanent commitment characteristic of treaties; declarations can be changed by a later Assembly and, consequently, they have a suppleness which may be highly desirable in areas of rapid changes" ('The Prospects for a Regime in Outer Space and International Organization', in M. Cohen (ed.), *Law and Politics in Space* (1964), p. 95, at p. 99).'

[119] B. Cheng, 'United Nations Resolutions on Outer Space: "Instant" International Customary Law?', 5 *Indian JIL* (1985), p. 23, at pp. 46–7; reprinted in Cheng (ed.), *International Law (1982)*, p. 237, at pp. 260–1 [Ch. 7 above, s. XI].

lutions, particularly unanimous resolutions, even though in the concrete cases in question, these resolutions did not quite succeed in doing so.

Thus without prejudice to the question whether he was right or not in regard to resolution 1721A, the rest of what he said was no more than a truism when the United States delegate to COPUOS' Legal Sub-Committee said:

When a General Assembly *proclaimed principles of international law*—as resolution 1721 (XVI) had done—and was adopted unanimously, it represented the law as generally accepted in the international community.[120]

This statement cannot but be a truism insofar as the General Assembly is actually 'proclaiming principles of international law'. Can this be denied?

The true position was well put by the Italian delegate earlier on in the same discussion, insofar as he was referring to what he considered to be a declaration of legally binding principles enunciated through a General Assembly resolution:

His delegation did not . . . feel that the binding force of the principles would be determined by the mere fact that they were enunciated in the form of a General Assembly resolution. *In international law, rules were binding primarily because States considered themselves bound by such rules, whatever their origin.* From that view point, recommendations of the General Assembly undoubtedly had binding force. In any case, recommendations of the General Assembly *had the function of identifying, and even of eliciting participation in the formation of, the rules* exacted by the awareness of the international community to certain basic needs—an awareness which was the primary and fundamental source of international law.'[121]

Rules of international law are binding because States considered themselves bound by them. The fact that they have been identified and enunciated by a General Assembly resolution cannot undermine their binding force. However, what is required is that the resolution must so identify whatever it is enunciating. Current discussions of the legal effects of General Assembly resolutions tend to treat their wording and content as all falling under one single category, when in fact this is far from the truth.

Thus in General Assembly resolution 96 (I) of 11 December 1946, adopted unanimously, the resolution reads:

The General Assembly . . . affirms that genocide is a crime under international law.[122]

In such a case—what I call, on account of its very clear-cut wording, a law-finding resolution—in the absence of evidence to the contrary, the General Assembly resolution can be regarded as sufficient evidence of an *opinio communis juris generalis*, a common *opinio juris* of all Members of the United

---

[120] A/AC.105/C.2/SR.20 (22.4.63), pp. 10–11; italics added.
[121] Ibid., p. 7; italics added.
[122] A/64/Add.1, p. 188; *UNYB* (1946–7), p. 254

Nations, that genocide is a crime under international law—whatever 'a crime under international law' may mean, but that is a different story.

The reason why it was said that in reality resolutions 1721A and 1962 fell short of law-finding resolutions was based on their purely recommendatory wordings.

No reference was made of resolution 1884 (XVIII) of 17 October 1963,[123] because there the wording is purely hortative. In it, it will be recalled, the General Assembly,

1. *Welcomes* the expressions by the Union of Soviet Socialist Republics and the United States of American of their intention not to station in outer space any objects carrying nuclear weapons or other kinds of weapons of mass destruction;
2. *Solemnly calls upon* all States:
   a. To refrain from placing in orbit around the earth any objects carrying nuclear weapons or any other kinds of weapons of mass destruction, installing such weapons on celestial bodies, or stationing such weapons in outer space in any other manner;
   b. To refrain from causing, encouraging or in any way participating in the conduct of the foregoing activities.

It is clear from the wording of the resolution itself that, at the time, neither the Soviet Union nor the United States was under a legal duty to refrain from the acts in question. They had merely announced their intention to do so. The resolution could hardly do more than to recommend solemnly that all States do likewise.

Insofar as resolution 1721 is concerned,[124] in its relevant part it says:

The General Assembly, . . . 1. *Commends* to States for their guidance in the exploration and use of outer space the following principles: . . . .

The words 'commends' and 'for their guidance' can hardly be construed as indicating an intention on the part of the States concerned of acknowledging that the principles, which are here stated as being merely 'for . . . guidance', are actually binding in law.

The title and the introductory part of resolution 1962 (XVIII)[125] are couched in a somewhat stronger language as follows:

Declaration of Legal Principles Governing the Activities of States in the Exploration and Use of Outer Space

The General Assembly,

    . . . .

Solemnly declares that in the exploration and use of outer space States should be guided by the following principles:

---

[123] See s. II.A.2. above [App. II.2 below].   [124] See s. II.A.1 above [App. II.1 below].
[125] See s. II.A.3 above [App. II.3 below].

. . . .

Although the title of the resolution claims the principles to be 'legal princi-ples', the wording of the introductory part nevertheless studiously avoids any pretension that they are legal principles which are already in force and legally binding; for it does not say that States 'shall be bound' by the following prin-ciples, only that they 'should be guided'. Consequently, on account of their wording, as Conclusion 10 has clearly stated, neither resolution 1721A nor resolution 1962 can be treated as law-finding. They cannot be said to be stat-ing binding rules of international law. Nor can they acquire greater binding force solely by reason of repetition, no matter how many times. As Professor Iain MacGibbon pointed out, 'however many times nothing was multiplied by, the result was still nothing.'[126]

However, the phraseology of resolution 1962, in the context in which it was formulated, namely, with an understanding clearly stated in COPUOS at the time that in due course the principles would be incorporated in a binding treaty, very much suggests that the Declaration stated principles that were intended by those approving them to become one day rules of general inter-national law. In this case, the resolution could be regarded as a statement of what Members of the United Nations considered to be not so much principles *de lege lata* (the law as it is) but principles *de lege ferenda* (the law as one would wish it to be).

Two points may be raised in this connection. First, these General Assembly resolutions served a useful purpose as representing an intermediary stage in the development of international space law by outlining preliminary agree-ment on the principles to be translated later into binding rules of international law, with the possibility for those States which wish to, actually to treat the principles elaborated as existing rules of international law in their own *opin-iones individuales juris generalis* which would further assist the formation of an *opinio generalis juris generalis* in the matter in due course.

Secondly, in assessing the significance of a given resolution, which is not unlike the assessment of any other piece of collective State practice as evidence of a general *opinio juris*, one has to take a number of factors into account. Apart from the definitiveness of the language used, there is the pattern of vot-ing. Mention has already been made of the fact that in principle COPUOS operates by consensus,[127] which enables the major powers to exercise more easily their due influence on the work of the Committee. However, the ordi-nary rule on voting in the United Nations is by a simple or qualified majority. Under Article 18 of the Charter, important questions in the General Assembly are decided by a two-thirds majority. In this connection, it may be of interest

---

[126] 'Means for the Identification of International Law', in B. Cheng (ed.), *International Law* (1982), p. 10, at p. 17.
[127] See s. III.B above.

to mention that it has been calculated that, as a result particularly of recent increases in membership in the United Nations, a two-thirds majority in the General Assembly can be made up of States which altogether represent *in toto* little more than 10 per cent of the world population, 4 per cent of the world's gross national product, and 3.5 per cent of the United Nations budget contributions. It is obvious that, at one end of the spectrum, a resolution adopted by such a majority would carry the minimum of weight in terms of political recommendation or probative force as evidence of either *lex lata* or *lex ferenda*, whilst, at the other end of the spectrum, a resolution carried unanimously would count much more in whatever message it is carrying. From this point of view, it is hardly surprising that much was made of the fact that the first three General Assembly resolutions relating to outer space were adopted unanimously.

Thus as it was said by the United Kingdom delegate to COPUOS' Legal-Sub-Committee:

Although as stated by the USSR delegation, resolutions of the General Assembly were not—save in the exceptional cases provided for in the Charter—binding upon Member States—a resolution, *if adopted unanimously*, would be most authoritative.'[128]

It may be noted that the United Kingdom delegate did not say that the resolution would be legally binding, but he accepted that it would be 'most authoritative'. In other words, it would be most authoritative for whatever message it is carrying: a *voeu*, as Assembly resolutions were said to express under the League of Nations Covenant, a recommendation, a political commitment, an expression of *opinio juris de lege ferenda* or even a statement of an *opinio juris de lege lata*.

Even the Soviet Union, which at the time in question was far from being enamoured of General Assembly resolutions, accepted that special significance might attach to unanimity. Thus when the draft declaration of principles was presented to the First Committee, the Soviet delegate appeared to have made an unanimous acceptance of the draft resolution by the General Assembly a condition of the Soviet undertaking to respect the principles it contained:

The Soviet Union . . . undertook also to respect the principles enunciated in the draft declaration if it were unanimously adopted.'[129]

It may be interesting to compare this statement with Professor G. Tunkin's doctrine of what he calls 'interconditionality' in what I would label a State's *opinio individualis juris generalis* in the process of the formation of rules of general international law. Expressing what may be regarded as the current orthodox Soviet view on the subject, Professor Tunkin says:

[128] A/AC.105/C.2/SR.17 (17.4.63), p. 9; and ibid./SR.24 (29.4.63), p. 13.
[129] A/C.1/SR.1342 (2.12.63), p. 161.

The concordance of the wills of states includes the *interconditionality of wills*, reflected in the fact that the consent of a state to recognize a particular norm as a norm of international law is given on condition of analogous consent by another or other states.[130]

In other words, in Soviet legal thinking, all *opiniones individuales juris generalis* are conditional, that is, conditional on acceptance of the rule in question by 'another or other States'. The import of the flexibility in the number of other States involved is not very clear, but presumably this flexibility caters for rules involving, in practice, only a limited number of States or even only one other State. Be that as it may, this concept would seem to turn all *opiniones individuales juris generalis* into conditional ones, in other words, *opiniones conditionales juris generalis*, conditioned on the rule being accepted by all other States or specific States. It may, however, be wondered whether, as a general proposition, this is true. For instance, the respective *opinio individualis juris generalis* that can be inferred, with opposability *vis-à-vis* the States concerned, from President Truman's proclamation of United States claims to its adjacent continental shelves in 1945, or Canada's enactment of its Arctic Waters Pollution Prevention Act in 1970 can hardly be regarded as conditional in any way on acceptance of the same rule by any other State.[131]

However, although ordinary *opinio juris* is not normally conditional—or may even not be allowed by general international law to be conditional—in the case of General Assembly resolutions, such a reservation, tacit or express, in any preparedness to accept the resolution is doubtless permissible and may well be present in the minds of many States when they vote in favour of a resolution. While basically such a resolution, except in the instances provided for in the Charter, is only recommendatory, and States are in law not bound by it, they may nevertheless if they so wish, be prepared to attach great weight to it if it were unanimously adopted, whether as a recommendation, a political commitment, a presentation of the law as they would like to see established or a statement of the law as they think it already is. Since such additional weight as a State may wish to lend to it is purely voluntary, the State is, therefore, free at the same time to attach any condition it likes.

The position can be quite different in the case of resolutions adopted by a majority vote, for instance, resolution 37/92 on Principles Governing the Use by States of Artificial Earth Satellites for International Direct Broadcasting adopted by the General Assembly on 10 December 1982 by 107 votes for, 13 votes against, and 13 abstentions.[132] It is interesting first to compare the wording of the relevant parts of this resolution with those of resolutions 1721 and 1962. In this case, the General Assembly:

---

[130] *Theory of International Law* (1974), p. 216. Italics added.
[131] See further Cheng, 'Nature and Sources of International Law', *loc. cit.* in n. 78 above, at pp. 223 ff.
[132] See s. II.A.4 above.

Taking into consideration that the operation of international direct broadcasting satellites will have significant international political, economic, social and cultural implications,

Believing that the establishment of principles for international direct television broadcasting will contribute to the strengthening of international co-operation in this field and further the purpose and principles of the Charter of the United Nations,

Adopts the Principles Governing the Use by States of Artificial Earth Satellites for International Direct Television Broadcasting set forth in the annex to the present resolution.

Unlike resolution 1961, there is no claim that these principles represent legal principles either *de lege lata* or even *de lege ferenda*. In this connection, it is significant that among the implications of the operation of international direct broadcasting satellites which were being taken into consideration in the adoption of the principles, its legal implications were conspicuously absent. Finally, the Principles were 'adopted', but there was no commendation or recommendation. The only ground stated in the resolution which lends any authority to the resolution is the 'belief' of the General Assembly that the 'establishment' of these principles will 'further the purposes and principles of the Charter of the United Nations'. Presumably by implication, the General Assembly also believed that their observance would also have the same effect. But it does not appear that one can thereby argue that the principles constitute an authoritative gloss on, or interpretation of, Articles 1 and 2 of the Charter on the purposes and principles of the United Nations as applied to this matter, or that non-observance of the principles would therefore be contrary to the purposes and principles of the United Nations. Nevertheless, these principles remain a General Assembly resolution and express what the General Assembly believes to be conducive to advancing the purposes and principles of the United Nations Charter. Notwithstanding any express recommendation, it presumably represents a recommendation of the Assembly, one which is not legally binding, but carries with it such political force as General Assembly resolutions are supposed to have. To the extent to which voting in the General Assembly represents State practice, it would appear that insofar as States voting for the resolution are concerned, this collective action is an additional factor which renders the resolution, not legally, but politically, that little bit more compelling. Speaking again not of its legal but only its political force, probably even those States that abstained or even voted against a resolution should pay some heed to it, once constitutionally adopted. In this connection, one should beware of the extremism of those who at the moment, because of their dislike or distrust of many of the resolutions adopted by the General Assembly, instead of analysing the problem dispassionately, tend to rubbish all resolutions of international institutions and disparage any suggestion which might conceivably weaken the assault. Such attacks can of course fall into exactly the same pitfall as some of the exaggerated claims made by the

United States and some American and other writers for General Assembly resolutions in the immediate post-war period. With resolution 37/92 for instance, these claims have now come home to roost. The whole episode is an object-lesson in the perils of engaging in tortuous legal gymnastics to gain immediate objectives, which often turn out to be of only short-term benefit, while causing long-term embarrassment. This type of exercise is often much favoured by self-styled 'dynamic' legal advisers who pride themselves in being always able, without any difficulty or qualms, to produce 'a solution to every problem,' unlike their 'timid' colleagues who see 'problems in every solution'. Some of them appear to be quite oblivious of the danger that a State's, like an individual's, credibility can be damaged by indulging too often in spurious legal contortions just as much as by the what might be regarded as the corresponding practice of distorting facts in order to get itself out of a tight corner seemingly preferred by the Soviet Union on occasions.[133]

Be that as it may, what is to be said later regarding the need for due representation to law-making no doubt applies also to political recommendations. Thus the very weak wording in the resolution itself, as well as the opposition of a large of number of States in the field in question to its adoption, hardly ensures that resolution 37/92 on international direct television broadcasting by artificial satellites will command close compliance. As the Japanese delegate to the United Nations Special Political Committee is recorded as having said at the time of the debate:

It was doubtful whether the resolution would be meaningful if it was adopted over the objections of certain countries.[134]

6. *Terminological Objections.*   Coming back to the problem of 'instant' general (*alias* customary) international law, certain objections are purely terminological. For example, it has been said that, 'instant' international *lex non scripta* (unwritten rules of international law) *si*, 'instant' customary international law *non*. But in Conclusion No. 6 in the article published in the *Indian Journal of International Law*[135], I already made it clear that from this point of view 'international customary law' and 'unwritten international law' were, in this regard, to be treated as synonymous. The reason why the term 'customary international law' was used instead of 'unwritten rules of international law' was simply because the former is the traditionally accepted definition of the portion of international law in question, as recognized, for instance, in Article 38(1)(*b*) of the Statute of the International Court of Justice, where the latter receives no mention at all. In any event, the substance of the matter is

---

[133] Cf., e.g., B. Cheng, 'The United Nations and Outer Space', 14 *CLP* (1961), p. 247, at pp. 268–72 on the RB–47 incident in 1960 [Ch. 6 above, s. V.B], and B. Cheng, 'The Destruction of KAL Flight KE007, and Article 3*bis* of the Chicago Convention', in J. W. E. Storm van 's Gravesande and A. van der Veen Vonk (eds.), *Air Worthy: Liber Amicorum honouring Professor Dr I.H. Ph. Diederiks-Verschoor* (1985), p. 59, esp. p. 54.

[134] A/SPC/37/SR.34 (22.11.82), p. 13.   [135] See s. V.J. 4 above.

whether international law rules can be created instantaneously; it does not advance the discussion by some fetishistic terminological diversion.

Along the same terminological path, yet others have pointed out that unwritten international law is not synonymous with 'customary' international law, inasmuch as there are unwritten treaties and general principles of law. In the first place, following what we have already made clear, treaties are not rules of international law.[136] Secondly, as regards general principles of law, the problem is far from being confined to 'unwritten international law'; for from both the practical and the theoretical points of view, 'customary international law' used in its broad sense has often also been considered as comprising the general principles of law. As long ago as 1953, I wrote:

> international custom or customary international law, understood in a broad sense, may include all that is unwritten in international law, i.e., both custom and general principles of law.[137]

In any event, even accepting that the term 'unwritten international law' might include unwritten treaties and general principles of law, as well as what now often goes under the name 'customary international law', that hardly is an objection to instant unwritten rules of international law; for one can certainly have instant treaties. Instant general principles of law also cannot be excluded. All this merely goes to show that much of the scepticism of, and stand-offishness *vis-à-vis*, the concept of instant general international law is not one of substance, but is simply a symptom of inherent conservatism in legal thinking reinforced in this instance by traditions inherited from municipal law, perhaps coupled with, in some instances, some facile suspicion that it is some 'third-world' device designed to attribute legally binding effect to General Assembly resolutions or to lend respectability to 'revolutionary' State practices not in conformity with traditional international law, such as the initial claims of some Latin-American States to an Exclusive Economic Zone (EEZ).

On the specific question of terminology, I wrote in 1982:

> As the words between brackets in my Conclusion 6 quoted above show, I was of course not unconscious of the 'inherent (verbal) contradiction' in such a phrase as 'instant custom.' The problem is that there is not a suitable name that is readily available. *General* international law is a possibility and the International Court of Justice has increasingly been using this term, but like *unwritten* international law, it comprises both general principles of law and what Article 38(1)(*b*) of the Statute of the International Court calls 'international custom.' My only justification for using such a phrase as 'instant customary law' is simply because this particular part of international law has been traditionally so denominated with the result that its meaning can be as easily recognised as, for instance, other inherently contradictory phrases such as 'maritime territory,' and 'the continental shelf beyond the continental margin.'

---

[136] See s. V.D above.   [137] Cheng, op. cit. in n. 80 above, p. 23.

This is not to say, however, that this description is satisfactory. Professor Jennings is absolutely right, therefore, when he says: 'The time has surely come to recognise boldly that it is not custom at all, and never was.'[138]

At the least, increasingly most of that part of international law which Article 38(1)(*b*) of the Court's Statute intends to cover is no longer based on 'custom'. Alternatively, it is possible to say that, in fact, the whole of this part of international law is constantly evolving, changing, and growing according to a living *opinio generalis juris generalis*, tuned to the ever changing needs of international society. Nowhere has this been so dramatically demonstrated as in the development of international space law.

VI. Conditions Governing International Rule-Making

The development of international space law in such a short time provides also a clear lesson on the conditions governing the successful conclusion of multilateral treaties, especially those aspiring to become in due course rules of general international law. In sum, three factors emerge as of prime importance, namely:

(i)   there must a felt need for the new rules;
(ii)   there has to be a propitious political climate;
(iii)   there has to be due representation of the interests involved.

A. Perceived Needs

First, a felt need. A telling example is the conclusion of the 1967 Space Treaty.[139] The Soviet Union proposed in 1962 that there should be a treaty on space law. The United States at first agreed only to have a General Assembly resolution. This resulted eventually in General Assembly resolution 1962 (XVIII) of 1963, setting out legal principles governing the activities of States in the exploration and use of outer space. The same resolution requested COPUOS to give consideration to 'incorporating in international agreement form, in the future as appropriate,' those legal principles. Negotiations towards a treaty went on desultorily for several years. As late as October 1965, the United States was still against a general treaty on space.[140]

Yet less than a year later, in September 1966, the United States considered that the need for such a treaty was 'all the more urgent because of man's recent strides towards landing on the moon'.[141] The most notable 'stride' early in

---

[138] Cheng, 'Nature and Sources of International Law', loc. cit. in n. 78 above, at p. 223. The reference to Professor R. Y. Jenning's remark is from his contribution on 'The Identification of International Law', in B. Cheng (ed.), *International Law* (1982), p. 3, at p. 6.

[139] See s. II.B.1 above.   [140] A/AC.105/PV.37–42, p. 32 (5.10.65).

[141] A/PV.1412 (Prov.) (22.9.66), p. 41. See also s. II.B.1 above.

1966 was the first ever 'soft' landing on the moon achieved on 3 February by the Soviet Union with its automatic station Luna IX. Success came after three failures in 1965. The Soviet Union scored another first on 31 March, with the launching of Luna X, which became the moon's first artificial satellite. The United States followed on 2 June 1966 with Surveyor I, which transmitted back to earth over 10,000 photographs of the surface of the moon, and Lunar Orbiter I, launched on 10 August. The Soviet Union launched Luna XI, another lunar satellite, on 24 August. The various lunar satellites were designed specifically to select suitable landing sites on the moon. Meanwhile, on 16 March, the United States also achieved a first when astronauts Neil Armstrong and David Scott successfully 'docked' their Gemini VIII spacecraft with an Agena target vehicle. The Gemini Project was directly connected with manned flight into space. Rendezvous techniques, dockings and activities outside the space vehicle were further tested with the successful launching of Gemini IX on 3 June, Gemini X on 18 July, and Gemini XI on 12 September. By then it was clear that no further technological barrier stood between man and the moon, and it was anyone's guess whether it was the Soviet Union or the United States that would be the first to send a man to the moon.

It is easy to see that, in the circumstances, it became vitally important for the two space powers in their own interests to reach an agreement on the legal principles involved in advance of man's landing on the moon.[142] President Johnson announced on 7 May 1966 that the United States would seek a treaty through the United Nations to prevent any nation from claiming sovereignty over the moon or any other celestial bodies and that the exploration thereof would be for peaceful purposes only. This announcement was transmitted to the United Nations on 9 May.[143] Consultation with the Soviet Union began on 11 May, and on 30 May, the Soviet Union requested that the matter be included in the agenda of the forthcoming session of the General Assembly. The preliminary negotiations took place in COPUOS, but the controversial issues were dealt with by direct negotiations between the two space powers, agreement between whom was announced on 8 December 1966. A 43-power draft resolution 'commending' the treaty to States was submitted to the First Committee on 15 December, and it reached the General Assembly on 19 December. The General Assembly adopted it on the same day. The Treaty was opened for signature on 27 January 1967 simultaneously in London, Moscow and Washington. It entered into force on 10 October 1967. Where there is a will, there is always a way!

That very year saw agreement reached on what became known as the 1968 Agreement on the Rescue of Astronauts, the Return of Astronauts and the Return of Objects Launched into Outer Space. That was also the year in

---

[142] Cf. USA, A/AC.105/PV.37–42, p. 32 (5.10.65); A/AC.105/C.2/SR.72 (12.9.66), p. 3; A/AC.105/PV.44 (19.9.66), p. 20; A/PV.1412 (Prov.) (22.9.66), p. 41.
[143] A/6327.

which the first fatal accidents in space exploration occurred. On 27 January, three United States astronauts died when fire broke out on board Apollo I before take-off. On 24 April, Colonel V. Kamorov of the Soviet Union perished in Soyuz I on landing. They were powerful reminders that accidents could occur. The result was that the Astronauts Agreement was reached in record time.[144]

While the making of such rules, whether conventional or general, depends on needs, such needs must also be perceived by the dominant section of society. Thus, notwithstanding the fact that non-space powers had clamoured almost from the start for a treaty to determine liability for damage caused by objects launched into space and to establish the procedure for recovery, that the United States was in favour of such a treaty from the beginning, and that the General Assembly was urging COPUOS practically every year to intensify its efforts to reach an agreement and was vainly setting one deadline after another for its completion, the Soviet Union, which maintained that such a treaty was superfluous, was never in a hurry to come to an agreement. In the end, it took COPUOS nine years from 1962 to 1971 to produce what later became the 1972 Convention on International Liability for Damage caused by Space Objects.[145]

A further illustration of this point is the question of delimiting the frontier between national airspace and outer space, between the zone where States exercise complete and exclusive territorial sovereignty and the zone where the exercise of such sovereignty by States is proscribed. From every point of view, an early settlement of this question in order to avoid future conflicts would seem called for. Yet, no doubt for the purposes of keeping all options open, the United States is blithely opposed to even discussing this problem, let alone resolving it, maintaining that there is no present need to do so.[146] The subject of delimitation lingers on as a perennial item in the agenda of COPUOS and its Legal Sub-Committee.

B. Propitious Political Climate

The second condition for successful rule-making, even in a technical field, is that there must be a propitious political climate. This has been seen time and again in the development of international space law in the United Nations, in both a negative and a positive manner. Thus one of the first major proposals regarding the future development of space law came from President Eisenhower in his address to the United Nations General Assembly on 22

---

[144] See s. II.B.2 above.   [145] See s. II.B.3 above.

[146] See further Cheng, 'The Legal Régime of Airspace and Outer Space: The Boundary Problem', loc. cit. in n. 5 above, at p. 323 [Ch. 14 below]; and B. Cheng, 'The Legal Status of Outer Space and Relevant Issues: Delimitation of Outer Space and Definition of Peaceful Uses', 11 *JSL* (1983), p. 89.

September 1960,[147] but coming in the wake of the U–2 (1 May 1960) and RB–47 (1 July 1960) incidents[148] and the collapse of the Paris Summit meeting as a result thereof, it could be taken up only after the change in Administration in the United States.

It was this change in Administration in the United States and a change in the political climate which allowed agreement to be reached between the Soviet Union and the United States, thus enabling General Assembly resolution 1721 (XVI) to be adopted on 20 December 1961, setting out, in the words of Mr Khrushchev in his message of 20 March 1962 to President Kennedy, 'the initial principles of space legislation'.[149]

The next major step was of course the adoption by the General Assembly on 13 December 1963 of resolution 1962 (XVIII) containing the Declaration of Legal Principles Governing the Activities of States in the Exploration and Use of Outer Space,[150] but this was possible only because agreement had, earlier on in that year, been reached on the Moscow partial Test Ban Treaty (5 August 1963).

The 1967 Space Treaty and the 1968 Astronauts Agreement were, at the time of their conclusion, as we have just seen, treaties urgently wanted by both space powers. In the case of the 1972 Convention on Liability for Damage caused by Space Objects, discussions of which had dragged on for years, it was openly acknowledged by both the United States and the Soviet Union that this had been made possible by the favourable political conditions that had recently emerged, particularly regarding co-operation in space matters between the two space powers. More specifically, as the United States delegate to COPUOS' Legal Sub-Committee pointed out, on, 'January 21, 1971, following intensive discussions, a delegation of the United States National Aeronautics and Space Administration and a Soviet delegation had initialled a document providing, *inter alia*, for the development of compatible space rendezvous and docking techniques, the exchange of lunar soil samples, etc.'[151]

Similarly, the efforts to draw up the Moon Treaty which languished in COPUOS for some seven years, suddenly blossomed and fructified all within the span of fifteen days.[152] Perhaps it was no coincidence that agreement was reached precisely fifteen days after the signature of the second Strategic Arms

---

[147] See Cheng, 'The United Nations and Outer Space', loc. cit. in n. 133 above, at p. 277 [Ch. 6 above, s. VI].

[148] See ibid., at pp. 262–72 [Ch. 6 above, s. V].   [149] See s. II.A.1 above.

[150] See s. II.A.3 above.

[151] A/AC.105/C.2/SR.152–169, p. 9 (SR.152). See further Cheng, 'Convention on International Liability for Damage Caused by Space Objects', loc. cit. in n. 23 above, at pp. 92 ff. [Ch. 11 below, s. III.F.5]. For text of USA–USSR Agreement on Co-operation in Exploration and Use of Outer Space, 21 Jan. 1971, see 10 *ILM* (1971), p. 617.

[152] See s. II.B.5 above.

Limitation Treaty (SALT–II) between the Soviet Union and the United States (18 June 1979).[153]

In general, therefore, a propitious climate is required in addition to all the other factors.

C. Due Representation of the Dominant Section

Finally, in the light of what we have said regarding the rôle of the dominant section of international society in the making of legal rules in the international legal order,[154] it will hardly be surprising to find that, in order to achieve results, there must be due representation of the dominant section in the process of elaborating such rules. Nowhere is this need for due representation more dramatically illustrated by the history of COPUOS.

COPUOS started life as the *Ad Hoc* Committee on the Peaceful Uses of Outer Space, an eighteen-member committee established by the General Assembly on 13 December 1958. The Soviet Union had originally proposed to the United States that space matters should be discussed directly between them. Alternatively, if the subject was to be studied by the United Nations, it put forward the *troika* principle that there should be a committee of eleven consisting of four Western powers, four Soviet-bloc countries and three 'neutrals,' thus in the proportion of 4:4:3. However, bearing in mind that the United States had an easy majority in the United Nations at the time and that admission to the United Nations was then strictly controlled, of which the two International Court of Justice Advisory Opinions on admission to the United Nations were merely the symptoms, it was perhaps to be expected that, in the eighteen-member *Ad Hoc* Committee that was actually established, the proportion of Western-bloc nations, Soviet-bloc nations and neutrals was 13:4:2. Mr Cabot Lodge, the United States delegate to the United Nations, during the discussions leading to the formation of the *Ad Hoc* Committee said:

There are no 'two sides' to outer space. There are not—and never have been—'two sides' in the United Nations . . . We do not . . . accept the idea of 'two sides'—and frankly, we don't understand it.[155]

The perhaps not very surprising result was that the three Soviet-bloc members boycotted the *Ad Hoc* Committee. Nor did the two neutral members attended its meetings. Needless to say, the *Ad Hoc* Committee achieved nothing. The following year, 1959, the General Assembly established COPUOS with an enlarged membership of twenty-four, divided in the proportion this

---

[153] See 18 *ILM* (1979), p. 1112, and further Cheng, 'The Moon Treaty', loc. cit. in n. 27 above, pp. 216–17 [Ch. 12 below, s. II.E].

[154] See ss. III.B and V.H.2. above.

[155] 24 Nov. 1958, United States Information Service (USIS), London, Official Text (25 Nov. 1958), p. 2; the account in GA (XIII), A/C.1/SR.994, p. 235, is slightly abridged.

time of 12:7:5. It may be of interest to observe that shortly before the meeting of the General Assembly in 1959, the Conference of Foreign Ministers recommended the formation of a ten-nation Committee on Disarmament to replace the previous five-power sub-committee. Whereas the latter was composed of the Soviet Union in the midst of four Western powers (Canada, France, the United Kingdom, and the United States), the ten-nation Disarmament Committee is composed of five NATO powers and five Warsaw-Pact powers.

However, the Soviet Union remained dissatisfied with the composition of the new COPUOS, and, moreover, wanted the unanimity rule, instead of the usual United Nations majority rule, to be applied in COPUOS, which would of course ensure that every member would in fact have the power of veto. COPUOS transacted no substantive business for nearly two years until a direct agreement between the Soviet Union and the United States led to the unanimous proposal from COPUOS that later became resolution 1721 (XVI). This resolution *inter alia* awarded four additional seats on COPUOS to the Soviet bloc, thus enlarging COPUOS membership to twenty-eight in the proportion of 12:11:5.[156]

No doubt as part of the same package deal between the United States and the Soviet Union, it was announced at the opening session of the now twenty-eight-member COPUOS that the Committee and its sub-committees would in future operate by consensus without vote,[157] thus in effect conceding the Soviet Union's second demand, unanimity. It was only then that COPUOS really began to function,[158] thus demonstrating that for the purpose of successfully developing new legal rules, there must be due representation of the dominant section in the field in question. The text is not one of simple military, political, or economic powers, but a functional one in relation to the subject-matter.

Due representation can present many facets. COPUOS membership has since been successively increased to thirty-seven in 1973, forty-seven in 1977 and fifty-three in 1980. This continuing widening of the membership of COPUOS may or may not have exceeded the optimum. One thing is certain: to the extent to which the dominant section of international society in this field becomes under-represented in the decision-making process, the end result may well be counter-productive. In many ways, this is illustrated by General Assembly resolution 37/92 on Principles Governing the Use by States of Artificial Earth Satellites for International Direct Television Broadcasting, which was adopted on 10 December 1982.[159]

---

[156] See s. III.A above.   [157] See s. III.B above.

[158] On the United Nations and outer space in general, see Cheng, 'The United Nations and Outer Space' and 'United Nations Resolutions on Outer Space', loc. cit. in respectively nn. 132 and 3 above [Chs. 6 and 7 above].

[159] A/RES/37/92 (4.2.83) [text reproduced as App. II.4 below].

In this case, the General Assembly adopted by majority vote the principles, on which consensus had not been reached within COPUOS. The vote in the Assembly was 107 for and 13 against, with 13 abstentions. The majority consisted essentially of States within the Soviet bloc, and the Group of 77. Most of the Western industrialized nations either voted against or abstained. These include the United States, Canada, all the then European Communities countries, Japan, and other countries which either already have or are about to have direct broadcasting satellite services.[160] As we have seen, General Assembly resolutions in themselves have no legally binding force. They may, depending upon the intention of the States concerned, and the way in which the States have expressed their intention, be used variously to evince an *opinio juris de lege lata*, an *opinio juris de lege ferenda*, a voluntary code of conduct, a *voeu*, or mere wishful thinking. Their impact either as a guide to probable future behaviour or a source for the future development of the law depends consequently in great measure on both the degree and intensity of the support they receive from the relevant dominant section in the real world outside the United Nations. The usefulness of resolutions which are rammed down the throat of the dominant section of international society by a purely numerical majority in the United Nations, whether from East or West, North or South, is more than dubious. As the New Zealand delegate to the General Assembly's Special Political Committee said:

the set of principles must have the support of all Member States, particularly the technologically advanced States, in order to be of real value.[161]

This is perhaps one of the major problems in international rule-making today: the distortion of the real weight of States in the making of such rules by the precept of 'one State one vote' which is based on a misrepresentation of the principle of equality of States.[162] It is hoped that this survey of the development of international space law through the United Nations has shown that successful rule-making in international law depends upon due representation being given to the relevant weight of States in any given subject-matter. Ultimately, it is a political issue, but if the validity of this proposition can be recognized, and recognized as being compatible with the principle of sovereign equality of States in international law, one would already be half way towards a more rational and realistic approach to international law-making in general.

---

[160] See s. II.A.4 above.
[161] A/SPC/37/SR.34 (22.11.82), p. 13; see further ss. II.A.4 and IV above.
[162] See ss. III.B and V.H.2 above.

PART III

UNITED NATIONS TREATIES
ON OUTER SPACE

9

The 1967 Space Treaty*

I. Introduction

The Chairman of the Legal Sub-Committee of the United Nations Committee on the Peaceful Uses of Outer Space, in opening the fifth session of the Legal Sub-Committee on 12 July 1966 pithily observed:

[I]n the three years since the adoption of the Declaration of Legal Principles Governing the Activities of States in the Exploration and Use of Outer Space [General Assembly resolution 1962 (XVIII)] little progress had been made towards ensuring that outer space was used for man's advancement and not for his destruction.[1]

Yet, scarcely five months later on 16 December 1966, he had the satisfaction of being able to announce to the First Committee of the General Assembly[2] that agreement had just been reached on a Treaty of Principles Governing the Activities of States in the Exploration and Use of Outer Space, Including the Moon and Other Celestial Bodies,[3] a treaty described by President Johnson as 'the most important arms control development since the limited test ban treaty of 1963'.[4] The treaty received the unanimous 'commendation' of the General Assembly on 19 December 1966,[5] was opened for signature by 'all States' on 27 January 1967 simultaneously at London, Moscow, and Washington, and came into force on 10 October 1967, having by then been signed by 93 States and ratified by 16, including all the depositary States.

II. The Background

The extraordinary speed at which the Space Treaty was concluded was due unquestionably to the need of such an agreement in advance of man's landing

* First published in 95 *JDI* (1968), pp. 532–645, in both English and French, the latter under the title 'Le Traité de 1967 sur l'Espace'. Reproduced by kind permission of the Director of the *Journal du Droit international (Clunet)*.

[1] A/AC.105/C.2/SR.57, pp. 2–3.

[2] A/C. 1/944 (16.12.66), pp. 2–3; A/C.1/SR.1491 (16.12.66), pp. 417–18.

[3] Hereinafter Space Treaty. For text, see Annex to A/RES/2222 (XXI), *Off. Rec. of the GA* (XXI), Suppl. No. 16 [reproduced as App. I.1 below].

[4] 55 *Dept. of State Bull.* (1966), p. 952; statement released on 8 Dec. 1966, when agreement was actually reached between the major space powers.

[5] Resolution 2222 (XXI), loc. cit. in n. 3 above; see also A/PV.1499 (Prov.), pp. 71–2.

on the moon.[6] By mid-1966, as the United States representative to the United Nations pointed out on 22 September 1966, the need was 'all the more urgent because of man's recent strides towards landing on the moon'.[7]

The most notable 'stride' early in 1966 was the first ever 'soft' landing on the moon achieved on 3 February by the Soviet Union with its automatic station Luna IX. Success came after three failures in 1965.[8] The United States followed on 2 June with Surveyor I, which transmitted back to earth over 10,000 photographs of the surface of the moon. The Soviet Union scored another first with the launching on 31 March of Luna X which became the moon's first artificial satellite. Luna X was later joined by the United States Lunar Orbiter I launched on 10 August, and the Soviet Luna XI on 24 August. All these satellites were designed specifically to select suitable landing sites on the moon. Meanwhile, on 16 March the United States also achieved a first when astronauts Neil Armstrong and David Scott successfully 'docked' their Gemini VIII spacecraft with an Agena target vehicle. The Gemini Project is directly connected with manned flight into space. Rendezvous techniques, docking, and activities outside the space vehicle were further tested with the successful launching of Gemini IX on 3 June, Gemini X on 18 July, and Gemini XI on 12 September. It would appear that by then it was already clear that no further technological barrier stood between man and the moon.

The first artificial earth satellite went into orbit in 1957. Although certain tentative steps were taken, including the setting up of first an Ad Hoc Committee,[9] and subsequently a Committee on the Peaceful Uses of Outer Space,[10] the United Nations, for several years to come, failed to make any significant headway in its attempt to play an active role in international co-operation in space activities. In fact, deadlock existed, due primarily to political differences between the two super-powers.[11]

However, not long before his office expired, President Eisenhower, addressing the General Assembly on 22 September 1960, made an important statement defining Unites States policy on outer space. Recalling the missed opportunity of the 1946 Baruch Plan on atoms for peace and the successful conclusion of the Antarctic Treaty the year before, he proposed:

1. We agree that celestial bodies are not subject to national appropriation by any claims of sovereignty.
2. We agree that the nations of the world shall not engage in warlike activities on these bodies.

    [6] Cf. USA, A/AC.105/PV.37–42, (5.10.65), p. 32; A/AC.105/C.2/SR.72 (12.9.66), p. 3; A/AC.105/PV.44 (19.9.66), p. 20; A/PV.1412 (Prov.) (22.9.66), p. 41.
    [7] A/PV.1412 (Prov.), p. 41.
    [8] Luna V launched on 9 May 1965; Luna VII, 4 Oct. 1965; Luna VIII, 3 Dec. 1966.
    [9] GA resolution 1348 (XIII) of 13 Dec. 1958.
    [10] Hereinafter Outer Space Committee. GA resolution 1472 (XIV) of 12 Dec. 1959.
    [11] On developments up to 1961, see the writer's 'The United Nations and Outer Space', 14 *CLP* (1961), p. 247 [Ch. 6 above].

3. We agree, subject to appropriate verification, that no nation will put into orbit or station in outer space weapons of mass destruction.
4. All launchings of space craft should be verified in advance by the United Nations.[12]

The significance of these proposals is brought out by the fact that, seven years later, except the requirements of verification, their underlying principles were all incorporated in the 1967 Space Treaty. Some of them had, however, previously found expression in various General Assembly resolutions.

The thaw in United Nations co-operation in outer space began in 1961.[13] Before the year was out, as Mr Khrushchev later said to President Kennedy in a message dated 20 March 1962 which on this point, though perhaps not formally accurate, was doubtless expressive of the political truth:

the Soviet Union and the United States found it possible to agree on the proposal about the initial principles of space legislation, which was then unanimously approved by all Members of the United Nations.[14]

Mr Khrushchev was of course referring to General Assembly resolution 1721 (XVI) of 20 December 1961 in which the General Assembly unanimously,

Commends to States for their guidance in the exploration of outer space the following principles:

(*a*) International law, including the Charter of the United Nations, applies to outer space and celestial bodies;

(*b*) Outer space and celestial bodies are free for exploration and use by all States in conformity with international law and are not subject to national appropriation.[15]

Subsequently, after the signing of the Moscow Test Ban Treaty on 5 August 1963, the Soviet Union and the United States further expressed their intention not to station in outer space any objects carrying nuclear weapons or other kinds of weapons of mass destruction. In its resolution 1884 (XVIII) of 17 October 1963, again unanimously adopted, the General-Assembly welcomed these statements and called on all States similarly not to do so.[16]

[12] A/PV.868 (22.9.1960), p. 45, at p. 48. According to the US State Department, item 4 of the proposal formed part of item 3, whilst item 4 should read: 'We press forward with a programme of international co-operation for constructive peaceful uses of outer space under the United Nations', which, in the procès-verbaux of the General Assembly became merely part of the speech. See further loc. cit. in n. 11, above, p. 277, n. 43 [Ch. 6 above, n. 142].

[13] See further loc. cit. in n. 11 above [Ch. 6 above]; for subsequent developments, see further the writer's 'United Nations Resolutions on Outer Space: "Instant" International Customary Law?', 5 *Indian JIL* (1965), p. 23 [Ch. 7 above].

[14] See loc. cit. in n. 13 above, p. 24, n. 6 [Ch. 7, n. 6].

[15] For resolution, see App. II.1 below. See further loc. cit. in n. 13 above, pp. 24 ff. [Ch. 7 above, s. III].

[16] Cf. item 3 of the Eisenhower proposal, n. 12 above. For resolution, see App. II.2 below.

In his message of 20 March 1962[17] to President Kennedy, Mr Khrushchev
also proposed the conclusion of two *treaties*, one a declaration of basic principles governing activities in space, the other an agreement on assistance to
and return of astronauts in distress. On 6 June 1962, drafts were submitted by
the Soviet Union to the Legal Sub-Committee.[18] On its part, the United States
on 4 June 1962 submitted a proposal[19] which envisaged the eventual conclusion of an agreement on liability for space vehicle accidents, but with seeming
inconsistency, suggested that the question of assistance to astronauts should
be dealt with by a General Assembly resolution,[20] and submitted its own proposal to this effect.[21] It was not until April 1963 that the United States agreed
to the principle of a separate agreement on assistance to astronauts.[22]

On the subject of an instrument setting out the basic principles governing
activities in space, however, the United States was adamant, and it submitted
its own proposal for a General Assembly resolution on 8 December 1962.[23] In
the end, at least insofar as the question of form was concerned, the United
States view prevailed. As regards questions of substance, although desultory
discussions took place in the Legal Sub-Committee, it was soon evident that
everything depended on the space powers and on their being able to reach
agreement on issues some of which lay outside the competence of the
Committee.

In the summer of 1963, the Moscow Test Ban Treaty was signed,[24] and a
series of arrangements were reached between the Soviet Union and the United
States on co-operation in outer space.[25] Soon afterwards, direct negotiations
began in earnest between the two space powers on the basic principles governing space activities, assisted, it would appear, by a few other members of
the Outer Space Committee. The resultant Declaration of Legal Principles
Governing the Activities of States in the Exploration and Use of Outer Space
was 'solemnly' and unanimously adopted by the General Assembly in its resolution 1962 (XVIII) of 13 December 1963.[26]

The main arguments advanced in favour of General Assembly resolutions
were speed, simplicity, and flexibility[27], qualities which can hardly be denied.
But, in addition, the more than dubious propositions were constantly being
put forward that General Assembly resolutions, especially if adopted unani-

---

[17] See n. 14 above.   [18] Respectively, A/AC.105/C.2/L.1, and A/AC.105/C.2/L.2.
[19] A/AC.105/C.2/L.4 (4.6.62).   [20] A/AC.105/C.2/SR.7 (7.6.62).
[21] A/AC.105/C.2/L.3 (8.6.62).   [22] A/AC.105/C.2/SR.25 (30.4.62).
[23] A/C.1/881. Meanwhile, the United Arab Republic had also submitted a draft code on 14
Sept. 1962 (A/AC.105/L.6), and the United Kingdom, a draft resolution on 4 Dec. 1962
(A/C.1/879).
[24] 5 Aug. 1963, 480 UNTS 43.
[25] Transmitted to the UN by letter of 22 Aug. 1963 from the permanent representatives of the
US and USSR (UN GAOR Annexes (XVIII) 28, p. 1).
[26] For resolution, see App. II.3 below. See further loc. cit. in n. 13 above, pp. 27–8 [Ch. 7 above,
s. VI].
[27] See further loc. cit. in n. 13 above, pp. 32–3 [Ch. 7 above, s. VII].

mously, were either as binding as treaties, or merely declaratory of international law.[28] That the General Assembly did not entirely share these views can
be seen from resolution 1963 (XVIII) adopted at the same time as resolution
1962. It recommended that the Outer Space Committee should give consideration to 'incorporating in international agreement form, in the future as
appropriate, the legal principles governing the activities of States in the exploration and use of outer space'. In the same resolution 1963 (XVIII), the
General Assembly requested the Outer Space Committee to press on with the
preparation of the draft agreements on liability and on assistance and
return.[29]

During the years that followed, a constant bone of contention in the Outer
Space Committee was whether priority should be given to the treaty on general principles or to the agreements on liability and assistance.[30] However,
even as late as October 1965, the United States was of the view that the 'appropriate' moment for converting resolution 1962 (XVIII) into treaty form had
not yet arrived. Speaking in the Outer Space Committee on 5 October 1965,
the United States representative said:

A suggestion has been made that we should yield priority to the codification in treaty
form of the Declaration of Legal Principles adopted by the General Assembly in 1963.
As members will recall from Ambassador Stevenson's statement at that time, the
United States attributes very important effects to that Declaration as it stands. We do
not think the Declaration requires re-statement in any new form. This is not to say that
work should not be done to embody in international agreements a statement of legal
obligations which Member States would undertake in giving specific effect to individual principles set forth in the Declaration. For instance, we are anxious to see completed the agreements on liability and assistance and return, which have now been in
preparation for eighteen months. And, as Ambassador Goldberg proposed in his
speech to the General Assembly on 23 September, we believe that the United Nations
should undertake, in advance of man-landings on the moon, the drafting of international rules to govern the exploration of celestial bodies.[31]

What the United States had in mind then was, therefore, not a general treaty
on space, but a special agreement on celestial bodies.

III. The Negotiations

The negotiations may be divided into five phases.

---

[28] For the writer's views on these propositions, see loc. cit. (1965) in n. 13 above on the concept
of so-called 'soft law' [Ch. 7 above]. Cf. the writer's comment in British Institute of International
and Comparative Law, *Current Problems in Space Law* (1966), p. 83, at pp. 84–5.

[29] See text to nn. 18–22 above.

[30] E.g., A/AC.105/C.2/SR.29–37 (9–26.3.64); USSR A/AC.105/PV.34 (5.11.64), p. 9.

[31] A/AC.105/PV.37–42 (5.10.65), p. 32.

A. Phase I

As mentioned before, with the landing of Luna IX on the moon on 3 February 1966, the need of such an agreement became all the more urgent.[32] Speaking from his ranch in Texas on 7 May 1966, President Johnson announced that the United States would seek a treaty through the United Nations to prevent any nation from claiming sovereignty over the moon or any other celestial bodies and that the exploration thereof would be for peaceful purposes only.[33] This announcement was transmitted to the United Nations on 9 May.[34] Consultations with the Soviet Union took place on 11 May when an outline of twelve points which, in the opinion of the United States, should be included in a 'celestial bodies treaty' was handed to the latter.[35] Thus began the first phase of the negotiations.

The response of the Soviet Union was prompt. On 30 May it requested the 'Conclusion of an international agreement on legal principles governing the activities of States in the exploration and conquest of the Moon and other celestial bodies' to be included in the agenda of the twenty-first session of the General Assembly[36]. The text of a Soviet draft treaty (USSR draft I) followed on 16 June 1966[37].

On the same day, the United States transmitted to the Chairman of the Outer Space Committee the text of a draft treaty (US draft I), together with a request that the Outer Space Legal Sub-Committee should be convened on 12 July to discuss the matter[38]. The Soviet Union had originally proposed that discussion of this topic should be begun in the General Assembly in the autumn, but general agreement was subsequently reached on an early meeting of the Legal Sub-Committee, and the Soviet draft treaty was transmitted to the Sub-Committee on the eve of its fifth session,[39] where the second phase of the negotiations was to take place.

[32] See text to n. 7 above.   [33] Cf. item 2 of the Eisenhower proposal, n. 12 above.
[34] A/6327.
[35] See letter of 16 June 1966 from the US representative to the Chairman of the Outer Space Committee, A/AC.105/32, p. 1. This outline probably accounts for some of the similarities in the subsequent US and USSR drafts. It contained twelve points, namely, 1. freedom of exploration; 2. non-appropriation; 3. freedom of and co-operation in scientific investigations; 4. reporting of findings; 5. open access to all areas; 6. non-militarisation; 7. jurisdiction of the launching State; 8. ownership of objects launched into space; 9. mutual assistance among astronauts; 10. avoidance of harmful contamination; 11. settlement of disputes; 12. final clauses.
[36] A/6341 (31.5.66). It will be noted that the initial Soviet proposal was also limited to the moon and other celestial bodies, and did not include outer space. In an accompanying letter from the Soviet Minister for Foreign Affairs, the Soviet Union outlined four principles on which the proposed treaty should be based, namely, 1. freedom and equality in exploration and use; 2. non-militarisation; 3. non-appropriation and exploration and use for the good of all mankind; 4. co-operation and mutual aid.   [37] A/6352. Hereinafter referred to as USSR draft I.
[38] A/AC.105/32, and Corr. 1; reproduced but for Corr. 1 (amending a clerical error in Art. 12 of the draft treaty) in Annex I of the Sub-Committee's Report on its fifth sessioin (12 July–4 Aug. 1966 and 12–16 Sept. 1966), A/AC.105/35. Hereinafter referred to as US draft I.
[39] A/AC.105/C.2/L.13 (11.7.66), reproduced in Annex I of the Sub-Committee's Report on its fifth session, A/AC.105/35.

B. Phase II

Thus when the fifth session of the Legal Sub-Committee opened on 12 July 1966, the Sub-Committee had before it both the Soviet draft and the United States draft.

A comparison of the two drafts shows that the Soviet draft was intended, as its title indicates, to be a general 'Treaty on Principles Governing the Activities of States in the Exploration and Use of Outer Space, the Moon and other Celestial Bodies', and, in this sense, may be regarded as in direct implementation of resolution 1963 (XVIII)[40]. From the substantive point of view, it largely reproduced the principles set forth in resolutions 1721,[41] 1884,[42] and 1962,[43] except in its Articles I and IV. Article I, in addition to reiterating paragraphs 1 and 2 of resolution 1962, laid down the principles of free access to all regions on celestial bodies and 'equal conditions' being accorded to States engaged in the exploration of outer space.[44] Article IV, in accord with President Johnson's proposal, was concerned with the non-militarization of celestial bodies.

The United States draft, on the other hand, was limited in scope to the moon and celestial bodies and formed, from this point of view, a new topic in the agenda of the Legal Sub-Committee. Instead of being a mere attempt to convert resolutions 1721, 1884, and 1962 into treaty form, which the United States presumably still considered unnecessary,[45] the United States draft was rather an adaptation of these resolutions to the special circumstances of the moon and other celestial bodies. Outer space was largely excluded from it.

The United States draft borrowed freely from the Antarctic Treaty of 1 December 1959. In addition to the principles of non-appropriation (Article 1) and non-militarization of celestial bodies (Articles 8 and 9), it provided for the reporting of activities on celestial bodies to the Secretary-General of the United Nations, publication of findings (Article 4), and free access to all areas of celestial bodies and all installations thereon at all times (Article 6). It enunciated the principles of freedom of (Article 2) and international co-operation in scientific investigations (Article 3), and laid down the duties of preventing harmful contamination of celestial bodies (Article 10), and of mutual assistance to one another's nationals engaged in activities on them (Article 5). Compulsory jurisdiction over all disputes was conferred on the International Court of Justice (Article 11).

In the general debate which followed in the Legal Sub-Committee, it soon became evident that the overwhelming opinion was in favour of a general treaty governing both outer space and celestial bodies. On the other hand, there was also general support for many of the novel features that were to be found in the United States draft.

[40] See n. 29 above.   [41] See n. 15 above.   [42] See n. 16 above.
[43] See n. 26 above.   [44] See s. VII.D below: Tracking Facilities.   [45] See n. 31 above.

The general debate ended in a spirit of great co-operativeness on the part of both space powers, each declaring its readiness to consider the possibility of incorporating in its own draft features not covered therein that appeared in the other's proposal.[46]

Thus, although some States still doubted the wisdom of a general treaty on the law of outer space at this stage of the development of astronautics,[47] the United States almost immediately agreed to enlarge the scope of the treaty to embrace not only celestial bodies, but also outer space,[48] thus abandoning its previous position on the subject[49]. Moreover, in the course of the discussions in the Legal Sub-Committee, the United States indicated its general preparedness to accept all proposals in the Soviet draft which merely incorporated the terms of previous General Assembly resolutions on outer space.

Similarly, almost from the start, the Soviet Union accepted the principles of freedom of, and international co-operation in, scientific investigations contained in the United States draft (Articles 2 and 3).[50] Moreover, while both the Soviet draft and the United States draft provided for free access to all areas of celestial bodies,[51] the Soviet Union was also prepared to accept, in principle, the United States proposal of free access to all installations thereon[52].

The result was that agreement was fairly quickly reached in the first part of the fifth session of the Legal Sub-Committee which met at Geneva from 12 July to 4 August 1966 on what subsequently became the first nine articles of the treaty, including the new and vital clause reserving celestial bodies exclusively to peaceful exploration and use, subject only to further discussion on whether, in Article IV(2) of the treaty, the word 'installations', was also to be included alongside of 'military bases and fortifications', and whether the use of military equipment was to be permitted in the peaceful exploration and use of celestial bodies[53].

Insofar as the substantive articles of the treaty were concerned, agreement had yet to be reached on *inter alia*, first, the Soviet proposal that each contracting State must grant equal rights,[54] subsequently limited to equal facilities for tracking space objects,[55] to all the other contracting States engaged in the exploration of outer space. Secondly, there was the question whether reporting of information on activities on celestial bodies should be compul-

---

[46] USSR, A/AC.105/C.2/SR.62 (19.7.66), pp. 10–11; USA, ibid., pp. 11–12.

[47] E.g. Belgium, A/AC.105/C.2/SR.61 (16.7.66), pp. 6–7.

[48] USA, A/AC.105/C.2/SR.63 (20.7.66), p. 2/3.   [49] See text to n. 31 above.

[50] USSE, A/AC.105/C.2/SR.63 (20.7.66), pp. 4–5.

[51] USSR draft Art. 1–2; USA draft Art. 6.

[52] USSR, A/AC.105/C.2/SR.63 (20.7.66), pp. 4–5; see s. VII.D below.

[53] See Report of the Legal Sub-Committee on the Work of its Fifth Session (12 July–4 Aug. 1966 and 12–16 Sept. 1966), A/AC.105/35, App. II.

[54] Under Art. I of USSR draft I; see n. 44 above.

[55] Revised Soviet draft, A/AC.105/C.2/WP.23/Corr.1 (29.7.66); see further s. VII.D below.

sory[56] or discretionary[57], and whether it should be made through the United Nations. Thirdly, there was the question whether free access to installations on celestial bodies should be permissible 'at all times'[58] or 'on the basis of reciprocity and under the condition that the time of the visit is to be agreed between the parties concerned'.[59] Fourthly, the position of international organizations engaged in space activities had yet to be clarified.[60] Lastly, insofar as the final clauses were concerned, there was the highly political problem whether the treaty should be open to 'all States'[61] or only members of the so-called United Nations family.[62]

When the Legal Sub-Committee, after a period of consultations, resumed its fifth session at New York on 12 September 1966, it became clear that except for States in the Soviet bloc, members of the Sub-Committee were generally unwilling to agree to the equivalent of an unconditional most-favoured-nation clause on tracking facilities. On the other hand, the Soviet Union now made it plain that it regarded this provision a *sine qua non* of the treaty.[63] Without an agreement on this article, it was not prepared to consider fresh proposals on the questions of dissemination of information and free access, on both of which the United States had meanwhile made important concessions. On this note, the Legal Sub-Committee ended its fifth session on 16 September 1966. This marked also the end of the second phase in the negotiations.

C. Phase III

No further progress was made when the Outer Space Committee itself met on 19 September.[64] Meanwhile, the United States on 17 September requested the subject to be included in the agenda of the twenty-first session of the General Assembly and submitted a revised draft of the treaty (US draft II)[65]. The twenty-first session of the General Assembly opened on 20 September. On 22

---

[56] US draft, Art. 4; USA A/AC.105/C.2/SR.64 (21.7.66), pp. 11–12; see further ss. VI.E and VII.C below.

[57] USSR, A/AC.105/C.2/SR.64 (21.7.66), pp. 12–13; ibid./5th Sess./WP.4 (21.7.66); see further ss. VI.E and VII.C below.

[58] US draft I, Art. 6; USA, A/AC.105/C.2/SR.70 (3.8.66), pp. 5–6; see further s. VI.D below.

[59] USSR, A/AC.105/C.2/SR.63 (20.7.66), pp. 4–5; see further s. VI.D below.

[60] See further s. V.G below.   [61] USSR draft I, Art. XI.

[62] US draft I, Art. 12: 'This Agreement shall be open for signature by States Members of the United Nations or any of the specialised agencies or Parties to the Statute of the International Court of Justice, or by any other State invited by the General Assembly of the United Nations to become a Party. Any such State which does not sign this Agreement may accede to it at any time.'

[63] See USA, A/AC.105/C.2/SR.73 (16.9.66), p. 4; USSR, ibid., pp. 6–7; see further s. VII.D below.

[64] See Report of the Committee, A/6431. The Report of the Legal Sub-Committee on the work of its session is included therein as Annex III, to which are appended *inter alia* the first US and USSR drafts of the treaty. See further n. 68 below.

[65] A/6392. Hereinafter referred to as US draft II. See further n. 68 below.

September during the general debate, the United States made the following offer to the Soviet Union on the question of tracking facilities:

If the Soviet Union desires to provide for tracking coverage from United States territory, we, on our part are prepared to discuss with Soviet representatives the technical and other requirements involved, with a view to reaching some mutually beneficial agreement; and our scientists and technical representatives can meet without delay.[66]

The United States representative added:

The outer space treaty is too important and too urgent to be delayed.[67]

Scarcely a fortnight later, on 4 October 1966, the Soviet Union submitted its own revised draft of the treaty (USSR draft II)[68] the terms of which show that the two major space powers had meanwhile not only reached a compromise on tracking facilities,[69] but also agreement on the preamble, the use of military equipment,[70] the scope of the obligation to publish information,[71] the conditions governing visits to installations on celestial bodies,[72] the position of international organisations engaged in space activities,[73] and the amendment clause[74]. The Soviet draft also revealed the remaining areas of disagreement, namely, the Soviet proposal that the treaty should be treated as establishing a conventional *jus cogens* as among the contracting States,[75] the Soviet refusal to accept the compulsory jurisdiction of the International Court of Justice,[76] and the Soviet insistence that the treaty should be open to 'all States'[77]. The period between the end of the fifth session of the Legal Sub-Committee[78] and the submission of Soviet draft II[79] may be regarded as the third phase of the negotiations, which was conducted directly between the two major space powers.

D. Phase IV

So was the fourth phase of the negotiations which lasted until 8 December when complete agreement was announced. The compromise consisted in dropping from the final text any reference to subsequent agreements[80] and the

---

[66] A/PV.1412 (Prov.) (22.9.66), p. 41.   [67] Ibid.

[68] A/6352/Rev.1. Hereinafter referred to as USSR draft II. A/6341, A/6352/Rev.1, A/6392, and A/6431, are all to be found *inter alia* in GAOR (XXI) agenda items 30, 89 and 91, Annexes.

[69] Art X of USSR draft II and of treaty; see further s. VII.D below.

[70] Art. II of USSR draft II; Art. IV of treaty; see further n. 53 above and s. VI.C below.

[71] Art XI of USSR draft II and of treaty; see further ss. VI.E and VII.C below.

[72] Art. XII of USSR draft II and of treaty; see further s. VI.D below.

[73] Art. XIII of USSR draft II and of treaty.

[74] US draft II, Art. 17; USSR draft II, Art. XVII; see further s. IX below.

[75] A/AC.105/C.2/5th Sess./WP.32 (13.9.66); USSR draft II, Art XIV; see further s. VIII below.

[76] US draft II, Art. 12; USSR draft II, Art. XV.

[77] US draft II, Art. 14; USSR draft II, Art. XVI.

[78] 16 Sept. 1966; see s. III.B above.   [79] 4 Oct. 1966; see n. 68 above.

[80] See n. 75 above and s. VIII below.

clause compromissoire[81], and in opening the treaty to 'all States'[82]. A withdrawal clause was also inserted.[83]

E. Phase V

The final phase, which took place once more in the United Nations was largely formal. The agreed text was submitted to the First Committee of the General Assembly on 15 December in a 43-power draft resolution,[84] which was adopted by the First Committee without objection on 17 December.[85] When the draft treaty reached the General Assembly on 19 December, a 'note of discord' was sounded by the representative of Tanzania, as he himself said. *Inter alia*, he complained, on this point not without some justification, that the General Assembly had been given too little time to consider the draft treaty, and suggested that the Assembly should only 'take note' of it. 'It is probable that the completed draft . . . has not yet been seen by many of the Foreign Offices of the delegations represented here.'[86] Nevertheless, he did not, he said, wish to stand in the way of the General Assembly which then proceeded unanimously to 'commend' the treaty in its resolution 2222 (XXI).[87] As has been mentioned before, the treaty was then opened for signature on 27

---

[81] See n. 76 above.

[82] Art. XIV:

1. This Treaty shall be open to all States for signature. Any State which does not sign this Treaty before its entry into force in accordance with paragraph 3 of this article may accede to it at any time.
2. This Treaty shall be subject to ratification by signatory States. Instruments of ratification and instruments of accession shall be deposited with the Governments of the United Kingdom of Great Britain and Northern Ireland, the Union of Soviet Socialist Republics, and the United States of America, which are hereby designated the Depositary Governments.
3. This Treaty shall enter into force upon the deposit of instruments of ratification by five Governments including the Governments designated as Depositary Governments under this Treaty.
4. For States whose instruments of ratification or access are deposited subsequent to the entry into force of this Treaty, it shall enter into force on the date of deposit of their instruments of ratification or accession.
5. The depositary Governments shall promptly inform all signatory and acceding States of the date of each signature, the date of deposit of each instrument of ratification of and accession to this Treaty, the date of its entry into force and other notices.
6. This Treaty shall be registered by the Depositary Governments pursuant to Article 102 of the Charter of the United Nations.

The exceptional character of this accession clause was referred to or emphasized by the United Kingdom, A/C.1/SR.1492 (17.12.66), p. 430 (para. 27); Italy, ibid., pp. 431–2 (para. 37); Japan, ibid./SR.1493 (17.12.66), p. 439 (para. 35). The following States made it clear that the signing or ratification of, or accession to, the treaty would in no way affect the status of an entity or regime on its recognition or non-recognition by other parties to the treaty; USA, A/C.1/SR.1492 (17.12.66), p. 428 (para. 9); United Kingdom, ibid., p. 430 (para. 27); Australia, ibid./SR.1493 (17.12.66), p. 438 (para. 22); Japan, ibid., p. 439 (para. 35).

[83] Art. XVI: 'Any State Party to the Treaty may give notice of its withdrawal from the Treaty one year after its entry into force by written notification to the Depositary Governments. Such withdrawal shall take effect one year from the date of receipt of this notification.' This clause first appeared in US draft I (Art. 16).

[84] A/AC.1/L.396, and Add. 1 and 2.   [85] A/AC.1/SR.1493 (17.12.66), p. 445 (para. 86).

[86] A/PV.1499 (Prov.) (19.12.66), p. 66.   [87] Ibid., pp. 71–2.

January 1967, and came into force on 10 October 1967[88] to take its place as the first chapter in the new *Corpus Juris Spatialis*.

IV. Cosmographical Scope and Definitions

As its title indicates, the treaty is intended to govern the activities of States 'in outer space, including the moon and other celestial bodies'.

A. Outer Space and Celestial Bodies

Attention may first be drawn to a few points of terminology. In contrast to previous General Assembly resolutions on outer space, such as resolutions 1721 and 1962, which speak of 'outer space and celestial bodies', thus distinguishing between 'outer space' and 'celestial bodies', the treaty includes 'celestial bodies' within the notion of 'outer space'.[89] This new terminology has at least three major disadvantages.

First, it has lost the use of a term with an accepted meaning, describing the space beyond terrestrial national space and between the myriad celestial bodies. Consequently, whenever reference has to be made to this area, some long-winded specification will now be required.

Secondly, there has been no gain in brevity; for notwithstanding the extended meaning it has given to the term 'outer space', the treaty specifies on practically every occasion,[90] that the term includes the moon and other celestial bodies[91]. This pleonasm is further aggravated by singling out the moon for special mention in most instances.

Thirdly, it sows the seeds of doubt and confusion wherever this habit of exemplicative particularization is not followed. It is hardly surprising, therefore, that the representative of Ceylon to the United Nations found it 'perplexing' that, in the vital Article IV of the treaty dealing with non-militarization, whereas sentences two and five mentioned the 'moon and other celestial bodies' without reference to outer space, sentences one and three spoke simply of 'celestial bodies' with no mention of the moon.[92] Two days later, at the General Assembly, he complained that he had asked the sponsors of the draft resolution for an explanation, but none was received,

---

[88] See text after n. 5 above.

[89] This phrase occurred in the first instance as a freak in Art. I(2) of USSR draft I; for elsewhere the phrase used was always 'outer space and celestial bodies'. The US draft I also mentioned celestial bodies, without reference to the moon. As Art. I of USSR draft I was the first article to be discussed, it set the precedent. Cf., for instance, India, A/AC.105/C.2/SR.63 (20.7.66), pp. 2–3; USA, ibid./SR.64 (21.7.66), p. 10 (amending Art. II to follow the terminology of Art. I).

[90] Except the preamble, Art. V(1), Art. VIII *in principio*, Art. XI *in principio*.

[91] No less than 25 times in all, including the title of the treaty; 7 times alone in Art. IX! See s. VII.E below.

[92] A/C.1/SR.1493 (17.12.66), p. 437 (para. 19).

and expressed the hope that no inference *a contrario* would be drawn from these omissions.[93] The answers are of course that the former omissions were deliberate,[94] while the latter were simply the result of hasty and sloppy draftsmanship, with the result that his hopes will at best be only partially fulfilled. Indeed, in the light of the preparatory work and because of the use of the word 'other', it may be assumed that, in principle, wherever the treaty refers merely to 'celestial bodies', the moon is also included.[95] For all the above reasons, it is submitted that it would be clearer and simpler in future space legislation to revert to the expression 'outer space *and* celestial bodies' and, unless the text or context indicates otherwise, these terms will be so used in this chapter. Outer space *and* celestial bodies taken together will be referred to as extraterrestrial space.

B. Definition of Outer Space

An even more important problem is the definition of outer space. The treaty establishes a special regime for outer space, fundamentally different from national airspace which is subject to the complete and exclusive sovereignty of the State. Consequently, as this writer had occasion to point out in 1960, the demarcation of the upper limit of national space and the beginning of outer space, 'while hitherto unimportant in air law, is one of the first and most important problems that have to be tackled in space law'.[96] It is the 'inevitable first step in any rational approach to the legal problems of outer space'.[97] However, for reasons which are not too difficult to fathom, there has been considerable reluctance on the part of States and the United Nations to discuss this problem.[98]

The Space Treaty has similarly avoided it, with the result that, unlike for instance the Antarctic Treaty where the treaty area is precisely defined in Article VI as that 'south of 60° South Latitude', it gives no indication from what height above the earth its provisions referring to outer space begin to operate.[99] The only pointer is contained in Article VII which, if the existence of a gap in its provisions is not to be admitted, seems to have committed itself

---

[93] A/PV.1499 (Prov.) (19.12.66), p. 71.   [94] See further s. VI below.

[95] Arts. I(2) *in fine*; IV(1), and IV(2) 2nd sentence; V(2); VIII.

[96] See the writer's 'From Air Law to Space Law', 13 *CLP* (1960), p. 228, at p. 230 [Ch. 3 above, s. II.A]; also the writer's 'Problems of Space Law', 7 *The Scientist* (1960), at p. 1256; 'The United Nations and Outer Space', 14 *CLP* (1961), p. 247, pp. 259 ff. [Ch. 6 above, s. IV]; ILA, *Report of the 50th Conference, Brussels* (1962), p. 50; Id., *Report of the 51st Conference, Tokyo* (1964), p. 638; the writer's 'The Extraterrestrial Application of International Law', 18 *CLP* (1965), p. 132 [Ch. 5 above, s. III.A]; ILA, *Report of the 52nd Conference, Helsinki* (1966), p. 166.

[97] Loc. cit. in n. 11 above, p. 262 [Ch. 6 above, s. IV *in fine*].

[98] See ibid., pp. 259–62 [s. IV]; and generally loc. cit in n. 96 above.

[99] On the position under international customary law, see the writer's 'The Extraterrestrial Application of International Law', 18 *CLP* (1965), p. 132, at pp. 144–8 [Ch. 5 above, s. III.A].

to the view that outer space begins immediately beyond airspace without any intermediate zone.

It is to the credit of the French delegation to the United Nations that it succeeded in introducing into the draft resolution of the General Assembly which commended the Space Treaty an additional paragraph (4(*b*)) requesting the Outer Space Committee to begin 'the study of questions relative to the definition of outer space'.[100] Ultimately, the demarcation can be carried out with authoritative effect only by agreement among governments.[101]

C. Urbi et Orbi

However, although the treaty is intended to regulate activities in outer space and on celestial bodies, it remains an instrument creating international rights inuring to, and obligations incumbent on, its contracting States on this planet. Certain provisions of the treaty, therefore, clearly relate to obligations of the contracting Parties on the earth, for instance, Article V on assistance to and return of astronauts 'in the event of accident, distress or emergency landing on the territory of another State Party or on the high seas'. During the discussions, France did raise the point whether it was 'desirable to refer to the terrestrial effects of space exploration in certain cases and not in others'.[102] While the point raised doubtless has substance, this situation is largely inevitable. What is clear is that the treaty intends to establish the legal framework of man's exploration and use of outer space and celestial bodies.

V. The Legal Regime of Outer Space and Celestial Bodies

A. The Extraterrestrial Application of International law

Doubts had from time to time been expressed before, and were often repeated during, the discussions leading to the Space Treaty,[103] whether international law was applicable to outer space and celestial bodies. Yet it is hardly open to doubt that the international legal system, which governs the conduct of States in their mutual relations, is not bound by the still ill-defined upper limit of national space, but follows States as they advance, four hundred years after Christopher Columbus, into another new world[104]. From this point of view,

---

[100] I.e., resolutioin 2222 (XXI); see France, A/PV.1499 (19.12.66), p. 61; see also Mexico, A/C.1/SR.1493 (17.12.66), p. 439 (para. 39).

[101] See *New Scientist*, loc. cit. in n. 96 above, p. 1257, and Cheng, loc. cit. in n. 99 above, at p. 152 [Ch. 5 above, s. V, *in fine*].

[102] A/AC.105/C.2/SR.66 (25.7.66), p. 11.

[103] E.g., France, A/AC.105/C.2/SR.57 (12.7.66), p. 16; ibid./SR.64 (21.7.66), p. 6; ibid./SR.69 (27.7.66), pp. 5–6; A/AC.105/PV.44 (19.9.66), pp. 38–43; Brazil, A/AC.105/C.2/SR.62 (19.7.66), pp. 7–8; ibid./SR.71 (4.8.66), pp. 16–18; A/C.1/SR.1492 (17.12.66), p. 432.

[104] See loc. cit. in n. 99 above [Ch. 5 above].

the treaty itself is but an example of the application of international treaty law to outer space and celestial bodies.

B. *Res Extra Commercium*

International law being applicable, the legal status of outer space and extraterrestrial bodies is determinable by reference to it. Thus, under international customary law, whilst outer space constitutes *res extra commercium*, that is to say, areas not subject to national appropriation, celestial bodies are *res nullius*, that is to say, areas which may be subject to national sovereignty.[105] As among contracting States, however, the status of the latter has now been changed. Under the treaty, both outer space and celestial bodies are declared *res extra commercium*, thus forestalling any possible recurrence of colonialism in extraterrestrial space, as some delegates did not fail to point out.[106] Article II stipulates:

Outer space, including the moon and other celestial bodies, is not subject to national appropriation by claim of sovereignty, by means of use or occupation, or by any other means.[107]

Furthermore, Article I, in its paragraphs 2 and 3, provides *inter alia*:

. . . Outer space, including the moon and other celestial bodies, shall be free for exploration and use by all States without discrimination of any kind, on a basis of equality and in accordance with international law, and there shall be free access to all areas of celestial bodies.
There shall be freedom of scientific investigation in outer space, including the moon and other celestial bodies . . .

Article I(2) of the treaty is derived via Article I(2) of Soviet draft I from paragraph 2 of resolution 1962, to which the Soviet draft added the words 'without discrimination of any kind'. Perhaps still slightly stunned, albeit at the same time relieved, by the timely discovery that what had appeared to be a fairly innocent sentence in the same draft Article I, ostensibly inspired by the same spirit of non-discrimination, turned out in reality to be a most-favoured-nation clause regarding the grant of tracking and other facilities,[108] the United Kingdom representative was frankly uneasy about this addition. After agreement had been reached on this article, he said:

The United Kingdom delegation did not fully understand what those words meant in the context or why they were needed, but had accepted them in order to reach

[105] See loc. cit. in n. 99 above, at pp. 143–8 [Ch. 5 above, s. III].
[106] Mongolia, A/AC.105/C.2/SR.62 (19.7.66), p. 9; Chile, A/C.1/SR.1492 (17.12.66), p. 432; Brazil, ibid., p. 432; Italy, A/PV.1499 (Prov.) (19.12.66), pp. 57–9/60: Treaty of Tordesillas of 1494 recalled which divided the then New World between Portugal and Spain.
[107] Substantially the same as resolution 1962, para. 3.
[108] See nn. 44, 54, 55, and 63 above, and s. VII.D below.

agreement. However, it could not accept the USSR proposal that States which provided facilities to another State for the observation of the flight of space objects should be obliged to extend the same facilities to all other Parties to the Treaty.[109]

However, like the freedom of the high seas, the freedom of outer space and celestial bodies for scientific investigation, exploration and use is merely a corollary of their status of *res extra commercium*. Similarly, Article III of the treaty simply spells out the logical consequence of the *ipso jure* applicability of international law to outer space and celestial bodies in stating:

States Parties to the Treaty shall carry on activities in the exploration and use of outer space, including the moon and other celestial bodies, in accordance with international law, including the Charter of the United Nations, in the interest of maintaining international peace and security and promoting international co-operation and understanding.[110]

In the discussions leading to the conclusion of the treaty, France indicated more than once that she was 'not altogether satisfied with the wording' of Article II of the treaty.[111] At one stage, her representative said:

I am thinking in particular of the risks of ambiguity between the principle of non-sovereignty—which falls under public law—and that of non-appropriation, flowing from private law.[112]

It is submitted, however, that the alleged ambiguity does not, in fact, exist. The concept of non-appropriation embodied in Article II is the same as that which has been traditionally applied to the high seas. It simply means that as among the contracting States, none will be entitled to exercise *territorial* jurisdiction, no matter on what basis, over any part of outer space or celestial bodies.[113]

As on the high seas, however, the exclusion of territorial jurisdiction from outer space and celestial bodies does not mean that either quasi-territorial jurisdiction or personal jurisdiction may also not be exercised.[114] Indeed, if outer space is not to become an area of lawlessness, it is necessary to ensure that some type of State jurisdiction is exercised there.[115]

---

[109] A/AC.105/C.2/SR.71 and Add. 1 (4.8.66), p. 5.

[110] Substantially the same as resolution 1962, principle 4.

[111] A/AC.105/C.2/SR.70 (3.8.66), p. 14.

[112] A/AC.105/PV.44 (19.9.66), p. 41; see further s. V.D below.

[113] On the division of State jurisdiction into territorial, quasi-territorial and personal, and the hierarchy of these three types of jurisdiction, see loc. cit. in n. 99 above, pp. 134–42 [Ch. 5 above, s. II].

[114] See further loc. cit. in n. 99 above [Ch. 5 above].

[115] Cf. some of the problems of a similar nature discussed in the writer's 'Crimes on Board Aircraft', 12 *CLP* (1959), pp. 177 ff.; see also Art. IX(1)(*e*) of the Antarctic Treaty, 1959, where provision is made for regulating the 'exercise of jurisdiction in Antarctica'.

C. Jurisdiction of the State of Registry

From this point of view, the Space Treaty seems to envisage that the prevailing jurisdiction in outer space and on celestial bodies will be the quasi-territorial jurisdiction of the State of registry of objects launched into outer space. Article VIII affirms:

A State Party to the Treaty on whose registry an object launched into outer space is carried shall retain jurisdiction and control over such object, and over any personnel there of, while in outer space or on a celestial body . . .[116]

Regarding this provision, attention may be drawn to the following points.

1. *Registration of Objects Launched into Space.* In the first instance, the treaty presupposes that all States parties to the treaty will maintain a registry of objects launched into space. Secondly, it assumes that objects launched into space will all first be registered. In fact, the application of a number of the provisions of the treaty depends on the registration of the spacecraft, namely, the exercise of jurisdiction (Article VIII), the return of space objects (Article VIII),[117] and the return of astronauts (Article V).[118]

Unlike the 1944 Chicago Convention on International Civil Aviation, the Space Treaty does not confer nationality on spacecraft,[119] or explicitly prohibit dual registration,[120] or provide for international registration,[121] although both dual registration and international registration of spacecraft would seem to fit in ill with the scheme of the treaty. On the other hand, Article XIII of the treaty appears explicitly to envisage the possibility of joint registration of spacecraft effected by two or more contracting States either directly or, notwithstanding the terminology used in the treaty, through joint bi- or multinational organizations.[122]

2. *Quasi-territorial Character of Jurisdiction.* The jurisdiction referred to in Article VIII is quasi-territorial rather than personal in character,[123] for it applies to not only the spacecraft but also any personnel on board, irrespective of their nationality. The quasi-territorial jurisdiction of the State of registry overrides, therefore, the personal jurisdiction of the national State, at least insofar as the power of enforcement or implementation ('jurisaction')[124] is concerned.

---

[116] For the rest of the article, see ss. V.d, and VII.F below.

[117] See s. VII.F below.   [118] See s. VII.F below.

[119] Cf. Chicago Convention, 1944, Art. 17. [On nationality of space objects, see Ch. 17 below].

[120] Chicago Convention, 1944, Art. 18.   [121] Chicago Convention, 1944, Art. 77.

[122] On analogous problems in the field of air law, discussed by the Air Law Committee of the International Law Association, ILA, *Report of the 52nd Conference, Helsinki* (1966), p. 228; the writer's Memorandum is reprinted under the title 'Nationality and Registration of Aircraft— Article 77 of the Chicago Convention', in 32 *JALC* (1966), p. 551; see further s. V.G below.

[123] See loc. cit. in n. 99 above [Ch. 5 above].

[124] On the division of jurisdiction into jurisfaction and jurisaction, see loc. cit. in n. 99 above, pp. 136–42 [Ch. 5 above, s. II.B].

Furthermore, this jurisdiction of the State of registry applies to these persons, not only when they are on board, but also when they are outside their vehicle.[125] The substitution of the word 'thereof' for 'thereon' found in paragraph 7 of resolution 1962 was intended to make this point explicit.[126] To the extent that they are members of the crew[127] of space vehicles, the treaty envisages therefore that all persons in outer space and on celestial bodies will be subject to the quasi-territorial jurisdiction of the State of registry of their respective spacecraft, irrespective of their own nationality. A Canadian member of a United States registered spacecraft will thus be subject to United States and not Canadian jurisdiction while in outer space and on celestial bodies.

3. *Overriding Character.* The jurisdiction of the State of registry not only overrides that of the national State of foreign members of the crew, but it appears implicitly to override also that of all other States which may be involved in the launching of the spacecraft, by being the only one to be mentioned in the treaty in this connexion. The entire operation of maintaining law and order in outer space and on celestial bodies, insofar as individuals are concerned, is consequently left in the hands of the respective States of registry. Tasks such as those of registering births, deaths, and marriages would also fall on them.

This being so, it would appear that whenever States engage in co-operative schemes for the conduct of space activities, joint registration, accompanied by satisfactory arrangements concerning the exercise of jurisdiction, is highly desirable, if they are not to find themselves burdened with various responsibilities under the treaty, but at the same time deprived of effective power to meet them.[128]

4. *Persons Other than Members of the Crew.* As soon as space exploration, let alone space utilization, reaches the point when space vehicles begin carrying persons other than members of the crew, or when stations on celestial bodies begin to be manned by persons brought up by spacecraft registered in different countries, then problems not resolved by the treaty will arise. It seems highly desirable that in the former case the treaty should either be amended or construed to mean that the jurisdiction of the State of registry extends to all persons on board whether or not members of the crew. In the latter case some system of delegation of authority might be worked out. In any event both problems deserve consideration by the Outer Space Committee under paragraph 4(*b*) of resolution 2222 whereby it is requested to begin the

---

[125] See USSR, A/AC.105/C.2/SR.66 (25.7.1866), p. 11: 'the text . . . covered both the object launched into space and its crew, whether the latter was inside or outside the object'.

[126] See Canada, ibid., p. 11.

[127] The terms personnel and crew seem to have been treated as synonyms, see n. 125 above.

[128] See further ss. V.F and V.G below; cf. also chs. 23 and 24 below.

study of questions relative to the 'utilisation of outer space and celestial bodies'.

D. Rights of Ownership and Exploitation

The above paragraph of the resolution was first proposed by France.[129] The French delegation was obviously concerned with the effect of Article II[130] on the future use and exploitation of outer space and celestial bodies. Speaking of the task which the proposed paragraph would impose on the Outer Space Committee, the French representative said:

That task was necessary because, while the principles established by the treaty would no doubt be easy to apply in the case of the exploration of space, their application would be more difficult when State activities involved exploitation, and particularly where simple occupation had to be distinguished from appropriation.[131]

Insofar as private rights are concerned, the second sentence of Article VIII provides:

Ownership of objects launched into outer space, including objects landed or constructed on a celestial body, and of their component parts, is not affected by their presence in outer space or on celestial body or by their return to the earth.[132]

However, inasmuch as there is to be no territorial jurisdiction, there can be no private ownership of parts of outer space or celestial bodies, which presupposes the existence of a territorial sovereign itself competent to confer titles of such ownership. In this sense, outer space and celestial bodies are not only not subject to national appropriation, but also not subject to appropriation under private law.[133]

However, separate from the problem of appropriating parts of outer space and celestial bodies is that of appropriating resources of outer space and celestial bodies. To the extent to which outer space and celestial bodies constitute *res extra commercium*,[134] by analogy with the rules underlying the freedom of the high seas, the appropriation of the natural resources thereof merely forms part of the freedom of exploration and use, and is not prohibited.

---

[129] See n. 100 above.   [130] See n. 112 above.

[131] A/C.1/SR.1492 (17.12.66), p. 430 (para. 22).

[132] For the first sentence, see n. 116 above; the third sentence, s. VII.F below.

[133] See Belgium, A/AC.105/C.2/SR.71 and Add. 1 (4.8.66), p. 7: 'His delegation had taken note of the interpretation of the term "non-appropriation" advanced by several delegations—apparently without contradiction—as covering both the establishment of sovereignty and the creation of titles to property in private law'; France, A/C.1/SR.1492 (17.12.66), p. 429 (para. 20): 'the prohibition of any claim to sovereignty or property rights in space'. See also n. 112 above. It is submitted, however, that non-appropriation under private law is merely the logical consequence of non-appropriation under international law. 'Non-appropriation' in the treaty refers to 'national appropriation' under international law.

[134] See s. V.B above.

But as the French delegation suggested,[135] the semi-permanent occupation of parts of outer space and especially celestial bodies for purposes of exploitation will pose problems which require further study and, if the example of the continental shelf is any guide, also further regulation.

E. 'Exploration and Use for the Benefit of All Countries'

But perhaps before this point is reached, even more complex problems will have arisen under Article I(1) of the treaty, if it is to be strictly interpreted and applied:

The exploration and use of outer space, including the moon and other celestial bodies, shall be carried out for the benefit and in the interests of all countries, irrespective of their degree of economic or scientific development . . .

The main part of this sentence originated in Soviet draft I had been adapted from paragraph 1 of resolution 1962. During the discussions, the Indian representative 'expressed some doubt as to whether it dealt with a specific legal obligation and, therefore, whether its inclusion in the body of the text was warranted'.[136] The Italian and French representatives actually suggested that it should be transferred to the preamble,[137] while a contrary view was expressed by the representative of Brazil,[138] who proposed the addition of the words: 'irrespective of the state of their scientific development'.[139]

Looking at the text as it stands, there seems to be no valid reason why it should not be treated as stating a binding legal obligation. If so, Article I(1) of the treaty must be regarded as superimposing on the freedom of exploration and use affirmed in Article I(2) a principle of far-reaching significance; for such exploration and use are permissible only to the extent to which they are 'for the benefit and in the interests of all countries'. While opinion may differ on what constitutes 'the interests of all countries' and compliance with this part of the obligation might have to rely largely on the good faith of the contracting States, the rest of the sentence is much more concrete in meaning. It strongly suggests that 'all States' have a legal right to the fruits of space exploration and use, by whomsoever carried out. It is hardly surprising, therefore, that the representative of Cyprus, in welcoming the treaty, hailed it as going:

beyond international law and the Charter, which regarded nations as independent sovereign agents, whereas the treaty saw mankind as a single entity.[140]

It is to be wondered, however, whether such optimism was justified. Insofar as the preparatory work of the treaty is concerned, the discussions which took

---

[135] See text to n. 131 above.
[136] A/AC.105/C.2/SR.63 (20.7.66), p. 11; cf. his earlier remark, ibid., p. 7.
[137] Italy, A/AC.105/C.2/SR.64 (21.7.66), pp. 4–5; France, ibid., p. 6.
[138] A/AC.105/C.2/SR.63 (20.7.66), p. 9.   [139] Ibid./SR.64 (21.7.66), p. 9.
[140] A/C.1/SR.1493 (17.12.66), p. 443 (para. 72).

place on several articles of the treaty clearly showed that its draftsmen hardly intended this part of Article I to be anything more than a declaration of principles from which no specific rights of a legal nature were to be derived, even though it might give rise to a moral obligation.

Thus, in order to persuade the Soviet Union to accept the United States proposal that there should be compulsory reporting of all space activities and all findings, the Canadian representative referred not only to this provision in the Soviet draft, but also to that which required States to regard astronauts as envoys of mankind.[141] The logic of this argument appears undeniable. The Hungarian representative who sought to refute it obviously found himself in a dilemma. On the one hand, he said:

States parties to the treaty would . . . be undertaking to explore space £or the benefit of all. It would follow from that that the results of such exploration would be accessible to all . . . Those States [i.e., the space powers] would be bound by a moral obligation and by a contractual obligation under the treaty as a whole to publish scientific data.[142]

On the other hand, he maintained that:

the publication of information should be at the discretion of the States which had made the greatest sacrifices to promote the exploration of space . . . The voluntary principle should be accepted, as it was in the case on the United Nations technical assistance programmes supported by voluntary contributions.[143]

In the end, the voluntary principle, suitably dressed up, was incorporated into Article XI of the treaty.[144]

Insofar as non-space powers are concerned, it may also be questioned whether it would necessarily be an unmixed blessing for them to insist on too literal an interpretation of Article I(1); for the tables can easily be turned. Thus one of the arguments adduced by the Soviet Union in favour of its proposal of a most-favoured-nation clause on the grant of tracking facilities was the principle that 'the exploration of outer space should be carried out in the interests of all mankind'.[145] The same argument was later used by the Bulgarian representative:

The Bulgarian delegation attached great importance to the principles stated in the first paragraph of Article I . . . , and particularly to the principle that the results achieved through space exploration and research were to benefit all mankind, not merely certain States or groups of States. It was satisfactory to find that principle stated in the operative part of the treaty and not merely in the preamble. While only the economically and scientifically advanced countries could afford the tremendous cost of space

---

[141] A/AC.105/C.2/SR.65 (22.7.66), p. 3; see further ss. VI.E, VII.C, and VII.F.1 below.
[142] A/AC.105/C.2/SR.65 (22.7.66), p. 4.   [143] Ibid.
[144] See n. 71 above, and ss. VI.E, and VII.C below.
[145] A/AC.105/C.2/SR.63 (20.7.66), p. 6.

research, all other States should make what contribution they could to an activity of common interest to all.[146]

In their turn, the non-space powers did not feel moved to grant such facilities unconditionally. That the 'benefit of all countries' clause in the treaty, apart from expressing a lofty and most desirable ideal, will be prayed in aid of all kinds of causes can be illustrated also by the duty to 'regard astronauts as envoys of mankind' imposed on contracting States by Article V of the treaty, together with the obligation to render them 'all possible assistance'. When questioned by the Austrian representative as to the precise meaning of 'envoys of mankind', the Soviet representative, while 'prepared to consider another form of words', was recorded as having said:

In his opinion, the expression used in the article served to justify the legal obligations it laid down.[147]

It can only be a matter of conjecture whether the Soviet preparedness to consider another form of words was not prompted by another remark of the Austrian representative; for, if astronauts were envoys of mankind, he wondered blandly 'whether States which were not space powers should not have a hand in the way astronauts were launched into space'.[148]

Indeed, the image which the draftsmen of the treaty seek to project that the exploration and use of outer space are being and shall ever be carried out primarily or even exclusively for the benefit of mankind rather than in the interests of individual States reminds one strongly of the discussion in the early days of the International Law Commission on the continental shelf. Getting somewhat weary with the constant invocation of the 'benefit of mankind' and the 'requirements of humanity' as reasons for parcelling out the world's continental shelves among the coastal States, Mr Amada wryly remarked:

The exploitation in question was mainly carried out for pecuniary gain.[149]

Mutatis mutandis, this observation applies with even greater force to the exploration of outer space, on which astronomical sums are being spent, except that the interests involved are what is still regarded in present-day international society as the highest for every State, namely, national security. Herein lies the significance of Article IV of the treaty, and the immediate importance of the treaty itself.[150]

---

[146] A/AC.105/C.2/SR.71 and Add. 1 (4.8.66), p. 23.
[147] A/AC.105/C.2/SR.58 (13.7.66), p. 9; see further s. VII.F.1 below.   [148] Ibid., p. 2/3.
[149] A/CN.4/SR.131, para. 13; see further the writer's 'International Law Commission', 5 *CLP* (1952), p. 251, at pp. 257 ff.
[150] See further s. VI below.

F. International Responsibility of States for Activities in Space and International Liability for Damage Caused

Whereas the Space Treaty recognizes the quasi-territorial jurisdiction in outer space and on celestial bodies of States of registry of space vehicles,[151] it imposes on contracting States international responsibility for all national activities outside terrestrial space, and international liability for all damage caused to other contracting States or their nationals. The relevant provisions are Articles VI and VII.

Article VI states:

States Parties to the Treaty shall bear international responsibility for national activities in outer space, including the moon and other celestial bodies, whether such activities are carried on by governmental agencies or by non-governmental entities, and for assuring that national activities are carried out in conformity with the provisions set forth in the present Treaty. The activities of non-governmental entities in outer space, including the moon and other celestial bodies, shall require authorisation and continuing supervision by the appropriate State Party to the Treaty. When activities are carried on in outer space, including the moon and other celestial bodies, by an international organisation, responsibility for compliance with this Treaty shall be borne both by the international organisation and by the States Parties to the Treaty participating in such organisation.

Article VII states:

Each State Party to the Treaty that launches or procures the launching of an object into outer space, including the moon and other celestial bodies, and each State Party from whose territory or facility an object is launched, is internationally liable for damage to another State Party to the Treaty or to its natural or juridical persons by such object or its component parts on the earth, in air space or in outer space, including the moon and other celestial bodies.

There has been much discussion as to the precise meaning of these provisions. It is submitted that what they amount to, in substance, is that all activities in space, whether carried on by a governmental or a non-governmental agency are deemed to be governmental activities involving direct State responsibility.[152] Insofar as the international liability of the State 'from whose territory or facility an object is launched' is concerned, this seems to be properly based on the decision of the Trail Smelter Arbitration Tribunal (1935) which affirmed the duty of every State at all times 'to protect other States against injurious acts by individuals from within its jurisdiction',[153] and held:

---

[151] See s. V.C. above.

[152] On the distinction between direct and indirect State responsibility and the principles governing direct State responsibility, see the writer's *General Principles of Law*, Part III, pp. 163 ff.

[153] Award II (1941), 3 *RIAA*, p. 1905, at p. 1963.

No State has the right to use or permit the use of its territory in such a manner as to cause injury . . . in or to the territory of another or the properties or persons therein, when the case is of serious consequence and the injury is established by clear and convincing evidence.[154]

During the discussions of the draft treaty, the Indian representative, speaking with reference to what later became Article VII of the treaty, said:

The word 'internationally' had not been explained, and would be acceptable to his delegation only if the Powers concerned made it clear that it meant 'absolutely'.[155]

It does not appear that such an assurance was ever given.[156] However, liability for damage caused by space activities had been the subject of a separate treaty which was being considered by the Legal Sub-Committee of the United Nations Outer Space Committee. By late 1965, it would appear that agreement had already been reached on the principle of absolute liability, though not on some of the exceptions to it.[157] But in itself, Article VII cannot be regarded as asserting the principle of absolute liability. It is merely the logical consequence of Article VI, though, as the *Trail Smelter Arbitration* shows, in many cases the line dividing them may be rather thin.

However, Article VII deals merely with damage caused by objects launched into space. It is not explicit as regards objects which fail to reach outer space. And it clearly does not cover damage caused by astronauts. For all such unregulated cases, it would seem necessary to fall back on Article VI on the international responsibility of the State concerned.

Among the many points which may be raised regarding Article VI is the meaning of 'national activities'. If the expression means State activities, whether carried on directly by governmental agencies or indirectly by non-governmental entities, then the article appears to be superfluous. It may mean, therefore, in addition to activities of the State, activities of all persons within its territorial, quasi-territorial[158] and personal jurisdiction[159]. But, inasmuch as the system of 'authorisation and continuing supervision' envisaged by Article VI can be effectively administered only by the State exercising territorial and quasi-territorial jurisdiction, rather than by the State exercising merely personal jurisdiction, it would appear that Article VI is not intended to include within the notion of 'national activities' those conducted by the

---

[154] Ibid., p. 1965; see further op. cit. in n. 152 above, pp. 83 ff., and 130.

[155] A/AC.105/C.2/SR.71 and Add. 1 (4.8.66), p. 8; cf. also Argentina, A/AC.105/C.2/SR.67 (25.7.66), p. 10.

[156] Cf. India, A/C.1/SR.1493 (17.12.66), p. 8 (para. 8).

[157] See Chairman, A/AC.105/C.2/SR.50 (28.9.65), p. 13.

[158] I.e., on ships and aircraft bearing the nationality of the State; see further loc. cit. in n. 113 above [Ch. 5 above, s. II].

[159] Primarily its nationals, individual or corporate, wherever they may be; see further loc. cit. in n. 113 above [Ch. 5 above, s. II].

nationals of a State when they are not within either its territorial or quasi-territorial jurisaction.[160]

Even so, it is not to be forgotten that whilst Article VIII explicitly recognizes only the jurisdiction of the State of registry, Article VI makes contracting States internationally responsible for national space activities, and Article VII imposes international liability on a contracting State which launches or procures the launching of a space object, as well on a contracting State from which or from the facility of which a space object is launched. Consequently, a State, unless it is also the State of registry, may be held responsible for activities in extraterrestrial space over which it has no jurisdiction recognized by the treaty, and liable for any damage resulting therefrom.[161] This situation certainly merits the urgent attention of the Legal Sub-Committee when it considers the question of international liability.

G. International Organizations

The position becomes even more complex in the case of international organizations. It may be recalled that under Article VI of the treaty, when space activities are carried on by an international organization, 'responsibility for compliance with this Treaty shall be borne both by the international organisation and by the States Parties to the Treaty participating in such organisation'.[162]

The question of international organizations is a general one, not specifically confined to the problem of liability. Already in 1965, it had taken up a great deal of the time of the Legal Sub-Committee when the Sub-Committee was discussing the draft agreement on liability.[163] The question is also one of great interest for the smaller and even most medium powers, inasmuch as their best chance to participate in the exploration and use of outer space is through co-operative efforts in international organizations,[164] such as the European Space Research Organization (ESRO), the European Space Vehicles Launchers Development and Construction Organization (ELDO), and the International Telecommunications Satellite Consortium (INTELSAT).

On the Soviet side, there are two objections to conceding any *locus standi* to international organizations in space activities, one political, the other juridical, to the extent to which it is possible to separate law from politics in Soviet eyes. From the political point of view, the Soviet Union looks upon some of

---

[160] Cf., however, Art. IX of the treaty (see s. VII.E below) where the responsibility of the State extends also to activities and experiments 'planned by . . . its nationals'. See also Ch. 24 below. On the distinction between jurisfaction and jurisaction, see loc. cit. in n. 99 above, pp. 136–42 [Ch. 5 above, s. II.B].

[161] See s. V.C.3, especially text to n. 128 above.   [162] See s. V.F above.

[163] A/AC.105/C.2/SR.52 (29.9.65), pp. 3 ff.

[164] Cf. Sweden, A/AC.105/C.2/SR.70 (3.8.66), pp. 11–13; Australia, ibid./SR.71 and Add.1 (4.8.66), pp. 14–16.

these organizations as mere instruments of United States aggressive or monopolistic designs.[165] From the juridical point of view, it and other States within the Soviet block adopt what may be regarded as an extremely cautious attitude towards treating international organizations as subjects of international law.[166] Here, indeed, is an important issue, which has been raised in relation to the operation of both ships[167] and aircraft[168], but which has as yet not been satisfactorily resolved by either the doctrine or the practice of international law.

Article VI of the treaty is derived from paragraph 5 of resolution 1962 via Article VI of the Soviet draft. General Assembly resolutions are mere recommendations, and they may be addressed to all and sundry. But as was immediately pointed out by the Austrian representative during the discussions of the draft, in a treaty, no obligations can, or may be imposed on international organizations without their being parties to the treaty or otherwise consenting.[169]

The Soviet Union recalled that at one time it had proposed that only States should be allowed to engage in space activities. The reference to international organizations in paragraph 5 of resolution 1962 and Article VI of its draft was, therefore, already a concession in that it thereby recognized the possibility of their engaging in space activities.[170] But this

did not mean that international organisations were being placed, from a legal point of view, on the same footing as States Parties to the Treaty. . . No State Party to the Treaty must be allowed to evade its responsibilities when it acted as a member of an international organisation.[171]

On the other hand, the view was voiced:

As a matter of simple justice, international organisations should not be bound by articles imposing obligations or governing their conduct unless they were entitled to the benefits provided in certain articles for those conducting space activities. [172]

---

[165] E.g., USSR, A/AC.105/PV.31 (3.11.64), pp. 3 ff.; 'ELDO . . . the rocket pool of the NATO countries'; ibid./PV.34 (5.11.64), pp. 2 ff.: Washington Agreements of 20 Aug. 1964 on Global Commercial Satellite Communications System establishing INTELSAT were said to be in furtherance of American Telephone and Telegraph Co.'s monopoly over telecommunications, and contrary to resolution 1962.

[166] Cf., e.g., the rather typical remark of the Romanian delegate that 'the rules of international law did not explicitly refer to international organisations', A/AC.105/C.2/SR.66 (25.7.66), p. 14.

[167] Cf. the Geneva High Seas Convention, 1958, Art. 6; and the problems raised in Prof. Francois' Report on the Right of International Organisations to Sail Vessels under their Flags, 2 *ILC Ybk* (1956), p. 102.

[168] See further loc. cit. n. 122 above.

[169] A/AC.105/C.2/SR.58 (13.7.66), pp. 2/3–4; ibid./SR.71 and Add. 1 (4.8.66), pp. 10–11; Canada, ibid./SR.66 (25.7.66), p. 14; Australia, ibid./SR.71 and Add. 1 (4.8.66), pp. 14–16.

[170] A/AC.105/C.2/SR.67 (25.7.66), p. 3.   [171] A/AC.105/C.2/SR.58 (13.7.66), p. 8.

[172] United Kingdom, A/AC.105/C.2/SR.66 (25.7.66), p. 13; see also France, ibid., p. 13; ibid./SR.70 (3.8.66), p. 15; Australia, ibid./SR.66 (25.7.66), p. 13, Sweden, ibid./SR.70 (3.8.66), p. 13.

And it was suggested that:

provision should be made in the treaty for international organisations either to accede to it or to share in the rights and obligations it created.[173]

While it was not thought 'that the rights granted to States under the treaty could apply in an identical manner to an international organisation; an international organisation could not, for example, have jurisdiction over an object launched into space or over its personnel,' it was said:

However, it would be inconceivable that an organisation set up by States Parties to the Treaty, which has undertaken to ensure that the organisation complied with the treaty, should not be entitled, for example, to the right of free exploration, mutual assistance and co-operation and the right to visit space vehicles.[174]

In the course of the discussions, the United Kingdom proposed that the following provision should be added to the treaty:

1. If an international organisation which conducts activities in outer space including the moon and other celestial bodies transmits to (the depositary authority) a declaration that it accepts and undertakes to comply with the provisions of this Treaty, all the provisions except articles . . . (here insert a reference to the articles concerning signature, ratification and accession by States), shall apply to the organisation as they apply to a State which is a Party to this Treaty.
2. The States Parties to the Treaty undertake to use their best endeavours to ensure that any international organisation which conducts such activities and of which they are constituent members is authorised to make and will make the declaration referred to in paragraph 1 of this article.
3. The States Parties to the Treaty shall take such steps as are open to them to ensure that any international organisation which conducts such activities and of which they are constituent members acts, subject to reciprocity, in accordance with the principles set out in this Treaty until such time as a declaration is made pursuant to paragraph 1 of this article.[175].

The United Kingdom proposal was rejected outright by the Soviet Union, 'because it would leave any international organisation free, after the conclusion of the treaty, to do exactly as it chose until it declared itself willing to comply with the principles of the treaty'.[176] It 'could lead to evasion of the

[173] Austria, A/AC.105/C.2/SR.71 and Add. 1 (4.8.66), p. 10. At one stage Italy proposed that the phrase 'A State Party to the Treaty' should be replaced by 'The Parties to the Treaty' in view of the possibility that a 'multilateral organisation might eventually engage in space activities', A/AC.105/C.2/SR.66 (25.7.66), p. 11; subsequently, however, it stated: 'The Treaty should take account of the present and future role of international organisations in space activities; it should not, however, place those organisations on the same footing as the States parties to the treaty', ibid./SR.70 (3.8.66), p. 10; see further nn. 174 and 180 below.

[174] Sweden, A/AC.105/C.2/SR.70 (3.8.66), p. 13; see also Italy, loc. cit. in n. 173 above, and n. 180 below; Iran, A/AC.105/C.2/SR.71 and Add. 1 (4.8.66), p. 25.

[175] A/AC.105/C.2/5th Sess./WP.17 (25.7.66); United Kingdom, A/AC.105/C.2/SR.67 (26.7.66), pp. 4–6.

[176] A/AC.105/C.2/SR.67 (25.7.66), p. 6.

treaty obligations by the creation of an international organisation in bad faith'.[177] In the words of the Indian delegate, 'Unlike the Soviet draft article VI, the new article proposed by the United Kingdom delegation created more difficulties than it solved'.[178]

Under Article VI of the Soviet draft which, with minor verbal modifications, became Article VI of the Space Treaty, the responsibility imposed on international organizations ultimately fell on those of their members which were parties to the treaty. It would in fact appear that members of international organizations engaged in space activities became jointly and severally liable for such activities. It would thus be entirely up to those members which became parties to the treaty to ensure that the responsibility of their organizations would be borne by the organization as a whole, and not by themselves alone. Where they were unable to do so, they would have no alternative but to withdraw from the organization. In the opinion of the Swedish representative, all this should be made explicit.[179] And the Italian representative proposed the following addition to the treaty:

The States Parties which conduct space activities through international organisations undertake that those activities will fully comply with the provisions of the Treaty.

A declaration to this effect may be transmitted by such an organisation to (the depositary authority). [180]

However, the Soviet representative announced at the penultimate meeting of the first part of fifth session of the Legal Sub-Committee:

The USSR was categorically opposed to the idea that international organisations should not be responsible for their activities in space unless they had made a declaration to that effect; moreover, it could not agree that such organisations should be placed on a footing of equality with parties to the treaty, which were sovereign States.[181]

The Australian representative commented:

To impose the obligation solely on the States parties to the treaty who were members of the international organisation and to leave everything else to the internal mechanism of the organisation, would amount to a refusal to treat an international organisation as a subject or object of international rights and duties [182],

[177] Cf. United Kingdom, A/AC.105/C.2/SR.71 and Add. 1 (4.8.66), p. 6.

[178] A/AC.105/C.2/SR.67 (25.7.66), p. 7.

[179] A/AC.105/C.2/SR.70 (3.8.66), p. 12: 'It was essential to include a very strict provision making States parties responsible for ensuring that any international organisation of which they were members complied with the treaty, so that they could not, as members of the organisation, escape the obligations they assumed under the treaty.'

[180] A/AC.105/C.2/5th Sess./WP.27 (3.8.66); A/AC.105/C.2/SR.70 (3.8.66), p. 10; the Italian representative had earlier apparently envisaged the possibility of international organizations becoming parties to the treaty, ibid./SR.66 (25.7.66), p. 11; see further n. 173 above.

[181] A/AC.105/C.2/SR.70 (3.8.66), p. 3.

[182] A/AC.105/C.2/SR.71 and Add. 1 (4.8.66), p. 16.

by which was meant doubtless 'a subject of international law or a bearer of international rights and duties'. The provision which was eventually inserted into the treaty as its Article XIII in fact reflects this view, though it opens the possibility for any contracting party which recognizes the international personality of a particular international organization to deal with it direct. Article XIII is worded as follows:

The provisions of this Treaty shall apply to the activities of States Parties to the Treaty in the exploration and use of outer space, including the moon and other celestial bodies, whether such activities are carried on by a single State Party to the Treaty or jointly with other States, including cases where they are carried on within the framework of international inter-governmental organisations.

Any practical questions arising in connexion with activities carried on by international inter-governmental organisations in the exploration and use of outer space, including the moon and other celestial bodies, shall be resolved by the States Parties to the Treaty either with the appropriate international organisation or with one or more States members of that international organisation, which are Parties to this Treaty.

In the present state of international law and society which, from this point of view, may be compared to the early stages in the development of corporate persons with limited liability in municipal law and society, it is difficult to see how such a solution can be easily avoided without giving rise to even more complex problems. While it is true that there is an increasing tendency to grant international personality to international organizations, this does not mean that all inter-governmental organizations established by States are *ipso facto* subjects of international law. Their international legal personality depends in the first instance on the consent of their members. But when they have been granted legal personality by their members, insofar as third States are concerned, notwithstanding the dictum of the International Court of Justice on 'objective international legal personality',[183] their legal personality need not be recognised by non-members unless the latter wish to.[184]

Whereas before its recognition as a separate international person, an international organization, whether binational or multinational, is basically a joint organization of States the rights and duties of which are collectively those of its members, once it is recognized, it has its own rights and duties separate from those of its members. It becomes, moreover, an entity with limited liability. In the absence of some international control, it is clear that third States will wish first to be satisfied with the willingness and especially the ability of an international organization to exercise its rights and discharge its duties before they grant it recognition. It is consequently difficult to see how they can

---

[183] *Reparations for Injuries* (1949), *ICJ Rep. 1949*, p. 174, at p.185. Cf. the writer's comments in 'International Law in the United Nations', 8 *YBWA* (1954), p. 170, at pp. 191–2.

[184] Herein lies the difference between the Space Treaty, and the precedents cited by Australia, A/AC.105/C.2/SR.71 and Add. 1 (4.8.66), p. 16, where the parties are either members of, or ready to recognize, the organizations concerned.

be called upon to subscribe in advance to a blanket recognition of the international legal personality of all intergovernmental organizations which other States may establish. Furthermore, to allow an international organization to join a treaty more or less on a basis of equality, when some[185] or all of its members need not be parties to it would be like allowing a group of persons to travel on the fare of a single passenger. All the non-parties to the treaty, members of the organization, will in fact be carried free, apart from what they have contributed towards the single fare[186].

VI. Partial Demilitarization of Outer Space and Non- Militarization of Celestial Bodies

A. Limited Demilitarization

By a coincidence, on the date the Space Treaty came into force, 10 October 1967, advance copies of the United Nations Secretary-General's Report on the effects of the possible use of nuclear weapons were being distributed[187] for publication on 23 October, the official date of issue. In this Report, prepared by a high-powered group of experts, it is said:

> There is one inescapable and basic fact. It is that the nuclear armouries which are in being already contain large megaton weapons every one of which has a destructive power greater than that of all the conventional explosive that has ever been used in warfare since the day gunpowder was discovered . . .
>
> . . . The exact number of nuclear warheads which may now exist in the world is not known, but it is quite certain that the arms race between the United States and the Union of Soviet Socialist Republics alone, has resulted in the production of weapons whose cumulative destructive power is certainly more than sufficient to eliminate all mankind.[188]

In its Conclusion, the Report points out that while national and international security must ultimately be sought in general and complete disarmament, all agreements on arms limitation will help to promote it.

That extraterrestrial space should be used exclusively for peaceful purposes has been the aim of the United Nations from the start. In previous years, however, attempts to discuss the matter within the Outer Space Committee or its Sub-Committees were always met with the answer that it lay with the Disarmament Commission.[189] That the super powers were finally able to reach some agreement on the subject and willing to put this agreement in

---

[185] Cf. Art. 6 of the Agreement on the Rescue of Astronauts, the Return of Astronauts, and the Return of Objects Launched into Outer Space, commended to States by the General Assembly on 19 Dec. 1967; see further n. 274, and Ch. 10 below.

[186] Cf. similar problems in the field of air law, loc. cit. in n. 122 above.

[187] A/6858 and Corr. 1.   [188] Paras. 1 and 81.

[189] See further loc. cit. in n. 11 above, pp. 272 ff. [Ch. 6 above, s. VI].

treaty form as Article IV of the Space Treaty certainly represents, therefore, a significant, albeit limited, step in that direction. From this point of view, in an age which suffers only too frequently from the dangers of 'double talk',[190] it is perhaps just as well that there is little attempt to disguise the limited scope of the demilitarization clause in the treaty, the text of which is as follows:

States Parties to the Treaty undertake not to place in orbit around the earth any objects carrying nuclear weapons or any other kinds of weapons of mass destruction, install any such weapons on celestial bodies, or station such weapons in outer space in any other manner.

The moon and other celestial bodies shall be used by all States Parties to the Treaty exclusively for peaceful purposes. The establishment of military bases, installations and fortifications, the testing of any type of weapons and the conduct of military manœuvres on celestial bodies shall be forbidden. The use of military personnel for scientific research or for any other peaceful purposes shall not be prohibited. The use of any equipment or facility necessary for peaceful exploration of the moon and other celestial bodies shall also not be prohibited.

Article IV is divisible into two clearly separate sections. The first consists in an agreement partially to demilitarize extraterrestrial space, including all celestial bodies; the second completely to demilitarize all celestial bodies.

B. Partial Demilitarization of Extraterrestrial Space

Inasmuch as artificial satellites which are able to complete at least one orbit round the earth are now generally deemed to be outside terrestrial space subject to national sovereignty and consequently to be in outer space,[191] the geographical or perhaps more correctly the cosmographical scope of Article IV(1) consists of all areas beyond terrestrial space. This interpretation is corroborated by Article I(1)(*a*) of the 1963 Moscow Nuclear Test Ban Treaty which forbids 'any nuclear weapon test explosion, or any other nuclear explosion' not only 'in the atmosphere' but also 'beyond its limits, including outer space'.[192]

Article IV(1) of the Space Treaty means that no contracting State is entitled to station nuclear weapons or other weapons of mass destruction anywhere in extraterrestrial space, including both outer space and celestial bodies. Insofar as those States which are also parties to the Test Ban Treaty are concerned, none is entitled to cause any nuclear explosion in the same area either.

---

[190] Cf. nn. 200 and 206 below.

[191] See loc. cit. in n. 99 above, at pp. 144 ff., esp. p. 146, n. 35 [Ch. 5 above, s. III.A, esp. n. 38].

[192] The words 'at any place under its jurisdiction or control' in Article I(1) of the Test Ban Treaty threaten almost to nullify the effect of the article insofar as extraterrestrial space is concerned, if it were not for the comprehensive language in Article I(2), because no part of it is subject to at least the territorial jurisdiction of the contracting States to the Space Treaty.

The view that the phrase 'or control' covers any place in outer space where a test is conducted (see, e.g., M. M. Whiteman, 11 *Digest of International Law* (1968), p. 791) appears highly disputable.

Even these two treaties taken together, however, do not make extraterrestrial space entirely nuclear-weapon-free. In particular, the transit through outer space of missiles with nuclear warheads, at present the ultimate weapon in the armouries of super powers, is not prohibited. Specifically, Article IV does not cover the so-called Fractional Orbital Bombardment System (FOBS), in which the missiles behave rather like an artificial satellite with a low orbit except that they are designed to re-enter the earth's atmosphere and home on their targets before they complete a single orbit.[193]

The very fact that missiles, whether of intercontinental or intermediate range, have to go through outer space to reach their targets explains why, at present, notwithstanding the expressed wishes of many States,[194] the super powers, in the absence of general disarmament, are unwilling to agree to limit outer space to peaceful uses only; for apart from the transit of missiles, outer space is now used extensively for military purposes. *Inter alia*, artificial satellites have proved themselves invaluable for military communications and navigation, as well as for photographic, electronic, and weather reconnaissance. And if the Soviet Union is developing the Fractional Orbital Bombardment System,[195] the United States is planning to spend $1,500,000,000 on its Manned Orbiting Laboratory (MOL) programme which, announced on 25 August 1965, must be regarded in the words of the *New York Times*, as 'an ambitious and potentially far-reaching military project'.[196]

The present position, therefore, is that outer space as such is militarily too important already to be demilitarized except as part of a general programme of disarmament. Both super powers made it clear that any attempt within the context of the space treaty to demilitarize outer space would simply make the treaty as a whole unacceptable to them.[197] The Indian delegate to the Legal Sub-Committee most ably and valiantly argued for total demilitarization,[198] but it was to no avail.

---

[193] On 3 Nov. 1967, Mr McNamara, the US Defense Secretary, announced that the Soviet Union appeared to have developed such a system.

[194] E.g. Argentina, A/AC.105/C.2/SR.63 (20.7.66), pp. 8–9; India, ibid./SR.65 (22.7.66), p. 11; Argentina, ibid./SR.66 (25.7.66), p. 3; India, ibid., pp. 5–6, 7; Iran, ibid., p. 7; Canada, ibid./SR.70 (3.8.66), pp. 13–14; India, ibid./SR.71 and Add. 1 (4.8.66), pp. 8–9; Austria, ibid., pp. 10–11; Japan, ibid., pp. 12–13; Brazil, ibid., pp. 16–18; Mexico, ibid., pp. 19–21; Iran, ibid., pp. 24–5; Brazil, A/C.1/SR.1492 (17.12.66), p. 432; India, A/C.1/SR.1493 (17.12.66), p. 436; Ceylon, ibid., p. 437; Kenya, ibid., p. 441; UAR, ibid., p. 442; Cyprus, ibid., p. 443; Burma, ibid., p. 444 (some slight misunderstanding regarding the scope of Art. IV); Ceylon, A/PV.1499 (Prov.) (19.12.66), pp. 68/70–1.

[195] See n. 193 above.

[196] *Keesing's*, 20998 A; 88 *Flight International* (1965 III), p. 468.

[197] Cf. USA, A/AC.105/C.2/SR.65 (22.7.66), pp. 9–10; USSR, ibid./SR.66 (25.7.66), pp. 6–7; on history of efforts to demilitarize space, see loc. cit. in n. 11 above, pp. 272–9 [Ch. 6 above, s. VI].

[198] See A/AC.105/C.2/SR.65 (22.7.66), p. 11; ibid./SR.66 (25.7.66), pp. 5–6, 7.

C. Non-militarization of Celestial Bodies

The wording of Article IV(2) of the Space Treaty is traceable to Article I of the 1959 Antarctic Treaty, which provides as follows:

1. Antarctica shall be used for peaceful purposes only. There shall be prohibited, *inter alia*, any measures of a military nature, such as the establishment of military bases and fortifications, the carrying out of military manœuvres, as well the testing of any type of weapons.
2. The present Treaty shall not prevent the use of military personnel or equipment for scientific research or for any other peaceful purpose.

In discussions on space activities in general and space law in particular, in order to fit the square peg of the already extensive use of outer space for military purposes[199] into the round and hitherto rather hollow concept of 'peaceful uses', there has unfortunately developed in some quarters the habit of interpreting the term 'peaceful' as applied to outer space as meaning 'non-aggressive' instead of 'non-military'.[200] From this point of view, Article I of the Antarctic Treaty is explicit in that 'any measures of a military nature' are '*inter alia*' prohibited. In many ways, the wording of the Antarctic Treaty remains superior, inasmuch as the various prohibited items enumerated are purely exemplicative. The original United States draft I was also exemplicative, though the examples used were more limited in character.[201] The wording of the second sentence in the present Article IV(2), which is based on Article IV of the Soviet draft,[202] unfortunately gives the impression of being a definite list of prohibited activities. Considerable discussions took place as to whether the word 'installations' and the words 'and equipment' should or should not be inserted in respectively the second and third sentences of Article IV(2). Finally, the United States agreed to the insertion of the word 'installations', and the Soviet Union to permitting the use of military equipment under conditions separately laid down in a new sentence.[203] For reasons which were not fully apparent, the Soviet Union was reluctant to follow the example of the Antarctic Treaty,[204] even though it was a party to the Antarctic Treaty, having signed it on 1 December 1959, and ratified it on 2 November 1960.

[199] See text to nn. 193–7 above.

[200] Cf. the present writer, in ILA, *Report of the 50th Conference, Brussels* (1962), p. 50; and the discussions that took place there, pp. 31 ff.; see also reference thereto, Hungary A/AC.105/C.2/SR.66 (25.7.66), pp. 3–4; see also n. 206 below.

[201] Art. 9. 'Celestial bodies shall be used for peaceful purposes only. All States undertake to refrain from conducting on celestial bodies any activities such as the establishment of military fortifications, the carry out of military manœuvres, or the testing of any type of weapons. The use of military personnel, facilities or equipment for scientific research or for any other peaceful purpose shall not be prohibited.'

[202] Itself derived probably from item 6 of the original US outline of an agreement handed to the Soviet Union on 11 May: '. . . Military fortifications, weapons tests, and military manoeuvres should be forbidden'; see loc. cit. in n. 35 above.

[203] See further nn. 53 and 70 above.   [204] A/AC.105/C.2/SR.65 (22.7.66), p. 11.

It is submitted, however, that of far more importance than the technical qualification or classification of personnel, equipment, and activities as military or civilian is the purpose for which they are employed. Instead of concentrating on the inclusion or exclusion of specific items, all or any of which, depending on circumstances or on the good faith of the parties, can probably be used for either peaceful or military purposes,[205] the draftsmen of the article could have with profit followed more closely Article I of the Antarctic Treaty in ensuring that the rest of the paragraph merely served to illustrate the basic principle laid down in its first sentence, namely, that all celestial bodies shall be used 'exclusively for peaceful purposes'. However, even in its present form, there is no doubt that this paragraph should be interpreted in good faith, and that no activity serving a military purpose should be pursued on celestial bodies.[206]

Table IX.1 SCOPE OF ARTICLE IV OF THE SPACE TREATY

OBJECTS AND ACTIVITIES PROHIBITED	AREA COVERED
Nuclear weapons and other weapons of mass destruction (para. 1)	In orbit around the earth, installed on celestial bodies, or stationed in outer space in any manner
Uses not for peaceful purposes (para. 2)	The moon and other celestial bodies **[NB: NOT THE SPACE BETWEEN CELESTIAL BODIES]**

D. Free Access to Installations on Celestial Bodies

In order to ensure that the demilitarization clause of the treaty is observed, the Antarctic Treaty incorporates an effective system of inspection by observers

---

[205] Cf. two highly interesting and apposite decisions by the German–United States Mixed Claims Commissioin (1922), on the meaning of 'military materials' and 'civilian population', in *Opinion Construing the Phrase 'Naval and Military Works and Materials'* (1924), 1 *Dec. and Op.*, p. 75, and the *Damson Case* (1925), ibid., p. 243; see further Cheng, *General Principles of Law*, p. 197, n. 20.

[206] From this point of view, what the Indian representative to the First Committee said cannot be regarded as correct. Criticizing the limited scope of Art. IV, he went on to say: 'the use of military personnel and any necessary equipment or facility was expressly permitted, and in circumstances where it was emphatically asserted that "peaceful" meant not "non-military" but merely "non-aggressive" ' (A/C.1/SR.1493 (17.12.66), p. 436 (para. 9)). The only reference to this subject was that of the Hungarian delegate to the Legal Sub-Committee (see n. 200 above), and all the latter did was to call for this point to be clarified. The absence of a definition of the world 'peaceful' in the treaty does not mean that the word should not be understood in its ordinary meaning, namely, 'non-military' as in the Antarctic Treaty.

designated by the original contracting States and other Parties conducting substantial scientific research activity in Antarctica. Article VII of the treaty provides *inter alia*:

3. All areas of Antarctica, including all stations, installations and equipment within those areas, and all ships and aircraft at points of discharge or embarking cargoes or personnel in Antarctica, shall be open at all times to inspection by any observers designated in accordance with paragraph 1 of this Article.

In order to assist such inspections, paragraph 5 of the same article requires each contracting State, at the time when the treaty enters into force for it, to inform other contracting Parties, and thereafter to give them notice in advance, of (*a*) all expeditions to and within Antarctica, on the part of its ships or nationals, and all expeditions to Antarctica organized in or proceeding from its territory; (*b*) all stations in Antarctica occupied by its nationals; and (*c*) any military personnel or equipment intended to be introduced by it into Antarctica for scientific research or other peaceful purposes.

In United States draft I, provisions were also made for all installations on celestial bodies to be open at all times to representatives of all States conducting activities there.[207] The Soviet Union accepted this proposal almost at once, except that it wished to substitute for 'at all times' the following condition:

on the basis of reciprocity under the condition that the time of the visit is to be agreed between the parties concerned.[208]

Considerable discussion on the condition introduced by the Soviet Union took place. In the first place, it was pointed out that if reciprocity meant that a contracting State might legitimately refuse access to its installations to any State which did not comply with its obligation to allow visits to its installations, then such a condition was already implicit in the United States draft and indeed in all treaties, and was consequently redundant.[209] If, on the other hand, reciprocity were to mean that a contracting State could legitimately refuse visits simply by making known its intention not to avail itself of this provision in the treaty, then the introduction of such a condition could easily nullify the obligation to allow free access.[210] All that the Soviet Union was prepared to say was that 'reciprocity should be understood in the traditional sense of the word in international law'.[211] Finally, the United States indicated that if the former interpretation of the word reciprocity were universally

---

[207] Art. 6.   [208] A/AC.105/C.2/SR.63 (20.7.66), pp. 4–5.
[209] Cf. Australia, A/AC.105/C.2/SR.63 (20.7.66), pp. 7–8; Canada, ibid./SR.64 (21.7.66), pp. 6–7; Lebanon, ibid., pp. 7–8.
[210] Cf. United Kingdom, A/AC.105/C.2/SR.63 (20.7.66), p. 9; Italy, ibid./SR.64 (21.7.66), pp. 4–5.
[211] A/AC.105/C.2/SR.64 (21.7.66), p. 9.

shared, it would be prepared to include the words 'on the basis of reciprocity'.[212]

As regards the condition that the time of the visit must be agreed upon in advance between the parties concerned, fear was expressed that this might either cause delay[213] or even imply 'a sort of veto'.[214] The Soviet Union, however, while it 'accepted fully the principle of open access'[215] made it clear that the 'at all times' condition was totally unacceptable[216], on the ground that it would be 'technically impossible to put into effect'[217] or at least 'physically difficult to apply'.[218] In answer to a question, the Soviet representative explained, however, that, in putting forward the Soviet proposal, he 'did not have in mind the conclusion of a supplementary agreement of a formal legal character; it would be a matter simply of agreeing on the date for a visit, to suit the convenience of the host government and the visitor.' Finally, taking into account various suggestions made by the different delegations in order to preserve the effective operation of the free access clause[219], the United States, when the suspended fifth session of the legal Sub-Committee reconvened on 12 September 1966, submitted a revised version of its draft Article 6,[220] which eventually became Article XII of the treaty:

All stations, installations, equipment and space vehicles on the Moon and other celestial bodies shall be open to representatives of other States Parties to the Treaty on a basis of reciprocity. Such representatives shall give reasonable advance notice of a projected visit, in order that appropriate consultations may be held and that maximum precautions may be taken to assure safety and to avoid interference with normal operations in the facility to be visited.

As the United States made it clear, however, 'for safety reasons, it was prepared to agree to the provision that advance notice must be given of a projected visit', but its agreement to this article was on the understanding that neither this requirement nor the condition of reciprocity implied any 'veto right'.[221] Like Article IV, Article XII of the treaty applies only to celestial bodies and not to outer space.

---

[212] A/AC.105/C.2/SR.70 (3.8.66), pp. 6–7.

[213] Mexico, A/AC.105/C.2/SR.63 (20.7.66), p. 8.

[214] USA, A/AC.105/C.2/SR.70 (3.8.66), p. 6.

[215] A/AC.105/C.2/SR.63 (20.7.66), p. 6; ibid./SR.70 (3.8.66), pp. 7–8.

[216] Cf. A/AC.105/C.2/SR.63 (20.7.66), p. 7.

[217] A/AC.105/C.2/SR.63 (20.7.66), p. 7.   [218] A/AC.105/C.2/SR.64 (21.7.66), p. 9.

[219] See e.g. Italy, A/AC.105/C.2/SR.64 (21.7.66), p. 5; ibid./SR.70 (3.8.66), pp. 8–10 (supported by Canada, ibid./SR.64 (21.7.66), pp. 13–14; Japan, A/AC.105/C.2/SR.64 (21.7.66), p. 8 (supported by the United States, ibid./SR.70 (3.8.66), pp. 3–7); Mexico, A/AC.105/C.2/SR.71 and Add.1 (4.8.66), pp. 19–21.

[220] A/AC.105/C.2/5th Sess./WP.32 (12.9.66).

[221] A/C.1/SR.1492 (17.12.66), p. 428 (para. 7); see also United Kingdom, ibid, p. 430 (para. 27).

E. Reporting of Space Activities

It will be recalled that the Antarctic Treaty provides for advance information on proposed activities in Antarctica to be given to all other contracting Parties in order to facilitate the treaty system of inspection.[222] The United States draft I also contained a similar provision in its Article 4, except that the information was to be communicated to the Secretary-General of the United Nations and need not be given in advance. In retrospect, it was perhaps unfortunate that this obligation was coupled to a duty also to publish the findings of such activities. The Antarctic Treaty too has such a provision in its Article III, but there the duty is only to do so 'to the greatest extent feasible and practicable'.

The United States regarded the obligation to make public information on activities on celestial bodies, as well as the obligation to allow free access to all installations on them, an important means to implement the 'principle of openness'.[223] Not only did a large number of States share the view that there should be a binding obligation to do so,[224] but many also wished it to be extended to activities in outer space.[225] The Soviet Union, on the other hand, was willing to make the information available only 'on a voluntary basis',[226] and its position was, as usual, strongly supported by all the States within the Soviet bloc in the Legal Sub-Committee[227] and, in this instance, also by the United Arab Republic.[228]

Except for a few delegates in the Legal Sub-Committee, such as the Indian[229] and the Japanese[230] representatives, however, most of the others concentrated their attention mainly on the second half of the United States proposal, namely, the duty of making results of space exploration freely available. The Japanese representative expressly referred to Article VII of the Antarctic Treaty and, together with the Indian representative, urged that the previous recommendation of the General Assembly contained in resolution 1721B (XVI) calling on all States to inform the United Nations of all launchings of objects into space should be incorporated into the treaty as a legal obligation.

---

[222] See s. VI.D above.   [223] A/AC.105/C.2/SR.64 (21.7.66), pp. 11–12.

[224] Japan, A/AC.105/C.2/SR.64 (21.7.66), pp. 13–14; Canada, ibid./SR.65 (22.7.66), pp. 3–4; ibid./SR.70 (3.8.66), pp. 13–14; Argentina, ibid./SR.65 (22.7.66), p. 4; United Kingdom, ibid., p. 5; Italy, ibid., p. 5; Brazil, ibid., p. 5; Australia, ibid., p. 7 (even if the scope *ratione materiae* of the obligation were to be more limited); Sweden, ibid./SR.70 (3.8.66), pp. 11–13; Austria, ibid./SR.71 and Add. 1 (4.8.66), pp. 10–11; Brazil, ibid., pp. 16–18; ibid./SR.75 (16.9.66), p. 11.

[225] India, A/AC.105/C.2/SR.64 (21.7.66), p. 13; Japan, ibid., pp. 13–14; Lebanon, ibid./SR.65 (22.7.66), pp. 4–5; Sweden, ibid./SR.70 (3.8.66), pp. 11–13; Mexico, ibid./SR.71 and Add. 1 (4.8.66), pp. 19–21.

[226] A/AC.105/C.2/5th Sess./WP.4 (21.7.66); A/AC.105/C.2/SR.64 (21.7.66), pp. 12–13.

[227] Hungary, A/AC.105/C.2/SR.65 (22.7.66), p. 4; Bulgaria, ibid., p. 6; Mongolia, ibid./SR.71 and Add. 1 (4.8.66), pp.11–12; Hungary, ibid., p. 22.

[228] A/AC.105/C.2/SR.65 (22.7.66), pp. 7–8.   [229] A/AC.105/C.2/SR.64 (21.7.66), p. 13.

[230] Ibid., pp. 13–14.

It seems a great pity that this suggestion, limited if necessary to merely objects launched onto celestial bodies, was not taken up; for it would doubtless help in enforcing the demilitarization clause of the treaty.[231] In the end, even though some delegations apparently felt that the United States had gone too far in meeting the Soviet view on the subject[232], when the Legal Sub-Committee resumed its fifth session in September 1966, the United States introduced a revised version of its draft article 4 in which parties to the treaty would report on activities on celestial bodies only 'to the greatest extent feasible and practicable', and which became Article XI of the Treaty.[233]

VII. International Co-operation and Mutual Assistance

A. The Principle of International Co-operation and Mutual Assistance

In the preamble to the treaty, the contracting Parties express their desire to contribute to broad international co-operation in the exploration and use of outer space for peaceful purposes. Furthermore, in the first sentence of Article IX, it is stated:

In the exploration and use of outer space, including the moon and other celestial bodies, States Parties to the Treaty shall be guided by the principle of co-operation and mutual assistance and shall conduct all their activities in outer space, including the moon and other celestial bodies, with due regard to the corresponding interests of all other States Parties to the Treaty . . .[234]

B. Scientific Investigations

The United States in Article 3 of its draft if proposed that:

States shall facilitate and encourage international co-operation in scientific investigations concerning celestial bodies.

In common with the majority of the other provisions in the treaty, the scope of this proposal was enlarged to include also outer space. In the treaty, this proposal became the second half of the third paragraph of Article I.[235] Although couched in mandatory form, this provision is more a statement of principle than one laying down specific obligations.[236] As such, it is supple-

---

[231] Cf. item 4 of the Eisenhower proposal, n. 12 above.

[232] As reported by USA, A/AC.105/C.2/SR.73 (16.9.66), p. 4; Brazil, ibid., p. 11.

[233] Ibid., pp. 3–4; see further s. VII.C below where the text of Art. XI is reproduced.

[234] For the rest of article, see s. VII.E below.

[235] Art. I(3): 'There shall be freedom of scientific investigation in outer space, including the moon and other celestial bodies, and States shall facilitate and encourage international co-operation in such investigation.'

[236] Cf. s. V.E above. It may be noted *en passant* that, as worded, Art. I(3) applies to all States, even non-parties to the treaty.

mented by at least two other statements of principle in the treaty, one of which is perhaps more obligatory than the other.

C. Dissemination of Information

The more obligatory of the two further statements of principle is to be found in Article XI:

In order to promote international co-operation in the peaceful exploration and use of outer space, States Parties to the Treaty conducting activities in outer space, including the moon and other celestial bodies, agree to inform the Secretary-General of the United Nations as well as the public and the international scientific community, to the greatest extent feasible and practicable, of the nature, conduct, locations and results of such activities. On receiving the said information, the Secretary-General of the United Nations should be prepared to disseminate it immediately and effectively.

As explained before,[237] the original intention of this provision, limited at first to activities on celestial bodies, was to serve a dual purpose, both to ensure the observance of the demilitarization provision of the treaty, and to disseminate the findings of space activities freely to the public and the international scientific community. In its final form, the scope of Article XI has been extended to extraterrestrial space as a whole, but, on account of Soviet objections, instead of laying down an unqualified obligation, Article XI merely requires Parties to the treaty to publish such information 'to the greatest extent feasible and practicable' or, in other words, according to their own discretion.[238] Inasmuch as there is no obligation to supply such information in advance, or promptly, or in full, Article XI can no longer be seriously considered as serving the first of its two originally intended functions. On the other hand, however imperfectly, it does constitute some acknowledgement of the principles stated in Article I(1) of the treaty, and provides a centralized channel of communication from which 'all countries, irrespective of their degree of economic or scientific development' will be able to benefit from at least some of the scientific fall-outs of space explorations.

D. Tracking Facilities

In Article I(1) of Soviet draft if of the treaty, there was found, after a rather pompous statement of principle,[239] the following provision:

The Parties to the treaty undertake to accord equal conditions to States engaged in the exploration of outer space.

In answer to a question as to its meaning, the Soviet representative explained that it was

---

[237] See s. VI.E above.   [238] See further s. V.E above.   [239] See n. 44, and s. V.E above.

based on his country's traditional position that the exploration of outer space should be carried out in the interests of all mankind. That sentence meant that if State A permitted State B to build a tracking station on its territory, State C, which was pursuing the same peaceful aims in space, should be given the opportunity to build a similar station on A's territory. *The provision, of course, would not affect the sovereign right of State A to refuse to grant such privileges to either State B or State C.*[240]

The background to this proposal must be found in the fact that while the Soviet Union was not anxious to allow foreign tracking stations in the Soviet Union,[241] it was keen on obtaining the same tracking facilities in foreign territories as the United States which at the time,[242] had them in 23 different countries, based on bilateral agreements. France and the European Space Research Organization also had established widespread tracking networks on a similar basis.[243] However, as the United States pointed out, the original Soviet draft was not merely a most-favoured-nation clause, but also a national treatment clause so that space powers must also grant one another national treatment[244]. Subsequently, the Soviet Union substituted for its original draft the following proposal, which doubtless expressed the Soviet intention more explicitly and more correctly:

States Parties to the Treaty will accord other States Parties to the Treaty conducting activities relating to the exploration and use of outer space equal conditions for observing the flight of space objects launched by those States.[245]

The Soviet proposal of such a most-favoured-nation clause on tracking rights received no support in the Legal Sub-Committee, except from States in the Soviet bloc.[246] In fact, there was stiff opposition from the non-space powers.[247] It was pointed out *inter alia* that such a provision would in fact

---

[240] A/AC.105/C.2/SR.63 (20.7.66), p. 6. Italics added.

[241] See President Kennedy's proposals to Mr Khrushchev on 17 Mar. 1962 and the latter's reply of 20 Mar. 1962; loc. cit. in n. 13 above, p. 26 [Ch. 7 above, s. IV].

[242] USSR, A/AC.105/C.2/SR.75 (16.9.64), pp. 6–7.

[243] On co-operation in tracking among members of the Soviet bloc, USSR, A/AC.105/PV.26 (27.10.66), p. 13.

[244] A/AC.105/C.2/SR.63 (20.7.66), p. 10.

[245] A/AC.105/C.2/5th Sess./WP.23/Corr.1 (29.7.66).

[246] Mongolia, A/AC.105/C.2/SR.71 (4.8.66), pp. 11–12; Hungary, ibid., pp. 21–22 (would enable all States 'to participate in space activities . . . intended to benefit all mankind'); Bulgaria, ibid., pp. 23–4 ('all other (i.e., non-space) States should make what contribution they could to an activity of common interest to all'); Hungary, ibid./SR.73 (16.9.66), p. 11; Bulgaria, ibid., pp. 12–13; Czechoslovakia, A/AC.105/PV.45 (19.9.66), pp. 18/20–23/25; Bulgaria, ibid., pp. 47–51.

[247] E.g. Brazil, A/AC.105/C.2/SR.63 (20.7.66), p. 9 (not acceptable); United Kingdom, ibid., p. 9 (obligation 'onerous'); Canada, ibid./SR.70 (3.8.66), pp. 13–14 ('imposed unequal obligations'); United Kingdom, ibid./SR.71 and Add. 1 (4.8.66), p. 5; Austria, ibid., pp. 10–11 (feasibility doubted); Japan, ibid., pp. 12–13 (not appropriate for multilateral agreement); Australia, ibid., pp. 14–16 (not acceptable); Brazil, ibid., pp. 16–18 (must depend on bilateral agreements); Mexico, ibid., pp. 19–21 (position not certain until obligations of space powers specified); Italy, ibid./SR.73 (16.9.66), pp. 7–8 (Soviet position on dissemination of information compared: 'same freedom of decision' logically required); Australia, ibid., pp. 8–9 (no unwillingness in principle, but bilateral regulation required); Japan, ibid., p. 9; Brazil, ibid., p. 11; Canada, ibid., pp. 11–12

discourage international co-operation,[248] and acceptance of the treaty itself.[249] It may be recalled that the second phase in the negotiations of the treaty broke down in the Outer Space Committee because of lack of agreement on the Soviet proposal.[250]

The third phase of the negotiations opened when the United States, in an attempt to break the deadlock, offered to discuss with the Soviet Union the possibility of establishing Soviet tracking facilities in United States territory.[251] This offer evidently bore fruit; for by the end of the third phase of the negotiations,[252] the Soviet draft II had modified its previous proposal[253] and contained a provision[254] almost identical to the present Article X which is worded as follows:

> In order to promote international co-operation in the exploration and use of outer space, including the moon and other celestial bodies, in conformity with the purposes of this Treaty, the States Parties to the Treaty shall consider on a basis of equality any requests by other States Parties to the Treaty to be afforded an opportunity to observe the flight of space objects launched by those States.
>
> The nature of such an opportunity for observation and the conditions under which it could be afforded shall be determined by agreement between the States concerned.

From the standpoint of the obligation imposed on contracting States, Article X of the Treaty probably goes no more than fractionally beyond Article 23(*e*) of the League of Nations Covenant, which was the object of interpretation by the Permanent Court of International Justice in the Advisory Opinion on *Railway Traffic between Lithuania and Poland* (1931).[255] There is certainly no obligation to grant such facilities in the absence of an agreement. Article X does not even amount to a *pactum de contrahendo* which would impose an obligation to enter negotiations in good faith with a view to reaching an agreement.[256] Subject to the 'principle of co-operation and mutual assistance' by which all States should be guided,[257] and such force as may be attributed to Article I(1) of the treaty,[258] a contracting State is entitled to adopt an equally negative attitude towards all requests for tracking facilities and accede to none. Its obligation consists merely in considering such requests from other contracting States 'on a basis of equality'. This is not a most-favoured-nation clause either, the operation of which is automatic and unconditional.[259] Here the grant of such facilities is not automatic, nor need

(lacked reciprocity); United Kingdom, ibid., p. 13; Canada, A/AC.105/PV.45 (19.9.66) pp. 11–13 (ditto); United Kingdom, ibid., pp. 23/25–29/30 (related matters ignored; lacked reciprocity); Belgium, ibid., pp. 29/30–33; Australia, A/C.1/SR.1493 (17.12.66), p. 437 (para. 22).

[248] Italy, A/AC.105/C.2/SR.70 (3.8.66), pp. 8–10; USA, A/AC.105/PV.44 (19.9.66), pp. 23/25.

[249] USA, A/AC.105/PV.44 (19.9.66), pp. 23/25.   [250] See s. III.B above.

[251] A/PV.1412 (Prov.) (22.9.66), p. 41; see n. 66 above.   [252] See s. III.C above.

[253] See text to n. 240 above.   [254] Soviet Draft II, Art. X.

[255] A/B 42, p. 419.   [256] See the writer's *General Principles of Law*, pp. 111, 117–18.

[257] See s. VII.A above.   [258] See s. V.E above.

[259] See G. Schwarzenberger, 'The Most-Favoured-Nation Standard in British State Practice', 22 *BYIL* (1945), p. 96.

it be unconditional. Furthermore, it would appear that neither the nature of the facility, nor the conditions under which it is to be granted, need be the same in every case. Finally, the change from the positive form of words in Soviet draft II, 'the conditions under which it [i.e., such opportunity].is to be afforded' to the present wording, 'the conditions under which it could be afforded,' though not very meaningful or even grammatical, does appear to indicate an intention to obviate any implication that such opportunities are to be granted on request, subject to agreement. This is probably what the United States delegate meant when he said that Article X, in its final form, 'properly incorporated the principle that each State which was asked to co-operate had the right to consider its legitimate interests in reaching its decision'.[260]

However, Article X does afford every space power a *locus standi* to address such requests to the other contracting States and a right to expect that these will be considered without discrimination.

E. Avoidance of Harmful Contamination or Interference

Obligations of an also somewhat indefinite character are to be found in Article IX of the treaty, the text of which is as follows:

In the exploration and use of outer space, including the moon and other celestial bodies, States Parties to the Treaty shall be guided by the principle of co-operation and mutual assistance and shall conduct all their activities in outer space, including the moon and other celestial bodies, with due regard to the corresponding interests of all other States Parties to the Treaty. States Parties to the Treaty shall pursue studies of outer space, including the moon and other celestial bodies, and conduct exploration of them so as to avoid their harmful contamination and also adverse changes in the environment to the earth resulting from the introduction of extraterrestrial matter and, where necessary, shall adopt appropriate measures for this purpose. If a State Party to the Treaty has reason to believe that an activity or experiment planned by it or its nationals in outer space, including the moon and other celestial bodies, would cause potentially harmful interference with activities of other States Parties in the peaceful exploration and use of outer space, including the moon and other celestial bodies, it shall undertake appropriate international consultations before proceeding with any such activity or experiment. A State Party to the Treaty which has reason to believe that an activity or experiment planned by another State Party in outer space, including the moon and other celestial bodies, would cause potentially harmful interference with activities in the peaceful exploration and use of outer space, including the moon and other celestial bodies, may request consultation concerning the activity or experiment.

The purpose which Article IX serves may be illustrated by the United States Project West Ford, which consisted in launching into orbit a belt of tiny

---

[260] A/C.1/SR.1492 (17.12.66), p. 429 (para. 9); see also Australia, ibid./SR.1493 (17.12.66), p. 437 (para. 22).

dipoles (needles) round the earth. In the first experiment, in October 1961, the needles did not disperse. The second, launched on 12 May 1963, went as planned. The first announcement of this plan, about August 1960, created grave concern and brought a great deal of protest. In September 1961, the International Council of Scientific Unions (ICSU) invited its Committee on Space Research (COSPAR) to examine any proposed experiments or other space activities that might have potentially undesirable effects on scientific activities and observations. In order to carry out this task, COSPAR established in May 1962 a Consultative Group on Potentially Harmful Effects of Space Experiments. In its Report submitted in May 1964,[261] the Consultative Group found *inter alia* that the actual experiments confirmed prior calculations that the specified belt would cause no harmful interference. But in view of initial uncertainties and the expressed fear that frequent launchings of far denser belts might be proposed, the problem was being kept under review. On the basis of this Report, COSPAR passed various resolutions calling on its members in future to give advance information on experiments of this sort and recommending measures to avoid contamination of celestial bodies. Since then, it would appear that the procedures of consultation through the COSPAR Consultative Group have been functioning satisfactorily.

This probably explains why the two major space powers were content with the procedure of consultation in the present Article IX which has been taken over via Article VIII of Soviet draft I from paragraph 6 of resolution 1962 (XVIII).

During the discussions in the Legal Sub-Committee, doubts were expressed by the Lebanese and Japanese delegates as to the effectiveness of the procedure. The former pointed out that while the article provided that consultation might be requested, it did not specify that the other Party must accede to the request.[262] The latter went further and proposed an amendment to the Soviet draft which would require any Party conducting any activity or experiment which might cause harmful interference, to give advance notice to the Secretary-General of the United Nations 'before proceeding with any such activity or experiment'.[263] In the opinion of the Soviet Union, however, since its draft already provided for the obligation of prior consultation, the duty to supply advance information, if not to the Secretary-General, at least to the other contracting States concerned, was implicit. Consequently, the Japanese amendment was unnecessary.[264] For the same reason, there was a duty to comply with requests for consultation.[265] Insofar as the United States was concerned, it seemed satisfied with the Soviet draft, and added: 'Care must be

---

[261] Reproduced in C. W. Jenks, *Space Law* (1965), pp. 402 ff.
[262] A/AC.105/C.2/SR.68 (27.7.66), p. 9.
[263] A/AC.105/C.2/5th Sess./WP.10; A/AC.105/C.2/SR.68 (16.7.66), pp. 5–6.
[264] A/AC.105/C.2/SR.68 (26.7.66), pp. 4–5.   [265] Ibid., p. 9.

taken . . . not to establish too rigid procedures, which might hinder research.'[266]

It is submitted that while the Soviet replies to the Japanese and the Lebanese delegates were technically correct, they appear to overlook the fact that the duty of prior consultation rested on the somewhat, though not entirely, subjective premise that the Party undertaking the experiment or activity 'had reason to believe' that it 'would cause potentially harmful interference'. In a situation similar to the United States Project West Ford where the United States had reason to believe that the experiment would cause no harmful interference, the point whether there is a duty of prior consultation under the treaty can easily be argued either way.

F. Assistance to and Return of Astronauts and Return of Objects Launched into Space

The problem of assistance to and return of astronauts is one to which the Soviet Union attaches a great deal of importance. Early in 1962 in reply to a message from President Kennedy, Mr Khrushchev proposed, in addition to a general treaty on space, the conclusion of a special agreement on the subject,[267] and a Soviet draft to this effect was introduced before the Legal Sub-Committee on 6 June 1962.[268] The draft applied also to the rescue of spaceships. One of the proposals which caused immediate concern was the exception clause in Article 7(2), excluding from the obligation to return space vehicles those designed 'for the collection of intelligence information in the territory of another State'.[269] Over the years, relatively little progress was made on the treaty.

For the purpose of resolution 1962, however, agreement was reached on what is now the first paragraph of Article V. The second paragraph on mutual assistance among astronauts was introduced by Soviet draft I,[270] while the third paragraph was added during the discussions in the Legal Sub-Committee on a proposal submitted by the United States.[271] The final text of Article V is as follows:

States Parties to the Treaty shall regard astronauts as envoys of mankind in outer space and shall render to them all possible assistance in the event of accident, distress, or emergency landing on the territory of another State Party or on the high seas. When astronauts make such a landing, they shall be safely and promptly returned to the State of registry of their space vehicle.

In carrying on activities in outer space and on celestial bodies, the astronauts of one State Party shall render all possible assistance to the astronauts of other States Parties.

---

[266] Ibid., p. 7.   [267] See loc. cit. in n. 13 above, p. 26 [Ch. 7 above, s. IV].
[268] A/AC.105/C.2/L.2.
[269] On the legal position of reconnaissance and surveillance satellites, see loc. cit. in n.11 above, pp. 262 ff. [Ch. 6 above, s. V].
[270] Art. IX.   [271] A/AC.105/C.2/SR.66 (25.7.66), p. 8.

States Parties to the Treaty shall immediately inform the other States Parties to the Treaty or the Secretary-General of the United Nations of any phenomena they discover in outer space, including the moon and other celestial bodies, which could constitute a danger to the life or health of astronauts.

In addition, the last sentence of Article VIII on objects launched into space provides:

Such objects or component parts found beyond the limits of the State Party to the Treaty on whose registry they are carried shall be returned to that State Party, which shall, upon request, furnish identifying data . . .[272]

Agreement on these provisions was reached in the Legal Sub-Committee without a great deal of discussion.[273] Several points, however, deserve further consideration. It may also be pointed out that discussions on an Agreement on the Rescue and Return of Astronauts and the Return of Objects Launched into Outer Space were brought to a successful conclusion on 15 December 1967, and the draft agreement received the unanimous commendation of the General Assembly on 19 December.[274] It was opened for signature on 22 April 1968.

1. *'Envoys of Mankind'*.   This rather florid expression was first introduced in resolution 1962. During the discussions on the treaty, the Lebanese delegate almost threw the cat among the pigeons when he suggested that the obligation in the treaty should arise only when astronauts were engaged in peaceful activities; for otherwise they would not be 'envoys of mankind'.[275] This point was, however, not taken up.

In 1965, in the Legal Sub-Committee, the Hungarian delegate put forward the view that the term 'envoys of mankind' implied that astronauts were immune from local jurisdiction, but that they should not enjoy such immunity if they were not engaged in peaceful activities.[276] It is more than dubious that one can read into the word 'envoy' a duty to grant astronauts jurisdictional immunity, and it is not surprising, therefore, that the Austrian delegate expressed his doubt whether the first part of the first sentence of Article V 'could give rise to a legal obligation'.[277] From the observation made subsequently by the Soviet delegate, it is quite clear that no special significance was to be attached to this expression. It merely 'served to justify the legal obligations' laid down in the rest of the article, and he would be 'prepared to consider another form of words provided that it did not complicate the text of the draft treaty'.[278] This expression has since been dropped from the subsequent special Agreement on Rescue and Return.[279]

---

[272] For the other parts of this article, see ss. V.C and V.D above.
[273] On Art. V, see A/AC.105/C.2/SR.66 (25.7.66), pp. 8–10; on Art. VIII, ibid., p. 11.
[274] Annex to resolution 2345 (XXII). See further Ch. 10. below.
[275] A/AC.105/C.2/SR.66 (25.7.66), p. 9; also Iran, ibid./SR.71 and Add. 1 (4.8.66), pp. 24–5.
[276] A/AC.105/C.2/SR.44 (Prov.) (22.9.65), pp. 8 ff.
[277] A/AC.104/C.2/SR.58 (13.7.66), p. 2/3.
[278] Ibid., pp. 8–9; see further text to nn. 147 and 148 above.   [279] See n. 274 above.

2. *On Whom Duties are Incumbent.* The duty to render all possible assistance to astronauts in distress lies first and foremost with the contracting States themselves. Although the first sentence of Article V is not very well drafted,[280] it seems that this duty extends to all astronauts wherever they may be and whatever their nationality. In addition, through the contracting States, a duty is imposed on all astronauts, while they are carrying on activities in outer space or on celestial bodies to render assistance to astronauts of other contracting States.[281] From this point of view, it seems a singular omission that the opportunity was not taken to lay a similar duty, as in air and maritime law in the case of safety of life at sea, through the contracting State, on ships and aircraft of their nationality. As regards the return of astronauts and objects launched into space, the duty appears to be an absolute one incumbent on all contracting States insofar as such astronauts and objects are within their jurisdiction.

3. *To Whom Astronauts and Objects are to be Returned.* In the Space Treaty, astronauts in an emergency landing, and space objects found, outside the State of registry of the space vehicle shall be returned to the State of registry. From this point of view, the nationality of the astronaut, the ownership of the object, the State by which or from which the space vehicle was launched appear all to be irrelevant. The proper application of Articles V and VIII of the Treaty, therefore, presupposes that every space vehicle of object will be registered before launching.[282] The position has, however, since been changed by the subsequent special Agreement on Rescue and Return,[283] which requires astronauts and space objects to be returned to 'representatives of the launching authority'.[284]

4. *Notification of Dangerous Phenomena.* The last paragraph of Article V of the Treaty originated in a United States proposal during the discussions in the first part of the fifth session of the Legal Sub-Committee.[285] The possibility of informing either the other contracting States or the Secretary-General of the

---

[280] Particularly in its use of the words 'or emergency landing on the territory of *another* State Party'.

[281] The subsequent Rescue and Return Agreement does not mention this duty; see n. 274 above.

[282] See s. V.C.1 above. [283] See n. 274 above.

[284] Arts. 4 and 5(3). Art. 6 of the agreement defines 'the launching authority' as follows: 'For the purpose of this Agreement, the term "launching authority" shall refer to the State responsible for launching, or, where an international intergovernmental organisation is responsible for launching, that organisation, provided that that organisation declares its acceptance of the rights and obligations provided for in this Agreement and a majority of the States members of that organisation are Contracting States to this Agreement and to the Treaty on Principles Governing the Activities of States in the Exploration and Use of Outer Space, including the Moon and Other Celestial Bodies.' This article represents a considerable step forward in recognizing the *locus standi* of international organizations in space activities, as compared with Art. XIII of the Space Treaty; see s. V.G above.

[285] A/AC.105/C.2/SR.66 (25.7.66), p. 11.

United Nations may be due to a desire that such information should reach the other contracting States as soon as possible, but it may also be due to the Soviet position, made clear at one point during the discussions, that it did not wish to see the Secretary-General of the United Nations

given functions which might be interpreted as playing a role in the application of the treaty by States.[286]

The Soviet Union did, however, relent to some extent on this point in regard to Article XI of the treaty.[287] Although Article V does not explicitly require the Secretary-General to disseminate the information transmitted to it, presumably it is implied that he is under a duty to do so. In any event, he can be said to be under a duty to do so on account of the last sentence of Article XI. As regards the question whether the imposition of such a duty on the Secretary-General conflicts with the *pacta tertiis* rule, it is probably possible to maintain that, as the United Nations General Assembly has 'commended' the draft treaty, it has also commended the discharge of this function to the Secretary-General.

VIII. Relationship with other Agreements and Amendment

A. Relationship with other Agreements

During the Legal Sub-Committee's discussions on the draft treaty, concern was frequently expressed that the conclusion of the Space Treaty should not prejudice the subsequent agreements on individual problems, particularly the two agreements on rescue and return of astronauts and on liability for damage caused to third parties, which had been on the agenda of the Sub-Committee for a number of years.[288] Several proposals to this effect were tabled, relating to individual articles in the draft treaty.[289] Subsequently, Australia proposed a general provision on the subject, worded as follows:

The provisions of this Treaty are adopted without prejudice to the negotiation of future specific agreements on the peaceful uses of outer space, including the Moon and other celestial bodies.[290]

On the other hand, the Soviet Union submitted the following text to the opposite effect:

---

[286] A/AC.105/C.2/SR.68 (26.7.66), pp. 7–8.   [287] See ss. VI.E and VII.C above.

[288] Cf. Austria, A/AC.105/C.2/SR.58 (13.7.66), pp. 2/3–4; Belgium, ibid./SR.61 (18.7.66), pp. 7–8; Inida, ibid./SR.66 (25.7.66), pp. 9–10; United Kingdom, ibid./SR.67 (25.7.66), p. 10; Australia, ibid., p. 11; Belgium, ibid., p. 11; Lebanon, ibid., p. 11; Mexico, ibid., p. 11.

[289] Australia, A/AC.105/C.2/SR.66 (25.7.66), p. 10; Japan, ibid./SR.67 (25.7.66), p. 10; India, A/AC.105/C.2/5th Sess./WP.21 (28.7.66); ibid./WP.22 (28.7.66).

[290] A/AC.105/C.2/5th Sess./WP.25 (1.8.66); see ibid./SR.71 and Add. 1 (4.8.66), pp. 14–16.

This Treaty shall not be construed as affecting the right of States Parties thereto to conclude any international agreements relating to the activities of States in the peaceful exploration and use of outer space, provided that such agreements do not conflict with the provisions of this Treaty.[291]

In the Legal Sub-Committee, the Australian proposal received substantial support.[292] Commenting on the Soviet proposal, which had the effect of establishing a conventional *jus cogens*, the Australian representative pointed out that it might for instance prevent an agreement between the parties to the Treaty to return astronauts to other than the State of registry of the space vehicle on account of Article V of the treaty.[293]

The Australian and the Soviet proposals came at the very end of phase II of the negotiations,[294] and it does not seem that adequate attention was given to the subject. Although the two proposals appear to be poles apart, their supporters were probably much less divided in substance. For while all would doubtless agree with the Soviet Union that individual parties to the treaty should not be able, by subsequent agreement between themselves, to depart from the basic principles of the treaty, such as those in its Articles II, III, and IV, it is to be wondered whether the Soviet Union in fact had in mind that the subsequent agreements to be concluded on liability, assistance, and return could in no way modify the rules contained in the treaty on those topics. Thus when the Soviet delegate introduced in the Legal Sub-Committee the provision on liability in Soviet draft I, he

confirmed that his delegation had put forward article VII without prejudice to any special agreement on the question of liability.[295]

He added later:

The agreements on liability and assistance should take article VII as their starting point and should refer to it, not vice versa. He thought it unnecessary to insert a special statement in a treaty indicating that article VII would not prejudice the agreements to be concluded on liability; no such statement had been included in the Declaration when the identical provision had been adopted. The members appeared to be generally agreed on that point.[296]

Although later, the Australian proposal did appear in United States draft II,[297] it is perhaps not without significance that the United States delegate at the same meeting of the Legal Sub-Committee at which Article VII of Soviet draft I was discussed did say:

---

[291] A/AC.105/C.2/5th Sess./WP.32 (13.9.66).
[292] Cf. India, A/AC.105/C.2/SR.71 and Add. 1 (4.8.66), pp. 8–9; USA, ibid./SR.73 (16.9.66), p. 5; Japan, ibid., p. 9; Belgium, ibid., p. 10; Brazil, ibid., p. 11; France, ibid., p. 11; United Kingdom, ibid., p. 13.
[293] A/AC.105/C.2/SR.73 (16.9.66), pp. 8–9.
[294] See s. III.B above.
[295] A/AC.105/C.2/SR.67 (25.7.66), p. 10.
[296] Ibid., p. 12.

He thought that the matter could be handled by an understanding manifested in the record that the provision was without prejudice to the subsequent negotiation of a specific agreement on liability.[298]

In the end, no provision on the subject was inserted in the final text of the treaty. The position may perhaps be taken to be precisely what the United States had suggested. This view in fact finds confirmation in the subsequent Agreement on Rescue and Return; inasmuch as, under this agreement, astronauts and space objects are no longer to be returned to the State of registry as required by the treaty, but to 'representatives of the launching authority'.[299]

B. Amendment

In view of the strong opposition shown by the Soviet Union to the Australian proposal,[300] it is rather surprising that it did not adopt a similar attitude towards the amendment clause[301] in the United States draft which, with minor modifications, became Article XV of the treaty:

Any State Party to the Treaty may propose amendments to this Treaty. Amendments shall enter into force for each State Party to the Treaty accepting the amendments upon their acceptance by a majority of the States Parties to the Treaty and thereafter for each remaining State Party to the Treaty on the date of acceptance by it.

It will be seen that this article permits a majority of the contracting States to amend the treaty with binding effect on those which accept the amendment. Nevertheless, it received relatively little attention during the discussions. However, some highly pertinent remarks were made by both speakers who did intervene. First, the Romanian representative pointed out that it hardly seemed appropriate that in a treaty designed to lay down basic principles governing activities in outer space, a situation could be created in which some States would be bound by one version of the treaty while others were bound by a different one.[302] To this, the Swedish representative added that, according to the present provision, 'it would be possible for amendments to come into force without the support of the space Powers'.[303] From this point of view, the amendment procedure of the Space Treaty differs from that of the Antarctic Treaty, under which the unanimous agreement of certain contracting States specified in the Treaty is required.[304]

---

[297] Art. 13.
[299] See n. 284 above.
[301] US draft I, Art. 15.
[304] Art. XII.

[298] A/AC.105/C.2/SR.67 (25.7.66), p. 11.
[300] See s. VIII.A above.
[302] A/AC.105/C.2/SR.69 (27.7.66), p. 4.   [303] Ibid.

IX. Conclusion

The Space Treaty was born from the need to determine the legal status of celestial bodies before man's landing on the moon, and based on a tacit agreement on the part of the super powers to forgo territorial claims and military activities on all celestial bodies. In comments on the treaty, of all its provisions, emphasis has rightly been placed most of the time on the demilitarization clause which, marking a step forward in mankind's search for total disarmament, lends the treaty special significance. However, the progress achieved is relatively limited; for total demilitarization applies only to celestial bodies the military usefulness of which is estimated to be negligible. Insofar as outer space is concerned, which is of vital military importance, the demilitarization clause extends only to prohibiting the stationing of nuclear weapons and other weapons of mass destruction, leaving present and potential military activities totally unaffected. If the whole of extraterrestrial space is to be effectively demilitarized, not only must this gap be closed, but there should also be adequate safeguards, including prior verification of all launchings, as suggested by the United States in 1960,[305] whether by the United Nations or by a specially constituted international agency.

In converting into legally binding rules non-binding norms contained in successive General Assembly resolutions on the legal regime of outer space and celestial bodies and on international co-operation in their exploration and use, the treaty now provides a proper legal framework for future activities of States in this New World of the space age. It is to be hoped that it will speedily be supplemented by agreements on specific problems, such as the definition of outer space, the implementation of the principle of international responsibility and liability, and the exploitation of celestial bodies. From this point of view, the impetus which the treaty gave to the conclusion of the special agreement on rescue and return of astronauts and the return of space objects is an encouraging pointer. Yet, in the long run, attention must be given not only to substantive rules, but also to the procedure of dispute settlement and the machinery of co-ordination, co-operation and, where necessary, supervision, if the international rule of law is truly to be established in outer space and on celestial bodies.

[305] See n. 12 above.

10

The 1968 Astronauts Agreement*

I. Introduction

Never before in the history of the United Nations has a request of the General
Assembly to one of its Sub-Committees to prepare the text of a multipartite
treaty been implemented with such alacrity as in the case of the 1968
Agreement on the Rescue of Astronauts, the Return of Astronauts and the
Return of Objects Launched into Outer Space. On 3 November 1967, the
General Assembly in its resolution 2260 (XXII) requested its Committee on
the Peaceful Uses of Outer Space 'to continue with a sense of urgency its work
on the elaboration of', *inter alia*, 'an agreement on assistance to and return of
astronauts and space vehicles'. Scarcely six weeks later, and before the
Twenty-Second Session of the Assembly was out, an agreed text[1] was circulated on 13 December 1967, at the request of the Soviet and United States delegations, to members of the Legal Sub-Committee of the Outer Space
Committee, which met on the 14th. On the 19th, the draft treaty reached the
General Assembly on the last day of its Twenty-second Session and at once
received the Assembly's commendation.[2]

   The agreement was opened for signature to 'all States' on 22 April 1968,
simultaneously in London, Moscow, and Washington,[3] and came into force
on 3 December 1968, upon ratification by the three depositary States.[4]

II. The Background

The year in which agreement was reached on this treaty, 1967, was also that
which saw the first casualties in space exploration. On 27 January, three

---

   * First published in 23 *YBWA* (1969), pp. 185–208, based on an address delivered before the
British Branch of the International Law Association on 18 Feb. 1969. Reproduced by kind permission of Sweet & Maxwell Ltd.

   [1] A/AC.105/C.2/L.28. On developments of space law in the United Nations up to 1961, see B.
Cheng, 'The United Nations and Outer Space', 14 *CLP* (1961), p. 247 [Ch. 6 above]; for subsequent developments, see 'United Nations Resolutions on Outer Space: "Instant" International
Customary Law?', 5 *Indian JIL* (1965), p. 23 [Ch. 7 above]; 'Le Traité de 1967 sur l'espace/The
1967 Space Treaty', 95 *JDI* (1968), p. 532 [Ch. 9 above].

   [2] Resolution 2345 (XXII) adopted by 115 votes to none, with no abstentions.

   [3] 47 States signed it that day. Signature not binding without ratification. For text, see Appendix
I.2 below.

   [4] Five ratifications required (Art. 7(3)). Previously ratified by Byelorussia, Ireland, and Nepal.

United States astronauts died when fire broke out on board Apollo I before take-off.[5] On 24 April, Colonel Vladimir Kamorov of the Soviet Union perished in Soyuz I on landing.[6]

When the Outer Space Legal Sub-Committee reconvened at Geneva for its Sixth Session on 19 June 1967, both accidents were referred to by the Soviet representative[7] in support of his argument that, among the various items on the agenda, namely, liability for damage caused by launching objects into space, assistance to astronauts, and definition and utilization of outer space, priority should be given to assistance to astronauts.[8] Insofar as the United States and especially most non-space powers were concerned, the problem of liability, being definitely more complex and at least equally important and urgent, ought to be dealt with first.[9] The Soviet Union has from the beginning attached the greatest importance to the conclusion of a binding international agreement on assistance to and return of astronauts.

Apart from the natural desire of space powers that their astronauts in distress should be given every possible assistance, the reasons for the Soviet Union's special concern with the problem of rescue and return of astronauts are not difficult to seek. First, whilst the United States, in support of its space activities, has a world-wide network of tracking and other facilities sited in its own territory and, thanks to numerous bilateral agreements, in a number of foreign countries, the Soviet Union does not. So anxious was the Soviet Union to obtain similar rights from third States that at one stage in the negotiation of the 1967 Space Treaty, it made equal treatment in this matter a *sine qua non* of the Treaty.[10] Secondly, the Soviet Union does not have the same resources as the United States for recovering returning spacecraft and astronauts from the high seas in all parts of the world. These factors account, at least partly, for the fact that so far all United States returning space vehicles and astronauts splash down on, and are recovered by United States naval vessels from, the high seas, while all Soviet ones land on Soviet territory. The net result is that the chances of Soviet astronauts requiring assistance from third States are, relatively speaking, much higher.

This point and the risks in space exploration were clearly illustrated in a third incident in 1967. The United States unmanned Biosatellite II was

---

[5] Lt.-Cols. Virgil Grissom and Edward White, and Cdr. Roger Chaffee. See *Flight* (2 Feb. 1967), p. 181.

[6] *Flight* (4 May 1967), p. 722: the straps of the parachute became twisted.

[7] A/AC.105/C.2/SR.75 (19.6.67), p. 6; see also ibid./SR.76 (20.6.67), p. 4.

[8] See also the same representative, M. Piradov, writing in *Pravda* on 21 Aug. 1967: 'The draft of this agreement [concerning the rescue of astronauts] . . . was put the first on the agenda at the insistence of the Soviet delegation. It is generally known that the great cause of exploration of outer space has already led to casualties . . .'; quoted in P.-H. Houben, 'A New Chapter of Space Law', *Netherlands ILR* (1968), p. 121, n. 4.

[9] See further text to nn. 22 ff., and 58 ff. below.

[10] See loc. cit. (1968) in n. 1 above, pp. 550 ff. [Ch. 9 above, text to nn. 55 ff.], and text to nn. 18 ff. below.

launched on 7 September 1967, to be brought back in three days' time. Owing to faulty communications and an imminent tropical storm in the recovery area in the Pacific, it was decided to terminate the flight 24 hours earlier. However, during the critical period of preparation for 'de-boost,' the space-craft took no notice of commands except those from ground stations in Australia. Thanks to contingency plans which had previously been made, the facilities in Australia were immediately brought into action and played a vital rôle in making the Biosatellite II mission a success.[11] The lesson was doubt-less not lost on Soviet scientists.

Furthermore, the imminence of man's landing on the moon,[12] and the pos-sibility of large manned stations in space and other space probes in the near future,[13] unquestionably made the Soviet Union even more anxious than before to bring about an international agreement on assistance to and the return of astronauts. The fact that the Soviet Union eventually agreed to the British proposal regarding international organizations[14] shows clearly how far the Soviet Union was prepared to go in order to do so.

In this connection, the coming into force on 10 October 1967, of the 1967 Space Treaty no doubt helped to create a favourable climate for such an agree-ment. From the United States point of view, although its need for such an agreement is not as great as that of the Soviet Union, being one of the two major space powers, it can but benefit from it. While in agreeing to give pri-ority to assistance in preference to liability it may incur the displeasure of some of its friends and allies, the opportunity of securing an agreement which provides for the unconditional return of astronauts and space objects,[15] of furthering its co-operation with the Soviet Union in space exploration,[16] and of being able to chalk up yet another treaty with the Soviet Union despite the Vietnam war, was not to be missed.[17]

III. The Preliminary Phases of Negotiations

A. Phase I: The 1963 Space Declaration

The idea of a treaty on assistance to and return of astronauts can be traced back to a proposal made by Prime Minister Khrushchev in his letter to

---

[11] *Flight* (23 Nov. 1967), p. 887.

[12] See loc. cit. (1968) in n. 1 above, pp. 534 ff. [Ch. 9 above, s. II. Background].

[13] Cf. Soviet Academician L. Sedov's Press interview in the autumn of 1967, when he referred to the risks involved and the need for international co-operation in such projects, *Flight* (14 Sept. 1967), p. 426; see also ibid. (21 Sept. 1967), p. 501.

[14] See text to nn. 32, 89 ff., and 105 below.

[15] See text after n. 24 below, and to nn. 33 ff., 39, and 110 ff. below.

[16] It is generally known that after the *Soyuz I* tragedy, the United States renewed its offer of co-operation, *Flight* (21 Sept. 1967), p. 501.

[17] Cf. also loc. cit. (1968) in n. 8 above, p. 122.

President Kennedy on 20 March 1962, in which he also suggested the conclusion of a general space treaty.[18] The thaw in space co-operation having begun, the Legal Sub-Committee of the Outer Space Committee, the latter set up in 1959, met for the first time on 28 May 1962. Both Soviet proposals were at once put forward, and drafts were later introduced.[19] The immediate United States reaction was one of agreement in principle but disagreement as regards procedure. The United States preferred to proceed by way of General Assembly resolutions and, in the matter of assistance and return, submitted a draft text[20] to this effect. In its view, the principles involved were so clear and simple that they did not require elaboration in a formal legal instrument.[21] On the other hand, the United States proposed that liability should be dealt with by an international agreement.[22] On this, the Soviet Union in turn thought otherwise on the ground that 'compensation would undoubtedly be payable.'[23] The Soviet position was supported by all the States of the Soviet bloc, while the United States's by most of the others. A deadlock was reached which was not resolved until about a year later towards the end of the Second Session of the Legal Sub-Committee when on 30 April 1963, agreement was reached that there should be a treaty for each of these topics.[24]

From the substantive point of view, while both the Soviet and United States drafts agreed in assistance being given to astronauts in distress, in such astronauts and their space vehicles being promptly returned to their launching State, and the launching State being responsible for the expenses incurred, the United States, supported by Australia, France, and the United Kingdom, could not agree to the conditions attached by the Soviet Union to the return of space vehicles, namely, (i) foreign spacecraft would be returned without delay only if they had identification marks and their launchings had been officially announced, and (ii) spacecraft containing devices for the collection of intelligence information would not be returned.

But the problem of assistance was overshadowed by that of liability which in turn was overshadowed by that of general principles of space law. No progress was possible on any of these three topics in 1962 or 1963 until suddenly, soon after the Moscow Test Ban Treaty of 5 August 1963, agreement was reached between the two super powers on a *Declaration of Legal Principles Governing the Activities of States in the Exploration and Use of Outer Space*. The agreed text was presented to the Outer Space Committee on

---

[18] See further loc. cit. (1965) in n. 1 above, pp. 26 ff. [Ch.7 above, s. IV].

[19] A/AC.105/C.2/L.1 (general treaty); A/AC.105/C.2/L.2 (assistance and return).

[20] A/AC.105/C.2/L.3 (8.6.62).

[21] See, e.g., A/AC.105/C.2/SR.1 (28.5.62), pp. 8–9. The US position was shared by Canada and the United Kingdom. Doubt on the legal effectiveness of General Assembly resolutions was, however, expressed by the French delegate; see A/AC.105/C.2/SR.9 (12.6.62), p. 2.

[22] A/AC.105/C.2/L.4 (4.6.62).   [23] A/AC.105/C.2/SR.14 (19.6.62), p. 3.

[24] A/AC.105/C.2/SR.25 (30.4.63).

22 November and unanimously adopted by the General Assembly on 13 December 1963, in its resolution 1962 (XVIII).

In the matter of assistance and return, the 1963 Space Declaration, which is a mere recommendation, contains the following provisions:

7. The State on whose registry an object launched into outer space is carried shall retain jurisdiction and control over such object, and any personnel thereon, while in outer space. Ownership of objects launched into outer space, and of their component parts, is not affected by their passage through outer space or by their return to the earth. Such objects or component parts found beyond the limits of the State of registry shall be returned to that State, which shall furnish identifying data upon request prior to return.

8. . . .

9. States shall regard astronauts as envoys of mankind in outer space, and shall render to them all possible assistance in the event of accident, distress, or emergency landing on the territory of a foreign State or on the high seas. Astronauts who make such a landing shall be safely and promptly returned to the State of registry of their space vehicle.[25]

B. Phase II: Marking Time

The General Assembly on 13 December 1963, also adopted unanimously resolution 1963 (XVIII) which 'recommended' that 'consideration should be given' to incorporating the principles of the 1963 Declaration in a treaty, and 'requested' the Outer Space Committee 'to arrange for the prompt preparation of draft international agreements on liability for damage caused by objects launched into outer space and on assistance to and return of space vehicles.'

During the years 1964–5, the major difference between the Soviet and the Western blocs in the Outer Space Committee was whether priority should be given to the draft treaty on general principles or to the draft agreements on liability and assistance.[26]

While this controversy continued, however, new drafts were submitted on liability and on assistance,[27] and useful discussions took place. Towards the end of 1964, when the Second Part of the Fourth Session of the Legal Sub-Committee ended on 23 October, it was able to report preliminary agreement on the Preamble of the draft agreement, as well as several articles.[28] However, compared to the 1963 Space Declaration, the only significant advance was

---

[25] On the legal effect of the 1963 Space Declaration, see further loc. cit. (1965) in n. 1 above [Ch. 7 above]. The text of the Declaration is reproduced in App. III.3 below.

[26] See loc. cit. (1968) in n. 1 above, pp. 542 ff. [Ch. 9 above, text after n.. 29].

[27] Soviet Union, A/AC.105/C.2/L.2/Rev. 1 and 2; USA, A/AC.105/C.2/L.9; Australia and Canada, suggested compromise, W.G.I./17/Rev.1 and W.G.I./30.

[28] Report of the Legal Sub-Committee on the Work of the Second Part of its Third Session, A/AC.105/21, Annex III.

agreement on the duty of the launching State to remove objects of a hazardous or deleterious nature.[29]

But four major points of disagreement between the Soviet and the Western blocs remained, only the last one of which was specifically related to the assistance agreement.

(i) *Universality of the treaty.* The United States proposed that the agreement should be open to all States of the so-called 'United Nations family'. The Soviet Union insisted on its being open to all States without restriction, including, for instance, the German Democratic Republic.[30]

(ii) *Dispute settlement by the International Court.* States of the Soviet bloc flatly rejected the United States proposal to confer obligatory jurisdiction on the International Court of Justice to hear disputes regarding the interpretation or application of the treaty.[31]

(iii) *Status of international organizations.* Many States indicated that they would be able to engage in space exploration or exploitation only through international organizations. The United States and most Western powers were in favour of treating international organizations engaged in space activities on the same footing as States. This was firmly resisted by the Soviet bloc for reasons both political ('ELDO equals NATO') and juridical ('international organizations not States').[32]

(iv) *Conditional return of space vehicles.* Without referring any longer to intelligence-gathering devices,[33] the revised Soviet draft at first subordinated the return of foreign spacecraft to the condition that they had been launched 'for purposes of *peaceful* exploration and use of outer space,' and that the launching State had 'officially announced the launch of these objects and the purposes of launching.'[34] Subsequently, the Soviet draft referred merely to 'foreign spaceships, satellites and capsules launched in accordance with the' 1963 Space Declaration.[35] Without going into the merits of these conditions or qualifications, the United States and many States of the Western bloc voiced the fear that, especially in the absence of an arbitral clause, these conditions would give rise to endless difficulties in practice. At this point, the Legal Sub-Committee in September 1965, finding itself in an impasse, moved on to the question of liability.

---

[29] Report of the Legal Sub-Committee on the Work of the Second Part of its Third Session, A/AC.105/21, Annex III, Art. 6(3)(b), since deleted, imposed a duty on the State announcing the launching which knew that the object might be of a hazardous or deleterious nature to notify the State of landing.

[30] Cf. loc. cit. (1968) in note 1 above, pp. 554 and 556, esp. nn. 77 and 82 [Ch. 9 above, nn. 77 and 82 and text thereto; see also further text to nn. 38 and 104 below.]

[31] See further text to nn. 38 and 111 below.

[32] See further loc. cit. (1968) in nn. 1 above, pp. 588–98 [Ch. 9 above, s. V.G].

[33] See text after n. 24 above. On the legality of using aircraft and spacecraft for reconnaissance purposes, see loc. cit. (1961) in n. 1 above, pp. 262 ff. [Ch. 6 above, s. V].

[34] See A/AC.105/C.2/L.2/Rev.1, Art. 9; also USSR, A/AC.105/C.2/SR.32 (12.3.64).

[35] A/AC.105/C.2/L.2/Rev.2, Art 6(2).

C. Phase III: The 1967 Space Treaty

The imminence of man's landing on the moon following the success early in 1966 of the 'soft' landing on the moon of Luna IX and Surveyor I led the United States in May 1966 urgently to propose to the Soviet Union the conclusion of a treaty on the legal status of *celestial bodies*.[36] This gave the Soviet Union the needed opportunity of pressing once again that priority should be given to a treaty on general principles governing *outer space and celestial bodies*.[37] The result was that the Outer Space Committee in 1966 turned its attention to a general treaty, an agreed text of which was presented to, and at once commended by, the General Assembly on 19 December.

Of the four controversial points which divided East and West in regard to the assistance agreement,[38] the first three were resolved in favour of the Soviet view. On the fourth point, the 1967 Space Treaty in essence reproduces paragraphs 7 and 9 of the 1963 Space Declaration as respectively its own Articles VIII and V. No condition is attached to the duty to return either astronauts or space vehicles, though this does not necessarily exclude a State from arguing that this duty is conditional on their mission being in conformity with the terms of the Treaty.[39]

On the initiatives of respectively the Soviet Union and the United States, the following two paragraphs were added to Article V of the Treaty:

In carrying on activities in outer space and on celestial bodies, the astronauts of one State Party shall render all possible assistance to the astronauts of other States Parties.

States Parties to the Treaty shall immediately inform the other States Parties to the Treaty or the Secretary-General of the United Nations of any phenomena they discover in outer space, including the moon and other celestial bodies, which could constitute a danger to the life or health of astronauts.

At the same time as approving the text of the draft Space Treaty, the General Assembly on 19 December also requested the Outer Space Committee to continue its work on the agreements on liability and assistance, to which a third item was added, namely, questions relating to the definition and utilization of outer space.

---

[36] See loc. cit. (1968) in n. 1 above, pp. 544 ff. [Ch. 9 above, s. III].

[37] Cf. text to n. 18 above.

[38] See text to nn. 30 ff. above. On the 1967 Space Treaty generally, see loc. cit. (1968) in n. 1 above [Ch. 9 above].

[39] See n. 25 above for text of paras. 7 and 9 of the 1963 Space Declaration [see also Appendix II.3 below]. Cf. the Lebanese suggestion that the duty should be conditional on the astronauts' mission being peaceful, which was, however, not taken up, A/AC.105/C.2/SR.66 (25.7.66), p. 9; also Iran, ibid./SR.71 & Add. 1 (4.8.66), pp. 24–5.

D. *Phase IV: More Haste Less Speed*

When the Sixth Session of the Legal Sub-Committee opened in June 1967, the Soviet Union, obviously anxious[40] to obtain an agreement on assistance to astronauts and concentrating on the bare essentials,[41] presented a revised draft of extreme brevity[42] which dealt solely with assistance to astronauts, and pressed for this topic to be given priority. At once the Sub-Committee became involved in discussing priorities and the scope of the assistance agreement. By omitting all references to space vehicles and even the return of astronauts, the Soviet draft avoided the issue whether the return of astronauts and space vehicles should be conditional or unconditional, but few outside the Soviet bloc relished the prospect of an agreement on rescue of astronauts alone. By the time the Session ended on 14 July, agreement was reached on only two articles, one on notification of accident, the other on assistance in the territory of a contracting State. When the Outer Space Committee met for its Tenth Session on 13 September, the Soviet Union, perhaps realizing that its plan had misfired, stated that it had no objection to completing its latest draft with provisions concerning the return of astronauts and space vehicles.[43] But otherwise no agreement was in sight.

Looking back at the records of the Legal Sub-Committee since its inception, one almost gets the impression that, at least during its formal proceedings, the Sub-Committee has spent more time discussing how it should carry out its work than on the substance of space law.

IV. The Critical Phase of Negotiations: a Common Pattern Followed

A common pattern underlies the work of the United Nations in its elaboration of the rules of space law: the predominance of the super-space powers. One of the reasons why the Legal Sub- Committee appears to spend more time on procedure than on substance is because the most critical part of the negotiations is always carried out behind the scenes directly between the two super powers. The rôle of the rest of the Legal Sub-Committee is reduced largely to that of commenting on proposals made by the superpowers by themselves, and ratifying whatever they have agreed on. From this point of view, the 1968 Astronauts Agreement has faithfully followed the established pattern.

Thus, the 1963 Space Declaration was preceded by two years of desultory discussions in the Legal Sub-Committee on a variety of topics. When, subsequent to the signing of the Moscow Test Ban Treaty on 5 August 1963, it appeared that agreement on outer space was possible between the two super

---

[40] See text to nn. 7 and 8, and n. 8 above.
[41] Cf. USSR, A/AC.105/C.2/SR.76 (20.6.67), p. 5: 'the absolute minimum'.
[42] A/AC.105/C.2/L.18.   [43] A/AC.105/PV.49 (13.9.67), p. 61.

powers, the Outer Space Committee, no sooner had it met in September 1963, adjourned to allow direct negotiations to take place between them, assisted and attended by a few unspecified States. The hope of the Outer Space Committee was not disappointed and, on 22 November 1963, it was presented with a draft which it dutifully forwarded to the First Committee. The latter in turn forwarded the draft, without disturbing a single comma, to the General Assembly, which adopted it by acclamation on 13 December.[44]

Very much the same situation occurred in the case of the 1967 Space Treaty. After another year of rather inconclusive discussion on assistance, liability, and especially priorities, the Legal Sub-Committee, when its Fifth Session opened in July 1966, brushed everything aside in order to consider the various drafts of a treaty on the legal regime of celestial bodies and outer space which the super powers had just submitted to it. Although it was able during its Fifth Session to comment on these drafts, the crucial negotiations took place directly between the two superpowers and behind the scenes. Agreement once reached, the text was submitted on Thursday, 15 December 1966, by a 43-power draft resolution directly to the First Committee, by-passing the Outer Space Committee. The draft was adopted without objection by the First Committee on Saturday. and received the unanimous commendation of the General Assembly on Monday. This time, there was at least a note of discord, if not a vote of dissent, registered by the delegate of Tanzania, who justifiably complained of the lack of time for consideration.[45]

Now, once more, the pattern has been repeated in the case of the Astronauts Agreement. It is true that in this case the subject had been on the agenda of, and discussed in, the Legal Sub-Committee for many years. However, when the Sixth Session of the Legal Sub-Committee ended on 14 July 1967, agreement seemed more remote than ever. Few, if any, would have guessed that of the two agreements the Outer Space Committee was requested on 3 November by the General Assembly in its resolution 2260 (XXII) urgently to elaborate, namely, liability and assistance, the latter would be singled out for priority treatment. Yet, once the superpowers decided to do so, there seemed little choice. A text[46] 'negotiated backstage'[47] was thrust upon the United Nations, which was given less than a week to consider and approve it.[48]

---

[44] See further loc. cit. (1965) in n. 1 above, pp. 28 ff. [Ch. 7 above, s. VI].

[45] See further loc. cit. (1968) in n. 1 above, pp. 556 ff. [Ch. 9 above, s. III.E].

[46] A/AC.105/C.2/L.28, circulated at the request of the Soviet Union and the United States on 13 Dec. 1967, the day before the opening of the Special Session of the Legal Sub-Committee.

[47] Phrase used by the Indian delegate, A/AC.105/C.2/SR.86 (14.12.67), p. 12. In his statement at the opening of the Special Session on 14 Dec. 1967, the Chairman of the Legal Sub-Committee remarked that 'a series of informal consultations had been held among members of the Sub-Committee' (ibid, p. 4). Apart from the Chairman, the British and French members were doubtless shown the text beforehand, or even consulted. *Inter alia*, the Indian (ibid., p. 12), Japanese (ibid., p. 10), Swedish (ibid., p. 20), and UAR members were not. They received the text only the previous day, and complained of the procedure followed.

[48] See text to nn. 1 and 2 above.

Whereas in the case of both the 1963 Space Declaration[49] and the 1967 Space Treaty,[50] the Legal Sub-Committee was by-passed, this time, probably in order to gain a modicum of support from its other members, it was at least spared this indignity. A Special Session was convened to meet on Thursday, 14 December, at 3.20 p.m. The draft reached it the previous day.[51] Members groaned, complained, protested and made reservations. Some wanted the matter deferred.[52] But generally they accepted the situation, and directed their efforts to making the most of the one and a half days at their disposal and to improving the text they had before them. They squeezed three meetings into Friday, and it was 10.10 p.m. before they reluctantly forwarded the draft to the Outer Space Committee. However, before they did so, they succeeded in doing what they were never in a position to do in the case of the 1963 Space Declaration and 1967 Space Treaty: they amended the text submitted jointly by the two major space powers on a number of points, including the very important one concerning international organizations.[53]

The Outer Space Committee itself, which had only the Saturday morning to consider the draft, also managed to make a few minor amendments to the text. This time, it was the turn of the First Committee to be by-passed, and the General Assembly received and approved the text on Tuesday, 19 December. Although the vote was again unanimous, on this occasion there was not merely a note of discord, but, taking into account not only what was said in the plenary, a chorus of discontent.

In the first place, many more delegates complained of the lack of time for proper consideration of the draft,[54] let alone consultation with their respective governments. In particular, it was pointed out that even in the limited time available to it, the Legal Sub-Committee and the Outer Space Committee were able to bring various improvements to the text of the draft,[55] while others emphasized that the consideration by the General Assembly of resolutions which had not been examined by one of the Main Committees and not been inscribed on the agenda in accordance with the rules of procedure should not be allowed to become a precedent.[56] In the end, a number of delegations,

---

[49] See text to nn. 18 ff. above.   [50] See text to nn. 35 ff. above.

[51] See complaints of Japanese and Swedish delegates, A/AC.105/C.2/SR.86 (14.12.67), pp. 10 and 20.

[52] Japan, A/AC.105/C.2/SR.86 (14.12.67), p. 11; India, ibid., p. 12; ;UAR, ibid., p. 15.

[53] See text to n. 32 above, and to nn. 89 ff. and 105 below.

[54] Japn, A/AC.105/C.2/SR.86 (14.12.67), p. 10; India, ibid., p. 12; Brazil, ibid., p. 14; Sierra Leone, A/AC.105/C.2/SR.87 (15.12.67), p. 5; Japan, A/AC.105/C.2/SR.89 (15.12.67), p. 6; France, A/AC.105/PV.52 (16.12.67), p. 32; France, A/PV.1640 (Prov.) (19.12.67), p. 41; Iran, ibid., p. 52; Burma, ibid., p. 56.

[55] India, A/AC.105/PV.52 (16.12.67), pp. 36–7; Iran, A/PV.1640 (Prov.) (19.12.67), p. 52.

[56] Ecuador, on behalf of a majority of the 'Latin American Group', A/PV.1640 (Prov.) (19.12.67), p. 47; Lebanon, ibid.

while they did not wish to vote against the draft treaty, at one stage or another reserved the position of their governments on the text.[57]

Secondly, while all the delegations, on humanitarian grounds, welcomed the agreement reached between the superpowers on assistance and return in principle, most considered that the liability agreement was at least no less important and urgent,[58] that it was complementary to the assistance agreement,[59] and some indicated that their governments might well not be able to consider acceptance of the assistance agreement without a satisfactory liability agreement,[60] or assurance from the space powers on liability.[61] The strong opinion of most of the delegations in the United Nations on this point accounts for the fourth operative paragraph of Resolution 2345 (XXII) calling on the Committee on the Peaceful Uses of Outer Space to complete urgently the preparation of the draft agreement on liability for damage caused by the launching of objects into outer space and, in any event, not later than the beginning of the twenty-third session of the General Assembly, and to submit it to the Assembly at that session. However, the General Assembly finding, at its twenty-third session, that the Outer Space Committee had not been able to comply with this request could do little except, in its Resolution 2453B (XXIII) of 20 December 1968, to extend the time limit to the twenty-fourth session of the General Assembly.

V. Space Powers v. Non-Space Powers

All these objections represent inherent obstacles to the agreement achieving wide acceptance, especially in the absence of a satisfactory liability agreement. While the liability agreement is of interest to both space powers and non-space powers, the obligations created by the Astronauts Agreement are primarily for the benefit of space powers.

---

[57] Japan, A/AC.105/C.2/SR.89 (15.12.67), p. 6; cf. Belgium, ibid.; Brazil, ibid, p. 9; Mexico, ibid.; India, A/AC.105/PV.52 (16.12.67), p. 38/40; Italy, ibid., pp. 41–2; Japan, ibid., p. 52; Burma, A/PV.1640 (Prov.) (19.12.67), p. 56; Sierra Leone, ibid., p. 61.

[58] United States, A/AC.105/C.2/SR.86 (14.12.67), p. 7; India, A/AC.105/C.2/SR.86 (14.12.67), p. 12; Canada, ibid., p. 16; Sweden, ibid., p. 19/20; Sierra Leone, A/AC.105/C.2/SR.87 (15.12.67), p. 5; Italy, ibid., p. 6; Belgium, p. 6; Austria, ibid., p. 9; United Kingdom, A/AC.105/C.2/SR.89 (15.12.67), p. 5; Canada, ibid., p. 6; United Kingdom, A/AC.105/PV.52 (16.12.67), p. 22; Sierra Leone, ibid., pp. 27–8/30; Australia, ibid., p. 46; Belgium, ibid., p. 55/57; Austria, ibid., p. 58; UAR, ibid., p. 66; France, A/PV.1640 (Prov.) (19.12.67), p. 42; Italy, ibid., p. 43; Iran, ibid., p. 53/55; Sierra Leone, ibid., p. 61.

[59] Iran, A/AC.105/C.2/SR.86 (14.12.67), p. 9; Japan, ibid., p. 11; Brazil, ibid, p. 14; UAR ibid., p. 15; Italy, A/AC.105/C.2/SR.87 (15.12.67), p. 6; Japan, A/AC.105/C.2/SR.89 (15.12.67), p. 5; Italy, A/AC.105/PV.52 (16.12.67), p. 41.

[60] Italy, A/AC.105/C.2/SR.87 (15.12.67), p. 6; A/AC.105/C.2/SR.89 (15.12.67), p. 6; Japan, A/AC.105/PV.52 (16.12.67), p. 41; Japan, ibid., p. 52; cf. condemnation of 'package deal', Bulgaria, A/AC.105/C.2/SR.86 (14.12.67), p. 9.

[61] Italy, A/PV.1640 (Prov.) (19.12.67), p. 46.

A number of States have remarked in the course of these discussions that, for humanitarian reasons, they would unhesitatingly give every assistance to astronauts in distress.[62] But this in itself is not an adequate reason why they should enter into legal obligations binding themselves on how they should discharge this essentially humanitarian task.

The Chairman of the Legal Sub-Committee, in presenting the draft agreement both before the Outer Space Committee and before the General Assembly, remarked: 'the text reflects a carefully designed balance between the legitimate interests of the party on whose territory the search and rescue operations are conducted and those of the launching authority.'[63] This is hardly true of the Agreement as a whole, though it may plausibly apply to efforts made in the Legal Sub-Committee to make Article 2 of the Agreement so. Article 2, which caused the most concern in the Legal Sub-Committee, illustrates the problems which a legally binding instrument can create for a contracting State.

Article 2 deals with rescue operations in the territory of a contracting Party. In the original draft its last two sentences were worded as follows:

If assistance by the launching authority would help to effect a prompt rescue or would contribute substantially to the effectiveness of search and rescue operations, *the Contracting Party shall co-operate with the launching authority* with a view to the effective conduct of search and rescue operations. Such operations shall be subject to the direction and control of the Contracting Party, which shall act in close and continuing consultation with the launching authority (italics added).

In introducing the draft agreement, the United States pointed out: 'It was likely that the views of the territorial party and the launching authority would coincide on the question whether, in a particular case, assistance by the launching authority would help to effect a prompt rescue or would contribute substantially to the effectiveness of search and rescue operations. In the unlikely event that they did not agree, the territorial party would of course have the final say in the matter.'[64]

Article 2 caused so much concern[65] that the United States had to repeat the above assurance that the territorial State had the 'final say' twice within two days.[66] Even so, as the Indian delegate said: 'Article 2 . . . did not make clear who would decide whether assistance by the launching authority would help . . . The implication was that the contracting parties should admit personnel

---

[62] See e.g. France, A/AC.105/PV.52 (16.12.67), p. 31; India, ibid., p. 36.

[63] A/AC.105/PV.52 (16.12.1968), p. 3; A/PV.1640 (Prov.) (19.12.1968), p. 36.

[64] A/AC.105/C.2/SR.86 (14.12.67), p. 8.

[65] See e.g. Iran, A/AC.105/C.2/SR.86 (14.12.67), pp. 9–10; India, ibid., p. 11; France, ibid., p. 13; ;Brazil, ibid., p. 14; Canada, ibid., p. 17; Sweden, p. 19/20; Australia, A/AC.105/C.2/SR.87 (15.12.67), p. 3; Sierra Leone, ibid., p. 5; Italy, ibid., p. 6; Argentina, ibid., p. 9; Mexico, ibid., p. 10.

[66] A/AC.105/C.2/SR.89 (15.12.67), p. 3; A/AC.105/PV.52 (16.12.67), pp. 9/10–11.

of the launching authority on their territory for search and rescue operations. That was a far-reaching obligation, with serious implications for a country's territorial sovereignty.'[67]

If regard is paid to some of the earlier Soviet[68] and United States[69] proposals on the subject, which respectively obliged the territorial State, if necessary, to require and even simply to permit the launching State to provide assistance, the above interpretation seems eminently natural. It was literally at the eleventh hour that a compromise was found. A French proposal was accepted which switched round the rôle of the launching authority and the territorial State in the third sentence so that it is now the launching authority which 'shall co-operate with the Contracting Party.'[70] Even with this amendment, however, some still felt it necessary to emphasize the statement of the United States delegate,[71] while others remained to the end unhappy.[72]

VI. Obligations of Contracting States

A. In Regard to Astronauts[73]

1. *Notification of Accidents.* A contracting State, on learning that an astronaut is in distress or has made an emergency landing anywhere other than in the territory of another State, shall immediately notify the launching authority or, if it cannot identify the launching authority, make a public announcement instead. At the same time, it must also notify the Secretary-General of the United Nations (Article 1).

2. *Search and Rescue in a Contracting State's Territory.* Under Article 2 contracting States undertake to 'take all possible steps' to rescue and assist astronauts in distress in territories under their jurisdiction, and to inform the launching authority and also the Secretary-General of the United Nations of the steps they are taking and their progress. The suggestion that, following Article 25 of the 1944 Chicago Convention on International Civil Aviation, a State should be bound only 'to provide such measures of assistance . . . as it finds practicable'[74] was not taken up. However, it was recognized that, not only in Article 2, but also in the first sentence of Article 3 and paragraphs 2

---

[67] A/AC.105/C.2/SR.86 (14.12.68), p. 12. [68] A/AC.105/C.2/L.2/Rev.2; Art. 3(3).
[69] A/AC.105/C.2/L.9: Art. 2(2). [70] A/AC.105/C.2/SR.89 (15.12.67), p. 3.
[71] Australia, A/AC.105/PV.52 (16.12.67), p. 47; Belgium, ibid., p. 56.
[72] E.g., Italy, A/AC.105/PV.52 (16.12.67), p. 42; Brazil, ibid., p. 61, and A/PV.1640 (Prov.) (19.12.67), p. 46.
[73] It is to be noted that except in the Preamble, the Agreement speaks always of 'the personnel of a spacecraft'—a term borrowed from an earlier Australian–Canadian proposal—in order to extend its benefits to all persons on board.
[74] France, A/AC.105/C.2/SR.86 (14.12.67), p. 13; cf. text to n. 85 below.

and 3 of Article 5, no State would be required to go beyond the limits of its capabilities.[75]

As has already been mentioned, in the original draft submitted by the major space powers, the contracting Parties were under a duty to co-operate with the launching authority in search and rescue operations in their own territories, but in the Legal Sub-Committee this duty was transformed into one incumbent on the launching authority to co-operate with the territorial State.[76]

3. *Landings in Areas not under the Jurisdiction of any State.* Article 3 applies to astronauts who have '*alighted* on the high seas or in any other place not under the jurisdiction of any State.'[77] 'Those Contracting Parties which are in a position to do so shall, if necessary, extend assistance in search and rescue operations for such personnel to assure their speedy rescue.' In reply to a question from the representative of Brazil,[78] the United States representative explained: 'it was not the intention of Article 3 to impose an obligation to assist in search and rescue operations on countries in the geographical vicinity to spacecraft which had alighted on the high seas or in any other place not under the jurisdiction of any State. It was intended mainly to allow for the possibility of a contracting party's ships being near the scene of the accident and therefore in a position to help with the rescue.'[79]

During the discussions, questions were raised whether the launching authority is itself obliged to assist in such search and rescue operations.[80] However, it is obvious from the text that a contracting State is merely to 'extend assistance' in search and rescue operations (presumably undertaken principally by the launching authority) and to do so only 'if necessary'. Nevertheless, Article 3 requires it to inform the launching authority and the Secretary-General of the United Nations of the steps it is taking and of their progress.

4. *Return of Astronauts.* If astronauts land in the territory of a contracting State or have otherwise been recovered by it, they shall, under Article 4, 'be safely and promptly returned to representatives of the launching authority.' Inasmuch as the 1967 Space Treaty requires its contracting Parties to return astronauts to the State of registry of the spacecraft,[81] a State party to both

[75] United States, A/AC.105/C.2/SR.86 (14.12.67), p. 21, confirming the Swedish delegate's understanding that the phrase 'meant action within the limits of the facilities at the contracting parties' disposal', ibid., p. 20. See also France, A/AC.105/PV.52 (16.12.67), p. 32: 'we cannot expect the impossible of anyone'. On Article 3, see s. VI.A.3 below; on Art. 5(2), see s. VI.B.2 below; on Art. 5(3), see s. VI.B.3 below.

[76] See text to nn. 64 ff. above, and text to n. 97 below.   [77] See text to n. 127 below.

[78] A/AC.105/C.2/SR.86 (14.12.67), p. 14.

[79] A/AC.105/C.2/SR.86 (14.12.67), pp. 20–1; it is doubtful if Art. 3 will fully achieve this purpose, see text to n. 128 below. On the required standard of assistance, see also text to n. 75 above.

[80] Sweden, A/AC.105/C.2/SR.86 (14.12.67), p. 20; ibid./SR.88 (15.12.67), p. 3; cf. United States affirmative reply, ibid., p. 3.

[81] Art. V(1). See futher text to nn. 25 and 38 above.

treaties can be faced with conflicting treaty obligations. The possibility of returning the astronauts to representatives of the launching authority instead of the launching authority itself,[82] on the other hand, greatly facilitates the task of the territorial State.[83]

B. In Regard to Space Objects

The obligations of contracting Parties in regard to objects launched into space are similar to, but less exacting than, those relating to astronauts.

1. *Notification of Landing.* If a contracting State learns that a space object has landed anywhere other than in the territory under the jurisdiction of another State it shall notify the launching authority and the Secretary-General of the United Nations. Article 5(1), however, does not require the notification to be immediate.[84] Moreover, the obligation is limited to objects which have 'returned to Earth,' excluding therefore celestial bodies.

2. *Recovery of Foreign Space Objects in Contracting State's Territory.* Upon request of the launching authority, the State of landing shall take 'such steps as it finds practicable[85] to recover the object' (Article 5(2)).

3. *Return of Space Objects.* Article 5(3) reproduces in substance the last sentence of Article VIII of the 1967 Space Treaty[86] except that the duty is now contingent on a request received from the launching authority. Moreover, upon a proposal made by the French delegate,[87] the State of landing, instead of returning the object, may simply hold it 'at the disposal of representatives of the launching authority.'[88]

VII. Duties of Launching Authority

A. Definition of Launching Authority

Article 6 defines the launching authority as 'the State responsible for launching, or, where an intergovernmental organisation is responsible for launching, that organisation, provided that that organisation declares its acceptance of

---

[82] Suggested by the French delegation, cf. United States, A/AC.105/C.2/SR.86 (14.12.67), p. 8.

[83] Cf. also loc. cit. (1968) in n. 8 above, pp. 126–7, in respect of States with no diplomatic relations. On whether the duty to return astronauts is absolute and unconditional, see further text to nn. 110 ff. below.

[84] Cf. Canada, A/AC.105/C.2/SR.86 (14.12.67), p. 17, drawing attention to the omission of this qualification which existed in previous drafts.

[85] Cf. text to nn. 74 and 75 above.

[86] I.e., para. 7 of the 1963 Space Declaration. See text to nn. 25 and 39 above. Cf. also text to n. 75 above.

[87] A/AC.105/C.2/SR.86 (14.12.67), p. 13; accepted, ibid., p. 21.   [88] Cf. text to n. 83 above.

the rights and obligations provided for in this Agreement and a majority of the States members of that organisation are Contracting Parties to this Agreement' and to the 1967 Space Treaty. The extension of the benefits of the Agreement to international organizations was proposed by the United Kingdom[89] in consultation with other European powers and Australia.[90] Its acceptance by the Soviet Union[91] represents a major concession on the part of the Soviet Union[92] to the views of what Ambassador Goldberg has described as the near-space powers and co-operative space powers.[93]

Another concession to the same interests is the shift from the notion of the State of registry, which is still central to the 1967 Space Treaty,[94] to the concept of the launching authority. This change dispenses with the need for registration and in particular with registration with a State which, in the case of an international organization being responsible for launching, can present problems.[95] The Agreement, however, fails to define what is meant by 'responsible.'[96]

B. Real or Apparent Duties

In form, the launching authority has five duties under the Agreement. In fact none of them is for the benefit of the territorial State, except possibly that under Article 5(4). This paragraph provides that if a contracting Party informs the launching authority that it has reason to believe that a space object discovered in its territory or recovered by it elsewhere is of a hazardous or deleterious nature, the launching authority 'shall immediately take effective steps, under the direction and control of the said Contracting Party, to eliminate possible danger of harm.' Even this duty may, however, be regarded as merely a method for the launching authority to discharge its obligation under international customary law not to cause damage to other States and to mitigate, and make reparation for, such damage as it may have caused.

The other apparent duties of the launching State consist in (i) co-operating with the territorial State in which its astronauts have landed in search and rescue operations,[97] (ii) providing assistance, if requested, in the recovery of its own space objects,[98] (iii) furnishing identifying data, if requested, prior to the

[89] A/AC.105/C.2/SR.86 (14.12.67), p. 13; supported by France, ibid., p. 13; Canada, ibid., p. 18; Sweden, ibid., pp. 19/20.
[90] Cf. United Kingdom, A/AC.105/PV.52 (16.12.67), pp. 23/25; France, ibid., pp. 32/35; Italy, ibid., p. 42; Australia, ibid., p. 47; Canada, ibid., p. 51; Belgium, ibid., p. 56; France, A/PV.1640 (Prov.) (19.12.67), p. 42; Ital, ibid., p. 44/45.
[91] At the same meeting, see A/AC.105/C.2/SR.86 (14.12.67), pp. 21–2.
[92] Cf. n. 32 above. [93] A/AC.105/PV.52 (16.12.67), p. 12.
[94] See loc. cit. (1968) in n. 1 above, pp. 568 ff. [Ch. 9 above, s. V.C].
[95] See ibid., especially n. 22 on p. 570 [Ch. 9 s. V.C.1].
[96] Question raised but not answered, Sierra Leone, A/AC.105/C.2/SR.87 (14.12.67), p. 5.
[97] Art. 2; see text to n. 63 ff. above on how this apparent duty was originally intended to be a right of the launching authority.
[98] Art. 5(3).

return of space objects,[99] and (iv) paying[100] for the expenses incurred in recovering and returning space objects, if it has requested the recovery and return of such objects.[101] It is not obliged to pay for the rescue and return of its astronauts.

VIII. Some General Observations

Apart from the inherent one-sidedness of the Agreement in the benefits it confers, which is obvious from the above survey,[102] the following general observations regarding the Agreement may be made.

A. The Personal and Temporal Scope of the Agreement and the Special Character of its Obligations

Following the 1967 Space Treaty,[103] the Agreement is open to 'all States'.[104] Under the United Kingdom amendment to Article 6,[105] an international organization may be considered a 'launching authority' under certain conditions, including a declaration by the organization concerned accepting the rights and obligations provided for in the Agreement. Yet, not being contracting parties, the rights and duties of such participating organizations can only be those of a 'launching authority' and not those of a contracting party.

As most of the obligations in the Agreement can only be discharged by territorial entities, i.e., States, if international organizations are parties to the Agreement, they would in fact be exempt from all such obligations. Moreover, insofar as the Agreement only stipulates that at least 'a majority' of the members of the participating organization must be parties to the Agreement, if the organzsation is a contracting party, it means that all the non-party members

---

[99] Art. 5(5).

[100] The present wording 'shall be borne by' was substituted for 'shall be reimbursed by' at the suggestion of France, A/AC.105/C.2/SR.86 (14.12.67), p. 13; supported by Canada, ibid., p. 17; accepted, ibid., pp. 21–2. It opens the possibility for the territorial State of requiring the launching authority to pay as work proceeds or even in advance. As this is precisely what the territorial State would be able to do if there is no Agreement, this shows that Article 5(5) can hardly be regarded a benefit in favour of the territorial State.

[101] Art. 5(5) does not expressly stipulate the condition stated in the text; but it limits the responsibility of the launching authority for expenses to those incurred under the Agreement, which does not require the territorial State to recover and return space objects unless requested by the launching authority to do so.

[102] See also n. 129 below.   [103] See text to nn. 30 and 38 above.

[104] United States, A/AC.105/C.2/SR.86 (14.12.67), p. 9, and A/AC.105/PV.52 (16.12.67), p. 11: no precedent, no implied recognition; see also Australia, A/AC.105/C.2/SR.87 (15.12.67), pp. 3–4; Canada, ibid./SR.86 (14.12.67), p. 18; France, ibid., p. 14; A/AC.105/PV.52 (16.12.67), pp. 33/35; A/PV.1640 (Prov.) (19.12.67), p. 42; Italy, A/AC.105/PV.52 (16.12.67), p. 42; United Kingdom, A/AC.105/C.2/SR.89 (15.12.67), p. 5; A/AC.105/PV.52 (16.12.67), p. 26. See further nn. 3 and 30 above.

[105] See text to nn. 89 ff. above.

would in fact benefit from the Agreement without being parties to it and bound by its obligations. These are some of the practical objections to international organizations being made equal parties to certain treaties.[106]

This objection is, however, not entirely applicable in this case, as the Agreement is not a synallagmatic one in which the parties promise to help one another in case of need. 'Prompted,' the Preamble says, 'by sentiments of humanity,' the parties to the Astronauts Agreement promise one another to help rescue and recover spacemen and spacecraft, *whether or not their national State or launching authority is a party to the treaty*. Article 6 consequently confers no extra benefits on non-parties. But this would not necessarily be true of a similar clause in another treaty.

While 'sentiments of humanity' may prompt States to conclude such an agreement for the rescue of astronauts, they appear much less compelling in relation to unmanned spacecraft, especially in the absence of a satisfactory liability agreement. Indeed, the Sierra Leone delegate rather acidly observed: 'Whereas in the case of the return of space vehicles only one object might be involved, the damage which it might cause might not only be incalculable but might also involve irreparably whole cities, whole cultures and whole civilisations.'[107]

It is in this light that the following oft-repeated French declaration is to be looked at: 'the text of the convention, as the French government understands it, applies in full only to flights that are experimental and scientific in nature. The rights of the signatory States must be fully reserved for the time when such flights may become utilitarian or commercial in character, at which time it will doubtless be necessary to negotiate a new convention.'[108]

Like the 1967 Space Treaty, the 1968 Astronauts Agreement is concluded for an indefinite duration, but parties may withdraw from it one year after its entry into force by giving a year's notice in writing to the depositary governments (Article 9). The amendment clause is also identical to that in the Space Treaty (Article 8).[109]

B. Duty to Return Astronauts and Space Objects: Absolute and Unconditional?

The question whether the duty to return astronauts and space objects is to be unconditional or not was what divided the Soviet Union and the United States from the beginning.[110] Indeed, it might be thought that the main attraction of the Astronauts Agreement for the United States is the establishment of

---

[106] See also loc. cit. (1968) in n. 1 185 above, pp. 588 ff. [Ch. 9 above, s. V.G].

[107] A/AC.105/PV.52 (16.12.67), p. 27; see also Australia, ibid., p. 46; Japan, A/AC.105/C.2/SR.86 (14.12.67), p. 11.

[108] A/PV.1640 (Prov.) (19.12.67), p. 42; see also A/AC.105/PV.52 (16.12.67), p. 33/35.

[109] See further loc. cit. (1968) in n. 1 above [Ch. 9 above].

[110] See text after n. 24, and text to nn. 33 ff. and 39 above.

an absolute and unconditional obligation to return astronauts and space objects, especially in the absence of a clause for the compulsory settlement of disputes by an independent body.[111] However, in the course of the discussions, France on three separate occasions and Austria twice asserted that Article 4 on 'the safe and prompt' return of astronauts was subject to respectively national 'legislation . . . concerning, for example, the right of asylum'[112] and 'the recognised principles of international relations which are reflected in Austria's traditional policy towards aliens.'[113] The United States in the Outer Space Committee made a special point of emphasizing that the obligation, like that in Article V of the 1967 Space Treaty,[114] was 'absolute and unconditional,'[115] but France reaffirmed her position once more in the plenary of the General Assembly.[116] On the basis of the Agreement as it is presently worded, the United States interpretation appears correct.[117] This is not to say, however, that a situation like that which arose after the Korean conflict in relation to Article 118 (on repatriation) of the 1949 Geneva Prisoners of War Convention might not arise.

It may be said that the obligation to return space objects is equally absolute and, once requested by the launching authority, is unconditional.[118] However, even though a proposal put forward by France that the return of space objects should be subject to the receipt of compensation for any damage caused[119] was not taken up, it might well be argued that the return of space objects under the 1968 Agreement, which does not need to be 'prompt,' may be subject, especially between parties to the 1967 Space Treaty, to the launching authority fulfilling at the same time its obligation to pay compensation for damage caused by its spacecraft under Article VII of the Space Treaty.[120]

More difficult is the problem raised by Japan: is a contracting party obliged to return a military space object? After indicating his government's concern at the reports of the development by the Soviet government of a 'fractional orbital bombardment system' (FOBS, which at one time used the Pacific as a firing range), the Japanese delegate said: 'The present draft agreement or any future agreement on rescue and return could not place an obligation on a contracting party to recover and return a space object intended primarily for the development of a bombardment system to be placed into any kind of orbit,

---

[111] See text after n. 35 above; cf. Italy, regretting the absence of such a clause, A/AC.105/C.2/SR.87 (15.12.67), p. 7; A/AC.105/PV.52 (16.12.67), p. 42.

[112] A/AC.105/C.2/SR.86 (14.12.67), p. 14; in subsequent statements, only national legislation as such was metnioned, ibid./SR.89 (15.12.67), p. 6; A/AC.105/PV.52 (16.12.67), p. 32.

[113] A/AC.105/C.2/SR.87 (15.12.67), p. 10; A/AC.105/PV.52 (16.12.67), p. 59/60.

[114] See text to nn. 25 and 39 above.   [115] A/AC.105/PV.52 (16.12.67), p. 66.

[116] A/PV.1640 (Prov.) (19.12.67), p. 41.

[117] Cf. *sic* Canada, A/AC.105/PV.52 (16.12.67), p. 51.

[118] See text to n. 86 above. See also n. 100 above on the possibility of requiring payment of expenses in advance.

[119] A/AC.105/C.2/SR.86 (14.12.67), p. 14; see also Japan, ibid., p. 11, and Sweden, ibid., p. 20.

[120] See loc. cit. (1968) in n. 1 above, pp. 582 ff. [Ch. 9 above, s. V.F].

whether fractional or not fractional.'[121] Maybe the solution lies in not entering into any such agreement rather than in making such assumptions.

C. Comparison with the 1967 Space Treaty and Cosmographical Scope of the Agreement

Much emphasis has been laid on the cosmic scope of the Agreement,[122] in particular its Articles 1, 3, 4, and 5, and this is sometimes considered an advance on the 1967 Space Treaty and almost a justification for the Agreement. It is true that the Agreement has now made it impliedly more specific in that the assistance provision (Article 3) extends also to areas such as Antarctica, and in that the return provision (Article 4) extends also to astronauts rescued from Antarctica, outer space and celestial bodies. In addition a clause has been added on giving notice of landings of spacecraft (Article 5(1)). But otherwise, both *ratione loci* and *ratione materiae*, the 1968 Agreement has added virtually nothing which cannot be deduced from Articles VI and VII of the Space Treaty,[123] from the latter's Articles VI and VII on the international responsibility and liability of the launching authority,[124] and from international customary law.[125]

While it is true that Article 3 of the Agreement now extends the duty to provide assistance in search and rescue operations to celestial bodies, the position is already adequately covered by Article V(2) of the Space Treaty on mutual assistance between astronauts,[126] except that the Treaty limits the assistance to be given to 'astronauts of other States Parties' to the Treaty.

On the other hand, the 1968 Agreement, in not reproducing Article V(2) of the Treaty, represents a retrograde step, for by restricting the scope of Article 3 to astronauts who have 'alighted', it no longer makes provision for assistance being given by one spacecraft to another spacecraft in outer space.[127] Moreover, it may be said that Article V(2) of the Space Treaty will in the long run be more effective, inasmuch as it is doubtful whether, in the absence of a specific provision, a State undertaking a duty to give assistance is obliged to compel those of its nationals who are not its officials or agents to carry out this duty. Except under Article V(2) of the Treaty, parties to both the Treaty and the Agreement are required to carry out their obligations only through their official agencies. From this point of view, it appears a great pity that

---

[121] A/AC.105/C.2/SR.86 (14.12.67), p. 11; see also Canada, ibid., p. 16.

[122] Soviet Union, A/AC.105/C.2/SR.86 (14.12.67), p. 5; United States, ibid., p. 7; France, ibid., p. 11; A/AC.105/PV.52 (16.12.67), p. 32; A/PV.1640 (Prov.) (19.12.67), p. 36.

[123] See text to nn. 25 and 39 above.

[124] See loc. cit. (1968) in n. 1 above, pp. 582 ff. [Ch. 9 above, s. V.F].

[125] See text to n. 23 above on liability for damage, text before n. 97 (s. VII.B above, first paragraph above) with reference to Article 5(4), and nn. 100 and 101 above with reference to Article 5(5).

[126] See text after n. 39 above.   [127] See text to n. 77 above.

neither the Treaty nor the Agreement imposes a duty, through the contracting States, on the masters of ships and commanders of aircraft of their nationality, to render all assistance in case of need to astronauts in distress.[128]

IX. How Not to Make a Treaty

The 1968 Astronauts Agreement may be said to provide a classic object lesson in how not to make a treaty. First, the haste in which the final text was prepared and rushed through the United Nations resulted in a very poorly conceived and drafted instrument, achieving virtually nothing and yet creating at the same time a host of unresolved problems and difficulties. Secondly, in an agreement the effectiveness of which depends on its wide acceptance, the benefits are so one-sidedly in favour of the space powers[129] (be they major, near-, or co-operative) that it is difficult to see why the non-space powers, which at least for the present represent the majority of States, even though they may be perfectly willing, on humanitarian grounds, to discharge the duties laid down in the Agreement, should legally divest themselves of all discretion as to how they are to be performed. Finally, the major space powers, by pushing this Agreement through ahead of the liability agreement in which all States are interested, and the non-space powers in particular, have only succeeded in convincing the latter that the surest way of ensuring that there will be a liability agreement and that its terms will be satisfactory, is not to ratify or accede to the Astronauts Agreement.

Under the circumstances, there is much to be said for a consolidated agreement on both assistance and liability so that there is a chance to reconsider the terms of rescue and return of astronauts and spacecraft and to produce a regime that will, in its operation, be at once more effective and more equitable to all concerned.

[128] See text to n. 79 above.
[129] It will not escape notice that, although the Legal Sub-Committee had reached tentative agreement in 1964 on a draft article that would require the State announcing the launching of a space object, and knowing that the object might be of a hazardous or deleterious nature, so to notify the State in which the object had landed. The final Agreement omitted to include even such an innocuous provision as this (see nn. 29 and 102 above).

11

The 1972 Convention on International Liability for Damage Caused by Space Objects*

I. Introduction

It took the United Nations Committee on the Peaceful Uses of Outer Space nine years from 1962 to 1971 to produce an agreement on international liability for damage caused by the launching of objects into space. The text of the draft convention elaborated by its Legal Sub-Committee and transmitted by it to the General Assembly of the United Nations was in due course endorsed by the latter in its resolution 2777 (XXIV) on 29 November 1971,[1] and opened for signature at London, Moscow, and Washington on 29 March 1972. The Convention received its fifth ratification on 1 September 1972 and, in accordance with its Article XXIV (3), entered into force on the same date.[2] The Convention contains 28 articles. There is what may be called an Optional Clause in Article XIX, at least as interpreted in paragraph 3 of General Assembly resolution 2777 (XXVI).[3] Some States have acted upon this interpretation and made declarations accepting in advance the decision of the Claims Commission under the Convention as binding.

II. Some Instances of Damage Caused by Space Objects

The subject of liability for space vehicle accidents was formally brought before the Outer Space Committee Legal Sub-Committee by the United States in June 1962.[4] In order to underscore the point that the subject was not only important, but also pressing, the United States was able on 14 September 1962, at a meeting of the Outer Space Committee, through its delegate, to

---

* First published in Nandasiri Jasentuliyana and Roy S. K. Lee, 1 *Manual on Space Law* (1979), pp. 83–172, with additions from the writer's 'Liability for Spacecraft', 23 *CLP* (1970), pp. 216–39. Reproduced by kind permission of respectively Oceana Publications, Inc., and Sweet & Maxwell Ltd.

[1] The vote was 93 to 0 with 4 abstentions. See n. 375 below.
[2] Text of the Convention is reproduced as Appendix I.3 below. See s. V.A.2 below.
[3] See text to n. 371 below.   [4] See s. III.A below.

produce a piece of metal weighing some fourteen pounds on the table in front of him. He said:

I should like to give you tangible evidence of what the United States believes is the need for early consideration of the practical problems of space law. Very early on the morning of 5 September 1962 a metal object weighing approximately twenty pounds landed on a street in Manitowoc, Wisconsin . . .[5]

According to calculations and observations carried out at the Smithsonian Laboratory, it was more than probable that the object was part of Sputnik IV, launched by the Soviet Union in May 1960. A piece was there and then offered to the Soviet delegate who, fearing a Greek gift, declined.[6] After a second and more discreet approach to the Soviet Embassy in Washington, the Embassy accepted it on 5 January 1963.[7]

Fortunately, no damage was caused on this occasion. But, with the ever-increasing number of objects which are being launched into space and orbiting the earth, there can be little doubt regarding the importance and urgency of the problem. Indeed, the Japanese delegate to the Committee's Legal Sub-Committee said on 4 July 1969:

He would point out to all those who thought that damage caused by the launching of objects into outer space was still a matter for the future that, according to the Japanese Press, a Japanese cargo boat off the coast of Siberia had been damaged on 5 June 1969 by fragments from a device launched into outer space and that five sailors had been injured.[8]

One year later, the year before agreement was finally reached on the subject, the United States once more brought to the notice of the United Nations the fact that it had just been showered by a very large number of fragments, presumably from vehicles launched by the Soviet Union, which had come down to earth on 28 August 1970. One of these fragments, which landed in the middle western part of the United States was said to weigh more than 650 pounds.[9]

Danger of not merely a physical nature was demonstrated by the United States Apollo XIII mission. The spacecraft, which was to have made a landing on the moon, carried with it a graphite cask containing 8.6 pounds of plutonium intended for a nuclear generator on the moon. An explosion in the service module caused the lunar landing mission to be abandoned. When the spacecraft returned to earth, it brought the cask back with it. The cask has never been traced. NASA hopefully believes that it fell into the Pacific some 600 nautical miles from the point where the three astronauts splashed down

---

[5] A/AC.105/PV.15, p. 33.

[6] Ibid., pp. 33–4; see further 82 *Flight* (20.9.62), p. 503 (photograph); 'Sputnik in Committee', ibid. (4.10.62), p. 570.

[7] 'Returned to Sender', 83 *Flight* (17.1.63), p. 97.

[8] A/AC.105/C.2/SR.131, p. 6.   [9] A/AC.105/PV.91–7, p. 111 (PV.97).

on 17 April 1970, and even now lies safely buried in the depth of the ocean. The incident made the risk of nuclear damage caused by space activities to third parties on the surface of the earth abundantly clear.[10]

Eight years later, a much more serious and dramatic warning came when Cosmos 954, a Soviet nuclear-powered satellite, which had been launched on 18 September 1977, began to drop from its orbit on 6 January 1978, as a result of 'unexplained decompression'. Cosmos 954 finally re-entered the earth's atmosphere on 24 January where it broke up and was scattered over a sparsely populated area in the North West Territories of Canada. The satellite was believed to have been used for 'open surveillance', by keeping track of United States naval craft and submarines, and its reactor, which provided it with the necessary power to make such observations, was thought to have contained up to 100 pounds of uranium 235. The accident caused a major alarm that there could be widespread radioactive contamination over the area affected. Fortunately although pieces of debris were recovered, extensive search operations did not appear to have revealed any serious injury, damage, or hazard. But the consequences could have been far worse. The costs of the search operations and other losses amounted altogether to a little over $6 million (Can.), for which Canada made a claim against the Soviet Union on 23 January 1979.[11]

III. The Long Haul Towards an Agreement

A. The Initial Phase: The United States, Belgian and Hungarian Drafts

The subject of liability for damage caused by space objects has been before the Outer Space Committee Legal Sub-Committee for almost as long as the Sub-Committee has been in existence. The Sub-Committee met for the first time on 28 May 1962.[12] A United States proposal on the subject was submitted on 4 June 1962.[13] The Soviet Union has from the beginning been more interested

---

[10] See the writer's letter to the Editor of *The Times* (London, 7.5.70), p. 13.

[11] *The Times* (London, 14.2.78), p. 6; *Keesing's* (19.5.78), p. 28984; 18 *ILM* (1979), 899: claim based *inter alia* on the 1972 Convention. Subsequently C$3 million paid by the Soviet Union on 2 Apr. 1981 in full settlement of the claim, 20 *ILM* (1981), p. 689.

[12] On developments in the United Nations in the field of space law up to 1961, see the writer's 'The United Nations and Outer Space', 14 *CLP* (1961), p. 247 [Ch. 6 above]; 'The Extraterrestrial Application of International Law', 18 *CLP* (1965), p. 132 [Ch. 5 above]; 'United Nations Resolutions on Outer Space: "Instant" International Customary Law?', 5 *Indian JIL* (1965), p. 23 [Ch. 7 above]; 'Le Traité de 1967 sur l'espace/The 1967 Space Treaty', 95 *JDI* (1968), 532 [Ch. 9 above]; and 'The 1968 Astronauts Agreement', 23 *YBWA* (1969), p. 185 [Ch. 10 above]. See also id., 'The United Nations and the Development of International Law Relating to Outer Space', 16 *Thesaurus Acroasium* (1990), p. 49 [Ch. 8 above].

[13] A/AC.105/C.2/L.4; a draft convention was later submitted on 9 Mar. 1964, A/AC.105/C.2/L.8. After the signing of the 1967 Space Treaty, this was replaced by a new draft, A/AC.105/C.2/L.19 (21.6.67).

in securing an agreement on the rescue and return of astronauts.[14] Consequently, it opposed the proposal on the ground that a liability agreement was superfluous, inasmuch as 'compensation would undoubtedly be payable'.[15] On the basis of the *Trail Smelter Arbitration* (1938, 1941)[16] and the *Corfu Channel Case* (Merits) (1949),[17] the Soviet statement was doubtless correct. But insofar as non-space powers were concerned, it was not sufficient that an obligation existed to pay compensation. It was essential that effective procedures should be established to ensure that compensation, equitable in amount, would in fact be promptly paid.[18]

No agreement was reached in the Legal Sub-Committee to work on a liability treaty until 30 April 1963.[19] The day before, a Belgian draft was submitted.[20] Consistent with its initial attitude, the Soviet Union never submitted a draft of its own, but a Hungarian draft was put in on 16 March 1964,[21] which, if not a Soviet draft by proxy, may at least be regarded as representative of the views of the Soviet bloc. Thus the three main standpoints were duly presented through this troika of three separate drafts and their amendments, which remained the basic working documents of the Legal Sub-Committee in its work on liability. At a later stage, these were supplemented by drafts submitted by India and Italy.[22] Comparative tables of some of these drafts exist.[23]

B. *The 1963 Declaration of Legal Principles*

Meanwhile, the United Nations had adopted on 13 December 1963 its Declaration on Legal Principles Governing the Activities of States in the Exploration and Use of Outer Space.[24] This Declaration, although not legally binding, is nevertheless important, inasmuch as it incorporates an agreed

[14] See further B. Cheng, 'The 1968 Astronauts Agreement', 23 *YBWA* (1969), p. 185 [Ch. 10 above].

[15] A/AC.105/C.2/SR.14, p. 3.   [16] 3 *RIAA*, p. 1905, at pp. 1963 ff.

[17] *ICJ Rep. 1949*, p. 4, especially at p. 22 *et passim*.

[18] As the General Assembly in its resolution 2601 (XXIV) of 16 Dec. 1969 'emphasizes, . . . the convention is intended to establish international rules and procedures concerning liability for damage caused by the launching of objects into outer space and to ensure, in particular, the prompt and equitable compensation for damage.'

[19] A/AC.105/C.2/SR.25.   [20] A/AC.105/C.2/L.7.   [21] A/AC.105/C.2/L.10.

[22] At the seventh session of the Legal Sub-Committee (1968), respectively A/AC.105/C.2/L.32 and Add. 1, and A/AC.105/C.2/L.40 and Corr. 1 and 2. See further *Report of the Legal Sub-Committee on the Work of its Seventh Session* (4–28.6.68), A/AC.105/45, para. 6; *Report of the Legal Sub-Committee on the Work of its Eighth Session* (9.6–4.7.69), A/AC.105/58, para. 17.

[23] For example, a comparative table of provisions contained in the proposals submitted by Belgium (A/AC.105/C.2/L.7/Rev.3), the United States (A/AC.105/C.2/L.19), and Hungary A/AC.105/C.2/L.10/Rev.1 and A/AC.105/C.2/L.24) is found in A/AC.105/C.2/W.2/Rev.4, which is annexed to *Report of the Legal Sub-Committee on the Work of its Seventh Session* (4–28.6.68), A/AC.105/45. A/AC.105/C.2/W.2/Rev.5 is a comparative table which includes not only five drafts, but also the texts and principles on which agreement has been reached at the eighth session of the Legal Sub-Committee.

[24] Resolution 1962 (XVIII); for text see App. II.3 below. See further Cheng, 'United Nations Resolutions on Outer Space', loc. cit. in n. 12 above [Ch. 7 above].

modus vivendi between the two major space powers regarding their activities in outer space, which was itself made possible by the successful conclusion of the Moscow Test Ban Treaty earlier that year.

This Declaration contains two principles on the matter under discussion, principles 5 and 8:

5. States bear international responsibility for national activities in outer space, whether carried on by governmental agencies or by non-governmental entities, and for assuring that national activities are carried on in conformity with the principles set forth in the present Declaration. The activities of non-governmental entities in outer space shall require authorization and continuing supervision by the State concerned. When activities are carried on in outer space by an international organization, responsibility for compliance with the principles set forth in this Declaration shall be borne by the international organization and by the States participating in it.

    . . .

8. Each State which launches or procures the launching of an object into outer space, and each State from whose territory or facility an object is launched, is internationally liable for damage to a foreign or to its natural or juridical persons by such object or its component parts on the earth, in airspace, or in outer space.[25]

C. Marking Time

For the Soviet Union, which had always insisted that the basic principles governing activities in outer space should be the subject of a binding international treaty rather than a non-binding General Assembly resolution, the 1963 Declaration was merely a step towards that goal.[26] During the next two years, the Legal Sub-Committee was primarily engaged in a continual debate on priorities, whether it should work first on a general treaty on outer space, or the draft agreement on assistance to astronauts, or the draft agreement on liability. On matters of substance, the discussions were slowly grinding to a halt over three issues common to all three draft treaties which stood between the Eastern Socialist camp from the Western bloc:[27]

(i) *universal participation*, i.e, whether the treaties should be open only to States members of the 'United Nations family' (West), or all States without restriction, including, for instance, the German Democratic Republic (East);[28]

---

[25] See further s. III.D below.

[26] See Cheng, 'The 1967 Space Treaty' loc. cit. in n. 12 above, at pp. 540 ff. [Ch. 9 above, text to nn. 17 ff.].

[27] See further Cheng, 'The 1968 Astronauts Agreement', loc. cit. in n. 12 above, at pp. 190–1 [Ch. 10 above, s. III.B.—Phase II].

[28] See Cheng, 'The 1967 Space Treaty', loc. cit. in n. 12 above, pp. 554 and 556, nn. 77 and 82 [Ch. 9 above, text to nn. 77 and 82 in particular and thereabouts].

(ii) *settlement of disputes* relating to interpretation and application by the International Court of Justice (West), or by negotiations alone (East);

(iii) *status of international organizations* engaged in space activities, i.e., whether (West) or not (East) they could participate in these treaties either actively or passively.[29]

D. The 1967 Space Treaty

Following the success of the technique of soft-landing on the moon early in 1966 which paved the way to the historic manned landings in 1969, both the Soviet Union and the United States became anxious to have a binding agreement on the legal regime of outer space, the moon, and other celestial bodies. The result was the 1967 Space Treaty,[30] in which the Soviet view prevailed on all the three points mentioned above, though some concession was made by the Soviet Union on the question of international organizations.

On liability, the 1967 Space Treaty incorporated textually, with minor verbal adjustments, paragraphs 5 and 8 of the 1963 Declaration[31] as respectively its own Articles VI and VII. The result is that, as among the contracting States, liability for damage caused by objects launched into space is governed by those two provisions of the Treaty.

However, those two provisions, though a useful step forward, are not entirely satisfactory. The principle of international responsibility established in Article VI has the desirable effect not only of confirming each State's direct responsibility for space activities conducted by its own agencies and officials,[32] but also of rendering the contracting States directly responsible for 'national activities' in outer space carried on by non-governmental entities.[33] But, inasmuch as the meaning of the expression 'national activities' is far from clear, a State may be held responsible for activities over which it has no jurisdiction or control.[34]

As regards Article VII, liability under it is sometimes assumed to be absolute and not based on fault, but the article itself refrains from saying so. While this assumption corresponds with the position under customary international law in respect of damage caused by space objects to third parties on the surface of the earth and celestial bodies, and to their aircraft in flight, it is questionable whether it applies equally to collision between space objects either in airspace or in outer space. Doubt exists also whether this article covers objects which fail to reach outer space. Furthermore, under this article,

---

[29] See ibid., pp. 588–98 [Ch. 9 above, s. V.G.—International Organizations].

[30] Ibid. For text, see App. I.1 below.   [31] See s. III.B above.

[32] On imputability of acts of governmental agencies to the State under international law, see Cheng, *General Principles of Law*, pp. 180–207.

[33] Cf. ibid., pp. 208 ff. on the principle of individual responsibility under which States would normally be responsible only for their own acts.

[34] Cf. Ch. 24 below.

potentially four States may be liable for any damage caused. How this liability is shared or divided among these States both *inter se* and *vis-à-vis* third States is not specified. Finally, most important of all, the Treaty does not provide for any procedure to ensure the speedy recovery of any compensation due.[35]

E. The 1968 Astronauts Agreement

In approving on 16 December 1966 the draft Space Treaty, the General Assembly of the United Nations requested the Outer Space Committee to continue its work on both the liability agreement and the agreement on the rescue and return of astronauts.[36] A year later, on 3 November 1967, it asked the Committee to do so 'with a sense of urgency'.[37] Insofar as the astronauts agreement was concerned, this time the Committee responded with unwonted alacrity and, with much opposition,[38] completed the agreement in record time so that the General Assembly was able to approve it a month and a half later on 19 December 1967.[39] The General Assembly at the same time asked the Committee to finish its work on the liability agreement not later than the beginning of the twenty-third session of the Assembly in 1968. For most countries, the early conclusion of the liability convention would be the *quid pro quo* for their co-operation in the adoption of the Astronauts Agreement.

F. The Final Phase

1. *The Five New Delhi Points.* But another year went by. On 20 December 1968, the General Assembly noted the delay with regret and extended the time-limit to the twenty-fourth session of the Assembly in 1969.[40] Certain informal consultations took place among various delegations[41] in November-December 1968 in New York, and in March 1969 in New Delhi.[42] Attention was focused on five issues which became known as the 'New Delhi points',

---

[35] On Arts. VI and VII, and the problem of international organizations in the 1967 Space Treaty, see further Cheng, 'The 1967 Space Treaty', loc. cit. in n. 12 above, pp. 582 ff. [Ch. 9 above, ss. V.F: International responsibility, and V.G: International organizations].

[36] Resolution 2222 (XXI).   [37] Resolutioin 2260 (XXII).

[38] As the negotiations on the liability treaty dragged on, delegates in the Outer Space Committee became more and more outspoken. The Indian delegate said the Astronauts Agreement 'had been imposed by the space Powers', A/AC.105/C.2/SR.123, p. 16; referring to the pledge of the space powers that they would next turn their efforts to the liability agreement, the Belgian delegate spoke of the impression of small and medium-sized countries 'that they have been deceived', A/AC.105/PV.70–8, p. 24 (PV.70). See also Sweden A/AC.105/PV.85–90, p. 68 (PV.87); Iran, ibid., p. 130 (PV.89).

[39] See Cheng, 'The 1968 Astronauts Agreement', loc. cit. in n. 12 above [Ch. 10 above]. For text, see App. I.2 below.

[40] Resolutioin 2453B (XXIII).

[41] Belgium, Hungary, India, the USSR, and the USA; see A/AC.105/58, p. 1, n. 1.

[42] See Indian Government Press Release of 22 Mar. 1969.

viz., (i) international organizations, (ii) nuclear damage, (iii) applicable law, (iv) limitation of liability, and (v) compulsory third party arbitration.

At the eighth session of the Legal Sub-Committee in 1969, the Soviet Union having agreed to the possibility of including nuclear damage in the draft agreement,[43] the Sub-Committee centred its discussions on the remaining four issues. So did the Outer Space Committee.[44] No agreement was possible, except that all were agreed that the various outstanding issues should be resolved 'in one package'.[45] The General Assembly on 16 December 1969 adopted resolution 2601B (XXIV) in which it 'expresses its deep dissatisfaction' at the six-year delay, and extended the time-limit by yet another year. Meanwhile, man has made his first landing on the moon on 21 July 1969.

2. *The Twin Outstanding Issues.*   The Outer Space Committee met in January 1970 and decided to hold consultations and negotiations in April 1970 at Geneva with a view to arriving at an agreement as soon as possible. By then, it would appear that the main stumbling blocks had reduced themselves to two. As the Chairman of the Outer Space Committee, who convened the consultations and negotiations, said afterwards in his Résumé subsequently communicated to the Chairman of the Legal Sub-Committee: 'An intensive exchange of views took place on the twin outstanding issues, settlement of claims and applicable law.'[46] But, as he also said: 'No agreement on texts was reached.'[47]

The ninth session of the Legal Sub-Committee met at Geneva from 9 June to 3 July 1970, and was devoted entirely to drafting the liability convention. It began by meeting in plenary and in the Working Group of the whole, concurrently with informal consultations. After two weeks, it established a Drafting Group of eight to deal with provisions which had been approved in substance by either the Working Group or the Sub-Committee itself, and to consider the structure of the convention, its preamble and its final clauses. At the end of the session, the Drafting Group produced a preamble with thirteen articles which received the approval of the Working Group and the Sub-Committee itself, although, in the case of certain delegations, subject to conditions and reservations. With minor modifications, these eventually became the present preamble, Articles I to XI, XIII, and XXIII.

What remained missing, in comparison with the final Convention, were particularly the provisions on applicable law, settlement of disputes, international organizations and the final clauses. Insofar as the last two topics were

---

[43] See s. V.C.2 below.

[44] *Report of the Committee on the Peaceful Uses of Outer Space on the Work of its 12th Session*, A/7621, para. 9; and Addendum to the above, A/7621/Add. 1.

[45] A/7621/Add. 1, para. 8(g); on nuclear damage, see s. V.C.2 below.

[46] *Report of the Legal Sub-Committee on the Work of its Ninth Session* (8.6–3.7.70), A/AC.105/85, Annex I, p. 2; the Résumé was transmitted by letter dated 27 Apr. 1970 (A/AC.105/C.2/8).

[47] Ibid.

concerned, in view of the compromise already achieved in the 1968 Astronauts Agreement where the Soviet bloc made concessions on the issue of international organizations,[48] while the Western powers, following what they had already done in the 1967 Space Treaty, gave way on that of participation by all States,[49] it would appear that by the end of 1969 they were no longer insoluble problems.[50]

Furthermore, it would seem that the question whether or not to set a ceiling on liability under the convention was also dropped, if not definitively, at least in principle, not long afterwards,[51] leaving thus only the twin issues of applicable law and settlement of disputes.

3. *Fade-out of Reported Discussions.* However, the official records of the Outer Space Committee and of its Legal Sub-Committee do not disclose how and when agreement had been reached on some of these controversial issues. Indeed, by this time, it was becoming increasingly difficult, from the official records, to discover what was going on in the Committee and its Legal Sub-Committee. The reasons were threefold.

First, seemingly for reasons of economy, a deliberate attempt was made to remove some of the discussions from the Legal Sub-Committee, summary records of the proceedings of which were issued, to the Working Group of the whole or the Drafting Group, after this had been established, for neither of which summary records were issued.[52]

Secondly, the Outer Space Committee and its Legal Sub-Committee, as seen above, had been encouraging informal consultations and negotiations, for which again no summary records would be issued. The most one would get

---

[48] See further Cheng, 'The 1968 Astronauts Agreement', loc. cit. in n. 12 above, pp. 191 and 202 [Ch. 10 above, ss. III.B, item (iii): Status of international organizations, and VII.A: Definition of launching authority].

[49] See further Cheng, 'The 1967 Space Treaty', loc. cit. in n. 12 above, pp. 554 and 556, especially nn. 77 and 82; as regards the 1968 Astronauts Agreement, see 'The 1968 Astronauts Agreement', loc. cit. in n. 12 above, pp. 191 and 204 [Ch. 9 above, text to nn. 77 and 82 and thereabouts; as regards the Astronauts Agreement, see Ch. 10 above, ss. III.B., item (iii)—Status of international organizations, and VII.A.—Definition of launching authority].

[50] See review by Chairman of Outer Space Committee referred to in n. 158 below, and *Addendum to the Report of the Committee on the Peaceful Uses of Outer Space on the Work of its 12th Session*, A/7621/Add. 1.

[51] The Chairman of the Legal Sub-Committee, in presenting the draft liability convention to the Outer Space Committee, said on 1 Sept. 1971 that this had been agreed upon 'at an early stage of the negotiations', A/AC.105/PV.98–106, p. 16 (PV.98), but this could have happened only after 1969 when even on 5 Dec. it was reported as an outstanding question, A/AC.105/PV.70–8, p. 160 (PV.78). Previously on 3 Dec. 1969, the Italian representative was saying that he regretted that 'no agreement has yet been reached because of the fact that *one* delegation finds itself in difficulty on this point' (ibid., p. 127 (PV.76); italics added). On 3 Sept. 1970, the Canadian delegate to the Outer Space Committee was still commenting that the issue remained to be 'resolved definitely', A/AC.105/PV.85–90, p. 89 (PV.87).

[52] Cf. *Report of the Legal Sub-Committee on the Work of its Ninth Session* (8.6–3.7.70), A/AC.105/85, para. 6.

would be a résumé like the one issued by the Chairman of the Outer Space Committee in April 1970.[53]

Thirdly, while it is far from unusual in international conferences for the most crucial negotiations to be conducted not only outside official meetings, but also in secret caucuses among delegations that consider themselves as 'the only ones that really matter', the major space powers, in negotiations on space treaties in the United Nations, have from the very beginning carried this practice almost to the point of contempt for the other members.[54] The drafting history of the liability convention, from this point of view, is no exception. Thus although the ninth session of the Legal Sub-Committee began on 8 June 1970, and was to have given priority to discussing the 'twin outstanding issues', as the Brazilian representative, who was also the Rapporteur of the Legal Sub-Committee, justifiably complained on 26 June, 'with three out of the four weeks of the session gone, the summary records contained no mention of those two cardinal questions to which it had been agreed to give priority.' He appealed 'to the members of the Sub-Committee to stop evading the discussions in plenary of the two important problems that it had been requested to solve'.[55] His complaint and appeal were promptly endorsed by the Chairman who said, that, despite 'repeated appeals by the chair at the beginning of each of the Sub-Committee's plenary meetings, no delegation had unfortunately seen fit in the course of those three weeks to ask to speak on those two essential questions'.[56]

4. *Retrogression and Deadlock.*　The truth was that, as it was later revealed, not only had the ninth session of the Legal Sub-Committee made no progress on the twin outstanding issues since the informal negotiations in April,[57] but fresh difficulties appeared also to have arisen with regard to those on which agreement was thought to have been reached.[58] Thus, on the question of international organizations, the Bulgarian delegation, for instance, introduced, on 12 June 1970,[59] a working paper[60] which, as the United Kingdom delegate immediately pointed out,[61] differed, on a material point, from the tentative agreement that had previously been reached in the Sub-Committee and which had been outlined in detail by the Chairman on 5 December 1969.[62] By deleting the requirement that all claims against an international organization must in the first place be presented to the organization, the Bulgarian delegation

---

[53] See n. 46 above.

[54] See further 'The 1968 Astronauts Agreement', loc. cit. in n. 12 above, pp. 193–7 [Ch. 10 above, s. IV: The Critical Phase of Negotiations: A Common Pattern Followed].

[55] A/AC.105/C.2/SR.132–51, p. 47 (SR.146).

[56] Ibid. The Brazilian delegation evidently felt sufficiently strongly about the issue to raise it again in the Outer Space Committee, A/AC.105/PV.85–90, pp. 119–20 (PV.89).

[57] Cf. Austria, A/AC.105/C.2/SR.132–51, p. 73 (SR.148).

[58] Cf. Belgium, ibid., p. 54 (SR.147).　　　　　　[59] Ibid., p. 15 (SR.136).

[60] PUOS/C.2/70/WG.1/CRP.2 and Corr. 1 (reproduced A/AC.105/85, Annex I, p. 9).

[61] A/AC.105/C.2/SR.132–51, p. 16 (SR.136).　　　　　　[62] See n. 50 above, and n. 158 below.

frankly admitted that this proposal was designed for the benefit of States which might 'not recognize the international intergovernmental organization responsible.'[63]

The deadlock which had evidently been reached was not broken at the thirteenth session of the Outer Space Committee which met in September 1970, notwithstanding exhortations to produce the liability convention in time for the General Assembly celebration of the twenty-fifth anniversary of the United Nations. The points at issue by this time had, however, become very clear. The majority of members insisted that, unless the twin issues were resolved, there would be no point in having a liability convention. They were prepared to give in on questions of form, but not on those of substance.

For them, the crux of the matter was that the convention must provide for full restoration of the victim to the position in which he would in all probability have been, had the accident not occurred, and that there should be, in the event of an accident, some effective procedure to establish the obligation of the launching State, including the precise amount of the compensation due, if any. The position of the Soviet Union,[64] supported by Bulgaria,[65] was that, if so, no agreement would be possible, and that one should simply sign a convention along the lines of those articles on which agreement had already been reached.

The delegates to the September 1970 session of the Outer Space Committee recognized that the Committee had arrived at an impasse. In evident exasperation, the French delegate suggested that perhaps it might be preferable for the Legal Sub-Committee to turn its attention to some other item on its agenda, such as the exploration and utilization of outer space,[66] which, it might perhaps be pointed out, was not one of the Soviet Union's favourite subjects.

5. *The Political Factor.* Some delegates expressed the view that what was lacking was the necessary 'political will',[67] and that what was needed was some 'political initiative'.[68] Although an Australian proposal to this effect[69] failed to be adopted in the Report of the Outer Space Committee for its Thirteenth Session,[70] a number of delegations clearly indicated that what ought to be done now was to appeal to the other four-fifths of the members of the United Nations in the General Assembly, who were not members of the Outer Space Committee, and ask the Assembly to issue some form of politi-

---

[63] A/AC.105/C.2/SR.132–51, p. 15 (SR.136); see also n. 357 below and text thereto on the joint Bulgaria, Hungary, USSR proposal on settlement of disputes, A/AC.105/C.2/L.76. The backsliding was by no means one-sided. See thus the Mexican proposal and the five-Western power proposal on international organizations, text to nn. 164 ff. below.

[64] Cf. A/AC.105/PV.85–90, pp. 79–85, especially p. 85 (PV.87).

[65] Cf. ibd., pp. 133–7 (PV.89). 　　　　　　[66] Ibid., p. 31 (PV.86).

[67] Brazil, ibid., p. 121 (PV.89). 　　　　　[68] Sweden, ibid., p. 69 (PV.87).

[69] A/AC.105/L.56/Add.2. 　　　　　　　　[70] Cf. A/AC.105/PV.91–7, pp. 23, 40 (PV.84).

cal guidance to the Outer Space Committee.[71] If the Czechoslovak[72] and Soviet delegates who spoke against the idea did not exactly scoff at it, the latter did point out that the majority could do what they liked, but, if pushed, the Soviet Union would simply 'not participate in such a convention', and 'such a convention would lose its point'.[73] What the Soviet delegate said was, of course, absolutely true of the real world outside the conference room, and Soviet delegates to the Outer Space Committee have from the outset never allowed those inside it to forget this elementary political truth for a single moment.

On 16 December 1970, the General Assembly, on the recommendation of its First Committee[74] and with eight members of the Soviet bloc voting against,[75] adopted by an overwhelming majority[76] resolution 2733B endorsing the view of the majority of the Outer Space Committee. Apart from urging the Committee to intensify its efforts to reach an agreement, resolution 2733B expressed the view that a condition of a satisfactory liability convention would be the inclusion of provisions ensuring the payment of a full measure of compensation to victims and effective procedures leading to the prompt and equitable settlement of claims.

But it would hardly be realistic to think that the guidance provided by the General Assembly in resolution 2733B, the strictures of the non-aligned countries on the delay in concluding the liability agreement contained in their Lusaka Declaration on Peace, Independence, Development, Co-operation and Democratization of International Relations (1970),[77] or the threat of some of the delegations at the tenth session of the Legal Sub-Committee in 1971 that, in the absence of a satisfactory liability convention, they would either not sign[78] or, if already a party, would reconsider their participation in the 1968 Astronauts Agreement,[79] would have in themselves either singly or put together been sufficient to bring about agreement on the liability convention at that session of the Legal Sub-Committee in the summer of 1971.

The crucial factor, as recognized by both the United States[80] and the Soviet Union[81] delegates at the very beginning of that session, was that favourable political conditions had since the last Assembly emerged, particularly

---

[71] See ibid., pp. 40 (Italy, 41 (Brazil), 43 (US), 48 (UK) (PV.94).

[72] Ibid., p. 45 (PV.94).　　　　　[73] Ibid., p. 47 (PV.94).

[74] In the First Committee, Czechoslovakia, Hungary and the USSR had submitted an amendment to the draft resolution, but the First Committee decided by 35 votes in favour to 23 against, with 37 abstentions, not to vote on the proposed amendment before proceeding to vote on the draft resolution.

[75] Bulgaria, Byelorussian SSR, Czechoslovakia, Hungary, Mongolia, Poland, Ukrainian SSR, USSR.

[76] The vote was 108 in favour, 8 against and 2 abstentions.

[77] Referred to by the Indian delegate, A/AC.105/C.2/SR.152–69, p. 22 (SR.154).

[78] E.g., France, ibid., p. 24 (SR.154). Cf. earlier statements to same effect, e.g., Belgium, A/AC.105/C.2/SR.132–51, p. 56 (SR.147); India, ibid., p. 77 (SR.149).

[79] E.g., Mexico, A/AC.105/C.2/SR.152–69, p. 82 (SR.162).

[80] Ibid., p. 9 (SR.152).　　　　　[81] Ibid., p. 22 (SR.154).

regarding co-operation in space matters between the two space powers. More specifically, as the United States delegate pointed out, on 'January 21, 1971, following intensive discussions, a delegation of the United States National Aeronautics and Space Administration and a Soviet delegation had initialled a document providing, *inter alia*, for the development of compatible space rendezvous and docking techniques, the exchange of lunar soil sample', etc.[82] The question of compatible space rendezvous and docking techniques was of special importance to the Soviet Union in the light of the launching of respectively 19 and 23 April 1971 of Salyut I and Soyuz 10 which successfully tested new docking equipment. This experiment, which some said put the USSR two years ahead of the United States on the road to manned space laboratories, coincided with the meeting of the twenty-fourth Soviet Communist Party Congress, where there was a call for 'piloted orbital stations', which were to be the Soviet answer to the United States man on the moon challenge.

But as Apollo 13 the previous year had shown, accidents can occur, and, while the benefits would obviously be mutual, the Soviet Union was evidently anxious to be able to call on the Americans for help in case one of its manned space stations were to develop a fault. Any such assistance would be very difficult, unless the docking mechanisms were compatible. Hence the significance of the NASA-Soviet Academy Agreement and the willingness to be co-operative.

On an even broader note, Mr Brezhnev's address to the twenty-fourth Soviet Communist Party Congress, not only mentioned co-operation with the United States in outer space, but also seemingly presaged the beginning of a period of East-West *détente*. Indeed, on the same day that Mr Brezhnev delivered his speech, the Soviet chief delegate to the 25-nation United Nations disarmament talks in Geneva unexpectedly adopted a hitherto rejected Western position on the outlawing of bacteriological weapons.

It was in this atmosphere that the tenth session of the Legal Sub-Committee met at Geneva on 7 June 1971. Although for two weeks the discussions in plenary were rather desultory, much like those of previous sessions, it was clear that something was in the air. Finally, at the beginning of the third week, a joint Belgium, Brazil, and Hungary proposal[83] was presented which, it immediately became clear, was based on some earlier package arrangement between the two major space powers.[84] The Canadian delegate, while congratulating the two major space powers on having achieved 'a meeting of minds' between them, was not exactly alone, although perhaps a little more outspoken than

---

[82] USA, A/AC.105/C.2/SR.152–69, p. 9 (SR.152). For text of agreement which, according to a NASA announcement of 31 Mar. 1971, had been confirmed by an exchange of letters between the Acting Administrator of NASA and the President of the Academy of Sciences of the USSR, see 10 *ILM* (1971), p. 617.

[83] A/AC.105/C.2/L.79, introduced on 22 June 1971 at the 162nd meeting of the Legal Sub-Committee, A/AC.105/C.2/SR.152–69, pp. 71 ff. (SR.162).

[84] Cf. Australia, ibid., p. 114 (SR.166).

the others, in saying that what might be good for the major space powers might not necessarily be in the interests of the others.[85] However, if a comparison is made with the drafting histories of the two previous United Nations treaties on space, it was quite remarkable that on this occasion the two major space powers actually allowed the joint draft based on their own package to be debated, added to, and amended—something quite unprecedented. By the standard of past practice, the Legal Sub-Committee this time also enjoyed an unwonted amount of time to finalize the convention.

6. *The Parturition.* In fact, however, it was given only a little over a week, in which time the Legal Sub-Committee performed the almost impossible by not only producing the final text of the draft convention, but also, in the process, improving the joint draft in various ways. Thus it succeeded actually in strengthening, albeit ever so slightly, the most fought over rule on the measure of compensation by a minor amendment[86] in the fourth paragraph of the preamble, the text of which had already been agreed upon previously. It managed to tighten up considerably the time-scale of the dispute settlement procedure in the joint draft, in the first place, by eliminating the intermediate Inquiry Commission stage which the joint proposal provided for between the diplomatic negotiations phase and the Claims Commission phase,[87] and secondly by introducing what is now paragraph 3 of Article XIX, which requires the Claims Commission to give its decision or award normally within a year. *Mirabile dictu*, the Legal Sub-Committee even contrived to reinforce, although only in a minimal fashion, the effect of the 'recommendatory award' by first adding that it shall be considered by the parties in good faith (Article XIX(2)),[88] and secondly requiring a copy of the decision or award to be delivered not only to each of the parties to the dispute, but also to the Secretary-General of the United Nations (Article XIX(4)).[89] These may all seem relatively trivial points, but at one time insistence on any of them might well have wrecked the convention.

Finally, at the eleventh hour, provisions were added allowing claims to be presented through the Secretary-General of the United Nations (Article IX *in fine*),[90] permitting expenses of the Claims Commission to be apportioned other than equally between the parties (Article XX *in fine*),[91] concerning assistance to States suffering large-scale damage (Article XXI),[92] and providing for

---

[85] Ibid., pp. 88 and 91 (SR.163). Canada eventually abstained in the vote on General Assembly resolution 2777 (XXVI): see n. 376 below.

[86] PUOS/C/2/WG(X)/L.2/Rev.1 (reproduced A/AC.105/94, p. 18). See n. 300 below.

[87] See n. 360 below.   [88] See n. 361 below.   [89] See n. 362 below.

[90] On 28 June 1971, by the Drafting Group, subject to the approval of the Working Group, upon a proposal of the United Arab Republic: see A/AC.105/94, p. 5. See also n. 327 below.

[91] See n. 363 below.

[92] On 29 June 1971. See A/AC.105/C.2/SR.152–69, p. 111 (SR.166).

possible review or revision of the convention after a number of years (Article XXVI).[93]

Having been hammered out by the Working Group on 28 June 1971, the final draft was considered by the Drafting Group on the same date. The following morning, it went back to the Working Group for approval, before it was formally adopted by the Legal Sub-Committee the same afternoon. From there, the draft convention moved to the Outer Space Committee, the First Committee of the General Assembly and the Assembly itself, which on 29 November 1971 in resolution 2777 (XXVI) requested the depositary governments to open it for signature.[94] From conception to actual coming into force, the Liability Convention took just a little over ten years (1962–72).

IV. Some Drafting Points

From the standpoint of legislative procedure or technique, it is interesting to observe that the Liability Convention is the first in the Outer Space Committee to have received scrutiny from both a Working Group of the whole and a Drafting Group. Neither the 1967 Space Treaty nor the 1968 Astronauts Agreement was allowed such luxuries.[95] Consequently, by comparison, the Liability Convention is a much better drafted document. However, attention needs to be drawn to certain dubious innovations in treaty drafting in which it has engaged.

The Drafting Group at the ninth session of the Legal Sub-Committee in 1970 adopted the following three principles in its work:

[93] Upon a joint proposal from Argentina, Austria, Brazil and Mexico of 18 June 1971, PUOS/C.2/DG(X)/WP.1 (reproduced A/AC.105/94, p. 29), together with an amendment suggested by India on 24 June 1971, PUOS/C.2/WG(X)L.2/Rev.1 (reproduced A/AC.105/94, p. 19): accepted into the Working Group draft of 28 June 1971, PUOS/C.2/WG(X)/2 (reproduced A/AC.105/94, pp. 21 ff.).

Art. XXVI provides:

Ten years after the entry into force of this Convention, the question of the review of this Convention shall be included in the provisional agenda of the United Nations General Assembly in order to consider, in the light of past application of the Convention, whether it requires revision. However, at any time after the Convention has been in force for five years, and at the request of one third of the States Parties to the Convention, and with the concurrence of the majority of the States Parties, a conference of the States Parties shall be convened to review this Convention.

The actual amendment procedure is found in Article XXV which is worded as follows:

Any State Party to this Convention may propose amendments to this Convention. Amendments shall enter into force for each State Party to the Convention accepting the amendments upon their acceptance by a majority of the States Parties too the Convention and thereafter for each remaining State Party on the date of acceptance by it.

[94] See n. 1 above.

[95] See Cheng, 'The 1967 Space Treaty', loc. cit. in n. 12 above, at pp. 544–58 [Ch. 9, above, s. III.—The Negotiations; id., 'The 1968 Astronauts Agreement', loc. cit. in n. 12 above, at pp. 188–99 [Ch. 10 above, ss. III–VI].

(a) in view of the fact that the term 'State' used in the draft Convention necessarily means a State Party to the Convention, it would be sufficient to use the term 'State' in substitution for the terms 'State Party to the Convention' and 'Contracting Party';

(b) whenever a term used in the draft Convention is identical with that in the Outer Space Treaty, the latter should be followed in all languages;

(c) throughout the draft Convention the term 'State presenting a claim' should be used in substitution for the terms 'claimant State', 'claimant' or 'presenting State', and the term 'launching State' in substitution for the term 'respondent' or 'respondent State'.[96]

Principle (b) is obviously sensible, and, had it been consistently followed, would have overridden Principle (a). In so far as Principle (c) is concerned, the tenth session of the Legal Sub-Committee reversed the first part of the principle and reverted to the expression 'the claimant State'. Whilst this does not seem to give rise to any difficulty, the same cannot be said of 'the State presenting a claim', if this expression is used instead throughout the Convention. Take, for instance, the case of an international organization which has suffered damage caused by a space object. If this organization has made a declaration in accordance with Article XXII(1), then it is, at least arguably, under the same Article, 'deemed' to be a 'claimant State' in the present terminology of the Convention. Consequently, under Article XIII of the Convention, which stipulates that compensation shall normally be paid 'in the currency of the claimant State',[97] the organization in question will be entitled to receive the compensation in so-to-speak 'its own currency' which, in such a case, again arguably, might be said to be the currency in which its budgets and finances are calculated. But had one said in Article XIII 'the currency of the State presenting the claim', as it had at one time been suggested[98] then the organization concerned which, under Article XXII(4) of the Convention can have its claim presented only by a member of the organization which is a party to the Convention, would only be entitled to receive the compensation in the currency of the State presenting the claim, unless the State which is presenting its claim on its behalf asks the compensation to be paid in the currency of the State from which compensation is due, as is permitted by Article XIII. Admittedly, the present wording of the Convention does not exclude entirely the same construction. It is arguable that, when an international organization has its claims presented through a contracting State, as is required under Article XXII(4), the expression 'the claimant State' in Article XIII, because of the rather ambiguous language of Article XXII(4), in fact refers not to the organization, but to the State which is presenting the claim on its behalf. It is

---

[96] *Report of the Legal Sub-Committee on the Work of its Ninth Session* (8.6–3.7.70), A/AC.105/85, p. 6 (para. 25).

[97] See s. VIII.C below.

[98] *Sic* in text approved by the ninth session of the Legal Sub-Committee A/AC.105/85, p. 9.

submitted, however, that such a construction would not be compatible with Article XXII(1) which unambiguously includes XIII among the provisions of the Convention applicable to international organizations, and which, therefore, has the effect of assimilating a claimant organization to a claimant State under Article XIII.

However, it is the first principle adopted by the Drafting Group that is the most questionable, inasmuch as it was explicitly based on a patently unsound premise, namely, that 'the term "State" used in the draft Convention necessarily means a State Party to the Convention', which was presumably an erroneous deduction from the principle *Pacta tertiis nec prosunt nec nocent*. In this respect, the Liability Convention represents the opposite to the 1929 Warsaw Convention on International Carriage by Air. The latter, which is a treaty subject to ratification, goes to the other extreme and, in its final clauses, calls signatory States High Contracting Parties, even before the signatory States have ratified the convention, with the result that in the English case *Philippson* v. *Imperial Airways, Ltd.*[99], Lords Atkin and Wright held that the term High Contracting Parties must be given the same meaning even in the substantive provisions of the convention. The *Philippson Case* caused so much concern that, when the Warsaw Convention was amended at The Hague in 1955, a new Article 40A was introduced in order to counteract it. But Article 40A was itself so badly drafted that the whole episode turns out to be a comedy of errors.[100]

Unfortunately, the draftsmen of the Liability Convention treated their very questionable assumption as axiomatic and did not, therefore, make them explicit; for if they had said in the Convention expressly that all references to States were to contracting States unless otherwise specified, then there would be no problem at all. In the absence of any such definition, the Convention must be interpreted as it stands.

In looking at the Convention, one finds that the Drafting Group failed to adhere to its own principle in the very introductory phrase of the Preamble; for the Convention begins with these words: 'The States Parties to this Convention . . .'[101] Furthermore, in Articles XXII, XXV, XXVI, and XXVII, the Convention is clearly not following the principle of the Drafting Group and resorts quite happily and without any seeming tautology to the expression 'States Parties to the Convention', whenever the occasion requires. Principle (a) of the Drafting Group cannot, therefore, be said to have been embraced by the Convention and to form one of its inarticulate drafting premises for the purpose of interpreting the Convention.

---

[99] [1939] A.C. 332.

[100] See further B. Cheng, 'High Contracting Parties in Air Law: *Philippson* v. *Imperial Airwyas, Ltd.* Revisited', *JBL* (1959), p. 30.

[101] Cf. text approved by the ninth session of the Legal Sub-Committee, as drafted by the Drafting Group, A/AC.105/85, p. 6.

Article XXIV(1) of the Convention, moreover, visibly demonstrates that the assumption on which Principle (a) of the Drafting Group was based must be false; for it says: 'This Convention shall be open to all States for signature. Any State which does not sign this Convention . .'. In this instance, the assumption obviously cannot be correct when it says that 'the term "State" used in the draft Convention necessarily means a State Party to the Convention'; for the 'States' in Article XXIV(1), not having signed the Convention, cannot possibly be 'States Parties to the Convention'.

From this point of view, Article XXI, which was introduced into the Convention at the eleventh hour and fifty-ninth minute,[102] is most interesting. The article provides that, if a space object causes a major disaster, 'the States Parties, and in particular the launching States, shall' consider rendering assistance 'to the State which has suffered the damage', upon its request. It goes on to say that 'the rights or duties of the States Parties under the Convention' are not affected. By its explicit references successively to 'the States Parties', 'the State' and then once more 'the States Parties', Article XXI makes a clear distinction between the two different expressions. Although, on account of the *Pacta tertiis* principle, the rights and obligations under Article XXI belong exclusively to 'States Parties', the benefit of the provision (i.e., being considered for assistance) inures to any 'State' victim of a major disaster caused by space objects, whether or not a party to the Liability Convention.[103]

What one finds in the Liability Convention is thus as follows. In the introductory phrase to its Preamble and in its Articles XXI, XXII, XXIV–XXVII, the Convention, like any normal treaty, designates a contracting party to the Convention as either a 'State Party' or a 'State Party to this (the) Convention', and uses the term 'State' by itself when the State is clearly not a party, as under Article XXIV, or can be either a contracting party or a non-contracting party as under Article XXI.

However, elsewhere in the Convention, the expressions 'States Parties', 'States Parties to the Convention', 'contracting Parties', or 'contracting States' are studiously avoided, and the terms 'States', 'claimant States', 'launching States' are used freely without either any general or any individual qualification that the States concerned need be parties to the Convention.

The question is, in the light of those provisions previously mentioned, how are these unqualified terms to be interpreted. The inevitable answer is that there will be uncertainty and confusion. For instance, under Article IX,[104] where a claimant State has no diplomatic relations with a launching State, it

---

[102] See text to n. 92 above, and s. IX below.

[103] Insofar as the *travaux préparatoires* are concerned, although the Moroccan delegate, whose delegation later put forward the proposal PUOS/C.2/WG(X)/L.4/Rev.1 (reproduced A/AC.105/94, p. 19) which subsequently became Article XXI, had initially spoken of the desirability of 'assistance between States parties', A/AC.105/C.2/SR.152–69, p. 57 (SR.160), neither the Moroccan proposal nor the final text says that the victim State has to be a contracting party.

[104] See s. X.B below.

may present a claim against the latter through 'another State'. The *Pacta ter-tiis* principle may ensure that the right to present a claim is conferred, and the obligation to receive it is imposed, only on parties to the Convention, but the drafting idiosyncrasy of the Liability Convention leaves it clearly uncertain whether the third State has also to be a party to the Convention.[105]

There is a much wider and more important problem which applies to all what may be called the normative or substantive, as opposed to the procedural or adjectival, provisions of the Convention, such as arguably paragraph 4 of the Preamble, Articles I–VII, XII, and XXI, to mention only the most obvious ones. It is quite conceivable that a non-party to the Convention, while, on account of the *Pacta tertiis* principle, it may not be able to rely upon these provisions as international treaty law *inter partes*, might put up a fairly plausible case that the contracting parties, having formulated these provisions in an absolute rather than contractual manner by reference to relations only among contracting parties, in fact treat them as statements of general international law, applicable even in the absence of a treaty. In other words, it might be argued that, in regard to these provisions, what the contracting States have in their mind is not only an *opinio obligationis conventionalis*, but also an *opinio juris generalis* or *consuetudinis*.[106]

Such a non-party might even draw a comparison with Article VII of the 1967 Space Treaty and point out that, under the Space Treaty, the international liability for damage caused by space objects laid down in the Treaty is expressly stated to be that of one State Party to the Treaty towards another State Party to the Treaty. By deleting this qualification, it can be plausibly argued, parties to the Liability Convention intend to state principles of general international law, especially in the light of the Drafting Group's Principle (b). Consequently, even though a non-party may not rely on the Convention as such, it may nevertheless invoke those normative provisions of the Convention which are worded in general terms as a matter of general international law. They represent 'instant' customary international law.[107]

Whatever may be the answer to such an argument, one may well ask what was the real reason which made the draftsmen of the Liability Convention reject the precedent set by the 1967 Space Treaty, which uses the term 'States

---

[105] In view of the fade-out of reported discussions mentioned under s. III.F.3 above, the records of the Legal Sub-Committee provides no clue to resolve this uncertainty. In favour of the interpretation that there is no such requirement, cf. Article XXII(4) which provides that the State by which the claim of an international organization is presented has to be 'a State party to this Convention'. For text of Article XXII(4), see text between nn. 166 and 167 below.

[106] Current literature on international law mostly fails to distinguish between different kinds of *opinio juris* on the importance of which see further 'United Nations Resolutions on Outer Space', loc. cit. in n. 12 above [Ch. 7 above, especially s. IX: 'Instant' Customary Law; see also the writer's 'Custom: The Future of General State Practice in a Divided World', in R. St. J. Macdonald and D. M. Johnston (eds.), *The Structure and Process of International Law* (1983), 513– 54, especially s. V: The Nature of Customary International Law. *Nota* Ch. 8, n. 71].

[107] Ibid.

Parties to the Convention', or that the 1966 Astronauts Agreement, which speaks of 'Contracting Parties'. Indeed, what caused them to forsake the legal experiences of centuries or one might even say millennia? Brevity could hardly have been the reason. To eliminate a few words merely for the sake of brevity at the cost of endless uncertainty and confusion would indeed be foolish.

As such folly is unthinkable of the very experienced delegates who have fashioned, in very difficult circumstances, an otherwise quite remarkable instrument, the real reason must be sought elsewhere. One suspects that it was probably related to the controversy that was going on in the Legal Sub-Committee on the place of international organizations in the Liability Convention. One can well imagine States, especially the space powers, being anxious that as many parties as possible, including international organizations, took part in the rescue and return of astronauts and space objects. None, therefore, objected to the use of the fairly neutral expression 'Contracting Party' in the 1968 Astronauts Agreement where international organizations were accorded greater recognition than in the 1967 Space Treaty.[108] But when it came to the Liability Convention, some States probably began to have second thoughts and refused to allow international organizations being even 'deemed', either directly or by inference, to be 'Contracting Parties' and still less 'States Parties to this Convention'.[109]

Whatever may have been the operative reason, this drafting innovation in the Liability Convention is one which other diplomatic conferences would do well to eschew.

V. Scope of the Liability Convention

A. Personal Scope

1. *Ecumenical Application?*   It has already been seen that, because of a drafting idiosyncrasy in the Liability Convention, a case can be made out that the normative or substantive provisions of the Convention which are formulated in general terms and not expressly stated to be applicable only as among contracting parties, are intended as statements of general international law of universal application, independently of the treaty.[110] Anyone who wishes to pursue this argument might even see support for it in paragraph 4 of the Preamble of the Convention and in the fact that the 1963 Declaration of Legal Principles from which the Liability Convention is in spirit derived[111] was addressed to all States, without there being required any treaty relationship.

---

[108] This is not to say that international organizations have been accorded the status of contracting parties in the Astronauts Agreement, regarding which see 'The 1968 Astronauts Agreements', loc. cit. in n. 12 above, at p. 204 [Ch. 10 above, s. VIII.A: The Personal and Temporal Scope of the Agreement].

[109] See further text to n. 170 below.   [110] See s. IV above.   [111] See s. III.B above.

Although the Convention must lie in the bed which its draftsmen have made for it, whether this argument represents the true intention of the authors of the Convention is more than doubtful.

Moreover, while some of the normative provisions of the Convention may in fact not be too different from rules of general or customary international law,[112] it will probably be difficult for a non-party to argue that even provisions of a procedural character such as those relating to the presentation of claims and the Claims Commission[113] have also acquired the character of general international law. However, notwithstanding the novel drafting technique of the Liability Convention, the *Pacta tertiis* principle will still prevent the invoking by, or application to, a non-party of a provision of the Convention, unless it can be proved to be expressive of a rule of general international law.

2. *Participation by 'all States'.*   Although the matter was initially not without controversy,[114] the Liability Convention, following the precedent set by the 1967 Space Treaty and the 1968 Astronauts Agreement, is open for signature or accession by 'all States' (Article XXIV(1)). Furthermore, as is also the case with the other two agreements,[115] by having three Depositary Governments (Article XXIV(2)), the Convention is in practice open to any State or government that is recognized by at least one of the three Depositary States, the United Kingdom, the United States, and the USSR. In strict law, however, the position should perhaps be otherwise. While all three treaties impose no restriction on where they may be signed, by the use of the conjunctive 'and' instead of the disjunctive 'or' when referring to the three Depositary Governments, they appear to require that instruments of ratification and accession are deposited with all three Depositary Governments. Such an interpretation runs counter to the original intention of securing the widest possible degree of participation[116] and the wording of Article XXIV itself.

3. *Relaxation of the Rule on Nationality of Claims.*   Under general international law, a State may present claims against another in respect of damage suffered by itself or its nationals, but not damage suffered by nationals of another State or by stateless persons.[117] This rule has been considerably relaxed under Article VIII of the Liability Convention which provides:

1.   A State which suffers damage, or whose natural or juridical persons[118] suffer damage, may present to a launching State a claim for compensation for such damage.

---

[112] Cf., e.g., text to nn. 15–17 above.   [113] See ss. X, and XI below.

[114] See text to nn. 28 and 49 above.

[115] 1967 Space Treaty, Art. XIV(2); 1968 Astronauts Agreement, Art. 7(2).

[116] See text to n. 28 above.

[117] See G. Schwarzenberger, 1 *International Law* (1957), pp. 590 ff.

[118] Although this paragraph is not altogether clear on the subject, it would appear from paragraphs 2 and 3 that by a State's 'natural or juridical persons', the Convention means natural or juridical persons possessing the nationality of the State in question. If so, it would not include officials of a State who do not have its nationality. See text to n. 174 below, regarding the protection of such officials.

2. If the State of nationality has not presented a claim, another State may, in respect of damage sustained in its territory by any natural or juridical person, present a claim to a launching State.
3. If neither the State of nationality nor the State in whose territory the damage was sustained has presented a claim or notified its intention of presenting a claim, another State may, in respect of damage sustained by its permanent residents, present a claim to a launching State.

As befits a victim-oriented convention, victims of damage caused by space objects have thus the possibility of recovering compensation through three separate channels, their national State, the State where the damage occurred or the State of which they are permanent residents. This means that a stateless victim, for instance, would be able to have his claim presented through either the territorial State or the State of which he is a permanent resident.

Article VIII appears to establish a hierarchy among the three States which may present a claim: the national State, the territorial State, and the State of permanent residence. Thus if the national State has already presented a claim, the other two may no longer do so; and if the territorial State has presented a claim, the State of permanent residence may no longer do so. In fact, the State of permanent residence may no longer present a claim, if either of the two preceding States has 'notified its intention of presenting a claim', although the Convention does not specify whether this means a notification addressed to the launching State. However, this hierarchy may be only apparent; for the article does not say that the State or States lower down the hierarchy may present a claim only if the State or States higher up in the hierarchy decides or decide not to present a claim. Had the Convention done so, then the State or States lower down in the hierarchy must, if not exactly wait for a decision to be taken by the State or States higher up in the hierarchy, at least delay its or their own claim sufficiently in order to give preceding State or States reasonable time to make up its or their mind. As the article is worded at present, there seems to be nothing to prevent even a State which is lowest in the hierarchy from presenting a claim before the States higher up in the hierarchy have made a decision wether or not to present a claim. For instance, in a given incident, a victim's State of permanent residence may, under Article VIII, arguably decide to pre-empt the prescribed order by jumping in first with its own claim before the State of nationality and the territorial State, provided that neither of them has yet presented a claim or notified its intention of doing so. But what happens if the State of nationality or the territorial State then decides to take up the claim? Would it be precluded from doing so, or, on the contrary, when it does put in a claim, would the State of permanent residence be obliged to withdraw its claim? Or would the two or even three claimant States become joined in the same proceeding within the meaning of Article XVII of the Convention?[119] The Convention is unclear on the subject; nor is

---

[119] See text to n. 367 below.

it entirely clear whether all the claimant States and launching States have to be contracting States to the Convention, although, on account of the *Pacta tertiis* principle, the answer to the last question is probably yes in all cases.[120]

4. *Exclusion of Nationals, Participants, and Invitees.* Article VII provides:

The provisions of this Convention shall not apply to damage caused by a space object of a launching State to:

(a) nationals of that launching State;

(b) foreign nationals during such time as they are participating in the operation of that space object from the time of its launching or at any stage thereafter until its descent, or during such time as they are in the immediate vicinity of a planned launching or recovery area as the result of an invitation by that launching State.

Paragraph (b) is an application of the principle *Volenti non fit injuria*, whilst paragraph (a) is an application of a basic principle of international law which, in normal circumstances, refrains from dealing with relations between a State and its nationals. At the ninth session (1970) of the Outer Space Legal Sub-Committee, Italy put forward a proposal which would have qualified paragraph (a) with the following:

unless they reside permanently in another State and have their principal domicile in that State.[121]

A hypothetical example adduced to support this proposal was the case of an Italian emigrant injured by an Italian space object in his new country.[122] The Italian proposal was not adopted.

A more difficult problem which has apparently not been dealt with by the Convention is the application of paragraph (a) when there are two or more launching States. Under Article I(c), in any launching, there can potentially be four different categories of launching States; within each category, there can, moreover, be more than one State.[123] At one time in its drafting history, the present Article VIII contained an additional paragraph 4 which said: 'No claim may be presented under this Convention in respect of the nationals of the respondent.'[124] This formula avoided the ambiguity of the generic term 'launching State', but, following the adoption of the three drafting principles of the Drafting Group,[125] it was changed to 'No claim may be presented under this Convention to a launching State in respect of nationals of that State.'[126]

---

[120] See s. IV above.

[121] PUOS/C.2/70/WG.1/CRP.7 (reproduced A/AC.105/85, Annx I, p. 11). 'Domicile' is here used in the civil law sense of residence.

[122] Ibid.: 'Grounds'.   [123] See s. V.A.5 below.

[124] See text approved by the Drafting Group, A/AC.105/C.2/WG(IX)/L.10 (reproduced A/AC.105/85, Annex I, p. 20, at p. 23).   [125] See s. IV above.

[126] Text as modified by the Drafting Group, PUOS/C.2/DG(IX)/R.3 (reproduced A/AC.105/85, Annex I, p. 29, at p. 31). See further s. V.A.4 below.

That paragraph was subsequently deleted, presumably because it was thought that it duplicated Article VII(a). On this basis, it is possible to argue that the use of the qualification 'that' in Article VII, as well as the drafting history of Article VIII, would seem to suggest that the Convention does not prevent either the territorial State or the State of permanent residence from presenting a claim in respect of damage caused to a foreigner injured by a space object launched by his own State, not to his national State (which is precluded by Article VII(a)), but to a co-launching State of which the victim is not a national. Opponents of this argument would probably say that, for purposes of the Convention, any damage caused by a space object would be deemed to have been caused, because of the principle of joint and several liability,[127] by each and every one of the launching States, when there are more than one, with the result that damage caused to the nationals of any of the launching States would be excluded by Article VII(a). The fact that the Convention has set out to be victim-oriented probably tilts the balance in favour of the former interpretation, although the rejection of the Italian proposal in turn tends to cast doubt on the conclusiveness of this consideration.

5. *The Party Liable.* The question has already been discussed whether the principles contained in the Liability Convention may be regarded *ipso jure*, because of the language of the Convention itself, as expressive of general international law.[128] Subject to that qualification, the Convention is basically applicable qua treaty only to its contracting parties and participating organizations. The Convention, in its Articles II, III, IV, and V, renders the 'launching State' liable for any damage which may be caused by a space object, the term 'launching State' being, under Article XXII of the Convention, applicable to certain international intergovernmental organizations. The position of international organizations in the Liability Convention is discussed in the next Section, but it should be mentioned forthwith that participating international organizations do not thereby become contracting parties to the Liability Convention.[129]

Article I(b) of the Convention explains that 'the term "launching" includes attempted launching'.

Article I (c) further provides:

The term 'launching State' means:

   (i)   A State which launches or procures the launching of a space object;

  (ii)   A State from whose territory or facility a space object is launched.

In this, the Liability Convention is merely following the example of Article VII of the Space Treaty, under which there can be, in any one case, four different

---

[127] See s. VII below.   [128] See s. V.A.1 above.
[129] See s. V.A.6 below, especially text to nn. 167 ff.

States or categories of States which may be simultaneously liable for damage caused by any object launched into outer space, namely:

(i)　　the State which launches the object;
(ii)　　the State which procures its launching;
(iii)　　the State from whose territory it is launched; and
(iv)　　the State from whose facility it is launched.

Although initially there was some discussion whether the liability of the last two categories of States was to be primary or secondary, eventually all four categories of States were, at least insofar as the Convention is concerned, treated on an equal footing.[130]

By attributing liability solely to the 'launching State', the Liability Convention seemingly ignores cases where damage may be caused by a space object that has not been launched by a State, or an organization deemed to be a State. While this may be literally true, the very comprehensive definition of the term 'launching State', especially by its inclusion of the last two categories of States mentioned above, probably means in practice, that the Convention covers all launchings of space objects within the territorial and quasi-territorial jurisdictions of any of the contracting State.[131]

6. *The Problem of International Organizations.*　　The problem of international organizations was one of the so-called New Delhi points which held up the convention for a number of years.[132] Behind an eminently practical problem lies a basic doctrinal difference of some importance. On the part of the so-called co-operative space powers, led particularly by the United Kingdom on the theoretical side and pushed from behind by Australia at a more down-to-earth level,[133] it was maintained that the separate personality of international organizations should be recognized,[134] that consequently an international organization should not be bound by the proposed agreement unless it made a declaration accepting the agreement,[135] and that, once it became a party, it benefited from the treaty even though some of its members were non-parties to the treaty and would remain unbound by its provisions.[136] The 1968 Astronauts Agreement was cited as the guiding precedent.[137]

---

[130]　See s. VII.A below.
[131]　See further text to n. 193 below, and also s. VII.A below, including text to n. 237.
[132]　See ss. III.C, III.F.2, and III.F.4 above.
[133]　E.g., United Kingdom, A/AC.105/C.2/SR.117, p. 12; ibid./SR.126, p. 7.
[134]　See Belgian draft, A/AC.105/C.2/L.7/Rev.3, Art. 6; United States draft, A/AC.105/C.2/L.19 and L.58, Art. V; Italian draft, A/AC.105/C.2/L.40/Rev.1, Art. 6; Belgium, France, Italy, Sweden and United Kingdom proposal, A/AC.105/C.2/L.60 and Add. 1; and, e.g., Australia, A/AC.105/C.2/SR.116, p. 4; Canada, ibid./SR.117, p. 3; Japan, ibid./SR.117, p. 9; United Kingdom, ibid./SR.120, pp. 2–3; *contra*: USSR, ibid./SR.105, p. 2.
[135]　E.g., United Kingdom, A/AC.105/C.2/SR.120, p. 6.
[136]　See e.g., joint proposal by Belgium, France, Italy, Sweden and the United Kingdom on international organizations, A/AC.105/C.2/L.60 and Add. 1; and further nn. 150 and 154 below.
[137]　E.g., Australia, A/AC.105/C.2/SR.120, p. 5; United Kingdom, ibid./SR.122, p. 6; see

On the other hand, many States within the Soviet bloc denied that international organizations had an existence separate from their members and maintained that the fact that a State conducted its space activities merely as a member of an international organization made no difference to its obligations under the agreement.[138] The 1967 Space Treaty was treated as the correct starting point.[139] Thus the Hungarian draft simply made international organizations and their members jointly and severally liable without further ado,[140] though subsequently, as a possible compromise, some States within the Soviet bloc were willing to accept[141] the so-called New Delhi principle that an international organization would become *ipso facto* bound by the treaty only if a majority of its members were parties to it.[142]

Neither view appears to be entirely correct. As regards the latter, the Advisory Opinion of the International Court of Justice on *Reparation for Injuries Suffered in the Service of the United Nations* (1949) has fully demonstrated the possibility of international organizations acquiring international legal personality.[143] However, as for the former view, the Court was obviously wrong in holding, contrary to the *pactum tertiis* principle now re-affirmed in Article 34 of the 1969 Vienna Convention on the Law of Treaties, that members of an international organization, if sufficiently numerous, were able to confer on their organization so-called objective international legal personality that could be invoked against non-members.[144]

On the one hand, it would amount to denying practically all States other than the super powers the opportunity of engaging in space activities if international organizations are placed beyond the pale of the various space treaties, and it would be downright iniquitous to impose on them the treaty obligations without the corresponding rights. On the other hand, it would be equally unreasonable to maintain that all parties to an international treaty must recognize the separate legal personality of any international organization which some of their co-parties may establish, and to accept it as a full and independent party to the treaty whenever it cares to make a declaration to this

---

further 'The 1968 Astronauts Agreement', loc. cit. in n. 12 above, at pp. 204 ff. [Ch. 10 above, s. VIII.A: The Personal and Temporal Scope].

[138] E.g., Romania, A/AC.105/C.2/SR.121, p. 2: 'not an entity in itself'; Bulgaria, ibid./SR.122, p. 5: 'no sociological reality'; cf., however, *contra*: Hungary, ibid./SR.96, p. 12; Czechoslovakia, ibid./SR.120, p. 6. But in the latter cases, both in fact denied the effects of such separate existence on 'practical grounds'.

[139] E.g., USSR, A/AC.105/C.2/SR.118, p. 5; Poland, ibic./SR.120, p. 8; USSR, ibid./SR.122, p. 11; see further Cheng, 'The 1967 Space Treaty', loc. cit. in n. 12 above, at p. 588 ff. [Ch. 9 above, s. V.G: International Organizations].

[140] A/AC.105/C.2/L.10/Rev.1 and Corr. 1, L.24 and Add. 1, Article VII. See also USSR and Bulgarian Working Paper, A/AC.105/C.2/L.67 and Add. 1. Bulgaria was harking back to this idea as late as June 1970 in its proposal PUOS/C.2/70/WG.1/CRP.2 and Corr. 1: see s. III.F.4 above, particularly nn. 60 and 63 and nn. 159, 163 below.

[141] E.g., Czechoslovakia, A/AC.105/C.2/SR.120, p. 6; Bulgaria, ibid./SR.122, p. 5.

[142] Cf. Indian draft treaty, A/AC.105/C.2/L.32/Rev.2, Art. XIII (1).

[143] *ICJ Rep. 1949*, p. 174, at p. 179.　　　　　　　　　　[144] Ibid., p. 185.

effect, without even an opportunity of satisfying themselves that it will be able to discharge all the obligations under the treaty. From this point of view, it has always to be remembered that international organizations even when recognized as international persons, nevertheless differ from States, not least because they have no territory, no population and in fact no resources of their own.[145] In fact, it is not inconceivable that, at the end of the day, an international organization is found to own no more than perhaps just a few typewriters! And, it is no answer to say simply that one is not a member of any bogus space organization of straw.[146] An international organization can become insolvent or even dissolved over night. In the absence of the appropriate civil and criminal legislation to protect the rights and interests of third parties, one is really back in the early days of limited liability companies in municipal law when they were looked at with suspicion and even treated as immoral. Another argument against allowing international organizations, without further qualification, to become full contracting parties to an international treaty is that it would not be fair to allow non-parties to a treaty to benefit from it through an international organization that has accepted the treaty, especially when the view is held that such non-parties remain not bound by the treaty even *pro tanto*.[147]

In the context of the liability agreement, the obvious starting point must be that an international organization is capable of acquiring international legal personality, but that it has no separate legal existence unless such legal personality has been granted by existing international persons through their consent or recognition. If not recognized by the other parties to the treaty, an international organization, though some or all of its members may be parties to the treaty, is *vis-à-vis* those other parties, incapable of bearing rights or duties under the treaty. To impose obligations upon it is in fact to recognize its separate legal personality. But if an international organization is to be recognized as an international person, it obviously cannot be bound by a treaty, unless it consents. Contrary to what has sometimes been maintained, this by no means opens the possibility of parties to a treaty evading their treaty obligations behind the screen of an international organization.

Two different situations must be clearly distinguished. First, in the event of an organization not being a party to the treaty, non-member States that are parties to the treaty are not obliged to recognize the separate legal personality of the organization. Member States parties to the treaty, therefore, remain bound by the treaty in respect of activities they conduct through their organization, in the same way as when they engage in joint ventures. If the treaty

---

[145] Cf. ICJ: *Reparation for Injuries* (1949), *ICJ Rep. 1949*, p. 174, at p. 179: to say that an organization is an international person '. . . is not the same thing as saying that it is a State, which it certainly is not, or that its legal personality and rights and duties are the same as those of a State.'

[146] E.g., Austrlia, A/AC.105/C.2/SR.96, p. 12.

[147] E.g., Australia, A/AC.105/C.2/SR.120, p. 5. See further nn. 150 and 154 below.

imposes on contracting parties joint and several liability for joint ventures,[148] then member States parties to the treaty would incur such liability for any and all the damage which the organization might cause, even though some of the members might not be parties to the treaty.[149] However, if the organization were to suffer damage, as the separate existence of the organization need not be recognized by non-members parties to the treaty, only those members of the organization that are parties to the treaty would be able to benefit from the treaty. In other words, only the interests of parties to the treaty would be protected, but not those of non-parties. Such imbalance as exists between the rights and duties of parties to the treaty that are members of non-party organization lies, therefore, in favour of the potential victims and there is consequently a built-in incentive for parties to the treaty to induce organizations of which they are members to become parties to the treaty, if allowed to do so. For the same reason, not to allow international organizations to become parties to space treaties or at least to be associated with them insofar as rights and obligations are concerned is to make it all the more difficult for small and medium powers to engage in space activities.

Secondly, if an international organization is allowed, and agrees, to become a party to the treaty or otherwise bound by it, then the separate legal personality of the organization is recognized by the other parties to the treaty. This implies that the rights and duties of the organization will be exercised and discharged, in the first instance at least, by the organization. But, inasmuch as international organizations are in reality associations of States which remain the basic units of international society, members of the organization must also be considered bound, at least ultimately, by the treaty insofar as activities of the organization are concerned, *whether or not they are parties to the treaty*.[150]

---

[148] See s. VII below.

[149] This was rightly pointed out by the Austrian delegate, A/AC.105/C.2/SR.120, p. 7, but somewhat surprisingly, this aspect of the problem received little attention during the discussions. This was probably due partly at least to the desire of the co-operative space powers to enable international organizations to take part in space activities and to make non-members recognize the separate existence of such organizations even when they were not parties to the treaty, and the desire of the Soviet bloc States, on the other hand, to subject such organizations to the treaty, whether parties to it or not.

[150] Cf. *sic*: Belgian draft, A/AC.105/C.2/L.7/Rev.3, Article 6; and see Italy, A/AC.105/C.2/SR.91, p. 14, and Italian draft A/AC.105/C.2/L.40/Rev.1, Art. 11. Although proceedings against non-party members were probably not envisaged in 1968 by Austria, Belgium, France, Sweden and the United Kingdom in their joint proposal of 13 June 1968 on international organizations (A/AC.105/C.2/L.41), by 1969 Austria (A/AC.105/C.2/SR.120, p. 7) and again Italy (ibid., p. 8) were willing to accept this consequence as a matter of principle, while the United Kingdom, France, Belgium and Canada were prepared to accept it only as a possible compromise (A/AC.105/C.2/SR.120, pp. 3–6), but Australia was not (ibid., p. 5). However, in the joint proposal put forward on 23 June 1969 by Belgium, France, Italy, Sweden and the United Kingdom, liability was not imposed on non-party members (A/AC.105/C.2/L.60 and Add. 1). See also Canada, A/AC.105/C.2/SR.126, p. 6. The fact that Belgium and Italy were sponsors of the June 1969 proposal shows how the views of States sometimes fluctuate in these discussions. See also nn. 151 and especially 154 below.

This being so, whether the liability of member States is deemed theoretically to have arisen *ab initio* or only after the organization has defaulted has little practical significance.[151] A more difficult problem is whether members should be held jointly and severally for the entire damage caused by the organization,[152] or only in proportion to their assessed membership contributions,[153] in case the organization is in default of its obligations. Arguments may be advanced in favour of either solution, though the very default of the organization probably tilts the balance in favour of the former,[154] especially in a so-called 'victim-oriented' treaty.

Progress on the subject of international organizations in the negotiations leading to the Liability Convention was slow. Certain points were provisionally agreed upon at respectively the sixth (1967)[155] and eighth (1969)[156] sessions of the Legal Sub-Committee, but none affected the substance of the matter.[157] During the twelfth session of the Outer Space Committee in 1969, extensive consultations took place under the chairmanship of Ambassador Haymerle, Chairman of the Committee. On 5 December 1969, at the last meeting of the twelfth session, he was able to report the following on the question of international organizations:

[151] In the joint proposal put forward by Austria, Belgium, France, Sweden and the United Kingdom on 13 June 1968 (A/AC.105/C.2/L.41), it was envisaged that the liability of members would arise if within six months of the presentation of the claim the organization had not carried out its obligations. See United Kingdom, A/AC.105/C.2/SR.120 (19 June 1969), p. 2. As a 'concession', the joint proposal put forward by Belgium, France, Italy, Sweden and the United Kingdom on 23 June 1969 (A/AC.105/C.2/L.60 and Add. 1) made members of the organization parties to the treaty liable *ab initio* subject in fact to the same condition. See further United Kingdom, A/AC.105/C.2/SR.122, p. 6. The practical consequences are virtually the same.

[152] E.g., Hungary, A/AC.105/C.2/SR.95, p. 11; India, ibid./SR.96, p. 17; USSR, ibid./SR.105, p. 2.

[153] E.g., France, A/AC.105/C.2/SR.91, p. 6; Australia, ibid./SR.96, p. 12; Italy, ibid./SR.116, p. 11; Iran, ibid./SR.117, p. 2.

[154] *Sic*: Belgian draft, A/AC.105/C.2/L.7/Rev.3, Art. 6 (both parties and non-parties); United States draft, A/AC.105/C.2/L.19 and L.58, Art. V(3) (only parties to the agreement); Hungarian draft, A/AC.105/C.2/L.10/Rev.1 and Corr. 1, L.24 and Add. 1, Art. VII (all members *ab initio*); Indian draft, A/AC.105/C.2/L.32/Rev.2, Art. XIII(3) (parties only); Belgium, France, Italy, Sweden and United Kingdom proposal, A/AC.105/C.2/L.60 and Add. 1, para. 3 (parties only).

[155] On the one hand, 'International organizations that launch objects into outer space should be liable under the Convention for damage caused by such objects', and on the other hand, damage caused to property of international organizations was included in the definition of damage compensable under the convention: *Report of the Legal Sub-Committee on the Work of its Sixth Session* (19.6–14.7.67), A/AC.105/37, para. 17.

[156] 'If damage is caused by a space object to the property of an international intergovernmental organization, the claim should be presented by one of the States members of the international intergovernmental organizations [*sic*; "organization"?] which are parties to this Convention': *Report of the Legal Sub-Committee on the Work of its Eighth Session* (9.6–4.7.69), A/AC.105/58, para. 22.

[157] The *Report of the Legal Sub-Committee for its Eighth Session*, ibid., para. 22, formulated the remaining difference as follows: 'No agreement was reached on the question whether the liability of the States members of the international organization that are parties to the liability convention (a) should be residual and arise only in the event of default by the international organization, or (b) should arise at the same time as the liability of the international organization.'

[I]t appears that, if all other problems in a dispute were settled, agreement might be possible under a provision which would be based on the following principles: the corresponding provisions of the convention would apply to an international intergovernmental organization which declared its acceptance of the rights and obligations provided for in the convention and if a majority of the States members of the organization are contracting parties to the convention and to the outer space Treaty.

The States members of such an organization which are contracting parties to the convention would take appropriate steps in the organization, with a view to the making of such a declaration.

If an international intergovernmental organization is liable for damage under the convention, claims must first be presented to the organization, and only when it has not paid the sum due within a specified period may the claim be presented to one or more States members which are contracting parties to the convention.

If damage is caused by a space object to the property of an international intergovernmental organization, the claim should be presented by one of the States members of the international intergovernmental organization which are parties to the convention.[158]

At the ninth session of the Legal Sub-Committee in 1970, proposals on international organizations were presented separately by Bulgaria,[159] and Mexico[160], and jointly by Belgium, France, Italy, Sweden and the United Kingdom.[161] To the five-power proposal, there was also an Indian amendment.[162]

All three proposals were based on the 1969 understanding, but each differed from it in some degree. The Bulgarian proposal went back on point 3 of the understanding by providing that 'the claim for compensation may be addressed to the organization itself or to one or more of its member States.' As the Bulgarian delegate frankly said in respect of the proposal of his delegation: 'It would have the advantage of avoiding any complications which might arise should the victim not recognize the international intergovernmental organization responsible.'[163] On the other hand, the Mexican proposal sought to improve on point 4 of the 1969 understanding by permitting an international organization to present its own claims.[164] In view of the known Soviet bloc attitude on the subject, exemplified by the latest Bulgarian proposal, it was little wonder that even the United Kingdom delegate did not think that the Mexican proposal would work 'without encountering considerable difficulties in practice'.[165]

Nor was the five-power proposal free from a certain amount of backsliding. Regarding point 2 of the 1969 understanding, the joint proposal merely said

---

[158] A/AC.105/PV.70–8, p. 163 (PV.78). See also A/7621/Add. 1, para. 8(h)(iv).
[159] PUOS/C.2/70/WG.1/CRP.2 and Corr. 1 (reproduced A/AC.105/85, Annex I, p. 9).
[160] PUOS/C.2/70/W.G.1/CRP.8 (reproduced (A/AC.105/85, Annex I, p. 11).
[161] PUOS/C.2/70/WG.1/CRP.11 (reproduced A/AC.105/85, Annex I, pp. 13–14).
[162] PUOS/C.2/70/WG.1/CRP.15 (reproduced A/AC.105/85, Annex I, p. 15).
[163] A/AC.105/C.2/SR.132–51, p. 15 (SR.136).
[164] Cf. Mexico, ibid., p. 19 (SR.137). [165] Ibid., p. 23 (SR.138).

that the contracting States members of the organization 'shall support in the organization the making of a declaration'. According to the United Kingdom delegate who introduced the joint proposal before the Legal Sub-Committee, 'That went as far as it appeared reasonably possible to go, as a legal matter.'[166] However, the Indian delegation in its amendment did succeed in finding a slightly more positive form of words which was closer to the 1969 understanding. There was also a further minor Indian amendment of an essentially verbal character to paragraph 1 of the joint proposal.

Subject to these two Indian amendments and certain other drafting changes, the joint proposal eventually became the present Article XXII.

The Liability Convention has gone a long way towards the recognition of the separate international legal existence and personality of international intergovernmental organizations which conduct space activities, provided that a majority of the members of the organization concerned are parties to the Liability Convention and the 1967 Space Treaty.

Such an organization may, upon its own decision, make a declaration accepting the rights and obligations provided for under the Convention, and all the provisions of the Convention, except Articles XXIV to XXVII (i.e., all the final clauses save one, namely, Article XXVIII), will then become applicable to it. The Convention does not specify any special form or procedure for the making of this declaration. For instance, no provision is made for it to be addressed to or deposited with the Depositary Governments. However, Article XXVIII having been rather pointedly left out of those provisions which are expressly stated to be not applicable to international organizations, one wonders whether Depositary Governments have a duty to treat international organizations which have made a declaration under Article XXII (which, for the sake of convenience, will be called 'participating organizations') as 'signatory and acceding States', and transmit to them duly certified copies of the Convention in accordance with the terms of Article XXVIII.

The exclusion of the application of the remainder of the final clauses of the Convention to participating organizations has, however, the definite effect of withholding from them the status of contracting parties to the Convention. Accordingly participating organizations cannot initiate or take part in reviews of the Convention under Article XXVI of the Convention;[167] nor can they propose amendments to the Convention under Article XXV.[168] In fact, the Convention is silent as to what happens to participating organizations when the Convention is amended. One can only conjecture that a fresh declaration will have to be made after a majority of the members of the organization concerned have become bound by the amendment. Can Article XXII be amended against the wishes of participating organizations? This can happen in practice, if members of participating organizations represent only a small minority

---

[166] A/AC.105/C.2/SR.132–51, p. 22 (SR.138).   [167] See n. 93 above.
[168] See n. 93 above.

among parties to the Convention and are not in a position to prevent such an amendment being adopted. In law, the answer would appear to be also in the affirmative, inasmuch as, under Article XXII, participating organizations have no say in the amendment process. From this point of view, participating organizations do not even enjoy the status of third parties which have accepted the rights and obligations of a treaty providing for rights and obligations for third parties; for in the latter case the rights and obligations may not be revoked or modified without the consent of the third parties concerned.[169]

Furthermore, as one goes through the final clauses, one may well ask whether participating organizations can terminate their participation. Under Article XXVII of the Convention,

Any State Party to this Convention may give notice of its withdrawal from the Convention one year after its entry into force by written notification to the Depositary Governments. Such withdrawal shall take effect one year from the receipt of this notification.'

But Article XXVII is not applicable to international organizations. Can a participating organization nevertheless withdraw the declaration which it has made under Article XXII? If so, there is, on the one hand, once more the question of form and procedure. There is, on the other hand, the additional question whether such withdrawal takes effect immediately or, by analogy with Article XXVII, only one year after it has been made. However, while the Convention provides no clue as to how these questions are to be answered, it is probably clear from Article XXII that, if a participating organization for one reason or another no longer meets the requirements for becoming a participating organization in the first place, it ceases forthwith being one.

But, while participating organizations are excluded from the application of all the final clauses except one and thereby denied the status of contracting parties to the Convention, in all other respects they have the same rights and duties as 'States' referred to in the Convention. One sees here the subtlety of the Drafting Group at work: Article XXII has avoided saying that references to 'contracting States' or 'contracting Parties' shall be deemed to apply to participating organizations. They are assimilated to 'States', but not 'contracting States'.[170]

In some ways, this assimilation is quite literal. Thus, notwithstanding a suggestion from the Mexican delegation to extend the protection of the Convention to not only the property of international organizations, but also the property and persons of their officials,[171] Article I(a) limits compensable damage, in the case of international organizations, to only their property.[172]

---

[169] Cf. Vienna Convention of the Law of Treaties, 1969, Arts. 25–7; PCIJ: *Free Zones Case* (1932), A/B 46.

[170] See s. IV above *in fine*.   [171] A/AC.105/C.2/SR.132–51, p. 19 (SR.137).

[172] See s. V.C.1 below.

But upon closer examination, it will be found that the same is true of States; for if the interpretation is correct that the phrase 'whose natural or juridical persons' in Article VIII(1) refers to persons possessing the nationality of the State concerned,[173] then a contracting State would also not be able to extend its protection to any of its officials who is not one of its nationals or permanent residents and who has suffered damage caused by a space object outside its territory.[174]

But the very fact that the Convention recognizes that a participating organization may have a claim of its own in respect of damage which it has itself suffered against even a non-member party to the Convention represents a very substantial shift in the position previously held by Soviet bloc States on the subject, even though Article XXII(4) provides that the claim has to be presented through a State member of the organization which is a party to the Convention. Inherent in this arrangement is the possibility that non-parties to the Convention may be benefiting from the Convention by being members of a participating organization, without incurring any corresponding obligations. The obligations of the Convention are incumbent only on the participating organization and, ultimately, on those members of the organization which are parties to the Convention.

The benefits of Article XXII of the Convention may be said to be almost exclusively on the side of members of such organizations. The fact that the participating organization is rendered liable for any damage which it may cause adds little to the rights of the victim under the Convention, except where members of the responsible organization that are parties to the Convention are all either practically insolvent or very prone to default in their obligations, and that the organization has other members which are not parties to the Convention but which are both anxious to see the organization honour its obligations and disposed to provide the necessary finances to enable it to do so.

The explanation is that, in view of Article V(1) of the Convention on joint ventures,[175] as long as the international organization which has caused damage by a space object has at least a member which is a contracting party to the Convention, the victim will always be able to hold that contracting State liable for the entire damage. Consequently, insofar as the principle of liability is concerned, the advantage of adding the organization to the list of those already jointly and severally liable for the damage is not very significant.[176]

As regards the presentation of the claim, the balance of benefits is again in favour of members of the organization, although there is no real disadvantage insofar as the victim or claimant State is concerned, except for what the Bulgarian proposal had in mind.[177] However, even here, on the analogy of

[173] See n. 118 above.　　　　　　　　[174] See s. V.A.3 above, especially n. 118 therein.
[175] See s. VII.A below.　　　　　　　[176] See n. 149 above and text thereto.
[177] See n. 163 above and text thereto.

inter-State relations, although, on account of Article XXII, contracting States to the Convention have no option but to recognize the international legal existence and personality of participating organizations, they have no duty to enter into 'diplomatic relations' with them. Article XXII(4) already sees to it that, where the participating organization is a claimant, it cannot present a claim directly to the launching State.[178]

Where a participating organization is the launching authority, presumably Article IX will allow any claimant State that does not wish to enter into 'diplomatic relations' with the organization to request 'another State to present its claim to that [organization] or otherwise represent its interests.' However, inasmuch as such a participating organization is unlikely, at least in the foreseeable future, to become a member of the United Nations, the claimant State, while this remains the case, will not be able to have its claim presented 'through the Secretary-General of the United Nations.'[179]

This raises also the question whether claims in respect of damage suffered by participating organizations may be submitted through the Secretary-General of the United Nations. The arguments that have been advanced to show that the phrase 'the claimant State' in Article XIII in relation to Article XXII(4) means the participating organization rather than the State presenting the claim[180] would seem equally applicable here. If so, the answer must be that claims under Article XXII cannot be submitted through the Secretary-General of the United Nations even when both the State presenting the claim and the launching State are members of the United Nations.

Finally, a word about the 'period of six months' referred to in Article XXII(3)(b). It should be realized that this period does not run from the date negotiations break down in any attempt to obtain compensation from a participating organization, but from the time when the claim has been established and the amount of compensation duly liquidated. Inasmuch as the claims procedure of the Convention can take as long as two years and six months from the date a claim is notified under Article XIV to the date the Claims Commission renders its decision or award under Article XIX(3),[181] the whole period by which the presentation of a claim to a member State of a participating organization may be delayed is, therefore, as much as three years. However, as by then both the principle and the amount of indebtedness have already been established in accordance with the terms of the Convention, it is submitted that, when the liability of members of a participating organization is invoked under Article XXII(3)(b), the decision or award of the Claims Commission which has rendered a decision or award as between the claimant State and the participating organization would have the same effect *vis-à-vis* members of the organization which are parties to the Convention as it has in regard to the organization, and there will be no need for the claimant State to

---

[178] For text of article, see text shortly after n. 166 above.　　　[179] See X.B below.
[180] See text to nn. 97 ff. above.　　　[181] See text shortly before n. 368 below.

re-start the whole cycle of the claims procedure once more. In this sense, it is possible to say that the effective delay caused by the interposition of an international organization in the settlement of a claim is in reality no more than six months.

Reference has previously been made to the fact that Article XXII represents a significant shift in the attitude of the Eastern European States towards international organizations in international legal relations. This shift, however, should not necessarily be interpreted as a concession merely towards small and medium space powers in the West which aspire to go into outer space on the back of international organizations; for such international organizations are gradually emerging also within the Soviet bloc in the form, for instance, of INTERSPUTNIK and INTERCOSMOS.[182] Indeed, one has only to compare the number of States at the eve of the First World War with that today in order to realize the increasingly pressing need for having international organizations with separate legal personality. The position is not unlike the transformation of a rural into an urban society. The significance of Article XXII of the Liability Convention lies in its being a major landmark in the response of the international society to this development.

B. Cosmographical Scope

At the time when the Convention was being drafted, there was considerable discussion as to the cosmographical scope of the proposed convention. It was argued that for the sake of simplicity, the convention should deal only with what in air law has come to be known as 'surface damage' on earth, extended in this case, to aircraft in flight, excluding thus damage occurring in outer space and on celestial bodies.[183]

However, as it has also been recalled, in this connection, Article VII of the 1967 Space Treaty provides that a launching State 'is internationally liable for damage to another State Party to the Treaty or to its natural or juridical persons by such object or its component parts *on the Earth, in airspace, or in outer space, including the moon and other celestial bodies*.'[184] The general view was that the proposed treaty should be universal in scope, though different rules might have to be applied in different environments.[185]

---

[182] Cf. A. S. Piradov (ed.), *International Space Law* (1976), pp. 228 ff., and Jasentuliyana and Lee, 1 *Manual*, Chs. XII (Yuri M. Kolossov, 'International System and Organization of Space Communication (INTERSPUTNIK)', p. 401), and XIII (Vladlen S. Vereshchetin, 'Agreement on Co-operation in the Exploration and Use of Outer Space for Peaceful Purposes (INTERCOSMOS)', p. 415).

[183] Cf. the limited agreement reached at the sixth session of the Legal Sub-Committee, A/AC.105/C.2/SR.93, p. 4; Austria ibid., pp. 2, 10; USA, ibid., pp. 10–11.

[184] Italics added.

[185] Cf. Italy, A/AC.105/C.2/SR.91, p. 13; Czechoslovakia (SR.93, p. 8); Iran (SR.93, p. 9); Belgium (SR.93, p. 9). See US change of view, SR.94, p. 5 and SR.95, p. 3: 'in all environments'; SR.95, p. 14: 'wherever caused'. Text approved, SR.97, pp. 6–7: 'A State which launches a space

Table XI.1 COSMOGRAPHICAL SCOPE OF THE LIABILITY CONVENTION

COSMOGRAPHICAL SCOPE AND LOCATION OF DAMAGE			CATEGORY OF DAMAGE CAUSED BY A SPACE OBJECT FOR WHICH A LAUNCHING STATE IS LIABLE
u	'on the surface of the earth'		Seeming all damage, as defined in Article I(a), without further restriction (Arts. II and IV(a))
n i v e r s	'else-where than on the surface of the earth'	in airspace	(1) 'damage caused . . . to aircraft in flight' (Arts. II and IV(a)) (2) 'damage . . . caused . . . to a space object of [another] launching State or to persons or property on board such a space object' (Art. III) (3) 'damage thereby being caused to a third State or to its natural or juridical persons . . . [in respect of] (a) . . . aircraft in flight . . . [or] (b) . . . a space object of the third State or . . . persons or property on board that space object' (Art. IV)
a l		in outer space, including the moon and other celestial bodies	(1) 'damage . . . caused . . . to a space object of [another] launching State or to persons or property on board such a space object' (Art. III) (2) 'damage thereby being caused to a third State or to its natural or juridical persons . . . [in respect of] . . . a space object of the third State or . . . persons or property on board that space object' (Art. IV)

    This view resulted eventually in the present Articles II and III, the combined effect of which, from the cosmographical point of view is that, although the scope of the Convention is in principle universal, its field of application in the different cosmographical environment differs as shown in Table XI.1.

    It will readily be seen that the category of damage caused by space objects 'elsewhere than on the surface of the earth' for which a launching is liable is

object shall be liable for damage caused to persons or property during the launching, transit or descent of such space objects, irrespective of the place in which the damage has occurred.' This text did not find its way into the Convention.

rather restrictive. In the first place, as was pointed out by the French delegate to the Legal Sub-Committee, there is a discrepancy between the wording of Article VII of the 1967 Space Treaty which speaks of damage 'on the earth', and that of Article II of the Liability Convention which limits its own sphere of operation to only damage caused 'on the surface of the earth or to aircraft in flight'.[186]

Secondly, insofar as damage caused in airspace is concerned, the Convention excludes all damage other than damage caused to aircraft in flight or to another spacecraft, either directly or indirectly, and all persons and property on board the other spacecraft.[187] As the French delegate to the Legal Sub-Committee remarked: 'Such damage, which his delegation regarded as extremely important, might take the form of the pollution or contamination of airspace and was likely to become an acute problem as a result of technical developments and the use of nuclear devices. His delegation accordingly considered that the words 'in airspace' should be inserted after the words 'of the earth' in Article II.'[188] The French proposal was, however, not taken up.

Finally, when it comes to outer space, including the moon and other celestial bodies, the Convention becomes even more restrictive. At the ninth session of the Legal Sub-Committee, Sweden did raise the question of installations and stations on the moon and other celestial bodies which might be damaged by a space object.[189] For that matter, the Liability Convention also does not cover the case of an astronaut injured by a space object, when he is outside his spacecraft either in outer space or on a celestial body, or a parachutist in airspace.

At the ninth session of the Legal Sub-Committee in 1970, the Italian delegation introduced a Working Paper which would have introduced the words 'or of celestial bodies' after 'on the surface of the earth' in Article II and thus covered all surface damage on celestial bodies.[190] However, Belgium, supported by France and the USSR, thought that the problem of possible damage to persons or property on the moon and other celestial bodies would be better dealt with in a separate convention,[191] and the matter does not appear to have been raised again.[192]

---

[186] A/AC.105/C.2/SR.132–51, p. 85 (SR.150).

[187] The difference in phraseology between Arts. II and III presumably does not mean that the Convention intends to exclude damage to persons and property on board aircraft in flight that might be directly injured or damaged by a space object, but such an argument cannot be excluded.

[188] A/AC.105/C.2/SR.132–51, p. 85 (SR.150); Mexico, ibid., p. 86 (SR.150); France, A/AC.105/PV.85–90, p. 27 (PV.86).

[189] A/AC.105/C.2/SR.132–51, p. 24 (SR.138); see also Italy, ibid., p. 25 (SR.138); Argentina, ibid., p. 25 (SR.138); Mexico, ibid., p. 29 (SR.138).

[190] PUOS/C.2/70/WG.1/CRP.12 (reproduced A/AC.105/85, Annex I, p. 14); A/AC.105/C.2/SR.132–51, p. 25 (SR.138).

[191] Belgium, A/AC.105/C.2/SR.132–51, p. 28 (SR.138); France, ibid., USSR, ibid., p. 29 (SR.138).

[192] The 1979 Moon Treaty has since mentioned the subject in its Art. 14(2), but only to postpone the issue for future arrangements. See Ch. 12 below.

Insofar as the cosmographical scope of launching activities is concerned, there is no cosmographical limitation on where a State may launch or secure the launching of a space object, or where a facility from which a space object is launched should be. Launching can take place, and launching facilities can be situated, not only in national territory, but also on or under the high seas, in outer space, or on a celestial body. Even as regards the concept of the territory from which a space object is launched under Article I(c)(ii), it is arguable that it extends possibly to ships, aircraft, and spacecraft under the quasi-territorial jurisdiction of a contracting State, whenever they are outside the territorial jurisdiction of any State.[193]

C. Material Scope

1. *Damage Defined.*   Agreement had previously been reached at the sixth session of the Legal Sub-Committee in 1967 on the meaning of damage under the Liability Convention. The following text was approved in 1969:

(a) the term 'damage' means loss of life, personal injury or other impairment of health; or loss of or damage to property of States or of persons, natural or juridical, or property of international organizations.[194]

This definition is identical to that found in Article I(a) of the Convention, except that the qualification 'intergovernmental' has now been added between 'international' and 'organization'.

No agreement was reached at the sixth session whether or not to include in the definition a reference to indirect damage and delayed damage.[195] At the seventh session in 1967, the majority of delegates regarded the matter—correctly, it is submitted[196]—as one of proximate or adequate causality which need not be expressed in the convention.[197] There remained, however, the problems of nuclear damage and applicable law, two of the 'New Delhi points'.[198]

2. *Nuclear Damage.*   Nuclear damage may be caused by a nuclear space device or by a space object damaging a nuclear installation. Nuclear damage

---

[193] See n. 131 above and text to n. 237 below. On the distinction between territorial and quasi-terriotiral jurisdiction, see 'The Extraterrestrial Application of International Law', loc. cit. in n. 12 above, at p. 133 ff. [Ch. 5 above, s. II: Position under General International Law].

[194] See *Report of the Legal Sub-Committee on the Work of its Sixth Session* (19.6–14.7.67), A/AC.105/37, para. 17; *Report of the Legal Sub-Committee on the Work of its Eighth Session* (9.6–4.7.69), A/AC.105/58, para. 26.

[195] *Report* A/AC.105/37, para. 17.

[196] See further Cheng, *General Principles of Law*, Ch. 10: 'The Principle of Proximate Causality', pp. 241–53.

[197] See A/AC.105/C.2/SR.103 *passim*; and para. 1 of Working Paper submitted by Japan, A/AC.105/C.2/L.61 and Corr. 1. See also s. VIII below.

[198] See s. III.F. above.

of the former type was excluded from the Hungarian draft.[199] Soviet bloc States long maintained that nuclear damage should be separately dealt with, either by a different instrument or by an amendment of the 1963 Vienna Convention on Nuclear Damage,[200] against the practically unanimous opposition of the other members of the Legal Sub-Committee. Especially as the 1963 Vienna Convention was considered inapplicable to such cases,[201] the latter States were unwilling to see such a crucial issue left unregulated by the proposed agreement.[202] The fear was voiced that there would be no incentive to conclude a separate treaty.[203] Finally, much to everyone's relief, the Soviet Union announced in 1969 its willingness to extend the scope of the convention to cover nuclear damage as part of any 'package deal' that might be reached.[204] Apollo 13 and Cosmos 954 clearly demonstrates the wisdom of not allowing nuclear damage to be excluded from the Convention.[205]

3. *Space Object.*   The Liability Convention regulates, as its title says, 'damage caused by space objects'. Article VII of the 1967 Space Treaty uses the expression 'the launching of an object into outer space', but the Liability Convention studiedly and studiously avoids this phrase and in its Article I(c) speaks instead of 'the launching of a space object'.

In the same Article, the Convention contents itself with saying under (d):

the term 'space object' includes component parts of a space object as well as its launch vehicle and parts thereof.

Article I(b) having already said that 'the term "launching" includes attempted launching', it is clear that the object need not have reached outer space, wherever outer space may begin from.

But the question is, must the object be one designed and calculated to reach outer space, as Italy[206] and Mexico[207] had suggested? However, obviously

---

[199] A/AC.105/C.2/L.10/Rev.1 and Corr. 1, L.24 and Add. 1, Art. I(1).

[200] E.g., USSR, A/AC.105/C.2/SR.92, p. 10; ibid./SR.93, p. 5; Poland, ibid./SR.93, p. 11; Hungary, ibid./SR.93, p. 13; USSR, ibid./SR.94, p. 4; Hungary, ibid./SR.94, p. 9.

[201] E.g., United Kingdom, A/AC.105/C.2/SR.93, p. 14; Belgium, ibid.; United Kingdom, ibid./SR.94, p. 4.

[202] See *passim* A/AC.105/C.2/SR.91–5; ibid./SR.106; ibid./SR.116–18. Japan was for a time uncommitted, primarily because it wished the relationship between the proposed agreement and existing treaties on nuclear liability to be clarified (see ibid./SR.91, p. 10; ibid./SR.125, pp. 2–3; and para. 5 of its Working Paper A/AC.105/C.2/L.61 and Corr. 1), but finally declared itself in favour of inclusion of nuclear damage, A/AC.105/C.2/PV.63, p. 21.

[203] USA, A/AC.105/C.2/SR.106, p. 6.

[204] A/AC.105/C.2/SR.118, p. 5; see previously, Czechoslovakia, ibid./SR.118, p. 2; subsequently, Bulgaria, ibid./SR.122, p. 5.

[205] See s. II above.

[206] See PUOS/C.2/70/WG.1/CRP.10/Rev.1 (reproduced A/AC.105, Annex I, p. 13); Italy, A/AC.105/C.2/SR.132–51, pp. 24–5 (SR.139); pp. 81–3 (SR.149).

[207] See PUOS/C.2/70/WG.1/CRP.14 (reproduced A/AC.105/85, Annex I, p. 15). See also definition of 'space object' in the Belgian draft, A/AC.105/C.2/L.7 (see n. 20 above), and Hungarian draft, A/AC.105/C.2/L.10 (see n. 21 above), as well as the Indian proposal, A/AC.105/C.2/WGII/20.

because the boundary of outer space was and still is a very sensitive issue with some States, this question was not taken up by the Legal Sub-Committee and it remains unanswered. This is a further refutation of the highly fashionable doctrine that no definition of outer space is required.[208]

The question was also asked by Sweden whether, especially in connection with Articles III and IV,[209] 'installations or stations on the surface of a celestial body' came under the definition of 'space objects', a question particularly relevant when they should become damaged by undisputed space objects.[210] But, notwithstanding the warning from the Argentine delegate that it 'was essential to avoid the error committed in the 1968 Agreement on the Rescue of Astronauts, in which even the term "astronaut" was not defined,'[211] the Convention did not even adopt the following joint proposal submitted by Argentina, Belgium and France which contained no mention of outer space:

'Space object' means any object made and intended for space activities.

For the purpose of this Convention, the term 'space object' also includes a launch vehicle and parts thereof, as well as all component parts on board, detached from or torn from the space object.[212]

The fact that the Convention, in this connection, lays emphasis on the act of launching, albeit this term includes also attempted launching, gives rise to the question whether there is a temporal scope of the concept of a 'space object'. Up to a point the question asked by the Swedish delegate shows that there comes a time when a space object ceases to be a space object, for instance, when it has become an installation on a celestial body.[213] Likewise, one may ask when does an object begin to be a space object, within the meaning of the Convention? From this point of view, the first part of the joint proposal submitted by Argentina, Belgium, and France, apart from other considerations, may already be said to be unsatisfactory inasmuch as it has no such temporal limits. For the purposes of the Convention, presumably damage caused by the explosion of a space rocket in a hangar is not covered by Article II. From this point of view, perhaps one of the clues to what the Convention has in mind is to be found in its Article VII(b). In the light of this article, the view may be put forward that a space object, whatever this may be,

---

[208] See Cheng, 'The United Nations and Outer Space', loc. cit. in n. 12 above, at pp. 259 ff., under 'Blind Spot in the Sky' [Ch. 6 above, s. IV]. See also B. Cheng, 'Legal Implications of Remote Sensing from Space', in European Space Agency, *Earth Observation from Space and Management of Planetary Resources'*, *Proceedings of an International Conference held at Toulouse 6–11 March 1978*, ESA SP–134 (1978), p. 597, under 2.3.1 [cf. Chs. 14 and 22, s. IV.A below].

[209] See ss. V.B above, and VI and VII below.

[210] A/AC.105/C.2/SR.132–51, p. 24 (SR.138).   [211] Ibid., p. 25 (SR.138).

[212] PUOS/C.2/70/WG.1/CRP.16 (reproduced A/AC.105/85, Annex I, p. 16). See Australia, A/AC.105/C.2/SR.106, p. 61, on the absence of any need for a definition, except to specify inclusion of component parts, etc. Cf. also United Kingdom, ibid., p. 56; Czechoslovakia, ibid., p. 57; Canada, ibid., pp. 58–9; India, ibid, p. 59.

[213] See n. 209 above.

is a space object within the meaning of the Convention only when it is in its operational state, i.e., 'from the time of its launching (or attempted launching) or at any stage thereafter until its descent', including at the one end the 'planned launching' phase and at the other end the 'recovery phase'.[214]

Finally, it is of interest to find that in the opinion of the United States, the Convention applies equally to military space objects.[215]

VI. Basis of Liability

It is generally assumed that under the 1963 Space Declaration[216], and the 1967 Space Treaty,[217] a State's liability for damage caused by space objects is absolute and not dependent on fault.[218] Insofar as surface damage on the surface of the earth is concerned, this would be in line with the 1952 Rome Convention on Damage Caused by Foreign Aircraft to Third Parties on the Surface.[219] The Belgian, United States, and Hungarian drafts were all agreed on the subject, except that the Hungarian draft initially excluded natural disaster.[220] However, in the summer of 1968 Hungary withdrew the exception of natural disaster.[221]

Subject to further discussions on the actual cosmographical scope of these provisions,[222] there was no great difficulty in reaching agreement in principle on the present Article II in 1967,[223] Articles III[224] and VI[225] in 1968, and Article IV in 1970[226]. The content of the relevant articles is summarized in Table XI.2.

---

[214] See s. V.A.1 and n. 185 above, and the text containing a temporal definition mentioned therein; see also Ch. 18 below: Definitional Issues.

[215] See US Senate, *Report from the Committee on Foreign Relations on the Convention on International Liability for Damage Caused by Space Objects*, 92d Congres, 2d Session, Executive Report No. 92–38 (1972), p. 7.

[216] See s. III.B above.   [217] See s. III.D above.

[218] *Pace* Professor Piradov, USSR, A/AC.105/PV.85–90, pp. 82–3 (PV.87); see nn. 15–17, and further s. III.D above, particularly *in fine*, and n. 219 below.

[219] 310 UNTS, p. 181; ICAO Doc. 7364; Cmd. 8886 (1953).

[220] Belgian draft, A/AC.105/C.2/L.2/Rev.3, Art. 1 (b); USA draft, A/AC.105/C.2/L.19 and L.58, Art. II (1); Hungarian draft,m A/AC.105/C.2/L.10, Art. VI, and Rev.1, Art. III. All three drafts were, moreover, in general agreement on following the various nuclear liability conventions rather than the 1952 Rome Convention on the grounds for exemption from liability, i.e., wilful misconduct rather than mere negligence on the part of the victim. See nn. 226 and 229 below.

[221] A/AC.105/C.2/SR.91, p. 3.   [222] See s. V.B above.

[223] *Report of the Legal Sub-Committee on the Work of its Sixth Session* (19.6–14.7.67), A/AC.105/37, para. 17, under 'Field of Application, para. 2.'

[224] *Report of the Legal Sub-Committee on the Work of its Seventh Session* (4–28.6.68), A/AC.105/45, para. 10 under 'Field of Application'. See further A/AC.105/C.2/SR.91, 92 and 94 *passim*.

[225] *Report of the Legal Sub-Committee on the Work of its Seventh Session*, loc. cit. in n. 224 above, para. 10.

[226] The relevant precedents for Art. VI(1) are the nuclear conventions rather than the 1952 Rome Convention on Surface Damage by aircraft; see nn. 219–20 above, and 229 below. See also *Report of the Legal Sub-Committee on the Work of its Ninth Session* (8.6–3.7.70), A/AC.105/85, paras. 20, 27, and A/AC.105/C.2/L.77 (reproduced ibid., Annex I, p. 4).

Table XI.2 BASIS OF LIABILITY UNDER THE LIABILITY CONVENTION

ABSOLUTE LIABILITY of launching State of space objects in respect of	**FAULT LIABILITY** of launching State of space objects for own fault or fault of persons for whom launching State responsible, in respect of
(1) damage caused *on the surface of the earth* (Art. II), or (2) damage caused to *aircraft in flight* (Art. II). In both instances, either (a) directly (Art. II), or (b) as a result of damage having been caused to a space object of another launching State or to persons or property on board such a space object (Art. IV(1)(a)).	damage caused *elsewhere than on the surface of the earth* (1) to a space object of another launching State (Art. III), or (2) to persons or property on board such a space object (Art. III). In both instances, either (a) directly (Art. III), or
Exoneration to the extent to which damage resulted wholly or partially from: (a) gross negligence, or (b) act or omission done with intent to cause damage, on the part of the claimant State or natural or juridical persons it represents (Art. VI(1)). *No exoneration*, however, if damage resulted from activities of launching State contrary to international law including, in particular, the United Nations Charter and the 1967 Space Treaty (Art. VI(2)).	(b) as a result of damage having been caused to a space object of yet another launching State or to persons or property on board such a space object (in such an event, the fault of either of the two States involved in the first incident or of persons for whom either of these two States is responsible [227] renders both States jointly and severally liable to the first-mentioned third State, the space object of which is damaged in the subsequent incident) (Art. IV(1), (1)(b) and (2)).

In the event of damage being caused elsewhere than on the surface of the earth to a space object of the launching State or to persons or property on board such a space object by a space object of another launching State, the latter shall be liable only if the damage is due to its fault or the fault of persons

[227] See s. V.B above.

for whom it is responsible.'[228] Article III is ambiguous. On the one hand, it can mean that a launching State is liable only to the extent of its fault. On the other hand, it can also mean that a State becomes liable for the totality of the damage as soon as it has been established that there is fault on its part, and there is a causal connection between this fault and the damage. In the event that the second alternative is the proper interpretation, there are two exceptions. First, if it is a case of joint and several liability under Article IV(1), then the two launching States in their relations *inter se* are liable, under Article IV(2), only 'to the extent to which they were at fault' (and 'if the extent of the fault of each of these States cannot be established, the burden of compensation shall be proportioned equally between them'). Secondly, under Article VI(1), the launching State may be able to gain exoneration in whole or in part. The express provisions on the subject found in Articles IV(2) and VI(1) would tend to support the latter interpretation, even though this might well not have been the intention of those who were drafting Article III, if they had turned their mind to the question.

Both paragraphs of Article VI contain ambiguities. In paragraph 1,[229] it is uncertain whether those encompassed in the phrase 'natural or juridical persons' whom a claimant State represents include all persons for whom, under Article VI of the 1967 Space Treaty, a claimant State may be responsible,[230] or only 'natural or juridical persons' in respect of damage caused to whom by a space object a claimant State is presenting a claim under the terms of the Convention. The Convention probably means the latter, but the former interpretation may be more consistent with Article VI of the 1967 Space Treaty.

In paragraph 2, the Convention first of all fails to distinguish between general international law and treaties. Secondly, by this provision, the Convention makes the relevant provisions of the United Nations Charter and the 1967 Space Treaty binding even on those States and participating international organizations which are not parties to them. Thirdly, the phrase 'in particular' suggests that there may be other treaties that have to be observed.

VII. Joint and Several Liability

A. Joint Launching

As has been mentioned before,[231] Article I(c) of the Liability Convention, following the example of Article VII of the 1967 Space Treaty, defines the 'launching State' as:

[228] In this connection, attention is drawn to Article VI of the 1967 Space Treaty, under which contracting parties are internationally responsible for 'national activities in outer space'; see s. III.D above, and Cheng, 'The 1967 Space Treaty', loc. cit. in n. 12 above, s. IV.6 [Ch. 9 above, s. V.F: International responsibility; see also Chs. 23 and 24 below].

[229] Cf. B. Cheng, 'Wilful Misconduct: From Warsaw to The Hague and from Brussels to Paris', 2 *AASL* (1977), p. 55.   [230] See n. 228 above, and n. 236 below.

[231] See s. V.A.5 above.

(i)   a State which launches or procures the launching of a space object;
(ii)   a State from whose territory or facility a space object is launched.

Although there appeared to have been some hesitation on the subject at one time in the negotiations,[232] by the end of the ninth session of the Legal Sub-Committee in 1970, agreement had already been reached on the present Article V(3):

A State from whose territory or facility a space object is launched shall be regarded as a participant in a joint launching. [233]

But in the light of Article I(c), this is either incomplete or tautological. However, in view of the existence of earlier proposals that the liability of States whose territory or facility had been used for the launching of a space object might be only secondary,[234] it is perhaps just as well to have an express provision to make the position clear.

What applies to Article I(c)(ii) must apply *a fortiori* to Article I(c)(i). Consequently, where there are four States falling into these four categories of launching States engaged in a launching, they are all launching States and each must be liable as such under the Convention, with the result that the principle of joint and several liability is already implicit in this all-embracing definition of the launching State.

Article V(3) makes this explicit; for it subjects all the four categories of the launching State, as defined under Article I(c), expressly to Article V(1) which provides:

Whenever two or more States jointly launch a space object, they shall be jointly and severally liable for any damage caused.

Of course, Article V(1) applies not only to the four categories of the launching State as such, but also to all the States which may find themselves within each of these four categories. In this sense, there is no reason why Article V would not apply to any contracting party to the Convention which is a member of any international organization that engages in any form of 'launching' within the meaning of Article I(c) and thus render that contracting party liable for any damage caused.[235]

The Liability Convention does not deal specifically with the responsibility of contracting States to the 1967 Space Treaty for national activities in space

---

[232] *Report of the Legal Sub-Committee on the Work of its Eighth Session* (9.6–4.7.69), A/AC.105/58, para. 26, n. 3; cf. the French proposal, A/AC.105/C.2/L.36/Rev.2, and the U.K. amendment, A/AC.105/C.2/L.38, and discussions thereon, A/AC.105/C.2/SR.91, 92, 95–97, and 104 *passim*.

[233] Art. V(3) of approved draft articles, *Report of the Legal Sub-Committee on the Work of its Ninth Session (8.6–3.7.70)*, A/AC.105/85, p. 8. Based apparently on a Working Paper submitted by the USSR, PUOS/C.2/70/WG.1/CRP.17 (reproduced A/AC.105/85, Annex I, p. 16). Cf., however, comment by Argentina, A/AC.105/C.2/SR.132–51, p. 39 (SR.143).

[234] See text to nn. 130 and 232 above.   [235] See s. V.A. 5 above.
[236] See nn. 228 and 230 above.

under Article VI of the Space Treaty.[236] But by making the State from the territory of which a space object is launched a launching State jointly and severally liable for any damage which such an object may cause, the Liability Convention covers all launchings from territories of the contracting parties, whether the authors of the launching are individuals or institutions, authorized or unauthorized, official or private, national or foreign, and the launching intentional or purely accidental. Moreover, it would not be difficult to argue that the concept of territory in this context extends to ships, aircraft or even spacecraft registered in a contracting State or otherwise belonging to it, whenever they are not under the territorial jurisdiction of another State.[237] Alternatively, they come under the category of facilities from which space objects are being launched.

Under Article V (2):

A launching State which has paid compensation for damage shall have the right to present a claim for indemnification to other participants in the joint launching. The participants in a joint launching may conclude agreements regarding the apportioning among themselves of the financial obligation in respect of which they are jointly and severally liable. Such agreements shall be without prejudice to the right of the State sustaining damage to seek the entire compensation due under this Convention from any or all of the launching States which are jointly and severally liable.[238]

In this connection, mention may be made to Article XXIII of the Convention the purpose of which is partly to facilitate any such agreements among the States concerned.[239] Article XXIII provides:

1. The provisions of this Convention shall not affect other international agreements in force in so far as relations between the States Parties to such agreements are concerned.
2. No provision of this Convention shall prevent States from concluding international agreements reaffirming, supplementing or extending its provisions.

B. *Damage Jointly Caused by Two or More Space Objects*

Reference has previously been made to Article IV of the Convention,[240] under which where one space object causes damage to another space object elsewhere than on the surface of the earth, both States concerned become jointly

---

[237] See nn. 131 and 193 above.

[238] This was derived from a USSR Working Paper, PUOS/C.2/70/WG.1/CRP.17 (reproduced A/AC.105/85, Annex I, p. 16), that linked it specifically to the State from whose territory or facility a space object was launched. See n. 233 above.

[239] Cf. Argentina, A/AC.105/C.2/SR.132–51, p. 87 (SR.150): 'He welcomed the inclusion as art. XIII [present Art. XXIII] of the Belgian proposal in document A/AC.105/C.2/L.72, which partly met Argentina's problem concerning the position of countries making available their territory or facilities under United Nations auspices. He would, however, have preferred a more explicit text'. It is evident that this article is intended very much to cover such cases.

[240] See s. VI above.

and severally liable to third States in respect of any damage which such third States may thereby have suffered.[241]

Paragraph 2 of the Article further provides that, without prejudice to the right of third States, the 'burden of compensation for the damage shall be apportioned between the first two States in accordance with the extent to which they were at fault; if the extent of the fault of each of these States cannot be established, the burden of compensation shall be apportioned equally between them.'

As regards the scope of Article IV(1), it has been suggested that presumably 'that could relate solely to cases of collision.'[242] Support for this view might be found in the fact that the following joint proposal submitted by Argentina, Belgium, France, Italy, and Mexico failed to be adopted:

The expression 'damage caused by a space object' means damage caused:
    (a) by any space object;
    (b) by any person on board a space object;
    (c) by any component part of a space object, parts on board, detached or torn from the space object, or the launch vehicle or parts thereof.[243]

But it might also be said that paragraph (c) is already covered by Article I(d) of the Convention, and paragraph (b) is subsumed under the concept of the space object, with the result that Article IV(1) of the Convention extends beyond mere collision to include cases where, for example, one space object is damaged by laser beams released from another space object either deliberately by persons on board or accidentally without human intervention simply because of a fault in the equipment on board the latter space object. Physical contact or collision between the two space objects or components thereof is not required.

However, Article IV would not seem applicable to the State which from the ground or from an aircraft causes, otherwise than by an object launched into space, the space object of another to fall, thereby causing damage to the space object of a third State in outer space, to an aircraft of a third State in flight or to property of a third State on the surface of the earth. The second State, if without fault, would not be liable either to the State of the third space object, but would incur absolute liability towards the State of the damaged aircraft and the third State on the surface of the earth. The international responsibility of the first State would have to be based on Article VI of the 1967 Space Treaty and general international law.

---

[241] The basis of liability differs depending on where the damage to the third State is caused: see s. VI above.

[242] Italy, A/AC.105/C.2/SR.132–51, p. 83 (SR.149).

[243] PUOS/C.2/70/WG.1/CRP.18/Rev.1 (reproduced A/AC.105/85, Annex I, p. 16).

VIII. Measure of Compensation

A. Applicable Law

The question of the applicable law was one of the most intractable problems in the drafting of the Liability Convention, together with compulsory third-party settlement of disputes, with which it was closely related.[244] The United States draft provided that 'compensation . . . shall be determined in accordance with applicable principles of international law, justice and equity.'[245] Under the Belgian draft, however, compensation should be 'assessed under the national law of the person injured (*lex patriae*), or if not, under applicable principles of international law,'[246] and under the Hungarian draft, 'a claim for damage may be advanced on the ground of loss of profits and moral damage whenever compensation for such damage is provided for by the law of the State liable for damage in general.'[247] A further system of applicable law was suggested by France, namely, the law of the place where the damage was caused (*lex loci*),[248] which, insofar as any national law was deemed applicable, was soon recognized by all the non-Soviet bloc delegates in the Legal Sub-Committee, with the addition of Romania,[249] as preferable to any other.[250] All these States, including Romania, were equally firm against the application of the law of the respondent State. After the New Delhi consultations, India proposed the following compromise:

> If there is agreement between the claimant and the respondent on the applicable law regarding the amount of compensation payable under this Convention, then that law should be applied. If the claimant and the respondent do not agree on the applicable law, the amount of compensation shall be determined in accordance with international law, taking into consideration the law of the claimant State and, where considered appropriate, the law of the respondent State. In case of conflict, international law shall prevail.[251]

Soviet bloc States other than Romania, which until then all insisted on the Hungarian draft, were prepared to accept the Indian proposal as a compro-

---

[244] See ss. III.F.2 ff. above.   [245] A/AC.105/C.2/L.19 and L.58, Art. IV.
[246] A/AC.105/C.2/L.7/Rev.3, Art. 2.
[247] A/AC.105/C.2/L.10/Rev.1 and Corr. 1, L.24 and Add. 1, Art. II.
[248] A/AC.105/C.2/SR.91, p. 8.
[249] A/AC.105/C.2/SR.100, p. 4; ibid./SR.116, p. 10; A/AC.105/PV.70-8, p. 131 (PV.76).
[250] E.g., United Kingdom, A/AC.105/C.2/SR.99, p. 10; Sweden, ibid./SR.100, p. 5; Italy, ibid./SR.100, pp. 5 and 10; Australia, ibid./SR.100, pp. 7-8; United Kingdom, ibid./SR.100, p. 9; Iran, ibid./SR.117, p. 2; Japan, ibid./SR.117, p. 9; Sweden, ibid./SR.117, p. 9; United Kingdom, ibid.,/SR.117, p. 11; Brazil, ibid./SR.118, p. 4; France, ibid./SR.121, p. 3; United Kingdom, ibid./SR.121, p. 10; Sweden, ibid./SR.121, p. 11; Austria, Belgium, Canada, Italy, Japan and Sweden in joint proposal, A/AC.105/C.2/L.62; Belgium (as compromise in joint proposal), A/AC.105/C.2/SR.122, p. 2; Sweden, ibid./SR.122, pp. 8-9, Romania, A/AC.105/PV.70-78, p. 131 (PV.76).
[251] A/AC.105/C.2/L.32/Rev.2, Art. VI.

mise,[252] but realizing that the Indian draft, especially with its reference to the law of the respondent, merely papered over the differences between the two sides without settling any of them, the other members of the Legal Sub-Committee, including Romania, were not ready to do so.[253]

The problem of applicable law, as more than one delegate had pointed out, was in reality a question of the extent to which victims of damage caused by space objects were to be compensated,[254] to which question that of the applicable law was merely a way of arriving at the answer. As the perceptive Lebanese delegate to the Outer Space Committee rightly said, this was a 'practical' matter. Different States chose different laws because they were pursuing different objectives. The Lebanese delegate, for instance, was saying, with a disarming frankness, that, from the standpoint of an under-developed country, which law was to apply—international law, the law of the claimant State, the law of the launching State—was really immaterial. What he wanted was simply the law that was the most favourable to the victim State.[255]

It was similarly for very pragmatic reasons that the Soviet Union, supported by its friends, insisted, for a number of years, on the inclusion of the law of the launching State. As a space power, it wished to avoid, in case of an accident, paying more than what it considered necessary. In order to justify their stand, the Soviet Union and its friends sometimes gave the matter the appearance of a high political content by constantly harping on the differences in 'juridical, economic and social systems' and the principle of State sovereignty, almost as if the matter was one which went to the heart of socialist economic and social systems.[256] It is a measure of the exasperation which some members of the Outer Space Committee were evidently feeling that the United States delegate, at one point, called the Soviet line of argument 'utter nonsense'.[257] He drew attention to the fact that, although the legal and social systems of Romania and the United States were as different as could be imagined, he had no difficulty in agreeing with the Romanian representative.[258]

The truth lies probably somewhere in between. On the one hand, the problem was not unconnected with differences in national laws. The plain fact is, as Soviet bloc States freely admitted, 'although [immaterial] . . . damage was

---

[252] E.g., USSR, A/AC.105/C.2/SR.118, p. 5; Hungary, ibid./SR.120, p. 10; ibid./SR.121, pp. 5–6; Bulgaria, ibid./SR.122, p. 4; USSR, ibid./SR.122, p. 10; Hungary, A/AC.105/PV.70–8, p. 123 (PV.76).

[253] E.g., United Kingdom, A/AC.105/C.2/SR.117, p. 11; Austria, ibid./SR.121, p. 7; Canada, ibid./SR.121, p. 9; United Kingdom, ibid./SR.121, p. 10; Sweden, ibid./SR.121, p. 11. See also n. 249 above.

[254] Cf. USSR, A/AC.105/PV.70–8, p. 96 (PV.75); Austria, A/AC.105/C.2/SR.132–51, p. 73 (SR.148).

[255] A/AC.105/PV.70–8, p. 102 (PV.75).

[256] Cf. Poland, A/AC.105/C.2/SR.132–51, p. 64 (SR.148); USSR, ibid., pp. 71–2 (SR.148); Mongolia, ibid., p. 74 (SR.148) Hungary, ibid., p. 75 (SR.149); USSR, A/AC.105/PV.85–90, p. 86 (PV.87).

[257] A/AC.105/PV.91–97, p. 75 (PV.95).   [258] Ibid., p. 76 (PV.95).

awarded in most laws, some socialist laws did not recognize it.'[259] On the other hand, this was not a difference which divided 'socialist' from 'bourgeois' legal systems. The English case of *Boys* v. *Chaplin*[260] shows that such variation in rules on measure of compensation may be quite widespread. In the *Boys Case*, there was a possibility of applying either the law of Malta or the law of England when deciding the question of damages. The law of Malta also did not compensate immaterial damage. If it had been applied, the plaintiff, who was injured in a motor car accident in Malta, would have recovered only £53. By applying English law, the court awarded him an additional £2,250. The case thus also illustrates the appreciable difference in practical terms which the applicable law can make.

Now the position of the Soviet bloc States was simply they were unwilling to pay compensation for such 'moral or immaterial damage', whatever happened.[261] Hence the Hungarian draft which made its payment dependent on the law of the respondent State.[262] Answering criticisms of the Soviet position, the Soviet delegate to the Outer Space Committee said in 1970:

I refer to the argument according to which the reference to the law of the respondent State is allegedly undesirable because in different countries there is a different standard of living. In other words, as we understand this argument, if the standard of living in the country which has suffered damage is lower than the standard of living in the respondent State, then the State that has suffered damage cannot claim to the same extent than as if the case were reversed, if the citizens of the respondent State were to be compensated.[263]

What the Soviet Union was complaining about in effect was that there would be a lack of reciprocity. If one were to forget for the moment the argument about the standard of living and come back to the difference in the law on damages, one can see that the Soviet contention is in a sense true. Let us assume, merely for the purpose of illustration, that the law of Malta on damages is the same as that of the Soviet Union, and the law of England the same as the United States or Wisconsin. Let us assume, further, that a United States space vehicle has injured a Soviet citizen in Leningrad, and a Soviet space vehicle has injured a United States citizen in Wisconsin,[264] each causing exactly the same amount of damage as was suffered by the plaintiff in *Boys* v. *Chaplin*. The Soviet delegate would be perfectly correct in saying that if one were to apply the *lex loci* and to ignore the law of the launching State, the Soviet citizen would receive only £53, while the United States citizen would receive £2,313.

---

[259] Hungary, A/AC.105/C.2/SR.99, p. 8.
[260] [1971] A.C.356. See also n. 272 below for fuller details on this case.
[261] See USSR, A/AC.105/C.2/SR.100, pp. 6–7.   [262] See n. 247 above.
[263] A/AC.105/PV.70–8, p. 97(PV.75).
[264] Example used by US delegate, ibid., p. 65 (PV.73).

But this, as the United Kingdom delegate had tried to explain in words of one syllable, would have been no more and no less than what the injured parties would normally have expected in all their fields of tort law, be they accidents on the road or in the air, in the woods of the Adirondacks or by the Moscow river.[265] The Belgian delegate was more outspoken and said that the idea of applying the law of the defendant State in such cases was 'contrary to the most elementary common sense.'[266] Indeed, it was not exactly certain how the Soviet bloc proposal was to work in practice. In the hypothetical case given above, was the Soviet Union saying that both victims should receive only £53? Under the Hungarian proposal, the answer must be a simple yes.

This was precisely what all the other States were afraid of; for it would mean, for most of them, that their own nationals, if injured, would be grossly under-compensated. What was wanted by them almost unanimously was integral reparation for any damage caused, otherwise described as *restitutio in integrum*,[267] full compensation, making the victim whole again, or putting him back in the situation in which in all probability he would have been, had the accident not occurred.[268] But many of these States, some perhaps persuaded by the eloquence of the Belgian delegate,[269] held the erroneous idea that the matter had little to do with public international law and that, in order to achieve their objective, private international law dictated the choice of the *lex loci delicti commissi*. A number of them committed the further mistake of either believing that public international law was, in this regard, vague and deficient,[270] or thinking that the fact space law was still 'embryonic'[271] had anything to do with the matter, as if the problem was specific to space law.

---

[265] Ibid., pp. 70 ff. (PV.74).   [266] Ibid., p. 21 (PV.70).

[267] *Pace* Roman law, in which the term had a very technical meaning. To be distinguished also from the restoration of the *status quo ante*, which merely restores the person to the position in which he found himself prior to the event in question, though one find that the two phrases were and are frequently used as if they were interchangeable. The difference becomes immediately apparent if one were to consider the appropriate reparation due to a fisherman whose fishing boat was illegally detained from the beginning to the end of the fishing season. To restore the *status quo ante*, if suffices merely to return the boat to him, but this would hardly make him whole again. See further Cheng, *General Principles of Law*, Ch. 9: 'The Principle of Integral Reparation'. Cf. text to nn. 275 and 288 below.

[268] E.g., USA, A/AC.105/PV.70–78, p. 65 (PV.75); Canada, A/AC.105/C.2/SR.132–51, p. 49 (SR.146); Sweden, ibid., p. 50 (SR.146); Mexico, ibid., p. 53 (SR.147); France, ibid., p. 57 (SR.147); Italy, ibid., p. 58 (SR.147); Romania, ibid., p. 59 (SR.147); Iran, ibid., p. 60 (SR.147); Japan, ibid., p. 62 (SR.148).

[269] Cf., e.g., A/AC.105/PV.70–8, pp. 20 ff. (PV.70).

[270] For example, Belgium, A/AC.105/C.2/SR.92, p. 13; United Kingdom, ibid./SR.99, p. 10 (opposite view held subsequently); Belgium, ibid./SR.117, p. 6; Argentina, ibid./SR.122, p. 7; France, ibid./SR.123, p. 3; Belgium, A/AC.105/PV.63, p. 4; France, A/AC.105/PV.85–90, p. 30 (PV.86); India, A/AC.105/C.2/SR.152–69, p. 117 (SR.166); *contra*: United Kingdom, A/AC.105/C.2/SR.100, p. 9; ibid./SR.121, p. 10; A/AC.105/C.2/SR.152–69, p. 92 (SR.163); Italy, A/AC.105/C.2/SR.132–51, p. 81 (SR.149); A/AC.105/C.2/SR.152–69, pp. 31 ff. (SR.156); 99 ff. (SR.164); 121 (SR.167).

[271] E.g., France, A/AC.105/C.2/SR.121, p. 3; cf. comment by United Kingdom, ibid., p. 10. See 'The Extraterrestrial Application of International Law', loc. cit. in n. 12 above [Ch. 5 above].

In the first place, this school of thought ignored the fact, even if one were to follow the technique and terminology of conflict of laws, that, in this case, public international law was the *lex fori*, and the answer to the question of the applicable law must be sought *in concreto* in public international law which has its own rules of private international law, and not merely *in abstracto* by reference to comparative conflict of laws.

Secondly, from the standpoint of comparative conflict of laws, the *lex loci* solution rather oversimplified matters. *Boys* v. *Chaplin*,[272] which seems an eminently reasonable decision, shows that in the modern world which is far more mobile than of yore, there may be—it is accepted that this probably occurs only in exceptional circumstances—connecting factors even more relevant than the *locus delicti* for the purpose of bringing about integral reparation.

Thirdly, as regards the adequacy of public international law in dealing with the problem, it suffices to point out, as the writer had occasion to do in 1970 while discussing the draft convention,[273] that international courts and tribunals have, in modern times, in many hundred of cases since the Jay Treaty arbitrations of 1794, never experienced any difficulty in assessing damages according to international law, and that anyone who has doubts on the amount of material available has only to consult Dr Majorie Whiteman's three monumental volumes on *Damages in International Law*, totalling 2,242 pages, published between 1937 and 1943.[274]

In fact, the Permanent Court of International Justice, in the *Chorzów Factory Case* (Merits) (1928), gave one of the best known expositions of the principle of integral reparation:

The essential principle contained in the actual notion of an illegal act—a principle which seems to be established by international practice and in particular by the decisions of arbitral tribunals—is that reparation must, as far as possible, wipe out all the consequences of the illegal act and re-establish the situation which would, in all probability, have existed if that act had not been committed. Restitution in kind, or, if this is not possible, payment of a sum corresponding to the value which a restitution in kind would bear; the award, if need be, of damages for loss sustained which would not be covered by restitution in kind or payment in place of it—such are the principles which should serve to determine the amount of compensation due for an act contrary to international law.[275]

---

[272] See n. 260 above. In this case, both parties were normally resident in England. The court's decision to apply English law in regard to the head of damages was affirmed by the Court of Appeal and the House of Lords.

[273] B. Cheng, 'Liability for Spacecraft', 23 *CLP* (1970), p. 216, at p. 232.

[274] Washington DC: GPO. See also Cheng, *General Principles of Law*, Ch. 9: The Principle of Integral Reparation, at pp. 233–40.

[275] PCIJ: A.17, p. 29. It is submitted that, without prejudice to the question of the characterization of damage caused by space objects, the principle of integral reparation applicable to international unlawful acts is equally applicable to it and to other cases of compensation for no-fault liability, whether absolute or strict, unless otherwise stipulated. It will be seen that this was the conclusion at which the Committee eventually arrived. See text to nn. 288–93 below, and Art. XII of the Convention.

Mention has previously been made of the original United States proposal under which compensation was to be determined in accordance with applicable principles of international law, justice and equity.[276] But the United States later switched over to the *lex loci* school,[277] on the ground that reference to international law was no longer a viable solution, because the Soviet Union had in fact destroyed its usefulness as an instrument of providing for prompt and equitable compensation by readily agreeing to the international law standard only with the cynical understanding that 'international law is merely what individual States Members of the international community says it is'.[278] Matters were not helped by such purely verbal compromises as the Indian proposal in which the laws of the claimant State and of the respondent State figured alongside of international law without any real consensus as to what it all meant.[279] The same applies to the following proposal of Belgium,[280] in which there was apparently a certain amount of Soviet interest:[281]

The indemnity which the respondent State will have to pay for damages in application of the present Convention will be determined in conformity with the agreed law between the claimant State and the respondent State. In the absence of such agreement the indemnity will be determined in conformity with international law and the law of the respondent State or the law of the claimant State at the choice of the latter.

To go back to the hypothetical example of the double accident in Leningrad and in Wisconsin,[282] the Belgian proposal means that not only will the United States citizen be able to recover £2,313, but the Soviet government will also be entitled to have United States or Wisconsin law applied to the case and receive £2,313 for the Soviet victim, notwithstanding the fact that, had the Soviet citizen suffered exactly the same injury because of the wheel of an aeroplane falling on him, or simply in a road accident in Leningrad, he would, under Soviet law, have received only £53. Such a result, while it would fulfil the objective of the Lebanese delegate if he meant by the maximum amount for the victim not just the maximum the victim normally expect to get,[283] but the maximum in absolute terms, would, however, offend the principle of integral reparation—assuming that one wishes to accept this principle as controlling; for it is part of this principle that the reparation for an unlawful act should not be allowed to become a source of enrichment for the injured person.[284]

However, this does not mean that, in no circumstances, in such a case, under the principle of integral reparation, would the law of the launching State be applicable. But it would be applicable by an international tribunal, in

---

[276] See n. 245 above.
[277] A/AC.105/PV.70–8, pp. 62–8 (PV.73); see also Italy, ibid., p. 127 (PV.76).
[278] A/AC.105/PV.91–7, p. 75 (PV.95).   [279] See n. 251 above.
[280] A/AC.105/PV.70–8, p. 115 (PV.76).
[281] Cf. USA, A/AC.105/C.2/SR.152–69, p. 10 (SR.152).
[282] See n. 264 above.   [283] See n. 255 above.
[284] See Cheng, *General Principles of Law*, at p. 236.

pursuance of the principle of integral reparation, not simply because the victim or claimant State requests it, but only if it could be shown that the victim was subject to the law of the launching State in this matter on other grounds and, therefore, entitled to the higher compensation which the law of the launching State provided for. Consequently, in not applying the law of the launching State, the victim would in fact have been deprived of the additional compensation which he would have received, and therefore not made whole. The possibility of such a situation arising cannot be entirely excluded.[285]

Unfortunately, the atmosphere, at one stage, was such that it was difficult for members of the Committee even to take one another's proposals at their face value. Thus the Soviet delegate at one point complained: 'On the question of the applicable law, the draft says one thing, whereas the sponsor says something that is quite different.'[286] That might well have been the reason why, especially in the absence of effective procedures for third-party settlement of disputes, the non-Soviet bloc States declined to entertain the following joint proposal put forward by Bulgaria, Hungary and the USSR in 1970:

The compensation which the respondent State shall be required to pay should be determined in accordance with international law having in view the aim to compensate according to the Convention the entire damage caused to a contracting party or to natural or juridical persons in respect of which this contracting party may present a claim.

If there is agreement on any other applicable law between the claimant and the respondent, then that law should be applied.[287]

Without direct reference to the three-power proposal and its mention of 'the entire damage', the following account by the Austrian delegate of the informal discussions that were then going on would seem to be related to them:

The idea had been put forward that the term 'full compensation' should be used rather than 'full reparation' and that the victim should be restored to the physical condition which had existed prior to the date of the damage [i.e., *status quo ante* (annotation added)], instead of restoring it to the condition that would have existed if the damage had not occurred [i.e., *restitutio in integrum* (annotation added)]. Many delegations—including his own—had objected to that idea because it excluded compensation for indirect damage, *lucrum cessans*, interest, etc. Once again no common ground had been found.[288]

---

[285] See n. 328 below, and text thereto. Cf. B. Cheng, 'The Rationale of Compensation for Expropriation', 44 *Grotius Society Transactions* (1958, 1959), p. 267, at p. 281, re non-discrimination. In fact, as pointed out there, ibid., pp. 289–91, the *Norwegian Shipowners Claims* (1922) (2 *HCR*, p. 40) can be regarded possibly as a case of the application of the national standard, when it is higher than the international standard. However, when transposed to the context of the Liability Convention, it shold not be automatically assumed that a national standard intended for domestic application is *ipso facto* applicable extraterritorially outside the country. See further under s. X.d below, and nn. 260 and 272 above.

[286] A/AC.105/PV.70–8, p. 97 (PV.75).

[287] A/AC.105/C.2/L.75 (reproduced A/AC.105/85, Annex I, p. 4).

[288] A/AC.105/C.2/SR.132–51, p. 73 (SR.148). See further n. 267 above.

Having by then become rather wary of simple verbal formulae with possible hidden meanings and uncontrollable glosses, Argentina, Canada, Japan, and Sweden decided in the summer of 1970 to resolve the matter by—to use the words of the Japanese delegate—spelling out in their proposal 'the essentials of the substantive principle which should serve as the basis for the measure of compensation.'[289] The sponsors were soon joined by Australia, Belgium, Italy, and the United Kingdom.[290] The eight-power proposal, in which one can clearly discern echoes of the *Chorzów Factory Case*[291] and antecedents of the present Article XII, was worded as follows:

The compensation which a launching State shall be liable to pay for damage under this Convention shall be based on the rule that each person, natural or juridical, State or international organization on whose behalf a claim is presented be restored in full to the condition equivalent to that which would have existed if the damage had not occurred. In giving effect to this rule account shall be taken of the law of the place where the damage occurred and of relevant principles of international law.

Although France did not formally become a co-sponsor, it firmly supported both the principle and the objective of the eight-power proposal. Its representative said:

As to the applicable law, his delegation could accept that there should be no reference to national law, or even to international law and the principle of justice and equity, provided that the convention included a clause to the effect that compensation would be based on the principle of fully restoring the victim to a situation equivalent to that which would have existed if the damage had not occurred. That, in his delegation's view, was the heart of the matter.[292]

It will be recalled that on this topic the majority in the Outer Space Committee eventually appealed to the General Assembly on the question of principle and was able to obtain an explicit guidance from the General Assembly in the form of resolution 2733B in which the General Assembly endorsed the view that the Convention should include provisions ensuring the payment of a full measure of compensation to victims.[293]

On the technical question as to how this was to be achieved, although Italy was one of the co-sponsors of the eight-power proposal, it remained convinced of the advantage of using the purely international law standard.[294] In

---

[289] Ibid., p. 62 (SR.148); see also Canada, ibid., p. 48 ff. (SR.146); Sweden, ibid., pp. 50 (SR.146), 70 (SR.148).

[290] A/AC.105/C.2/L.74 and Adds. 1 and 2 (reproduced A/AC.105/85, Annex I, p. 3).

[291] See n. 275 above. It should be noted, however, that both the joint proposal and the Liability Convention have failed to include the qualification 'in all probability' so wisely used by the Court in the *Chorzów Factory Case*. See further Cheng, *General Principles of Law*, Ch. 10: 'The Principle of Proximate Causality', pp. 241–53.

[292] A/AC.105/C.2/SR.132–51, p. 57 (SR.147); see also Austria, ibid., p. 72 (SR.148); India, ibid., p. 77 (SR.149).

[293] See s. III.F.5 above.   [294] A/AC.105/C.2/SR.132–51, p. 81 ff. (SR.149).

fact, it would appear that the Italian delegation played an active part in the United States putting forward, after extensive consultations, the following proposal, which omitted all references to national law.[295] It will readily be seen that this proposal is substantially the same as the present Article XII. The only difference consists in deleting from the United States draft the words in round brackets and substituting for them in the final text those in square brackets. The changes are all of a purely drafting nature.

The compensation which the launching State shall be liable to pay for damage under this Convention shall be determined in accordance with international law and the principles of justice and equity, in order to provide (full) [such] reparation in respect of the damage (and thus) [as will] restore the person, natural or juridical, State or international organization on whose behalf the claim is presented to the condition (equivalent to that) which would have existed (had) [if] the damage [had] not occurred.

The United States proposal later, with some of the stylistic changes indicated above already made, became embodied in the joint Belgium, Brazil, and Hungary proposal presented to the tenth session of the Legal Sub-Committee in 1971.[296] From there, with the remainder of the above indicated changes incorporated, it became the present Article XII.

A number of delegations, however, regretted, some in rather strong terms, the omission of references to the *lex loci*.[297] The Italian delegate provided a learned and patient exposition of the law on the subject, assuring his colleagues that international law was fully equipped to achieve the objective stated in the article, and citing as authority *inter alia* the *Chorzów Factory Case*.[298] From this point of view, it is of interest to observe that Hungary, one of the joint sponsors of the three-power proposal that incorporated the United States draft Article XII, in defending the full capability of international law to cope with the problem of measure of damages, cited not only the *Chorzów Factory Case* decided by the Permanent Court of International Justice, but also the *Corfu Channel Case* (Compensation) (1949) decided by the International Court of Justice.[299]

Finally, reference should be made to the last minute amendment of the

[295] A/AC.105/C.2/SR.132–51, p. 79 ff. (SR.149); A/AC.105/PV.85–90, pp. 10 ff., at pp. 17–18 (PV.85).

[296] A/AC.105/C.2/L.79, see n. 83 above.

[297] E.g., India, A/AC.105/PV.85–90, p. 66 (PV.87); Sweden, ibid., pp. 68–9 (PV.87); Romania, ibid., p. 125 (PV.89); Iran, ibid., p. 131 (PV.89); Sweden, A/AC.105/C.2/SR.152–69, p. 27 (SR.155); Japan, ibid., p. 78 (SR.162); Canada, ibid., p. 88 (SR.163); Austria, ibid., pp. 101–2 (SR.164); Sweden, ibid., p. 113 (SR.166); India, ibid., p. 117 (SR.166).

[298] A/AC.105/C.2/SR.152–69, pp. 31 ff. (SR.156); 99 ff. (SR.164); 121 (SR.167). See also Belgium, ibid., pp. 71–4 (SR.162); United Kingdom, ibid., p. 92 (SR.163).

[299] A/AC.105/C.2/SR.152–69, p. 77 (SR.162). The judgment in the *Corfu Channel Case* (Compensation) (1949), between Albania and the United Kingdom *ICJ Rep. 1949*, p. 244, was adopted by 12 votes to 2, the two dissenting votes being those of Judge Krylov of the USSR and the Ad Hoc Judge appointed by Albania, Professor Ečer of Czechoslovakia.

fourth paragraph of the Preamble,[300] based on an Australian proposal, as amended by Belgium. In the words of the Australian delegate:

His delegation had . . . wanted to see in the draft convention some reflection of the spirit of General Assembly resolution 2733B (XXV) and it considered that that had now been achieved through the amendment of the fourth preambular paragraph, which should be read in conjunction with article XII dealing with applicable law.[301]

The present paragraph 4 reads as follows:

Recognising the need to elaborate effective international rules and procedures concerning liability for damage caused by space objects and to ensure, in particular, the prompt payment under the terms of this Convention of a full and equitable measure of compensation to victims of such damage.

Thus starting from the initial United States draft,[302] the question of the applicable law in the Liability Convention has come full circle. However, in the process, the article has probably succeeded in clarifying its own meaning by, on the one hand, cleansing itself of some of the ambiguous glosses which at one time or another sought to attach themselves to it, and, on the other hand, fortifying itself with a statement of its underlying principle both in the article itself and in paragraph 4 of the Preamble. The latter serves also as a reminder of the relation between the measure of compensation and effective procedures for establishing liability and assessing damages.

B. Limitation of Liability

One of the issues which remained unresolved for a long time in the drawing up of the Liability Convention was whether the proposed convention should contain a limit of liability.[303] It was perhaps slightly paradoxical that the United States—which insisted 'as a matter of principle' that INTELSAT (albeit 'an organization which is exploiting outer space for commercial purposes') should not be allowed to limit its liability[304]—should be the only advocate in the Legal Sub-Committee of such a limit.[305] The Soviet bloc attitude was reflected in the evolution of the Hungarian draft which originally provided for

---

[300] See n. 86 above.

[301] A/AC.105/C.2/SR.152–69, p. 115 (SR.166); see alsoo Italy, ibid., p. 121 (SR.167).

[302] See n. 245 above.

[303] See s. III.F.1 and n. 51 above.

[304] See Statement of 8 Sept. 1969 of the United States delegate to the Preparatory Committee of the Plenipotentiary Conference on Definitive Arrangements for INTELSAT (June–July 1969), PC (II)34, p. 4. See further B. Cheng, 'Communications Satellites', 24 *CLP* (1971), p. 211, at pp. 243 ff.; 'INTELSAT: The Definitive Arrangements', *Essays on International Law in Honour of Krishna Rao* (Ed. by M. K. Nawaz) (1975), p. 256 [Ch. 21 below].

[305] See Art. VIII of the United States draft, A/AC.105/C.2/L.19 and L.58. It should, however, be mentioned that the limit was only applicable to claims under the Convention, without prejudice to liability and claim outside the Convention.

the possibility of limitation of liability,[306] but this provision was deleted in 1967.[307]

In support of its proposal, the United States cited the various nuclear liability conventions. Referring to the limits in these conventions, as well as those in its domestic law and bilateral agreements, the United States indicated its readiness to accept the highest of these, namely, $500 million.[308] The United States attitude was doubtless dictated by the need of obtaining the consent of the Senate before the United States President could ratify a treaty of this nature.[309] None of the other delegates in the Legal Sub-Committee favoured limitation of liability, though some was prepared, as a practical concession, to agree to having a limit, provided it were sufficiently high.[310] The United States appears to have dropped its insistence on a limit sometime in 1970.[311]

C. Currency In Which Compensation Is To Be Paid

Article XIII of the Convention provides:

Unless the claimant State and the State from which compensation is due under this Convention agree on another form of compensation, the compensation shall be paid in the currency of the claimant State or, if that State so requests, in the currency of the State from which compensation is due.[312]

This provision appears to have been derived from a Working Paper submitted to the ninth session of the Legal Sub-Committee by Bulgaria and Hungary,[313] and is consistent with the Soviet bloc attitude on applicable law. It also bears some resemblance to the Belgian compromise proposal on applicable law, in which apparently the Soviet Union evinced some interest,[314] and has very much the same effect, *mutatis mutandis*.

This provision did not provoke much discussion in the Legal Sub-Committee. But if the Convention is to work equitably, in the event the claimant chooses to be paid in the currency of the State from which the

---

[306] A/AC.105/C.2/L.10, Art. II(1).   [307] A/AC.105/C.2/L.24/Add. 1.

[308] A/AC.105/C.2/SR.106, p. 2; 'billion' in line 3 should read 'million'. There is an outside limit of $560 million (see s. 170(e) of United States Atomic Energy Act 1954 cf. OECD, *Nuclear Legislations* (1967), p. 77).

[309] Cf. Canada, A/AC.105/C.2/SR.106, pp. 4–5.

[310] E.g., Italy, A/AC.105/C.2/SR.91, p. 12; Canada, ibid./SR.92, p. 12; Australia, ibid./SR.100, p. 8; France, ibid., p. 11 (if favoured by majority); Australia, ibid./SR.116, p. 3; Argentina, ibid., p. 9 (if favoured by majority); Czechoslovakia, ibid./SR.118, p. 2 (prepared to compromise; but see ibid./SR.121, p. 4); France, ibid./SR.123 (not less than $500 million, and if activities in conformity with international law); UAR, ibid./SR.123, p. 14; Lebanon, A/AC.105/PV.70–8, p. 133 (PV.76).

[311] See n. 51 above.

[312] See s. IV above, *in principio*, in relation to the application of this provision to participating organizations.

[313] PUOS/C.2/70/WG.1/CRP.3 (reproduced A/AC.105/85, Annex I, p. 9).

[314] See nn. 280 and 281 above.

compensation is due, it must say so before the final amount has been determined. Otherwise, Article XIII can easily lend itself to abuse, in view particularly of the artificiality of some exchange rates.

IX. Assistance to Victim State Facing Large-Scale Danger

Article XXI was introduced into the Liability Convention at the eleventh hour,[315] upon a Moroccan proposal.[316] It provides:

If the damage caused by a space object presents a large-scale danger to human life or seriously interferes with the living conditions of the population or the functioning of vital centres, the States Parties, and in particular the launching State, shall examine the possibility of rendering appropriate and rapid assistance to the State which has suffered the damage, when it so requests. However, nothing in this Article shall affect the rights or obligations of the States Parties under this Convention.

Morocco had originally envisaged the provision, partly at least, as a form of restitution in kind[317] that would be of particular importance to countries with limited resources.[318] But in essence the provision was treated primarily as a humanitarian one,[319] perhaps providing a counterpart to the 1968 Astronauts Agreement.[320] The wording of the Article, which pointedly leaves out the qualification 'Parties' when referring to 'the State which has suffered the damage', suggests that, whatever may be said about the rest of the Convention,[321] Article XXI, like the 1968 Astronauts Agreement,[322] contains in fact an obligation which is not strictly synallagmatic in the sense that it merely obliges the contracting parties to consider giving assistance to one another in case of need. The obligation, although binding only *inter partes*, is to do so in respect of *any* State which has suffered the damage, whether a contracting State or not.

This said, it must be recognized at the same time that the obligation specified in Article XXI, even in regard to the launching State, can hardly be considered as very onerous. As a matter of fact, the obligation is not even to

---

[315] See n. 92 above.

[316] PUOS/C.2/WG(X)/L.4/Rev.1, submitted on 25 June 1971 (reproduced A/AC.105/94, p. 19). See Morocco, A/AC.105/C.2/SR.152–69, p. 109 (SR.165). Morocco had previously suggested the idea informally: see ibid., pp. 57 (SR.160), 96 (SR.163). Supported by France, ibid., p. 109 (SR.165); Brazil, ibid., and Australia, ibid. It was presumably upon a comment of the Australian delegate that the words 'or is likely to present' in the original Moroccan proposal after the word 'presents' were deleted. These words could have been relevant in the 1978 Cosmos 954 incident: see text to n. 11 above.

[317] See *Chorzów Factory Case* (Merits) (1928), loc. cit. in n. 275 above.

[318] Morocco, A/AC.105/C.2/SR.152–69, p. 57 (SR.160).

[319] Cf. France and Brazil, ibid., p. 109 (SR.165).   [320] Cf. Morocco, ibid.

[321] See s. IV above, text to nn. 102 ff.

[322] See 'The 1968 Astronauts Agreement', loc. cit. in n. 12 above, at p. 204 [Ch. 10 above, s. VIII.A].

consider giving assistance, but merely to consider the *possibility* of giving assistance. The obligation, if one can still justifiably use the term, is thus twice removed from actually giving assistance.[323]

X. Presentation of Claims

A. Personal Scope

Who may present claims under the Liability Convention in respect of damage caused to whom is a question which has already been examined in Section V.A above, to which reference may be made.

B. Diplomatic Channels

Article IX provides:

A claim for compensation for damage shall be presented to a launching State through diplomatic channels. If a State does not maintain diplomatic relations with the launching State concerned, it may request another State to present its claim to that launching State or otherwise represent its interests under this Convention. It may also present its claim through the Secretary-General of the United Nations, provided the claimant State and the launching State are both Members of the United Nations.

The question has already been raised whether the third State through which a claimant State may have its claim presented and interests represented under Article IX has also to be a party to the Liability Convention.[324] Mention has also been made of the fact that, inasmuch as space organizations are unlikely, in the foreseeable future, to become members of the United Nations, claims against participating organizations will, while this remains the case, not be able to be presented through the Secretary-General of the United Nations.[325] The converse question whether participating organizations may present their claims via the presenting State through the Secretary-General has also been considered before.[326]

The fact that the Convention has been drafted by the United Nations is presumably sufficient authority for the Secretary-General to accept the task entrusted to it by Article IX, but the utility of this second route for the presentation of claims, which was introduced into the Convention at the last minute, upon a proposal of the United Arab Republic,[327] is dubious. Among other things, the Secretary-General can hardly be expected 'otherwise' to

---

[323] Is there a duty to request assistance? Would failure to do so through gross negligence bring Art. VI into operation? Cf. W. F. Foster, 'The Convention on International Liability for Damage Caused by Space Objects', 10 *Canadian YBIL* (1972), p. 137, at p. 178.

[324] See text to n. 105 above. [325] See text to n. 179 above.

[326] See text to n. 180 above. [327] See n. 90 above.

represent the interests of the claimant State. In fact the wording of Article IX makes it quite clear that the Convention does not expect him to do so.

C. Time-limits

Under Article X:

1. A claim for compensation for damage may be presented to a launching State not later than one year following the date of the occurrence of the damage or the identification of the launching State which is liable.
2. If, however, a State does not know of the occurrence of the damage or it has not been able to identify the launching State which is liable, it may present a claim within one year following the date on which it learned of the aforementioned facts; however, this period shall in no event exceed one year following the date on which the State could reasonably be expected to have learned of the facts through the exercise of due diligence.

3. The time-limits specified in paragraphs 1 and 2 of this Article shall apply even if the full extent of the damage may not be known. In this event, however, the claimant State shall be entitled to revise the claim and submit additional documentation after the expiration of such time-limits until one year after the full extent of the damage is known.

D. Local Remedies

Under general international law, before a State may present a diplomatic claim against another State in respect of damage allegedly suffered by its nationals in the latter State, the nationals must have first exhausted all available local remedies. Article XI of the Liability Convention dispenses with this requirement without, however, depriving the claimant State and natural and juridical persons whom it might represent, of the opportunity of resorting to such remedies where they exist:

1. Presentation of a claim to a launching State for compensation for damage under this Convention shall not require the prior exhaustion of any local remedies which may be available to a claimant State or to natural or juridical persons it represents.
2. Nothing in this Convention shall prevent a State, or natural or juridical persons it might represent, from pursuing a claim in the courts or administrative tribunals or agencies of a launching State. A State shall not, however, be entitled to present a claim under this Convention in respect of the same damage for which a claim is being pursued in the courts or administrative tribunals or agencies of a launching State or under another international agreement which is binding on the States concerned.

While discussing the issue of applicable law, the question was raised whether a claimant State might be able to benefit from the law of the launching State in those cases where the law of the launching State may be more generous in its treatment of the victim.[328] Prima facie, a possible way of achieving this result might be for the victim to bring his claim before the courts or administrative tribunals or agencies of the launching State. This would be particularly appropriate where a State has laws for compensating victims of damage caused by its own space objects, wherever the damage may have occurred.

Under the Convention, the fact that a claimant has resorted to local remedies and found them wanting by international law standards would not prevent his claim from being afterwards presented in accordance with the terms of the Convention. The same cannot, however, be said necessarily of remedies provided for in another international agreement. Much would depend upon the nature of such remedies. If the other treaty provides for a binding arbitral or juridical decision under international law, then there might well be *res judicata* which would preclude the claim from being presented again before another international law forum,[329] Article XXIII of the Convention notwithstanding.[330]

XI. Third-Party Settlement of Claims

This was the last and probably the most crucial issue which held up the conclusion of the Liability Convention. Both the Belgian draft[331] and the United States draft[332] provided for compulsory arbitration of claims which were not settled by negotiations within a given time. The Hungarian draft also contained a clause[333] providing for the establishment of a 'committee of arbitration' to be 'set up by the two States on a basis of parity,' without, however, specifying a time limit. On this basis, the Legal Sub-Committee at its sixth session in 1967 agreed provisionally that:

If a claim presented under the Convention is not settled within six months from the date on which the applicant (presenting) (claimant) State completes its documentation, the applicant (presenting) (claimant) State may refer the matter to an arbitral commission.[334]

In yet another cautionary tale for budding negotiators, it was soon discovered that the Hungarian proposal involved no more than a negotiating committee on which both sides would be equally represented.[335] In his

---

[328] See n. 285 above and text thereto.
[329] See Cheng, *General Principles of Law*, Ch. 17: 'The Principle of *Res Judicata*', pp. 336–72.
[330] See text to nn. 239 ff. above.
[331] A/AC.105/C.2/L.7/Rev.3, Art.4.   [332] A/AC.105/C.2/L.19 and L.58, Art. X.
[333] A/AC.105/C.2/L.10/Rev.1 and Corr. 1, L.24 and Add. 1, Art. XI.
[334] *Report of the Legal Sub-Committee on the Work of its Sixth Session* (19.6–14.7.67), A/AC.105/37, para. 17, under 'Arbitration in the event of dispute'.
[335] Cf., e.g., USA, A/AC.105/C.2/SR.101, p. 16; Italy, ibid., France, ibid., p. 18.

explanation, the Hungarian delegate to the Sub-Committee drew an apparently ad hoc distinction between arbitration and 'super-arbitration'.[336] The
latter, involving an impartial third arbiter and a binding decision, he and all
his colleagues from the Soviet bloc resolutely rejected for a variety of reasons,
mostly of a political nature.[337]

The root of the difference was simply that States within the Soviet bloc, particularly the Soviet Union, together with one or two other States,[338] had
always been unwilling, especially in inter-State relations, to give up the right
of auto-interpretation in favour of compulsory third-party settlement.[339]
They just did not want to give up an iota of their freedom to interpret and
apply the agreement and the law as they themselves saw fit. The other States
on the Legal Sub-Committee, however, especially in their position as potential victim-States, rightly regarded compulsory third-party settlement of
claims as the most crucial element of the proposed agreement, without which
the agreement would hardly be worth having.[340]

By the end of 1960, it was accepted that the dispute settlement procedure
would fall into the following three stages:

(i)   diplomatic negotiations;
(ii)   a parity conciliation or inquiry commission; and

[336] Ibid., pp. 20–1; this rather unorthodox terminology was later abandoned, ibid., p. 24.

[337] USSR, ibid., p. 16: 'realistic'; Hungary, ibid., p. 21: 'political problems were involved'; ibid.,
p. 24: at least 'had political aspects'; USSR, ibid./SR.128, p. 10: 'States with different social and
legal systems and with a different approach to international relations'.

[338] Brazil, ibid./SR.118, p. 3; but see ibid./SR.124, p. 4, where Brazil announced its willingness
to accept compulsory third-party settlement on financial aspects of claims, though not in regard
to other disputes.

[339] Cf. Hungary, ibid./SR.121, p. 5: 'No settlement could be imposed on a sovereign State
against its wishes'; Poland, ibid./SR.132–51, p. 64 (SR.148); 'incompatible with . . . sovereignty'.
These States were later to have the United Nations Declaration on Principles of International
Law Concerning Friendly Relations and Co-operation among States in Accordance with the
Charter of the United Nations (General Assembly resolution 2625 (XXV)) in its draft and final
forms quoted at them by Sweden, ibid./SR.132–51, p. 51 (SR.146); United Kingdom,
ibid./SR.152–69, p. 19 (SR.154); Sweden, ibid., p. 28 (SR.155). The relevant passage in the
Declaration says: 'Recourse to, or acceptance of, a settlement procedure freely agreed to by States
with regard to existing or future disputes to which they are parties shall not be regarded as incompatible with sovereign equality.'

[340] See, e.g., Australia, A/AC.105/C.2/SR.101, p. 14; United Kingdom, ibid., p. 15; India, ibid.,
p. 16 (financial aspects only); Italy, ibid., p. 17; France, ibid., p. 18; Sweden, ibid., p. 19; Austria,
ibid., p. 22; Australia, ibid./SR.116, pp. 3–4; France, ibid., p. 7; Canada, ibid./SR.117, p. 4;
Belgium, ibid., p. 6; Japan, ibid., p. 9; United Kingdom, ibid., p. 11; Italy, ibid./SR.123, pp. 4–5;
Australia, ibid., p. 6; USA, ibid., p. 8; Argentina, ibid.,/SR.124, p. 3; Iran, ibid./SR.126, p. 2;
France, A/AC.105/PV.64, p. 19/20; Italy, ibid., p. 32; Sweden, ibid., p. 48/50; United Kingdom,
ibid., p. 56, ibid./PV.74, pp. 6–7; Canada, A/AC.105/C.2/SR.132–51, pp. 49–50 (SR.146); Austria
(reporting that 'the majority of delegations wished the decision to be final and binding'), ibid., p.
72 (SR.148); United Kingdom, A/AC.105/C.2/SR.152–69, p. 19 (SR.154); India, ibid., p. 23
(SR.154); Lebanon, ibid., p. 26 (SR.155); Sweden, ibid., p. 28 (SR.155); Iran, ibid., p. 39 (SR.157);
Mexico, ibid., pp. 82–3 (SR.162); Canada, ibid., p. 89 (SR.163); Austria, ibid., p. 101 (SR.164);
Canada, ibid., p. 111 (SR.166); Japan, ibid., p. 112 (SR.166); Sweden, ibid., p. 114 (SR.166);
Australia, ibid., p. 115 (SR.166); etc.

(iii)   a tripartite arbitral commission.[341]

The crux of the problem was the effect to be given to the arbitral commission. Basically, what the majority wanted was that, in the event of a claim arising, there should be:

(A) some machinery, involving an independent third party whose voice should be decisive, that,

(B) notwithstanding any lack of co-operation on the part of the respondent State,

    (i)   could be established,

    (ii) could function, and

    (iii) could arrive at a conclusion which would

        (a)   resolve the question of liability, and

        (b)   if liability was established, determine the amount of compensation due,

(C) with time-limits set at every stage so that there would be an absolute *dies ad quem*, by which time no amount of delaying tactics on the other side would be able to prevent a definitive conclusion from being reached, and

(D) last but not least, with the decision treated as final and binding.[342]

An eight-power proposal along these lines was formally submitted to the ninth session of the Legal Sub-Committee in 1970.[343]

Realizing that the last point was the kernel of the stumbling-block, members of the Committee were deploying all their ingenuity in trying to find a way round it. If hair was being split in the process, it was being done under an electron microscope. Every conceivable compromise was thought of. Thus, instead of a legally final and obligatory decision,[344] reference was made to a decision which was only 'final and binding', without specifying in what way it was binding.[345] There was talk also of an award that was 'final', but only morally and politically 'binding', which could be reinforced, if necessary, by an undertaking 'to abide by the award', or simply to consider it. Its moral and political effect could also be strengthened by the requirement that the award had to state its reasons, or be published, or transmitted to the Secretary-General of the United Nations.[346] And why not an award that was just 'final'?[347] Further yet down the line, there were those who suggested that the

[341] Cf. France, A/AC.105/PV.70–9, p. 110 (PV.76).

[342] Cf., e.g., the understanding found in the Explanatory Note appended to the joint 8-power proposal referred to in n. 343 below.

[343] Argentina, Australia, Belgium, Canada, Italy, Japan, Sweden, United Kingdom, A/AC.105/C.2/L.74 and Adds. 1 and 2 (reproduced A/AC. 105/85, Annex I, p. 3).

[344] Cf. Belgium A/AC.105/PV.70–8, pp. 154–5 (PV.78); Canada, A/AC.105/C.2/SR.132–51, pp. 49–50 (SR.146); Sweden, ibid., p. 51 (SR.146).

[345] E.g., France, A/AC.105/PV.70–8, p. 110 (PV.76); Lebanon, ibid., p. 135 (PV.76).

[346] Italy, ibid., p. 129 (PV.76); A/AC.105/C.2/SR.152–69, pp. 33 (SR.156), 99–100 (SR.164).

[347] Lebanon, A/AC.105/PV.70–8, p. 135 (PV.76), not as proposal, but merely a suggestion that that was the least the Brazilian could have offered (see n. 348 below).

final and binding effect of the conclusions should be optional,[348] that the whole arbitration procedure should be optional,[349] until we reach the point where the suggestion was that the arbitral phase should be eliminated altogether.[350]

The impasse which the Legal Sub-Committee had reached by the end of its ninth session in the summer of 1970 was revealed by the Belgian delegate in his account of the informal discussions that were then going on:

Appreciating the arguments of those who had invoked such considerations as the sovereignty and equality of States, his delegation, in the spirit of compromise, had thought it could be satisfied with what had been called a decision that was binding, not legally, but from the political and, as it were, moral standpoints. It was regrettable that certain delegations had even been able to accept that minimum, and were also raising objections to the publication of decisions. It was legitimate to ask, in the circumstances, what remained of the principle that the convention should be oriented towards a prompt and equitable compensation of the victim as recommended by the General Assembly.[351]

Reference has previously been made to the fact that, instead of making progress, the ninth session of the Legal Sub-Committee was in danger of slipping backwards in its negotiations.[352]

From this point of view, it may be relevant to mention that, soon after the Belgian delegate, the French representative reiterated in plenary the compromise proposal of a final, but not legally binding, recommendation or conclusion which, however, must state its reasons and be published.[353] At the next meeting, the Bulgarian representative, Professor Anguelov, actually welcomed the French proposal, and seemed quite happy with it. He even added:

The French representative had rightly stressed the need to publish and give the grounds for the recommendation so as to strengthen their moral and political effect. The recommendations or conclusions would be regarded as final, and not subject to appeal . . .[354]

But at the very next meeting the following morning, the Bulgarian Alternate, Monsieur Koltchakov, from the Ministry of Foreign Affairs, took the floor, instead of Professor Anguelov,[355] and presented[356] jointly with Hungary and the USSR a proposal[357] which eliminated the arbitral stage in

---

[348] Brazil, A/AC.105/PV.70–8, p. 112 (PV.76).   [349] Romania, ibid., p. 131 (PV.76).
[350] Joint Bulgaria, Hungary, USSR proposal, A/AC.105/C.2/L.76 (reproduced A/AC.105/85, Annex I, p. 4).
[351] A/AC.105/C.2/SR.132–51, p. 55 (SR.147).   [352] See s. III.F.4 above.
[353] A/AC.105/C.2/SR.132–51, p. 57 (SR.147).   [354] Ibid., pp. 67–8 (SR.148).
[355] Ibid., pp. 78–9 (SR.149).
[356] A comparison of the head notes of meetings 148 and 149 (ibid., pp. 61 and 75 respectively) will show that the proposal in question, A/AC.105/C.2/L.76, was not yet before the former meeting, but was among the papers to be considered by the latter.
[357] A/AC.105/C.2/L.76 (reproduced A/AC.105/85, Annex I, p. 4).

the dispute settlement procedure altogether and left it to the parties in dispute to decide whether they wished to make the conclusions of the parity conciliation commission final and binding or not.

The deadlock was not broken until a year later when on 21 June 1971 the joint Belgium, Brazil and Hungary proposal was presented,[358] which dealt exclusively with the twin outstanding issues of applicable law and settlement of disputes. As has been mentioned before,[359] the Legal Sub-Committee was in fact able, on the question of the settlement of disputes, to make a number of changes to the joint proposal, including:

(a) the telescoping of the whole procedure into two stages by eliminating the Inquiry Commission,[360]

(b) the introduction in the present Article XIX(2) of the clause 'which the parties shall consider in good faith'[361] after the words 'recommendatory award',

(c) a new paragraph 3 in the present Article XIX which requires the Claims Commission to render its award, in principle, not later than one year from the date of its establishment,

(d) the addition of the second sentence in the present Article XIX, providing for the Secretary-General of the United Nations, as well as the parties in dispute, receiving a copy of any decision or award which might be given under the Convention,[362]

(e) the option now given to the Claims Commission in Article XX, if the Commission so decides, to apportion the Commission's expenses otherwise than equally between the parties, as is customary in international arbitrations.[363]

As finally adopted, the relevant provisions of the Convention on the settlement of claims are contained in Articles XIV to XX.

It may be interjected here that the draftsmen of the Liability Convention have, in Articles XV and XVI(1), wisely avoided the trap into which the Peace Treaties of 1947 with Bulgaria, Hungary, and Romania fell into the hands of the International Court of Justice in the *Interpretation of Peace Treaties* (2nd Phase) (1950).[364] A slight difference exists, however, between Article XVI(1)

[358] See n. 83 above and text thereto.   [359] See s. III.F.6 above.

[360] Cf. Australia, A/AC.105/C.2/SR.132–51, p. 66 (SR.148); deletion proposed by Lebanon, ibid./SR.152–69, p. 79 (SR.162); see Argentina, ibid., p. 94 (SR.163); Morocco, ibid., p. 95 (SR.163); Romania, p. 97 (SR.163); France, ibid., p. 97 (SR.193); see Italy, ibid., p. 101 (SR.164).

[361] Upon an Indian proposal, PUOS/C.2/WG(X)/L.2/Rev.1 (reproduced A/AC.105/94, p. 18). See also Lebanon, A/AC.105/C.2/SR.152–69, p. 81 (SR.162); Sweden, ibid., p. 98 (SR.163); Canada, Mexico, United Kingdom, per Sweden, ibid.; Italy, ibid., p. 100 (SR.164); Morocco, ibid., p. 109 (SR.165).

[362] India, ibid., p. 118 (SR.166).

[363] Lebanon, ibid., p. 80 (SR.162); Argentina, ibid., p. 95 (SR.163); Morocco, ibid., p. 95 (SR.163). cf. comments by India, ibid., p. 118 (SR.166).

[364] *ICJ Rep. 1950*, p. 221; see Cheng, *General Principles of Law*, pp. 151 ff.

and what could have otherwise happened under the 1947 Peace Treaties if the Court's Advisory Opinion had, in its second phase, followed Judge Read's Dissenting Opinion.[365] Leaning over backwards in order to be fair, Article XVI(1), as well as Article XVII in similar circumstances, in the event of one of the parties failing to appoint one of the three members of the Claims Commission, in fact disqualifies the member appointed by the other side and makes the Chairman sit alone as a single-member Commission, instead of allowing the member appointed by the other party to sit with the Chairman, who in such an event will enjoy a casting vote. The practical result is probably very much the same.

The first part of Article XVII follows the precedent set by Article 31 of the Statute of the International Court of Justice relating to the composition of the Court in the event of several parties sharing the same interest.[366] The second part of Article XVII follows the same principle as Article XVI.

One of the principal objectives of the dispute settlement provisions of the Convention from Article XIV to Article XX is to enable a claimant State, in the absence of a settlement through diplomatic negotiations a year after the claim has been notified to the launching State, to initiate an independent process which will be able, with, but if necessary without, the co-operation of the launching State, to arrive at a definitive conclusion on the question of liability and the quantum of compensation payable, if any, determined in accordance with the terms of the Convention. The whole procedure, from the notification of the claim to the final decision or award, unless the Commission finds it necessary to extend the period, should not take longer than two years and six months (i.e., one year under Article XIV, four months plus two months under Article XV(2), and one year under Article XIX(3)). In the case of a participating international organization being the defendant, the process may take an additional six months.[367] At the latest by the end of this period, be it 30 or 36 months, the claimant State is more or less guaranteed that it will receive an authoritative pronouncement on whether its claim is valid under the Convention and, if so, exactly how much, in the opinion of the Commission, the launching State owes it in order to make it whole again within the meaning of Article XII. Because the Convention deals with a rather exceptional situation, the claimant State, in such circumstances, if the Commission so decides, may not even have to share half of the expenses 'in regard to' the Commission, as it would normally be expected to do in international arbitrations.[368]

In so far as the effect of the end result of the work of the Commission is concerned, reference has already been made to the travail experienced by the

[365] *ICJ Rep. 1950*, p. 221, at pp. 231 ff.

[366] Particularly Art. 31(5) which is worded as follows: 'Should there be several parties in the same interest, they shall, for the purpose of the preceding provisions, be reckoned as one party only. Any doubt upon this point shall be settled by the decision of the Court.'

[367] See text to n. 181 above.   [368] See nn. 91 and 363 above.

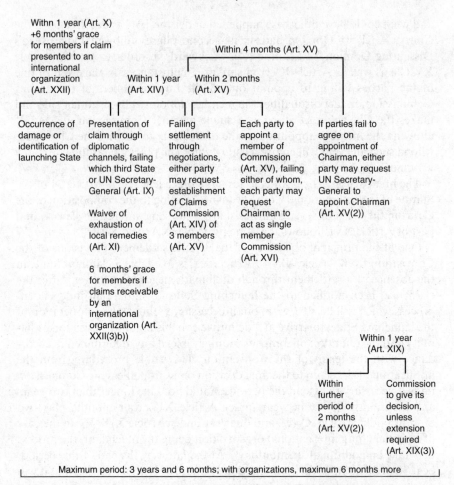

**Figure XI.1. TIME SCALE IN THE SETTLEMENT OF DISPUTES UNDER
THE 1972 LIABILITY CONVENTION**

Legal Sub-Committee in arriving at the present compromise.[369] As it now
stands, Article XIX appears to make a distinction between a decision, when
the conclusion is binding, and an award, when it is merely 'recommendatory',
and in order to avoid confusion, this distinction is here adhered to, although
from the terminological point of view, it would be wrong to assume that an
award is any the less binding than a decision. In fact, between the two, the
word 'decision' is probably more neutral than 'award'.

---

[369] See text from n. 341 to n. 358 above.

However, in both cases, the findings of the Commission are 'final', and, as was said by Professor Anguelov, 'not subject to appeal'.[370] Apart from this, their legal status is deliberately ambiguous. On the one hand, if the parties have so agreed, the findings become legally binding on them. As has been mentioned before, although there seems to be no explicit basis for it, the General Assembly in its resolution 2777 (XXVI) has somehow read into Article XIX(2) an Optional Clause similar to Article 36(2) of the Statute of the International Court of Justice, and consequently in its paragraph 3:

Notes that any State may, on becoming a party to the Convention, declare that it will recognize as binding in relation to any other State accepting the same obligation, the decision of the Claims Commission concerning dispute to which it may become a party.[371]

This is not to say, however, that in the absence of any provision to this effect in the Convention, such declarations cannot be made. Like declarations made under the Optional Clause of the Statute of the International Court of Justice, these declarations have the effect of offers that are subject to acceptance, which occurs when one of the States concerned requests the establishment of a Claims Commission under Article XIV. Once accepted, they can no longer be amended or withdrawn.

As with declarations to be made by participating organizations under Article XXII,[372] the General Assembly resolution gives no indication of the form and procedure to be followed if a contracting State wishes to make such a declaration under Article XIX. As regards form and content, such a State would do well to consult declarations under the Optional Clause of the Statute of the Court, the drafting of which has developed into a fine art. Insofar as procedure is concerned, those States that have already done so have obviously assumed that any such declaration should be deposited with the Depositary Governments,[373] which in turn will have to notify all signatory and acceding States accordingly, under Article XXIV, as a matter of 'other notices'.

However, for reasons which have already been fully explained,[374] in the absence of agreement between the parties, the findings of the Claims Commission, although still final and not subject to appeal, constitute only a 'recommendatory award'. In fact, Canada, Iran, Japan and Sweden felt so strongly over this point that they abstained in both the First Committee and in the General Assembly, when the vote was taken to approve the draft Convention, which was otherwise adopted in both bodies *nemine contradicente*.[375]

---

[370] See text to n. 254 above.
[372] See s. V.A.6 above, *in medio*.
[374] See text from n. 337 to n. 340 above.

[371] See n. 3 above.
[373] See s. V.A.2 above.

[375] See nn. 1 and 85 above. The position of Canada, Japan, and Sweden was made clear already at the tenth session of the Legal Sub-Committee. See Canada, A/AC.105/C.2/SR.152–69, p. 111 (SR.166); Japan, ibid., p. 112 (SR.166); Sweden, ibid., p. 114 (SR.166). Cf. also Mexico, ibid., p. 82 (SR.162); Austria, p. 101 (SR.164); Australia, ibid., p. 115 (SR.166).

What is the legal status of a 'recommendatory award'? In the circumstances and in the spirit in which it has been reached, the compromise incorporated in Article XIX is quite exceptional. As a genus, however, 'recommendatory awards' are not entirely unknown in international law. The Advisory Opinions of the International Court of Justice and of its predecessor the Permanent Court of International Justice immediately come to mind, even though they may belong to a slightly different species. Then there are the reports of the International Commissions of Inquiry under respectively the 1899 and 1907 Hague Conventions on the Pacific Settlement of International Disputes. One of the best known Commissions of Inquiry was that which resolved the *Dogger Bank Case* (1905) between Great Britain and Russia. It is interesting to note that, in that case, Russia accepted the findings of the Commission without demur and paid Great Britain damages to the extent of some $300,000.[376]

Finally, mention may be made of various bilateral agreements which in case of a dispute cannot be resolved through negotiations, refer it to some independent body or person for a report or sometimes even an advisory report. The view has been expressed that such 'advisory reports are, according to international practice, in all but name arbitral awards'.[377]

With the express obligation incumbent on parties to the dispute to consider the 'recommendatory award' in good faith and the other items incorporated in Article XIX in order to enhance its moral and political standing,[378] it is indeed to be hoped that parties to the Liability Convention will conform to this time-honoured practice, which would do no more than to meet the legitimate expectations of all those who laboured so hard over a period of nine years to secure this agreement.

---

[376] Scott, 1 *HCR*, p. 403. See from this point of view also the *I'm Alone Case* (1935) between Great Britain and the United States, 2 *RIAA*, p. 1609. The Agreement between the two States only provided for claims to be referred to a joint commission, and for '[e]ffect [to] be given to the *recommendations* contained in any such joint report' from the commissioiners (Art. IV of the Treaty of 23 Jan. 1924, ibid., at p. 1611; italics added).

[377] See Cheng, *The Law of International Air Transport*, p. 458, where *inter alia* the *clause compromissoire* in the first Bermuda Agreement of 1946 between the United Kingdom and the United States is discussed, and where, besides the *I'm Alone Case* (see n. 376 above), reference is also made to the case of the *British Claims in the Spanish Zone of Morocco* (1924/5) (2 *RIAA*, p. 615). Cf. also the new Air Services Agreement of 1977 between the same two countries, generally known as the Bermuda II Agreement, under Art. 17(7) of which, 'Each Contracting Party shall, consistent with its national law, give full effect to any decision or award of the arbitral tribunal. In the event that one Contracting Party does not give effect to any decision or award, the other Contracting Party may take such proportionate steps as may be appropriate.' There is no other provision regarding the effect of the decision or award.

[378] See nn. 346, 353, 361, and 362 above.

XII. Conclusion

As a purely legal document, the Liability Convention may not be very remarkable. Placed, however, in its political context, it is an important international legal landmark. Here, it suffices to recall some of its salient features.

The relaxation of the rule on the nationality of claims[379] is an innovation of considerable interest, which may with profit be copied in other treaties concerned with the protection of the individual.

Secondly,[380] the way in which international organizations have been allowed to participate in the Convention without actually becoming contracting parties represents also a significant breakthrough on both the doctrinal and practical fronts, especially in international relations on a world scale. A reasonable solution representing a point of convergence of many different, and sometimes extreme, views appears to have been worked out, and its practical operation will obviously be watched with interest.

The controversy over the question of applicable law[381] may doctrinally speaking have been a storm in a tea cup, but in this case the storm did reveal that a number of strange matters had apparently succeeded in getting into the cup. As the cup contained the blood stream of the Convention, it was perhaps just as well that it went through this clarification and purification process. The new provision has been prepared under the full glare of world publicity, with every particle of it thoroughly analysed and documented and it has been provided with an unusual number of safeguards all calculated to ensure that its content and meaning will, this time, be crystal clear and absolutely unmistakable. The draftsmen have indeed done everything that can be reasonably expected of them. Whether Article XII will now succeed in giving the Liability Convention the vital force it is intended to have in ensuring to every victim—in the words of the Preamble—'a full and equitable measure of compensation', will depend on more than the mere wording of the treaty itself. No treaty, however well drafted, will be effective, unless the parties observe it in good faith.

The same applies all the more to the claims settlement procedure in the Liability Convention.[382] From the standpoint purely of legal technique, the machinery provided for in the Convention is far from being the most effective. But the remarkable thing here, like the case of the dog that dances on its hind legs, is not how well it performs, but that it exists at all. The Liability Convention, from this point of view, is a very notable achievement. Moreover, for reasons which have already been explained, the modest procedure, in appearance, laid down in the Convention for the settlement of claims may, in

---

[379] See s. V.A.3 above.   [380] See s. V.A.6 above.   [381] See s. VIII.A above.
[382] See s. XI above.

effect, be, again given good faith and a modicum of good will, more effective than some of its critics would give it credit for.

All in all, the Liability Convention is a treaty which all the members of the Outer Space Committee and its Legal Sub-Committee may look back with some satisfaction and even pride. Their labour has been rewarded by a convention which not only forms an important chapter in the emergent *corpus juris spatialis*, but also deserves an honourable mention in the annals of international treaty law. All it needs now is to be observed in good faith.

12

The Moon Treaty: Agreement Governing the Activities of States on the Moon and other Celestial Bodies within the Solar System other than the Earth*

I. Introduction

The Agreement Governing the Activities of States on the Moon and Other Celestial Bodies, to give the instrument its official title, was throughout its long period of gestation, always referred to as the Moon Treaty,[1] by which name, on account of, if nothing else, its brevity, the treaty will no doubt continue to be generally known in practice. This agreement, which was opened for signature on 18 December 1979, has the distinction of being the first treaty to give effect in international law to the concept of 'the common heritage of mankind'. In effect the United Nations Committee on the Peaceful Uses of Outer Space (COPUOS) which drafted the moon treaty has stolen a march on the Third United Nations Conference on the Law of the Sea (UNCLOS III) which at the time was still, Laocoön-like, wrestling with the concept.[2] To the hitherto tripartite division in international law of the world into (i) national territory, (ii) *res nullius*, i.e. areas which may be acquired as national territory, and (iii) *res extra commercium*, i.e. areas which by law are not susceptible of national appropriation, there is now a fourth category, (iv) the common heritage of mankind, areas which are not only in themselves not subject to national appropriation in a territorial sense, but the fruits and resources of which are also deemed to be the property of mankind at large. For this reason, however hastily and hence poorly put together, the Moon Treaty deserves the most general attention.

* First published in 33 *CLP* (1980), pp. 213–37, and Corrigenda. Reproduced by kind permission of Sweet & Maxwell.

[1] Cf. e.g., the Table of Contents of the Report of the United Nations Committee on the Peaceful Uses of Outer Space (COPUOS) for its 22nd Session (18 June to 3 July 1979), at which agreement was finally reached on the Agreement, continued to refer to it under II.A.7 as 'Draft treaty relating to the moon', following simply the wording of item 4(g) of the Committee Agenda for the 22nd Session (UN Doc. A/34/20, pp. iii and 2). For text see App. I.5 below.

[2] Cf. UNCLOS III, Revised Informal Composite Negotiating Text (RICNT) for the 8th Session produced in 1979, UN Doc. A/CONF.62/WP.10/Rev. 1; reproduced in 18 *ILM* (1979), p. 686.

II. The Drafting History

A. Background

In order to understand the history of the Moon Treaty, it is necessary to go back to the initial stages in the development of space law. From the very beginning, the non-space powers wanted to have a share of the fruits of space exploration and exploitation in the form of scientific knowledge, technology and in due course other material or pecuniary benefits, apart from their desire to ban colonialism from, and the militarization of, outer space and celestial bodies. However, all that they succeeded in achieving, nay, all that they were granted by the space powers, in the all-important 1967 Treaty on Outer Space was to make the whole of outer space, including the moon and other celestial bodies, *res extra commercium*, which, while it precludes the space powers from appropriating territorially portions of outer space, the moon or celestial bodies, leaves them free, notwithstanding views to the contrary, nevertheless to appropriate their resources.[3] Although the moon and celestial bodies have been reserved exclusively for peaceful use under the 1967 Treaty, outer space as such has only been partially demilitarized.[4] The 1967 Treaty left many non-space powers unsatisfied. The question of the utilization of outer space remained on the agenda of successive meetings of the Legal Sub-Committee of the Outer Space Committee, and proposals continued to be made after 1967 concerning the activities on and resources coming from the moon and other celestial bodies.[5]

B. The Argentine Initiative

In 1969 man landed on the moon. The following year, Argentina presented to the Legal Sub-Committee a Draft Agreement on the Principles Governing Activities in the Use of the Natural Resources of the Moon and Other Celestial Bodies,[6] the first article of which boldly proclaims that 'the natural resources of the Moon and other celestial bodies shall be the common heritage of mankind,' benefits derived from the use of which shall be made avail-

---

[3] See further B. Cheng, 'Le Traité de 1967 sur l'espace/The 1967 Space Treaty', 95 *JDI* (1968), p. 532, especially pp. 564–8, and pp. 576–82 [Ch. 9 above, ss. V.B: Res Extra Commercium, and V.E: Exploration and Use for the Benefit of All Countries]; cf. however, e.g. M G. Marcoff, *Traité de droit international public de l'espace* (1973), pp. 665 ff.

[4] See Cheng, loc. cit. in n. 3 above, under V [Ch. 9 above, s. VI: Partial Demilitarization of Outer Space].

[5] See, e.g., 8th Session of Legal Sub-Committee (1969), proposals made by Poland, A/AC.105/C.2/L.53; Argentina, A/AC.105/C.2/L.54; France, A/AC.105/C.2/L.64; Argentina and Poland, A/AC.105/C.2/L.66 (replacing A/AC.105/C.2/L.53 and L.54); Argentina, France and Poland, A/AC.105/C.2/L.69: all reproduced in *Report of Legal Sub-Committee on its 8th Session* (9.6–4.7.69), A/AC.105/58, Annex I, pp. 4–7.

[6] A/AC.105/L.71 and Corr. 1.

able to all in order to promote higher standards of living, and economic and social development. The draft furthermore distinguishes between resources used *in situ* and those brought back to the earth.[7]

C. The Soviet Proposal

In what can only be regarded as a move to head off the Argentine initiative, the Soviet Union on 27 May 1971 proposed the addition of a new item on the agenda of the forthcoming Session of the United Nations General Assembly, namely, the Preparation of an International Treaty Concerning the Moon. On 5 June 1971, it submitted its own draft moon treaty.[8] In contrast to the Argentine draft, the Soviet proposal (i) applied only to the moon but not to other celestial bodies, and (ii) did not deal with the problems of resources. These were two of the issues which held up agreement on the treaty for seven years. In fact, the Soviet draft hardly went beyond elaborating some of the provisions of the 1967 Space Treaty. On 29 November 1971, the General Assembly adopted Resolution 2779 (XXVI) in which, among other things, it took note of the Soviet Draft, and requested the Outer Space Committee and its Legal Sub-Committee to consider, as a matter of priority, the question of a moon treaty.

D. The Initial Élan Soon Met with an Impasse

As a result of this procedural manœuvre, when the Legal Sub-Committee met the following spring, the Soviet draft, in preference to the Argentine proposal, became the basis of its discussion as well as that of the Working Group set up by it to consider the matter.[9] The Working Group went about its job with great gusto. Apart from the Soviet and Argentine proposals, it received no fewer than sixteen proposals from the United States, and nine from various other countries.[10] In less than a month, the Legal Sub-Committee was already able to approve a preliminary draft of 21 articles, which, in form at least, correspond roughly to the 21 articles of the final treaty.[11] However, many of the articles contained elements between square brackets indicating that no agreement on them had yet been reached.

---

[7] See Arts. 3, 4, and 5. See further also the Argentine delegate, Mr Cocca, A/AC.105/C.2/SR.154 (9.6.71), pp. 19–21; ibid./SR.168 (30.6.71), pp. 144–5; also Argentine delegate Mr Delpech, A/AC.105/C.2/SR.190 (4.5.72), pp. 41–3.

[8] A/8391 and Corr. 1 and annex.

[9] See *Report of the Legal Sub-Committee on its 11th Session (10.4–5.5.72)*, A/AC.105/101, para. 18, an Annex 1. The Soviet proposal took precedence over the Argentine one because it was a proposal presented to the General Assembly and the subject of a General Assembly resolution, whilst the Argentine one was merely one presented to the Legal Sub-Committee.

[10] Ibid.   [11] Ibid., para. 21.

While the 1973 (12th) Session of the Legal Sub-Committee succeeded in improving the wording of some of the articles in the preliminary draft,[12] it soon became clear that three fundamental issues proved insoluble: (i) the scope of the treaty, (ii) the timing of the information to be furnished on missions to the moon, and (iii) the question of the natural resources of the moon. In brief, mainly on the ground that it was premature to do so, the Soviet Union, supported by some other delegations, was opposed to (i) extending the treaty to celestial bodies other than the moon,[13] and (ii) including provisions in the treaty concerning the resources of the moon.[14] Furthermore, it was not disposed to provide advance information on missions to the moon, as opposed to information on 'completed missions'.

While informal and behind-the-scenes discussions no doubt took place continually,[15] officially, notwithstanding successive calls from the General Assembly, some of great urgency,[16] little progress was made by the Legal Sub-Committee in its various sessions from 1973 to 1979 inclusive, although a Working Paper[17] submitted to the 17th (1978) Session of the Legal Sub-Committee and containing the text of a tentative draft agreement elaborated by the Austrian delegate who had been chairing a series of informal consultations[18] was generally regarded as very promising. Thus the Soviet government, in a wide-ranging communication sent in the summer of 1978 to the United Nations concerning the importance of the 1967 Space Treaty, said:

> The complete unwillingness of some countries to abandon the introduction of the concept of 'common heritage' into the new treaty threatens to make it impossible to conclude the treaty. There is, however, a good basis for compromise in the constructive proposal put forward by the Austrian delegation at the 1978 session of the Legal Sub-Committee . . .[19]

However, while the 18th Session of the Legal Sub-Committee, which met from 12 March to 6 April 1979, devoted considerable time to the Austrian Working

[12] See *Report of the Legal Sub-Committee on its 12th Session (26.3–20.4.73)*, A/AC.105/115, para. 17.

[13] E.g., Japan, A/AC.105/C.2/SR.187 (2.5.72), pp. 3–4; USSR, ibid., p. 8; Hungary, ibid. p. 14; Poland, ibid. p. 15; Egypt, ibid./SR.188 (3.5.72), p. 19; Bulgaria, ibid. p. 29; Czechoslovakia, ibid. p. 30.

[14] E.g., USSR, A/AC.105/C.2/SR.187 (2.5.72), p. 8; Hungary, ibid. p. 14; Poland, ibid. p. 16; France, ibid./SR.188 (3.5.72), p. 26; Bulgaria, ibid. p. 29; Czechoslovakia, ibid. p. 31; Mongolia, ibid./SR.190 (4.5.72), p. 42.

[15] Cf. e.g., N. M. Matte, 'Legal Principles Relating to the Moon,' in Jasentuliyana and Lee (eds.), 1 *Manual*, p. 253, at pp. 267–8.

[16] Resolutions 2915 (XXVII) of 9 Nov. 1972; 3182 (XXVIII) of 18 Dec. 1973; 3234 (XXIX) of 12 Nov. 1974; 3388 (XXX) of 18 Nov. 1975; 31/8 of 8 Nov. 1976; 32/196A of 20 Dec. 1977 and 33/16 of 10 Nov. 1978.

[17] A/AC.105/C.2/WG1(1978)/WP.2 (3.4.78); see A/AC.105/218, Annex I, p. 2.

[18] See *Report of the Legal Sub-Committee on its 18th Session (13.3–7.4.78)*, Annex I, para. 4.

[19] *Importance of the Treaty on Principles Governing the Activities of States in the Exploration and Use of Outer Space for the Development of International Co-operation in the Practical Application of Space Technology*, A/AC.105/219 (15.5.78), p. 35.

Paper, agreement appeared to be no nearer,[20] so much so that further consideration of the matter almost seemed futile.

E. The Mystery and Miracle of Birth

When the Outer Space Committee itself later opened its 22nd Session on 18 June 1979, its chairman, referring to what happened in the Legal Sub-Committee earlier in the year, said with remarkable frankness in his opening speech:

Indeed, the end result of the work was not altogether encouraging, and we have to face this fact quite squarely . . . [P]rogress by the Sub-Committee on the outstanding issues will take place only as Member States display an active desire and, let me say, a somewhat stronger political will to achieve the necessary compromises . . . In this connexion, the time might even have come for us to reassess our respective positions in order to see whether we cannot really bridge this gap. And if, in all honesty, we find ourselves unable to do so, the time might also have come to devote our energies—at least for the time being—to other important areas of concern which deserve our attention.[21]

It was with this advice ringing in their ears that the Committee established an informal working group of the whole under the chairmanship of Mr Gyula K. Szelei (Hungary) to consider the matter. The Working Group held four meetings between 26 June and 3 July 1979. Under the new system of shunting most discussions to groups whose proceedings, in the name of economy, are not published, the public is in fact debarred from knowing what happened then.[22] The next time one encounters a reference to the moon treaty in the verbatim records of the Outer Space Committee is a cryptic six-line report that 'Subsection 7 of section A of chapter II' entitled 'Draft Treaty relating to the Moon' in the draft report of the Committee (A/AC.105/L.113/Add.1) had been adopted by consensus without a vote.[23] It is only when one turns to the actual report of the Committee that one finds recorded in the most factual manner:

The Committee, having thus completed its work on this item decided to submit, to the General Assembly at its thirty-fourth session, for consideration, final adoption and opening for signature, the draft agreement governing the activities of States on the moon and celestial bodies . . .[24]

---

[20] See *Report of the Legal Sub-Committee on its 18th Session (12.3–6.4.79)*, Annex III.

[21] A/AC.105/PV.190 (18.6.79), pp. 7–8.

[22] See further B. Cheng, 'Convention on International Liability for Damage Caused by Space Objects', in Jasentuliyana and Lee (eds.), 1 *Manual*, p. 83, at pp. 89–90 [Ch. 11 above, s. III.F.3: Fade-out of Reported Discussions].

[23] A/AC.105/PV.203 (3.7.79), p. 6.

[24] *Report of COPUOS on its 22nd Session (1979)*, A/34/20, para. 66.

The draft agreement sponsored by 38 delegations was adopted by the Special Political Committee of the General Assembly on 2 November 1979,[25] and by the General Assembly itself on 5 December 1979 in Resolution 34/68,[26] in both cases by consensus without a vote. The Agreement was opened for signature by the Secretary-General of the United Nations on 18 December 1979.

In view of the absence of official records, it can only be a matter for speculation what supplied the political will referred to by the Chairman of the Outer Space Committee on 18 June 1979 that caused the seemingly barren and frustrating labour of seven years suddenly to bloom and fruit all within the span of fifteen days. The answer may well be found in the second Strategic Arms Limitation Treaty (SALT–II) which, by a coincidence, was signed also on 18 June 1979. It was not without significance that in his speech at the closing meeting of the 1979 session of the Outer Space Committee after the text of the draft moon treaty had been approved, the delegate from the German Democratic Republic said:

My delegation wishes to underline the idea . . . that implementation of the SALT–II Agreement . . . and its spirit will have a positive bearing on the peaceful use of outer space.[27]

Indeed, in the subsequent meetings of the Special Political Committee, whenever the draft moon treaty was mentioned, while most other delegations extolled its adoption of the concept of the common heritage of mankind, those from the Soviet bloc preferred to lay emphasis on the re-affirmation of the demilitarization of the moon and bodies in Article 3.[28] In fact, for the super powers the political and military aspects of the regulation of outer space can weigh much more than its economic side. Thus when the 1967 Space Treaty was concluded what President L. B. Johnson chose to emphasize was that it was 'the most important arms control development since the limited test ban treaty of 1963.'[29]

III. Scope of the Agreement

A. Cosmographical Scope

1. *Extension to Other Celestial Bodies in the Solar System, Other Than the Earth.* The exact cosmographical scope of the moon treaty was unresolved virtually until the eleventh hour. Consequently, all the substantive provisions

---

[25] See A/SPC/34/SR.20 (2.11.79), paras. 9 and 10; *Report of the Special Political Committee*, A/34/664, paras. 8 and 9.

[26] A/34/PV.89 (Prov.), pp. 7–10.   [27] A/AC.105/PV.203 (3.7.79), pp. 19–20.

[28] See, e.g., Germany Democratic Republic, A/SPC/34/SR.15 (29.10.79), para. 47; Ukrainian SSR, ibid./SR.18 (1.11.79), para. 49. cf. also USSR, loc. cit., in n. 19 above, p. 34.

[29] See loc. cit. in n. 3 above, at p. 534 [Ch. 9 above, n. 4 and text thereto].

of the treaty refer only to the moon. In the final text, their application has been extended by Article 1(1) to all 'other celestial bodies within the solar system, other than the earth, except in so far as specific legal norms enter into force with respect to any of these celestial bodies,' by which are meant presumably norms of international law binding on the States Parties concerned.

In order to take this extension into account, the Preamble does refer in its various paragraphs to 'the moon and other celestial bodies,' except, however, in its second and fourth paragraphs, where the moon alone is mentioned. The omission of the words 'the other celestial bodies' in paragraph 2 is no doubt intentional inasmuch as it refers to the moon 'as a natural satellite of the earth,' but their omission in paragraph 4 which expresses the desire of the contracting States 'to prevent the moon from becoming an area of international conflict' is capable of giving rise to all kinds of speculations.

At all events, this form of drafting obviously was not to the entire satisfaction of all the delegations to the Outer Space Committee which, when approving the text of the agreement, decided to adopt the following interpretative understanding:

The Committee agreed that by virtue of Article 1, paragraph 1, the principle contained in Article XI, paragraph 1, would also apply to celestial bodies in the solar system other than the earth and to its natural resources.[30]

The problem of such excess of caution in regard to an individual provision in the Agreement is that it can throw doubt on all the other provisions. Except for the preambular paragraph 4, it is submitted that such doubts would not be justified and, following the definition incorporated in Article 1, all references to the moon hereinafter in relation to the Agreement will have the meaning attributed to it by Article 1, unless otherwise indicated.

2. *Inclusion of Orbits and Trajectories.* Article 1(2) provides:

For the purposes of this Agreement reference to the moon shall include orbits around or other trajectories to or around it.

In adopting the text of the draft Agreement, the Outer Space Committee recorded its agreement that:

the trajectories and orbits mentioned in Article 1, paragraph 2, do not include trajectories and orbits of space objects in earth orbits only and trajectories of space objects between the earth and such orbits.[31]

Immediately after the adoption of the text of the draft Agreement, the United States delegate to the Outer Space Committee, Mr S. Neil Hosenball, added in this connection:

---

[30] *Report of the Committee on the Peaceful Uses of Outer Space on its 22nd Session (1979),* A/34/20, para. 62. It may be mentioned that as finally approved by the General Assembly the article numbers in the Agreement have been changed from Roman to Arabic.

[31] Ibid., para. 63.

In regard to the phrase 'earth orbit only', the fact that a space object in earth orbit also is in orbit around the sun does not bring the space objects which are only in earth orbit within the scope of this treaty; and a space object orbiting the moon, while the moon orbits the earth as well as the sun, is in fact within the scope of this treaty.[32]

There was apparently no dissent. The United States statement implicitly recognizes that the sun itself is within the scope of the Agreement.

3. *Exclusion of Extraterrestrial Materials Reaching Earth by Natural Means.* Following a proposal made by the United Kingdom in 1972,[33] the Agreement provides in its Article 1(3) that it 'does not apply to extraterrestrial materials which reach the surface of the earth by natural means'.

B. Personal Scope

The Moon Treaty, under its Article 19, is open for signature, ratification, and accession 'by all States'. Following the example set by the 1975 Convention on Registration of Objects Launched into Outer Space,[34] the Secretary-General of the United Nations acts as the depositary authority.

As with the previous four treaties in the field of outer space drawn up by the United Nations, the provisions of the Moon Treaty, except the Final Clauses, are applicable to international intergovernmental organizations which conduct space activities, if the organizations concerned declare their acceptance of the rights and obligations provided for in the Agreement and if a majority of the States members of the organizations concerned are States Parties to the Agreement and to the 1967 Space Treaty.[35]

C. Temporal Scope

The Moon Treaty has been concluded for an indefinite period. Parties are entitled, under Article 20, to give notice of withdrawal which takes effect one year from the date of the receipt of the notice. It may be amended at any time if a majority of the States Parties so wish, with effect, however, only upon those States Parties which accept the amendment (Article 17). Ten years after the entry into force of the Agreement, the question whether it requires revision will be placed on the provisional agenda of the United Nations General Assembly. Nevertheless at any time after the Agreement has been in force for

---

[32] A/AC.105/PV.203 (3.7.79), p. 26. Repeated by US delegate to Special Political Committee, A/SPC/34/SR.19 (1.11.79), para. 22.

[33] A/AC.105/C.2(XI)/WP.24 (20.4.72).   [34] General Assembly Res. 3235 (XXIX), annex.

[35] Art. 16; see further Cheng, loc. cit. in n. 3 above, pp. 588 ff. [Ch. 9 above, s. V.G: International Organizations]; B. Cheng, 'The 1968 Astronauts Agreement', 23 *YBWA* (1969), p. 185, pp. 204–5 [Ch. 10 above, s. VIII.A: Personal and Temporal Scope]; B. Cheng, 'Convention on International Liability for Damage Caused by Space Objects', in Jasentuliyana and Lee (eds.), 1 *Manual* (1979), p. 83 [Ch. 11, above, s. V.A.6: International Organizations]. See also Convention on Registration of Objects Launched into Outer Space, 14 Jan. 1975, Art. VII.

five years, the Secretary-General of the United Nations, as depositary, shall, at the request of one third of the States Parties to the Agreement and with the concurrence of the majority of the States Parties, convene a conference of the States Parties to review the Agreement. A review conference will also consider the question of the implementation of Article 11(5) on the establishment of an international regime to govern the exploitation of the natural resources of the moon, in the light of relevant technological developments,[36] as well as the question of the adequacy of the rules on liability.[37]

IV. The Common Heritage of Mankind

A. The Hub of the Agreement

The focal point and in fact the very *raison d'être* of the Agreement for many States is its Article 11(1) which declares:

The moon and its natural resources are the common heritage of mankind, which finds expression in the provisions of this Agreement, in particular in paragraph 5 of this article.

Such a declaration was what was sought by the initial 1970 Argentine proposal. On the other hand, the opposition which the concept of the common heritage of mankind provoked on the part of the Soviet Union, at least until agreement was reached on the SALT–II Agreement, was one of the principal reasons why the conclusion of the Moon Treaty was delayed until 1979.

In order to understand this provision, it is necessary to recall the background of the treaty.[38] At the dawn of the space age, many had hoped that outer space would be used only for peaceful purposes and in the interest of all mankind. As mentioned before, what was granted to them in the Outer Space Treaty of 27 January 1967 was rather limited.[39] By a coincidence later the same year, on 17 August 1967, Ambassador Arvid Pardo, on behalf of the Permanent Mission of Malta to the United Nations, proposed the inclusion in the agenda of the 22nd Session of the General Assembly of an item entitled: 'Declaration and Treaty Concerning the Reservation Exclusively for Peaceful Purposes of the Sea-Bed and of the Ocean Floor, Underlying the Seas Beyond the Limits of Present National Jurisdiction, and the Use of their Resources in the Interests of Mankind.' An accompanying memorandum explained why it was necessary to declare the sea-bed and ocean floor 'a common heritage of mankind,'[40] and to draw up a treaty to implement this concept. For those

---

[36] Art. 18; see also s. IV.L below: An International Regime.
[37] Art. 14(2); see also s. IV.M below: Liability for Damage Caused.
[38] See s. II.A above: Background.   [39] See text to n. 4 above.
[40] UN Doc. A/6695 (18.8.67). See also G. Weissberg, 'International Law Meets the Short-Term National Interest: The Maltese Proposal on the Sea-bed and Ocean Floor', 19 *ICLQ* (1969), p. 41.

countries which either directly themselves or indirectly on account of their nationals are interested in actually exploiting the resources of the ocean floor, someone has just opened Pandora's box. For the developing countries, the concept appears as manna from heaven.

Thus the United Nations General Assembly on 15 December 1969 adopted Resolution 2574D by 62 votes in favour (primarily developing nations), 28 against (industrialized nations), with 28 abstentions, declaring a moratorium on sea-bed exploitation.[41] The following year, on 17 December 1970, in Resolution 2749 (XXV), the General Assembly 'solemnly declare[d]':

The sea-bed and ocean floor, and the subsoil thereof, beyond the limits of national jurisdiction (hereinafter referred to as the area), as well as the resources of the area, are the common heritage of mankind.[42]

General Assembly resolutions are, however, mere recommendations and are not legally binding.[43] It has been left to the Third United Nations Conference on the Law of the Sea (UNCLOS III) to draw up an international treaty to translate this concept into treaty law, and to set up 'the Authority' to 'organise and control activities in the Area'. UNCLOS III held its organizational session in New York in December 1973 and its first substantive session in Caracas from 20 June to 29 August 1974.[44] Meanwhile, the Argentine proposal had already launched the campaign to apply the concept to the moon and other celestial bodies. In the end, the space lawyers proved to be the first to succeed in turning a corner of the universe into, in law, a common heritage of mankind, whatever this phrase may mean.[45]

One of the Soviet objections to the adoption of this concept, from the purely technical and legal point of view, was probably its lack of legal definition and the consequential danger of alleged rules and obligations being deduced from it in time to come. In a Working Paper submitted to the 1973 session of the Legal Sub-committee on the question, the Soviet Union explained: 'What is involved is not so much the terminology as the essence of the problem.'[46] In this sense, the virtue of the 1978 Austrian Working Paper lay in its stabilizing the content of the concept by spelling it out and in its confining the concept solely to this Agreement. It was saying in effect that the

[41] UN DOC. A/RES/2574D (XXIV), 9 *ILM* (1970), p. 422.

[42] UN. DOC. A/RES.2749 (XXV), 10 *ILM* (1971), p. 220.

[43] See B. Cheng, 'United Nations Resolutions on Outer Space: "Instant" International Customary Law?', 5 *Indian JIL* (1965), p. 23, esp. pp. 33–5 [Ch. 7 above, esp. s. VIII: Effects of General Assembly Resolutions].

[44] Cf. A. O. Adede, 'The System for Exploitation of the "Common Heritage of Mankind" at the Caracas Conference,' 69 *AJIL* (1975), p. 31.

[45] For the position in the law of the sea at the time, see UNCLOS III, Revised Informal Composite Negotiating Text (RICNT), A/CONF.62/WP.10/Rev.1 (28.4.79), 18 *ILM* (1979), p. 686.

[46] *Report of the Legal Sub-Committee on its 12th Sessioin (26.3–20.4.73)*, A/AC.105/115, Annex I, p. 24.

concept consisted in no more and no less than the totality of the substantive obligations laid down in the Agreement itself. The Austrian draft had provided in its Article Xl(l):

For the purposes of this Agreement, the moon and its natural resources shall be considered the common heritage of mankind, which finds its expression in the relevant provisions of this Agreement and in particular in paragraph 5 of this article.[47]

The Moon Treaty in the text of its Article 11(1), by deleting the initial prepositional phrase—for the purposes of this Agreement—and changing the verb in the main clause—shall be—to the present indicative—are—Parties to the Agreement presumably intend to treat Article 11(1) as declaratory of the existing legal position, but, because of the adjectival clause which qualifies the concept, they will nevertheless be precluded from reading into the treaty rights or obligations which do not find 'expression in the provisions of this Agreement, in particular in paragraph 5 of' Article 11. In this sense, the concept of the common heritage of mankind as used in the Moon Treaty, instead of being a ready-made package of rights and duties under general international law, is no more than a label for the bundle of provisions in the Agreement creating a new type of territorial status. These provisions will now be briefly examined.

B. International Law, Peace, Security, Co-operation, Understanding, Well-being, Progress and Development

Articles 2 and 4 provide that all activities on the moon shall be carried out in accordance with international law, as well as, particularly in its exploration and use, a host of rather platitudinous and legally unenforceable exhortations which largely repeat Articles I and IX of the 1967 Space Treaty,[48] designed to promote international peace, security, co-operation, understanding, well-being, progress and development.

C. Non-militarization

Article 3 repeats Article IV(2) of the 1967 Treaty by providing that the 'moon shall be used by all States Parties exclusively for peaceful purposes,' and should have, therefore, the same effect as the latter which, it is submitted, means total non-militarization and the prohibition of all military activities. However, the United States persists in wishing to interpret 'peaceful' as meaning 'non-aggressive' instead of 'non-military.'[49] Article 15 more or less repeats

[47] A/AC.105/C.2/WG.I(1978)/WP.2 (3.4.78), reproduced in A/AC.105/218, Annex I, p. 2.

[48] See further Cheng, loc. cit. in n. 3 above, especially ss. IV.1, 2 and 5, and VI.1 [Ch. 9 above, ss. V.A, V.B, and V.e, and VII.A]; see also Art. 6(3).

[49] The US delegate to the Outer Space Committee Mr Hosenball made this clear after the adopting of the text of the Agreement, A/AC.105/PV.203 (3.7.79), p. 22. On Art. IV(2) of the 1967 Space Treaty, see further Cheng, loc. cit. in n. 3 above, s. V.3; on the US attitude, see further ibid., p. 606 [Ch. 9 above, s. VI.C: Non-militarisation of Celestial Bodies].

Article XII of the 1967 Space Treaty on the right of mutual inspection, but makes it explicit that this right is to ensure compliance with the treaty. Article 15 has, moreover, dispensed with the condition of reciprocity.[50]

In relation to Article 3(2) which provides: 'Any threat or use of force or any other hostile act or threat of hostile act on the moon is prohibited,' the United Kingdom delegate made the rather puzzling statement in the Special Political Committee that the United Kingdom had agreed to the reference to 'any other hostile act or threat of hostile act' on the understanding that the treaty—and consequently the prohibition—related only to the moon and not to the earth.[51] Under Article 2(4) of the United Nations Charter, the use or threat of force in international relations in any manner inconsistent with the purposes and principles of the Charter is already illegal. What then are these hostile acts or threats of hostile acts which, so it would seem, would be lawful on earth according to the United Kingdom Government, but unlawful on the moon? It is, therefore, interesting to find that the French, when signing the Moon Treaty, attached the following explanation to their signature:

France is of the view that the provisions of Article 3, paragraph 2, of the Agreement relating to the use or threat of force cannot be construed as anything other than a reaffirmation, for the purpose of the field of endeavour covered by the Agreement, of the principle of the prohibition of the threat or use of force, which States are obliged to observe in their international relations, as set forth in the UN Charter.[52]

D. Non-appropriation

1. *No National Appropriation.* Article 11(2) repeats the prohibition of national appropriation of any portion of the moon in Article 11 of the 1967 Space Treaty, which in itself, it is submitted, does not prohibit the appropriation of the resources of the moon.[53]

2. *No Proprietary Right over Surface, Subsurface or Natural Resources in Place.* Under Article 11(3):

Neither the surface nor the subsurface of the moon, nor any part thereof or natural resources in place, shall become property of any State, international intergovernmental or non-governmental organisation, national organisation or non-governmental entity or of any natural person. The placement of personnel, space vehicles, equipment, facilities, stations and installations on or below the surface of the moon, including structures connected with its surface or subsurface, shall not create a right of ownership over the surface or subsurface of the moon or any areas thereof. The fore-

---

[50] On Art. XII of the Space Treaty, see Cheng, loc. cit. in n. 3 above, s. V.4 [Ch. 9 above, s. VI.D: Free Access]; on mutual inspection under the Moon Treaty, see further s. K below.

[51] A/SPC/34/SR.19 (1.11.79), para. 42.

[52] As subsequently quoted in Nandasiri Jasentuliyana, 'The Moon Treaty', in id. (ed.), *Maintaining Outer Space for Peaceful Uses* (1984), p. 121, at p. 131.

[53] See Cheng, loc. cit. in n. 3 above, s. IV.2 [Ch. 9 above, s. V.B: *Res Extra Commercium*].

going provisions are without prejudice to the international régime referred to in paragraph 5 of this article.

It will be noted that the prohibition, in regard to natural resources, applies only to those 'in place.'

E. Freedom of Scientific Investigation

While the 1967 Space Treaty in its Article 1(3) asserts a general freedom of scientific investigation in outer space, Article 6(1) of the Moon Treaty which declares the moon to be the common heritage of mankind paradoxically refers only to the freedom of 'all States Parties'. The Moon Treaty has, however, settled a controversy which had arisen over the proper interpretation of Article II of the 1967 Space Treaty regarding non-appropriation, at least for the purposes of the Moon Treaty itself. Article 6(2) provides that in carrying out or in the course of scientific investigations, States Parties enjoy the following rights:

(i) *Collection of samples.* They 'have the right to collect on and remove from the moon samples of its mineral and other substances'. Although the treaty avoids using the term, they become in fact property of the States Parties concerned and 'may be used by them for scientific purposes.' However, the Treaty commends to States Parties the desirability of making a portion of samples available to others for scientific purposes.

(ii) *Use of lunar substances for support of missions.* States Parties may also 'use mineral and other substances of the moon in quantities appropriate for the support of their missions'.

F. Freedom of Exploration and Use Without Discrimination

Article 11(4), in furtherance of Article 4(1), proclaims that 'States Parties have the right to exploration and use of the moon without discrimination . . .' Article 8(1) says they may do so 'anywhere on or below its surface . . .' They may, in particular, according to Article 8(2):

(a) Land their space objects on the moon and launch them from the moon;
(b) Place their personnel, space vehicles, equipment, facilities, stations and installations anywhere on or below the surface of the moon.[54]

These may also be moved freely. Care is to be taken to avoid interference with the activities of other States Parties. In case of interference, consultations shall take place in accordance with Article 15(2) and (3) (Article 8(3)).

---

[54] Presumably also over it, either in orbit or, where there is an atmosphere, aeronautically, bearing in mind that the Agreement is applicable, apart from the moon, also to other celestial bodies within the solar system, other than the earth (Art. 1(1)).

G. Freedom to Establish Manned and Unmanned Stations

Under Article 9, manned and unmanned stations may be established subject to the following provisos:

(i) only the area required for the station may be used;
(ii) immediate notification of the location and purpose to the Secretary-General of the United Nations;
(iii) annual report to the Secretary-General;
(iv) free access to all areas of the moon of other States Parties not obstructed.

H. Legal Status of Personnel, Space Vehicles, Equipment, Facilities, Stations, and Installations

1. *No Ownership over Surface or Subsurface.* The placement of personnel, space vehicles, stations, and so forth creates no right of ownership over the surface or the subsurface of the moon or any area thereof.[55]

2. *Jurisdiction and Ownership.* Such items remain under the jurisdiction of their respective States Parties and, in the case of space vehicles, equipment, facilities, stations, and installations, their ownership is not affected by their presence on the moon.[56] The Moon Treaty is unclear as to what it means by a State's personnel. This can be taken to refer to astronauts that are its nationals. If so, Article 12(1) of the Moon Treaty is at variance with Article VIII of the 1967 Space Treaty which confers jurisdiction on the State of registry of the vehicle to which the personnel belong. If the Moon treaty has in mind also the State of registry of the vehicle, then it would have failed to clarify the position of an astronaut who no longer forms part of the personnel of a space vehicle. Is the State which exercises jurisdiction over him his national State or the State controlling the station to which he is attached?

3. *Return of Space Objects.* Vehicles, installations and equipment found in places other than their intended location shall be dealt with in accordance with Article 5 of the 1968 Astronauts Agreement.[57]

4. *Safety Measures.* States Parties shall adopt all practicable measures to safeguard the life and health of persons on the moon and treat them in accordance with the Astronauts Agreement.[58]

---

[55] Art. 11(3); see further s. IV.D.2 above.
[56] Art. 12(1). See further Cheng, loc. cit. in n. 3 above, s. IV.3 [Ch. 9 above, s. V.C: Jurisdiction of the State of Registry.]
[57] Art. 12(2); see further B. Cheng, 'The 1968 Astronauts Agreement', 23 *YBWA* (1969), p. 185, pp. 201 ff. [Ch. 10 above, s. VI.B: In Regard to Space Objects].
[58] Art. 10(1).

5. *Distress.*   States Parties shall offer shelter to persons in distress on the moon in their lunar facilities.[59]

6. *Emergency.*   In the event of an emergency, involving a threat to human life, States Parties may use the facilities of other States Parties on the moon. Prompt notification shall be made to the Secretary-General of the United Nations or the State Party concerned.[60]

7. *Accidents.*   Article 13 provides:

A State Party which learns of the crash landing, forced landing or other unintended landing on the moon of a space object, or its component parts, that were not launched by it, shall promptly inform the launching State Party and the Secretary-General of the United Nations.

It seems that this provision could have with advantage been extended to knowledge of all accidents occurring on the moon.[61]

I. Various Duties of States Parties

1. *Information on Missions.*   Article 5(1) requires States Parties to provide the Secretary-General of the United Nations, the international scientific community and the public with information on their activities on the moon. An early attempt to require that such information should be provided 'well in advance of launching'[62] was strongly resisted by the Soviet Union. The present obligation to provide information 'as soon as possible' and, like that under Article XI of the 1967 Space Treaty,[63] only 'to the greatest extent feasible and practicable' leaves the States Parties a great deal of discretion.

2. *Advance Information.*   Exceptions are made in the first place where a State Party becomes aware that another State Party plans to operate simultaneously in the same area, in which case it shall promptly inform the other State of the timing of and plans for its own operation (Article 5(2)). Secondly, under Article 7(2), States Parties shall, to the maximum extent feasible, notify the United Nations Secretary-General in advance of all placements by them of radioactive materials on the moon and of the purpose of such placements.

---

[59] Art. 10(2). On distress, see Cheng, *General Principles of Law*, pp. 75–7.

[60] Art. 12(3). The 'or' is to provide for cases where there is no diplomatic relations between the Parties concerned, although having made use of the facilities of another, it seems a little churlish not to inform the other party direct, where ownership is known, cf. Art. 13 where 'and' is used. Art. 12(3) is in any event merely declaratory of the recognized plea of necessity (*Notstand*) in general international law, which involves a duty to reimburse benefits received or damage caused. See further Cheng, *General Principles of Law*, pp. 69–77.

[61] Cf. Art. 1 of the 1968 Astronauts Agreement, which would appear to cover this situation and to be much better drafted. See Ch. 10 above, s. VI.A.1: Notification of Accidents.

[62] Cf. US Working Paper, A/AC.105/C.2(XI)/WP.3 (11.4.72), reproduced A/AC.105/101, Annex I, p. 8.

[63] Cf. Cheng, loc. cit. in n. 3 above, s. V.4 [Ch. 9 above, s. VI.E: Reporting of Space Activities].

3. *Report of Dangerous Phenomena or Organic Life.* Article 5(3) slightly enlarges the obligation under Article V(3) of the 1967 Space Treaty by requiring States Parties to report any phenomena they may discover which could endanger human life or health, as well as any indication of organic life.

4. *Environmental Preservation.* Under Article 7, States Parties are under an obligation to take measures to protect the environment in their exploration and use of the moon, and to inform the Secretary-General of the United Nations of measures being adopted by them. As mentioned before, they are also, to the maximum extent feasible, to notify him in advance of all placements by them of radio-active materials on the moon and the purposes of such placements. Thought is given to the possibility of establishing international scientific preserves. To that end, States Parties are asked to report areas of special scientific interest to the Secretary-General and other States Parties. The 1979 Session of the Outer Space Committee said in its Report that in the discussions before the draft treaty was adopted,

the Committee agreed that Article VII is not intended to result in prohibiting the exploitation of the natural resources which may be found on celestial bodies other than the earth but, rather, that such exploitation will be carried out in such a manner as to minimize any disruption or adverse effects to the existing balance of the environment.[64]

5. *Report on the Discovery of Natural Resources.* In order to facilitate the establishment of the international regime for the management of the natural resources of the moon, States Parties are under an obligation to inform the United Nations Secretary-General, the public and the international scientific community, to the greatest extent feasible and practicable, of any natural resources they may discover on the moon (Article 11(6)).

J. State Responsibility for National Activities

Following the precedent set by Article VI of the 1967 Space Treaty, Article 14(1) of the Moon Treaty holds States Parties directly responsible for national activities on the moon. Like the Space Treaty, however, it fails to specify whether this responsibility extends only to activities within a State's territorial jurisdiction and quasi-territorial jurisdiction, or whether it applies also to activities carried out from outside its territory by its nationals acting without its authority and even contrary to its laws.[65]

K. Mutual Supervision

Article 15 recognizes that '[e]ach State Party may assure itself that the activities of other States Parties . . . are compatible with the provisions of this

---

[64] A/34/20, para. 65.
[65] Cf. Cheng, loc. cit. n n. 3 above, s. IV.6 [Ch. 9 above, s. V.F: International Responsibility].

Agreement' and consequently allows the States Parties freely to visit the facilities of one another on the moon, subject to reasonable notice and the taking of maximum precautions to assure safety, and to avoid undue interference, but, unlike Article XII of the 1967 Space Treaty, no longer subject to the condition of reciprocity.[66]

In case of disagreement, Article 15 provides for, in the first instance, consultation between the States Parties concerned, and, in case of an impasse, unilateral recourse to the Secretary-General of the United Nations for assistance, without seeking the consent of the other Party concerned, in order to resolve the controversy. The same procedure applies to mutual interference on the moon (Article 8(3)).

L. An International Regime

The crux of the concept of the common heritage of mankind is probably that at some stage a purely normative framework no longer suffices and an institutional structure is required. Thus, while the present rules of the Moon Treaty will be adequate during the exploration phase of lunar activities, the contracting States recognize that something more will be needed once it becomes possible to exploit the resources of the moon. A crucial element of the concept of the common heritage of mankind as incorporated in the Moon Treaty is, therefore, the undertaking of the States Parties, under Article 11(5), 'to establish an international regime, including appropriate procedures, to govern the exploitation of the natural resources of the moon as such exploitation is about to become feasible.'

Article 11(7) provides:

The main purposes of the international régime to be established shall include:
(a) The orderly and safe development of the natural resources of the moon;
(b) The rational management of those resources;
(c) The expansion of opportunities in the use of those resources;
(d) An equitable sharing by all States Parties in the benefits derived from those resources, whereby the interests and needs of the developing countries, as well as the efforts of those countries which have contributed either directly or indirectly to the exploration of the moon, shall be given special consideration.

Under Article 18, the question of setting up the international regime will be considered at any conference convened to review the Agreement. The question of convening such a conference will automatically be included in the provisional agenda of the United Nations General Assembly ten years after the entry into force of the Agreement. But such a conference can be convened at any time after the Agreement has been in force for five years, if requested by

---

[66] See further ibid., s. V.4 [Ch. 9 above, s. VI.D: Free Access].

one third of the States Parties and this request meets with the concurrence of a majority of the States Parties.[67]

M. Liability for Damage Caused

In the event of damage caused on the moon, the Agreement appears to rely on the rules on liability found in the 1967 Space Treaty,[68] and the 1972 Liability Convention.[69] But it recognizes that detailed arrangements may become necessary as a result of more extensive activities on the moon. Under Article 14, it leaves the matter to be discussed at the next review conference.[70]

V. Some Concluding Remarks

From the purely formal point of view, the Agreement is perhaps one of the most poorly drafted among the five treaties that have emanated from the United Nations Outer Space Committee, outdoing even the 1968 Astronauts Agreement.[71] First, the extraordinary extension which the treaty has given to the word moon is likely to give rise to a great deal of confusion. Secondly, the various provisions appear to have been assembled together in no particular order. In 1974, the United States did suggest a rearrangement of the articles in order to bring about greater 'clarity and coherence,'[72] but the proposal fell on deaf ears.

From the substantive point of view, it is true that the treaty has proclaimed the moon and all the celestial bodies within the solar system other than the earth the common heritage of mankind. But what does this amount to? Much of the concept, as defined in the Agreement, would seem to consist in rules already found in the 1967 Space Treaty, the 1968 Astronauts Agreement, and the 1972 Liability Convention.

The crucial problem is of course that of resources. In the light of the United Nations General Assembly resolution declaring a moratorium on the exploitation of the resources of the sea-bed and ocean floor,[73] as soon as the draft moon treaty was approved by the United Nations Outer Space Committee, a major controversy developed in the United States as to whether the moon treaty imposed a similar moratorium. Almost immediately after the

---

[67] See s. III.C above: Temporal Scope.
[68] See Cheng, loc. cit. in n. 3 above, IV.6 [Ch. 9 above, s. V.F: International Responsibility].
[69] Cf. further loc. cit. in n. 22 above [Ch. 11 above, esp. s. V.B: Cosmographical Scope]. It should be noted that during the discussions leading to the drawing up of the 1972 Liability Convention, the question of injury to astonauts and damage to installations and stations on the moon or other celestial bodies caused by a space object was raised, but not specifically dealt with. See text to Ch. 11, n. 189.
[70] See s. III.C above: Temporal Scope.   [71] See Ch. 10 above.
[72] A/AC.105/C.2/L.91, and Corr. 1 (6.5.74), reproduced in A/AC.105/133, Annex I, p. 2.
[73] See text to n. 41 above.

vote had been taken in the Outer Space Committee on the draft moon treaty, Mr Hosenball, the United States delegate (and also General Counsel of NASA) said:

The draft agreement—and I am particularly pleased about this, as a member of the National Aeronautics and Space Administration (NASA)—as part of the compromises made by many delegations, places no moratorium upon the exploitation of the natural resources on celestial bodies, pending the establishment of an international régime. This permits orderly attempts to establish that such exploitation is in fact feasible and practicable, by making possible experimental beginnings and, then, pilot operations, a process by which we believe we can learn if it will be practicable and feasible to exploit the mineral resources of such celestial bodies.[74]

This view was, however, challenged by Mr Leigh S. Ratiner, a Washington attorney who served for many years as a member of the United States delegation to UNCLOS III. In a prepared statement presented on behalf of the L–5 Society, an organization interested in the utilization of the potential of space, to the Sub-Committee on Space Science and Applications of the Committee on Science and Technology of the United States House of Representatives on 6 September 1979, Mr Ratiner said:

it is my very strong view that the moon treaty in its present form imposes a *de facto* moratorium on private enterprise use of outer space in connection with the development of natural resources.[75]

Mr Ratiner stated a little later:

it should also be noted that not only as a practical matter, but also as a legal matter, the moon treaty can be deemed to be a moratorium.[76]

Quoting the above passage from Mr Hosenball's statement, Mr Ratiner further asked rhetorically:

Can there be any doubt, Mr Chairman, that the American delegate has made it clear by his statement that the treaty does not permit exploitation itself?[77]

What is the correct position? First, it is necessary to clarify the meaning of the word exploitation. Insofar as the treaty is concerned, the word has the

---

[74] A/AC.105/PV.203 (3.7.79), p. 22; see also the speech of the US delegate to the Special Political Committee, Mr Petree, A/SPC/34/SR.19 (1.11.79), para. 25: 'The draft Treaty placed no moratorium on the exploitation of the natural resources of celestial bodies by States or their nationals.'

[75] *International Space Activities 1979*. Hearings before the Sub-Committee on Space Science and Application of the Committee on Science and Technology, US House of Representatives 96th Cong. 1st Sess. Sept. 5 and 6, 1979 [No. 50], p. 100, at p. 108.

[76] Ibid.

[77] Ibid. In both instances where Mr Hosenball had used the word 'exploitation', Mr Ratiner's quotation of it used the word 'exploration'. However, this does not appear to affect Mr Ratiner's argument in any way. See, moreover, Mr Ratiner's oral testimony, where the same passage was correctly quoted, ibid. p. 115.

meaning attributed to it particularly in Article 11(5) which provides for an international regime to be established when 'exploitation is about to become feasible.'[78] Exploitation in this context would seem to go beyond mere 'exploration and use' and involve the systematic appropriation or utilization of the natural resources of the moon for commercial or other practical purposes. It was doubtless in this sense that Mr Ratiner used the term, and also in this sense that Mr Hosenball used the word the second time in the above quoted passage, when he spoke of 'orderly attempts to establish that *such exploitation is in fact feasible and practicable.*' However, when he referred to 'exploitation' the first time in the same passage, he was using the word, if not in a different, at least in a wider, sense to include 'experimental beginnings' and 'pilot operations', which correspond more to what the treaty calls exploration. It is possible to use the term in an even wider sense, as did, for example, Mr Petree the United States delegate to the Special Political Committee when he said:

The draft Treaty placed no moratorium on the *exploitation* of the natural resources of celestial bodies by States or their nationals, but it did provide that any such *exploitation* must be carried out in accordance with article XI, paragraph 7, and article VI, paragraph 2.[79]

In including activities under Article 6(2), which would be what the treaty calls 'exploration and use', within the meaning of 'exploitation', he would of course be correct in saying that the treaty imposed no moratorium on exploitation, inasmuch as such activities are expressly authorized by the treaty.[80] But the question remains whether the treaty imposes a moratorium on 'exploitation' within the meaning of Article 11(5).

In order to answer this question, one must start from the beginning, which is the premise laid down by the treaty in its Article 11(2) precluding the private ownership of 'natural resources *in place*.'[81] The treaty, insofar as resources are concerned, next provides in its Article 11(8):

All the activities with respect to the natural resources of the moon shall be carried out in a manner compatible with the purposes specified in paragraph 7 of this article and the provisions of article 6, paragraph 2, of this Agreement.

It follows from this provision that the handling of the natural resources of the moon must come under either one or the other of these two headings, i.e. either scientific investigation under Article 6(2),[82] or utilization and appropriation in accordance with the purposes of the international regime to be established as set out in Article 11(7).[83] If this interpretation is correct and it is

---

[78] See s. IV.L. above.
[79] A/SPC/34/SR.19 (1.11.79), para. 25; italics added. Mr Hosenball in his reply to written Question 7 put to him by the House of Representatives Sub-Committee on Space Science and Application used the word exploitation seemingly in the same way: see loc. cit. in n. 75 above, p. 99.
[80] See s. IV.E above.   [81] See s. IV.D.2 above.   [82] See s. IV.E above.
[83] See s. IV.L above.

submitted that it is, then the 'right of exploration and use' under Article 11(4)[84] does not confer any additional right in relation to natural resources, but is concerned only with the modalities of exploration and use, such as landing, take off, emplacement of personnel, the establishment of manned and unmanned stations and so forth.[85]

Insofar as Article 6(2) is concerned, it is clear, as has been mentioned before, that there can be no question of a moratorium. Indeed, Mr Hosenball was no doubt right when he said:

article XI, paragraph 8, by referring to article VI, paragraph 2, makes it clear that the right to collect samples of natural resources is not infringed upon and that there is no limit to the right of States Parties to utilize, in the course of scientific investigations, such quantities of those natural resources found on celestial bodies as are appropriate for the support of their mission.[86]

As to Article 11(7), it seems that, although this paragraph states the main purposes of the international regime to be established, it potentially governs three different situations. In the first place, on the assumption that exploitation has become feasible and an international regime has been duly established, it is obvious that the regime will have to comply with the principles laid down in Article 11(7).

Secondly, it seems clear from Article 11(8) that Article 11(7) is applicable also to the type of pre-exploitation operations mentioned by Mr Hosenball on which, so it would appear, the treaty has laid down no moratorium. That there could be operations not covered by the regime and that such operations would nonetheless come under Article 11(7) were points clearly envisaged by Mr Petree when he said:

Article XI, paragraph 7, provided a framework for such exploitation since even exploitation undertaken by a State Party or its nationals *outside the context of the proposed régime* would have to be compatible with the provisions of that paragraph.[87]

This also leads to the third possibility, namely, the situation that would exist when exploitation within the meaning of Article 11(5) is already feasible, but, because of the impossibility of reaching an agreement, no international regime has been established. By the nature of things, the setting up of the regime needs another treaty. The obligation undertaken by States under Article 11(5) is no more than a *pactum de contrahendo*, which means that States Parties are obliged only to negotiate in good faith with a view to reaching agreement on such a regime, but not bound to reach agreement willy-nilly at whatever cost.[88] Mr Hosenball, in the quoted speech, said in this connection:

[84] See s. IV.F above.   [85] See ss. IV.F and IV.G above.
[86] Loc. cit. in n. 74 above, p. 22. Similarly, US delegate to Special Political Committee, loc. cit. in 79 above.
[87] Loc. cit. n. 79 above, para. 25; italics added.
[88] See Cheng, *General Principles of Law*, pp. 111 n. 27, 117–8. See also Mr Hosenball in his Reply to Written Question 8, loc. cit. in n. 75 above, p. 99.

My government will, when and if these negotiations for such a régime are called for, under Article XI and XVIII, make every effort to see that the régime is successfully negotiated.[89]

Mr Petree was more explicit before the Special Political Committee. Having said his government would 'make a good-faith effort' to ensure such negotiations were 'successfully concluded,' he added:

Each of the participants in the conference on such a régime would, of course, have to evaluate any treaty emerging from the conference in the light of their own national interests. For his country, that would require a treaty which was balanced and reasonable and which met with the approval of the United States Senate.[90]

The possibility that, when the time comes, there will be no international regime can, therefore, hardly be discounted.

If this happens, is there a moratorium on exploitation? While States which advocate the maximum sharing of the benefits of exploitation would no doubt favour an affirmative reply, an objective analysis of the treaty and its history inclines one, alas, to the opposite conclusion. First, the treaty itself indicates no such moratorium. Secondly, a joint proposal put forward by Egypt, India, and Nigeria in 1974 which would have permitted only 'exploration for experimental purposes'[91] was not accepted. Thirdly, in the light of the controversial nature of the General Assembly resolution calling for a moratorium on the exploitation of the resources of the sea-bed and ocean floor,[92] the twice repeated assertion of United States delegates during the drafting of the treaty that there was no moratorium on exploitation—which assertion not being contradicted[93]—must be taken as expressive of the views of those who drafted the treaty. However, even in this situation, which Mr Petree's statement can well be read as also covering, the principles of Article 11(7) apply.

---

[89] Loc. cit. in n. 74 above.   [90] Loc. cit. in n. 79 above, para. 24.

[91] A/AC.105/C.2/L.97; reproduced in A/AC.105/133, Annex I, p. 14.

[92] See text to n. 41 above.

[93] See n. 74 above and text thereto. In his prepared statement presented to the Sub-Committee on Space Science and Applications of the US House of Representatives Committee on Science and Technology on 6 Sept. 1979, Mr Hosenball indicated that one of the reasons why the 1979 session of the Outer Space Committee was able to reach a consensus on the Moon Treaty was 'the agreement of the developing countries not to insist on a provision imposing a moratorium on the exploitation of natural resources pending the establishment of an international régime to govern such exploitation' (loc. cit. in n. 75 above, p. 82, at p. 84). There is, however, for the reasons given above (see n. 22 above and text thereto), no record of such an agreement and it is to be wondered if any such informal understanding can be treated as part of the *travaux préparatoires* of the treaty. As to the statements made by the United States representatives to the Legal Sub-Committee of the Outer Space Committee in 1972 and 1973 and quoted by Mr Hosenball in his statement (loc. cit. in n. 75 above, at p. 85) it may be pointed out that (i) they must be considered as being somewhat remote in time to the final agreement to be in any way regarded as conclusive as to the proper interpretation of the treaty, and (ii) they have been much abbreviated in the summary records issued by the United Nations (see respectively, A/AC.105/C.2/SR.188 (3.5.72), p. 31; ibid./SR.205 (19.4.73), p. 112).

Table XII.1 EXPLORATION, USE AND EXPLOITATION OF THE NATURAL RESOURCES OF THE MOON

1. Moon not subject to national appropriation (Art. 11(2)) **2. No right of ownership over moon's surface, subsurface, or natural resources *in place* (Art. 11(3))** **3. Equal right to explore and use moon (Art. 11 (4))** **4. Activities with respect to moon's natural resources governed by Art. 11(8), which in turn refers to compatibility and conformity with following provisions:**			
Art. 6(2) permits, in scientific investigation, (a) collection and removal of samples, and	**Art. 11(7)** which specifies the main purposes of the international regime to be established, including (a) orderly and safe development, (b) rational managment, (c) expansion of opportunities in use of sources, and (d) equitable sharing of benefits.		
(b) use of natural resources for support of mission.	**Exploitation not yet feasible**	**Exploitation feasible**	
		International regime established (Art. 11(5))	Lack of agreement on an international regime
Imposes no moratorium	No mortorium on experimental and pilot schemes	Exploitation to be under the authority of the regime	*Semble*: no moratorium on exploitation, provided Art. 11(7) complied with

In that connection, what, in referring to Article 11(7), Mr Petree went on to say is significant:

The latter [i.e., Article 11(7)] also provided an incentive for exploitation, for it decreased States' and private entities' doubts about the advisability of embarking on the costly exploitation of the moon's natural resources and recognized that equitable sharing of the benefits deriving therefrom required that special consideration be given both to those who had contributed directly to the exploration of the moon and to the developing countries and those who had indirectly contributed to the moon's exploration. Already, under existing international co-operation in other areas of space explorations, States which had expended large resources on developing space systems to exploit space applications had shared the benefits equitably within the international community.[94]

One reading of this statement would be that space powers are already sharing the benefits of space applications equitably with the rest of the international community so that no dramatic changes are to be expected when Article 11(7) is being applied or even under the international regime itself, at least insofar as the sharing of benefits is concerned.

This is not to say, however, that an international regime will not be established, or, when established, will not have a substantial impact on the exploitation of the natural resources of the moon and other celestial bodies and be of major significance to international law as a whole. But just as the conclusion of the moon treaty was a matter of political will, so also will be its implementation . Whether the new concept of the common heritage of mankind introduced by the treaty develops into a shining reality or degenerates into a myth will depend on whether in the years to come the States Parties display the necessary will to comply with not only the letter of the treaty, but also its spirit.

[94] Loc. cit. in n. 79 above, para. 25.

PART IV

OUTER SPACE, ASTRONAUTS, AND SPACE OBJECTS

13

Outer Space: The International Legal Framework—the International Legal Status of Outer Space, Space Objects, and Spacemen*

I. The Legal Status of Outer Space and of Celestial Bodies and the Definition and Delimitation of Outer Space under General International Law

A. A Matter of International Law

In order to avoid any misunderstanding, let it be said at the very outset that space law, as it now exists, is not an independent legal system. It is merely a functional classification of those rules of international law and of municipal law relating to outer space, natural or man-made objects in outer space, spacemen, and man's activities in outer space. In our present discussion, we are in fact concerned only with those rules of public international law which, by defining the legal status of outer space, space objects and spacemen, provide the international legal framework for the activities of States and of their astronauts in outer space.

B. The Nature of International Law

In view of the utter confusion which appears to prevail in the doctrine of international law at the moment as to what international law really is, it may perhaps be well to lay bare the premises on which our discussion is to be based. Its object is primarily to review analytically and critically the *lex lata* and any emergent *lex lata*. Where we discuss *leges ferendae*, it would be realistic ones which we would be prepared to suggest to any government or table at any diplomatic conference, and not the kind which people would enunciate for their idealistic or ideological effect but which, if perchance called upon to implement, they might well recoil from in practice. The term international law refers, therefore, to an existing and operative system of law made on this

* Lectures delivered at the Institute of Public International Law and International Relations, University of Thessaloniki in Sept. 1979, and first published in 10 *Thesaurus Acroasium* (1981), pp. 41–106. Reprinted by kind permission of the Institute, publishers of *Thesaurus Acroasium*.

planet by the subjects of international law, i.e., States and other entities endowed with international legal personality, to regulate their interrelations, and not to some philosophy, however worthy, which lives only in the mind of its proponents and adherents who lack the requisite political power to turn its tenets into legal norms. Such a positivist approach has sometimes been criticized as one of moral anaesthesia, but such critics are not unlike the medieval theologians who considered medical studies to be a betrayal of the Faith and of His healing powers.

C. The Personal Scope of the Rules of the International Legal System

The international legal system comprises, for purposes relevant to the present discussion, two groups of rules, first those of *general international law* (a term used here synonymously with customary international law *sensu lato*) which are binding on all the subjects of international law, and secondly those created by *treaties* which are binding only on their contracting parties. Notwithstanding frequent assertions or assumptions to the contrary, a treaty, however numerous its contracting parties, cannot as such create rights or duties for non-parties without their consent, a point now happily re-affirmed in Article 34 of the 1969 Vienna Convention on the Law of Treaties, although as Article 38 of the same Convention says nothing precludes a rule established in a treaty from becoming binding on third parties as a rule of general international law. But, as the *North Sea Continental Shelf Cases* (1969) have shown, whether a treaty rule has become a rule of general international law is an issue which must be established in respect of each individual rule by reference to general State practice and not by reference merely to the number of States parties to the treaty in question.[1]

In discussing any topic of international law, it is consequently important always clearly to distinguish the legal position on the level of the general law common to all the subjects of international law, and that on the level of treaties which affects only those that are parties to the relevant treaties. This is particularly important in the field of space law where the applicable rules of general international law might at first sight appear to be few and where there have been concluded a number of multilateral treaties under the auspices of the United Nations.[2] In this connection, it is hardly necessary to point out that the United Nations has no legislative authority, that the resolutions of its General Assembly do not *per se* create rules of general international law,[3] and are not, contrary to a fairly prevalent view, in themselves legally binding except in United Nations organizational and budgetary matters.

---

[1] *ICJ Rep. 1969*, p. 3; see further s. I.J below.   [2] See further ss. I.J and II below.
[3] See B. Cheng, 'United Nations Resolutions on Outer Space: "Instant" International Customary Law?', 5 *Indian JIL* (1965), p. 23 [Ch. 7 above], and s. I.I below.

D. The Cosmographical Scope of the Rules of the International Legal System

When man first penetrated into outer space, the fear was sometimes voiced that he would be entering a legal vacuum. Even today, the United Nations, whenever it finds an opportunity, likes to assert the applicability of international law, including the Charter of the United Nations, to outer space. In fact, international law knows no inherent geographical limits and extends to the activities of the subjects of international law in outer space from the very beginning.[4]

Table XIII.1 THE PERSONAL AND COSMOGRAPHICAL SCOPE OF RULES OF THE INTERNATIONAL LEGAL SYSTEM

	GENERAL INTERNATIONAL LAW	**TREATIES**
PERSONAL SCOPE	Applicable to all subjects of international law	Applicable only between contracting States
COSMO-GRAPHICAL SCOPE	In principle, applicable without geographical limits, and extend to outer space and celestial bodies from the very beginning	

E. Territorial Delimitation of State Competence: a Prime Function and a Major Premise of International Law

Notwithstanding views to the contrary frequently expressed sometimes even by the most eminent authorities, what was said by Judge Max Huber in the *Palmas Arbitration* (1928) remains totally valid today:

The development of the national organisation of States during the last few centuries and, as a corollary, the development of international law, have established this principle of the exclusive competence of the State in regard to its own territory in such a way as to make it the point of departure in settling most questions that concern international relations . . . [T]erritorial sovereignty belongs always to one, or in exceptional circumstances to several States, to the exclusion of all others. The fact that the functions of a State can be performed by any State within a given zone is, on the other hand, precisely the characteristic feature of the legal situation pertaining in those parts of the globe which, like the high seas or lands without a master, cannot or do not yet form the territory of a State.

[4] See further B. Cheng, 'The Extraterrestrial Application of International Law', 18 *CLP* (1965), p. 132 [Ch. 5 above].

Territorial sovereignty is, in general, a situation recognised and delimited in space, either by so-called natural frontiers as recognised by international law or by outward signs of delimitation that are undisputed, or else by legal engagements entered into between interested neighbours, such as frontier conventions, or by acts of recognition of States within fixed boundaries . . .

. . . [I]t serves to divide between nations the space upon which human activities are employed, in order to assure them at all points the minimum of protection of which international law is the guardian.[5]

International law assumes, therefore, that the world will be divided spatially into three different categories of territory, namely, (i) national territory, over which one State (or very exceptionally two or more) exercises territorial sovereignty, to the exclusion of all others; (ii) territories which *cannot* be made the territory of a State (*territorium extra commercium*), such as the high seas; and (iii) territories which are not under the sovereignty of a recognized subject of international law but which are capable of being acquired by any State in accordance with the rules of international law governing the acquisition of territory: in other words, they are merely *not yet* the territory of any State (*territorium nullius*). To be added to this traditional tripartite classification mentioned by Judge Huber in his Award, is the new category about to be introduced into international law by the Moon Treaty 1979, namely, (iv) territories which constitute 'the common heritage of mankind' and are excluded from national appropriation (*territorium commune humanitatis*).

While *territorium extra commercium* and *territorium commune humanitatis* share the same characteristic that they cannot be territorially appropriated by any State, they differ in that the former is essentially a negative concept, whereas the latter is a positive one. In the former, in time of peace, as long as a State respects the exclusive quasi-territorial jurisdiction[6] of other States over their own ships, aircraft, and spacecraft, general international law allows it to use the area or even to abuse it more or less as it wishes, including the appropriation of its natural resources, closing large parts of it for weapon testing and military exercises, and even using it as a cesspool for its municipal and industrial sewage. The emergent concept of the common heritage of mankind, on the other hand, still lacks precise definition. Basically it wishes to convey the idea that the management, exploitation and distribution of the natural resources of the area in question are matters to be decided upon by the international community and are not to be left to the initiative and discretion of individual States or their nationals.[7]

Once the areas of the world have been so classified, the main function particularly of general international law is to determine and regulate the competence of States in each of the several categories of territory: namely, what States may or may not do in their own territory, in the territories of other

---

[5] 2 *RIAA*, p. 829 at pp. 838–9.   [6] See further s. I.F below.
[7] See further s. II.B below.

Table XIII.2 SPATIAL CLASSIFICATION OF WORLD TERRITORY UNDER INTERNATIONAL LAW

National Territory	Territorium Extra Commercium	Territorium Nullius	Common Heritage of Mankind

States, in *territorium extra commercium*, in *territorium nullius* and in territories that constitute the common heritage of mankind. It will be readily perceived that the functional classification of activities of States into those that are lawful and those are unlawful follows—and not precedes—spatial delimitation. To do otherwise would be to put the cart before the horse. Under general international law, there are in fact few activities of States that are either universally lawful or universally unlawful. Thus the answer to the question for instance, whether a State may arrest a foreign vessel or not for monitoring its electronic defence installations will depend not on the nature of the act but primarily on the *locus*, of both the act and the arrest, i.e., whether the act of intelligence-gathering and the arrest are carried out in a State's own territory, in the territory of another State, on the high seas, in no man's land, or in an area which is the common heritage of mankind; and secondarily on the relationship between the State and the vessel, i.e., on whether the ship has the nationality of the State.

F. Nature, Scope, and Limits of State Jurisdiction[8]

In order to understand fully what has just been said, one has to understand the nature of State jurisdiction and its scope and limits. In international law, States are recognized as having three types of jurisdiction, that over its own territory, that over its own ships, aircraft, and spacecraft (in fact, one may perhaps say, any means of transport which is designed for travel in areas not subject to the territorial jurisdiction of any State, i.e., *territorium nullius*, *territorium extra commercium*, or common heritage of mankind, and which has a special relationship with the State through ownership, nationality, registration, or any other recognized link), and that over its own nationals, be they natural or legal persons. These are respectively known as territorial, quasi-territorial, and personal jurisdictions.

Each type of jurisdiction is further divisible into the power of the State on the one hand to enact laws and make legally binding decisions, including judicial decisions, applicable to its territory, its means of transport and its nationals (*jurisfaction*) and its power on the other hand to actually implement and

---

[8] See further B. Cheng, 'The Extraterrestrial Application of International Law', 18 *CLP* (1965), p. 132 [Ch. 5 above].

enforce such laws and decisions (*jurisaction*). Over those who are subject to its jurisdiction, whether territorial, quasi-territorial, or personal, a State's jurisfaction is universal in its cosmographical scope, with the result that an object of international law can frequently be simultaneously subject to the jurisfactions of many States, as when for instance a Spartan is on board an Utopian ship in Arcadian territory. He is at one and the same time under the jurisfactions of Arcadia (territorial), Utopia (quasi-territorial) and Sparta (personal). Different States' jurisfactions can, without causing any difficulty, be concurrent. In contradistinction to jurisfaction, States' jurisactions must at all times be exclusive. In order to avoid any conflict of jurisactions, which can almost be said to be its prime function, international law, in addition to delimiting areas of State competence spatially as we have described above, establishes a hierarchy among the three types of jurisaction, whenever they overlap, with territorial jurisaction overriding both quasi-territorial and personal jurisactions, and quasi-territorial jurisaction overriding personal jurisaction. Thus, for as long as the Spartan mentioned in the above example remains on board the Utopian vessel within Arcadian territory, he is subject exclusively to Arcadian territorial jurisaction. As soon as the ship has left Arcadian waters and is on the high seas, he is subject exclusively to Utopia's quasi-territorial jurisaction. And, if he leaves the ship to live on a desert island belonging to no State, he will be under the exclusive personal jurisaction of his own State, Sparta.

It will readily be seen that what has just been said applies *mutatis mutandis* to outer space and celestial bodies, to spacecraft and to spacemen, and why it has been necessary to dwell first on these very basic and fundamental concepts of international law.

Table XIII.3 STATE JURISDICTION: TYPES, ELEMENTS AND HIERARCHY

TYPE	TERRITORIAL		QUASI-TERRITORIAL		PERSONAL	
ELEMENT	Juris-faction	Juris-action	Juris-faction	Juris-action	Juris-faction	Juris-action
HIER-ARCHY AND PRECED-ENCE	JURIS-FACT-ION	On a par with other types of juris-faction		On a par with other types of juris-faction		On a par with other types of juris-faction	
	JURIS-ACTION		First		Second		Third

G. Functional versus Spatial Delimitation of Outer Space

It will also be seen why it is not possible for us to share the view that it is not necessary or may not even be desirable to demarcate outer space from national airspace. Such a view is held by those who have become known as the functionalists, for whom a space activity is either lawful or unlawful. If lawful, it may be conducted; if unlawful, it may not. The nature of the activity determines its legality (hence functionalism); the *locus*, the place where the activity is carried out, is irrelevant. If States, who are the makers of international law, are generally in agreement that this is the legal position, so be it. But as the example given above of a State arresting a foreign vessel for monitoring its electronic defence installations illustrates, this is not how international law operates.

Thus the monitoring of the electronic defence installations of a foreign State is in itself neither illegal nor legal. It is not a matter of 'functional' determination. Its legality depends, in the first place, upon the *locus*. Carried out in areas subject to the overriding jurisaction of the State under observation, the latter is entitled to make the act illegal and have its law in the matter enforced. Thus on 1 May 1960, the Soviet Union shot down a United States U–2 reconnaissance aircraft while it was flying over the Soviet Union, and tried, convicted, and imprisoned its pilot. The United States accepted the lawfulness of the Soviet action. However, if the same activity was carried out where the State being observed had no such jurisaction, then the act would not be illegal under international law and the latter State would in fact be violating international law if it tried to interfere with it. Thus when, two months later on 1 July 1960, the Soviet Union shot down another United States reconnaissance aircraft, an RB–47, this time over the high seas, the United States protested and took the matter to the Security Council of the United Nations. The Soviet Union eventually accepted implicitly the illegality of its action by returning to the United States the two survivors from the RB-47, without attempting to try them for espionage.[9]

What is true of reconnaissance by aircraft applies to reconnaissance, as such, by satellites. Whether such reconnaissance is lawful or not under international law depends, therefore, in the first instance on whether the reconnaissance is within the territory of the State under observation or outside. This depends in turn on the height to which a State's sovereignty over the airspace above its territory can be said to extend. The issue of such a spatial division between national airspace and outer space cannot be avoided by simply asserting that reconnaissance by satellites is in itself either legal or illegal no matter where conducted (functional delimitation). Whoever maintains a

---

[9] See further B. Cheng, 'The United Nations and Outer Space', 14 *CLP* (1961), p. 247, at pp. 262 ff. [Ch. 6 above, s. V: Reconnaissance and Surveillance Satellites, and the distinction therein made between penetrative and peripheral reconnaissance].

conclusion differing from that under general international law has the burden of proving that such an exception to the general rule exists. No proof has been adduced to show either that such reconnaissance, even if conducted in the national airspace of another State, is lawful, or that, even if conducted clearly in outer space, it would still be illegal, although allegations of this nature have from time to time been made in furtherance invariably of the particular interests of the States concerned.

H. The Legal Status of Outer Space and Celestial Bodies under General International Law

Insofar as the legal status of outer space under general international law is concerned, writing on the subject of 'International Law and High Altitude Flights: Balloons, Rockets and Man-Made Satellites' in an article published three months before Sputnik I, this writer said:

> [I]n view of the fact that assertions of national sovereignty at extreme heights become increasingly less definable and meaningful even for States of continental dimensions, all that may be said is that a not unreasonable conjecture is that States will subject the whole of outer space to the same régime as the high seas.[10]

This writer also stated at the same time:

> On the other hand, States may not perhaps object to treating other planets and stars, including their atmospheric space, as *res nullius*, capable of appropriation through effective occupation by individual States.[11]

Under general international law, prima facie, outer space as such is, like the high seas, *extra commercium*, while celestial bodies, being *terrae firmae* and no different from, for instance, the so called 'New World' when Christopher Columbus landed there, are *res nullius* capable of being lawfully occupied by States.

How far has this position changed since the beginning of the space age? The first point to be examined would be the effect of the two resolutions unanimously adopted by the General Assembly of the United Nations on respectively 20 December 1961 and 13 December 1963, namely resolution 1721A (XVI) and resolution 1962 (XVIII), which, in themselves, are, in law, without binding force.

I. United Nations General Assembly Resolutions

Resolution 1721A (XVI) of 20 December 1961 commends to States 'for their guidance' not only the principle that international law applies to outer space,

---

[10] 6 *ICLQ* (1957), p. 487, at pp. 493–4 [Ch. 2 above, s. IV: Legal Status of Flight Space].
[11] Ibid., at p. 493 [Ch. 2 above, s. IV].

a principle which, for reasons that I have already explained, can only be regarded as declaratory, but also that 'outer space and celestial bodies are . . . not subject to national appropriation'. In resolution 1962 (XVIII), the General Assembly adopted a Declaration of Legal Principles Governing the Activities of States in the Exploration and Uses of Outer Space and 'solemnly declare[d] that in the exploration and use of outer space States should *be guided* by the principles incorporated in the Declaration'.[12] Principle 3 provides:

Outer space and celestial bodies are not subject to national appropriation by claim of sovereignty, by means of use or occupation, or by any other means.

The question which requires examination is the extent to which this principle enunciated by the United Nations General Assembly in these two resolutions can be said to have brought about a change in existing general international law. The answer in the final analysis must be, on the whole, in the negative.

To start with, General Assembly resolutions, except in budgetary and internal organizational matters, are merely recommendations and have no legally binding force. Secondly, the language which both resolutions have used is not such as would estop members of the United Nations, even those who have voted for them, from denying that the principles which these resolutions incorporate are legally binding; for the resolutions have merely adopted these principles *for the guidance* of States. The United Nations at most expect States to *be guided* by them, it does not say that States are *legally bound* by them. It would indeed be more loyalist than the king to go beyond the wording and expectation of the resolutions themselves. Thirdly, the various undertakings to respect these principles given by member States at the time of the adoption of these resolutions were given mostly on the very assumption that these resolutions were mere recommendations. Two or three States, however, having declared that they regarded these principles as declaratory of general international law, might perhaps be precluded from denying their binding character in their *inter se* relations. Finally, it may be said that possibly the only binding element attached to these principles (rather than the resolutions) is to be found in the prior agreements between the two super-space powers which made these resolutions possible. These prior agreements represent *modi vivendi* between the super powers regarding outer space, and the one preceding resolution 1962 incorporates, it would appear, also a *pactum de contrahendo* to translate eventually the principles embodied in the Declaration into binding treaty provisions, as was eventually done in 1967.[13]

While these two resolutions may not have in themselves affected the legal position concerning the legal status of outer space and celestial bodies, and

---

[12] Italics added. For text of resolutions 1721A and 1962 see App. II.1 and II.3 below.
[13] See s. II.A below.

that celestial bodies remain in principle susceptible of appropriation, the *modi vivendi* between the super powers may lead them, and the two resolutions may lead others, not to recognize any claims to sovereignty put forward either individually by States or collectively through intergovernmental agencies. In view of the decisive importance of foreign recognition in consolidating titles to territory, especially recognition by the dominant section of international society, this policy of the super powers, if adhered to in practice, may effectively prevent the establishment of territorial sovereignty on celestial bodies. All this amounts, however, to no more than saying that the principle of non-appropriation of celestial bodies enunciated in resolutions 1721A and 1962 may in time, if adhered to and upheld by the generality of States, including both super powers, become a rule of general international law.

In recent years, this trend has been reinforced by the 1967 Treaty on Principles Governing the Activities of States in the Exploration and Use of Outer Space, including the Moon and Other Celestial Bodies and the 1979 Agreement Governing the Activities of States on the Moon and Other Celestial Bodies.[14]

J. Effect of Multilateral Treaties on General International Law

At this stage only the legal effect of these treaties on the legal status of outer space and of celestial bodies under general international law will be examined. From this point of view, the 1969 Vienna Convention on the Law of Treaties has happily refuted a fallacy which has in recent decades gained a great deal of currency, namely, multilateral treaties amount to general international law. Article 34 of the Vienna Convention categorically provides:

A treaty does not create either obligations or rights for a third State without its consent.

What is true of course is stated in Article 38:

Nothing in articles 34 to 37 precludes a rule set forth in a treaty from becoming binding upon a third State as a customary rule of international law, recognised as such.

The *North Sea Continental Shelf Cases* (1969)[15] decided by the International Court of Justice show clearly that multilateral treaties as such have no claim to being recognized as conclusive evidence of rules of general international law[16]. All that can be said with certainty is that a considerable number of States have as among themselves by treaties modified the rule concerning the status of celestial bodies, and that they may well decline to recognize any claim to celestial bodies or portions thereof put forward even by

---

[14] See further s. II below.   [15] *ICJ Rep. 1969*, p. 3.
[16] Cf. R. R. Baxter, 'Multilateral Treaties as Evidence of Customary International Law', 41 *BYIL* (1965–6), p. 275; or his later 'Treaties and Custom', 129 Hague *Recueil* (1970–1), p. 25.

non-parties, with the result that a rule of customary international law prohibiting the national appropriation of celestial bodies is possibly emerging, while such a rule exists already in respect of outer space from the very beginning of the space age.

K. Demarcation of Outer Space from National Airspace

We have already seen that in international law, spatial delimitation of the different parts of the world is necessary in order to determine which State is entitled to exercise which type of State jurisdiction in respect of which territory, means of transport or person.[17] We have also seen that under customary international law, outer space constitutes *res extra commercium* which is not subject to national appropriation or the territorial jurisdiction of any State[18]. Now, it is a well recognized principle of general international law confirmed in multilateral treaties, first in the 1919 Paris Convention for the Regulation of Aerial Navigation and, after the Second World War, in the 1944 Chicago Convention on International Civil Aviation that every State exercises complete and exclusive sovereignty over the airspace above its territory.[19] So it is clear that reckoning from the surface of the earth upwards, we have first a zone, the airspace, over which, if this zone is over the territory of a State, that State exercises complete and exclusive sovereignty, and beyond this zone outer space in which the exercise of such territorial sovereignty is precluded. How it can be argued that these two zones need not in law be clearly demarcated has always remained a great mystery to me. But for a number of years the United Nations Committee on Outer Space, following the footsteps of its predecessor the *Ad Hoc* Committee, not only decided to close its eyes to the issue, but also tried to rationalize and justify its so doing.[20]

However, when it comes to determining where does national airspace end and where does outer space begin under general international law the task proves very difficult. Writing on the subject a year before Sputnik I, this writer said:

The matter appears . . . supremely vague, and there can be no doubt that an international agreement fixing a precise upper limit to airspace sovereignty at a definite height, be it 100, 200, 500 or 1,000 kilometres, would be infinitely preferable. But such an agreement requires the consent of the States concerned and would be binding only on those States which have agreed to it. In view of the utter failure among States to reach agreement even on the much more mature and well-established subject of the inner and outer limits of the territorial sea, once thought to be the ripest topic for international codification, the chances of any international agreement on the upper limit of

---

[17] See ss. E–G above.   [18] See s. H above.
[19] See further Cheng, *The Law of International Air Transport*, pp. 120 ff.
[20] See further B. Cheng, 'The United Nations and Outer Space', 14 *CLP* (1961), p. 247, at pp. 259–62 [Ch. 6 above, s. IV: Blind Spot in the Sky].

the territorial airspace would appear to be more than remote. Perforce, the only criterion available and acceptable is the physical limit of the earth's atmosphere, however, uncertain and ill-defined this may be.[21]

Nine years later in 1965, there was already sufficient State practice for a more precise determination to be made of the applicable rule under customary international law. This writer wrote then:

At a time before space flights began, the present writer, on the basis of geophysical factors, had estimated the upper limit of airspace to lie at a height of between 500 and 1,000 kilometres (i.e., between 310 and 620 miles) above the surface of the earth. Since then, it appears that a general practice has grown up among States interpreting airspace as meaning space in which navigation by conventional aircraft is possible and outer space as space where artificial satellites are able to orbit, thus bringing the frontier down to approximately 50 miles, with a possible margin of 25 miles either way. This development may be regarded either as the interpretation of an existing rule of international law by the practice of States, or the emergence of a new rule of international customary law modifying a previous one.

The evidence for saying that States now accept a fairly low limit of territorial space is their attitude towards the problem of the right of passage of orbiting satellites and, particularly, towards reconnaissance satellites. A careful scrutiny of the discussion on outer space in the United Nations reveals that States appear to be in general agreement, that orbiting satellites in their orbits never enter airspace and, therefore, the problem of the right of passage through foreign territorial airspace does not arise, except possibly during launching and re-entry.[22]

From this evidence, it was therefore possible to conclude that outer space under general international law would at least begin from the lowest point reached by an artificial satellite, in other words, the lowest perigee ever achieved. For this reason, the International Law Association at its 53rd Conference in Buenos Aires in 1968, at a joint session on Air Law and Space Law, approved a resolution adopting the lowest perigee achieved by any artificial satellite on 27 January 1967, when the 1967 Space Treaty was opened for signature, as marking the beginning of outer space for the purpose of interpreting the term 'outer space' in the Space Treaty.[23]

The adoption of this resolution does not, as I said at the previous conference of the International Law Association at Helsinki in 1966, when speaking in support of a similarly drafted resolution introduced by Professor D. Goedhuis,[24] mean the adoption of the so-called 'perigee rule',

---

[21] B. Cheng, 'Recent Developments in Air Law', 9 *CLP* (1956), p. 208, at pp. 214–15 [Ch. 1 above, s. III: The Upper Limits of Airspace].

[22] B. Cheng, 'The Extraterrestrial Application of International Law', 18 *CLP* (1965), p. 132, at pp. 145–6; nn. omitted [Ch. 5 above, s. III.A: Outer Space].

[23] ILA, *Report of the 53rd Conference, Buenos Aires* (1968), pp. 110 ff.

[24] ILA, *Report of the 52nd Conference, Helsinki* (1966), p. 200: 'The International Law Association, considers that the *practice* of States is consistent with the view that air sovereignty does not extend as far as the lowest perigee of any satellite so far placed in orbit.'

that is to say, determination of the frontier between national space and outer space by means of the lowest perigee of any satellite which has been, or may hereafter be, put into orbit. This draft Resolution . . . is essentially a statement of fact. It impliedly records a limited consensus of States on this subject which appears to have crystallized at this juncture, namely, the general agreement which appears to exist among States that all existing satellites orbit in outer space, i.e., space which, in their view, is not subject to national appropriation. From this consensus is drawn the essentially negative conclusion that States consider that airspace sovereignty in no event extends as far as the lowest perigee of any satellite *so far placed in orbit.* This statement does not say that this consensus will *necessarily* extend to all future satellites.

Secondly, it does not purport to fix definitely a precise boundary between outer space and national space. It does not even define the existing upper limit of airspace sovereignty. It merely says that this upper limit definitely does not lie outside the point indicated in the draft Resolution. Consequently, this upper limit may be lower, but not higher, than that stated in the draft Resolution . . .[25]

It follows from the draft resolution put forward at Helsinki or that adopted in Buenos Aires in 1968 that, in the present state of general international law, we have possibly in fact three layers of space above the surface of the earth:

First, there is that layer of a State's superincumbent space closest to the surface of the earth which is incontrovertibly subject to national sovereignty. There is, secondly, beyond the point stated in the draft Resolution, the vast space which is equally incontrovertibly, not subject to national sovereignty or appropriation. But . . . there is, thirdly, an intermediate zone of uncertainty lying below the point stated in the draft Resolution and above the undisputed zone of national airspace, in which, at a height that is not yet clearly defined, lies the actual boundary line between national space and outer space.[26]

Relatively uncertain though what may be called 'the lowest perigee so far achieved by any unchallenged satellite' test may appear, it does help considerably to reduce the utter confusion which appears still to reign in this subject. What I said at the Helsinki Conference of the International Law Association in 1966 remains true:

At present, not only among laymen, but even among some of those who interest themselves in the subject, there is still much speculation as to where airspace sovereignty ends and where outer space begins: 50 miles, 75 miles, 100 miles, 500 miles, or even *ad infinitum.* Now, if I recall rightly, the lowest perigee of artificial satellites so far placed in orbit is 80 odd miles above the mean sea level.[27]

More recently, the subject is at long last being more actively examined by the Outer Space Committee of the United Nations, and detailed studies have been prepared or presented by the Secretariat.[28] The accompanying Diagram of artificial earth satellites with lowest perigee heights launched between 4

---

[25] Ibid., pp. 166–7.   [26] Ibid., p. 167.   [27] Ibid., p. 167.
[28] See e.g. *The Question of the Definition and/or the Delimitation of Outer Space,* A/AC.105/C.2/7 (1970), and Id./Add. 1 (1977).

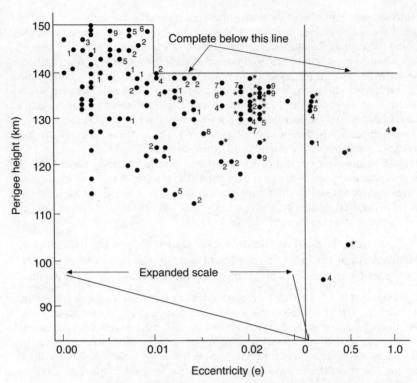

Source: UN GA COPUOS, Study on Altitudes of Artificial Earth Satelites
(Working paper presented by the Secretariat), A/AC.105/164
(6.1.76), Annex II, p. 2.

**Figure XIII.1. ARTIFICIAL SATELLITES WITH LOWEST PERIGEE HEIGHTS
LAUNCHED BETWEEN 4 OCTOBER 1957 AND 4 NOVEMBER 1975**

October 1957 and 4 November 1975 is taken from the background paper on
Study on Altitudes of Artificial Earth Satellites[29] presented by the Secretariat
in 1976 to the Outer Space Committee. As the diagram clearly shows, in the
course of eighteen years since Sputnik I first went into orbit on 4 October
1957, the lowest perigee achieved so far is that of the United Kingdom
Skynet–IIA (1974) at 96 kilometres (approximately 60 miles), and that excepting this and another one at 104 kilometres, all the other satellites have perigees
above the 110 kilometre line (approximately 68 miles).[30] On this basis, one

[29] A/AC.105/164 (1976), Annex II, p. 2.

[30] On some of these figures, see comments in B. Cheng, 'Legal Implications of Remote
Sensing', *Earth Observations from Space and Management of Planetary Resources: Prc. Int. Conf.
organised by CNES and ESA, Toulouse, March 1978* (ESA SP–134) (1978), p. 597, at p. 601, col.
1 [cf. Ch. 14 below, ss X and XI].

can, in applying 'the lowest perigee so far achieved by any unchallenged satellite' test, say that at 96 kilometres one is definitely in outer space. Should one have doubts and wonder if a lone Skynet is not that proverbial one swallow which does not make a summer, then the 110-kilometre line should satisfy even the most sceptical.

Over the years, there has been increasing support among States for the views expressed here. Even the Soviet Union has finally come round to this view, and at the Eighteenth Session of the Legal Sub-Committee of the United Nations Committee on the Peaceful Uses of Outer Space submitted a working paper entitled 'Approach to the solution of the problems of the delimitation of airspace and outer space'[31] in which the Soviet Union proposed first the recognition of the region above 100 (110) kilometres altitude from the sea level of the earth as outer space, and secondly, the establishment by treaty of a boundary between airspace and outer space at an altitude not higher than 100 (110) kilometres above sea level. What the Soviet Union has packaged with its proposal, however, is a right of passage through a State's national airspace for foreign space objects. The last of the Soviet proposal is likely to prove to be, if not a bone of contention, at least a matter for some very hard bargaining between space powers and non-space powers, inasmuch as under general international law, there is no such right of passage and there is insufficient practice to infer any general acquiescence on the part of States in such a right.

Nevertheless, it needs to be mentioned that there are still some States, including notably the United States, which are in favour of a functional approach or wait-and-see approach. The functional approach has obvious appeals for space powers insofar as, once a space activity has been proclaimed lawful (and there is hardly anyone there capable of verifying or, still less, challenging a space power's own pronouncement on the subject), it will not depend on the consent of third States even when such space objects go through the latter's airspace. The functional approach also leaves States with the possibility of not making up their mind for the moment on where the boundary should be.

L. The Geostationary Orbit

Such deliberate ambivalence can, however, be a two-edged sword. Taking advantage of the fact that there is at present no clear-cut delimitation of outer space from national airspace, eight equatorial States, namely, Brazil, Colombia, Congo, Ecuador, Indonesia, Kenya, Uganda, and Zaire, at their first meeting at Bogotá on 3 December 1976, issued a declaration laying claims to the geostationary orbit. The geostationary orbit, also known as the

---

[31] A/AC.105/C.2/L.121 (28.3.79), reproduced in A/AC.105/240, Annex IV, p. 6.

synchronous orbit, is a circular orbit above the equator at a height of just over 36,000 km (22,300 miles). An artificial satellite placed in this orbit would be circling the earth at such a speed that, to an observer on the earth, the satellite would appear to be stationary over a given spot on the earth's equator. This orbit has obvious advantages, but unfortunately by its nature can only accommodate a limited number of satellites, and is, therefore, reckoned to be a limited resource.[32]

The Bogotá Declaration says in part:

. . . Equatorial countries declare that the geostationary synchronous orbit is a physical fact linked to the reality of our planet because its existence depends exclusively on its relation to gravitational phenomena generated by the earth, and that is why it must not be considered part of the outer space. Therefore, the segments of geostationary synchronous orbit are part of the territory over which Equatorial States exercise their national sovereignty . . .

. . . [T]he Equatorial countries meeting in Bogotá have decided to proclaim and defend on behalf of their peoples, the existence of their sovereignty over this natural resource . . .

Both the physics and the law of the Bogotá Declaration are open to question. But the mere fact that such a claim can be seriously made by States and that those who consider it unnecessary to demarcate outer space from national space are not in a position categorically to refute such a claim because the latter are themselves unable or unwilling to say where outer space begins is merely one of the many chickens of functionalism which are now gradually coming home to roost. Before long, it will be the turn of those States which object to certain types of satellites, such as those that engage in remote sensing, to claim sovereignty over national space above the usual heights at which such satellites orbit so as to subject them to the consent and control of the States overflown but not necessarily to exclude them.[33]

II. The Legal Status of Outer Space and Celestial Bodies Under Multilateral Treaties

Two multilateral treaties, both drafted by the United Nations Committee on the Peaceful Uses of Outer Space, specifically deal with the legal status of outer space and celestial bodies. The first, and by far the most important among all the treaties concerning outer space drafted by the United Nations, is the Treaty on Principles Governing the Activities of States in the Exploration and Use of Outer Space, including the Moon and other Celestial Bodies. It was opened for signature in London, Moscow, and Washington on

[32] See further B. Cheng, 'Communications Satellites', 24 *CLP* (1971), p. 211, at p. 212 [Ch. 21 below, s. II.B].

[33] See further loc. cit. in n. 30 aove, at p. 600, col. 2 ff. (para. 2.3.1.) [cf. Ch. 22 below, s. VI.A].

27 January 1967, and entered into force on 10 October 1967.[34] The second one is the Agreement Governing the Activities of States on the Moon and Other Celestial Bodies, the text of which was finally agreed upon without fanfare at the 22nd session of the United Nations Outer Space Committee in June–July 1979[35]. These two treaties will be examined successively, insofar as they affect the legal status of outer space and celestial bodies.

A. The 1967 Space Treaty

1. *The Extraterrestrial Application of International Law and of the Charter of the United Nations.*   Article III of the 1967 Space Treaty provides:

States Parties to the Treaty shall carry on activities in the exploration and use of outer space, including the moon and celestial bodies, in accordance with international law, including the Charter of the United Nations, in the interest of maintaining international peace and security and promoting international co-operation and understanding.

Article III has in fact three parts. First, it affirms that international law has to be complied with by States Parties to the Treaty in their activities in outer space and on celestial bodies. For reasons which have already been explained, this is merely confirmatory of existing international law.[36]

Secondly, it says that international law includes the Charter of the United Nations. This is only a half-truth. Again, we have already seen why multilateral treaties cannot *ipso facto* be considered integral parts of general international law.[37] This is true even of the United Nations Charter, although this does not exclude certain provisions of the Charter being declaratory of general international law and others having, by general consent, acquired the force of general international law. Although often erroneously said to have this effect, Article 2(6) of the Charter does not purport to make the Charter binding on non-members. The obligation in Article 2(6) is laid on the organization and not on non-members, and the organization can only discharge its task in accordance with international law and international law does not confer on the organization the power to impose obligations on non-parties without their consent. However, by virtue of Article III of the Space Treaty, contracting Parties which are not members of the United Nations have thereby consented to be bound by the Charter insofar as their activities in outer space are concerned.

The third part of Article III is ambiguous. First, it can mean that States Parties must always conduct their space activities in the interest of

---

[34] See further B. Cheng, 'Le Traité de 1967 sur l'espace/The 1967 Space Treaty', 95 *JDI* (1968), 532, for a detailed analysis of the Treaty [Ch. 9 above].

[35] See further B. Cheng, 'The Moon Treaty', 33 *CLP* (1980), p. 213, for a detailed analysis of the Agreement [Ch. 12 above].

[36] See s. I.D above.   [37] See s. I.J above.

maintaining international peace and security and promoting international co-operation and understanding. Secondly, it may serve merely to explain why States Parties must comply with international law, including the Charter of the United Nations. Thirdly, the Charter of the United Nations has to be complied with only insofar as it affects international peace and security and the promotion of international co-operation and understanding.

On the whole, except insofar as non-members of the United Nations are concerned, Article III appears to add little to the obligations of the contracting Parties under general international law and under treaties to which they are already parties.

2. *Prohibition of Appropriation of Outer Space or Celestial Bodies.* Under Article II of the Space Treaty,

Outer space, including the moon and other celestial bodies, is not subject to national appropriation by claim of sovereignty, by means of use or occupation, or by any other means.

Article II of the Space Treaty has turned the whole of outer space, including the moon and other celestial bodies, into *res extra commercium*. Insofar as outer space *sensu stricto* is concerned, i.e., the void between all the celestial bodies, what we shall call the outer void space, Article II has merely confirmed its legal status under general international law.

As regards the moon and other celestial bodies, Article II has the effect, as among the contracting States, of transforming them from *res nullius* (their status under general international law)[38] to *res extra commercium*.

Indeed, the concept of non-appropriation embodied in Article II is the same as that which has been traditionally applied to the high seas. It simply means that, as among the contracting States, none will be entitled to exercise *territorial* jurisdiction, no matter on what basis, over any part of outer space or of celestial bodies. As on the high seas, however, the exclusion of territorial jurisdiction does not mean that either quasi-territorial jurisdiction or personal jurisdiction may also not be exercised.[39] If outer space is not to become an area of lawlessness, it is in fact necessary to ensure that some type of State jurisdiction is exercised.[40]

Inasmuch as there is to be no territorial jurisdiction in outer space and on celestial bodies, there can also be no private ownership of parts of outer space or celestial bodies, which presupposes the existence of a territorial sovereign itself competent to confer titles of such ownership. In this sense, outer space and celestial bodies are not only not subject to national appropriation, but also not subject to appropriation under private law.[41]

However, separate from the problem of appropriating parts of outer space and of celestial bodies is that of appropriating resources of outer space and of

[38] See s. I.H above.
[40] See further s. IV below.
[39] On State jurisdiction, see further s. I.F above.
[41] See further s. II.B.4.b below.

celestial bodies. To the extent to which outer space and celestial bodies constitute *res extra commercium*, by analogy with the rules underlying the freedom of the high seas, the appropriation of the natural resources thereof merely forms part of the freedom of exploration and use,[42] and is, notwithstanding eminent views to the contrary, not prohibited under the 1967 Space Treaty.

However, even though appropriation, whether by States or by individuals, of parts of outer space and of celestial bodies is prohibited, if any part thereof, especially in the case of celestial bodies, is subjected to prolonged occupation, for instance, for the purpose of exploitation, complicated legal problems are bound to arise. Some of these problems are illustrated in the problem sheet annexed to this chapter[43]. It does not appear that they have been resolved by the 1979 Moon Treaty either.[44]

3. *Freedoms of Scientific Investigation, Exploration, Use, and Access.* It is stipulated in Article I(2) and (3):

> Outer space, including the moon and other celestial bodies, shall be free for exploration and use by all States without discrimination of any kind, on a basis of equality and in accordance with international law, and there shall be free access to all areas of celestial bodies.
>
> There shall be freedom of scientific investigation in outer space, including the moon and other celestial bodies . . .

Inasmuch as Article II of the Space Treaty has made the whole of outer space, including the moon and other celestial bodies, *res extra commercium*, and Article III has confirmed that international law is applicable to the entire area, the above provisions are largely tautological. However, the inclusion of 'exploration and use', as well as 'scientific investigations', among the freedoms of outer space does reinforce the interpretation that Article II of the Space Treaty places no obstacle in the way of commercial or industrial exploration and use of outer space and celestial bodies, contrary to the views of some commentators.[45]

At the end of the previous Section,[46] mention was made of possible legal complications arising from prolonged occupation of, particularly, parts of celestial bodies through exploration or use. Such occupation can easily come into conflict with the 'free access' principle which is inherent in the concept of non-appropriation and *res extra commercium* and which is reaffirmed in Article I(2). The problem has been made slightly more complicated for lack of clear precedents, inasmuch as the position on land is somewhat different from that on the high seas. That, notwithstanding Article II, some such occupation is not precluded by the Treaty can be seen from Article XII:

---

[42] See further ss. II.A.3 and II.B below.   [43] See Annex at the end of this chapter.
[44] See s.II.B.6 below.   [45] See, however, s. II.B below.   [46] See II.A.2 above.

All stations, installations, equipment and space vehicles on the moon and other celestial bodies shall be open to representatives of other States Parties to the Treaty on a basis of reciprocity. Such representatives shall give reasonable advance notice of a projected visit, in order that appropriate consultations may be held and that maximum precautions may be taken to assure safety and to avoid interference with normal operations in the facility to be visited.

The exercise of the right of free access is thus in certain cases subject to conditions. Unless further international regulations are made, the hypothetical example given in the problem sheet annexed to the present chapter[47] shows how in practice complications can easily arise.

4. *Promotion of International Co-operation.*

(a) *Preambular desire.* The fourth paragraph of the Preamble of the Treaty speaks of the desire of the contracting Parties 'to contribute to broad international co-operation in the scientific as well as the legal aspects of the exploration and use of outer space for peaceful purposes'. What actually has been incorporated in the Treaty in implementation of this desire remains much more in the realm of declarations of intentions than firm legal commitments.

(b) *Scientific investigations.* In Article I(3), the Treaty, having enunciated the principle of the freedom of scientific investigation in outer space, continues:

. . . and States shall facilitate and encourage international co-operation in such investigation.

It is more than doubtful whether a contracting State would be entitled, under this Article to demand, for instance, to take part, as of right, in scientific investigations being undertaken by another State Party. In fact, for reasons which will become even more apparent when we examine Article I(1), this whole article belongs much more to the preamble than to the body of the treaty.[48] Further confirmation of this assessment of the concrete value of this laudable principle of international co-operation may be found in the fact that three further provisions in the Treaty are in explicit implementation of this principle. Yet only in one of them is there even any suggestion of a truly binding obligation.

(c) *Protection of the environment.* Ironically, in the first of the three provisions in which the strongest binding element is to be found, Article IX of the Treaty speaks of the contracting States being 'guided by the principle of co-operation and mutual assistance', rather than of their being 'bound' by it.

Article IX does, however, lay down certain obligations and confer certain rights in the interest of protecting the environment, albeit all of extreme lightweight. It provides:

---

[47] At the end of this chapter.   [48] See s. II.A.5 below.

In the exploration and use of outer space, including the moon and celestial bodies, States Parties to the Treaty shall be guided by the principle of co-operation and mutual assistance and shall conduct all their activities in outer space, including the moon and other celestial bodies, with due regard to the corresponding interests of all other States Parties to the Treaty. States Parties to the Treaty shall pursue studies of outer space, including the moon and other celestial bodies, and conduct exploration of them so as to avoid their harmful contamination and also adverse changes in the environment of the earth resulting from the introduction of extraterrestrial matter and, where necessary, shall adopt appropriate measures for this purpose. If a State Party to the Treaty has reason to believe that an activity or experiment planned by it or its nationals in outer space, including the moon and other celestial bodies, would cause potential harmful interference with activities of other States Parties in the peaceful exploration and use of outer space, including the moon and other celestial bodies, it shall undertake appropriate international consultations before proceeding with any such activity or experiment. A State Party to the Treaty which has reason to believe that an activity or experiment planned by another State Party in outer space, including the moon and other celestial bodies, would cause potentially harmful interference with activities in the peaceful exploration and use of outer space, including the moon and other celestial bodies, may request consultation concerning the activity or experiment.

The duties and rights involved amount hardly to even *obligatio imperfecta.*

(d) *Opportunities to observe flights.* Those who harbour illusions regarding Article I of the Space Treaty would do well to ponder over Article X; for if Article I were to contain any truly binding legal obligation, Article X would not be necessary and should certainly not be in such watered-down wording which merely confirms that no real legal rights or duties flow from Article 1. Article X says:

In order to promote international co-operation in the exploration and use of outer space, including the moon and other celestial bodies, in conformity with the purposes of this Treaty, the States Parties to the Treaty shall consider on a basis of equality any requests by other States Parties to the Treaty to be afforded an opportunity to observe the flight of space objects launched by those States.

The nature of such an opportunity for observation and the conditions under which it could be afforded shall be determined by agreement between the States concerned.

(e) *Dissemination of information.* What has just been said is further confirmed by Article XI and its history. Article XI provides:

In order to promote international co-operation in the peaceful exploration and use of outer space, States Parties to the Treaty conducting activities in outer space, including the moon and other celestial bodies, agree to inform the Secretary-General of the United Nations as well as the public and the international scientific community, *to the greatest extent feasible and practicable,* of the nature, conduct, locations and results of such activities. In receiving the said information, the Secretary-General of the United Nations should be prepared to disseminate it immediately and effectively.[49]

---

[49] Italics added.

The words which have been italicized reduce whatever obligation this Article might have contained to a matter which lies purely within the discretion of the space power concerned. To some extent, this has resulted from the naïvety and greed of the non-space powers. If the non-space powers had merely asked for information on the nature of space flights for the purpose of ensuring compliance with the demilitarization provisions of the Treaty, along the lines of Article VII(5) of the 1959 Antarctic Treaty, they might have succeeded in obtaining a more binding provision. By including the divulgence of also the 'results' of space exploration, they were truly 'asking for the moon'. The inevitable result is an absolutely supine provision, which in due course proves to be even an embarrassment. The latter has come about because some non-space powers are now desperately trying to prevent space powers, whose remote sensing of their natural resources they are powerless to prevent at least from releasing the results of such remote sensing to the world at large.[50]

5. *The Benefit and Interests of all Countries.* The 1967 Space Treaty in the third paragraph of its Preamble records the *belief* of the States Parties:

that the exploration and use of outer space should be carried on for the benefit of all peoples irrespective of the degree of their economic or scientific development.'

No doubt in pursuance of this belief, the Treaty begins in the first paragraph of its first Article thus:

The exploration and use of outer space, including the moon and other celestial bodies, shall be carried out for the benefit and in the interests of all countries, irrespective of their degree of economic and scientific development, and shall be the province of all mankind.

Looking at the text as it stands, there seems to be no valid reason why it should not be treated as stating a binding legal obligation. If so, Article I(1) of the Treaty must be regarded as superimposing on the freedom of exploration and use affirmed in Article I(2) a principle of far-reaching significance; for such exploration and use are permissible only to the extent to which they are 'for the benefit and in the interests of all countries'. While opinion may differ on what constitutes 'the interests of all countries' and compliance with this part of the obligation might have to rely largely on the good faith of the contracting States, the rest of the sentence is much more concrete in meaning. It strongly suggests that 'all States' have a legal right to the fruits of space exploration and use, by whomsoever carried out.

Such an interpretation, while it may be literally valid, hardly accords with the drafting history of the 1967 Treaty, the intention of the Parties, or the other provisions in the Treaty. Whatever has already been said regarding the

---

[50] See further loc. cit. in n. 30 above, at pp. 605–6; and the Convention on the Transfer and Use of Data of the Remote Sensing of the Earth from Outer Space, Moscow, 19 May 1978, signed by a number of Eastern bloc States, UN Doc. A/33/162 (29.6.78).

lack of binding effect of the principle of international co-operation[51] in general and the pseudo-obligation in Article XI to share the results of space exploration and use in particular,[52] applies *a fortiori* to the sharing of all the fruits of space exploration and use. From the legal point of view, Article I(1) of the Space Treaty is at best a joint expression of intention, conferring no legal rights and imposing no real obligations. However, this intention has been carried one stage further in the 1979 Moon Treaty.

B. The 1979 Moon Treaty

1. *The Moon and Celestial Bodies within the Solar System Declared the Common Heritage of Mankind.* Although the proper title of the treaty is the Agreement governing the Activities of States on the Moon and other Celestial Bodies, the Agreement will properly always be known as the Moon Treaty, because in its preparatory stage it was always so known and this in turn because the extension of the cosmographical scope of the treaty to other celestial bodies within the solar system excluding the earth (Article 1(1)) was undertaken only at the last moment.[53] On account of this last minute decision, the draftsmen of the treaty did not even have time to modify all the provisions in the treaty. Instead, this extension was made simply by introducing a definitional provision (Article 1(1)) under which:

The provisions of this Agreement relating to the moon shall also apply to other celestial bodies within the solar system, other than the earth, except in so far as specific legal norms enter into force with respect to any of these celestial bodies.

The same extension applies consequently to all quotations from, and references to, the treaty herein contained, unless otherwise specified.

For many, although by no means all, United Nations Members, the greatest achievement, and the very *raison d'être*, of the Moon Treaty is the recognition of the principle by the contracting Parties that the moon and other celestial bodies within the solar system, except the earth, and all their natural resources 'are the common heritage of mankind'. For the first time in the history of international law, a genuine '*territorium commune humanitatis*' belonging to an entirely new category of territory has been created.

However, this was not achieved without difficulty. Opposition to the introduction of the new concept of the 'common heritage of mankind', on the ground among other things that it was amorphous, was one of the main factors which held up the conclusion of the treaty for many years. The day was ultimately saved by the so-called Austrian formula now found in the crucial Article 11(1) which enunciates the principle of the common heritage of

---

[51] See s. II.A.4 above.　　　　　　　　　　　　[52] See s. II.A.4.e above.
[53] Concerning the whole of s. B., see further B. Cheng, 'The Moon Treaty', 33 *CLP* (1980), p. 213 [Ch. 12 above].

mankind not as a ready-made legal concept but merely as a shorthand expression to cover a host of norms detailed in the treaty itself. Article 11(1) provides:

The moon and its natural resources are the common heritage of mankind, *which finds its expression in the provisions of this Agreement*, in particular in paragraph 5 of this article.[54]

Space permits only a brief enumeration of the main tenets of this concept as conceived in the Moon Treaty.

2. *International Law, Peace, Security, Co-operation, Understanding, Well-being, Progress, and Development.* Under Articles 2 and 4, all activities on the moon shall be carried out in accordance with international law, as well as, particularly in its exploration and use, a number of rather platitudinous and legally unenforceable exhortations, which largely repeat Articles I and IX of the 1967 Space Treaty,[55] calculated to promote international peace, security, co-operation, understanding, well-being, progress and development.

3. *Non-militarization.* Article 3 deals with demilitarization and largely repeats Article IV of the 1967 Space Treaty[56].

4. *Non-appropriation.*

    a. *No national appropriation.* Article 11(2) of the Moon Treaty repeats Article II of the Space Treaty.[57]

    b. *No proprietary rights over surface, subsurface or natural resources in place.* Under Article 11(3):

Neither the surface nor the subsurface of the moon, nor any part thereof or natural resources *in place*, shall become property of any State, international intergovernmental or non-governmental organisation, national organisation or non-governmental entity or of any natural person. The placement of personnel, space vehicles, equipment, facilities, stations and installations on or below the surface of the moon, including structures connected with its surface or subsurface, shall not create a right of ownership over the surface or subsurface of the moon or any areas thereof. The foregoing provisions are without prejudice to the international régime referred to in paragraph 5 of this article.[58]

5. *Freedom of scientific investigation.* While the 1967 Space Treaty in its Article I(3) asserts a general freedom of scientific investigation in outer space presumably for *all States*,[59] paradoxically Article 6(1) of the Moon Treaty, which proclaims the moon the common heritage of *mankind*, asserts this freedom only for 'all States *Parties*'. Article 6 of the Moon Treaty goes, however, some way in resolving the controversy surrounding the proper interpretation

---

[54] Italics added.
[56] See further s. III below.
[58] Italics added.
[55] See ss. II.A.4.e and II.A.5 above.
[57] See s. II.A.2 above.
[59] See s. II.A.3 above.

of Article II of the 1967 Space Treaty insofar as natural resources are concerned.[60] Article 6(2) provides that, in carrying out, or in the course of, scientific investigations, States Parties shall be entitled to collect samples and to use the natural resources of the moon for supporting their missions.

6. *Freedom of Exploration and Use Without Discrimination.* Article 11(4) likewise proclaims the freedom of exploration and use only in respect of the States Parties. Article 8(2) confirms their right to land space objects on the moon and to launch them from there, as well as their right to place their personnel, space vehicles, equipment, facilities, stations, and installations anywhere on or below the surface of the moon. Article 9 further recognizes the right of States Parties to establish manned and unmanned stations on the moon, subject to certain provisos. The Agreement has not, however, resolved all possible jurisdictional problems[61]

7. *An International Regime.* A crucial problem with the concept of the common heritage of mankind is that, at some stage, a purely normative framework no longer suffices, and an institutional structure becomes necessary. Thus, while the present rules of the Moon Treaty will probably be adequate during the exploration phase of lunar activities, the contracting States recognize that something more will be needed once exploitation of the resources of the moon or celestial bodies becomes possible. An essential element of the concept of the common heritage of mankind incorporated in the Moon Treaty is, therefore, as Article 11(1) recognizes,[62] the undertaking of the States Parties, under Article 11(5), 'to establish an international regime, including appropriate procedures, to govern the exploitation of the natural resources of the moon as such exploitation is about to become feasible'.

Article 11(7) provides:

The main purposes of the international regime to be established shall include:
(a) The orderly and safe development of the natural resources of the moon;
(b) The rational management of those resources;
(c) The expansion of opportunities in the use of those resources;
(d) An equitable sharing by States Parties in the benefits derived from those resources, whereby the interests and needs of the developing countries, as well as the efforts of those countries which have contributed, either directly or indirectly to the exploration of the moon, shall be given special consideration.

The most difficult problem which is likely to arise with the Moon Treaty will be the establishment of the international regime, which under Article 11(5), will be by means of a fresh agreement to be concluded in due course when the exploitation of the natural resources of the moon and celestial bodies is about to become feasible. Insofar as the international regime is concerned, the

---

[60] See text to n. 42 above.
[61] See further text to n. 43 above, and the Annex to this chapter below.
[62] See II.B.1 above *in fine*.

Moon Treaty is no more than a *pactum de contrahendo*. If, when the time comes, the contracting Parties engage in good faith in negotiating the new treaty but genuinely cannot reach agreement, there will be, without any breach of the Moon Treaty, no international regime.

The only consolation is perhaps to be found in Article 11(8):

All the activities with respect to the natural resources of the moon shall be carried out in a manner compatible with the purposes specified in paragraph 7 of this article and the provisions of article 6, paragraph 2, of this Agreement.

This means that, subject to the exceptions made in respect of scientific investigations,[63] the natural resources of the moon and celestial bodies can be explored, used or exploited[64] only in accordance with the purposes of the international regime specified in Article 11(7) and quoted above. However, while the wording of Article 11(7) and (8) is sufficiently concrete and specific to distinguish these provisions from the mere declarations of intention in, say, Article I of the 1967 Space Treaty, and to make them legally binding, whether, in practice, these provisions will amount to very much, in the absence of an institution to oversee their implementation, is an open question.

III. The Demilitarization of Outer Space and of Celestial Bodies

Demilitarization, partial or total, is entirely a matter of treaty law.

A. The 1963 Partial Nuclear Test Ban Treaty

Under Article I(l) of the Treaty of 5 August 1963 banning Nuclear Weapon Tests in the Atmosphere, in Outer Space and Under Water:

Each of the Parties to this Treaty undertakes to prohibit, to prevent and not to carry out any nuclear weapon test explosion, or any other nuclear explosion, *at any place under its jurisdiction or control*:

(a) in the atmosphere; *beyond its limits, including outer space* . . . ; or
(b) *in any other environment* if such explosion causes radioactive debris to be present outside the territorial limits of the State under whose jurisdiction or control such explosion is conducted . . .[65]

The outcome of the *Nuclear Tests Case*[66] brought before the International Court of Justice would seem to suggest by implication that the Treaty cannot yet be regarded as declaratory of general international law, apart from the fact

---

[63] See s. II.B.5 above *in fine*.
[64] On the question whether the Agreement involves a moratorium on exploitation, see loc. cit. in n. 53 above, pp. 228 ff. [Ch. 12 above, s. V: Some Concluding Remarks].
[65] Italics added.   [66] *ICJ Rep. 1974*, p. 253.

that Article IV(2) of the Test Ban Treaty expressly allows withdrawal, albeit subject to conditions.

The words 'at any place under its jurisdiction or control', while under-standable when applied to the duty of States to prohibit and prevent others carrying out such tests, are a little unfortunate when referring to the duty of contracting States not to carry out such tests themselves. The view that the phrase 'or control' covers any place in outer space where a test is conducted[67] appears highly disputable. However, the situation is probably saved by sub-paragraph (b) and the very comprehensive language of Article I(2):

Each of the Parties to this Treaty undertakes furthermore to refrain from causing, encouraging, or in any way participating in, the carrying out of any nuclear weapon test explosion, or any other nuclear explosion, anywhere which would take place in any of the environments described, or have the effect referred, to, in paragraph I of this article.

B. United Nations General Assembly resolution 1884 (XVIII) of 17 October 1963

The meaning and purely exhortative effect[68] of the following resolution of the General Assembly are self-evident:

. . .

Determined to take steps to prevent the spread of the arms race to outer space,

1. *Welcomes* the expressions by the Union of Soviet Socialist Republics and the United States of America of their intention not to station in outer space any objects carrying nuclear weapons or other kinds of weapons of mass destruction;

2. *Solemnly calls upon* all States:

(a) To refrain from placing in orbit around the Earth any objects carrying nuclear weapons or any other kinds of weapons of mass destruction, installing such weapons on celestial bodies, or stationing such weapons in outer space in any other manner;

(b) To refrain from causing, encouraging or in any way participating in the conduct of the foregoing activities.

The agreement between the super powers which underlies their joint expres-sions of intention recorded in paragraph I of the resolution is of course the key to Article IV of the 1967 Space Treaty.

C. The 1967 Space Treaty

1. *Article IV.* It will readily be seen that Article IV of the Space Treaty springs from the above agreement between the two principal super powers and is in accord with their general desire not to see nuclear weapons left lying

---

[67] M. M. Whiteman, 11 *Digest of International Law* (1968), p. 791. Cf. s. III.D below.
[68] See s. I.I above.

about all over the world.[69] In many ways, Article IV is probably, from the political point of view the most important article in the whole treaty. President L. B. Johnson's immediate comment on the 1967 Treaty was that it was 'the most important arms control development since the limited test ban treaty of 1969'.[70] Article IV is worded as follows:

> States Parties to the Treaty undertake not to place in orbit around the earth any objects carrying nuclear weapons or any other kinds of weapons of mass destruction, instal such weapons on celestial bodies, or station such weapons in outer space or in any other manner.
>
> The moon and other celestial bodies shall be used by all States Parties to the Treaty exclusively for peaceful purposes. The establishment of military bases, installations and fortifications, the testing of any type of weapons and the conduct of military manoeuvres on celestial bodies shall be forbidden. The use of military personnel for scientific research or for any other purposes shall not be prohibited. The use of any equipment or facility necessary for peaceful exploration of the moon and other celestial bodies shall also not be prohibited.

Article IV is thus clearly divided into two parts. The first consists in an agreement partially to demilitarize extraterrestrial space, including all celestial bodies; the second completely to demilitarize all celestial bodies.

2. *Partial Demilitarization of Extraterrestrial Space.*   Article IV(I) of the Space Treaty means that no contracting State is entitled to station nuclear weapons or other weapons of mass destruction anywhere in extraterrestrial space, including both outer space and celestial bodies. Insofar as those States which are also parties to the Partial Test Ban Treaty are concerned, nor are they entitled to cause any nuclear explosion in the same area.

Even these two treaties taken together, however, do not make extraterrestrial space entirely nuclear-weapon-free. In particular, the transit through outer space of missiles with nuclear warheads, at present the status symbol and the ultimate weapon in the armouries of the great powers, is not prohibited. In fact, functionalists would even have us believe that, insofar as the targets of any such missiles are on earth and not in outer space, they have nothing to do with space law, even though they physically pass through what spatialists would definitely regard as outer space.[71] This is an additional reason why the military and those that defer to them prefer the functionalists.

More specifically, as worded at present, Article IV(l) does not cover the so-called Fractional Orbital Bombardment System (FOBS) in which the missiles behave rather like an artificial satellite with a low orbit except that they are designed to re-enter the earth's atmosphere and home on their targets before they complete a single orbit.

---

[69] See also the subsequent 1971 Treaty on the Prohibition of the Emplacement of Nuclear Weapons and other Weapons of Mass Destruction on the Sea-Bed and the Ocean Floor and in the Subsoil Thereof, London, Moscow, Washington DC (1971), 955 UNTS 115.

[70] 55 *Dept. of State Bulletin* (1966), p. 952.   [71] See further ss. I.K above, and IV.C.1 below.

In any event, apart from the mere transit of military missiles, the many vital rôles played by outer space from the military point of view, including reconnaissance, communications, geodesy, and navigational satellites, render it much too important to States to be totally demilitarized, unless as part of a general programme of disarmament. During the drafting stage of the Space Treaty, some delegates did call for its total demilitarization, but both super powers made it quite clear that any attempt within the context of the treaty then being drafted wholly to demilitarize outer space would simply make the treaty unacceptable to them. Consequently, even as among the contracting States to the 1967 Space Treaty, except for the stationing of nuclear weapons and other weapons of mass destruction, outer space may be freely used for military purposes, subject of course always to the observance of international law and the Charter of the United Nations.[72]

3. *Non-militarization of Celestial Bodies.* The wording of Article IV (2) of the Space Treaty is traceable to Article I of the Antarctic Treaty which provides as follows:

1. Antarctica shall be used for peaceful purposes only. There shall be prohibited, *inter alia*, any measures of a military nature, such as the establishment of military bases and fortifications, the carrying out of military manoeuvres, as well as the testing of any type of weapons.
2. The present Treaty shall not prevent the use of military personnel or equipment for scientific research or for any other peaceful purposes.

In discussions on space activities in general and space law in particular, in order to fit the square peg of the already extensive use of outer space for military purposes into the politically hallowed concept of 'peaceful uses', there has unfortunately developed in some quarters the habit of interpreting the term 'peaceful' as applied to outer space as meaning 'non-aggressive' instead of 'non-military'. From this point of view, Article I of the Antarctic Treaty is explicit in that 'any measures of a military nature' are '*inter alia*' prohibited. In many ways, the wording of the Antarctic Treaty is superior, inasmuch, as the various prohibited items enumerated are purely exemplificative. For reasons which remain obscure, the Soviet Union was reluctant to follow the example of the Antarctic Treaty. However, even in its present form, it is clear that, as among the contracting Parties, no activity whatsoever serving a military purpose should be pursued on celestial bodies. Celestial bodies, including the moon, have been totally demilitarized.[73]

---

[72] See s. II.A.1 above.
[73] For an example of the many borderline cases that must remain, see the problem annexed to this chapter. As regards free access to installations on celestial bodies and the supply of information on space activities for the purpose of ensuring compliance with the provisions of the Treaty, see ss. II.A.3 *in fine* and II.A.4.e above. See also s. III.E below.

D. The 1977 Geneva Convention on the Prohibition of Military or any other Hostile Use of Environmental Modification Techniques

The first two articles of the Treaty set out its principal provisions and are self-explanatory:

Article I
1. Each State Party to this Convention undertakes not to engage in military or any other hostile use of environmental modification techniques having widespread, long-lasting or severe effects as the means of destruction, damage or injury to any other State Party.
2. Each State Party to this Convention undertakes not to assist, encourage or induce any State, group of States or international organisation to engage in activities contrary to the provisions of paragraph I of this article.
Article II
As used in article I, the term 'environmental modification technique' refers to any technique for changing—through the deliberate manipulation of natural processes—the dynamics, composition or structure of the Earth, including its biota, lithosphere, hydrosphere and atmosphere, or of *outer space*.[74]

From the standpoint of legislative drafting, it is interesting to observe that the 1977 Geneva Convention, when referring to the indirect responsibility of States for the acts of others in areas subject to its jurisdiction and control, has learnt to avoid the pitfall in the Partial Test Ban Treaty.[75] Article IV provides:

Each State Party to this Convention undertakes to take measures it considers necessary in accordance with its constitutional processes to prohibit and prevent any activity in violation of the provisions of the Convention anywhere under its jurisdiction or control.

This is obviously also what the Test Ban Treaty has in mind.

E. The 1979 Moon Treaty[76]

1. *Article 3.*   Under Article 3 of the Moon Treaty:

1. The moon shall be used by all States Parties exclusively for peaceful purposes.
2. Any threat or use of force or any other hostile act or threat of hostile act on the moon is prohibited. It is likewise prohibited to use the moon in order to commit any such act or to engage in any such threat in relation to the earth, the moon, spacecraft, the personnel of spacecraft or man-made space objects.
3. States Parties shall not place in orbit around or other trajectory to or around the moon objects carrying nuclear weapons or any other kinds of weapons of mass destruction or place or use such weapons on or in the moon.
4. The establishment of military bases, installations and fortifications, the testing of any type of weapons and the conduct of military manoeuvres on the moon shall be

---

[74] Italics added; 16 *ILM* (1977), p. 88.   [75] See s. III.A above.
[76] See further s. II.B above, especially as regards the cosmographical scope of the Treaty.

forbidden. The use of military personnel for scientific research or for any other peaceful purposes shall not be prohibited. The use of any equipment or facility necessary for peaceful exploration and use of the moon shall also not be prohibited.

Article 3 largely repeats Article IV of the Space Treaty,[77] especially Article IV(2), although in a rather mumbled way. The only new element is to be found in paragraph 2, which from this point of view, goes beyond not only the 1967 Space Treaty, but also Article 2(4) of the United Nations Charter, where the prohibition of the use or the threat of force is only 'against the territorial integrity or political independence of any State, or in any other manner inconsistent with the Purposes of the United Nations'. In the Moon Treaty the prohibition is absolute, and one wonders whether the kind of situation envisaged in the annex to this chapter[78] would fall foul of Article 3.

Moreover, Article 3 prohibits not only the use and threat of force, but also 'any other hostile act or threat of hostile act'. The phraseology used is reminiscent of the 1977 Geneva Convention on Environmental Modification Techniques which, it will be recalled, speaks of 'military or any hostile use' of such techniques[79]. It will also be noted that the use of the moon and other celestial bodies for such acts of force or hostile acts or threats of either against a variety of targets is prohibited.

The United States continues, however, to interpret 'peaceful' to mean 'non-aggressive'.

2. Mutual Supervision. Article 15 of the Moon Treaty recognizes that '[e]ach State Party may assure itself that the activities of the States Parties . . . are compatible with the provisions of this Agreement' and consequently allows the States Parties freely to visit the facilities of one another on the moon, subject to reasonable notice and the taking of maximum precautions to assure safety, and to avoid undue interference, but, unlike Article XII of the 1967 Space Treaty, no longer to the condition of reciprocity.[80]

In case of disagreement, Article 15 provides for, in the first instance, consultation between the States Parties concerned, and, in case of an impasse, unilateral recourse to the Secretary-General of the United Nations for assistance, without seeking the consent of the other Party concerned, in order to resolve the controversy. The same procedure applies, under Article 8(3), to mutual interference on the moon and other celestial bodies. This consultation and conciliation procedure would seem, therefore, to be applicable, on both counts, to the situation outlined in the annex[81], were the Moon Treaty applicable.

---

[77] See s. III.C above, especially s. III.C.3.   [78] See Annex at end of this chapter.
[79] See s. III.D above.
[80] See ss. II.A.3 and n. 73 above. Article 5 of the Moon Treaty also provides for the supply of information concerning the exploration and use of the moon and other celestial bodies; see ss. II.A.4.e and n. 73 above.
[81] See Annex at end of this chapter.

IV. The Legal Status of Space Objects and of Spacemen

A. The 1967 Space Treaty

1. *Articles V and VIII.* The 1967 Space Treaty contains two specific provisions on the status of space objects and spacemen. They are respectively Articles VIII and V. Under Article VIII:

A State Party to the Treaty on whose registry an object launched into outer space is carried shall retain jurisdiction and control over such object, and over any personnel thereof, while in outer space or on a celestial body. Ownership of objects launched into outer space, including objects landed or constructed on a celestial body, and of their component parts is not affected by their presence in outer space or on a celestial body or by their return to the Earth. Such objects or component parts found beyond the limits of the State Party to the Treaty on whose registry they are carried shall be returned to that State Party, which shall, upon request, furnish identifying data prior to their return.

As regards spacemen, Article V provides:

States Parties to the Treaty shall regard astronauts as envoys of mankind in outer space and shall render to them all possible assistance in the event of accident, distress, or emergency landing on the territory of another State Party or on the high seas. When astronauts make such a landing, they shall be safely and promptly returned to the State of registry of their space vehicle.

In carrying on activities in outer space and on celestial bodies, the astronauts of one State Party shall render all possible assistance to the astronauts of other States Parties.

States Parties to the Treaty shall immediately inform the other States Parties to the Treaty or the Secretary-General of the United Nations of any phenomena they discover in outer space, including the moon and other celestial bodies, which could constitute a danger to the life or health of astronauts.

2. *Registration of Objects Launched into Space.* It results from the above provisions that, first, the Treaty presupposes that all States parties to the treaty will maintain a registry of objects launched into space. Secondly, it assumes that objects launched into space will all first be registered. In fact, the application of a number of the provisions of the treaty depends on the registration of the spacecraft, namely, the exercise of jurisdiction (Article VIII), the return of space objects (Article VIII), and the return of astronauts (Article V).

Neither assumptions would of course be true under general international law in the absence of the treaty. Nor were these assumptions relied upon in the 1968 Astronauts Agreement,[82] or the 1972 Liability Convention.[83] Under customary international law, the quasi-territorial jurisdiction over a space object

---

[82] See further s. IV.B.1 below.

[83] See further B. Cheng, 'Convention on International Liability for Damage Caused by Space Objects', in Jasentuliyana and Lee (eds.), 1 *Manual* (1979), p. 83, at pp. 102 ff. [Ch. 1 above, ss. V.A.5 and 6].

will no doubt be attributed by reference to what the International Court of Justice has in the *Nottebohm Case* termed the 'genuine link',[84] which, in the absence of registration, could, for instance, be ownership.[85] Instead of referring to the State of registry, the 1968 Astronauts Agreement and the 1972 Liability Convention preferred respectively the 'launching authority' (Article 6) and the 'launching State' (Article I(c)) as defined in these two treaties. Notwithstanding the 1975 Registration Convention,[86] the 1979 Moon Treaty[87] has refrained from using the State of registry link and has instead reverted to the 'launching State' (Article 13) and possibly ownership (Article 12) test.

3. *Quasi-territorial Character of Jurisdiction.*   Whether the test be ownership, registration, a functional one of responsibility for launching (e.g., 'the launching authority' under the Astronauts Agreement), or an arbitrary one as defined in a treaty (e.g., 'the launching State' as defined in the 1972 Liability Convention), the need for having such a test arises from the practical one of having to link every space object to a subject of international law. On the one hand, this is necessary in order to ensure that rules of international law established to govern the exploration and use of space will in fact be complied with. The rights and duties flowing from these rules of international law are those of the State to which such objects are attributed, it being obvious that such objects, not being subjects of international law, are themselves not directly subject to these rules, or bound by them.

On the other hand, international law acknowledges the special relationship between such objects and the State concerned by recognizing that the latter retains jurisdiction and control over such objects wherever they may be. This is precisely what Article VIII of the 1967 Space Treaty has done, although the position is probably the same under customary international law. Whether or not one were to label this relationship as nationality is really of no great significance.

Inasmuch as space objects may carry persons and are likely to spend most of their time in areas not subject to the territorial jurisdiction of any State,[88] the jurisdiction referred to in Article VIII is quasi-territorial in character; for it applies not only to the spacecraft, but also to any personnel on board, irrespective of their nationality. The quasi-territorial jurisdiction of the State of registry overrides, therefore, the personal jurisdiction of the national State of the individuals, at least insofar as the concrete power of implementation and enforcement (jurisaction) is concerned.

Furthermore, under Article VIII, this jurisdiction of the State of registry applies to the crew, not only when they are on board, but also when they are

---

[84] *ICJ Rep. 1955*, p. 20.
[85] Cf. B. Cheng, 'State Ships and State Aircraft', 11 *CLP* (1958), p. 225.
[86] See further s. IV.C below.   [87] See further s. IV.D below.   [88] See s. I.F above.

outside their space vehicle. The substitution of the word 'thereof' for 'thereon', which was the expression used in paragraph 7 of General Assembly resolution 1962, was intended to make this point explicit.

Mention has previously been made of the incompleteness of the analogy of the high seas for the situation on celestial bodies.[89] The flag State of ships exercise a similar quasi-territorial jurisdiction. But during the time when a ship is on the high seas, persons on board do not normally wander away from the ship. Cases of the crew of a ship taking a swim in the waters of the high seas and then becoming involved in a fight in such waters with the crew of another ship of a different nationality doing the same thing are, shall we say, on the whole rather uncommon. However, similar incidents on celestial bodies between crew members from different spacecraft can certainly not be ruled out.[90]

4. *Ownership of Space Objects.* The question of ownership over space objects and their components is essentially a matter of municipal law to be decided, in case of need, by reference to ordinary rules of private international law. All that Article VIII is saying is that such ownership shall not be affected 'by their presence in outer space or on a celestial body or by their return to the Earth'. This does not mean that such objects cannot become *res derelicta*, while in outer space or on their return to the earth, because their owners have abandoned them by losing their *animus domini* over them. In fact, there is an abundance of such debris in outer space. Moreover, a fair quantity has survived the earth's atmosphere on re-entry.

5. *Return of Space Objects.*   Article VIII of the Space Treaty makes it a legal duty to return all space objects found beyond the (presumably territorial) limits of the State of registry, subject only to the condition that the State of registry might be requested to furnish identifying data first. In practice, a State may often have no interests in the fragments from a spent satellite that have survived re-entry, and it is not unknown for a launching State to decline proffered fragments rather like a Greek gift, suspecting that they might be accompanied by a claim for compensation for damage caused by such fragments. The return of space objects is further regulated in the 1968 Astronauts Agreement.[91]

6. *Astronauts Envoys of Mankind.*   It follows from Article VIII of the Space Treaty, that, as among contracting States to the Treaty, astronauts, while in outer space and on celestial bodies, are under the quasi-territorial jurisdiction of the spacecraft to which they belong, irrespective of their own nationality, and whether or not they are on board the spacecraft.

Article V of the Space Treaty begins with the injunction that 'State Parties shall regard astronauts as envoys of mankind in outer space'. The rather florid

---

[89] See ss. II.A.2 and II.B.6 above.   [90] Cf. Problem annexed to this chapter.
[91] See ss. IV.B.3.b and IV.B.3.c below.

expression 'the envoys of mankind' was first introduced in General Assembly resolution 1962, and seemed to find favour particularly with the Soviet Union. During the negotiating stage of the Space Treaty, the representative from Hungary did put forward once the view that as 'envoys' astronauts should enjoy jurisdictional immunity. On another occasion, the representative from Austria wistfully queried, as astronauts were designated envoys of mankind, 'whether States which were not space powers should not have a hand in the way astronauts were launched into space'. One can only wonder whether it was not this remark that led the Soviet representative eventually to say that this phrase merely 'served to justify the legal obligations' in the rest of the article, and that he would be 'prepared to consider another form of words provided that it did not complicate the text of the draft treaty'.[92] In other words, this expression has no special legal significance. It has been dropped from the 1968 Astronauts Agreement onwards.

7. *Assistance To and Return of Astronauts.*   The remainder of Article V of the 1967 Space Treaty is fairly straightforward. Astronauts of one State Party owe assistance to those of other State Parties. States Parties shall render them assistance in case of emergency landing. Deserving a special mention is the fact that astronauts involved in an emergency landing are to be returned not to their national State, but to the State of registry.

B. The 1968 Astronauts Agreement

1. *Unilateral Character.*   The 1968 Agreement on the Rescue of Astronauts, the Return of Astronauts and the Return of Objects Launched into Outer Space was drawn up in great haste, under heavy pressure from the space powers, particularly the Soviet Union, and in the shadow of the first fatal accidents in space flight.[93] The obligations of the contracting States, which are essentially one-sided in favour of astronauts and hence the space powers, are summarized below.

2. *Duties in Regard to Astronauts.*
   (a) *Notification of accidents.* A contracting State, on learning that an astronaut is in distress or has made an emergency landing anywhere other than in the territory of another State, shall immediately notify the launching authority or, if it cannot identify the launching authority, make a public announcement instead. At the same time, it must also notify the Secretary-General of the United Nations (Article 1). The Agreement, in its definition of the 'launching authority' does not go beyond saying that it is the State (or organization) 'responsible for launching' (Article 6).

[92] A/AC.105/C.2/SR.58 (13.7.66), pp. 8–9.
[93] For a detailed analysis of this Agreement, see B. Cheng, 'The 1968 Astronauts Agreement', 23 *YBWA* (1969), p. 185 [Ch. 10 above].

(b) *Search and rescue in a contracting State's territory*. Under Article 2, contracting States undertake to 'take all possible steps' to rescue and assist astronauts in distress in territories under their jurisdiction, and to inform the launching authority and also the Secretary-General of the United Nations of the steps they are taking and their progress. However, it was recognized in the *travaux préparatoires* that neither in Article 2 nor in the first sentence of Article 3, or paragraphs 2 and 3 of Article 5 would any contracting State be required to go beyond the limits of its capabilities.

(c) *Landings in areas not under the jurisdiction of any State*. Article 3 applies to astronauts who have '*alighted* on the high seas or in any other place not under the jurisdiction of any State'.[94] 'Those Contracting Parties which are in a position to do so shall, if necessary, extend assistance in search and rescue operations for such personnel to assure their speedy rescue'. They are at the same time required, as under Article 2, to 'inform the launching authority and the Secretary-General of the United Nations of the steps they are taking and of their progress'.

(d) *Return of astronauts*. If astronauts land in the territory of a contracting State or have otherwise been recovered by it, they shall, under Article 4, 'be safely and promptly returned to representatives of the launching authority'. Inasmuch as the 1967 Space Treaty requires its contracting Parties to return astronauts to the State of registry of the spacecraft,[95] a State party to both treaties can be faced with conflicting treaty obligations. The possibility of returning the astronauts to representatives of the launching authority rather than the launching authority itself, on the other hand, can facilitate the task of the territorial State.

3. *Duties in Regard to Space Objects.*   These are similar to, but less exacting than, those relating to astronauts.

(a) *Notification of landing*. If a contracting State learns that a space object has landed anywhere other than in the territory under the jurisdiction of another State, it shall notify the launching authority and the Secretary-General of the United Nations. Article 5(1), however, does not require the notification to be immediate. Moreover, the obligation is limited to objects which have 'returned to Earth', excluding thus celestial bodies.[96]

(b) *Recovery of foreign space objects in contracting State's territory*. Upon request of the launching authority, the State of landing shall take 'such steps as it finds practicable to recover the object' (Article 5(2)).

(c) *Return of space objects*. Article 5(3) reproduces in substance the last sentence of Article VIII of the 1967 Space Treaty,[97] except that the duty is now contingent on a request from the launching authority. Moreover, upon a proposal made by the French delegate, the State of landing, instead of returning

---

[94] Italics added.   [95] See IV.A.7 above.   [96] See s. IV.D below.
[97] See ss. IV.A.1 and IV.A.5 above.

the object, may simply hold it 'at the disposal of representatives of the launching authority'. Expenses for recovering and returning space objects made at the request of the launching authority are to be borne by the launching authority (Article 5(5)), which apparently is not responsible for the expenses incurred by other contracting States in rescuing and returning its astronauts.

C. The 1975 Registration Convention

1. *Registrable Objects.* Article I of the 1975 Convention on Registration of Objects launched into Outer Space defines 'space objects', for the purposes of the Convention, as including 'component parts of a space object as well as its launch vehicle and parts thereof'. Article II(1) says that, 'When a space object *is launched into earth orbit or beyond*, the launching State shall register the space object . . .'[98] Unlike the 1972 Liability Convention, the 1975 Registration Convention does not say that 'launching includes attempted launching'. Although there has been before and since the 1975 Convention persistent demands for advance information on space exploration and use, it would appear arguable that under the Convention, registration is required only if the object *has been* launched into earth orbit or beyond (whether entirely successfully or not, i.e., into the planned orbit or trajectory or not).[99]

Furthermore, it follows from Article II(1) that only objects that have been so launched are registrable. In other words, objects which merely transit outer space, such as sounding rockets and ballistic missiles, would not be included, although how far this narrow definition of space object is applicable beyond the Registration Convention is more than questionable.[100] However, in this connection, there seems to be no reason why FOBS, which is designed to go into earth orbit though not to complete it,[101] should not come under the Registration Convention.

2. *National Register.* Under Article II:

1. When a space object is launched into earth orbit or beyond, the launching State shall register the space object by means of an entry in an appropriate registry which it shall maintain

. . . .

3. The contents of each registry and the conditions under which it is maintained shall be determined by the State of registry concerned.

Article I, following the example of the 1972 Liability Convention, defines, for the purpose of the Convention, the 'launching State' as meaning:

(i) A State which launches or procures the launching of a space object;
(ii) A State from whose territory or facility a space object is launched.

[98] Italics added.
[99] Cf. also the 1979 Moon Treaty which appears to confirm this view; see s. IV.D below.
[100] Cf. s. III.C.2 above.   [101] See ibid.

A launching State can, therefore, be any one of four different States: the State that launches; the State that procures the launching; the State from whose territory a space object is launched; the State from whose facility a space object is launched.

Article II(2) provides:

> Where there are two or more launching States in respect of any such space object, they shall jointly determine which one of them shall register the object in accordance with paragraph 1 of this article, bearing in mind the provisions of article VIII of the Treaty on Principles Governing the Activities of States in the Exploration and Use of Outer Space, including the Moon and Other Celestial Bodies, and without prejudice to appropriate agreements concluded or to be concluded among the launching States on jurisdiction and control over the space object and over any personnel thereof.

Article II (2) has to some extent taken over the system of joint registration of aircraft devised by the International Civil Aviation Organisation, but in a rather abbreviated form. What the Registration Convention has done is to say to the States concerned in such cases that they should designate one of them to be the State of registry for the purpose of the Registration Convention and, so it would seem, also Article VIII of the 1967 Space Treaty.[102] In this, the Registration Convention has followed the example of the 1944 Chicago Convention on International Civil Aviation in the matter of aircraft and the 1958 Geneva Convention on the High Seas in the matter of ships in seeking to avoid dual or multiple registration of space objects. With single registration, only one set of laws, that of the State of registry, will be applicable on board on a quasi-territorial basis.

Insofar as the last part of Article II(2) commencing with the words 'without prejudice' is concerned, it would seem that arrangements among the launching States can only affect their relations *inter se*, but cannot prejudice the position of third States, particularly other contracting Parties to the 1967 Space Treaty, which will be entitled to recognize only the jurisdiction and control of the State of registry.

3. *Institutional Register.* Even since the 1968 Astronauts Agreement, every treaty drawn up by the United Nations concerning outer space has allowed international intergovernmental organizations a majority of the members of which are parties to the treaty in question and the 1967 Space Treaty to enjoy the rights and assume the obligations provided in the treaty if they were to make a declaration accepting such rights and obligations. The Registration Convention is no exception (Article VII).

In this case, however, certain difficulties arise. The Convention, literally interpreted, permits any international organization which fulfils the conditions laid down in its Article VII to establish a register for the registration of space objects launched by it. In fact, it is obliged to do so.

---

[102] See s. IV.A.1 above.

The first difficulty which is likely to arise is that, inasmuch as there is no provision similar to Article VII of the Registration Convention in the 1967 Space Treaty, such an institutional registration would be quite meaningless under Article VIII of the Space Treaty. Even if one were able to overcome this difficulty, at least among parties to the Registration Convention, there is a second and more obstinate one which consists in the lack of State jurisdiction on the part of present-day international intergovernmental organizations. As international organizations, they have neither the legislative authority nor the law enforcement machinery to enable them to exercise quasi-territorial jurisdiction over spacecraft of their registry. If in due course they become so endowed, then they are no longer intergovernmental organizations, but have transformed themselves into federal States or incipient federal States, in which case, they should accede to the Treaty like any other State. The whole idea of institutional registration is ill-conceived,[103] unless it be of a secondary nature such as the United Nations register discussed below. The only practical way out would be for an international organization to register its spacecraft with one of its member States.

4. *United Nations Register.*   The Registration Convention provides, in addition to the national register for also a United Nations register maintained by the Secretary-General (Article III). The prime purpose of the former would appear to be the identification of the State which exercises quasi-territorial jurisdiction over a space object., The latter, by collecting, recording, and making available, through open access, certain basic data concerning every space object recorded in a national register, seeks to assist in the identification of all space objects in general and individual space objects in particular.[104]

Under Article IV (1):

Each State of registry shall furnish to the Secretary-General of the United Nations, as soon as practicable, the following information concerning each space object carried on its registry:
   (a) Name of launching State or States;
   (b) An appropriate designator of the space object or its registration number;
   (c) Date and territory or location of launch;
   (d) Basic orbital parameters, including:
       (i)   Nodal period,
       (ii) Inclination,
       (iii) Apogee, and
       (iv) Perigee;
   (e) General function of the space object.

---

[103] Cf. B. Cheng, 'Nationality of Aircraft operated by Joint or International Agencies', *YBASL* (1966), pp. 5–31; 'Nationality and Registration of Aircraft—Article 77 of the Chicago Convention', *JALC*, 32 (1966), pp. 551–63; 'Memorandum on Nationality and Registration of Aircraft', ILA, *Report of the 52nd Conference, Helsinki* (1966) pp. 268–82.
[104] Cf. Preamble, para. 8.

5. *Designation or Registration Mark.* Inspired by perhaps maritime and aeronautical precedents, many States are keen to see space objects carrying on them some identification mark. Others point out that in the vast expanse of outer space, such marks are not very meaningful, that space objects are usually identified by tracking or other means, and that in any event there are technical difficulties in devising external markings that would survive re-entry into the earth's atmosphere.

The present Article V of the Registration Convention represents a compromise between these views:

Whenever a space object launched into earth orbit or beyond is marked with the designator or registration number referred to in article IV, paragraph 1 (*b*), or both, the State of registry shall notify the Secretary-General of this fact when submitting the information regarding the space object in accordance with Article IV. In such case, the Secretary-General of the United Nations shall record this notification in the Register.

D. The 1979 Moon Treaty

Article 5(1) of the Moon Treaty, without reference to the 1975 Registration Convention, more or less confirms that registration of space objects with the United Nations can be carried out after launching.[105]

. . . Information on the time, purposes, locations, orbital parameters and duration shall be given in respect of each mission to the moon *as soon as possible after launching* . . .[106]

The information referred to here corresponds to that specified in Article IV(1) of the Registration Convention.[107] It is not clear, however, whether, when both Conventions are applicable, two separate notifications are required, one under each Convention.

Article 12(1) more or less repeats Article VIII of the 1967 Space Treaty[108] in saying:

States Parties shall retain jurisdiction and control over their personnel, space vehicles, equipment, facilities, stations and installations on the moon. The ownership of space vehicles, equipment facilities, stations and installations shall not be affected by their presence on the moon.

It will be noted, however, that the Moon Treaty has rather pointedly omitted references to registration, thus creating a source of confusion; for, *inter alia*, while the possessive 'their' can imply ownership and thus be applied without too much difficulty to space vehicles and so forth, its application to 'personnel' can mean a variety of different things.

---

[105] Cf. s. IV.C.1 above.   [106] Italics added.   [107] See s. IV.C.4 above.
[108] See s. IV.A.1 above.

For the rest, the Moon Treaty does not appear to be able to make up its mind whether to incorporate the whole of the 1968 Astronauts Agreement by reference or to borrow bits from it. This adds to the confusion which further contributes to making the Moon Treaty a monument of sloppy draftsmanship.

Thus Article 13 of the Moon Treaty reduces the twelve-line Article 1 of the Astronauts Agreement[109] to four lines and adapts it to crash landings on the moon. Again, it ignores the Registration Convention and requires notification to be made to the 'launching State Party', forgetting that whilst 'the launching authority' as used in the Astronauts Agreement is defined in that Agreement, the term 'launching State' is not defined in the Moon Treaty. Does 'launching State Party' mean the 'launching authority' as defined in the Astronauts Agreement,[110] or the 'launching State' as defined in the Liability Convention or Registration Convention,[111] or neither?

Under Article 12(2), space vehicles, installations and equipment on the moon 'found in places other than their intended location' are to be dealt with in accordance with Article 5 of the Astronauts Agreement, thus incorporating Article 5 of the latter Agreement into the Moon Treaty by reference and making it binding on parties to the Moon Treaty even if they are not parties to the Astronauts Agreement.

But in the case of persons on the moon and other celestial bodies, Article 10 merely provides that 'any person on the moon' shall be regarded as an 'astronaut' within the meaning of Article V of the 1967 Space Treaty, and 'part of the personnel of a spacecraft' within the meaning of the Astronauts Agreement. This provision may marginally widen the scope of these two treaties, although even this is dubious, but it does not place such persons under the protection of these two treaties unless the contracting Parties to the Moon Treaty concerned are already parties to these other two treaties. In other words, in this instance, neither the Space Treaty nor the Astronauts Agreement has been incorporated by reference into the Moon Treaty.

Instead, the Moon Treaty seems to prefer its own provisions concerning assistance to persons on the moon and celestial bodies. Thus:

Article 10

1. States Parties shall adopt all practicable measures to safeguard the life and health of persons on the moon . . .

2. States Parties shall offer shelter in their stations, installations, vehicles and other facilities to persons in distress on the moon.

Article 12

. . .

3. In the event of an emergency involving a threat to human life, States Parties may use the equipment, vehicles, installations, facilities or supplies of other States Parties

---

[109] See ss. IV.B.2.a and IV.B.3.a above.   [110] See s. IV.B.2.a above.
[111] See s. IV.C.2 above.

on the moon. Prompt notification of such use shall be made to the Secretary-General of the United Nations or State Party concerned.

The right provided for in Article 12(3) exists already in general international law under the plea of necessity, except that in such cases the law normally requires compensation to be paid for objects consumed or damaged.[112] Whether compensation is required under Article 12 or not is an open question. The article does, however, appear to be a little mean in not requiring the State Party whose property has been so used to be informed in all cases.

Annex: Problem to be Examined

State Prima has discovered Cupidium in the Sea of Tranquillity on the moon. Cupidium, a material not found on the earth or elsewhere on the moon, while it can be used also for the production of energy, is capable of producing the most powerful weapon known to man. Prima, through a wholly State-owned corporation incorporated in Prima, the Priman Lunar Enterprise (PLE), has erected a fence enclosing the entire area in the Sea of Tranquillity where Cupidium is likely to be found, named the place the Priman Tranquillity Science Centre (PTSC), and begun to mine and to process Cupidium on the moon. State Seconda, another major space power, protests that the fencing off of a part of the Sea of Tranquillity is a violation of the 1967 Space Treaty, demands to inspect the installations at PTSC and asserts that its lunar base, the State University of Seconda Space Centre Lunar Station (SUSSCLS), is entitled to work the PTSC mines on the same terms as PLE. Twenty-four hours after notice having been served of a projected visit, ten Secondan astronauts from SUSSCLS arrive at the entrance of PTSC. A fight with the PLE guards at PTSC breaks out and an astronaut on each side is killed. Each side, moreover, has captured an astronaut of the other side whom it accuses as having killed one of its members, and whom it wishes to bring back to the earth for trial.

State Tertia, a non-space power, maintains at the General Assembly of the United Nations that the mining and processing of Cupidium on the moon, whether by PLE, SUSSCLS, Prima or Seconda, constitute violations of the 1967 Space Treaty, unless they be for the account of all countries, in which case the mineral must be distributed equally among all the States of the world, or handed over to the United Nations as trustees of mankind.

Prima, Seconda, and Tertia are all members of the United Nations and parties to the 1967 Space Treaty. Consider also the situation where all the States concerned are parties to the 1979 Moon Treaty, but, for lack of agreement, the international regime cannot be established.

---

[112] See Cheng, *General Principles of Law*, pp. 69–77.

14

The Legal Regime of Airspace and Outer Space: the Boundary Problem Functionalism versus Spatialism: the Major Premises*

I. Introduction

In the subject index to the book *Law and Public Order in Space* (1963) by Professors Myers S. McDougal, Harold D. Lasswell, and Ivan A. Vlasic, there is to be found the following entry:

Boundary between outer space and airspace (a comedy of errors).

This entry is typical of the often pungent wit and humour with which the authors in the text of their masterly work exposed what appeared to them to be the fallacy and even folly of those who sought to draw a boundary—or to borrow a graphic expression from their at times rather esoteric terminology, a horizontal sheet—between airspace and outer space—people who have since been dubbed the spatialists. Instead, the authors firmly nailed to their mast the flag of functionalism—which goes well in any event with the authors' New Haven policy-oriented approach to international law pioneered by Professor McDougal. The following excerpt was quoted from an article by Professors McDougal and Lipson published in 1958 in the *American Journal of International Law* 'predict[ing] that':

with the growing awareness of the difficulties entailed by fixed lines or putative horizontal sheets and of the factors that do and should affect policy, the problem will *transform itself from one of boundaries to one of activities*, in an appropriate pattern of

* First published in 5 *AASL* (1980), pp. 323–61, with some additional material taken from 'The Legal Status of Outer Space and Relevant Issues: Delimitation of Outer Space and Definition of Peaceful Use', 11 *JSL* (1983), p. 89, at pp. 89–98. See also the writer's contribution in Centre for Research of Air and Space Law, *Earth-Oriented Space Activities and Their Legal Implications: Proceedings of the Symposium held on October 15–16, 1981* (1983), pp. 230–74, on 'For Delimiting Outer Space' in a Debate on 'Delimitation of Airspace and Outer Space: Is It Necessary?', forming part of the Symposium. Reprinted with the kind concurrence of the McGill University Institute and Centre of Air and Space Law, publishers of the *Annals of Air and Space Law* and of *Earth-Oriented Space Activities and Their Legal Implications*, and by kind permission of the *Journal of Space Law*, in respect of 'The Legal Status of Outer Space and Relevant Issues'.

reciprocities and (potential) retaliations; and the now vexed *question of the legal 'status' of outer space will be discarded* for practical purposes, as the *question of 'status' was discarded* when negotiations *on the use of airspace* came to the point of concrete agreement.[1]

Thus from the dawn of the space age all those who deal with the question of defining outer space have been neatly divided into those who are spatialists and those who are functionalists. In this long drawn out discussion, often not without comic ironies, many have taken part: writers and speakers on space law and international law, government delegates, learned societies, governments, the United Nations and some of its specialized agencies.

In the United Nations, the functionalists, backed initially by both major space powers, to whose interests it was not to have boundaries which might restrict their freedom to get into space (whether for peaceful or military purposes) without let or hindrance, handsomely won the first rounds, starting with the 1959 Report of the *Ad Hoc* Committee on the Peaceful Uses of Outer Space which did not consider that the topic called for priority consideration.[2] In 1966, the spatialists, however, can perhaps be said to have managed to win a round—albeit only on points and probably only by a split decision among the judges at that—when the General Assembly, at least as a gesture to Mexico and some other countries which had asked for outer space to be defined in the then draft Outer Space Treaty, decided in resolution 2222 (XXI) to request the Outer Space Committee to study the problem. But the fortune of the spatialists was and still is hardly helped by a complete lack of agreement among themselves. In addition to those who wish simply to delimit outer space from national airspace, there are those who advocate tri-zonal or pluri-zonal solutions. As regards the method for fixing the lower limit and/or the upper limit of national airspace, there are probably as many criteria as there are speakers or writers on the subject: gravitational effect, effective control, actual lowest perigee of orbiting satellites, theoretical lowest perigee of orbiting satellites, the von Karman line, limit of air drag, limit of air flight, the atmosphere and its various layers, an absolutely arbitrary height (e.g., one-thousandth of the distance measured on a meridian of the earth from the equator to the pole (100 kilometres) or one-hundredth of the earth's radius (64 kilometres—Canadian suggestions), and so forth.[3] The way the Legal Sub-Committee of the Outer Space Committee first dealt with the request from the General Assembly to study the problems was to pass it on to the Scientific and Technical Sub-Committee of the Outer Space Committee. The latter, after due consideration, replied *inter alia* in 1967:

---

[1] At pp. 352–3. Italics added. Cf. Bin Cheng's review of *Law and Public Order in Space* in 16 *University of Toronto LJ* (1965), p. 210.

[2] See B. Cheng, 'The United Nations and Outer Space', 14 *CLP* (1961), p. 247, at pp. 259–62 [Ch. 6 above, s. IV: Blind Spot in the Sky].

[3] See further works cited in nn. 12, 13 and 14 below.

there was consensus in the Scientific and Technical Sub-Committee that it is not possible at the present time to identify scientific or technical criteria which would permit a precise and lasting definition of outer space.[4]

The ball was firmly back in the court of the Legal Sub-Committee, a majority of the members of which appears to accept that it is now up to the Legal Sub-Committee to find a legal definition.

Over the years, however, in the Legal Sub-Committee, probably the only place where States are more or less obliged to express a view on the subject, the functionalists, notwithstanding their initial dominance and their subsequent widening the scope of their terms of reference to include the definition of not only the functions of activities, but also the functions of vehicles, have been losing ground. The Italians, for instance, have seemingly long been spatialists. Already in 1958, their representative on the First Committee of the General Assembly, Professor Ambrosini, advocated that national sovereignty should be limited to 'atmospheric space' which, he estimated, extended to 'approximately a hundred kilometres from the surface of the earth'.[5] Gradually more and more States shifted from the functional to the spatial approach. A clear example is Belgium, which, previously functionalist, in a paper it submitted in 1976 changed its mind and suggested a 100 kilometre line.[6] While the Soviet Union at the time appeared to make light of the Belgian suggestion on the ground that it was avowedly arbitrary, what must be regarded as an important landmark from this point of view was when in 1979 the Soviet Union itself introduced the following working paper[7] on 'Approach to the solution of the problems of the delimitation of airspace and outer space':

1. The region above 100 (110) kilometres altitude from the sea level of the earth is outer space.

2. The boundary between airspace and outer space shall be subject to agreement among States and shall subsequently be established by a treaty at an altitude not exceeding 100 (110) kilometres above sea level.

3. Space objects of States shall retain the right to fly over the territory of other States at altitudes lower than 100 (110) kilometres above sea level for the purpose of reaching orbit or returning to earth in the territory of the launching State.

It is not improbable that this change in attitude, as it appears to have been suggested,[8] of the Soviet Union and of the Soviet bloc States, as well as some other States, might have been, if not caused, at least precipitated, by the claim to the geostationary orbit at 36,000 kilometres made by the equatorial States

---

[4] UN GA, *Off. Rec.*, 22nd Session, agenda item 32, A/6804, annex II, para. 36.

[5] A/C.1/PV.982 (12.11.58), p. 56.

[6] A/AC.105/C.2/L.76, presented to the 13th Session of the Scientific and Technical Sub-Committee of the Outer Space Committee.

[7] A/AC.105/C.2/L.121 (reissued version of 28.3.79); see further s. XI below.

[8] Cf. A. Górbiel, *Legal Definition of Outer Space* (1980), p. 12.

in the Bogotá Declaration of 3 December 1979.[9] At the 1979 meeting of the Legal Sub-Committee, the Japanese delegate seemed to have been the only one still wearing the functional approach upon his sleeve,[10] although the United States, followed by the United Kingdom, the Federal Republic of Germany, and some others, continued to argue against at least, any immediate need for a boundary between airspace and outer space. The principal reasons advanced by the United States delegate were:

(i) the inability of most countries to monitor such an altitude boundary;
(ii) the lack of adequate examination of the relevant scientific, legal, technical, and political factors;
(iii) the possible inhibiting and even stifling effect of a fixed boundary on future efforts to explore and use outer space.[11]

The debate thus continues, both in the United Nations and in the doctrine. Much of this debate has been ably chronicled by the United Nations Secretariat in the background paper which, at the request of the Legal Sub-Committee, it produced in 1970 on *The Question of the Definition and/or the Delimitation of Outer Space*,[12] to which there is an addendum dated 21 January 1977.[13] The narrative is recapitulated and brought up to date in Professor A. Górbiel's clear and succinct *Legal Definition of Outer Space*.[14] There is little point in going over the same ground again here.

The controversy, especially on the doctrinal level is, however, unlikely to be resolved unless the premises and bases of both schools of thought have been laid bare. From this point of view, the theory of functionalism has already been much explored. Thus Professor N. M. Matte, who first applied this notion in 1952 to the right in municipal law of the owner of land over the superjacent space,[15] devoted an entire monograph to developing a comprehensive theory of functionalism, which was directed specifically at this problem but which was deemed also applicable throughout the international legal system.[16] The same task probably remains to be undertaken on behalf of spatialism. Meanwhile, what will be attempted here is to go back to the very fundamentals of international law in the hope that this will enable us to understand better the major premises of both spatialism and functionalism and thus to see the problem of a boundary between airspace and outer space in a clearer perspective.

---

9 See further s. XII below.   10 A/AC.105/C.2/SR.314 (2.4.79), p. 3.
11 A/AC.105/C.2/SR.316 (4.4.79), p. 2.   12 A/AC.105/C.2/7.
13 A/AC.105/C.2/7/Add. 1.   14 Published by the University of Łódź, 1980, 77 pp.
15 '*À qui appartient le milieu aérien?*' 12 *Revue du Barreau du Québec* (1952), p. 227.
16 *Deux frontières invisibles: De la mer territoriale à l'air 'territoriale'* (1964).

II. A Matter of International Law

In the first place, it should be pointed out that in speaking of 'the legal regime of airspace and outer space: the boundary problem', one is referring to the boundary problem in the regime of airspace and outer space under *public international law*. Contrary to a view which has sometimes been advanced, there is no such thing as an independent legal system known as space law free-wheeling in outer space. Space law is merely a functional classification of those rules of international law and of municipal law relating to outer space, natural and man-made objects in outer space, astronauts and man's activities in outer space or affecting outer space. In other words, there are only rules of inter-national space law and rules of space law belonging to the various municipal legal systems. The functional grouping and treatment of all the rules of space law of either an individual legal system, or of all legal systems, together have obvious scientific and practical advantages, a fact, in this and numerous other fields of study, often called by some writers, especially on the Continent, as the autonomy of their subjects. However, this functional classification should not obscure the reality of the situation in terms of separate binding legal systems. The present discussion is limited to international space law, because in the matter of boundaries between airspace and outer space it is international law which is controlling. Municipal law comes into the picture only insofar as it throws light on the situation in international law.

III. The Nature of International Law

A. Law Man-made and Not Preordained

In view of the utter confusion which appears to prevail in the doctrine of inter-national law at the moment as to what international law really is, it may

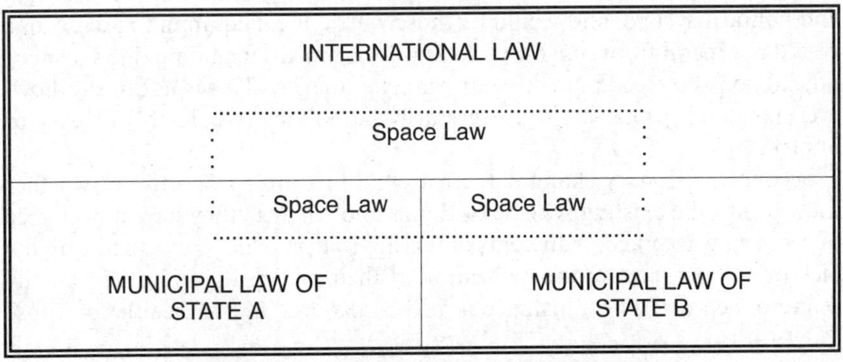

INTERNATIONAL LAW	
Space Law	
Space Law	Space Law
MUNICIPAL LAW OF STATE A	MUNICIPAL LAW OF STATE B

Figure XIV.1. THE NATURE OF SPACE LAW

perhaps be well very briefly to make clear at the outset this writer's views. While this writer fully accepts that law is an instrument to an end, he does not see it as an instrument with a predetermined content, as do both the naturalists of yore and some modern social-science oriented international lawyers. For the former, law has a predetermined content, because its source is preordained, by God, by human nature, by the right reason or by some other factor. For the latter, the content of law not only should be, but in fact is predetermined at every point by its preselected goal. To whichever point one wishes a society to go, everything in that society, including law not only in its general direction, but also in its every particular and at all times, must be mobilized to take it there. 'Scientific' methods will decide from case to case the best route. That route, without further ado, is then 'the' law.

Given their premises, both schools are perfectly reasonable, logical or even irrefutable. But need one say that neither life nor law is pure reason or pure logic, for the simple reason that man is neither the one nor the other? Another approach would be to look at law as a concrete social phenomenon of a normative character, the content of which varies from society to society but can be established, verified, scrutinized, and described, warts and all, by any detached observer in a totally objective manner, as would any scientist or clinician.[17] In speaking of international law, one will, therefore, be referring primarily to the *lex lata* such as it really exists in international society.

B. Lex Lata and Lex Ferenda

It is obvious, however, that in considering any legal problem, one is likely to be drawn into discussing not only the law as it is (*lex lata*), but also proposals for its development or reform, the *lex ferenda* (the law as one would like to see it reformed). For present purposes, proposals of changes in the law (*de lege ferenda*), on the assumption that they are all technically excellent and inherently desirable, may be said to fall broadly into three categories. First, feasible changes: these try to take into account the realities within the existing legal and political system, and would be those which, if called upon to advise, one would not recoil from suggesting to any government, including one's own, or official body engaged in making or changing the law. This is not to say, however, that such proposals will necessarily be politically palatable or easy to implement.

Secondly, visionary changes: these are put forward irrespective of whether they fit into the existing scheme of things and whether they have any chance of ever being accepted. Adherents of this approach are not concerned with the lack of any prospect of the realization of their proposals, and often happily point to such writers, for instance, as de Lacroix or St Pierre the titles of whose

---

[17] Cf. B. Cheng, 'The Role of Law in Society: East and West, National and International', *Chinese University Bulletin* (Hong Kong, Winter 1978), p. 15; and s. IV.B below.

works on world reform (though mostly unread—one may perhaps add) continue to be ritually cited in text books from century to century.

Thirdly, revolutionary changes: since the Second World War when the prestige of international law reached its nadir, schools of thought have sprung up which virtually treat the *lex lata* of international law as irrelevant and concentrate on 'meaningful' rules of *lex ferenda*, which presuppose a radical change in the structure of international society and probably also in human nature. In fact, one almost detects certain affinity between followers of this approach and 'direct action' groups that are so much part of the contemporary scene in their rejection of the 'establishment' (i.e., the *lex lata*) and the substitution of their own 'authority' in its place. The *lex ferenda* they have in mind is, for at least some of them, *the law*.

It may well be that all three types of *lex ferenda* have their place in international law. However, in order to assess their practical relevance, what is required is to bear in mind the process by which international law is created. Here again, there are now so many views on the subject that it becomes necessary to restate the position.

IV. Personal Scope of International Law

A. General International Law and Treaties

The international legal system comprises, for purposes relevant to the present discussion, two groups of rules, first those of *general international law* (a term used here synonymously with customary international law *sensu lato*)[18] which are binding on all the subjects of international law, and secondly those created by *treaties* which are binding only on their contracting parties. Notwithstanding frequent assertions to the contrary, a treaty, however numerous its contracting parties, cannot as such create rights of duties for non-parties without their consent, a point now happily re-affirmed in Article 24 of the 1969 Vienna Convention on the Law of Treaties, although as Article 38 of the same Convention says, nothing precludes a rule established in a treaty from becoming binding on third parties as a rule of general international law. But, as the *North Sea Continental Shelf Cases* (1969)[19] have shown, whether a treaty rule has become a rule of general international law is an issue which must be established in respect of each individual rule by reference to general State practice and not by reference merely to the number of States to the treaty in question, however numerous.

In discussing any topic of international law, it is consequently important always to distinguish clearly between the legal position on the level of the general law common to all the subjects of international law, and that on the level

---

[18] See further B. Cheng, *General Principles of Law*, p. 23.　　　[19] *ICJ Rep. 1969*, p. 3.

of treaties which affect only those that are parties to the relevant treaties. This is particularly important in the field of space law where the applicable rules of general international law might at first sight appear to be few and where there have been concluded a number of multilateral treaties under the auspices of the United Nations. In this connection, it is hardly necessary to point out that, notwithstanding the number of States Parties to the United Nations Charter, the Charter as such is not part of general international law, that the United Nations has no legislative authority, and that, contrary to a fairly prevalent view, the resolutions of its General Assembly are not in themselves legally binding even among United Nations members, except in internal organizational or budgetary matters.[20]

B. Subjects and Makers af International Law

1. *International Law A Horizontal Legal System.* Who are the subjects of international law and by whom are the rules of international law made? From this point of view, international law is known as a horizontal legal system, as opposed to municipal legal systems, which are almost invariably hierarchical systems. In hierarchical systems, one has legislative, judicial, and executive authorities *above* the subjects of the legal system. In a horizontal legal system, the subjects of the legal system are themselves the law-givers, judges, and law-enforcement officers, except where they have by treaty or otherwise agreed to delegate such powers to another State or to some third parties. This being the case, unless a State had consented to third-party settlement of disputes, it is legally entitled to hold on to its own interpretation of the law, unless it can be persuaded to do otherwise—the phenomena of auto-interpretation. Hence the main method of settlement of disputes is by negotiation.

2. *States Remaining the Typical Subjects of International Law.* In international society, the subjects of international law remain, notwithstanding many opinions to the contrary, States and other entities recognized by States as being endowed with international legal personality. Such other entities at present include the Holy See and a number of inter-State organizations, but do not include, despite fallacious conclusions drawn from piracy, war crime trials, and supranational institutions such as the European Communities and the European Commission and Court of Human Rights, the ordinary individual, although if existing subjects of international law so wish they can confer international legal personality on any entity, including individuals, albeit with effect only *vis-à-vis* the recognizing States themselves. Pirates and war criminals are simply withdrawn from the ordinary protection of their national States. As regards supranational law, it is in fact a form of federal law.

---

[20] See further B. Cheng, 'United Nations Resolutions on Outer Space: "Instant" International Customary Law?', 5 *Indian JIL* (1965), p. 23 [Ch. 7 above].

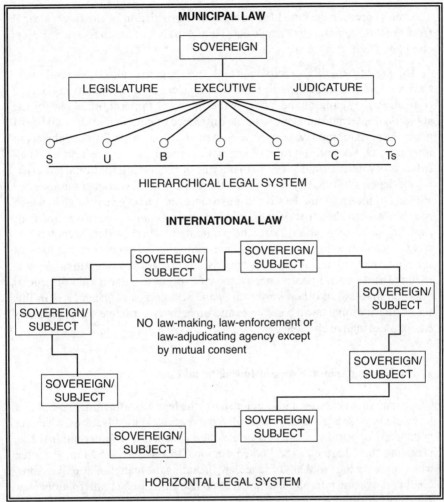

**Figure XIV.2. DIFFERENCE IN THE STRUCTRE OF INTERNATIONAL LAW
AND MUNICIPAL LAW**

Nationals of members of supranational institutions are placed directly under
the law of a functional federation, i.e., federation in a specific field. They have
not become subjects of international law.

3. *Making of Treaties.*   Insofar as treaties are concerned only subjects of
international law can enter into them, and, as has already been mentioned
before, they bind only those that are parties to them, unless the rules they
incorporate have become rules of general international law. Furthermore,
unless a State is a party to the 1969 Vienna Convention on the Law of Treaties

and has, moreover, accepted the compulsory jurisdiction of the International Court of Justice under its Article 66(a) in the matter of *jus cogens*, a State has complete freedom of treaty.

4. *Making of General International Law.* As regards rules of general international law, it is hoped that it is sufficiently clear by now that, as in the case of treaties, they can only be made by the subjects of international law for the subjects of international law, with the difference of course that the making of general international law requires a consensus of the generality of subjects of international law and the rules of general international law are binding on all subjects of international law. Whether a rule of general international law exists or not depends ultimately on whether there is a general consensus among the subjects of international law as to its existence, an *opinio generalis juris*, which is to be distinguished from what is in truth only an *opinio generalis obligationis conventionalis*, such would exist where a treaty has been widely accepted and where the contracting parties would naturally share a general recognition of the binding character of the treaty provisions qua treaty obligations. What is required is a general acceptance of the rule in question as a rule of general international law, in other words, an *opinio generalis juris generalis*.[21] In this sense, international law is a concrete and objectively verifiable social phenomena of a normative character.[22]

V. The Cosmographical Scope of International Law

When man first penetrated into outer space, the fear was sometimes voiced that he would be entering a legal vacuum. Even today, the United Nations, whenever it finds an opportunity, likes to assert the applicability of international law, including the Charter of the United Nations, to outer space. Many a writer, when approaching problems of space law, including the matter of boundary, proceeds as if existing international law is of no relevance. In fact, international law knows no inherent geographical limits and extends to the activities of the subjects of international law in outer space from the very beginning.[23]

VI. Territorial Delimitation of State Competence a Prime Function and a Major Premise of International Law

Notwithstanding views to the contrary frequently expressed sometimes by even the most eminent authorities, what was said by Judge Max Huber in the *Palmas Arbitration* (1928) remains totally valid today:

---

[21] See 5 *Indian JIL* (1965), at p. 45 [Ch. 7 above, s. XI: Conclusions].   [22] See s. III.A above.
[23] See further B. Cheng, 'The Extraterrestrial Application of International Law', 18 *CLP* (1965), p. 132 [Ch. 5 above].

Table XIV.1 THE PERSONAL AND COSMOGRAPHICAL SCOPE OF THE RULES OF THE INTERNATIONAL LEGAL SYSTEM

RULES OF THE INTERNATIONAL LEGAL SYSTEM		
SCOPE	GENERAL INTERNATIONAL LAW	TREATIES
P E R S O N A L — CREATION	Only by subjects of international law	
	By the generality of subjects developing an *opinio generalis juris generalis*	By specific agreement between the contracting parties
P E R S O N A L — APPLICATION	Applicable to all subjects of international law (*erga omnes*)	Applicable only between the contracting parties (*inter partes*)
COSMOGRAPHICAL	In principle, applicable without geographical limits, and extend to outer space and celestial bodies from the very beginning	

The development of the national organisation of States during the last few centuries and, as a corollary, the development of international law, have established this principle of *exclusive competence of the State in regard to its own territory* in such a way as to make it the point of departure in settling most questions that concern international relations . . . [T]erritorial sovereignty belongs always to one, or in exceptional circumstances to several States, to the exclusion of all others. The fact that *the functions of a State can be performed by any State within a given zone* is, on the other hand, precisely the *characteristic* feature of the legal situation pertaining in those parts of the globe which, like the *high seas or lands without a master, cannot or do not yet form the territory of a State.*

Territorial sovereignty is, in general a situation *recognised and delimited in space*, either by so-called natural frontiers as recognised by international law or outward signs of delimitation that are undisputed, or else by legal engagements entered into between interested neighbours, such as frontier conventions, or by acts of recognition of States within fixed boundaries . . . [I]t serves to *divide between nations the space upon which human activities are employed*, in order to assure them at all points the minimum of protection of which international law is the guardian.[24]

International law assumes, therefore, that the world (including outer space and celestial bodies)[25] will be divided spatially ('divide between nations the space upon which human activities are employed') into three different categories of territory,[26] namely:

---

[24] *2 RIAA*, p. 829, at pp. 839–9. Italics added.   [25] See s. V. above.

[26] Notwithstanding its etymology, the word (derived from *terra*, land) is now used (e.g., maritime territory) and is used in international law to refer to any area or space delimited either two

(i) *national territory*, over which one State (or in exceptional circumstances two or more) exercises *territorial sovereignty*, 'to the exclusion of all others';

(ii) *territorium extra commercium*, territory which 'cannot . . . form the territory of a State', such as the high seas; and

(iii) *territorium nullius*, 'lands without a master', which 'do not yet form the territory of a State'. In other words, these are territories that are not under the sovereignty of a recognized subject of international law but which are capable of being acquired by any State in accordance with the rules of international law governing acquisition of territory.

In addition to the tripartite classification of territory mentioned by Judge Huber in his Award, a new category has now been officially introduced into international law by the 1979 Moon Treaty, namely:

(iv) the common heritage of mankind (*territorium commune humanitatis*),[27] which so far exists only at the level of treaty law.

While *territorium extra commercium* and *territorium commune humanitatis* share the same characteristic that they cannot be territorially appropriated by any State, they differ in that the former is essentially a negative concept, whereas the latter is a positive one. In the former, in time of peace, as long as a State respects the exclusive quasi-territorial jurisdiction[28] of other States over their own ships, aircraft and spacecraft, general international law allows it to use the area or even to abuse it more or less as it wishes, including the appropriation of its natural resources, closing large parts of such space for weapon testing and military exercises, and even using such areas as a cesspool for its municipal and industrial sewage. The emergent concept of the common heritage of mankind, on the other hand, while it still lacks precise definition, wishes basically to convey the idea that the management, exploitation and distribution of the natural resources of the area in question are matters to be decided by the international community (or simply by the contracting parties?—as in the Moon Treaty!) and are not to be left to the initiative and discretion of individual States or their nationals.[29]

Table XIV.2 SPATIAL CLASSIFICATION OF WORLD TERRITORY UNDER INTERNATIONAL LAW

NATIONAL TERRITORY	*TERRITORIUM EXTRA COMMERCIUM*	*TERRITORIUM NULLIUS*	COMMON HERITAGE OF MANKIND

dimensionally or three dimensionally, physically or merely geometrically on a map or a legal instrument, especially for purposes of international law or relations.

[27] See further B. Cheng, 'The Moon Treaty: Agreement Governing the Activities of States on the Moon and Other Celestial Bodies within the Solar System other than the Earth, December 18, 1979', 33 *CLP* (1980), p. 213 [Ch. 12 above].

[28] See s. VII below.   [29] See further loc. cit. in n. 27 above [Ch. 12 above].

The function of this spatial classification is precisely, as Judge Huber has said, 'to divide between nations the space upon which human activities are employed, in order to assure them at all points the minimum of protection of which international law is the guardian.' The way this is done is for international law to determine and regulate the competence of States in each of the several categories of territory, or, to put the matter in other words, to determine and regulate what States may or may not do in their own territory, in the territories of other States, in *territorium extra commercium*, in *territorium nullius* and in territories that constitute the common heritage of mankind.

It will be readily perceived, therefore, that the functional classification of activities of States into those that are lawful and those that are unlawful *follows*—and *not precedes*—spatial delimitation. Contrary to the view of some functionalists, spatialism does not mean doing away with a functional classification of what is a lawful activity and what is not, but to apply a functional test without regard to where an activity takes place is not only to put the cart before the horse, but to dispense with the horse. Under general international law, there are in fact few activities of States that are either universally lawful or universally unlawful. Most of the time, it depends on where an activity is carried out. Thus the answer to the question, for instance, whether a State may arrest a foreign vessel or not for monitoring its electronic defence installations will depend not on the nature of such actions but primarily on the *locus*, i.e., on whether the act of intelligence-gathering and the arrest are carried out in a State's own territory, in the territory of another State, on the high seas, in no man's land, or in an area which is the common heritage of mankind; and secondarily on the relationship between the State and the vessel, i.e., on whether the ship has the nationality of the State, has no nationality or has a foreign nationality.[30]

VII. Nature, Scope, and Limits of State Jurisdiction[31]

In order to understand what has just been said fully, one has to understand the nature, scope, and limits of State jurisdiction, which, to go back to the *Palmas Case*, is in fact the power, recognized by international law, of a State 'to perform the functions of a State'. One of the main functions of international law, as created by States, is to regulate the powers of the different States in the world, which are the subjects of international law, to perform respectively the functions of a State *vis-à-vis* the various objects of international law in the world. Objects of international law comprise every object, person, entity, and anything else in the world, or even the universe, that is not a

---

[30] See further text to nn. 42 and 44 below.
[31] See further B. Cheng, 'Crimes on Board Aircraft' 12 *CLP* (1959), p. 177; and loc. cit. in n. 23 above [Ch. 5 above].

subject of international law. The power of the State over different objects of international law varies, above all *ratione loci*, according to whether one is speaking of national territories, or any of three other types of territory. Over a State's own territory, as the *Palmas Case* points out, a State's power is in principle complete and exclusive, subject of course to international law. By the same token, no State is entitled to exercise the power of a State within the territories of other States. In areas which, for one reason or another, have not yet been, or in law cannot be, appropriated by any State, no State can exercise the same kind of power over such areas as it exercises over its own territory, but, in such areas, every State enjoys and may exercise certain State powers over such other objects of international law, such as ships, aircraft, and physical or corporate persons, that are recognized as belonging to it by reason primarily, albeit not exclusively, of their nationality. Thus even outside national territories, all persons, whether physical or corporate, their activities, their properties, and possessions, wherever they may be, come under the jurisdiction and control of one or another of the various subjects of international law. Consequently, through these various subjects of international law, international law is able to reach and regulate all human activities throughout the world. This is the way how international law is enabled, in Judge Huber's words, to assure human activities 'at all points the minimum of protection' of which it is the guardian. Whether we think this protection to be adequate or beneficial is an entirely different matter. Furthermore, this is also the way how international law, by demarcating and regulating the respective competences of States, avoids conflicts between them when they are 'performing the functions of a State', thus rendering international law a coherent system without internal conflicts or contradictions.

In international law, States are recognized as having three types of jurisdiction:

(i) *Territorial jurisdiction*. This is the jurisdiction to which a State is normally entitled over its own territory, territory under its sovereignty.

(ii) *Quasi-territorial jurisdiction*. This is the jurisdiction of a State over its own ships, aircraft, spacecraft and, one may perhaps say, any other means of transport which is designed for travel in areas not subject to the territorial jurisdiction of any State (i.e., *territorium extra commercium*, *nullius*, or *commune humanitatis*) and which has a special relationship with the State concerned through ownership, nationality, registration, or any other recognized link.

(iii) *Personal jurisdiction*. This is the jurisdiction of a State over its own nationals, be they natural or legal persons, excluding, however, ships and aircraft even though they may be endowed with nationality.

Each type of jurisdiction is further divisible into two elements:

(i) *Jurisfaction*. This is the normative power of a State to enact laws, take decisions, and, if need be, administratively or judicially to interpret such laws and decisions with legally binding effect. It is essentially a normative power to establish legally obligatory norms. The essence of this power, where a State enjoys it, is that the norms so established under it are recognized by international law as lawful, valid and hence applicable.

(ii) *Jurisaction*. This is a State's power concretely and physically to 'perform the functions of a State', be they legislative, judicial or executive. It may thus, under this power, hold legislative assemblies, conduct judicial inquiries, carry out arrests, or establish armed forces. Where it has this power, such activities would be permissible and lawful in the eyes of international law. They would not be, where it does not have such power.

Over those who are subject to its jurisdiction, whether territorial, quasi-territorial or personal, a State's *jurisfaction* is *universal* in its cosmographical scope, with the result that an object of international law can frequently be subject simultaneously to the jurisfactions of many States, as, for instance, when a United States national is on board a Polish ship docked in a United Kingdom port, whom the United States is seeking to extradite back to the United States on a charge of contempt of Congress.[32] He is at one and the same time subject to the laws and authority (hence *jurisfactions*) of the United Kingdom (territorial), Poland (quasi-territorial) and the United States (personal). Different States' jurisfactions can, without causing any difficulty, be *concurrent*, and they may also be exercised concurrently. Thus, If they so wish, all the three States concerned will have the right under international law to issue warrants for his arrest.

In contradistinction to jurisfaction, while jurisactions may also be concurrent, the right to exercise jurisaction cannot be. The power of States under international law to exercise *jurisactions* must at all time be *exclusive*. In order to avoid any conflict of jurisactions, the avoidance of which can be said to be one of its prime functions, international law, in addition to delimiting areas of State competence spatially as we have described above, establishes a *hierarchy* among the three types of jurisaction, whenever they overlap, with territorial jurisaction overriding both quasi-territorial and personal jurisaction, and quasi-territorial overriding personal jurisaction. Thus, in the above example, as long as the Polish ship remains within United Kingdom territory, the United States national on board is subject exclusively to United Kingdom territorial jurisaction. As soon as the ship has left the United Kingdom territory and is on the high seas, he is subject exclusively to the quasi-territorial jurisaction of Poland. And, if he leaves the ship to live on a desert island belonging to no State, he will be under the exclusive personal jurisaction of the United States.

It will readily be seen that what has just been said on a two-dimensional level applies *mutatis mutandis* also to three-dimensional spaces, and why it has

---

[32] Cf. the *Eisler Case. The Times* (London), 16 May 1949, p. 4, col. 7, and 28 May 1949, p. 2, col. 1.

been necessary to dwell first on these very basic and fundamental concepts of international law. In order further to explain the concept of State jurisdiction as analysed above, a tabular presentation of the concept which first appeared in the article on 'The Extraterrestrial Application Of International Law' in Volume 18 of *Current Legal Problems* (1965),[33] is here reproduced, although the theory itself was first put forward in 1959.[34]

VIII. The Policy Behind, and Function of, International Law's Spatialism

The primarily spatial approach of international *lex lata* and its three-tier classification of State jurisdiction, whatever their defects, have the great merit, from the practical point of view, of providing, where the system is implemented, an unambiguous framework for the solution of all international legal disputes which may exist or arise. The framework supplies an agreed starting point—which in the solution of any legal problem is always the most crucial factor—for dealing with any potential conflict of States' legal powers.

First and foremost, starting from the level of co-existence, no State may overstep the limits of its own jurisaction and infringe the sphere of jurisaction of the same rank of another (the principle), unless authorized by a rule of international law (exception). For example, unless so authorized whether by customary law or a treaty, no State may perform the function of a State in the territory of another (co-existence of territorial jurisactions), or on or over the high seas interfere with the ships or aircraft of another (co-existence of quasi-territorial jurisactions).

Secondly, where a State's jurisaction is the prevailing one, then, again unless there is a rule of international law or a treaty providing for the contrary (exception), all persons within the sphere of that State's jurisaction are subject to it (principle).

Thirdly, in the situation envisaged immediately above, again subject to the same exception, the principle is that the State of which the jurisaction is the prevailing one is entitled to do as it pleases.

Once the framework has been provided, it becomes possible for States through the development of rules of general law and of treaties to modify the initial principles in order to regulate specific activities. Such rules can help transform international relations from passive co-existence through active co-existence, co-operation, collaboration and supranationalism, to, if the States so wish, federalism and a unitary State, at which point international law will bow out and be replaced by a system of municipal law.

But until that point is reached, international law, that is to say, States who make international law, simply cannot afford to jettison the basic framework

---

[33] P. 132, at pp. 138–9 [Ch. 5 above].   [34] See loc. cit. in n. 31 above.

Table XIV.3 State Jurisdiction

TYPE	TERRITORIAL		QUASI-TERRITORIAL		PERSONAL	
Object	*Terra firma* (terrestrial or extraterrestrial) including adjacent maritime belt, subsoil and superjacent space		Ships, aircraft and spacecraft		Individuals, corporate bodies and business enterprises	
Material Scope	In respect of the whole territory, including all its resources, all persons and things therein, and the extraterritorial activities of all such persons, whether individual or corporate		In respect of the craft themselves and all persons and things therein, including the activities of such persons, individual or corporate, whether on board the craft or elsewhere		In respect of individuals, corporate bodies and business enterprises, and all property, rights and legal interests belonging to them, wherever they may be	
Source	*International customary law*: sovereignty, law of war and *status mixtus*, including self-defence and reprisals. *Treaties* with, and *recognition* or *acquiescence* of, other international persons, e.g., protectorates, leased, mandated and trust territories		State jurisdiction over flag-craft and pirate vessels *jure gentium*. Right to flag under *international customary law* may be based on nationality of owner or charterer, other 'genuine link', and registration. It may also be derived from *consent, recognition* or *acquiescence* of other international persons		*International customary law*: State jurisdiction over nationals, including corporate bodies and business enterprises endowed with nationality, other persons owing allegiance, and pirates *jure gentium*. *Treaties* with, and *recognition* or *acquiescence* of, other international persons, e.g., jurisdiction over protected persons	
Element	Jurisfaction	Jurisfaction	Jurisfaction	Jurisfaction	Jurisfaction	Jurisfaction
Hierarchy and Precedence (*Jurisfaction*)	On a par with other types of jurisfaction		On a par with other types of jurisfaction		On a par with other types of jurisfaction	
Hierarchy (*Jurisaction*)		First		Second		Third
Precedence (*Jurisaction*)		In case of conflict, overrides quasi-territorial and personal jurisaction		In case of conflict, gives way to territorial jurisaction but overrides personal jurisaction		In case of conflict, gives way to both territorial and quasi-territorial jurisaction
Geographical Scope	Limitless (terrestrial and extra-terrestrial)	National territory of a State, other territory for the international relations of which it is responsible, and territory under its *occupatio pacifica* or *bellica*	Limitless (terrestrial and extraterrestrial)	Over flag-craft anywhere outside territories subject to the territorial jurisaction of other recognized international persons	Limitless (terrestrial and extra-terrestrial)	Over all individuals, corporate bodies and business enterprises subject to a State's personal jurisdiction outside territories or craft subject to the territorial or quasi-territorial jurisaction of other recognized international persons
Relevance to Space Law	Extraterrestrially applicable	Stresses the urgent need of clearly delimiting national space from outer space. Will also apply extraterrestrial territories, once sovereignty established and recognized in accordance with existing rules of international law	Extraterrestrially applicable	Applicable to national spacecraft in outer space	Extraterrestrially applicable	Applicable to nationals and other persons or entities subject to a State's personal jurisdiction even when they are in outer space

of the international legal system which, for all its faults, provides, with all this talk about law being legitimate community expectations, for all concerned and not only those steeped in some specific jurisprudence, a ready reckoner to find an answer to every international legal problem, even one which has never arisen before, albeit the answer may not be the most equitable. The party who invokes a principle has the presumption of the law in his favour (cf. *The Lotus* (1927));[35] the party who invokes an exception has the burden of proving its existence, failure to discharge which means that his claim fails. This is how international law achieves its 'logical plenitude' (*logische Geschlosenheit des Rechtes*) by clearly laying down the initial premises, and is thus enabled to avoid any *lacuna*—gap in the law.

What the New Haven school of policy-oriented jurisprudence fails to do is to give sufficient importance to the macro-policy of international law which is to provide such a framework so that, in every situation, everyone knows exactly where he stands, and there is no need for him to wait for the 'decision-makers' to make up their mind *ad hoc*—and most probably also retrospectively and, alas, *ad hominen*—whether what he has done or is doing is lawful or not lawful policywise. Basically, the New Haven school goes in for micro-policy implementation: law to be individually tailored for each case. This is not law, but equity which, as Aristotle has already pointed out, is justice (read alternatively policy) in the individual case.[36] The quality of equity *contra legem* practised in a municipal legal system depends, as experience has shown, ultimately on the person of the *praetor* or the chancellor. In a horizontal and auto-interpretative legal system like international law, what it really means is that the superpowers will be able to do what they like in the name of natural law or justice (read alternatively, inclusive interests or policy).

In the excerpt quoted above from an article by Professors McDougal and Lipson, it was said:

... the now vexed question of the legal 'status' of outer space will be discarded for practical purposes, as the question of 'status' was discarded when negotiations on the use of airspace came to the point of concrete agreement.[37]

Here the premise of the analogy is patently faulty, because in agreements on the use of airspace, notably bilateral air services agreements, the 'status' of territorial sovereignty over national airspace is never for a minute absent from the minds of the parties. This status is what makes the agreement necessary; this status also renders it impossible to avoid all sorts of not always very seemly or functional bargaining in the negotiations; this status conditions the interpretation and implementation of these agreements, all matters unregulated by the agreements remaining completely within the discretion of the

---

[35] PCIJ, A.10.

[36] See further B. Cheng, 'Justice and Equity in International Law', 8 *CLP* (1965), p. 185.

[37] See text on n. 1 above.

territorial sovereign unless there is a rule of general international law or another agreement governing the subject; last but not least all these agreements are terminable at relatively short notice with the result that parties to such agreements would be very unwise to ignore the ever-present Damoclean sword of a closed air frontier which can come down almost at any time at the drop of a hat.[38]

This situation may not be functionally the most conducive to what might be regarded as the 'rational' development of international civil aviation, but without the spatial starting point of national sovereignty over airspace, it would indeed be difficult at the present stage of international relations to know exactly where else to start. A solely functional approach of allowing the airlines to fly wherever there is traffic, while seemingly most rational can, in the present what economists would call conditions of very imperfect competition, lead easily to the entire industry being completely dominated, if not for ever monopolized, by a few strong carrier nations. Interestingly enough, such nations have always been championing the cause of complete freedom of the air.[39] The parallel between aeronautics and astronautics, seen here in a perspective somewhat different from that of the learned authors quoted above, should certainly not be overlooked by those interested in the definition of outer space.

In all probability, many so-called functionalists, in not giving adequate consideration to the major premises of international law, are, maybe unconsciously, still very much influenced by municipal law thinking. In domestic law, in the generality of cases whether an act committed within the State is lawful or unlawful depends primarily on a 'functional' determination by the law of that State without reference to where it takes place. However, this is from a wholly parochial standpoint.

Without considering the problems of conflict of laws and international criminal law in the sense of crimes committed in different countries, one needs only to think of the laws of federal States. To say that spatialism should give way to functionalism in international law or in international space law would be like saying, in a nominally federal State, that everything should be treated as a federal matter to be governed directly by federal law. This would eliminate at a stroke all the rights and laws of the constituent states or provinces which after all are only a form of spatialism. In the same way, functionalism in the matter of defining outer space, by asserting that, insofar as 'lawful' space activities (their 'lawfulness' being no doubt defined in the end by the mere say-so of the major space powers) are concerned, they may be conducted anywhere in the world without spatial restriction, is in effect implying that such activities may be carried on even in the national airspace of other States.

[38] See further B. Cheng, *The Law of International Air Transport* (1962), Ch. 4.2.A, and Part III; cf. also B. Cheng, 'From Air Law to Space Law', 13 *CLP* (1960), p. 228, at pp. 228–42 [Ch. 3 above, s. I: Airspace Sovereignty.]

[39] See B. Cheng, *The Law of International Air Transport* (1962), esp. Ch. 13.

Under functionalism, States would, therefore, lose the right which they have by reason of their sovereignty, to control or in any way interfere with self-styled 'lawful' foreign space activities in their national airspace.

If international space lawyers still wish to cling to their municipal concepts, the analogy they should conjure up should certainly not be national criminal law, bearing in mind that international law is essentially a system of civil law. International criminal law in the sense of rules forming that part general international law which render specific acts of States or individuals criminal offences under general international law and punishable by the international community as a whole hardly exists.[40] If analogy there must be, the closest would be to the right of ownership. What one can do with or in one's own property does not mean necessarily that one can do it to or in others' properties, at least not without their consent or permission.

It is probably true that in an ideal world, in Utopia, there will be no frontiers nor any need for frontiers, just as there will be no need for locked doors, and perhaps even no place for individual ownership. Everything will be regulated functionally on a global and the most sensible basis. But until that day is reached, some form of spatialism, of which being able to call one's home one's castle is but another manifestation, is still perceived rightly or wrongly by most people, whether as individuals or groups, and seemingly most animals, as what satisfies best their instinct and needs of self-preservation.

In any event, this is the basis on which States—these territorially organized entities—have built the law to regulate their interrelations for centuries. It may well be that they are all mistaken. But what is not believed to be feasible is to develop rules in a tiny corner of international law in a way which, however laudable in the abstract, is contrary to the basic framework of the international legal system. Nor do I think one can or should try to achieve such an objective by so-to-speak a sleight-of-hand without States realizing what they have been led to accept. And without acceptance by the subjects of international law either in treaties or as rules of general international law, proposals *de lege ferenda* will always remain just that.

IX. Functional versus Spatial Delimitation of Outer Space

If there is great dissension among the spatialists on the exact method of delimiting outer space and/or national airspace,[41] functionalists can also be divided into different categories, unified only by their common belief that spatial delimitation is either not required at all or not required for the present:

---

[40] Cf. G. Schwarzenberger, 'The Problem of an International Criminal Law', 3 *CLP* (1950), p. 263.
[41] See text to n. 3 above.

(i) Spatial delimitation not required at all:

    (a) Astronautics can be regulated by reference solely to the nature of the activities;

    (b) Astronautics can be regulated by reference solely to the nature of the activities and the nature of the space objects;

(ii) Spatial delimitation not required at present and astronautics can be adequately regulated at present by either (i)(a) or (i)(b) above.

The essence of the functionalists' argument is that the *locus* of an act need be of no moment to its legality or illegality, which can be determined solely by reference to its nature. But as the example given above of the arrest by a State of a foreign vessel for monitoring its electronic defence installations illustrates, this is simply not how international *lex lata* operates.[42] In international law, the monitoring of the electronic defence installations of a foreign State, which is being done all the time, is in itself neither illegal nor legal. It is not a matter of 'functional' determination. Its legality depends, first and foremost, upon the *locus*. Carried out in the territory of the observing State, it must be eminently lawful. Carried out outside the territory of the observed State, such as on the high seas, it remains perfectly lawful and in fact is done every day.

But if carried out in areas subject to the overriding jurisaction of the State under observation, the latter is fully entitled to make the act illegal under its own law and have its law in the matter enforced. This is true in two-dimensional, as well as in three-dimensional, space. Thus on 1 May 1960, the Soviet Union shot down a United States U–2 reconnaissance aircraft while it was flying over the Soviet Union, and had its pilot tried, convicted, and imprisoned. The United States accepted the lawfulness of the Soviet action without demur, and called off all further U–2 flights over the Soviet Union.

However, if the *same activity* was carried out where the State being observed had no such jurisaction, then the act would not be illegal under international law and the latter State would in fact be violating international law if it tried to interfere with it. Thus when, two months later on 1 July 1960, the Soviet Union shot down another United States reconnaissance aircraft, an RB–47, this time over the high seas, the United States protested and took the matter to the Security Council of the United Nations. The Soviet Union in due course implicitly admitted the illegality of its action by returning to the United States the two survivors from the RB–47 without attempting to try them for espionage.[43]

What is true of reconnaissance by ships and by aircraft applies equally to reconnaissance, as such, by satellites. Whether such reconnaissance is lawful

---

[42] See text to nn. 30 above, and 44 below.

[43] See further B. Cheng, 'The United Nations and Outer Space', 14 *CLP* (1961), p. 247, at pp. 262 ff. [Ch. 6 above, s. V: Reconnaissance and Surveillance Satellites], and the distinction therein made between penetrative and peripheral reconnaissance.

or not under international law depends, therefore, in the first instance on whether the reconnaissance is within the territory of the State under observation or is outside it. This will depend in turn on the height to which a State's sovereignty over the airspace above its territory, a point that is common ground, can be said to extend. The issue of such a spatial division between national airspace (which is subject to the sovereignty of the subjacent State) and outer space (which is, probably under general international law as well as under the 1967 Space Treaty, *res extra commercium* incapable of national appropriation) cannot be avoided by simply *asserting* that reconnaissance by satellites is itself legal or illegal no matter where conducted (functional delimitation). Whoever maintains a conclusion differing from that under general international law has the burden of proving that such an exception to the general rule exists. No proof has been adduced to show either that such reconnaissance, even if conducted in the national space of another State, is lawful, or that, even if conducted clearly in outer space, it would still be illegal, although both allegations have from time to time been made in furtherance invariably of the particular interests of the State concerned.

The statement has sometimes also been made that no great harm has arisen out of the lack of a general agreement on the precise outer limit of the territorial sea and the same should be true of territorial space, but this ignores the fact that, although there is no general agreement, the precise limit of the territorial sea claimed by the coastal State is always known. Functionalists should, from this point of view, ponder over the hypothetical situation where a coastal State does not claim a specific spatial limit and only asserts a functional right to prohibit all acts in its 'adjacent sea' that it considers inimical to its national security. From this point of view, much may be learnt from the *Pueblo Incident* (1968) where the dispute concerning the North Korean seizure of a United States vessel arose not so much out of the nature of the activity of the ship in question which was reconnaissance, as from doubts regarding the spatial delimitation of competence of the North Korean authorities to make the seizure (whether their authority extended to 3 miles or 12 miles, non-recognition by the United States of the North Korean 12-mile limit without, however, asserting such non-recognition, and the lack of definition of the phrase 'contiguous waters' in the Korean Armistice Agreement) and the actual *locus* of both the vessel and its arrest.[44]

Indeed, the lesson of the *Pueblo* should also not be ignored by those who are only wait-and-see functionalists. While not denying that spatial delimita-

[44] Cf. 'The *Pueblo* Seizure: Facts, Law Policy', *ASIL Proc.* (1969), p. 1. Dr W. E. Butler, one of the two principal speakers, said that he was assuming the rôle of the 'devil's advocate'. It seems reasonable to think, therefore, that the other principal speaker Mr G. H. Aldrich was merely doing what he had been invited to do, i.e., putting forward as forcefully as possible the US case. Both statements, particularly the latter, should be read very much in the light of Professor Lissitzyn's searching 'interrogation'.

[45] See text to n. 9 above, and s. XII below.

tion will be required, they maintain that the time has not yet come to make such a delimitation. From this point of view, the present line-up of States may even suggest, apart from possibly other motives, a difference of cultural origin. In this regard, while there is much to be said for the pragmatism of what the Continentals would call the 'Anglo-Saxons' in letting sleeping dogs lie and the Common Law approach of even letting them have one free bite when they wake up, the *Pueblo*, the geostationary orbit,[45] remote sensing,[46] and other factors would seem to suggest that in practice, especially when it is recognized that one will have to do it in due course, it would be more prudent to try and slip the muzzle on the animal while all the issues are still dormant than to wait till the divergent interests of all the nations have hardened.

X. The Limit Between Outer Space and Territorial Space

If it is remembered that the geographical or cosmographical scope of international law is unlimited,[47] it will then become apparent that the question of a limit between outer space and territorial space, even at the threshold of the space age, would be governed already by the *lex lata*, however vague and uncertain this may be. This point does not appear, however, to be always fully realized. Yet, to embark on schemes of 'progressive development of international law' *de lege ferenda* without investigating the *lex lata* is not unlike starting building work on previously uninspected grounds or sites. From this point of view, it is also not to be forgotten that what is international *lex lata* is the law as made by the subjects of international law and not simply what appeals to one as the most logical, reasonable, or desirable.[48] What one has to do consequently is to seek out such evidence as can be found of the *opinio generalis juris generalis* of the subjects of international law in the matter.[49]

Thus when in 1956, the year before Sputnik I, I wrote on the subject, what I tried to do was not to make a 'proposal', but to find out what *lex lata* existed on the subject at the time. On the basis of Article 1 of the 1944 Chicago Convention on International Civil Aviation which, following the precedent set by the 1919 Paris Convention on the Regulation of Aerial Navigation, asserts the complete and exclusive sovereignty of 'every State' over the 'airspace' ('*espace atmosphérique*' in the authentic French text of the Paris Convention) above its territory, and which is generally accepted by States as stating general international law, and relying on the authority of the Permanent Court of International Justice in the *Eastern Greenland Case* (1932) in the matter of

---

[46] See further B. Cheng, 'Legal Implications of Remote Sensing', *Earth Observations from Space and Management of Planetary Resources: Proc. Int. Conf. organized by CNES and ESA, Toulouse, March 1978* (ESA SP–134) (1978), p. 597, under s. 2.3.1: Raising the Limit of Territorial Space [cf. Ch. 22 below, s. VI.A].

[47] See s. V above.   [48] See further ss. II and IV above.

[49] See further ss. IV.B.3 and IV.B.4 above.

interpretation,[50] I consequently arrived at the conclusion, according to such evidence as was available, that territorial sovereignty extended to the upper limit of 'airspace', which, insofar as it was possible to ascertain from scientific evidence, appeared to lie at a height of between 500 and 1,000 kilometres (i.e., between 310 and 620 miles) above the surface of the earth. Such a limit being vague and uncertain which could become a source of controversy, I ventured to suggest that *de lege ferenda* it would be preferable if States could, by an international agreement, fix a precise upper limit to airspace sovereignty at a definite height, be it at 100, 200, 500 or 1,000 kilometres.[51] Even with hindsight, it is difficult to see why it was 'curious' or self-contradictory to have done so, as some writers have alleged.

General international law, being in reality the *opinio generalis juris generalis* of the subjects of international law at any moment, is not static. Thus relying on the same methodology, I found nine years later in 1965 that there was already sufficient evidence in State practice to make a more precise determination of the applicable rule under the then prevailing general international law. I wrote:

At a time before space flights began, the present writer, on the basis of geophysical factors, had estimated the upper limit of airspace to lie at a height of between 500 and 1,000 kilometres (i.e., between 310 and 620 miles) above the surface of the earth. Since then, it appears that a general practice has grown up among States interpreting airspace as meaning space in which navigation by conventional aircraft is possible and outer space as space where artificial satellites are able to orbit, thus bringing the frontier down to approximately 50 miles (80 km), with a possible margin of 25 miles (40 km) either way. This development may be regarded either as the interpretation of an existing rule of international law by the practice of States, or the emergence of a new rule of international customary law modifying a previous one.

The evidence for saying that States now accept a fairly low limit of territorial space is their attitude towards the problem of the right of passage of orbiting satellites and, particularly, towards reconnaissance satellites. A careful scrutiny of the discussion on outer space in the United Nations reveals that States appear to be in general agreement that orbiting satellites in their orbits never enter airspace and, therefore, the problem of the right of passage through foreign territorial airspace does not arise, except possibly during launching and re-entry.[52]

This view provided at least in part the theoretical basis for the following draft resolution proposed by Professor D. Goedhuis to a joint session on Air Law and Space Law at the 1966 Helsinki Conference of the International Law Association:

---

[50] Interpreting the meaning of the term Greenland used in various diplomatic documents, the Court held: 'The natural meaning of the term is its geographical meaning' (A/B 53, at p. 52).

[51] See further Cheng, 'Recent Developments in Air Law' (1956), 9 *CLP*, p. 208, at pp. 208–15 [Ch. 1, ss. II and III: The Definition and Upper Limits of Airspace]; and 'From Air Law to Space Law', 13 ibid. (1960), p. 228 [Ch. 3, s. II: Airspace Sovereignty].

[52] Loc. cit. in n. 23 above, at pp. 145–6; nn. omitted [Ch. 5 above, s. III.A: Outer Space].

The International Law Association considers that the practice of States is consistent with the view that air sovereignty does not extend as far as the lowest perigee of any satellite so far placed in orbit.[53]

As I said at the time, speaking as chairman of the Air Law Committee in support of the draft resolution, its adoption would not mean the acceptance of the so-called 'perigee rule', sometimes referred to as the technological criterion,

that is to say, determination of the frontier between national space and outer space by means of the lowest perigee of any satellite which has been, or may hereafter be, put into orbit. This draft Resolution . . . is essentially a statement of fact. It impliedly records a limited consensus of States on this subject which appears to have crystallized at this juncture, namely, the general agreement which appears to exist among States that all existing satellites orbit in outer space, i.e., space which, in their view, is not subject to national appropriation. From this consensus is drawn the essentially negative conclusion that States consider that airspace sovereignty in no event extends as far as the lowest perigee of any satellite *so far placed in orbit*. The statement does not say that this consensus will *necessarily* extend to all future satellites.

Secondly, it does not purport to fix definitely a precise boundary between outer space and national space. It does not even define the existing upper limit of airspace sovereignty. It merely says that this upper limit definitely does not lie outside the point indicated in the draft Resolution. Consequently, this upper limit may be lower, but not higher, than that stated in the draft Resolution . . .[54]

It follows from the draft resolution, which I regard as a correct statement of the international *lex lata* not only in 1965 or 1966 but also even now, that in the present state of general international law, we have in fact three layers of space above the surface of the earth. As I went on to say then in Helsinki:

First, there is that layer of a State's superincumbent space closest to the surface of the earth which is incontrovertibly subject to national sovereignty. There is, secondly, beyond the point stated in the draft Resolution, the vast space which is equally incontrovertibly not subject to national sovereignty or appropriation. But . . . there is, thirdly, an intermediate zone of uncertainty lying below the point stated in the draft

[53] See ILA, *Report of the 52nd Conference, Helsinki* (1966), pp. 160–85, 191–201. A modified version of this draft resolution was adopted at the subsequent conference held in Buenos Aires in 1968: see ILA, *Report of the 53rd Conference, Buenos Aires* 91968), pp. 110 ff.

[54] ILA, *Report of the 52nd Conference, Helsinki* (1966), pp. 166–7. The ILA resolution adopted at Buenos Aires in 1968 basically reflects this view, albeit limiting the use of the term to the 1967 Treaty, which by then had come into force, and pegging it to the date the Treaty was opened for signature. It reads:

. . . the term 'outer space' as used in the Treaty . . . should be interpreted so as to include all space at and above the lowest perigee achieved by the 27th January 1967, when the Treaty was opened for signature, by any satellite put into orbit, without prejudice to the question whether it may or may not later be determined to include any part of space below such perigee.

See ILA, *Report of the 53rd Conference, Buenos Aires* (1968), p. xxii. See also the discussion at the joint Air and Space Law session, ibid., pp. 103–12.

Resolution and above the undisputed zone of national airspace, in which, at a height that is not yet clearly defined, lies the actual boundary line between national space and outer space,[55] . . .

What has just been said does not, however, coincide with the so-called tri-zonal approach which is basically a proposal *de lege ferenda* that between territorial space and outer space, there could or should be an intermediate zone of a legal status different from either territorial space or outer space. Such evidence as exists does not support the view that States accept any of the several variants of the tri-zonal proposals. On the contrary, the majority appear to consider that outer space lies immediately outside territorial space, even though they usually refrain from committing themselves directly or explicitly on where the boundary is to be found, as do the various space treaties, leaving us hence with the uncertainty with which we are faced.

The question has sometimes been asked what would be the purpose of making an affirmation of the state of the law based on 'the lowest perigee so far achieved by any unchallenged satellite', in view of the residue of uncertainty which it still contains. The answer would be that, first, this is a statement of fact and it is not possible to go beyond what the evidence would warrant in any attempt to seek greater precision. Secondly, such a statement, if expressly accepted by States, would already contribute much to reducing the existing margin of uncertainty. In this regard, what I said in 1966 remains apposite today:

At present, not only among laymen, but even among some of those who interest themselves in the subject, there is still much speculation as to where airspace sovereignty ends and where outer space begins: 50 miles, 75 miles, 100 miles, 500 miles, or even *ad infinitum*. Now, if I recall rightly, the lowest perigee of artificial satellites so far placed in orbit is 80 odd miles above the mean sea level.

Therefore, if this Resolution is adopted, it will remove a great deal of this speculation, albeit not entirely. It confirms the existence of a maximum height beyond which no State is entitled to extend its airspace sovereignty, without saying, however, that a State is necessarily entitled to extend its sovereignty to this height.[56]

The only qualification to be made is that, since then, further information has become available on the height of perigees. The accompanying diagram of artificial earth satellites with lowest perigee heights launched between 4 October 1957 and 4 November 1975 is taken from the background paper on *Study on Altitudes of Artificial Earth Satellites*[57] presented by the United Nations Secretariat to the Outer Space Committee. As the diagram clearly shows, in the course of eighteen years since Sputnik I first went into orbit on 4 October 1957, the lowest perigee achieved so far is that of the United Kingdom Skynet–IIA (1974) at 96 kilometres, and that excepting this and

---

[55] ILA, *Report of the 52nd Conference, Helsinki* (1966), p. 167; italics added.
[56] Ibid., p. 167.   [57] A/AC.105/164 (1976), Annex II, p. 2.

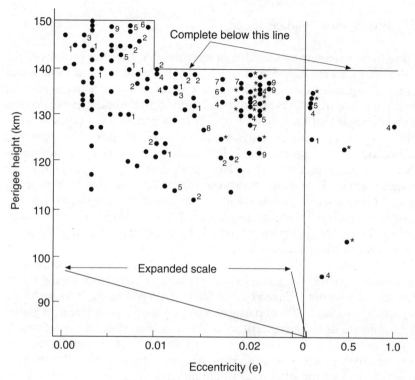

Source: UN GA COPUOS, Study on Altitudes of Artificial Earth Satelites
(Working paper presented by the Secretariat), A/AC.105/164
(6.1.76), Annex II, p. 2.

**Figure XIV.3. DIAGRAM OF ARTIFICIAL SATELLITES WITH LOWEST
PERIGEE HEIGHTS LAUNCHED BETWEEN 4 OCTOBER 1957 AND 4
NOVEMBER 1975**

another one at 104 kilometres, all the other satellites have perigees above the
110 kilometre line.[58] On this basis, one can, in applying 'the lowest perigee so
far achieved by any unchallenged satellite' test, say that at 96 kilometres one
is definitely in outer space. Should one have doubts and wonder if a lone
Skynet is not that proverbial one swallow which does not make a summer,
then the 110-kilometre line should satisfy even the most sceptical. Above this
height one is definitely in outer space, according to *lex lata*.

---

[58] On some of these figures, see comments in Cheng, loc. cit. in n. 46 above, at p. 601, col. 1.

XI. The 1979 Soviet Working Paper

It should be apparent by now that at least the first two propositions of the 1979 Soviet working paper[59] in many ways correspond with the views which have been expressed above. In this regard, I would, however, prefer to have the word 'definitely' inserted in proposition 1 of the Soviet working paper in order to make it clear that the height of 100 (110) kilometres is not necessarily the definitive starting point of outer space, even though this is in some way implied in the Soviet proposition 2. For reasons which I have been advancing since 1956 and some of which have been recalled here, I consider that it would be useful either (i) to have an express affirmation, possibly by a properly worded General Assembly 'law-finding' resolution,[60] clarifying as much as possible the position of the existing law on the extent of either outer space or territorial space, or (ii) preferably to have a general international treaty defining the precise boundary between the two zones.

What is difficult is the Soviet proposition 3. *De lege lata*, it is more than questionable whether one can speak of space objects 'retaining' the right to fly through the territorial space of other States. *De lege ferenda*, it might be too restrictive to secure a right of passage merely for the purpose of reaching orbit or returning to earth 'in the territory of the launching State'; for space objects might, for instance, be launched from and return to *territorium extra commercium*, such as the high seas. However, once the principle of passage is accepted, perhaps the latter issue would no longer represent an insurmountable obstacle.

The real issue is the very right of passage itself, especially if one is thinking not merely of a right similar to the right under general international law of 'innocent passage' for ships through foreign territorial seas, which incidentally does not apply to aircraft, whether civil or State, in the air or on the water, but of a right, such as that currently being discussed in the Third United Nations Conference on the Law of the Sea (UNCLOS III), of 'transit passage' for both civil and State aircraft, as well as all ships, through foreign international straits and archipelagic sea lanes and air routes. Here, it should perhaps be made clear in the first place that under general international law, land-locked States, contrary to a view which has frequently been expressed, have no legal right of passage through the territory of other States to the high seas.[61] By analogy, land-locked countries have no such right of transit for its space objects on their way to or back from outer space through the territorial space of other States. Nor can a rule of customary international law be said to have

---

[59] See text to n. 7 above.

[60] See Cheng, loc. cit. in n. 20 above, at pp. 37–40, and Conclusions 8 and 9 at p. 46 [Ch. 7 above, s. IX: 'Instant' Customary Law, and Conclusions 8 and 9 in s. XI].

[61] German–Venezuelan Mixed Commission (1903): *Faber Case, Ven. Arb. 1903*, p. 600, at pp. 629–30; see further Cheng, *General Principles of Law*, p. 69.

grown up granting such a right. Consequently, in order to create such a right, the agreement of the States flown over will, just as in aerial flights, have to be obtained.[62] Here, as in aviation, it is most unlikely that in negotiating such rights, States will discard from their minds the fact that it is within their discretion whether or not to grant such a right of transit.

While among space powers or near-space powers, such a right, in the expectation of reciprocity, may be easily granted, the same can hardly be said of States which have no aspiration to go into space. The price the latter will exact will probably be proportionate to their strategic importance for the passage of space objects. In any event, if air law is anything to go by, it is most likely that States will wish to distinguish between military and non-military space objects, and, amongst the latter, possibly between commercial and non-commercial, and between nuclear and non-nuclear space objects.[63] In this way, as in other fields of international law, the functional approach is brought into use, once the spatial framework of State competence has been established.

Such functional criteria having been created by reference to either the nature of the activity or the nature of the space object, the next hurdle would be to provide methods of verification. Now that States, at least those which are parties to the 1975 Convention on Registration of Object Launched into Outer Space,[64] are already committed to the principle of registering space objects with the United Nations, this hurdle may perhaps not be as formidable as before. In this regard, it will no doubt be worthwhile considering the system of international safeguards, institutional and otherwise, that have been developed in the field of international nuclear law,[65] even if recent events seem to suggest that they might not be entirely effective.

The path towards the successful delimitation of outer space from territorial space is doubtless narrow and stony, but the establishment of a precise legal framework, consonant with the basic principles of international law, for the future activities of States in outer space will, it is still believed, remove a source of potentially dangerous conflicts between States, and furthermore afford some safeguard of the rights and interests of non-space powers which otherwise are likely to be eroded by incipient customs based on the almost complete freedom of action at present of the space powers.

In fact, it is time that one recognizes the likely effects of the functionalist approach on airspace sovereignty. What the functionalists are really saying is that, insofar as space flights are concerned, the concept of airspace

---

[62] See Cheng, loc. cit. in n. 38 above, Index, under 'Transit right'.

[63] See further Cheng, loc. cit. in n. 38 above, at pp. 238–9 [Ch. 3 above, s. II.C: Privileges Exchanged].

[64] See B. Cheng, 'Outer Space: The International Legal Framework—The International Legal Status of Outer Space, Space Objects and Spacemen', 10 *Thesaurus Acroasium* (1981), p. 41, pp. 98–102 [Ch. 13 above, s. IV.C: The 1975 Registration Convention].

[65] See further B. Cheng, 'International Co-operation and Control: From Atoms to Space', 15 *CLP* (1962), p. 228 [Ch. 4 above].

sovereignty is irrelevant. In other words, whatever may be the effects of the principle of airspace sovereignty on other matters, such as aerial navigation, it is simply not applicable to space flights. What they are saying is that, if a space activity is authorized by international law, then the flight may thereby take place within the airspace of another State. This ignores the fact that when people reckon a particular space activity to be compatible with international law, say military reconnaissance, what they have in mind is such activity when conducted in *outer space*, but never for a moment thereby a right for military reconnaissance satellites to pass through the national airspace of other States, and maybe even to operate there while on their way. The effect of the functionalist doctrine, which is relied upon by the wait-and-seers allegedly only as a temporary expedient, is, therefore, the gradual erosion leading to the eventual abolition of the rule of airspace sovereignty in favour of space activities and space vehicles recognized as lawful by international law in *outer space*. Therefore, the functionalists are not really non-believers in the spatial approach. All that they are saying is that, insofar as a State's space activities are concerned, other States' airspace sovereignty begins and ends at sea level; in other words, it no longer exists.

International law is not made by the will of international lawyers. It is made by the will of States. If States wish to create a right of either innocent or transit passage for space flights through the airspace of other States, or if they wish to abolish airspace sovereignty of States altogether in favour of foreign space flights, they are perfectly entitled to attempt to do so.

There are, however, two things which may be said in this connection. First, if States wish to do any of these things, it behoves them, especially those which consider themselves leader nations, to do so openly, and not through some legal sleight-of-hand, which in the long run can only undermine respect for international law. While some such tactics may not be uncommon sometimes in municipal law, the arrogance, insensitivity, and deviousness which they imply when resorted to in the international arena can in fact be very harmful to a State's international image and relations.

Secondly, in the light of what is happening, it becomes all the more necessary for all States and scholars to examine much more closely than hitherto what is meant by permissible and non-permissible space activities. Does permissibility mean solely permissibility in outer space, or does it imply also a right of passage for such activities through, or even permissibility of such activities in, what other States would normally consider to be their national airspace? This merely shows the inevitability of the delimitation issue, however hard the functionalists and the wait-and-seeists may wish to dodge it. If permissibility means strictly the former, then delimitation becomes a prerequisite and, therefore, a priority issue. But if it is to be given the latter meaning, as the space powers, whether major or minor, whether spatialist, functionalist, or wait-and-seeist, seem now to imply, then this appears to be high time for the other States to take a closer interest in the precise nature of these activities before a right of way is created through their national airspace in favour of these activities, or even a right to operate there.

XII. The Geostationary Orbit

As an epilogue to this 'comedy of errors', a telling example may be given of the disadvantage which may spring from the functionalist or wait-and-see approach to the problem of delimitation. This is the claim of the equatorial States to the geostationary orbit, which possibly prompted the Soviet Union to bring forth its 1979 proposal.[66]

The geostationary orbit, also known as the synchronous orbit, is a circular orbit above the equator at a height of approximately 36,000 kilometres (22,300 miles). An artificial satellite placed in this orbit would be circling the earth at such a speed that, to an observer on the earth, the satellite would appear to be stationary over a given spot on the earth's equator. This orbit has obvious advantages, but unfortunately, by its nature, can only accommodate a limited number of satellites, and is, therefore, reckoned to be a limited resource.[67]

Taking advantage of the fact that there is at present no clear-cut delimitation of outer space from national, space, eight equatorial States, namely, Brazil, Colombia. Congo, Ecuador, Indonesia, Kenya, Uganda, and Zaire, at their first meeting at Bogotá on 3 December 1976, issued a Declaration laying claims to the respective sectors of the geostationary orbit above their territory.

The Bogotá Declaration says in part:

... Equatorial countries declare that the geostationary synchronous orbit is a physical fact linked to the reality of our planet because its existence depends exclusively on its relation to gravitational phenomena generated by the earth, and that is why it must not be considered part of outer space. Therefore, the segments of geostationary synchronous orbit are part of the territory over which Equatorial States exercise their national sovereignty ... [T]he Equatorial countries meeting in Bogotá have decided to proclaim and defend on behalf of their peoples, the existence of their sovereignty over this natural resource ...

Both the physics and the law of the Bogotá Declaration are open to question. But the mere fact that such a claim can be seriously made by States and that those who consider it unnecessary to delimit outer space from national space are not in a position categorically to refute such a claim because the latter are themselves unable or unwilling to say where outer space begins is merely one of the many chickens of the functionalist and wait-and-see

[66] See text to n. 9 above.

[67] See further B. Cheng, 'Communications Satellites', 24 *CLP* (1971), p. 211, at p. 212 [Ch. 21 above, s. II.B: Geostationary and Other Orbits].

approach which are now coming home to roost. Before long, it could well be the turn of those States which object to certain types of satellites, such as those that engage in remote sensing, to claim sovereignty over national space above the usual heights at which such satellites orbit so as, not necessarily to exclude them, but to subject them to the consent and control of the States overflown.[68]

[68] See Cheng, loc. cit. in n. 46 above, pp. 600–1, s. 2.3.1: Raising the Limit of Territorial Space [cf. Ch. 22 below, s. VI.A].

15

The Legal Status of Astronauts*[1]

I. Notion

The 1967 Treaty on Principles Governing the Activities of States in the exploration and Use of Outer Space (the Outer Space Treaty)[2] is the first multilateral treaty to use the term 'astronaut' (Article V(1)). Though used from time to time, the term has not been defined in any of the multilateral treaties on outer space sponsored by the United Nations. It is descriptive rather than technical, and refers to any person who ventures into outer space or who travels on board a spacecraft.[3] Soviet practice favours the expression 'cosmonaut'.[4]

II. General International Law

Under general international law, there are scarcely any specific rules relating to astronauts. Such rules that exist are derived from the premise (i) that international law is inherently applicable to outer space,[5] (ii) that outer space, including the moon and other celestial bodies, is in law no longer subject to national appropriation, and (iii) that, therefore, its legal régime is analogous to the basic status of the high seas,[6] shorn of any special rules appropriate only to the latter.

* First published in Bernhardt (ed.), 11 *Ency. PIL* (1989), pp. 40–3. Reproduced by kind permission of Elsevier Science Publishers B.V.

[1] See B. Cheng, *General Principles of Law as Applied by International Courts and Tribunals* (1953, 1987); 'The Extraterrestrial Application of International Law', 18 *CLP* (1965), p. 132 [Ch. 5 above], 'Le Traité de 1967 sur l'espace/The 1967 Space Treaty', 95 *JDI* (1968), 532 [Ch. 9 above]; 'The Astronauts Agreement', 23 *YBWA* (1969), p. 185 [Ch. 10 above]; 'Outer Space: The International Legal Framework—The International Legal Status of Outer Space, Space Objects and Spacemen', 10 *Thesaurus Acroasium* (1981), p. 41 [Ch. 13 above]. For the rest of the list of further references, see Bibliography V.C below.

[2] App. I.1 below.

[3] See further B. Cheng, 'Spacecraft, Satellites and Space Objects', in Bernhardt (ed.), 11 *Ency. PIL* (1989), p. 309 [Ch. 16 below].

[4] See A. S. Piradov (ed.), *International Space Law* (1976), p. 103.

[5] See Cheng, 'The Extraterrestrial Application of International Law', loc. cit. in n. 1 above [Ch. 5 above].

[6] See Cheng, 'Outer Space: The International Legal Framework, loc. cit. in n. 1 above [Ch. 13 above].

On that basis, astronauts of whatever nationality are subject to the full jurisdiction (jurisfaction as well as jurisaction) of the territorial State, while they are within its territory, including its airspace, whether or not actually on board their spacecraft. In addition, they are subject to the quasi-territorial jurisdiction to prescribe (jurisfaction) of the State of registry (or launching State) of the space vehicle they are in, as well as the personal jurisfaction of their respective national States. As soon as a space vehicle leaves the airspace of the territorial State and reaches outer space, the astronauts on board come under the full jurisdiction of the State of registry, while remaining under the personal jurisfaction of their national States. Once they have definitely left the space vehicle without any intention of returning thereto, they would be subject solely to the jurisdiction of their respective national States.[7]

On the same basis, astronauts in distress should also benefit from the rules of general international law founded on the general principle of law on necessity as in the case of ships in distress.[8]

Whether some of the rules concerning astronauts developed in multilateral treaties relating to outer space by the United Nations, to the extent to which they differ from the above rules, have or have not crystallized into rules of general international law is open to question.

III. Treaty Rules

A. Jurisdictional Issues

The Outer Space Treaty lays down in its Article VIII:

A State Party to the Treaty on whose registry an object launched into outer space is carried shall retain jurisdiction and control over such object, and over any personnel thereof, while in outer space or on a celestial body . . .

This provision was taken over almost verbatim from paragraph 7 of the 1963 General Assembly Declaration of Legal Principles Governing the Activities of States in the Exploration of Outer Space (Resolution 1962 (XVIII)).[9] Article VIII, however, changed the word 'thereon' in paragraph 7 to 'thereof', in order to show that the rule is applicable to personnel outside as well as inside the space object.[10]

---

[7] See Cheng, 'The Extraterrestrial Application of International Law', loc. cit. in n. 1 above [Ch. 5 above]; B. Cheng, 'Outer Space: The International Legal Framework', loc. cit. in n. 1 above, pp. 93–5 [Ch. 13 above, s. IV.A.3]; and B. Cheng, 'The Legal Régime of Airspace and Outer Space: The Boundary Problem—Functionalism *versus* Spatialism: The Major Premises', 5 *AASL* (1980), p. 323, pp. 335–8 [Ch. 14 above, s. VI].

[8] See Cheng, *General Principles of Law*, pp. 69–77.   [9] App. II.3 below.

[10] See Cheng, 'The 1967 Space Treaty', loc. cit. in n. 1 above, pp. 570–2 [Ch. 9 above, s. V.C.2: Quasi-territorial Character of Jurisdiction].

The interpretation of Article VIII is not straightforward. On the face of it, Article VIII makes no provision for persons who do not form part of the personnel ('équipage' in the French text of the 1968 Agreement on the Rescue of Astronauts, the Return of Astronauts and the Return of Objects Launched into Outer Space (Astronauts Agreement),[11] Articles 1–4) of a space object, for instance, passengers or visitors from another spacecraft. Article VIII should, however, be regarded as merely confirmatory of general international law rather than establishing a special regime in derogation, and hence excluding the application, of general international law. What it confirms, when it refers to 'jurisdiction and control over such object', is the quasi-territorial jurisdiction of the State of registry over the spacecraft and all persons thereof as well as thereon, irrespective of their nationality. Such jurisdiction clearly extends, therefore, to all passengers and visitors, invited or uninvited. When Article VIII goes on to say, 'and over any personnel thereof', this should be treated as exemplificative of the preceding statement rather than as qualifying it. Otherwise, when the personnel of one spacecraft visits another, Article VIII would cause a conflict of jurisdictions derived from two parts of the same provision.

In the light of this interpretation and of the change from 'on' to 'of' previously mentioned, it is possible to say that, under Article VIII, as under general international law, the State of registry retains quasi-territorial jurisdiction over all persons belonging to the space object both inside and outside the space object, for as long as they can be regarded as still belonging, or being attached, to the space object.

This would cover not only those who go on space walks outside a spacecraft, but also those who move about on the moon or other celestial bodies, provided that they belong to an object launched into space.

Article 12(1) of the 1979 Agreement Governing the Activities of States on the Moon and Other Celestial Bodies (Moon Treaty)[12] provides:

States Parties shall retain jurisdiction and control over their personnel, vehicles, equipment, facilities, stations and installations on the moon . . .

This poses no problem provided that the 'personnel' in question belong to objects launched into space by the States Parties, and further provided, in this context, that moon stations and installations, whatever their nature, are accepted as 'objects launched into outer space'.

Otherwise, there is a problem; for, unless such personnel either belong to a space object registered in a State Party or are nationals of a State Party, the State of registry or nationality has no jurisdiction (respectively quasi-territorial or personal) to 'retain' over such personnel. The point is that there can be no third source of jurisdiction over such personnel other than territorial jurisdiction. Particularly on *terra firma* which is 'not subject to national

---

[11] App. II.2 below.   [12] App. I.5 below.

appropriation', such as the moon, the recognition of any form of State juris-diction over a piece of land with some kind of structure on it that does not strictly qualify as 'an object launched into space', and the extension of that jurisdiction to any person either working there as 'personnel' or, what would be even more the case, merely being within that piece of land would come close to creating some form of territorial sovereignty.

B. Humanitarian Provisions

In another borrowing from General Assembly Resolution 1962 (XVIII), the 1967 Space Treaty, in its Article V(1), reproduces almost verbatim paragraph 9 of the Resolution. Article V(1) provides:

States Parties to the Treaty shall regard astronauts as envoys of mankind in outer space . . .

Initially, some tentative attempt was made to infer jurisdictional immunities for astronauts by reason of their having been called 'the envoys of mankind'. But it was most probably the wistful question whether, in that case, mankind should perhaps have a say in the way they were launched into space which quickly brought the response that it was only a figure of speech. This phrase has not appeared in any of the subsequent multilateral treaties on space spon-sored by the United Nations.[13]

The rest of Article V, and the subsequent Astronauts Agreement, as well as Articles 10 and 12(3) of the Moon Treaty, are all designed to provide assis-tance to, and for the search and rescue of, astronauts in the event of accident, distress or emergency landing outside their intended country, as well as for their safe return to the State of registry of their vehicle or to the launching authority.

IV. Evaluation and Prospective

The legal status of astronauts is governed by general international law and specific treaty provisions, many of which are of a humanitarian character. Existing treaty provisions on the jurisdictional issues are far from clear or ade-quate. Much further work requires to be done.

The development of permanent or semi-permanent manned space stations makes this all the more urgent. This is especially so in the case of multina-tional manned stations, such as that planned between the United States, Europe, Japan, and Canada and scheduled to come into operation in 1996. In

---

[13] See Chang, 'The 1967 Space Treaty', loc. cit. in n. 1 above, pp. 632–4 [Ch. 9 above, s. VII.F.1: 'Envoys of Mankind']; 'Outer Space: The International Legal Framework', loc. cit. in n. 1 above, pp. 95–6 [Ch. 13 above, s. IV.A.6: Astronauts Envoys of Mankind].

the latter case, further co-ordination among the participating States is needed in order to settle the many problems of jurisdiction, including applicable law and enforcement, on board a structure which will comprise objects launched into space by, or at least on behalf of, a number of States each registering its own element. Article II(2) of the 1975 Convention on Registration of Objects Launched into Outer Space (the Registration Convention)[14] envisages such a situation, but leaves the method of dealing with it entirely to the States concerned.

The jurisdictional problem regarding manned stations on the moon and other celestial bodies is probably even harder to resolve, in view of the difficulties of avoiding any semblance of 'national appropriation' if exclusive jurisdiction is granted to any State over any piece of land on *terra firma*.

As space exploration and exploitation further develop, separate rules will need to be evolved for different categories of astronauts engaged in diverse activities, such as operating crew, other personnel, passengers, visiting missions, rescue missions, salvage teams. Moreover, what would be their position when astronauts not only engage in commercial transportation into outer space, but also plan to make regular landings in the territory of other States?

As the experience in air law has shown, and in view particularly of the principle of international responsibility for national space activities laid down in Article VI of the 1967 Space Treaty, States involved in space urgently need to regulate the activities of their spacecraft and astronauts in outer space, and to extend the applicability of their domestic law, including their general criminal law, and the jurisdiction of their courts to outer space.

States should give early attention to these problems unilaterally, bilaterally, or multilaterally either without or within the United Nations Committee on the Peaceful Uses of Outer Space.

[14] App. I.4 below.

16

Legal Status of Spacecraft, Satellites, and Space Objects*[1]

I. Notion

A. Spacecraft and Space Vehicles

Spacecraft and space vehicles appear to have been treated as synonymous terms in treaties relating to outer space concluded under the auspices of the United Nations. While the 1967 Treaty on Principles Governing the Activities of States in the Exploration and Use of Outer Space, including the Moon and Other Celestial Bodies (Space Treaty)[2] speaks in its Article V of astronauts and their 'space vehicle', the 1968 Agreement on the Rescue of Astronauts, the Return of Astronauts and the Return of Objects Launched into Outer Space, April 22, 1968 (Astronauts Agreement)[3] prefers in its various provisions to refer to the 'personnel of a spacecraft' (Articles 1(1), 2, 3, and 4). Article 3(2) of the 1979 Agreement Governing the Activities of States on the Moon and Other Celestial Bodies, (Moon Treaty)[4] also refers to 'spacecraft' and 'the personnel of spacecraft'. The 1967 Space Treaty in its Article XII distinguishes 'space vehicles' on celestial bodies from 'stations, installations, [and] equipment', to which the Moon Treaty consistently adds 'facilities' (Articles 8(1)(b), 10(2), 11(3), 12(1), (3), 15).

It would appear that the terms 'space vehicle' and 'spacecraft' have been used primarily to designate any device designed to move, or to be stationed, in space or on celestial bodies, whether manned or unmanned. However, the question can be asked whether the plain reference to 'vehicles' without the qualification 'space' in Articles 9(2), 10(2), and 12(2) and (3) of the Moon

* First published in Bernhardt (ed.), 11 *Ency. PIL* (1989), pp. 309–17. Reproduced by kind permission of Elsevier Science Publishers B.V.

[1] See B. Cheng, 'Crimes on Board Aircraft', 12 *CLP* (1959), pp. 177–207; 'The Extraterritorial Application of International Law', 18 *CLP* (1965), pp. 132–52 [Ch. 5 above]; 'Le Traité de 1967 sur l'espace/The 1967 Space Treaty', 95 *JDI* (1968), 532 [Ch. 9 above]. 'The Legal Régime of Airspace and Outer Space: The Boundary Problem—Functionalism versus Spatialism: The Major Premises', 5 *AASL* (1980), pp. 323–61 [Ch. 14 above]; 'Outer Space: The International Legal Framework—The International Legal Status of Outer Space, Space Objects and Spacemen', 10 *Thesaurus Acroasium* (1981) pp. 41–106 [Ch. 13 above]; 'The Legal Status of Outer Space and Relevant Issues: Delimitation of Outer Space and Definition of Peaceful Use', 11 *JSL* (1983), pp. 89–105. For the rest of the list of further references, see Biliography V.C below.

[2] App. I.1 below.   [3] App. I.2 below.   [4] App. I.5 below.

Treaty indicates a differentiation between vehicles capable of space flight and those capable only of locomotion on celestial bodies. The formulation of, for instance, Article 12(1) of the Moon Treaty, where the expressions 'space vehicles' and 'vehicles' are used in the same paragraph, would seem to suggest that no such distinction is intended, and that the qualifier 'space' is sometimes dropped when reference is made to vehicles on celestial bodies, on the assumption seemingly that all such vehicles on celestial bodies would *ipso facto* be space vehicles.

B. Satellites

None of the treaties relating to outer space concluded under the auspices of the United Nations has occasion to refer to artificial earth satellites, although the Preamble of the Moon Treaty does mention the 'moon, as a natural satellite of the earth'. There are also references in two of the treaties to objects placed 'in orbit around the earth' or 'in earth orbit' (Space Treaty, Article IV(1); the 1975 Convention on Registration of Objects Launched into Outer Space (Registration Convention),[5] Article V).

It is, of course, also possible to have artificial satellites placed around celestial bodies other than the earth. In fact, Article 3 of the Moon Treaty prohibits the placing of nuclear weapons, or any other kinds of weapons of mass destruction 'in orbit around' the moon. However, most other treaties, such as those establishing the International Telecommunications Satellite Organisation 'INTELSAT' and the International Maritime Satellite Organisation (INMARSAT), where the term 'satellite' is much used, take for granted that, especially in their context, the description 'satellite', if unqualified, refers to an artificial earth satellite. Neither treaty includes 'satellite' among the terms defined in the agreement.

C. Space Objects

From the legal standpoint, 'space object' is, in current practice, the generic term used to cover spacecraft, satellites, and in fact anything that human beings launch or attempt to launch into space, including their components and launch vehicles, as well as parts thereof. This practice appears to have been well established by the 1967 Space Treaty (Articles VII and VIII), the 1972 Convention on International Liability for Damage Caused by Space Objects (Liability Convention)[6], and the Registration Convention. In respect of State jurisdiction, registration and liability, the rules operate by reference primarily to 'space objects'. The fact that Article 3(2) of the Moon Treaty mentions spacecraft and man-made space objects separately when it refers to

---

[5] App. I.4 below.   [6] App. I.3 below.

'the earth, the moon, spacecraft, [and] the personnel of spacecraft or man-made space objects', is intended no doubt to facilitate the reference to 'personnel of spacecraft' and is not believed to imply thereby that spacecraft do not constitute 'man-made space objects'.

The expression 'space object' is, however, not specifically defined in any of the conventions relating to outer space established under the auspices of the United Nations, notwithstanding efforts to do so in the negotiations leading to the Liability Convention and the Registration Convention. As referred to in Articles VII and VIII of the 1967 Space Treaty, for example, it denotes simply 'an object launched into outer space', which, in the terminology of the treaty, includes the moon and other celestial bodies.

Under Article I(b) of the Liability Convention, ' "launching" includes attempted launching'. That definition appears to be generally applicable in the determination of what is a space object. The 1967 Space Treaty, in its Article VIII, appears to subsume under the term 'space objects' not only 'their component parts', but also 'objects landed or constructed on a celestial body'. Whilst the Astronauts Agreement still refers separately and expressly to 'component parts' of a space object (Article 5), both the Liability Convention (Article 1(d)) and the Registration Convention (Article 1(b)) provide in identical fashion:

The term 'space object' includes component parts of a space object as well as its launch vehicle and parts thereof.

Without using exactly the same wording, Article 12(1) of the Moon Treaty appears to do no more than to echo Article VIII of the Space Treaty in providing:

States Parties shall retain jurisdiction and control over their personnel, vehicles, equipment, facilities, stations and installations on the moon. The ownership of space vehicles, equipment, facilities, stations and installations shall not be affected by their presence on the moon.

These items all come no doubt under the description 'man-made space objects' in Article 3(2) of the same treaty.

In sum, therefore, the term space object designates any object which humans launch, attempt to launch or have launched into outer space. It embraces satellites, spacecraft, space vehicles, equipment, facilities, stations, installations and other constructions, including their components, as well as their launch vehicles and parts thereof.

II. Freedom of Exploration and Use

Article II of the 1967 Space Treaty which declares outer space, including the moon and other celestial bodies, not subject to national appropriation can probably be accepted now as merely declaratory of general international law. As a result, there is freedom in the exploration and use of outer space by means of satellites, spacecraft and other objects launched into outer space or constructed in outer space or on the moon and other celestial bodies, as well as 'free access to all areas of celestial bodies' (Article 1(2) and (3)).

In the Moon Treaty, as its Article 1 says, reference in the treaty to the moon applies also 'to other celestial bodies within the solar system, other than the earth', except when otherwise stated. In relation to the Moon Treaty, this practice will also be followed here. As among the Treaty's contracting States, which declare the moon and its natural resources the common heritage of mankind (Article 11(1)), the freedom of their space objects to land on the moon, to be launched from it, to be placed on or below its surface, or to move and be moved over or below its surface is clearly preserved (Article 8). Article 9 specifically provides that States parties may establish manned and unmanned stations on the moon, although it lays down at the same time certain restrictions and regulations relating to them, including the need of preserving free access to all areas of the moon.

III. Prohibited Objects

Under Article IV of the 1967 Space Treaty:

States Parties to the Treaty undertake not to place in orbit around the earth any objects carrying nuclear weapons or any other kinds of weapons of mass destruction, install such weapons on celestial bodies, or station such weapons in outer space in any other manner.

The moon and other celestial bodies shall be used by all States Parties to the Treaty exclusively for peaceful purposes. The establishment of military bases, installations and fortifications, the testing of any type of weapons . . . on celestial bodies shall be forbidden. The use of military personnel for scientific research or for any other peaceful purposes shall not be prohibited. The use of any equipment or facility necessary for peaceful exploration of the moon and other celestial shall . . . not be prohibited.

Controversy exists as to whether the adjective 'peaceful' in the second paragraph, particularly as found in the first sentence of that paragraph, means 'non-military' or merely 'non-aggressive'. There is also a very prevalent misconception that the first sentence of the second paragraph applies also to outer space as such, and not merely to the 'moon and other celestial bodies'. This may well be one of the reasons why some States insist on interpreting the word 'peaceful' to mean merely 'non-aggressive'.[7]

---

[7] See Cheng, loc. cit. (983) in n. 1 above, at pp. 98–105 [Ch. 19 below].

A very similar provision in relation to the moon and other celestial bodies within the solar system other than the earth exists in the Moon Treaty (Article 3).

IV. Jurisdiction and Ownership

Article VIII of the 1967 Space Treaty provides:

. . . Ownership of objects launched into outer space, including objects landed or constructed on a celestial body, and of their component parts, is not affected by their presence in outer space or on a celestial body or by their return to the earth . . .

As quoted above, Article 12(1) of the Moon Treaty contains a very similar statement. Insofar as the ownership of space objects is concerned, these two provisions may be regarded as merely declaratory of the position under general international law. However, they do not appear to preclude States from abandoning those of their space objects which have outlived their usefulness. In fact debris in space is becoming a serious problem.

Article VIII of the 1967 Space Treaty further provides:

A State Party to the Treaty on whose registry an object launched into outer space is carried shall retain jurisdiction and control over such object, and over any personnel thereof, while in outer space or on a celestial body . . .

At first sight, Article 12(1) of the Moon Treaty, as quoted above, in saying that

States Parties shall retain jurisdiction and control over their personnel, vehicles, equipment, facilities, stations and installations on the moon . . .

may appear to have slightly extended the scope of Article VIII of the 1967 Space Treaty. However, if regard is had to the latter's use of the expression 'retain', and its immediate reference thereafter to continued ownership of 'objects landed or constructed on a celestial body', suggest that this provision in the Moon Treaty is a mere amplification of Article VIII of the Space Treaty, without modifying it. At the same time, the use of the possessive pronoun 'their' in the Moon Treaty may also give rise to the interpretation that the Moon Treaty attributes jurisdiction and control according to the nationality of the personnel, and the ownership of the vehicles, equipment, facilities, stations and installations on the moon, instead of the registration of the space object as provided for in the Space Treaty.

Insofar as space objects are concerned, inasmuch as outer space and celestial bodies can now probably all be reckoned to be *res extra commercium* under general international law, the above provisions can, with perhaps only some slight reservation relating to registration, also be taken to be declaratory of general international law, especially as both provisions use the expression 'retain'. Since there can now be no territorial sovereignty in outer space or on celestial bodies, there can also be no exercise of territorial jurisdiction there. Consequently, such jurisdiction that States exercise over their space objects will be quasi-territorial in character, that is, of the same nature as that over their own ships and aircraft. It applies not only to the object as such, but also to all things and persons on board. In case of concurrence or conflict, quasi-territorial jurisaction overrides personal jurisaction.[8]

Under general international law, ships and aircraft fall under the quasi-jurisdiction of States on account of their nationality which they acquire through domestic law by reason either of their ownership by nationals of a State (as in the case of British ships), or (as is more generally the case) of their being registered in a State. Although Article VIII of the 1967 Space Treaty appears to presuppose that all objects launched into outer space will have been placed on some State register, this assumption is not implied in either the Astronauts Agreement or the Liability Convention. The latter treaties studiously eschew any reference to the State of registry. They speak always of the 'launching authority' or the 'launching State', which can mean altogether four separate States; for it refers to the State that launches or procures the launching of a space object, or a State from whose territory or facility a space object is launched. In fact, the problem of registration of space objects was not resolved until eight years after the 1967 Space Treaty by the Registration Convention. It would appear that where there is no registration, jurisdiction will probably follow ownership, as the Moon Treaty seems to envisage when, in its Article 12(1), it speaks of States parties retaining jurisdiction over 'their' vehicles, equipment, and so forth on the moon.

The 1967 Space Treaty lays down certain limitations on the exercise of the State of registry's jurisdiction over its 'stations, installations, equipment and space vehicles on the moon and other celestial bodies' in providing in its Article XII that these facilities:

shall be open to representatives of other States Parties to the Treaty on a basis of reciprocity. Such representatives shall give advance notice of a projected visit, in order that appropriate consultations may be held and that maximum precautions may be taken to assure safety and to avoid interference with normal operations in the facility to be visited.

As among contracting States to the Moon Treaty, a similar provision exists, albeit no longer subject to the condition of reciprocity, for the express purpose of enabling contracting parties to assure themselves that the treaty is being complied with (Article 15).

In a slightly opposite direction, there is now increasingly talk of safety or 'keep-out' zones around space objects.[9]

---

[8] See Cheng, loc. cit. (1965) in n. 1 above, p. 132, pp. 134–48 [Ch. 5 above, s. II: Position under General International Law].

[9] See F. K. Schwetje, 'Protecting Space Assets: A Legal Analysis of "Keep-out Zones" ', 15 *JSL* (1987), pp. 131–46.

V. Registration and Legal Status

One of the concerns of States which fear that they or their nationals may be victims of damage caused by foreign space objects is how to establish the identity of such space objects and therefrom the identity of the launching State or States responsible. Initially by analogy with ships and aircraft, many were thinking in terms of requiring identification marks to be displayed on space objects. However, the special characteristics of space flight, together with the fact that space objects that return to earth to cause damage have most often already disintegrated into relatively small fragments, soon brought about the realization that perhaps it would be more helpful if details of individual space objects, including their planned and actual orbits and trajectories, were generally and readily accessible.

For this purpose, as well as for the purpose of providing the scientific community and the public at large with the fruits of space exploration, and the other contracting States with some means of monitoring whether the treaty provisions are being observed or not, all that the 1967 Space Treaty has succeeded in persuading the States parties to undertake is a vague promise to inform the United Nations Secretary-General as well as the public and the international scientific community, 'to the greatest extent feasible and practicable,' of the nature, conduct, location and results of their exploration and use of outer space (Article XI). Previously, the General Assembly in Resolution 1721 (XVI) (20 December 1961) did call upon States launching objects into orbit or beyond promptly to inform the United Nations of such launchings, and asked the Secretary-General to establish a public registry to record them. However, such reporting, though it nominally still continues, is voluntary and incomplete.[10]

It was not until 1975 that a system of mandatory reporting was established by the Registration Convention. The Convention provides for two levels of registration: national or domestic registration and United Nations registration.

A. National Registration

National or domestic registration may be further distinguished.

1. *State Register.* Under Article II(1) of the Registration Convention:

When a space object is launched into earth orbit or beyond, the launching State shall register the space object by means of an entry in an appropriate registry which it shall maintain . . .

[10] See C. S. Sheldon II and B. M. DeVoe, 'United Nations Registry of Space Vehicles', 13 *Space Law Colloquium* (1970), pp. 127–41; and UN Secretary-General, *Report on Application of the Convention on Registration of Objects Launched into Outer Space*, A/AC.105/382 (2.3.87).

The Convention has avoided joint registration. Instead, Article II(2) provides:

Where there are two or more launching States in respect of any such space object, they shall jointly determine which one of them shall register the object in accordance with paragraph 1 of this article, bearing in mind the provisions of article VIII of the Treaty on Principles Governing the Activities of States in the Exploration and Use of Outer Space, including the Moon and Other Celestial Bodies, and without prejudice to appropriate agreements concluded or to be concluded among the launching States on jurisdiction and control over the space object and over any personnel thereof.

Under Article II(3), the State of registry has complete discretion as to how the register is operated.

2. *Institutional Register.* As a result of Article VII of the Registration Convention, which allows certain qualified international intergovernmental organizations conducting space activities that make a declaration accepting the rights and obligations of the Convention to become quasi-parties to the Convention, such quasi-parties are also entitled to have their own registers.

In such instances, inasmuch as no international organizations conducting space activities has yet been endowed with the power or capability of exercising quasi-territorial jurisdiction, where an organization has registered a space object, the United Nations Legal Counsel has apparently ruled, in response to an inquiry from the European Space Agency (ESA), that arrangements may be made by the organization with one of its members to extend the latter's jurisdiction and control to the object registered.[11]

B. United Nations Register

In addition to the domestic registers maintained by States or international organizations, entry on which will have the effect, directly or, at least it is to be hoped, as a concomitant thereof, of determining the State which exercises quasi-territorial jurisdiction over a space object, the Registration Convention requires the Secretary-General of the United Nations to maintain a United Nations' Register (Article III). States, as well as international organizations, maintaining domestic registers are obliged to furnish the Secretary-General, 'as soon as practicable' various items of information concerning space objects carried on their registers, including, where applicable, the designators or registration numbers borne by such objects, to supply him 'from time to time' with additional information, and to notify him 'to the greatest extent feasible and as soon as practicable' of previously reported artificial earth satellites 'no longer . . . in earth orbit' (Articles IV and V).

[11] See G. Lafferanderie, 'L'application, par l'Agence Spatiale Européenne, de la Convention sur l'immatriculation des objets lancés dans l'espace extra-atmosphérique', 11 *AASL* (1986), p. 229, at pp. 231–2; cf. Cheng, loc. cit. (1981) in n. 1 above, at pp. 100–1 [Ch. 13 above, s. IV.C.3: Institutional Register]. See also Ch. 24 below s. II.I on Art. II(2).

C. Legal Status

Are space objects, like ships and aircraft, endowed with nationality? In the drafting of the various treaties relating to outer space, there has been seemingly an almost deliberate and concerted attempt to avoid any reference to the concept of nationality. Registration is deemed sufficient to provide the link between these objects of international law and the subjects of international law, failing which the act of launching or even ownership would seem to be considered adequate. This approach represents an interesting experiment, which may in time prove that the concept of nationality as applied even to ships and aircraft does no more, upon final analysis, than to serve as the denomination of the special relationship that exists between subjects of international law and certain categories of objects of international law, provided of course that the applicable substantive rules, including that conferring quasi-territorial jurisdiction on the owner's State or the State of registry as the case may be, remain clearly established and create no uncertainty in practice. If international civil aviation is any guide, nationality can sometimes prove an emotive insignia causing difficulties that are legally at times complicated to resolve.

VI. Liability for Damage Caused

States are liable for damage caused by their space objects to other States and their nationals, including, in certain circumstances, the latter's space objects. As among the respective contracting parties, the subject is regulated by *inter alia* Article VII of the 1967 Space Treaty, the Liability Convention, and Article 14(2) of the Moon Treaty.[12]

VII. Return of Stray Objects

Article VIII of the 1967 Space Treaty, after stating that the ownership of space objects is not affected by their presence in outer space or on a celestial body or by their return to the earth, goes on to say:

Such objects or component parts found beyond the limits of the State Party to the Treaty on whose registry they are carried shall be returned to that State Party, which shall, upon request, furnish identifying data prior to their return.

---

[12] See further B. Cheng, 'Convention on International Liability for Damage Caused by Space Objects', in Jasentuliyana and Lee (eds.), 1 *Manual* (1979), p. 83 [Ch. 11 above]; 'The Moon Treaty: Agreement Governing the Activities of States on the Moon and Other Celestial Bodies within the Solar System other than the Earth, December 18, 1979', 33 *CLP* (1980), p. 213 [Ch. 12 above]; and Chs. 23–4 below.

This article has been further elaborated by Article 5 of the Astronauts Agreement, which has in turn been extended by Article 12(1) of the Moon Treaty to '[v]ehicles, installations and equipment or their component parts [on the moon] found in places other than their intended location.'

Under Article 5(1) of the Astronauts Agreement, contracting States undertake to notify both the launching State (whether a contracting party or not) and the Secretary-General of the United Nations if they receive information or discover that a space object or its component parts has returned to earth in territories under their jurisdiction or on the high seas or in any other place not under the jurisdiction of any State. Article 13 of the Moon Treaty provides for a similar duty in regard to forced landings of space objects on the moon, but appears to impose such a duty only if the launching State is a contracting party. This limitation is inoperative, however, if a State is a party to both treaties, inasmuch as the moon must be considered as a place not under the jurisdiction of any State, within the meaning of Article 5(1) of the Astronauts Agreement. In such a case, the wider duty under the Astronauts Agreement prevails.

VIII. Evaluation and Prospective

Inasmuch as space objects are intended to operate in areas which are not subject to the territorial sovereignty or jurisdiction or any State, it is only natural that space law should wish to attach such objects to States and other international persons so that thereby they become subject to both the regulations and protection of international law. It is also natural that space law should have followed the examples of the law of the sea and of air law in attributing to the State of registry quasi-territorial jurisdiction.

One of the first things that States sending objects into space, especially manned spacecraft or space stations, must take care to do is to exercise this jurisdiction and extend their domestic laws, especially their general criminal law, and the jurisdiction of their courts to such space objects. Otherwise, as demonstrated in many cases in civil aviation,[13] one may find, in any given case, that actually no system of criminal law is applicable on board, and that what otherwise would be considered as criminal offences will as a result go unpunished. In due course, the extension of other rules of municipal law to space objects and space activities, such as those on intellectual and industrial property, carriage, and a host of other matters, will also be required.[14]

However, the specific nature of space flights means that many problems cannot and should not be resolved merely by analogy. Furthermore, as the

---

[13] See Cheng, loc. cit (1959) in n. 1 above.
[14] Cf. various authors, 'Determination of Applicable Law to Living and Working in Outer Space', 23 *Space Law Colloquium* (1981), p. 187.

exploration and use of outer space progress, many of the existing rules may need to be clarified, adjusted, or supplemented.

A. Definitional and Classificatory Problems

In the first place, there are definitional and classificatory problems with regard to space objects. What is a space object? Such an object said to be an object launched, or attempted to be launched, into 'outer space, including the moon and other celestial bodies'. In view, however, of the current resistance of many States, including major space powers, to any attempt even to discuss the problem of defining and delimiting outer space, does one know where, in law, outer space begins?[15] Are meteorological sounding rockets, for instance, space objects? If it were said that sounding rockets at least are aimed at the upper space, whether or not 'outer space', would not attempts be made to deny that inter-continental ballistic missiles which are aimed at targets on earth and not intended to be launched into outer space are space objects, although they traverse what, even in the absence of any definition, most people would regard as outer space?

If, instead of outer space, one refers to earth orbit or beyond, the question then arises whether there need be at least an intention that the object complete an entire orbit. The projected British Aerospace Horizontal Take-Off and Landing (HOTOL) aerospace plane and the United States planned National Aero-Space Plane (NASP), code-named the X–30, for instance, would travel only part of their way in earth orbit. In any event, even if such objects qualify as space objects, as do doubtless at present the United States and Soviet space shuttles and will in due course shuttles of other States, they are really amphibian craft. It will fall on the International Civil Aviation Organisation (ICAO), in association with the United Nations Committee on the Peaceful Uses of Outer Space (COPUOS), to study the problems relating particularly to the status and regulation of such space vehicles after their re-entry into the earth's atmosphere, when they behave like, and fall under existing definitions of, aircraft.

B. Registration and Jurisdictional Problems

Registration and jurisdictional problems are obviously linked closely together. In the case of the shuttles, the question arises whether foreign payloads need to be separately registered. The practice of the United States' National Aeronautics and Space Administration (NASA) is to make the answer dependent on whether the payload is intended to be 'separated in Earth orbit from the Shuttle'. On this basis, it regarded ESA's Spacelab, which drew its supplies

---

[15] See Cheng, loc. cit. (1980) in n. 1 above [Ch. 14 above].

from the shuttle and remained all the time within the shuttle, as merely a part of the latter and did not agree to its being separately registered, causing Europe thus to lose jurisdiction and control.[16] On the other hand, where a separately registered space object is in due course to be separated from the shuttle, that object and its personnel will, before separation, be under the jurisdictions of both its State of registry and the State of registry of the shuttle. In such a case, the question may well be asked: Which jurisdiction prevails?

The same question applies to the projected multinational, permanently manned International Space Station, involving the United States, Canada, ESA as well as its nine member States, and Japan. If the various elements belonging to the so-called 'Four Partners' are to be separately registered in different States, as in fact it has been so decided, which country will have jurisaction when an astronaut from a module registered in one State visits a module registered in another State? Is the substitution of the personal jurisaction of the astronaut's national State for the quasi-territorial jurisaction of the State of registry of the element in which the astronaut is present likely to function smoothly?

The problem becomes even more complicated, when unmanned and, particularly, manned stations are established on the moon, especially if constructed from materials brought up to the moon by spacecraft registered in different States. Is a station on the moon entitled to be separately registered? In that event, how far will the jurisdiction exercised by the State of registry be different from territorial jurisdiction? Even if a State were a party to the Moon Treaty, would the safeguards under Article 9, such as limited areas, reports to the Secretary-General of the United Nations, and free access, be adequate to distinguish sufficiently such occupation from appropriation, however temporary? States which have not accepted the Moon Treaty would not be subject even to such restrictions.

Article II(2) of the Registration Convention appears to permit contracting States, when two or more of them jointly launch a space object which is then registered with one of them, to conclude 'appropriate agreements' among them 'on jurisdiction and control over the space object and over any personnel thereof'. Whilst this provision seemingly has the merit of affording the States concerned the maximum of flexibility in the matter, it may well be open to question whether, in the light of Article VIII of the 1987 Space Treaty, once an object has been registered, States have any discretion to alter the link between registration and jurisdiction. If, in practice, Article VIII is to be so interpreted as to permit unfettered discretion to States to make alternative arrangements, uncertainty in any concrete case as to which State actually enjoys jurisdiction and control is bound to arise. This is underscored by the

---

[16] See G. Lafferranderie, 'La station spatiale', in J. Dutheil de la Rochère (ed.), *Droit de l'espace* (1988), p. 147, at p. 172, n. 29.

fact that the Registration Convention does not even require such arrangements to be reported to the United Nations and recorded in its register. The view of the United Nations Legal Counsel that similar arrangements may be made by international organizations for jurisdiction over space objects registered with them to be exercised by one of their members will inevitably lead to further erosion of the rule that jurisdiction and registration go hand in hand.

C. Identification of Space Objects

The Registration Convention was concluded for the purpose, among other things, of assisting States in identifying space objects that threaten their rights or which may have already caused them damage, and of inducing a degree of openness in space activities so that their conformity with international law and treaty obligations may be monitored. What has just been said already throws doubt on the extent to which registration will fulfill these hopes. Furthermore, not only has the Convention failed to require advance registration of projected launches of space objects, but it also provides in its Article IV merely that contracting States need furnish the Secretary-General with the necessary information 'as soon as practicable' after the event. In practice, the United Nations is informed often only after considerable delay; and some objects are registered more than once, whilst others not at all, especially so-called non-functional objects.[17] Moreover, under the heading, 'general function of the space object', the information provided, in the majority of cases, is singularly cryptic.[18]

In the controversy whether there is need, or even urgent need, to define outer space from national airspace, while the so-called spatialists maintain that there is, the so-called functionalists argue that there is not.[19] The latter contend that outer space can be regulated by reference simply to the function of space objects and the nature of space activities. If the present system of registration of space objects is any guide, it is more than doubtful whether such regulations would prove very meaningful.

Matters are made worse by the fact that, as at present, the State of registry of a space object, which should be exercising 'jurisdiction and control' over it under Article VIII of the 1967 Space Treaty, need not necessarily be the State actually exercising them. Moreover, neither the State of registry nor the State actually exercising jurisdiction and control need necessarily be the State which, under Article VI of the 1967 Space Treaty, is internationally responsible for its activities.[20] Perhaps, in due course, one may need in space law to turn, after all, to the concept of nationality.

---

[17] See UN Secretary-General, op. cit. in n. 10 above.
[18] See A. J. Young, 'A Decennial Review of the Registration Convention', 9 *AASL* (1986), pp. 287–308.   [19] See Cheng, loc. cit. (1980) in n. 1 above [Ch. 14 above].
[20] See B. Cheng, 'Space Activities, Responsibility and Liability for', in Bernhardt (ed.), 11 *Ency. PIL* (1989), pp. 299–303 [cf. Chs. 23 and 24 below].

17

Nationality for Spacecraft?*

I. Subjects and Objects of International Law

International law distinguishes between *subjects* of international law and *objects* of international law. Subjects of international law are entities endowed with international legal personality. International legal personality is the legal capacity to bear and to exercise rights and to incur and to carry out obligations under international law. Those who are capable of doing so are subjects of international law. Today the primary *subjects* of international law are States, namely territorially organized entities which are, and which are recognized as, sovereign and independent. However, other entities, such as intergovernmental international organizations and, in principle, even individuals and non-governmental organizations, may also, by the consent of or recognition by existing international persons, be endowed with international legal personality and made subjects of international law.[1]

Everyone and everything that does not possess that capacity is an *object* of international law incapable of bearing rights or obligations under international law. Included in this category are territories, the ordinary persons, whether natural or corporate, and other objects, animate or inanimate.

Two of the most important functions of international law are first that of maintaining the status quo, as well as of providing peaceful means to bring about changes, in the allocation of objects of international law among the subjects of international law, and secondly that of ensuring proper demarcation of the powers of the subjects of international law over objects of international law, as well as of laying down rules for the peaceful resolution of possible conflicts in the exercise of such powers.

---

* First published in T. L. Masson-Zwaan and P. M. J. Mendes de Leon (eds.), *Air and Space Law: De Lege Ferenda—Essays in honour of Henri A. Wassenbergh* (1992), pp. 202–17. Reproduced with kind permission from Kluwer Law International.

[1] See further B. Cheng, 'Custom: The Future of General State Practice in a Divided World', in R. St. J. Macdonald and D. M. Johnston (eds.), *The Structure and Process of International Law* (1983), p. 513, at p. 516–9 under 'International Legal Order a Voluntary and Cooptative System' (N.B.: in the book, pp. 545 and 546 have been transposed, and are wrongly paginated); and B. Cheng, 'Introduction to Title I: Subjects of International Law', in M. Bedjaoui (ed.), *International Law: Achievements and Prospects* (1991), pp. 23–40.

II. Territories and Territorial Sovereignty

It is currently fashionable among some space lawyers to play down the importance of the spatial division of territories, but anyone with any acquaintance of international law and relations would recognize that the first and foremost problem on the minds of all States is the certainty, security and inviolability of their own frontiers, followed by a clear knowledge of the geographical limits of the others' legal powers—in other words, of everyone's competence *ratione loci*.[2]

In the *Palmas Island Arbitration* (1928) between the Netherlands and the United States, the sole arbitrator Judge M. Huber, speaking of territorial sovereignty being the right of a State, in regard to a portion of the globe, 'to exercise therein to the exclusion of any other State, the functions of a State', went on to say:

The development of the national organisation of States during the last few centuries and, as a corollary, the development of international law, have established this principle of the exclusive competence of the State in regard to its own territory in such a way as to make it the point of departure in settling most questions that concern international relations.[3]

Referring to the law as it was at the time of the arbitration, Judge Huber pointed out that the world was divided into three types of territory: (i) national territory under the exclusive jurisdiction of the national State over the whole area and all persons and things found therein, (ii) territory that belongs to no State or other international person but is capable of being reduced to sovereignty ('no man's land' or *territorium nullius*), and (iii) territory, such as the high seas, that belongs to no State and is, in law, as such not subject to appropriation, though its resources are (*territorium extra commercium* or 'territory not susceptible of appropriation'). To these three traditional categories of territory must now be added a fourth, namely, (iv) the common heritage of mankind of which not only the area as such, but also its resources, is not subject to individual appropriation. An example of this new category is the 1979 Moon Treaty which, as among the contracting States, declares the moon and the other celestial bodies within the solar system other than the earth the common heritage of mankind.

---

[2] See further B. Cheng, 'The Legal Régime of Airspace and Outer Space: The Boundary Problem—Functionalism *versus* Spatialism: The Major Premises', 5 *AASL* (1980), p. 323 [Ch. 14 above].

[3] 2 *RIAA*, p. 829, at p. 838.

III. The Distribution of Objects of International Law among Subjects of International Law and International Law's Major Premises

The first and most important distribution of objects of international law among the subjects of international law is territorial, a distribution made by historical struggles or accommodations among States rather than by any superior authority or the law. Once these territorially organized entities have been established and mutually recognized as full members of the international legal order, each, apart from asserting full authority over its *national* territory and all persons and things within it and agreeing to certain areas of the world being treated as *territorium extra commercium* or even common heritage of mankind, is entitled also to claim additional objects of international law as its own by attributing to them its national imprint—its nationality.

This spatial division of the world and the subsequent allocation to States of the other objects of international law form the fundamental premises in the legal regulation of the relations between States, which are remarkable in the neatness of their structure. Within national territory, the presumption is in favour of the freedom of each State to act as it pleases unless there is a rule of international law or a legally binding treaty provision limiting that freedom of action.[4] By the same token, the presumption is against any State being entitled to exercise territorial jurisdiction in the territory of another State, unless there is a rule of international law or an applicable treaty provision permitting it. In areas not subject to the territorial sovereignty of any State, be they *territorium nullius, territorium extra commercium* or the common heritage of mankind, the presumption is in favour of a State exercising jurisdiction over entities possessing its nationality, while against its being entitled to exercise jurisdiction over entities of foreign nationality, always subject to specific rules of general international law or applicable treaty provisions to the contrary.

IV. The Concept of Nationality

Nationality denotes a special legal bond recognized by international law between a State and various *objects* of international law, be they human beings, corporate bodies or inanimate objects. By conferring its nationality on an object of international law, a State claims and treats the latter as a component of the national community. Under general international law, a State, on the one hand, retains its authority—its jurisdiction—over its nationals even when they are outside its territory. On the other hand, a State's nationals, including their property, continue to receive its protection when they are

---

[4] See PCIJ: *The Lotus* (1927), A.10, p. 18.

abroad, in particular *vis-à-vis* other States. Any injury to one of its nationals by a foreign State is an injury to the State itself.[5]

Traditionally, nationality has been granted to individuals, bodies corporate, ships,[6] and aircraft[7]. Over the centuries, general international law has evolved a number of specific rules regarding the rights which a State is entitled to claim *vis-à-vis* other States in respect of individuals, corporations, ships and aircraft possessing its nationality, as well as the duties which at the same time it owes them. In addition a State may have concluded agreements with other States securing from the latter specific benefits or treatments for its nationals, or assuming specific duties. A State has a right to expect other States to treat its nationals in accordance with these rules of international law and all applicable treaty provisions, and at the same time a duty to fulfil any obligation towards other States that may be incumbent upon it in this regard, including its obligation to ensure that any restrictions imposed on its nationals are duly enforced.

The concept of nationality is thus not just a simple symbol without any significance. It represents a number of assumptions and carries with it a number of legally recognized consequences, which dovetail into a complex of other well established rules of international law. It is also the normal conduit through which benefits can be conferred and restrictions imposed on objects of international law through their respective national States by either general international law or by treaties, and the customary channel whereby international law reaches out to individual objects of international law.

V. Nationality and the Three Types of State Jurisdiction

From the standpoint of international law, the division or distribution of State powers throughout the world is very clear, and is designed, as much as possible, to avoid possible conflicts in the exercise of such powers. General international law divides State sovereignty and its manifestations, namely, State jurisdictions, into three types: *territorial* jurisdiction, *quasi-territorial* jurisdiction, and *personal* jurisdiction.

How general international law seeks to avoid conflicts of State jurisdiction is first to restrict each type of a State's jurisdiction to a very specific category of objects of international law, all stamped with the particular national character of that State. Thus normally a State enjoys exclusive *territorial jurisdiction* only over its own national territory, including all persons and things

---

[5] See PCIJ: *Mavrommatis Palestine Concessions* (Jd.) (1924), A.12.

[6] Cf. Art. 91 of the United Nations Convention on the Law of the Sea, 1982, which, although [at the time of writing] it is not yet in force, may already, especially in this regard, be considered to be declaratory of general international law, provides: '. . . Ships have the nationality of the State whose flag they are entitled to fly . . .'

[7] Art. 17 of the 1944 Chicago Convention on International Civil Aviation provides: 'Aircraft have the nationality of the State in which they are registered'.

therein, and enjoys exclusive extraterritorial jurisdiction only over its own nationals.

However by the nature of things, the extraterritorial jurisdiction which a State possesses under international law over ships and aircraft of its nationality differs somewhat from that over individuals or bodies corporate that are its nationals. This difference springs from the fact that the former are means of transport which often carry large numbers of persons and cargo through parts of the world, such as in particular the high seas, which are not subject to the territorial sovereignty and hence the laws of any State. It follows that unless the national State of the ship or aircraft is recognized to have special authority over these craft, lawlessness may prevail when they are, for instance, on or over the high seas. Consequently, the jurisdiction which the national State exercises over ships and aircraft of its nationality is wider than that over individuals or bodies corporate that also have its nationality. Jurisdiction over the former applies to not only the craft themselves but also all persons and things on board, whilst jurisdiction over the latter applies only to the persons themselves, whether individual or corporate, and indirectly through them to their property. Hence, the former type of State jurisdiction is termed quasi-territorial, whilst the latter personal. The term quasi-territorial is used not because ships and aircraft are considered integral parts of the national territory as they sometimes were so thought of long ago, but simply because a State's jurisdiction over ships and aircraft of its nationality is more akin to territorial jurisdiction than personal jurisdiction.

This authority which the State exercises over these respective objects of international law is recognized by other States and protected by international law. However, as Judge Huber said in the *Palmas Case*, 'This right has as corollary a duty.' In the case of exclusive territorial jurisdiction over national territory, the duty consists in, in the words of the same arbitrator, 'the obligation to protect within the territory the rights of other States'.[8]

The same applies *mutatis mutandis* to a State's quasi-territorial and personal jurisdictions over ships, aircraft, and persons of its nationality. To the extent to which general international law or special treaty provisions impose an obligation on a State to ensure that those under its authority, including ships, aircraft, and persons of its nationality, behave in a certain way, a State is internationally responsible for seeing that they do so behave, at least to the extent of its legal capability of doing so.

VI. The Two Elements of State Jurisdiction

Mention has just been made of the possibility that a State's responsibility for the conduct of those of its nationality may be limited by the extent of its legal

[8]   3 *RIAA*, p. 829, at p. 839.

capability to enforce its laws in their regard. This is because at times a State's quasi-territorial jurisdiction and personal jurisdiction over its nationals may have to give way to the jurisdiction of another State. International law has in fact a very neat way of resolving potential conflicts of State jurisdiction. It does so first of all by dividing State jurisdiction into separate elements. This distinction is not always fully appreciated, and there is often much confusion over so-called concurrent jurisdiction. The two elements of State jurisdiction are *jurisfaction* and *jurisaction*.[9]

On the one hand, *jurisfaction* represents the normative element of State jurisdiction which entitles a State to make laws or take decisions, including judicial decisions, with legally binding effect within its own territory or world-wide extraterritorially. *Jurisaction*, on the other hand, represents the concrete element of State jurisdiction which enables a State physically to carry out the functions of a State by setting up machinery to make laws and to take decisions, or actually to implement and to enforce its laws and decisions.

Subject to limits, international law permits the jurisfactions of different States to be concurrent with the result that, for example, a national of State A on board a ship of the nationality of State B which is berthed in a harbour in State C is at one and the same time under the jurisfactions and laws of all three States. The same is not true of jurisaction. International law establishes a strict hierarchy among jurisactions. In case of concurrence, territorial jurisaction overrides both quasi-territorial and personal jurisactions, whilst quasi-territorial jurisaction overrides personal jurisaction. Thus, in the above example, while the ship is in harbour, the territorial jurisaction of State C prevails over the quasi-territorial jurisaction of States B and the personal jurisaction of State A. When the ship moves onto the high seas, the quasi-territorial jurisaction of the flag State of the ship prevails, and if the person lands on a territory that belongs to no State, only his national State is entitled to exercise personal jurisaction over him. This represents the basic position in international law, which is subject to modification by specific rules of general international law, such as those on piracy, and special agreements between States. But these are exceptions that prove the rule.

The system of hierarchy among jurisactions means that normally at any given time and place, there can be only one State that is entitled actually to exercise jurisaction, thus obviating any conflict at least in the actual and physical exercise of State powers.

This hierarchy of jurisactions does not mean, however, that laws of the national State of ships, aircraft, and persons are thereby abrogated or annulled if such ships, aircraft, or persons are in the territory of another State. Such laws remain binding because jurisfactions can be concurrent. It is only

---

[9] On the notion of State jurisdiction, see B. Cheng, 'Crimes on Board Aircraft', 12 *CLP* (1959), p. 177, and B. Cheng, 'The Extraterrestrial Application of International Law', 18 *CLP* (1965), p. 132 [Ch. 5 above].

the national State's jurisaction that is in abeyance, which will immediately reassert itself as soon as these ships, aircraft, or persons are no longer under a superior foreign jurisaction.

Thus, although it is true that a State may not be able to enforce its laws in respect of ships, aircraft, and persons of its nationality while they are under a superior foreign jurisaction, it regains this capability when they remove themselves or *are removed* from such superior foreign jurisaction. To the extent to which the rights of a foreign State might be affected by a failure of a State to enforce its laws in regard to its nationals, including ships and aircraft of its nationality, while it might not be held responsible for such a failure if these nationals are effectively under a superior foreign jurisaction at the time, its ultimate responsibility may depend on what efforts it makes to regain control, for instance, through voluntary repatriation or extradition of its nationals from under a superior foreign jurisaction. From this point of view, while it is true that *ad impossibile nemo tenetur* (i.e., no one is held liable for not doing what is objectively the impossible), it is hardly necessary to recall what the arbitral tribunal said in the *Alabama Arbitration* (1872):

The government of Her Britannic Majesty cannot justify itself for a failure in due diligence on the plea of insufficiency of the legal means which it possessed.[10]

In the case of *The Alabama* the requisite legal means were within the power of the State to make available. Thus, to the extent to which it is by employing due diligence possible, or it is within the power of a State through due diligence to make it possible for it, to enforce its laws in regard to its subjects, who are linked to it by the concept of nationality, in order to ensure its observance through them of its international obligations that are of such a nature that they can be breached by acts or omissions of its nationals, a State is under general international law responsible to other subjects of international law entitled to expect those obligations to be respected, for any breach of those obligations. An example would the breach by fishing fleets of a State's nationality of fishing quotas agreed with another State. This point is of particular relevance in understanding the extent of a contracting State's obligations under Article VI of the Space Treaty, as will be seen later.

All in all, it would appear that general international law, in the concept of nationality whether applied to inanimate objects or to persons, has developed a system which is clear, logical and consistent in its structure, and well tried and well-understood by all concerned in its operation. It is found, in practice, to minimize conflict and confusion. This is not to say that it is entirely free of problems, such as problems arising from double nationality or statelessness, but those are exceptions, in fact exceptions that prove the rule.

---

[10] Moore, 1 *International Arbitrations*, p. 495, at p. 656. For a discussion of the *Alabama Arbitration* on this point and the maxim *Ad impossibile nemo tenetur*, see Cheng, *General Principles of Law*, pp. 221–3, 227 n. 30, and Ch. 8 generally.

VII. Space Objects and Nationality

However, up to now, space law has carefully eschewed the concept of nationality in regard to space objects. All the treaties relating to space developed under the auspices of the United Nations have avoided this concept. A number of factors may have contributed to this. Among them, the following have probably all played a rôle: the novelty of the situation combined with fear of the unknown; preoccupation with ensuring absolute State responsibility; the anxiety of many States that they would not be able to afford to engage in space activities individually and could do so only co-operatively, through international joint efforts or membership of specialized international organizations, in which case it might have been thought that the concept of nationality might be difficult to apply; lack of anticipation that space activities would so soon be undertaken to such an extent by non-governmental entities; plus perhaps certain difficulties which were at the time being encountered with the concept of nationality in air law which led eventually to the adoption of a new Article 83*bis* to the 1944 Chicago Convention on International Civil Aviation in September 1980.[11]

Whatever may have been the reason, States have so far refrained from conferring nationality on spacecraft. Instead, in the various multilateral treaties relating to outer space drawn up under the auspices of the United Nations, they have resorted to a number of other devices.

VIII. The UN Sponsored Treaties on Space

In the 1967 Treaty on Principles Governing the Activities of States in the Exploration and Use of Outer Space (the Space Treaty), firstly Article VI makes 'States Parties to the Treaty . . . bear international responsibility for national activities in outer space . . . , whether such activities are carried on by governmental agencies or by non-governmental entities.' Secondly, Article VII renders four categories of States that may be associated with the launching of a space object 'internationally liable for damage to another State Party to the Treaty or to its natural or juridical persons by such object'. The four categories of State that may be liable are: (i) the State that 'launches . . . an object into outer space'; (ii) the State that 'procures the launching'; (iii) the State

---

[11] The Chicago Convention lays down various duties on the State of registry of an aircraft. This causes problems when aircraft are being leased, chartered or interchanged to operators of another country for long periods of time, when it becomes impracticable for the State of registry to perform those duties. Art. 83*bis* permits those duties by agreement to be transferred to another contracting State, with effect on other contracting parties to the Chicago Convention, provided that the agreement has been registered with and made public by the Council of the International Civil Aviation Organization or directly communicated to the other contracting State or States.

'from whose territory . . . an object is launched'; and (iv) the State from whose 'facility' an object is launched. Thirdly, Article VIII provides that the State of registry of a space object 'shall retain jurisdiction and control over such object, and over any personnel thereof, while in outer space or on a celestial body'. Fourthly, under Article IX, if a State Party 'has reason to believe that an activity or experiment planned by it *or its nationals* . . . would cause potentially harmful interference with activities of other States Parties . . . , it shall undertake appropriate international consultations . . .' Registration and not nationality has thus been chosen as the link establishing a State's jurisdiction over a space object, although various other connecting factors have also been used in relation to other matters.

The 1968 Agreement on the Rescue of Astronauts, the Return of Astronauts and the Return of Objects Launched into Outer Space (the Astronauts Agreement), unlike the Space Treaty, is the first multilateral treaty relating to space concluded under the auspices of the United Nations to recognize the possible independent legal existence of international organizations engaged in space activities (Article 6). Possibly for this reason it avoids any reference even to registration of space objects, not to mention nationality. Space objects and astronauts in distress shall be returned to 'the launching authority' which is defined as simply the State or 'international intergovernmental organization' 'responsible for launching', provided, in the case of an international organization, that it meets the conditions laid down in Article 6 of the Agreement.

The 1972 Convention on International Liability for Damage Caused by Space Objects (the Liability Convention), which spells out the conditions under which States (or maybe only States Parties?) may be held liable for damage caused by space objects follows to some extent the Astronauts Agreement. Going perhaps ever further than the Astronauts Agreement, it not only acknowledges the possible separate legal existence of international intergovernmental organizations engaged in space activities and permits them to become a kind of associate parties to the treaty, but also works out in detail the position of such organizations in the event of their becoming either claimants or respondents in claims arising under the Convention (Article XXII). The party liable under the Convention for damage caused by space objects is the 'launching State' and a 'launching State' is defined as '(i) A State which launches or procures the launching of a space object; (ii) A State from whose territory or facility a space object is launched.' Under Article XXII of the Convention, insofar as the substantive provisions of the Convention are concerned, the term 'States' applies also to international intergovernmental organizations, provided that such organizations satisfy certain conditions. Once again, the Convention avoids all references to registration.

Registration did not come to its own until the 1975 Convention on Registration of Objects Launched into Outer Space (the Registration

Convention), sometimes dubbed the 'Surprise Convention'. Article I of the Convention defines the 'launching State' in exactly the same terms as the Liability Convention, whilst its Article VII likewise permits international intergovernmental organizations that fulfil certain conditions, through a declaration of acceptance, to share the same rights and duties as parties to the Convention. Article II of the Convention provides:

1. When a space object is launched into earth orbit or beyond, the launching State shall register the space object . . . in an . . . registry which it shall maintain . . .

2. Where there are two or more launching States in respect of any such space object, they shall jointly determine which one of them shall register the object . . . , *bearing in mind* the provisions of article VIII of the [Space] Treaty . . . , and *without prejudice* to appropriate agreements concluded or to be concluded among the launching States on jurisdiction and control over the space object and over any personnel thereof.[12]

The Convention further provides that there shall be a United Nations Register, in which shall be recorded various information with which the State of Registry shall supply the Secretary-General. It should perhaps be noted that under Article II, States, when concluding agreements among them to arrange which State shall exercise jurisdiction and control over an space object jointly launched by them, need only to 'bear in mind' Article VIII of the Space Treaty. Article VIII is thus regarded as merely optional. Moreover, information regarding such arrangements need not be recorded in the national register nor supplied to the United Nations.

What has just been said appears applicable equally to space objects registered with one of the recognized international intergovernmental organizations that have accepted the rights and obligations of the Registration Convention under its Article VII, when they launch space objects jointly with one or more States. In a letter dated 19 September 1975 from Mr E. Suy, the Legal Counsel of the United Nations, addressed to Mr H. Kaltenecker, Deputy Director of the European Space Agency (ESA) in charge of International Affairs, the former stated *inter alia*:

Where an international intergovernmental organization launches a space object jointly with one or more States, the provisions of paragraph 2 of Article II are relevant. In other words, the organization and the States may enter into appropriate agreement on jurisdiction and control over the space object and over any personnel thereof, if it is decided that the organization should register the space object.[13]

What happens in such cases, as in other cases of joint launching, is that, under the Registration Convention, arrangements may be made to provide for the space object to be registered in State A and jurisdiction and control to be

---

[12] Italics added.
[13] I am grateful to Monsieur G. Lafferanderie, Legal Adviser of the European Space Agency, for kindly supplying me with a copy of this letter.

exercised in State B. A discrepancy can thus lawfully exist between registration and jurisdiction, notwithstanding Article VIII of the Space Treaty.

A perhaps unintended result of Article II of the Registration Convention is that it opens the door to the possibility of having the equivalent of 'flags of convenience' in space. In any event, since there is no provision for any such arrangements under Article II to be registered, notified to third States or given any publicity, much confusion can arise as to which State has jurisdiction and control over a given space object and consequently which system of law is applicable on board. Third parties can easily be misled, and Article VIII of the Space Treaty loses all credibility in all cases of joint launching. From this point of view, space law can at least take a leaf from Article 83*bis* of the 1944 Chicago Convention on International Civil Aviation, where permitted deviations from the Convention by separate agreement between members are not effective *vis-à-vis* other parties to the Convention unless they have been communicated directly to other members or been registered with, and made public by, the International Civil Aviation Organization.[14]

Four years after the Registration Convention, the Agreement Governing the Activities of States on the Moon and Other Celestial Bodies (the Moon Treaty) was adopted in 1979. No explicit reference is made to registration. Instead, Article 12 provides *inter alia*:

1. States Parties shall retain jurisdiction and control over their personnel, vehicles, equipment, facilities, stations and installations on the moon. The ownership of space vehicles, equipment, facilities, stations and installations shall not be affected by their presence on the moon.

2. Vehicles, installations and equipment or their component parts found in places other than their intended location shall be dealt with in accordance with article 5 of the [Astronauts] Agreement . . .

Now, in accordance with Article 5 of the Astronauts Agreement, such objects should be returned to the 'launching authority'. This being the case, one wonders whether in paragraph 1, when the Moon Treaty refers to the State retaining jurisdiction, it is referring to the owner-State, the launching authority, or the State of registry. In any case, no provision has been made specifically for stations and installations on the moon to be, as such, registered, apart from registration of the various component parts, unless they are launched onto the moon as complete and individual units. It would appear to follow that, when components of a station have been launched by, and are registered in, different States, more than one State would be simultaneously exercising jurisdiction over a station, each over the component part registered with it, unless of course the Moon Treaty has in mind that whichever State owns or operates the station shall alone exercise jurisdiction and control over it, irrespective of

---

[14] See n. 11 above.

whether or not various parts of the station may have been launched by, and are registered in, different States.

Article 12 of the Moon Treaty is highly ambiguous. In referring to States Parties' 'facilities, stations and installations', it can well be using the criterion of ownership by the State or by nationals, physical or corporate, for the attribution of jurisdiction and control over such objects, thus brushing aside the link of registration. In fact, the Moon Treaty appears to extend this criterion to persons on the moon and other celestial bodies in the solar system other than the earth; for Article 12 also speaks of States Parties retaining jurisdiction and control over 'their personnel' directly and independently of the spacecraft to which the personnel belong. This would seem to be a departure from the Space Treaty, the Astronauts Agreement and the Registration Convention which appear all to submit the personnel of a spacecraft, even when they may be outside a spacecraft, to the jurisdiction of the State exercising jurisdiction over the spacecraft. However, in speaking of 'personnel', instead of 'nationals', the Moon Treaty would seem to base jurisdiction over such persons not on their nationality, but perhaps on their being employed or controlled by the State, on the nationality of their employer, or the nationality of the owners or operators of the facilities, stations or installations to which these personnel are attached.

If this is what the Moon Treaty has in mind, there are dangerous implications. The danger consists in States either directly or through their nationals, by establishing facilities, stations and installations on the moon, in effect exercising the equivalent of territorial jurisdiction over the premises of such facilities, stations, and installations. The saving grace is perhaps that seemingly, although by no means certain, under Article 12 of the Moon Treaty, any personnel belonging to other States Parties who happen to be present in such facilities, stations, and installations would remain under the jurisdiction and control of their 'own' State.

IX. Inconsistencies, Ambiguities, and Pitfalls

Problems arising from the space treaties sponsored by the United Nations in this regard do not stop there. Article VI of the Space Treaty appears to assimilate all 'national activities' carried out by 'non-governmental entities' to activities of 'governmental agencies', at least from the standpoint of international responsibility. From this point of view, in regard to 'national activities in outer space by non-governmental entities', parties to the treaty assume three separate and different obligations, the exact extent of which is not altogether clear.

First, States parties are obliged to ensure that national activities by non-governmental entities, as well as government agencies, are 'carried out in conformity with the provisions of the present Treaty'.

Secondly, States parties are obliged to subject activities of non-governmental entities to 'authorization and continuing supervision'. The extent to which this duty of supervision goes and the exact implications of this duty are not entirely clear and depend largely on the third obligation. Thirdly, States parties 'bear international responsibility for national activities in outer space . . . by non-governmental entities', in the same way as for those by 'governmental agencies'. Two interpretations of this assumption of direct State responsibility for non-governmental activities are possible: (i) this responsibility exists solely for what would be breaches of rules of international law and international obligations of the States parties, were the non-governmental activities governmental activities; (ii) this responsibility exists even in respect of breaches of rules and obligations under domestic and private law, such as contracts and intellectual property, in what would be a total assimilation of such non-governmental activities to governmental activities.

Since the parties' responsibility is qualified as 'international', perhaps interpretation (i) is closer to the intention of the parties, but interpretation (ii) cannot be altogether excluded. Moreover, further complications arise from the interpretation of the expression 'national activities'.

Such activities include obviously activities by governmental agencies. As regards activities by non-governmental entities, opinions seem to differ. The United States[15] and Sweden[16], in their domestic legislation, extend their control and supervision to all space activities within their territory, as well as those of their nationals outside their country. The United Kingdom, however, in its Outer Space Act 1986,[17] following perhaps the example of Article IX of the Space Treaty, refers only to United Kingdom nationals even in the United Kingdom.

However, to the extent that responsibility should go hand in hand with control, it would appear that it should extend to all areas, objects, and persons over which a State enjoys jurisdiction, i.e., to all activities conducted within national territory, on board or from ships and aircraft of a State's nationality, as well as those by its nationals, wherever such ships, aircraft or nationals may be. Whilst such responsibility may be held in abeyance while such ships, aircraft and nationals are under an overriding jurisaction, responsibility may nevertheless arise if a State does not use due diligence in seeking to regain its effective jurisaction over such objects or persons in order to comply with its international obligation. From this point of view, Article IX of the Space Treaty and the several national laws may all be found wanting, especially now that launching space objects from the air is more than just a possibility.

[15] Commercial Space Launch Act, 49 USC App. 2601 (1988).
[16] Swedish Space Activities Act of 1982 (1982:963). The Act is supplemented by a decree, Decree on Space Activities (1982:1069). See J. Reifarth, 'Nationale Weltraumgesetze in Europa', 36 *ZLW* (1987), p. 11.
[17] 1986, c. 38.

'National activities' must include activities conducted by all persons within a State's jurisdiction, (whether territorial, quasi-territorial, or personal), wherever they may be and whatever their nationality.

Insofar as space objects are concerned, Article VIII of the Space Treaty links jurisdiction to registration, without, however, specifying whether all space objects have to be registered and the consequences of non-registration. But, as has been mentioned before, both the Astronauts Agreement and the Liability Convention avoid any mention of registration and use the concept of the 'launching authority' or the 'launching State' instead, as the connecting factor between a space object and a subject of international law.

Inasmuch as Article VIII of the Space Treaty places the personnel of a space object within the jurisdiction of the State of registry, this jurisdiction appears somewhat similar to the quasi-territorial jurisdiction enjoyed by flag-States of ships and aircraft over their ships and aircraft. However, Article VIII, in avoiding the concept of nationality, when it specifies only personnel as being within the jurisdiction of the State of registry, raises the question whether this jurisdiction is exactly the same as that of flag-States over ships and aircraft, inasmuch as no mention has been made of other persons that may be on board, such as passengers. A straightforward grant of nationality to space objects in accordance with well-established rules of international law would have avoided any such ambiguity or *lacunae*.

The present arrangement gives rise to further problems. In specifying deliberately that the State of registry retains jurisdiction over the personnel *of* a spacecraft rather than *on board* a spacecraft in order to cover the astronaut engaged in a space or moon walk outside the spacecraft, Article VIII of the Space Treaty leaves in doubt the status of personnel of a spacecraft registered in State A when visiting a spacecraft registered in State B (when in outer space). A literal reading of Article VIII would mean that such personnel would remain under the jurisdiction of State A, thus preventing State B or, for that matter, the commander of the spacecraft being visited from exercising jurisdiction over the visitor who may be going berserk. If the traditional concept of nationality were used, the quasi-territorial jurisaction of State B would override the concurrent personal jurisaction of State A, and there would be no problem.

The position is further complicated by the fact, which has already been mentioned before,[18] that in the light of Article II of the Registration Convention, even as among contracting States, Article VIII of the Space Treaty is not regarded as mandatory with the result that, especially in joint launches, changes may be made at will by agreement between the parties concerned without the consent of the other contracting parties or their knowledge. In this regard, one may be permitted to wonder whether Article 5(2) of

---

[18] See text to n. 13 above and thereabouts.

the 1988 Intergovernmental Agreement (IGA) between the United States, ESA on behalf of its members, Japan, and Canada on the Permanently Manned Civil Space Station is intended to be an interpretation or a modification of Article VIII of the Space Treaty when it provides:

Pursuant to Article VIII of the Outer Space Treaty and Article II of the Registration Convention, each Partner shall retain jurisdiction and control over the elements it registers in accordance with paragraph 1 above and over personnel in or on the Space Station *who are its nationals* . . .[19]

Although Article 5(2) purports to follow Article VIII of the Space Treaty, yet by deliberately departing from the latter's wording, it creates additional problems. Instead of placing both the element and its personnel under the jurisdiction of the State of registry, it appears to separate the two. The element, seemingly excluding all persons on board who either form part of its personnel or happen to be there, comes under the jurisdiction of the State of registry, whilst persons who are nationals of partners of the Space Station come under their respective national States. The jurisdiction of the national State of the individuals supersedes the jurisdiction of the State of registry. But then what happens to a person who is not a national of any of the partners? What happens to a national of one partner who forms part of the personnel of an element registered with another partner, or who simply visits it and commits what appears to be an offence there? In any case, where do all these leave Article VIII of the Space Treaty? In addition, the matter is further complicated by Article 22(2) of the Intergovernmental Agreement which confers a kind of special 'extra-element' jurisdiction on the United States over non-United States nationals on or in a non-United States element in certain circumstances.

Finally, the Moon Treaty has completely befuddled the whole area by seemingly introducing jurisdictional links based on ownership, operational control, or even employment, in addition to launching and registration.

X. Re-thinking Required

What is clear from this brief survey of in particular the provisions of the various United Nations treaties on outer space in the way they have dealt with the relationship between subjects of international law and space objects, while studiously avoiding the concept of nationality, is the tangled mess of inconsistencies, ambiguities, and pitfalls in which they have landed themselves. Part of the explanation for this situation may perhaps be found in the fact that these treaties were drawn up primarily during the period when space activities were still very much in the exploration stage and were thought to be capable

---

[19] Italics added.

of being undertaken for a long time to come only by States either individually or through international organizations, with private enterprise being treated only as a distant possibility. In particular, the question which private persons involved in space, their activities, their means of transport, and their hardware should be allocated to the jurisdiction and control of which subjects of international law has not received the degree of attention which the rapid developments in space show that it now urgently deserves.

XI. Nationality for Space Objects

All in all, what seems needed is serious reconsideration whether, after all, especially since commercial and private activities in outer space have now fully taken off,[20] it would not be best to revert to the well-established concept of nationality in linking space objects to the subjects of international law. Nationality would denote that the national State enjoys quasi-territorial jurisdiction, including quasi-territorial jurisaction, over any space object bearing its nationality, including all persons and things on board or constructively on board. This quasi-territorial jurisaction would override all concurrent personal jurisactions of the national States of any foreigners who may be on board, but would give way to the territorial jurisaction of any State in which the space object may land intentionally or by accident. Such nationality may depend on registration, as is the case with aircraft, or on a combination of either registration or ownership, as is the case with ships[21]. However, since a convention on registration already exists, registration would probably prove simpler. Obviously some modification of both Article VIII of the Space Treaty and the Registration Convention will be necessary, although arguably such modifications might be accomplished by *de facto* amendments through subsequent practice accompanied with the requisite *opinio generalis juris generalis*[22]. This can be accomplished even instantaneously, if States are so minded.[23]

---

[20] Cf. B. Cheng, 'The Commercial Development of Space: The Need for New Treaties', 19 *JSL* (1991), p. 17 [Ch. 25 below].

[21] In most countries, the nationality of ships depends on registration. The nationality of British ships depends, however, on ownership. British ships are ships owned by British nationals, irrespective of registration. See B. Cheng, 'State Ships and State Aircraft', 11 *CLP* (1958), p. 225.

[22] See Cheng (1983), loc. cit. in n. 1 above, at pp. 533 ff.

[23] On the concept of instant 'customary' or general international law, see B. Cheng, 'United Nations Resolutions on Outer Space: "Instant" International Customary Law?', 5 *Indian JIL* (1965), p. 23 [Ch. 7 above]; R. Y. Jennings, 'The Identification of International Law', in Cheng (ed.), *International Law* (1982), p. 3, esp. pp. 4–6; and R. R. Baxter, 'Treaties and Custom', Hague *Recueil* (1970–I), p. 25, at pp. 44, 67, and *passim*. Regrettably, it has sometimes been dismissed rather offhandedly without further ado as a simple contradiction in terms by those who obviously have little notion of the true nature of what Art. 38.1.(b) of the Statute of the International Court of Justice designates as, and what international lawyers out of tradition habitually call, 'international custom', and who, moreover, either have not read the article at all or, if they have read it,

Nationality of spacecraft may also assist in resolving, if not wholly at least in part, some of the problems in the interpretation of Article VI of the Space Treaty on international responsibility for 'national activities' in outer space. Activities of, or from on board, space objects bearing a State's nationality will clearly form part of 'national activities' which require 'the authorization and continuing supervision' of the national State and for which the national State, under Article VI of the Space Treaty, shall bear 'international responsibility'.

Nationality for spacecraft would sweep away much of the confusion which now prevails regarding jurisdiction over space objects, confusion inherent in the various treaties on outer space which has been made more confounded by *inter alia* Article II of the Registration Convention. Yet as Article 83*bis* of the Chicago Convention shows,[24] once the cobweb of confusion has been cleared away, and the premises on which further rules and arrangements are to be built have been made clear and firm by adopting well-tried concepts, there is nothing to prevent alternative arrangements from being made to meet special requirements, provided that such arrangements are effective only between the parties concerned, unless third parties have agreed thereto through prior or subsequent consent.

In legal relations, international as well as national, public as well as private, there is everything to be said for clarity, consistency, and knowability. It is submitted that nationality for space objects will be an effective step in that direction.

have completely failed to grasp its meaning, or even bigotedly refused to go beyond the oxymoron and to consider the reasoning with care and objectivity.

[24] See n. 11 above.

18

Definitional Issues in Space Law: 'Space Objects', 'Astronauts', and Related Expressions*

I. Introduction

Space law has grown up at an extremely fast rate in a very short time. Much of international space law has been developed through the United Nations, principally in the form of the five treaties that it has drafted and presented to States for their acceptance.

These are the Treaty on Principles Governing the Activities of States in the Exploration and Use of Outer Space, including the Moon and Other Celestial Bodies of 27 January 1967 (the Space Treaty), the Agreement on the Rescue of Astronauts, the Return of Astronauts and the Return of Objects Launched into Outer Space of 22 April 1968 (the Astronauts Agreement), the Convention on International Liability for Damage Caused by Space Objects of 29 March 1972 (the Liability Convention), the Convention on Registration on Objects Launched into Outer Space of 14 January 1975 (the Registration Convention), and the Agreement Governing the Activities of States on the Moon and Other Celestial Bodies of 5 December 1979 (the Moon Treaty) .

Owing partly to the speed of the development of astronautics, and partly to a lack of co-ordination, some of the terms and phraseology used in these treaties are increasingly being seen as, if not exactly inconsistent, at least ambiguous, confusing, or inadequate. Among these terms are 'space objects' and 'astronauts', and some of their related expressions, such as 'personnel of spacecraft'.

This chapter seeks to unravel the meanings of these terms in international space law, especially in the context of the several treaties relating to outer space elaborated by the United Nations.[1]

---

* First published in 34 *Space Law Colloquium* (1991), pp. 17–27.

[1] Cf. B. Cheng, 'Astronauts', in Bernhardt (ed.), 11 *Ency. PIL* (1989), pp. 40–3 [Ch. 15 above]; Id., 'Spacecraft, Satellites and Space Objects', *ibid.*, pp. 309–17 [Ch. 16 above]; G. Lafferanderie, 'Pour une charte de l'astronaute', 12 *AASL* (1987), pp. 263–77; Various authors, 'Legal Status of Artificial Space Objects', 24 *Space Law Colloquium* (1981), pp. 82–115; A. Górbiel, 'Space Objects in International Law', 21 *Il Diritto Aereo* (1982), pp. 75–89.

II. 'Space Objects' and Related Expressions

A. *'Space Objects' and 'Objects Launched into Outer Space'*

The expression 'object launched into outer space' is one of the most commonly used in the various United Nations sponsored treaties relating to outer space. It is found, for example, in Article VIII of the Space Treaty. The Space Treaty also speaks of the 'launching of' 'objects' into outer space (Article VII). Although the question was discussed during the drafting of the Liability Convention, no real definition was adopted apart from what is to be found in Article 1(d).[2] For the moment, we may perhaps equate 'space object' with 'object launched into outer space'.

On this assumption, the various treaties drafted by the United Nations appear superficially to be fairly consistent, inasmuch as the term 'space object' figures in all of them. Thus the Astronauts Agreement in both its Title and paragraph 1 of its Preamble speaks of 'objects launched into outer space', while its Article 5 repeatedly uses the term 'space object'. The Liability Convention too adheres most faithfully to the term 'space object', and includes it in its Title.

This is, however, no longer true when one comes to the subsequent Registration Convention and the still later Moon Treaty.

B. *'Non-Space Objects' Launched into Outer Space?*

In the Registration Convention one finds initially the term 'space object' in a number of its provisions (Preamble, paragraphs 4, 7; Articles I, II, IV, V, VI), and the phrase 'objects launched into outer space' in the Title of the Convention and in several paragraphs of its Preamble (2, 3, 5, 6, 8). This leads one to believe that the two expressions are used interchangeably, as in previous treaties.

However, paragraph 5 of the Preamble refers to 'space objects launched into outer space'. One wonders, therefore, whether there are objects launched into outer space that are not 'space objects', and whether the two expressions 'space objects' and 'objects launched into outer space' are in fact conterminous. The specific reference to *'space* objects launched into outer space' in paragraph 5 of the Preamble is echoed in the most crucial article in the Convention, namely, its Article II. Article II(1) seemingly makes a similar distinction between 'object' and 'space object' when it requires only *'space* objects launched into *earth orbit or beyond'* to be registered.

---

[2] See B. Cheng, 'Convention on International Liability for Damage Caused by Space Objects', in Jasentuliyana and Lee (eds.), 1 *Manual*, p. 83, at pp. 116–7 [Ch. 11 above, s.V.C.3: Space Object]. Cf. also the following definition proposed by Australia and Canada in 1964: ' "Space Object" means an object or any of its component parts which a launching State has launched or attempted to launch into outer space', A/AC.105/C.2/SR.106, p. 67.

The phrase 'launched into earth orbit or beyond' has doubtless come from the precursor of the Registration Convention, namely, Part B of the General Assembly Resolution 1721 (XVI) of 20 December 1962. This resolution established a voluntary system of registration of launchings. States which launched 'objects into orbit or beyond' were 'called upon' to provide the United Nations, which was to establish a registry, with information regarding the launching. The Registration Convention has, therefore, merely followed the precedent set in 1962 by Resolution 1721 in those very early days of astronautics. It has, however, slightly modified the terminology of the Resolution.

First, instead of merely referring to 'orbit and beyond', it now says 'earth orbit and beyond', which is more precise, but which in effect would not appear to make much difference. Basically, the use of this formula, in either form, is to exclude from the need of registration 'space objects' that are not being 'launched into earth orbit or beyond'.

Typical examples of what this formula intends to exempt from registration would be sounding rockets and ballistic missiles, which (or the payload of which) are not placed in any orbit but are intended either to return to the vicinity of the launch site or to land on their target on the earth. However, this formula would not appear to exempt objects such as the aerospace craft that are currently being discussed or the, at one time mooted, fractional orbital bombs (FOBS), provided that they do achieve at some stage a velocity which would have enabled them to complete at least a single orbit, even if in fact they were made to return before doing so. These would then all be, to use the phraseology of the Registration Convention, 'launched into earth orbit'. The Convention does not say that a space object must be intended to *complete* an orbit before it needs to be registered. The position here should not be confused with that under Article IV of the Space Treaty on the prohibition of stationing weapons of mass destruction in outer space. There the article speaks of placing such weapons 'in orbit *around* the earth' or *stationing* them there in any other manner.

C. *'Object' versus 'Space Object'*

Secondly, and this is of particular interest here, the Registration Convention has added before the word 'object' the qualifier 'space' and, under its Article II(1) a duty to register exists only '[w]hen a *space* object is launched into earth orbit or beyond'.

The question that immediately springs to mind is, is there a distinction between an 'object launched into earth orbit or beyond' and a *'space* object launched into earth orbit or beyond'? Now, under Article IV(1) of the Space Treaty, Parties 'undertake not to place in orbit around the earth any *objects* carrying nuclear weapons or any other kinds of weapons of mass destruction'.

The Moon Treaty contains a similar provision in its Article 3(3) applicable to all celestial bodies within the solar system other than the earth. Other instances of the use of the description 'object' without any qualification exist in the various treaties sponsored by the United Nations, such as Articles VII and VIII of the Space Treaty, the Title of the Astronauts Agreement and paragraph 1 of its Preamble, and the Title and paragraphs 2, 3, 6 and 8 of the Preamble of the Registration Convention itself.

Does Article II(1) of the Registration Convention really intend to say that a distinction exists between simple 'objects launched into earth orbit and beyond' as distinguished from 'space objects launched into earth orbit launched into earth orbit and beyond'? Does it, therefore, on the basis of the wording of Article IV of the Space Treaty and, in anticipation, Article 3(3) of the Moon Treaty, mean that 'objects' which are launched 'into earth orbit' around the earth or around any of the celestial bodies within the solar system carrying non-nuclear weapons which are not capable of 'mass destruction', such as a non-nuclear anti-satellite device, need not be registered?

If this were the intention, does it mean that the Registration Convention, its contracting parties, its draftsmen, namely, COPUOS, and its sponsors, namely, the United Nations' General Assembly, also intend that, in all the other treaties relating to outer space, there is a similar distinction between 'space objects' and simple 'objects launched into space'?

If this were so, does it mean that, whereas, on the one hand, under Article VII of the Space Treaty, contracting States are 'internationally liable for damage' caused by any 'object' they launch into space, on the other hand, under the Liability Convention, contracting States would only be liable for damage caused by '*space* objects' they launch into outer space; for the latter treaty uses consistently the expression 'space object'?

But whether all concerned wish to make such a distinction generally or merely for the purpose of Article II(1) of the Registration Convention, the distinction appears to be one without any difference. The reason is that neither the Registration Convention nor any of the other treaties relating to outer space sponsored by the United Nations provide any clue as to what may be the difference between an 'object' launched into outer space and an 'space object launched into outer space.'

One is consequently given no help by this formula in the Registration Convention in one's search for a definition of 'space object' or a clarification of its meaning. For the moment, one is driven back to the simple paraphrase 'object launched into outer space'.

D. 'Outer Space' versus 'Earth Orbit and Beyond'

It is possible that the addition of the qualifier 'space' to the phrase 'object launched into earth orbit or beyond' in Article II(1) of the Registration

Convention is intended to avoid the use of the expression 'outer space' while referring to orbits around the earth, at a time when doubt exists still as to the boundary of outer space, especially since this form of words is derived from that first used in 1962 in General Assembly Resolution 1721.

In this regard, it may be said that the formulas 'launched into orbit or beyond' and 'launched into earth orbit or beyond' are by no means clear. Much depends upon the specific meaning that is attributed to the expressions 'orbit', 'earth orbit' and particularly 'beyond'. Does such a formula mean to refer to only any object being launched into any orbit around the earth as well as any that having circumnavigated the earth in an earth orbit are propelled at a tangent to some part of outer space *beyond* that orbit, or does it mean simply that the object must be launched to some part of outer space *beyond* a height where an artificial earth satellite is able, or has been shown to be able, to orbit the earth? The former interpretation might exempt from registration, no doubt contrary to the intention of the Registration Convention, a space object on a trajectory that takes it straight out of the solar system without first entering into an earth orbit. The latter would, again very much contrary to the intention of the Registration Convention, include within the requirement of registration, objects which are launched beyond the lowest perigee height feasible for, or ever reached by, a satellite intending to complete, or having completed, an orbit around the earth; for, if so, sounding rockets or intercontinental ballistic missiles (ICBMs) that exceed such heights would require to be registered.

Or does this formula intend to say simply 'into earth orbit or anywhere in outer space beyond earth orbit', in other words, into any orbit around the earth or to anywhere beyond the farthest orbit around the earth? Put it another way: unless it is beyond the farthest orbit around the earth, it would have to be in some kind of earth orbit. Whilst such an interpretation or formulation would take care of both types of situation mentioned above, it may not quite cover the case of a space object which is on a direct trajectory for the moon. Should it also be exempted from registration?

However, this is much more a problem of registration. Insofar as the question of any possible distinction that may exist between 'object' and 'space object' is concerned, it does not appear that Article II(1) of the Registration Convention intends to draw any such distinction.

Similarly, instead of pointing to any possible difference that may exist between 'objects launched into outer space' and 'space objects launched into earth orbit or beyond', this article really serves to confirm that 'objects launched into earth orbit or beyond' are in fact '*space* objects', and thereby implies that outer space does begin where satellites are capable of completing a full or whole orbit around the earth, since it is calling any object that is capable of going into any earth orbit, even one with the lowest possible perigee a '*space* object'.

In sum, Article II(1) of the Registration Convention merely limits the requirement of registration to certain 'space objects'. It leaves intact the definition of space objects as simply 'objects launched into outer space' implied in fact in all the treaties relating to outer space sponsored by the United Nations.

E. Where is Outer Space?

If a 'space object' is simply an 'object launched into outer space', the question then arises, Where is outer space? This raises of course the perennial problem of the boundary of outer space that has been with us from even before the beginning of the space age. The question is still awaiting an agreed and authoritative solution, primarily because of the refusal of certain powers even to have it discussed, let alone resolved.[3] It is indeed ludicrous that so many years after the Space Treaty which clearly distinguishes, for instance, in its Article VII between what happens 'on the earth, in air space or in outer space', one is supposed to be still officially ignorant of, or indifferent to, where in law airspace ends and outer space begins.

However, notwithstanding the obscurantist and arrogant attitude of some super powers, since the first artificial earth satellite went into space in 1957, State practice has confirmed the rapid emergence of a rule of general international law which recognizes that all satellites that have hitherto been in orbit around the earth have, during the whole time they have been in orbit, remained in outer space and that they have not, while in orbit, at any time entered or violated the airspace of any State. It follows that at the altitude of the lowest perigee of the orbits of these satellites one must, in the eyes of general international law, already be in outer space. This point, as we have just seen, is in fact confirmed by Article II(1) of the Registration Convention. Any object that is 'launched into earth orbit'—any earth orbit, including the lowest—is *per se* a '*space* object'.

Technically the lowest perigee so far of any artificial satellite that has gone around the earth at least once is at 96 kilometres above the surface of the earth. The next one is at 104 kilometres. Although those may be isolated cases, there have been a fair number of artificial earth satellites with perigees between 110 and 130 kilometres. Above 130 kilometres, the number grows quite rapidly. On the basis of this evidence, it appears possible, insofar as general international law is concerned, irrespective of the opinion of geophysicists or astronautical engineers, just as the outer limit of a State's territorial sea is ultimately not dependent on the views of marine scientists or engineers, to maintain that, without prejudice to the question where in law airspace ends and outer space actually begins, one is arguably in outer space when one

---

[3] See B. Cheng, 'The Legal Status of Outer Space and Relevant Issues: Delimitation of Outer Space and Definition of Peaceful Use', 11 *JSL* (1983), p. 89, at pp. 89–98.

reaches 96 kilometres above the earth, clearly so at 110 kilometres, and definitely so at 130 kilometres.[4]

This being the case, it is possible to define a space object as any object that is being launched, or has been launched, into those heights and beyond, whether or not into earth orbit. Objects being launched beyond those heights are, in the eyes of general international law, being launched 'into outer space'.

This means that sounding rockets, ICBMs and any other objects which are being launched to those minimum heights and beyond are space objects. It is of interest to observe from this point of view that the United States does not exclude military space objects from the 1972 Liability Convention.[5]

F. From What Moment?

From what moment does an object become a space object? Whilst obviously a term can be given a specific meaning in a given treaty, some idea may nevertheless be gained from the various treaties relating to outer space sponsored by the United Nations as to what they think is the general answer to this question.

Thus, if one examines Article VII of the Space Treaty, one finds that it speaks of each State party 'that launches or procures the launching of an object into outer space' and each State party 'from whose territory or facility an object launched' being internationally liable for damage caused 'by such object'. A similar form of words is to be found in Article I(c) of the Liability Convention and Article I(a) of the Registration Convention in the definition of the 'launching State'.

It would appear from this phraseology that when the rest of the respective treaties is referring to 'space objects', reference would be made to objects that are being launched as well as those already launched into outer space. In other words, the objects need not have reached outer space. This means that an object destined for outer space comes within the notion of 'space object' at the latest from the moment that its launching commences. Unless this were the interpretation, Article VII of the Space Treaty, and all relevant provisions of both the Astronauts Agreement and of the Liability Convention would not apply to objects that fail to reach outer space. This would obviously be contrary to the intention of the draftsmen of and contracting parties to the respective treaties.

This view finds support in both Article I(b) and Article VII of the Liability Convention. The former provides very explicitly that ' "launching" includes

---

[4] See B. Cheng, 'The Legal Régime of Airspace and Outer Space: The Boundary Problem—Functionalism *versus* Spatialism: The Major Premises', 5 *AASL* (1980), p. 323, esp. at 356 [Ch. 14 above, s. X: The Limit between Outer Space and Territorial Space].

[5] See US Senate, *Report from the Committee on Foreign Relations on the Convention on International Liability for Damage Caused by Space Objects*, 92d Congress, 2d Session, Executive Report No. 92–38 (1972), p. 7.

attempted launching', whilst the latter excludes from the scope of the Convention foreign nationals who participate in the operation of space object 'from the time of its launching or at any stage thereafter'. The following inferences can be drawn from Article VII: (i) prior to launching, the object would not be considered a space object, and regulation by the Convention of that period is not necessary, as the Convention deals only with liability for damage caused by 'space objects'; (ii) 'from the time of its launching', such an object would have become a 'space object' which, but for this exclusion in Article VII(b), would fall within the scope of the Convention. Under Article I(b), any object that is the object of a failed launching would nevertheless be an object that was being launched into outer space and hence a space object.

G. Non-Man-Made Space Objects?

The Moon Treaty in its Article 3(2) refers to 'man-made space objects', thus raising the question whether all 'space objects' have to be man-made or whether there are 'man-made' and 'non-man-made' space objects. For instance, would a non-man-made object launched into outer space be nevertheless a 'space object' for the purpose of the Liability Convention or, for that matter, under any of the other treaties relating to outer space sponsored by the United Nations?

It is submitted that there is no real distinction in the various treaties between man-made and non-man-made objects that have been launched into outer space, including the moon and other celestial bodies, provided of course that they have been launched by human agency, and the introduction of the reference to 'man-made space objects' in Article 3(2) of the Moon Treaty is perhaps not altogether felicitous.

This phrase 'man-made space objects' occurs in paragraph 2 of Article 3 of the Treaty which prohibits not only '[a]ny threat or use of force or any other hostile act or threat of hostile act on the moon', but also 'the use of the moon in order to commit any such act or to engage in any such threat in relation to the earth, the moon, spacecraft, the personnel of spacecraft or man-made space objects'. The authors of the treaty, in referring to 'man-made space objects' here, obviously have in mind such objects as an unmanned communications satellite in outer space, but it is not believed that they intend to exclude from this prohibition the use of the moon to threaten the existence of, for instance, a colony of animals on board a space station in outer space. To regard them as 'the personnel' of the space station would be putting too much of a strain on the language. Perhaps a more precise formulation of what the Treaty calls 'man-made space objects' would be 'objects launched into outer space by humans' or 'other objects launched into outer space by humans', after having just mentioned 'spacecraft and the personnel of spacecraft'.

H. 'Space Vehicles' and 'Spacecraft'

Article V of the Space Treaty mentions astronauts and their 'space *vehicle*'. The Astronauts Agreement seems to prefer the expression 'the personnel of a *spacecraft*' (Articles 1, 2, 3, and 4). The Moon Treaty, which is perhaps not the best drafted of treaties, uses, it would appear rather indiscriminately, both expressions. Articles 8, 11, 12, and 15 refers to 'space vehicles', sometimes side by side with simple 'vehicles', whilst its Article 3(2) speaks of 'spacecraft, the personnel of spacecraft'.

All in all, it would appear from their frequently linked references to astronauts and personnel that space vehicles and spacecraft are simply space objects actually carrying, or capable of carrying, persons and/or cargo. At least at present, they do not occupy a legal category of their own, although in due course they and other means of transport in space, such as space tugs and space shuttles, may all require special regulation. At the moment, Article VIII of the Space Treaty is quite happy to refer to 'any personnel' of an 'object launched into outer space'.

I. Space Objects and Paraphernalia

What is the material scope of the notion of 'space objects'?

1. *Component Parts.* In various provisions of the treaties relating to outer space sponsored by the United Nations, reference to space objects includes their component parts. For example, in the Space Treaty this is the case in Article VII on damage caused to third parties, and in Article VIII on ownership of objects in outer space, and the return of stray objects. Insofar as stray objects are concerned, the various treaties consistently include component parts. Thus in addition to Article VIII of the Space Treaty, mention may be made of Article 5 of the Astronauts Agreement and Article 13 of the Moon Treaty. Both the Liability Convention (Article I(d)) and the Registration (Article I(b)) include within the term 'space object' 'component parts of a space object.'

The express inclusion of 'component parts' in all the instances mentioned above may give rise to the argument that component parts are not automatically included. However, it may perhaps be equally maintained that such specification has been made out of an abundance of caution and that reference to a 'space object' automatically includes its components. On balance, the latter interpretation would seem more convincing, unless of course the context indicates otherwise.

2. *'Launch Vehicle and Parts Thereof'*. Article I(d) of the Liability Convention and Article I(b) of the Registration Convention include not only

the component parts of a space object within the term 'space object', but also 'its launch vehicle and parts thereof'. Their inclusion in the context of the Liability Convention is natural. Their inclusion in the Registration Convention hinges largely on one of the key *raisons d'être* of the Convention, namely, registration would assist in the identification of space objects or fragments thereof that have either caused damage to third parties or simply strayed into their territories. This is made clear both in the Preamble and especially in Article VI of the Convention. In both instances, the intention is no doubt to include the launch vehicle and parts thereof within the scope of the treaty.

Once more, the question arises whether references to 'space objects' include automatically their 'launch vehicle and parts thereof'. Once again, the answer would appear to be in the affirmative, unless the context indicates otherwise. With or without the hindsight of the Liability Convention, it seems clear that Article VII of the Space Treaty on liability for damage caused to third parties by an 'object launched into outer space' intends to include damage caused by the object's 'launch vehicle and parts thereof', whether or not designed to reach outer space themselves.

Furthermore, in the light of Article VIII of the Space Treaty, only by regarding the launch vehicle thereof as an integral part of the space object would it be brought under the jurisdiction and control of the State of registry. From this point of view, it is interesting to observe that, on account of the Convention's Article I(b), registration of a space object under the Registration Convention automatically includes its 'component parts . . . as well as its launch vehicle and parts there'.

3. *Space Objects and Payloads.* The position is less straightforward when it comes to payloads on board space objects, insofar as registration is concerned. The Registration Convention is silent on the subject. In the case of the shuttle operated by the United States National Aeronautics and Space Administration (NASA), according to the practice of NASA, the answer to the question whether foreign payloads have to be separately registered depends on whether the payload is intended to be 'separated in Earth orbit from the Shuttle'. On this basis, NASA regarded the European Space Agency's (ESA) Spacelab, which drew its supplies from and remained at all times within the shuttle, as merely a part of the latter and did not agree to its being separately registered.[6] If the payload were to be separated and to have an independent existence, then it would be a separate space object and would need to be separately registered with the appropriate State or international organization. If not, the payload would simply be what Article III of the

---

[6] See G. Lafferranderie, 'L'application par l'Agence Spatiale Européenne de la Convention sur l'immatriculation des objets lancés dans l'espace extra-atmosphérique', 11 *AASL* (1988), p. 229, at p. 172, n. 29.

Liability Convention calls 'property on board' a space object, forming part of that space object and would not be an independent space object. This would in fact apply to all items of property on board.

J. Objects Landed or Constructed on a Celestial Body

This leads to the problem of the legal status of what Article VIII of the Space Treaty has already referred to, namely, 'objects landed or constructed on a celestial body'. It provides:

Ownership of objects launched into outer space, including objects landed or constructed on a celestial body, and of their component parts, is not affected by their presence in outer space or on a celestial body or by their return to the earth.

The second paragraph of Article IV of the Space Treaty prohibits the 'establishment of military bases, installations and fortifications' on celestial bodies, but permits the 'use of any equipment or facility necessary for peaceful exploration of the moon and other celestial bodies.' Similar provisions to the above exist in respectively Articles 12 (1) and 3(4) of the Moon Treaty.

Reference is made in Article XIII of the Space Treaty to 'stations, installations, equipment and space vehicles on the moon' which shall be open to representatives of other States Parties on a basis of reciprocity. To the list of space vehicles, equipment, facilities, stations, manned and unmanned, installations, the Moon Treaty has further added structures (Article 11(3)), supplies (Article 12(3)), and mere vehicles without the qualifier 'space' (Articles 9(2), 10(2), 12(1, 2, and 3)).

Whilst both the Space Treaty and the Moon Treaty stipulate that ownership over all such items and their component parts shall not be affected by their presence in outer space or their return to the earth, the Space Treaty is otherwise silent as to their position in international law.

The Moon Treaty in its Article 12(1) provides, however:

States Parties shall retain jurisdiction and control over their personnel, vehicles, equipment, facilities, stations and installations on the moon.

The term 'vehicle' here presumably means vehicles other than the space vehicle which transported these items to the moon, since in the subsequent sentence, Article 12(1) in relation to ownership refers specifically to 'space vehicles, equipment, facilities, stations and installations'. The term space vehicle appears also in several other articles of the Moon Treaty (Articles 8(2), 11(3), 12(1), 15(1)), whilst 'vehicle' without qualification is used in a number of others (Articles 9(2), 10(2), 12(2 and 3)).

The omission of the qualifier 'space' before 'vehicle' in the first sentence of Article 12(1) relating to jurisdiction, and its use in the second sentence relating to ownership may at first sight appear to be strange. This may perhaps be explained by the fact that the original space vehicle would already, by virtue of its registration and Article VIII of the Space Treaty, be under the jurisdiction of the State of registry.

Be that as it may, a number of problems are raised by Article 12(1) of the Moon Treaty. Leaving aside for the moment the problem of personnel, the immediate question in the present context is whether the various items enumerated there are 'space objects' and, if so, whether they are separate and independent space objects distinct in legal identity from the space object that brought these items to the moon.

The problem may have to be divided three ways. First, to the extent to which these items still belong to the space vehicle that brought them to the moon, albeit temporarily landed on the moon, they remain part of that space object under the jurisdiction of the State of registry of that space object. In this sense, the use of the expression 'retain jurisdiction' becomes meaningful, inasmuch as the State of registry had jurisdiction over them while they were on board the space vehicle. In that case, the word 'their' must be understood not in the sense of ownership, but to mean items hitherto under their jurisdiction.

Secondly, what is the position of items which are no longer attached to the space vehicle that brought them to the moon? These can be items that have been brought up to the moon by a spacecraft registered in one State, but has since been transferred to the ownership and control of another State or the nationals of another State. Or they can be items which have been brought up by a number of different space vehicles and which are being used quite separately from and independently of those space vehicles, for example, in the construction or equipping of a manned or unmanned station. In the case of such a station, are the various parts of the station to remain parts of the different space objects that brought them to the moon and consequently under the jurisdiction of their respective States of registry? Is this what Article 12(1) means when it says that States Parties retain jurisdiction over their stations on the moon? Or is it the intention of Article 12(1) to refer to ownership or control, and to stipulate that jurisdiction and control shall lie with the States Parties that own or operate the station?

In the case of the 1988 Agreement between the United States, member States of ESA, Japan, and Canada for the development of a permanently manned civil space station in outer space, the parties have chosen a variant of the former course and decided that they would register their respective elements in the station separately. However, in the case of the Moon Treaty as regards stations on the moon, whilst the former solution is not precluded, the latter would seem to be more in accord with the intention of the authors of the treaty. But then from where has the owner/operator derived such jurisdiction? It would not be from Article VIII of the Space Treaty. The more immediate question in our context is whether the moon station is a separate and distinct space object. If the practice of NASA mentioned above is any guide, since the raw materials for the construction of the station are no longer part of the original space vehicles, the station would be a separate space object.[7] If that is the case, then both the Registration and the Moon Treaty may be said to suffer from a slight omission; for if such an item were to be a separate space object, which otherwise might not be under the effective jurisdiction of any State for want of registration, then both treaties should treat it as a separate space object and provide for its registration.

Article II(1) of the Registration may well be expanded to include 'space objects constructed or installed in outer space, including the moon and other celestial bodies' among the items to be registered, whilst the Moon Treaty should stipulate that stations and installations on the moon are to be registered by the States which (or non-governmental entities under the jurisdiction of which) procure, finance, or carry out the construction of such stations and installations or own or operate them. Once this is done, presumably 'vehicles, equipment, facilities, structures and supplies' on the moon would simply form part of the space vehicle that brought them to the moon, or part of a moon station or installation and, together with their parent station or installation, come under the jurisdiction of the State of registry of the station or installation.

The third part of the problem is merely a variation on the previous one, in which it was assumed that all the parts and raw materials for the station and installation had been brought up from the earth and had consequently been 'launched into outer space'. There is, however, a possibility that such stations or installations, whether in outer space as such or on a celestial body, may be constructed wholly from what Article 1(3) of the Moon Treaty calls 'extraterrestrial materials'. When that happens, there appears to be no valid reason why what has just been said about extraterrestrial stations and installations constructed and equipped with materials brought out from the earth should not apply, except perhaps to specify that reference is to stations and installations constructed by humans.

This being the case, our definition of space objects may have to be expanded to include also 'stations and installations constructed by humans in outer space or on the moon or other celestial bodies'.

K. Until What Moment?

Does a space object ever cease to be space object and, if so, when? In the first place, Article 5 of the Astronauts Agreement, for example, repeatedly uses

---

[7] The question whether 'installations or stations on the surface of a celestial body' came under the definition of 'space objects' was in fact raised by the Swedish delegate during discussions in the UN leading eventually to the Liability Convention (A/AC.105/C.2/SR.132–51, p. 24 (SR.138), but no decision was taken on the subject. See further B. Cheng, loc. cit. in n. 2 above, pp. 116–7 [Ch. 11 above, s. V.C.3: Space Object].

phrases such as 'a space object or its component parts discovered in territory under its [that of a contracting State other than the launching authority] jurisdiction', whilst the Liability Convention in its Article II talks of 'damage caused by its [a contracting State's] space object on the surface of the earth or to aircraft in flight'. The continued reference to space objects that have returned to the earth as space objects in both these conventions merely echoes Articles VII and VIII of the Space Treaty, where the broad principles subsequently elaborated in these conventions were first enunciated. Article VIII of the Space Treaty in fact further provides quite explicitly that ownership of space objects and their component parts 'is not affected . . . by their return to the earth'.

Presumably, therefore, a space object does not cease to be a space object, and its component parts do not cease to be the component parts of a space object and in particular its component parts, merely by the fact that they have returned to earth. One can probably say that they do not cease to be such until perhaps they have been dismantled or otherwise disposed of.

Thus, insofar as the duty to return stray space objects or their component parts is concerned under either Article VIII of the Space Treaty or under the Astronauts Agreement, there is no apparent time limit. There is no inherent reason why those provisions should not apply to fragments discovered five, ten or even fifty years after their descent.

The time frame of the Liability Convention is, however, somewhat different. Appeal may once again be made to Article VII(b) of the Convention. The temporal scope of application of the Convention probably coincides with what is described there in a different context as 'from the time of its [the space object's] launching or at any stage thereafter until its descent'. Damage caused by a space object's, including its component parts', descent would obviously be included within the scope of the Convention, even if Article X of the Convention does set a time limit of a year from the discovery of the occurrence of the damage or from when it should have been discovered for the presentation of a claim. But this does not affect that status of the fragment or component part as a part of a space object. Moreover, what would not be included within the scope of the Liability Convention or Article VII of the Space Treaty would be damage which has no relationship to the launching of a space object. Thus, notwithstanding the fact that an artificial satellite in a museum that has been to outer space and back probably still ranks as a space object. If that satellite were to fall from its support and cause injury to a visitor to the museum, that accident would not come under either the Liability of the Convention or Article VII of the Space Treaty. Liability is related to the launching of a space object and its aftermath, including operation and recovery, and not to its ownership or possession. It is separate in that respect from the status of an object as a space object.

L. Non-functional Objects and Debris

Finally there remain two problems of a rather topical character. First, are non-functional space objects, i.e., space objects which are no longer working, still space objects? Secondly, what is the legal status of debris?

Insofar as the first question is concerned, there is no reason to think that non-functional space objects are no longer space objects. The definition of space object is not related to the object's use or usefulness. Going back to the Moon Treaty's reference in its Article 3(2) to 'man-made space objects', one can only say that a lump of rock launched into outer space for no reason at all but for the fun of it must still be considered a space object. Whether and, if so, how non-functional space objects in outer space, especially those which hinder other users of outer space, should be regulated is a different issue beyond the scope of this chapter.

The same applies to debris. Fragments of a space object that fall on the earth are certainly treated as parts of that space object, and are given exactly the same status as the whole object, were the object to come back in one piece. This is the case in both the Astronauts Agreement and the Liability Convention. Nothing in any of the other treaties suggests otherwise, or that shattered fuel tanks or flakes of paint from space objects in outer space should be treated any differently.[8] The same could probably be said also of refuse generated in space, under the heading of objects made by humans in space, although deliberate and harmful release of refuse in space would doubtless come under Article IX of the Space Treaty and Article 7 of the Moon Treaty relating to harmful contamination.

The problem of non-functional space objects and debris is causing increasing concern. One of the unresolved legal issues in the way of a solution appears to be that of ownership. Are other States legally entitled to move or remove such objects? Confining ourselves merely to this issue, it may be suggested that a practice can be developed for States to 'disown' such objects by an entry in the national register which is notified to the United Nations and recorded in the United Nations register. Such 'disowned space objects' may then lawfully be moved or removed by anyone. A further practice can at the same time be developed, maturing in due course perhaps into a legally binding rule, to the effect that failure to 'disown' such objects ranks automatically as 'fault' within the meaning of Article III of the Liability Convention with the result that damage caused by 'undisowned' non-functional space objects or debris to another State's space object even elsewhere than on the surface of

---

[8] Cf. a very sensible joint proposal put forward by Argentina, Belgium, and France during the discussions leading in due course to the Liability Convention, albeit eventually not adopted because of the general disinclination to adopt definitions: 'For the purpose of this Convention the term "space object" also includes a launch vehicle and parts thereof, as well as all component parts on board, detached from or torn from the space object' (PUOS/C.2/70/WP.1/CRP.16 (reproduced as Annex I in A/AC.105/85, p. 16)).

the earth would in effect also involve absolute liability. If this is deemed too drastic a solution, at least a regime of presumed fault can be established.

III. 'Astronauts' and Related Expressions

The notion of astronauts is included here merely because it is often related to that of space objects.

As such, the term 'astronauts' probably poses little problem. Although literally it means persons who sail among the stars, and the term cosmonauts favoured by the Soviet Union those who navigate the universe, in practice both terms are used simply to describe those who venture extraterrestrially to outer space, including the moon and other celestial bodies, whether or not beyond interplanetary space.

Problems arise rather with some of the related expressions. First of all, Article V of the Space Treaty says that States Parties shall regard astronauts 'as envoys of mankind'. However, it was soon recognized that this was no more than a figure of speech without really any legal significance.[9]

Next, Article VIII of the Space Treaty deliberately avoids the familiar concept of nationality for space objects and stipulates that the State of registry of a space object 'shall retain jurisdiction and control over such object, and over any *personnel thereof*'. The ordinary meaning of 'personnel' would mean the crew of the space object, including anyone engaged in some service in the functioning of the space object. Article VIII has thus the effect of leaving the position of all persons on board who do not form part of the *personnel* of the space object, such as passengers or visitors from another space object, unclear. Under Article VIII they do not come under the jurisdiction of the State of registry of the space object.[10]

A similar problem exists in the Astronauts Agreement. The Preamble of the Agreement follows the terminology used in Article V of the Space Treaty and refers to assistance being given to 'astronauts' and the return of 'astronauts'. In the body of the treaty, however, the Agreement speaks all the time of the 'personnel of a spacecraft' (Articles 1, 2, 3, and 4) with the result that the duty of rescue and return of astronauts under the Agreement, unlike that under Article V of the Space Treaty, does not extend, strictly speaking, to astronauts who are not part of the 'personnel' of a spacecraft.

Although the Moon Treaty occasionally uses the term 'personnel' sometimes by itself (Articles 8(2), 9(2) 11(3), 12(1)) and sometimes in the expression 'personnel of spacecraft' (Article 3(2)), both the Liability Convention and the Moon Treaty have avoided the pitfall that exists in Article VIII of the Space

---

[9] See B. Cheng, 'Le Traité de 1967 sur l'espace/The 1967 Space Treaty', 95 *JDI* (1968), p. 532, at pp. 532–4 [Ch. 9 above, s. VII.F.1: 'Envoys of Mankind'].

[10] See ibid., at p. 572 [Ch. 9 above, s. V.C.4: Persons Other than Members of the Crew].

Treaty and in the Astronauts Agreement. The Liability Convention, instead of speaking of personnel, consistently refers to 'persons . . . on board' a space object (Articles III, IV(1)).

The Moon Treaty likewise uses the expression 'person'. In fact, it provides explicitly in its Article 10:

1. States Parties shall adopt all practicable measures to safeguard the life and health of persons on the moon. For this purpose they shall regard any person on the moon as an astronaut within the meaning of article V of the [Space] Treaty . . . and as part of the personnel of a spacecraft within the meaning of the [Astronauts] Agreement.

States Parties shall offer shelter in their stations, installations, vehicles and other facilities to persons in distress on the moon. [11]

Article 10 of the Moon Treaty and the Liability Convention thus show up the shortcoming of using the term 'personnel' of either a space object or of a moon station when in reality the intention is to refer to everyone present. From this point of view, in time even the use of such terms as astronauts or cosmonauts would seem obsolete insofar as they carry the connotation of navigation. To do so would in due course be . . . archaic, misleading, and even erroneous as if we were nowadays to refer to all who fly or simply travel by air as aeronauts or aviators. In future, the use of a general term such as 'persons' would seem far more appropriate, at least until such time as it becomes necessary further to distinguish between different categories of persons, such as commander, various types of crew, licensed or unlicensed, research scientists, visitors, passengers and so forth.

IV. Conclusions

In the light of the various treaties relating to outer space concluded under the auspices of the United Nations, it would appear that the term 'space object' covers any object launched by humans into outer space, as well as any component part thereof, together with its launch vehicle and parts thereof. Objects launched into earth orbit and beyond are *ipso facto* regarded as space objects. This confirms the view that, in accordance with State practice, outer space can be said, in international law, to begin arguably at an altitude of 96 kilometres above the earth, clearly so at 110 kilometres, and definitely so at 130 kilometres. Space objects may be man-made or non-man-made. Terms such as space vehicles or spacecraft cover merely different forms of space object, mainly

---

[11] See also Art. 12(3): 'In the event of . . . a threat to human life . . .', and B. Cheng, 'The Moon Treaty: Agreement Governing the Activities of States on the Moon and Othger Celestial Bodies within the Solar System other than the Earth, December 18, 1979', 33 *CLP* (1980), p. 213 [Ch. 12 above].

those used as a means of conveyance. Payloads which are not to be off-loaded and are not thus to acquire a separate existence would remain part of the space object.

An object becomes a space object from the moment of its being launched, including any attempted launching, until it is dismantled or otherwise disposed of, after what may be called the recovery phase of its life.[12] The term space object covers both functional and non-functional objects and extends to all items of property on board as well as any debris and refuse originating from a space object both while in space or when scattered anywhere on landing. As a contribution to the solution of the problem of non-functional space objects and debris clustering up outer space, it is suggested that at least a practice, if not a binding rule, should be developed whereby States 'disown' such objects by entries in the relevant registers so that they may be freely moved or removed by others. Damage caused to other States' functioning space objects by undisowned non-functional space objects or debris should then lead to an at least rebuttable, if not irrebuttable, presumption of fault on the part of the launching authority.

It is furthermore suggested that stations and installations constructed by humans in outer space or on celestial bodies should be considered as independent space objects, especially when such stations or installations have a separate existence independent of the space vehicle(s) which have brought the materials for their construction to outer space, or when they have been constructed from extraterrestrial materials. As at present, the legal status of extraterrestrial stations and installations constructed from materials not launched from the earth or not launched in one piece or by a single launching authority, especially those on celestial bodies, is not specifically or clearly determined.

Insofar as the term astronauts is concerned, it now probably covers all who travel to outer space. However, it has been found that the expression 'personnel of a space object' often fails to convey what is in fact intended, namely, all persons on board or attached to a space object, whether or not forming part of its personnel. The use of the term 'persons', which is found in the more recent treaties, would seem to be far more accurate, unless of course it is intended specifically to refer to the personnel of a space object. It is submitted that in due course the more general reference to persons is likely to replace the use of terms like astronauts or cosmonauts which will in time appear archaic and inapt. In time, needs may arise for specific designations, as in air and shipping law and other fields of life.

---

[12] See Cheng, loc. cit. in n. 2 above, at p. 117 [Ch. 11 above, s. V.C.3: Space Object].

PART V

MILITARY USE
OF OUTER SPACE

19

Definitional Issues in Space Law: the 'Peaceful Use' of Outer Space, including the Moon and other Celestial Bodies*

I. Issue Requiring Wider Discussion

Insofar as definitional issues in space law are concerned, there is one the present development of which gives rise to grave anxiety. This is the definition of the term 'peaceful', particularly as used in Article IV(2) of the 1967 Treaty on Principles Governing the Activities of States in the Exploration and Use of Outer Space, Including the Moon and Celestial Bodies (Space Treaty), and Article 3(a) of the 1979 Agreement Governing the Activities of States on the Moon and Other Celestial Bodies (Moon Treaty). The current development, if unchecked, can produce serious consequences in many fields of international law. It, therefore, deserves wide attention and discussion, which should not be confined merely to the specialists.[1]

II. The Vogue of 'Peaceful Use'

Insofar as pre-1967 Space Treaty general international law was concerned, there was certainly no specific rule relating to the military use of outer space, the moon and other celestial bodies other than those which were applicable to any other areas of *res extra commercium* or *res nullius*. This meant that their military use was in principle permitted, subject only to the observance of the ordinary rules of international law and, as among members of the United Nations, those to be found in the Charter of the United Nations, such as its Article 2(4).[2]

---

* Adapted from the second half of a paper on 'The Legal Status of Outer Space and Relevant Issues: Delimitation of Outer Space and Definition of Peaceful Use', first published in 11 *JSL* (1983), pp. 89–105. Reproduced by kind permission of *Journal of Space Law*.

[1] On the dangers of compartmentalized learning and knowledge, see I. Brownlie, 'Problems of Specialisation', in Cheng (ed.), *International Law*, p. 109.

[2] 'All Members shall refrain in their international relations from the threat or use of force against the territorial integrity or political independence of any State, or in any other manner inconsistent with the Purposes of the United Nations.'

However, especially in the heady atmosphere of the initial period of man's first entry into space, there was a very strong and highly emotional, albeit not very realistic, sentiment among many people, and even governments, that outer space and celestial bodies should be used only for genuinely peaceful purposes and the common benefit of mankind. Proposals to this effect were made respectively by the United States in 1957 and the Soviet Union in 1958.[3] Such proposals in the early days of the space age are reminiscent of similar ones a decade before in the field of nuclear energy, including the 1946 United States Atoms for Peace Plan.[4] From this point of view, the very name given by the United Nations to its organs dealing with space matters is indicative of this pious hope. Thus in 1958 it set up the *Ad Hoc* Committee on the *Peaceful Uses of Outer Space*, and the following year the Committee on the *Peaceful Uses of Outer Space* (COPUOS), the latter remaining the main United Nations organ concerned with outer space. Moreover, various resolutions passed by the General Assembly on outer space during this period, such as Resolution 1348 (XIII) of 13 December 1959, Resolution 1472 (XIV) of 12 December 1959, Resolution 1721 (XVI) of 20 December 1961, Resolution 1802 (XVII) of 19 December 1962, all referred to the 'peaceful uses of outer space'.

It was in the midst of all this that the United States in 1958 adopted the National Aeronautics and Space Act[5] which, *inter alia*, set up the National Aeronautics and Space Administration (NASA). In Section 101, sub-section (a), it is provided:

The Congress declares that it is the policy of the United States that activities in space should be devoted to peaceful purposes for the benefit of mankind.

In this connection, two further factors may be mentioned. First, the 1958 National Aeronautics and Space Act was passed in the very infancy of space flights. Secondly, the late 'fifties also marked the beginning of the Soviet Union's campaign under Premier Khrushchev of 'peaceful co-existence', both as a result of, and in response to, which everything one did then was given the vogue label of 'peace'. The fervour and fever were such that it was reported that the Soviet Ambassador to the United Kingdom had ordered 100 rose bushes of the variety 'Peace' to be planted in the ambassadorial country residence. However, inevitably, much of this movement was sheer window-dressing. Thus often, without necessarily altering what one was doing, one found oneself no longer engaged in war studies, but first in defence, and then better still in peace studies. The old adage, *Si vis pacem, para bellum* (If you desire peace, prepare for war) was given a new twist.

---

[3] See B. Cheng, 'The United Nations and Outer Space', 14 *CLP* (1961), p. 247, nn. 54, 55 [Ch. 6 above, nn. 54, 55].

[4] See B. Cheng, 'International Co-operation and Control: From Atoms to Space', 15 *CLP* (1962), p. 228, esp. pp. 233–4 [Ch. 4 above, esp. 2. IV.A: International Institutions].

[5] P.L. 85–568; 72 Stat. 426.

III. The United States Interpretation of 'Peaceful Use'

However, the military potential of space technology soon became more and more apparent. It would seem that it was against this background that the peculiar United States interpretation of the word 'peaceful' was born. The official United States position, backed more often than not by United States writers, as well as some foreign ones, has from almost the very beginning of the space era till even now, been that 'peaceful' means 'non-aggressive' and not 'non-military'.

Thus, in a statement made before the First Committee of the United Nations on 3 December 1962, Senator Gore, representing the United States, said:

It is the view of the United States that outer space should be used only for peaceful— that is, non-aggressive and beneficial—purposes. The question of military activities in space cannot be divorced from the question of military activities on earth. To banish these activities in both environments we must continue our efforts for general and complete disarmament with adequate safeguards. Until this is achieved, the test of any space activities must not be whether it is military or non-military, but whether or not it is consistent with the United Nations Charter and other obligations of law.[6]

What Senator Gore said was perfectly understandable, even if his use of words was not necessarily defensible. The United States was not prepared without further ado to accept legal restraints on the use of outer space for 'military' purposes, but it would of course abide by its obligations under the United Nations Charter and other obligations of law in not using outer space for 'aggressive' purposes. Insofar as the substance of what Senator Gore said is concerned, it can hardly be faulted; for, as we have seen, there was nothing in general international law or even the Charter of the United Nations which obliged States not to use outer space for military purposes. In fact, that remains the position even today.[7]

However, by seeking not to ride against the tide of popular opinion on the 'peaceful use' of outer space, and bearing in mind possibly Section 101(a), of the 1958 National Aeronautics and Space Act, the United States was putting its foot on the slippery slope of distorting the meaning of 'peaceful' by interpreting it as 'non-aggressive' and not 'non-military'.

Those who defend the United States use of the word 'peaceful' often point to the impossibility of separating 'military' from 'non-military' activities, seemingly under the impression that there exists some clear-cut and universally recognized and immediately recognizable distinction between

---

[6] A/C.1/PV.1289 (3.12.62), p. 13. Regarding the Soviet attitude, see n. 12 below.
[7] See further B. Cheng, 'The Military Use of Outer Space in International Law', in E. G. Bello and Prince Bola A. Ajibola, San (eds), 1 *Essays in Honour of Judge Taslim Olawale Elias* (1992), p. 63 [Ch. 20 below].

'aggressive' and 'non-aggressive' space activities. One wonders in this context whether partisans of this view have a ready definition of what paragraph 9 of the Preamble of the 1967 Space Treaty would designate as 'propaganda designed or likely to provoke or encourage any threat to the peace, breach of the peace, or act of aggression'.

But it is clear from what Senator Gore said that he had no difficulty in distinguishing between military and non-military activities. In fact, while the United States National Aeronautics and Space Act of 1958 says that it is the 'policy of the United States that activities in space should be devoted to peaceful purposes for the benefit of all mankind', it does not specify that they should be *exclusively* for peaceful purposes. Moreover, the policy in question is not confined to United States activities in space, but activities in space in general. In other words, Section 101(a) does no more than state a general objective to be pursued by the United States internationally as well as domestically. It is by no means a legal limitation on the type of activity the United States is entitled to engage in outer space.

Besides, the 1958 Act clearly distinguishes between space activities which come under the 'civilian agency' NASA and 'activities peculiar to or primarily associated with the development of weapons systems, military operations, or the defence of the United States (including the research and development necessary to make effective provision for the defence of the United States)' which 'shall be the responsibility of . . . the Department of Defence'. So the distinction is not between 'peaceful' and 'military', but between 'civilian' or 'civil'[8] on the one hand and 'military' and 'defence' on the other hand. But this is pure semantics; for, in substance, it is the same distinction. This is not to say that there are no problems in demarcating clearly between 'military' and 'non-military'. But, contrary to the contention of those who defend the United States use of the word 'peaceful', in saying that, in practice, it is not possible to separate the military from the non-military, such a distinction, described as one between 'defence' (i.e., military) and 'civilian' (i.e., non- military) lies at the very foundation of the United States National Aeronautics and Space Act itself.

IV. Article IV of the 1967 Space Treaty

Reference has previously been made to the use of the expression 'peaceful uses' of outer space in various resolutions of the United Nations General Assembly in the early sixties,[9] and to the attitude of the superpowers to the

---

[8] Cf. also, 'Description of a Presidential Directive on National Space Policy, The White House, June 20, 1978', *Space Law. Selected Basic Documents*, 2d ed., Senate Comm. on Commerce, Science and Transportation, 95th Cong., 2d Sess. 559 (Comm. Print 1978).

[9] See n. 13 below.

complete demilitarization of outer space in isolation from the question of disarmament in general.[10] From this point of view, the exact title of General Assembly Resolution 1962 (XVIII) of 13 December 1963, which is the precursor of the subsequent 1967 Space Treaty, and that of the 1967 Treaty itself are interesting. The former is the Declaration of Legal Principles Governing the Activities of States in the Exploration and Use of Outer Space, the latter Treaty on Principles Governing the Activities of States in the Exploration and Use of Outer Space, including the Moon and Other Celestial Bodies. In neither case, is the word 'peaceful' included in the title, although in paragraph 4 of both, the desire 'to contribute to broad international co-operation in the scientific as well as in the legal aspects of exploration and use of outer space for peaceful purposes' is expressed. But this is really not all that different from Section 101(a) of the United States National Aeronautics and Space Act of 1958.

Nowhere, however, in the 1967 Space Treaty, is outer space in the narrow sense of the term, i.e., the void in between all the celestial bodies, or what I call the 'outer void space', confined to 'peaceful uses' only.

The relevant provision is Article IV which provides:

States Parties to the Treaty undertake not to place in orbit around the earth any objects carrying nuclear weapons or any other kinds of weapons of mass destruction, install such weapons on celestial bodies, or station such weapons in outer space in any other manner.

The moon and other celestial bodies [*N.B.: no reference to outer space*] shall be used by all States Parties to the Treaty exclusively for peaceful purposes. The establishment of military bases, installations and fortifications, the testing of any type of weapons and the conduct of military manoeuvres on celestial bodies shall be forbidden. The use of military personnel for scientific research or for any other peaceful purposes shall not be prohibited. The use of any equipment or facility necessary for peaceful exploration of the moon and other celestial bodies shall also not be prohibited.[11]

From the standpoint of international law and according to its rules on treaty interpretation, the structure and interpretation of Article IV are fairly clear. The article is divided into two parts.

A. Partial Demilitarization of Earth Orbits and of Outer Space in the Wide Sense of the Term

Cosmographically, *ratione loci*, or if one wishes, spatially, paragraph 1 of Article IV, notwithstanding the omission of any specific reference to the moon, is applicable to (i) earth orbits, without prejudice to the question

[10] See n. 6 above.
[11] See B. Cheng, 'Le Traité de 1967 sur l'espace/The 1967 Space Treaty', 95 *JDI* (1968), 532, pp. 598–616 [Ch. 9, s. VI: Partial Demilitarization of Outer Space and Non-Militarization of Celestial Bodies].

whether or not they are in outer space, and (ii) using the expression favoured in the 1967 Space Treaty, 'outer space, including the moon and other celestial bodies', as a whole, i.e., outer space in the wide sense of the term (*sensu lato*).

Materially, *ratione materiae*, or, to use the 'in' word, functionally, it prohibits the installation or stationing of 'any objects carrying nuclear weapons or any other kinds of weapons of mass destruction' in any of those places mentioned above or 'in any other manner'. But, subject to what is provided for in paragraph 2 of the same article, *nothing in Article IV(1) itself* prohibits the stationing of any other type of weapons in outer space, including the moon and other celestial bodies, or in fact the use of outer space, including the moon and celestial bodies, for military purposes in any other way. Insofar as Article IV(1) is concerned, apart from the stationing of nuclear weapons and weapons of mass destruction, outer space as a whole has not been demilitarized at all. Such demilitarization as it stipulates, in the form of the prohibition of the stationing of nuclear weapons and weapons of mass destruction, is strictly partial. Attempts made during the drafting of the 1967 Space Treaty by some delegations to bring about a complete demilitarization of outer space were clearly rejected by both super powers.[12] In other words, under both general international law and Article IV(1) of the 1967 Space Treaty, States are perfectly entitled to use the whole of outer space for military purposes, bar the stationing of nuclear weapons and weapons of mass destruction.

B. Complete Demilitarization of the Moon and Other Celestial Bodies

Paragraph 2 of Article IV, on the other hand, is quite different, different in both its cosmographical and its material scope. Cosmographically, it applies only to 'the moon and other celestial bodies'. Specifically and pointedly, it does not refer to the outer void space as such, i.e., the space in between the celestial bodies. Materially, it demilitarizes all celestial bodies other than the earth.

Article IV of the 1967 Space Treaty owes much to President Eisenhower's proposal presented to the United Nations in 1960.[13] In making his proposal, he recalled specifically the Antarctic Treaty of the previous year, even though neither superpower seemed inclined to apply the Antarctica model bodily to the whole of outer space.[14]

Article I of the Antarctic Treaty is very similar to Article IV(2) of the 1967 Space Treaty and is, therefore, very helpful in clarifying the latter's meaning. It states:

1.   Antarctica shall be used for peaceful purposes only. There shall be prohibited, *inter alia*, any measures of a military nature, such as the establishment of military

---

[12] Cf. A/AC.105/C.2/SR.65 (22.7.66), pp. 9–10 (USA); ibid./SR.66 (25.7.66), pp. 6–7 (USSR).

[13] GAOR, GA(XV) A/PV.868 (22.9.60), p. 45, at p. 48. See also Cheng, loc. cit. in n. 3 above, n. 43 on p. 277 [Ch. 6 above, n. 142].

[14] See n. 12 above.

bases and fortifications, the carrying out of military manoeuvres, as well as the testing of any type of weapons.

2. The present Treaty shall not prevent the use of military personnel or equipment for scientific research or for any other peaceful purpose.

Three points emerge clearly from Article I of the Antarctic Treaty, which *mutatis mutandis* appear fully applicable also to Article IV(2) of the 1967 Space Treaty:

(i) 'peaceful' means non-military;

(ii) references to military installations, military manoeuvres and so forth in the provision are exemplificative and not exhaustive;

(iii) the possibility of using military personnel and equipment for scientific research or other peaceful purposes in no way invalidates point (i) above.

Regarding the last point, there has been a great deal of misunderstanding, resulting in frequent allegations that the last sentence of Article IV(2) of the Space Treaty merely highlights the hollowness of the whole paragraph. But this is not so. In this connection, the following quotation from the decision of Edwin B. Parker, umpire in the United States–German Mixed Claims Commission (1922), in *Opinion Construing the Phrase 'Naval and Military Works or Materials' as Applied to Hull Losses and Also Dealing with Requisitioned Dutch Ships* (1924), in relation to events which took place during World War I, is highly pertinent. It shows clearly that the test of whether an activity or an equipment is of a military character is essentially a functional one and not one of nominal status:

The taxicabs privately owned and operated for profit in Paris during September, 1914, were in no sense military materials; but when these same taxicabs were requisitioned by the Military Governor of Paris and used to transport French reserves to meet and repel the oncoming German army, they became military materials, and so remained until redelivered to their owners. The automobile belonging to the United States assigned to its President and constitutional commander-in-chief of its Army for use in Washington is in no sense military materials. But had the same automobile been transported to the battlefront in France or Belgium and used by the same President, it would have become a part of the military equipment of the Army and as such impressed with a military character.[15]

Thus if the same automobile is subsequently to be sent either to Antarctica or to the moon to carry out scientific research, the same equipment, although it may still belong to the Army, would not be 'impressed with a military character', and its use would be perfectly lawful under both treaties, provided there is no abuse which, of course, is a different matter, inasmuch as it would no longer be a matter of treaty interpretation, but one of treaty violation.

---

[15] *Dec. and Op.*, p. 75, at p. 97.

V. United States Interpretation of the Term 'Peaceful' in Relation to Article IV: Needless, Wrong, and Potentially Noxious

A. United States Interpretation Needless

In the light of what has been said in regard to the proper interpretation of Article IV of the 1967 Space Treaty, it is quite unnecessary for the United States to interpret, or rather to misinterpret, the term 'peaceful' in Article IV(2) of the Space Treaty as meaning 'non-aggressive' and not 'non-military' in order to enable itself to use outer space in the narrow sense of the term for military purposes, as do in fact both super powers and a few other States by means of observational, communications, meteorological, geodetic, and other types of satellites, space vehicles, or space stations. All States Parties to the 1967 Space Treaty remain entitled to do so both under the Treaty and under general international law,[16] unless of course they become so tangled up by their functional definition of outer space that they do not know where outer space is.

It has sometimes been suggested that since the United States has for many years used the term 'peaceful' in relation to outer space to mean 'non-aggressive' and not 'non-military', and has encountered no opposition or protest, this usage must be deemed to have been accepted by other States.[17] But this reasoning is invalid, inasmuch as there is no call for other States to protest for as long as the United States has violated no rule of international law or any of its treaty obligations. That some States wish to give their legitimate activities some fancy description such as 'beneficial', 'the greatest', or 'peaceful', is something which is quite immaterial to others, who are entitled simply to dismiss such action as eccentric, propagandist, or simply as a case of legal malapropism. Neither the law nor their legal position can thereby be changed.

The present United States interpretation of the word 'peaceful' in relation to Article IV of the Space Treaty is quite needless for as long as, of course, the United States does not seek to apply it to Article IV(2). The United States position is all the more incomprehensible inasmuch as there is no evidence to suggest that the United States intends to conduct military activities on the moon and other celestial bodies.

[16] See in this regard, H. G. Darwin, 'The Outer Space Treaty', 42 *BYIL* (1967), p. 278, at p. 284: 'There is no provision requiring that outer space shall be used for peaceful purposes only. Even at the time of the Declaration of Legal Principles, several delegations regretted the absence of such a provision . . . the Soviet representative . . . said, "The Declaration did not, and indeed could not, touch the use of space for military purposes . . ." (GAOR, 18th Session, 1st Committee, 1342nd Meeting, 2.12.62, p. 161).' Henry Darwin was then a Legal Adviser of the British Foreign Office. He obviously understood 'peaceful' to mean 'non-military'. He became in due course Deputy Legal Adviser and the Second Legal Adviser at the Foreign and Commonwealth Office.

[17] Cf. Tanja L. Zwaan, 'The Law Governing Outer Space Activities', *Europolis* (July–August 1987), p. 24.

B. United States Interpretation Wrong

The present United States interpretation of the word 'peaceful' to mean merely 'non-aggressive' would simply be wrong if applied to Article IV(2) of the Space Treaty, which is where the word appears in Article IV. The same would be true if applied to Article 3 of the 1979 Moon Treaty which likewise provides that all celestial bodies within the solar system other than the earth 'shall be used by all States Parties exclusively for peaceful purposes.'[18]

Among various reasons, the simplest is that any such interpretation would render the first sentence of Article IV(2) of the Space Treaty completely meaningless and redundant, and cannot, therefore, be valid. The elementary explanation is that 'aggressive' acts are contrary to international law and the Charter of the United Nations, particularly Article 2(4) of the Charter,[19] not only on the moon and on other celestial bodies, but also anywhere in the universe. Insofar as Parties to the 1967 Space Treaty are concerned, they specifically undertake in Article III of the Treaty that:

States Parties to the Treaty shall carry on activities in the exploration and use of outer space, including the moon and celestial bodies, in accordance with international law, including the Charter of the United Nations . . .

Aggressive acts would, therefore, be prohibited in outer space as a whole and it would consequently be absolutely superfluous in Article IV(2) specifically to provide that 'the moon and other celestial bodies shall be used . . . exclusively for *non-aggressive* purposes'. Is anyone seriously suggesting that because Article IV(2) does not mention outer space, i.e., outer space in the narrow sense of the term, States Parties to the 1967 Space Treaty may, therefore, freely engage in 'aggressive' acts in outer void space? The conclusion is inescapable that, if the word 'peaceful' in Article IV(2) is to have any meaning at all, it must bear its plain meaning of 'non-military' and can certainly not mean 'non-aggressive'.

C. United States Interpretation Potentially Noxious

For as long as the United States restricts its idiosyncratic interpretation of the word 'peaceful' to some non-existent limitation on the military use of the outer void space, perhaps no more harm is done than the emperor preening himself in his non-existent clothes. But this rather whimsical interpretation carries with it seeds of serious consequences.

The United States is a party to the Antarctic Treaty. It is also a party to many multilateral and bilateral agreements for international co-operation in

---

[18] See B. Cheng, 'The Moon Treaty: Agreement Governing the Activities of States on the Moon and Other Celestial Bodies within the Solar System other than the Earth, December 18, 1979', 33 *CLP* (1980), p. 213 [Ch. 12 above].

[19] See n. 2 above.

nuclear matters, under which nuclear materials, equipment, and facilities which have been transferred from one contracting party to another contracting party may be used by the latter only for 'peaceful purposes'.[20] Is the United States prepared to allow the word 'peaceful' in these treaties to be interpreted by the other parties as meaning also 'non-aggressive' and not 'non-military'? Is that the reply that the United States is getting from some of the States which have already misused the nuclear assistance they have received in order to make bombs, non-aggressive bombs no doubt? If not, it should not take them long to learn what is the interpretation of the word 'peaceful' favoured by the United States, unless the United States itself takes immediate steps to revise its attitude in the matter.

VI. Conclusion

The United States occupying as it does a pre-eminent position in the world, its *opinio juris* must obviously carry great weight in the formation of rules of general international law. However, in regard to both the question of delimitation of outer space and the interpretation of the expression 'peaceful', particularly in relation to the 1967 Space Treaty, the United States has persisted in attitudes it took up at the very beginning of the space age. It is hoped that at least a case has been made to show that its rather strange interpretation of the word 'peaceful' to mean 'non-aggressive' and not 'non-military', harbours serious consequences for international law. It is to be hoped that the issues it raises will not only be given some serious thought by the United States, and by space lawyers and general international lawyers everywhere, but will also receive the attention of the public at large; for some things may be too important to be left entirely in the hands of government officials and lawyers alone.

---

[20] See Cheng, loc. cit. in n. 4 above, at pp. 233 ff. [Ch. 4 above, esp. ss. IV ff.].

20

The Military Use of Outer Space and International Law*

I. Preliminary Observations

It may be helpful at the outset to make certain preliminary observations, which may assist in understanding my approach to the subject.

(i) In referring to the law, States and the inter-State society (and their legal advisers) have in mind essentially or, in all probability, exclusively human-made laws. Human-made law does not emanate from on high, but is made by humans, representing thus the will of those who make it.

(ii) No law is self-executing. It is viable only if, as a system, it is on the whole, willingly or grudgingly through favour or fear, wanted, supported, complied with, and, in case of breach, more than likely to be enforced by the dominant (prevailing) section of society in which it operates.[1]

(iii) Law consequently, in general, represents the will of the dominant section in society, namely, the section that has the intention, the will, and the capability (which need not necessarily be military, but may be economic, religious, moral or other means of persuasion or forms of power) of making its will prevail.

(iv) From the legal point of view, international society is horizontal in structure, instead of being organized hierarchically as in municipal (i.e., national) societies where the State exercises sovereign legislative, judicial, and law-enforcement powers over the subjects. In international society, States, the primary subjects of the international legal system, remain essentially their own law-makers, judges and law enforcement officers. There is no super State above them.

(v) The fact that States are essentially their own law-makers and law-enforcement officers means that what the ordinary individual in the street may regard as unmistakably an unmitigated evil in international life cannot be simply legislated away by some fiat from on high. It can only be made unlawful by the consent of the States concerned in the form of treaties or by the

* First published in E. G. Bello and Bola A. Ajibola, San (eds.), 1 *Essays in Honour of Judge Taslim Olawale Elias* (1992), pp. 63–75. Reproduced with kind permission from Kluwer Law International.

[1] See B. Cheng, 'The Contribution of Air and Space Law to the Development of International Law', 39 *CLP* (1986), p. 181 [Epilogue below].

concurrence of the generality of States, including the dominant section of international society, in the form of general international law or what is traditionally called customary international law.[2] This applies to the banning or limitation of weapons in outer space no less than to any other matter.

(vi) The fact that States are essentially their own judges, being legally entitled not to allow disputes to which they are parties being subjected to even the process of third-party settlement unless they agree to do so, leads to the emergence of three separate grades of international law: 1. auto-interpretative—the grade of international law applied by States when they have more or less made up their mind not to let disputes in which they may be involved be adjudicated upon by third parties; 2. justiciable—that applied by them when they are already committed, or are at least in principle agreeable, to submit, if necessary, to third-party arbitrament both the facts and the law involved in disputes to which they are or may subsequently become parties; and 3. judicial—that as applied by international courts and tribunals. Basically it is the same international law, but the auto-interpretative grade is subjective, volatile, and highly susceptible to the effect of power and to abuse.[3]

(vii) Legal rules are generally polysemous, in the sense that they are usually capable of a number of possible interpretations within a permissible range. Auto-interpretation not only accentuates the polysemous character of the law, but can also subject it to abuse.

(viii) In concrete situations, auto-interpretation applies not only to the law, but also to the facts of the case.

(ix) Rules of international law, including treaties on sensitive issues, such as arms limitation, usually operate on the auto-interpretative level. The military use of outer space is a prime example.

(x) In this chapter, an examination will be made of the law as it is, including treaties that are in force, but not proposals that have not yet been adopted.[4]

II. Relevant Rules of General International Law

Contrary to a view which has not completely disappeared, outer space and celestial bodies are, in inter-State relations, from the very beginning subject to

[2] See B. Cheng, 'Custom: The Future of General State Practice in a divided World', in R. St. J. Macdonald and D. M. Johnston (eds.), *The Structure and Process of International Law* (1983), p. 513. N.B.: in the book, pp. 545 and 546 have been transposed, and are wrongly paginated.

[3] See B. Cheng, 'Flight from Justiciable to Auto-interpretative International Law: From the Jay Treaty to the Shultz Letter', *Liber Amicorum Elie Van Bogaert* (1985), p. 1.

[4] For some of the proposals *de lege ferenda*, see V. Kopal, 'Concerns Expressed in the United Nations over the Military Uses of Outer Space', in N. Jasentuliyana (ed.), *Maintaining Outer Space for Peaceful Uses: Proceedings of a Symposium* (1984), p. 59, and papers on various aspects of the problem by Bhupendra Jasani, D. Goedhuis, Robert W. Buchheim, Sune Danielsson, Boris Mayorsky, Ogunsola Ogunbanwo and Karl-Heinz Böckstiegel in Part 4 (Prospects for Further Demilitarization) of the Proceedings, pp. 219 ff.

international law, and not a virgin slate for which every rule has to be newly fashioned and hence can be created from fresh thoughts and attitudes free from the contamination of terrestrial strives and conflicts.[5]

At the initial stage of the space age, celestial bodies, including the moon, were simply *territorium nullius*, subject to appropriation by States through effective occupation under the ordinary rules of international law governing acquisition of territory. At the present moment, the rule first envisaged in General Assembly resolution 1721A (XVI) of 20 December 1961 and then incorporated in Article II of the 1967 Space Treaty that outer space, including the moon and celestial bodies, is not subject to national appropriation can probably be regarded as having become a rule of general international law.[6]

Not being *terra firma*, outer space as such or any portion thereof, has, probably from the very beginning, not been subject to national appropriation under general international law. This rule has since been reinforced by a consensus that Article II of the 1967 Space Treaty is now probably only declaratory of general international law.

This status of outer space and of celestial bodies of being not subject to national appropriation, puts them into the category of *territorium extra commercium* under general international law, the prime example of which hitherto were the high seas.

Consequently, under general international law, outer space and celestial bodies now share the basic legal condition of the high seas, without, however, the special rules that pertain solely to the high seas. In brief, this means that the starting point for any discussion of the legal status of outer space and of celestial bodies is that they are open to use (and possibly even abuse or misuse) by all States and their nationals. As long as the freedom of other States to use them is not interfered with, insofar as general international law is concerned, there are no specific restrictions, in peacetime, on the testing or deployment of weapons, target practice, dumping of waste in outer space or on the moon and other celestial bodies, or generally on their military use. Nor have any special rules of general international law been developed specifically governing the use of outer space, the moon and other celestial bodies for military purposes in time of war or armed conflict, especially—God forbid—global ones, when dominance in outer space will no doubt be of vital importance. Such restrictions as exist are to be found in treaties.

---

[5] See B. Cheng, 'The Extraterrestrial Application of International Law', 18 *CLP* (1965), p. 132 [Ch. 5 above].

[6] See B. Cheng, 'Outer Space: The International Legal Framework—The International Legal Status of Outer Space, Space Objects and Spacemen', 10 *Thesaurus Acroasium* (1981), p. 41, at pp. 75–6 [Ch. 13 above, s. II.A.2: Prohibition of Appropriation].

III. Treaties Restricting the Military Use of Outer Space

It has to be remembered first that treaties are binding only when they are in force, save to the extent to which they are merely declaratory of general international law, in which case it is the latter and not the treaty that binds. Secondly, as the 1969 Vienna Convention on the Law of Treaties has now happily confirmed in its Articles 34 and 38, treaties are binding only on contracting parties or those that have otherwise consented to them, unless the provisions in question have become rules of general international law through general acceptance.

A. The 1963 Partial Nuclear Test Ban Treaty

Article I the 1963 Nuclear Test Ban Treaty provides:

(1) Each of the Parties to this Treaty undertakes to prohibit, to prevent and not to carry out any *nuclear weapon test explosion, or any other nuclear explosion*, at any place under its jurisdiction or control:
    (a) in the atmosphere; *beyond its limits, including outer space*; . . . ; or
    (b) in any other environment if such explosion causes radioactive debris to be present outside the territorial limits of the State under whose jurisdiction or control such explosion is conducted . . .
(2) Each of the Parties to this Treaty undertakes furthermore to refrain from causing, encouraging, or in any way participating in, the carrying out of any nuclear weapon test explosion, or any other nuclear explosion, anywhere which would take place in any of the environments described, or have the effect referred to, in paragraph 1 of this Article.[7]

Insofar as States parties to the Treaty are concerned and for as long as they remain parties to it (the Treaty is subject to denunciation, albeit only in 'extraordinary' circumstances[8]), on the face of it, the use of 'nuclear explosions' in outer space, whether against satellites or against missiles or for any other purpose, such as the disruption of telecommunications, is prohibited. So is the testing of such weapons, as well as any aiding or abetting of the carrying out of such explosions or tests. However, there can be a number of reservations.

First, some nuclear States, including France and the People's Republic of China, are not parties to the Treaty. Furthermore, as has already been mentioned, the Treaty is subject to denunciation.

---

[7] Italics added.
[8] Although Article IV(1) of the Treaty says, 'This Treaty shall be of unlimited duration', the second paragraph provides: 'Each Party shall in exercising its national sovereignty have the right to withdraw from the Treaty if it decides that extraordinary events, related to the subject matter of this Treaty, have jeopardized the supreme interests of its country. It shall give notice of such withdrawal to all other Parties to the Treaty three months in advance.'

Secondly, among the contracting States, certain ambiguities exist. It is arguable that the expression 'nuclear explosion' applies only to so-to-speak naked nuclear explosions, but not to small enclosed nuclear explosions which may be used to supply energy to gamma-ray, X-ray or other type of laser weapons in space without producing a 'nuclear explosion' or causing radioactive debris to be present in the environment outside the weapon. It hardly needs to be mentioned that nuclear powered spacecraft are already commonplace.

It might further be argued that, in the light of the title of the Treaty, the intention of the Treaty is essentially to ban *nuclear tests* in time of peace. It is not as such intended to regulate the use of nuclear weapons in time of war or its equivalent under any other name. Witness from this point of view the world's nuclear arsenals.

B. The 1967 Space Treaty

Article IV of the Space Treaty states:

States Parties to the Treaty undertake not to place in orbit around the earth any objects carrying nuclear weapons or any other kinds of weapons of mass destruction, install such weapons on celestial bodies, or station such weapons in outer space in any other manner.

The *moon and other celestial bodies* shall be used by all States Parties to the Treaty *exclusively for peaceful purposes*. The establishment of military bases, installations and fortifications, the testing of any type of weapons and the conduct of military manoeuvres *on celestial bodies* shall be forbidden. The use of military personnel for scientific research or for any other peaceful purposes shall not be prohibited. The use of any equipment or facility necessary for peaceful exploration of the moon and other celestial bodies shall also not be prohibited.[9]

Several points need be noted in connection with Article IV of the Space Treaty.[10]

(i) The Treaty constantly uses the expression, 'outer space, including the moon and celestial bodies'. In general, therefore, for the purpose of the Treaty, 'outer space' includes 'celestial bodies', and 'celestial bodies' include 'the moon'.

(ii) It would follow that Article IV(2) which limits the use of 'the moon and other celestial bodies' to 'exclusively' 'peaceful purposes', does not apply to outer space in the narrow sense of the term, meaning the void between celestial bodies, which, in order to avoid confusion and for the sake of brevity, we shall hereinafter refer to as the 'outer void space'. In other words, notwithstanding a great deal of wishful thinking, misunderstanding, propaganda, and

---

[9] Italics added.
[10] See B. Cheng, 'Le Traité de 1967 sur l'espace/The 1967 Space Treaty', 95 *JDI* (1968), p. 532, at pp. 598–617 [Ch. 9 above, esp. s. VI: Partial Demilitarization of Outer Space and Non-Militarization of Celestial Bodies].

sometimes even misrepresentation, *the 1967 Treaty has not reserved outer space as a whole for use exclusively for peaceful purposes*. The erroneous belief that the whole of outer space has been restricted to use for 'peaceful purposes' only has probably contributed to the misinterpretation of the term 'peaceful'.[11]

(iii) The omission of a reference to the moon in the second sentence of Article IV(2), where 'celestial bodies' alone are mentioned is not regarded as significant, for reasons which have already been given, namely, in the terminology of the Treaty, the term 'celestial bodies' includes the moon.

However, it cannot be precluded that, for those intent on doing so, this omission may well be seized upon, together with some of the other factors mentioned below, as justification to establish military bases, installations, and fortifications, to test weapons and to conduct military manœuvres on the moon,[12] subject only to the prohibitions found in Article IV(1).[13]

(iv) There is a difference of opinion as to whether the first sentence of the second paragraph is all-controlling and, therefore, the rest of the paragraph purely exemplificative, or the first sentence is merely introductory and the rest of the paragraph alone operative. Depending on the interpretation one chooses, even if the word 'peaceful' is interpreted as meaning 'non-military', the construction, for instance, of a mine on the moon or other celestial bodies for the excavation of valuable minerals for the manufacture of space weapons, or of a factory for such manufacture could be regarded as either prohibited or allowed.[14] If the 1959 Antarctic Treaty is any guide,[15] it is submitted that the former interpretation is more in accordance with the intention of the parties.

(v) A fundamental rift exists in the interpretation of the word 'peaceful',[16] which carries with it far-reaching consequences. Some maintain that 'peaceful' means 'non-military', while others argue that it means 'non-aggressive'.

According to the former, who base themselves on the traditional use of the term as exemplified in the 1959 Antarctic Treaty and the numerous treaties on international co-operation in the peaceful uses of nuclear energy,[17] the moon

[11] See B. Cheng, 'The Legal Status of Outer Space and Relevant Issues: Delimitation of Outer Space and Definition of Peaceful Use', 11 *JSL* (1983), p. 89 [cf. Ch. 19 above].

[12] Cf. Jasentuliyana, 'The Moon Treaty', in op. cit. in n. 4 above, p. 121, at p. 130.

[13] See (viii) below.

[14] Cf. e.g., M. Menter, 'Peaceful Uses of Outer Space and National Security', 17(3) *International Lawyer* (1983), p. 581, at pp. 583–4. Note also how the author, in common with many other United States writers, appears to apply the restriction of 'peaceful uses' to the whole of outer space and then, by interpreting the word 'peaceful' to mean really 'peacetime' or 'non-aggressive', to seek to demonstrate that the Treaty will not jeopardize national security. See e.g. also E. R. Finch, 'Outer Space for "Peaceful Purposes" ', 54 *American Bar Association Journal* (1968), p. 365.

[15] Art. I(1) of the Antarctic Treaty provides expressly: 'Antarctica shall be used for peaceful purposes only. There shall be prohibited, *inter alia*, any measure of a military nature . . .' What is enumerated in the second sentence is clearly by way of examples.

[16] See loc. cit. in n. 11 above.

[17] See B. Cheng, 'International Co-operation and Control: From Atoms to Space', 15 *CLP* (1962), p. 228 [Ch. 4 above].

and other celestial bodies are completely demilitarized under the 1967 Space Treaty.

According to the latter interpretation, espoused by the United States and under its influence by its NATO allies, Article IV(2) of the Treaty, except for the prohibitions which it specifically mentions, continues to permit the moon and other celestial bodies to be used for military purposes, as long as these purposes are 'non-aggressive'. This interpretation, which may well have been inspired by the erroneous belief that Article IV(2) applies also to the outer void space, the void between celestial bodies beyond terrestrial national space,[18] renders the first sentence of Article IV(2) totally superfluous, inasmuch as aggressive acts are prohibited in any event under both general international law and Article 2(4), as well as Chapter VII, of the United Nations Charter, the latter forbidding even the threat thereof.[19]

(vi) The 'non-aggressive' interpretation, combined with the interpretation that the second sentence of Article IV(2) is not applicable to the moon,[20] would allow the moon to be used fully for military purposes, including the establishment of moon-based anti-satellite (ASAT) and other weapons, except those prohibited under Article IV(1).[21]

(vii) To the extent to which the 'non-aggressive' interpretation of the word 'peaceful' is prompted by the fear that, otherwise, the 1967 Treaty might deny the military use of the whole of outer space to contracting States for even purely defensive purposes, this fear is totally unfounded, inasmuch as the *limitation to use exclusively for peaceful purposes*, as has been mentioned before, *applies only to the moon and other celestial bodies and does not apply to the vast empty space in between.*[22]

(viii) The only specific limitation placed on the use of the outer void space (i.e., the empty space between celestial bodies beyond terrestrial national space) for military purposes in the Space Treaty is that found in Article IV(1), namely, the prohibition of the stationing, including the placing in earth and presumably any other orbit, of 'nuclear weapons or any other kinds of weapons of mass destruction' anywhere in outer space, including the moon and other celestial bodies. This renders compulsory among the contracting States what was a stated policy of the United States and the Soviet Union as communicated to the United Nations, and one urged upon all States by the UN General Assembly in its Resolution 1885 of 17 October 1993, but neither Article IV nor the Treaty as a whole imposes any other restriction on the military use of the outer void space. It follows that, insofar as the 1967 Space Treaty is concerned, *the outer void space as such* can be used for any military activity that is compatible with general international law and the Charter of the United Nations, as long as no 'nuclear weapons or any other kind of

---

[18] Cf. (ii) and n. 14 above.
[19] Cf. M. Lachs, 'Opening Address', in op. cit. in n. 4 above, p. 5, at p. 7.
[20] See (iii) above.   [21] See (viii) below.   [22] See (ii) above.

weapons of mass destruction' are *stationed* there, including being placed there in earth orbit. Subject to this limitation and such constraints as may be found in general international law, the Charter of the United Nations, and any other treaty commitments, contracting States to the 1967 Space Treaty, even under the interpretation that 'peaceful' means 'non-military' and not 'non-aggressive', would, therefore, remain perfectly entitled to conduct any military activity, including research, experiments, exercises, and manœuvres, in outer void space, and to test, deploy and station there any number of military reconnaissance satellites, early warning satellites, meteorological satellites, communications satellites, geodetic satellites, navigation satellites, anti-satellite weapons (ASAT), ballistic missile defence (BMD) systems, permanently manned space stations, and any other kind of weaponry or device, all either partly or exclusively for military purposes.

If this is not enough, the use of the phrase 'any *other* kind of weapons of mass destruction' suggests that what the Treaty has in mind may not necessarily be nuclear weapons as such, but only nuclear weapons that cause 'mass destruction'. Provided, therefore, that they do not cause *mass* destruction, whatever mass destruction may be interpreted to mean,[23] it might conceivably be argued, though perhaps not convincingly because of the express wording of the provision, that the stationing in outer void space of, for example, mini-nuclear space mines, with very limited impact, would not be prohibited under the Space Treaty, even when 'peaceful' is interpreted to mean 'non-military', although their testing and use in peacetime may contravene, for those States that are parties to it, the Partial Nuclear Test Ban Treaty.[24]

Moreover, in addition to what has already been said in connection with the Test Ban Treaty, this interpretation of the words 'any other kind of weapons of mass destruction' would further reinforce the contention that Article IV(1) is no obstacle to the stationing in outer void space of *nuclear powered weapons*, such as X-ray lasers,[25] provided that their use does not entail 'mass' (i.e., large-scale) 'destruction',[26] and for those that are parties to the Partial Nuclear Test Ban Treaty, the causing of any radioactive debris in the environment.

Furthermore, it should be pointed out that what the parties have agreed to refrain from in Article IV(1) is simply to station such weapons in outer space,

---

[23] The United Nations Commission for Conventional Armaments resolved on 12 Aug. 1948 that 'weapons of mass destruction should be defined to include atomic explosive weapons, radioactive material weapons, lethal chemical and biological weapons, and any weapons developed in the future which have characteristics comparable in destructive effect to those of the atomic bomb or other weapons mentioned above', UN S/C.3/32/Rev.1 (18.8.48). It should, however, be remembered that this was only a working definition and recommendation, and cannot be regarded as a binding definition of the expression under general international law, and still less an authoritative or authentic interpretation of the 1967 Space Treaty.

[24] See s. III.A above.   [25] See ibid.

[26] Cf. Eilene Galloway, 'International Institutions to Ensure Peaceful Uses of Outer Space', in op. cit. in n. 4 above, p. 143, at p. 156: 'mass destruction is large-scale destruction of either life or property or both . . .'; and see n. 23 above.

including celestial bodies. They have not agreed to refrain from either (a) using any kind of weapon in outer void space or (b) sending any kind of weapon to their target through outer void space. The 1967 Treaty is certainly no obstacle to the passage through outer void space on their way to their targets of land-to-land, sea-to-land or air-to-land ballistic missiles with nuclear warheads. And, unless one is governed by the Partial Nuclear Test Ban Treaty, even the exploding of a nuclear warhead in outer void space by a missile fired from the earth, whether land-, sea- or air-based, as long as it is not space-based, is not covered by Article IV(1) of the Space Treaty, though it may contravene other rules of international law. From this point of view, as has been suggested, it might even be argued that, on account of its title, which is Treaty Banning Nuclear Weapon Tests in the Atmosphere, in Outer Space and Under Water, the Test Ban Treaty governs merely the testing of weapons but not their use, which is subject only to such rules as exist in general international law or applicable treaties on the use of force or on the use of weapons, although such an interpretation would be contrary to the text of the Treaty. The prohibition in its Article I applies expressly not only to 'nuclear weapon test explosion', but also 'any other nuclear explosion'.

A further point that may be noted in this connection is that, whilst the stationing of weapons of mass destruction in outer space is prohibited by the 1967 Space Treaty, nothing prevents the stationing of such weapons in a State's own territory, including its national airspace, provided they are not in earth orbit. Since there is no agreed delimitation of the boundary between national airspace and outer space, a question which the United States does not wish even to see discussed, this can be an added source of conflict.[27]

(ix) In sum, it can be seen that, contrary to the fear that national security would be impaired if it were otherwise, the adoption of the 'non-military' interpretation of the word 'peaceful' in Article IV of the Space Treaty, will still leave the contracting parties with almost complete freedom to use outer void space (i.e., the empty space between celestial bodies beyond terrestrial national space) for military purposes, except the stationing there of weapons of mass destruction, something which does not appear to provide any strategic or tactical advantage and which no space power seems to be thinking of undertaking. It is much safer to store such weapons in the security of one's own territory, or to have a few of them carried in nuclear submarines lurking, hopefully undetected, somewhere around the world, than to leave them, for everyone to see, like sitting ducks, in their orbit where they may easily be disabled or destroyed by one's enemy. Under the 'non-military' interpretation of

---

[27] See B. Cheng, 'The Legal Régime of Airspace and Outer Space: The Boundary Problem— Functionalism *versus* Spatialism: The Major Premises', 5 *AASL* (1980), p. 323 [Ch. 14 above]; 'For Delimiting Outer Space', in McGill University Center for Research of Air and Space Law, *Proceedings of the Symposium on Earth-oriented Space Activities and Their Legal Implications, Montreal, 1981* (1983), p. 230; 'The Legal Status of Outer Space and Relevant Issues: Delimitation of Outer Space and Definition of Peaceful Use', 11 *JSL* (1983), p. 89.

the word 'peaceful', the moon and other celestial bodies will, however, be completely demilitarized by the 1967 Space Treaty. For those who embrace the interpretation that 'peaceful' means 'non-aggressive' and especially those who wish to exploit what is no more than a stylistic ellipsis in the second sentence of Article IV(2), what has been said of outer void space would be true also of the moon. For them, the only real restrictions laid down by Article IV(2) are the establishment of military bases, installations, testing of weapons and the conduct of military manœuvres on *celestial bodies other than the moon* and the earth. As, outside the earth, the moon is the only celestial body that has remotely any possible military use, this construction renders Article IV(2) utterly devoid of any meaning or practical effect.

Table XX.1 ARTICLE IV OF THE 1967 SPACE TREATY ON THE MILITARY USE OF OUTER SPACE

OBJECTS AND ACTIVITIES PROHIBITED	AREA COVERED
Nuclear weapons and other weapons of mass destruction (para. 1)	In orbit around the earth, installed on celestial bodies, or stationed in outer space in any manner
Uses not for peaceful purposes (para. 2)	The moon and other celestial bodies **[NB: NOT THE SPACE BETWEEN CELESTIAL BODIES]**

C. The 1977 Geneva Convention on the Prohibition of Military or any other Hostile Use of Environmental Modification Techniques

Suffice it to say that this Treaty, which prohibits the use of environmental modification techniques 'as the means of destruction, damage or injury to any other State Party', is applicable to outer space.[28]

D. The 1979 Moon Treaty

Six points may be made in this regard in relation to the Moon Treaty.[29]

---

[28] 16 *ILM* (1977) p. 88; cf. C. Q. Christol, 'The Convention on the Prohibition of Military or Any Other Hostile Use of Environmental Modification Techniques', in op. cit. in n. 4 above, p. 189.
[29] See further B. Cheng, 'The Moon Treaty', 33 *CLP* (1980), p. 213 [Ch. 12 above], and loc. cit. in n. 6 above, at pp. 90–2 [Ch. 13 above, s. III.E: The 1979 Moon Treaty].

(i) It should be noted that under Article 1(1) of the Moon Treaty, reference to the moon in the Treaty applies also to 'other celestial bodies within the solar system, other than the earth'. The same extension applies accordingly to references to provisions of the Moon Treaty in this chapter and particularly this section.

(ii) For those who believe that Article IV(2) of the 1967 Space Treaty lays down a binding rule totally demilitarizing the moon and other celestial bodies, Article 3(1) and (4) of the Moon Treaty in particular, and the Treaty as a whole do little more than to reiterate that provision of the Space Treaty, except perhaps to clarify the omission of the reference to the moon in the second sentence of the latter by making it clear now that the enumerated prohibitions under the Moon Treaty apply to the moon no less than to all other celestial bodies within the solar system apart from the earth. However, those who place significance on the omission of any explicit reference to the moon in the second sentence of Article IV(2) of the Space Treaty may seek to argue that this is not so much a clarification as an extension of those restrictions by the new treaty to the moon. For those of them who also embrace the 'non-aggressive' interpretation of the word 'peaceful' in Article IV(2) of the Space Treaty, this means in any event no more than that, for those States bound by the Moon Treaty, the specific prohibitions laid down in Article IV(2) of the Space Treaty now apply, for those who are bound by the Moon Treaty, also to the moon, as well as to other celestial bodies.

(iii) In introducing a prohibition in its Article 3(2) on the threat or use of force or of hostile act on the moon, or the use of the moon in order to commit any such acts or to engage in any such threats in relation to 'the earth, the moon, spacecraft, the personnel of spacecraft or man-made space objects', the Moon Treaty could be regarded as doing no more than to re-iterate the basic principle underlying Article 2(4) of the United Nations Charter, whilst at the same time gilding the lily of 'peaceful purposes' in its Article 3(1). Otherwise, the question may well be asked whether Article 3(2) has the effect of implying that such acts are only prohibited 'on the moon', but permitted elsewhere. Article 3(2) could, however, be interpreted as applicable also to the acts on the moon of persons acting under authority delegated to them by a State, for instance, the commander of a spacecraft in relation to astronauts or spacecraft of that State, or even to acts of private individuals. If so, the implementation of this provision may well give rise to some not necessarily anticipated problems, such as the consequences under international law of violations of this provision.

(iv) Article 3(3) of the Moon Treaty simply repeats Article IV(1) of the Space Treaty with special reference to the moon. The only addition possibly is the prohibition of the placing of nuclear weapons or other kinds of weapons of mass destruction in a trajectory to the moon.

(v) Article 15 of the Moon Treaty confers a right of mutual supervision on the contracting Parties, including a right to visit one another's space vehicles, equipment, installations, and so forth on the moon, in order to ensure compliance with the Treaty. This right, while still subject to 'reasonable advance notice', is no longer subject to 'reciprocity', as under Article XII of the 1967 Space Treaty. Moreover, failing an amicable settlement of any differences between the contracting States arising from the exercise or attempted exercise of this right, any party to the dispute may seek the assistance of the UN Secretary-General, 'without seeking the consent of any other State Party concerned, in order to resolve the controversy'.

(vi) The Moon Treaty, though in force, has so far been accepted by only a few States none of which is a significant space power. It does not appear that it is likely to play a major rôle in the regulation of the military use of outer space.

E. The 1972 Treaty between the United States and the Soviet Union on the Limitation of Anti-Ballistic Missile Systems (ABM Treaty), and the 1974 Protocol

Even on the assumption that it has completely demilitarized the moon and other celestial bodies, we have seen that the 1967 Space Treaty still leaves wide open the possibility of the use of every kind of weapon in outer void space, and the possibility of stationing them there, except nuclear weapons and other kinds of weapons of mass destruction. However, certain restrictions exist in the relations between the United States and the Soviet Union regarding anti-ballistic systems, by virtue of the 1972 ABM Treaty between them on the Limitation of Anti-Ballistic Missile Systems.[30] Under Article V(1):

Each Party undertakes not to develop, test, or deploy ABM systems or components which are *sea-based, air-based, space-based, or mobile land-based*.[31]

Attached to the Treaty is a document setting out 'Agreed Interpretations and Unilateral Statements on ABM Treaty . . .'[32] Under the heading (b) *Common Understandings*, sub-heading (D) *Mobile ABM Systems*, it would seem clear that what the parties envisaged was that the provisions of the Treaty 'rule out the deployment of ABM launchers and radars which were not permanent fixed types', i.e., permanently fixed on earth. On the face of it, the ABM Treaty specifically prohibits *air-based* and *space-based*, as well as sea-based and mobile land-based, ABM systems, insofar as the contracting States are concerned.

However, it has sometimes been observed that, on controversial issues, especially when their legal position is not very strong, the two super powers appear usually each to follow a set pattern of behaviour. On the one hand Soviet government pronouncements tend not infrequently to play conjuring

[30] 11 *ILM* (1972), p. 784. [31] Italics added. [32] 11 *ILM* (1972), p. 796.

tricks with facts, as they did, for instance, in the 1960 RB–47 incident involving the shooting down of a United States reconnaissance aircraft,[33] and the
1983 Korean Air Lines case when Soviet fighters shot down a civilian air-
liner.[34] This foible, which is not uncommon to totalitarian regimes, may be
due to their ability to manipulate their own media and opinion at home, and
their habit of doing so becoming second nature, oblivious of the fact that foreign media and public opinion abroad cannot be so easily controlled. On the
other hand, United States government lawyers are prone from time to time to
indulge in some kind of legal acrobatics, as, for example, in their defence of
the United States interception of an Egyptian aircraft over the high seas in
1985 after the *Archille Lauro* hijacking,[35] and their interpretation of the word
'peaceful' in Article IV(2) of the Space Treaty.[36] From the purely legal point
of view, the tragedy is that very often crude and forced arguments are arro-
gantly advanced, with apparently scant regard to their consequences for the
country's long-term legal position, even when more subtle and plausible ways
may, with a little effort, sometimes be found to achieve the desired objective,
thus giving rise to the distinct impression that relatively little importance is
attached to legal argumentation in the process of decision-making and deci-
sion-presentation.[37] On the level of auto-interpretative international law, such
antics, whether with facts or with the law, are extremely difficult to control.

In order to justify the US Administration's programme of Strategic Defense
Initiative (SDI) in relation to the ABM Treaty, to the extent to which it is not
going to be fixed land-based, various arguments have been advanced in the
United States.

The first argument in favour of SDI takes advantage of the polysemous
character of the law, and maintains that *research* is not *development* and still
less *testing* or *deployment*, which alone are prohibited by the treaty. While
there is no doubt a distinction between what is purely research and development, there can also be research which is hardly distinguishable from development. In any event, this argument will not allow the programme to proceed
beyond what can distinctly no longer be called research and what is clearly on
the road of development.

[33] See B. Cheng, 'The United Nations and Outer Space', 14 *CLP* (1961), p. 247, at pp. 286–72
[Ch. 6 above, s. V.B: Peripheral Reconnaissance].

[34] See B. Cheng, 'The Destruction of KAL Flight KE007 and Article 3*bis* of the Chicago
Convention', in J. W. E. Storm van 's Gravesande and A. van der Veen Vonk (eds.), *Air Worthy.
Liber Amicorum Honouring Professor Dr I. H. Ph. Diederiks-Verschoor* (1985), p. 47.

[35] See B. Cheng, 'Aviation, Criminal Jurisdiction and Terrorism: The Hague
Extradition/Prosecution Formula and Attacks at Airports', in B. Cheng and E. D. Brown (eds.),
*Contemporary Problems of International Law: Essays in honour of Georg Schwarzenberger on his
eightieth birthday* (1988), p. 25, at pp. 48–9.

[36] See s. III.B, (v) above, and Cheng, loc. cit. in n. 10 above [Ch. 9 above].

[37] It is not uninteresting to find Senator D. P. Moynihan, commenting on the contemporary
Washington DC scene, said: 'The idea of international law *had* faded. But just as important, in
the 1980s it had come to be associated with weakness in foreign policy. Real men did not cite
Grotius' (*On the Law of Nations* (1990), p. 7, original italics).

A second argument relies on paragraph [E] (often erroneously designated as paragraph D) of the *Initialed Statements* among the *Agreed Interpretations*. This calls for consultation under the established procedure of the Treaty on 'specific limitations' on ABM systems which 'are created in the future' 'based on other physical principles' 'capable of substituting for' existing ABM missiles, launchers, or radars. This paragraph which is specifically designed 'to insure fulfillment of the obligation not to deploy ABM systems and their components except as provided in Article III of the Treaty', is now invoked virtually to nullify the treaty when ABM systems 'based on other physical principles' become possible. Such an interpretation, paradoxically called 'broad interpretation', is using what is a mere 'agreed interpretation', not to interpret it, but to override a clear provision in the Treaty itself. Moreover, it hardly accords with what appears to be the original and true intention of the parties.[38]

Thirdly, the interpretation placed by Mr Abraham Sofaer, Legal Adviser to the State Department, on the ABM Treaty, relying heavily but not exclusively on paragraph [E] of the Initialed Statements among the Agreed Interpretations (what he calls agreed statement D) appears in fact to be an extreme form of the doctrine of *clausula rebus sic stantibus*, to wit, a treaty applies for as long as things remain as they stood at the time of its conclusion.[39] Such extreme forms of the doctrine are highly dangerous and can easily rebound on their user.

Fourthly, another argument in law has sometimes been mentioned, although not in so many words and not directly in justification of the SDI, namely, the Latin maxim *Inadimplenti non est adimplendum*, in other words, non-fulfilment of a treaty obligation is justifiable in regard to a contracting party who fails to fulfil his part of the bargain. The specific charges are first that the Soviet Union's radar station at Krasnoyarsk is in violation of the ABM Treaty, and subsequently that the Soviet Union itself had been developing alternative ABM systems for many years, something which the Soviet Union has since tardily acknowledged. Such belated admissions under pressure can hardly be regarded as a feather in the Soviet cap of trustworthiness in treaty compliance. However, in the circumstances, the Treaty might perhaps be said to have undergone a *de facto* amendment by subsequent common practice,[40] which now permits development of, as well as research on, alternative ABM systems, including space-based ones, by both parties.

---

[38] Cf. paragraph (A)(3) ('Future ABM Systems) of Secretary of State William Roger's letter of 10 June 1972 transmitting the ABM Treaty to President R. Nixon, which was attached to President Nixon's Letter of Transmittal of the Treaty to the Senate dated 13 June 1972, 11 *ILM* (1972), p. 923.

[39] 26 *ILM* (1987), p. 283.

[40] On interpretation of treaties through subsequent practice, see International Court of Justice, *Temple of Preah Vihear Case* (1962), *ICJ Rep. 1962*, p. 6; and 1969 Vienna Convention on the Law of Treaties, Art. 31(3)(b). Re radar station, see below Ch. 22, n. 64.

IV. Concluding Remarks

This leads us to the crux of the problem of arms control: verification and the degree of good faith that one partner in any such arrangement is entitled and able to expect from the other or others in its compliance.

For a number of years, the Soviet Union has been making proposals for the complete banning of weapons in space. With the Soviet Union's track record of playing games with facts, it is perhaps not surprising that others are sceptical of Greek gifts, fearing not only what may be no more than a hollow propaganda stunt, but also what may prove to be a deadly trap.

Among recent Soviet moves are the bringing forth of these proposals before the United Nations Committee on the Peaceful Uses of Outer Space (COPUOS) and the Soviet plan for a world space organization (WSO).[41] These moves raise another problem, and bring back memories of the very early days of COPUOS when the Soviet Union was in a minority there, as well as in the General Assembly. The Soviet Union then pointedly refused to discuss matters of disarmament in COPUOS, maintaining that they fell strictly within the competence of the Disarmament Committee, and fought hard against resolving principles of space law by General Assembly resolutions.[42]

The tables have now been turned. If the Soviet Union still does not have an assured majority in COPUOS or in the General Assembly, the United States does, however, from time to time find itself in a minority in these bodies. The United States is consequently not unnaturally chary of having such matters discussed in COPUOS, instead of the Conference on Disarmament or bilateral negotiations, and of leaving such issues to be dealt with by yet another international organization where its freedom of action to say the least may be subject to all kinds of collective pressure.

In any meaningful law-making, three conditions are vital: (i) perceived need; (ii) propitious climate; and (iii) due representation of the dominant section.[43]

It is probably correct to say that, at this moment, the climate is not unpropitious, with various treaties on disarmament and on outer space cooperation having recently been concluded between the United States and the Soviet Union. What is now required is that the super-space powers themselves should clarify in their own mind what they really need and want and are

---

[41] See UN Doc. A/AC.105/L.171 (13.6.88), Soviet proposal on Basic Provisions of the Charter of a World Space Organization.

[42] See loc. cit. in n. 33 above, at pp. 272–9 [Ch. 6 above, s. VI: Demilitarization and Disarmament]; and 'United Nations Resolutions on Outer Space: "Instant" International Customary Law?', 5 *Indian JIL* (1965), p. 23, at pp. 27–30 [Ch. 7 above, ss. V and VI: Treaty v. Resolution, and Superpower Dominance].

[43] See B. Cheng, 'The United Nations and the Development of International Law Relating to Outer Space', 16 *Thesaurus Acroasium* (1990), p. 49, at pp. 113–21 [Ch. 8 above, s. VI: Conditions Governing International Rule-Making]; and Epilogue below, s. IV.

willing to give up, that there should be sufficient guarantees that agreements will be kept in good faith, and that, in any arrangement or organization to be set up, States' interests, capability, responsibility, and their gains and concessions in real terms, are all duly taken into account.

Meanwhile, the question may be raised whether the best tactic to be used in international relations is to resort to legal acrobatics or the deliberate distortion of facts. Thus the United States re-interpretation of the word 'peaceful' to mean merely 'peacetime' or 'non-aggressive', and its refusal to discuss the question of the boundary between airspace and outer space, as well as certain other rather strained methods of treaty interpretation, are not only making lucid discussions of the problems of outer space difficult, but may also render the rules of international law on many other issues dangerously unclear.[44] To take a recent example, the United States interpretation of the word 'peaceful' may thus cause serious soul searching on the part of the other partners to the Permanently Manned *Civil* Space Station programme, when these partners come to determine for themselves whether a contemplated use by others of an element which they have provided is or is not for 'peaceful purposes'.[45]

On the other hand, the Soviet Union may have some way to go yet to gain full credibility in its good faith in the observance of rules of international law and treaty obligations, without which chances of success in meaningful arms control in outer space, as in many other fields, will remain precarious.

---

[44] See Conclusion No. 6 of the 1984 United Nations University Symposium on Maintaining Outer Space for Peaceful Uses which refers to existing 'divergences of interpretation' and points to the desirability of 'a coherent use of definitions and terms', op. cit. in n. 4 above, p. 3.

[45] See Agreement Among the Government of the United States of America, Governments of Member States of the European Space Agency, the Government of Japan, and the Government of Canada on Cooperation in the Detailed Design, Development, Operation, and Utilization of the Permanently Manned Civil Space Station, 1988, Arts. 9(8)(b) and 14(1).

PART VI

COMMERCIAL USES
OF OUTER SPACE
AND INTERNATIONAL LAW

21

Communications Satellites*

I. Introduction

When the idea of relaying communications by artificial earth satellites was put forward in 1945,[1] it appeared to verge on science fiction. Yet, less than 25 years later, on 21 July 1969, thanks to artificial satellites (which made transoceanic television transmission possible for the first time), live pictures of man's first landing on the moon were brought by television to an estimated audience of 500 million people in virtually all parts of the world.[2] Satellites have added a new dimension to telecommunications. Little wonder that the United Nations General Assembly in its Resolution 1721 D (XVI) of 20 December 1961, expressed the view that:

communication by means of satellites should be available to the nations of the world as soon as practicable on a global and non-discriminatory basis.

II. Types and Systems of Communications Satellites

A. Passive and Active Communications Satellites

Passive communications satellites are mere reflectors of radio waves. Examples are Echo I and Echo II launched by the United States in 1960 and 1964 respectively. Though simple in concept, passive communications satellites, if nothing else, require more elaborate earth stations. Almost all the operational and planned communications satellites are *active communications satellites* which can receive, amplify, and retransmit radio signals. They are like radio towers in the sky.

---

* First published in 24 *CLP* (1971), pp. 211–45, with the relevant sections replaced by 'INTELSAT—The Definitive Arrangements', first published in M. K. Nawaz (ed.), *Essays on International Law in Honour of Krishna Rao* (1975), pp. 156–69. The former article reproduced by kind permission of Sweet & Maxwell Ltd., and the latter by kind permission of the Indian Society of International Law.

[1] A. C. Clarke, 'Extraterrestrial Relays', *Wireless World* (1945), p. 305.

[2] For an account of this broadcast, see Hearings on *Assessment of Space Communications Technology* before the Sub-Committee on Space Science and Applications of the US House of Representatives Committee on Science and Astronautics, 91st Cong., 1st Sess., Dec. 16–19, 1969 (1970), p. 144.

B. Geostationary and Other Orbits

All the early satellites, including Telstar I which transmitted the first ever live television pictures across the Atlantic on 13 July 1962, were placed in low *elliptical orbits* so that, relative to the earth, they were moving constantly and could link earth stations in any given part of the world for only limited periods. The same would be true of a low *circular orbit*. A succession of satellites is required in order to provide continuity.

Continuity can alternatively be assured by placing a satellite in a *synchronous* or *geostationary orbit*, which is a circular orbit above the equator at a height of just over 22,300 miles (36,000 km). Such a satellite would appear to an observer on the earth as if it were stationary. A satellite at this height is able to provide round-the-clock communications between earth stations belonging to the systems within an area covering 40 per cent of the earth's surface, known as its footprint. Three geostationary satellites, strategically placed, can cover the entire planet, with the exception of regions above latitude 75° south or north.

This is the basis of the INTELSAT global satellite system which has satellites over the Atlantic, the Indian, and the Pacific Oceans. The first satellite in this system Early Bird (later renamed INTELSAT I) was launched on 6 April 1965. The global system was first achieved on 1 July 1969.

Partly at least because geostationary satellites cannot reach the polar regions, the Soviet Union in its Molnya system favours a long elliptical orbit having its apogee in the northern hemisphere at a height of 24,500 miles (40,000 km.). The Molnya satellites take about twelve hours to circle the globe. The first was launched on 23 April 1965. It is estimated that, in principle, three such satellites would be enough to provide uninterrupted 24-hour service, and about fifteen satellites in co-ordinated orbits to provide worldwide service. The Molnya system was originally designed primarily for domestic use, but it also provides communications facilities with certain other countries such as France and Cuba. Orbita is the name of the earth station network operated in conjunction with the Molnya satellites.[3]

---

[3] See UN, *Practical Benefits of Space Exploration* (1969), pp. 19 ff. summarizing papers on Orbita and Molnya I submitted by Soviet scientists to the UN Conference on the Exploration and Peaceful Uses of Outer Space, Vienna, 1968, and published in UN, *Space Exploration and Applications* (1969); N. I. Tchistiakov, 'Evolution of Satellites and Orbits', in UNESCO, *Communication in the Space Age* (1968), pp. 138 ff.; J. Voge, 'Les applications des satellites de télécommunications,' in Centre national de la recherche scientifique, *Les télécommunications par satellites* (1968), p. 24; R. Brown, *Telecommunications* (1969).

MAP XXI.1 THE INTELSAT SYSTEM IN 1970

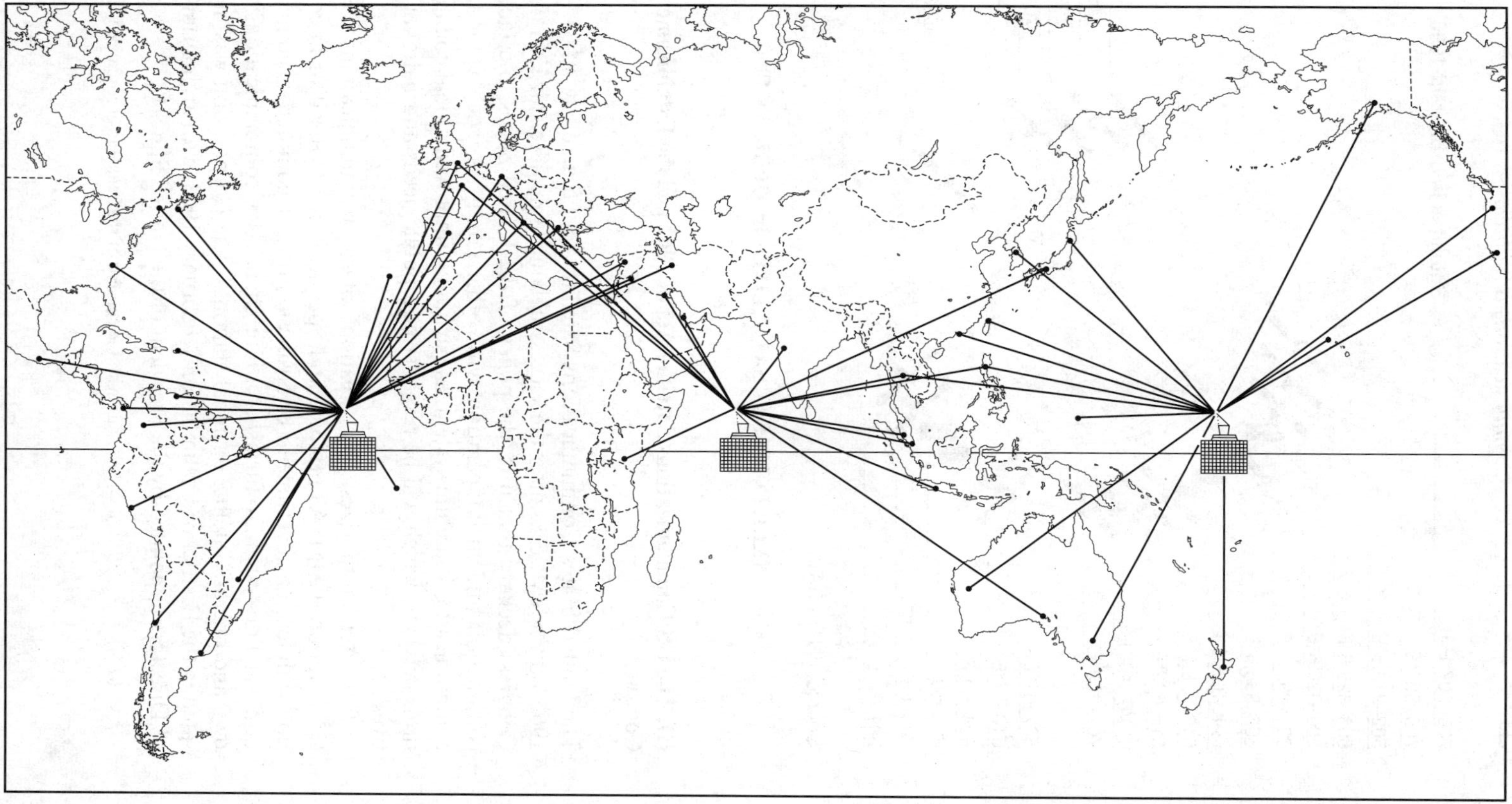

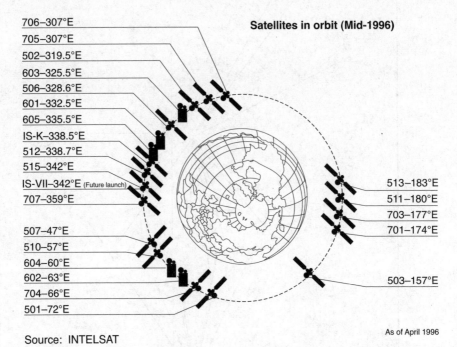

706–307°E
705–307°E
502–319.5°E
603–325.5°E
506–328.6°E
601–332.5°E
605–335.5°E
IS-K–338.5°E
512–338.7°E
515–342°E
IS-VII–342°E (Future launch)
707–359°E
507–47°E
510–57°E
604–60°E
602–63°E
704–66°E
501–72°E

Satellites in orbit (Mid-1996)

513–183°E
511–180°E
703–177°E
701–174°E

503–157°E

As of April 1996

Source: INTELSAT

Figure XXI.1. INTELSAT SATELLITES IN ORBIT IN 1996

III. The US Communications Satellite Act of 1962 and the Establishment of Comsat

The United States Communications Satellite Act became law on 31 August 1962, only a few weeks after the successful launching of Telstar I. In this Act, Congress declares that it is 'the policy of the United States to establish, in conjunction and in cooperation with other countries, . . . a commercial communications satellite system, as part of an improved global communications network, which will be responsive to public needs and national objectives . . .'[4]

The Act authorizes the creation of a Communications Satellite Corporation (COMSAT) to own and operate, either by itself or in conjunction with foreign governments or business entities, a commercial communications satellite system; to furnish, for hire, channels of communications; and to own and operate satellite terminal stations.[5] The Corporation was incorporated in the District of Columbia on 1 February 1963, with an interim Board of Directors appointed by the President of the United States.[6]

---

[4] s. 102 (*a*).   [5] s. 305 (*a*).   [6] By and with the consent of the Senate in accordance with s. 302.

The Corporation is, however, not an agency or establishment of the United States government.[7] The Act authorizes the Corporation to issue shares of capital stock, 50 per cent of which are to be reserved for authorized United States communications common carriers, the remainder for sale to the public.[8] Under the 1962 Act, as amended in 1969, out of the fifteen directors, eight are elected by the Series I (public) shareholders, four by the Series II (carrier) shareholders, and three appointed by the President of the United States with the advice and consent of the Senate.

Although the Communications Satellite Act proclaims that COMSAT is a private corporation, subject to appropriate governmental regulations,[9] and 'will not be an agency or establishment of the United States Government,'[10] it seems obvious from the Act and from the presence of three government-appointed directors on the Board, that COMSAT is the chosen instrument of the United States in the provision, with or without the participation of foreign governments or interests, of 'a commercial communications satellite system, as part of an improved global communications network . . . responsive to public needs and national objectives . . .'[11]

No sooner had it been established than COMSAT proceeded apace with plans to discharge its intended rôle, including the launching in 1965 of Early Bird, the first step towards a global communications satellite system.

IV. INTELSAT: The Interim Arrangements

A. Creation

Meanwhile, in May 1963, a European Conference on Satellite Communications (CETS) was created, and met for the first time in London in July 1963. The European States resolved to negotiate jointly with the United States, and a series of talks with NASA representatives took place in 1963. It soon became clear that, because of the wide technological gap between them, the European States had little alternative but to join the Americans and to do so very much on their terms.[12]

The result was the conclusion at Washington on 20 August 1964, of two separate agreements, first, the Agreement establishing Interim Arrangements

---

[7] s. 301.   [8] s. 304.   [9] s. 102 (c).   [10] s. 301.

[11] Cf. *inter alia*, s. 201 (*a*)(2), Presidential review of activities; s. 201 (*a*)(4), Presidential supervision of COMSAT relationships with foreign governments or entities; s. 201 (*b*), NASA co-operation with and assistance to COMSAT; ss. 301, 302, initial establishment of the corporation; s. 303, directors; s. 305, purposes and powers of the corporation; s. 402, foreign relations; s. 404, reports to President and Congress. See also COMSAT, *Annual Report 1964* (1965), p. 13, cols. 1–2.

[12] Cf. Council of Europe, Consultative Assembly, Committee on Science and Technology Report on *Long-term prospects of space exploration for Europe* (rapporteur: Mrs Maxsein), Doc. 2517 (16.1.69), pp. 34 ff. See also a British Postmaster-General White Paper on *Satellite Communications* (1964) presented to Parliament in 1964, Cmnd. 2436.

for a Global Commercial Communications Satellite System and, secondly, the Special Agreement concluded pursuant to Article II of that Agreement.[13] A year later, a Supplementary Agreement on Arbitration was established on 4 June 1965.[14]

The United States government, in publishing the 1964 Interim Agreement and Special Agreement in its Treaties and Other International Acts Series, committed a rather embarrassing *lapsus calami* when it entitled the document, 'Communications Satellite System (COMSAT)' on the cover and 'Multilateral Communications Satellite System (COMSAT)' on the inside title page. The title International Telecommunications Satellite Consortium (INTELSAT) was adopted on 28 October 1965, and appears on copies of TIAS No. 5646 reprinted in January 1967.[15] [16]

Legally, it is open to question whether INTELSAT has any corporate existence.[17] Structurally, there are three levels to INTELSAT.

B. Inter-Governmental Level

There is first the inter-governmental level. Under Article XII of the Interim Agreement, the treaty is open for signature or accession by the government of any State which is a member of the International Telecommunication Union. As of 1 January 1971, 77 States were parties to the Interim Agreement. However, the powers and functions of the participating States appear to be limited to laying down the basic rules of the consortium in the Interim Agreement, the Special Agreement and the Supplementary Agreement. They have nothing further to do except each to designate either itself or a 'communications entity', which may be public or private, to become a signatory of the Special Agreement (the parties to which hereinafter referred to as 'signatories').[18] Indeed, under its Article 15, the Special Agreement may even be amended without reference to the participating States. Furthermore, participating States, as such, have no *locus standi* in arbitration proceedings instituted under the Supplementary Agreement.[19]

C. Inter-Signatory Level

The consortium begins to take shape from this level onwards. The so-called 'space segment' (that is to say, the communications satellites and their supporting installations and facilities)[20] of INTELSAT is 'owned in undivided

---

[13] UKTA No. 12 (1966), Cmnd. 2940.   [14] UKTS No. 71 (1967), Cmnd. 3375.
[15] TIAS 5646—US Government Printing Office (1964).
[16] See R. R. Colino, 'INTELSAT: Doing Business in Space', 6 *Columbia J. of Transnational L.* (1967), p. 17, at p. 19, n. 6.
[17] Cf. Colino, ibid., at pp. 42 ff.   [18] Art. II.   [19] Art. 2(*c*).
[20] See Interim Agreement, Art. I(*b*)(i): 'the term "space segment" comprises the communications satellites and the tracking, control, command and related facilities and equipment required to support the operation of the communications satellites,' i.e., not including earth stations.

shares by the signatories to the Special Agreement in proportion to their respective contributions to the costs of . . . the space segment'.[21] The percentages of contributions are set forth in the Annex to the Special Agreement.[22] The governing body of INTELSAT is the Interim Communications Satellite Committee (ICSC or Interim Committee), composed of 'one representative from each of the signatories to the Special Agreement whose quota is not less than 1.5 per cent, and one representative from any two or more signatories to the Special Agreement whose combined quotas total not less than 1.5 per cent and which have agreed to be so represented.'[23]

The Interim Committee is responsible for calling up funds within a limit of US$200 million.[24] It may decide on 'additional contributions'[25] up to $300 million without reference, and in excess of that sum only after a special conference of the signatories.[26] A signatory 'may assume the obligation to pay all or part of its quota of any such additional contribution,' but is not required to do so.[27]

The Committee is generally responsible for the establishment and operation of the space segment.[28] In particular it approves the programme for the launching of satellites,[29] establishes standards for approval of earth stations,[30] fixes utilization charges,[31] approves the investment quotas of new signatories,[32] approves budgets by major categories,[33] exercises supervision over contracts exceeding certain sums to be concluded by COMSAT,[34] and approves the appropriate compensation to be agreed upon with COMSAT for its services as manager.[35]

The Interim Agreement provides that the Interim Committee 'shall endeavour to act unanimously.' Failing agreement, the Committee decides by a majority of the votes cast.[36] However, in all matters of relevance, a system of weighted voting applies: 'any decision must have the concurrence of representatives whose total votes exceed the vote of the representative with the largest vote by not less than 12.5.'[37] In certain circumstances, the percentage may be reduced to 8.5.[38]

[21] Interim Agreement, Art. III.

[22] Special Agreement, Art. 3.

[23] Interim Agreement, Art. IV(*b*).

[24] Interim Agreement, Art. VI(*a*).

[25] See Art. V(*c*)(vi).

[26] Interim Agreement, Art. VI(*b*).

[27] Interim Agreement, Art. VI(*c*); cf. Colino, loc. cit. in n. 16 above, p. 42, n. 78, who sets out the arguments for and against interpreting the mandatory ceiling as being $200m. or $300m. In the writer's opinion, the expression 'additional contributions' has the same meaning in Arts. V(*c*)(vi), VI(*b*) and VI(*c*), and includes contributions in excess of $200m. See also para. 15 of the United Kingdom White Paper on *Satellite Communications* (1964) which evidently regards contributions within the $200m. to $300m. range as optional, Cmnd. 2436, p. 7.

[28] Interim Agreement, Art. IV(*a*).

[29] Special Agreement, Art. 10(*d*).

[30] Interim Agreement, Art. VII.

[31] Special Agreement, Art. 9.

[32] Interim Agreement, Art. XII.

[33] Interim Agreement, Art V(*c*)(iii); Special Agreement, Art. 12(*a*).

[34] Special Agreement, Art. 10(*b*) and (*c*).

[35] Interim Agreement, Art. V(*c*)(xiv); Special Agreement, Arts. 5(*c*) and 9(*b*).

[36] See Interim Agreement, Art. V(*c*).

[37] Interim Agreement, Art. V(*c*).

[38] Interim Agreement, Art. V(*d*) and (*e*).

A frequent criticism of INTELSAT is that COMSAT, the United States designated signatory, was initially allocated by the Special Agreement a quota of 61 per cent.[39] Even though this quota has been reduced on account of the increased number of participants, Article XII(c) of the Interim Agreement ensures that COMSAT's quota will never be allowed to fall below 50.63 per cent.[40] The result is that not only has COMSAT negatively a right of veto, but also its views will prevail if supported by an additional 12.5 per cent of the quotas. Sometimes, only another 8.5 per cent is required.

D. Managerial Level

The situation is all the more unsatisfactory as the Interim Agreement makes COMSAT the manager of INTELSAT.[41] In other words, the dominant member of the governing body is also the operating agency of the consortium. In reply to criticisms, it is sometimes said that this is not unheard of in business or industry. But with INTELSAT there is the political element which is not to be overlooked; for COMSAT is not only a corporation created by and subject to United States law, but also one that enjoys a very special relationship with the United States government.[42]

V. INTERSPUTNIK

The structure of INTELSAT has not infrequently been the subject of comment by Soviet representatives and writers.[43] It may thus be of interest to compare it with the draft agreement communicated to the United Nations by a number of communist countries (Bulgaria, Cuba, Czechoslovakia, Hungary, Mongolia, Poland, Romania, USSR) on the establishment of an international satellite communications system called INTERSPUTNIK.[44] As yet, it is merely a plan.

---

[39] The proportion was related to expected use of the system estimated on the basis of relevant 1968 long-distance telephone traffic, cf. Colino, loc. cit. in n. 16 above, at p. 41: 'the European members' quota was set at a total of 30.5% and the remaining 8.5% was allotted among Australia, Canada and Japan.' Cf. nn. 46, and 133 below.

[40] This result is hidden behind the rather obscure wording of Art. XII(c) which, when suitably translated, means that the minimum COMSAT quota = 61/100 (100 - 17) = 50.63%. COMSAT is more explicit in its *Annual Report 1964* (1965): 'The Corporation's ownership interest can in no event be reduced to a percentage less than 50.6%, by admission of additional participants or otherwise' (p. 12, col. 3).

[41] Art. VIII.   [42] See text to nn. 9–11 above.

[43] See, e.g., I. Cheprov, 'Global or American Space Communications System', *Int. Aff. (Moscow)* (12:1964), p. 69; V. Aldoshin, 'Outer Space Must be a Peace Zone', ibid. (Moscow) (12:1968), p. 38; V. S. Vereshchetin, 'International Space Communications Systems', 13 *Space Law Colloquium* (1970), p. 259. Cf. S. E. Doyle, 'International Satellite Communications and the Law', 11 *McGill LJ* (1965), p. 137; R. R. Colino, 'An Answer to Dr Vereshchetin', 13 *Space Law Colloquium* (1970), p. 246.

[44] UN Doc. A/AC.105/46 (1968); see also S. E. Doyle, 'An Analysis of the Socialist States' Proposal for Intersputnik', 15 *Villanova LR* (Fall, 1969), p. 83.

Unlike INTELSAT, INTERSPUTNIK would not be limited to ITU members, but would be open to all States.[45] Members' contributions would be proportionate to their use of communications channels,[46] but their quotas would have no effect on their voting power. The precise way in which these quotas would be set out was left to be determined subsequently, as were also the ceiling of total contributions and the technical programme.[47] INTERSPUTNIK would be a legal person[48] and have two principal organs, namely, a council representing member States ('the governing body') and a secretariat ('the permanent executive and administrative organ'), headed by a Director-General.[49] Every member would have one representative, each with one vote, on the Council. Decisions would be taken by a two-thirds majority of members of the Council.[50] The Council would 'elect' the Director-General and his deputy[51] for a term of four years, after which they would be eligible for re-election.[52] Under Article 7(5), 'The Council shall be the organ which takes all the steps necessary to ensure that the [technical] programme . . . is carried out in good time,' but the Council meets in regular session only once a year and would hardly be in a position to run a communications system. Three possibilities exist.

First, as the draft agreement now stands, it is possible to leave the future structure of INTERSPUTNIK as an operating agency entirely to the Council.[53]

The second possibility under the proposal is to leave everything to the Director-General.[54] In this case, the relationship, from the functional point of view, between the Council and the Director-General in INTERSPUTNIK would be very similar to that between the Interim Council and the manager in INTELSAT,[55] though from the institutional point of view, the position would be very dissimilar inasmuch as, in the case of INTERSPUTNIK, the Director-General would be an international civil servant.

A third possibility under the proposal would be for INTERSPUTNIK to operate the system[56] in a rather notional fashion; for the proposed agreement envisages that INTERSPUTNIK need not own the space segment itself, but

---

[45] Art. 2. In other words, entities such as East Germany, Communist China, North Korea and North Vietnam would no longer be excluded.

[46] Art. 9. Cf. nn. 39 above, and 136 below.   [47] Art. 9.

[48] Art. 5(4). It is not clear if this means merely municipal legal personality or also international legal personality. Cf. n. 17 above, regarding INTELSAT.

[49] Art. 6.   [50] Art. 7.   [51] Art. 7.   [52] Art. 8.

[53] See esp. Arts. 6(2) and 7(5)(*a*).

[54] Cf. Art. 6 'executive organ'; also Art. 8(4) on carrying out the Council's decisions.

[55] Cf., e.g., Art. 7(5) on the function of the Council with Art. V of the Interim Agreement of INTELSAT.

[56] Although under Art. 5(2) the organization appears obliged to 'operate the outer-space network,' this function seems to be regarded as consisting merely in 'assigning communications channels both to member States and to other . . . users.' All other functions presumably may be contracted out to other agencies or member States.

may lease it from member States.[57] If terms from maritime and air law may be borrowed, such leases might be either 'wet' or 'dry,' i.e., with or without the necessary operating personnel. In the former case, such leases might well turn out to be in effect management agreements. This would in fact fit in well with the preamble and Article 1 of the draft agreement, according to which the rôle of the organization would be more to 'co-ordinate' national efforts than truly to own and operate a communications system itself.

In view of its lacunary nature, it would be interesting to know what chances the sponsors of the INTERSPUTNIK plan thought it would have of being widely adopted or even adopted at all in its present form. However, it and some of its 'democratic' trappings have doubtless propaganda value. Insofar as third States are concerned, they provide an obvious leverage for obtaining a better bargain from the United States in the protracted negotiations to reach the long-promised Definitive Arrangements on INTELSAT.[58] In fact, some of the INTERSPUTNIK features have found their way into the draft Definitive Arrangements.

VI. INTELSAT: the Definitive Arrangements

A. The Long Haul Towards Agreement

As its name implies, the Interim Agreement of INTELSAT was meant to be temporary. Article IX of the Agreement envisages the establishment of definitive arrangements by 1 January 1970.[59] Pursuant to this Article, the United States government convened a conference in Washington, D.C., in February 1969. Sixty-seven of the then sixty-eight member States took part. Observers from the United Nations, the International Telecommunication Union and 29 non-member States, including the Soviet Union, also attended. The conference recessed on 21 March after establishing an intersessional Preparatory Committee. The Preparatory Committee held three sessions in 1969.[60] The

---

[57] Cf. Art. 3(2) and (4), and Art. 5(1).

[58] Cf. Council of Europe, Consultative Assembly, Committee on Science and Technology, Report on *Long-term Prospects of Space Exploration for Europe*, Doc. 2517 (16.1.69), pp. 37–8.

[59] Art. IX(*b*), which lays down certain principles to be retained in the definitive arrangements, is an interesting example of one treaty seeking to control the contents of that which replaces it. While no contracting party may unilaterally depart from its treaty obligations, there is little doubt that, provided that all the parties are in agreement, an existing treaty may be revised in any way which the parties please. Cf. S. H. Lay and H. J. Taubenfeld, *The Law Relating to Activities of Man in Space* (1970), p. 126, col. 2.

[60] July, Sept., and Nov.–Dec. The negotiations were regarded as confidential. On the work of the Preparatory Committee during its first two sessions, and especially the US position, including the fourteen-State draft (Doc. PC (II)/45), the sponsors of which subsequently became known as the PC-45 Group, see T. E. Donahue, Jr, Director, International Agreements Division, COMSAT, 'A Discussion of the Positions Taken by the United States in the Negotiations of Definitive Arrangements for INTELSAT', 12 *Space Law Colloquium* (1969), p. 30.

On the position of most of the western European members of INTELSAT, which submitted the

resumed Plenipotentiary Conference which met early in 1970 was faced with two sets of proposals,[61] and little progress was made until the delegations of Australia and Japan submitted a proposed compromise package settlement, Doc. 93. Doc. 93 which received widespread support was, however, couched in a number of general principles. When the Conference adjourned on March 20, it established an Intersessional Working Group to draft a single text reflecting Doc. 93. The Group held 125 meetings before issuing its report on 31 December 1970.[62] While certain issues remained to be resolved by the Plenipotentiary Conference, which would meet early in 1971, it was expected that the Definitive Arrangements would be signed before 1971 was out. In fact, after more than two years of technical and arduous negotiations, agreement was finally reached the following year, and the Definitive Arrangements for the International Telecommunications Satellite Organization (also to be known as INTELSAT)[63] were adopted on 21 May 1971 at the Resumed Plenipotentiary Conference convened for this purpose in Washington, D.C., and later opened for signature on 20 August 1971,[64] exactly seven years to the day after the opening for signature and coming into force of the Interim Arrangements. Fifty-four States signed the Definitive Arrangements on that day.

When the Definitive Arrangements come into force, the new INTELSAT will take the place of the International Telecommunications Satellite Consortium (also INTELSAT), the Global Commercial Communications Satellite System which since 1965 has brought the world televised moon walks, newscasts, Olympics plus telephone calls, telegrams and news dispatches from one continent to another.

B. Structure of the Definitive Arrangements

The Definitive Arrangements consist of two agreements: (i) the intergovernmental *Agreement*, the contracting parties to which are States and are known as the *Parties*, and (ii) the *Operating Agreement*, which may be signed by either the contracting States themselves or their designated telecommunications entities. The parties to the Operating Agreement, whether they be States or their designated telecommunications entities, are known as the *Signatories*.[65]

---

alternative sixteen-delegation draft in Doc. PC (III)/54 and which later became known as the PC-54 Group, cf. statement made by the British Minister of State, Foreign and Commonwealth Office (Mr Frederick Mulley) in the House of Commons on 25 July 1969 (787 H.C. Deb. 5 s., cols. 2368–2369). See also UK House of Commons, *Thirteenth Report from the Estimates Committee, Session 1966–67, Space Research and Development* (1967), pp. xviii–xix, xxviii.

[61] See previous n.   [62] IWG(III)/Doc. 170.
[63] See Art. I(*a*) of the Agreement.   [64] 10 *ILM* (1971), p. 909.

[65] Reference without further qualification hereinafter to Parties and Signatories will consequently be automatically to parties to respectively the definitive Agreement and the Operating Agreement. Moreover, the provisions of the Agreement are numbered in capital Roman letters, those of the Operating Agreement in arabic numerals. References so shown are automatically to the respective treaties without further specification, unless otherwise indicated.

Appended to the intergovernmental Agreement are four Annexes: A. on the functions of the Secretary-General; B. setting out the functions and guidelines for the Management Services Contract; C. Provisions on Procedures relating to Settlement of Disputes; and D. Transitional Arrangements. They all form part of the Agreement.

C. Corporate Aspects

1. *Aims and Objectives.* The preamble of the Agreement States the aims and objectives of the contracting Parties as being the establishment of 'a single global commercial communications satellite system' accessible to 'all peoples'[66] 'as part of an improved global telecommunications network,' and the provision of 'for the benefit of mankind . . . the most efficient and economic facilities possible consistent with the best and most equitable use of the radio frequency spectrum and of orbital space.'[67] The main purpose of the new INTELSAT is 'to continue and carry forward on a definitive basis . . . the global commercial communications satellite system' created by the Interim Agreement.[68]

2. *Scope of Activities.*

(a) *Public telecommunications and specialized services.* Article III(*a*) of the definitive Agreement defines the 'prime objective' of INTELSAT as 'the provision, on a commercial basis, of the space segment required for *international public telecommunications services* . . . on a non-discriminatory basis to all areas of the world.' Paragraph (*b*) subsumes under this notion also domestic services between territories separated by areas not under the jurisdiction of the State concerned, and subject to the approval of the Meeting of Signatories upon the advice of the Board of Governors, domestic services between areas between which, because of exceptional natural barriers, no viable terrestrial wideband facilities can be established.

As long as its main objective is not impaired, INTELSAT shall also provide facilities for other *domestic public telecommunications services*.[69] Furthermore, provided that the efficient and economic operation of the INTELSAT space segment for its prime objective is not prejudiced, INTELSAT may also, on request and subject to appropriate terms, cater for non-military *specialized telecommunications services*, domestic or international,

---

[66] Cf. 'all States' in preamble of Interim Agreement. The change is designed to include entities other than States, such as the United Nations; see further s. VI.G below: Free Access for the United Nations?

[67] Note the addition of the words 'and of orbital space' when comparing the text with the preamble of the Interim Agreement. The space in the synchronous equatorial orbit used by the geostationary satellites of INTELSAT and the radio frequency spectrum are both definitely limited natural resources, and may even be regarded as scarce resources. See also s. VIII.A and B below.

[68] Art. II(*a*).   [69] Art. III(*c*).

such as those for purposes of navigation,[70] or provide *satellites and associated facilities separate from the INTELSAT space segment* for (i) domestic public telecommunications services of contracting Parties, (ii) international public telecommunications services between contracting Parties, and (iii) non-military specialized services.[71] The use of the INTELSAT space segment and the provision of satellites and facilities separate from the INTELSAT space segment for specialized telecommunications services are, in addition, subject to authorizations from the Assembly of Parties under Article VII(*c*)(iv) of the Agreement, after consultation, in appropriate cases, with the Specialized Agencies of the United Nations directly concerned.[72]

(b)'*A single system*.' The expression 'a single system' in the preamble of the Interim Agreement has been relied upon as the basis for maintaining that members of INTELSAT are obliged not to be parties to any other global system.[73] It is doubtful, however, whether in the absence of a clear undertaking, such a phrase in the preamble of a treaty is sufficient to create so important an obligation. Insofar as the Interim Agreement is concerned, the Interim Council found the Agreement no barrier to either the Franco-German Project Symphonie or the proposed Canadian domestic satellite system and limited itself to co-ordinating the frequencies to be used in order to avoid harmful interference.

It may not be entirely fair, but Soviet writers[74] have not failed to contrast the proposed INTERSPUTNIK's alleged tolerance of rival satellite communications systems[75] with the United States proposal at the initial stage of the negotiations of the Definitive Arrangements to the effect that INTELSAT members that were to join or even use a rival system could be expelled.[76]

The preamble of the definitive Agreement continues to refer to the aim of achieving 'a single global commercial telecommunications satellite system,' but Article XIV clearly recognizes the possibility of contracting Parties and persons within their jurisdiction intending to 'establish, acquire or utilise' alternative facilities. Four different situations are envisaged according to the degree of concern to INTELSAT: (i) services for 'national security

[70] Art. III(*d*); see n. 108 below. Art I(*h*) defines 'space segment' as follows: ' "space segment" means the telecommunications satellites, and the tracking, telemetry, command, control, monitoring and related facilities and equipment required to support the operation of these satellites.'
[71] Art. III(*e*); see n. 108 below.   [72] Art. III(*f*).
[73] See Colino, loc. cit. in n. 16 above, p. 40; cf. P. You, *Le préambule des traités internationaux* (1941).
[74] E.g., Vereshchetin, op. cit. in n. 43 above.
[75] Art. 5(3), which merely indicates, however, that INTERSPUTNIK would co-ordinate its activities with ITU and such other systems, without expressly stating that INTERSPUTNIK members would be able freely to participate in such rival systems. The article only acknowledges the undeniable fact that, if established, INTERSPUTNIK would not be the only system in existence, and co-ordination would be required.
[76] Plenipotentiary Conf., Doc. 10, US draft, Art. VIII; see also Donahue, Jr, loc. cit. in n. 60 above, p. 36. Cf. also a similar article proposed by the United States in the negotiations of the Interim Agreement, Colino, loc. cit. (1967) in n. 16 above, p. 40, n. 68.

purposes';[77] (ii) domestic public telecommunications services;[78] (iii) specialized telecommunications services;[79] and (iv) international public telecommunications services.[80]

Situation (i) is outside INTELSAT's jurisdiction. In the other three cases, INTELSAT has only a co-ordinative rôle, discharged by the Board of Governors directly in situation (ii), and in the remaining two cases by the Assembly of Parties, taking into account the advice of the Board of Governors. In each case, prior consultation with the organization is required, in the case of the Assembly of Parties through the Board of Governors, and the relevant organ will express its findings, in the form of recommendations, on the technical compatibility of the alternative facilities with the use of the radio frequency spectrum and orbital space by the existing and planned INTELSAT space segment. In situation (iv), which affects the prime objective of INTELSAT, the objects of the consultation and of the findings shall include the avoidance of 'significant economic harm to the global system of INTELSAT,' but even in this case INTELSAT's findings remain recommendatory and not binding.

3. *Legal Status.* Unlike the interim INTELSAT,[81] the definitive INTELSAT has both international and municipal legal personality.[82] It directly owns the INTELSAT space segment,[83] and all the property, rights, and liabilities previously belonging to the signatories to the Special Agreement under the Interim Arrangements, as well as all those that may be acquired or incurred in future.[84]

The organization shall have headquarters of its own, and its property, activities and officers shall enjoy fiscal and jurisdictional immunities. The headquarters are to be in Washington, DC. Immunities and privileges will be the subject of a separate Headquarters Agreement with the host State and a general protocol among the contracting Parties.[85]

4. *Membership.* The preamble to, and Article XIX(a)(ii) of, the Agreement, state explicitly that investment in and membership of INTELSAT shall be open to members of the International Telecommunication Union. However, this would not preclude a party to the Interim Agreement from joining the definitive INTELSAT,[86] or oblige a member of the definitive INTELSAT to withdraw because of a change in its status with regard to the ITU.[87]

Members of INTELSAT may voluntarily withdraw.[88] Withdrawal of a Party to the Agreement entails simultaneous withdrawal of the corresponding Signatory to the Operating Agreement.[89] If a Signatory withdraws,[90] the

---

[77] Para. (g).   [78] Para. (c); cf. n. 69 above.   [79] Para. (e); cf. n. 70 above.
[80] Para. (d); see s. VI.C.2.a above.   [81] See n. 17 above.
[82] Art. IV.   [83] Art. V(a); Art. 3(b).   [84] Art. 3(a) and (b).
[85] Art. XV; see also Art. XIV(b).   [86] Art. XIX(a)(i).   [87] Art. XVI(n).
[88] Art. XVI(a).   [89] Art. XVI(d).   [90] Cf. Art. XVI(a)(i).

corresponding member must assume itself the capacity of a Signatory, or designate a new Signatory, or withdraw from INTELSAT.[91]

For non-compliance with the Agreement, a Party may be expelled from INTELSAT by the Assembly of Parties.[92] The rights of a Signatory may be suspended by the Board of Governors for breaches of either the Agreement or the Operating Agreement. On the recommendation of the Board of Governors, the Meeting of Signatories may expel a Signatory.[93] Neither Agreement uses, however, the word 'expel'; the euphemism 'deemed to have withdrawn' is used instead. Suspension applies only to the rights of a Signatory, but not its obligations and liabilities.[94] In the case of withdrawal or expulsion, the rights of representation and voting cease and no further obligations or liabilities will be incurred after receipt of the notice of withdrawal or the approval of the recommendation to expel; all pre-existing commitments, obligations, and liabilities, however, remain until discharged.[95]

D. Institutional Structure

The definitive Agreement endows INTELSAT with four organs: (i) the Assembly of Parties; (ii) the Meeting of Signatories; (iii) the Board of Governors; and (iv) an executive organ, responsible to the Board of Governors.[96] Doubtless as a result of the delicate balance achieved in the Definitive Arrangements, it is expressly provided that, except as authorized under the Agreements, no organ may interfere with the discharge of the functions attributed to another organ,[97] even though the Assembly of Parties is designated 'the principal organ of INTELSAT.'[98] The first three named are, however, enjoined to pay due consideration to the views of one another.[99] There is a transitional period of six years before the last named, i.e., the executive organ, attains its permanent form.

1. *Assembly of Parties.*   This is the plenary and 'premier'[100] organ of INTELSAT, in which all the contracting States are represented on the basis of each Party having one vote, irrespective of investment quota. Decisions on matters of substance are taken by a two-thirds majority of the representatives present and voting; those on procedure by a simple majority.[101] Ordinary meetings should in principle be held every two years.[102]

---

[91] Art. XVI(e).   [92] Art. XVI(b)(i).
[93] Art. XVI(b)(ii) and (c). Arrears with dues can also bring about automatic suspension.
[94] Art. XVI(h); see also para. (i).   [95] Art. XVI(g), (i), and (k).
[96] Art. VI(a).   [97] Art. VI(b).   [98] Art. VII(a).
[99] Art. VI(c); repeated in Arts. VII(b), VIII(a), IX(b).

[100] Thus referred to in the compromise package Doc. 93 submitted by Australia and Japan to the Resumed Plenipotentiary Conference in 1970 that formed the basis of the subsequent Definitive Arrangements. See further text following n. 61 above). However, Doc. 93 also made clear the separateness and independence of especially the two plenary organs.

[101] Art. vII(a) and (f).   [102] Art. VII(d) and (e).

According to the Agreement, '[t]he Assembly of Parties shall give consideration to those aspects of INTELSAT which are primarily of interest to the Parties as sovereign States.'[103] On matters of general policy, it only formulates recommendations.[104]

Its main functions and powers as defined in the Agreement are as follows: (i) to decide on measures to be taken to prevent INTELSAT from infringing any multilateral treaty which has been accepted by at least two-thirds of the Parties;[105] (ii) to approve amendments to the Agreement, which shall enter into force when accepted by a specially qualified majority;[106] (iii) to propose, express its views, and make recommendations on amendments to the Operating Agreement;[107] (iv) to authorize the use of the INTELSAT space segment, or the provision of separate satellites and facilities, for specialized telecommunications services;[108] (v) to express its findings, in the form of recommendations, with respect to the intended establishment, acquisition or utilization, of space segment separate from the INTELSAT facilities;[109] (vi) to review the general rules established by the Meeting of Signatories on (a) approval of earth stations, (b) allotment of space segment capacity, and (c) rates of utilization charges, in order to ensure the application of the principle of non-discrimination;[110] (vii) to consider complaints submitted to it by Parties;[111] (viii) to decide on the expulsion of Parties;[112] (ix) to decide on questions of formal relationship between INTELSAT and other subjects of international law;[113] (x) to establish a list of experts from which presidents of arbitral tribunals are to be selected;[114] (xi) to confirm the appointment of the Director-General by the Board of Governors;[115] and (xii) to adopt the organizational structure of the executive organ.[116]

2. *Meeting of Signatories.* This is the plenary meeting of all the Signatories to the Operating Agreement.[117] As the financial interest in INTELSAT is vested in the Signatories to the Operating Agreement rather than in the

---

[103] Art. VII(*b*).

[104] Art. VII(*c*)(i), see also Art. VII(*c*)(vi) concerning reports presented by the Meeting of Signatories and the Board of Governors.

[105] Art. VII(*c*)(ii); see further text to n. 197 ff. below.

[106] Art. VII(*c*)(ii); Art. XVII: the majority may consist of either two-thirds of the contracting States representing at least two-thirds of the total investment shares, *or* 85% of the total number of contracting States regardless of the amount of investment shares.

[107] Art. VII(*c*)(iii).   [108] Art. VII(*c*)(iv), and text to nn. 70–1 above.

[109] Art. VII(*c*)(vii); see s. VI.C.2.b above.

[110] Art. VII(*c*)(v). Presumably the Assembly has the power to revise the said rules and not merely to remit them back to the Meeting of Signatories. The French and Spanish texts speak of 'la révision' and 'Revisar.' See also n. 126 below.

[111] Art. VII(*c*)(x). Presumably this can lead ultimately to the expulsion of a Party; see next n.

[112] Art. VII(*c*)(viii); see s. VI.C.4 above: Membership.   [113] Art. VII(*c*)(ix).

[114] Art. VII(*c*)(xi).

[115] Art. VII(*c*)(xii). It is not clear what happens if the Assembly refuses to confirm the appointment. Cf. Art. XII(i). See also n. 148 below.

[116] Art. XVII(*c*)(xiii); Art. XII(*h*); see also n. 160 below.   [117] Art. VIII(*a*).

Parties to the Agreement,[118] this is also a kind of shareholders' meeting, except that voting strength in the Meeting of Signatories, unlike that in the Interim Committee,[119] no longer depends on the investment quota. Each Signatory has only one vote. Decisions on matters of substance are taken by a two-thirds majority of the representatives present and voting; those on procedural matters by a simple majority.[120] An ordinary meeting shall be held in every calendar year.[121]

Those functions within INTELSAT which may have political or international implications having been attributed to the Assembly of Parties;[122] the functions of the Meeting of Signatories as laid down in Article VIII(*b*) of the definitive Agreement relate essentially to internal matters of high policy.

The Meeting of Signatories receives annual reports, annual financial statements, and future programmes from the Board of Governors, and expresses views on them.[123] It in turn reports on the implementation of general policies, the activities and the long-term programme of INTELSAT to the Assembly of Parties and to the Parties.[124]

Whenever the Meeting of Signatories has to act in matters affecting the operational activities of INTELSAT, it does so after taking note of the recommendation of the Board of Governors. Thus the Meeting of Signatories decides on any increase that may be recommended by the Board of Governors in the financial ceiling of the Signatories' net capital contributions as specified in the Operating Agreement.[125] It establishes general rules, upon the recommendation of and for the guidance of the Board of Governors, concerning (i) the approval of earth stations; (ii) the allotment of INTELSAT capacity; and (iii) rates of utilization charge.[126] Having regard to the advice of the Board of Governors, it also approves the assimilation of certain domestic telecommunications services to international services for the operations of INTELSAT.[127]

The Meeting of Signatories is the organ to which complaints are to be addressed by Signatories, and non-Signatory users, through the Board of Governors.[128] It also expels Signatories for failure to comply with their obligations.[129]

Finally, the Meeting of Signatories has important functions connected with the representation of Signatories on the Board of Governors,[130] and has to

---

[118] Art. V(*a*), (*b*) and (*c*); Art. 3(*c*).   [119] See text to nn. 36 ff. above.

[120] Art. VIII(*e*).   [121] Art. VIII(*c*).   [122] See text to n. 103 above.

[123] Art. VII(*b*)(i) and (iii).   [124] Art. VIII(*b*)(viii).

[125] Art. VIII(*b*)(iv). The capital ceiling of the definitive INTELSAT is set initially at US$500 million, with discretion in the Board of Directors to increase this ceiling or any subsequently established ceiling by 10%; see Operating Agreement, Art. 5.

[126] Art. VIII(*b*)(v); see also n. 110 above.

[127] Art. VIII(*b*)(ix); see also s. VI.C.2 above: Public telecommunications and specialised services.

[128] Art. VIII(*b*)(vii).

[129] Art. VIII(*b*)(vi); see also Art. XVI and s. VI.C.4 above: Membership.

[130] Arts. VIII(*b*)(xi); IX(*b*)(ii) and (iv). See s. VI.D.3 below, text to n. 134.

consider and express views on the report of the Board of Governors to the Assembly of Parties on permanent management arrangements.[131] It shall also express its views and make recommendations on proposed amendments to the Agreement,[132] and consider and take decisions on proposed amendments to the Operating Agreement. Amendments to the Operating Agreement, once approved, shall come into force when accepted by either two-thirds of the Signatories representing at least two-thirds of the total investment shares, or 85 per cent of the total number of Signatories, regardless of the amount of investment shares.[133]

3. *Board of Governors.*   This will be the governing body of the new INTEL-SAT. The basic idea[134] is that the Board shall be composed of approximately 20 members, each representing a Signatory or group of Signatories, whose investment share is not less than a given minimum, which minimum is in turn adjusted annually by the Meeting of Signatories in order to maintain this figure of twenty. In addition, a maximum of five seats, distributed on a geographical basis,[135] are reserved on the Board for groups of Signatories not otherwise represented.

The voting procedure of the INTELSAT Interim Committee was much criticized. Under the Definitive Arrangements, voting in the Board of Governors remains related directly to the Signatories' voting investment shares, which are now explicitly based on 'the utilisation of the INTELSAT space segment for public telecommunications services' specifically defined in the Agreement.[136] However, unlike in the Interim Committee, 'no representative may cast more than 40 per cent of the total voting participation represented on the Board of Governors.' Any voting power in excess of 40 per cent is equally distributed among the other representatives who will consequently always represent a minimum of 60 per cent of the total voting participation.[137]

In order that in the new INTELSAT no single participant, or even two or three participants can freely make or veto decisions in the organization, the Definitive Arrangements many times use the dual procedure of deciding mat-

---

[131] Art. VIII(*b*)(x); see also text to nn. 159 ff. below.   [132] Art. VIII(*b*)(ii).

[133] Art. VIII(*b*)(ii), and Operating Agreement, Art. 22(*d*).   [134] Art. IX(*a*)–(*d*).

[135] Spread among the five regions established at the 1965 Montreaux ITU Plenipotentiary Conference for election to the International Frequency Registration Board, namely, (i) The Americas, (ii) Western Europe, (iii) Eastern Europe and Northern Asia, (iv) Africa, and (v) Asia and Australasia.

[136] Art. IX(*f*) and (*h*); see s. VI.C.2.a above, and cf. nn. 39 and 46 above. On how investment shares are to be calculated, see Operating Agreement, Art. 6. The minimum investment share is 0.05% (Art. 6(*h*)). It should be noted that a Signatory's *voting* investment share is not necessarily the same as its *actual* investment share. The latter according to Art. 6(*a*) of the Operating Agreement is 'equal to its percentage of *all use* of the INTELSAT space segment by all Signatories' (italics added). Voting shares, on the other hand, depend solely on utilization for specific telecommunications services as defined in the Agreement. This difference was clearly stated in the Australia–Japan package proposal (Doc. 93, 8.3.70; see text following n. 61 above).

[137] Art. IX(*g*)(iv).

ters either by a heavily weighted majority subject to some numerical qualification, or by a quasi-total numerical majority with little or no regard to the
amount of investment or utilization of INTELSAT facilities.[138] Thus a quo-
rum for any meeting of the Board of Governors consists of either a majority
of the Board representing at least two-thirds of the total voting participation
of all Signatories and groups of Signatories represented on the Board, or else
the total number constituting the Board of Governors minus three, regardless
of the amount of voting participating they represent.[139] Moreover, the Board
of Governors, though enjoined like the Interim Committee, to act unanimously whenever possible, may, if need be, on substantive questions, decide
either by a vote in favour cast by at least four members having at least two-
thirds of the total voting participation on the Board, or else by an affirmative
vote cast by at least the total number constituting the Board of Governors
minus three, regardless of voting participation. Procedural questions are
decided by a simple majority, each Governor having one vote.[140]

Like the Interim Committee,[141] the Board of Governors 'shall have the
responsibility for the design, development, construction, establishment, operation and maintenance of the INTELSAT space segment.' In discharging this
responsibility, it shall, *inter alia*,[142] adopt policies regarding the segment,
finances, procurement procedures, and rights in inventions; lay down the terms
and conditions governing the approval of earth stations, allotment of space segment capacity, access to the space segment by entities not under the jurisdiction
of any of the contracting Parties; and establish the rates of utilization charge. It
approves procurement contracts and the access of non-standard earth stations
to the space segment. It appoints the Secretary-General and, subject to confirmation by the Assembly of Parties, also the Director-General. It may remove
them both from office for cause on its own authority.[143] It determines the number and conditions of employment of all posts on the executive organ upon the
recommendation of its head, and approves the appointment of senior officers.
It shall, in case of need, designate a senior officer in the executive organ as
Acting Secretary-General[144] or Acting Director-General, as the case may be,
and negotiate with the United States a headquarters agreement to be submitted
to the Assembly of Parties for decision.

The Board of Governors also approves the INTELSAT budget and pre-
pares annual reports and financial statements for submission to the Meeting
of Signatories, as well as reports and recommendations on such other matters
as it deems appropriate.[145]

---

[138] See text to nn. 106 and 133 above.   [139] Art. IX(*i*).
[140] Art. IX(*i*). Thus even the largest shareholder would still require an extra 26⅔% of voting
participation to have a motion carried. It would have no veto. Cf. s. IV.C above, Inter-Signatory
Level, *in fine*, as regards the interim INTELSAT.
[141] Interim Agreement, Art. IV(*a*). See n. 28 above.   [142] See Art. X.
[143] Art. XI(*b*)(iii); see n. 115 above.   [144] Arts. X(*a*)(xix), XI(*d*)(i), and XII(*d*)(i).
[145] Art. X(*a*)(iii), (xiv), and (xvi).

4. *Executive Organ.*

(a) *Permanent structure.* The Definitive Agreement provides that not later than six years after its entry into force the executive organ of INTELSAT shall be headed by a Director-General.[146] When appointed, the Director-General will be the chief executive and the legal representative of INTELSAT, and will be directly responsible to the Board of Governors for the performance of all management functions.[147] He is appointed by the Board, subject to confirmation by the Assembly of Parties, but may be removed from office for cause by the Board on its own authority.[148] The Director-General will contract out to one or more entities technical and operational functions 'to the maximum extent practicable'. Such entities may be of various nationalities, or may be an 'international corporation owned and controlled by INTELSAT.'[149]

(b) *Transitional management arrangements.* The definitive Agreement in its Article XII(*a*)(i) provides that '[a]s a matter of priority after entry into force of this Agreement, the Board of Governors shall . . . appoint the Secretary-General and authorize the necessary support staff.' Though the Agreement is not very clear on the subject, it would appear that the Secretary-General and his support staff constitute the executive organ referred to in the Definitive Arrangements during the transitional period.[150] Annex A to the Agreement sets out in great detail the functions of the Secretary-General, but they are confined exclusively to Annex A.[151]

The Board of Governors must. also as a matter of priority, arrange a 'management services contract' between COMSAT, which is referred to as 'the management services contractor,' and INTELSAT for the performance of technical and operational management services for INTELSAT for a period of six years beginning from the entry into force of the definitive Agreement.[152] Elaborate guidelines for the management services contract are laid down in Annex B to the definitive Agreement.

The definitive Agreement provides that a Director-General shall be appointed and assume office one year before the end of the management services contract with COMSAT or by 31 December 1976, whichever is earlier.[153] Until the Director-General assumes office, COMSAT will operate under the direct authority of the Board of Governors, and will negotiate and sign contracts on behalf of INTELSAT within the area of its responsibilities.[154] The Secretary-General, although the legal representative of INTELSAT and

---

[146] Art. XI(*a*).   [147] Art. XI(*b*)(i).   [148] Art. XI(*b*)(iii).   [149] Art. XI(*c*)(ii).

[150] Art. XII(*b*), (*c*), and (*d*)(i) and (ii) all speak of the executive organ during the transitional period, but Art. XII(*g*) and (*h*) seem to suggest that the 'organizational structure' of the executive organ would only be defined towards the end of the transitional period. The latter provisions probably intend to refer to the definitive rather than the initial structure of the executive organ.

[151] See Art. XII(*b*).   [152] Art. XII(*a*)(ii), and (*e*).

[153] Art. XII(*i*). On the appointment of the Director-General, see text to nn. 115, 143, and 146 above.

[154] Art. XII(*e*).

responsible to the Board of Governors for the performance of management services, does so only outside COMSAT's sphere of responsibilities. He is expressly precluded from exercising a supervisory rôle over COMSAT as the management services contractor, or interposing himself between the latter and the Board.[155] It is particularly in this that the office of the Secretary-General differs from that of the Director-General; once the Director-General assumes office, the management services contractor will be responsible to the Board of Directors 'through the Director-General,'[156] and will be under his supervision.[157] Apart from this, however, presumably the Director-General must continue to observe the terms of the management services contract with COMSAT until the six-year period runs out.[158]

At the same time, the definitive Agreement lays down a strict time-table for the Board of Governors to initiate studies and submit recommendations on 'the most efficient and effective permanent management arrangements,'[159] for the Assembly of Parties to act on these recommendations,[160] and for the Director-General to carry them out so that they will be 'fully implemented not later than the end of the sixth year after the entry into force of this Agreement.'[161]

E. Settlement of Disputes

Article XVIII of the Agreement and Article 20 of the Operating Agreement deal with the settlement of disputes. Annex C to the former establishes the procedure. The principle of compulsory arbitration and the procedure of Annex C apply to legal disputes arising under the Agreement and the Operating Agreement between the Parties,[162] between the Signatories[163] and between INTELSAT on the one hand and the Parties or the Signatories on the other.[164] The principle of compulsory arbitration applies also to such disputes with former Parties and former Signatories. In the former case Annex C also applies, provided the former Party agrees; in the latter, it applies only if both disputants so agree.[165] Arbitration is optional between Parties and Signatories.[166] Disputes between INTELSAT and COMSAT under the management services contract are to be settled in accordance with the Rules

---

[155] Art. XII(*b*).   [156] Art. XII(*e*)(ii).   [157] Art. XII(*i*).

[158] See further Transitional Provisions in Annex D to the Agreement, esp. para. 2 on Management, *in fine*; and n. 152 above.

[159] Art. XII(*a*)(iii), and (*f*).   [160] Art. XII(*g*) and (*h*).   [161] Art. XII(*i*).

[162] Art. XVIII(*a*). Insofar as the Operating Agreement is concerned, this covers only disputes arising under Arts. 14(*c*) and 15(*c*).

[163] Operating Agreement, Art. 20(*a*).

[164] Agreement, Art. XVIII(*a*); Operating Agreement, Art. 20(*a*). Insofar as disputes between Parties and INTELSAT are concerned, this is subject to the qualification referred to in n. 162 above.

[165] Agreement, Art. XVIII(*b*); Operating Agreement, Art. 20(*b*).   [166] Art. XVIII(*a*).

of Conciliation and Arbitration of the International Chamber of Commerce.[167]

F. Entry into Force

Under Article XX of the Agreement, the Agreement enters into force 60 days after it has been accepted by two-thirds of the Parties to the Interim Agreement as of the date upon which it is opened for signature, provided (i) such two-thirds represent at least two-thirds of the investment shares under the Special Agreement, and (ii) the Operating Agreement has been correspondingly signed. However, the Agreement also provides that it shall not enter into force less than eight months or more than eight (20 April 1972) months after the date it is opened for signature (20 August 1971).[168] Thus the effective date by which the requisite number of unconditional acceptance of the Definitive Arrangements must be received is 60 days prior to 20 February 1973. Should the Definitive Arrangements fail to come into force, the Interim Arrangements would continue to apply.

G. Free Access for the United Nations?

The United Nations on 4 March 1969 submitted a memorandum to the Plenipotentiary Conference on Definitive Arrangements for INTELSAT, the concluding sentence of which was as follows:

The Conference may . . . wish to endorse, in the operative part of the Definitive Agreement, the principle that the United Nations should enjoy *permanent free-of-charge multiple access* to the INTELSAT system for both operational *and information* requirements . . .[169]

The Intersessional Working Group set up a United Nations Study Subgroup to examine the request. In his Report, the Chairman summarized the conclusions as follows:

. . . of the fifteen delegations who attended the meetings of the UNSG, seven were opposed to the request of the United Nations as a matter of principle, three expressed interest in studying the request with regard to the United Nations peace-keeping operations, two were in favour of the request and three did not enunciate a position.[170]

The United Nations may well have good reasons based on its past experience to wish to have direct, instantaneous and 'reliable' means of communi-

---

[167] Agreement Annex B, 2(*g*). Those arising between the date of entry into force of the Operating Agreement and the effective date of the contract shall be submitted to arbitration in accordance with Annex C to the Agreement (see Annex to Operating Agreement, para. 3).

[168] Art. XX(*a*).

[169] Doc. Com.I/31; italics added. Additional documents were later submitted.

[170] IWG(III)/Doc. 114 (9.12.70), p. 2.

cation with its field missions engaged in peace-keeping operations, and INTELSAT, especially when reasonably priced mobile earth stations become available, can ideally provide such a channel independent of the local telephone or teleprinter exchange. However, the request was over-ambitious in trying to cover practically all United Nations telecommunications requirements. Moreover, and most important of all, no truly valid reason was advanced why the United Nations should be allowed to use the system free-of-charge. Article 4(*b*) of the Operating Agreement of INTELSAT now provides explicitly that 'all . . . users . . . shall pay appropriate utilisation charges.'[171] However, in a resolution adopted on 21 May 1971 by the Resumed Plenipotentiary Conference, the Conference recommended:

. . . that the Secretary-General of INTELSAT study the request in detail with the United Nations Secretary-General and submit the result of the study to the Board of Governors which will transmit it together with its views to the first session of the Assembly of Parties for decision.[172]

VII. Direct Broadcast Satellites

Closely allied to communications satellites are direct broadcast satellites. This is a subject that has greatly interested UNESCO and the United Nations Outer Space Committee. Much hope has indeed been pinned on direct broadcast satellites by those who see in them a means of tackling some of the educational, cultural, and social problems in the developing countries.

According to studies carried out by a Working Group of the United Nations Space Committee, direct broadcasting of television signals into existing, unaugmented home receivers on an operational basis was not foreseen for the period 1970–85. On the other hand, direct broadcast of television into either augmented home receivers or augmented community receivers could become feasible technologically by the middle of the 1970s. Of the two systems, the latter would be much simpler and cheaper to install and operate.[173]

After having by agreement dated 2 October 1967 established a Joint Study Group to study the project, the Department of Atomic Energy of the Government of India and NASA of the United States signed on 18 September

---

[171] Arguments have sometimes been advanced based on Art. I(1) of the 1967 Space Treaty. Insofar as Art. I(1) of the Space Treaty is concerned, cf. B. Cheng, 'Le Traité de 1967 sur l'espace/The 1967 Space Treaty', 95 *JDI* (1968), p. 532, at pp. 576 ff. [Ch. 9 above, s. V.E: Exploration and Use for the Benefit of All Countries]. Then there is also the question whether the United Nations may be regarded *simpliciter* as the personification of 'all countries'. Cf. also INTER-SPUTNIK plan, Art. 10(2): 'Communications channels shall be made available for use against payment . . .'

[172] Doc. 207 (as amended): 10 *ILM* (1971), p. 964.

[173] Report of the Working Group on Direct Broadcast Satellites on its first session, Annex III to Addendum to the Report of the Committee on the Peaceful Uses of Outer Space, A/7621/Add.1 (1969), pp. 10–11.

1969, a Memorandum of Understanding concerning the India/USA ITV Satellite Experiment Project. Under this Agreement, NASA would position an appropriate satellite within view of India as early as possible, while the Indian Department of Atomic Energy 'will arrange for the transmission of instructional TV programs from its earth station at Ahmedabad to the satellite for broadcast to appropriate receivers provided and sited by Indian agencies in villages in India. The number of receivers contemplated is approximately 5,000, to be widely distributed.'[174] Perhaps, if nothing else, this Project would be able to tell whether the result justified the enormous cost involved.

VIII. Some General Legal Problems

A. ITU and Communications Satellites

The International Telecommunication Union (ITU) is the specialized agency of the United Nations responsible for the allocation and control of radio frequencies.[175] In 1963 at Geneva its Extraordinary Administrative Radio Conference for Space Radiocommunication purposes met to allocate frequencies for satellite communications. From the United States point of view, this was done just in time for the newly formed COMSAT to go into business.[176]

However, apart from other shortcomings in the ITU regulatory machinery,[177] the 1963 Conference proceeded on the usual 'first-come, first-served' principle which is not necessarily the most equitable when applied to one of the world's most scarce natural resources.[178] The first commercial communications satellite ever launched was originally named Early Bird. If the early birds were not to be allowed to pick the available frequency spectrum bare, some hard thinking and effective action would be required at the 1971 World Administrative Radio Conference for Space Telecommunications, and especially at the 1973 ITU Plenipotentiary Conference.[179]

What has just been said applies equally to direct and semi-direct broadcasting satellites, a subject which ITU was not able effectively to take up in 1963. In that connection, a more than merely technical problem may arise

---

[174] The text of the Oct. 1967 Agreement and the Sept. 1969 Agreement are reproduced in *Assessment of Space Communications Technology* (1970), cited in n. 2 above, pp. 15–20; see also UNESCO, op. cit. in n. 3 above, and further text to nn. 180 ff. below, and DBS in Index.

[175] See B. Cheng, 'The United Nations and Outer Space', 14 *CLP* (1961), p. 247, at pp. 250 ff. [Ch. 6 above, s. III: Radio Frequency: Allocation and Control].

[176] Cf. N. Jasentuliyana, 'Regulatory Functions of ITU in the field of Space Telecommunications', 34 *JALC* (1968), p. 62, at pp. 72 ff.

[177] Cf. J. H. Glaser, '*Infelix* ITU', 23 *Federal Bar J.* (1963), p. 1; D. M. Leive, *International Telecommunications and International Law* (1970), pp. 283 ff.

[178] Cf. E. N. Valters, 'Perspectives in the Emerging Law of Satellite Communication', 5 *Stanford J. of International Studies* (1970), p. 53, at pp. 76 ff.

[179] See also Leive, op. cit. in n. 177 above, pp. 241 ff.

concerning the interpretation of Article 7, § 1(1) of the 1959 Radio Regulations:

The establishment and use of broadcasting stations (sound broadcasting and television broadcasting stations) on board ships, aircraft or any other floating or airborne objects outside national territories is prohibited.[180]

Although it might be argued that Article 7 was designed to outlaw so-called 'pirate' radio and television stations,[181] its object may equally be said to be the exclusion of all broadcasting stations outside national territories. From the textual point of view, the answer depends on whether a satellite may be regarded as a 'floating object'.

But even if the above provision were deemed inapplicable, the question would still remain how far should direct broadcast from foreign satellites outside national territory be subject to national or international control, especially from the standpoint of programme content. Among suggestions put forward in the UN Outer Space Committee Working Group on Direct Broadcast Satellites was one that would subject such broadcasts to the prior consent of the State concerned. Others, without going so far, had in mind some form of international regulation or an international good conduct code.[182] But this would be well beyond the competence of the ITU and some alternative machinery would have to be devised.

B. Freedom and Non-Appropriation of Outer Space and the Problem of the Synchronous Equatorial Orbit

Under Articles I and II of the 1967 Space Treaty, outer space and celestial bodies shall be 'free for exploration and use by all States' and are 'not subject to national appropriation by claim of sovereignty, by means of use or occupation, or by any other means.'[183]

---

[180] Leive, op. cit. in n. 177 above, p. 244, n. 56, considers that this Regulation is restricted to 'shipboard or airborne faciltiies,' excluding satellites. However, the Japanese government in its comment on the Reports of the UN Outer Space Committee Working Group on Direct Broadcasting Satellites by no means excluded the possibility of Art. 7 being so applicable (A/AC.105/79 (7.4.70), pp. 5–6). The very existence of the European Agreement for the Prevention of Broadcasts Transmitted from Stations outside National Territories, 22 Jan. 1965, Cmnd. 2616 (1965) is a reminder that ITU Regulations lack sanction. Cf. also S. E. Doyle, 'Communication Satellites', 55 *California LR* 91967), p. 431, at p. 447.

[181] Leive, ibid.

[182] See *Report of the Second Session of the Working Group on Direct Broadcast Satellites,* A/AC.105/66 (12.8.69), pp. 6–8; see also, *inter alia,* working papers submitted by Canada and Sweden, ibid./59 (20.6.69), pp. 17 ff., which warned that 'the lack of globally accepted principles could constitute a serious limiting factor in the use of direct satellite broadcasting' (p. 19); France, ibid./62 (30.6.69), pp. 3 ff.; Australia, ibid./63 (30.6.69), pp. 1 ff.; United Kingdom, ibid./65 (18.8.69), pp. 6 ff. For an American view, see A. Chayes and L. Chazen, 'Policy Problems in Direct Broadcasting from Satellites,' 5 *Stanford J. of International Studies* (1970), p. 4. See Index, DBS.

[183] On the controversy concerning their interpretation, cf. ILA, *Report of the 54th Conference, The Hague* (1970), pp. 422–41: Space Law Committee Report.

It is submitted that the prohibition of national appropriation applies merely to territorial appropriation of portions of outer space and celestial bodies, but not to appropriation of their natural resources. The possibility of exploiting such resources is precisely part of the freedom of outer space.[184]

However, this freedom means in practice 'first come, first served'. It has already been seen, in regard to radio frequencies, that the ITU procedure which merely regulates the application of this principle is becoming more and more unsatisfactory. A closely analogous problem is the synchronous equatorial orbit for geostationary satellites.[185] The number of satellites it can accommodate is obviously not unlimited. This number is further reduced by considerations such as the need for separation in order to avoid harmful interference and the risk of collision, as these satellites tend to drift. Moreover, of all available 'parking places' or 'slots', some are more advantageous than others, for technical, commercial, or other reasons. For instance, relatively few parking slots above the Indian Ocean will be able to afford a simultaneous view of both Britain and Japan. It is hardly surprising, therefore, that in their Reports to the United Nations Committee on the Peaceful Uses of Outer Space in 1970, both the Committee's Scientific and Technical Sub-Committee[186] and its Working Group on Direct Broadcast Satellites expressed the view that 'the geostationary orbit was a limited natural resource'.[187]

The French government, in a Working Paper submitted to the Working Group on Direct Broadcast Satellites, suggested:

... the rule of non-appropriation contained in Article II [of the Space Treaty] quoted above in itself implies a limitation on the complete freedom of States in space. In fact, the very use of geostationary satellites can be regarded as an 'appropriation' of the equatorial orbit, which is a privileged portion of space. In return for such *de facto* occupation, the State responsible for the satellite should agree to submit to certain rules ...[188]

The United States representative in the working group in making a long statement refuting this assertion[189] appears to have taken it too literally; for the French were obviously not arguing that any State that put a satellite into synchronous orbit was violating the Space Treaty. As an obviously well-informed commentator has pointed out:

The debate has matured during the past several months with an emerging emphasis by the United States on the freedom of national action contrasting with the French con-

---

[184] See further Cheng, loc. cit. in n. 171 above, at pp. 564 ff. [Ch. 9 above, ss. V.B: Res Extra Commercium, and V.D: Rights of Ownership and Exploitation].

[185] See s. II.B above: Geostationary and Other Orbits.   [186] A/AC.105/82.

[187] See *Report of the Committee on the Peaceful Uses of Outer Space*, A/8020 (1970), paras. 37 and 53.

[188] A/AC.105/62 (30.6.69), pp. 3–4.

[189] Quoted in Valters, loc. cit. in n. 178 above, at pp. 66–7; proceedings in working groups not normally published.

cept of 'parking slots' as an international resource. The acceptance of the French view would facilitate any future international legal regulation of the use of orbital 'parking slots', as well as other aspects of outer space use.[190]

Article IX of the 1967 Space Treaty does provide:

In the exploration and use of outer space, including the moon and other celestial bodies, States Parties to the Treaty shall be guided by the principle of co-operation and mutual assistance and shall conduct all their activities in outer space, including the moon and other celestial bodies, with due regard to the corresponding interests of all other States Parties to the Treaty . . .

However, in the absence of concrete provisions in the Treaty regarding the implementation of this principle, except that consultation may be required when potential harmful interference is feared,[191] it is difficult to see how to avoid what the French called the '*de fact* occupation' of all the best parking slots in the geostationary orbit by the early birds. The subject of the geostationary orbit is on the agenda of the ITU 1971 World Administrative Radio Conference for Space Telecommunications.[192] Yet, under the existing International Telecommunication Convention, the ITU probably could do little more than to fend harmful interference off the 'first come' and the 'first served', for otherwise the matter might well be regarded as outside the competence of the ITU.[193] If so, unless the basic principles and procedure can be altered, it may be better if alternative rules were established and the matter placed in other hands.

C. Governmental Responsibility for Activities in Space

Under Article VI of the 1967 Space Treaty,

States Parties to the Treaty shall bear international responsibility for national activities in outer space, including the moon and other celestial bodies, whether such activities are carried on by governmental agencies or by non-governmental entities, and for assuring that national activities are carried out in conformity with the provisions set forth in the present Treaty. The activities of non-governmental entities in outer space . . . shall require authorization and continuing supervision by the appropriate State Party to the Treaty. When activities are carried on by an international organisation, responsibility for compliance with this Treaty shall be borne both by the international

---

[190] Ibid. p. 67.

[191] See remainder of Art. IX, and also Cheng, loc. cit. in n. 171 above, pp. 626 ff. [Ch./ 9 above, s. VII.E: Avoidance of Harmful Contamination or Interference].

[192] See text to n. 179 above.

[193] See Art. 4 of the Convention, 1959. Cf., however, Art. 13 of the Operating Agreement of the INTELSAT Definitive Arrangements, in which INTELSAT is required 'to give consideration' to ITU recommendations in the establishment and operation of the space segment and earth stations. Se also text to n. 67, and text following n. 80 above.

organisation and by the States Parties to the Treaty participating in such organisation.[194]

On the assumption that all the States concerned are also parties to the 1967 Space Treaty, how is this provision to be applied to the interim INTELSAT, the definitive INTELSAT and the proposed INTERSPUTNIK? From this point of view, the expression 'national activities in outer space' is far from clear or satisfactory.[195]

As has been mentioned before, the interim INTELSAT is probably a joint venture of the participating States in outer space, without separate legal personality.[196] Each participating State is consequently responsible for ensuring that the Space Treaty is observed in all the interim INTELSAT activities, although it is difficult to see how any of them, except the United States, is in a very effective position to do so. The Signatories to the Special Agreement are, of course, also carrying on activities in space. To the extent to which participating States themselves are not also the Signatories, they must authorize and supervise the activities of their designated Signatory. Parties and Signatories are, therefore, all under a positive duty to ensure that the consortium as a whole acts in conformity with the Treaty. In case they fail to do so, they would have committed a breach of the Treaty, and must be held responsible for it. The only way to avoid an otherwise inevitable conflict of obligations, when such a conflict threatens, is to withdraw from either the one or the other. On the managerial level, the matter is simpler, even though it might conceivably be argued that as manager of INTELSAT, COMSAT's activities are international rather than national. There is in fact little doubt that, being a creation of a United States statute and incorporated in the United States, COMSAT's activities in space have to be authorized and supervised by the United States which, under the Treaty, is responsible for its activities to all the other contracting parties to the 1967 Space Treaty.

Although the definitive INTELSAT has been established as an intergovernmental organization, and the proposed INTERSPUTNIK is intended to be one, both endowed with separate legal personality, the position of their member States would in fact not be very different from that of participating States of the interim INTELSAT. Ultimately, it is the member States that are responsible for ensuring that the organization complies with the Treaty.

In the Definitive Arrangements for INTELSAT, Article VII(c)(ii) of the Agreement specifically entrusts the Assembly of Parties with the function and power:

---

[194] See further Cheng, loc. cit. in n. 171 above, at pp. 582 ff. [Ch. 9 above, s. V.F: International Responsibility].
[195] Ibid., at p. 586 [Ch. 9 above, last two paragraphs of s. V.F].
[196] See n. 17 above.

To determine that measures should be taken to prevent the activities of INTELSAT from conflicting with any general multilateral convention that is consistent with this Agreement and which is adhered to by at least two-thirds of the Parties.[197]

It should be noted that the said Agreement places its own terms above those of any other treaty so that, in case of conflict, the Agreement has to be applied. It is only within these limits that the Assembly of Parties has the task of avoiding breaches of other multilateral treaties to which at least two-thirds of the member States are parties. As has been said in regard to the interim INTEL-SAT, ultimately the only way out for any State which is unable to prevent an international organization of which it is a member from actually heading for a collision course with a treaty to which it is a party would be to withdraw either from the organization or from the treaty. Although some of the States which advocate separate legal personality for INTELSAT in the Definitive Arrangements appear to think so, member States would in fact not be able to shield behind the corporate veil of the organization.

In both the INTERSPUTNIK plan and the Definitive Arrangements for INTELSAT, besides the organization and the member States, there are, as in the case of the interim INTELSAT, the national States of the independent contractors which will also be responsible, as such, for the activities in space of their own nationals. Under the Space Treaty, they would not only have to authorize such activities, but also to keep them under 'continuing supervision'. This may in practice give rise to difficulties.

D. Liability for Damage

Under Article VII of the 1967 Space Treaty:

Each State Party to the Treaty that launches or procures the launching of an object into outer space . . . and each State Party from whose territory or facility an object is launched is internationally liable for damage to another State Party to the Treaty or to its natural or juridical persons by such object or its component parts on the earth, in airspace or in outer space . . .

The United Nations Outer Space Committee has been working for a number of years on a draft Convention on International Liability for Damage Caused by Space Objects.[198] As the draft now stands, the basic principle underlying Article VII of the Space Treaty remains unaffected. It has, however, been made clear that liability means absolute liability without fault, except in case of damage caused elsewhere than on the surface of the earth.[199]

[197] See n. 105 above. On the position of international organizations engaged in space activities, see Cheng, loc. cit. in n. 171 above, at pp. 588 ff. [Ch. 9 above, s. V.G: International Organizations].

[198] See further the B. Cheng, 'Liability for Spacecraft,' 23 *CLP* (1970), p. 216 [see Ch. 11 above for an anlysis of the 1972 Convention on International Liability for Damage Caused by Space Objects].

[199] See Draft Convention, Arts. II, III and IV, Annex IV to *Report of the Committee on the Peaceful Uses of Outer Space* (1970), A/8020, p. 29 [see n. 198 above, *in fine*].

Moreover, where two or more States jointly launch a space object, they shall be jointly and severally liable.[200] This includes the State from whose facility or territory a space object is launched.[201]

In the case of the interim INTELSAT, it would appear that all the participating States must be considered jointly and severally liable under the draft convention, and most probably also under the 1967 Space Treaty.[202] Their liability cannot be limited either by their investment quota, or for that matter by the total estimated costs of INTELSAT during the interim period of US$200 million or an outside limit of US$300 million referred to in Article VI of the Interim Agreement.[203] In addition, the United States is liable also in its capacity as the launching State and as the State responsible for COMSAT, without any limitation of liability.[204] Maybe this explains why in the negotiations of the Definitive Arrangements, the United States strongly insisted that INTELSAT should not be allowed to limit its liability for damage caused to third parties.[205] In Article 18(*b*) of the Operating Agreement, it is now provided that, notwithstanding any ceiling which may be established to capital contributions, Signatories shall pay to INTELSAT in proportion to their investment shares such sums as may be required in order to meet INTELSAT liabilities incurred as a result of its activities, as may be determined by decision of a competent tribunal or agreed to by the Board of Governors. INTELSAT's, as well as its Signatories' liability for damage caused to third parties on the surface will consequently be unlimited.[206]

In the case of the India/USA ITV Satellite Experiment Project, both India, as the State procuring the launching of the satellite, and the United States, as the State launching it, would be liable for damage caused by the satellite used.[207]

In connection with liability, reference should also be made to Article 13 of the interim INTELSAT's Special Agreement:

Neither the Corporation as Signatory or manager, nor any other Signatory as such, shall be liable to any other Signatory for loss or damage sustained by reason of a failure or breakdown of a satellite at or after launching or a failure or breakdown of any other portion of the space segment.

[200] Art. V(1). [201] Art. V(3).
[202] See Cheng, loc. cit. in n. 171 above, pp. 582 ff. [Ch. 9 above, s. V.F: International Responsibility and Liability for Damage Caused.]
[203] See text to nn. 24 ff. above.
[204] Cf. remarks of S. E. Doyle, J. A. Johnson, and R. K. Woetzel in *ASIL Proc.* (1967), pp. 44–6.
[205] See Cheng, loc. cit. (1970) in n. 198 above, p. 234 [cf. Ch. 11 above, s. VIII.B: Limitation of Liability].
[206] Neither the Agreement nor the Operating Agreement provides for the contingency of one of the Signatories, which may be non-governmental entities, not being able to meet its liabilities. See further Cheng, loc. cit. (1970) in n. 198 above, pp. 223 ff. on the problem of international organizations in relation to liability; and p. 234–5 on the problem of limitation of liability in the draft convention on liability [cf. Ch. 11 above, ss. V.6 and VIII.B].
[207] See nn. 174, 200, and 201 above.

Although the wording of this article is not entirely clear, it is submitted that it in no way refers to surface damage envisaged by Article VII of the Space Treaty or the convention on liability for damage caused by space objects. Article 13 is, from this point of view, akin to Article 33 of the 1959 International Telecommunication Convention under which:

Members and Associate Members accept no responsibility towards users of the international telecommunication services, particularly as regards claims for damages.

What is referred to in Article 13 of the Special Agreement is consequently loss or damage sustained as a result of failure or breakdown in the actual telecommunication services. This is now made clear in Article 18(*a*) of the definitive INTELSAT's Operating Agreement which denies liability 'for loss or damage sustained by reason of any unavailability, delay or faultiness of telecommunications services . . .'

IX. Postlude

This chapter has sought to outline the major institutional as well as legal problems involved in the use of communications satellites for commercial or instructional purposes, especially those in the organization and activities of INTELSAT. These activities break new grounds, inasmuch as they constitute the first experiment in the commercial exploitation of the resources of outer space. The experience gained in this first experiment is bound to have an important effect on the future development of space law, which must henceforth concern itself not only with the provision of a legal framework for scientific exploration, but also with ensuring that in the exploitation of the natural resources of outer space and celestial bodies the welfare of mankind and of nations large and small is safeguarded.

Legal and Commercial Aspects of Data Gathering by Remote Sensing*

I. Introduction: Remote Sensing in Perspective

'Data gathering by remote sensing' may sound highly technical and even very esoteric, but like Monsieur Jourdain, the character from Molière's *Bourgeois gentilhomme*, who did not realize that he had been speaking prose for over forty years, all of us, except those who are unsighted, have been doing it all our lives. Remote sensing is simply the collection of information from a distance[1] about an object or an area without any direct physical contact. As has been pointed out, '[t]he most obvious example of a remote sensor and closest to man is his eyes. The eyes visually sense information from the world around us'.[2]

There in a nutshell is the problem before us. We only have to compare the advantages enjoyed by a person endowed with eyesight and good hearing with the disabilities of a person deprived of them, or the advantages of a person being able to enhance his eyesight and hearing with optical, electronic and other means, such as binoculars, telescopes, radars, infrared cameras, and ultra-sensitive microphones, with the handicaps of his rivals who do not have the same facilities. At the same time, we should also think of the many ways and devices people resort to in order to prevent themselves, their property or what they may be doing from being seen or heard by others, and the length to which they may go in doing so. Curtains, gates, fences, walls, guards, tarpaulins, camouflage, prohibited areas, lead-lined rooms, 'Datastop' glass to screen computers from stray emissions,[3] and so forth. In addition, we have laws that protect privacy, intellectual and industrial property, official secrets, as well as

---

* First published in Chia-Jui Cheng and P. Mendes de Leon (eds.), *The Highways of Air and Space Law over Asia* (1992), pp. 49–76, with some additional material taken from the paper on 'Legal Implications of Remote Sensing from Space', in European Space Agency, *Proceedings of an International Conference on Earth Observation from Space and Management of Planetary Resources, Toulouse, 1978* (ESA SP–134), p. 597. The former article reproduced with kind permission from Kluwer Law International, and the latter with kind concurrence from ESA.

[1] Cf. e.g., E. C. Barrett and L. F. Curtis, *Introduction to Environment Remote Sensing* (1976), p. 3: 'Remote sensing is the observation of a target by a device separate from it by some distance.'

[2] United Nations Institute for Disarmament Research (UNIDIR), *Disarmament: Problems related to Outer Space* (1987), p. 11.

[3] See 'Spy-proof Glass to Beat the Hackers', *The Times* (London, 17 Jan. 1991), p. 25, cols. 2–5.

laws against trespass, nuisance, peeping Toms, and espionage, whether industrial, political, or military.

II. Hitherto a State's Territory is its Castle

Let us now look at this scenario not from the perspective of individuals, but
in terms of States. Until the advent of the space age, States have been able to
guard their secrets thanks to the concept of national sovereignty, which covers not only their land territory, but also a maritime belt along their coast and
the whole of the airspace above their territory, both land and maritime. A
State's territory is its castle. No one is allowed to enter it without its permission, and, inside, it is entitled to do exactly what it likes unless there is a rule
of international law restricting its freedom of action.[4] Since international law
is in fact made by States, they have hardly strained themselves in imposing
restrictions upon their own freedom of action. The only major concession in
our present context which they either deem worthwhile making to their
mutual benefit or have had to make in face of overwhelming pressure from the
maritime powers is probably the right of innocent passage which they have to
accord to foreign ships through their territorial seas. But they have always
maintained their right to subject the entry of foreign aircraft, civilian as well
as military, to their airspace to authorization, with the result that although
aviation has added an extra dimension to the problem of States in controlling
what goes on in their territory, their grip in law and in fact remains unaltered,
so much so that from the legal point of view the world resembles a series of
immense airtight petroleum storage tanks representing the various national
States with their three-dimensional sovereignty.[5]

This airtightness of national territory was only recently dented, albeit ever
slightly, by the introduction of the right of transit passage and archipelagic sea
lanes passage.[6] But even there, foreign ships and aircraft are supposed only to
pass through 'solely for the purpose of continuous and expeditious transit',[7]
without prying—not even scientific research or survey without prior authorization, although curiously Article 40 of the UN Convention on the Law of
the Sea mentions only ships but not aircraft.[8] This can give rise to the *a*

---

[4] See *Palmas Island Case* (1928), 2 *RIAA*, p. 821, at pp. 838–9; PCIJ: *The Lotus Case* (1927), Ser. A, No. 10, at p. 18.

[5] See Fig. XXII.1: The Legal Status of Territory.

[6] UN Convention on the Law of the Sea, 1982, Part III, Section 2, and Part IV, Arts. 53 and 54. Even before the Convention came into force, many of its provisions, including, it would appear, those mentioned above, were already claimed to have become rules of general international law.

[7] Ibid., Art. 38(2). See also Art. 53(3) which has added 'unobstructed' to the description of the transit and 'in the normal mode' to the passage.

[8] 'During transit passage, foreign ships, including marine scientific research and hydrographic survey ships, may not carry out any research or survey activities without the prior authorization

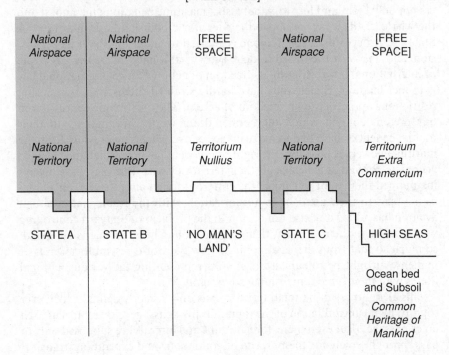

THE MOON AND OTHER CELESTIAL BODIES WITHIN THE
SOLAR SYSTEM OTHER THAN THE EARTH
Common Heritage of Mankind
(under Moon Treaty)

OUTER SPACE, INCLUDING THE MOON AND OTHER CELESTIAL BODIES
Territorium Extra Commercium
[FREE SPACE]

| National Airspace | National Airspace | [FREE SPACE] | National Airspace | [FREE SPACE] |

| National Territory | National Territory | Territorium Nullius | National Territory | Territorium Extra Commercium |

| STATE A | STATE B | 'NO MAN'S LAND' | STATE C | HIGH SEAS |

Ocean bed and Subsoil

Common Heritage of Mankind

Figure XXII.1. THE LEGAL STATUS OF TERRITORY

contrario interpretation that aerial survey and even exploration by aircraft are permitted, although this is unlikely to have been the intention of the parties, inasmuch as the right is strictly for transit and the area traversed forms part of the national territory of the coastal State or States concerned.

of the States bordering straits.' Art. 40 applies *mutatis utandis* to archipelagic sea lanes passage by virtue of Art. 54.

III. The EEZ and the Continental Shelf: the Scramble for Natural Resources, and the Exclusive Right to Explore and Exploit Them

The position regarding the continental shelf and the Exclusive Economic Zone (EEZ) is more ambiguous, neither of which is, strictly speaking, part of a State's national territory.[9]

First, the continental shelf. Article 77(1) of the UN Convention on the Law of the Sea recognizes that the coastal State 'exercises over the continental shelf *sovereign rights* for the purpose of *exploring* it and exploiting its natural resources', but paragraph 1 of the next article makes it clear that these rights 'do not affect the *legal status* of the superjacent waters or of the *airspace* above those waters'[10] Whilst drilling on the continental shelf is subject to the coastal State's authorization and regulation,[11] and marine scientific research '*on* the continental shelf' subject to its consent,[12] remote sensing by aircraft of the resources of the seabed and subsoil of the continental shelf and of the resources of the superjacent waters would seem to be perfectly compatible with the Convention. However, a contrary thesis can no doubt be advanced on the basis that Article 77(2) of the 1982 Convention, following the wording of Article 2(2) of the 1958 Geneva Convention on the Continental Shelf, lays down that the coastal State's right of 'exploring it and exploiting its natural resources' is 'exclusive'.

Whatever it is, there is little doubt that States have, since the Second World War, been increasingly seeking to extend their right to explore and exploit the natural resources of what used to be international spaces, and to claim *exclusive* rights at that. Thus after the continental shelf came the exclusive economic zone, over which the coastal State claims 'sovereign rights for the purpose of *exploring* and exploiting . . . the natural resources, . . . and with regard to other activities for the economic exploitation and *exploration* of the zone . . .'[13]. However, Article 56(1) of the Law of the Sea Convention does say that these rights exist '*[i]n* the exclusive economic zone'. The same applies to

---

[9] President Reagan's Proclamation of 10 Mar. 1983 of the United States' EEZ is explicit on the subject: '. . . the Exclusive Economic Zone remains an area beyond the territory and territorial sea of the United States . . .' (22 *ILM* (1983), p. 465. The Reagan Proclamation follows closely the provisions of the UN Convention on the Law of the Sea on this subject.

[10] Italics added. See also the 1958 Geneva Convention on the Continental Shelf which uses exactly same language in its Arts. 2 and 3 respectively.

[11] Ibid., Art. 81.

[12] Art. 246(2). The juxtaposition of 'in the exclusive economic zone and on the continental shelf' makes it clear that the article is speaking of the location of the research and not of the object or subject of the research. This is even clearer in Art. 5(8) of the 1958 Geneva Continental Shelf Convention which provides: 'The consent of the coastal State shall be obtained in respect of any research concerning the continental shelf *and undertaken there*' (italics added). Moreover, its Art. 1 states explicitly: 'The exploration of the continental shelf and the exploitation of its natural resources [by the coastal State or authorized by it] must not . . . result in any interference with fundamental oceanographic or other scientific research carried out with the intention of open publication.'

[13] Ibid., Art. 56(1)(a). Italics added.

marine scientific research. Article 246(2) only requires research '*in* the exclusive economic zone' to be subject to the consent of the coastal State, but would appear to exclude from this requirement research *on*, that is, regarding, the EEZ, conducted, say, from the air.

With respect to the EEZ, it is probably true that a contrary argument might be advanced based on the fact that Article 58(1) of the Law of the Sea Convention appears to have reserved to the aircraft of other States merely a right of 'overflight' over the EEZ, but perhaps the simple truth is that, as the word 'overflight' itself would seem to imply, the negotiators of the Law of the Sea Convention, even without regard to the restrictions on their mandate, were probably so immersed in discussing the sea and its seabed and subsoil and their resources, that they just did not give too much thought to activities in the air and beyond, apart from the right of transit passage.

However what the above excursion into the domestic and national scene as well as that into the law of the sea does show is that traditionally individuals and States insist on and have been able to achieve a great degree of privacy regarding their own affairs and resources, and of late, especially since the Second World War, instead of moving towards greater liberalization in the exploration and exploitation of natural resources, States have in concert encroached more and more on what used to be international spaces, first the continental shelf and then the EEZ, claiming the natural resources in these areas as their own and effectively reducing by an appreciable margin the size of the high seas. These developments cannot all be ascribed simply to the whims and doings of developing countries with their repeated 'slogan-matic' assertions through General Assembly resolutions of permanent national sovereignty over national natural resources. Although by no means the first claim by a State to the seabed and subsoil of areas outside its territorial sea and their natural resources, the 1945 Proclamation by President Truman marked effectively the beginning of the continental shelf doctrine. The United States was not the originator of the idea of the EEZ. However, notwithstanding the fact that the United States has otherwise very much spurned the UN Convention on the Law of the Sea, the United States was among the first to embrace the EEZ part of the Convention as stating general international law. This was done when President Reagan proclaimed the establishment of a United States Exclusive Economic Zone on 10 March 1983, three months to the day after the conclusion of the UN Convention.[14] This social, political, and general legal background is well worth remembering when one approaches the problem of remote sensing from outer space,[15] if we are not to be carried away in our thinking by our single-minded enthusiasm for outer space.[16]

[14] 22 *ILM* (1983), p. 461.

[15] See further W. E. Morris, 'Marine Remote Sensing and International Law', 30 *Space Law Colloquium* (1987), p. 350.

[16] Cf. I. Brownlie, 'Problems of Specialisation', in Cheng (ed.), *International Law* (1982), p. 109.

IV. Arrival of the Space Age: Roof Ripped off the Castle?

Similarly, although the United Nations General Assembly in its 1986 Resolution on the Principles Relating to Remote Sensing of the Earth from Outer Space defined remote sensing as the sensing of the earth's surface 'for the purpose of improving natural resources management, land use and the protection of the environment',[17] one would be taking, through rose tinted glasses, a wholly Cyclopean view of the subject if one were to pretend that this is all there is to remote sensing. This is particularly so because, as it has been said, 'the gap between the capabilities of civilian and military satellites is now rapidly narrowing'[18] Indeed, the arrival of the space age has wrought havoc with the cocoon and, if one wishes, with our image of the huge petroleum storage tanks in which States were hitherto able to enclose themselves.

The impact of the space age on the age-old cocoon was dramatically demonstrated in 1960. On 1 May 1960, the United States sent a U–2 reconnaissance aircraft over the Soviet Union, thus infringing the privacy and sovereignty of the Soviet Union by remote sensing photographically what was going on with all the military parades on a May Day in the Soviet Union. The flight began from Peshawar in Pakistan and was planned to fly all the way through the heart of the Soviet Union from its south-eastern corner to its north-western part including Archangel and Murmansk before landing at Bodö in Norway.[19] The Soviet Union was, however, able somehow to shoot down the aircraft when it was over Sverdlovsk about halfway on its flight across the Soviet Union in order, from the Soviet point of view, to protect its privacy and sovereignty. The right of the Soviet Union under international law to shoot down the aircraft and subsequently to try and, when found guilty, to imprison the pilot was not challenged by the United States. President Eisenhower accepted United States responsibility for the flight and promised the Soviets that no more U–2s would be flown over the Soviet Union.[20] However, the United States could by then afford to make that promise without too much harm to its 'open-skies' policy and programme of 'surveillance' from above of what was going on inside the Soviet Union and certain other countries; for it had already begun using reconnaissance satellites to gather military and other useful data from outer space. Not surprisingly, the Soviet Union protested that the use of military reconnaissance satellites was illegal. Going back to our petroleum storage tank analogy, the arrival of the space

[17] Resolution 41/65, 3 Dec. 1986; text of resolution reproduced as Appendix II.5 below. See further text to nn. 52 and 66 ff. below.

[18] B. Jasani and C. Larsson, 'Security Implications of Remote Sensing', *Space Policy* (Feb. 1988), p. 46, at p. 46.

[19] For an account of the mission by the pilot in question, see F. G. Powers, *Operation Overflight* (1970).

[20] See B. Cheng, 'The United Nations and Outer Space', 14 *CLP* (1961), p. 247, at pp. 264–8 [Ch. 6 above, s. V.A: Penetrative Reconnaissance].

age was as if the lid on the tank was suddenly ripped off. And, if we can change the image, it was like opening up an ant-hill with all the ants inside scurrying round wondering how to cover themselves and their secrets and stores.

From the layman's point of view, there was perhaps indeed little difference between reconnaissance by a foreign aircraft and that by a foreign satellite, between the U–2 and a reconnaissance satellite. The purpose and effect of their flight overhead remained the same. All that had happened in practice was that the United States had moved their remote sensors a few hundred kilometres up. But the question for us is whether *in law* these few hundred kilometres made a difference.

V. Data Gathering from Outer Space under General International Law

In order to answer this question, two distinctions must first be made, and a problem resolved.

The first distinction is the legal status of different parts of the world. Traditionally, there were only three categories: national territory, lands belonging to no State but capable of being reduced to sovereignty (*territorium nullius*), and areas under no sovereign and not capable of being subjected to sovereignty (*territorium extra commercium*). The 1979 Moon Treaty has officially introduced into international law a fourth category, namely, areas that constitute the 'common heritage of mankind'.[21] For convenience, *territorium nullius*, *territorium extra commercium* and the common heritage of mankind may be called 'international spaces' as distinguished from 'national territory', which is an area under the exclusive and complete sovereignty of a State, whereas international spaces are where no such sovereignty, more specifically territorial sovereignty, exists.

The second distinction that has to be made is between 'penetrative reconnaissance' and 'peripheral reconnaissance', or, if one wishes, between penetrative data gathering and peripheral data gathering. The legal distinction between these two types of data gathering was dramatically illustrated by

Table XXII.1 CLASSIFICATION OF WORLD TERRITORY UNDER INTERNATIONAL LAW

NATIONAL TERRITORY	TERRITORIUM EXTRA COMMERCIUM	TERRITORIUM NULLIUS	COMMON HERITAGE OF MANKIND
	(International spaces)		

[21] See B. Cheng, 'The Moon Treaty', 33 *CLP* (1980), p. 213 [Ch. 12 above].

comparing the U–2 incident that has just been mentioned with another shooting down by the Soviet Union of an unarmed United States reconnaissance aircraft two months later, the RB–47, off the Soviet coast on the Barents Sea. At first, the Soviet Union, thinking that the United States would not know exactly where the aircraft was when it was shot down, maintained that the United States had broken its promise and that the RB–47 was shot down when it penetrated into Soviet airspace. However, when the United States was able to prove that the unarmed RB–47 was at all times over the high seas and that it was intercepted, pursued, and actually shot down by Soviet fighters over the high seas, the Soviet Union backed down. The two pilots, who were able to bale out, were picked up from the sea by the Soviets who made no attempt subsequently to put them on trial. They were returned early the following year to the United States.

A comparison of the U–2 and the RB–47 incidents brings out clearly the distinction in law between what I have called 'penetrative reconnaissance' and 'peripheral reconnaissance'. Penetrative data gathering or data gathering by going into the territory of another State, whether of data concerning that State or concerning a third State, will always be subject to the laws and, if required, the permission of the territorial State. If practised by one State on another State without the latter's authorization, it would be a violation of the latter's territorial sovereignty and illegal under international law. Peripheral data gathering from international spaces, whether of data in international spaces or of data elsewhere, including data in national territories, is permissible under international law, and any interference with this right by another State, as happened in the RB–47 case, would be contrary to international law.[22]

We now have the major premise for answering the question whether data gathering by artificial satellites is lawful. The major premise in this syllogism is that whilst data gathering from international spaces is lawful, data gathering by one State in the territory of another State, including the latter's national airspace, without the latter's permission, tacit or express, is unlawful.[23] Legality depends thus not upon the nature of the act (*pace* the functionalists), but upon its location or, in other words, its *locus*.[24] The answer to our question turns, therefore, on the minor premise of the syllogism, Where are these data gathering satellites located, in international space or national space? Now, as a matter of practice, the military reconnaissance satellites are mostly

---

[22] On the U–2 and RB–47 incidents and the distinction between these two types of reconnaissance, see further loc. cit. in n. 20 above, at pp. 262–72 [Ch. 6 above, s. V: Reconnaissance and Surveillance]. See also B. Cheng, 'Legal Implications of Remote Sensing from Space', in ESA, *Proceedings of an International Conference on Earth Observation from Space and Management of Planetary Resources, Toulouse, 1978*, (ESA SP–134), p. 597, at p. 599.

[23] See Table XXII.2: Permissibility of Remote Sensing under General International Law.

[24] See B. Cheng, 'The Legal Régime of Airspace and Outer Space: The Boundary Problem— Functionalism *versus* Spatialism: The Major Premisses', 5 *AASL* (1980), p. 323 [Ch. 14 above].

Table XXII.2 PERMISSIBILITY OF REMOTE SENSING UNDER GENERAL INTERNATIONAL LAW

OBJECT TO BE SENSED	REMOTE SENSING TO BE CARRIED OUT BY STATE A — LOCUS					
	FROM TERRITORY SUBJECT TO NATIONAL SOVEREIGNTY			FROM TERRITORY NOT SUBJECT TO NATIONAL SOVEREIGNTY (INTERNATIONAL SPACES)		
				FROM TERRITORIUM EXTRA COMMERCIUM		FROM TERRITORIUM NULLIUS
	FROM STATE A	FROM STATE B	FROM STATE C	FROM HIGH SEAS, INCLUDING SUPERJACENT AIRSPACE	FROM OUTER SPACE, INCLUDING CELESTIAL BODIES	
STATE A	free	consent of State B	consent of State C	free	free	free
STATE B	free	consent of State B	consent of State C	free	free	free
STATE C	free	consent of State B	consent of State C	free	free	free
HIGH SEAS	free	consent of State B	consent of State C	free	free	free
OUTER SPACE, INCLUDING CELESTIAL BODIES	free	consent of State B	consent of State C	free	free	free

Plate XXII.1. Satellite picture of a Soviet shipyard with an aircraft carrier under construction in two sections.

Source: *Jane's Defence Weekly* (1984).

several hundred kilometres above the surface of the earth, and the generality of earth resources observation satellites closer to 1,000 kilometres up.[25] There may be some that are geosynchronous, in which case they would be at the geostationary orbit at a height of 36,000 kilometres above the equator.

The next questions then are, first, whether at these heights one is in outer space or could one be still in national space, and, secondly, what is the legal status of outer space? To answer the second question first, it seems now possible to say that Article II of the 1967 Space Treaty[26] which declares outer space, including the moon and other celestial bodies, not subject to national appropriation (in other words, *territorium extra commercium*) has passed already into the realm of general international law. Outer space, therefore, may now be said to form part of international space.

What is more difficult is the first question which raises once more the vital issue, where does outer space begin? The United States in particular has consistently led the opposition to any discussion of this topic, relying either on the so-called functional approach or sometimes on a supremely arrogant attitude that States with no space capability need not bother their little heads about this problem.[27] However, general State practice has probably confirmed that, in the opinion of the generality of States, all satellites that have so far been able to complete one orbit around the earth are to be considered to be operating in outer space. This would indicate that in their opinion or, to put it another way, it is the *opinio generalis juris generalis* of States,[28] that outer space begins in any event from about 100 or 110 kilometres above the surface of the earth, because this is about the lowest perigee reached by any orbiting satellite so far.[29] This would then put all existing military reconnaissance and earth resources observation satellites in international space. The conclusion from this syllogism is, therefore, that data gathering as such by such satellites is in itself lawful under international law.

---

[25] See Jasani and Larsson, loc. cit. in n. 18 above, Table 1 on p. 47 which gives details of 'Characteristics of some past, current and future sensors on military reconnaissance and civil Earth resources satellites', including designation, altitude, spatial resolution, spectral region and date of launch.

[26] See B. Cheng, 'Le Traité de 1967 sur l'espace/The 1967 Space Treaty', 95 *JDI* (1968), 532, at pp. 564–76 [Ch. 9 above, s. V: Legal Regime of Outer Space and Celestial Bodies].

[27] See further B. Cheng, 'The Legal Status of Outer Space and Relevant Issues: Delimitation of Outer Space and Definition of Peaceful Use', 11 *JSL* (1983), p. 89 [cf. Ch. 14 above].

[28] On *opinio juris* and the formation of rules of general (*alias* customary) international law, see B. Cheng, 'Custom: The Future of General State Practice in a Divided World', in R. St. J. Macdonald and D. M. Johnston (eds.), *The Structure and Process of International Law* (1983), p. 513, at pp. 530–50. N.B.: in the book, pp. 545 and 546 have been transposed, and are wrongly paginated. See too Ch. 8. s. V.H above: Formation of General International Law.

[29] See further Cheng, loc. cit. in n. 24 above, at pp. 350–6 [Ch. 14 above, especially s. X: Limit between Outer Space and Territorial Space].

VI. Three Qualifications

This conclusion is, however, subject to three qualifications.[30]

A. *Extension of National Space*

The equatorial States in the Bogotá Declaration of 3 December 1976 tried to claim for themselves the respective segments of the geostationary orbit above their territory in what may be regarded as a vertical application of the sector principle.[31] While their claim may have gained little credence, we have seen that coastal States have in recent years, with the acquiescence of the land-locked countries, thus by general consensus, succeeded in severely encroaching on international space in extending the permissible limit of their territorial seas to twelve nautical miles, and in conferring on themselves sovereign rights over their continental shelves and their EEZ. It has to be remembered that international law is still essentially a law made by States for States.[32] For as long as States persist in failing to come to some general agreement clearly delimiting the boundary between territorial space and outer space, and some States in refusing even to discuss the issue,[33] there is in law nothing to prevent States that are most concerned with foreign satellites remote-sensing their territories from taking advantage of the situation and, if nothing else merely as tactical move, and similarly extending their national space to beyond where these data gathering satellites operate. The result would be that it could be claimed that such satellites are operating within their territorial space and could in future continue to do so only subject to their consent. For information, the perigee and apogee heights of Landsat–I launched on 22 July 1972 are respectively 897 and 917 kilometres, and those of Landsat–II launched on 22 January 1975 901 and 915 kilometres.[34]

B. *Domestic Criminalization of Acts in Space*

Assuming that those States that wish to fail to establish national sovereignty beyond the height of the lowest perigee achieved so far by any orbiting artificial earth satellite, a second line of argument might be that which was once often voiced by the Soviet Union and some East European countries in the

---

[30] On all three qualifications, see further Cheng, loc. cit. (1978) in n. 22 above, at pp. 600–2.

[31] See loc. cit. in n. 24 above, at pp. 359–60 [Ch. 14 above, s. XII: The Geostationary Orbit].

[32] Cf. B. Cheng, 'The Military Use of Outer Space in International Law', in E. G. Bello and Prince Bola A. Ajibola, San (eds.), 1 *Essays in Honour of Judge Taslim Olawale Elias* (1992), p. 63, at pp. 63–4 [Ch. 20 above s. I: Preliminary Observations].

[33] See loc. cit. in n. 24 above [Ch. 14 above].

[34] ITU, 'Table of Artificial Satellites Launched between 1957 and 1976', 44–II *Telecommunication J.* (1977). Also separately published, pp. 168, and 204. The international numbers of the two satellites are respectively: 1972–58–A and 1975–4–A.

United Nations. They used to maintain that espionage, no matter where it was carried out, was contrary to international law and the Charter of the United Nations, and that space objects and astronauts involved in such 'illegal' activities would place themselves outside the pale of the various space treaties.[35] But this argument is not very convincing, and in any event appears to have been dropped by the Soviet Union from about the time of the 1968 Astronauts Agreement.[36]

A legally more feasible way for a State which objects to being sensed would be to adopt domestic laws to make the sensing of its natural resources and any of the related processes, including the dissemination and use of the information derived therefrom, without its authorization, offences under its own law, wherever in the world the offences may have been committed. The decision of the Permanent Court of International Justice in the case of *The Lotus* (1927)[37] shows that international law seemingly allows States, subject to specific rules of international law to the contrary, to criminalize acts committed outside their territory, provided that they do not enforce such laws until the person in question is within their territory or, to be more precise, under their effective jurisaction.[38] In fact, the enactment of some such legislation would seem the necessary preliminary step to any State raising objections to remote sensing; for unless the gathering of such data and the dissemination and use of the information derived therefrom are illegal when carried out within the territory of the State, there would seem little ground for saying that they would be illegal when conducted outside. Thus a review by States of their domestic laws in this regard in the light of the new technology may well be a matter of some urgency.

C. The Principle of Good Neighbourliness

For the rest, States, at least under existing international law, may have to reply on the principle of good neighbourliness, which, from this point of view, is probably more apposite than the principle of unjust enrichment. The latter, based doubtless on analogy with United States domestic law, where the concept has been occasionally applied to unauthorized prospecting for oil or minerals,[39] was suggested in the United Nations Secretary-General's

[35] Cf., e.g., USSR/ A/C.1/SR.1289 (3.12.62), p. 216; Czechoslovakia, A/C.1/SR.1294 (7.12.62), p. 238; Bulgaria, A/C.1/SR.1296 (10.12.62), p. 246; USSR,A/C.1/C.2/SR.17 (17.4.63), p. 7; Hungary A/AC.105/C.2/SR.26 (1.5.63), p. 4. See further B. Cheng, 'The Extraterrstrial Application of International Law', 18 *CLP* (1965), p. 132, p. 148 [Ch. 5 above, s. III.A: Outer Space, penultimate paragraph].

[36] See B. Cheng, 'The 1968 Astronauts Agreement', 23 *YBWA* (1969), p. 185, at pp. 205–8 [Ch. 10 above, s. VIII.B: Duty to Return Astronauts and Space Objects Absolute and Uncondtiiona?].

[37] PCIJ: Ser. A, No. 10.

[38] On the distinction between jurisfaction and jurisaction, see loc. cit. in n. 35 above, at pp. 136–42 [Ch. 5 above, s. II.B].

[39] See *Shell Petroleum Corp.* v. *Scully*, 71 F.2d 772 (5th Cir. 1934); *Piccu* v. *Fohs Oil Co.*, 222 La. 1068, 64 So. 2d 434 (1953). Cf. H. DeSaussure, 'Remote Sensing by Satellite: What Future for an International Regime?', 71 *AJIL* (1977), p. 707, aty pp. 715–16.

Background Paper of 1973.[40] However, the principle of unjust enrichment, though useful in determining the quantum of damages, requires a normative element to render the enrichment unjust in the first place.[41] The principle of good neighbourliness would provide the requisite legal rule of conduct.

Under Article 74 of the United Nations Charter, Member States agree that their policy in respect seemingly of all territories under their jurisdiction 'must be based on the general principle of good-neighbourliness, due account being taken of the interests and well-being of the rest of the world, in social economic and commercial matters.' There is no reason why this principle does not apply to data gathering from outer space. In fact, Article III of the 1967 Space Treaty reaffirms the applicability of the United Nations Charter to activities in outer space. Although the import of the principle may not be altogether clear, its relevance to remote sensing is patent, especially in relation to the problems of dissemination and misuse of remote sensing data and information.

While there may be some uncertainty regarding the precise scope and content of the principle enshrined in Article 74 of the Charter, it is arguable that, at least on the level of judicial international law, i.e., international law as applied by international courts and tribunals,[42] the principle of good-neighbourliness as a principle of general international law has been already affirmed, and its application exemplified, in such cases as the 1941 decision of the *Trail Smelter* Arbitral Tribunal set up by agreement (1935) between Canada and the United States,[43] and the decisions of the International Court of Justice in the *Corfu Channel Case* (Merits) (1949)[44] and the *Fisheries Jurisdiction Case* (1974) between the United Kingdom and Iceland.[45] In the first two cases, compensation was awarded for damage caused by what might be termed unneighbourly conduct. In the last mentioned case, what had to be found, said the Court, was an 'equitable solution'. This is doubtless what one should seek in all international issues, including all differences regarding remote sensing.

VII. Remote Sensing: Capability and Uses

The most sophisticated remote sensors used in outer space are doubtless the military ones, but information about them is not usually available. However,

---

[40] *Background Paper by the Secretary-General Assessing United Nations Documents and Other Pertinent Data Related to the Subject of Remote Sensing of the Earth by Satellites*, A/AC.105/118 (1973), ch. IV, para. 198.

[41] On the application of the principle of unjust enrichment in international law, see B. Cheng, 'Justice and Equity in International Law', 8 *CLP* (1955), p. 185, at pp. 195–202.

[42] Cf. loc. cit. in n. 32 above, F, at p. 64 [Ch. 20 above, s. I: Preliminary Observations (vi)].

[43] 3 *RIAA*, p. 1905, at p. 1965.   [44] *ICJ Rep. 1949*, p. 4, at p. 22.

[45] *ICJ Rep. 1974*, p. 3, at pp. 30–1.

one is given a glimpse of what satellites are capable of by a photograph which first appeared in *Jane's Defence Weekly* in August 1984, and which was subsequently reproduced the same week in *The Times* newspaper.[46] It was a picture of the Soviet shipyard at Nikolaiev on the Black Sea showing clearly and in some detail the Soviet Navy's first 75,000-ton nuclear-powered aircraft carrier under construction in two sections. This was a picture taken, it would appear, by a United States KH–11satellite some years previously from a height of, it is believed, 800 kilometres. A number of similar images have obviously been taken. Technology has no doubt much improved since then. In any event, critical military reconnaissance pictures would be taken from a height of maybe 250 kilometres. At that distance it is said that the satellite picture would be like a photograph taken from 50 metres away. The resolution can be as high as 0.3 or even 0.25 metre. In other words, if one were to put a car licence plate on the ground, one could recognize it from the satellite picture as a licence plate, even though, as yet, one would not be able really to read the number.[47]

It is hardly surprising, therefore, that the initial reaction of many countries to data gathering from outer space was one of suspicion, apprehension, fear, and probably even hostility. The Soviet Union in particular, which has always been a closed society, at the beginning vehemently denounced military reconnaissance by satellites as spying and hence illegal and even criminal. However, as the Soviets perfected their technique, the denunciation became more and more muted until it ceased altogether. A tacit recognition of its lawfulness first appeared in the 1972 Treaty between the United States and the Soviet Union on the Limitation of Anti-Ballistic Missile Systems,[48] generally known as the ABM Treaty. When Article XII of the Treaty states that the parties shall each use 'national technical means of verification at its disposal in a manner consistent with generally recognized principles of international law' in order to assure itself of the other's compliance with the treaty, it obviously has in mind reconnaissance satellites among other means. This receives confirmation, should confirmation be required, in the 1987 Treaty between the same two States on the Elimination of their Intermediate-range and Shorter-range Missiles, generally known as the IFN Treaty.[49] Article XII of the IFN Treaty also refers specifically to the use by each party of what the treaty calls 'national technical means of verification at its disposal' to ensure compliance with the treaty. Even though in both instances the treaty does add 'in a manner consistent with generally recognized principles of international law', both in the context of Article XII itself, and in the article-by-article analysis of the

[46] London, 8 Aug. 1984, p. 26, cols. 1–6.
[47] See British Broadcasting Corporation (BBC) Horizon, *Coming in From the Cold* (Transcript of television programme transmitted 28 Jan. 1991) (1991), pp. 9–10.
[48] 11 *ILM* (1972), p. 784; US President's message of transmittal to the Senate, ibid., p. 923.
[49] 27 *ILM* (1988), p. 84.

latter treaty by the United States Department of State, it is quite clear that these 'national technical means' 'include reconnaissance satellites'.[50] Military reconnaissance satellites have not only become simply a fact of international life that States just have to learn to live with, but also a vital instrument in the process of arms control and the preservation of international peace.

There are, however, many other types of data gathering from outer space, for example, meteorological satellites, geodetic, and geodynamics satellites. Satellite pictures of the weather are now taken for granted. And there is now much talk of the possible establishment of a Mediasat, a satellite that will serve to gather news and news pictures for the media.[51]

An area of remote sensing that has caused more discussion than perhaps even military reconnaissance is data gathering from outer space of the earth's natural resources and its environment. As has been mentioned before, some would even confine the use of the term exclusively to this type of remote sensing, like the 1986 General Assembly Resolution on the Principles Relating to Remote Sensing of the Earth from Outer Space[52] However, in view of, first, the multiple use to which remote sensing from outer space can be, and are now being, put and secondly, because of the ever decreasing gap between the capabilities of military and civilian sensors,[53] it becomes less and less realistic to restrict the discussion of the legality of remote sensing to merely earth-resources satellites as if the other uses of data gathering from outer space do not exist.

Be that as it may, the remote sensing of the earth's natural resources and its environment is economically and environmentally a development doubtless of the greatest importance. Landsat–I (initially known as ERTS or Earth Resources Technology Satellite) launched on 22 July 1971 by the United States heralded the beginning of the United States Landsat programme devoted to this purpose. Landsat–I was followed by others in the series and by earth resources satellites or sensors launched, or being planned, by other countries or groupings, such as the Soviet Union, the People's Republic of China, France, India, Japan and the European Space Agency. These natural resources sensors can tell you almost everything about what is on land or in the water, as well as a great deal that is below the surface. Remote sensing can provide accurate, detailed and, given the resources, almost instant information, which is not otherwise available or at least not easily available, on topographic features, including inaccessible jungles and mountain ranges, geological structure, soil types, crop species, crop health and crop yield, mineral resources, hydrocarbon resources, water resources, water pollution,

---

[50] 27 *ILM* (1988), p. 199, at p. 221.

[51] See, for instance, R. Dalbello, 'The Legal and Political Implications of Media Newsgathering from Space', 30 *Space Law Colloquium* (1987), p. 79; G. P. Sloup, 'Mediasat, Gray Reconnaissance, and the New United Nations Principles on Remote Sensing', ibid., p. 385.

[52] See text to n. 17 above and to nn. 66 ff. below.   [53] See n. 18 above and text thereto.

coastal changes, ice floes and icebergs, and marine resources. Such information is obviously of tremendous value to national economic planning and the exploitation by either the State or by individuals of the natural resources of the world, including agriculture and forestry, fishery, and mining, as well as many related activities, such as shipping, cartography, the planning of transcontinental highways, and so forth.

At the same time, all information of this nature will clearly have important practical and commercial bearings. Among recent developments is, for instance, the use of satellites to guide fishing vessels to the best fishing grounds. But such information in the hands of foreign, especially hostile, governments can also have important political and even military consequences.

For many countries, in particular developing countries, which of late have been asserting so hard their permanent sovereignty over their national natural resources, earth resources remote sensing means that their precious natural resources, the exploration of which was hitherto legally at least under their exclusive control, would be an open book to all States with remote sensing capability. This capacity, together with the perhaps even more demanding capability of processing, analysing, and interpreting the data garnered from remote sensing, is at present technologically and financially beyond the reach of many or most if not all of them—in any event directly and individually. Added to this is a general fear for their national security, not only from the economic point of view, but also military, political, technological, and even environmental. Little wonder they were seriously alarmed by the prospect that they might be denied vital information about their country which others have acquired through remote sensing.

The other side of the coin was that initially the United States was willing to give away free the data gathered by Landsat to any country that would put up a ground station to which the information could be downlinked directly, but the added fear was then that not only would such information be in the possession of the sensing States, but might also easily fall into the hands of hostile or simply unscrupulous third parties, be they State or private.

However, in time the many benefits of natural resources remote sensing came to be realized. Apart from their inability to undo what was already a *fait accompli*, especially on the military side, many nations, without themselves having direct remote sensing capabilities, were soon put in the position of having to decide whether to keep the cake or to eat it, whether to oppose remote sensing of their territories by others or to accept it. In the end, as with data gathering from outer space in general, they have on the whole accepted it as a fact of life and turned their efforts to damage-control, while seeking to benefit from it as much as possible.

VIII. Commercialization and Commercial Prospects

In 1984, the United States passed the Land Remote Sensing Commercialization Act.[54] The Landsat system was transferred from the National Aeronautics and Space Administration (NASA) to the National Oceanic and Atmospheric Administration (NOAA) and the Department of Commerce was authorized to transfer it to private ownership and control. A licence was in due course awarded to EOSAT (Earth Observation Satellite Co.), a company formed (September 1985) by a consortium of RCA and Hughes Aircraft.[55] EOSAT images cost from $50 to $200 each depending on their enhancement and quality.[56] EOSAT provided the first images of the Chernobyl nuclear disaster. Its images are also credited with having identified Libya's poison gas plant at Rabta.[57]

EOSAT was in fact antedated by Spot–Image formed in 1981 to sell to the public data collected by the French remote sensing satellite SPOT (*Satellite probatoire pour l'observation de la terre*). SPOT–1 was successfully launched on 22 February 1986. SPOT–1 has a higher resolution (10 metres panchromatic and twenty metres multispectral) than the current Landsats (thirty metres)[58], and was consequently able to up-stage EOSAT with its much clearer, albeit later (because it was not passing over the Soviet Union at the time) pictures of the Chernobyl accident. Its images, which include many of military facilities in various countries,[59] are freely available at £1,500 a time. There is a complete catalogue. Spot–Image, based in Toulouse, has a subsidiary in the United States, Spot–Image Corporation (SI Corp).

Hot on the heels of SPOT–1 were the Soviets who created in 1987 Soyuzkarta to sell images collected from its various satellite systems, SALYUT, MIR, METEOR, COSMOS. Some of the images are said to have 'perhaps five or six metre resolution',[60] and are being offered at competitive prices. Another Soviet agency that also offers for sale remote sensing imageries is Glavkosmos.[61]

[54] 15 USC §4200 (Supp. IV 1986).

[55] See Hamilton DeSaussure, 'Remote Sensing Satellite Regulation by National and International Law', 15 *Rutgers Computer & Technology LJ* (1989), p. 351, at pp. 363 ff.

[56] *The World in Space* (Chipman ed., 1982), pp. 270, 380, quoted in DeSaussure, loc. cit. in n. 55 above, at p. 353.

[57] See W. Kennedy (EOSAT) on the BBC Horizon television programme, op. cit. in n. 47 above, at p. 18, who may seem also to have implied that current EOSAT satellites have a resolution of 15 metres. Speaking of this particular image, he said: 'Now it is commercially available, any nation can order this image, take the information from it and be able to target this facility within 15 metres.'

[58] See C. Jung, 'Capacité et limite du satellite SPOT dans le domaine de la surveillance', in McGill University Centre for Research in Air and Space Law, *Space Surveillance for Arms Control and Verification: Options, Symposium Proceedings 1987*, p. 5.

[59] See, e.g., Sloup, loc. cit. in n. 51 above, nn. 1 and 3 on p. 391.

[60] Prof. P. Zimmerman in the BBC Horizon TV programme, op. cit. in n. 47 above, at p. 17.

[61] See Jasani and Larsson, loc. cit. in n. 18 above, p. 48. The article contains reproductions of several satellite photographs and images obtained from Soyuzkarta, SPOT–1, and Landsat.

The trade in remote sensing images is expected to be joined in due course by Japan, with its MOS–1 and 2, India (IRS–1a, 1B and 1C), the European Space Agency in co-operation with Canada (ERS–1), Canada (RADARSAT), and no doubt others. The competition in the market place is getting keener and keener and the United States is said to be beginning to offer military quality images, except where their sale is precluded by national security.[62]

With all these activities going on, the commercial prospects of remote sensing itself can be easily gauged, from research and development, through manufacture and actual operation, to data processing, data analysing, data interpretation, and data dissemination, without counting the commercial possibilities of exploiting the knowledge gained from data gathered from outer space. Peter Norris, Vice-President of EOSAT, speaking at a symposium in 1987, referred to forecasts 'that the overall dollar value of remote sensing as a business will approach $6.6 billion . . . over the next ten years, of which $4.5 billion will be in value-added services.'[63]

Commercialization is now irreversible. The trend towards greater availability of images of higher and higher resolution is probably also inevitable. With commercially available images having shown their ability among other things to discover and reveal the existence and location of Libya's chemical plants and the Soviet secret radar station in Siberia built in violation of the 1972 US–USSR Anti-Ballistic Missile Treaty,[64] for many nations, remote sensing in general and perhaps commercialized remote sensing in particular, pose a potentially serious threat to both their economic and their military security. Their natural resources and their economic and military installations are now there for all to see. For those who have not the capability either individually or in co-operation with others to engage in remote sensing, the question then is, can one avoid being sensed and, if not, how to control the damage?

IX. United Nations Principles on Remote Sensing

The United Nations Committee on the Peaceful Uses of Outer Space (COP-UOS) discussed the subject for 15 years from 1971 onwards.[65] Finally a set of 15 principles was adopted by consensus on 3 December 1986 by the General

[62] See among others M. Bourély, 'Legal Problems Posed by the Commercialization of Data Collected by the European Remote Sensing Satellite ERS–1', 16 *JSL* (1988), p. 129.

[63] P. M. E. Norris, 'Commercial Opportunities in Earth Observation from Space', in McGill University Centre for Research of Air and Space Law, op. cit. in n. 58 above, p. 19.

[64] After the United States spotted that the Soviet Union had built a radar in Siberia in violation of the ABM Treaty (for reference, see n. 48 above), it refused to publish the satellite image, and released only an artist's impression. The Soviet Union denied any violation. Shortly after SPOT–1 went into orbit, Media Network in Stockholm acquired unclassified pictures which clearly indicated its existence and location. See BBC Horizon, op. cit, in n. 47 above, pp. 14–15.

[65] For an analysis of the many problems encountered in the negotiations, see Cheng, loc. cit. (1978) in n. 22 above, s. 3: Proposals to Regulate Remote Sensing.

Assembly under the title of Principles Relating to Remote Sensing of the Earth from Outer Space.[66]

It should be pointed out in the first place that this instrument took the form of a General Assembly resolution and not, as was hoped by some States, a treaty, with the result that the principles, instead of being intended to constitute rules legally binding upon those that subscribe to them, are merely guidelines.[67]

Secondly, Principle I(a) makes it clear that the principles are applicable only to remote sensing 'of the Earth's surface . . . for the purpose of improving natural resource management, land use and protection of the environment'. Other types of remote sensing are, therefore, not covered by these principles. Principle I(e), however, extends the geographical scope of application of some of the principles beyond merely outer space by defining 'remote sensing activities' as 'the operation of remote sensing space systems, primary data collection and storage stations, and activities in processing, interpreting, and disseminating the processed data'. Much if not necessarily all of the operations of data collection, storage, processing, interpretation and dissemination would be on earth rather than in outer space, although not all the principles apply to 'remote sensing activities'. Some apply to only 'remote sensing' as such.

Turning to the contents of these principles, one finds that many of them are merely re-affirmations of existing rules of international law or provisions of existing treaties, such as Principle III on the need to respect international law, the United Nations Charter, the 1967 Space Treaty and the relevant instruments of the International Telecommunication Union. Certain provisions of the 1967 Space Treaty have been given special emphasis, such as its Article I in Principle IV with added provisos on respect for the principle of States' 'permanent sovereignty . . . over their own wealth and natural sources' and not conducting remote sensing 'in a manner detrimental to the legitimate rights and interests of the sensed State', which sounds like an application of the principle of good neighbourliness. Principle IX reminds States of their duties under Article IV of the Registration Convention and Article XI of the 1967 Space Treaty to inform the United Nations Secretary-General of their space activities, and urges them, to the extent they can, to let other States, 'particularly any developing country that is affected by the programme', have any relevant information they may have requested. Principle XIV recalls Article VI of the Space Treaty on international responsibility for national space activities, with a rather cryptic additional sentence saying: 'This principle is without prejudice to the applicability of the norms of international law on State responsibility for remote sensing activities'. The term 'remote sensing activi-

---

[66] UN GA Resolution 41/65. For text see App. II.5.

[67] See further B. Cheng, 'United Nations Resolutions on Outer Space: "Instant" International Customary Law?', 5 *Indian JIL* (1965), p. 23 [Ch. 7 above].

Table XXII.3 PRINCIPLES RELATING TO REMOTE SENSING OF THE EARTH FROM OUTER SPACE
General Assembly Resolution A/RES/41/65 of 3 December 1986

SUBJECT	PARTICULARS	PRINCIPLE
REAFFIRMATION OF APPLICABLE RULES AND PRINCIPLES	* Respect of IL, UN Charter, Space Treaty, ITU	III
	* Freedom of outer space	IV
	* International responsibility	XIX
	* Respect of other States' sovereignty over resources and their rights and interests	IV
	*Art. XI of Space Treaty, Registration Convention	IX
SAFEGUARD OF CERTAIN COMMON INTERESTS	* Interests of all countries, and needs of developing ones	II, IV, IX, XII, XIII
	* Promote environmental protection	X
	* Prompt information re pending natural disaster	XI
PARTICIPATION, CO-OPERATION & TECHNICAL ASSISTANCE	*Opportunity for participation	V
	* Co-operation in data collection, storage, processing and interpretation	VI
	* Technical assistance	VII
PERMISSIBILITY OF SENSING	* High seas *sensu stricto*	—
	* Continental shelf, EEZ, etc.	—
	* Territory of a foreign State	Cf. IV, XII, XIII
DISSEMINATION OF PRIMARY DATA & ANALYSED INFORMATION	* Resources outside national jurisdictions	Cf. IX
	* Resources of a foreign State:	
	—To sensed State	XII
	—To the public or third States	IX
INTERESTS OF SENSED STATE	* Regard for legitimate rights and interests	IV
	* Access to primary and processed data, and available analysed information	XII
	* Right to request consultation and opportunity for participation	XIII
INSTITUTIONAL ASPECTS	* UN Secretary-General to be kept informed	IX
	* UN to play co-ordinating rôle	VIII
SETTELEMT OF DISPUTES	* Normal procedure (no special ones)	XV

ties', as we have just seen, is, under these principles, not necessarily conterminous with 'remote sensing' as such.

Then there are some principles designed to promote certain common interests, such as Principle II on the benefits of all countries and the particular needs of developing nations, and Principles X and XI on the protection of the Earth's natural environment and the prevention of natural disasters. Under Principles X and XI, sensing States that have information of any phenomenon harmful to the environment or of any impending natural disaster are to disclose such information to the States concerned.

Principles V, VI, VII, and XIII basically encourage States to enter cooperative arrangements, particularly with regard to data collection, storage, processing and interpretation, to permit participation, especially when requested by States whose territories are being sensed, and to make available technical assistance.

The crux of the problem concerning remote sensing which took COPUOS fifteen years to arrive at a set of mere guidelines remains the conflict between those who champion the principle of sovereignty, particularly the so-called permanent sovereignty over national natural resources and those who champion the principle of the freedom of outer space and the freedom to disseminate information.

The problem can be reduced to four separate issues: permissibility, access, dissemination to third parties, and use.

First, permissibility. The opening bid by the sovereignty school was succinctly put in Article V of the Argentina/Brazil draft: 'States parties shall refrain from undertaking activities of remote sensing of national resources belonging to another State party, including the resources located in maritime areas under national jurisdiction, *without the consent of the latter*'.[68] This would have included the natural resources of not only a State's territory, but also its continental shelf and its EEZ. The Principles as adopted rejected not only the notion of prior consent but also that of prior consultation.[69] The only

---

[68] Argentina and Brazil: Treaty on Remote Sensing—Draft Basic Articles, A/C.1/1047. Italics added.

[69] Cf. UN GA Resolution 37/92 on Principles Governing the Use by States of Artificial Earth Satellites for International Direct Television Broadcasting, adopted by the General Assembly on 10 Dec. 1982. Sections G (Principle 10) and J (Principles 13–15) establish a duty and right to consult, whilst Principle 14 even subjects the establishment of an international DBS TV service to prior agreement(s) with the receiving State(s). This resolution, the text of which is reproduced in the Appendix (II.4), contrary to the usual COPUOS practice of operating by consensus, was adopted by a majority vote in the General Assembly of 107 in favour to 13 against (which included the Federal Republic of Germany, Italy, Japan, Luxembourg, United Kingdom and United States), with 13 abstentions (which included Australia, Canada and France). In the case of remote sensing, France proposed in 1973 that 'every State whose territory or territorial sea is affected by remote sensing shall receive prior notification thereof from the State, States or international organization responsible for such activity' (France: Draft Principles Governing Remote Sensing, A/AC.105/L.69, para. 4). This suggestion was, however, not repeated in the joint proposal which France later submitted together with the Soviet Union the following year (France

reference to consultation—not prior consultation—with the sensed State, and here the reference is to 'territory' without mention of 'maritime areas under national jurisdiction', is to be found in Principle XIII. A sensed State (not one *to be* sensed) may request consultation in order to seek 'opportunities for participation' and ways of enhancing 'mutual benefits', opportunities which sensing States are in any event encouraged by Principle V to afford to others. Principle V makes it clear, moreover, that participation 'shall be based . . . on equitable and mutually acceptable terms'. Insofar as the Principles are concerned, therefore, stripped of all the verbiage about respect for this and respect for that, the bottom line is that data gathering from outer space directed at any object anywhere on earth is permissible.

Secondly, access. As regards access to data gathered from outer space by remote sensing, a distinction has to be made between data concerning areas outside the territorial jurisdiction of any State, such as the high seas, and data concerning the sensed State. Insofar as the former category of data is concerned, all three principal drafts before COPUOS contained provisions on access by all States, whether free,[70] on 'equal and mutually acceptable terms',[71] or 'on an equitable, timely and non-discriminatory basis'.[72] However, the 1986 Principles remain completely silent on the subject, unless one can subsume it under Principle IX which more or less repeats Article XI of the 1967 Space Treaty.

Perhaps the only thing that the potentially sensed and non-sensing States managed to get out of the whole 15–year exercise is to be found in Principle XII:

As soon as the primary data and the processed data concerning the territory under its jurisdiction are produced, the sensed State shall have access to them on a non-discriminatory basis and on reasonable cost terms. The sensed State shall also have access to the available analysed information concerning the territory under its jurisdiction in the possession of any State participating in remote sensing activities on the same basis and terms, particular regard being given to the needs and interests of the developing countries.

Even in the final stages of the discussions, there were attempts on the one hand to enhance the position of the sensed State by giving it priority access, and on the other hand to diminish it by limiting such obligation, be it only moral or political, to doing what is 'feasible and practicable'. These attempts were, however, dropped in the end. Perhaps all that Principle XII amounts to now

and USSR: Draft Principles Governing Remote Sensing, A/AC.105/C.2/L.99). Interestingly, the French proposal, unlike the joint Argentina/Brazil draft (see n. 68 above), made no reference to either the continental shelf or the EEZ, which, strictly speaking, do not form part of the 'territory' of the coastal State. See in this regard, n. 9 above and text thereto.

[70] Argentina/Brazil draft, loc. cit.in n. 68 above, Art. XII.
[71] France/USSR draft, loc. cit. in n. 69 above, para. 6.
[72] COPUOS, *Legal Implications of Remote Sensing: United States Working Paper on the Development of Additional Guidelines*, A/AC.105/C.2/L.103 (1975), para. V.

is that a State taking part in the remote sensing of the territory under the jurisdiction of another State should not withhold from that State any of the primary or processed data, or any of the available analysed information that is in its possession, concerning that State. Such data and information should be made available to it on a 'non-discriminatory basis and on reasonable cost terms', with special consideration being given to developing countries. In this regard, particular difficulties may arise over 'analysed information' which often may no longer be in the hands of the sensing State. Moreover, such information may carry a great deal of independent input, creating problems of ownership and intellectual property rights. A similar problem may arise regarding also primary and processed data when remote sensing has been commercialized, but this can probably be overcome in the authorization and licensing process.

Thirdly, dissemination to third parties. Another item of great concern to the developing countries and not necessarily them alone was the dissemination of data concerning their natural resources to third parties, although some of them may have been hoisted by their own petard in having pushed for the adoption of Article XI of the 1967 Space Treaty, under which space Powers are asked 'to the greatest extent feasible and practicable' to share with the world the results of their space activities.

Be that as it may, Article IX of the Argentina/Brazil draft, for instance, held strongly to the view that a State acquiring 'information relating to the natural resources of another State . . . through remote sensing shall neither divulge such information nor transmit or transfer it in any manner to a third State, international organization or private entity, without the *express authorization* of the party to which the natural resources belong . . .'[73] On the other hand, there were States, principally the industrialized nations, which held equally strongly to the policy of free dissemination.[74] In fact, the United States has, since the launch of its Landsat–I in 1972, made available data with resolution of 30 metres (instantaneous field of view–IFOV) to all purchasers on an equal basis and without obtaining the permission of the countries being sensed.[75]

---

[73] For support, see, e.g., among COPUOS members in discussions in the Legal Sub-Committee at its 16th (1977) Session, Chile, A/AC.105/C.2/SR.269 (17.3.77), para. 4; Iran, ibid./SR.270 (18.2.77), para. 13; India, ibid./SR.270 (18.3.77), para. 32; Mexico, ibid./SR.271 (21.3.77), para. 14; Indonesia, ibid./SR.272 (22.3.77), para. 16; German Democratic Republic, ibid./SR.272 (22.3.77), para. 27; Egypt, ibid./SR.272 (23.3.77), para. 7.

[74] E.g., among COPUOS members in discussions in the Legal Sub-Committee at its 16th (1977) session, Italy, A/AC.105/C.2/SR.269 (13.3.77), para. 14; United Kingdom, A/AC.105/C.2/SR.269 (17.3.77), para. 21; Federal Republic of Germany, A/AC.105/C.2/SR.270 (18.3.77), para. 8; Japan, A/AC.105/C.2/SR.272 (22.3.77), para. 11; Sweden 1977, A/AC.105/C.2/SR.272 (22.3.77), para. 22; USA, A/AC.105/C.2/SR.273 (23.3.77), para. 17.

[75] See Jasani and Larsson, loc. cit. in n. 18 above, p. 58.

In between stood the Soviet Union which, supported by a number of East European countries,[76] suggested[77] that it might be possible on the basis of some technical criterion such as spatial resolution to divide remote sensing data into those of a global/regional character on the one hand and those of a local character on the other. The former would be so general that they could not possibly affect national sovereignty or security and would, therefore, require no special regulation, whilst specific rules should be developed for data, for instance, of spatial resolution superior to 50 metres. In the latter case, the rule proposed in the France/USSR draft, pursuant to its acknowledgement of a State's right to dispose of information concerning its resources,[78] was that such information acquired through remote sensing by another State would not be made 'public without the clearly expressed consent of the State to which the natural resources belong'.[79]

In this connection, it may be of interest to note that in 1978 a number of socialist countries[80] signed a Convention on the Transfer and Use of Data of the Remote Sensing of the Earth from Outer Space adopting precisely the above principle. Under Article IV of the treaty, the consent of the sensed State is required for the dissemination of any data where the specific resolution is better than 50 metres, whilst Article V prohibits the dissemination of information derived from remote sensing relating to the natural resources or the economic potential of the sensed State.[81]

However, this idea was not accepted in the United Nations principles, nor a subsequent French compromise distinguishing between 'primary data' and 'analysed information' with a more liberal attitude towards the former,[82] and limiting the requirement of consent merely to processed data of resolution of 10 metres and better.[83]

The Principles adopted in 1986 contain nothing specific at all on the subject of dissemination of data to third parties. Apart from the rather guarded

[76] E.g., among COPUOS member in discussions in the Legal Sub-Committee at its 16th (1977) Session, Hungary, A/AC.105/C.2/SR.271 (21.3.77), para. 17; Czechoslovakia, ibid./SR.272 (22.3.77), para. 5; Bulgaria, ibid./SR.273 (25.3.77), para. 2; Poland, ibid./SR.273 (25.3.77), para. 7.

[77] USSR working paper submitted to the 13th (1976) Session of the Scientific and Technical Sub-Committee, A/AC.105/C.1/L.81. See also USSR additional working paper submitted the following session (1977), ibid./L.94.

[78] France/USSR draft, loc. cit. in n. 69 above, para. 2.   [79] Ibid., para. 5(b).

[80] Cuba, Czechoslovakia, the German Democratic Republic, Hungary, Mongolia, Poland, Romania, and the USSR.

[81] See W. E. Mounts, 'Marine Remote Sensing and International Law', 30 *Space Law Colloquium* (1987), p. 350, at p. 355. Also the sensing State must not in any circumstances use the acquired data to the detriment of the sensed State.

[82] France, A/AC.105/PV.173 (23.6.77), p. 12.

[83] France had earlier submitted two working papers on the subject, A/AC.105/C.1/L.86 in 1976 and A/AC.105/C.1/L.93 in 1977. In the latter, France had proposed: 'The dissemination of any processed "information" prepared by methods giving a spatial resolution of one decameter or less and obtained after processing of raw data collected by any type of satellite borne sensor shall require the prior consent of the State concerned or sensed' (para. 5).

concessions on opportunities for participation and mutual benefits under Principle XIII and access to primary and processed data as well as to 'available analysed information' under Principle XII, the sensed State has been given no special treatment at all, except perhaps the very vague safeguard found in Principle IV. Principle IV provides that remote sensing activities shall be conducted among other things on the basis of respect for the principle of full and permanent sovereignty of States and peoples over their own wealth and natural resources, and 'shall not be conducted in a manner detrimental to the legitimate rights and interests of the sensed State'. But all this is subject to auto-interpretation.[84]

The only saving grace to Principle IV is, whatever this amounts to, that, since it refers all the time to 'remote sensing activities', it, in accordance with the definition of the term 'remote sensing activities' in Principle I, applies not only to 'the operation of remote sensing space systems, primary data collection and storage stations', but also to 'activities in processing, interpreting and *disseminating the processed data*'[85]. However, this definition leaves out the *use of the data*, on which the Principles are in fact silent.

In sum those who are apprehensive that data gathering from outer space by others might work to their detriment or that the data gathered from outer space might be misused by either the sensing State or by third parties to their detriment can probably find only scant comfort from the United Nations Principles.

For protection, it appears that their best safeguard is still to be found in Article VI of the 1967 Space Treaty whereby States Parties are rendered internationally responsible for 'national activities in outer space'.[86] This article is re-affirmed in Principle XIV. But arguably Principle XIV appears to have limited the application of Article VI of the Space Treaty to activities connected with 'operating remote sensing satellites', while leaving the remaining activities to be regulated only by the ordinary 'norms of international law on State responsibility'.[87] Here we would have to go back to what we have said before

---

[84] On the three grades of international law, auto-interpretative, justiciable and judicial, see B. Cheng, 'Nature and Sources of International Law', in Cheng (ed.), *International Law*, p. 201, at pp. 209–15; and 'Flight from Justiciable to Auto-interpretative International Law: from the Jay Treaty to the Shultz Letter', in *Liber Amicorum Elie Van Bogaert* (1985), p. 3, at pp. 14–18. See also below, Index, international law (grades).   [85] Italics added.

[86] This is not to say that Art. VI of the 1967 Space Treaty is necessarily very clear as to its meaning. See further B. Cheng, 'Space Activities, Responsibility and Liability For', in Bernhardt (ed.), 11 *Ency. PIL* (1989), pp. 299–303 [cf. Ch. 24 below].

[87] *Sic* Marietta Benkö and G. Gruber, 'The UN Committee on the Peaceful Uses of Outer Space: Adoption of Principles of Remote Sensing of the Earth from Outer Space and Other Recent Developments', 36 *ZLW* (1987), p. 24; *contra* V. Kopal, 'Principles relating to Remote Sensing of the Earth from Outer Space', 30 *Space Law Colloquium* (1987), p. 322, pp. 326–7. It should further be noted that Art. VI of the 1967 Space Treaty extends in any event only to 'national activities *in outer space*' (italics added). Unless Art. VI can be interpreted to include within a State's 'international responsibility' all the consequences of 'national activities in outer space', even when such consequences involve additional human intervention on earth outside of outer space, a General Assembly resolution would not be legally capable of so extending its scope of application. See further Cheng, loc. cit. in n. 86 above.

regarding the three qualifications to the right of States under international law to conduct remote sensing from outer space.[88]

At the end of the day then, insofar as inter-State relations are concerned, subject to specific treaty obligations, the law on data gathering from outer space remains largely as it was with its three qualifications, namely, extension of the limit of national space, criminalization under domestic law of harmful acts committed outside the country, and appeal to the principle of good neighbourliness. This being the case, one wonders from this point of view whether the latest offering from COPUOS is really worth 15 years of labour. One is wistfully reminded of Aesop's fable of *The Mountain in Labour*,[89] or, as put so succinctly by Horace: *Parturiunt montes, nascetur ridiculus mus.*[90]

[88] See n. 30 above and text thereto.

[89] As found in Phædrus, *Fables*, Bk. iv, fab. 22, 1. 1: 'A mountain was in labour, sending forth frightful groans, and there was the highest expectation throughout the land. But it brought forth only a mouse.'

[90] Horace, *Ars Poetica*, 1. 139: 'The mountains are in labour, and a ridiculous mouse will be born'.

23

International Responsibility and Liability for Launch Activities*

I. Introduction

It was only in 1957 that Sputnik I succeeded in being the first object launched from this planet to reach outer space. Yet today the launching of objects into space, although not quite yet, promises soon to be almost a daily occurrence. Responsibility and liability for launch activities consequently deserve our close attention.

In examining the problem of international responsibility and liability for launch activities, it is necessary to clarify the meaning of these different terms used, namely, international responsibility, international liability and launch activities.

II. Launch Activities

A. Meaning of 'Launch Activities'

The phrase 'launch activities' means here in reality the act of launching a space object. For the sake of clarity, the 1972 Liability Convention[1] has added in its Article 1(b):

The term 'launching' includes attempted launching.

The question then is, What is a space object?

---

* First published in 20 *ASL* (1995), pp. 297–310, being a paper presented at the *International Symposium on the Use of Air and Space at the Service of World Peace and Prosperity*, Beijing, 21–3 Aug. 1995, held jointly by the Peking University; the Asian Institute of International Air and Space Law, Soochow University, Taipei; the International Institute of Air and Space Law, Leiden University; and the Institute of Air and Space Law, McGill University, Montreal. Reproduced with kind permission from Kluwer Law International.

[1] Convention on International Liability for Damage Caused by Space Objects, London, Moscow and Washington, 1972, 961 UNTS 187 [App. I.3 below]. See B. Cheng, 'Convention on International Liability for Damage Caused by Space Objects', in Jasentuliyana and Lee (eds.), 1 *Manual* (1979), pp. 83–172 [Ch. 11 above].

B. *Meaning of 'Space Object'*

The expression 'space object' is not specifically defined in any of the conventions relating to outer space established under the auspices of the United Nations, notwithstanding efforts to do so in the negotiations leading to the 1972 Liability Convention and the 1975 Registration Convention.[2] As referred to in Articles VII and VIII of the 1967 Space Treaty,[3] for example, it denotes simply 'an object launched into outer space', which, in the terminology of the treaty, includes the moon and other celestial bodies in outer space.

From the legal standpoint, 'space object', in current practice, is the generic term used to cover spacecraft, satellites, and in fact anything that human beings launch or attempt to launch into space. This practice appears to have been well established by the 1967 Space Treaty (Articles VII and VIII), the 1972 Liability Convention, and the 1975 Registration Convention. The fact that Article 3(2) of the Moon Treaty[4] mentions spacecraft and man-made space objects separately when it refers to 'the earth, the moon, spacecraft, the personnel of spacecraft or man-made space objects', is intended no doubt to facilitate the reference to 'personnel of spacecraft' and is not believed to imply thereby that spacecraft do not constitute 'man-made space objects'. Moreover, although in the context of the Moon Treaty, it makes sense to refer specifically to man-made objects, a more precise specification would be 'man-launched space object', or 'object launched into outer space by humans', rather than 'man-made space object'; for there seems to be no valid reason why an object launched into space must be 'man-made'—an artefact. If for some reason, a piece of naturally formed rock is launched into outer space, why should it not be accepted as a space object, or the component of a space object?

Whilst the Astronauts Agreement[5] still refers separately and expressly to 'component parts' of a space object (Article 5), both the Liability Convention (Article 1(d)) and the Registration Convention (Article 1(b)) provide in identical fashion:

[2] Convention on Registration of Objects Launched into Outer Space, New York, 1975, 1023 UNTS 15 [App. I.4 below]. See B. Cheng, 'Outer Space: The International Legal Framework—The International Legal Status of Outer Space, Space Objects and Spacemen', 10 *Thesaurus Acroasium* (1981), p. 41, at pp. 98–102 [Ch. 13 above, s. IV.C: The Registration Convention].

[3] Treaty on Principles Governing the Activities of States in the Exploration and Use of Outer Space, including the Moon and Other Celestial Bodies, London, Moscow and Washington, 1967, 610 UNTS 205 [App. I.1 below]. See B. Cheng, 'Le Traité de 1967 sur l'espace/The 1967 Space Treaty', 95 *JDI* (1968), pp. 532–645 [Ch. 9 above].

[4] Agreement Governing the Activities of States on the Moon and Other Celestial Bodies, New York, 1979, 1363 UNTS 3 [App. I.5 below]. See B. Cheng, 'The Moon Treaty', 33 *CLP* (1980), pp. 213–37 [Ch. 12 above].

[5] Agreement on the Rescue of Astronauts, the Return of Astronauts and the Return of Objects Launched into Outer Space, London, Moscow and Washington, 1968, 672 UNTS 119 [App. I.2 below]. See B. Cheng, 'The 1968 Astronauts Agreement', 23 *YBWA* (1969), pp. 185–208 [Ch. 10 above].

The term 'space object' includes component parts of a space object as well as its launch vehicle and parts thereof.

In addition, the 1967 Space Treaty, in its Article VIII, appears to subsume under the term 'space objects' not only 'their component parts', but also 'objects landed or constructed on a celestial body'.

Furthermore, the Liability Convention makes it clear in its Article 1(b):

The term 'launching' includes attempted launching.

In sum, therefore, the term space object designates any object which humans launch, attempt to launch or have launched into outer space, including the moon and other celestial bodies. The term includes the components of a space object, as well as its launch vehicle and parts thereof.[6]

C. Where Begins Outer Space?

Now comes the question, where is outer space? We know where the terrestrial moon is, and more or less where most, if not all, the other celestial bodies are, but at what point are we in outer space? In view of the persistent resistance of many States, including major space powers, to any attempt even to discuss the problem of defining and delimiting outer space, does one know where, *in law*, outer space begins?

There are basically three schools of thought on the subject: (i) the spatialists who believe that there must logically be in law a clearly determined upper limit to national space and a clearly determined base-line marking the beginning of outer space, (ii) the functionalists who dispute the need for or even the possibility of such a delimitation, and who believe that the lawfulness or unlawfulness of space activities should be determined solely by the nature of the activity or of the vehicle; and (iii) the you-don't-need-to-know school who claim that those who need to know already know where outer space is, but feel that there is really no need for the rest of us to bother ourselves with such problems. They prefer that the question not be raised, and still less discussed.

The latter two schools often take shelter behind the argument that geophysicists are unable, from the scientific point of view, to point to any specific line separating airspace from outer space, and in any case even if such a line were drawn it would be meaningless to most people. However, this argument either betrays ignorance of or deliberately ignores what States have done for centuries in drawing invisible boundary lines on the sea which separate their territorial seas from the high seas, lines the precise location of which is impos-

---

[6] See further B. Cheng, 'Spacecraft, Satellites and Space Objects', in Bernhardt (ed.), 11 *Ency. PIL* (1989), pp. 309–17 [Ch. 16 above]; and 'Definitional Issues in Space Law: "Space Objects", "Astronauts" and Related Expressions', 34 *Space Law Colloquium* (1991), pp. 17–27 [Ch. 18 above].

sible to determine except through detailed maps of the coast and by reference to the legislation of the coastal State.

In fact, notwithstanding the obscurantist stance of the latter two schools, State practice indicates that there is already an acknowledged baseline of outer space, inasmuch as all States appear to accept that all the artificial satellites that are orbiting the earth or have orbited the earth are or were doing so in outer space, with the result that it is possible to say that according to the general *opinio juris* of States outer space begins at least from the point of the lowest perigee of any artificial earth satellite so far recorded. In putting this proposition forward, it may need to be emphasized that this is not to adopt what has sometimes be called 'the lowest perigee rule' either in the sense that the baseline of outer space coincides with the lowest *theoretical* perigee of artificial earth satellites, or in the sense that it will vary with the lowest perigee that may be achieved at any time in the future. The above conclusion is based on the actual practice of States evidencing what they accept to be the law at this moment. In the absence of any successful protest by any State that any of the artificial earth satellites so far launched into earth orbit has actually violated its national space or airspace sovereignty, and in the light of express acknowledgements by some States that all existing artificial earth satellites were orbiting in outer space, the conclusion must be that there exists already a rule of general international law recognizing the lowest perigee of any existing or past artificial earth satellites as marking the beginning of outer space. In absolute terms, this point may be put at 94 kilometres from the surface of the earth. Conservatively, the figure may be put at 100 or 110 kilometres. This is, however, always subject to the proviso that States may at any time, like what they have done with regard to the breadth of the territorial sea, wish to claim a higher or lower limit, or tacitly or expressly agree on a specific limit separating national space from outer space.[7]

D. Meaning of 'Launching of Objects into Outer Space'

This being the case, there remains the question of the meaning of the phrase, 'launching of object into outer space'. First, must the intention be that the object enters some orbit in space, or remains somewhere in space, for instance, on the moon or into deep space? In the former event, must it at least complete, or be intended to complete, an orbit? Or is it sufficient that the object

---

[7] See further B. Cheng, 'The Legal Régime of Airspace and Outer Space: The Boundary Problem—Functionalism *versus* Spatialism: The Major Premises', 5 *AASL* (1980), p. 323 [Ch. 14 above]; 'For Delimiting Outer Space', in McGill University Center for Research of Air and Space Law, *Proceedings of the Symposium on Earth-oriented Space Activities and Their Legal Implications, Montreal, 1981* (1983), pp. 230–74; and 'The Legal Status of Outer Space and Relevant Issues: Delimitation of Outer Space and Definition of Peacefull Use', 11 *JSL* (1983), pp. 89–105; reprinted 9 *Revista del Centro de Investigación y Difusión Aeronáutico-Espacial* (1984), pp. 71–99.

penetrates into outer space, such as, for instance, meteorological sounding rockets that go straight up into outer space with a payload that comes straight down, or intercontinental ballistic missiles that traverse outer space in order to reach their target on earth, or fractional orbital bombs that enter into an earth orbit but do not complete it before re-entering the earth's atmosphere in order to reach their target? The fact that the United States considers ballistic missiles to fall under the 1972 Liability Convention[8] may be cited as evidence for the proposition that any object that reaches or is intended to reach outer space is a space object in the eyes of international space law. From this point of view, it would seem that aerospace craft fall within the definition of space object for as long as they operate as a spacecraft. All this merely shows how necessary it is to have a clear idea where outer space begins.

Now, how about objects that do not reach outer space? We know that, as used for instance in the Liability Convention, 'launching' includes attempted launching. From that point of view, there is no doubt that the ill-fated space-craft Challenger which in 1986 so tragically and dramatically exploded soon after lift-off was a space object, but how about rockets or missiles which are not designed to reach outer space and never reach outer space. The clearest example would be a rocket fired from a life boat to a vessel in distress at sea, but one can also think of the many amateur rockets, including the first ever liquid-fuel rocket, that fired by the pioneer rocketeer Robert H. Goddard on 16 March 1926, which travelled only a few hundred feet.[9] For that matter, the highest point reached by the German V–2 was only about 50 miles (80 kilo-metres) before its trajectory started to bend earthwards.[10] It is submitted that all rockets and missiles which are not designed or intended to reach outer space and which in fact do not penetrate into outer space are not space objects. Consequently, the launch of such objects would not be the launching of a space object, and, therefore, fall outside the present inquiry. In interna-tional law, responsibility and liability for their launch would be a matter of general international law, and not one of international space law.

---

[8] See e.g. Statement of Mr Harry H. Almond, Jr, Office of the General Counsel for the US Department of Defense, before the US Senate Foreign Relations Committee, appended to the Committee's Report on the Convention on International Liability for Damage Caused by Space Objects, Ex. Rept. 92–38, 4 Oct. 1972, p. 7; also letter of 6 Sept. 1972 from David M. Abshire, Assistant Secretary for Congressional Relations, US Department of State, to the Chairman of the Foreign Relations Committee, *ibid.*, p. 8, at p. 9.

[9] G. V. Groves, *Space Travel* (1959), pp. 56–60.

[10] Groves, op. cit. in n. 9 above, p. 9. The highest point reached by those captured V–2's fired after the war into the highest regions of the earth's atmosphere by the Americans was 133 miles (213 km), ibid., p. 75.

III. Responsibility and Liability Distinguished

A. Responsibility

The term 'responsibility', derived from the Latin *respondere* (to answer), means primarily answerability or accountability. At the most basic level, in the present context, it can mean simply authorship of an act or omission. Thus in paragraph 6 of the UN Security Council Resolution 487 (1981) of 19 June 1981 condemning the Israeli raid on the Iraqi nuclear research centre at Tammuz, the Security Council expressed the view that 'Iraq is entitled to appropriate redress for the destruction it has suffered, responsibility for which has been acknowledged by Israel'.[11] Here responsibility means no more than that of authorship, a factual situation, since Israel had strongly maintained that its action was lawful and denied any liability. But, on the premise that human beings are masters of their own will and hence of their own actions, responsibility is a notion commonly associated with all systems of norms of human behaviour, moral, religious or legal, in the sense that people are answerable for the conformity of their own actions with the applicable norm or norms. Thus it has been held that Article 231 of the Versailles Treaty in naming Germany and her allies responsible 'for all the loss and damage to which the Allied and Associated Governments and their nationals have been subjected as a consequence of the war', it did no more than affirm the *moral responsibility* of Germany and her allies. In other words, judged by *moral* norms, they were the causes of all the loss and damage suffered by the Allies and associated powers and their nationals during the First World War, and they were *only morally* answerable for such loss and damage.[12] In law, responsibility would mean therefore that, judged by legal norms, one is considered to be the author of a given act or omission, and to be the cause of all what, in law, are regarded as the consequences of that act or omission. One is consequently answerable for such action or omission being in conformity with the law, and also answerable for its consequences.

B. Liability

In the case of a breach of a legal rule causing damage to another, legal responsibility entails a legal obligation incumbent on the author of the breach to make integral reparation to the victim for the damage so caused in order to restore the position to what it probably would have been had the breach not taken place.[13] The author of the breach becomes 'liable' for the

[11] UN Doc. S/RES/487 (1981), reproduced in 20 *ILM* (1981), p. 993.
[12] German-United States Mixed Claims Commission (1922): *Administrative Decisions No II* (1923), *Dec. & Op.*, p. 5, at p. 15. See further Cheng, *General Principles of Law*, pp. 164–5.
[13] See PCIJ, *Chorzów Factory Case* (Merits), (1928), A. 17, pp. 29 and 47. Cf. Cheng, op. cit., in n. 12, 1 above, pp. 233–40.

damage.[14] In French, the same word '*responsabilité*', sometimes, though not necessarily, qualified as *responsabilité legale,* is used, thus not differentiating in terminology, albeit in fact and in law, between 'responsibility' and 'liability'. Liability represents merely one aspect of responsibility and a consequence of responsibility in case the person responsible breaches an obligation that is incumbent upon it and, in doing so, causes damage to another.

C. State Responsibility

Insofar as international law is concerned, State responsibility is ordinarily divided into direct State responsibility and the so-called indirect State responsibility.[15] Direct State responsibility refers to responsibility for its own acts. Since States can only act through its servants and agents, these are then acts of its servants and agents performed in their official capacity, which are thus imputable to it as its own acts. Indirect State responsibility is strictly speaking not a case of State responsibility as such. It describes in reality an international legal obligation to protect foreign States and their nationals, as well as their property, within its jurisdiction, particularly territorial jurisdiction, from injurious acts committed by persons who are not servants or agents of the State acting in their official capacity, acting individually or in groups of any number, from mobs to revolutionaries. The duty is not absolute, but consists only in the use of due diligence, in accordance with prevailing international standards, in preventing, suppressing, and repressing such injurious acts. Failure to do so by whether the legislative, executive or judicial branch of the State involves in fact the direct responsibility of the State, since failures by its officials will be imputed to the State as its own acts.

D. Individual, Assumed, and Legally Imposed Responsibility

Thus, States, like individuals, are normally responsible only for their own acts or omissions, and, in law, liable only for damage caused by their own unlawful acts or omissions. However, in addition, in all legal systems responsibility for other people's acts or omissions, as well as liability for damage, however caused, and by whomsoever caused, whether wrongfully or not wrongfully, may be voluntarily assumed or legally imposed.[16] These may be called assumed and imposed responsibilities. They can also apply to responsibilities and liabilities for given situations or results which might occur.

International space law has made use of many of these notions and devices. Under the 1967 Space Treaty and the 1979 Moon Treaty, the contracting States have, irrespective of their obligations under general international law,

---

[14] Cf. 1967 Space Treaty, Art. VII.   [15] See Cheng, op. cit. in n. 12, 1 above, p. 201.
[16] See further Cheng, op. cit., in n. 12, 1 above, Part III: The Concept of Responsibility.

assumed special obligations regarding their responsibility for the launching of space objects, and their liability for damage caused by space objects.

IV. Responsibility for Space Activities

A. General International Law

As mentioned above, States are directly responsible merely for their own acts. They are thus responsible for their own space activities, wherever they may be conducted. Insofar as acts of those who are not their servants or agents are concerned, States have merely a duty to use due diligence to protect other States and their nationals according to international standards. In fact, this duty of indirect responsibility clearly exists only in areas subject to the effective territorial jurisdiction of the State concerned, particularly a State's own territory where its jurisaction[17] prevails. Whether such responsibility extends to places and persons subject merely to its quasi-territorial or personal jurisdiction, or even effective jurisaction, such as ships, aircraft, or persons, whether natural or legal, outside its territory is, to say the least, in present State practice somewhat uncertain. For example, States have to be coaxed by the 1963 Tokyo Convention[18] to extend their criminal law to aircraft of their registration when flying outside the national territory, and piracy is dealt with directly by international law.

B. Treaty Rules—the 1967 Space Treaty

1. *Article VI.* Following the principle first envisaged in paragraph 5 of the 1963 Declaration of Legal Principles Governing the Activities of States in the Exploration and Use of Outer Space[19], Article VI of the 1967 the Space Treaty, provides:

States Parties to the Treaty shall bear international responsibility for national activities in outer space, including the moon and other celestial bodies, whether such

---

[17] On the division of State jurisdiction in international law into jurisfaction (the normative power of a State in international law to enact laws, make judicial pronouncements and adopt other decisions with legally binding effect) and jurisaction (a State's power in international law to set up machinery to make, implement and enforce, and physically to make, implement and enforce its laws, judicial pronouncements and other legally binding decisions; in other words, actually to exercise the functions of a State), see B. Cheng, 'Crimes on Board Aircraft', 12 *CLP* (1959), p. 177, at pp. 181–6; and 'The Extraterrestrial Application of International Law', 18 *ibid.* (1965), pp. 132–52 [Ch. 5 above].

[18] Convention on Offences and Certain other Acts Committed on Board Aircraft, Tokyo, 1963, ICAO Doc. 8364; 704 UNTS 219. See Cheng, loc. cit. (1959) in n. 17 above; Royal Aeronautical Society, *Report on Crimes and Offences on Board Aircraft for Submission to the Minister of Aviation* (Mimeographed, 1962); Sir Richard Wilberforce (as he then was), 'Crime in Aircraft', 67 *Journal of the Royal Aeronautical Society* (1963), p. 175.

[19] UN GA Res. 1962 (XVIII), 13 Dec. 1963 [App. II.3 below].

activities are carried on by governmental agencies or by non-governmental entities, and for assuring that national activities are carried out in conformity with the provisions set forth in the present Treaty. The activities of non-governmental entities in outer space, including the moon and other celestial bodies, shall require authorization and continuing supervision by the appropriate State Party to the Treaty. When activities are carried on in outer space, including the moon and other celestial bodies, by an international organization, responsibility for compliance with this Treaty shall be borne both by the international organization and by the States Parties to the Treaty participating in such organization.

A similar provision is to be found in Article 14 of the 1979 the Moon Treaty.

2. *Assumption of Direct Responsibility for Non-governmental Space Activities.* Such a provision is highly innovatory in international law. Under the first sentence of Article VI, States parties to the treaty would seem to have thereby assumed direct responsibility for acts which in law would otherwise not be imputable to them, i.e., space activities of non-governmental entities. Here, it would appear that the description 'non-governmental' refers only to the government of the State, but does not necessarily exclude activities by foreign governments, especially foreign governments acting *jure gestionis*, provided that the activities in question can be classified as the former State's 'national activities'. Such non-governmental activities are to be treated as if they were activities of the respective States themselves, which, as a result, accept the legal consequences of such an assumption of responsibility. On this basis, it seems that the second sentence and the second part of the first sentence of Article VI do not exhaust the scope of this responsibility as stated in the first part of the first sentence, and that the Treaty has merely singled out certain specific duties among all the consequences flowing from the contracting States' responsibility for express mention and emphasis. In other words, it does not appear possible to limit this responsibility merely to requiring authorization, instituting supervision and assuring conformity with the provisions of the 1967 Treaty.

In fact, it is probably possible to have a narrow and a wide interpretation of the first sentence of Article VI of the Space Treaty where States assume direct responsibility for national activities in outer space carried on by non-governmental entities.

Under the narrow interpretation, as partially implied by the second half of the first sentence, one would equate space activities carried on by non-governmental entities with governmental activities only in respect of the State's obligations under international law, obligations not only under the Space Treaty, but also under general international law. It extends to all acts and omissions by non-governmental entities which, if they had been committed by governmental agencies, would have engaged the international responsibility and liability of the State towards other States, including their nationals.

The wide interpretation would apply this assimilation even to private law responsibilities, liabilities, and obligations of the non-governmental entities, such as, for instance, failure to pay the launching charges, at least in regard to foreign States and their nationals.

Whilst the former interpretation would be normal under general international law in respect of obligations assumed by a State in the sense that it is obliged to ensure their observance by all those effectively under its jurisdiction, the latter interpretation would go beyond the usual position in international law, but it is not an impossible interpretation. However, even had the authors of the Treaty envisaged this possibility in 1967 when non-governmental space activities were regarded still as most exceptional, such an interpretation would need serious reconsideration today.

3. *'National Activities'.*   Inasmuch as space objects are objects that penetrate into outer space, and the penetration or attempted penetration of outer space constitutes consequently an activity in outer space, it follows that the launching and attempted launching of space objects form part of that activity 'in outer space' and fall under the first sentence of Article VI. Contracting States, therefore, bear international responsibility for launchings that qualify as being 'national', whether carried on by themselves or by non-governmental entities.

There are those, including the United Kingdom in its Outer Space Act 1986, who are of the view that the phrase 'national activities' means solely activities of a State and its nationals.[20] Up to a point, they are able to rely on the wording of IX of the Space Treaty, which speaks of 'an activity . . . planned by it or its nationals'. It is submitted that this interpretation cannot be correct because it is at once both too narrow and too broad.

It is too restrictive inasmuch as it excludes activities by foreigners within its territory. The United States Commercial Space Launch Act of 1984, as amended in 1988, for instance, is more prudent in submitting within its ambit not only launch activities, including the operation of a launch site, of United States citizens, but also those of any person, irrespective of nationality, within the United States.[21] It also excludes activities carried on by, or by persons on board, ships, aircraft, and spacecraft under its flag or registration, especially when such craft are outside the territorial jurisdiction of any State and are, therefore, within the sole operative jurisdiction (or more specifically the effective jurisaction) of the flag State. If the territorial State or flag State in such circumstances are not internationally responsible for space activities carried on in their territory or by craft or by persons on board craft in areas not under the territorial jurisdiction of any State, no other State would in fact be

---

[20] See Preamble and s. 2. See also B. Cheng, 'Whose Parking Space Is It Anyway? Mapping Out a Legal Minefield in the Celestial Outlands', *The Times Higher Educational Supplement* (30 May 1986, No. 789), p. 14, cols. 3–5, and p. 15, cols. 1–5.

[21] 49 USCS App., s. 2605.

able to control such activities. The Treaty could hardly have intended such a result.

At the same time, to confine national activities solely to those of a State and its nationals is too broad an interpretation, because nationals can often be under the operative jurisdiction (effective jurisaction) of another State. It would seem most unlikely that States would have wished to assume responsibility over activities which they are not in a position to control.

The most reasonable interpretation would seem, therefore, the one which renders all States Parties internationally responsible for activities in space—including launching—carried on by itself, wherever it may be, and those carried on by whomsoever within their jurisdiction, including their territorial, quasi-territorial, and personal jurisdiction. Thus in addition to activities carried on by a State's nationals wherever they may be, and those by any person within a State's territory, one should include within the notion of 'national activities' also those by, or on board, ships and aircraft of a State's nationality, wherever these ships or aircraft may be and irrespective of the nationality of the persons involved. To these, one may add, in any event as among parties to the 1967 Space Treaty, also activities by, or by personnel of, space objects under a State's registry. Since Article VIII of the Space Treaty speaks of the State of registry 'retaining' its jurisdiction and control over such objects and their personnel, 'while in outer space or on a celestial body', it implies that such jurisdiction exists before such objects and their personnel enter outer space, and is not restricted to the period when they are in it. Consequently, its responsibility covers their activities wherever carried on.

Insofar as nationals and means of transport capable of operating in areas outside the territorial jurisdiction of any State, as well as those on board, are concerned, inasmuch as no one can be held responsible for doing the impossible (*nemo tenetur ad impossibile*),[22] States may be exempt from their responsibility if such persons or means of transport happen to be under the effective jurisdiction of another State and it proves impossible, notwithstanding its efforts in good faith, to bring them within its effective jurisdiction, through extradition or other lawful means. The last proviso is necessary in order to prevent the use of havens or flags of convenience in order to avoid the obligations under the Treaty. There is a possibility of this happening under the present system.

4. *Scope of Responsibility.*   Among possible duties incumbent on the contracting Parties to the Space Treaty responsible for national activities in outer space, the 1967 Treaty specifies that which obliges the Parties to assure 'that national activities are carried out in conformity with the provisions set forth in the . . . Treaty.' It follows that all launch activities of the contracting States, whether carried out by themselves or by non-governmental entities, will have to

---

[22] See Cheng, op. cit. in n. 12, 1 above, pp. 222, 223, and 227.

conform to the Treaty. It may be recalled that relevant provisions in this connection include, but are not limited to, Article II on non-appropriation of outer space, Article III on obligation to comply with 'international law, including the Charter of the United Nations', Article IV about weapons of mass destruction, Article V on assistance to astronauts, Article VIII on return of stray space objects, Article IX on avoidance of 'harmful contamination' and 'adverse changes in the environment of the earth resulting from the introduction of extraterrestrial matter', and Article XII on opening stations on celestial bodies to representatives of other contracting States, subject to reciprocity.

Since Article III of the Treaty obliges States Parties to conduct launch activities 'in accordance with international law', the first sentence of Article VI of the 1967 Space Treaty has consequently the effect of requiring all contracting Parties to the Treaty to ensure that all launchings of space objects for which they are responsible, whether carried on by themselves or by non-governmental entities, will conform, in addition, on account of the international law rule of *pacta sunt servanda*, with all other treaty obligations incumbent on the contracting Parties relating to outer space activities, including the launchings of space objects.

5. *'The appropriate State Party'.* Insofar as the second sentence of Article VI of the Space Treaty is concerned, there is much controversy on the identity of what the Treaty calls the 'appropriate State Party' which has the obligation of subjecting the 'activities of non-governmental entities in outer space' to 'authorization and continuing supervision'. All non-governmental launchings must consequently be authorized and supervised.

There are several views as to which country is the 'appropriate State Party'. First, since the Treaty uses the singular in referring to the appropriate State, it has been argued that there can be only one single appropriate State. A possible and in fact very plausible candidate would be the State of registry, envisaged under Article VIII of the Treaty. The fact that the relevant provision in Article VI follows that concerning the national State being internationally responsibility for such activities as if they were its own suggests that the 'appropriate State Party' is none other than the State Party that bears international responsibility for these activities.

However, since, as has been pointed out before, a number of States may be actually and potentially responsible for a single space activity, the view has also been expressed that there may be several appropriate States. Moreover, as we shall soon see, a number of States Parties may be not only responsible but also liable for damage caused by a given non-governmental activity leads one to think that all these States would wish to exercise control in the form of authorization and supervision of pertinent non-governmental space activities, including launchings; for otherwise they would fail to exercise control over activities for which they may be held responsible and liable. That under the

Treaty more than one State can be responsible and liable for a given space activity in fact finds support in both Article XIII of the 1967 Treaty, and the last sentence of Article VI itself. The former provides:

The provisions of this Treaty shall apply to the activities of States Parties . . . , whether such activities are carried on by a single State Party . . . or jointly with other States, including cases where they are carried on within the framework of international inter-governmental organizations . . .

The latter states:

When activities are carried on in outer space . . . , by an international organization, responsibility for compliance with this Treaty shall be borne both by the international organization and by the States Parties to the Treaty participating in such organization.

The result is that each of the Parties involved can be reckoned as the 'appropriate State Party'. Consequently, there can be a number of 'appropriate States Parties'.

It has to be recognized at the same time, however, that if all non-governmental space activities require to be authorized and supervised by all the States which are concerned with their responsibility and liability for them, matters can become very complicated, especially if the various States were to act independently of one another.

There is no reason why the States Parties may not act jointly in granting the authorization and in exercising the supervision. Or they may even by consent arrange for one of them to do so. In this connection, it may be of interest to find that in the UN General Assembly's Resolution 1962 (XVIII) of 13 December 1963 on Declaration of Legal Principles Governing the Activities of States in the Exploration and Use of Outer Space, the precursor of the Space Treaty, principle 5, which is the equivalent of the Treaty's Article VI, used the expression 'State concerned'. It was only at the last minute in the drafting of the Space Treaty that it was changed to 'the appropriate State'. Clearly, as we have seen, many a State may be concerned with a given launching or space activity, but it is not impossible for them to choose one among them as the appropriate State to exercise the required control of authorization and supervision, just as it is possible, especially in the light of Article II(2) of the 1975 Registration Convention, for two or more States involved in a launching to arrange for one of them to be the State of Registry.

Bearing in mind Article VIII of the Treaty which confers jurisdiction and control on the State of registry, there may be much to be said for the States concerned to entrust the control of authorization and supervision to the State of registry, but there is equally nothing to prevent them from separating the two functions and entrusting the duty of authorization and supervision to a contracting State other than the State of registry. However, the latter arrangement may, in practice, be difficult to operate.

The possibility of entrusting another State in a joint launching or space activity with the task of authorization and supervision, as well as the responsibility of ensuring compliance with international obligations is in fact clearly envisaged in the United Kingdom Outer Space Act 1986 which provides in its section 3(2)(*b*) that a United Kingdom licence is not required,

for activities in respect of which it is certified by Order in Council that arrangements have been made between the United Kingdom and another country to secure compliance with the international obligations of the United Kingdom.[23]

What cannot be entirely excluded is the possibility of a kind of haven or flag of convenience being created, since there appears to be no restriction on what States may arrange. However, what needs to be borne in mind in any such arrangement is that it in no way absolves any of the States Parties involved from either their responsibility under the first sentence of Article VI of the Space Treaty, or their liability for damage under either Article VII of the Space Treaty or under the 1972 Liability Convention. Consequently, all the States involved will need to ensure that both the State of Registry and the State of authorization and control, be they one and the same or two separate States, will discharge their duties in such a way as to obviate any risk of their international responsibility or liability being involved—or at least being involved without adequate recourse or remedy.

Examples of some such arrangements include the agreements between China and the United Kingdom concerning the launching by the China Great Wall Industry Corporation of Asiasat–1, Asiasat–2, Apstar–1 and Apstar–2, in which the Chinese government assumes liability for any damage to third States or their nationals under the 1967 Space Treaty, the 1972 Liability Convention and general international law 'during the launch phase (from ignition of the launch vehicle to the separation of the satellite from the launch vehicle)'.[24]

What is perhaps interesting is the above agreements between China and the United Kingdom is the fact that whereas China agrees to indemnify the United Kingdom in respect of any liability for damage caused during the launch phase of the various satellites, no stipulation is made regarding possible indemnification of China by the United Kingdom in respect of damage which may be caused by those satellites subsequent to the launch phase. As we shall presently see, the satellites having been launched from both Chinese territory, and from a Chinese facility, China is one of the launching States which

---

[23] See also United States' Commercial Space Launch Act, 1984, as amended in 1988, 49 USCS App., s. 2605(a)(3)(A).

[24] Exchange of Notes between the United Kingdom and China concerning Liability for Damage arising during the Launch Phase of the Asiasat Satellite, Peking, 26 Mar. 1990 and 2 Apr. 1990, UKTS No. 7 (1993), Cm. 2138; the same concerning Liability for Damage during the Launch Stage of the Apstar–1, Apstar–2, and Asiasat–2 Satellites, Peking, 28 June 1994, UKTS No. 7 (1995), Cm. 2737.

are, under both Article VII of the Space Treaty and under the Liability Convention, internationally liable for any damage caused by those satellites throughout their entire career. The absence of an indemnification clause in favour of China would appear to be an oversight on the part of China.

V. Liability for Space Activities

A. General International Law

With reference primarily to a State's liability for damage caused to foreign States, including damage to their territory, nationals, and property, by objects which it has launched into outer space or which have been launched by non-governmental entities from its territory, several rules of general international law may be applicable.

First, consideration may be given to the rule quoted with approval by the arbitral tribunal in the *Trail Smelter Arbitration* (1935, 1941):

A State owes at all times a duty to protect other States against injurious acts by individuals from within its jurisdiction.[25]

In the *Corfu Channel Case* (Merits) (1949), the International Court of Justice also spoke of 'every State's obligation not to allow knowingly its territory to be used for acts contrary to the rights of other States'.[26] What applies to the acts of individuals within the territory of a State applies all the more to the acts of the State itself. However, the word 'knowingly' in the *Corfu Channel* decision indicates that State responsibility in such cases remains based on fault.[27]

It is debatable whether there is yet in international law a general rule, as opposed to treaty provisions, imposing no-fault liability on States for damage caused by their ultra-hazardous activities.[28] However, it may be argued that in certain fields, including space activities, the underlying principles of certain widely accepted treaties may have already passed into the realm of general international law.

B. Treaty Rules

1. *The 1967 Space Treaty.* Following essentially the principle first enunciated in paragraph 8 of General Assembly Resolution 1962 (XVIII), Article VII of the Outer Space Treaty provides:

---

[25] 3 *RIAA*, p. 1905, at p. 1963.   [26] *ICJ Rep. 1949*, p. 4, at p. 22.

[27] See Cheng, op. cit. in n. 12, 1 above, p. 231, n. 44.

[28] Cf. C. W. Jenks, 'Liability for Ultra-Hazardous Activities in International Law', 117 Hague *Recueil* (1966-I), pp. 99–200; Karl Zemanek, 'Causes and Forms of International Liability', in B. Cheng and E. D. Brown (eds.), *Contemporary Problems of International Law: Essays in Honour of Georg Schwarzenberger* (1988), p. 319, II.3: Liability for acts not prohibited by international law, pp. 324–6.

Each State Party to the Treaty that launches or procures the launching of an object into outer space, including the moon and other celestial bodies, and each State Party from whose territory or facility an object is launched is internationally liable for damage to another State Party to the Treaty or to its natural or juridical persons by such object or its component parts on the earth, in airspace or in outer space, including the moon and other celestial bodies.

This article, in regard to the launch of any space object and in relation to other contracting parties to the Treaty, creates the possibility of four separate contracting States being simultaneously and, it would appear, jointly and severally liable for any damage which the space object may cause, namely, (i) the State that launches the space object, (ii) the State that procures its launching, (iii) the State from whose territory the object is launched, and (iv) the State from whose facility it is launched. Doubt remains, however, as to the precise interpretation of the phrase 'internationally liable', and in particular whether the article implies fault or no-fault liability. Concern exists also regarding the procedure of enforcing this liability.

2. *The 1968 Astronauts Agreement.*　The 1968 Astronauts Agreement provides in its Article 5(4) that:

a Contracting Party which has reason to believe that a space object or its component parts discovered in territory under its jurisdiction, or recovered in territory under its jurisdiction, or recovered by it elsewhere, is of a hazardous or deleterious nature may so notify the launching authority.

The launching authority is defined in Article 6 as the State or appropriate international intergovernmental organization responsible for launching. In case of notification, the launching authority 'shall immediately take effective steps, under the direction and control of the said Contracting Party, to eliminate possible danger of harm'. The Agreement makes no reference to possible compensation or any other obligation on the part of the launching authority.

3. *The 1972 Liability Convention.*　The treaty that specifically tackles the problem of damage caused by space objects is the 1972 Liability Convention. The Convention first of all makes clear that 'damage' means loss of life, personal injury or other impairment of health; or loss of or damage to property . . .', the phrase 'launching State' refers to the same circle of States that the Space Treaty has in mind, and the term 'space object' includes component parts of a space object as well as its launch vehicle and parts thereof' (Article I). It follows from the definition of the launching State that, in addition to the State which launches or procures the launching of a space object, the State from whose facility or territory a non-governmental space object is launched is automatically liable for any damage which the object may cause to other contracting States or their nationals, irrespective of the principle of national responsibility under Article VI of the Outer Space Treaty. However, in view of

Article VI of the Space Treaty, whenever reference is made to a State, it applies also to ships, aircraft and persons, whether natural or corporate, of its nationality, inasmuch as their space activities would constitute 'national activities'. What is rather unclear here is whether the term territory includes ships and aircraft of a State's nationality. However, if they are used for the launching of space objects, they would probably all fall into the category of facility. In regard to non-governmental launch facilities, what is also not clear is whether the decisive factor is the nationality of the owner or that of the operator. The United States Commercial Space Launch Act seems to regard the nationality of the operator of the launch site as alone relevant.[29]

Under Article V of the Liability Convention, all the States participating in a joint launching will be jointly and severally liable. The position of international intergovernmental organizations conducting space activities is set out in Article XXII.

The Convention is not applicable to damage caused to nationals of the launching State or foreign nationals participating in the operation of the space object (Article VII), but there is no exclusion of damage caused by either nuclear material or military space objects,[30] nor any ceiling to the launching State's liability.

The Convention establishes the launching State's absolute liability[31] for damage caused by its space objects on the surface of the earth or to aircraft in flight (Article II), except to the extent to which such damage has been caused by the gross negligence or an act or omission on the part of the victim or of the claimant State done with intent to cause damage (Article VI(1)). Liability for damage done elsewhere rests on fault (Article III).

Article IX of the Convention prescribes that the presentation of claims under the Convention by contracting States against one another shall be through diplomatic channels (Article IX) whether the claims be on their own behalf, or on behalf of their nationals (Article VIII). In an interesting innovation, the Convention permits a State, if the State of nationality has not presented a claim, to present a claim to a launching State in respect of damage sustained in its territory by any natural or juridical person, and in default of such a claim, a third State may present claims in respect of damage sustained by its permanent residents (Article VIII).

The most notable achievements of the Convention consists in establishing a system of compulsory third-party settlement of disputes (Articles X to XIX). This system, albeit its decisions are not binding unless the parties have so agreed, is able, even when faced with a total lack of co-operation from one of

---

[29] 49 USCS App., s. 2605(1) and (2).   [30] See n. 8 above.

[31] On the notion of absolute liability and related concepts, see B. Cheng, 'A Reply to Charges of Having Inter Alia Misused the Term Absolute Liability in Relation to the 1966 Montreal Inter-Carrier Agreement in my Plea for an Integrated System of Aviation Liability', 6 *AASL* (1981), pp. 3–13.

the parties, to lead, within a prescribed time scale, to a final and recommendatory award, based on international law, on both the merits of the claim and the amount of compensation, if any, payable. The parties are under a duty to consider such an award in good faith.[32]

VI. Summary

Clarification of Terms

1. First, it is necessary to clarify the meaning of various terms, particularly: international responsibility, international liability, and launch activities.
2. 'Launch activities' means basically the launching of space objects, including attempted launching.
3. 'Space object' means object, including components, launch vehicles, and parts thereof, which humans launch, attempt to launch, or have launched into space, including the moon and other celestial bodies.
4. As to where outer space begins, there are three schools of thought: first, the spatialists who believe in the need in law to have a boundary separating national airspace from outer space; secondly, the functionalists who disagree and believe that space activities can be regulated without such a boundary; and thirdly, the 'you-don't-need-to-know' school who do not wish to see the question raised and still less discussed.
5. In practice, since no State has ever claimed that any of the satellites that have orbited the earth has infringed its national airspace, it is possible to say that in international law outer space begins at least from the height above the earth of the lowest perigee of any existing or past artificial satellite that has orbited the earth without encountering any valid protest.
6. 'Launching of object into space' means consequently the launching or attempted launching of an object designed and intended to penetrate into outer space—i.e., above the height as defined above, whether or not in any orbit, and for whatever length of time. Any such object is a 'space object'.
7. Objects which are not designed or intended to enter outer space and which in fact do not penetrate into outer space are not space objects for the purpose of international space law.

Responsibility and Liability Distinguished

A. *Responsibility*
8. At its most basic level, responsibility can mean simply a factual relation of authorship. As human beings are deemed to be masters of their own will and actions, responsibility implies a person's answerability for his or her own acts

---

[32] See further Cheng, loc. cit. in n. 1 above.

according to relevant normative systems of behaviour, be they social, moral, religious, legal, or otherwise.
9. In law, responsibility (*responsabilité* in French) implies answerability for one's conduct being in conformity with applicable legal norms.

B. *Liability*
10. In law, breaches of applicable legal norms causing damage to another create liability, which consists in an obligation to make integral reparation to the other person for the damage caused. In French, no special term is used to describe this aspect of responsibility, and the same term *responsabilité* is used, sometimes qualified, though not necessarily, as *responsabilité legale*.

C. *State responsibility*
11. State responsibility is sometimes divided into direct State responsibility and indirect State responsibility. The former refers to a State's responsibility for governmental acts, i.e., acts or omissions of any of its servants or agents acting in their capacity as government officials. Such acts are imputed to the State as the State's own acts, since States can act only through their servants and agents. The so-called indirect State responsibility is in reality an obligation incumbent on a State to exercise due diligence to protect primarily foreign States, their nationals, and their property against injurious acts committed within that State's jurisdiction, particularly territorial jurisdiction. Its responsibility is engaged only if its servants and agents fail to discharge this duty of the State, and is in fact a case of a State's direct responsibility for the failures of its servants and agents which are imputable to the State as the State's own acts.

D. *Individual, assumed and legally imposed responsibility and liability*
12. States, like individuals, are normally responsible and liable only for their own acts and omissions, including those of their servants and agents which are imputable to them. However, in all legal systems, persons may either voluntarily assume additional responsibilities and liabilities, or have responsibilities and liabilities imposed on them by law.

Responsibility for Space Activities

A. *General international law*
13. Under general international law, a State would be directly responsible for its own space activities wherever they may be conducted.
14. Under general international law, States would incur only indirect State responsibility for space activities carried on by non-governmental entities, and this probably only for activities in areas subject to their territorial jurisdiction.
15. It is debatable whether States owe the same duty to protect foreign States

and their nationals in respect of non-governmental acts committed by or from ships, aircraft, and spacecraft bearing their flag, or by their nationals, when such craft and nationals are outside of the territorial jurisdiction.

B. *Treaty Rules—The 1967 Space Treaty*

1. *Article VI*
16. The most important treaty provision regarding international responsibility for space activities is Article VI of the 1967 Space Treaty. A similar provision exists in the 1979 Moon Treaty.

2. *Assumption of direct State responsibility for non-governmental space activities*
17. Under Article VI of the Space Treaty, the contracting States, in addition to their responsibility for their own space activities, have assumed direct State responsibility for national activities in outer space carried on by non-governmental entities. Here it would appear that the description 'non-governmental' simply means the government of the State, but does not necessarily exclude activities by foreign governments, especially foreign governments acting *jure gestionis*, provided that the activities in question can be classified as the former State's 'national activities'.
18. It is possible to have a narrow and a wide interpretation of Article VI. Under the narrow interpretation, as partially implied by the second half of the first sentence, the State assumes responsibility merely for ensuring that such activities conform with rules of international law relating to such activities as if they were its own activities. Under the wide interpretation, the State would be internationally responsible even for the private law obligations of the non-governmental entities carrying on space activities as if they were its own activities, such as for instance failure to pay the launching charges.

3. *'National activities'*
19. There is much divergence in opinion as to what constitutes 'national activities'. Based on the principle that whatever activity that is subject to its effective jurisdiction and therefore not under the control of any other State, or, in the absence of effective control by another State, reasonably capable of being brought back under its effective jurisdiction, it is submitted that the following constitute 'national activities' within the meaning of Article VI of the Space Treaty:

a. A State's own activities, wherever conducted;
b. Activities, by whomsoever conducted, within its effective jurisaction, whether territorial, quasi-territorial, or personal. This means in effect, activities (i) by whomsoever conducted within a State's territory, (ii) by or

by persons on board ships, aircraft, or spacecraft of its nationality or registration, when they are outside the territorial jurisdiction of any State, and (iii) those of its nationals, physical or corporate, when outside the territorial or quasi-territorial jurisdiction of any other State;

c. Activities by or on board craft of its nationality or registration, or by its nationals, wherever they may be, if it is reasonably practicable for it to bring them back to within its effective jurisdiction.

4. *Scope of responsibility*

20. Among the responsibilities of the contracting States, Article VI of the Space Treaty specifies the duty to ensure that all 'national activities in outer space' including all launchings of space objects, will conform with the 1967 Space Treaty (which contains a number of specific obligations), the United Nations Charter, and international law. Since international law contains the principle of *pacta sunt servanda*, this means that the State must also ensure that national activities, even by non-governmental entities, will comply with all its relevant treaty obligations.

5. '*The appropriate State Party*'

21. Article VI of the Space Treaty specifies that non-governmental space activities, which would include all launchings of space objects, require to be authorized and supervised by 'the appropriate State Party'.

22. There is much discussion as to which country is the 'appropriate State Party'. The fact that the Treaty uses the singular in referring to the appropriate State has given rise to the view that there can be only one single appropriate State. However, when two or more States Parties are involved in a launching, each incurs the same obligation to subject the activity to authorization and supervision, with the result that there can be several appropriate States Parties. Besides, since probably all the States involved are internationally responsible and liable for the said activity, each will have an interest in making sure that the activity is properly controlled and supervised.

23. However, nothing in the Treaty appears to prevent States, if more than one are involved in a space activity, to make arrangements for the designation of one of them to act on their joint behalf in subjecting that activity to authorization and continuing supervision. What cannot be entirely excluded is the possibility of a kind of haven or flags of convenience being created. However, it has to be remembered that such arrangements would not absolve any of the States concerned from the responsibility and liability incumbent on them under the Treaty. For this reason, it is important for all the parties involved to ensure that the designated State carries out the control effectively, and that there is a well thought out system of allocation of responsibility, and of mutual waivers and indemnification.

Liability for Space Activities

A. *General international law*
24. On the basis of authorities such as the *Trail Smelter Arbitration* and the *Corfu Channel Case*, it appears that States' liability for damage caused by their space objects and those launched from its territory by non-governmental entities may still be based on fault, although it is arguable that the treaty rules which have since been developed in this field have already been received into general international law.

B. *Treaty Rules*

1. *The 1967 Space Treaty*
25. Under Article VII of the Space Treaty, in launching a space object, four States can be internationally liable for any damage caused. These are the State that launches, the State that procedures the launching, the State from whose territory the object is launched, and the State from whose facility it is launched. However, where more than one State is involved, although it is presumed that their liability will be joint and several, the Treaty is not explicit. Nor is it clear whether this liability is absolute or based on fault. There is no clarification of the meaning of the phrase 'internationally liable', or of the procedure how claims are to be made or, in case of dispute, settled.

2. *The 1968 Astronauts Agreement*
26. Under the 1968 Astronauts Agreement, the launching authority (which is not specifically defined apart from the statement that it is the 'State responsible for launching') has the duty of eliminating possible danger of harm from space objects or their components which have come down elsewhere than intended, if it is notified by the State of landing that it is believed that they are of a hazardous or deleterious nature.

3. *The 1972 Liability Convention*
27. The 1972 Liability Convention has defined the meaning of the terms 'damage', 'launching', 'launching State', and 'space object', and clarified the position of international intergovernmental organizations engaged in space activities. It has confirmed the principle of joint and several liability, when two or more States are involved.
28. The 1972 Convention excludes damage to nationals, and foreigners participating in the operation. Nuclear damage and damage by military space objects are not excluded from the Convention, which moreover places no ceiling on the amount of compensation which may be due.
29. States incur absolute liability for damage caused on the surface of the earth and to aircraft in flight, except where there is gross contributory

negligence or where there is intent to cause damage. Liability for damage caused elsewhere depends on fault.

30. Claims for compensation are presented through diplomatic channels, and may be done by States on behalf of their nationals, or residents if the damage occurred within their territory, or their permanent residents.

31. Perhaps the greatest achievement of the Liability Convention is the incorporation of a system of third-party settlement of claims, in case of dispute, on the basis of international law, within a prescribed time scale by the end of which a final decision has to be reached on the merits of the claim and the amount of compensation, if any, payable, even though the award is only recommendatory, unless the parties agree that it should be binding.

24

International Responsibility and Liability of States for National Activities in Outer Space, Especially by Non-governmental Entities*

I. Introduction

International space law has come a long way since man first succeeded in penetrating into space in 1957. However, much of it has developed piecemeal, and some of the key treaties in this field were drawn up at the beginning of the space age when the pace of development in space technology and the use which might be made of outer space were relatively difficult to gauge, and when it was envisaged that probably for some time to come space activities would be undertaken primarily by State agencies, and that such activities would remain largely in the field of exploration. Furthermore, the very thought of space flight in those early days filled a world still largely dazed with wonderment also with a sense of awe, very much uncertain as to what lay in wait in the outer space into which, for the first time since his existence, man had only just succeeded in penetrating. It is, therefore, no great surprise to find that almost from the start, most States have subscribed to the principle, albeit by treaty, although most probably in the case of almost all of them with the conviction that it is also one of general international law, that States bear international responsibility for national activities in outer space, carried on whether by State agencies or by non-governmental entities, and international liability for damage caused by space objects launched by them or their components. This wholesale assumption of direct State responsibility and international liability for the acts of non-governmental entities is quite unprecedented.[1] Since then, activities in outer space have long entered the era

---

* First published in R. St. J. Macdonald (ed.), *Essays in Honour of Wang Tieya* (1993), pp. 145–63, with some additional material taken from B. Cheng, 'Space Activities, Responsibility and Liability For', in Bernhardt (ed.), 11 *Ency. PIL* (1989), pp. 299–303. The former article reproduced with kind permission from Kluwer Law International, and the latter with kind permission from Elsevier Science Publishers B.V.

[1] On 'assumed' responsibility, see Cheng, *General Principles of Law*, pp. 165–8, and 'direct' State responsibility, see ibid., p. 201.

of exploitation and commercial use, including in particular commercial exploitation by non-governmental entities. The implications of this situation on the principle of direct international responsibility and liability for national activities in outer space appear to be still little appreciated. The legal position in any event is somewhat obscure, especially since not all the relevant multilateral treaties on outer space are necessarily consistent on the subject. It merits careful examination.

II. Jurisdiction

A. Relevance of State Jurisdiction

In any discussion of the problems of international responsibility and liability relating to national activities in outer space, especially by non-governmental entities, the most important task is to identify the country or countries that exercise jurisdiction over the space object or station and those involved. This is because the system or systems of law and State authority normally and directly applicable to the space object and to those involved would be those of the State or States to the jurisdiction or jurisdictions of which the space object and those involved are subject under international law.

B. Types of State Jurisdiction

State jurisdiction[2] in international law is divisible into three types and each type is divisible into two elements. The three types of State jurisdiction are:

(i)   Territorial jurisdiction, which is the jurisdiction enjoyed by a State over its own territory, and all persons and things within it;
(ii) Quasi-territorial jurisdiction, which is the jurisdiction enjoyed by a State over ships and aircraft of its nationality, and all persons and things on board; and
(iii) Personal jurisdiction, which is the jurisdiction enjoyed by a State over its nationals, whether natural or corporate persons.

C. Elements of State Jurisdiction

Each type of State jurisdiction has two elements: jurisfaction and jurisaction. Jurisfaction represents the normative element of State jurisdiction which entitles a State to make laws or take decisions, including judicial decisions, with legally binding effect within its own territory or world-wide extraterritorially.

---

[2] On the notion of State jurisdiction, see B. Cheng, 'Crimes on Board Aircraft', 12 *CLP* (1959), p. 177; and B. Cheng, 'The Extraterrestrial Application of International Law', 18 *CLP* (1965), p. 132, at pp. 134–48 [Ch. 5 above, ss. II.A and B: Types and Elements of State Jurisdiction].

Jurisaction represents the concrete element of State jurisdiction which enables a State physically to carry out the functions of a State by setting up machinery to make laws and to take decisions, or by actually taking steps to implement and to enforce its laws and decisions.

D. Concurrence and Hierarchy of Jurisdictions

It follows from what has just been said that there can often be a concurrence of jurisdictions even in fairly normal circumstances. Thus a person on board a foreign ship which is anchored in the port of a third State would simultaneously be under the jurisdictions of three separate States: (i) the territorial jurisdiction of the territorial State, (ii) the quasi-territorial jurisdiction of the flag-State of the ship, and (iii) the personal jurisdiction of his national State.

International law removes any problem which might possibly arise from this overlapping of jurisdiction by establishing an order of precedence among the concurrent jurisactions, whilst permitting concurrent jurisfactions to co-exist. Insofar as jurisaction is concerned, international law prescribes that, in the event of concurrence, territorial jurisaction overrides both quasi-territorial and personal jurisactions, whilst quasi-territorial jurisaction overrides personal jurisaction.

However, what is important to remember is that in all such cases, even where the flag State of a ship or aircraft, or the national State of a person may not be able to exercise its jurisaction because of the concurrence of an overriding jurisaction, its jurisfaction remains, and its laws and judicial pronouncements continue to apply, because international law establishes no hierarchy among jurisfactions so that they can happily co-exist side by side.

E. Possible Confusion in Existing Space Law

What has just been said is the position under general international law. However, the various treaties relating to outer space concluded under the auspices of the United Nations, in avoiding the traditional concept of nationality for space objects and space vehicles, have created a certain amount of confusion, especially as these treaties have not been entirely consistent.[3]

F. The 1967 Space Treaty

Thus the 1967 Space Treaty on Principles Governing the Activities of States in the Exploration and Use of Outer Space, including the Moon and Other

---

[3] See further B. Cheng, 'Spacecraft, Satellites and Space Objects', in Bernhardt (ed.), 11 *Ency. PIL* (1989), pp. 309–17 [Ch. 16 above], and 'Definitional Issues in Space Law: "Space Objects", "Astronauts" and Related Expressions', 34 *Space Law Colloquium* (1991), pp. 17–31 [Ch. 18 above].

Table XXIV.1 HIERARCHY OF TYPES AND ELEMENTS OF STATE JURISDICTION

		STATE JURISDICTION					
TYPES		**TERRITORIAL**		**QUASI-TERRITORIAL**		**PERSONAL**	
ELEMENTS		Juris-faction	Juris-action	Juris-faction	Juris-action	Juris-faction	Juris-action
H I E R A R C H Y	**JURIS-FACTION**	On a par with the other two		On a par with the other two		On a par with the other two	
	JURIS-ACTION		1		2		3

Celestial Bodies (the Space Treaty),[4] the key treaty on outer space, eschews all mention of the concept of nationality and, in its Article VIII, attributes jurisdiction and control over objects launched into space and their personnel to the State of registry. Article VIII provides:

A State Party to the Treaty on whose registry an object launched into outer space is carried shall retain jurisdiction and control over such object, and over any personnel thereof, while in outer space or on a celestial body. Ownership of objects launched into outer space, including objects landed or constructed on a celestial body, and of their component parts, is not affected by their presence in outer space or on a celestial body or by their return to the earth. Such objects or component parts found beyond the limits of the State Party to the Treaty on whose registry they are carried shall be returned to that State Party, which shall, upon request, furnish identifying data prior to their return.

This provision is by no means clear in its implications.

(i) Nationality or a specific regime?[5]
Does Article VIII, while avoiding the use of the term, mean nevertheless that space objects have the nationality of the State of registry and have consequently *mutatis mutandis* the same status of ships and aircraft of a State's nationality, over which and over all persons and things on board the flag State

---

[4] See B. Cheng, 'Le Traité de 1967 sur l'espace/The 1967 Space Treaty', 95 *JDI* (1968), pp. 432–645 [Ch. 9 above].

[5] See further B. Cheng, 'Nationality for Spacecraft?', in T. L. Masson-Zwaan and P. M. J. Mendes de Leon (eds.), *Air and Space Law: De Lege Ferenda* (1992), pp. 203–17 [Ch. 17 above].

exercises quasi-territorial jurisdiction? Or has Article VIII established a special regime for space objects, in accordance with which the State of registry 'shall retain jurisdiction and control' not only over any space object registered with it, but also 'over any personnel thereof, while in outer space or on a celestial body', even when such personnel is outside the said space object? The expression 'personnel thereof' was deliberately chosen by the Treaty in lieu of 'personnel thereon'. By studiously avoiding any reference to nationality and using instead the phraseology it has chosen, it would appear that the Space Treaty has indeed intended to create a special regime for space objects applicable among the contracting States, different from the traditional one applicable to ships and aircraft of a State's nationality under general international law.

In that case, among the unresolved problems is that of the status, for instance, of a member of one space station visiting another space station registered in a different State. Will he remain under the jurisdiction of the State of registry of the space object to which he belongs, or will he come under the jurisdiction of the State of registry of the space object which he is visiting? Under the traditional concept of nationality of ships and aircraft, the quasi-territorial jurisaction of the vehicle will override the personal jurisaction of the national State of the astronaut. Under the Space Treaty, the personnel of a space object is seemingly said to remain, while a personnel of that space object, under the jurisaction of its State of registry, even when he is on board a spacecraft registered in another State. Is this so?

(ii) What if spacecraft not registered?
In view of the special regime set up by Article VIII, another question that may well be asked is, what happens if a spacecraft is not registered with any State? The Space Treaty does not provide that all space objects must be registered, and there was no international agreement on registration until eight years later when the Registration Convention was concluded in 1975.[6] The Registration Convention provides for a national registry and a United Nations registry. While the duty of domestic registration appears to be more or less immediate, registration with the United Nations needs to take place only 'as soon as practicable' and, in practice, is often long delayed and even not done at all. Moreover, not every party to the Space Treaty needs to be a party to the Registration Convention. It is true, however, that, under Article VIII of the Space Treaty, jurisdiction and control depend upon domestic and not United Nations registration. The Space Treaty would appear to have left the unregistered space object in limbo.

---

[6] See s. II.H below.

G. The 1968 Astronauts Agreement

The Astronauts Agreement[7] uses neither the concept of nationality nor that of registration. It seems to link space objects and astronauts to the 'launching authority'. As a result, on the one hand, under the Astronauts Agreement, if a space object or one of its component parts, or a crew member of a manned space object were, on its or his return to earth, to come down, in an emergency, in the territory of another contracting State, they would have to be returned to the 'launching authority'. On the other hand, under respectively Articles V[8] and VIII of the Space Treaty, 'astronauts' in distress should be returned to the State of registry of their vehicle, and space objects or their component parts that have gone astray should likewise be returned to their State of registry.

However, if the above-mentioned crew member were being ferried back by a spacecraft launched by a State other than the State of registration of his own space station and does not form part of the personnel of the spacecraft of which he is a mere passenger, the Astronauts Agreement is not applicable, because the Agreement applies only to the 'personnel' of a spacecraft.[9] This is not the case with Article V of the Space Treaty, which merely speaks of 'astronauts'. But, even under the Space Treaty, it may be a moot question whether he should be returned to the State of registry of the spacecraft he is on (Article V) or to the State of registry of the spacecraft of which he is a crew member, forming part of its 'personnel' (Article VII). In other words, should Article V or Article VIII apply? Inasmuch as he would then no longer be 'in outer space or on a celestial body' (Article VIII), the former is probably applicable on the basis that the spacecraft he was on is his 'space vehicle' under Article V of the Treaty, although the alternative solution is also sustainable.

H. Jurisdiction under the 1975 Registration Convention

The Registration Convention[10] has to some extent resolved the discrepancy between the Space Treaty and the Astronauts Agreement by stipulating in its Article II(1) that space objects 'launched into earth orbit or beyond' are to be

---

[7] See B. Cheng, 'The 1968 Austronauts Agreement', 23 *YBWA* (1969), pp. 185–208 [Ch. 10 above].

[8] Art. V(1):

States Parties to the Treaty shall regard astronauts as envoys of mankind in outer space and shall render to them all possible assistance in the event of accident, distress, or emergency landing on the territory of another State Party or on the high seas. When astronauts make such a landing, they shall be safely and promptly returned to the State of registry of their space vehicle.

[9] See Art. 2.

[10] See B. Cheng, 'Outer Space: The Internationl Legal Framework—The International Legal Status of Outer Space, Space Objects and Spacemen', 10 *Thesaurus Acroasium* (1981), p. 41, at pp. 98–102 [Ch. 13 above, s. IV.C: The Registration Convention].

registered by their respective 'launching State'. However, much of the good work is undermined when its Article I defines a 'launching State' as:

(i)   A State which launches or procures the launching of a space object;
(ii) A State from whose territory or facility a space object is launched.

It follows that any space object can easily have four launching States for the purpose of the Registration Convention, namely, the State which *launched* it, the State that *procured its launching*, the State from whose *territory* it was launched, and the State from whose *facility* it was launched. In the light of Article VI of the Space Treaty, it is likely, although not certain, that when the Registration Convention speaks of States, it could mean also the national State of private persons, natural or corporate, because of the principle of international responsibility for national activities in space established by Article VI of the Space Treaty. Thus a State would be one of the launching States, if the launching of a space object was effected or procured by a private person, whether natural or corporate, that bears its nationality.[11] This plethora of 'launching States' renders uncertain which State is under a duty to register a specific space object.

I. Article II(2) of the Registration Convention

The good work achieved by Article II(1) of the Registration Convention in requiring space objects to be registered thus making it possible, at least in principle, to identify the State which exercises jurisdiction and control over it, is perhaps more than undone by the subsequent paragraph. Where there are more than one launching State in any launching operation, a situation which, as has been seen, can easily occur, Article II(2) of the Registration Convention provides:

Where there are two or more launching States in respect of any such space object, they shall jointly determine which one of them shall register the object in accordance with paragraph 1 of this article, bearing in mind the provisions of article VIII of the Treaty on Principles Governing the Activities of States in the Exploration and Use of Outer Space, including the Moon and Other Celestial Bodies, and without prejudice to appropriate agreements concluded or to be concluded among the launching States on jurisdiction and control over the space object and over any personnel thereof.

In the first place, Article II(2) now makes it clear, almost in so many words, that the linkage in Article VIII of the Space Treaty between registration on the one hand and jurisdiction and control on the other is not mandatory. Contracting States need only 'bear it in mind'. Where there is more than one State involved in the launching, registration is without prejudice to the question as to which of the States involved is going to exercise jurisdiction and control over the space object. This is going to be a source of great confusion.

---

[11] See further s. III, X below.

Jurisdiction, as we have seen, implies the power of a State to apply its laws to an entity and to enforce such laws. The system created by Article VIII of the Space Treaty, although it falls short of the concept of nationality, at least makes it relatively easy to identify the country the laws and authority of which are to apply to a given spacecraft, namely, the State of registry. Now under Article II(2) of the Registration Convention, a space object can be registered in State A, but the State exercising authority over it and the laws applicable on board, including criminal law, health regulations, safety regulations, intellectual property, industrial property, and so forth, could be those of State B. Article II(2) of the Registration Convention and the possible disjunction between registration and jurisdiction which it apparently permits, while they afford the advantage of flexibility, produce also some not necessarily foreseen or desirable consequences.

First, Article II(2) cancels out whatever certainty Article II(1) of the Registration Convention, in conjunction with Article VIII of the Space Treaty, may have brought to the question of which State has jurisdiction over a given space object.

Secondly, to make confusion more confounded, the Registration Convention does not require whatever arrangements that may have been made regarding jurisdiction to be recorded in either the national register or the United Nations register.

Thirdly, Article II(2) even seems to suggest that these arrangements can be altered freely by the parties during the life time of the space object. It speaks of 'agreements concluded or *to be* concluded'.

Fourthly, although Article II(2) is technically not applicable to situations where there is only one launching State, there is in fact nothing to prevent such a launching State or its nationals associating itself or themselves with another State or its nationals in the project.[12] In other words, the door is wide open to those intending to engage in space activities to create, if they so wish, if not actual flags of convenience, inasmuch as no nationality and consequently no 'flag' is involved, at least the equivalent of flags of convenience, tax havens, and possibly other havens in space law. Perhaps the only qualification to what has just been said is that in space law this situation cannot be brought about simply by associating foreign nationals with a project, because the co-operation of the various States concerned is required, which have to conclude the necessary agreements regarding registration, jurisdiction and control.

Finally, the view has been expressed by the Legal Counsel of the United Nations that:

---

[12] Cf., for example, S. Kiley, 'Loophole helps Tonga build a Satellite Empire in Space', *Sunday Times* (London), 20 Sept. 1990, s. 1, p. 15, cols. 4–8, reporting that Tongasat in Tonga, which was laying claim to the last sixteen slots in the geostationary orbit over the Pacific, was announcing in a news release that it was 'welcoming investors', presumably from abroad.

Where an international intergovernmental organization launches a space object jointly with one or more States, the provisions of paragraph 2 of Article II are relevant. In other words, the organization and the States may enter into appropriate agreement on jurisdiction and control over the space object and over any personnel thereof, if it is decided that the organization should register the space object.[13]

This further widens the flexibility that has just been mentioned.

It follows that on account of both the actual wording of Article II(2) of the Registration Convention and the way in which it seems to have been interpreted in practice, namely, that the launching States can freely determine which of them is to register a space object and which of them, not necessarily the same State, is to exercise jurisdiction over it, Article VIII of the Space Treaty now serves at best as a presumption. It certainly can no longer be relied upon to indicate for certain which State in fact has jurisdiction over a given space object. Such a system may well have the advantage of flexibility, but it carries with it inevitably the seeds of uncertainty, confusion and possible abuse. Below is an illustration of what can happen under Article II(2) of the Registration Convention.

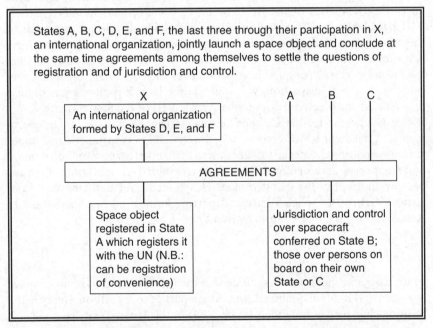

States A, B, C, D, E, and F, the last three through their participation in X, an international organization, jointly launch a space object and conclude at the same time agreements among themselves to settle the questions of registration and of jurisdiction and control.

X — An international organization formed by States D, E, and F

A   B   C

AGREEMENTS

Space object registered in State A which registers it with the UN (N.B.: can be registration of convenience)

Jurisdiction and control over spacecraft conferred on State B; those over persons on board on their own State or C

Figure XXIV.1. REGISTRATION CONVENTION: POSSIBLE EFFECTS OF ARTICLE II(2)

[13] Letter of 19 Sept. 1975 from Mr E. Suy to Mr H. Kaltenecker, Deputy Director in charge of International Affairs of the European Space Agency. I am grateful to Mr G. Lafferranderie, Legal Adviser of ESA, for this information.

In 1988 the United States, Member States of the European Space Agency (ESA), Japan, and Canada signed an Agreement on a Permanently Manned Civil Space Station (Intergovernmental Agreement or IGA). This Agreement provides for the establishment of a space station with several sections, called elements, each registered with one of the partners—ESA in the case of the European States. It affords a clear illustration of the point that, as a result of the kind of flexibility created by Article II(2) of the Registration Convention, it is no longer possible, in any joint launching of a space object, to rely on its registration and Article VIII of the Space Treaty, in order to determine the applicable law and jurisdiction. Article 5(2) of the Agreement states:

Pursuant to Article VIII of the Outer Space Treaty and Article II of the Registration Convention, each Partner shall retain jurisdiction and control over the elements it registers in accordance with paragraph 1 above and over personnel in or on the Space Station *who are its nationals* . . .[14]

Thus, notwithstanding its proclaimed adherence to Article VIII of the Space Treaty by recognizing that each State of registry retains jurisdiction and control over the element that is on its registry, this provision, presumably on the basis of Article II(2) of the Registration Convention, has modified Article VIII by subtracting from such jurisdiction individuals who are nationals of the other partners. Consequently when personnel of any one of the partners 'who are its nationals' are in or on an element registered with another partner, the former partner's personal jurisdiction over such nationals, including presumably personal jurisaction, will override the latter's partner's jurisdiction over its element which it enjoys under Article VIII of the Space Treaty.

The position is further complicated by Article 22(2) of the Intergovernmental Agreement which confers, albeit in special circumstances and under various conditions, a special jurisdiction to the United States over non-United States nationals in or on non-United States registered elements of the manned base or attached to the manned base. This is then a further departure from Article VIII of the Space Treaty, a departure authorized presumably under Article II(2) of the Registration Convention.

J. The 1979 Moon Treaty

In the case of a space object stationed on the moon instead of in outer space as much, and if all the States concerned are parties to the Moon Treaty,[15] the position changes again. Under Article 12(1) of the Moon Treaty,

States Parties shall retain jurisdiction and control over their personnel, vehicles, equipment, facilities, stations and installations on the moon . . .

---

[14] Italics added.
[15] See B. Cheng, 'The Moon Treaty', 33 *CLP* (1980), pp. 213–37 [Ch. 12 above].

The meaning of this provision is far from clear. In addition to the uncertainty as to which State is exercising jurisdiction over which space object, the Moon Treaty appears to have provided other connecting factors, namely ownership or contracts of employment. It speaks of jurisdiction and control of States Parties 'over their personnel', and so forth. It is possible, however, that the Moon Treaty means to say no more than that being on the moon does not alter the jurisdiction position of personnel, installations, stations, and so on, They retained the status they had prior to their arrival or installation on the moon.

However, if a space station on the moon is built from materials, and its staff comprises persons, brought up to the moon by spacecraft subject to the jurisdictions of a number of different States, the application of Article 12(1) can be very problematic. Do such persons remain under the jurisdiction of the State of registry of the space vehicle that ferried them to the moon or do they come under the jurisdiction of the State that exercises jurisdiction and control over the moon station? But which State or States that exercise jurisdiction and control over the moon station—the different States of registry on board whose spacecraft the materials of the space station have been brought to the moon, or any State which may happen to own, operate, or hire the personnel of the station? In such cases, perhaps the flexibility of Article II(2) of the Registration Convention can once more be invoked in order to allow the different States concerned to agree to transfer their jurisdiction to one or more of them. Once again, no provision is made, in such an event, for information on even the existence of any such arrangement to be given. Consequently, in such cases, registration loses much of its significance for the purpose of identifying the State exercising jurisdiction and control over a space object.

All in all, it does appear that the present position of the law relating to jurisdiction over space objects is highly unsatisfactory. It is inconsistent and unclear, leading to uncertainty, confusion, and possibly abuse. Yet, the problem of jurisdiction is pivotal in determining the authorities of which State exercise control over, and which system of law is applicable to, a given space object, a question of special relevance in the case of manned space stations, whether in outer space or on any celestial body. The question is of interest not merely to third States. It is in fact of crucial importance to all those States which may be found to be engaged in 'activities in outer space' or which may come within the definition of 'launching States'. The reason is that, unless they exercise effective jurisdiction and control, or have made adequate and effective arrangements to see that such jurisdiction and control are exercised, over all the activities for which they may be held responsible and for any damage caused for which they may be held liable, they can easily incur such responsibility and liability without even realizing it simply through failure to ensure that such jurisdiction and control are exercised.

III. International Responsibility and the Appropriate State[16]

A. Article VI of the Space Treaty

Article VI of the Space Treaty provides:

States Parties to the Treaty shall bear international responsibility for national activities in outer space, including the moon and other celestial bodies, whether such activities are carried on by governmental agencies or by non-governmental entities, and for assuring that national activities are carried out in conformity with the provisions set forth in the present Treaty. The activities of non-governmental entities in outer space, including the moon and other celestial bodies, shall require authorization and continuing supervision by the appropriate State Party to the Treaty. When activities are carried on in outer space, including the moon and other celestial bodies, by an international organization, responsibility for compliance with this Treaty shall be borne both by the international organization and by the States Parties to the Treaty participating in such organization.

Article II(2) of the Registration Convention reminds States that jointly launch a space object to 'bear in mind' Article VIII of the Space Treaty when deciding which of them is to register the object. In fact what is equally important is for them to bear in mind Article VI; for they will have to rely on the State chosen to ensure that they will not be found in breach of the international responsibility that is incumbent on them under Article VI. A provision very similar to Article VI of the Space Treaty is Article 14 of the Moon Treaty.

B. Extent of Responsibility

What is the extent of a State's responsibility under Article VI? Insofar as a State's own acts are concerned the problem is a straightforward one of direct State responsibility, which a State would incur in any event under general international law. The position of non-governmental activities gives rise, however, to some uncertainties. In regard to non-governmental activities, Article VI seems to have laid down three separate obligations incumbent upon States parties to the Treaty:

(i)   They must through 'the appropriate State Party to the Treaty' subject such national activities to 'authorization and continuing supervision';
(ii)   They must ensure that 'national activities are carried out in conformity with the provisions set forth in the present Treaty'; and
(iii) They 'shall bear international responsibility' for national activities.

The use of the singular by Article VI when referring to the 'appropriate State' seems to suggest that in the case of a joint launching, the States con-

---

[16] See also B. Cheng, 'Space Activities, Responsibility and Liability For', Bernhardt (ed.), 11 *Ency. PIL* (1989), pp. 299–303 [cf. Ch. 23 above].

cerned may by agreement delegate the responsibility of authorization and supervision to one of them.[17] However, especially in the light of the last sentence in Article VI, this would not relieve the other States of their 'international responsibility' and, in the event of damage, consequential liability, which are in effect joint and several. Such responsibility and liability could arise, for example, in case such non-governmental activities were to commit acts which, if committed by a State Party would constitute infringements of the provisions of the Space Treaty. It may be recalled that relevant provisions in this connection include, but are not limited to, Article II on non-appropriation of outer space, Article III on obligation to comply with 'international law, including the Charter of the United Nations', Article IV about weapons of mass destruction, Article V on assistance to astronauts, Article VIII on return of stray space objects, Article IX on avoidance of 'harmful contamination' and 'adverse changes in the environment of the earth resulting from the introduction of extra-terrestrial matter', and Article XII on opening stations on celestial bodies to representatives of other contracting States, subject to reciprocity.

Therefore, in any arrangement between two or more States jointly launching a space object to designate one of them to register the space object and to assume sole responsibility for authorization and continuing supervision, it becomes essential that suitable provisions are made regarding their, in effect, joint and several international responsibility and consequential liability.

Whilst the first two duties undertaken by contracting States in Article VI are fairly straightforward, what is not clear at all in this article is the extent of the overall 'international responsibility' which the contracting States have undertaken in respect of national space activities carried on by non-governmental entities. It is probably possible to have either a wide interpretation or a narrow interpretation.

The narrow interpretation would assimilate space activities carried on by non-governmental entities with governmental activities only in respect of the State's obligations under international law *vis-à-vis* other States, not only under the Space Treaty, but also under general international law. The activities would comprise all acts and omissions by such non-governmental entities which, if they had been committed by governmental agencies, would have engaged the international responsibility and liability of the State towards other States, including their nationals.

The wide interpretation would extend this assimilation and responsibility even to liabilities, both civil and criminal, under municipal law, of such

---

[17] The United Kingdom Outer Space Act 1986 envisages this possibility in its s. 3(2)(b), under which it is provided that a UK licence is not required 'for activities in respect of which it is certified by Order in Council that arrangements have been made between the United Kingdom and another country to secure compliance with the international obligations of the United Kingdom'. See also United States' Commercial Space Launch Act 1984, as amended in 1988, 49 USCS App., s. 2605(a)(3)(A).

non-governmental entities, including thus criminal, contractual and tortious liabilities, at least in regard to foreign States and their nationals.

Whilst the former interpretation would be normal under general international law in respect of obligations assumed by a State in the sense that it is obliged to ensure their observance by all those effectively under its jurisdiction, the latter interpretation would go beyond the usual position in international law, but it is not an impossible interpretation. However, even had the authors of the Treaty envisaged this possibility in 1967 when non-governmental space activities were regarded still as most exceptional, such an interpretation would need serious reconsideration today.

C. *Meaning of 'National Activities'*

The next question is, What is meant by 'national activities'? Article IX of the Space Treaty, in setting out the responsibility of contracting States to avoid potential 'harmful interference with the activities of other States Parties in the peaceful exploration and use of outer space', prescribes, where there is this possibility, a duty of prior 'international consultation' not only in regard to a State's own planned activities, but also those of 'its nationals'. No mention is made of space activities that might be carried on by foreigners from a State's territory, or from ships and aircraft of a State's nationality. Is this all that is meant by 'national activities' in Article VI, namely, activities by a State and its nationals, and theirs alone? The United Kingdom Outer Space Act of 1986 appears to think so, in applying the Act only to United Kingdom nationals, natural or corporate, wherever they may be.[18] However, the United States Commercial Space Launch Act of 1984, as amended in 1988, is more prudent in submitting within its ambit not only launch activities, including the operation of a launch site, of United States citizens, but also those of any person, irrespective of nationality, within the United States.[19]

In fact, to be totally comprehensive, national activities should include all activities by whomsoever carried on within the jurisdiction of a State, including its territorial jurisdiction, quasi-territorial jurisdiction and personal jurisdiction. Thus, in addition to activities carried on by a State's nationals wherever they may be, and those by any person within a State's territory, one should include within the notion of 'national activities' also those by, or on board, ships and aircraft of a State's nationality, wherever these ships or aircraft may be and irrespective of the nationality of the persons involved. To these, one may add, in any event as among parties to the 1967 Space Treaty, also activities by, or by personnel of, space objects under a State's registry.

---

[18] See Preamble and s. 2. See also B. Cheng, 'Whose Parking Space Is It Anyway? Mapping Out a Legal Minefield in the Celestial Outlands', *The Times Higher Educational Supplement* (30 May 1986, No. 789), p. 14, cols. 3–5, and p. 15, cols. 1–5.
[19] 49 USCS App., s. 2605.

Table XXIV.2 THE MEANING OF 'NATIONAL ACTIVITIES' IN ARTICLE VI OF THE 1967 SPACE TREATY

'NATIONAL ACTIVITIES' COMPRISE ACTIVITIES CARRIED ON		
BY WHOM?		**WHERE?**
A. By governmental agencies		Anywhere
B. By non-governmental entities	1. nationals, natural or juridical	Anywhere
	2. ships or aircraft of a State's nationality, or any person on board, or, under Art. VIII of the Space Treaty, by space objects on a State's registry or any personnel thereof	Anywhere
	3. any person, natural or juridical	Within national territory

Since Article VIII of the Space Treaty speaks of the State of registry 'retaining' its jurisdiction and control over such objects and their personnel, 'while in outer space or on a celestial body', it implies that such jurisdiction exists before such objects and their personnel enter outer space, and is not restricted to the period when they are in it. Consequently, its responsibility covers their activities wherever carried on. The position may be summed up as in Table 2.

From this point of view, the reformulation of the second sentence of Article VI of the Space Treaty by the Moon Treaty in its Article 14(1) is an improvement. It says:

. . . States Parties shall ensure that non-governmental entities under their jurisdiction shall engage in activities on the moon only under the authority and continuing supervision of the appropriate State Party . . .

It follows from what has been said above that, although Article VI of the Space Treaty uses the singular when it submits national activities in outer space by non-governmental entities to the 'authorization and continuing supervision by *the appropriate State Party* to the Treaty', there are potentially a number of States which may need to ensure that the requisite regime of authorization and continuing supervision be established in order to permit them to carry out their obligation under Article VI of the Treaty. It also follows that any space object may find itself needing authorization from, and coming under the continuing supervision of, more than one State. In such an event, an obviously desirable course would be for the States in question to come to some arrangement in order to simplify the procedure, at least as among themselves, even though such arrangements would not be effective *vis-à-vis* third States, without their consent.[20] Of course, it will also be incumbent upon the States concerned to ensure that the arrangements made are fully adequate and effective.

However, as we have indicated before,[21] a State may have jurisdiction over an entity, but not necessarily have effective jurisaction, as happens when a person or a ship of its nationality is, by being in a foreign country, not under its effective jurisaction. Thus, while it is quite right that all the States enjoying jurisdiction over the author of an activity should bear responsibility, nevertheless if the regime established is to be effective, it is believed that a State should especially be held responsible not only when the person carrying on the activity is within its effective jurisaction but also when it is within its capability to bring that person within its effective jurisaction either voluntarily or through extradition. To the extent to which a State is internationally responsible, it is also liable for repairing the consequences of any failure to measure up to its responsibility.[22]

IV. Liability for Damage Caused by Space Objects

A. Liability of the Launching State

It is generally accepted that the 1972 Convention on International Liability for Damage Caused by Space Objects (Liability Convention)[23] is an elaboration of the principle of international liability for damage caused by space objects established in Article VII of the Space Treaty.[24] The 1979 Moon Treaty, while recognizing that further arrangements may be necessary in due

[20] See further B. Cheng, 'The Commercial Development of Space: The Need for New Treaties', 19 *JSL* (1991), pp. 17–44, esp. pp. 36–40 [Ch. 26 below, s. X: Who is Responsible for Whom and What Under Aricle VI?].

[21] See s. II.D above.

[22] On the duty to make integral reparation as a consequence of responsibility, see Cheng, *General Principles of Law*, pp. 233–40. See also ibid., chs. 8 and 10 on respectively 'The Principle of Fault' and 'The Principle of Proximate Causality', pp. 218–32 and 241–53, regarding the limits of responsibility.

[23] See B. Cheng, 'Convention on International Liability for Damage Caused by Space Objects', in Jasentuliyana and Lee (eds.), 1 *Manual* (1979), pp. 83–172 [Ch. 11 above].

[24] Space Treaty, Art. VII:

Each State Party to the Treaty that launches or procures the launching of an object into outer space, including the moon and other celestial bodies, and each State Party from whose territory or facility an object is launched is internationally liable for damage to another State Party to the Treaty or to its natural or juridical persons by such object or its component parts on the earth, in airspace or outer space, including the moon and other celestial bodies.

course concerning liability for damage caused on the moon, meanwhile seems content to rely on the 1972 Liability Convention.[25]

Under the 1972 Convention, a launching State incurs absolute liability in respect of damage caused by its space objects 'on the surface of the earth or to aircraft in flight', but only fault liability for damage 'caused elsewhere than on the surface of the earth to a space object of [another] launching State or to persons or property on board such a space object'. Under the Liability Convention 'damage' is defined in Article I as 'loss of life, personal injury or other impairment of health, or loss of or damage to property . . .' The position of damage to astronauts who are not on board a space object, such as astronauts on the moon or in a space walk, is not entirely clear. Nor is it clear whether, like in air law, the operator of an aircraft is liable not only for damage caused by the aircraft to third parties on the surface, but also for damage caused by persons and objects falling from the aircraft. Since the Convention does apply to 'component parts of a space object as well as its launch vehicle and parts thereof' (Article 1(d)), there is no problem where something that escaped from it can be regarded as one of its component parts. The question whether the Convention also applies to things escaping from a space object that is not a component part of it is, however, uncertain. But if the escaped item is, for example, a cargo of dangerous substances, then perhaps the case might be regarded as a violation of Article IX of the Space Treaty on harmful contamination or the consequence of engaging in an ultra hazardous activity involving an obligation to make reparation under general international law. In any event, whether it be absolute liability or fault liability, or liability under the Space Treaty or under general international law, this liability falls on the launching State *vis-à-vis* other States, irrespective of whether the space object belongs to the State itself or to non-governmental entities.

B. Meaning of 'launching State'

Both Article VII of the Space Treaty and the Liability Convention recognize that, in any given launch of a space object, there can be four States that will collectively qualify as the 'launching State'. Thus Article I of the Liability Convention provides:

(c) The term 'launching State' means:
(i)   A State which launches or procures the launching of a space object;
(ii)   A State from whose territory or facility a space object is launched.

Although this article divides the categories of potential States involved into two, on closer examination, it will be seen that there are really four:

(i)   the State that launches;

[25] Art. 14(2).

(ii)   the State that procures the launching;

(iii)   the State from whose territory a space object is launched; and

(iv)   the State from whose facility it is launched.

In view of Article VI of the Space Treaty, whenever reference is made to a State, it applies also to ships, aircraft and persons, whether natural or corporate, of its nationality. What is rather unclear here is whether territory includes ships and aircraft of a State's nationality, which, however, if used for the launching of space objects, would probably fall in any case under the category of facility. In regard to non-governmental launch facilities, what is not clear is whether the decisive factor is the nationality of the owner or the nationality of the operator, were the owner and operator of different nationalities. The United States Commercial Space Launch Act seems to regard the nationality of the operator of the launch site as alone relevant.[26]

Under Article V of the Liability Convention, all the States participating in a joint launching will be jointly and severally liable.

V. Assessment of The International Law Situation and its Consequences

It follows from the above survey of particularly the various multilateral treaties relating to outer space concluded under the auspices of the United Nations that a number of States may be internationally responsible and liable for the activities of a space object. For that reason, particularly in the case of a non-governmental object, it would be necessary for all the governments involved, and not just a single so-called 'appropriate State', to exercise such supervision and control, by providing the requisite regulations, restrictions, obligations, machinery and safeguards, as would ensure as much as possible that (i) they, the States themselves, would be able effectively to fulfil their responsibility and to prevent any liability from arising, and that (ii) should liability be incurred, they would be fully indemnified by the parties concerned.

We have also seen that if there are several States involved in any given space activity, there will be a choice not only as to the State where the space object is to be registered, but also as to the State whose jurisdiction and laws are to apply to the space object in outer space. However, notwithstanding such arrangements, *vis-à-vis* third States, the international responsibility and international liability of the several States will remain.

Under Article VI of the Space Treaty, all the States of which a given space activity may be said to constitute a 'national activity in space' will be internationally responsible for:

(i)   the authorization and continuing supervision of the said activity,

[26]   49 USCS App., s. 2605(1) and (2).

(ii)   ensuring that the space object or any person involved with it, does noth-
        ing which may constitute a breach by any of the States concerned of
        their international obligations under general international law, the
        Charter of the United Nations and the Space Treaty, which *inter alia*
        contains provisions against harmful contamination of the environment,
        and more ambiguously,
(iii)   any act of commission or omission of the space object or by those
        involved as if it were committed by an agency of the States themselves.

In concrete terms, the States which are thus internationally responsible
include all the States that enjoy jurisdiction over some aspect of the launching
of a space object and its operation, whether this jurisdiction be territorial,
quasi-territorial or personal. In practice, it is possible for arrangements to be
made among the States responsible in order to carry out the authorization
and supervision of the project, but the different States remain individually
responsible towards third States.

In addition, under the Space Treaty and the Liability Convention, it would
appear that States are internationally and directly liable for damage caused
not only by their own space objects, but, on account of the principle of international responsibility for national activities in space, also for damage caused
by objects launched into outer space by non-governmental entities. Thus any
State the nationals of which launch or procure the launching of the spacecraft
on board of which a space object is located, the State the nationals of which
operate, and possibly also the State the nationals of which own, the facility
from which a space object is launched, as well as any State from the territory
of which a space object is launched, are all jointly and severally liable internationally to third States for damage caused to them or their nationals by the
space object or any of its components. Whether, under the Liability
Convention, this liability extends to dangerous substances not forming component parts of a space object escaping from a space object is uncertain.
However, liability may arise under Article IX of the Space Treaty on contamination of the environment, and possibly also under general international law
for ultra hazardous activity.

In view of these potential responsibilities and liabilities which various
States may incur in any space activity undertaken by non-governmental entities, it is not surprising that States, in making provision for the licensing and
control of space activities should require the participants to take out adequate
insurance and to impose upon them the duty to indemnify the State against
any claim which might be made against it under international agreements.[27]

Furthermore, in view of the multitude of States which may be responsible
and hence liable in any given case, it would seem essential that the States

[27] E.g., United Kingdom's Outer Space Act 1986, s. 18; US Commercial Space Launch Act,
1984 as amended in 1988, 49 USCS App., s. 2615.

concerned arrive at some arrangement in advance regarding jurisdiction and control, as well as the apportionment of liability should it arise. While such arrangements may not be effective *vis-à-vis* third States, they can be very useful *inter se*. But general international law needs also to be much clearer on the subject in order to have a more certain starting point in dealing with situations of this kind.[28]

VI. Need to Extend Domestic Laws to Space

International law governs relations among States and often regulates the conduct of their subjects in areas of serious international concern. However, the law that immediately regulates the conduct of these subjects is municipal law, i.e., the internal law of States. Space activities have now expanded to such an extent that States must give serious consideration, as some States have already begun to do, to extending their domestic laws to outer space. This is because most systems of municipal law are designed to apply domestically within the territory of the State, and often have no extra-territorial application, with the result that, like in the early days of civil aviation, aircraft flying over the high seas or no man's land were frequently without any system of general criminal law applicable on board.[29] The same is now true of spacecraft. In order to ensure that activities on board space stations are conducted according to the usual standards applicable within a State, the necessary rules and regulations must be extended to activities in outer space. This would cover not only general criminal law, but also specialized regulations such as those pertaining to intellectual and industrial property, health, safety, experiments on animals, product liability, and so forth; for the world, including the non-governmental commercial and industrial world, is no longer only terrestrial, but well and truly cosmic.

---

[28] See further Cheng, loc. cit. in n. 20 above.
[29] See further Cheng, loc. cit. (1959) in n. 2 above.

25

The Commercial Development of Space: the Need for New Treaties*

I. Introduction

Ten years and six days after man first reached outer space, the Treaty on Principles Governing the Activities of States in the Exploration and Use of Outer Space, including the Moon and Other Celestial Bodies (the Space Treaty) entered into force on 10 October 1967.[1] The intention of the United Nations, to which goes the credit of securing agreement on this treaty, was that it should establish a legal framework for man's exploration and use[2] of outer space, a framework to be supplemented by subsequent agreements as man's exploration and use of outer space further develop. So far, four more treaties have been concluded through the United Nations,[3] namely, the 1968 Agreement on the Rescue of Astronauts, the Return of Astronauts and the Return of Objects Launched into Outer Space (the Astronauts Agreement),[4] the 1972 Convention on International Liability for Damage Caused by Space Objects (the Liability Convention),[5] the 1975 Convention on Registration of Objects Launched into Outer Space (the Registration Convention),[6] and the

* Adapted from a keynote address delivered on 17 Aug. 1990 at a seminar on *The Cape York Space Port: The Legal and Business Issues*, organized by the Convenor of the Queensland group of the International Law Association (Australian Branch) Peter Baston, Esq., at Cairns, North Queensland, Australia, in conjunction with the 64th Conference of the ILA in Australia, and first published in 19 *JSL* (1991), pp. 17–44. Reproduced by kind permission of the *Journal of Space Law*.

[1] See B. Cheng, 'Le Traité de 1967 sur l'espace/The 1967 Space Treaty', 95 *JDI* (1968), p. 532 [Ch. 9 above].

[2] The term 'use' is here used in its broad meaning as to include 'exploitation', although theoretically it is possible, as the Moon Treaty has perhaps done, to distinguish between exploration, use and exploitation. See M. Bourély, 'La commercialisation des activités spatiales: aspects juridiques', 37 *Annales de l'Université des sciences sociales de Toulouse* (1989), p. 43, at p. 53.

[3] See further B. Cheng, 'The United Nations and the Development of International Law Relating to Outer Space', 16 *Thesaurus Acroasium* (1990), p. 49 [Ch. 8 above].

[4] See B. Cheng, 'The 1968 Astronauts Agreement', 23 *YBWA* (1969), p. 185 [Ch. 10 above].

[5] See B. Cheng, 'Convention on International Liability for Damage Caused by Space Objects', in Jasentuliyana and Lee (eds.), 1 *Manual* (1979), p. 83 [Ch. 11 above].

[6] See B. Cheng, 'Outer Space: The International Legal Framework—The International Legal Status of Outer Space, Space Objects and Spacemen', 10 *Thesaurus Acroasium* (1981), p. 41, pp. 98–102 [Ch. 13 above, s. IV.C: The Registration Convention]; and B. Cheng, 'Spacecraft, Satellites and Space Objects', in Bernhardt (ed.), 11 *Ency. PIL* (1989), p. 309 [Ch. 16 above, s. V: Registration].

1979 Agreement Governing the Activities of States on the Moon and Other Celestial Bodies (the Moon Treaty).[7] In addition, the United Nations' General Assembly has since the last mentioned treaty adopted *inter alia* two resolutions relating to the use of outer space, to wit, the 1982 resolution 37/92 on Principles Governing the Use by States of Artificial Earth Satellites for International Direct Broadcasting, and the 1986 resolution 41/65 on Remote Sensing[8]. At the same time, there are a number of multilateral and bilateral treaties relating to outer space concluded outside the United Nations, such as the treaties establishing the International Telecommunications Satellite Organization (INTELSAT),[9] the International Maritime Satellite Organization (INMARSAT), and the European Space Agency (ESA), and those between the Soviet Union and the United States on co-operation in space[10]. Participation in some of the multilateral treaties are open to more or less all States and certain international organizations; in others it may be limited to specific groups or parties, such as the 1988 Intergovernmental Agreement (IGA) on the Permanent Manned Civil Space Station among the governments of the United States, member States of ESA, Japan, and Canada.

International society and international law have no centralized legislature with power to promulgate rules binding on States. Contrary to a widely held fallacy, general international law (otherwise known as customary international law) has been applicable to outer space from the very beginning, at least insofar as relations between States are concerned.[11] However, general international law as applied to outer space provides only the basic ground rules, which need to be supplemented with additional and detailed norms as the need arises. In the absence of an international legislature, treaties fulfil the rôle of contract and imperfectly that of legislation in domestic law. As the 1969 Vienna Convention on the Law of Treaties makes it clear in its Articles 34 and 38, treaties are legally binding only on those who have agreed to them, although this does not mean that treaty provisions cannot evolve into rules of general international law when and if so recognized by the generality of States. At the moment, the surest and most effective way of creating legally binding rules applicable in space is through treaties.

Although many human endeavours are undertaken for their own sake, such as the scaling of Everest, man's entry into outer space was not only accompa-

---

[7] See B. Cheng, 'The Moon Treaty', 33 *CLP* (1980), p. 213 [Ch. 12 above].

[8] See B. Cheng, 'Legal and Commercial Aspects of Data Gathering by Remote Sensing', in Chia-Jui Cheng and Pablo Mendes de Leon (eds.), *The Highways of Air and Space Law over Asia* (1992), p. 49 [Ch. 22 above, s. IX: Un Principles on Remote Sensing].

[9] See B. Cheng, 'Communications Satellites', 24 *CLP* (1971), p. 211 [Ch. 21 above].

[10] One of the most recent agreements is the Agreement on Co-operation in the Exploration and Use of Outer Space for Peaceful Purposes, 15 Apr. 1987, 26 *ILM* (1987), p. 622.

[11] See B. Cheng, 'The Extraterrestrial Application of International Law', 18 *CLP* (1965), p. 132 [Ch. 5 above].

nied by unprecedented excitement but also attended by great expectations. As the Preamble to the 1967 Space Treaty says, it opened 'great prospects'.

While outer space's military potential will always remain uppermost in the minds of governments,[12] its commercial prospects surely cannot be far behind. Indeed more than ten years before man's entry into space, Arthur C. Clarke, in his seminal article on *Extraterrestrial Relays*,[13] was already pointing to the possibility of what has now turned out to be one of the biggest industries in outer space. The pace of commercial development in outer space is such that less than twenty years after Clarke's article and at least two years before the text of the Outer Space Treaty was adopted by the United Nations General Assembly[14], an international treaty was signed[15] by no fewer than 45 countries setting up a Global Commercial Communications Satellite System, the International Telecommunications Satellite Consortium, which is the predecessor of the present International Telecommunications Satellite Organization, both known as INTELSAT. INTELSAT in 1990 had well over 100 member States.

The experience of INTELSAT teaches us that the commercial development of outer space is likely in many cases to be an international effort which, moreover, has to be fitted into the international legal framework that is now gradually being built up through either the United Nations or the practice of States, beginning, as we have seen, especially with the 1967 Space Treaty. The purpose of this chapter is to examine what, if any, further treaties may now be required, or even urgently required, in view of present and future commercial developments in outer space.

II. Relevance of International Law for Commercial Space Activities

International law, including international treaties, is of particular significance for commercial activities in space on account of the basic international legal framework established by the 1967 Space Treaty for the exploration and use of outer space. From this point of view, the most relevant provision is its Article VI, which provides:

---

[12] Cf. B. Cheng, 'The Military Use of Outer Space in International Law', in E. G. Bello and Prince Bola A. Ajibola, San (eds.), 1 *Essays in Honour of Judge Taslim Olawale Elias* (1992), p. 63 [Ch. 20 above].

[13] *Wireless World* (1945), p. 305.

[14] Although the treaty was not opened for signature until 27 Jan. 1967, the text was adopted by the General Assembly on 19 Dec. 1966. See further B. Cheng, 'Le Traité de 1967 sur l'espace/The 1967 Space Treaty', 95 *JDI* (1968), p. 532, at pp. 544 ff. [Ch. 9 above, s. III: The Negotiations].

[15] Agreement establishing Interim Arrangement for a Global Commercial Communications Satellite System, Washington, 20 Aug. 1964–20 Feb. 1965. See further B. Cheng, 'Communications Satellites', 24 *CLP* (1971), p. 211 [Ch. 21 above].

States Parties to the Treaty shall bear international responsibility for national activities in outer space, including the moon and other celestial bodies, whether such activities are carried on by governmental agencies or non-governmental entities, and for assuring that national activities are carried out in conformity with the provisions set forth in the present Treaty. The activities of non-governmental entities in outer space, including the moon and other celestial bodies, shall require authorization and continuing supervision by the appropriate State Party to the Treaty. When activities are carried on in outer space, including the moon and other celestial bodies, by an international organization, responsibility for compliance with this Treaty shall be borne both by the international organization and by the States Parties to the Treaty participating in such organization.

Some may claim, probably not without justification, that this article has already passed, through general acceptance, from being a mere treaty provision binding only upon the parties into the realm of general international law binding on all States.[16] In any event, under Article VI, unlike in any other field of commercial activities, all commercial national activities in outer space (which, following the Treaty, will here always be used to include the moon and other celestial bodies, unless otherwise stated), whether carried on, as the Treaty says, by governmental agencies or non-governmental entities, either directly or through international organizations, are, as among the contracting States, insofar as responsibility towards one another, including one another's nationals, is concerned, to be treated as activities of the State, for which the State bears direct State responsibility.[17] This means that contracting States have a critical interest in regulating, as well as, under the Space Treaty, a duty to control and supervise, private national space activities in order to ensure that these activities conform to their obligations under the Treaty, under international law, and under the Charter of the United Nations.[18] It means also that the simplest way of regulating commercial space activities internationally is by means of international law, including treaties. Furthermore, this means that all those involved in commercial space activities need to be directly concerned and fully conversant with all the relevant rules of international space law, including all the pertinent treaties.

[16] On the metamorphosis of treaty provisions into rules of general international law, see Cheng, 'Custom', in R. St. J. Macdonald and D. M. Johnston (eds.), *The Structure and Process of International Law* (1983), p. 513, at pp. 532–33. N.B.: in the book, pp. 545 and 546 have been transposed and are wrongly paginated.

[17] See B. Cheng, 'Space Activities, Responsibility and Liability, For', in Bernhardt (ed.), 11 *Ency. PIL* (1989), p. 299 [cf. Ch. 24 above; see also Ch. 23], and s. III below.

[18] See Art. III of the Space Treaty, which requires all States Parties to carry on space activities 'in accordance with international law, including the Charter of the United Nations'.

III. Where Begins Outer Space?[19]

We talk of space law and of outer space, but where does outer space begin? Ever since the beginning of the space age, this question has been asked. However, for reasons best known to itself, but probably through self-interest as the leading space power, the United States has consistently refused even to have the subject discussed. In its stance, it is assisted by the so-called 'functionalist school' of international space lawyers who believe that all one has to do is to regulate space activities. According to them, one need not, or even should not, try to define where outer space begins, as is advocated by the so-called 'spatialists' who believe that the boundary question between national airspace and outer space should be settled as a matter of priority.

The functionalists' argument is in reality based on false premises; for, insofar as international law is concerned, the initial and most fundamental level of classification is spatial (to avoid the issue and call it 'zonal' is merely to play with words) which precedes, and in fact determines, any functional classification whether an activity is lawful or not lawful. International law first of all divides the world traditionally into three categories of territory, namely, (i) national territory, over which States exercise complete and exclusive sovereignty, (ii) *territorium nullius*, or 'no-man's land', i.e., territory which belongs to no State and which is capable of being appropriated by States under the rules of international law, and (iii) *territorium extra commercium*, or 'territory outside commerce', i.e., territory which belongs to no State and is, under international law, not subject to appropriation by States or their nationals, though its resources are. The high seas are the prime example of *territorium extra commercium*. Article II of the Space Treaty has now added outer space, including the moon and other celestial bodies, to this category. Lately, a fourth category has been created by treaty, namely, (iv) territory that constitutes a 'common heritage of mankind' where neither the area itself nor its resources may be individually appropriated by States or their nationals for their own benefit. The Moon Treaty was the first multilateral treaty to give recognition to this new category by declaring the moon and other celestial bodies within the solar system other than the earth the common heritage of mankind[20].

The legality of an act under international law depends in many instances not upon the nature of the act itself but upon where it takes place. This is because, whereas, on the one hand, within the territory of a State the legal presumption is that a State is entitled to regulate everything that goes on within it and the legality of an act depends ultimately upon the law of that State, on the other hand in all the other categories of territory the presumption is

[19] See further B. Cheng, 'The Legal Régime of Airspace and Outer Space: The Boundary Problem', 5 *AASL* (1980), p. 323 [Ch. 14 above].
[20] The Moon Treaty, Art. 11(1). See further B. Cheng, 'The Moon Treaty', 33 *CLP* (1980), p. 213 [Ch. 12 above].

against any State having such a right except over its own nationals, and ships, aircraft and spacecraft of its own registry. The presumption is in fact in favour of freedom of activity by all States and their nationals, unless there is a rule of international law against it. Take for instance military reconnaissance conducted by aircraft of State A of military installations in State B. The question is not whether military reconnaissance is functionally a permitted activity under international law. The answer depends on where it takes place. On the one hand, from State A, from above no-man's land, from above the high seas and from what may be a common heritage of mankind, it would all be lawful. It becomes unlawful, on the other hand, only if conducted without authorization inside the territory of State B.[21] The position of space activities is not greatly dissimilar.

What the functionalists are advocating is in effect to brush aside the rule and existence of sovereignty over national airspace in favour of space activities.[22] For non-space powers to embrace it is to renounce part of their territorial sovereignty in favour of other States' space activities. However, even for space powers, the acceptance of such a doctrine can be an act of highly short-sighted complacency; for in claiming that their space objects have a right to operate freely in foreign airspace, they would also be renouncing a part of their sovereignty over their own airspace. Reciprocity is the cornerstone of international law. The tables can easily be turned one day, and the space activities of other States in one's own airspace may prove highly intrusive. When that happens, States that now embrace functionalism or an arrogant policy of you-don't-need-to-know may well rue their erstwhile craftiness and complacency.

That space powers would like to have a more or less free hand in the airspace of other States for their space activities is, however, not confined only to those who embrace functionalism. The Soviet Union which, after some initial vacillation, converted to spatialism, in its working paper submitted to the United Nations Committee on the Peaceful Uses of Outer Space (COPUOS) in 1987,[23] while proposing the definition by treaty of a boundary between airspace and outer space not exceeding 100 (110) kilometres above sea level, added:

Space objects of States shall retain the right to fly over the territory of other States at altitudes lower than 100 (110) kilometres above sea level for the purpose of reaching orbit or returning to earth in the territory of the launching State.[24]

---

[21] See B. Cheng, 'The United Nations and Outer Space', 14 *CLP* (1961), p. 247, at pp. 262–72 [Ch. 6 above, s. V. Reconnaissance and Surveillance Satellites].

[22] See further B. Cheng, 'The Legal Régime of Airspace and Outer Space: The Boundary Problem', 5 *AASL* (1980), p. 323, at pp. 341–6 [Ch. 14 above, s. VIII: The Policy Behind, and Function of, International Law's Spatialism].

[23] A/C.105/C.2/L.121 (reissued version of 28.3.79).

[24] See further B. Cheng, 'The Legal Régime of Airspace and Outer Space: The Boundary Problem', 5 *AASL* (1980), p. 323, at pp. 356 ff. [Ch. 14 above, s. XI: The 1979 Soviet Working Paper].

The Soviet Union is correct in seeing the logical and legal necessity that there must be a clear and definite, albeit not necessarily definitive and inalterable, boundary between airspace and outer space defined by treaty. It is, however, not quite straightforward when it tries to suggest that there exists already a legal right of passage for space objects ('shall retain the right'), under general international law, through the airspace of other States 'for the purpose of reaching orbit or returning to earth'. There is no evidence that such a right exists. Indeed, what guarantee is there that, if a South Korean space object on its return to earth tomorrow were to fly through Soviet airspace, by a coincidence, successively over both the Kamchatka Peninsula and the Sakhalin Island along more or less the same route as that of Korean Airline's ill-fated flight KE007 on the fateful night of 31 August–1 September 1983, it would be accorded safe passage?[25]

IV. Need to Delimit Airspace

In any event, all these merely go to show that, if commercial space flights were to develop, it is essential that the question of boundary between airspace and outer space should be clearly defined by a treaty, as well as the position of space objects which, either by design or by accident, find themselves in or in transit through foreign airspace. From this point of view, the Soviet proposal of 100 or alternatively 110 kilometres is probably very close to the existing position under general international law in accordance with current State practice which regards all satellites so far in orbit to be in outer space.[26]

However, just as in the case of the territorial sea, the maximum breadth of which is now accepted in the 1982 United Nations Convention on the Law of the Sea as twelve nautical miles[27] instead of the customary three, there is nothing in law to prevent the generality of States from agreeing now to either a higher or a lower limit than 100 (110) kilometres, or, having agreed to one now, from subsequently agreeing to raise or to lower it.

The main thing for those contemplating entry into the commercial development of space is the need for some assurance of at least a modicum of certainty in the law. The danger for them of the major space powers wishing to keep all the options open by refusing to make clear where their territorial

---

[25] See B. Cheng, 'The Destruction of KAL Flight KE007, and Article 3*bis* of the Chicago Convention', in J. W. E. Storm van 's Gravesande and A. van der Veen Vonk (eds.), *Air Worthy: Liber Amicorum Honouring Professor Dr. I. H. Ph. Diederiks-Verschoor* (1985), p. 49.

[26] See further B. Cheng, 'The Legal Régime of Airspace and Outer Space: The Boundary Problem', 5 *AASL* (1980), p. 323, at pp. 350–6 [Ch. 14 above, s. X: The Limit between Outer Space and Territorial Space].

[27] Art. 3. At the time of writing in 1991, the 1982 Convention (Law of the Sea Convention) was not yet in force, but many of its provisions had already been by then recognized as stating rules of current general international law. The Convention has since entered into force on 16 Nov. 1994.

airspace, over which they have in law absolute control, ends, and where outer space, over which legally they have absolutely no such right, begins, lies in such powers abruptly deciding on an alternative option. One may suddenly find one day that one's spacecraft is impounded or even destroyed for allegedly trespassing in some State's national airspace. Many a complete enterprise can be ruined simply because a major power has changed its mind about the height of its national airspace. This has happened before with maritime frontiers. Certainty is essential.

V. Need to Regularize Status of Space Objects in Foreign Airspace

Once a boundary has been fixed, assuming the height is such that space objects on their way to, and their return from, outer space may occasionally fly through other States' airspace, then from the standpoint of space flights, it would obviously be desirable if the position of space objects in foreign airspace were at the same time clearly defined. By analogy with air law and the law of the sea, various options exist. The starting point is that States exercise complete and exclusive sovereignty over the airspace above their territory[28] with the result that no foreign space objects may fly through it without the permission of the subjacent State. However, in air law, after distinguishing between civil and State aircraft,[29] States have been fairly liberal in granting transit rights to foreign civil aircraft.[30] The grant is made in either bilateral or multilateral treaties, without treating it as a matter of right under general international law. In the law of the sea, foreign merchant ships have traditionally enjoyed a legal right of innocent passage through a State's territorial seas, a right which has now been extended to all foreign government ships, apparently including foreign warships, if not already by the 1958 Geneva Convention on the Territorial Sea,[31] then definitely by the 1982 United

[28] See Chicago Convention on International Civil Aviation (Chicago Convention), 1944, Art. 1. There is sometimes a notion that this article states a rule exclusively for the purpose of aviation or air law: see H. L. van Traa-Engelman, *Commercial Utilization of Outer Space—Legal Aspects* (1989), p. 38. Both the history and the wording of the article make it clear that the contracting States are merely stating a rule of general international law. See B. Cheng, 'From Air Law to Space Law', 13 *CLP* (1960), p. 228, at pp. 228–42 [Ch. 3 above, s. II: Airspace Sovereignty]; and further Cheng, *The Law of International Air Transport*, p. 120.
[29] See 1944 Chicago Convention, Art. 3, and B. Cheng, 'International Law and High Altitude Flights: Balloons, Rockets and Man-Made Satellites', 6 *ICLQ* (1957), p. 487, at pp. 495–501 [Ch. 2 above, ss. VI.A and B: State and Civil Flight Craft].
[30] Cf. B. Cheng, 'From Air Law to Space Law', 13 *CLP* (1960), p. 228, at pp. 238–42 [Ch. 3 above, s. II.C: Privileges Exchanged].
[31] See s. III of the Convention. The express extension of the application of s. III.A, which contains Art. 14 on innocent passage, to government ships in s. III.C is not found in s. III.D on warships, thus giving rise to a possible argument *a contrario* that Art. 14 is not applicable to warships, although the position is unclear.

Nations Convention on the Law of the Sea.[32] This right of innocent passage does not, however, apply to aircraft, civil or military. But as a result of a great deal of horse-trading, the 1982 Convention, even before its entry into force, seems already to have introduced into general international law a new rule, that of a right of transit passage through straits used for international navigation,[33] and a right of archipelagic sea lanes passage,[34] for 'all ships and aircraft', whether civil or military, subject to only minimal control by the coastal State or States.

The 1979 Soviet proposal, in its third paragraph, appears to be fishing for the recognition by treaty of a right under general international law similar to the rather unfettered 'right of transit passage' for space objects to transit foreign airspace, which will, therefore, need no further consent from the territorial State. It is questionable whether the generality of States will be agreeable to such a solution. What may be achievable is a multilateral agreement similar in nature, though not necessarily in detail, to the International Air Services Transit Agreement or Article 5 of the Chicago Convention on International Civil Aviation, both of 1944, in air law.[35] In such a treaty, States can grant one another the right of (innocent) passage for their (civil) space objects and those of their nationals on their way to outer space (or only when to 'earth orbit and beyond' as Article II of the Registration Convention says), and on their return to earth. The exercise of this right can be subjected to specific limitations and conditions, such as compliance with international law and regulations, and being civil space objects engaged in activities exclusively for peaceful (i.e., non-military) purposes.[36] Such a right would be particularly useful in the case of aerospace craft, or in certain circumstances even the shuttle, but it can also be of benefit to other types of spacecraft. In the absence of a multilateral treaty, such a right would have to be secured bilaterally.

VI. Urgent Need to Clarify a Number of other Terms and Concepts

What has just been said raises at least two concepts which, from the standpoint of commercial development, are among those that are in urgent need of clarification. One is the meaning of peaceful purposes, the other that of space object. Others include a number of points arising from Article VI of the Space

---

[32] Cf. s. 3 with s. III of the 1958 Geneva Territorial Sea Convention as referred to in the previous n. No similar *a contrario* argument can now be made. Under s. 3.C, warships and government ships appear together to benefit directly from Art. 17 on the right of innocent passage.

[33] Part III, s. 2, Arts. 37–44.   [34] Arts. 53–4.

[35] See B. Cheng, 'From Air Law to Space Law', 13 *CLP* (1960), p. 228, at pp. 238–42 [Ch. 3 above, s. II.C: Privileges Exchanged]; and Cheng, *The Law of International Air Transport* pp. 193 ff., and 291 ff.

[36] Cf. B. Cheng, 'From Air Law to Space Law', 13 *CLP* (1960), p. 228, at pp. 244–9 [Ch. 3 above, s. IV: Conditions to be fulfilled by Flightcraft, their Crews and Passengers].

Treaty, especially when read in conjunction with related instruments, such as the Liability Convention and the Registration Convention. F. K. Nielsen, the American Commissioner on the Mexican-United States General Claims Commission (1923) once said:

An inaccurate use of terminology may sometimes be of but little importance, and discussion of it may be merely a quibble. But accuracy of expression becomes important when it appears that inaccuracy is due to a confusion of thought in the understanding or application of proper rules or principles of law.'[37]

VII. Peaceful Purposes[38]

Nowhere is what has just been said more apposite than with regard to the word 'peaceful' in the 1967 Space Treaty. In numerous treaties relating to nuclear energy[39] and more particularly in the 1959 Antarctic Treaty, Article I of which[40] was in particular very much in the minds of those who drew up the 1967 Space Treaty, the word 'peaceful' is used in contradistinction to 'military'.[41] At the time the 1967 Space Treaty was being discussed, there was much clamour that outer space should only be used for 'peaceful', i.e., non-military purposes. The then only two space powers both played to the gallery by claiming that all their space activities, including the most important one at the time, namely, military reconnaissance, were 'peaceful'. On the one hand, the Soviet Union, used to controlling the media—at least at home—and distorting facts, simply denied that it ever engaged in such internationally 'illegal' activity as spying on anyone, especially not from outer space, even though it was obviously indulging in it. Its satellites were all said to be for 'scientific research'. It would say that only the Americans were guilty of 'spying' from space and that they must be stopped at once. On the other hand, the United States which, since the days of President Eisenhower's abortive 'Open Sky'

---

[37] US–Mexican Gen. Claims Commission (1923): *International Fisheries Co. Case* (1931), *Opinions of Commissioners* (1931) p. 207, at pp. 265–6.

[38] See further B. Cheng, 'The Legal Status of Outer Space and Relevant Issues: Delimitation of Outer Space and Definition of Peaceful Uses', 11 *JSL* (1983), p. 89, at pp. 98–105 (cf. Ch. 19 above].

[39] See further B. Cheng, 'International Co-operation and Control: From Atoms to Space', 15 *CLP* (1962), p. 228 [Ch. 4 above].

[40] Art I:

1. Antarctica shall be used for peaceful purposes only. There shall be prohibited *inter alia*, any measures of a military nature, such as the establishment of military bases and fortifications, the carrying out of military manoeuvres, as well as the testing of any type of weapons.

2. The present treaty shall not prevent the use of military personnel or equipment for scientific research or for any other peaceful purpose.

[41] See further B. Cheng, 'Le Traité de 1967 sur l'espace/The 1967 Space Treaty', 95 *JDI* (1968), p. 532, at pp. 598–616, esp. pp. 604–8 [Ch. 9 above, s. VI, esp. sub-s. C: Non-militarization of Celestial Bodies; see also Ch. 20 above].

Plan, has been euphemistically dubbing U–2 and similar flights over others' territories as mere 'aerial surveillance' for 'peaceful purposes', cheerfully distorts the term 'peaceful' to mean any activity that is 'non-aggressive'. These tactics enabled both the Soviet Union and the United States blithely to maintain to the world that all their activities in outer space, notwithstanding the deployment of their military reconnaissance satellites, were exclusively 'for peaceful purposes'. Now that the Soviet Union admits, albeit implicitly, to using reconnaissance satellites, its position is somewhat ambiguous. However, the rest of the world, in a supreme mixture of Machiavellian worldliness and naïve self-deception, has ever since made believe that outer space is being used only for peaceful purposes.

But those who drafted the 1967 Outer Space Treaty were not so naïve and they were much more careful with their words. Contrary to the pronouncements of many a politician and even eminent commentator, the 1967 Space Treaty nowhere lays down a legal obligation upon its contracting parties to use the whole of outer space only for 'peaceful purposes'. Some have referred to the Preamble, but, leaving aside the question whether the preamble of a treaty can have such a far-reaching effect, all that the Preamble says is that how nice it would be to explore and use outer space for peaceful purposes. It does not say that outer space may be used only for 'peaceful purposes'.

The only provision in the 1967 Treaty which limits the use of any part of outer space to 'exclusively . . . peaceful purposes' is to be found in the second paragraph of Article IV, but, in very explicit terms, it applies only to 'the moon and other celestial bodies'. A simple comparison of the two paragraphs of Article IV, and a careful examination of the history and wording of the 1967 Treaty will show that this restriction does not apply to paragraph 1, and hence does not apply to the empty space between all the celestial bodies (unfortunately the Space Treaty has deprived us of a simple description of this vast area). In paragraph 1, the only obligation is not to leave any nuclear weapons or other kinds of weapons of mass destruction lying around in outer space either in earth orbit or 'in any other manner'. Otherwise, contracting States are perfectly free to have in this vast void (which we shall call the outer void space) any type and any number of military space objects, including reconnaissance and communications satellites, as well as any kind of defensive or even offensive weapons, provided that they are neither nuclear nor falling within the category of weapons of mass destruction.

However, the United States, prompted it would appear by an initial misreading of the Treaty and the erroneous belief that the restriction of use for 'exclusively peaceful purposes' extends not only to the moon and other celestial bodies, but also to the whole of outer space between such celestial bodies, flying in the face of the international acceptation of the word 'peaceful' as evidenced by the nuclear energy treaties, the Antarctic Treaty and in fact the clear wording of the 1967 Space Treaty itself, insists that 'peaceful' in Article IV(2) means not 'non-military', but 'non-aggressive'.[42] The simple fact that the United States interpretation has the effect of making the first sentence of Article IV(2) of the Space Treaty meaningless and redundant shows that it cannot be correct. The Soviet Union opposes it. Friends and allies of the United States, some having been bullied or duped into accepting the United States interpretation, mostly suffer it in silence, sorrow, and despair.

This is not the place to go further into the subject,[43] except to say that clarification of the meaning of this term, and of the scope of its application in outer space, by means of an international agreement is of vital importance to future commercial development in outer space. In the absence of such clarification, one can easily find that what one is geared up to do, is actually doing or has just done is out of the blue branded as a violation of the law because it is not 'for peaceful purposes'. The State or States responsible under Article VI of the Space Treaty would also be immediately involved and made responsible for this 'violation'. In this connection, reference may be made to the first sentence of Article 1 and the last sentence of Article 14(1) of the 1988 Agreement between the United States, member States of the European Space Agency, Japan, and Canada on a Permanently Manned *Civil* Space Station:

> Article 1. Object and Scope.
> 1. The object of this Agreement is to establish a long-term international cooperative framework among the Partners, . . . , for the detailed design, development, operation, and utilization of a permanently manned civil Space Station for peaceful purposes, in accordance with international law . . .
> Article 14. Evolution.
> 1. . . . The Space Station together with its additions of evolutionary capability shall remain a civil station, and its operation and utilization shall be for peaceful purposes, in accordance with international law.

It will be observed that here at least the partners of the United States in this joint venture have succeeded, albeit in perhaps a somewhat roundabout way, in making it clear that by 'peaceful purposes' they mean civil, i.e., non-military, projects, even if the United States may still have some reservation on the subject.[44] A general and more explicit agreement on the subject is urgently required.

---

[42] An interesting parallel is the way in which the words 'States' and 'nation' have acquired in the United States meanings different from, and almost opposite to, their original and currently international acceptation. The *e pluribus unum* aspiration and notion of one 'nation' forged from peoples of many different origins has over the years been, so to speak, secularized to denote simply what the rest of the world would call a 'State', whilst the term 'state' carries a somewhat vague connotation of being merely a component part of a 'nation' with a different set of laws and zip code or perhaps just where one lives or has a house. It would be just as unreasonable to try to foist such altered meanings of words upon the rest of the world.

[43] See further B. Cheng, 'The Legal Status of Outer Space and Relevant Issues', 11 *JSL* (1983), p. 89, at pp. 98 ff. [cf. Ch. 19 above].

[44] In an Exchange of Notes dated 19/20 Sept. 1988 between the Chief US Negotiator and the Head of the European Governments' Delegation to the International Space Station Negotiations,

VIII. Status of Space Objects[45]

Another term or group of terms which require clarification, definition and standardization are 'space objects' and related expressions and notions. The various treaties at present speak, seemingly without much discrimination, of space vehicles, spacecraft, space objects, man-made space objects, objects launched into outer space and so forth. In addition, one has satellites, artificial satellites, manned and unmanned stations, elements, component parts, launch vehicles, and, particularly in relation to the moon and celestial bodies, installations, constructions, vehicles, equipment, facilities, and so forth.

Unless these and related terms and notions are urgently clarified and defined, and their usage standardized, much confusion will arise. It will be difficult both for the regulators to regulate and for those who have to comply with the regulations to comply. The matter is further complicated by the fact that, since territorial sovereignty has been banned from outer space[46] and, with it, territorial jurisdiction, the overriding jurisdiction in outer space now is quasi-territorial jurisdiction[47]. Under Article VIII of the Space Treaty, this quasi-territorial jurisdiction appears to be anchored on the registration of a space object. Article VIII of the Space Treaty provides:

A State Party to the Treaty on whose registry an object launched into outer space is carried shall retain jurisdiction and control over such object, and over any personnel thereof, while in outer space or on a celestial body. Ownership of objects launched into outer space, including objects landed or constructed on a celestial body, and of their component parts, is not affected by their presence in outer space or on a celestial body

the latter confirmed as correct the former's 'automatic reservation' that not only 'the United States has the right to use its elements, as well as its allocations of resources derived from the Space Station infrastructure, for national security purposes', but also '[w]ith respect to such uses of these elements and resources, the decision whether they may be carried out under the Agreement will be made by the United States.' But the latter also added that: 'I should like to confirm that, with respect to the use of elements of the permanently manned civil Space Station provided by Europe, the European Partner will be guided by Article II of the Convention establishing the European Space Agency' (Texts reproduced in ESA, *Proceedings of the Colloquium on Manned Space Stations—Legal Issues* 145–6 (1990), pp. 145–6.) Art. II of the ESA Convention states very clearly:

The purpose of the Agency shall be to provide for and to promote, *for exclusively peaceful purposes*, co-operation among European States in space research and technology and their space applications, with a view to their being used for scientific purposes and for operational space applications systems . . . [italics added].

[45] B. Cheng, 'Spacecraft, Satellites and Space Objects', in Bernhardt (ed.), 11 *Ency. PIL* (1989), p. 309 [Ch. 16 above, and see also Ch. 18].

[46] 1967 Space Treaty, Art. II: 'Outer space, including the moon and other celestial bodies, is not subject to national appropriation by claim of sovereignty, by means of use or occupation, or by any other means.' See B. Cheng, 'Le Traité de 1967 sur l'espace/The 1967 Space Treaty', 95 *JDI* (1968), p. 532, at pp. 564–98 [Ch. 9 above, s. V: Legal Regime of Outer Space and Celestial Bodies].

[47] On State jurisdiction in outer space, see further B. Cheng, 'The Extraterrestrial Application of International Law', 18 *CLP* (1965), p. 132 [Ch. 5 above].

or by their return to the earth. Such objects or component parts found beyond the limits of the State Party to the Treaty on whose registry they are carried shall be returned to that State Party, which shall, upon request, furnish identifying data prior to their return.

Assuming that 'space object' is the most comprehensive term which includes 'spacecraft', 'space vehicles', and 'artificial satellites', the first question that requires elucidation is what is a space object, and when does an object begin and cease, if ever, to qualify and begin to qualify as a space object.

The Registration Convention in its Article II only requires space objects 'launched into earth orbit or beyond' to be registered. No doubt on this basis, the Swedish Space Activities Act of 1982,[48] for example, does not consider the launching of sounding rockets a space activity. Is a sounding rocket, which may well go up to 500 kilometres above the surface of the earth, nevertheless a space object? Does it benefit from the Astronauts Agreement? On the international level, is its launching nonetheless a national activity in outer space, for which the 'national' State bears internationally responsibility under Article VI of the Space Treaty? Does the sounding rocket come under the Treaty's Article VII on the liability of the launching State for damage caused by objects launched 'into outer space'? Is it subject to the Liability Convention, which simply refers to 'space object'? Is being launched 'into outer space' the decisive criterion? Or 'into earth orbit and beyond'? Where is outer space any way? One comes back to the problem of delimitation of outer space. In any event, the wording of Article II of the Registration Convention, in requiring only space objects 'launched into earth orbit or beyond' to be registered, does not appear to preclude that there may be space objects which are not launched into earth orbit or beyond. They simply need not be registered.

A not entirely dissimilar but much more thorny problem is that of ballistic missiles which are aimed at targets in outer space or which traverse outer space in order to reach targets on earth. As has been mentioned before, in the field of aviation, the Chicago Convention frankly and modestly limits itself to international civil aviation, leaving aircraft used in military, customs, and police services severely alone.[49] Up to a point, one is still in the rather euphoric honey-moon period of space exploration and use, and one likes to foster and wallow in the myth that outer space is being used by everyone only for 'peaceful purposes', notwithstanding all the military hardware that are already there or that may hereafter be sent up there; for they are, after all— ours at least—all 'non-aggressive'. Do they all come under the various United Nations treaties on outer space? The fact that no military space object seems

---

[48] (1982: 963). The Act is supplemented by a Decree (1982: 1069). See J. Relfarth, 'Nationale Weltraumgesetze in Europea', 36 *ZLW* (1987), p. 11.

[49] Art. 3. See further B. Cheng, 'International Law and High Altitude Flights: Balloons, Rockets and Man-Made Satellites', 6 *ICLQ* (1957), p. 487, at pp. 495–8 [Ch. 2 above, s. VI.A: State Flight Craft].

so far to have found its way into the United Nations register can of course be interpreted in many different ways. It is, however, interesting to observe that the United States accepts that military space objects are not excluded from the 1972 Liability Convention.[50] Does this mean that all military space objects, including ballistic missiles, come under all the general international law and applicable treaty rules on space objects? Moreover, what is the status of shuttles and aerospace craft when they are in airspace? Then there is the enormous problem of debris in outer space.

And when, if ever, does a space object or fragment of a space object cease to be a space object—an object 'launched into space'? What is the interrelationship between registration, ownership, liability and jurisdiction in regard to debris? Can space objects become *res derelicta* through the State of registry formally de-registering them, if they are registered objects? Can such abandonment and de-registration have any effect on the launching State's liability? Can one encourage prompt registration, and at the same time help solve the quandary over ownership of disused space objects and other junks in other space, by declaring that all objects which have not been registered with the United Nations within so many days, weeks or months of their launch are to be treated like stray dogs without a licence that can be disposed of by anyone, without prejudice, however, to the launching State's liability for any damage which such objects may cause to third parties. Whether or not States have the will to go this far, it is evident that, for the sake of all the parties concerned, the notion and status of 'space object' urgently need to be clearly defined.

IX. Space Objects and Jurisdiction

The question of jurisdiction in relation to space objects is no clearer. Article VIII of the Space Treaty, as we have seen, appears to attach jurisdiction to registration. However, it also speaks of the State of registry 'retaining' jurisdiction and control over the space object 'while [it is] in outer space or on a celestial body', suggesting that such jurisdiction and control exist both before it enters outer space and, in view especially of Article VIII's second and third sentences, after its return to earth. However, presumably, an object does not become a space object, at the earliest, until it is launched or is at least being prepared for launching into outer space. Its status as a space object, at present, certainly does not appear to date from either national or United Nations registration, as, notwithstanding calls for this to be done, the Registration

---

[50] US Senate, *Report from the Committee on Foreign Relations on the Convention on International Liability for Damage Caused by Space Objects*, 92d Congress, 2d Session, Executive Report No. 92–38, (1972), p. 7; see further B. Cheng, 'Convention on International Liability for Damage Caused by Space Objects', in Jasentuliyana and Lee (eds.), 1 *Manual* (1979), p. 83, at pp. 116–7 [Ch. 11 above, s. V.C.3: Space Object].

Convention does not really require that registration be made prior to launching,[51] and, in practice, registration with the United Nations is often long delayed.

But does Article VIII of the Space Treaty nevertheless have the effect of making jurisdiction dependent on registration? In this regard, it may be pointed out that, although the rules of registration of space objects were finally agreed upon in 1975, in the intervening years, two other treaties concerned with outer space concluded under the auspices of the United Nations eschewed any reference to registration. The 1968 Astronauts Agreement speaks only of the 'launching authority', whilst the 1972 Liability Convention only of the 'launching State'. The former defines the 'launching authority' as either the State or an appropriate international organization 'responsible for launching' the space object,[52] whereas the latter is more explicit in defining a 'launching State' as a State (or appropriate international organization) which launches or procures the launching of a space object, or one from whose territory or facility a space object is launched.[53] In other words, in a given launch, there can be four separate States or organizations all falling within the definition of the 'launching State'. For example, if State A requests State B to launch one of State A's satellites from a facility owned by State C located in State D, all four States A, B, C, and D will be launching States for that launch, and all four States will be jointly and severally liable for any damage caused by that space object.[54]

Now, does the term 'launching authority' in the Astronauts Agreement have the same meaning as 'launching State' in the Liability Convention? It may be observed that, whilst Article VIII of the Space Treaty says that ownership is not affected by space objects having been launched into outer space, on the one hand, Article VIII prescribes that strayed space objects found should be returned to the State of registry, whereas, on the other hand, the Astronauts Agreement provides that they should be, upon request, returned to the launching authority or held at the disposal of its representatives.[55] No mention is made of either the owner or his national State. In any event, there is need to straighten out the discrepancy between the two treaties. Now that the Registration Convention has been fairly widely accepted, probably there is no more inhibition in making the State of registry the principal or even sole connecting factor, apart from the matters of international responsibility and international liability.

[51] Cf. Arts. II, and especially IV.

[52] Art. 6. See B. Cheng, 'The 1968 Astronauts Agreement', 23 *YBWA* (1969), p. 185, at p. 202 [Ch. 10 above, s. VII.A: Definition of Launching Authority; cf. also Ch. 23 above].

[53] Art. 1(*c*). See B. Cheng, 'Convention on International Liability for Damage Caused by Space Objects', in Jasentuliyana and Lee (eds.), 1 *Manual* (1979), p. 83, at pp. 102–12 [Ch. 1 above, s. V.A.5 and 6: The Party Liable and the Problem of International Organizations].

[54] Arts. II and V. See Cheng, loc. cit. in previous n., at pp. 119–22 [Ch. 11 above, s. VII: Joint and Several Liability]. Cf. also Art. VII of the 1967 Space Treaty.

[55] Art. 5(3).

In fact, there is probably much to be said for going back to the traditional concept of nationality in space law[56] which would create a direct and visible link between registration and jurisdiction; for at the moment, notwithstanding Article VIII of the Space Treaty, registration and jurisdiction are not always tied together as stated in that article. This is especially true when space objects are being launched jointly by several States either directly or indirectly, through or together with an international organization. Article II of the Registration Convention seemingly permits the States concerned, after registering the space object with one of them, to conclude 'appropriate agreements' among them 'on jurisdiction and control over the space object and over any personnel thereof'. All that they are asked to do is to 'bear[. . .] in mind the provisions of Article VIII' of the Space Treaty.

Although Article II of the Registration Convention appears to have the merit of affording the States concerned the maximum of flexibility in the matter, it may well be open to question whether, in the light of Article VIII of the Space Treaty, once an object has been registered, States have any discretion to alter the link between registration and jurisdiction. If, in practice, Article VIII is to be so interpreted as to permit States unfettered discretion to make alternative arrangements, uncertainty in any concrete case is bound to arise as to which State actually enjoys jurisdiction and control over a space object, with all the attending consequences, such as which State's law is applicable to it and on board. This is particularly so since the Registration Convention does not even require such arrangements to be reported to the United Nations and recorded in its register. In this connection, the view which has been expressed by the United Nations General Counsel to the European Space Agency that similar arrangements may be made by international organizations, for jurisdiction and control over space objects registered with them to be exercised by one of their members or any of the States with which such organizations may have jointly launched a given space object,[57] will inevitably lead to further erosion of the rule that jurisdiction and registration go hand in hand. Notwithstanding some of problems connected with the concept of nationality in aviation and shipping and the important rôle played by international organizations in the exploration and use of outer space, it does appear that there is much to be said for a new arrangement introducing the concept of

[56] See further B. Cheng, 'Nationality for Spacecraft?', in T. L. Masson-Zwaan and P. M. J. Mendes de Leon (eds.), *Air and Space Law: De Lege Ferenda* (1992), p. 203 [Ch. 17 above].

[57] I am grateful to Monsieur G. Lafferranderie, Legal Adviser of the European Space Agency, for the text of the letter of 19 Sept. 1975 from Mr E. Suy, the Legal Counsel of the United Nations, to the Agency's Deputy Director in charge of International Affairs Mr H. Kaltenecker, regarding the application of the Registration Convention to international intergovernmental organizations, in which the former stated *inter alia*:

Where an international intergovernmental organization launches a space object jointly with one or more States, the provsiions of paragraph 2 of Article II are relevant. In other words, the organization and the States may enter into appropriate agreement on jurisdiction and control over the space object and over any personnel thereof, if it is decided that the organization should register the space object.

nationality to space law in order to tie jurisdiction and control over space objects to registration and to remove the many uncertainties which now exist in this field.

Such a move is useful in other ways. At present neither Article VIII of the Space Treaty nor the 1979 Moon Treaty is very helpful over the status of objects on celestial bodies, including constructions, installations, equipment, facilities, vehicles, and stations, manned or unmanned. Both treaties dwell on ownership being unchanged. The Moon Treaty seemingly even links jurisdiction and control to ownership.[58] This creates uncertainty and is probably contrary to Article VIII of the Space Treaty. If the experience with the shuttle is any guide, whilst payloads which remain on board in outer space are not separately registered, those which are going to be separated from the shuttle are individually registered.[59] Clarification of when a space object needs to be registered and endowed with nationality together with all the attending consequences, and when it need not be, should prove of great practical importance to all those intending to be involved in commercial development in outer space; for *inter alia* jurisdiction is directly related to the question which system of law is applicable. At present the situation leaves a great deal of uncertainty in the regulatory regime, uncertainty which can present unnecessary risks for those concerned.

X. Who is Responsible for Whom and What Under Article VI of the Space Treaty?

The introduction of the familiar concept of nationality may also help to clarify the operation of Article VI of the Space Treaty which makes the contracting States internationally responsible for 'national activities in outer space'. Differences of opinion appear to have arisen over the interpretation of whose activities, apart from those carried on by a State's own agencies, constitute 'national activities' and consequently require 'authorization and continuing supervision' in accordance with Article VI.[60] Whilst both the United States [61] and Sweden,[62] in their space legislation, extend their control and supervision

---

[58] Art. 12(1). See B. Cheng, 'The Moon Treaty', 33 *CLP* (1980), p. 213, at pp. 224–5 (Ch. 12 above, s. IV.H.2: Jurisdiction and Ownership].

[59] Cf. G. Lafferranderie, 'L'application, par l'Agence Spatiale Européenne, de la Convention sur l'immatriculation des objets lancés dans l'espace extra-atmosphérique', 11 *AASL* (1986), p. 229; same, 'La station spatiale', in J. Dutheil de la Rochère (ed.), *Droit de l'espace* (1988), p. 147, at p. 172, n. 29.

[60] Cf. H. Bittlinger, 'Private Space Activities: Questions of International Responsibility', 30 *Space Law Colloquium* (1987), p. 191; K. Tatsuzawa, 'The Regulation of Commercial Space Activities by the Non-Governmental Entities in Space Law', 31 *Space Law Colloquium* (1988), p. 341.

[61] Commercial Space Launch Act 1984, and 1988 amendments, 49 USCS App., ss. 2601 ff.

[62] See n. 48 above.

to all space activities within their territory, as well as those of their nationals outside the country, the United Kingdom in its Outer Space Act 1986,[63] basing itself on the rather complacent belief that foreigners are unlikely to engage in space activities in the United Kingdom and probably also on what can only be regarded as a slip of the pen in Article IX of the Space Treaty which refers only to 'nationals', applies such control only to space activities of United Kingdom nationals, wherever they may be.[64]

International agreement is necessary in order to clarify and unify the notion of 'national activities' and who is 'the appropriate State' responsible for 'authorization and continuing supervision' under Article VI of the Space Treaty; for otherwise it can be very confusing and risky for those who wish to engage in commercial development in space. From the standpoint of the latter, it would of course be desirable if there were only one State and one authority involved. However, from the standpoint of the rest of the world and that of the governments concerned, especially in the light of the Liability Convention which renders all the States involved in the launch of a space object liable for any damage which it may cause, it would be in the interest of any State that may be held internationally responsible or liable that it has a say in controlling such activities.

The position is clearer if one has a proper understanding of the rules governing State jurisdiction.[65] There are basically two elements to State jurisdiction and three different types. The three types of State jurisdiction are: (i) *territorial* jurisdiction which is what a State exercises over its territory; (ii) *quasi-territorial* jurisdiction over its ships, aircraft, and space objects wherever they may be; and (iii) *personal* jurisdiction over its nationals, again wherever they may be. Each type of jurisdiction has two elements: (i) *jurisfaction*, which is the normative power of a State to legislate, and to make other legally binding decisions, including judicial pronouncements, if necessary *in absentia*, with not only territorial, but, if need be, also extraterritorial effect, and (ii) *jurisaction*, namely, the power of a State actually and physically to implement, enforce, and carry out laws, judgments, and other binding decisions. Now, whereas *jurisfaction* of different types of State jurisdiction can co-exist so that a person can simultaneously be under his own national law, the law of the flag-State of the ship he happens to be on, and the law of the country where the ship happens to be moored, there is a definite hierarchy in *jurisaction* so that, in case of conflict, territorial jurisaction overrides quasi-territorial and personal jurisactions, whilst quasi-territorial jurisaction overrides personal jurisaction.

---

[63] 1986 c. 38.

[64] S. 2; see also B. Cheng, 'Whose Parking Space Is It Anyway? Mapping Out a Legal Minefield in the Celestial Outlands', *The Times Higher Educational Supplement* (30 May 1986), p. 14.

[65] See further B. Cheng, 'The Extraterrestrial Application of International Law', 18 *CLP* (1965), p. 132, at pp. 134 ff. [Ch. 5 above, s. II: General International Law].

Since responsibility must perforce go hand in hand with control, all the States having jurisdiction should logically be held internationally responsible, but at any given time and place, insofar as non-governmental activities are concerned, the only State actually to be held responsible should be the State exercising the overriding jurisaction. This would be (i) the territorial State if the activity occurs within the territory of a State, (ii) the flag-State or State of registry if it occurs on board a ship, an aircraft, or a spacecraft outside the territory of any State, and (iii) the national State if the activity is carried on by a national, whether an individual or a corporate person, in territories without a sovereign, or on board a stateless ship, aircraft or spacecraft outside the territory of any State. However, to the extent to which other States have concurrent jurisdiction over the activity, even though for the moment their jurisaction may be overridden by that of another, they really should also have an international responsibility for 'assuring that national activities are carried out in conformity with the' Space Treaty, with international law, and with any other specific international obligations. This is because their own jurisaction can or may subsequently, either in the normal course of events or by deliberate action, become the operative one. This can happen, for instance, when the ship of a State's registry on which the activity takes place moves from a foreign harbour onto the high sea, or when the foreign State where its nationals have been carrying on such activities grants the request to have them expelled or extradited. When their jurisaction becomes or can be made effective, then their responsibility will also operate. Without this residuary responsibility, the burden of supervision and control can be easily evaded by resorting to flags of convenience or 'responsibility havens'. The result is that, under Article VI of the Space Treaty, notwithstanding the use of the definite article in it, far from there being only one 'appropriate State' having an interest in subjecting a given space activity to authorization and continuing supervision, there may be several 'appropriate' States.[66]

From the standpoint of those concerned with the commercial development in space, the position is obviously complicated, cumbersome, and highly unsatisfactory, inasmuch as, in certain cases, authorization may have to be obtained from more than one State. In fact, in addition to the States which have just been mentioned, the State from whose 'facility' a space object is being launched may also wish to exercise control over the activity in view of its liability under the Liability Convention for any damage which the object may cause. Moreover, on account of Article VI of the Space Treaty, the national State of the owner of a space object or of a facility may also be at risk, even when the space object is launched, or the facility operated, by another State or nationals of another State from or in a foreign country.

---

[66] See further B. Cheng, 'Space Activities, Responsibility and Liability For', in Bernhardt (ed.), 11 *Ency. PIL* (1989), pp. 299–303 [cf. Ch. 24 above].

One way of alleviating the lot of private parties that wish to engage in activities in space and at the same time simplifying the task of the various governments involved would be for the governments concerned or likely to be concerned either bilaterally or multilaterally to come to some agreement whereby at least administratively the licensing process can be handled through a single State. As among the contracting States themselves, some arrangements regarding liability, with at least certain parties being held harmless, could no doubt also be made. In this regard, a leaf may perhaps be taken from the 1944 Chicago Convention on International Civil Aviation, under Article 83*bis* of which member States of the International Civil Aviation Organization (ICAO) are allowed by agreement to transfer certain functions and duties they have under the Convention as States of registry to other member States when one of their aircraft has been leased, chartered or interchanged to an operator of the latter. The United Kingdom Outer Space Act 1986, in its section 3(2)(b), in fact envisages some such possibility when it provides:

(2) A licence is not required,

   (a) ...
   (b) for activities in respect of which it is certified by Order in Council that arrangements have been made between the United Kingdom and another country to secure compliance with the international obligations of the United Kingdom.

Under Article 83*bis* of the Chicago Convention, once such an arrangement has been notified to and published by the ICAO Council or been directly communicated to the other contracting State(s) concerned, the State of registry is relieved of its responsibility in respect of the duties and functions transferred. It is to be questioned whether States would be prepared to go so far in any similar arrangement relating to Article VI of the Space Treaty. In any event, any such arrangement can only be a measure of convenience and facilitation among the contracting parties, with effects limited strictly to themselves. They cannot affect the rights and duties of third States without their consent, a long established rule of international law, since unequivocally confirmed in Article 34 of the 1969 Vienna Convention on the Law of Treaties.

Among such a welter of States, if the introduction of the concept of nationality to space objects can, as in the case of aircraft and the generality of ships, ensure a direct connection between registration, nationality and jurisdiction, and, coupled with a system of compulsory entry of this information in the various registers, thereby create some certainty and transparency as to which State is actually exercising jurisdiction and control over which object, or which element in a complex of space objects, it would doubtless be a boon to all concerned.

While clarifying the notion of 'national' in the phrase 'national activities in outer space', it would be useful at the same time to elucidate the meaning of the second half of the phrase, namely, 'activities in outer space', as well as the extent of a State's responsibility. This question has been raised, for instance, particularly in relation to remote sensing and the problem of the subsequent processing, interpretation and dissemination of the data which take place on this planet rather than 'in outer space'. The United Nations General Assembly resolution 41/65 adopted in 1986 defines the term 'remote sensing activities' in such a way as to encompass the whole cycle of operations, including the dissemination of the processed data. However, the resolution is far from clear regarding the extent of States' responsibility. In fact, its Principle XIV, while recalling Article VI of the Space Treaty, merely says:

States operating remote sensing satellites shall bear international responsibility for *their* activities,

even though it goes on to say later on:

irrespective of whether such activities are carried out by governmental or non-governmental entities or through international organizations to which such States are parties. This principle is without prejudice to the applicability of the norms of international law on State responsibility for remote sensing activities.

The wording of Principle XIV lends itself to the possible interpretation that it construes Article VI of the Space Treaty, when applied to compliance with the resolution, as holding a State responsible merely for its *own* activities, whether or not carried out directly by itself, and not for its *national* activities as the term is generally understood, such as remote sensing activities of private entities under its effective jurisdiction. It would seem that it is referring State responsibility for the latter activities to general international law rather than to Article VI of the Space Treaty. This impression is reinforced by the resolution's Principle XII which limits, what may be called, the equitable interest of a sensed State to 'have access to the available analysed information concerning the territory under its jurisdiction' 'on a non-discriminatory basis and on reasonable cost terms' merely to information 'in the possession of any State participating in remote sensing activities'. This interest does not seem, therefore, to extend to information in the hands of nationals of a State, especially when the State did not itself participate in gathering, processing, or analysing the original data. However, in relation to remote sensing carried out either directly or indirectly by a State, it would seem that the expression 'activities in outer space' includes also the logical consequences of such activities, whether such consequences occur in outer space or on earth. Whether this construction of Article VI of the Space Treaty is correct is open to question.[67]

The problem is probably even more complex in the case of direct broadcasting satellites. Does the responsibility assumed by States under Article VI

---

[67] See further B. Cheng, 'Legal and Commercial Aspects of Data Gathering by Remote Sensing', in Chia-Jui Cheng and Pablo Mendes de Leon (eds.), *The Highways of Air and Space Law over Asia* (1992), p. 49 [Ch. 22 above].

extend to the content of broadcasts made by private concerns under their jurisdiction, at least to the same extent as if the broadcasts were made by the States themselves, or are States merely obliged to ensure that the broadcasting activity is carried out in accordance with international law and pertinent international agreements?[68] Also does it extend to, for instance, private claims for breach of copyrights and neighbouring rights?

The same kind of questions apply *mutatis mutandis* to other private and commercial activities in outer space, such as the manufacturing industry, salvage claims, and so forth.

XI. Extension of National Laws to Space

Speaking of copyrights and private claims, one is reminded of the urgent need to persuade all the States concerned to take the necessary steps to extend the relevant parts of their national laws to outer space. As is well known, Article II of the Space Treaty provides:

Outer space, including the moon and other celestial bodies, is not subject to national appropriation by claim of sovereignty, by means of use or occupation, or by any other means.[69]

What this means is that there is no territorial sovereignty or territorial jurisdiction in outer space. Consequently, following what has been said previously regarding State jurisdiction, the only jurisdictions permitted in outer space are the quasi-territorial ones of States of registry of space objects and the personal ones of national States of individuals or corporations. This being the case, since, if the experience of air law is any guide, the laws, especially criminal laws, of most countries are essentially territorial in nature applicable only within their national territories, it may be necessary by treaty, paradoxical as it may seem, to commit States to extend their laws to their spacecraft and other space objects when they are outside national territory, especially in outer space, and possibly also to their nationals when in outer space.

An example in air law in this direction is the 1963 Tokyo Convention on Offences and Certain Other Acts on Board Aircraft.[70] For the purpose of furthering commercial development in outer space, it will be necessary to urge

---

[68] See also M. N. Taishoff, *State Responsibility and the Direct Broadcast Satellite* (1987). Taishoff does not appear, however, to distinguish clearly the responsibility of States under Art. VI of the Space Treaty from their liability under its Art. VII and the Liability Convention. See, e.g., p. 175 in particular.

[69] See further B. Cheng, 'Le Traité de 1967 sur l'espace/The 1967 Space Treaty', 95 *JDI* (1968), p. 532, at pp. 564–98 [Ch. 9 above, s. V: Legal Regime of Outer Space and Celestial Bodies].

[70] See further B. Cheng, 'Crimes on Board Aircraft', 12 *CLP* (1959), pp. 177–202; Royal Aeronautical Society, *Report on Crimes and Offences on Board Aircraft for Submission to the Minister of Avaiation* (mimeographed, 1962), 33 pp.; B. Cheng, 'Aviation Security: Safeguarding International Civil Aviation Against Acts of Unlawful Interference', Lloyd's of London Press, *Speakers' Papers for Lloyd's of London Press International Civil Avaiation Conference No. 6,*

and, if possible, to bind States to extend not only their criminal law, but also the scope of their laws on, for instance, intellectual and industrial property to works, products, and inventions produced in outer space. The United States has already taken a lead in this direction.[71] A treaty somewhat along the lines of the Tokyo Convention may be necessary. Other areas where an international effort to encourage the extension of national laws to outer space would be highly desirable may well include taxation, employer's liability, safety regulations, product liability,[72] experiments on live animals, and so forth. However, as one commentator has quite rightly remarked, unification of substantive law by treaty may not always be desirable inasmuch as such efforts, even when they succeed, can easily, like the Warsaw system, lead to the fossilization of the lowest common denominator of all the different national laws.[73] However, an international treaty that would resolve potential problems of private international law relating to activities in outer space[74] would be of obvious attraction to future commercial development. Moreover, in the wake of the news that the Soviet astronauts in August 1990 brought back 23 pure crystals grown in outer space, each worth $1 million,[75] no doubt an international agreement, following the lead set by a United States federal statute in 1982, to allow items from outer space duty free entry,[76] would be warmly welcomed by those thinking of similar enterprises.

Montreal, 1984 [1985], pp. 35–44; B. Cheng, 'International Legal Instruments to Safeguard International Air Transport: The Conventions of Tokyo, The Hague, Montreal, and a New Instrument Concerning Unlawful Violence at International Airports', in International Institute of Air and Space Law, University of Leyden, and others, *Conference Proceedings: Aviation Security, The Hague, 1987* (1987), pp. 23–46; B. Cheng, 'Aviation, Criminal Jurisdiction and Terrorism: The Hague Extradition/Prosecution Formula and Attacks at Airports', in B. Cheng and E. D. Brown (eds.), *Contemporary Problems of International Law: Essays in honour of Georg Schwarzenberger on his eightieth birthday* (1988), pp. 25–52.

[71] See 18 USCA, ss. 7(6) and (7) whereby the United States extended its jurisdiction in 1981 to '[a]ny vehicle used or designed for flight or navigation in space and on the registry of the United States pursuant to the [Space Treaty and the Registration Convention], while that vehicle is in flight . . .', and in 1984 to '[a]ny place outside the jurisdiction of any nation with respect to an offense by or against a national of the United States'. See further P. Dann, 'The Future Rôle of Municipal Law in Regulating Space-Related Activities', in T. L. Zwaan (ed.), *Space Law: Views of the Future* (1988), p. 125, at p. 131; G. Lafferranderie, 'The United States Proposed Patent in Space Legislation—An International Perspective', 18 *JSL* (1990), p. 1; S. Gorove, 'The Growth of Domestic Space Law: A U.S. Example', 18 *JSL* (1990), p. 99. Cf. also B. Packwood (by direction of), *Policy and Legal Issues Involved in the Commercialization of Space* (US Senate Committee on Commerce, Science, and Transportation print) (1983).

[72] Cf. B. Cheng, 'Product Liability, with Special Reference to Aeronautics', in [Brazilian] Ministério da Aeronáutica, Centro Téchnico Aeroespacial, Instituto Tecnolólogico de Aeronáutica, *1° Seminário sobre Responsabilidade Civil do Fabricante, 11 e 12 de julho de 1983, São José dos Campos* (1984), pp. 5–36.

[73] See Dann, loc. cit. in n. 71 above, pp. 131–2; see also B. Cheng, 'Sixty Years of the Warsaw Convention: Airline Liability at the Crossroads', 38 *ZLW* (1989), p. 319, esp. pp. 319–20, and 39 ibid. (1990), p. 3.

[74] See H. DeSaussure, 'An Integrated Legal System for Space', 6 *JSL* (1978), p. 179, at p. 191.

[75] *The Times* (London), 10 Aug. 1990, p. 20, cols. 1–2.

[76] See A. Dula, 'Material Processing as a Subject of Space Law', 28 *Space Law Colloquium* (1985), pp. 224–7.

XII. Dispute Settlement, International Civil Space Organization, and an International Regime for the Moon?

There remain a number of areas where international agreements would be desirable from the standpoint of commercial development in outer space. In the first place, apart from the Liability Convention,[77] none of the other treaties on outer space concluded under the auspices of the United Nations contains a proper dispute settlement procedure. Various organizations have been working on the subject.[78] Mention may, for instance, be made of the highly comprehensive First Draft of a Convention on the subject drawn up by the International Law Association Space Law Committee under the rapporteurship of Professor K. -H. Böckstiegel.[79]

During the negotiations of the Moon Treaty, proposals were made for the establishment of an international space authority,[80] and for a number of years, the Soviet Union has been advocating the setting up of a World Space Organization.[81] As to the Moon Treaty,[82] it is really a political document, with a hotchpotch of provisions mostly culled from previous treaties. Whether it will ever gain sufficient support from the main space powers to turn its basic principles into rules of general international law is still an open question. As among its contracting States, it has done little for commercial exploitation of the moon and other celestial bodies. In the first place, it has placed restrictions on exploitation and at least raised doubt whether there is a moratorium on exploitation. Secondly, it has cast a long shadow over any enterprise on celestial bodies by postulating the future existence of an unknown international regime yet to be established which will take over the management of their natural resources as soon as their exploitation 'is about to become feasible'[83]. If we are to have an international regime, perhaps it would be desirable to have it sooner than later.

However, whether in the form of intergovernmental or non-governmental entities, it is certain there will be in the years to come an increasing number of international commercial agencies or consortia involved in the exploration, use and exploitation of outer space. From this point of view, the many co-operative arrangements that already exist, such as INTELSAT and

[77] See B. Cheng, 'Convention on International Liability for Damage Caused by Space Objects', in Jasentuliyana and Lee (eds.), 1 *Manual* (1979), p. 83, at pp. 135–42 [Ch. 11 above, s. XI: Third Party Settlement of Claims].

[78] See van Traa-Engelman, op. cit. in n. 28 above, Ch. XI, pp. 251 ff., including n. 14.

[79] For text of the First Draft, see ILA, *Report of the 61st Conference, Paris* (1984), p. 334; refer also to p. 376. The final Draft, at the time of writing, had not yet been presented.

[80] A/AC.105/C.2/SR.190 (4.5.72), p. 42; see also A/AC.105/PV.169 (21.6.77), pp. 48–50.

[81] A/41/470 (1986), pp. 34–8.

[82] See further B. Cheng, 'The Moon Treaty', 33 *CLP* (1980), p. 213 [Ch. 12 above].

[83] Art. 11. See further Cheng, loc. cit. in previous n., at pp. 227–8 [Ch. 12 above, s. IV.L: An International Regime].

INMARSAT,[84] can no doubt all provide useful pointers as to how such operations may be undertaken.

Looking further afield, it may be said that the establishment of an international space organization, perhaps called, in view now of the United States seeming acceptance, albeit with some reservation, of the term 'civil'[85], the International Civil Space Organization, devoted solely to international co-operation in the exploration and use, including commercial exploitation, of outer space for truly peaceful (i.e., non-military) purposes, along perhaps the lines of the International Civil Aviation Organization[86] or the International Maritime Organization, is only a matter of time.

XIII. Conditions Governing International Rule-Making

In a survey I made in 1986 of the development of international law in the light of the history of air law and space law since their inception, I arrived at the conclusion that there were three essential conditions governing the successful making of rules of international law, including the successful conclusion of treaties. These conditions are:

(i)   perceived needs on the part of the States concerned;
(ii) propitious political climate; and
(iii) due representation of the dominant section of international society having special concern in the subject matter.[87]

Insofar as the last point is concerned, it is interesting to observe that a commentator from the Soviet Union, where the principle of equality of States is often harped upon whenever it is in the Soviet interest to do so, recently remarked:

From a policy perspective, of particular importance is the fact that any attempt to establish a new space order can only be successful if it is based on a realistic assessment of existing power structures within the international community.[88]

Both in the negotiation of the various treaties that we have suggested and in the actual structure of any International Civil Space Organization that may be set up, this point needs to be carefully taken into account, while bearing fully in mind the aspirations and needs of the developing countries, and the

---

[84] See further B. Cheng, 'Communications Satellites', 24 *CLP* (1971), p. 211 [Ch. 21 above].

[85] See n. 44 above and text thereto.

[86] Cf. Cheng, *The Law of International Air Transport*, Part I: The Institutional and Legal Framework.

[87] See B. Cheng, 'The Contribution of Air and Space Law to the Development of International Law', 39 *CLP* (1986), p. 181 [Epilogue below].

[88] G. M. Danilenko, 'The Progressive Development of Space Law: New Opportunities and Restraints', in Zwaan (ed.), op. cit. in n. 71 above, p. 102.

desirability of involving them to a much greater extent than hitherto in space activities.[89]

As regards a propitious political climate, the Berlin Wall, symbolizing the Iron Curtain, has now dramatically fallen and we are at the moment witnessing the warmest relationship between the two major space powers and between countries within what used to be called the Eastern and Western blocs. The barometer reads 'Fair-set'. As the saying goes, one should make hay while the sun shines.

Finally, perceived need. We have, I hope, seen in this survey why, as commercial development in outer space gathers pace, there is a need, and, in many cases, an urgent need, for the new international agreements we have discussed. It is earnestly to be hoped that our perception in the matter will not fall on deaf ears, but will be shared by all the powers that be.

---

[89] Cf. K.-H. Böckstiegel, 'Prologue', in Zwaan, op. cit. in n. 71 above, p. 1, at p. 2; I. H. Diederiks-Verschoor, 'Implications of Commercial Activities in Outer Space, especially for the Developing Countries', 17 *JSL* (1989), p. 115; D. E. D. Gaggero, 'Developing Countries and 'Space', 5 *Space Policy* (1989, p. 107; S. Gorove, 'Space Commercialization: Roles of Developing Countries [account of a symposium held in Nashville, Tennessee, on 5–10 Mar. 1989]', 17 *JSL* (1989), p. 66.

EPILOGUE

The Contribution of Air and Space Law to the Development of International Law*

I. Introduction

Although the first aircraft took to the air in 1783,[1] and the first multilateral international treaty relating specifically to aviation, albeit military aviation, was signed in 1899,[2] both international air law and international space law are essentially products of the twentieth century. The latter came into being in fact only in the second half of the twentieth century.[3] Yet these two branches of international law have, in this relative short span of time, probably contributed more to the understanding and development of general international law than any other branch of international law.

II. The Sources of International Law

First, the unprecedented speed at which air law and space law have developed since Kitty Hawk (1903) and Sputnik I (1957) throws very revealing light on the whole question of the sources of international law.[4] In particular, it provides a unique insight into the nature of what has hitherto been traditionally termed customary international law. In the *European Commission of the*

* First published in 39 *CLP* (1986), pp. 181–210. Reproduced by kind permission of Sweet & Maxwell Ltd.

[1] The Montgolfier brothers' hot air balloons. See further B. Cheng, 'The Right to Fly', 42 *Grotius Society Transactions 1956* (1958), p. 99.

[2] Hague Declaration I (1899); this was pre-dated by a year by the first bilteral international agreement, that between Austria-Hungary and Germany of 8 June and 2 Nov. 1898 on the legal status of military balloons flying over the frontier; see E. Riesch, 'Das erste Luftfahrtakbommen der Welt', 10 *Archiv für Luftrecht* (1940), p. 41. There was an even earlier document relating to dispatch-bearers carried over enemy lines by balloons not being treated as spies in Art. 22(3) of the 1874 Draft Brussels Declaration concerning the Laws and Customs of War (A. P. Higgins, *The Hague Peace Conference* (1909), p. 273), but the 1874 Draft Declaration was never ratified. A similar provision is found in the subsequent 1899 Hague Convention II on the Laws and Customs of War on Land, Art. 29, ibid., p. 206, but, in both instances, the reference to aircraft is only incidental.

[3] See B. Cheng, 'Recent Developments in Air Law', 9 *CLP* (1956), p. 208 [Ch. 1 above], and 'International Law and High Altitude Flights: Balloons, Rockets and Man-Made Satellites', 6 *ICLQ* (1957), p. 487 [Ch. 2 above].

[4] D. H. N. Johnson, in his lectures on *Rights in Air Space* (1965), p. 4, said: 'A separate "Space Law" is indeed being elaborated under our very eyes. The process of its elaboration . . . provides a fascinating, up-to-date and practical means of checking the many theories that exist about the "sources of international law"', but did not pursue this topic further, as it was outside the scope of his lectures.

Danube Advisory Opinion before the Permanent Court of International Justice, Judge Negulesco in his Dissenting Opinion went as far as saying:

> . . . an international custom . . . can only be established by a continuous practice from time immemorial and by a reciprocal conviction of the lawfulness of the exercise of the right in question . . .[5]

Whilst probably few would now share Judge Negulesco's extreme view requiring, before a rule of general international law can be said to exist, immemorial usage to evidence it, the conventional view remains that the formation of rules of international customary law is slow, while the making of rules of international law by means of treaties is more direct and expeditious.

A. Treaty Making can be a Slow Process

The experience in international air and space law has shown that this is not necessarily so. In the first place, the negotiation of a multilateral treaty can be an extremely prolonged process. Thus the United Nations Committee on the Peaceful Uses of Outer Space (COPUOS), or more precisely its Legal Sub-Committee spent nine years (1967–71) drafting a 28-article Convention on International Liability for Damage Caused by Space Objects.[6] The 21-article Moon Treaty took the same amount of time (1970–9).[7] But even when agreement has been reached on a treaty and the treaty has been signed, the signatures are usually subject to ratification. The ratifications can often be long delayed, and may not be forthcoming at all. For instance, the United Kingdom signed the 1948 Geneva Convention on the International Recognition of Rights in Aircraft in 1948.[8] Only in 1968, exactly 20 years later, did it adopt the necessary legislation in order to enable the Government to ratify the treaty.[9] But up to now, nearly another 20 years later, the United Kingdom is still not a party to it, and there has been no further sign that it might ratify the Convention in the near future.

In the case of the Geneva Convention, the treaty has actually come into force, albeit without the United Kingdom. But in many cases, the lack of ratifications can hold up the very coming into force of a treaty for a long time. Thus in the early fifties a number of parties to the 1929 Warsaw Convention for the Unification of Certain Rules relating to International Carriage by Air[10] wanted to amend it. Agreement was finally reached at The Hague in

---

[5] (1927) PCIJ: B.14, p. 6, at p. 114.

[6] See B. Cheng, 'Convention on International Liability for Damage Caused by Space Objects', in Jasentuliyana and Lee (eds.), 1 *Manual* (1979), p. 83, at pp. 84–94 [Ch. 11 above, s. III: The Long Haul Towards an Agreement].

[7] See B. Cheng, 'The Moon Treaty', 33 *CLP* (1980), p. 213, at pp. 214–8 [Ch. 12 above, s. II: The Drafting History].

[8] ICAO Doc. 7620.   [9] Civil Aviation Act 1968, ss. 16–18.

[10] UKTS No. 11 (1933), Cmd. 4284.

1955, in the form of the 1955 Hague Protocol to Amend the Warsaw Convention.[11] The principal object of the Hague Protocol was to remedy what was perceived as an injustice in the original Warsaw Convention, an injustice to passengers injured or killed in aviation accidents occurring in the course of international carriage by air. This was because, since the gold clause in the Warsaw Convention was no longer allowed to operate freely according to the true value of gold, but had to follow everywhere its artificial official price, the limits set by the Convention to the passengers' right of recovery became, in the eyes of many, extremely low. The Hague Protocol required 30 ratifications to bring it into effect. Many States were at first unwilling to ratify the Protocol unless the United States were to do so. But the United States was hesitant, because it considered the revised limit still far too low. It did not sign the Protocol until some nine months after the Conference. Eventually it became clear that the United States was not going to ratify the Protocol after all. But even then it took the other States a long time to decide that they would bring the Protocol into force without the United States. It was only in 1963, that is, eight years after the adoption of the Protocol, that the thirtieth ratification which was needed to bring the Protocol into force, was finally received. The United Kingdom further delayed its ratification until 1967,[12] in other words, twelve years after the Hague Conference.

The refusal of the United States to ratify the Hague Protocol and the bringing into force of the Hague Protocol without the United States, together with the subsequent unilateral action of dubious legality taken by the United States in the form of the 1966 Montreal intercarrier Agreement,[13] made the situation of the passenger who suffers injuries in the course of international carriage by air one pregnant with confusion and anomalies which grievously offend one's sense of distributive justice.[14]

At this point, it may be possible between parentheses to mention the contribution of the 1929 Warsaw Convention on International Carriage by Air to the development of the so-called international uniform law, that is, uniform rules of domestic law brought about through international agreement. It is a tribute to the genius of those who drafted the Warsaw Convention that the essential structure of the Convention, drawn up in the infancy of the aviation industry, remains unchanged after over 50 years and unaffected by even the supersonic age. It has probably more contracting parties than any other treaty establishing international uniform law, with over 130 States or territories. Among the few States that have not accepted the Warsaw system, those whose

---

[11] ICAO Doc. 7632.

[12] See Carriage by Air (Convention) Order 1967 (S.I. 1967 No. 478).

[13] See B. Cheng, 'Air Transport Law: National and International', para. 1.5, in National Consumer Council, *Air Transport and the Consumer, a need for change?* (1986), p. 208, at pp. 209–10.

[14] See B. Cheng, 'Compensation for Airline Passenger Death and Injury. The Future of the Warsaw Convention', 71 *J. of the Royal Aeronautical Society* (1967), p. 501.

airlines become involved in a major accident on an international flight soon realize their mistake and join the fold, as did Turkey in 1978, shortly after the tragic loss of a Turkish Airlines aircraft outside Paris. Moreover, the rules it establishes for 'international carriage' have often been extended by the contracting States to 'non-international carriage'. Furthermore, the Warsaw system is still used sometimes as a model for legal regulation of other forms of transport. An example is the 1974 Athens Convention on Carriage of Passengers and their Luggage by Sea. The Warsaw system is thus the example *par excellence* of the benefits of international uniform law: the elimination of problems of conflict of laws and of jurisdictions, and the removal of the inconveniences inherent in the diversity of national laws in areas of the law which carry inevitable foreign elements.[15] It should certainly be borne in mind when the time comes to consider the elaboration of rules to regulate commercial carriage to and in outer space.

But the refusal of the United States to ratify the 1955 Hague Protocol, together with subsequent actions on the part of the United States and others to salvage the resultant situation, caused the pristine uniformity of the original Warsaw system to be fragmented into a number of haphazard variations and permutations that do violence to distributive justice. The several excrescences on the original Warsaw Convention can cause passengers in similar situations who would have been treated alike by the Convention to receive very different treatments for no particular rhyme or reason.[16] The fact that passengers are not really made aware of these discrepancies in their treatment is nothing short of scandalous. Consequently, the 1955 Hague Protocol, instead of having eradicated the injustice it sought to remove, has itself brought in its train additional causes of injustice, and this is largely because of the cumbersome procedure of rule-making by means of treaties.

The upshot is the conclusion of yet another treaty, the 1971 Guatemala City Protocol to amend the Warsaw Convention as Amended at The Hague.[17] The Guatemala City Protocol hopes to reunify the law of international carriage by air by agreeing to a very high limit of liability for passenger injuries which would be acceptable to the United States.

In order to ensure that this revision and reunification will not take place without United States participation, the Guatemala City Protocol not only requires 30 ratifications before it comes into force, but it also stipulates in effect, if not expressly, that among these ratifications there must be that of the United States (Article XX). Subsequently, it appeared that the United States might not ratify this Protocol either. So in the 1975 Montreal Additional Protocol No. 3,[18] to amend the 1971 Guatemala City Protocol the signatories

---

[15] See B. Cheng, 'Fifty Years of the Warsaw Convention: Where Do We Go from Here?', 28 *ZLW* (1975), p. 945. For text of Athens Convention, see 14 *ILM* (1975), p. 945.

[16] See Cheng, loc. cit. in nn. 13, 14, and 15 above.   [17] ICAO Doc. 8932.

[18] ICAO Doc. 9147. See also 22 *ILM* (1983), p. 13.

boldly decided that they would bring the substance of the 1971 Protocol into effect, with or without the United States. To do this, they introduced a novel method of in effect bringing into force a treaty without following the relevant provisions of that treaty. What they did was *inter se* to treat the substantive provisions of that treaty as if they had come into effect (Articles V and VII) and to provide that the amendment Protocol would come into force without the special condition in the original treaty (Article VIII).

The United Kingdom ratified the 1975 Montreal Additional Protocol No. 3 on 5 July 1984, but by the beginning of 1986, there were still only six ratifications to the Guatemala City Protocol as such, and seven to Montreal Additional Protocol No. 3. Consequently, fifteen years after the conclusion of the Guatemala City Protocol, the prospect of rectifying the injustice already perceived then to be in need of correction appears as remote as ever, notwithstanding the fact that the United Kingdom has already ratified the relevant international convention and enacted the necessary domestic legislation[19] to put the Protocol into effect in United Kingdom domestic law, when the Protocol itself comes into force.

Treaty-making can not only be a long drawn out process, but treaties are also, seemingly contrary to a belief which appears to be very prevalent in the United States and perhaps North America generally, not capable, as such, of binding non-parties, no matter how many States may have accepted them. Thus with regard particularly to hijacking of aircraft, the United States tried hard in the late sixties to stem the traffic to Cuba without having to talk directly to the Castro regime. In due course, a conference was convened in December 1970 at The Hague to draw up what emerged as the 1970 Hague Convention for the Suppression of Unlawful Seizure of Aircraft.[20] However, as perhaps was to be expected, Cuba was not at the conference. Nor has Cuba ever signed, ratified, or acceded to the Convention. In the end, no doubt with the help of the Canadian government which signed an Agreement with Cuba on the same date,[21] the United States had to negotiate and eventually sign on 15 February 1973 with the Castro government, through intermediaries, a Memorandum of Understanding on the Hijacking of Aircraft and of Vessels in practically identical terms.[22]

But, before that, Canada and the United States, from 1970 onwards, had tried extremely hard, albeit in vain, to bring about international schemes that would enforce, even against non-contracting States, the rules evolved in the 1963 Tokyo Convention on Offences and Certain other Acts Committed on Board Aircraft,[23] the 1970 Hague Convention on

[19] Carriage by Air and Road Act 1979. [20] ICAO Doc. 8920.
[21] Canadian Department of External Affairs, Canada Communiqué No. 19 (15 Feb. 1973).
[22] 12 *ILM* (1973), p. 370.
[23] ICAO Doc. 8364. Regarding the Tokyo Convention, and the Hague and Montreal Conventions also referred to in the text, see B. Cheng, 'International Legal Instruments to Safeguard International Air Transport: The Conventions of Tokyo, The Hague, Montreal, and a

Hijacking,[24] and the 1971 Montreal Convention on Sabotage,[25] by the majority decision of a group established by the contracting parties to a new sanctions convention.[26] The shelving of these schemes by the International Civil Aviation Organization (ICAO)[27] and the repudiation of any such ideas by the ICAO Extraordinary Assembly and diplomatic conference which met in Rome in 1973[28] are clear vindications of the well-established principle of international law on the law of treaties clearly acknowledged in Article 34 of the 1969 Vienna Convention on the Law of Treaties[29]: 'A treaty does not create either obligations or rights for a third State without its consent.'

The confirmation of this principle by the practice of States is of course no great revelation, but it does highlight the difference between treaties and customary international law as 'sources' of international law. Indeed, it lends strong support to the view that the term rules of international law should be reserved for norms of the international legal order which are applicable to all the subjects of international law, whilst treaty provisions, being norms which are applicable only between the contracting parties, are mere treaty obligations and not 'rules of international law'. Hence, contrary to the pure consensualist position which regards treaties as the principal sources of international law, being based on the express consent of States, treaties are in fact not sources of international law with rules binding on all (*erga omnes*), but only sources of international legal obligations with rules binding on only the contracting parties (*inter partes*).[30] This has sometimes been erroneously taken to imply some diminution in the status of treaty provisions involving some impairment to its binding effect. This is of course not so. It merely clarifies the situation by distinguishing these two categories of norms within the international legal system.

New Instrument Concerning Unlawful Violence at International Airports', in International Institute of Air and Space Law, University of Leyden, and others, *Conference Proceedings: Aviation Security, The Hague, 1987* (1987), pp. 23–46.

[24] Convention for the Suppression of Unlawful Seizure of Aircraft, The Hague (ICAO Doc. 8920). See also B. Cheng, 'The Hague Convention on Hijacking of Aircraft 1970—The Legal Aspects', 76 *Aeronautical J.* (1972), pp. 529–35; in German, 22 *ZLW* (1973), pp. 223–33.

[25] Convention for the Suppression of Unlawful Acts Against the Safety of Civil Aviation, Montreal (ICAO Doc. 8966).

[26] See Canadian–US draft in Appendix D to ICAO Doc. LC/SC CR: Report 27/4/71 and ICAO Doc. 9090–LC/169, Legal Committee 29th (Special) Session, Montreal, Jan. 1973, for further variants of this proposal.

[27] See A. W. G. Kean, B. Cheng, and Sir Frederick Tymms, 'The Latest on Hijacking', 77 *Aeronautical J.* (1973), p. 338.

[28] See ICAO, *International Conference on Air Law, Rome 1973*, Minutes and Documents, ICAO Doc. 9225.

[29] 8 *ILM* (1969), p. 679.

[30] See G. G. Fitzmaurice, 'Some Problems regarding the Formal Sources of International Law', *Symbolae Verzijl* (1958), p. 153, at p. 157; C. Parry, *The Sources and Evidences of International Law* (1965), pp. 28 ff.; D. P. O'Connell, 1 *International Law* (1965), pp. 22 ff.; B. Cheng, 'On the Nature and Sources of International Law', in Cheng (ed.), *International Law*, p. 202, at pp. 229 ff.; Cheng, 'Custom', in R. St. J. Macdonald and D. M. Johnston (eds.), *The Structure and Process of International Law* (1983), p. 513, at pp. 526 ff. N.B.: in the book, pp. 545 and 546 have been transposed, and are wrongly paginated.

What has so far been said does not mean that treaties, especially bilateral treaties, cannot sometimes be concluded very quickly. Many are. However, experience in the field of air and space law shows clearly, on the one hand, that treaties are by no means as simple or as expeditious an instrument for the creation of binding obligations in international law as it is often assumed.

B. Emergence of Rules of General International Law can be Instantaneous

By contrast, it has been demonstrated that what is commonly called 'customary international law' need not necessarily be based on prolonged usage or any usage at all.

Thus whilst there was some initial hesitation in the doctrine of international law at the beginning of the century[31] and on the part of some States,[32] the principle that every State exercises complete and exclusive sovereignty over the airspace above its territory was quickly recognized, especially with the approach of the First World War and the passing of the doctrine of *laissez faire, laissez passer*.[33]

It is significant that by 1919, the Paris Convention on the Regulation of Aerial Navigation,[34] in its Article 1, proclaimed the principle of airspace sovereignty no longer as one accepted contractually among the contracting parties, but as one which they were simply taking note of and reaffirming.

But probably the most dramatic example of the rapid or almost instantaneous creation of a body of rules of general international law is to be found in the development of rules relating to man's exploration and exploitation of outer space. All of a sudden, States had to take position regarding the many novel situation which man's penetration into outer space has transformed from the purely theoretical and speculative to the actual and the practical. Among the problems which had to be faced with various degrees of urgency were the upper limit of national sovereignty, the lawfulness of satellite flights in relation to the sovereign rights of the subjacent States (their mere overflights and the various activities in which they may be engaged, such as photo-reconnaissance, remote sensing, and direct broadcasting), the legal status of outer space and of celestial bodies, the possibility of territorial sovereignty in

---

[31] Cf. P. Fauchille who, in his celebrated draft code on 'Régime juridique des aérostats' submitted to the Institut de Droit International in 1902, suggested in its Art. 7 that '*L'air est libre*', thus launching the doctrine of 'free air'. What was implied was of course that airspace was free.

[32] In 1914, the British Government, in a note to Switzerland, while expressing its regret for a violation of Swiss airspace by British aircraft, added that this 'should not be interpreted as a recognition by His Majesty's Government of the existence of an air sovereignty' (J. Kroell, *Traité de droit international public aérien* (1934), p. 37, n. 4, cited in P. H. Sand, G. N. Pratt, and J. T. Lyon, *An Historical Survey of the Law of Flight* (1961), p. 12). However, at the 1910 Paris Conference on International Aviation, it was the British Government that unequivocally supported the sovereignty principle, whilst the French and the Germans paid lip service to the freedom of the air (D. H. N. Johnson, *Rights in Air Space* (1965), p. 23).

[33] See Cheng, *Law of International Air Transport*, p. 120.					[34] 11 LNTS, p. 173.

outer space or on celestial bodies, the military and peaceful uses of outer space and celestial bodies, jurisdiction over space vehicles and astronauts, and a host of many others.

In a span of less than 30 years since Sputnik I, the responses which States had quickly to find to these novel problems have together by now already built up a substantial corpus of international space law. The ways in which this has been done provide a telling demonstration of how rules of general international law come into existence, in almost laboratory or hot-house conditions.

To take just the example of the legality of mere overflights by artificial satellites, which is almost a sequel to the question of airspace sovereignty 50 years earlier, experience in space law shows that rules of general international law do not come into existence as the result of a tacit agreement—a form of multilateral or even universal *pactum tacitum*.

Thus, when Lord Hailsham, in the name of the United Kingdom government, said in the House of Lords in 1959, 'Her Majesty's Government consider that sovereignty over space above national territory cannot extend indefinitely upwards . . .',[35] this was a unilateral expression of the view of the United Kingdom on the law in question. It was not part of a general tacit agreement. Nor could the United Kingdom at that stage be said to be following any general prolonged usage. It was simply an example of an *opinio individualis juris generalis*, a State's individual opinion or recognition (that can be quoted against it) of what the content is of a given rule of general (international) law. Where there are only isolated instances of such *opinio individualis*, a rule of general international law cannot be said to have come into existence.

General international law is formed when there is a sufficient number of *opiniones individuales juris generalis* among States to constitute together an *opinio generalis juris generalis*—a general *opinio juris* among States as to what is the content of a rule of general international law. Thus a little over two years later, the Canadian delegate to the United Nations Outer Space Committee was already able to say:

Under the concept of outer space now being developed, as long as a spacecraft stays within outer space it is safely proceeding in an area which we might describe as the 'high seas' of the air.[36]

What is required is a general consensus, not a consensus in the sense of a contractual *consensus ad idem*, a meeting of wills creating a tacit agreement, but a number of identical *opiniones individuales juris generalis* running in parallel. This consensus can be established by tracing the individual attitudes of

[35] 216 H.L. Deb. 5s., col. 975.
[36] UN Doc. A/AC.105/PV.4 (21.3.62), p. 26. The statement was not very well put, but what he clearly meant was that all satellites in orbit were beyond national airspace, in other words, in outer space.

States, but there is nothing to prevent it from being expressed through other channels, such as General Assembly resolutions or international treaties, as has been done in a number of instances in the field of space law. What has to be clearly understood is that in such cases, what causes the rules to be legally binding would not be the General Assembly resolutions as such (which except in internal, including budgetary, matters are merely recommendatory) or, *vis-à-vis* third States, the treaties (which are binding only between the parties), but the *opinio generalis juris generalis* of States to the effect that the rules in question are rules of general international law.

The development of space law has clearly shown that the crucial factor in determining whether a rule of general international exists is this *opinio generalis juris generalis* of States. In a horizontal society such as the international society, where States are their own law-givers, no more is required to bring a rule of general international law into existence than this *opinio generalis juris generalis*.

From this point of view, three lessons stand out. First, rules of general international law are developed by States in a deliberate and well-considered manner according to what may be termed—to borrow Judge de Lacharrière's phraseology—the carefully thought out 'external legal policies' of States *vis-à-vis* given situations[37] and not, as some would have it, by States following in a half-dazed fashion some 'initial error' committed by themselves or others.

Secondly, contrary to the view of those who deny the possibility of establishing the *opinio juris* of States in saying either that States can have no mind of their own, or that it is not possible to fathom the mind of a legal person, there is really no difficulty in deducting from either the British or the Canadian statements quoted above what the attitude of the State concerned is. The mistake is to confuse *opinio juris* with the motives of a State. *Opinio juris* in international law is no more and no less than the attitude of a State on a point of international law that may be inferred from its words or actions of such a character that the inference is in law *opposable* to it, i.e., that it may be invoked against it.

Lastly, contrary to the growth of customary law in domestic law where the subjects of the law have no power to make the law, and where it takes time for a general practice accepted as binding first to establish itself and then to receive the force of law from either the legislator or the judge (hence in municipal law *opinio juris* means rather a conviction of being *legally obliged* by essentially a pre-existing rule), international law in the international legal system, where the subjects of the law are themselves the law-givers, coincides simply with what States collectively accept as law at any given moment, whether written or unwritten. The term *opinio juris* is thus used in international law with a slightly different meaning from that in municipal law. Instead of being

---

[37] Guy de Lacharrière, *La politique juridique extérieure* (1983).

essentially passive and retrospective, looking back from the standpoint of a subject of the legal system to what has traditionally been accepted as legally binding, in international law *opinio juris* is the view of the law of a State, in its combined capacities of legislator, judge and subject all rolled into one, which takes into account not only what has been the situation and the law in the past, but also the present and the future needs and interests of the State in accordance with, within the limits of one's power position in the world, one's own 'external legal policies'. In this sense, international law is a truly living law which can shift in content from day to day in order to meet, for example, in the field we are now discussing, the challenge arising from man's venture into new frontiers.

What we have been examining is what Article 38(1)(*b*) of the Statute of the International Court of Justice calls 'international custom', i.e. general international law binding on all the subjects of the international legal order. Whether we call it general international law or international custom is merely a matter of words, but it would be sheer grammatolatry to ignore the true nature of general international law, which forms the basic infrastructure of the international legal system, simply because the Statute has followed the tradition and called it 'custom', and to argue that, therefore, we must look no further than what can be exegetically be derived from the literal and strict meaning of 'custom'. 'The time has surely come', as Judge Jennings said, 'to recognise boldly that it is not custom at all, and never was'.[38] The truth is that there is no reason why rules of general (*alia* 'customary') international law cannot arise instantaneously.[39]

III. The Rôle of the Dominant Section in the Making of Rules of General International Law

One of the main controversial points regarding the formation of rules of general international law is whether what is required is the concurrence of all the subjects of international law, as the consensualists maintain, or only of the views of the generality or majority of States. In this regard too, experience in the air and space law field provides useful insight.

From this point of view, what occurs in multilateral treaty-making is instructive. It will be recalled that earlier we referred to the special position occupied by the United States in the field of carriage by air. We have seen that States were reluctant to ratify the 1955 Hague Protocol without the United

---

[38] R. Y. Jennings, 'The Identification of International Law', in Cheng (ed.): *International Law*, p. 3, at p. 6.
[39] See B. Cheng, 'United Nations Resolutions on Outer Space: "Instant" International Customary Law?', 5 *Indian JIL* (1965), p. 23 [Ch. 7 above], and Cheng, loc. cit. (1982) and (1983) in n. 30 above.

States, and that the participation of the United States became one of the conditions for the coming into force of the 1971 Guatemala City Protocol.[40] Even when this special condition has been deleted, leaving merely the requirement of any 30 States ratifying the 1975 Montreal Additional Protocol No. 3 in order to bring both the 1975 and, in effect if not in law, the 1971 Protocols into force, the number of ratifications in 1986, eleven years after Montreal 1975, had not yet one-third of that required.

Why? It is not because the United States is a superpower, whether in a military or a political sense. It is simply because the United States occupies such a pre-eminent position in the field of international carriage by air, both as consumer and supplier, that the revision of the widely accepted treaty rules on international carriage by air would, without United States participation, lose a great deal of its impact and usefulness. This shows that, irrespective of the field of international activity in question, what one needs in order that such activity be effectively regulated by given rules of the international legal order, is that those accepting these rules must include what the International Court of Justice in the *North Sea Continental Shelf Cases* called, those States 'whose interests are specially affected'.[41]

What is clear is that in the enactment of legal norms within the international legal order, whether those of general international law or those in multilateral treaties, States do not carry equal weight.[42] In this regard, it may be pointed out that ultra-consensualists in international law tend to apply the principle of equality of States not only the position of States before the law, as one should if the Rule of Law were to prevail, but also to their rôle in the making of the law.[43] But even in those systems of municipal law where the principle of the Rule of Law and of equality before the law has been scrupulously observed, universal suffrage has never been regarded as legally an indispensable element. There is no reason why it necessarily be in international law.

This weighting of States in the formation of legal norms in the international legal order is further demonstrated most dramatically in the field of space law. Space law accentuated this phenomenon because at the beginning of space exploration, there were only two States with space capabilities, the Soviet Union and the United States.

Thus, the year after Sputnik I (1957), the General Assembly of the United Nations established an eighteen-member *Ad Hoc* Committee on the Peaceful Uses of Outer Space, which was transformed the year after (1959) into the Committee on the Peaceful Uses of Outer Space (COPUOS) with an enlarged membership of 24 and a mandate of two years. But it was another two years later, in 1961, that COPUOS began work in earnest and produced General Assembly Resolution 1721 (XVI), the first substantive General Assembly

---

[40] See s. II.A above.   [41] *ICJ Rep. 1969*, pp. 3, 42, and 43.
[42] See also Judge Tanaka, ibid., at p. 176.
[43] Cf. G. Tunkin, *Theory of International Law* (1974), p. 128.

resolution on the legal aspects of space exploration. This resolution also continued the existence of COPUOS and further enlarged its membership to 28.

Among the factors which enabled the further-enlarged COPUOS to work were first, as we shall see later, its changed composition and secondly, its decision from the beginning that it and its sub-committees would not use majority votes, but would proceed by consensus.[44] This, in a sense, gave every member a veto. But, as it was stressed by almost all the delegates, the essential point was agreement between the two space powers. The India delegate was merely voicing a general sentiment when he said:

This was a wise decision because no solution which is not acceptable to the two space powers can be implemented.[45]

At one stage in the career of COPUOS, at a time when the United States was still commanding an easy majority in the United Nations and its various committees, the United States hinted that the Committee and its sub-committees should revert to the normal majority rule of United Nations organs. The Soviet delegate, even though what he had in mind was no doubt primarily the positive votes of both super powers and not just the vote of the United States, said with candour and a great deal of truth in the 28-member committee:

twenty-six signatures on this document would have no value; there must be twenty-eight signatures. Even if all of us, including the Soviet Union, the countries of Asia, Africa and Latin America—which are in principle in favour of signing the declaration—sign, if there is no signature of the United States, the whole endeavour would have no result. It is clear that without agreement of the United States it is impossible to resolve such a problem.[46]

The operative part of this statement is the last sentence: 'without agreement of the United States it is impossible to resolve such a problem'. And as it was a question of space law, what was true of the United States was also true of the Soviet Union. But this certainly would not be true of every member of the 28-strong Committee, and still less of every member of the United Nations. In law-making, some States are definitely more equal than others.

In practice, this was clearly shown by the manner in which the various United Nations General Assembly resolutions promoting the development of space law were arrived at.

Especially in the early days of space exploration, the substantive provisions of each and every one of the resolutions were based primarily on direct agreement between the two space powers. Thus in the case of the first of these resolutions, namely Resolution 1721 (XVI) adopted by the General Assembly

[44] Statement of Chairman, A/AC.105/PV.2 (19.3.62), p. 4.
[45] A/AC/105/PV.13 (13.9.62), p. 7; cf. also Poland, A/AC/105/C.2/SR.6 (6.2.62), p. 6; USSR, A/AC/105/PV.15 (14.9.62), p. 29.
[46] A/AC/105/PV.15 (14.9.62), p. 28.

on 20 December 1961, although the draft was nominally submitted by all the members of COPUOS, according to Mr Khrushchev's message of 20 March 1962 to President Kennedy, it really stemmed from an agreement between the two space powers.[47]

As for Resolution 1962 (XVIII) adopted by the General Assembly on 13 December 1963, which contained the Declaration of Legal Principles Governing the Activities of States in the Exploration and Use of Outer Space, the precursor of the 1967 Space Treaty, what happened was that when the fourth session of COPUOS opened on 9 September 1963, it was clear that agreement between the two space powers on the basic legal issues in the exploration and use of outer space was imminent. As a result, the Committee held only four meetings and then adjourned, leaving the two space powers to continue their negotiations, assisted and attended by a few others. It would appear that after agreement had been reached between the two space powers, the original intention was to bring the text from what the French delegate pointedly called the 'secluded places' where it had been negotiated, straight to the First Committee of the General Assembly, thus bypassing COPUOS. It was subsequently decided, however, that the proposal would 'make a stop' in COPUOS in order, it would appear, to collect the signatures of all the other members of the Committee. To this end, the Committee met on 22 November 1963 with the understanding seemingly that no amendment would be entertained. At this meeting, the Indian delegate, presumably one of the select few chosen to attend the behind-the-scene negotiations of the space powers, said: 'Many of the points in dispute between the space powers have been cleared up and an agreed paper is now before us.'[48]

In the event, the proposal was adopted unanimously first by COPUOS, then by the First Committee and finally by the General Assembly itself without a word being changed or a comma disturbed, to become Resolution 1962 (XVIII).

What one finds in this case, therefore, is a resolution which purports to state the 'legal principles governing the activities of States in the exploration and use of outer space' being in essence drafted exclusively by agreement between the, then only two, space powers. The other members of the United Nations and of the world virtually took no part in determining either their content or their formulation. Whilst it is true that at the time, only the two super powers had space capabilities, yet even then many others had the potential of acquiring such capabilities. Moreover, a number of the principles in the resolution

---

[47] In his message, Mr Khrushchev said: 'I regard as a positive fact that at the XVIth session of the United Nations General Assembly, the Soviet Union and the United States found it possible to agree on the proposal about the initial principles of space legislation, which was then unanimously approved by all the Members of the United Nations' (A/AC.105/2). See also Soviet delegate, A/C.1/SR.1214 (11.12.61), p. 268 (para. 12).

[48] A/AC/105/PV.24, p. 21; repeated in substance in Committee I, A/C.1/SR.1343 (3.12.63), p. 168.

were applicable to all States, including those which had no space pretensions whatsoever, such as the principle governing liability for damage caused by objects launched into space. Furthermore, even before the resolution was adopted, the view had already been expressed by some that '[t]he legal principles contained in [the draft resolution] reflected international law as it was currently accepted by Member States.'[49] If so, this means that rules of general international law intended for general application were being drawn up by agreement exclusively by two States.

It may be said in this case that what was agreed upon by these two States was nevertheless adopted unanimously by the General Assembly of the United Nations with the result that, whatever may be the effect of General Assembly resolutions in general and this resolution in particular, this resolution did receive the approbation of all the members of the United Nations. And, probably for this reason, there were States which attached great importance to the fact that this was a resolution that had been adopted unanimously.[50]

In the first place, however, this does not take into account the fact that United Nations membership is still not universal. Switzerland remains a notable exception, upon which a rule of general international law would no doubt be regarded as binding, but to which a General Assembly resolution, whether unanimously adopted or not, would simply be *res inter alios acta* without any legal effect on her whatsoever. Secondly, to reason in this way is to ignore the reality of the situation. Thus one has only to look at the next substantive General Assembly resolution on outer space, namely Resolution 2222 (XXI) adopted on 19 December 1966.[51]

This was the resolution which 'commended' the text of the treaty on outer space drawn up by COPUOS to 'all States' for their signature, ratification and accession. The treaty was based substantially on the Declaration in Resolution 1962 (XVIII). Although this time, there was some more discussion in COPUOS on the text of the draft treaty, which became in due course the 1967 Space Treaty, the crucial issue at all times was whether the provisions were acceptable to the Soviet Union and the United States, and much of the negotiation took place directly between them. Once they were able to reach agreement, then the rest became largely a formality. Agreement was announced on 8 December, 1966. A 43-power draft resolution incorporating the agreed text was submitted on 15 December 1966. It came before the first Committee on 17 December, and the Plenary of the General Assembly on 19 December 1966. One can but sympathize with the Tanzanian delegate to the

---

[49] E.g., Canada, A/C.1/SR/1346 (5.12.63), p. 189.

[50] E.g., USA, A/AC.105/C.2/SR.20 (22.4.63), pp. 10–11; see, however, the last four paragraphs of this section.

[51] See B. Cheng, 'Le Traité de 1967 sur l'espace/The 1967 Space Treaty', 95 *JDI* (1968) [Ch. 9 above]. The texts of the various treaties relating to outer space concluded through the United Nations are reproduced in the Appendix below.

General Assembly when he sounded, as he said he wanted to do, a 'note of discord', in complaining that the General Assembly had been given too little time to consider the draft treaty. 'It is probable,' said he, 'that the completed draft . . . has not yet been seen by many of the Foreign Offices of the delegations represented here.'[52] In this case, he did not wish to stand in the way of the General Assembly which then proceeded to adopt the resolution unanimously. Yet, with due respect to the States concerned, would it have mattered very much had Tanzania and some of the States whose Foreign Offices had not yet had a chance of seeing a complete text of the draft treaty or resolution abstained or even voted against the resolution?

Not really, as long as there was a two-thirds majority for the resolution to be adopted. What was legally relevant in this instance was not the size of the vote. What was to become legally binding was the treaty and not the resolution, and what would make the treaty legally binding were the requisite signatures and ratifications. The treaty requires only five ratifications in order to come into force, but these must include the ratifications by the three depositary governments, namely, the Soviet Union, the United Kingdom, and the United States.[53]

Whilst in principle the treaty will be binding only on those States that are parties to it, there are nevertheless provisions in the treaty which purport to be legal rules of a general nature applicable *erga omnes*, or what the International Court of Justice in the *North Sea Continental Shelf Cases* called of 'a fundamentally norm-creating character such as could be regarded as forming the basis of a general rule of law.'[54] A typical example is Article II which provides:

Outer space, including the moon and other celestial bodies, is not subject to national appropriation by claim of sovereignty, by means of use or occupation, or by any other means.

There is much evidence to indicate that many States, parties to the Treaty, believe Article II to be declaratory of general international law. The question then is how does such a provision in a treaty transform itself into a rule of general international law with binding effect even on non-parties. That this is legally feasible is clearly acknowledged in Article 38 of the 1969 Vienna Convention on the Law of Treaties which provides:

Nothing in Articles 34 to 37 precludes a rule set forth in a treaty from becoming binding upon a third State as a customary rule of international law, recognised as such.

What is required for this to happen is that there must be a sufficient number of States which believe Article II to be not merely a treaty provision, but also a rule of general international law (in order words, there must be a

---

[52] UN Doc. A/PV.1499 (Prov.) (19.12.66), p. 66.   [53] Art. XIV(3).
[54] *ICJ Rep. 1969*, p. 3, at p. 42. This is not necessarily to agree with the Court's terminology. Even purely contractual provisions create norms, albeit only *inter partes*.

substitution towards it on the part of States of what would otherwise be merely an *opinio obligationis conventionalis*—acceptance of the binding character of a rule as a matter of treaty obligation—by an *opinio juris generalis*—acceptance of the binding character of a rule as a matter of general [international] law). In addition, there must be included among them enough States which have the intention, the ability and the will to uphold Article II as a rule of general international law. What we need, therefore, are not only States which are willing themselves to observe Article II, but also States which will be willing and able effectively to challenge any breach thereof by others. In other words, rules of general international law are made and sustained by the will of the dominant section of international society in each individual case.

In this connection, it is interesting to contrast Article II of the 1967 Space Treaty which prohibits any national appropriation of outer space, including the moon and other celestial bodies, thus giving outer space the status of *res extra commercium* in international law, with the more ambitious attempt in the 1979 Moon Treaty to declare the moon and other celestial bodies within the solar system other than the earth, as well as their resources, 'the common heritage of mankind'.[55] Now, both the Space Treaty and the Moon Treaty were drafted, at least nominally, by COPUOS. Both went through the same procedure for adoption by the General Assembly, and each was adopted by the General Assembly by consensus without a vote. Both require only five ratifications to come into force. The only apparent difference, from the procedural point of view, is that the Moon Treaty, unlike the Space Treaty, does not require the ratification by any specified State. Both treaties are now in force. The Moon Treaty actually came into force on 11 July 1984, then having been ratified by Austria, Chile, the Netherlands, the Philippines, and Uruguay.

However, without any disrespect to any of these five countries, if it is claimed that since the Moon Treaty is now in force, the moon and other celestial bodies in the solar system other than the earth have thereby, as a matter of general international law valid and binding *erga omnes*, been transformed into the common heritage of mankind, such a claim will hardly be credible.

In contrast, disregarding what effect General Assembly Resolution 1721 (XVI) may or may not have in the matter, the moment the Space Treaty came into force on 10 October 1976, when the three depositary States ratified it simultaneously, if it was claimed there and then that Article II of the Space Treaty placing outer space and celestial bodies beyond national appropriation had become also a rule of general international law, such an assertion would in all probability have been valid. But it is quite evident that this effect could have sprung from the mere fact that when the Space Treaty came into force, there were seventeen parties to it instead of there being only five to the Moon

---

[55] See loc. cit. in n. 7 above [Ch. 12 above].

Treaty; for, to borrow what the Soviet delegate said in a slightly different context,[56] in the case of a rule of this nature, its acceptance by the United States and the Soviet Union is of crucial importance. And yet this would certainly not be true of just any or every member of international society.

All this points to the conclusion that in the making of rules of international law, the weight of States certainly is not equal. Unanimity is not required. What is needed is that the preponderant weight of States should be behind a given norm before it can be pronounced a rule of general international law. How the weight of different States is to be calculated varies with the subject matter and probably from case to case, if it can be calculated with precision at all; but the important point if we are to understand the process of international law-making is openly to recognize that this difference does exist and may legitimately be taken into account, instead of treating it as heretical or taboo, because it seemingly flies in the face of the principle of sovereign equality.

IV. Conditions Governing International Rule-Making

In both air law and space law, a good number of treaties have been concluded establishing rules binding on the contracting parties, some of which, as we have seen, have developed into rules of general international law. An examination of history of these treaties provides interesting insight into the conditions governing the development of these rules, especially treaty rules, on a multilateral basis. In sum, three factors emerge as of prime importance, namely:

(i)   there must be a felt need for the new rules;
(ii)   there has to be a propitious political climate;
(iii) following especially what we have been saying just now, there has to be due representation of the interests involved.

A. Perceived Need

First, a felt need. A telling example is the conclusion of the 1967 Space Treaty. The Soviet Union proposed in 1962 that there should be a treaty on space law.[57] The United States at first agreed only to have a General Assembly resolution. This resulted eventually in General Assembly resolution 1962 (XVIII) of 1963 setting out legal principles governing the activities of States in the exploration and use of outer space. The same resolution requested COPUOS to give consideration to 'incorporating in international agreement

---

[56] See n. 46 before.
[57] Mr Khrushchev's letter of 20 Mar. 1962 to President Kennedy; see n. 47 above.

form, in the future as appropriate', those legal principles. Negotiations towards a treaty went on desultorily for several years. As late as October 1965, the United States was still against a general treaty on space.[58]

Yet less than a year later, in September 1966, the United States considered that the need for such a treaty was 'all the more urgent because of man's recent strides towards landing on the moon'.[59] The most notable 'stride' early in 1966 was the first ever 'soft' landing on the moon achieved on 3 February by the Soviet Union with its automatic station Luna IX. Success came after three failures in 1965. The Soviet Union scored another first on 31 March, with the launching of Luna X, which became the moon's first artificial satellite. The United States followed on 2 June 1966 with Surveyor I, which transmitted back to earth over 10,000 photographs of the surface of the moon, and Lunar Orbiter I launched on 10 August. The Soviet Union launched Luna XI, another lunar satellite, on 24 August. The various lunar satellites were designed specifically to select suitable landing sites on the moon. Meanwhile, on 16 March, the United States also achieved a first when astronauts Neil Armstrong and David Scott successfully 'docked' their Gemini VIII space-craft with an Agena target vehicle. The Gemini Project was directly connected with manned flight into space. Rendezvous techniques, docking, and activities outside the space vehicle were further tested with the successful launching of Gemini IX on 3 June, Gemini X on 18 July, and Gemini XI on 12 September. By then it was clear that no further technological barrier stood between man and the moon, and it was anyone's guess whether it was the Soviet Union or the United States that would be the first to send a man to the moon.

In the circumstances, it became vitally important for the two space powers to reach an agreement on the legal principles involved in advance of man's landing on the moon.[60] President Johnson announced on 7 May 1966 that the United States would seek a treaty through the United Nations to prevent any nation from claiming sovereignty over the moon or any other celestial bodies and that the exploration thereof would be for peaceful purposes only. This announcement was transmitted to the United Nations on 9 May.[61] Consultation with the Soviet Union began on 11 May, and on 30 May the Soviet Union requested that the matter be included in the agenda of the forth-coming session of the General Assembly. The preliminary negotiations took place in COPUOS, but the controversial issues were dealt with by direct nego-tiations between the two space powers, agreement between whom was announced on 8 December 1966. A 43-power draft resolution 'commending' the treaty to States was submitted to the First Committee on 15 December,

---

[58] UN Doc. A/AC.105/PV.37–42 (5.10. 65), p. 32.
[59] UN Doc. A/PV.1412(Prov.) (22.9.66), p. 41.
[60] Cf. USA, UN Doc. A/AC.105/PV.37-42 (5.10.65), p. 32; A/AC.105/C.2/SR.72 (12.9.66), p. 3; A/AC.105/PV.44 (19.9.66), p. 20; A/PV.1412 (Prov.) (22.9.66), p. 41.
[61] UN Doc. A/6327.

and it reached the General Assembly on 19 December. The General Assembly adopted it on the same date. The Treaty entered into force less than a year after on 10 October 1967.[62] Where there's a will, there's a way.

That very year saw agreement reached on what became known as the 1968 Agreement on the Rescue of Astronauts, the Return of Astronauts and the Return of Objects Launched into Outer Space. That was also the year in which the first casualties in space exploration occurred. On 27 January, three United States astronauts died when fire broke out on board Apollo I before take-off. On 24 April, Colonel V. Kamorov of the Soviet Union perished in Soyuz I on landing. They were powerful reminders that accidents could occur. The result was that the Astronauts Agreement was reached in record time.[63]

Other examples of States acting quickly in response to perceived needs are the 1970 Hague Convention on aircraft hijacking, officially known as the Convention for the Suppression of Unlawful Seizure of Aircraft,[64] and the 1971 Montreal Convention on sabotage of aircraft, officially known as the Convention for the Suppression of Unlawful Acts Against the Safety of Civil Aviation.[65] The former was in response to the rising tide of aircraft hijacking, the number of which rose from six in 1967, to 58 in 1968, and 82 in 1969. The latter was designed to combat the increasing wave of aerial sabotage, including, in 1970, the blowing up of a Swissair aircraft in mid-air, shortly after take-off from Zurich.[66]

However, such needs must also be perceived by the dominant section. Thus notwithstanding the fact that non-space powers had clamoured almost from the start for a treaty to determine liability for damage caused by objects launched into space and to establish the procedure for recovery, that the United States was in favour of such a treaty from the beginning, and the general Assembly urged COPUOS practically every year to intensify its efforts to reach an agreement and vainly set deadlines time and again, the Soviet Union, which maintained that such a treaty was superfluous, was never in a hurry to come to an agreement. In the end, it took COPUOS nine years from 1962 to 1971 to produce what later became the 1972 Convention on International Liability for Damage Caused by Space Objects.[67]

A further illustration of this point is the question of delimiting the frontier between national airspace and outer space, between the zone where States exercise complete and exclusive territorial sovereignty and the zone where the exercise of such sovereignty by States is proscribed. From every point of view, an early settlement of this question in order to avoid future conflicts would seem called for. Yet, no doubt for the purpose of keeping all its options open,

---

[62] See loc. cit. in n. 51 above [Ch. 9 above].

[63] See further B. Cheng, 'The 1968 Astronauts Agreement', 23 *YBWA* (1969), p. 185 [Ch. 10 above].

[64] See n. 24 above.   [65] See n. 25 above.

[66] See B. Cheng, 'Hijacking and Sabotage', 25 *New Society* (1973), p. 270.

[67] See loc. cit. in n. 6 above [Ch. 11 above].

the United States is opposed even to discussing this problem, let alone resolving it, maintaining that there is no present need to do so.[68]

B. *Propitious Climate*

The second condition for successful international rule-making, even in a technical field, is that there must be a propitious political climate. This has been seen time and again in the field of air and space law, in both a negative and a positive manner. Thus one of the first major proposals regarding the future development of space law came from President Eisenhower in his address to the United Nations General Assembly on 22 September 1960,[69] but coming in the wake of the U–2 (1 May 1960) and RB–47 (1 July 1960) incidents[70] and the collapse of the Paris Summit meeting, it could be taken up only after the change in Administration in the United States.

It was this change in Administration in the United States and a change in the political climate which allowed agreement to be reached between the Soviet Union and the United States, thus enabling General Assembly Resolution 1721 (XVI) to be adopted on 20 December 1961, setting out, in the words of Mr Khrushchev in his message of 20 March 1962 to President Kennedy, 'the initial principles of space legislation'.[71]

The next major step was of course the adoption by the General Assembly on 13 December 1963 of resolution 1962 (XVIII) containing the Declaration of Legal Principles Governing the Activities of States in the Exploration and Use of Outer Space,[72] but this was possible only because agreement had, earlier on in that year, been reached on the Moscow partial Test Ban Treaty (5 August 1963).

The 1967 Space Treaty and the 1968 Astronauts Agreement were treaties, at the time of their conclusion, urgently wanted by both space powers.[73] But in the case of the 1972 Convention on Liability for Damage Caused by Space Objects, discussions on which had been bogged down for years, and agreement on which was finally reached only in 1971, it was openly acknowledged by both the United States and the Soviet Union that this had been made possible by the favourable political condition that had recently emerged, particularly regarding co-operation in space matters between the two space powers. More specifically, as the United States delegate pointed out, on 'January 21,

---

[68] See B. Cheng, 'The Legal Régime of Airspace and Outer Space: The Boundary Problem—Functionalism *versus* Spatialism: The Major Premises', 5 *AASL* (1980), p. 323 [Ch. 14 above]; and 'The Legal Status of Outer Space and Relevant Issues: Delimitation of Outer Space and Definition of Peaceful Uses', 11 *JSL* (1983), p. 89.

[69] See B. Cheng, 'The United Nations and Outer Space', 14 *CLP* (1961), p. 247, at p. 277 [Ch. 6 above, s. VI: Demilitarization and Disarmament, *in fine*].

[70] See ibid., at pp. 262–72 [Ch. 6 above, s. V: Reconnaissance and Surveillance].

[71] See n. 47 above.   [72] See text after n. 47 above.

[73] See s. IV.A above: Perceived Need.

1971, following intensive discussions, a delegation of the United States National Aeronautics and Space Administration and a Soviet delegation had initialled a document providing *inter alia*, for the development of compatible space rendezvous and docking techniques, the exchange of lunar soil samples, . . .'[74]

Similarly, the efforts to draw up the Moon Treaty which languished in COPUOS for some seven years, suddenly blossomed and fructified all within the span of fifteen days.[75] Perhaps it was no coincidence that agreement was reached precisely fifteen days after the signature of the second Strategic Arms Limitation Treaty (SALT-II) between the Soviet Union and the United States (18 June 1979).[76]

In general, therefore, a propitious climate is required in addition to all the other factors.

C. Due Representation of the Dominant Section

Finally, in the light of what we have said regarding the rôle of the dominant section of international society in the making of legal rules in the international legal order, it will hardly be surprising to find that, in order to achieve results, there must be due representation of the dominant section in the process of elaborating such rules. This is amply demonstrated by the successful exercise of quasi-legislative powers by the Council of the International Civil Aviation Organization (ICAO). The Council is an elective organ of 33 in an organization with a membership of nearly 160. On the Council, two-thirds of the members represent States of chief importance in international civil aviation or making the largest contribution in providing facilities for international air navigation.[77] The Council formulates by a majority vote rules, regulations and procedures for international aviation principally in the form of Annexes to the Chicago Convention, which are revised from time to time as need arises, and of which there are now eighteen. Member States are under a duty to notify the Council of any differences between their own practice and the international standards set out in these Annexes. In this way, international civil aviation benefits from a unified body of rules and regulations, which are often observed even by non-members.[78] The success of the ICAO from this point of view, it is submitted, springs no doubt largely from the fact that the dominant section in international civil aviation is allowed to play the leading rôle in the discharge of the Organization's quasi-legislative function.

[74] See Cheng, loc. cit. in n. 6 above, at pp. 91–3 [Ch. 11 above, s. III.F.5: The Political Factor]. For text of USA-USSR Agreement on Co-operation in Exploration and Use of Outer Space, 21 Jan. 1971, see 10 *ILM* (1971), p. 617.

[75] See Cheng, loc. cit. in n. 7 above, at pp. 216–8 [Ch. 12 above, s. II.E: The Mystery and Miracle of Birth].

[76] 18 *ILM* (1979), p. 1112.   [77] See Cheng, loc. cit. in n. 33 above, pp. 45 ff.

[78] See further ibid., pp. 63 ff.; also T. B. Buergenthal, *Law-Making in ICAO* (1969); C. S. Rhyne, A. R. Mutuc, and R. J. H. Sands, *Law-Making Activities of ICAO* (1976).

The need for due representation is probably more dramatically illustrated by the history of COPUOS which has done much in the development of space law.

COPUOS started life as the *Ad Hoc* Committee on the Peaceful Uses of Outer Space, an eighteen-member committee established by the General Assembly on 13 December 1958. The Soviet Union had originally proposed to the United States that space matters should be discussed directly between them. Alternatively, if the subject was to be studied by the United Nations, it put forward the *troika* principle that there should be a committee of eleven consisting of four Western powers, four Soviet-bloc countries and three 'neutrals', thus, in the proportion of 4:4:3. However, bearing in mind that the United States had then an easy majority in the United Nations and that admission to the United Nations was then strictly controlled, of which the two International Court of Justice Advisory Opinions on admission to the United Nations[79] were merely the symptoms, it was perhaps to be expected that, in the eighteen-member *Ad Hoc* Committee that was actually established, the proportion of Western-bloc nations, Soviet-bloc nations, and neutrals was 13:4:2. Mr Cabot Lodge, the United States delegate to the United Nations, during the discussions leading to the formation of the *Ad Hoc* Committee, in resisting the Soviet move, said:

There are no 'two sides' to outer space. There are not—and never have been—'two sides' in the United Nations . . . We do not . . . accept the idea of 'two sides'—and, frankly, we don't understand it.[80]

The perhaps not very surprising result was that the three Soviet-bloc members boycotted the *Ad Hoc* Committee. Nor did the two neutral members attend its meetings. Needless to say, the *Ad Hoc* Committee achieved nothing. The following year, 1959, the General Assembly established COPUOS with an enlarged membership of 24, divided in the proportion this time of 12:7:5. It may be of interest in passing to observe that shortly before the meeting of the General Assembly in 1959, the Conference of Foreign Ministers recommended the formation of a ten-nation Committee on Disarmament to replace the previously five-power sub-committee. Whereas the latter was composed of the Soviet Union in the midst of four Western powers Canada, France, the United Kingdom, and the United States (i.e., 4:1), the ten-nation Disarmament Committee of five NATO powers and five Warsaw-Pact powers (i.e., 5:5). Space had definitely introduced a new dimension to the world's balance of power.

---

[79] ICJ: *Admission of a State to the United Nations* (1948) Adv. Op., *ICJ Rep. 1947–8*, p. 57; *Competence of Assembly Regarding Admission to the United Nations* (1950) Adv. Op., *ICJ Rep. 1950*, p. 4.

[80] 24.11.58, USIS (London), Off. Text (25.11.58), p. 2; the account in UN Doc. GA (XIII), A/C.1/SR.994, p. 235, is slightly abridged.

The Soviet Union remained dissatisfied with the composition of the new 12:7:5 COPUOS, and, moreover, wanted the unanimity rule, instead of the usual United Nations majority rule, to be applied in COPUOS, which would of course ensure that every member would in fact have the power of veto. COPUOS transacted no substantive business for nearly two years until a direct agreement between the Soviet Union and the United States led to the unanimous proposal from COPUOS that later became Resolution 1721 (XVI). This resolution *inter alia* awarded four additional seats on COPUOS to the Soviet bloc, thus enlarging COPUOS membership to 28 in the proportion of 12:11:5.[81]

No doubt as part of the same package deal between the United States and the Soviet Union, it was announced at the opening session of the now 28-member COPUOS that the Committee and its sub-committees would in future operate by consensus without vote,[82] thus in effect conceding the Soviet Union's second demand for unanimity. It was only then that COPUOS really began to function,[83] thus demonstrating that for the purpose of successfully developing new legal rules, there must be due representation of the dominant section in the field in question. As in the case of the United States in the matter of international carriage by air,[84] the test is not one of simple military, political or economic powers, but a functional one in relation to the subject-matter.

Due representation can present many facets. COPUOS membership has since been successively increased to 37 in 1973, 47 in 1977, and 53 in 1980. This continuing widening of the membership of COPUOS may or may not have exceeded the optimum. But one thing is certain: to the extent to which the dominant section of international society in this field becomes under-represented in the decision-making process, the end result may well be counter-productive. In many ways, this is illustrated by General Assembly resolution 37/92 on Principles Governing the Use by States of Artificial Earth Satellites for International Direct Television Broadcasting, which was adopted on 10 December 1982.[85]

In this case, the General Assembly adopted by majority vote the Principles, on which consensus had not been reached within COPUOS. The vote was 107 for and 13 against, with 13 abstentions. The majority consisted essentially of States within the Soviet bloc, and those from the Group of 77. Most of the Western industrialized nations either voted against or abstained. These include the United States, Canada, all the European Communities countries, Japan, and other countries which either already have or are about to have

---

[81] See text to n. 47 above.   [82] See n. 44 above.

[83] On the United Nations and outer space, see further Cheng, loc. cit. in nn. 39 and 69 above [Part II above].

[84] See paras. 2 ff. of s. II.A, and paras. 2–3 of s. III above.

[85] UN Doc. A/RES/37/92 (4.2.83); 22 *ILM* (1983), p. 451.

direct broadcasting satellite services.[86] General Assembly resolutions in themselves have no legally binding force. They may, depending upon the intention of the States concerned, and the way in the States have expressed their intention, be used differently to evince an *opinio juris de lege lata*, an *opinio juris de lege ferenda*, a voluntary code of conduct, a *voeu*, or mere wishful thinking. Their impact either as a guide to probable behaviour or a source for the future development of the law depends consequently in great measure on both the degree and intensity of the support they receive from the relevant dominant section in the real world outside the United Nations. The usefulness of resolutions which are rammed down the throat of the dominant section of international society by a purely numerical majority in the United Nations, whether from East or West, North or South, is more than dubious.[87]

This is perhaps one of the major problems in international rule-making today: the distortion of the real weight of States in the making of such rules by the precept of 'one State, one vote' which is based on a misrepresentation of the principle of equality of States,[88] or an unwarranted anthropomorphization of the State and the fallacious transposition to it of the principle of 'one person, one vote', which incidentally, on account of the vastly divergent population sizes of States, is itself a repudiation of the latter principle. It is hoped that this survey of the process in the making of air and space law has shown that successful rule-making in international law depends upon due representation being given to the relevant weight of States in any given subject-matter. Ultimately, it is a political issue, but if the validity of this proposition can be recognized, and recognized as being compatible with the principle of the sovereign equality of States in international law, one would already be half way towards a more rational and realistic approach to international law making in general.

V. *Varia*

Space does not permit a review of each and every individual contribution of air and space law to the development of international law. In addition to what we have examined, it is hoped that we shall have just enough room simply to mention a few more.

In the first place, from a general point of view, attention may be drawn to the sheer volume of rules of international law, including a vast conventional

---

[86] See 22 *ILM* (1983), p. 451, n. *.

[87] In 'Nature and Sources of International Law' (loc. cit. in n. 30 above), I mentioned: 'The present low value of General Assembly resolutions is due probably in no small measure to the fact that, at a rough count, a two-thirds majority for adopting a resolution can be mustered by Member States representing *in toto* little more than 10 per cent of the world population, 4 per cent of the world's gross national product, and 3.5 per cent of the United Nations budget contributions' (p. 227).

[88] See text to nn. 42 ff. above.

and institutional superstructure, which have developed in both fields. Mention has already been made of the successful system of international uniform law represented by the Warsaw system of rules on international carriage by air,[89] and the quasi-legislative rôle of ICAO in the standardization of rules, regulations, and procedures in international civil aviation.[90]

From the standpoint of international legal personality, the recognition which has been given to that of international organizations in the various space treaties, despite initial Soviet opposition, has been a notable achievement.[91]

As regards the domain of international law, space law has added a whole new dimension to the geographical scope of international law by extending it to the entire universe.[92] The 1979 Moon Treaty also has the distinction of being the first multilateral treaty to recognize the concept of the common heritage of mankind, by applying it to the moon and other celestial bodies within the solar system other than the earth.[93]

In the field of State jurisdiction, both air law and space law have done much to clarify the notion of the different types and the different elements of State jurisdiction.[94] The 1963 Tokyo Convention on Offences and Certain Other Acts Committed on Board Aircraft is designed to remove gaps in the exercise of State jurisdiction in respect of aircraft, especially when they are flying over areas not subject to the jurisdiction of any State, such as the high seas.[95] For its part, the 1970 Hague Convention for the Suppression of Unlawful Seizure of Aircraft has created a model for the implementation of the principle *aut dedere, aut punire* in relation to individuals guilty of offences universally condemned.[96] It is a model that has been followed by many other conventions.[97]

In treaty law, perhaps the most notable innovation is the possibility permitted in a number of space treaties for international organizations to acquire a status very similar to that of being States parties to them—not just being parties, but parties as if they were States. This was first introduced in the 1968

---

[89] See text after n. 14 above.   [90] See s. IV.C above, *in principio*.

[91] See n. 98 below, and text thereto.

[92] See B. Cheng, 'The Extraterrestrial Application of International Law', 18 *CLP* (1965), p. 132 [Ch. 5 above].

[93] See Cheng, loc. cit. in n. 7 above [Ch. 12 above].

[94] See B. Cheng, 'Crimes On Board Aircraft', 12 *CLP* (1959), p. 177; and loc. cit. in n. 92 above [Ch. 5 above].

[95] See n. 23 above.

[96] See n. 24 above; and further B. Cheng, 'Aviation, Criminal Jurisdiction and Terrorism: The Hague Extradition/Prosecution Formula and Attacks at Airports', in B. Cheng and E. D. Brown (eds.), *Contemporary Problems of International Law: Essays in honour of Georg Schwarzenberger on his eightieth birthday* (1988), p. 25.

[97] See, e.g., Convention on the Prevention and Punishment of Crimes against Internationally Protected Persons, including Diplomatic Agents, New York, 1973, 13 *ILM* (1974), p. 41; European Convention on the Suppression of Terrorism, Strasbourg, 1976, 15 *ILM* (1976), p. 1272; International Convention Against the Taking of Hostages, New York, 1979, 18 *ILM* (1979), p. 1456.

Astronauts Agreement, and represented a major concession on the part of the Soviet Union to the views of those countries which have been described as near-space powers and co-operative space powers, and whose hope of being able to into space lies mainly in doing so through international organizations.[98]

In the field of State responsibility, mention should be made of the highly novel principle introduced by Article VI of the 1967 Space Treaty. This provision makes every contracting State directly responsible, as the article says, 'for national activities in outer space . . . whether such activities are carried on by governmental agencies or by non-governmental entities'.[99] Under Article VII of the 1967 Space Treaty and under the 1972 Liability Convention, the contracting States are also made directly and absolutely liable for any damage which may be caused by objects launched into space not only by themselves, on behalf of themselves, or from their own facilities, but also by anyone launching such objects from within their territory.[100] In order to ensure the observance of rules of international law, which now increasingly seek to regulate the activities of individuals, there is a great deal of scope for the application of this concept elsewhere. In this connection, there is an interesting and, in some ways, corresponding development in the field of international carriage by air, where the concept of absolute liability is increasingly gaining favour.[101]

Finally, in the law of international institutions, mention has already been made to the successful rule-making rôle of ICAO and COPUOS.[102] On the judicial level, at a time when invocation of equity for the solution of international differences is in vogue, attention may be drawn to the complaints procedure before the ICAO Council, provided for by the multilateral International Air Services Transit Agreement (Article II, section 1) and the International Air Transport Agreement (Article IV, section 2), both of 1944.

---

[98] Art. 6 (see Cheng, loc. cit. in n. 63 above, at p. 202 [Ch. 10 above, s. VII.A: Definition of Launching Authority]); cf. also Art. XIII of the 1967 Space Treaty (see Cheng, loc. cit. in n. 51 above, at pp. 588–98 [Ch. 9 above, s. V.G.: International Organizations]), Art. XXII of the 1972 Liability Convention (see Cheng, loc. cit. in n. 6 above, at pp. 103–12 [Ch. 11 above, s. V.A.6: International Organizations]), Art. VII of the 1975 Registration Convention (see B. Cheng, 'Outer Space: The International Legal Framework—The International Legal Status of Outer Space, Space Objects and Spacemen', 10 *Thesaurus Acroasium* (1981), p. 41, at pp. 100–1 [Ch. 13 above, s. IV.C.3: Institutional Register]), and Art. 16 of the 1979 Moon Treaty (see Cheng, loc. cit. in n. 7 above, at p. 219 [Ch. 12 above, s. III.B: Personal Scope]).

[99] See Cheng, loc. cit. in n. 51 above, at pp. 582–8 [Ch. 9 above, s. V.F: International Responsibility].

[100] See ibid., and Cheng, loc. cit. in n. 6 above, at pp. 102–3 [Ch. 11 above, s. V.A.5: The Party Liable].

[101] See nn. 13, 14, and 15 above; B. Cheng, 'A Reply to Charges of Having *Inter Alia* Misused the Term Absolute Liability' 6 *AASL* (1981), p. 3.

[102] See s. IV.C above, para. 1; n. 51 above, and text following it. See also ch. 8 above: The UN and the Development of International Space Law.

In such cases, the ICAO Council is given an equity jurisdiction, which is backed by sanctions.[103]

From a somewhat different angle, reference may be made to the highly original International Telecommunications Satellite Organization (INTELSAT),[104] and the International Maritime Satellite Organization (INMARSAT),[105] which have created international organizations that successfully engage in commercial and public services of a highly technical nature. They may well serve as models for other international enterprises.

VI. Closing Remarks

Within the course of a century, air law and space law have pushed the geographical boundaries of international law first from the surface of the earth to the skies, and then from the skies to the whole of the universe. They have quickly built upon the infrastructure of the general law, which automatically extends to these new frontiers, impressive superstructures of new rules, regulations, procedures and international organizations. They have done so largely because they had to break entirely new grounds, and, perhaps more than any other branch of international law, they have constantly to meet new challenges in the form of either advances in science and technology or ever changing social and economic needs.

In our survey of their contribution to the development of international law as a whole, we have perforce, because of the sheer size of the subject, been able to do so, in part, no more than to list some areas of significance. It is to be hoped, however, that enough has been said to give at least some indication of the substantial contribution which these two new subjects have been able to bring, by their many innovations and by the new insight which they provide, to practically every sphere of the international legal system. It is particularly to be hoped that even the brief exploration of the formative process in these two branches of the law such as that which has just been made is able to show that its further study can greatly help us in achieving a better understanding of the roots and workings of international law as a whole, which may in turn enable us to bring about a more realistic and effective international legal order.

---

[103] See Cheng, op. cit. in n. 33 above, at p. 455; and 'Dispute Settlement in Bilateral Air Transport Agreements', in K.-H. Böckstiegel (ed.), *Dispute Settlement of Space Law Disputes* (1970), p. 97, at pp. 110–11.

[104] See B. Cheng, 'Communications Satellites', 24 *CLP* (1971),m p. 211 [Ch. 21 above].

[105] See N. Jasentuliyana, 'INMARSAT', in Jasentuliyana and Lee (eds.), op. cit. in n. 6 above, p. 439.

APPENDIX

Appendix

I. TREATIES RELATING TO OUTER SPACE CONCLUDED UNDER THE AUSPICES OF THE UNITED NATIONS

1. TREATY ON PRINCIPLES GOVERNING THE ACTIVITIES OF STATES IN THE EXPLORATION AND USE OF OUTER SPACE INCLUDING THE MOON AND OTHER CELESTIAL BODIES. London, Moscow, and Washington, 27 January 1967.[106]

The States Parties to this Treaty,

Inspired by the great prospects opening up before mankind as a results of man's entry into outer space,

Recognizing the common interest of all mankind in the progress of the exploration and use of outer space for peaceful purposes,

Believing that the exploration and use of outer space should be carried on for the benefit of all peoples irrespective of the degree of their economic or scientific development,

Desiring to contribute to broad international co-operation in the scientific as well as the legal aspects of the exploration and use of outer space for peaceful purposes,

Believing that such co-operation will contribute to the development of mutual understanding and to the strengthening of friendly relations between States and peoples,

Recalling resolution 1962 (XVIII), entitled 'Declaration of Legal Principles governing the Activities of States in the Exploration and Use of Outer Space' which was adopted unanimously by the United Nations General Assembly on 13 December 1963,

Recalling resolution 1884 (XVIII), calling upon States to refrain from placing in orbit around the earth any objects carrying nuclear weapons or any other kinds of weapons of mass destruction or from installing such weapons on celestial bodies, which was adopted unanimously by the United Nations General Assembly on 17 October 1963,

Taking account of United Nations General Assembly resolution 110 (II) of 3 November 1947, which condemned propaganda designed or likely to provoke or encourage any threat to the peace, breach of the peace or act of aggression, and considering that the aforementioned resolution is applicable to outer space,

[106] Adopted on 19 Dec. 1966, opened for signature on 27 Jan. 1967, entered into force on 10 Oct. 1967. UN GA resolution 2222 (XXI) annex; 610 UNTS 205; UKTS No. 10 (1968), Cmnd. 3519; 18 UST 2410, TIAS No. 6347.

Convinced that a Treaty on Principles Governing the Activities of States to the Exploration and Use of Outer Space, including the Moon and Other Celestial Bodies, will further the purposes and principles of the Charter of the United Nations,

Have agreed on the following:

Article I

The exploration and use of outer space, including the moon and other celestial bodies, shall be carried out for the benefit and in the interests of all countries, irrespective of their degree of economic or scientific development, and shall be the province of all mankind.

Outer space, including the moon and other celestial bodies, shall be free for exploration and use by all States without discrimination of any kind, on a basis of equality and in accordance with international law, and there shall be free access to all areas of celestial bodies.

There shall be freedom of scientific investigation in outer space, including the moon and other celestial bodies, and States shall facilitate and encourage international co-operation in such investigation.

Article II

Outer space, including the moon and other celestial bodies, is not subject to national appropriation by claim of sovereignty, by means of use or occupation, or by any other means.

Article III

States Parties to the Treaty shall carry on activities in the exploration and use of outer space, including the moon and other celestial bodies, in accordance with international law, including the Charter of the United Nations, in the interest of maintaining international peace and security and promoting international co-operation and understanding.

Article IV

States Parties to the Treaty undertake not to place in orbit around the earth any objects carrying nuclear weapons or any other kinds of weapons of mass destruction, install such weapons on celestial bodies, or station such weapons in outer space in any other manner.

The moon and other celestial bodies shall be used by all States Parties to the Treaty exclusively for peaceful purposes. The establishment of military bases, installations and fortifications, the testing of any type of weapons and the conduct of military manœuvres on celestial bodies shall be forbidden. The use of military personnel for scientific research or for any other peaceful purposes shall not be prohibited. The use of any equipment or facility necessary for peaceful exploration of the moon and other celestial bodies shall also not be prohibited.

Article V

States Parties to the Treaty shall regard astronauts as envoys of mankind in outer space and shall render to them all possible assistance in the event of accident, distress, or emergency landing on the territory of another State Party or on the high seas. When astronauts make such a landing, they shall be safely and promptly returned to the State of registry of their space vehicle.

In carrying on activities in outer space and on celestial bodies, the astronauts of one State Party shall render all possible assistance to the astronauts of other States Parties.

States Parties to the Treaty shall immediately inform the other States Parties to the Treaty or the Secretary-General of the United Nations of any phenomena they discover in outer space, including the moon and other celestial bodies, which could constitute a danger to the life or health of astronauts.

Article VI

States Parties to the Treaty shall bear international responsibility for national activities in outer space, including the moon and other celestial bodies, whether such activities are carried on by governmental agencies or by non-governmental entities, and for assuring that national activities are carried out in conformity with the provisions set forth in the present Treaty. The activities of non-governmental entities in outer space, including the moon and other celestial bodies, shall require authorization and continuing supervision by the appropriate State Party to the Treaty. When activities are carried on in outer space, including the moon and other celestial bodies, by an international organization, responsibility for compliance with this Treaty shall be borne both by the international organization and by the States Parties to the Treaty participating in such organization.

Article VII

Each State Party to the Treaty that launches or procures the launching of an object into outer space, including the moon and other celestial bodies, and each State Party from whose territory or facility an object is launched, is internationally liable for damage to another State Party to the Treaty or to its natural or juridical persons by such object or its component parts on the Earth, in airspace or in outer space, including the moon and other celestial bodies.

Article VIII

A State Party to the Treaty on whose register an object launched into outer space is carried shall retain jurisdiction and control over such object, and over any personnel thereof, while in outer space or on a celestial body. Ownership of objects launched into outer space, including objects landed or constructed on a celestial body, and of their component parts, is not affected by their presence in outer space or on a celestial body or by their return to the Earth. Such objects or component parts found beyond the limits of the State Party to the Treaty on whose registry they are carried shall be returned to that State Party, which shall, upon request, furnish identifying data prior to their return.

Article IX

In the exploration and use of outer space, including the moon and other celestial bodies, States Parties to the Treaty shall be guided by the principle of co-operation and mutual assistance and shall conduct all their activities in outer space, including the moon and other celestial bodies, with due regard to the corresponding interests of all other States Parties to the Treaty. States Parties to the Treaty shall pursue studies of outer space, including the moon and other celestial bodies, and conduct exploration of them so as to avoid their harmful contamination and also adverse changes in the environment of the Earth resulting from the introduction of extraterrestrial matter and, where necessary, shall adopt appropriate measures for this purpose. If a State Party to the Treaty has reason to believe that an activity or experiment planned by it or its nationals in outer space, including the moon and other celestial bodies, would cause potentially harmful interference with activities of other States Parties in the peaceful exploration and use of outer space, including the moon and other celestial bodies, it shall undertake appropriate international consultations before proceeding with any such activity or experiment. A State

Party to the Treaty which has reason to believe that an activity or experiment planned by another State Party in outer space, including the moon and other celestial bodies, would cause potentially harmful interference with activities in the peaceful exploration and use outer space, including the moon and other celestial bodies, may request consultation concerning the activity or experiment.

Article X

In order to promote international co-operation in the exploration and use of outer space, including the moon and other celestial bodies, in conformity with the purposes of this Treaty, the States Parties to the Treaty shall consider on a basis of equality any requests by other States Parties to the Treaty to be afforded an opportunity to observe the flight of space objects launched by those States.

The nature of such an opportunity for observation and the conditions under which it would be afforded shall be determined by agreement between the States concerned.

Article XI

In order to promote international co-operation in the peaceful exploration and use of outer space, States Parties to the Treaty conducting activities in outer space, including the moon and other celestial bodies, agree to inform the Secretary-General of the United Nations as well as the public and the international scientific community, to the greatest extent feasible and practicable, of the nature, conduct, locations and results of such activities. On receiving the said information, the Secretary-General of the United Nations should be prepared to disseminate it immediately and effectively.

Article XII

All stations, installations, equipment and space vehicles on the moon and other celestial bodies shall be open to representatives of other States Parties to the Treaty on a basis of reciprocity. Such representatives shall give reasonable advance notice of a projected visit, in order that appropriate consultations may be held and that maximum precautions may be taken to assure safety and to avoid interference with normal operations in the facility to be visited.

Article XIII

The provisions of this Treaty shall apply to the activities of States Parties to the Treaty in the exploration and use of outer space, including the moon and other celestial bodies, whether such activities are carried on by a single State Party to the Treaty or jointly with other States, including cases where they are carried on within the framework of international intergovernmental organizations.

Any practical questions arising in connection with activities carried on by international intergovernmental organizations in the exploration and use of outer space, including the moon and other celestial bodies, shall be resolved by the States Parties to the Treaty either with the appropriate international organization or with one or more States members of that international organization, which are Parties to this Treaty.

Article XIV

1. This Treaty shall be open to all States for signature. Any State which does not sign this Treaty before its entry into force in accordance with paragraph 3 of this article may accede to it at any time.

2. This Treaty shall be subject to ratification by signatory States. Instruments of ratification and instruments of accession shall be deposited with the Governments of the United Kingdom of Great Britain and Northern Ireland, the Union of Soviet Socialist Republics and the United States of America, which are hereby designated the Depositary Governments.

3. This Treaty shall enter into force upon the deposit of instruments of ratification by five Governments including the Governments designated as Depositary Governments under this Treaty.

4. For States whose instruments of ratification or accession are deposited subsequent to the entry into force of this Treaty, it shall enter into force on the date of the deposit of their instruments of ratification or accession.

5. The Depositary Governments shall promptly inform all signatory and acceding States of the date of each signature, the date of deposit of each instrument of ratification of and accession to this Treaty, the date of its entry into force and other notices.

6. This Treaty shall be registered by the Depositary Governments pursuant to Article 102 of the Charter of the United Nations.

Article XV

Any State Party to the Treaty may propose amendments to this Treaty. Amendments shall enter into force for each State Party to the Treaty accepting the amendments upon their acceptance by a majority of the States Parties to the Treaty and thereafter for each remaining State Party to the Treaty on the date of acceptance by it.

Article XVI

Any State Party to the Treaty may give notice of its withdrawal from the Treaty one year after its entry into force by written notification to the Depositary Governments. Such withdrawal shall take effect one year from the date of receipt of this notification.

Article XVII

This Treaty, of which the English, Russian, French, Spanish and Chinese texts are equally authentic, shall be deposited in the archives of the Depositary Governments. Duly certified copies of this Treaty shall be transmitted by the Depositary Governments to the governments of the signatory and acceding States.

IN WITNESS WHEREOF the undersigned, duly authorized, have signed this Treaty.

DONE in triplicate, at the cities of London, Moscow and Washington, the twenty-seventh day of January, one thousand nine hundred and sixty-seven.

2. AGREEMENT ON THE RESCUE OF ASTRONAUTS, THE RETURN OF ASTRONAUTS, AND THE RETURN OF OBJECTS LAUNCHED INTO OUTER SPACE. London, Moscow, and Washington, 22 April 1968.[107]

The Contracting Parties,

Noting the great importance of the Treaty on Principles Governing the Activities of States in the Exploration and Use of Outer Space, including the Moon and Other Celestial Bodies, which calls for the rendering of all possible

---

[107] Adopted on 19 Dec. 1967, opened for signature on 22 Apr. 1968, entered into force on 3 Dec. 1968, UN GA resolution 2345 (XXII) annex; 672 UNTS; 119 UKTS No. 56 (1969), Cmnd. 3997; 19 UST 7570, TIAS No. 6577.

assistance to astronauts in the event of accident, distress or emergency landing, the prompt and safe return of astronauts, and the return of objects
launched into outer space,

   Desiring to develop and give further concrete expression to these duties,

   Wishing to promote international co-operation in the peaceful exploration
and use of outer space,

   Prompted by sentiments of humanity,

   Have agreed on the following:

Article 1

Each Contracting Party which receives information or discovers that the
personnel of a spacecraft have suffered accident or are experiencing conditions of distress or have made an emergency or unintended landing in territory under its jurisdiction or on the high seas or in any other place not under
the jurisdiction of any State shall immediately:

   (a) notify the launching authority or, if it cannot identify and immediately
communicate with the launching authority, immediately make a public
announcement by all appropriate means of communication at its disposal;

   (b) notify the Secretary-General of the United Nations, who should disseminate the information without delay by all appropriate means of communication at his disposal.

Article 2

If, owing to accident, distress, emergency or unintended landing, the personnel of a spacecraft land in territory under the jurisdiction of a Contracting
Party, it shall immediately take all possible steps to rescue them and render
them all necessary assistance. It shall inform the launching authority and also
the Secretary-General of the United Nations of the steps it is taking and of
their progress. If assistance by the launching authority would help to effect a
prompt rescue or would contribute substantially to the effectiveness of search
and rescue operations, the launching authority shall co-operate with the
Contracting Party with a view to the effective conduct of search and rescue
operations. Such operations shall be subject to the direction and control of the
Contracting Party, which shall act in close and continuing consultation with
the launching authority.

Article 3

If information is received or it is discovered that the personnel of a spacecraft have alighted on the high seas or in any other place not under the jurisdiction of any State, those Contracting Parties which are in a position to do so shall, if necessary, extend assistance in search and rescue operations for such personnel to assure their speedy rescue. They shall inform the launching authority and the Secretary-General of the United Nations of the steps they are taking and of their progress.

Article 4

If, owing to accident, distress, emergency or unintended landing, the personnel of a spacecraft land in territory under the jurisdiction of a Contracting Party or have been found on the high seas or in any other place not under the jurisdiction of any State, they shall be safely and promptly return to representatives of the launching authority.

Article 5

1. Each Contracting Party which receives information or discovers that a space object or its component parts has returned to Earth in territory under its jurisdiction or on the high seas or in any other place not under the jurisdiction of any State, shall notify the launching authority or the Secretary-General of the United Nations.

2. Each Contracting Party having jurisdiction over the territory on which a space object or its component parts has been discovered shall, upon the request of the launching authority and with assistance from that authority if requested, take such steps as it finds practicable to recover the object or component parts.

3. Upon request of the launching authority, objects launched into outer space or their component parts found beyond the territorial limits of the launching authority shall be returned to or held at the disposal of representatives of the launching authority, which shall, upon request, furnish identifying data prior to their return .

4. Notwithstanding paragraphs 2 and 3 of this article, a Contracting Party which has reason to believe that a space object or its component parts discovered in territory under its jurisdiction, or recovered by it elsewhere, is of a hazardous or deleterious nature may so notify the launching authority, which

shall immediately take effective steps, under the direction and control of the said Contracting Party, to eliminate possible danger of harm.

5. Expenses incurred in fulfilling obligations to recover and return a space object or its component parts under paragraphs 2 and 3 of this article shall be borne by the launching authority.

Article 6

For the purposes of this Agreement, the term 'launching authority' shall refer to the State responsible for launching, or, where an international inter-governmental organization is responsible for launching, that organization, provided that that organization declares its acceptance of the rights and oblig-ations provided for in this Agreement and a majority of the States members of that organization are Contracting Parties to this Agreement and to the Treaty on Principles Governing the Activities of States in the Exploration and Use of Outer Space, including the Moon and Other Celestial Bodies.

Article 7

1. This Agreement shall be open to all States for signature. Any State which does not sign this Agreement before its entry into force in accordance with paragraph 3 of this article may accede to it at any time.

2. This Agreement shall be subject to ratification by signatory States. Instruments of ratification and instruments of accession shall be deposited with the Governments of the United Kingdom of Great Britain and Northern Ireland, the Union of Soviet Socialist Republics and the United States of America, which are hereby designated the Depositary Governments.

3. This Agreement shall enter into force upon the deposit of instruments of ratification by five Governments including the Governments designated as Depositary Governments under this Agreement.

4. For States whose instruments of ratification or accession are deposited subsequent to the entry into force of this Agreement, it shall enter into force on the date of the deposit of their instruments of ratification or accession.

5. The Depositary Governments shall promptly inform all signatory and acceding States of the date of each signature, the date of deposit of each instrument of ratification of and accession to this Agreement, the date of its entry into force and other notices.

6. This Agreement shall be registered by the Depositary Governments pur-suant to Article 102 of the Charter of the United Nations.

Article 8

Any State Party to the Agreement may propose amendments to this Agreement. Amendments shall enter into force for each State Party to the Agreement accepting the amendments upon their acceptance by a majority of the States Parties to the Agreement and thereafter for each remaining State Party to the Agreement on the date of acceptance by it.

Article 9 ·

Any State Party to the Agreement may give notice of its withdrawal from the Agreement one year after its entry into force by written notification to the Depositary Governments. Such withdrawal shall take effect one year from the date of receipt of this notification.

Article 10

This Agreement, of which the English, Russian, French, Spanish and Chinese texts are equally authentic, shall be deposited in the archives of the Depositary Governments. Duly certified copies of this Agreement shall be transmitted by the Depositary Governments to the governments of the signatory and acceding States.

IN WITNESS WHEREOF the undersigned, duly authorized, have signed this Agreement.

DONE in triplicate, at the cities of London, Moscow and Washington, the twenty-second day of April, one thousand nine hundred and sixty-eight.

3. CONVENTION ON INTERNATIONAL LIABILITY FOR DAMAGE CAUSED BY SPACE OBJECTS. London, Moscow, and Washington, 29 March 1972.[108]

The States Parties to this Convention,

Recognizing the common interest of all mankind in furthering the exploration and use of outer space for peaceful purposes,

Recalling the Treaty on Principles Governing the Activities of States in the Exploration and Use of Outer Space, including the Moon and Other Celestial Bodies,

---

[108] Adopted on 29 Nov. 1971, opened for signature on 29 Mar. 1972, entered into force on 1 Sept. 1972. UN GA resolution 2777 (XXVI) annex; 961 UNTS 187; UKTS No. 16 (1974), Cmnd. 5551; 24 UST 2389; TIAS 7762.

Taking into consideration that, notwithstanding the precautionary measures to be taken by States and international intergovernmental organizations involved in the launching of space objects, damage may on occasion be caused by such objects,

Recognizing the need to elaborate effective international rules and procedures concerning liability for damage caused by space objects and to ensure, in particular, the prompt payment under the terms of this Convention of a full and equitable measure of compensation to victims of such damage,

Believing that the establishment of such rules and procedures will contribute to the strengthening of international co-operation in the field of the exploration and use of outer space for peaceful purposes,

Have agreed on the following:

Article I

For the purposes of this Convention:

(*a*) The term 'damage' means loss of life, personal injury or other impairment of health; or loss of or damage to property of States or of persons, natural or juridical, or property of international intergovernmental organizations;

(*b*) The term 'launching' includes attempted launching;

(*c*) The term 'launching State' means:

　(i) A State which launches or procures the launching of a space object;

　(ii) A State from whose territory or facility a space object is launched;

(*d*) The term 'space object' includes component parts of a space object as well as its launch vehicle and parts thereof.

Article II

A launching State shall be absolutely liable to pay compensation for damage caused by its space object on the surface of the earth or to aircraft in flight.

Article III

In the event of damage being caused elsewhere than on the surface of the earth to a space object of one launching State or to persons or property on board such a space object by a space object of another launching State, the latter shall be liable only if the damage is due to its fault or the fault of persons for whom it is responsible.

Article IV

1. In the event of damage being caused elsewhere than on the surface of the earth to a space object of one launching State or to persons or property on board such a space object by a space object of another launching State, and of damage thereby being caused to a third State or to its natural or juridical persons, the first two States shall be jointly and severally liable to the third State, to the extent indicated by the following:

(*a*) If the damage has been caused to the third States on the surface of the earth or to aircraft in flight, their liability to the third State shall be absolute;

(*b*) If the damage has been caused to a space object of the third State or to persons or property on board that space object elsewhere than on the surface of the earth, their liability to the third State shall be based on the fault of either of the first two States or on the fault of persons for whom either is responsible.

2. In all cases of joint and several liability referred to in paragraph 1 of this article, the burden of compensation for the damage shall be apportioned between the first two States in accordance with the extent to which they were at fault; if the extent of the fault of each of these States cannot be established, the burden of compensation shall be apportioned equally between them. Such apportionment shall be without prejudice to the right of the third State to seek the entire compensation due under this Convention from any or all of the launching States which are jointly and severally liable.

Article V

1. Whenever two or more States jointly launch a space object, they shall be jointly and severally liable for any damage caused.

2. A launching State which has paid compensation for damage shall have the right to present a claim for indemnification to other participants in the joint launching. The participants in a joint launching may conclude agreements regarding the apportioning among themselves of the financial obligation in respect of which they are jointly and severally liable. Such agreements shall be without prejudice to the right of a State sustaining damage to seek the entire compensation due under the Convention from any or all of the launching States which are jointly and severally liable.

3. A State from whose territory or facility a space object is launched shall be regarded as a participant in a joint launching.

Article VI

1. Subject to the provisions of paragraph 2 of this Article, exoneration from absolute liability shall be granted to the extent that a launching State establishes that the damage has resulted either wholly or partially from gross negligence or from an act or omission done with intent to cause damage on the part of a claimant State or of natural or juridical persons it represents.

2. No exoneration whatever shall be granted in cases where the damage has resulted from activities conducted by a launching State which are not in conformity with international law including, in particular, the Charter of the United Nations and the Treaty on Principles Governing the Activities of States in the Exploration and Use of Outer Space, including the Moon and Other Celestial Bodies.

Article VII

The provisions of this Convention shall not apply to damage caused by a space object of a launching State to:

(*a*) nationals of that launching State;

(*b*) foreign nationals during such time as they are participating in the operation of that space object from the time of its launching or at any stages thereafter until its descent, or during such time as they are in the immediate vicinity of a planned launching or recovery area as the result of an invitation by that launching State.

Article VIII

1. A State which suffers damage, or whose natural or juridical persons suffer damage, may present to a launching State a claim for compensation for such damage.

2. If the State of nationality has not presented a claim, another State may, in respect of damage sustained in its territory by any natural or juridical person, present a claim to a launching State.

3. If neither the State of nationality nor the State in whose territory the damage was sustained has presented a claim or notified its intention of presenting a claim, another State may, in respect of damage sustained by its permanent residents, present a claim to a launching State.

Article IX

A claim for compensation for damage shall be presented to a launching State through diplomatic channels. If a State does not maintain diplomatic relations with the launching State concerned, it may request another State to present its claim to that launching State or otherwise represent its interests under this Convention. It may also present its claim through the Secretary-General of the United Nations, provided the claimant State and the launching State are both Members of the United Nations.

Article X

1. A claim for compensation for damage may be presented to a launching State not later than one year following the date of the occurrence of the damage or the identification of the launching State which is liable.

2. If, however, a State does not know of the occurrence of the damage or has not been able to identify the launching State which is liable, it may present a claim within one year following the date on which it learned of the aforementioned facts; however, this period shall in no event exceed one year following the date on which the State could reasonably be expected to have learned of the facts through the exercise of due diligence.

3. The time-limits specified in paragraphs 1 and 2 of this Article shall apply even if the full extent of the damage may not be known. In this event, however, the claimant State shall be entitled to revise the claim and submit additional documentation after the expiration of such time-limits until one year after the full extent of the damage is known.

Article XI

1. Presentation of a claim to a launching State for compensation for damage under this Convention shall not require the prior exhaustion of any local remedies which may be available to a claimant State or to natural or juridical persons it represents.

2. Nothing in this Convention shall prevent a State, or natural or juridical persons it might represent, from pursuing a claim in the courts or administrative tribunals or agencies of a launching State. A State shall not, however, be entitled to present a claim under this Convention in respect of the same damage for which a claim is being pursued in the courts or administrative tribunals or agencies of a launching State or under another international agreement which is binding on the States concerned.

Article XII

The compensation which the launching State shall be liable to pay for damage under this Convention shall be determined in accordance with international law and the principles of justice and equity, in order to provide such reparation in respect of the damage as will restore the person, natural or juridical, State or international organization on whose behalf the claim is presented to the condition which would have existed if the damage had not occurred.

Article XIII

Unless the claimant State and the State from which compensation is due under this Convention agree on another form of compensation, the compensation shall be paid in the currency of the claimant State or, if that State so requests, in the currency of the State from which compensation is due.

Article XIV

If no settlement of a claim is arrived at through diplomatic negotiations as provided for in Article IX, within one year from the date on which the claimant State notifies the launching State that it has submitted the documentation of its claim, the parties concerned shall establish a Claims Commission at the request of either party.

Article XV

1. The Claims Commission shall be composed of three members: one appointed by the claimant State, one appointed by the launching State and the third member, the Chairman, to be chosen by both parties jointly. Each party shall make its appointment within two months of the request for the establishment of the Claims Commission.

2. If no agreement is reached on the choice of the Chairman within four months of the request for the establishment of the Commission, either party may request the Secretary-General of the United Nations to appoint the Chairman within a further period of two months.

Article XVI

1. If one of the parties does not make its appointment within the stipulated period, the Chairman shall, at the request of the other party, constitute a single-member Claims Commission.

2. Any vacancy which may arise in the Commission for whatever reason shall be filled by the same procedure adopted for the original appointment.

3. The Commission shall determine its own procedure.

4. The Commission shall determine the place or places where it shall sit and all other administrative matters.

5. Except in the case of decisions and awards by a single-member Commission, all decisions and awards of the Commission shall be by majority vote.

Article XVII

No increase in the membership of the Claims Commission shall take place by reason of two or more claimant States or launching States being joined in any one proceeding before the Commission. The claimant States so joined shall collectively appoint one member of the Commission in the same manner and subject to the same conditions as would be the case for a single claimant State. When two or more launching States are so joined, they shall collectively appoint one member of the Commission in the same way. If the claimant States or the launching States do not make the appointment within the stipulated period, the Chairman shall constitute a single-member Commission.

Article XVIII

The Claims Commission shall decide the merits of the claim for compensation and determine the amount of compensation payable, if any.

Article XIX

1. The Claims Commission shall act in accordance with the provisions of Article XII.

2. The decision of the Commission shall be final and binding if the parties have so agreed; otherwise the Commission shall render a final and recommendatory award, which the parties shall consider in good faith. The Commission shall state the reasons for its decision or award.

3. The Commission shall give its decision or award as promptly as possible and no later than one year from the date of its establishment, unless an extension of this period is found necessary by the Commission.

4. The Commission shall make its decision or award public. It shall deliver a certified copy of its decision or award to each of the parties and to the Secretary-General of the United Nations.

Article XX

The expenses in regard to the Claims Commission shall be borne equally by the parties, unless otherwise decided by the Commission.

Article XXI

If the damage caused by a space object presents a large-scale danger to human life or seriously interferes with the living conditions of the population or the functioning of vital centres, the States Parties, and in particular the launching State, shall examine the possibility of rendering appropriate and rapid assistance to the State which has suffered the damage, when it so requires. However, nothing in this article shall affect the rights or obligations of the States Parties under this Convention.

Article XXII

1. In this Convention, with the exception of Articles XXIV to XXVII, references to States shall be deemed to apply to any international intergovernmental organization which conducts space activities if the organization declares its acceptance of the rights and obligations provided for in this Convention and if a majority of the States members of the organization are States Parties to this Convention and to the Treaty on Principles Governing the Activities of States in the Exploration and Use of Outer Space, including the Moon and Other Celestial Bodies.

2. States members of any such organization which are States Parties to this Convention shall take all appropriate steps to ensure that the organization makes a declaration in accordance with the preceding paragraph.

3. If an international intergovernmental organization is liable for damage by virtue of the provisions of this Convention, that organization and those of its members which are States Parties to this Convention shall be jointly and severally liable; provided, however, that:

(*a*) any claim for compensation in respect of such damage shall be first presented to the organization;

(*b*) only where the organization has not paid, within a period of six months, any sum agreed or determined to be due as compensation for such damage, may the claimant State invoke the liability of the members which are States Parties to this Convention for the payment of that sum.

4. Any claim, pursuant to the provisions of this Convention, for compensation in respect of damage caused to an organization which has made a declaration in accordance with paragraph 1 of this Article shall be presented by a State member of the organization which is a State Party to this Convention.

Article XXIII

1. The provisions of this Convention shall not affect other international agreements in force in so far as relations between the States Parties to such agreements are concerned.

2. No provision of this Convention shall prevent States from concluding international agreements reaffirming, supplementing or extending its provisions.

Article XXIV

1. This Convention shall be open to all States for signature. Any State which does not sign this Convention before its entry into force in accordance with paragraph 3 of this article may accede to it at any time.

2. This Convention shall be subject to ratification by signatory States. Instruments of ratification and instruments of accession shall be deposited with the Governments of the United Kingdom of Great Britain and Northern Ireland, the Union of Soviet Socialist Republics and the United States of America, which are hereby designated the Depositary Governments.

3. This Convention shall enter into force upon the deposit of the fifth instrument of ratification.

4. For States whose instruments of ratification or accession are deposited subsequent to the entry into force of this Convention, it shall enter into force on the date of the deposit of their instruments of ratification or accession.

5. The Depositary Governments shall promptly inform all signatory and acceding States of the date of each signature, the date of deposit of each instrument of ratification of and accession to this Convention, the date of its entry into force and other notices.

6. This Convention shall be registered by the Depositary Governments pursuant to Article 102 of the Charter of the United Nations.

Article XXV

Any State Party to this Convention may propose amendments to this Convention. Amendments shall enter into force for each State Party to the Convention accepting the amendments upon their acceptance by a majority of the States Parties to the Convention and thereafter for each remaining State Party to the Convention on the date of acceptance by it.

Article XXVI

Ten years after the entry into force of this Convention, the question of the review of this Convention shall be included in the provisional agenda of the United Nations General Assembly in order to consider, in the light of past application of the Convention, whether it requires revision. However, at any time after the Convention has been in force for five years, and at the request of one third of the States Parties to the Convention, and with the concurrence of the majority of the States Parties, a conference of the States Parties shall be convened to review this Convention.

Article XXVII

Any State Party to this Convention may give notice of its withdrawal from the Convention one year after its entry into force by written notification to the Depositary Governments. Such withdrawal shall take effect one year from the date of receipt of this notification.

Article XXVIII

This Convention, of which the English, Russian, French, Spanish and Chinese texts are equally authentic, shall be deposited in the archives of the Depositary Governments. Duly certified copies of this Convention shall be transmitted by the Depositary Governments to the governments of the signatory and acceding States.

IN WITNESS WHEREOF the undersigned, duly authorized, have signed this Convention.

DONE in triplicate, at the cities of London, Moscow and Washington, this twenty-ninth day of March, one thousand nine hundred and seventy-two.

4. CONVENTION ON REGISTRATION OF OBJECTS LAUNCHED INTO OUTER SPACE. New York, 14 January 1975.[109]

The States Parties to this Convention,

Recognizing the common interest of all mankind in furthering the exploration and use of outer space for peaceful purposes,

Recalling that the Treaty on Principles Governing the Activities of States in the Exploration and Use of Outer Space, including the Moon and Other Celestial Bodies of 27 January 1967 affirms that States shall bear international responsibility for their national activities in outer space and refers to the State on whose registry an object launched into outer space is carried,

Recalling also the Agreement on the Rescue of Astronauts, the Return of Astronauts and the Return of Objects Launched into Outer Space of 22 April 1968 provides that a launching authority shall, upon request, furnish identifying data prior to the return of an object it has launched into outer space found beyond the territorial limits of the launching authority,

Recalling further that the Convention on International Liability for Damage Caused by Space Objects of 29 March 1972 establishes international rules and procedures concerning the liability of launching States for damage caused by their space objects,

Desiring in the light of the Treaty on Principles Governing the Activities of States in the Exploration and Use of Outer Space, including the Moon and Other Celestial Bodies, to make provision for the national registration by launching States of space objects launched into outer space,

Desiring further that a central register of objects launched into outer space be established and maintained, on a mandatory basis, by the Secretary-General of the United Nations,

Desiring also to provide for States Parties additional means and procedures to assist in the identification of space objects,

Believing that a mandatory system of registering objects launched into outer space would, in particular, assist in their identification and would contribute to the application and development of international law governing the exploration and use of outer space,

Have agreed on the following:

---

[109] Adopted on 29 Nov. 1971, opened for signature on 29 Mar. 1972, entered into force on 1 Sept. 1972. UN GA resolution 3235 (XXIX) annex; 1023 UNTS 15; UKTS No. 70 (1978), Cmnd. 7271; 28 UST 695; TIAS 8480.

Article I

For the purposes of this Convention:

(*a*) The term 'launching State' means:

  (i) A State which launches or procures the launching of a space object;

  (ii) A State from whose territory or facility a space object is launched;

(*b*) The term 'space object' includes component parts of a space object as well as its launch vehicle and parts thereof;

(*c*) The term 'State of registry' means a launching State on whose registry a space object is carried in accordance with article II.

Article II

1. When a space object is launched into earth orbit or beyond, the launching State shall register the space object by means of an entry in an appropriate registry which it shall maintain. Each launching State shall inform the Secretary-General of the United Nations of the establishment of such a registry.

2. Where there are two or more launching States in respect of any such space object, they shall jointly determine which one of them shall register the object in accordance with paragraph 1 of this article, bearing in mind the provisions of article VIII of the Treaty on Principles Governing the Activities of States in the Exploration and Use of Outer Space, including the Moon and Other Celestial Bodies, and without prejudice to appropriate agreements concluded or to be concluded among the launching States on jurisdiction and control over the space object and over any personnel thereof.

3. The contents of each registry and the conditions under which it is maintained shall be determined by the State of registry concerned.

Article III

1. The Secretary-General of the United Nations shall maintain a Register in which the information furnished in accordance with article IV shall be recorded.

2. There shall be full and open access to the information in this Register.

Article IV

1. Each State of registry shall furnish to the Secretary-General of the United Nations, as soon as practicable, the following information concerning each space object carried on its registry:

(*a*) name of launching State or States;

(*b*) an appropriate designator of the space object or its registration number;

(*c*) date and territory or location of launch;

(*d*) basic orbital parameters, including:

    (i) nodal period,

    (ii) inclination,

    (iii) apogee,

    (iv) perigee;

(*e*) general function of the space object.

2. Each State of registry may, from time to time, provide the Secretary-General of the United Nations with additional information concerning a space object carried on its registry.

3. Each State of registry shall notify the Secretary-General of the United Nations, to the greatest extent feasible and as soon as practicable, of space objects concerning which it has previously transmitted information, and which have been but no longer are in earth orbit.

Article V

Whenever a space object launched into earth orbit or beyond is marked with the designator or registration number referred to in article IV, paragraph 1(*b*), or both, the State of registry shall notify the Secretary-General of this fact when submitting the information regarding the space object in accordance with article IV. In such case, the Secretary-General of the United Nations shall record this notification in the Register.

Article VI

Where the application of the provisions of this Convention has not enabled a State Party to identify a space object which has caused damage to it or to any of its natural or juridical persons, or which may be of a hazardous or deleterious nature, other States Parties, including in particular States possessing space monitoring and tracking facilities, shall respond to the greatest extent feasible to a request by that State Party, or transmitted through the Secretary-General on its behalf, for assistance under equitable and reasonable conditions in the identification of the object. A State Party making such a request shall, to the greatest extent feasible, submit information as to the time, nature and circumstances of the events giving rise to the request. Arrangements under which such assistance shall be rendered shall be the subject of agreement between the parties concerned.

Article VII

1. In this Convention, with the exception of articles VIII to XII inclusive, references to States shall be deemed to apply to any international intergovernmental organization which conducts space activities if the organization declares its acceptance of the rights and obligations provided for in this Convention and if a majority of the States members of the organization are States Parties to this Convention and to the Treaty on Principles Governing the Activities of States in the Exploration and Use of Outer Space, including the Moon and Other Celestial Bodies.

2. States members of any such organization which are States Parties to this Convention shall take all appropriate steps to ensure that the organization makes a declaration in accordance with paragraph 1 of this article.

Article VIII

1. This Convention shall be open to all States for signature by all States at United Nations Headquarters in New York. Any State which does not sign this Convention before its entry into force in accordance with paragraph 3 of this article may accede to it at any time.

2. This Convention shall be subject to ratification by signatory States. Instruments of ratification and instruments of accession shall be deposited with the Secretary-General of the United Nations.

3. This Convention shall enter into force among the States which have deposited instruments or ratification on the deposit of the fifth such instrument with the Secretary-General of the United Nations.

4. For States whose instruments of ratification or accession are deposited subsequent to the entry into force of this Convention, it shall enter into force on the date of the deposit of their instruments of ratification or accession.

5. The Secretary-General shall promptly inform all signatory and acceding States of the date of each signature, the date of deposit of each instrument of ratification of and accession to this Convention, the date of its entry into force and other notices.

6. This Convention shall be registered by the Depositary Governments pursuant to Article 102 of the Charter of the United Nations.

Article IX

Any State Party to this Convention may propose amendments to the Convention. Amendments shall enter into force for each State Party to the

Convention accepting the amendments upon their acceptance by a majority of the States Parties to the Convention and thereafter for each remaining State Party to the Convention on the date of acceptance by it.

Article X

Ten years after the entry into force of this Convention, the question of the review of this Convention shall be included in the provisional agenda of the United Nations General Assembly in order to consider, in the light of past application of the Convention, whether it requires revision. However, at any time after the Convention has been in force for five years, at the request of one third of the States Parties to the Convention and with the concurrence of the majority of the States Parties, a conference of the States Parties shall be convened to review this Convention. Such review shall take into account in particular any relevant technological developments, including those relating to the identification of space objects.

Article XI

Any State Party to this Convention may give notice of its withdrawal from the Convention one year after its entry into force by written notification to the Secretary-General of the United Nations. Such withdrawal shall take effect one year from the date of receipt of this notification.

Article XII

The original of this Convention, of which the Arabic, Chinese, English, French, Russian and Spanish texts are equally authentic, shall be deposited with the Secretary-General of the United Nations who shall send certified copies thereof to all signatory and acceding States.

IN WITNESS WHEREOF the undersigned, being duly authorized thereto by their respective Governments, have signed this Convention, opened for signature at New York on the fourteenth day of January, one thousand nine hundred and seventy-five.

5. AGREEMENT GOVERNING THE ACTIVITIES OF STATES ON THE MOON AND OTHER CELESTIAL BODIES. New York, 18 December 1979.[110]

The States Parties to this Agreement,

Noting the achievements of States in the exploration and use of the moon and other celestial bodies,

Recognizing that the moon, as a natural satellite of the earth, has an important role to play in the exploration of outer space,

Determined to promote on the basis of equality the further development of co-operation among States in the exploration and use of the moon and other celestial bodies,

Desiring to prevent the moon from becoming an area of international conflict,

Bearing in mind the benefits which may be derived from the exploitation of the natural resources of the moon and other celestial bodies,

Recalling the Treaty on Principles Governing the Activities of States in the Exploration and Use of Outer Space, including the Moon and Other Celestial Bodies, the Agreement on the Rescue of Astronauts, the Return of Astronauts and the Return of Objects Launched into Outer Space, the Convention on International Liability for Damage Caused by Space Objects, and the Convention on Registration of Objects Launched into Outer Space,

Taking into account the need to define and develop the provisions of these international instruments in relation to the moon and other celestial bodies, having regard to further progress in the exploration and use of outer space,

Have agreed on the following:

Article 1

1. The provisions of this Agreement relating to the moon shall also apply to other celestial bodies within the solar system, other than the earth, except in so far as specific legal norms enter into force with respect to any of these celestial bodies.

2. For the purposes of this Agreement reference to the moon shall include orbits around or other trajectories to or around it.

---

[110] Adopted on 5 Dec. 1979, opened for signature on 18 Dec. 1979, entered into force on 11 July 1984. UN GA resolution 34/68; 1363 UNTS 3; 18 *ILM* (1979) 1434.

Article 2

All activities on the moon, including its exploration and use, shall be carried out in accordance with international law, in particular the Charter of the United Nations, and taking into account the Declaration on Principles of International Law concerning Friendly Relations and Co-operation among States in accordance with the Charter of the United Nations, adopted by the General Assembly on 24 October 1970, in the interest of maintaining international peace and security and promoting international co-operation and mutual understanding, and with due regard to the corresponding interests of all other States Parties.

Article 3

1. The moon shall be used by all States Parties exclusively for peaceful purposes.

2. Any threat or use of force or any other hostile act or threat of hostile act on the moon is prohibited. It is likewise prohibited to use the moon in order to commit any such act or to engage in any such threat in relation to the earth, the moon, spacecraft, the personnel of spacecraft or man-made space objects.

3. States Parties shall not place in orbit around or other trajectory to or around the moon objects carrying nuclear weapons or any other kinds of weapons of mass destruction or place or use such weapons on or in the moon.

4. The establishment of military bases, installations and fortifications, the testing of any type of weapons and the conduct of military manœuvres on the moon shall be forbidden. The use of military personnel for scientific research or any other peaceful purposes shall not be prohibited. The use of any equipment or facility necessary for peaceful exploration and use of the moon shall also not be prohibited.

Article 4

1. The exploration and use of the moon shall be the province of all mankind and shall be carried out for the benefit and in the interests of all countries, irrespective of their degree of economic or scientific development. Due regard shall be paid to the interests of present and future generations as well as to the need to promote higher standards of living and conditions of economic and social progress and development in accordance with the Charter of the United Nations.

2. States Parties shall be guided by the principle of co-operation and mutual assistance in all their activities concerning the exploration and use of the moon. International co-operation in pursuance of this Agreement should be as wide as possible and may take place on a multilateral basis, on a bilateral basis or through international intergovernmental organizations.

Article 5

1. States Parties shall inform the Secretary-General of the United Nations as well as the public and the international scientific community, to the greatest extent feasible and practicable, of their activities concerned with the exploration and use of the moon. Information on the time, purposes, locations, orbital parameters and duration shall be given in respect of each mission to the moon as soon as possible after launching, while information on the results of each mission, including scientific results, shall be furnished upon completion of the mission. In the case of a mission lasting more than sixty days, information on conduct of the mission, including any scientific results, shall be given periodically, at thirty-day intervals. For missions lasting more than six months, only significant additions to such information need be reported thereafter.

2. If a State Party becomes aware that another State Party plans to operate simultaneously in the same area of or in the same orbit around or trajectory to or around the moon, it shall promptly inform the other State of the timing of and plans for its own operations.

3. In carrying out activities under this Agreement, States Parties shall promptly inform the Secretary-General, as well as the public and the international scientific community, of any phenomena they discover in outer space, including the moon, which could endanger human life or health, as well as of any indication of organic life.

Article 6

1. There shall be freedom of scientific investigation on the moon by all States Parties without discrimination of any kind, on the basis of equality and in accordance with international law.

2. In carrying out scientific investigations and in furtherance of the provisions of this Agreement, the States Parties shall have the right to collect on and remove from the moon samples of its mineral and other substances. Such samples shall remain at the disposal of those States Parties which caused them to be collected and may be used by them for scientific purposes. States Parties shall have regard to the desirability of making a portion of such samples avail-

able to other interested States Parties and the international scientific community for scientific investigation. States Parties may in the course of scientific investigations also use mineral and other substances of the moon in quantities appropriate for the support of their missions.

3. States Parties agree on the desirability of exchanging scientific and other personnel on expeditions to or installations on the moon to the greatest extent feasible and practicable.

Article 7

1. In exploring and using the moon, States Parties shall take measures to prevent the disruption of the existing balance of its environment, whether by introducing adverse changes in that environment, by its harmful contamination through the introduction of extra-environmental matter or otherwise. States Parties shall also take measures to avoid harmfully affecting the environment of the earth through the introduction of extraterrestrial matter or otherwise.

2. States Parties shall inform the Secretary-General of the United Nations of the measures being adopted by them in accordance with paragraph 1 of this article and shall also, to the maximum extent feasible, notify him in advance of all placements by them of radioactive materials on the moon and of the purposes of such placements.

3. States Parties shall report to other States Parties and to the Secretary-General concerning areas of the moon having special scientific interest in order that, without prejudice to the rights of other States Parties, consideration may be given to the designation of such areas as international scientific preserves for which special protective arrangements are to be agreed upon in consultation with the competent bodies of the United Nations.

Article 8

1. States Parties may pursue their activities in the exploration and use of the moon anywhere on or below its surface, subject to the provisions of this Agreement.

2. For these purposes States Parties may, in particular:

(*a*) Land their space objects on the moon and launch them from the moon;

(*b*) Place their personnel, space vehicles, equipment, facilities, stations and installations anywhere on or below the surface of the moon.

3. Activities of States Parties in accordance with paragraphs 1 and 2 of this article shall not interfere with the activities of other States Parties on the

moon. Where such interference may occur, the States Parties concerned shall undertake consultations in accordance with article 15, paragraphs 2, and 3, of this Agreement.

Article 9

1. States Parties may establish manned and unmanned stations on the moon. A State Party establishing a station shall use only that area which is required for the needs of the station and shall immediately inform the Secretary-General of the United Nations of the location and purposes of that station. Subsequently, at annual intervals that State shall likewise inform the Secretary-General whether the station continues in use and whether its purposes have changed.

2. Stations shall be installed in such a manner that they do not impede the free access to all areas of the moon of personnel, vehicles and equipment of other States Parties conducting activities on the moon in accordance with the provisions of this Agreement or of article 1 of the Treaty on Principles Governing the Activities of States in the Exploration and Use of Outer Space, including the Moon and Other Celestial Bodies.

Article 10

1. States Parties shall adopt all practicable measures to safeguard the life and health of persons on the moon. For this purpose they shall regard any person on the moon as an astronaut within the meaning of article V of the Treaty on Principles Governing the Activities of States in the Exploration and Use of Outer Space, including the Moon and Other Celestial Bodies and as part of the personnel of a spacecraft within the meaning of the Agreement on the Rescue of Astronauts, the Return of Astronauts and the Return of Objects Launched into Outer Space.

2. States Parties shall offer shelter in their stations, installations, vehicles and other facilities to persons in distress on the moon.

Article 11

1. The moon and its natural resources are the common heritage of mankind, which finds its expression in the provisions of this Agreement, in particular in paragraph 5 of this article.

2. The moon is not subject to national appropriation by any claim of sovereignty, by means of use or occupation, or by any other means.

3. Neither the surface nor the subsurface of the moon, nor any part thereof or natural resources in place, shall become property of any State, international intergovernmental or non-governmental organization, national organization or non-governmental entity or of any natural person. The placement of personnel, space vehicles, equipment, facilities, stations and installations on or below the surface of the moon, including structures connected with its surface or subsurface, shall not create a right of ownership over the surface or the subsurface of the moon or any areas thereof. The foregoing provisions are without prejudice to the international régime referred to in paragraph 5 of this article.

4. States Parties have the right to exploration and use of the moon without discrimination of any kind, on the basis of equality and in accordance with international law and the terms of this Agreement.

5. States Parties to this Agreement hereby undertake to establish an international régime, including appropriate procedures, to govern the exploitation of the natural resources of the moon as such exploitation is about to become feasible. This provision shall be implemented in accordance with article 18 of this Agreement.

6. In order to facilitate the establishment of the international régime referred to in paragraph 5 of this article, States Parties shall inform the Secretary-General of the United Nations as well as the public and the international scientific community, to the greatest extent feasible and practicable, of any natural resources they may discover on the moon.

7. The main purposes of the international régime to be established shall include:

(a) The orderly and safe development of the natural resources of the moon;

(b) The rational management of those resources;

(c) The expansion of opportunities in the use of those resources;

(d) An equitable sharing by all States Parties in the benefits derived from those resources, whereby the interests and needs of the developing countries, as well as the efforts of those countries which have contributed either directly or indirectly to the exploration of the moon, shall be given special consideration.

8. All the activities with respect to the natural resources of the moon shall be carried out in a manner compatible with the purposes specified in paragraph 7 of this article and the provisions of article 6, paragraph 2, of this Agreement.

Article 12

1. States Parties shall retain jurisdiction and control over their personnel, vehicles, equipment, facilities, stations and installations on the moon. The

ownership of space vehicles, equipment, facilities, stations and installations shall not be affected by their presence on the moon.

2. Vehicles, installations and equipment or their component parts found in places other than their intended location shall be dealt with in accordance with article 5 of the Agreement on the Rescue of Astronauts, the Return of Astronauts and the Return of Objects Launched into Outer Space.

3. In the event of an emergency involving a threat to human life, States Parties may use the equipment, vehicles, installations, facilities or supplies of other States Parties on the moon. Prompt notification of such use shall be made to the Secretary-General of the United Nations or the State Party concerned.

Article 13

A State Party which learns of the crash landing, forced landing or other unintended landing on the moon of a space object, or its component parts, that were not launched by it, shall promptly inform the launching State Party and the Secretary-General of the United Nations.

Article 14

1. States Parties to this Agreement shall bear international responsibility for national activities on the moon, whether such activities are carried on by governmental agencies or by non-governmental entities, and for assuring that national activities are carried out in conformity with the provisions set forth in this Agreement. States Parties shall ensure that non-governmental entities under their jurisdiction shall engage in activities on the moon only under the authority and continuing supervision of the appropriate State Party.

2. States Parties recognize that detailed arrangements concerning liability for damage caused on the moon, in addition to the provisions of the Treaty on Principles Governing the Activities of States in the Exploration and Use of Outer Space, including the Moon and Other Celestial Bodies and the Convention on International Liability for Damage Caused by Space Objects may become necessary as a result of more extensive activities on the moon. Any such arrangements shall be elaborated in accordance with the procedure provided for in article 18 of this Agreement.

Article 15

1. Each State Party may assure itself that the activities of other States Parties in the exploration and use of the moon are compatible with the provi-

sions of this Agreement. To this end, all space vehicles, equipment, facilities, stations and installations on the moon shall be open to other States Parties. Such States Parties shall give reasonable advance notice of a projected visit, in order that appropriate consultations may be held and that maximum precautions may be taken to assure safety and to avoid interference with normal operations in the facility to be visited. In pursuance of this article, any State Party may act on its own behalf or with the full or partial assistance of any other State Party or through appropriate international procedures within the framework of the United Nations and in accordance with the Charter.

2. A State Party which has reason to believe that another State Party is not fulfilling the obligations incumbent upon it pursuant to this Agreement or that another State Party is interfering with the rights which the former State has under this Agreement may request consultations with that State Party. A State Party receiving such a request shall enter into such consultations without delay. Any other State Party which requests to do so shall be entitled to take part in the consultations. Each State Party participating in such consultations shall seek a mutually acceptable resolution of any controversy and shall bear in mind the rights and interests of all States Parties. The Secretary-General of the United Nations shall be informed of the results of the consultations and shall transmit the information received to all States Parties concerned.

3. If the consultations do not lead to a mutually acceptable settlement which has due regard for the rights and interests of all States Parties, the parties concerned shall take all measures to settle the dispute by other peaceful means of their choice appropriate to the circumstances and the nature of the dispute. If difficulties arise in connection with the opening of consultations or if consultations do not lead to a mutually acceptable settlement, any State Party may seek the assistance of the Secretary-General, without seeking the consent of any other State Party concerned, in order to resolve the controversy. A State Party which does not maintain diplomatic relations with another State Party concerned shall participate in such consultations, at its choice, either itself or through another State Party or the Secretary-General as intermediary.

Article 16

With the exception of articles 17 to 21, references in this Agreement to States shall be deemed to apply to any international intergovernmental organization which conducts space activities if the organization declares its acceptance of the rights and obligations provided for in this Agreement and if a majority of the States members of the organization are States Parties to this Agreement and to the Treaty on Principles Governing the Activities of States in the Exploration and Use of Outer Space, including the Moon and Other Celestial Bodies. States members of any such organization which are States Parties to this Agreement shall take all appropriate steps to ensure that the organization makes a declaration in accordance with the foregoing.

Article 17

Any State Party to this Agreement may propose amendments to the Agreement. Amendments shall enter into force for each State Party to the Agreement accepting the amendments upon their acceptance by a majority of the States Parties to the Agreement and thereafter for each remaining State Party to the Agreement on the date of acceptance by it.

Article 18

Ten years after the entry into force of this Agreement, the question of the review of this Agreement shall be included in the provisional agenda of the General Assembly of the United Nations in order to consider, in the light of past application of the Agreement, whether it requires revision. However, at any time after the Agreement has been in force for five years, the Secretary-General of the United Nations, as depositary, shall, at the request of one third of the States Parties to the Agreement and with the concurrence of the majority of the States Parties, convene a conference of the States Parties to review this Agreement. A review conference shall also consider the question of the implementation of the provisions of article 11, paragraph 5, on the basis of the principles referred to in paragraph 1 of that article and taking into account in particular any relevant technological developments.

Article 19

1. This Agreement shall be open for signature by all States at United Nations Headquarters in New York.

2. This Agreement shall be subject to ratification by signatory States. Any State which does not sign this Agreement before its entry into force in accordance with paragraph 3 of this article may accede to it at any time. Instruments of ratification or accession shall be deposited with the Secretary-General of the United Nations.

3. This Agreement shall enter into force on the thirtieth day following the date of deposit of the fifth instrument of ratification.

4. For each State depositing its instrument of ratification or accession after

the entry into force of this Agreement, it shall enter into force on the thirtieth day following the date of deposit of any such instrument.

5. The Secretary-General shall promptly inform all signatory and acceding States of the date of each signature, the date of deposit of each instrument of ratification of and accession to this Agreement, the date of its entry into force and other notices.

Article 20

Any State Party to this Agreement may give notice of its withdrawal from the Agreement one year after its entry into force by written notification to the Secretary-General of the United Nations. Such withdrawal shall take effect one year from the date of receipt of this notification.

Article 21

The original of this Agreement, of which the Arabic, Chinese, English, French, Russian and Spanish texts are equally authentic, shall be deposited with the Secretary-General of the United Nations, who shall send certified copies thereof to all signatory and acceding States.

IN WITNESS WHEREOF the undersigned, being duly authorized thereto by their respective Governments, have signed this Agreement, opened for signature at New York on 18 December 1979.

II. UNITED NATIONS GENERAL ASSEMBLY RESOLUTIONS ADOPTING PRINCIPLES ON THE EXPLORATION AND USE OF OUTER SPACE

1. INTERNATIONAL CO-OPERATION IN THE PEACEFUL USES OF OUTER SPACE[111]

The General Assembly,

Recognizing the common interest of mankind in furthering the peaceful uses of outer space and the urgent need to strengthen international co-operation in this important field,

Believing that the exploration and use of outer space should be only for the betterment of mankind and to the benefit of States irrespective of the stage of their economic or scientific development,

---

[111] Resolution 1721 A (XVI) of 20 Dec. 1961.

1. *Commends* to States for their guidance in the exploration and use of outer space the following principles:

(*a*) International law, including the Charter of the United Nations, applies to outer space and celestial bodies;

(*b*) Outer space and celestial bodies are free for exploration and use by all States in conformity with international law and are not subject to national appropriation;

2. *Invites* the Committee on the Peaceful Uses of Outer Space to study and report on the legal problems which may arise from the exploration and use of outer space.

2. QUESTION OF GENERAL AND COMPLETE DISARMAMENT[112]

The General Assembly,

Recalling its resolution 1721 A (XVI) of 20 December 1961 in which it expressed the belief that the exploration and use of outer space should be only for the benefit of mankind,

Determined to take steps to prevent the spread of the arms race to outer space,

1. *Welcomes* the expressions by the Union of Soviet Socialist Republics and the United States of America of their intention not to station in outer space any objects carrying nuclear weapons or other kinds of weapons of mass destruction;

2. *Solemnly calls upon* all States:

(*a*) To refrain from placing in orbit around the earth any objects carrying nuclear weapons or any other kinds of weapons of mass destruction, installing such weapons on celestial bodies, or stationing such weapons in outer space in any other manner;

(*b*) To refrain from causing, encouraging or in any way participating in the conduct of the foregoing activities.

3. DECLARATION OF LEGAL PRINCIPLES GOVERNING THE ACTIVITIES OF STATES IN THE EXPLORATION AND USE OF OUTER SPACE[113]

The General Assembly,

Inspired by the great prospects opening up before mankind as a result of man's entry into outer space,

Recognizing the common interest of all mankind in the progress of the exploration and use of outer space for peaceful purposes,

Believing that the exploration and use of outer space should be carried on for the betterment of mankind and for the benefit of States irrespective of their degree of economic or scientific development,

---

[112] Resolution 1884 (XVIII) of 17 Oct. 1963.
[113] Resolution 1962 (XVIII) of 13 Dec. 1963.

Desiring to contribute to broad international co-operation in the scientific as well as in the legal aspects of exploration and use of outer space for peaceful purposes,

Believing that such co-operation will contribute to the development of mutual understanding and to the strengthening of friendly relations between nations and peoples,

Recalling its resolution 110(II) of 3 November 1947, which condemned propaganda designed or likely to provoke or encourage any threat to the peace, breach of the peace, or act of aggression, and considering that the aforementioned resolution is applicable to outer space,

Taking into consideration its resolution 1721(XVI) of 20 December 1961 and 1802(XVII) of 14 December 1962, adopted unanimously by the States Members of the United Nations,

Solemnly declares that in the exploration and use of outer space States should be guided by the following principles:

1. The exploration and use of outer space shall be carried on for the benefit and in the interests of all mankind.

2. Outer space and celestial bodies are free for exploration and use by all States on a basis of equality and in accordance with international law.

3. Outer space and celestial bodies are not subject to national appropriation by claim of sovereignty, by means of use or occupation, or by any other means.

4. The activities of States in the exploration and use of other space shall be carried on in accordance with international law, including the Charter of the United Nations, in the interest of maintaining international peace and security and promoting international co-operation and understanding.

5. States bear international responsibility for national activities in outer space, whether carried on by governmental agencies or by non-governmental entities, and for assuring that national activities are carried on in conformity with the principles set forth in the present Declaration. The activities of non-governmental entities in outer space shall require authorization and continued supervision by the State concerned. When activities are carried on in outer space by an international organization, responsibility for compliance with the principles set forth in this Declaration shall be borne by the international organization and by the States participating in it.

6. In the exploration and use of outer space, States shall be guided by the principle of co-operation and mutual assistance and shall conduct all their activities in outer space with due regard for the corresponding interests of other States. If a State has reason to believe that an outer space activity or experiment planned by it or its nationals would cause potentially harmful interference with activities of other States in the peaceful exploration and use of outer space, it shall undertake appropriate international consultations before proceeding with any such activity or experiment. A State which has

reason to believe that an outer space activity or experiment planned by another State would cause potentially harmful interference with activities in the peaceful exploration and use of outer space may request consultation concerning the activity or experiment.

7. The State on whose registry an object launched into outer space is carried shall retain jurisdiction and control over such object, and any personnel thereon, while in outer space. Ownership of objects launched into outer space, and of their component parts, is not affected by their passage through outer space or by their return to the earth. Such objects or component parts found beyond the limits of the State of registry shall be returned to that State, which shall furnish identifying data upon request prior to return.

8. Each State which launches or procures the launching of an object into outer space, and each State from whose territory or facility an object is launched, is internationally liable for damage to a foreign State or to its natural or juridical persons by such object or its component parts on the earth, in air space, or in outer space.

9. States shall regard astronauts as envoys of mankind in outer space, and shall render to them all possible assistance in the event of accident, distress, or emergency landing on the territory of a foreign State or on the high seas. Astronauts who make such a landing shall be safely and promptly returned to the State of registry of their space vehicle.

4. PRINCIPLES GOVERNING THE USE BY STATES OF ARTIFICIAL EARTH SATELLITES FOR INTERNATIONAL DIRECT TELEVISION BROADCASTING.[114]

The General Assembly,

Recalling its resolution 2916(XXVII) of 9 November 1972, in which it stressed the necessity of elaborating principles governing the use by States of artificial earth satellites for international direct television broadcasting, and mindful of the importance of concluding an international agreement or agreements,

Recalling further its resolutions 3182(XXVIII) of 18 December 1973, 3234(XXIX) of 12 November 1974, 3388(XXX) of 18 November 1975, 31/8 of November 1976, 32/196 of 20 December 1977, 33/16 of 10 November 1978, 34/66 of 5 December 1981 in which it decided to consider at its thirty-seventh session the adoption of a draft set of principles governing the use by States of artificial earth satellites for international direct television broadcasting,

Noting with appreciation the efforts made in the Committee on the Peaceful Uses of Outer Space and its Legal Sub-Committee to comply with the directives issued in the above-mentioned resolutions,

Considering that several experiments of direct broadcasting by satellite have

[114] Resolution 37/92 of 10 Dec. 1982.

been carried out and that a number of direct broadcasting satellite systems are operational in some countries and may be commercialized in the very near future,

Taking into consideration that the operation of international direct broadcasting satellites will have significant international political, economic, social and cultural implications,

Believing that the establishment of principles for international direct television broadcasting will contribute to the strengthening of international co-operation in this field and further the purposes and principles of the Charter of the United Nations,

Adopts the Principles Governing the Use by States of Artificial Earth Satellites for International Direct Television Broadcasting set forth in the annex to the present resolution.

ANNEX

Principles Governing the Use by States of Artificial Earth Satellites for International Direct Television Broadcasting

A. Purposes and objectives

1. Activities in the field of international direct television broadcasting by satellite should be carried out in a manner compatible with the sovereign rights of States, including the principle of non-intervention, as well as with the right of everyone to seek, receive and impart information and ideas as enshrined in the relevant United Nations instruments.

2. Such activities should promote the free dissemination and mutual exchange of information and knowledge in cultural and scientific fields, assist in educational, social and economic development, particularly in the developing countries, enhance the qualities of life of all peoples and provide recreation with due respect to the political and cultural integrity of States.

3. These activities should accordingly be carried out in a manner compatible with the development of mutual understanding and the strengthening of friendly relations and co-operation among all States and peoples in the interest of maintaining international peace and security.

B. Applicability of international law

4. Activities in the field of international direct television broadcasting by satellite should be conducted in accordance with international law, including

the Charter of the United Nations, the Treaty on Principles Governing the Activities of States in the Exploration and Use of Outer Space, including the Moon and Other Celestial Bodies, of 27 January 1967, the relevant provisions of the International Telecommunication Convention and its Radio regulations and of international instruments relating to friendly relations and co-operation among States and to human rights.

C. Rights and benefits

5. Every State has an equal right to conduct activities in the field of international direct television broadcasting by satellite and to authorize such activities by persons and entities under its jurisdiction. All States and peoples are entitled to and should enjoy the benefits from such activities. Access to the technology in this field should be available to all States without discrimination on terms mutually agreed by all concerned.

D. International co-operation

6. Activities in the field of international direct television broadcasting by satellite should be based upon and encourage international co-operation. Such co-operation should be the subject of appropriate arrangements. Special consideration should be given to the needs of the developing countries in the use of international direct television broadcasting by satellite for the purpose of accelerating their national development.

E. Peaceful settlement of disputes

7. Any international dispute that may arise from activities covered by these principles should be settled through established procedures for the peaceful settlement of disputes agreed upon by the parties to the dispute in accordance with the provisions of the Charter of the United Nations.

F. State responsibility

8. States should bear international responsibility for activities in the field of international direct television broadcasting by satellite carried out by them or under their jurisdiction and for the conformity of any such activities with the principles set forth in this document.

9. When international direct television broadcasting by satellite is carried

out by an international intergovernmental organization, the responsibility referred to in paragraph 8 above should be borne both by that organization and by the States participating in it.

G. Duty and right to consult

10. Any broadcasting or receiving State within an international direct television broadcasting satellite service established between them requested to do so by any other broadcasting or receiving State within the same service should promptly enter into consultations with the requesting State regarding its activities in the field of international direct television broadcasting by satellite, without prejudice to other consultations which these States may undertake with any other State on that subject.

H. Copyright and neighbouring rights

11. Without prejudice to the relevant provisions of international law, States should co-operate on a bilateral and multilateral basis for protection of copyright and neighbouring rights by means of appropriate agreements between the interested States or the competent legal entities acting under their jurisdiction. In such co-operation they should give special consideration to the interests of developing countries in the use of direct television broadcasting for the purpose of accelerating their national development.

I. Notification to the United Nations

12. In order to promote international co-operation in the peaceful exploration and use of outer space, States conducting or authorizing activities in the field of international direct television broadcasting by satellite should inform the Secretary-General of the United Nations, to the greatest extent possible, of the nature of such activities. On receiving this information, the Secretary-General should disseminate it immediately and effectively to the relevant specialized agencies, as well as to the public and the international scientific community.

J. Consultations and agreements between States

13. A State which intends to establish or authorize the establishment of an international direct television broadcasting satellite service shall without

delay notify the proposed receiving State or States of such intention and shall promptly enter into consultation with any of those States which so requests.

14. An international direct television broadcasting satellite service shall only be established after the conditions set forth in paragraph 13 above have been met and on the basis of agreements and/or arrangements in conformity with the relevant instruments of the International Telecommunication Union and in accordance with these principles.

15. With respect to the unavoidable overspill of the radiation of the satellite signal, the relevant instruments of the International Telecommunication Union should be exclusively applicable.

5. PRINCIPLES RELATING TO REMOTE SENSING OF THE EARTH FROM OUTER SPACE[115]

The General Assembly,

Recalling its resolution 3234 (XXIX) of 12 November 1974, in which it recommended that the Legal Sub-Committee of the Committee on the Peaceful Uses of Outer Space should consider the question of the legal implications of remote sensing of the Earth from space, as well as its resolutions 3388(XXX) of 18 November 1975, 31/8 of 8 November 1976, 32/196 A of 20 December 1977, 33/16 of 10 November 1978, 34/66 of 5 December 1979, 35/14 of 3 November 1980, 36/35 of 18 November 1981, 37/89 of 10 December 1982, 38/80 of 15 December 1983, 39/96 of 14 December 1984 and 40/162 of 16 December 1985, in which it called for a detailed consideration of the legal implications of remote sensing of the Earth from space, with the aim of formulating draft principles relating to remote sensing.

Having considered the report of the Committee on the Peaceful Uses of Outer Space on the work of its twenty-ninth session and the text of the draft Principles Relating to Remote Sensing of the Earth from Space, annexed thereto,

Noting with satisfaction that the Committee on the Peaceful Uses of Outer Space, on the basis of the deliberations of its Legal Sub-Committee, has endorsed the text of the draft Principles Relating to Remote Sensing of the Earth from Space,

Believing that the adoption of the Principles Relating to Remote Sensing of the Earth from Space will contribute to the strengthening of international co-operation in this field,

Adopts the Principles Relating to Remote Sensing of the Earth from Space set forth in the annex to the present resolution.

[115] Resolution 41/65, 3 Dec. 1986.

ANNEX

Principles relating to Remote Sensing of the Earth from Space

Principle I

For the purposes of these principles with respect to remote sensing activities:

(*a*) The term 'remote sensing' means the sensing of the Earth's surface from space by making use of the properties of electromagnetic waves emitted, reflected or diffracted by the sensed objects, for the purpose of improving natural resources management, land use and protection of the environment;

(*b*) The term 'primary data' means those raw data that are acquired by remote sensors borne by a space object and that are transmitted or delivered to the ground from space by telemetry in the form of electromagnetic signals, by photographic film, magnetic tape or any other means;

(c) The term 'processed data' means the products resulting from the processing of the primary data, needed in order to make such data usable;

(*d*) The term 'analysed information' means the information resulting from the interpretation of processed data, inputs of data and knowledge from other sources;

(*e*) The term 'remote sensing activities' means the operation of remote sensing space systems, primary data collection and storage stations, and activities in processing, interpreting and disseminating the processed data.

Principle II

Remote sensing activities shall be carried out for the benefit and in the interests of all countries, irrespective of their degree of economic, social or scientific and technological development, and taking into particular consideration the needs of the developing countries.

Principle III

Remote sensing activities shall be conducted in accordance with international law, including the Charter of the United Nations, the Treaty on Principles Governing the Activities of States in the Exploration and Use of Outer Space, including the Moon and Other Celestial Bodies, and the relevant instruments of the International Telecommunication Union.

Principle IV

Remote sensing activities shall be conducted in accordance with the principles contained in article I of the Treaty on Principles Governing the Activities of States in the Exploration and Use of Outer Space, including the Moon and Other Celestial Bodies, which, in particular provides that the exploration and use of outer space shall be carried out for the benefit and in the interests of all countries, irrespective of their degree of economic or scientific development, and stipulates the principle of freedom of exploration and use of outer space on a basis of equality. These activities shall be conducted on the basis of respect for the principle of full and permanent sovereignty of all States and peoples over their own wealth and natural resources, with due regard to the rights and interests, in accordance with international law, of other States and entities under their jurisdiction. Such activities shall not be conducted in a manner detrimental to the legitimate rights and interests of the sensed State.

Principle V

States carrying out remote sensing activities shall promote international co-operation in these activities. To this end, they shall make available to other States opportunities for participation therein. Such participation shall be based in each case on equitable and mutually acceptable terms.

Principle VI

In order to maximize the availability of benefits from remote sensing activities, States are encouraged through agreements or other arrangements, to provide for the establishment and operation of data collecting and storage stations and processing and interpretation facilities, in particular within the framework of regional agreements or arrangements wherever feasible.

Principle VII

States participating in remote sensing activities shall make available technical assistance to other interested States on mutually agreed terms.

Principle VIII

The United Nations and the relevant agencies within the United Nations system shall promote international co-operation, including technical assistance and co-ordination in the area of remote sensing.

Principle IX

In accordance with article IV of the Convention on Registration of Objects Launched into Outer Space and article XI of the Treaty on Principles Governing the Activities of States in the Exploration and Use of Outer Space, including the Moon and Other Celestial Bodies, a State carrying out a programme of remote sensing shall inform the Secretary-General of the United Nations. It shall, moreover, make available any other relevant information to the greatest extent feasible and practicable to any other State, particularly any developing country that is affected by the programme, at its request.

Principle X

Remote sensing shall promote the protection of the Earth's natural environment. To this end, States participating in remote sensing activities that have identified information in their possession that is capable of averting any phenomenon harmful to the Earth's natural environment shall disclose such information to States concerned.

Principle XI

Remote sensing shall promote the protection of mankind from natural disasters. To this end, States participating in remote sensing activities that have identified processed data and analysed information in their possession that may be useful to States affected by natural disasters, or likely to be affected by impending natural disasters, shall transmit such data and information to States concerned as promptly as possible.

Principle XII

As soon as the primary data and the processed data concerning the territory under its jurisdiction are produced, the sensed State shall have access to them on a non-discriminatory basis and on reasonable cost terms. The sensed State shall also have access to the available analysed information concerning the territory under its jurisdiction in the possession of any State participating in remote sensing activities on the same basis and terms, taking particularly into account the needs and interests of the developing countries.

Principle XIII

To promote and intensify international co-operation, especially with regard to the needs of developing countries, a State carrying out remote sensing of the Earth from space shall upon request, enter into consultation with a State whose territory is sensed in order to make available opportunities for participation and enhance the mutual benefits to be derived therefrom.

Principle XIV

In compliance with article VI of the Treaty on Principles Governing the Activities of States in the Exploration and Use of Outer Space, including the Moon and Other Celestial Bodies, States operating remote sensing satellites shall bear international responsibility for their activities and assure that such activities are conducted in accordance with these principles and the norms of international law, irrespective of whether such activities are carried out by governmental or non-governmental entities or through international organizations to which such States are parties. This principle is without prejudice to the applicability of the norms of international law on State responsibility for remote sensing activities.

Principle XV

Any dispute resulting from the application of these principles shall be resolved through the established procedures for the peaceful settlement of disputes.

6. PRINCIPLES RELEVANT TO THE USE OF NUCLEAR POWER SOURCES IN OUTER SPACE[116]

The General Assembly,
Having considered the report of the Committee on the Peaceful Uses of Outer Space on the work of its thirty-fifth session and the text of the Principles

---

[116] Resolution 47/68, 14 Dec. 1992.

Relevant to the Use of Nuclear Power Sources in Outer Space as approved by the Committee and annexed to its report,

Recognizing that for some missions in outer space nuclear power sources are particularly suited or even essential owing to their compactness, long life and other attributes,

Recognizing also that the use of nuclear power sources in outer space should focus on those applications which take advantage of the particular properties of nuclear power sources,

Recognizing further that the use of nuclear power sources in outer space should be based on a thorough safety assessment, including probabilistic risk analysis, with particular emphasis on reducing the risk of accidental exposure of the public to harmful radiation or radiative material.

Recognizing the need, in this respect, for a set of principles containing goals and guidelines to ensure the safe use of nuclear power sources in other space,

Affirming that this set of Principles applies to nuclear power sources in outer space devoted to the generation of electric power on board space objects for non-propulsive purposes, which have characteristics generally comparable to those of systems used and missions performed at the time of the adoption of the Principles,

Recognizing that this set of Principles will require future revision in view of emerging nuclear-power applications and of evolving international recommendations on radiological protection,

Adopts the Principles Relevant to the Use of Nuclear Power Sources in Outer Space as set forth below.

Principle 1. Applicability of international law

Activities involving the use of nuclear power sources in outer space shall be carried out in accordance with international law, including in particular the Charter of the United Nations and the Treaty on Principles Governing the Activities of States in the Exploration and Use of Outer Space, including the Moon and Other Celestial Bodies.

Principle 2. Use of terms

1. For the purpose of these Principles, the terms 'launching State' and 'States launching' mean the State which exercises jurisdiction and control over a space object with nuclear power sources on board at a given point in time relevant to the principle concerned.

2. For the purpose of principle 9, the definition of the term 'launching State' as contained in that principle is applicable.

3. For the purposes of principle 3, the terms 'foreseeable' and 'all possible' describe a class of events or circumstances whose overall probability of occurrence is such that it is considered to encompass only credible possibilities for purposes of safety analysis. The term 'general concept of defence-in-depth' when applied to nuclear power sources in outer space refers to the use of design features and mission operations in place of or in addition to active systems, to prevent or mitigate the consequences of system malfunctions. Redundant safety systems are not necessarily required for each individual component to achieve this purpose. Given the special requirements of space use and of varied missions, no particular set of systems or features can be specified as essential to achieve this objective. For the purposes of paragraph 2(*d*) of principle 3, the term 'made critical' does not include actions such as zero-power testing which are fundamental to ensuring system safety.

Principle 3. Guidelines and criteria for safe use

In order to minimize the quantity of radioactive material in space and the risks involved, the use of nuclear power sources in outer space shall be restricted to those space missions which cannot be operated by non-nuclear energy sources in a reasonable way.

1. General goals for radiation protection and nuclear safety

(*a*) States launching space objects with nuclear power sources on board shall endeavour to protect individuals, populations and the biosphere against radiological hazards. The design and use of space objects with nuclear power sources on board shall ensure, with a high degree of confidence, that the hazards, in foreseeable operational or accidental circumstances, are kept below acceptable levels as defined in paragraphs 1(*b*) and (*c*).

Such design and use shall also ensure with high reliability that the radioactive material does not cause a significant contamination of outer space.

(*b*) During the normal operation of space objects within nuclear power sources on board, including re-entry from the sufficiently high orbit as defined in paragraph 2(*b*), the appropriate radiation protection objective for the public recommended by the International Commission on Radiological Protection shall be observed. During such normal operation there shall be no significant radiation exposure.

(*c*) To limit exposure in accidents, the design and construction of the nuclear power source systems shall take into account relevant and generally accepted international radiological protection guidelines.

Except in cases of low-probability accidents with potentially serious radiological consequences, the design for the nuclear power source systems shall, with a high degree of confidence, restrict radiation exposure to a limited geographical region and to individuals to the principal limit of 1 mSv in a year for some years, provided that the average annual effective dose equivalent over a lifetime does not exceed the principal limit of 1 mSv in a year.

The probability of accidents with potentially serious radiological consequences referred to above shall be kept extremely small by virtue of the design of the system.

Future modifications of the guidelines referred to in this paragraph shall be applied as soon as practicable.

(*d*) Systems important for safety shall be designed, constructed and operated in accordance with the general concept of defence-in-depth. Pursuant to this concept, foreseeable safety-related failures or malfunctions must be capable of being corrected or counteracted by an action or a procedure, possibly automatic.

Other measures shall also be take to raise the level of safety.

2. Nuclear reactors

(*a*) Nuclear reactors may be operated:

   (i)   On interplanetary missions;

   (ii) In sufficiently high orbits as defined in paragraph 2(*b*);

   (iii) In low-Earth orbits if they are stored in sufficiently high orbits after the operational part of their mission.

(*b*) The sufficiently high orbit is one in which the orbital lifetime is long enough to allow for a sufficient decay of the fission products to approximately the activity of the actinides. The sufficiently high orbit must be such that the risks to existing and future outer space missions and of collision with other space objects are kept to a minimum. The necessity for the parts of a destroyed reactor also to attain the required decay time before re-entering the Earth's atmosphere shall be considered in determining the sufficiently high orbit altitude.

(*c*) Nuclear reactors shall use only highly enriched uranium 235 as fuel. The design shall take into account the radioactive decay of the fission and activation products.

(*d*) Nuclear reactors shall not be made critical before they have reached their operating orbit or interplanetary trajectory.

(*e*) The design and construction of the nuclear reactor shall ensure that it cannot become critical before reaching the operating orbit during all possible events, including rocket explosion, re-entry, impact on ground or water, submersion in water or water intruding into the core.

(*f*) In order to reduce significantly the possibility of failures in satellites with nuclear reactors on board during operations in an orbit with a lifetime less than in the sufficiently high orbit (including operations for transfer into the sufficiently high orbit), there shall be a highly reliable operational system to ensure an effective and controlled disposal of the reactor.

3. Radioisotope generators

(*a*) Radioisotope generators may be used for interplanetary missions and other missions leaving the gravity field of the Earth. They may also be used in Earth orbit if, after conclusion of the operational part of their mission, they are stored in a high orbit. In any case ultimate disposal is necessary.

(*b*) Radioisotope generators shall be protected by a containment system that is designed and constructed to withstand the heat and aerodynamic forces of re-entry in the upper atmosphere under foreseeable orbital conditions, including highly elliptical or hyperbolic orbits where relevant. Upon impact, the containment system and the physical form of the isotope shall ensure that no radioactive material is scattered into the environment so that the impact area can be completely cleared of radioactivity by a recovery operation.

Principle 4. Safety assessment

1. A launching State as defined in principle 2, paragraph 1, at the time of launch shall, prior to the launch, through co-operative arrangements, where relevant, with those which have designed, constructed, or manufactured the nuclear power sources, or will operate the space object, or from whose territory or facility such an object will be launched, ensure that a thorough and comprehensive safety assessment is conducted. This assessment shall cover as well all relevant phases of the mission and shall deal with all systems involved, including the means of launching, the space platform, the nuclear power source and its equipment and the means of control and communication between ground and space.

2. This assessment shall respect the guidelines and criteria for safe use contained in principle 3.

3. Pursuant to article XI of the Treaty on Principles Governing the Activities of States in the Exploration and Use of Outer Space, including the Moon and Other Celestial Bodies, the results of this safety assessment, together with, to the extent feasible, an indication of the approximate intended time-frame of the launch, shall be made publicly available prior to each launch, and the Secretary-General of the United Nations shall be informed on how States may obtain such results of the safety assessment as soon as possible prior to each launch.

Principle 5. Notification of re-entry

1. Any State launching a space object with nuclear power sources on board shall in a timely fashion inform States concerned in the event this space object is malfunctioning with a risk of re-entry of radioactive materials to the Earth.

The information shall be in accordance with the following format:
  (a) System parameters:
  (i)   Name of launching State or States, including the address of the authority which may be contacted for additional information or assistance in case of accident;
  (ii) International designation;
  (iii) Date and territory or location of launch;
  (iv) Information required for best prediction of orbit lifetimes, trajectory and impact region;
  (v)   General function of spacecraft;
  (b) *Information on the radiological risk of nuclear power source(s)*:
  (i)   Type of nuclear power source: radioisotopic/reactor;
  (ii) The probable physical form, amount and general radiological characteristics of the fuel and contaminated and/or activated components likely to reach the ground. The term 'fuel' refers to the nuclear material used as the source of heat or power.

This information shall also be transmitted to the Secretary-General of the United Nations.

2, The information, in accordance with the format above, shall be provided by the launching State as soon as the malfunction has become known. It shall be updated as frequently as practicable and the frequency of dissemination of the updated information shall increase as the anticipated time of re-entry into the dense layers of the Earth's atmosphere approaches so that the international community will be informed of the situation and will have sufficient time to plan for any national response activities deemed necessary.

3. The updated information shall also be transmitted to the Secretary-General of the United Nations with the same frequency.

Principle 6. Consultations

States providing information in accordance with principle 5 shall, as far as reasonably practicable, respond promptly to requests for further information or consultations sought by other States.

Principle 7. Assistance to States

1. Upon the notification of an expected re-entry into the Earth's atmosphere of a space object containing a nuclear power source on board and its components, all States possessing space monitoring and tracking facilities, in the spirit of international co-operation, shall communicate the relevant information that they may have available on the malfunctioning space object with

a nuclear power source on board to the Secretary-General of the United Nations and the State concerned as promptly as possible to allow States that might be affected to assess the situation and take any precautionary measures deemed necessary.

2. After re-entry into the Earth's atmosphere of a space object containing a nuclear power source on board and its components:

(*a*) The launching State shall promptly offer and, if requested by the affected State, provide promptly the necessary assistance to eliminate actual and possible harmful effects, including assistance to identify the location of the area of impact of the nuclear power source on the Earth's surface, to detect the re-entered material and to carry out retrieval or clean-up operations;

(*b*) All States, other than the launching State, with relevant technical capabilities and international organizations with such technical capabilities shall, to the extent possible, provide necessary assistance upon request by an affected State.

In providing the assistance in accordance with subparagraphs (*a*) and (*b*) above, the special needs of developing countries shall be taken into account.

Principle 8. Responsibility

In accordance with article VI of the Treaty on Principles Governing the Activities of States in the Exploration and Use of Outer Space, including the Moon and Other Celestial Bodies, States shall bear international responsibility for national activities involving the use of nuclear power sources in outer space, whether such activities are carried on by governmental agencies or by non-governmental entities, and for assuring that such national activities are carried out in conformity that Treaty and the recommendations contained in these Principles. When activities in outer space involving the use of nuclear power sources are carried on by an international organization, responsibility for compliance with the aforesaid Treaty and the recommendations contained in these Principles shall be borne both by the international organization and by the States participating in it.

Principle 9. Liability and compensation

1. In accordance with article VII of the Treaty on Principles Governing the Activities of States in the Exploration and Use of Outer Space, including the Moon and Other Celestial Bodies, and the provisions of the Convention on International Liability for Damage Caused by Space Objects, each State which launches or procures the launching of a space object and each State from whose territory or facility a space object is launched shall be interna-

tionally liable for damage caused by such space objects or their component parts. This fully applies to the case of such a space object carrying a nuclear power source on board. Whenever two or more States jointly launch such a space object, they shall be jointly and severally liable for any damage caused, in accordance with article V of the above-mentioned Convention.

2. The compensation that such States shall be liable to pay under the aforesaid Convention for damage shall be determined in accordance with international law and the principles of justice and equity, in order to provide such reparation in respect of the damage as will restore the person, natural or juridical, State or international organization on whose behalf a claim is presented to the condition which would have existed if the damage had not occurred.

3. For the purposes of this principle, compensation shall include reimbursement of the duly substantiated expenses for search, recovery and clean-up operations, including expenses for assistance received from third parties.

Principle 10. Settlement of disputes

Any dispute resulting from the application of these Principles shall be resolved through negotiations or other established procedures for the peaceful settlement of disputes, in accordance with the Charter of the United Nations.

Principle 11. Review and revision

These Principles shall be reopened for revision by the Committee on the Peaceful Uses of Outer Space no later than two years after their adoption.

Bibliography

I. Bibliographies

Halket, T. O., F. A. Savage, L. D. Ahearn, R. L. Anglin, B. A. Carigmyle, B. L. Fisher and V. Leister, 'Bibliography of the Law of Outer Space', 22 *Jurimetrics Journal of Law, Science and Technology* (1982), pp. 195–238.

Institute of Advanced Legal Studies, University of London, *Union List of Air and Space Law Literature in the Libraries of Oxford, Cambridge and London* (2nd ed., London, 1975).

Kehrberger, H. P., *Legal and Political Implications of Space Research: A Selective Bibliography* (Hamburg, 1965).

Li, Kuo Lee (ed.), *World Wide Space Bibliography* (Montreal, 1978) and supplements, 1977–86, 1987 and 1988 (Montreal, 1987, 1988, 1989).

Magraw, D. B., and Theresa Ketler (eds), 'Law Relating to Outer Space: A Bibliography—Part I', 19 *The International Lawyer* (1985), 1391–1427; 'Part II', 20 ibid. (1986), pp. 399–421.

Morris, L., *Bibliography of Air and Space Law Materials* (Melbourne, 1978).

Rawnsley, L. S., and J. D. McWhirter, 'Space Law Bibliography', in S. Gorove (ed.), 3 *United States Space Law* (1987), pp. 1–280.

United Nations, *A Bibliography on the Law of Outer Space—Preliminary Edition* (1958).

——, Office for Outer Space Affairs, in cooperation with the International Institute of Space law, *Space Law: A Bigliography—Cumulative Index of the proceedings of colloquiums of the International Institute of Space Law 1958–1994* (New York, 1996).

Vanderdoe, N. A. C., S. Hobe, and M. Sude (eds.), *Inventory of Space Related Materials Available at ESA Headquarters* (1988).

II. Collected Documents

Böckstiegel, K. -H., and Benkö, M. (eds.), *Space Law: Basic Legal Documents* (2 vols., loose-leaf, Dordrecht, 1990–).

Gorove, S., *Cases on Space Law* (University, MS 38677, 1966).

—— (ed.), *United States Space Law—National and International Regulation* (Dobbs Ferry, NY, 1995)

Leanza, U., *The Future of International Telecommunications: The Legal Regime of Telecommunications by Geostationary Orbit Satellite* (4 vols., 1992).

United Nations: *The United Nations Treaties and Principles on Outer Space*, A/AC.105/572 and Corr. 1 (UN, 1994).

US Senate, Committee on Commerce, Science and Transportation: *Space Law and Related Documents* (US GPO, 1990).

III. Journals

Aeronautical Journal, The (Royal Aeronautical Society)
Aerospace (Royal Aeronautical Society)
AIR & Space LAW
Annuals of Air and Space Law
Aviation Week & Space Technology
Chronique des activités spaciales: aspects politiques et juridiques (Institut de droit comparé de l'Université Panthéon-Assas (Paris II))
ESA Bulletin
Journal of Space Law
Korean Journal of Air and Space Law
Revista de la Sociedad Venezolana de Derecho Aeronautico y Espacial (SOVEDA)
Revista del Centro de Investigación y Difusion Aeronautico-Espacial (CIDA, Montevideo)
Revue Française de Droit Aérien et Spatial
Revue Générale de l'Air et Espace
Space Communications Journal
Space News
Space Policy
Telecommunications & Space Journal
Zeitschrift für Luft- und Weltraumrecht

IV. General Books, Symposia, and Articles

American Assembly, *Outer Space: Prospects for Man and Society* (Englewood Cliffs, N.J., 1962).

Andem, M. N., *International Legal Problems in the Peaceful Exploration and Use of Outer Space* (Rovaniemi, 1992).

Bhatt, S., *Legal Controls of Outer Space* (New Delhi, 1973).

Böckstiegel, K. -H. (ed.), *Handbuch des Weltraumrechts* (Köln, 1991).

Bogaert, E. R. C. van, *Aspects of Space Law* (Deventer, 1986).

British Institute of International and Comparative Law: *Current Problems in Space Law: A Symposium* (London, 1966).

Chaumont, Ch., *Le droit de l'espace. Que sais-je?* (Paris, 1970).

Cheng, B., 'Problems of Space Law', 7 *The New Scientist* (1960), 1256–8.

Cheng, C. J. (ed.), *The Use of Airspace and Outer Space for all Mankind in the 21st Century* (The Hague, 1995).

Cheng, C. J., and Mendes de Leon, P. (eds.), *The Highways of Air and Outer Space over Asia* (Dordrecht, 1992).

Christol, Carl Q., *The Modern International Law of Outer Space* (New York, 1982).

——, *Space Law: Past, Present, and Future* (Deventer, 1991).

Cohen, M. (ed.), *Law and Politics in Space* (Montreal, 1964).

Cooper, J. C., *Exploration in Aerospace Law: Selected Essays* (ed. I. A. Vlassic; Montreal, 1968).

Dutheil de la Rochère, J. (ed.), *Droit de l'espace* (Paris, 1988).

Fasan, E.: *Weltraumrecht* (Mainz, 1965).

Fawcett, J. E. S.: *International Law and the Uses of Outer Space* (Manchester, 1968).

——, *Outer Space: New Challenges to the Law and Policy* (Oxford, 1984).

Francoz Rigalt, A., *Curso Monográfico de Derecho Espacial* (Mexico, 1977).

Gal, G., *Space Law* (New York and Leyden, 1969).

Gorove, S., *Studies in Space Law: Its Challenges and Prospects* (Leyden, 1977).

——, *Developments in Space Law* (Dordrecht, 1991).

Haley, A. G., *Space Law and Government* (New York, 1963).

Hosenball, S. N., 'NASA and the Practice of Space Law', 13 *JSL* (1985), 1–7.

International Astronautical Federation, International Institute of Space Law, *Colloquium on the Law of Outer Space* [*Space Law Colloquium*] (Washington DC, 1963 ff.).

Jasentuliyana, N. (ed.), *Space Law: Development and Scope* (Westport, Conn., 1992).

—— and Lee, R. S. K. (eds.): *Manual on Space Law* (4 vols.; New York and Alphen aan den Rijn, 1979–81).

Jenks, C. W., *Space Law* (London, 1965)

Lachs, M., *The Law of Outer Space* (Leiden, 1972).

Lay, S. G., and Taubenfeld, H. J., *The Law Relating to Activities of Man in Outer Space* (New Haven, 1963).

McDougal, M. S. Lasswell, H. D., and Vlassic, I. A., *Law and Public Order in Space* (Chicago, 1970).

McGill University, Centre for Research of Air & Space Law, *Earth-Oriented Space Activities and Their Legal Implications*. Proceedings of the Symposium held on October 15–16, 1981. (Montreal, 1981).

McMahon, J. E., 'Legal Aspects of Outer Space', 38 *BYIL* (1962), 339–99.

Marcoff, M. G., *Traité de Droit International Public de l'Espace* (Fribourg, 1973).

Martin, P. M., *Le droit de l'espace. Que sais-Je?* (Paris, 1991).

——, *Droit des activités spatiales* (Paris, 1992).

Masson-Zwaan, T. L., and Mendes de Leon, P. M. J., *Air and Space Law: De Lege Ferenda—Essays in Honour of Henri A. Wassenbergh* (Dordrecht, 1992).

Matte, N. M., *Aerospace Law* (London, Toronto, and Paris, 1969, 1977).

——, *Space Police and Programmes Today and Tomorrow: The Vanishing Duopole* (Montreal, 1980).

—— (ed.), *Space Activities and Implications: Where From and Where To at the Threshold of the 80's* (Montreal, 1981).

Miklitz, H. W., and Reich, N., *Legal Aspects of European Space Activities* (Baden-Baden, 1989).

Nozari, F., *The Law of Outer Space* (Stockholm, 1973).

Ogunbanwo, O. O., *International Law and Outer Space Activities* (The Hague, 1975).

Peyrefitte, L., *Droit de l'espace* (Paris, 1993).

Piradov, A. S. (ed.), *International Space Law* (Moscow, 1976).

Quadri, R., 'Droit international cosmique', 98 Hague *Recueil* (1959–III), 505–98.

Račič, O., *Osbivba Načela Kosmičkog Prava [Basic Principles of Space Law]* (Beograd, 1972). With Summary in English and Russian.

Reynolds, G., and Merges, R., *Outer Space: Problems of Law and Policy* (San Diego, CA, 1989).

Reijnen, G. C., *Legal Aspects of Outer Space* (Utrecht, 1976).

United Nations, *Space Exploration and Applications: Papers Presented at the UN Conference on the Exploration and Peaceful Uses of Outer Space, Vienna, 14–27 August 1968* [UNISPACE] (2 vols, UN, Sales No. E.69.I.16).

——, *Practical Benefits of Space Exploration* (UN Sales No. E.69.I.25).

——, *The World in Space: A Survey of Space Activities and Issues prepared for UNISPACE 82* (ed. R. Chipman; Englewood Cliffs, NJ, 1982).

——, *International Space Programmes and Policies, Proceedings of the Second United Nations Conference on the Exploration and Peaceful Uses of Outer Space* (UNISPACE 2) (eds. N. Jasentuliyana, and R. Chipman; New York, 1984).

——, *Report of the Second UN Conference on the Exploration and Peaceful Uses of Outer Space, Vienna, 9–21 August 1982* [UNISPACE 82] (A/CONF.101/10 (31.8.82).

——, *List of Conclusions and Recommendations of the Second UN Conference on the Exploration and Peaceful Uses of Outer Space* (A/CONF.101/11 (18.10.82), and Corr. 1 (2.11.82).

United States Senate, *Space Law*. A Symposium prepared at the Request of Honorable Lyndon B. Johnson, Chairman, Special Committee on Space and Astronautics, 85th Congress, 2nd Sess, December 31, 1958. (Washington, 1959).

——, *Legal Problems of Space Exploration: A Symposium*. Prepared for the use of the Committee on Aeronautical and Space Sciences, US Senate. 87th Congress, 1st Sess., Senate, Doc. No. 26. (Washington 1961)).

Universidad Nacional Autonoma de Mexico and International Institute of Air and Space Law, Leiden University, *Latin American Conference on International Air Transport and Activities in Outer Space* (Leiden, 1989).

Vereschchetin, V., *International Cooperation in Outer Space: Legal Problems* (Moscow, 1977).

——, Vasilevskaya, E., and Kamenetskaya, E, *Outer Space: Politics and Law* (Moscow, 1987).

Wadegaonkar, D., *The Orbit of Space Law* (London, 1984).

Wassenbergh, H. A., *Principles of Outer Space in Hindsight* (Dordrecht, 1991).

Williams, S. M., *Derecho Internacional Contemporaneo: La Utilizacion del Espacio Ultraterrestre* (Buenos Aires, 1990).

Zukov, G. P, and Kolosov, Y., *International Space Law* (New York, 1984).

Zwaan, T. L., and others (eds.), *Space Law: Views of the Future* (Deventer, 1988).

V. Analytical Bibliography

A. International Law and Space Law

Böckstiegel, H. -H. (ed.), *Settlement of Space Law Disputes* (Köln, 1979).

——, 'Convention on the Settlement of Space Law Disputes', 26 *Space Law Colloquium* (1983), 179–89.

Bourély, M. G., 'The Contributions made by International Organizations to the Formation of Space law', 10 *JSL* (1982), 159–68.

Bouchez, L. J., 'The Concept of Effectiveness as Applied to Territorial Sovereignty over Sea-Area, Air Space and Outer Space', 9 *Netherlands ILR* (1962), 151–82.

Cheng, B., 'Inter Astra Silent Leges? Prolegomena to Jural Cartography', 30 *GLIM* (1961), 18–22.

Christol, C. Q., 'Methodology and the Development of International Space Law', in University of Padjadjaran, Bandung, Indonesia, *Hukum Ankasa Dan Perkembangannya* (1989), 19–28.

Cooper, J. C., 'High Altitude Flights and National Sovereignty', 4 *ILQ* (1951), 411–8.

Czabafi, I. A., *The Concept of State Jurisdiction in International Law* (The Hague, 1971).

DeSaussure, H., 'Toward a Law for Space Transport. The Maritime Analogy', 14 *Lincoln LR* (1977), 707–24.

Diederiks-Verschoor, I. H. Ph., 'Similarities and Differences between Air and Space Law Primarily in the Field of Private International Law', 172 Hague *Recueil* (1982), 317–423.

Górbiel, A, *Outer Space in International Law* (Lódź, 1981).

Herczeg, I., 'Space Law and General International Law', 16 *Space Law Colloquium* (1974), 3–8.

Jasentuliyana, ., 'Ensuring Equal Access to the Benefits of Space Technologies for all Countries', 10 *Space Policy* (1994), 7–18.

Jessup, P. C., and Taubenfeld, H. J., *Controls for Outer Space and the Antarctica Analogy* (New York, 1959).

Katzenbach, N. D. (paper by), and commentators, 'Sharable and Strategic Resources: Outer Space, Polar Areas and the Oceans', *ASIL Proc.* (1959), 206–12.

Konstantinov, E., *The Principle of Sovereignty over the Airspace in Contemporary International Law* (Sofia, 1983). In Russian.

Kopal, V., 'Analogies and Differences in the Development of the Law of the Sea and the Law of Outer Space', 28 *Space Law Colloquium* (1985), 151–5.

Kovalev, F. N., and Cheprov, I. I., 'Artificial Satellites and International Law', *Soviet YBIL* (1958), 129–49.

Matte, N. M. (ed.), *Space Activities and Emerging International Law* (Montreal, 1984).

Meyer, A., 'Airspace Sovereignty and Outer Space Developments', 14 *ZLW* (1965), 296–311.

Milde, M., 'Considerations on Legal Problems of Space above National Territory', 5 *Review of Contemporary Law* (1958), 5–22.

Nesgos, P. D., 'The Proposed International Sea-Bed Authority as a Model for the Future Outer Space International Régime', 5 *AASL* (1980), 549–73.

Peng, Ming-Min, 'Le vol à haute altitude et l'art. 1 de la Convention de Chicago', 6 *RFDA* (1952), 390–404.

Reijnen, G. C. M., *Utilization of Outer Space and International Law* (Amsterdam, 1981).

Rode-Verschoor, I. H. Ph., 'Observations on Comparing the Responsibility for Damage Caused by Space Craft and that Caused by Nuclear Installations and Nuclear Powered Ships', 4 *Space Law Colloquium* (1961), 329–35.

Stovitz, C. J.and Loomis, T., 'Space Law: Lessons Learnt from the Antarctic'. 28 *Space Law Colloquium* (1985), 165–71.

Various authors, 'Interrelationship between Air and Space Law', 26 *Space Law Colloquium* (1983), 67–103.

Vereshchetin, V. S., and Danilenko, G. M., 'Custom as a Source of International Law of Outer Space', 13 *JSL* (1985), 22–35.

White, I. L., *Decision-making for Space: Law and Politics in Air, Sea and Outer Space* (Indiana, 1970).

Williams, S. M., 'The Role of Equity in the Law of Outer Space', 5 *International Relations* (1975), 776–99.

B. The United Nations and Space Law

Benkö, M., and Schrogl, K. U., (eds.), *Space Law in the United Nations* (Dordrecht, 1985).

——— and ——— (eds.), *International Space Law in the Making. Current Issues in the UN COPUOS* (Gif-sur-Yvette, 1993).

Bourély, M., 'The Contribution Made by International Organizations to the Formation of Space Law', 10 *JSL* (1982), 139–55.

Carver, J. H., 'The Scientific and Technical Sub-committee of the United Nations Committee on the Peaceful Uses of Outer Space', 5 *JSL* (1977), 17–27.

Christol, C. Q., 'The United Nations and the Development of International Law— Unanimous Resolutions of the General Assembly Dealing with Outer Space', 23 *Proceedings of the Institute of World Affairs, San Diego, California, 19 August 1965*, 213–19.

Galloway, E. M., 'Consensus Decisionmaking by the United Nations Committee on the Peaceful Uses of Outer Space', 7 *JSL* (1979), 3–14.

Górbiel, A, *International Organizations and Outer Space Activities* (Lódź, 1984).

Jankowitch, P., 'Contribution of the United Nations Committee on the Peaceful Uses of Outer Space: an Overview', 5 *JSL* (1977), 7–15.

Jasentuliyana, N., 'Treaty Law and Outer Space: Can the United Nations Play an Effective Rôle?', 11 *AASL* (1986), 219–27.

———, 'Space Law and the United Nations', 17 *AASL* (1992–II), 127–55.

Johnson, D. H. N., 'The Effects of Resolutions of the United Nations', 32 *BYIL* (1955–6), 97–122.

Kopal, V., 'Evolution of the Main Principles of Space Law in the Institutional Framework of the United Nations', 12 *JSL* (1984), 12–25.

Simsarian, J., 'Outer Space Co-operation in the United Nations', 57 *AJIL* (1963), 854–67.

United Nations, *Space Exploration and Applications; Papers presented at the United Nations Conference on the Exploration and Peaceful Uses of Outer Space, Vienna, 14–27 August 1968* [UNISPACE] (2 vols., UN Sales No. E.69.I.16).

———, *Practical Benefits of Space Exploration* (UN Sales No. E.69.I.25).

———, *The United Nations and Outer Space* (New York, 1977).

———, *Report of the Second UN Conference on the Exploration and Peaceful Uses of Outer Space, Vienna, 1982* [UNISPACE 82], A/CONF.101/10 (31.8.82).

———, *List of Conclusions and Recommendations of the Second UNISPACE 82, Note by the Secretariat*, A/CONF.101/11 (18.10.82), and Corr. 1 (2.11.82).

———, *The Implications of Establishing an International Satellite Monitoring Agency* (New York, 1983).

———, *International Space Programmes and Policies—Proceedings of the Second UN Conference on the Exploration and Peaceful Uses of Outer Space (UNISPACE), Vienna, Austria, August 1982* (eds. N. Jasentuliyana, and R. Chipman; New York, 1984).

——, *Space Activities of the United Nations and International Organizations*, A/AC105/521 (UN Sales No. E.92.I.30, New York, 1992).

Various authors, 'Legal Aspects of Space Activities of Organizations of the United Nations System and Other International Organizations', 36 *Space Law Colloquium* (1993), 3–122.

C. United Nations Treaties on Outer Space

Bourély, M. G., 'Is it Necessary to Re-Negotiate the Convention on Registration?', 31 *Space Law Colloquium* (1988), 227–33.

Christol, C. Q., 'The Common Heritage of Mankind Provisions of the December 5, 1979 Moon Treaty', 6 *Annuaire de Droit Maritime et Aérien* (1982), 429–63.

——, 'Article 2 of the 1967 Principles Treaty Revisited', 9 *AASL* (1984), 217–65.

Courteix, S., 'L'Accord régissant les activités des États sur la lune et les autres corps célestes', 25 *AFDI* (1979), 203–22.

Darwin, H. G., 'The Outer Space Treaty', 42 *BYIL* (1967), 278–89.

Foster, W. F., 'The Convention on International Liability for Damage Caused by Space Objects', 19 *Can. YBIL* (1972), 137–85.

Gaggero, E. D., and Ripoll, R. P., 'Accord régissant les activités des États sur la lune et autres corps célestes', 5 *AASL* (1980), 449–80; in Spanish 5 *Revista Uruguaya de Derecho Internacional* (1980), 123–66.

Galloway, E., *Agreement on the Rescue of Astronauts, the Return of Astronauts and the Return of Objects Launched into Outer Space, Text of Agreement and Analysis*, Senate Committee on Aeronautical and Space Sciences, 90th Cong. 2d Sess. 12 (1968).

——, 'Agreement Governing the Activities of States on the Moon and other Celestial Bodies', 5 *AASL* (1980), 481–508.

Goedhuis, D., 'Conflicts in the Interpretation of the Leading Principles of the Moon Treaty of 5 December 1979', 28 *Netherlands ILR* (1981), 14–29.

Gutiérrez Espada, C., ' "Reservas" Propuestas en el Congreso de los Diputados al Convenio sobre Responsabilidad internacional por Daños causados por objetos espaciales', 3 *Anales de Derecho, Universidad de Murcia* (1982), 79–90.

Hall, R. C., 'Rescue and Return of Astronauts on Earth and in Outer Space', 63 *AJIL* (1969), 197–210.

Hurwitz, B. A., *State Liability for Outer Space Activities in Accordance with the 1972 Convention on International Liability for Damage Caused by Space Objects* (Dordrecht, 1992).

Jacquemin, G., 'Le Traité du 27 janvier 1967 sur les principes devant régir l'exploration de l'espace et celui du 22 avril 1968 sur l'assistance des astronautes, leur signification et leur portée', 25 *RFDA* (1971), 257–68.

Jasentuliyana, N., 'Article 1 of the Outer Space Treaty Revisited', 17 *JSL* (1989), 129–44.

—— and Lee, 1 *Manual* contains *inter alia* contributions on the several treaties by P. G. Dembling (Space Treaty, 1–51), R. S. K. Lee (Astronaut Agreement, 53–81), B. Cheng (Liability Convention, 83–172), A. A. Cocca (Registration Convention, 173–93, and N. M. Matte (draft Moon Treaty, 253–82).

Kiss, A. C., 'L'Accord sur le retour et le sauvetage des astronautes et la restitution des objets launcés dans l'espace extra-atmosphérique', 14 *AFDI* (1968), 736–46.

Lafferranderie, G., 'L'application, par l'Agence Spatiale Européenne, de la Convention sur l'immatriculation des objets lancés dans l'espace extra-atmosphérique', 11 *AASL* (1986), 229–36.

Rajski, J., 'Convention on International Liability for Damage Caused by Space Objects', 17 *Space Law Colloquium* (1974), 245–59.

Rothblatt, M. A., and Samara, N. A., 'Legal Consequences of the Registration Convention for Space Platforms, Space Stations and Space Habitats', 28 *Space Law Colloquium* (1985), 192–8.

UN Secretary-General, *Report on Application of the Convention on Registration of Objects Launched into Outer Space*, A/AC.105/382 (2.3.87).

US Senate, *Convention on International Liability for Damage Caused by Space Objects: Report from the Committee on Foreign Relations*. 92d Cong., 2d Sess., Executive Rept. No. 92–38.

Various authors, 'Interpretation of the Space Treaty'. 10 *Space Law Colloquium* (1967), 105–71.

Williams, S. M., 'The "Surprise" Convention on the Registration of Space Objects', 28 *ZLW* (1979), 122–9.

Young, A. J., 'A Decennial Review of the Registration Convention', 9 *AASL* (1986), 287–308.

D. *Outer Space, Astronauts and Space Objects*

Baker, H. A., *Space Debris: Legal and Policy Implications* (Dordrecht, 1989).

Böckstiegel, K. -H. (ed.), *Space Stations—Legal Aspects of Scientific and Commercial Use in a Framework of Transatlantic Cooperation* (Cologne, 1985).

—— (ed.), *Environmental Aspects of Activities in Outer Space* (Cologne, 1988).

—— (ed.), *Manned Space Flight* (Cologne, 1993).

Cheng, B., 'Crimes on Board Aircraft', 12 *CLP* (1959), 177–207.

——, 'Nationality of Aircraft Operated by Joint or International Agencies', 2 *YBASL* (1966) 5–31.

——, 'Nationality and Registration of Aircraft Operated by International Operating Agencies', in ILA, *Report of the 53rd Conference Buenos Aires* (1968), 147–56.

Cooper, J. C., 'Flight-space and the Satellites', 7 *ICLQ* (1958), 82–91.

Csabafi, I., *The Concept of State Jurisdiction in International Space Law* (The Hague, 1971).

Danilenko, G. M., 'The Concept of the "Common Heritage of Mankind" in International Law', 13 *AASL* (1988), 247–65.

European Space Agency, *Space Debris* (Paris, 1988).

——, *Proceedings of an International Colloquium on the Manned Space Station: Legal Issues. Paris, 7–8 November 1989* (ESA SP–305, Paris, 1990).

Galloway, E., 'The Space Station: United States Proposal and Implementation', 14 *JSL* (1986), 14–39.

Goedhuis, D., 'Problems of Frontiers of Outer Space and Air Space', 174 Hague *Recueil* (1982–I), 371–407.

Górbiel, A., *Legal Status of Outer Space—Status prawny Kosmosu* (Lódź, 1977).

——, *Les aspects juridiques internationaux de l'utilisation de l'orbite géostationnaire* (Lódź, 1979).

——, *Legal Definitions of Outer Space* (Lódź, 1980).

——, 'Space Objects in International Law', 21 *Il Diritto Aereo* (1982), 75–89.

Gorove, S., 'The Geostationary Orbit: Issues of Law and Policy', 73 *AJIL* (1979), 444–61.

—— (ed.), *The Space Shuttle and the Law* (1980).

——, 'The Space Shuttle: Some of its Features and Legal Implications', 6 *AASL* (1981), pp. 381–98.

——, 'Definition Issues Pertaining to "Space Object', 37 *Space Law Colloquium* (1994), 87–98

Guyenne, T. D. (ed.), *International Colloquium on Manned Space Stations—Legal Issues* (ESA, Paris, 1990).

Hall, R. C., 'Rescue and Return of Astronauts on Earth and in Outer Space', 63 *AJIL* (1969), 197–210.

He, Qizhi, 'The Problem of Definition and Delimitation in Outer Space', 10 *JSL* (1982), 157–63.

Jasentuliyana, N., and Chipman, R., 'The Current Legal Régime of the Geostationary Orbit and Prospects for the Future', 17 *Acta Astronautica* (1988), 599–606.

Kish, J., *The Law of International Spaces* (Leiden, 1973).

Kopal, V., 'The Question of Defining Outer Space', 8 *JSL* (1980), 154–73.

——, 'Issues Involved in Defining Outer Space, Space Object and Space Debris', 34 *Space Law Colloquium* (1991), 38–44.

Kwon, Yeong-Mo, 'Review of ITU Registration for Koreasat', 7 *Korean JASL* (1995), 299–320.

Lachs, M., 'Outer Space, the Moon and other Celestial Bodies', in Bedjaoui, M. (ed.), *International Law: Achievements and Prospects*. (Paris and Dordrecht, 1991), 959–74.

Lafferranderie, G., 'Pour une charte de l'astronaute', 12 *AASL* (1987), 263–277.

Masson-Zwaan, T. L., 'The Spaceplane and the Law', 19 *JSL* (1991), 60–6.

Menter, M., 'Jurisdiction Over Man-Made Orbital Satellites', 1 *JSL* (1974), 19–25.

O'Brien, J. E., 'The US/International Space Station', 15 *JSL* (1987), 35–41.

Perek, L., 'Scientific Criteria for the Delimitation of Outer Space', 5 *JSL* (1977), 111–24.

Roth, A. D., *La prohibition de l'appropriation et les régimes d'accès aux espaces extra-terrestres* (Paris, 1992).

Sheldon II, C. S., and DeVoe, B. M., 'United Nations Registry of Space Vehicles', in 13 *Space Law Colloquium* (1970). 127–41.

Sloup, G. P., 'The "Aerospace Vehicle" as a Legal Concept—On Final Approach?', 8 *AASL* (1983), 433–42.

Schwetje, F. K., 'Protecting Space Assets: A Legal Analysis of "Keep-out Zones"', 15 *JSL* (1987), 131–46;

Smith, D. D., *Space Stations: International Law and Policy* (Colorado, 1979).

US Congress, Office of Technology Assessment, *Space Stations and the Law: Selected Legal Issues—Background Paper* (OTA–BP–ISC–41) (Washington DC, 1986).

——, *Orbiting Debris: A Space Environmental Problem—Background Paper* (OTA–BP–ISC–72) (Washington DC, 1990).

Various authors, 'Scientific and Legal Aspects of Large Systems in Space: Problems and Prospects', 22 *Space Law Colloquium* (1979), 263–89.

——, 'Determination of Applicable Law to Living and Working in Outer Space', in 23 *Space Law Colloquium* 1980), 187–279.

——, 'Legal Status of Artificial Space Objects', in 24, *Space Law Colloquium* (1981), 89–115.

——, 'Legal Aspects of Large Space Stations', 27 *Space Law Colloquium* (1984), 225–76.

——, 'Legal Problems of Registration of Space Objects', 28 *Space Law Colloquium* (1985), 173–207.

Verplaetse, J. G., 'On the Definition and the Legal Status of Spacecraft', 29 *JALC* (1963), 131–140.

Young, A. J., *Law and Policy in the Space Station Era* (Dordrecht, 1989).

E. Military Use of Outer Space

Almond, H. M., Jr., 'Peaceful Purposes and Peaceful Activities', 29 *Space Law Colloquium* (1986), 1–10.

——, 'Peaceful Purposes: Precision, Ambiguity or Confusion', 31 *Space Law Colloquium* (1988), 1–5.

Alves, P. G., *Prevention of an Arms Race in Outer Space: A Guide to the Discussion in the Conference on Disarmament* (UNDIR, 1991).

——, *Access to Outer Space Technologies: Implications for International Security* (UNDIR, 1992).

Bakotić, B., 'Outer Space—Region of War?', 30 *Space Law Colloquium* (1987), 12–4.

Brownlie, I., 'The Maintenance of International Security in Outer Space', 40 *BYIL* (1964), 1–31.

Cheng, B., 'Legal Controls of the Military Uses of Spacecraft', in British Institute of International and Comparative Law, *Current Problems in Space Law* (1966), 83–5.

Christol, C. Q., 'Arms Control and Disarmament in Space: The Rough Road to Vienna 1984', *Space Policy* (1985), 26–48, and 263–88.

Donay, P., 'The Military Use of Outer Space: Implications for International Law', in Branch, H. G. (ed.), *Technology, Armaments Dynamics and Disarmament* (London, 1989), 471–5.

Doyle. S. E., *Civil Space Systems: Implication for International Security* (UNIDIR, 1993).

Goedhuis, D., 'Some Observations on the Attitude of West-European Governments to the Development of Defensive Weapons in Outer Space', 15 *JSL* (1987), 101–8.

Górbiel, A., 'Towards the Entire Demilitarization of Outer Space', 18 *Postepy Astronautyki* (1985), 25–56.

Grable, C. L., *Space Weapons and the Strategic Defense Initiative* (Iowa, 1991).

Haeck, L., 'Le droit de la guerre spatiale', 16 *AASL* (1991), 307–40.

He, Qizhi, 'Towards Legal Control of Space Arms, a Difficult Process', 1 *Arms Control and Disarmament in Outer Space* (1985), 125–41.

Hurwitz, B. A., *The Legality of Space Militarization* (Amsterdam, 1986).

Jasani, B., *Outer Space—A New Dimension of the Arms Race* (New York, 1982).

——, *Space Weapons and International Security* (Oxford, 1987).

—— (ed.), *Peaceful and Non-Peaceful Uses of Space* (New York, 1991).

Jasentuliyana, N. (ed.), *Maintaining Outer Space for Peaceful Uses* (The Hague, 1984).

Kennedy, K. C., 'Treaty Interpretation by the Executive Branch: The ABM Treaty and "Star Wars" Testing and Development', 80 *AJIL* (1986), 854–77.

Kries, W. v., 'International Space Law Implications of the U.S. SDI and ASAT Programs: The Current Legal Debate', 35 *ZLW* (1986), 310–8.

Kubbi, B. W. (ed.), *Die militarishe Eroberung des Weltraums* (2 vols., Frankfurt, 1990).

Lellouche, P. (ed.), *Satellite Warfare: A Challenge for the International Community* (UNIDIR, 1987).

Markov, M. G., 'The juridical meaning of the term "Peaceful" in the 1967 Space Treaty', 11 *Space Law Colloquium* (1968), 30–5.

Matte, N. M. (ed.), *Arms Control and Disarmament in Outer Space* (4 vols., Montreal, 1985–91).

——, 'Military Uses of Outer Space and the 1967 Outer Space Treaty', in Storm van 's Gravesande, J. W. E., and van der Veen Vonk, A. (eds), *Air Worthy* (Deventer, 1985), 117– 34.

Meyer, A., 'Interpretation of the term "Peaceful" in the light of the Space Treaty', 11 *Space Law Colloquium* (1968), 24–9.

Noorden, W. v., 'IMMARSAT Use by Armed Forces: A Question of Treaty Interpretation'. 23 *JSL* (1995), 1–17.

Piradov, A. S., and Maiorsky, B. G., 'On the Question of the Non-Use of Force in Outer Space and from Space Against the Earth', 27 *Space Law Colloquium* (1984), 349–53.

Scoville, Jr., H., and Tsipis, K., *Can Space Remain a Peaceful Environment?* (Stanley Foundation, 1978).

Sloup, G. P., 'Arms Control Verification: The Poor Person's Approach', 29 *Space Law Colloquium* (1986), 77–83.

Stares, P. B., *The Militarization of Space: US Policy, 1945–1984* (New York, 1985).

Stutzle, W., Jasani, B., and Cowen, R. (eds.), *The ABM Treaty: To Defend or not to Defend* (Oxford, 1987).

UNIDIR, *Disarmament: Problems Related to Outer Space* (UN, 1987).

Various authors, 'Legal Aspects of Maintaining Outer Space for Peaceful Purposes', 29 *Space Law Colloquium* (1986), 1–99; 30 ibid. (1987), 1–120; 31 ibid. (1988), 1–88.

Vlasic, L. A., 'Disarmament Decade, Outer Space and International Law', 26 *McGill LJ* (1981), 135–206.

Zhukov, G., 'On the question of the interpretation of the term "Peaceful Use of Outer Space" contained in the Space Treaty', 11 *Space Law Colloquium* (1968), 36–9.

F. Commercial Uses of Outer Space and International Law

Achilleas, P., *La télévision par satellite, aspects juridiques internationaux* (Paris, 1995).

American Society of International Law: 'International Co-operation in Satellite Communications Systems' (Addresses by J. A. Johnson, R. K. Woetzel, and L. R. Marks, and report on panel discussion by P. F. Patman), *ASIL Proc.* (1967), 24–49.

Baker, H. A., 'Liability for Damage Caused in Outer Space by Space Refuse', 13 *AASL* (1988), 183–227.

Balsano, A. M., 'Space Technology and International Cooperation—The Role of Intellectual Property', 20 *ASL* (1995), 177–88.

Bender, R., *Space Transport Liability* (The Hague, 1995).

Böckstiegel, K. -H., 'Space Law—Changes and Expectations at the Turn to Commercial Space Activities', 8 *Forum Internationale* (1986), 3–28.

—— (ed.), *Die Produkthaftung in der Luft- und Raumfahrt* (Köln, 1978).

Bourély, M., 'Quelques particularités du régime de la responsabilités du fait des activités spatiales', 15 *AASL* (1990), 251–74.

Bogaert, E. R. C. van, 'The Political Impact of Remote Sensing', in Storm van's Gravesande, J. W. E., and A. van der Veen Vonk, *Air Worthy* (Deventer, 1985), 35–46.

Boyle, A. E., 'State Responsibility and International Liability for Injurious Consequences of Acts Not Prohibited by International Law: A Necessary Distinction?', 39 *ICLQ* (1980), 1–26.

Brown, R., *Telecommunications: The Blooming Technology* (London, 1969).

Burnett, D. J., and Schroeder, F. O., 'Developments in US Bilateral Launch Service Agreements', 19 *ASL* (1994), 326–31.

Catalano Sgrosso, G., *La Responsabilitá degli Stati per le attività svolte nello Spazio Extra-atmosferico* (Padova, 1990).

Centre National de la Recherche Scientifique, Groupe de Travail sur le Droit de l'Espace, *Les télécommunications par satellites: aspects juridiques* (Paris, 1968).

Chayes, A., Fawcett, J., Ito, M, Kiss, A. C., and others, *Satellite Broadcasting* (London, 1973).

Cheli, S., and Tuinder, P. H., 'European Space Police, Institutional Developments', 21 *ASL* (1996), 48–61.

Cheng, B., 'Whose Parking Space Is It Anyway? Mapping Out a Legal Minefield in the Celestial Outlands', *The Times Higher Educational Supplement* (No. 708, 30 May 1986), 14–5.

——, 'Liability Regulations Applicable to Research and Invention in Outer Space and their Commercial Exploitation', in Mosteshar, S. (ed.), *Research and Invention in Outer Space: Liability and Intellectual Property Rights* (Dordrecht, 1995), 71–94.

Christol, C. Q., 'International Liability for Damage Caused by Space Objects', 74 *AJIL* (1980), 346– 71.

——, 'Remote Sensing and International Space Law', 19 *JSL* (1988), 21–44.

Cocca, A. A., *El Derecho a Communicarse/The Right to Communicate.* (Cordoba, 1983).

Codding, Jr., G. A., and Rutkowski, A. M., *The ITU in a Changing World* (Dedhm, MA, 1982).

Cohen, A. F., 'Cosmos 954 and the International Law of Satellite Accidents', *Yale JIL* (1984), 78–91.

Colino, R. R., *The INTELSAT Definitive Arrangements* (EBU, Geneva, 1973).

Cordoba House of Cultural Foundation, Council of Advanced International Studies, *Round Table on Legal Framework of Economic Activity in Space*. (Cordoba, 1982).

DeSaussure, H., 'Remote Sensing by Satellite: What Future for an International Regime?', 71 *AJIL* (1977), 707–24.

Diederiks-Verschoor, I. H. Ph., 'Implications of Commercial Activities in Outer Space, Especially for the Developing Countries', 17 *JSL* (1989), 115–27.

——, 'Legal Aspects Affecting Telecommunications Activities in Space', 1 *Telecommunications & Space Journal* (1994), 81–91.

—— and Gormley, W. P., 'The Future Legal Status of Nongovernmental Entities in

Outer Space: Private Individuals and Companies as Subjects and Beneficiaries of International Space Law', 5 *JSL* (1977), 125–55.

Dunk, F. von der, 'Satellite Communications in the European Community', in *Issues in International Air and Space Law, and in Commercial Law: Essays in Commemoration of Prof. Dr. Doo Hwan Kim's Sixtieth Birthday* (1994), 317–64.

——, 'Commercial Space Activities: An Inventory of Liability, An Inventory of Problems', 37 *Space Law Colloquium* (1994), 161–71.

DYP Group, *The London Space Insurance Conference, 28 & 29 September 1993* (London, 1993).

European Space Agency, *Earth Observation from Space and Management of Planetary Resources*. Proceedings of an international conference, Toulouse 6–11 March 1978. ESA SP–134. (Paris, 1978).

Fenema, H. P. van, 'Cooperation and Competition in Space Transportation', 19 *ASL* (1994), 81–8.

Finch, E. R., 'Outer Space Liability: Past, Present, Future', 14 *International Lawyer* (1980), 12–127.

—— and Moore, A. L., *Astrobusiness: A Guide to the Commerce and Law of Outer Space* (New York, 1985).

Fisher, D. I., *Prior Consent to International Direct Satellite Broadcasting* (Dordrecht, 1990).

Galloway, E., 'United States National Space Legislation on the Exploration and Use of Outer Space for Peaceful Purposes', 30 *Space Law Colloquium* (1987), 32–41.

Galloway, J. F., *The Politics and Technology of Satellite Communications* (Lexington, Mass., 1972).

Gantt, J. B., 'The Commercialization of Space—Twenty Years of Experience', 12 *JSL* (1994), 109–35.

Goedhuis, D., 'Legal Aspects of the Utilisation of Outer Space', 17 *Netherlands ILR* (1970), 25–50.

He, Qizhi, 'Legal Aspects of Commercialization of Space Activities', 15 *AASL* (1990), 333–42.

——, 'Policy and Legal Implications of Asia-Pacific Space Cooperation', 19 *ASL* (1994), 207–10.

Hurwitz, B. A., *State Liability for Outer Space Activities* (Dordrecht, 1992).

Jakhu, R. S., 'Direct Broadcasting via Satellite and a New Information Order', 8 *Syracuse JIL & Commerce* (1981), 375–90.

Jenks, C. W., 'Liability for Ultra-Hazardous Activities in International Law', 117 Hague *Recueil* (1966–I), 99–200.

Kim, Doo Hwan, 'A Study for the Liability of the Compensation for Damages Caused by Space Debris', 7 *Korean JASL* (1995), 224–63.

Kildow, J. T., *INTELSAT: Policy-Maker's Dilemma* (Farnborough, 1973).

Lafferranderie, G., *Le statut juridique du satellite des télécommunications: Les télécommunications par satellite* (Paris, 1968).

Leive, D. M., *International Telecommunications and International Law: The Regulation of the Radio Spectrum* (Leyden, 1970).

Lyall, F., *Law and Space Telecommunications* (Dartmouth, 1989).

McLucas, J. L., and Sheffield, C. (eds.), *Commercial Operations in Space: 1980–2000* (American Astronautical Society, 1981).

McWhinney, E., *The International Law of Communications* (Leyden, 1971).

Magdelenat, J. L., 'The Major Issues in the "Agreed" Principles on Remote Sensing', 9 *JSL* (1981), 111–20.

Matte, N. M., and DeSaussure, H. (eds.), *Legal Implications of Remote Sensing from Outer Space* (Leyden, 1976).

Meredith,, P. L., and Robinson, G. S., *Space Law: A Case Study for the Practitioner: Implementing a Telecommunications Satellite Business Concept* (Dordrecht, 1992).

Mosteshar, S. (ed.), *Research and Invention in Outer Space: Liability and Intellectual Property Rights* (Dordrecht, 1995).

National Legal Center for the Public Interest (ed.), *American Enterprise, The Law and the Commercial Use of Space* (2 vols., Washington DC, 1986).

Nesgos, P. D., 'The Practice of Commercial Space Law', 17 *AASL* (1992–II), 177–85.

Noorden, W. v., 'Space Communications to Aircraft: A New Development in International Space Law', 15 *JSL* (1987), 25–34, 147–60.

—— and Dann, P. J., 'Public and Private Enterprise in Satellite Telecommunications: The Example of INMARSAT', 29 *Space Law Colloquium* (1986), 193–7.

——, 'Land Mobile Satellite Communications: a Further Development in International Space Law', 17 *JSL* (1989), 6–11, 103–13.

Queeney, K. M., *Direct Broadcast Satellites and the United Nations* (Alphen on the Rheim, 1978).

Peyreffitte, L., 'The Legal Regime of Remote Sensing of the Earth from Space', 24 *Space Law Colloquium* (1991), 286–97.

RANN/Office of Exploratory Research and Problem Assessment, *A Global Satellite Observation System for Earth Resources: Problems and Prospects*. A Report to the [US] National Science Foundation. NSF–RA–X–75–014. Washington DC.

Riddick, D., 'Why does Tonga own Outer Space', 19 *ASL* (1994), 15–29.

Salkeld, R., Patterson, D., and Grey, J. (eds.), *Space Transportation System 1980–2000* (American Institute of Aeronautics and Astronautics, 1978).

Schönbeck, J., 'Die Resolution der Vereinten Nationen vom 10 Dezember 1982 über Prinzipien für das direkte Satellitenfernsehen', 32 *ZLW* (1983), 16–31.

Sirkin, A. M. (ed.), *Resource Sensing from Space: Prospects for Developing Countries* (Washington DC, 1977).

Smith, D. D., *Communication via Satellite: A Vision in Retrospect* (Leyden, 1976).

Smith, M. L., *International Regulation of Satellite Communication* (Dordrecht, 1990).

Smits, J. M., *Legal Aspects of Implementing International Telecommunication Links* (Dordrecht, 1991).

Snow, M. S., *The International Telecommunications Satellite Organisation (INTEL-SAT)* (Baden-Baden, 1987).

Tatsuzawa, K., *Legal Aspects of Space Commercialization* (Tokyo, 1992).

Théraulaz, J. D., *Droit de l'espace et responsabilité* (Lausanne, 1971).

Traa-Engelman, H. L. van, *Commercial Utilization of Outer Space: Law and Practice* (Dordrecht, 1993).

UNESCO (ed.), *Communication in the Space Age: The use of satellite by the mass media* (Paris, 1968).

United States Congress, Office of Technology Assessment, *International Cooperation and Competition in Civilian Space Activities.* Washington DC, GPO. 1985. OTA–ISC–239.

Various authors, 'Commercialization of Space Activities', 29 *Space Law Colloquium* (1986), 154–204.

——, 'The United Nations and Legal Principles of Remote Sensing', 30 ibid. (1987), 268–418.

——, 'Legal Implications of Space Commercialization', 33 ibid. (1990), 3–130.

——, 'Legal Aspects of Space Insurance', 36 ibid. (1993), 187–228.

Wassenbergh, H. A., 'The Law Governing International private Commercial Activities of Space Transportation', 21 *JSL* (1993), 97–121.

Wenk, E., *Radio Frequency Control in Space* (Washington DC, 1960).

White, R. L., and H. M., *The Law and Regulation of International Space Communication* (Boston, 1988).

Wiewiorowska, K., 'Some Problems of State Responsibility in Outer Space Law', 7 *JSL* (1979), 23–38.

Williams, S. M., *Telecommunicaciones por Satelites* (Buenos Aires, 1981).

Index

Italic numbers denote reference to illustrations